Essentials *of* Investments

The McGraw-Hill/Irwin Series in Finance, Insurance, and Real Estate

Stephen A. Ross
Franco Modigliani Professor of Finance
and Economics
Sloan School of Management
Massachusetts Institute of Technology
Consulting Editor

FINANCIAL MANAGEMENT

Block, Hirt, and Danielsen
Foundations of Financial Management
Sixteenth Edition

Brealey, Myers, and Allen
Principles of Corporate Finance
Twelfth Edition

Brealey, Myers, and Allen
**Principles of Corporate Finance,
Concise**
Second Edition

Brealey, Myers, and Marcus
Fundamentals of Corporate Finance
Eighth Edition

Brooks
FinGame Online 5.0

Bruner
**Case Studies in Finance: Managing
for Corporate Value Creation**
Sixth Edition

Cornett, Adair, and Nofsinger
Finance: Applications and Theory
Third Edition

Cornett, Adair, and Nofsinger
M: Finance
Third Edition

DeMello
Cases in Finance
Second Edition

Grinblatt (editor)
**Stephen A. Ross, Mentor: Influence
through Generations**

Grinblatt and Titman
**Financial Markets and Corporate
Strategy**
Second Edition

Higgins
Analysis for Financial Management
Eleventh Edition

Ross, Westerfield, Jaffe, and Jordan
Corporate Finance
Eleventh Edition

Ross, Westerfield, Jaffe, and Jordan
**Corporate Finance: Core Principles
and Applications**
Fourth Edition

Ross, Westerfield, and Jordan
Essentials of Corporate Finance
Ninth Edition

Ross, Westerfield, and Jordan
Fundamentals of Corporate Finance
Eleventh Edition

Shefrin
**Behavioral Corporate Finance:
Decisions That Create Value**

INVESTMENTS

Bodie, Kane, and Marcus
Essentials of Investments
Tenth Edition

Bodie, Kane, and Marcus
Investments
Eleventh Edition

Hirt and Block
**Fundamentals of Investment
Management**
Tenth Edition

Jordan and Miller
**Fundamentals of Investments:
Valuation and Management**
Seventh Edition

Stewart, Piros, and Heisler
**Running Money: Professional
Portfolio Management**

Sundaram and Das
Derivatives: Principles and Practice
Second Edition

FINANCIAL INSTITUTIONS
AND MARKETS

Rose and Hudgins
**Bank Management and Financial
Services**
Ninth Edition

Rose and Marquis
Financial Institutions and Markets
Eleventh Edition

Saunders and Cornett
**Financial Institutions Management:
A Risk Management Approach**
Eighth Edition

Saunders and Cornett
Financial Markets and Institutions
Sixth Edition

INTERNATIONAL FINANCE

Eun and Resnick
International Financial Management
Seventh Edition

REAL ESTATE

Brueggeman and Fisher
Real Estate Finance and Investments
Fifteenth Edition

Ling and Archer
**Real Estate Principles: A Value
Approach**
Fourth Edition

FINANCIAL PLANNING AND
INSURANCE

Allen, Melone, Rosenbloom, and
Mahoney
**Retirement Plans: 401(k)s, IRAs,
and Other Deferred Compensation
Approaches**
Eleventh Edition

Altfest
Personal Financial Planning
Second Edition

Kapoor, Dlabay, and Hughes
**Focus on Personal Finance:
An Active Approach to Help You
Develop Successful Financial Skills**
Fifth Edition

Kapoor, Dlabay, and Hughes
Personal Finance
Eleventh Edition

Walker and Walker
**Personal Finance: Building Your
Future**
Second Edition

Essentials *of* Investments

Eleventh Edition

ZVI BODIE
Boston University

ALEX KANE
University of California, San Diego

ALAN J. MARCUS
Boston College

To our wives and eight wonderful daughters

ESSENTIALS OF INVESTMENTS, ELEVENTH EDITION

Published by McGraw-Hill Education, 2 Penn Plaza, New York, NY 10121. Copyright © 2019 by McGraw-Hill Education. All rights reserved. Printed in the United States of America. Previous editions © 2017, 2013, and 2010. No part of this publication may be reproduced or distributed in any form or by any means, or stored in a database or retrieval system, without the prior written consent of McGraw-Hill Education, including, but not limited to, in any network or other electronic storage or transmission, or broadcast for distance learning.

Some ancillaries, including electronic and print components, may not be available to customers outside the United States.

This book is printed on acid-free paper.

1 2 3 4 5 6 7 8 9 0 LWI 21 20 19 18

ISBN 978-1-26-001392-4
MHID 1-260-01392-8

Portfolio Manager: *Chuck Synovec*
Product Developer: *Allison Carroll*
Marketing Manager: *Natalie King*
Market Development Manager: *Trina Mauer*
Content Project Managers: *Angela Norris and Fran Simon*
Buyer: *Sandy Ludovissy*
Design: *Matt Diamond*
Content Licensing Specialists: *Lorraine Buczek*
Cover Image: *Paul Taylor/Getty Images*
Compositor: *SPi Global*

All credits appearing on page or at the end of the book are considered to be an extension of the copyright page.

Library of Congress Cataloging-in-Publication Data

Names: Bodie, Zvi, author. | Kane, Alex, 1942- author. | Marcus, Alan J., author.
Title: Essentials of investments / Zvi Bodie, Boston University, Alex Kane,
   University of California, San Diego, Alan J. Marcus, Boston College.
Description: Eleventh edition. | New York, NY : McGraw-Hill Education, [2019]
Identifiers: LCCN 2018023993 | ISBN 9781260013924 (alk. paper)
Subjects: LCSH: Investments.
Classification: LCC HG4521 .B563 2019 | DDC 332.6—dc23
LC record available at https://lccn.loc.gov/2018023993

The Internet addresses listed in the text were accurate at the time of publication. The inclusion of a website does not indicate an endorsement by the authors or McGraw-Hill Education, and McGraw-Hill Education does not guarantee the accuracy of the information presented at these sites.

mheducation.com/highered

Zvi Bodie

Boston University

Professor of Finance and Economics at Boston University School of Management

Zvi Bodie is Professor Emeritus at Boston University. He holds a PhD from the Massachusetts Institute of Technology and has served on the finance faculty at the Harvard Business School and MIT's Sloan School of Management. He has published widely in scholarly and professional journals on pension investment strategy and life-cycle asset-liability matching. In 2007 the Retirement Income Industry Association gave him its Lifetime Achievement Award for applied research.

Alex Kane

University of California, San Diego

Professor of Finance and Economics at the Graduate School of International Relations and Pacific Studies at the University of California, San Diego

Alex Kane holds a Ph.D. from the Stern School of Business of New York University and has been Visiting Professor at the Faculty of Economics, University of Tokyo; Graduate School of Business, Harvard; Kennedy School of Government, Harvard; and Research Associate, National Bureau of Economic Research. An author of many articles in finance and management journals, Professor Kane's research is mainly in corporate finance, portfolio management, and capital markets.

Alan J. Marcus

Boston College

Mario J. Gabelli Professor of Finance at the Carroll School of Management, Boston College

Alan Marcus received his Ph.D. from MIT, has been a Visiting Professor at MIT's Sloan School of Management and Athens Laboratory of Business Administration, and has served as a Research Fellow at the National Bureau of Economic Research, where he participated in both the Pension Economics and the Financial Markets and Monetary Economics Groups. Professor Marcus also spent two years at the Federal Home Loan Mortgage Corporation (Freddie Mac), where he helped to develop mortgage pricing and credit risk models. Professor Marcus has published widely in the fields of capital markets and portfolio theory. He currently serves on the Research Foundation Advisory Board of the CFA Institute.

Brief Contents

Contents

A Note from the Authors . . .

The past three decades witnessed rapid and profound change in the investment industry as well as a financial crisis of historic magnitude. The vast expansion of financial markets during this period was due in part to innovations in securitization and credit enhancement that gave birth to new trading strategies. These strategies were in turn made feasible by developments in communication and information technology, as well as by advances in the theory of investments.

Yet the crisis was also rooted in the cracks of these developments. Many of the innovations in security design facilitated high leverage and an exaggerated notion of the efficacy of risk transfer strategies. This engendered complacency about risk that was coupled with relaxation of regulation as well as reduced transparency that masked the precarious condition of many big players in the system.

Of necessity, our text has evolved along with financial markets. We devote considerable attention to recent breathtaking changes in market structure and trading technology. At the same time, however, many basic *principles* of investments remain important. We continue to organize the book around one basic theme—that security markets are nearly efficient, meaning that you should expect to find few obvious bargains in these markets. Given what we know about securities, their prices usually appropriately reflect their risk and return attributes; free lunches are few and far apart in markets as competitive as these. This starting point remains a powerful approach to security valuation. While the degree of market efficiency is and will always be a matter of debate, this first principle of valuation, specifically that in the absence of private information prices are the best guide to value, is still valid. Greater emphasis on risk analysis is the lesson woven into the text.

This text also places great emphasis on *asset allocation.* We prefer this emphasis for two important reasons. First, it corresponds to the procedure that most individuals actually follow when building an investment portfolio. Typically, you start with all of your money in a bank account, only then considering how much to invest in something riskier that might offer a higher expected return. The logical step at this point is to consider other risky asset classes, such as stocks, bonds, or real estate. This is an asset allocation decision. Second, in most cases the asset allocation choice is far more important than specific security-selection decisions in determining overall investment performance. Asset allocation is the primary determinant of the risk-return profile of the investment portfolio, and so it deserves primary attention in a study of investment policy.

Our book also focuses on investment analysis, which allows us to present the practical applications of investment theory and to convey insights of practical value. We provide a systematic collection of Excel spreadsheets that give you tools to explore concepts more deeply. These spreadsheets are available as part of the Connect resources for this text and provide a taste of the sophisticated analytic tools available to professional investors.

In our efforts to link theory to practice, we also have attempted to make our approach consistent with that of the CFA Institute. The Institute administers an education and certification program to candidates seeking designation as a Chartered Financial Analyst (CFA). The CFA Institute curriculum represents the consensus of a committee of distinguished scholars and practitioners regarding the core of knowledge required by the investment professional. We continue to include questions from previous CFA exams in our end-of-chapter problems as well as CFA-style questions derived from the Kaplan-Schweser CFA preparation courses.

This text will introduce you to the major issues of concern to all investors. It can give you the skills to conduct a sophisticated assessment of current issues and debates covered by both the popular media and more specialized finance journals. Whether you plan to become an investment professional or simply a sophisticated individual investor, you will find these skills essential.

Zvi Bodie
Alex Kane
Alan J. Marcus

Organization of the Eleventh Edition

Essentials of Investments, Eleventh Edition, is intended as a textbook on investment analysis most applicable for a student's first course in investments. The chapters are written in a modular format to give instructors the flexibility to either omit certain chapters or rearrange their order. The highlights in the margins describe updates and important features in this edition.

This part lays out the general framework for the investment process in a nontechnical manner. We discuss the major players in the financial markets and provide an overview of security types and trading mechanisms. These chapters make it possible for instructors to assign term projects analyzing securities early in the course.

Includes sections on securitization, the roots of the financial crisis, and the fallout from the crisis.

Extensive coverage of the rise of electronic markets, algorithmic and high-speed trading, and changes in market structure.

Includes coverage of innovations in exchange-traded funds.

This part contains the core of modern portfolio theory. For courses emphasizing security analysis, this part may be skipped without loss of continuity.

All data are updated and available on the web through the Connect resources. The data are used to discuss risk management and tail risk.

Introduces simple in-chapter spreadsheets that can be used to compute investment opportunity sets and the index model.

Includes single-factor as well as multifactor models.

Considers evidence both supporting and refuting efficient markets.

Contains extensive treatment of behavioral finance and provides an introduction to technical analysis.

This is the first of three parts on security valuation.

Includes material on sovereign credit default swaps.

Contains spreadsheet material on duration and convexity.

This part is presented in a "top-down" manner, starting with the broad macroeconomic environment before moving to more specific analysis.

Discusses how international political developments such as the sovereign debt crisis can have major impacts on economic prospects.

Contains free cash flow equity valuation models as well as a discussion of the pitfalls of discounted cash flow models.

Includes a top-down rationale for how ratio analysis can be organized to guide one's analysis of firm performance.

This part highlights how these markets have become crucial and integral to the financial universe and are major sources of innovation.

Offers thorough introduction to option payoffs, strategies, and securities with embedded options.

Includes an introduction to risk-neutral valuation methods and their implementation in the binomial option-pricing model.

This part unifies material on active management and is ideal for a closing-semester unit on applying theory to actual portfolio management.

Rigorous development of performance evaluation methods.

Provides evidence on political risk as well as the benefits of international diversification.

Updated assessment of hedge fund performance and the exposure of hedge funds to "black swans."

Employs extensive spreadsheet analysis of the interaction of taxes and inflation on long-term financial strategies.

Modeled after the CFA Institute curriculum, also includes guidelines on "How to Become a Chartered Financial Analyst."

Pedagogical Features

Learning Objectives

Each chapter begins with a summary of the chapter learning objectives, providing students with an overview of the concepts they should understand after reading the chapter. The end-of-chapter problems and CFA questions are tagged with the corresponding learning objective.

Chapter Overview

Each chapter begins with a brief narrative to explain the concepts that will be covered in more depth. Relevant websites related to chapter material can be found in Connect. These sites make it easy for students to research topics further and retrieve financial data and information.

You learned in Chapter 1 that the process of building an investment portfolio usually begins by deciding how much money to allocate to broad classes of assets, such as safe money market securities or bank accounts, longer-term bonds, stocks, or even asset classes such as real estate or precious metals. This process is called *asset allocation*. Within each class, the investor then selects specific assets from a more detailed menu. This is called *security selection*.

Each broad asset class contains many specific security types, and the many variations on a theme can be overwhelming. Our goal in this chapter is to introduce you to the important features of broad classes of securities. Toward

short-term, marketable, liquid, low-risk debt securities. Money market instruments sometimes are called *cash equivalents*, or just *cash* for short. Capital markets, in contrast, include longer-term and riskier securities. Securities in the capital market are much more diverse than those found within the money market. For this reason, we will subdivide the capital market into three segments: longer-term debt markets, equity markets, and derivative markets in which options and futures trade.

We first describe money market instruments. We then move on to debt and equity securities. We explain the structure of various stock market indexes in this chapter because market benchmark portfolios play an important

Key Terms in the Margin

Key terms are indicated in color and defined in the margin the first time the term is used. A full list of key terms is included in the end-of-chapter materials.

Publicly Traded Companies

initial public offering (IPO)
First public sale of stock by a formerly private company.

When a private firm decides that it wishes to raise capital from a wide range of investors, it may decide to *go public*. This means that it will sell its securities to the general public and allow those investors to freely trade those shares in established securities markets. This first issue of shares to the general public is called the firm's **initial public offering (IPO)**. Later, the firm may go back to the public and issue additional shares. A *seasoned equity offering* is the sale of additional shares in firms that already are publicly traded. For example, a sale by Apple of new shares of stock would be considered a seasoned new issue.

Numbered Equations

Key equations are called out in the text and identified by equation numbers. These key formulas are listed at the end of each chapter. Equations that are frequently used are also featured on the text's end sheets for convenient reference.

be necessary to provide an after-tax return equal to that of municipals. To derive this value, we set after-tax yields equal and solve for the *equivalent taxable yield* of the tax-exempt bond. This is the rate a taxable bond would need to offer in order to match the after-tax yield on the tax-free municipal.

$$r_{\text{taxable}}(1 - t) = r_{\text{muni}} \qquad (2.1)$$

or

$$r_{\text{taxable}} = \frac{r_{\text{muni}}}{1 - t} \qquad (2.2)$$

Thus, the equivalent taxable yield is simply the tax-free rate divided by $1 - t$. Table 2.2 presents equivalent taxable yields for several municipal yields and tax rates.

On the MARKET FRONT

THE LIBOR SCANDALS

LIBOR was designed initially as a survey of interbank lending rates but soon became a key determinant of short-term interest rates with far-reaching significance. More than $350 trillion of derivative contracts have payoffs tied to it, and many trillion dollars of loans and bonds with floating interest rates linked to LIBOR are currently outstanding. LIBOR is quoted for loans in five currencies (the U.S. dollar, yen, euro, U.K. pound, and Swiss franc) for maturities ranging from a day to a year, although three months is the most common.

However, LIBOR is not a rate at which actual transactions occur; instead, it is just a survey of "estimated" borrowing rates, and this has made it vulnerable to manipulation. Several large banks are asked to report the rate at which they *claim* they can borrow in the interbank market. Outliers are trimmed from the sample of responses, and LIBOR is calculated as the average of the mid-range estimates.

Over time, several problems surfaced. First, it appeared that many banks understated the rates at which they claimed they could borrow in an effort to make themselves look financially stronger. Other surveys that asked for estimates of the rates at which *other* banks could borrow resulted in higher values. Moreover, LIBOR did not seem to reflect current market conditions. A majority of LIBOR submissions were unchanged from day to day even when other interest rates fluctuated, and LIBOR spreads showed surprisingly low correlation with other measures of credit risk.

Even worse, once the market came under scrutiny, it emerged that participating banks were colluding to manipulate their LIBOR

wanted to see higher or lower submissions. Members of this informal cartel essentially set up a "favor bank" to help each other move the survey average up or down depending on their trading positions.

More than $6 billion of fines have been paid, among them, Deutsche Bank ($2.5 billion), UBS ($1.5 billion), Royal Bank of Scotland ($1.1 billion), Rabobank ($1 billion), and SocGen ($600 million). But government fines may be only the beginning. A federal appeals court in 2016 ruled that private lawsuits involving antitrust violations may proceed. Borrowers paying an interest rate tied to LIBOR argue that they were harmed by the collusion of participating banks to coordinate rates.

Several reforms have been suggested and some have been implemented. The British Bankers Association, which until recently ran the LIBOR survey, yielded responsibility for LIBOR to British regulators. LIBOR quotes in less active currencies and maturities, where collusion is easier, have been eliminated. More substantive proposals would replace the survey rates with ones based on actual, verifiable transactions—that is, real loans. British regulators have expressed their wish to phase out LIBOR by 2021. Two primary contenders to replace it are SONIA (Sterling Overnight Interbank Average Rate), an overnight interest rate in the U.K. market and, for U.S. dollar rates, the rate on repurchase agreements on Treasury securities.

These proposals leave some important questions unanswered. For example, if LIBOR is phased out, what will happen to LIBOR-based long-term contracts with maturities that extend beyond 2021? For example, LIBOR is the most common index for adjustable rate mortgages, most of which have maturities of 30 years

---

On the Market Front Boxes
Current articles from financial publications such as *The Wall Street Journal* are featured as boxed readings. Each box is referred to within the narrative of the text, and its real-world relevance to the chapter material is clearly defined.

CONCEPT check	**2.5**	Reconsider companies XYZ and ABC from Concept Check Question 2.4. Calculate the percentage change in the market value–weighted index. Compare that to the rate of return of a portfolio that holds $500 of ABC stock for every $100 of XYZ stock (i.e., an index portfolio).

Concept Checks
These self-test questions in the body of the chapter enable students to determine whether the preceding material has been understood and then reinforce understanding before students read further. Detailed Solutions to the Concept Checks are found at the end of each chapter.

EXAMPLE 2.4

Value-Weighted Indexes

To illustrate how value-weighted indexes are computed, look again at Table 2.3. The final value of all outstanding stock in our two-stock universe is $690 million. The initial value was $600 million. Therefore, if the initial level of a market value–weighted index of stocks ABC and XYZ were set equal to an arbitrarily chosen starting value such as 100, the index value at year-end would be 100 × (690/600) = 115. The increase in the index would reflect the 15% return earned on a portfolio consisting of those two stocks held in proportion to outstanding market values.

Unlike the price-weighted index, the value-weighted index gives more weight to ABC. Whereas the price-weighted index fell because it was dominated by higher-priced XYZ, the value-weighted index rose because it gave more weight to ABC, the stock with the higher total market value.

Note also from Tables 2.3 and 2.4 that market value–weighted indexes are unaffected by stock splits. The total market value of the outstanding XYZ stock increases from $100 million to $110 million regardless of the stock split, thereby rendering the split irrelevant to the performance of the index.

Numbered Examples
Numbered and titled examples are integrated in each chapter. Using the worked-out solutions to these examples as models, students can learn how to solve specific problems step-by-step as well as gain insight into general principles by seeing how they are applied to answer concrete questions.

Excel Integration

Excel Applications

Since many courses now require students to perform analyses in spreadsheet format, Excel has been integrated throughout the book. It is used in examples as well as in this chapter feature which shows students how to create and manipulate spreadsheets to solve specific problems. This feature starts with an example presented in the chapter, briefly discusses how a spreadsheet can be valuable for investigating the topic, shows a sample spreadsheet, and asks students to apply the data to answer questions. These applications also direct the student to the Web to work with an interactive version of the spreadsheet. The spreadsheet files are available for download in Connect; available spreadsheets are denoted by an icon. As extra guidance, the spreadsheets include a comment feature that documents both inputs and outputs. Solutions for these exercises are located on the password-protected instructor site only, so instructors can assign these exercises either for homework or just for practice.

Excel application spreadsheets are available for the following:

Chapter 3:	Buying on Margin; Short Sales
Chapter 11:	Immunization; Convexity
Chapter 15:	Options, Stock, and Lending; Straddles and Spreads
Chapter 17:	Spot-Futures Parity
Chapter 18:	Performance Measurement; Performance Attribution
Chapter 19:	International Diversification

Spreadsheet exhibit templates are also available for the following:

Chapter 5:	Spreadsheet 5.1
Chapter 6:	Spreadsheets 6.1–6.6
Chapter 10:	Spreadsheets 10.1 & 10.2
Chapter 11:	Spreadsheets 11.1 & 11.2
Chapter 13:	Spreadsheets 13.1 & 13.2
Chapter 16:	Spreadsheet 16.1
Chapter 21:	Spreadsheets 21.1–21.10

EXCEL APPLICATIONS: Buying on Margin

This spreadsheet is available in Connect

The Excel spreadsheet model below makes it easy to analyze the impacts of different margin levels and the volatility of stock prices. It also allows you to compare return on investment for a margin trade with a trade using no borrowed funds.

	A	B	C	D	E	F	G	H
1								
2			Action or Formula for Column B	Ending St Price	Return on Investment		Ending St Price	Return with No Margin
3								
4	Initial Equity Investment	$10,000.00	Enter data		−42.00%			−19.00%
5	Amount Borrowed	$10,000.00	(B4/B10)−B4	$20.00	−122.00%		$20.00	−59.00%
6	Initial Stock Price	$50.00	Enter data	25.00	−102.00%		25.00	−49.00%
7	Shares Purchased	400	(B4/B10)/B6	30.00	−82.00%		30.00	−39.00%
8	Ending Stock Price	$40.00	Enter data	35.00	−62.00%		35.00	−29.00%
9	Cash Dividends During Hold Per.	$0.50	Enter data	40.00	−42.00%		40.00	−19.00%
10	Initial Margin Percentage	50.00%	Enter data	45.00	−22.00%		45.00	−9.00%
11	Maintenance Margin Percentage	30.00%	Enter data	50.00	−2.00%		50.00	1.00%
12				55.00	18.00%		55.00	11.00%
13	Rate on Margin Loan	8.00%	Enter data	60.00	38.00%		60.00	21.00%
14	Holding Period in Months	6	Enter data	65.00	58.00%		65.00	31.00%
15				70.00	78.00%		70.00	41.00%
16	**Return on Investment**			75.00	98.00%		75.00	51.00%
17	Capital Gain on Stock	−$4,000.00	B7*(B8−B6)	80.00	118.00%		80.00	61.00%
18	Dividends	$200.00	B7*B9					
19	Interest on Margin Loan	$400.00	B5*(B14/12)*B13					
20	Net Income	−$4,200.00	B17+B18−B19			LEGEND:		
21	Initial Investment	$10,000.00	B4			Enter data		
22	Return on Investment	−42.00%	B20/B21			Value calculated		

Excel Questions

1. Suppose you buy 100 shares of stock initially selling for $50, borrowing 25% of the necessary funds from your broker; that is, the initial margin on your purchase is 25%. You pay an interest rate of 8% on margin loans.

   a. How much of your own money do you invest? How much do you borrow from your broker?

   b. What will be your rate of return for the following stock prices at the end of a one-year holding period? (i) $40; (ii) $50; (iii) $60.

End-of-Chapter Features

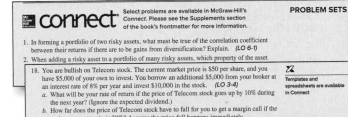

1. In forming a portfolio of two risky assets, what must be true of the correlation coefficient between their returns if there are to be gains from diversification? Explain. *(LO 6-1)*

2. When adding a risky asset to a portfolio of many risky assets, which property of the asset

18. You are bullish on Telecom stock. The current market price is $50 per share, and you have $5,000 of your own to invest. You borrow an additional $5,000 from your broker at an interest rate of 8% per year and invest $10,000 in the stock. *(LO 3-4)*

   Templates and spreadsheets are available in Connect

   a. What will be your rate of return if the price of Telecom stock goes up by 10% during the next year? (Ignore the expected dividend.)

   b. How far does the price of Telecom stock have to fall for you to get a margin call if the maintenance margin is 30%? Assume the price fall happens immediately.

Problem Sets

We strongly believe that practice in solving problems is a critical part of learning investments, so we provide a good variety. We have arranged questions by level of difficulty.

Excel Problems

Select end-of-chapter questions require the use of Excel. These problems are denoted with an icon. Templates and spreadsheets are available in Connect.

KAPLAN SCHWESER

10. A market order has: *(LO 3-2)*
    a. Price uncertainty but not execution uncertainty.
    b. Both price uncertainty and execution uncertainty.
    c. Execution uncertainty but not price uncertainty.

KAPLAN SCHWESER

11. Where would an illiquid security in a developing country *most likely* trade? *(LO 3-3)*
    a. Broker markets.
    b. Electronic crossing networks.
    c. Electronic limit-order markets.

Kaplan-Schweser Problems

Each chapter contains select CFA-style questions derived from the Kaplan-Schweser CFA preparation courses. These questions are tagged with an icon for easy reference.

CFA Problems

1. The following multiple-choice problems are based on questions that appeared in past CFA examinations.

   a. A bond with a call feature: *(LO 10-4)*
   (1) Is attractive because the immediate receipt of principal plus premium produces a high return.
   (2) Is more apt to be called when interest rates are high because the interest saving will be greater.
   (3) Will usually have a higher yield to maturity than a similar noncallable bond.
   (4) None of the above.

   CFA® PROBLEMS

CFA Problems

We provide several questions from past CFA exams in applicable chapters. These questions represent the kinds of questions that professionals in the field believe are relevant to the practicing money manager. Appendix B, at the back of the book, lists each CFA question and the level and year of the CFA Exam it was included in, for easy reference when studying for the exam.

WEB *master*

1. Go to the website for The Walt Disney Co (DIS) and download its most recent annual report (its 10-K). Locate the company's Consolidated Balance Sheets and answer these questions:
   a. How much preferred stock is Disney authorized to issue? How much has been issued?
   b. How much common stock is Disney authorized to issue? How many shares are currently outstanding?
   c. Search for the term "Financing Activities." What is the total amount of borrowing listed for Disney? How much of this is medium-term notes?
   d. What other types of debt does Disney have outstanding?

2. Not all stock market indexes are created equal. Different methods are used to calculate various indexes, and different indexes will yield different assessments of "market perfor-

Web Master Exercises

These exercises are a great way to allow students to test their skills on the Internet. Each exercise consists of an activity related to practical problems and real-world scenarios.

Supplements

MCGRAW-HILL *CONNECT*®

Less Managing. More Teaching. Greater Learning.
McGraw-Hill *Connect* is an online assignment and assessment solution that connects students with the tools and resources they'll need to achieve success.

McGraw-Hill *Connect* helps prepare students for their future by enabling faster learning, more efficient studying, and higher retention of knowledge.

McGraw-Hill *Connect* Features
Connect offers a number of powerful tools and features to make managing assignments easier, so faculty can spend more time teaching. With *Connect,* students can engage with their coursework anytime and anywhere, making the learning process more accessible and efficient. *Connect* offers you the features described below.

Simple Assignment Management
With *Connect,* creating assignments is easier than ever, so you can spend more time teaching and less time managing. The assignment management function enables you to:

- Create and deliver assignments easily with selectable end-of-chapter questions and Test Bank items.
- Streamline lesson planning, student progress reporting, and assignment grading to make classroom management more efficient than ever.
- Go paperless with the eBook and online submission and grading of student assignments.

Smart Grading
When it comes to studying, time is precious. *Connect* helps students learn more efficiently by providing feedback and practice material when they need it, where they need it. When it comes to teaching, your time also is precious. The grading function enables you to:

- Have assignments scored automatically, giving students immediate feedback on their work and side-by-side comparisons with correct answers.
- Access and review each response; manually change grades or leave comments for students to review.
- Reinforce classroom concepts with practice tests and instant quizzes.

Instructor Library
The *Connect* Instructor Library is your repository for additional resources to improve student engagement in and out of class. You can select and use any asset that enhances your lecture.

This library contains information about the book and the authors, as well as all of the instructor supplements for this text, including:

- **Instructor's Manual** Revised by Nicholas Racculia, St. Vincent College, this instructional tool provides an integrated learning approach revised for this edition. Each chapter includes a Chapter Overview, Learning Objectives, and Presentation of Material that outlines and organizes the material around the PowerPoint Presentation.

- **Solutions Manual** The Solutions Manual, carefully revised by the authors with assistance from Nicholas Racculia, contains solutions to all basic, intermediate, and challenge problems found at the end of each chapter.

- **Test Bank** Prepared by Jon Farlin, Ohio Dominican University, the Test Bank contains more than 1,200 questions and includes over 300 new questions. Each question is ranked by level of difficulty (easy, medium, hard) and tagged with the learning objective, the topic, AACSB, and Bloom's Taxonomy, which allows greater flexibility in creating a test. The Test Bank is assignable within Connect and available as a Word file or within EZ Test Online.

- **PowerPoint Presentations** These presentation slides, developed by Nicholas Racculia, contain figures and tables from the text, key points, and summaries in a visually stimulating collection of slides. These slides follow the order of the chapters, but if you have PowerPoint software, you may customize the program to fit your lecture.

Diagnostic and Adaptive Learning of Concepts: LearnSmart and SmartBook

LEARNSMART® Students want to make the best use of their study time. The LearnSmart adaptive self-study technology within *Connect* provides students with a seamless combination of practice, assessment, and remediation for every concept in the textbook. LearnSmart's intelligent software adapts to every student response and automatically delivers concepts that advance students' understanding while reducing time devoted to the concepts already mastered. The result for every student is the fastest path to mastery of the chapter concepts. LearnSmart:

- Applies an intelligent concept engine to identify the relationships between concepts and to serve new concepts to each student only when he or she is ready.
- Adapts automatically to each student, so students spend less time on the topics they understand and practice more those they have yet to master.
- Provides continual reinforcement and remediation, but gives only as much guidance as students need.
- Integrates diagnostics as part of the learning experience.
- Enables you to assess which concepts students have efficiently learned on their own, thus freeing class time for more applications and discussion.

SMARTBOOK® SmartBook®, powered by LearnSmart, is the first and only adaptive reading experience designed to change the way students read and learn. It creates a personalized reading experience by highlighting the most impactful concepts a student needs to learn at that moment in time. As a student engages with SmartBook, the reading experience continuously adapts by highlighting content based on what the student knows and doesn't know. This ensures that the focus is on the content he or she needs to learn, while simultaneously promoting long-term retention of material. Use SmartBook's real-time reports to quickly identify the concepts that require more attention from individual students—or the entire class. The end result? Students are more engaged with course content, can better prioritize their time, and come to class ready to participate.

Student Study Center

The *Connect* Student Study Center is the place for students to access additional resources. The Student Study Center:

- Offers students quick access to lectures, course materials, eBooks, and more.
- Provides instant practice material and study questions, easily accessible with LearnSmart and SmartBook.
- Gives students access to the Excel templates and files that accompany the text.

Student Progress Tracking

Connect keeps instructors informed about how each student, section, and class is performing, allowing for more productive use of lecture and office hours. The progress-tracking function enables you to:

- View scored work immediately and track individual or group performance with assignment and grade reports.
- Access an instant view of student or class performance relative to learning objectives.

Lecture Capture through Tegrity Campus

For an additional charge, Lecture Capture offers new ways for students to focus on the in-class discussion, knowing they can revisit important topics later. This can be delivered through Connect or separately. See below for more details.

For more information about Connect, go to **connect.mheducation.com** or contact your local McGraw-Hill sales representative.

TEGRITY CAMPUS: LECTURES 24/7

Tegrity Campus is a service that makes class time available 24/7 by automatically capturing every lecture in a searchable format for students to review when they study and complete assignments. With a simple one-click start-and-stop process, you capture all computer screens and corresponding audio. Students can replay any part of any class with easy-to-use browser-based viewing on a PC or Mac.

Educators know that the more students can see, hear, and experience class resources, the better they learn. In fact, studies prove it. With Tegrity Campus, students quickly recall key moments by using Tegrity Campus's unique search feature. This search helps students efficiently find what they need, when they need it, across an entire semester of class recordings. Help turn all your students' study time into learning moments immediately supported by your lecture.

To learn more about Tegrity, watch a 2-minute Flash demo at **http://tegritycampus.mhhe.com.**

Assurance of Learning Ready

Many educational institutions today are focused on the notion of *assurance of learning,* an important element of many accreditation standards. *Essentials of Investments,* Eleventh Edition, is designed specifically to support your assurance-of-learning initiatives with a simple, yet powerful, solution.

Each chapter in the book begins with a list of numbered learning objectives, which also appear in the end-of-chapter problems. Every Test Bank question for *Essentials of Investments* maps to a specific chapter learning objective in the textbook. Each Test Bank question also identifies the topic area, level of difficulty, Bloom's Taxonomy level, and AACSB skill area. You can use our Test Bank software, *EZ Test Online,* or *Connect* to easily

search for learning objectives that directly relate to the learning objectives for your course. You can then use the reporting features of *EZ Test* to aggregate student results in similar fashion, making the collection and presentation of assurance-of-learning data simple and easy.

AACSB Statement

McGraw-Hill/Irwin is a proud corporate member of AACSB International. Understanding the importance and value of AACSB accreditation, *Essentials of Investments,* Eleventh Edition, recognizes the curricula guidelines detailed in the AACSB standards for business accreditation by connecting selected questions in the Test Bank to the general knowledge and skill guidelines in the AACSB standards.

The statements contained in *Essentials of Investments,* Eleventh Edition, are provided only as a guide for the users of this textbook. The AACSB leaves content coverage and assessment within the purview of individual schools, the mission of the school, and the faculty. While *Essentials of Investments,* Eleventh Edition, and the teaching package make no claim of any specific AACSB qualification or evaluation, we have labeled selected questions according to the six general knowledge and skills areas.

McGraw-Hill Customer Care Contact Information

At McGraw-Hill, we understand that getting the most from new technology can be challenging. That's why our services don't stop after you purchase our products. You can e-mail our Product Specialists 24 hours a day to get product-training online. Or you can search our knowledge bank of Frequently Asked Questions on our support website. For Customer Support, call **800-331-5094** or visit www.mhhe.com/support. One of our Technical Support Analysts will be able to assist you in a timely fashion.

Acknowledgments

We received help from many people as we prepared this book. An insightful group of reviewers commented on this and previous editions of this text. Their comments and suggestions improved the exposition of the material considerably. These reviewers all deserve special thanks for their contributions.

Anna Agapova *Florida Atlantic University, Boca Raton*

Sandro C. Andrade *University of Miami*

Bala Arshanapalli *Indiana University Northwest*

Rasha Ashraf *Georgia State University*

Anand Bhattacharya *Arizona State University, Tempe*

Randall S. Billingsley *Virginia Polytechnic Institute and State University*

Howard Bohnen *St. Cloud State University*

Paul Bolster *Northeastern University*

Lyle Bowlin *University of Northern Iowa*

Brian Boyer *Brigham Young University*

Nicole Boyson *Northeastern University*

Ben Branch *University of Massachussets, Amherst*

Thor W. Bruce *University of Miami*

Timothy Burch *University of Miama, Coral Gables*

Alyce R. Campbell *University of Oregon*

Mark Castelino *Rutgers University*

Greg Chaudoin *Loyola University*

Ji Chen *University of Colorado, Denver*

Joseph Chen *University of California, Davis*

Mustafa Chowdhury *Louisiana State University*

Ron Christner *Loyola University, New Orleans*

Shane Corwin *University of Notre Dame*

Brent Dalrymple *University of Central Florida*

Praveen Das *University of Louisiana, Lafayette*

Diane Del Guercio *University of Oregon*

David C. Distad *University of California at Berkeley*

Gary R. Dokes *University of San Diego*

James Dow *California State University, Northridge*

Robert Dubil *University of Utah, Salt Lake City*

John Earl *University of Richmond*

Jeff Edwards *Portland Community College*

Peter D. Ekman *Kansas State University*

John Elder *Colorado State University*

Richard Elliott *University of Utah, Salt Lake City*

James Falter *Franklin University*

Philip Fanara *Howard University*

Joseph Farinella *University of North Carolina, Wilmington*

Greg Feigel *University of Texas, Arlington*

James F. Feller *Middle Tennessee State University*

James Forjan *York College*

Beverly Frickel *University of Nebraska, Kearney*

Ken Froewiss *New York University*

Phillip Ghazanfari *California State University, Pomona*

Eric Girard *Siena College*

Richard A. Grayson *University of Georgia*

Greg Gregoriou *SUNY, Plattsburgh*

Richard D. Gritta *University of Portland*

Anthony Yanxiang Gu *SUNY Geneseo*

Deborah Gunthorpe *University of Tennessee*

Weiyu Guo *University of Nebraska, Omaha*

Pamela Hall *Western Washington University*

Thomas Hamilton *St. Mary's University*

Bing Han *University of Texas, Austin*

Yvette Harman *Miami University of Ohio*

Gay Hatfield *University of Mississippi*

Larry C. Holland *Oklahoma State University*

Harris Hordon *New Jersey City University*

Stephen Huffman *University of Wisconsin, Oshkosh*

Ron E. Hutchins *Eastern Michigan University*

David Ikenberry *University of Illinois, Urbana-Champaign*

A. Can (John) Inci *Florida State University*

Victoria Javine *University of Southern Alabama*

Nancy Jay *Mercer University*

Richard Johnson *Colorado State University*

Douglas Kahl *University of Akron*

Richard J. Kish *Lehigh University*

Tom Krueger *University of Wisconsin, La Crosse*

Donald Kummer *University of Missouri, St. Louis*

Merouane Lakehal-Ayat *St. John Fisher College*

Reinhold P. Lamb *University of North Florida*

Angeline Lavin *University of South Dakota*

Hongbok Lee *Western Illinois University*

Kartono Liano *Mississippi State University*

Jim Locke *Northern Virginia Community College*

John Loughlin *St. Louis University*

David Louton *Bryant College*

David Loy *Illinois State University*

Christian Lundblad *Indiana University*
Robert A. Lutz *University of Utah*
Laurian Casson Lytle *University of Wisconsin, Whitewater*
Leo Mahoney *Bryant College*
Herman Manakyan *Salisbury State University*
Steven V. Mann *University of South Carolina*
Jeffrey A. Manzi *Ohio University*
James Marchand *Westminster College*
Robert J. Martel *Bentley College*
Linda J. Martin *Arizona State University*
Stanley A. Martin *University of Colorado, Boulder*
Thomas Mertens *New York University*
Edward Miller *University of New Orleans*
Michael Milligan *California State University, Fullerton*
Rosemary Minyard *Pfeiffer University*
Walter Morales *Louisiana State University*
Mbodja Mougoue *Wayne State University*
Shabnam Mousavi *Georgia State University*
Majed Muhtaseb *California State Polytechnic University*
Deborah Murphy *University of Tennessee, Knoxville*
Mike Murray *Winona State University*
C. R. Narayanaswamy *Georgia Institute of Technology*
Walt Nelson *Missouri State University*
Karyn Neuhauser *SUNY, Plattsburgh*
Mike Nugent *SUNY Stonybrook*
Raj Padmaraj *Bowling Green University*
Elisabeta Pana *Illinois Wesleyan University*
John C. Park *Frostburg State University*
Percy Poon *University of Nevada, Las Vegas*
Robert B. Porter *University of Florida*
Dev Prasad *University of Massachusetts, Lowell*
Rose Prasad *Central Michigan University*
Elias A. Raad *Ithaca College*
Murli Rajan *University of Scranton*
Kumoli Ramakrishnan *University of South Dakota*
Rathin Rathinasamy *Ball State University*
Craig Rennie *University of Arkansas*
Cecilia Ricci *Montclair University*
Craig Ruff *Georgia State University*
Tom Sanders *University of Miami*
Jeff Sandri *University of Colorado, Boulder*
David Schirm *John Carroll University*
Chi Sheh *University of Houston*
Ravi Shukla *Syracuse University*
Allen B. Snively, Jr. *Indiana University*
Andrew Spieler *Hofstra University*
Kim Staking *Colorado State University*
Edwin Stuart *Southeastern Oklahoma State University*
George S. Swales *Southwest Missouri State University*
Paul Swanson *University of Cincinnati*
Bruce Swensen *Adelphi University*
Glenn Tanner *University of Hawaii*

John L. Teall *Pace University*
Anne Macy Terry *West Texas A&M University*
Donald J. Thompson *Georgia State University*
Steven Thorley *Brigham Young University*
James Tipton *Baylor University*
Steven Todd *DePaul University*
Michael Toyne *Northeastern State University*
William Trainor *Western Kentucky University*
Andrey Ukhov *Indiana University, Bloomington*
Cevdet Uruk *University of Memphis*
Joseph Vu *DePaul University*
Jessica Wachter *New York University*
Joe Walker *University of Alabama at Birmingham*
Richard Warr *North Carolina State University*
William Welch *Florida International University*
Russel Wermers *University of Maryland*
Andrew L. Whitaker *North Central College*
Howard Whitney *Franklin University*
Alayna Williamson *University of Utah, Salt Lake City*
Michael E. Williams *University of Texas at Austin*
Michael Willoughby *University of California, San Diego*
Tony Wingler *University of North Carolina*
Annie Wong *Western Connecticut State University*
David Wright *University of Wisconsin, Parkside*
Richard H. Yanow *North Adams State College*
Tarek Zaher *Indiana State University*
Allan Zebedee *San Diego State University*
Zhong-guo Zhou *California State University, Northridge*
Thomas J. Zwirlein *University of Colorado, Colorado Springs*

For granting us permission to include many of their examination questions in the text, we are grateful to the CFA Institute.

A special thanks goes to the talented experts who help us develop and review the instructor materials and online content in Connect and LearnSmart, including Vincent Muscolino, Anna Kovalenko, James Forjan, Hyuna Park, John Farlin, Marc-Anthony Isaacs, Nicholas Racculia, and Dongmei Li.

Much credit is also due to the development and production team of McGraw-Hill Education: Chuck Synovec, Executive Portfolio Manager; Allison McCabe, Product Developer; Fran Simon, Core Project Manager; Angela Norris, Assessment Project Manager; Natalie King, Marketing Manager; Dave O'Donnell, Marketing Specialist; Beth Thole, Content Licensing Specialist, and Matt Diamond, Designer.

Finally, once again, our most important debts are to Judy, Hava, and Sheryl for their unflagging support.

Zvi Bodie
Alex Kane
Alan J. Marcus

Elements of Investments

Even a cursory glance at *The Wall Street Journal* reveals a bewildering collection of securities, markets, and financial institutions. But although it may appear so, the financial environment is not chaotic: There is rhyme and reason behind the vast array of financial instruments and the markets in which they trade.

These introductory chapters provide a bird's-eye view of the investing environment. We will give you a tour of the major types of markets in which securities trade, the trading process, and the major players in these arenas. You will see that both markets and securities have evolved to meet the changing and complex needs of different participants in the financial system.

Markets innovate and compete with each other for traders' business just as vigorously as competitors in other industries. The competition between NASDAQ, the New York Stock Exchange (NYSE), and several other electronic and non-U.S. exchanges is fierce and public.

Trading practices can mean big money to investors. The explosive growth of online electronic trading has saved them many millions of dollars in trading costs. On the other hand, some worry that lightning-fast electronic trading has put the stability of security markets at risk. All agree, however, that these advances will continue to change the face of the investments industry, and Wall Street firms are scrambling to formulate strategies that respond to these changes.

These chapters will give you a good foundation with which to understand the basic types of securities and financial markets as well as how trading in those markets is conducted.

Investments: Background and Issues

Learning Objectives

LO 1-1 Define an investment.

LO 1-2 Distinguish between real assets and financial assets.

LO 1-3 Explain the economic functions of financial markets and how various securities are related to the governance of the corporation.

LO 1-4 Describe the major steps in the construction of an investment portfolio.

LO 1-5 Identify different types of financial markets and the major participants in each of those markets.

LO 1-6 Explain the causes and consequences of the financial crisis of 2008.

investment

Commitment of current resources in the expectation of deriving greater resources in the future.

An **investment** is the *current* commitment of money or other resources in the expectation of reaping *future* benefits. For example, an individual might purchase shares of stock anticipating that the future proceeds from the shares will justify both the time that her money is tied up as well as the risk of the investment. The time you will spend studying this text (not to mention its cost) also is an investment. You are forgoing either current leisure or the income you could be earning at a job in the expectation that your future career will be sufficiently enhanced to justify this commitment of time and effort. While these two investments differ in many ways, they share one key attribute that is central to all investments: You sacrifice something of value now, expecting to benefit from that sacrifice later.

This text can help you become an informed practitioner of investments. We will focus on investments in securities such as stocks, bonds, or derivative contracts, but much of what we discuss will be useful in the analysis of any type of investment. The text will provide you with background in the organization of various securities markets, will survey the valuation and risk management principles useful in particular markets, such as those for bonds or stocks, and will introduce you to the principles of portfolio construction.

Broadly speaking, this chapter addresses three topics that will provide a useful perspective for the material that is to come later. First, before delving into the topic of "investments," we consider the role of financial assets in the economy. We discuss the relationship between securities and the "real" assets that actually produce goods and services for consumers, and we consider why financial assets are important to the functioning of a developed economy. Given this background, we then take a first look at the types of decisions that confront investors as they assemble a portfolio of assets. These investment decisions are made in an environment where higher returns usually can be obtained only at the price of greater risk and in which it is rare to find assets that are so mispriced as to be obvious bargains. These themes—the risk-return trade-off and the efficient pricing of financial assets—are central to the investment process, so it is worth

pausing for a brief discussion of their implications as we begin the text. These implications will be fleshed out in much greater detail in later chapters.

We provide an overview of the organization of security markets as well as the various players that participate in those markets. Together, these introductions should give you a feel for who the major participants are in the securities markets as well as the setting in which they act. Finally, we discuss the financial crisis that began playing out in 2007 and peaked in 2008. The crisis dramatically illustrated the connections between the financial system and the "real" side of the economy. We look at the origins of the crisis and the lessons that may be drawn about systemic risk. We close the chapter with an overview of the remainder of the text.

1.1 REAL ASSETS VERSUS FINANCIAL ASSETS

The material wealth of a society is ultimately determined by the productive capacity of its economy, that is, the goods and services its members can create. This capacity is a function of the **real assets** of the economy: the land, buildings, equipment, and knowledge that can be used to produce goods and services.

In contrast to such real assets are **financial assets** such as stocks and bonds. Such securities are no more than sheets of paper or, far more likely, computer entries and do not directly contribute to the productive capacity of the economy. Instead, these assets are the means by which individuals in well-developed economies hold their claims on real assets. Financial assets are claims to the income generated by real assets (or claims on income from the government). If we cannot own our own auto plant (a real asset), we can still buy shares in Ford or Toyota (financial assets) and, thereby, share in the income derived from the production of automobiles.

While real assets generate net income to the economy, financial assets simply define the allocation of income or wealth among investors. Individuals can choose between consuming their wealth today or investing for the future. If they choose to invest, they may place their wealth in financial assets by purchasing various securities. When investors buy these securities from companies, the firms use the money so raised to pay for real assets, such as plant, equipment, technology, or inventory. So investors' returns on securities ultimately come from the income produced by the real assets that were financed by the issuance of those securities.

The distinction between real and financial assets is apparent when we compare the balance sheet of U.S. households, shown in Table 1.1, with the composition of national wealth in the United States, shown in Table 1.2. Household wealth includes financial assets such as bank accounts, corporate stock, or bonds. However, debt securities, which are financial assets of the households that hold them, are *liabilities* of the issuers of those securities. For example, a bond that you treat as an asset because it gives you a claim on interest income and repayment of principal from Toyota is a liability of Toyota, which is obligated to make these payments.

real assets
Assets used to produce goods and services.

financial assets
Claims on real assets or the income generated by them.

TABLE 1.1	Balance sheet of U.S. households

Assets	$ Billion	% Total	Liabilities and Net Worth	$ Billion	% Total
Real assets					
Real estate	$ 26,528	24.6%	Mortgages	$ 9,994	9.3%
Consumer durables	5,418	5.0	Consumer credit	3,765	3.5
Other	485	0.4	Bank and other loans	998	0.9
Total real assets	$ 32,431	30.1%	Other	348	0.3
			Total liabilities	$ 15,104	14.0%
Financial assets					
Deposits	$ 10,369	9.6%			
Life insurance reserves	1,368	1.3			
Pension reserves	22,259	20.6			
Corporate equity	15,874	14.7			
Equity in noncorp. business	11,249	10.4			
Mutual fund shares	7,875	7.3			
Debt securities	5,239	4.9			
Other	1,244	1.2			
Total financial assets	75,478	69.9	Net worth	$ 92,805	86.0%
Total	$107,910	100.0%		$107,910	100.0%

Note: Column sums may differ from total because of rounding error.

Source: *Flow of Funds Accounts of the United States,* Board of Governors of the Federal Reserve System, March 2017.

TABLE 1.2	Domestic net worth

Assets	$ Billion
Commercial real estate	$18,335
Residential real estate	33,061
Equipment and intellectual property	8,449
Inventories	2,523
Consumer durables	5,418
Total	$67,786

Note: Column sums may differ from total because of rounding error.

Source: *Flow of Funds Accounts of the United States,* Board of Governors of the Federal Reserve System, March 2017.

Your asset is Toyota's liability. Therefore, when we aggregate over all balance sheets, these claims cancel out, leaving only real assets as the net wealth of the economy. National wealth consists of structures, equipment, inventories of goods, and land.[1]

---

[1] You might wonder why real assets held by households in Table 1.1 amount to $32,431 billion, while total real assets in the domestic economy (Table 1.2) are far larger, at $67,786 billion. A big part of the difference reflects the fact that real assets held by firms, for example, property, plant, and equipment, are included as *financial* assets of the household sector, specifically through the value of corporate equity and other stock market investments. Similarly, Table 1.2 includes assets of noncorporate businesses. Finally, there are some differences in valuation methods. For example, equity and stock investments in Table 1.1 are measured by market value, whereas plant and equipment in Table 1.2 are valued at replacement cost.

We will focus almost exclusively on financial assets. But you shouldn't lose sight of the fact that the successes or failures of the financial assets we choose to purchase ultimately depend on the performance of the underlying real assets.

Are the following assets real or financial?

a. Patents
b. Lease obligations
c. Customer goodwill
d. A college education
e. A $5 bill

CONCEPT check 1.1

1.2 FINANCIAL ASSETS

It is common to distinguish among three broad types of financial assets: debt, equity, and derivatives. **Fixed-income** or **debt securities** promise either a fixed stream of income or a stream of income that is determined according to a specified formula. For example, a corporate bond typically would promise that the bondholder will receive a fixed amount of interest each year. Other so-called floating-rate bonds promise payments that depend on current interest rates. For example, a bond may pay an interest rate that is fixed at two percentage points above the rate paid on U.S. Treasury bills. Unless the borrower is declared bankrupt, the payments on these securities are either fixed or determined by formula. For this reason, the investment performance of debt securities typically is least closely tied to the financial condition of the issuer.

Nevertheless, debt securities come in a tremendous variety of maturities and payment provisions. At one extreme, the *money market* refers to fixed-income securities that are short term, highly marketable, and generally of very low risk, for example, U.S. Treasury bills or bank certificates of deposit (CDs). In contrast, the fixed-income *capital market* includes long-term securities such as Treasury bonds, as well as bonds issued by federal agencies, state and local municipalities, and corporations. These bonds range from very safe in terms of default risk (for example, Treasury securities) to relatively risky (for example, high-yield or "junk" bonds). They also are designed with extremely diverse provisions regarding payments provided to the investor and protection against the bankruptcy of the issuer. We will take a first look at these securities in Chapter 2 and undertake a more detailed analysis of the fixed-income market in Part Three.

Unlike debt securities, common stock, or **equity,** in a firm represents an ownership share in the corporation. Equityholders are not promised any particular payment. They receive any dividends the firm may pay and have prorated ownership in the real assets of the firm. If the firm is successful, the value of equity will increase; if not, it will decrease. The performance of equity investments, therefore, is tied directly to the success of the firm and its real assets. For this reason, equity investments tend to be riskier than investments in debt securities. Equity markets and equity valuation are the topics of Part Four.

Finally, **derivative securities** such as options and futures contracts provide payoffs that are determined by the prices of *other* assets such as bond or stock prices. For example, a call option on a share of Intel stock might turn out to be worthless if Intel's share price remains below a threshold or "exercise" price such as $35 a share, but it can be quite valuable if the stock price rises above that level.[2] Derivative securities are so named because their values *derive* from the prices of other assets. For example, the value of the call option will depend on the price of Intel stock. Other important derivative securities are futures and swap contracts. We will treat these in Part Five.

Derivatives have become an integral part of the investment environment. One use of derivatives, perhaps the primary use, is to hedge risks or transfer them to other parties. This is done successfully every day, and the use of these securities for risk management is so commonplace

fixed-income (debt) securities

Pay a specified cash flow over a specific period.

equity

An ownership share in a corporation.

derivative securities

Securities providing payoffs that depend on the values of other assets.

---

[2] A call option is the right to buy a share of stock at a given exercise price on or before the option's expiration date. If the market price of Intel remains below $35 a share, the right to buy for $35 will turn out to be valueless. If the share price rises above $35 before the option expires, however, the option can be exercised to obtain the share for only $35.

that the multitrillion-dollar market in derivative assets is routinely taken for granted. Derivatives also can be used to take highly speculative positions, however. Every so often, one of these positions blows up, resulting in well-publicized losses of hundreds of millions of dollars. While these losses attract considerable attention, they do not negate the potential use of such securities as risk management tools. Derivatives will continue to play an important role in portfolio construction and the financial system. We will return to this topic later in the text.

Investors and corporations regularly encounter other financial markets as well. Firms engaged in international trade regularly transfer money back and forth between dollars and other currencies. In London alone, $2 trillion of currency is traded each day in the market for foreign exchange, primarily through a network of the largest international banks.

Investors also might invest directly in some real assets. For example, dozens of commodities are traded on exchanges such as those of the CME Group (parent company of the Chicago Mercantile Exchange and several other exchanges). You can buy or sell corn, wheat, natural gas, gold, silver, and so on.

Commodity and derivative markets allow firms to adjust their exposure to various business risks. For example, a construction firm may lock in the price of copper by buying copper futures contracts, thus eliminating the risk of a sudden jump in the price of its raw materials. Wherever there is uncertainty, investors may be interested in trading, either to speculate or to lay off their risks, and a market may arise to meet that demand.

1.3 FINANCIAL MARKETS AND THE ECONOMY

We stated earlier that real assets determine the wealth of an economy, while financial assets merely represent claims on real assets. Nevertheless, financial assets and the markets in which they trade play several crucial roles in developed economies. Financial assets allow us to make the most of the economy's real assets.

The Informational Role of Financial Markets

Stock prices reflect investors' collective assessment of a firm's current performance and future prospects. When the market is more optimistic about the firm, its share price will rise. That higher price makes it easier for the firm to raise capital and therefore encourages investment. In this manner, stock prices play a major role in the allocation of capital in market economies, directing capital to the firms and applications with the greatest perceived potential.

Do capital markets actually channel resources to the most efficient use? At times, they appear to fail miserably. Companies or whole industries can be "hot" for a period of time (think about the dot-com bubble that peaked and then collapsed in 2000), attract a large flow of investor capital, and then fail after only a few years. The process seems highly wasteful.

But we need to be careful about our standard of efficiency. No one knows with certainty which ventures will succeed and which will fail. It is therefore unreasonable to expect that markets will never make mistakes. The stock market encourages allocation of capital to those firms that appear *at the time* to have the best prospects. Many smart, well-trained, and well-paid professionals analyze the prospects of firms whose shares trade on the stock market. Stock prices reflect their collective judgment.

You may well be skeptical about resource allocation through markets. But if you are, then take a moment to think about the alternatives. Would a central planner make fewer mistakes? Would you prefer that Congress make these decisions? To paraphrase Winston Churchill's comment about democracy, markets may be the worst way to allocate capital except for all the others that have been tried.

Consumption Timing

Some individuals are earning more than they currently wish to spend. Others, for example, retirees, spend more than they currently earn. How can you shift your purchasing power from high-earnings to low-earnings periods of life? One way is to "store" your wealth in financial assets. In high-earnings periods, you can invest your savings in financial assets such as stocks and bonds. In low-earnings periods, you can sell these assets to provide funds for your consumption needs. By so doing, you can "shift" your consumption over the course of your lifetime, thereby allocating your consumption to periods that provide the greatest satisfaction. Thus, financial markets allow individuals to separate decisions concerning current consumption from constraints that otherwise would be imposed by current earnings.

Allocation of Risk

Virtually all real assets involve some risk. When Toyota builds its auto plants, for example, it cannot know for sure what cash flows those plants will generate. Financial markets and the diverse financial instruments traded in those markets allow investors with the greatest taste for risk to bear that risk, while other, less risk-tolerant individuals can, to a greater extent, stay on the sidelines. For example, if Toyota raises the funds to build its auto plant by selling both stocks and bonds to the public, the more optimistic or risk-tolerant investors can buy shares of stock in Toyota, while the more conservative ones can buy Toyota bonds. Because the bonds promise to provide a fixed payment, the stockholders bear most of the business risk but reap potentially higher rewards. Thus, capital markets allow the risk that is inherent to all investments to be borne by the investors most willing to bear it.

This allocation of risk also benefits the firms that need to raise capital to finance their investments. When investors are able to select security types with the risk-return characteristics that best suit their preferences, each security can be sold for the best possible price. This facilitates the process of building the economy's stock of real assets.

Separation of Ownership and Management

Many businesses are owned and managed by the same individual. This simple organization is well suited to small businesses and, in fact, was the most common form of business organization before the Industrial Revolution. Today, however, with global markets and large-scale production, the size and capital requirements of firms have skyrocketed. For example, at the end of 2016, General Electric listed on its balance sheet more than $50 billion of property, plant, and equipment and total assets in excess of $350 billion. Corporations of such size simply cannot exist as owner-operated firms. GE actually has over 500,000 stockholders with an ownership stake in the firm proportional to their holdings of shares.

Such a large group of individuals obviously cannot actively participate in the day-to-day management of the firm. Instead, they elect a board of directors that in turn hires and supervises the management of the firm. This structure means that the owners and managers of the firm are different parties. This gives the firm a stability that the owner-managed firm cannot achieve. For example, if some stockholders decide they no longer wish to hold shares in the firm, they can sell their shares to other investors, with no impact on the management of the firm. Thus, financial assets and the ability to buy and sell those assets in the financial markets allow for easy separation of ownership and management.

How can all of the disparate owners of the firm, ranging from large pension funds holding hundreds of thousands of shares to small investors who may hold only a single share, agree on the objectives of the firm? Again, the financial markets provide some guidance. All may agree that the firm's management should pursue strategies that enhance the value of their shares. Such policies will make all shareholders wealthier and allow them all to better pursue their personal goals, whatever those goals might be.

Do managers really attempt to maximize firm value? It is easy to see how they might be tempted to engage in activities not in the best interest of shareholders. For example, they might engage in empire building or avoid risky projects to protect their own jobs or overconsume luxuries such as corporate jets, reasoning that the cost of such perquisites is largely borne by the shareholders. These potential conflicts of interest are called **agency problems** because managers, who are hired as agents of the shareholders, may pursue their own interests instead.

agency problems

Conflicts of interest between managers and stockholders.

Several mechanisms have evolved to mitigate potential agency problems. First, compensation plans tie the income of managers to the success of the firm. A major part of the total compensation of top executives is typically in the form of shares or stock options, which means that the managers will not do well unless the stock price increases, benefiting shareholders. (Of course, we've learned that overuse of options can create its own agency problem. Options can create an incentive for managers to manipulate information to prop up a stock price temporarily, giving them a chance to cash out before the price returns to a level reflective of the firm's true prospects. More on this shortly.) Second, while boards of directors have sometimes been portrayed as defenders of top management, they can, and in recent years increasingly have, forced out management teams that are underperforming. Third, outsiders such as security analysts and large institutional investors such as mutual funds or pension funds monitor the firm closely and make the life of poor performers at the least uncomfortable. Such large investors today hold about half of the stock in publicly listed firms in the United States.

Finally, bad performers are subject to the threat of takeover. If the board of directors is lax in monitoring management, unhappy shareholders in principle can elect a different board. They can do this by launching a *proxy contest* in which they seek to obtain enough proxies (i.e., rights to vote the shares of other shareholders) to take control of the firm and vote in another board. Historically, this threat was usually minimal. Shareholders who attempt such a fight have to use their own funds, while management can defend itself using corporate coffers.

However, in recent years, the odds of a successful proxy contest have increased along with the rise of so-called activist investors. These are large and deep-pocketed investors, often hedge funds, that identify firms they believe to be mismanaged in some respect. They can buy large positions in shares of those firms, and then campaign for slots on the board of directors and/or for specific reforms. One estimate is that since the end of 2009, about 15% of the firms in the S&P 500 have faced an activist campaign, and that activists have taken share positions in about half of the S&P 500 firms. In 2014, nearly three-quarters of proxy votes were won by dissidents.[3]

Aside from proxy contests, the real takeover threat is from other firms. If one firm observes another underperforming, it can acquire the underperforming business and replace management with its own team. The stock price should rise to reflect the prospects of improved performance, which provides an incentive for firms to engage in such takeover activity.

EXAMPLE 1.1

Activist Investors and Corporate Control

Here are a few of the better known activist investors, along with a sample of their recent initiatives.

- Carl Icahn. One of the earliest and most combative of activist investors. Challenged Apple to increase repurchases and cash distributions to investors.
- William Ackman, Pershing Square. Took large positions in JC Penney, Valeant Pharmaceuticals, and Kraft Foods with a view toward influencing management practice.
- Nelson Peltz, Trian. Pushed General Electric to return capital to shareholders, for example, through stock buybacks, and more closely align executive compensation with firm performance.
- Dan Loeb, Third Point. Pressured Nestlé to sell its stake in L'Oreal as well as other "nonessential" holdings.
- Jeff Smith, Starboard Value. Pushed for Staples and Office Depot to merge. The firms agreed, but the merger ultimately was blocked on antitrust grounds.

Corporate Governance and Corporate Ethics

We've argued that securities markets can play an important role in facilitating the deployment of capital resources to their most productive uses. But market signals will help to allocate capital efficiently only if investors are acting on accurate information. We say that markets need to be *transparent* for investors to make informed decisions. If firms can mislead the public about their prospects, then much can go wrong.

---

[3] "An investor calls," *The Economist* , February 7, 2015.

Despite the many mechanisms to align incentives of shareholders and managers, the three years from 2000 through 2002 were filled with a seemingly unending series of scandals that collectively signaled a crisis in corporate governance and ethics. For example, the telecom firm WorldCom overstated its profits by at least $3.8 billion by improperly classifying expenses as investments. When the true picture emerged, it resulted in the largest bankruptcy in U.S. history, at least until Lehman Brothers smashed that record in 2008. The next-largest U.S. bankruptcy was Enron, which used its now notorious "special purpose entities" to move debt off its own books and similarly present a misleading picture of its financial status. Unfortunately, these firms had plenty of company. Other firms such as Rite Aid, HealthSouth, Global Crossing, and Qwest Communications also manipulated and misstated their accounts to the tune of billions of dollars. And the scandals were hardly limited to the United States. Parmalat, the Italian dairy firm, claimed to have a $4.8 billion bank account that turned out not to exist. These episodes suggest that agency and incentive problems are far from solved.

Other scandals of that period included systematically misleading and overly optimistic research reports put out by stock market analysts (their favorable analysis was traded for the promise of future investment banking business, and analysts were commonly compensated not for their accuracy or insight but for their role in garnering investment banking business for their firms) and allocations of initial public offerings (IPOs) to corporate executives as a quid pro quo for personal favors or the promise to direct future business back to the manager of the IPO.

What about the auditors who were supposed to be the watchdogs of the firms? Here too, incentives were skewed. Recent changes in business practice made the consulting businesses of these firms more lucrative than the auditing function. For example, Enron's (now defunct) auditor Arthur Andersen earned more money consulting for Enron than auditing it; given its incentive to protect its consulting profits, it should not be surprising that it, and other auditors, were overly lenient in their auditing work.

In 2002, in response to the spate of ethics scandals, Congress passed the Sarbanes-Oxley Act to tighten the rules of corporate governance. For example, the act requires corporations to have more independent directors, that is, more directors who are not themselves managers (or affiliated with managers). The act also requires each CFO to personally vouch for the corporation's accounting statements, provides for an oversight board to oversee the auditing of public companies, and prohibits auditors from providing various other services to clients.

1.4 THE INVESTMENT PROCESS

An investor's *portfolio* is simply his collection of investment assets. Once the portfolio is established, it is updated or "rebalanced" by selling existing securities and using the proceeds to buy new securities, by investing additional funds to increase the overall size of the portfolio, or by selling securities to decrease the size of the portfolio.

Investment assets can be categorized into broad asset classes, such as stocks, bonds, real estate, commodities, and so on. Investors make two types of decisions in constructing their portfolios. The **asset allocation** decision is the choice among these broad asset classes, while the **security selection** decision is the choice of which particular securities to hold *within* each asset class.

"Top-down" portfolio construction starts with asset allocation. For example, an individual who currently holds all of his money in a bank account would first decide what proportion of the overall portfolio ought to be moved into stocks, bonds, and so on. In this way, the broad features of the portfolio are established. For example, while the average annual return on the common stock of large firms since 1926 has been about 12% per year, the average return on U.S. Treasury bills has been less than 4%. On the other hand, stocks are far riskier, with annual returns (as measured by the Standard & Poor's 500 Index) that have ranged as low as −46% and as high as 55%. In contrast, T-bill returns are effectively risk free: You know what interest rate you will earn when you buy the bills. Therefore, the decision to allocate your investments to the stock market or to the money market where Treasury bills are traded will have great ramifications for both the risk and the return of your portfolio. A top-down

asset allocation

Allocation of an investment portfolio across broad asset classes.

security selection

Choice of specific securities within each asset class.

investor first makes this and other crucial asset allocation decisions before turning to the decision of the particular securities to be held in each asset class.

security analysis

Analysis of the value of securities.

Security analysis involves the valuation of particular securities that might be included in the portfolio. For example, an investor might ask whether Merck or Pfizer is more attractively priced. Both bonds and stocks must be evaluated for investment attractiveness, but valuation is far more difficult for stocks because a stock's performance usually is far more sensitive to the condition of the issuing firm.

In contrast to top-down portfolio management is the "bottom-up" strategy. In this process, the portfolio is constructed from securities that seem attractively priced without as much concern for the resultant asset allocation. Such a technique can result in unintended bets on one or another sector of the economy. For example, it might turn out that the portfolio ends up with a very heavy representation of firms in one industry, from one part of the country, or with exposure to one source of uncertainty. However, a bottom-up strategy does focus the portfolio on the assets that seem to offer the most attractive investment opportunities.

1.5 MARKETS ARE COMPETITIVE

Financial markets are highly competitive. Thousands of well-backed analysts constantly scour securities markets searching for the best buys. This competition means that we should expect to find few, if any, "free lunches," securities that are so underpriced that they represent obvious bargains. There are several implications of this no-free-lunch proposition. Let's examine two.

The Risk-Return Trade-Off

Investors invest for anticipated future returns, but those returns rarely can be predicted precisely. There will almost always be risk associated with investments. Actual or realized returns will almost always deviate from the expected return anticipated at the start of the investment period. For example, in 1931 (the worst calendar year for the market since 1926), the stock market lost 46% of its value. In 1933 (the best year), the stock market gained 55%. You can be sure that investors did not anticipate such extreme performance at the start of either of these years.

Naturally, if all else could be held equal, investors would prefer investments with the highest expected return.[4] However, the no-free-lunch rule tells us that all else cannot be held equal. If you want higher expected returns, you will have to pay a price in terms of accepting higher investment risk. If any particular asset offered a higher expected return without imposing extra risk, investors would rush to buy it, with the result that its price would be driven up. Individuals considering investing in the asset at the now-higher price would find the investment less attractive. The price will rise until its expected return is no more than commensurate with risk. At this point, investors can anticipate a "fair" return relative to the asset's risk, but no more.

risk-return trade-off

Assets with higher expected returns entail greater risk.

Similarly, if returns were independent of risk, there would be a rush to sell high-risk assets. Their prices would fall (improving their expected future rates of return) until they eventually were attractive enough to be included again in investor portfolios. We conclude that there should be a **risk-return trade-off** in the securities markets, with higher-risk assets priced to offer higher expected returns than lower-risk assets.

Of course, this discussion leaves several important questions unanswered. How should one measure the risk of an asset? What should be the quantitative trade-off between risk (properly measured) and expected return? One would think that risk would have something to do with the volatility of an asset's returns, but this guess turns out to be only partly correct. When we mix assets into diversified portfolios, we need to consider the interplay among assets and the

---

[4] The "expected" return is not the return investors believe they necessarily will earn, or even their most likely return. It is instead the result of averaging across all possible outcomes, recognizing that some outcomes are more likely than others. It is the average rate of return across possible economic scenarios.

effect of diversification on the risk of the entire portfolio. *Diversification* means that many assets are held in the portfolio so that the exposure to any particular asset is limited. The effect of diversification on portfolio risk, the implications for the proper measurement of risk, and the risk-return relationship are the topics of Part Two. These topics are the subject of what has come to be known as *modern portfolio theory*. The development of this theory brought two of its pioneers, Harry Markowitz and William Sharpe, Nobel Prizes.

Efficient Markets

Another implication of the no-free-lunch proposition is that we should rarely expect to find bargains in the security markets. We will spend all of Chapter 8 examining the theory and evidence concerning the hypothesis that financial markets process all available information about securities quickly and efficiently, that is, that the security price usually reflects all the information available to investors concerning the value of the security. According to this hypothesis, as new information about a security becomes available, the price of the security quickly adjusts so that at any time, the security price equals the market consensus estimate of the value of the security. If this were so, there would be neither underpriced nor overpriced securities.

One interesting implication of this "efficient market hypothesis" concerns the choice between active and passive investment-management strategies. **Passive management** calls for holding highly diversified portfolios without spending effort or other resources attempting to improve investment performance through security analysis. **Active management** is the attempt to improve performance either by identifying mispriced securities or by timing the performance of broad asset classes—for example, increasing one's commitment to stocks when one is bullish on the stock market. If markets are efficient and prices reflect all relevant information, perhaps it is better to follow passive strategies instead of spending resources in a futile attempt to outguess your competitors in the financial markets.

If the efficient market hypothesis were taken to the extreme, there would be no point in active security analysis; only fools would commit resources to actively analyze securities. Without ongoing security analysis, however, prices eventually would depart from "correct" values, creating new incentives for experts to move in. Therefore, in Chapter 9, we examine challenges to the efficient market hypothesis. Even in environments as competitive as the financial markets, we may observe only *near*-efficiency, and profit opportunities may exist for especially insightful and creative investors. This motivates our discussion of active portfolio management in Part Six. Nevertheless, our discussions of security analysis and portfolio construction generally must account for the likelihood of nearly efficient markets.

passive management
Buying and holding a diversified portfolio without attempting to identify mispriced securities.

active management
Attempting to identify mispriced securities or to forecast broad market trends.

1.6   THE PLAYERS

From a bird's-eye view, there would appear to be three major players in the financial markets:

1. Firms are net demanders of capital. They raise capital now to pay for investments in plant and equipment. The income generated by those real assets provides the returns to investors who purchase the securities issued by the firm.
2. Households typically are suppliers of capital. They purchase the securities issued by firms that need to raise funds.
3. Governments can be borrowers or lenders, depending on the relationship between tax revenue and government expenditures. Since World War II, the U.S. government typically has run budget deficits, meaning that its tax receipts have been less than its expenditures. The government, therefore, has had to borrow funds to cover its budget deficit. Issuance of Treasury bills, notes, and bonds is the major way that the government borrows funds from the public. In contrast, in the latter part of the 1990s, the government enjoyed a budget surplus and was able to retire some outstanding debt.

Corporations and governments do not sell all or even most of their securities directly to individuals. For example, about half of all stock is held by large financial institutions such as pension funds, mutual funds, insurance companies, and banks. These financial institutions stand between the security issuer (the firm) and the ultimate owner of the security (the individual investor). For this reason, they are called *financial intermediaries.* Similarly, corporations do not directly market their securities to the public. Instead, they hire agents, called investment bankers, to represent them to the investing public. Let's examine the roles of these intermediaries.

Financial Intermediaries

Households want desirable investments for their savings, yet the small (financial) size of most households makes direct investment difficult. A small investor seeking to lend money to businesses that need to finance investments doesn't advertise in the local newspaper to find a willing and desirable borrower. Moreover, an individual lender would not be able to diversify across borrowers to reduce risk. Finally, an individual lender is not equipped to assess and monitor the credit risk of borrowers.

For these reasons, **financial intermediaries** have evolved to bring together the suppliers of capital (investors) with the demanders of capital (primarily corporations and the federal government). These financial intermediaries include banks, investment companies, insurance companies, and credit unions. Financial intermediaries issue their own securities to raise funds to purchase the securities of other corporations.

For example, a bank raises funds by borrowing (taking deposits) and lending that money to other borrowers. The spread between the interest rates paid to depositors and the rates charged to borrowers is the source of the bank's profit. In this way, lenders and borrowers do not need to contact each other directly. Instead, each goes to the bank, which acts as an intermediary between the two. The problem of matching lenders with borrowers is solved when each comes independently to the common intermediary.

Financial intermediaries are distinguished from other businesses in that both their assets and their liabilities are overwhelmingly financial. Table 1.3 presents the aggregated balance sheet of commercial banks, one of the largest sectors of financial intermediaries. Notice that the balance sheet includes only very small amounts of real assets. Compare Table 1.3 to the aggregated balance sheet of the nonfinancial corporate sector in Table 1.4, for which real assets are about half of all assets. The contrast arises because intermediaries simply move funds from one sector to another. In fact, the primary social function of such intermediaries is to channel household savings to the business sector.

Other examples of financial intermediaries are investment companies, insurance companies, and credit unions. All these firms offer similar advantages in their intermediary role. First, by pooling the resources of many small investors, they are able to lend considerable sums to large borrowers. Second, by lending to many borrowers, intermediaries achieve significant diversification, so they can accept loans that individually might otherwise be too risky. Third, intermediaries build expertise through the volume of business they do and can use economies of scale and scope to assess and monitor risk.

Investment companies, which pool and manage the money of many investors, also arise out of economies of scale. Here, the problem is that most household portfolios are not large enough to be spread among a wide variety of securities. It is very expensive in terms of brokerage fees and research costs to purchase one or two shares of many different firms. Mutual funds have the advantage of large-scale trading and portfolio management, while participating investors are assigned a prorated share of the total funds according to the size of their investment. This system gives small investors advantages they are willing to pay for via a management fee to the mutual fund operator.

Investment companies also can design portfolios specifically for large investors with particular goals. In contrast, mutual funds are sold in the retail market, and their investment philosophies are differentiated mainly by strategies that are likely to attract a large number of clients.

Like mutual funds, *hedge funds* also pool and invest the money of many clients. But they are open only to institutional investors such as pension funds, endowment funds, or wealthy

financial intermediaries

Institutions that "connect" borrowers and lenders by accepting funds from lenders and loaning funds to borrowers.

investment companies

Firms managing funds for investors. An investment company may manage several mutual funds.

TABLE 1.3   Balance sheet of FDIC-insured commercial banks and savings institutions

Assets	$ Billion	% Total	Liabilities and Net Worth	$ Billion	% Total
Real assets			**Liabilities**		
Equipment and premises	$ 120.2	0.7%	Deposits	$12,894.7	76.8%
Other real estate	10.9	0.1	Debt and other borrowed funds	1,170.9	7.0
Total real assets	$ 125.2	0.7%	Federal funds and repurchase agreements	233.7	1.4
			Other	611.1	3.6
			Total liabilities	$14,910.4	88.9%
Financial assets					
Cash	$ 1,810.0	10.8%			
Investment securities	3,559.5	21.2			
Loans and leases	9,183.9	54.7			
Other financial assets	1,059.2	6.3			
Total financial assets	$15,612.5	93.0%			
Other assets					
Intangible assets	$ 350.4	2.1%			
Other	692.1	4.1			
Total other assets	$ 1,042.5	7.2%	Net worth	$ 1,869.8	11.1%
Total	$16,780.2	100.0%		$16,780.2	100.0%

Note: Column sums may differ from total because of rounding error.

Source: Federal Deposit Insurance Corporation, **www.fdic.gov**, March 2017.

TABLE 1.4   Balance sheet of U.S. nonfinancial corporations

Assets	$ Billion	% Total	Liabilities and Net Worth	$ Billion	% Total
Real assets			Liabilities		
Equipment and intellectual property	$ 6,936	16.6%	Bonds and mortgages	$ 6,299	15.1%
Real estate	13,319	31.9	Bank loans	985	2.4
Inventories	2,280	5.5	Other loans	1,140	2.7
Total real assets	$22,535	54.0%	Trade debt	2,146	5.1
			Other	7,495	17.9
			Total liabilities	$18,065	43.3%
Financial assets					
Deposits and cash	$ 1,070	2.6%			
Marketable securities	1,011	2.4			
Trade and consumer credit	2,800	6.7			
Other	14,344	34.3			
Total financial assets	19,224	46.0	Net worth	$23,694	56.7%
Total	$41,759	100.0%		$41,759	100.0%

Note: Column sums may differ from total because of rounding error.

Source: *Flow of Funds Accounts of the United States,* Board of Governors of the Federal Reserve System, March 2017.

individuals. They are more likely to pursue complex and higher-risk strategies. They typically keep a portion of trading profits as part of their fees, whereas mutual funds charge a fixed percentage of assets under management.

Economies of scale also explain the proliferation of analytic services available to investors. Newsletters, databases, and brokerage house research services all engage in research to be sold to a large client base. This setup arises naturally. Investors clearly want information, but with

On the MARKET FRONT

SEPARATING COMMERCIAL BANKING FROM THE INVESTMENT BANKING INDUSTRY

Until 1999, the Glass-Steagall Act prohibited banks from both accepting deposits and underwriting securities. In other words, it forced a separation of the investment and commercial banking industries. But when Glass-Steagall was repealed, many large commercial banks began to transform themselves into "universal banks" that could offer a full range of commercial and investment banking services. In some cases, commercial banks started their own investment banking divisions from scratch, but more commonly they expanded through merger. For example, Chase Manhattan acquired J. P. Morgan to form JPMorgan Chase. Similarly, Citigroup acquired Salomon Smith Barney to offer wealth management, brokerage, investment banking, and asset management services to its clients. Most of Europe had never forced the separation of commercial and investment banking, so their giant banks such as Credit Suisse, Deutsche Bank, HSBC, and UBS had long been universal banks. Until 2008, however, the stand-alone investment banking sector in the U.S. remained large and apparently vibrant, including such storied names as Goldman Sachs, Morgan Stanley, Merrill Lynch, and Lehman Brothers.

But the industry was shaken to its core in 2008, when several investment banks were beset by enormous losses on their holdings of mortgage-backed securities. In March, on the verge of insolvency, Bear Stearns was merged into JPMorgan Chase. On September 14, 2008, Merrill Lynch, also suffering steep mortgage-related losses, negotiated an agreement to be acquired by Bank of America. The next day, Lehman Brothers entered into the largest bankruptcy in U.S. history, having failed to find an acquirer who was able and willing to rescue it from its steep losses. The next week, the only two remaining major independent investment banks, Goldman Sachs and Morgan Stanley, decided to convert from investment banks to traditional bank holding companies. In so doing, they became subject to the supervision of national bank regulators such as the Federal Reserve and the far tighter rules for capital adequacy that govern commercial banks.[5] The firms decided that the greater stability they would enjoy as traditional banks, particularly the ability to fund their operations through bank deposits and access to emergency borrowing from the Fed, justified the conversion. These mergers and conversions marked the effective end of the independent investment banking industry—but not of investment banking. Those services are now supplied by the large universal banks.

Today, the debate about the separation between commercial and investment banking that seemed to have ended with the repeal of Glass-Steagall has come back to life. The Dodd-Frank Wall Street Reform and Consumer Protection Act places new restrictions on bank activities. For example, the Volcker Rule, named after former chairman of the Federal Reserve Paul Volcker, prohibits banks from "proprietary trading," that is, trading securities for their own accounts, and restricts their investments in hedge funds or private equity funds. The rule is meant to limit the risk that banks can take on. While the Volcker Rule is less restrictive than Glass-Steagall had been, both are motivated by the belief that banks enjoying federal guarantees should be subject to limits on the sorts of activities in which they can engage. Proprietary trading is a core activity for investment banks, so limitations on this activity for commercial banks reintroduces a separation between their business models. However, the limitations on such trading have elicited push-back from the industry, which argues that they have resulted in a brain drain of top traders from banks into hedge funds.. The debate on the separation of commercial and investment banking continues.

---

small portfolios to manage, they do not find it economical to personally gather all of it. Hence, a profit opportunity emerges: A firm can perform this service for many clients and charge for it.

Investment Bankers

Just as economies of scale and specialization create profit opportunities for financial intermediaries, these economies also create niches for firms that perform specialized services for businesses. Firms raise much of their capital by selling securities such as stocks and bonds to the public. Because these firms do not do so frequently, however, **investment bankers** that specialize in such activities can offer their services at a cost below that of maintaining an in-house security issuance division.

investment bankers

Firms specializing in the sale of new securities to the public, typically by underwriting the issue.

Investment bankers advise an issuing corporation on the prices it can charge for the securities issued, appropriate interest rates, and so forth. Ultimately, the investment banking

---

[5] For example, a typical leverage ratio (total assets divided by bank capital) at commercial banks in 2008 was about 10 to 1. In contrast, leverage at investment banks reached 30 to 1. Such leverage increased profits when times were good but provided an inadequate buffer against losses and left the banks exposed to failure when their investment portfolios were shaken by large losses.

firm handles the marketing of the security in the **primary market,** where new issues of securities are offered to the public. In this role, the banks are called *underwriters.* Later, investors can trade previously issued securities among themselves in the so-called **secondary market.**

For most of the last century, investment banks and commercial banks in the U.S. were separated by law. While those regulations were effectively eliminated in 1999, until 2008 the industry known as "Wall Street" still comprised large, independent investment banks such as Goldman Sachs, Merrill Lynch, or Lehman Brothers. But that stand-alone model came to an abrupt end in September 2008, when all the remaining major U.S. investment banks were absorbed into commercial banks, declared bankruptcy, or reorganized as commercial banks. The nearby box presents a brief introduction to these events.

Venture Capital and Private Equity

While large firms can raise funds directly from the stock and bond markets with help from their investment bankers, smaller and younger firms that have not yet issued securities to the public do not have that option. Start-up companies rely instead on bank loans and investors who are willing to invest in them in return for an ownership stake in the firm. The equity investment in these young companies is called **venture capital (VC).** Sources of venture capital include dedicated venture capital funds, wealthy individuals known as *angel investors,* and institutions such as pension funds.

Most venture capital funds are set up as limited partnerships. A management company starts with its own money and raises additional capital from limited partners such as pension funds. That capital may then be invested in a variety of start-up companies. The management company usually sits on the start-up company's board of directors, helps recruit senior managers, and provides business advice. It charges a fee to the VC fund for overseeing the investments. After some period of time, for example, 10 years, the fund is liquidated and proceeds are distributed to the investors.

Venture capital investors commonly take an active role in the management of a start-up firm. Other active investors may engage in similar hands-on management but focus instead on firms that are in distress or firms that may be bought up, "improved," and sold for a profit. Collectively, these investments in firms that do not trade on public stock exchanges are known as **private equity** investments.

primary market

A market in which new issues of securities are offered to the public.

secondary market

Markets in which previously issued securities are traded among investors.

venture capital (VC)

Money invested to finance a new, privately held firm.

private equity

Investments in companies whose shares are not traded in public stock markets.

1.7   THE FINANCIAL CRISIS OF 2008

This chapter has laid out the broad outlines of the financial system, as well as some of the links between the financial side of the economy and the "real" side, in which goods and services are produced. The financial crisis of 2008 illustrated in a painful way the intimate ties between these two sectors. We present in this section a capsule summary of the crisis, attempting to draw some lessons about the role of the financial system as well as the causes and consequences of what has become known as *systemic risk.* Some of these issues are complicated; we consider them briefly here but will return to them in greater detail later in the text once we have more context for analysis.

Antecedents of the Crisis

In early 2007, most observers thought it inconceivable that within two years the world financial system would be facing its worse crisis since the Great Depression. At the time, the economy seemed to be marching from strength to strength. The last significant macroeconomic threat had been from the collapse of the high-tech bubble in 2000–2002. But the Federal Reserve responded to an emerging recession by aggressively reducing interest rates. Figure 1.1 shows that Treasury bill rates dropped drastically between 2001 and 2004, and the LIBOR rate (LIBOR is an acronym for the London Interbank Offer Rate), which is the interest

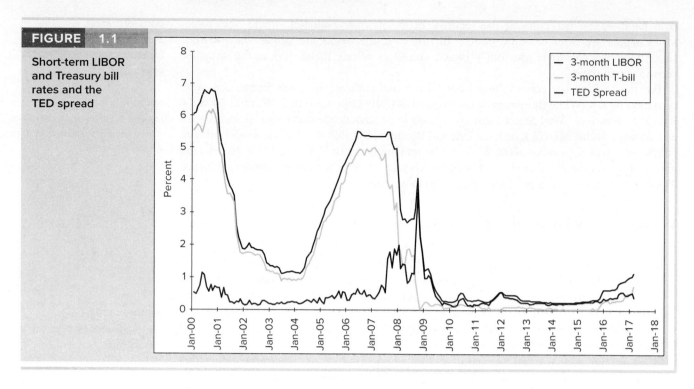

rate at which major money-center banks lend to each other, fell in tandem.[6] These actions appeared to have been successful, and the recession was short-lived and mild.

By mid-decade the economy was once again apparently healthy. While the stock market had declined substantially between 2001 and 2002, Figure 1.2 shows that it reversed direction just as dramatically beginning in 2003, fully recovering all of its post-tech-meltdown losses within a few years. Of equal importance, the banking sector seemed healthy. The spread between the LIBOR rate (at which banks borrow from each other) and the Treasury bill rate

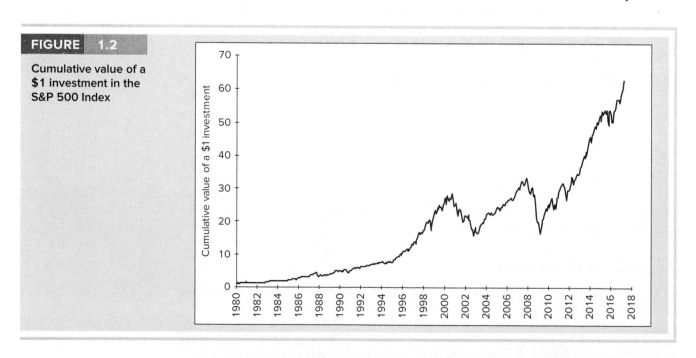

[6] The London Interbank Offer Rate is a rate charged in an interbank lending market outside the U.S. (largely centered in London). The rate is typically quoted for three-month loans.

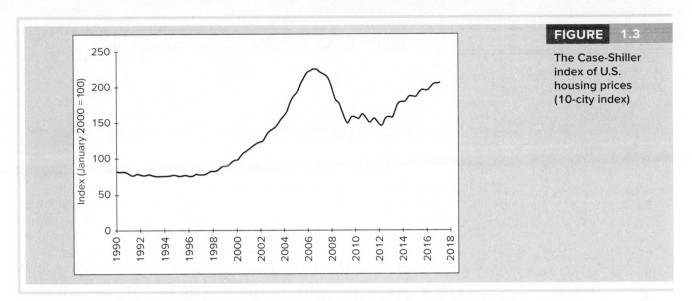

FIGURE 1.3

The Case-Shiller index of U.S. housing prices (10-city index)

(at which the U.S. government borrows), a common measure of credit risk in the banking sector (often referred to as the *TED spread*),[7] was only around 0.25% in early 2007 (see the blue line in Figure 1.1), suggesting that fears of default or "counterparty" risk in the banking sector were extremely low.

The combination of dramatically reduced interest rates and an apparently stable economy fed a historic boom in the housing market. Figure 1.3 shows that U.S. housing prices began rising noticeably in the late 1990s and accelerated dramatically after 2001 as interest rates plummeted. In the 10 years beginning 1997, average prices in the U.S. approximately tripled.

But confidence in the power of macroeconomic policy to reduce risk, the impressive recovery of the economy from the high-tech implosion, and particularly the housing price boom following the aggressive reduction in interest rates may have sown the seeds for the debacle that played out in 2008. On the one hand, the Fed's policy of reducing interest rates had resulted in low yields on a wide variety of investments, and investors were hungry for higher-yielding alternatives. On the other hand, low volatility and optimism about macroeconomic prospects encouraged greater tolerance for risk in the search for these higher-yielding investments. Nowhere was this more evident than in the exploding market for securitized mortgages. The U.S. housing and mortgage finance markets were at the center of a gathering storm.

Changes in Housing Finance

Prior to 1970, most mortgage loans would come from a local lender such as a neighborhood savings bank or credit union. A homeowner would borrow funds for a home purchase and repay it over a long period, commonly 30 years. A typical thrift institution would have as its major asset a portfolio of these long-term home loans, while its major liability would be the accounts of its depositors. This landscape began to change in the 1970s when Fannie Mae (FNMA, or Federal National Mortgage Association) and Freddie Mac (FHLMC, or Federal Home Loan Mortgage Corporation) began buying large quantities of mortgage loans from originators and bundling them into pools that could be traded like any other financial asset. These pools, which were essentially claims on the underlying mortgages, were soon dubbed "mortgage-backed securities," and the process was called **securitization.** Fannie and Freddie quickly became the behemoths of the mortgage market, between them buying more than half of all mortgages originated by the private sector.

Figure 1.4 illustrates how cash flows passed from the original borrower to the ultimate investor in a mortgage-backed security. The loan originator, for example, the savings and

securitization

Pooling loans into standardized securities backed by those loans, which can then be traded like any other security.

---

[7] *TED* stands for "Treasury-Eurodollar spread." The Eurodollar rate in this spread is, in fact, LIBOR.

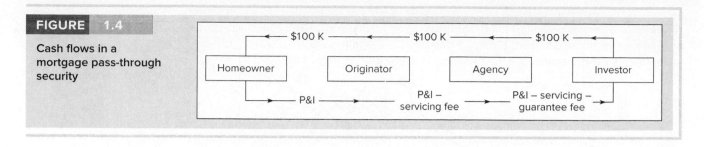

loan, might make a $100,000 loan to a homeowner. The homeowner would repay principal and interest (P&I) on the loan over 30 years. But then the originator would sell the mortgage to Freddie Mac or Fannie Mae and recover the cost of the loan. The originator could continue to service the loan (i.e., collect the monthly payments from the homeowner) for a small servicing fee, but the loan payments net of that fee would be passed along to the agency. In turn, Freddie or Fannie would pool the loans into mortgage-backed securities and sell the securities to investors such as pension funds or mutual funds. The agency (Fannie or Freddie) typically would guarantee the credit or default risk of the loans included in each pool, for which it would retain a guarantee fee before passing along the rest of the cash flow to the ultimate investor. Because the mortgage cash flows were passed along from the homeowner to the lender, to Fannie or Freddie, and finally to the investor, the mortgage-backed securities were also called *pass-throughs.*

Until the last decade, the vast majority of the mortgages that had been securitized into pass-throughs were held or guaranteed by Freddie Mac or Fannie Mae. These were low-risk *conforming* mortgages, meaning that eligible loans for agency securitization couldn't be too big and homeowners had to meet underwriting criteria establishing their ability to repay the loan. For example, the ratio of loan amount to house value could be no more than 80%.

Conforming loans were pooled almost entirely through Freddie Mac and Fannie Mae, but once the securitization model took hold, it created an opening for a new product: securitization by private firms of *nonconforming* "subprime" loans with higher default risk. One important difference between the government-agency pass-throughs and these so-called private-label pass-throughs was that the investor in the private-label pool would bear the risk that homeowners might default on their loans. Thus, originating mortgage brokers had little incentive to perform due diligence on the loan *as long as the loans could be sold to an investor.* These investors, of course, had no direct contact with the borrowers and could not perform detailed underwriting concerning loan quality. Instead, they relied on borrowers' credit scores, which steadily came to replace conventional underwriting.

A strong trend toward low-documentation and then no-documentation loans entailing little verification of a borrower's ability to carry a loan soon emerged. Other subprime underwriting standards also quickly deteriorated. For example, allowed leverage on home loans (as measured by the loan-to-value ratio) rose dramatically. By 2006, the majority of subprime borrowers purchased houses by borrowing the *entire* purchase price! When housing prices began falling, these highly leveraged loans were quickly "underwater," meaning that the house was worth less than the loan balance, and many homeowners decided to "walk away" or abandon their homes—and their loans.

Adjustable rate mortgages (ARMs) also grew in popularity, quickly becoming the standard in the subprime market. These loans offered borrowers low initial or "teaser" interest rates, but these rates eventually would reset to current market interest yields, for example, the Treasury bill rate plus 3%. While many of these borrowers had "maxed out" their borrowing capacity at the teaser rate, as soon as the loan rate was reset, their monthly payments would soar, especially if market interest rates had increased.

Despite these obvious risks, the ongoing increase in housing prices over the last decade seemed to have lulled many investors into complacency, with a widespread belief that continually rising home prices would bail out poorly performing loans. But starting in 2004, the ability of refinancing to save a loan began to diminish. First, higher interest rates put payment pressure on homeowners who had taken out adjustable rate mortgages. Second, as Figure 1.3 shows, housing prices peaked by 2006, so homeowners' ability to refinance a loan using built-up equity in the house declined. Mortgage default rates began to surge in 2007, as did losses on mortgage-backed securities. The crisis was ready to shift into high gear.

Mortgage Derivatives

One might ask: Who was willing to buy all of these risky subprime mortgages? Securitization, restructuring, and credit enhancement provide a big part of the answer. New risk-shifting tools enabled investment banks to carve out AAA-rated securities from original-issue "junk" loans. Collateralized debt obligations, or CDOs, were among the most important and eventually damaging of these innovations.

CDOs were designed to concentrate the credit (i.e., default) risk of a bundle of loans on one class of investors, leaving the other investors in the pool relatively protected from that risk. The idea was to prioritize claims on loan repayments by dividing the pool into senior versus junior slices called *tranches*. The senior tranches had first claim on repayments from the entire pool. Junior tranches would be paid only after the senior ones had received their cut. For example, if a pool was divided into two tranches, with 70% of the pool allocated to the senior tranche and 30% allocated to the junior one, the senior investors would be repaid in full as long as 70% or more of the loans in the pool performed, that is, as long as the default rate on the pool remained below 30%. Even with pools composed of risky subprime loans, default rates above 30% seemed extremely unlikely, and thus senior tranches were commonly granted the highest (i.e., AAA) rating by the major credit rating agencies, Moody's, Standard & Poor's, and Fitch. Large amounts of AAA-rated securities were thus carved out of pools of low-rated mortgages.

Of course, we know now that these ratings were wrong. The senior-subordinated structure of CDOs provided less protection to senior tranches than investors anticipated. When housing prices across the entire country began to fall in unison, defaults in all regions increased and the hoped-for benefits from diversifying loans geographically never materialized.

Why had the rating agencies so dramatically underestimated credit risk in these subprime securities? First, default probabilities had been estimated using historical data from an unrepresentative period characterized by a housing boom and an uncommonly prosperous economy. Moreover, the ratings analysts had extrapolated historical default experience to a new sort of borrower pool—one without down payments, with exploding payment loans, and with low- or no-documentation loans (sometimes dubbed *liar loans*). Past default experience was largely irrelevant given these profound changes in the market. Moreover, there was excessive optimism about the power of cross-regional diversification to minimize risk.

CONCEPT check **1.2**

When Freddie Mac and Fannie Mae pooled conforming mortgages into securities, they guaranteed the underlying mortgage loans against homeowner defaults. In contrast, there were no guarantees on the mortgages pooled into subprime mortgage–backed securities, so investors bore the exposure to credit risk. Were either of these arrangements necessarily a better way to manage and allocate default risk?

Credit Default Swaps

In parallel to the CDO market, the market in *credit default swaps* also exploded in this period. A credit default swap, or CDS, is in essence an insurance contract against the default of one or more borrowers. (We will describe these in more detail in Chapter 10.) The purchaser of the swap pays an annual premium (like an insurance premium) for the protection from credit risk. Credit default swaps became an alternative method of credit enhancement, seemingly allowing investors to buy subprime loans and insure their investments. But, in practice, some swap issuers ramped up their exposure to credit risk to unsupportable levels, without sufficient capital to back those obligations. For example, the large insurance company AIG alone sold more than $400 billion of CDS contracts on subprime mortgages.

The Rise of Systemic Risk

By 2007, the financial system displayed several troubling features. Many large banks and related financial institutions had adopted an apparently profitable financing scheme: borrowing short term at low interest rates to finance holdings in higher-yielding, long-term, illiquid[8] assets and treating the interest rate differential between their assets and liabilities as economic profit. But this business model was precarious: By relying primarily on short-term loans for their funding, these firms needed to constantly refinance their positions (i.e., borrow additional funds as the loans matured), or else face the necessity of quickly selling off their less liquid asset portfolios, which would be difficult in times of financial stress. Moreover, these institutions were highly leveraged and had little capital as a buffer against losses. Large investment banks on Wall Street in particular had sharply increased leverage, which added to an underappreciated vulnerability to refunding requirements—especially if the value of their asset portfolios came into question. Even small portfolio losses could drive their net worth negative, at which point no one would be willing to extend them loans.

Another source of fragility was widespread investor reliance on credit protection through products like CDOs. Many of the assets underlying these pools were illiquid, hard to value, and highly dependent on forecasts of future performance of other loans. In a widespread downturn, with rating downgrades, these assets would prove difficult to sell.

systemic risk

Risk of breakdown in the financial system, particularly due to spillover effects from one market into others.

This new financial model was brimming with **systemic risk,** a potential breakdown of the financial system when problems in one market spill over and disrupt others. When lenders such as banks have limited capital, and are afraid of further losses, they may rationally choose to hoard their capital instead of lending it out to customers such as small firms, thereby exacerbating funding problems for their customary borrowers.

The Shoe Drops

By fall of 2007, housing prices were in decline (Figure 1.3), mortgage delinquencies increased, and the stock market entered its own free fall (Figure 1.2). Many investment banks, which had large investments in mortgages, also began to totter.

The crisis peaked in September 2008. On September 7, the giant federal mortgage agencies Fannie Mae and Freddie Mac, both of which had taken large positions in subprime mortgage–backed securities, were put into conservatorship. (We will have more to say on their travails in Chapter 2.) The failure of these two mainstays of the U.S. housing and mortgage finance industries threw financial markets into a panic. By the second week of September, it was clear that both Lehman Brothers and Merrill Lynch were on the verge of bankruptcy. On September 14, Merrill Lynch was sold to Bank of America. The next day, Lehman Brothers, which was denied equivalent treatment, filed for bankruptcy protection. Two days later, on September 17, the government reluctantly lent $85 billion to AIG, reasoning that its failure would have been highly destabilizing to the banking industry, which was holding massive amounts of its credit guarantees (i.e., CDS contracts). The next day, the Treasury unveiled its first proposal to spend $700 billion to purchase "toxic" mortgage-backed securities.

A particularly devastating fallout of the Lehman bankruptcy was on the "money market" for short-term lending. Lehman had borrowed considerable funds by issuing very short-term unsecured debt called *commercial paper.* Among the major customers in the commercial paper were money market mutual funds, which invest in short-term, high-quality debt of commercial borrowers. When Lehman faltered, fear spread that these funds were exposed to losses on their large investments in commercial paper, and money market fund customers across the country rushed to withdraw their funds. In turn, the funds rushed out of commercial paper into safer and more liquid Treasury bills, essentially shutting down short-term financing markets.

---

[8]*Liquidity* refers to the speed and the ease with which investors can realize the cash value of an investment. Illiquid assets, for example, real estate, can be hard to sell quickly, and a quick sale may require a substantial discount from the price at which the asset could be sold in an unrushed situation.

The freezing up of credit markets was the end of any dwindling possibility that the financial crisis could be contained to Wall Street. Larger companies that had relied on the commercial paper market were now unable to raise short-term funds. Banks similarly found it difficult to raise funds. (Look back to Figure 1.1, where you will see that the TED spread, a measure of bank insolvency fears, skyrocketed in 2008.) With banks unwilling or unable to extend credit to their customers, thousands of small businesses that relied on bank lines of credit also became unable to finance their normal business operations. Capital-starved companies were forced to scale back their own operations precipitously. The unemployment rate rose rapidly, and the economy was in its worst recession in decades. The turmoil in the financial markets had spilled over into the real economy, and Main Street had joined Wall Street in a bout of protracted misery.

The crisis was not limited to the United States. Housing markets throughout the world fell and many European banks had to be rescued by their governments, which were themselves heavily in debt. As the cost of the bank bailouts mounted, the ability of these governments to repay their own debts came into doubt. In this way, the banking crisis spiraled into a sovereign debt crisis.

Greece was the hardest hit. Its government debt of about $460 billion was considerably more than its annual GDP. In 2011 it defaulted on debts totaling around $130 billion. Despite a series of rescue packages from the European Union, the European Central Bank, and the International Monetary Fund, it was still on shaky ground in 2017.

The Dodd-Frank Reform Act

The crisis engendered many calls for reform of Wall Street. These eventually led to the passage in 2010 of the Dodd-Frank Wall Street Reform and Consumer Protection Act, which proposed several mechanisms to mitigate systemic risk.

The act calls for stricter rules for bank capital, liquidity, and risk management practices, especially as banks become larger and their potential failure would be more threatening to other institutions. With more capital supporting banks, the potential for one insolvency to trigger another could be contained. In addition, when banks have more capital, they have less incentive to ramp up risk, as potential losses will come at their own expense and not the FDIC's.

Dodd-Frank also attempts to limit the risky activities in which banks can engage. The so-called Volcker Rule, named after former chairman of the Federal Reserve Paul Volcker, limits a bank's ability to trade for its own account and to own or invest in a hedge fund or private equity fund.

The incentives of the bond rating agencies are also a sore point. Few are happy with a system that has the ratings agencies paid by the firms they rate. The act creates an Office of Credit Ratings within the Securities and Exchange Commission to oversee the credit rating agencies.

It is still too early to know which, if any, of these reforms will stick. The implementation of Dodd-Frank is still subject to considerable interpretation by regulators, and the act is still under attack by some members of Congress. Regardless of the final outcome, the crisis surely has made clear the essential role of the financial system in the functioning of the real economy.

1.8   OUTLINE OF THE TEXT

The text has six parts, which are fairly independent and may be studied in a variety of sequences. Part One is an introduction to financial markets, instruments, and trading of securities. This part also describes the mutual fund industry.

Part Two is a fairly detailed presentation of "modern portfolio theory." This part of the text treats the effect of diversification on portfolio risk, the efficient diversification of investor portfolios, the choice of portfolios that strike an attractive balance between risk and return, and the trade-off between risk and expected return. This part also treats the efficient market hypothesis as well as behavioral critiques of theories based on investor rationality.

Parts Three through Five cover security analysis and valuation. Part Three is devoted to debt markets and Part Four to equity markets. Part Five covers derivative assets, such as options and futures contracts.

Part Six is an introduction to active investment management. It shows how different investors' objectives and constraints can lead to a variety of investment policies. This part discusses the role of investment management in nearly efficient markets, considers how one should evaluate the performance of managers who pursue active strategies, and takes a close look at hedge funds. It also shows how the principles of portfolio construction can be extended to the international setting.

SUMMARY

- Real assets create wealth. Financial assets represent claims to parts or all of that wealth. Financial assets determine how the ownership of real assets is distributed among investors.
- Financial assets can be categorized as fixed-income (debt), equity, or derivative instruments. Top-down portfolio construction techniques start with the asset allocation decision—the allocation of funds across broad asset classes—and then progress to more specific security-selection decisions.
- Competition in financial markets leads to a risk-return trade-off, in which securities that offer higher expected rates of return also impose greater risks on investors. The presence of risk, however, implies that actual returns can differ considerably from expected returns at the beginning of the investment period. Competition among security analysts also results in financial markets that are nearly informationally efficient, meaning that prices reflect all available information concerning the value of the security. Passive investment strategies may make sense in nearly efficient markets.
- Financial intermediaries pool investor funds and invest them. Their services are in demand because small investors cannot efficiently gather information, diversify, and monitor portfolios. The financial intermediary, in contrast, is a large investor that can take advantage of scale economies.
- Investment banking brings efficiency to corporate fund raising. Investment bankers develop expertise in pricing new issues and in marketing them to investors. By the end of 2008, all the major stand-alone U.S. investment banks had been absorbed into or had reorganized themselves into bank holding companies. In Europe, where universal banking had never been prohibited, large banks had long maintained both commercial and investment banking divisions.
- The financial crisis of 2008 demonstrated the links between the real and the financial sides of the economy and the importance of systemic risk. Systemic risk can be limited by transparency that allows traders and investors to assess the risk of their counterparties, capital requirements to prevent trading participants from being brought down by potential losses, frequent settlement of gains or losses to prevent losses from accumulating beyond an institution's ability to bear them, incentives to discourage excessive risk taking, and accurate and unbiased analysis by those charged with evaluating security risk.

KEY TERMS

active management, 11	investment, 2	securitization, 17
agency problems, 7	investment bankers, 14	security analysis, 10
asset allocation, 9	investment companies, 12	security selection, 9
derivative securities, 5	passive management, 11	systemic risk, 20
equity, 5	primary market, 15	venture capital (VC), 15
financial assets, 3	private equity, 15	
financial intermediaries, 12	real assets, 3	
fixed-income (debt)	risk-return trade-off, 10	
securities, 5	secondary market, 15	

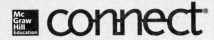

PROBLEM SETS

1. What are the differences between equity and fixed-income securities? *(LO 1-5)*
2. What is the difference between a primary asset and a derivative asset? *(LO 1-1)*
3. What is the difference between asset allocation and security selection? *(LO 1-4)*
4. What are agency problems? What are some approaches to solving them? *(LO 1-3)*
5. What are the differences between real and financial assets? *(LO 1-2)*
6. How does investment banking differ from commercial banking? *(LO 1-5)*
7. For each transaction, identify the real and/or financial assets that trade hands. Are any financial assets created or destroyed in the transaction? *(LO 1-2)*
   a. Toyota takes out a bank loan to finance the construction of a new factory.
   b. Toyota pays off its loan.
   c. Toyota uses $10 million of cash on hand to purchase additional inventory of spare auto parts.
8. Suppose that in a wave of pessimism, housing prices fall by 10% across the entire economy. *(LO 1-2)*
   a. Has the stock of real assets of the economy changed?
   b. Are individuals less wealthy?
   c. Can you reconcile your answers to (a) and (b)?
9. Lanni Products is a start-up computer software development firm. It currently owns computer equipment worth $30,000 and has cash on hand of $20,000 contributed by Lanni's owners. For each of the following transactions, identify the real and/or financial assets that trade hands. Are any financial assets created or destroyed in the transaction? *(LO 1-2)*
   a. Lanni takes out a bank loan. It receives $50,000 in cash and signs a note promising to pay back the loan over three years.
   b. Lanni uses the cash from the bank plus $20,000 of its own funds to finance the development of new financial planning software.
   c. Lanni sells the software product to Microsoft, which will market it to the public under the Microsoft name. Lanni accepts payment in the form of 2,000 shares of Microsoft stock.
   d. Lanni sells the shares of stock for $70 per share and uses part of the proceeds to pay off the bank loan.
10. Reconsider Lanni Products from Problem 9. *(LO 1-2)*
    a. Prepare its balance sheet just after it gets the bank loan. What is the ratio of real assets to total assets?
    b. Prepare the balance sheet after Lanni spends the $70,000 to develop its software product. What is the ratio of real assets to total assets?
    c. Prepare the balance sheet after Lanni accepts the payment of shares from Microsoft. What is the ratio of real assets to total assets?
11. What reforms to the financial system might reduce its exposure to systemic risk? *(LO 1-6)*
12. Examine the balance sheet of commercial banks in Table 1.3. *(LO 1-2)*
    a. What is the ratio of real assets to total assets?
    b. What is that ratio for nonfinancial firms (Table 1.4)?
    c. Why should this difference be expected?
13. Why do financial assets show up as a component of household wealth, but not of national wealth? Why do financial assets still matter for the material well-being of an economy? *(LO 1-2)*

14. Discuss the advantages and disadvantages of the following forms of managerial compensation in terms of mitigating agency problems, that is, potential conflicts of interest between managers and shareholders.   *(LO 1-3)*
    a. A fixed salary.
    b. Stock in the firm that must be held for five years.
    c. A salary linked to the firm's profits.

15. Oversight by large institutional investors or creditors is one mechanism to reduce agency problems. Why don't individual investors in the firm have the same incentive to keep an eye on management?   *(LO 1-3)*

16. Wall Street firms have traditionally compensated their traders with a share of the trading profits they generated. How might this practice have affected traders' willingness to assume risk? What is the agency problem this practice can engender?   *(LO 1-3)*

17. Why would you expect securitization to take place only in highly developed capital markets?   *(LO 1-6)*

18. What would you expect to be the relationship between securitization and the role of financial intermediaries in the economy? For example, what happens to the role of local banks in providing capital for mortgage loans when national markets in mortgage-backed securities become highly developed?   *(LO 1-6)*

19. Give an example of three financial intermediaries, and explain how they act as a bridge between small investors and large capital markets or corporations.   *(LO 1-5)*

20. Firms raise capital from investors by issuing shares in the primary markets. Does this imply that corporate financial managers can ignore trading of previously issued shares in the secondary market?   *(LO 1-4)*

21. The average rate of return on investments in large stocks has outpaced that on investments in Treasury bills by about 8% since 1926. Why, then, does anyone invest in Treasury bills?   *(LO 1-1)*

22. You see an advertisement for a book that claims to show how you can make $1 million with no risk and with no money down. Will you buy the book?   *(LO 1-1)*

WEB *master*

1. Log on to **finance.yahoo.com** and enter the ticker symbol "RRD" in the *Get Quotes* box to find information about R.R. Donnelley & Sons.
   a. Click on company *Profile*. What is Donnelly's main line of business?
   b. Now go to *Statistics*. How many shares of the company's stock are outstanding? What is the total market value of the firm? What were its profits in the most recent fiscal year?
   c. Look up the major *Holders* of the company's stock. What fraction of total shares is held by insiders?
   d. Now go to *Analyst* Opinion. What is the average price target (i.e., the predicted stock price of the Donnelly shares) of the analysts covering this firm? How does that compare to the price at which the stock is currently trading?
   e. Look at the company's balance sheet under the *Financials* tab. What were its total assets at the end of the most recent fiscal year?

2. Visit the website of the Securities and Exchange Commission, **www.sec.gov.** What is the mission of the SEC? What information and advice does the SEC offer to beginning investors?

3. Now visit the website of the Financial Industry Regulatory Authority, **www.finra.org.** What is its mission? What information and advice does it offer to beginners?

4. Now visit the website of the IOSCO, **www.iosco.org.** What is its mission? What information and advice does it offer to beginners?

1.1 *a.* Real

    b. Financial

    c. Real

    d. Real

    e. Financial

1.2 The central issue is the incentive and ability to monitor the quality of loans both when originated and over time. Freddie and Fannie clearly had incentive to monitor the quality of conforming loans that they had guaranteed, and their ongoing relationships with mortgage originators gave them opportunities to evaluate track records over extended periods of time. In the subprime mortgage market, the ultimate investors in the securities (or the CDOs backed by those securities), who were bearing the credit risk, should not have been willing to invest in loans with a disproportional likelihood of default. If they properly understood their exposure to default risk, then the (correspondingly low) prices they would have been willing to pay for these securities would have imposed discipline on the mortgage originators and servicers. The fact that they were willing to hold such large positions in these risky securities suggests that they did not appreciate the extent of their exposure. Maybe they were led astray by overly optimistic projections for housing prices or by biased assessments from the credit reporting agencies. While in principle either arrangement for default risk could have provided the appropriate discipline on the mortgage originators, in practice the informational advantages of Freddie and Fannie probably made them the better "recipients" of default risk. The lesson is that information and transparency are some of the preconditions for well-functioning markets.

Asset Classes and Financial Instruments

Learning Objectives

LO 2-1 Describe the differences among the major assets that trade in money markets and in capital markets.

LO 2-2 Describe the construction of stock market indexes.

LO 2-3 Calculate the profit or loss on investments in options and futures contracts.

Y ou learned in Chapter 1 that the process of building an investment portfolio usually begins by deciding how much money to allocate to broad classes of assets, such as safe money market securities or bank accounts, longer-term bonds, stocks, or even asset classes such as real estate or precious metals. This process is called *asset allocation*. Within each class, the investor then selects specific assets from a more detailed menu. This is called *security selection*.

Each broad asset class contains many specific security types, and the many variations on a theme can be overwhelming. Our goal in this chapter is to introduce you to the important features of broad classes of securities. Toward this end, we organize our tour of financial instruments according to asset class.

Financial markets are traditionally segmented into money markets and capital markets. Money market instruments include short-term, marketable, liquid, low-risk debt securities. Money market instruments sometimes are called *cash equivalents,* or just *cash* for short. Capital markets, in contrast, include longer-term and riskier securities. Securities in the capital market are much more diverse than those found within the money market. For this reason, we will subdivide the capital market into three segments: longer-term debt markets, equity markets, and derivative markets in which options and futures trade.

We first describe money market instruments. We then move on to debt and equity securities. We explain the structure of various stock market indexes in this chapter because market benchmark portfolios play an important role in portfolio construction and evaluation. Finally, we survey the derivative security markets for options and futures contracts. A selection of the markets, instruments, and indexes covered in this chapter appears in Table 2.1.

2.1   THE MONEY MARKET

The **money market** consists of very short-term highly marketable debt securities. Many of these securities trade in large denominations and so are out of the reach of individual investors. Money market mutual funds, however, are easily accessible to small investors. These mutual funds pool the resources of many investors and purchase a wide variety of money market securities on their behalf.

> **money markets**
>
> Include short-term, highly liquid, and relatively low-risk debt instruments.

Treasury Bills

U.S. **Treasury bills** (T-bills, or just bills, for short) are the most marketable of all money market instruments. T-bills represent the simplest form of borrowing. The government raises money by selling bills to the public. Investors buy the bills at a discount from the stated maturity value. At the bill's maturity, the government pays the investor the face value of the bill. The difference between the purchase price and the ultimate maturity value constitutes the investor's earnings.

> **Treasury bills**
>
> Short-term government securities issued at a discount from face value and returning the face amount at maturity.

T-bills are issued with initial maturities of 4, 13, 26, or 52 weeks. Individuals can purchase them directly from the Treasury or on the secondary market from a government securities dealer. T-bills are highly liquid; that is, they are easily converted to cash and sold at low transaction cost and with little price risk. Unlike most other money market instruments, which sell in minimum denominations of $100,000, T-bills sell in minimum denominations of only $100, although $10,000 denominations are far more common. While the income earned on T-bills is taxable at the federal level, it is exempt from state and local taxes, another characteristic distinguishing bills from other money market instruments.

Figure 2.1 is a partial listing of T-bills from *The Wall Street Journal Online* (look for the *Markets* tab, then *Market Data*, then *Rates,* and finally *Treasury Quotes*). Rather than providing prices of each bill, the financial press reports yields based on those prices. You will see yields corresponding to both bid and asked prices. The *asked price* is the price you would have to pay to buy a T-bill from a securities dealer. The *bid price* is the slightly lower price you would receive if you wanted to sell a bill to a dealer. The *bid–asked spread* is the difference in these prices, which is the dealer's source of profit.

The first two yields in Figure 2.1 are reported using the *bank-discount method.* This means that the bill's discount from its maturity, or face, value is "annualized" based on a 360-day year and then reported as a percentage of face value. For example, for the highlighted bill maturing on October 12, 2017, days to maturity are 177 and the yield under the column labeled "ASKED" is given as .895%. This means that a dealer was willing to sell the bill at a discount from face value of .895% × (177/360) = .440%. So a bill with $10,000 face value could be

TABLE 2.1	Financial markets and indexes	
The money market	**The bond market**
Treasury bills	Treasury bonds and notes
Certificates of deposit	Federal agency debt
Commercial paper	Municipal bonds
Bankers' acceptances	Corporate bonds
Eurodollars	Mortgage-backed securities
Repos and reverses	**Equity markets**
Federal funds	Common stocks
Brokers' calls	Preferred stocks
Indexes	**Derivative markets**
Dow Jones averages	Options
Standard & Poor's indexes	Futures and forwards
Bond market indicators	Swaps
International indexes	

MATURITY	DAYS TO MATURITY	BID	ASKED	CHG	ASKED YIELD
June 8, 2017	51	0.730	0.720	unch.	0.731
August 17, 2017	121	0.793	0.783	−0.010	0.795
October 12, 2017	177	0.905	0.895	−0.028	0.911
December 7, 2017	233	0.928	0.918	−0.023	0.936
March 29, 2018	345	0.988	0.978	−0.020	1.000

purchased for $10,000 × (1 − .0044) = $9,956.00. Similarly, on the basis of the bid yield of .905%, a dealer would be willing to purchase the bill for $10,000 × (1 − .00905 × 177/360) = $9,955.504. Because prices and yields are inversely related, the higher bid *yield* reported in Figure 2.1 implies a lower bid *price*.

The bank discount method for computing yields has a long tradition, but it is flawed for at least two reasons. First, it assumes that the year has only 360 days. Second, it computes the yield as a fraction of face value rather than of the price the investor paid to acquire the bill.[1] An investor who buys the bill for the asked price and holds it until maturity will see her investment grow over 177 days by a multiple of $10,000/$9,956.00 = 1.004419, for a gain of .4419%. Annualizing this gain using a 365-day year results in a yield of .4419% × 365/177 = .911%, which is the value reported in the last column, under "asked yield." This last value is called the Treasury bill's *bond-equivalent yield.*

Certificates of Deposit

A **certificate of deposit** (CD) is a time deposit with a bank. Time deposits may not be withdrawn on demand. The bank pays interest and principal to the depositor only at the end of the fixed term of the CD. CDs issued in denominations larger than $100,000 are usually negotiable, however; that is, they can be sold to another investor if the owner needs to cash in the certificate before it matures. Short-term CDs are highly marketable, although the market significantly thins out for maturities of three months or more. CDs are treated as bank deposits by the Federal Deposit Insurance Corporation, so they are insured for up to $250,000 in the event of a bank insolvency.

Commercial Paper

The typical corporation is a net borrower of both long-term funds (for capital investments) and short-term funds (for working capital). Large, well-known companies often issue their own short-term unsecured debt notes directly to the public, rather than borrowing from banks. These notes

are called **commercial paper** (CP). Sometimes, CP is backed by a bank line of credit, which gives the borrower access to cash that can be used if needed to pay off the paper at maturity.

CP maturities may range up to 270 days, but most often, they are issued with maturities of less than one or two months in denominations of multiples of $100,000. Therefore, small investors can invest in commercial paper only indirectly, through money market mutual funds.

CP is considered to be a fairly safe asset, given that a firm's condition presumably can be monitored and predicted over a term as short as one month. CP trades in secondary markets and so is quite liquid. Most issues are rated by at least one agency such as Standard & Poor's. The yield on CP depends on its time to maturity and credit rating.

While most CP historically was issued by nonfinancial firms, in the years leading up to the financial crisis, there was a sharp increase in so-called *asset-backed commercial paper* issued

---

[1]Both of these "errors" were dictated by computational simplicity in the days before computers. It is easier to compute percentage discounts from a round number such as face value than from purchase price. It is also easier to annualize using a 360-day year, since 360 is an even multiple of so many numbers.

by financial firms such as banks. This short-term CP typically was used to raise funds for the issuing firm to invest in other assets, most notoriously, subprime mortgages. These assets in turn were used as collateral for the CP—hence the label "asset-backed." This practice led to many difficulties starting in 2007 when those subprime mortgages began defaulting. The banks found themselves unable to issue new CP to refinance their positions as the old paper matured.

Bankers' Acceptances

A **banker's acceptance** starts as an order to a bank by a bank's customer to pay a sum of money at a future date, typically within six months. At this stage, it is like a postdated check. When the bank endorses the order for payment as "accepted," it assumes responsibility for ultimate payment to the holder of the acceptance. At this point, the acceptance may be traded in secondary markets much like any other claim on the bank. Bankers' acceptances are considered very safe assets, as they allow traders to substitute the bank's credit standing for their own. They are used widely in foreign trade where the creditworthiness of one trader is unknown to the trading partner. Acceptances sell at a discount from the face value of the payment order, just as T-bills sell at a discount from par value.

banker's acceptance
An order to a bank by a customer to pay a sum of money at a future date.

Eurodollars

Eurodollars are dollar-denominated deposits at foreign banks or foreign branches of American banks. By locating outside the United States, these banks escape regulation by the Federal Reserve Board. Despite the tag "Euro," these accounts need not be in European banks, although that is where the practice of accepting dollar-denominated deposits outside the United States began.

Most Eurodollar deposits are for large sums, and most are time deposits of less than six months' maturity. A variation on the Eurodollar time deposit is the Eurodollar certificate of deposit, which resembles a domestic bank CD except it is the liability of a non-U.S. branch of a bank, typically a London branch. Firms also issue Eurodollar bonds, that is, dollar-denominated bonds outside the U.S., although such bonds are not a money market investment by virtue of their long maturities.

Eurodollars
Dollar-denominated deposits at foreign banks or foreign branches of American banks.

Repos and Reverses

Dealers in government securities use **repurchase agreements**, also called **repos** (RPs), as a form of short-term, usually overnight, borrowing. The dealer sells securities to an investor on an overnight basis, with an agreement to buy back those securities the next day at a slightly higher price. The increase in the price is the overnight interest. The dealer thus takes out a one-day loan from the investor. The securities serve as collateral for the loan.

A *term repo* is essentially an identical transaction, except the term of the implicit loan can be 30 days or more. Repos are considered very safe in terms of credit risk because the loans are collateralized by the securities. A *reverse repo* is the mirror image of a repo. Here, the dealer finds an investor holding government securities and buys them with an agreement to resell them at a specified higher price on a future date.

repurchase agreements (repos)
Short-term sales of securities with an agreement to repurchase the securities at a higher price.

Brokers' Calls

Individuals who buy stocks on margin borrow part of the funds to pay for the stocks from their broker. The broker in turn may borrow the funds from a bank, agreeing to repay the bank immediately (on call) if the bank requests it. The rate paid on such loans is usually about one percentage point higher than the rate on short-term T-bills.

Federal Funds

Just as most of us maintain deposits at banks, banks maintain deposits of their own at the Federal Reserve Bank, or the Fed. Each member bank of the Federal Reserve System is required to maintain a minimum balance in a reserve account with the Fed. The required balance depends on the total deposits of the bank's customers. Funds in the bank's reserve account are called **Federal funds** or *Fed funds*. At any time, some banks have more funds than required at

Federal funds
Funds in the accounts of commercial banks at the Federal Reserve Bank.

THE LIBOR SCANDALS

LIBOR was designed initially as a survey of interbank lending rates but soon became a key determinant of short-term interest rates with far-reaching significance. More than $350 trillion of derivative contracts have payoffs tied to it, and many trillion dollars of loans and bonds with floating interest rates linked to LIBOR are currently outstanding. LIBOR is quoted for loans in five currencies (the U.S. dollar, yen, euro, U.K. pound, and Swiss franc) for maturities ranging from a day to a year, although three months is the most common.

However, LIBOR is not a rate at which actual transactions occur; instead, it is just a survey of "estimated" borrowing rates, and this has made it vulnerable to manipulation. Several large banks are asked to report the rate at which they *claim* they can borrow in the interbank market. Outliers are trimmed from the sample of responses, and LIBOR is calculated as the average of the mid-range estimates.

Over time, several problems surfaced. First, it appeared that many banks understated the rates at which they claimed they could borrow in an effort to make themselves look financially stronger. Other surveys that asked for estimates of the rates at which *other* banks could borrow resulted in higher values. Moreover, LIBOR did not seem to reflect current market conditions. A majority of LIBOR submissions were unchanged from day to day even when other interest rates fluctuated, and LIBOR spreads showed surprisingly low correlation with other measures of credit risk.

Even worse, once the market came under scrutiny, it emerged that participating banks were colluding to manipulate their LIBOR submissions to enhance profits on their derivatives trades. Traders used emails and instant messages to tell each other whether they wanted to see higher or lower submissions. Members of this informal cartel essentially set up a "favor bank" to help each other move the survey average up or down depending on their trading positions.

More than $6 billion of fines have been paid, among them, Deutsche Bank ($2.5 billion), UBS ($1.5 billion), Royal Bank of Scotland ($1.1 billion), Rabobank ($1 billion), and SocGen ($600 million). But government fines may be only the beginning. A federal appeals court in 2016 ruled that private lawsuits involving antitrust violations may proceed. Borrowers paying an interest rate tied to LIBOR argue that they were harmed by the collusion of participating banks to coordinate rates.

Several reforms have been suggested and some have been implemented. The British Bankers Association, which until recently ran the LIBOR survey, yielded responsibility for LIBOR to British regulators. LIBOR quotes in less active currencies and maturities, where collusion is easier, have been eliminated. More substantive proposals would replace the survey rates with ones based on actual, verifiable transactions—that is, real loans. British regulators have expressed their wish to phase out LIBOR by 2021. Two primary contenders to replace it are SONIA (Sterling Overnight Interbank Average Rate), an overnight interest rate in the U.K. market and, for U.S. dollar rates, the rate on repurchase agreements on Treasury securities.

These proposals leave some important questions unanswered. For example, if LIBOR is phased out, what will happen to LIBOR-based long-term contracts with maturities that extend beyond 2021? For example, LIBOR is the most common index for adjustable rate mortgages, most of which have maturities of 30 years. And because SONIA is only an overnight rate, what will replace the LIBOR benchmark for longer maturities?

---

the Fed. Other banks, primarily big New York and other financial center banks, tend to have a shortage of Federal funds. In the Federal funds market, banks with excess funds lend to those with a shortage. These loans, which are usually overnight transactions, are arranged at a rate of interest called the *Federal funds rate.*

Although the Fed funds market arose primarily as a way for banks to transfer balances to meet reserve requirements, today the market has evolved to the point that many large banks use Federal funds in a straightforward way as one component of their total sources of funding. Therefore, the Fed funds rate is simply the rate of interest on very short-term loans among financial institutions. While most investors cannot participate in this market, the Fed funds rate commands great interest as a key barometer of monetary policy.

The LIBOR Market

London Interbank Offer Rate (LIBOR)

Lending rate among banks in the London market.

The **London Interbank Offer Rate (LIBOR)** is the premier short-term interest rate quoted in the European money market and serves as a reference rate for a wide range of transactions. It was designed to reflect the rate at which banks lend among themselves. While such interbank lending has declined substantially in recent years, particularly at longer maturities, LIBOR remains a crucial benchmark for many financial contracts. For example, a corporation might borrow at a rate equal to LIBOR plus two percentage points. Hundreds of trillions of dollars of loans, mortgages, and derivative contracts are tied to it.

LIBOR and similar rates called Euribor (European interbank offer rate) and Tibor (Tokyo interbank offer rate) are quoted in major currencies (for example, the U.S. dollar, the British pound, the yen, the euro) for terms ranging from overnight to several months. However, they are all based on surveys of rates reported by participating banks rather than actual transactions.

MONEY MARKET FUNDS AND THE FINANCIAL CRISIS OF 2008

Money market funds are mutual funds that invest in the short-term debt instruments that comprise the money market. They are required to hold only short-maturity debt of the highest quality: The average maturity of their holdings must be maintained at less than three months. Because of this very conservative investment profile, money market funds typically experience extremely low price risk. Investors for their part usually acquire check-writing privileges with their funds and often use them as a close substitute for a bank account. This is feasible because the funds almost always maintain share value at $1 and pass along all investment earnings to their investors as interest.

Until 2008, only one fund had "broken the buck," that is, suffered losses large enough to force value per share below $1. But when Lehman Brothers filed for bankruptcy protection on September 15, 2008, several funds that had invested heavily in its commercial paper suffered large losses. The next day, Reserve Primary Fund, the oldest money market fund, broke the buck when its value per share fell to only $0.97.

The realization that money market funds were at risk in the credit crisis led to a wave of investor redemptions similar to a run on a bank. Fearing further outflows, the U.S. Treasury announced that it would make federal insurance available to money market funds willing to pay an insurance fee. This program would thus be similar to FDIC bank insurance. With the federal insurance in place, the outflows were quelled.

However, the turmoil in Wall Street's money market funds had already spilled over into "Main Street." Fearing further investor redemptions, money market funds became afraid to commit funds even over short periods, and their demand for commercial paper effectively dried up. Firms throughout the economy had come to depend on those markets as a major source of short-term finance to fund expenditures ranging from salaries to inventories. Further breakdown in the money markets would have had an immediate crippling effect on the broad economy.

To end the panic and stabilize the money markets, the federal government decided to guarantee investments in money market funds. The guarantee did in fact calm investors and end the run, but it put the government on the hook for a potential liability of up to $3 trillion—the assets held in money market funds at the time.

U.S. regulators have since approved a series of reforms to reduce the risks of runs on these funds. Institutional money market funds (those servicing institutions rather than retail investors) are required to "float" the prices of their shares based on the value of their assets rather than maintain a fixed $1 value per share. This limits the incentive during a crisis for investors to compete to be the first to withdraw funds while share prices are maintained at a nonsustainable level of $1. In addition, funds will have the authority to either limit redemptions or impose redemption fees of up to 2% if a fund's assets fall by more than 30%. Finally, the rules call for enhanced transparency, with greater disclosure of asset values, portfolio composition, and liquidity.

With interbank lending recently sparse, and in light of a major scandal in the LIBOR market in 2012, the search for a replacement is on.

British regulators have proposed phasing out LIBOR by 2021. They propose a replacement rate called SONIA (Sterling Overnight Interbank Average Rate), which is an overnight interest rate at which actual transactions take place. U.S. regulators have proposed that U.S. dollar LIBOR be replaced by the rate on repurchase agreements on Treasury securities.

The 2012 scandal involving the fixing of LIBOR deeply shook these markets and highlighted the considerable shortcomings of survey-based benchmarks. The nearby box discusses those events.

Yields on Money Market Instruments

Although most money market securities are low risk, they are not risk-free. The securities of the money market promise yields greater than those on default-free T-bills, at least in part because of their greater relative risk. Investors who require more liquidity also will accept lower yields on securities, such as T-bills, that can be more quickly and cheaply sold for cash. Figure 2.2 shows that bank CDs, for example, consistently have offered a yield premium over T-bills. Moreover as Figure 2.2 shows that premium increases with economic crises such as the energy price shocks associated with the OPEC disturbances, the stock market crash in 1987, the collapse of Long-Term Capital Management in 1998, and the financial crisis of 2008–2009. If you look back to Figure 1.1 in Chapter 1, you'll see that the TED spread, the difference between the LIBOR rate and the Treasury bill rate, also peaked during the financial crisis.

Money market funds are mutual funds that invest in money market instruments and have become major sources of funding to that sector. The nearby box discusses the fallout of the financial crisis on those funds.

FIGURE 2.2

Spread between three-month CD and T-bill rates

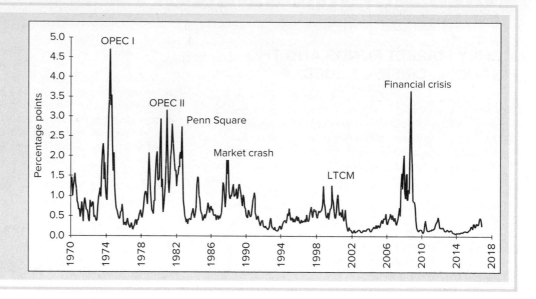

2.2   THE BOND MARKET

The bond market is composed of longer-term borrowing or debt instruments than those that trade in the money market. This market includes Treasury notes and bonds, corporate bonds, municipal bonds, mortgage securities, and federal agency debt.

These instruments are sometimes said to comprise the *fixed-income capital market,* because most of them promise either a fixed stream of income or stream of income that is determined according to a specified formula. In practice, these formulas can result in a flow of income that is far from fixed. Therefore, the term "fixed income" is probably not fully appropriate. It is simpler and more straightforward to call these securities either debt instruments or bonds.

Treasury Notes and Bonds

Treasury notes or bonds

Debt obligations of the federal government with original maturities of one year or more.

The U.S. government borrows funds in large part by selling **Treasury notes and bonds**. T-notes are issued with original maturities ranging up to 10 years, while T-bonds are issued with maturities ranging from 10 to 30 years. Both bonds and notes may be issued in increments of $100 but far more commonly trade in denominations of $1,000. Both bonds and notes make semiannual interest payments called *coupon payments,* so named because in precomputer days, investors would literally clip a coupon attached to the bond and present it to receive the interest payment.

Figure 2.3 is an excerpt from a listing of Treasury issues. The highlighted bond matures in May 2020. The coupon income or interest paid by the bond is 1.5% of par value, meaning that for a $1,000 face value bond, $15 in annual interest payments will be made in two semiannual installments of $7.50 each.

FIGURE 2.3

Listing of Treasury bond issues

Source: *The Wall Street Journal Online*, April 18, 2017.

Maturity	Coupon	Bid	Asked	Change	Asked yield to maturity
April 15, 2019	0.875	99.3828	99.3984	0.0547	1.182
May 31, 2020	1.500	100.3047	100.3203	0.1719	1.394
May 31, 2022	1.875	100.6797	100.6953	0.3750	1.732
February 15, 2031	5.375	136.5313	136.5938	1.1797	2.275
February 15, 2043	3.125	105.4531	105.4844	1.5313	2.824
February 15, 2047	3.000	103.1797	103.2109	1.5313	2.840

The bid price of the highlighted bond, which matures in May 2020, is 100.3047. (This is the decimal equivalent of 100 $^{39}/_{128}$. The minimum *tick size,* or price increment in the Treasury-bond market, is generally $^{1}/_{128}$ of a point.) Although bonds are typically traded in denominations of $1,000 par value, prices are quoted as a percentage of par. Thus, the bid price should be interpreted as 100.3047% of par, or $1,003.047 for the $1,000 par value bond. Similarly, the ask (equivalently, asked) price at which the bond could be purchased from a dealer is 100.3203% of par, or $1,003.203. The .1719 change means that the asked price on this day increased by .1719% of par value (equivalently, by $^{22}/_{128}$ of a point) from the previous day's close. Finally, the yield to maturity based on the asked price is 1.394%.

The *yield to maturity* reported in the last column is a measure of the annualized rate of return to an investor who buys the bond for the asked price and holds it until maturity. It accounts for both coupon income as well as the difference between the purchase price of the bond and its final value of $1,000 at maturity. We discuss the yield to maturity in detail in Chapter 10.

What were the bid price, asked price, and yield to maturity of the 1.875% May 2022 Treasury bond displayed in Figure 2.3? What was its asked price the previous day?

CONCEPT
c h e c k
2.1

Inflation-Protected Treasury Bonds

The natural place to start building an investment portfolio is at the least risky end of the spectrum. Around the world, governments of many countries, including the United States, have issued bonds that are linked to an index of the cost of living in order to provide their citizens with an effective way to hedge inflation risk.

In the United States, inflation-protected Treasury bonds are called *TIPS* (Treasury Inflation Protected Securities). The principal amount on these bonds is adjusted in proportion to increases in the Consumer Price Index. Therefore, they provide a constant stream of income in real (inflation-adjusted) dollars, and the real interest rates you earn on these securities are risk-free if you hold them to maturity. We return to TIPS bonds in more detail in Chapter 10.

Federal Agency Debt

Some government agencies issue their own securities to finance their activities. These agencies usually are formed for public policy reasons to channel credit to a particular sector of the economy that Congress believes is not receiving adequate credit through normal private sources.

The major mortgage-related agencies are the Federal Home Loan Bank (FHLB), the Federal National Mortgage Association (FNMA, or Fannie Mae), the Government National Mortgage Association (GNMA, or Ginnie Mae), and the Federal Home Loan Mortgage Corporation (FHLMC, or Freddie Mac).

Although the debt of federal agencies was never explicitly insured by the federal government, it had long been assumed that the government would assist an agency nearing default. Those beliefs were validated when Fannie Mae and Freddie Mac encountered severe financial distress in September 2008. With both firms on the brink of insolvency, the government stepped in and put them both into conservatorship, assigned the Federal Housing Finance Agency to run the firms, but did in fact agree to make good on the firm's bonds. (Turn back to Chapter 1 for more discussion of the Fannie and Freddie failures.)

International Bonds

Many firms borrow abroad and many investors buy bonds from foreign issuers. In addition to national capital markets, there is a thriving international capital market, largely centered in London.

A *Eurobond* is a bond denominated in a currency other than that of the country in which it is issued. For example, a dollar-denominated bond sold in Britain would be called a *Eurodollar bond.* Similarly, investors might speak of Euroyen bonds, yen-denominated bonds sold outside Japan. Since the European currency is called the *euro,* the term *Eurobond* may be confusing. It is best to think of them simply as international bonds.

In contrast to bonds that are issued in foreign currencies, many firms issue bonds in foreign countries but in the currency of the investor. For example, a Yankee bond is a dollar-denominated bond sold in the U.S. by a non-U.S. issuer. Similarly, Samurai bonds are yen-denominated bonds sold in Japan by non-Japanese issuers.

Municipal Bonds

municipal bonds

Tax-exempt bonds issued by state and local governments.

Municipal bonds ("munis") are issued by state and local governments. They are similar to Treasury and corporate bonds, except their interest income is exempt from federal income taxation. The interest income also is usually exempt from state and local taxation in the issuing state. Capital gains taxes, however, must be paid on munis if the bonds mature or are sold for more than the investor's purchase price.

There are basically two types of municipal bonds. *General obligation bonds* are backed by the "full faith and credit" (i.e., the taxing power) of the issuer, while *revenue bonds* are issued to finance particular projects and are backed either by the revenues from that project or by the municipal agency operating the project. Typical issuers of revenue bonds are airports, hospitals, and turnpike or port authorities. Revenue bonds are riskier in terms of default than general obligation bonds.

An *industrial development bond* is a revenue bond that is issued to finance commercial enterprises, such as the construction of a factory that can be operated by a private firm. In effect, this device gives the firm access to the municipality's ability to borrow at tax-exempt rates, and the federal government limits the amount of these bonds that may be issued.[2] Figure 2.4 plots outstanding amounts of industrial revenue bonds as well as general obligation municipal bonds.

Like Treasury bonds, municipal bonds vary widely in maturity. A good deal of the debt issued is in the form of short-term *tax anticipation notes* that raise funds to pay for expenses before actual collection of taxes. Other municipal debt may be long term and used to fund large capital investments. Maturities range up to 30 years.

The key feature of municipal bonds is their tax-exempt status. Because investors pay neither federal nor state taxes on the interest proceeds, they are willing to accept lower yields on these securities.

An investor choosing between taxable and tax-exempt bonds needs to compare after-tax returns on each bond. An exact comparison requires the computation of after-tax rates of return with explicit recognition of taxes on income and realized capital gains. In practice, there is a simpler rule of thumb. If we let t denote the investor's combined federal plus local

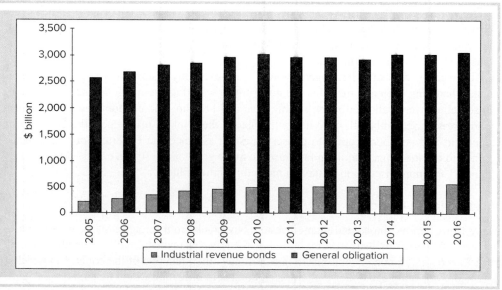

FIGURE 2.4

Outstanding tax-exempt debt

Source: *Flow of Funds Accounts of the United States,* Board of Governors of the Federal Reserve System, March 2017.

[2]A warning, however. Although interest on industrial development bonds usually is exempt from federal tax, it can be subject to the alternative minimum tax if the bonds are used to finance projects of for-profit companies.

TABLE 2.2	Equivalent taxable yields corresponding to various tax-exempt yields				
	Tax-Exempt Yield				
Marginal Tax Rate	**1%**	**2%**	**3%**	**4%**	**5%**
20%	1.25%	2.50%	3.75%	5.00%	6.25%
30	1.43	2.86	4.29	5.71	7.15
40	1.67	3.33	5.00	6.67	8.33
50	2.00	4.00	6.00	8.00	10.00

marginal tax rate and $r_{taxable}$ denote the total before-tax rate of return available on taxable bonds, then $r_{taxable}(1 - t)$ is the after-tax rate available on those securities.[3] If this value exceeds the rate on municipal bonds, r_{muni}, the investor does better holding the taxable bonds. Otherwise, the tax-exempt municipals provide higher after-tax returns.

One way of comparing bonds is to determine the interest rate on taxable bonds that would be necessary to provide an after-tax return equal to that of municipals. To derive this value, we set after-tax yields equal and solve for the *equivalent taxable yield* of the tax-exempt bond. This is the rate a taxable bond would need to offer in order to match the after-tax yield on the tax-free municipal.

$$r_{taxable}(1 - t) = r_{muni} \qquad (2.1)$$

or

$$r_{taxable} = \frac{r_{muni}}{1 - t} \qquad (2.2)$$

Thus, the equivalent taxable yield is simply the tax-free rate divided by $1 - t$. Table 2.2 presents equivalent taxable yields for several municipal yields and tax rates.

This table frequently appears in the marketing literature for tax-exempt mutual bond funds because it demonstrates to high-tax-bracket investors that municipal bonds offer attractive equivalent taxable yields. Each entry is calculated from Equation 2.2. If the equivalent taxable yield exceeds the actual yields offered on taxable bonds, then after taxes the investor is better off holding municipal bonds. The equivalent taxable interest rate increases with the investor's tax bracket; the higher the bracket, the more valuable the tax-exempt feature of municipals. Thus, high-bracket individuals tend to hold municipals.

We also can use Equation 2.1 or 2.2 to find the tax bracket at which investors are indifferent between taxable and tax-exempt bonds. We solve Equation 2.1 for the tax bracket at which after-tax yields are equal. Doing so, we find the cutoff tax bracket to be:

$$t = 1 - \frac{r_{muni}}{r_{taxable}} \qquad (2.3)$$

Thus, the yield ratio $r_{muni}/r_{taxable}$ is a key determinant of the attractiveness of municipal bonds. The higher the yield ratio, the lower the cutoff tax bracket, and the more individuals will prefer to hold municipal debt.

[3]The combined federal plus state tax rate depends on whether state taxes are deductible at the federal level. For individuals who take the standard deduction, state taxes do not affect federal taxes. Neither does an increase in state taxes affect the federal taxes of those who are already taking the $10,000 maximum deduction for state and local taxes. For these investors, the combined tax rate is simply the sum of the federal and state rates. For example, if your federal tax rate is 28% and your state tax rate is 5%, your combined tax rate would be 33%. However, if state taxes are (on the margin) deductible for federal taxes, then the combined tax rate reflects the fact that you owe taxes only on interest income *net* of state taxes. You therefore pay federal taxes on Interest × $(1 - t_{state})$. Your after-tax income on each dollar of municipal interest would be $(1 - t_{federal}) \times (1 - t_{state})$. In our example, your after-tax proceeds on each dollar earned would be $(1 - .28) \times (1 - .05) = .684$, which implies a combined tax rate of $1 - .684 = .316$, or 31.6%.

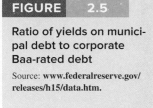

FIGURE   2.5

Ratio of yields on municipal debt to corporate
Baa-rated debt

Source: www.federalreserve.gov/
releases/h15/data.htm.

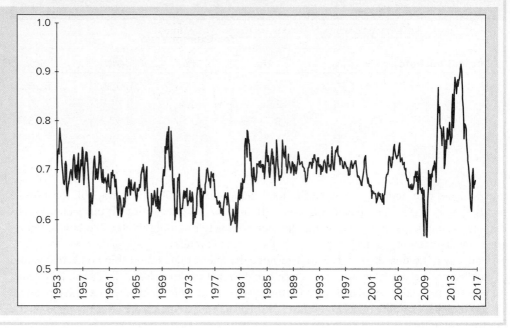

As a rough guide to the cutoff tax bracket, Figure 2.5 plots the ratio of 20-year municipal debt yields to the yield on Baa-rated corporate debt. The default risk on these bonds may be roughly comparable in many periods but certainly will fluctuate over time. For example, the sharp run-up in the ratio in 2011–2013 probably reflects increased concern at the time over the precarious financial condition of several states and municipalities, leading to higher credit spreads on their bonds.

EXAMPLE 2.1

*Taxable versus
Tax-Exempt Yields*

Figure 2.5 shows that for most of the last 60 years, the ratio of tax-exempt to taxable yields fluctuated around .70. What does this imply about the cutoff tax bracket above which tax-exempt bonds provide higher after-tax yields? Equation 2.3 shows that an investor whose combined tax bracket (federal plus local) exceeds $1 - .70 = .30$, or 30%, will derive a greater after-tax yield from municipals. As we pointed out, however, it is difficult to control precisely for differences in the risks of these bonds, so this calculation must be taken as approximate.

**CONCEPT
check   2.2**

Suppose your combined tax bracket is 30%. Would you prefer to earn a 6% taxable return or a 4% tax-free yield? What is the equivalent taxable yield of the 4% tax-free yield?

Corporate Bonds

corporate bonds

Long-term debt issued by private corporations typically paying semiannual coupons and returning the face value of the bond at maturity.

Corporate bonds are the means by which private firms borrow money directly from the public. These bonds are structured much like Treasury issues in that they typically pay semiannual coupons over their lives and return the face value to the bondholder at maturity. Where they differ most importantly from Treasury bonds is in risk.

Default risk is a real consideration in the purchase of corporate bonds. We treat this issue in considerable detail in Chapter 10. For now, we distinguish only among secured bonds, which have specific collateral backing them in the event of firm bankruptcy; unsecured bonds, called *debentures,* which have no collateral; and subordinated debentures, which have a lower priority claim to the firm's assets in the event of bankruptcy.

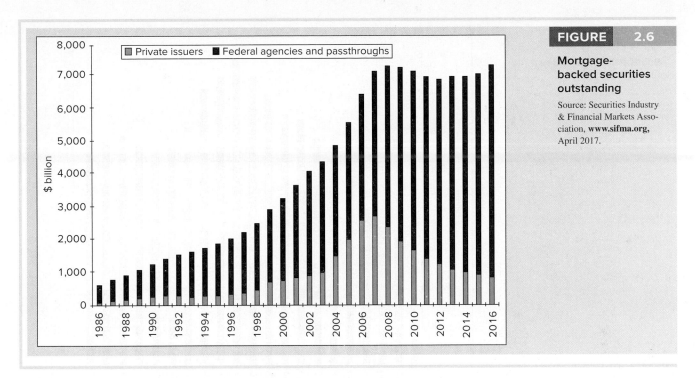

FIGURE 2.6

Mortgage-backed securities outstanding

Source: Securities Industry & Financial Markets Association, **www.sifma.org**, April 2017.

Corporate bonds sometimes come with options attached. *Callable bonds* give the firm the option to repurchase the bond from the holder at a stipulated call price. *Convertible bonds* give the bondholder the option to convert each bond into a stipulated number of shares of stock. These options are treated in more detail in Part Three.

Mortgage and Asset-Backed Securities

Using mortgage-backed securities, almost anyone can invest in a portfolio of mortgage loans, and these securities have become a major component of the fixed-income market.

As described in Chapter 1, a *mortgage-backed security* is either an ownership claim in a pool of mortgages or an obligation that is secured by such a pool. Most pass-throughs traditionally comprised *conforming mortgages,* which meant that the loans had to satisfy certain underwriting guidelines (standards for the creditworthiness of the borrower) before they could be purchased by Fannie Mae or Freddie Mac. In the years leading up to the financial crisis, however, a large amount of *subprime mortgages,* that is, riskier loans made to financially weaker borrowers, were bundled and sold by "private-label" issuers. Figure 2.6 illustrates the explosive growth of these securities, at least until the crisis.

In an effort to make housing more affordable to low-income households, the government-sponsored enterprises were encouraged to buy subprime mortgage securities. These loans turned out to be disastrous, with trillion-dollar losses spread among banks, hedge funds, and other investors, as well as Freddie and Fannie, which lost billions of dollars on the subprime mortgages they had purchased. You can see from Figure 2.6 that, starting in 2007, the market in private-label mortgage pass-throughs began to shrink rapidly.

Despite these troubles, few believe that securitization itself will cease, although practices in this market are likely to remain far more conservative than in previous years, particularly with respect to the credit standards that must be met by the ultimate borrower. Indeed, securitization has become an increasingly common staple of many credit markets. For example, it is now common for car loans, student loans, home equity loans, credit card loans, and even debt of private firms to be bundled into pass-through securities that can be traded in the capital market. Figure 2.7 documents the rapid growth of nonmortgage asset-backed securities, at least until 2007. After the financial crisis, the market contracted considerably, but the asset-backed market is still substantial.

FIGURE   2.7

Asset-backed securities outstanding

Source: Securities Industry & Financial Markets Association, **www.sifma.org.**

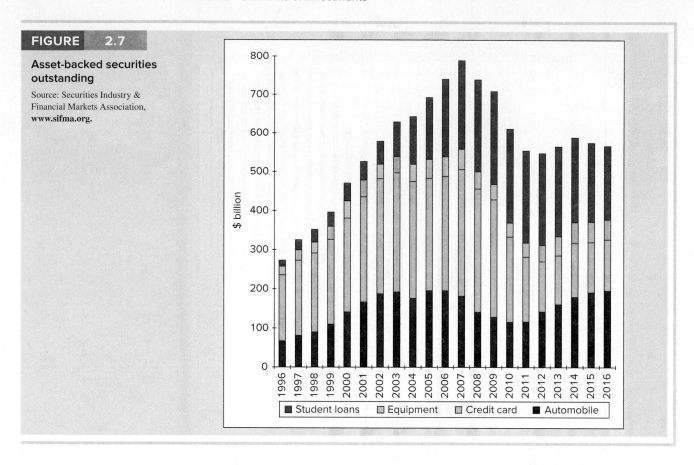

2.3   EQUITY SECURITIES

Common Stock as Ownership Shares

common stocks

Ownership shares in a publicly held corporation. Shareholders have voting rights and may receive dividends.

Common stocks, also known as equity securities, or equities, represent ownership shares in a corporation. Each share of common stock entitles its owners to one vote on any matter of corporate governance put to a vote at the corporation's annual meeting and to a share in the financial benefits of ownership (e.g., the right to any dividends that the corporation may choose to distribute).[4]

A corporation is controlled by a board of directors elected by the shareholders. The board, which meets only a few times each year, selects managers who run the corporation on a day-to-day basis. Managers have the authority to make most business decisions without the board's approval. The board's mandate is to oversee management to ensure that it acts in the best interests of shareholders.

The members of the board are elected at the annual meeting. Shareholders who do not attend the annual meeting can vote by proxy, empowering another party to vote in their name. Management usually solicits the proxies of shareholders and normally gets a vast majority of these proxy votes. Thus, management usually has considerable discretion to run the firm as it sees fit, without daily oversight from the equityholders who actually own the firm.

We noted in Chapter 1 that such separation of ownership and control can give rise to "agency problems," in which managers pursue goals not in the best interests of shareholders. However, several mechanisms are designed to alleviate these agency problems. Among these are compensation schemes that link the success of the manager to that of the firm; oversight by the board of directors as well as outsiders such as security analysts, creditors, or large institutional investors; the threat of a proxy contest in which unhappy shareholders attempt to replace the current management team; or the threat of a takeover by another firm.

---

[4]Sometimes a corporation issues two classes of common stock, one bearing the right to vote, the other not. Because of their restricted rights, the nonvoting stocks sell for a lower price, reflecting the value of control.

The common stock of most large corporations can be bought or sold freely on one or more stock markets. A corporation whose stock is not publicly traded is said to be *private*. In most privately held corporations, owners of the firm also take an active role in its management. Takeovers generally are not an issue.

Characteristics of Common Stock

The two most important characteristics of common stock as an investment are its residual claim and its limited liability features.

Residual claim means stockholders are the last in line of all those who have a claim on the assets and income of the corporation. In a liquidation of the firm's assets, the shareholders have claim to what is left after paying all other claimants, such as the tax authorities, employees, suppliers, bondholders, and other creditors. In a going concern, shareholders have claim to the part of operating income left after interest and income taxes have been paid. Management either can pay this residual as cash dividends to shareholders or reinvest it in the business to increase the value of the shares.

Limited liability means that the most shareholders can lose in event of the failure of the corporation is their original investment. Shareholders are not like owners of unincorporated businesses, whose creditors can lay claim to the personal assets of the owner—such as houses, cars, and furniture. In the event of the firm's bankruptcy, corporate stockholders at worst have worthless stock. They are not personally liable for the firm's obligations: Their liability is limited.

CONCEPT check 2.3

a. If you buy 100 shares of GE common stock, to what are you entitled?
b. What is the most money you can make over the next year?
c. If you pay $30 per share, what is the most money you could lose over the year?

Stock Market Listings

Figure 2.8 presents key trading data for a small sample of stocks traded on the New York Stock Exchange. The NYSE is one of several markets in which investors may buy or sell shares of stock. We will examine issues of trading in these markets in the next chapter.

To interpret Figure 2.8, consider the listing for General Electric, the last listed stock. The table provides the ticker symbol (GE), the closing price of the stock ($29.20), and its change (−.03) from the previous trading day. Over 19 million shares of GE traded on this day. The table also provides the highest and lowest price at which GE has traded in the last 52 weeks. The .96 value in the DIV column means that the last quarterly dividend payment was $0.24 per share, which is consistent with annual dividend payments of $0.24 × 4 = $0.96. This corresponds to a dividend yield (i.e., annual dividend per dollar paid for the stock) of .96/29.20 = .0329, or 3.29%.

The dividend yield is only part of the return on a stock investment. It ignores prospective *capital gains* (i.e., price increases) or losses. Shares in low-dividend firms presumably offer greater prospects for capital gains, or investors would not be willing to hold these stocks in their portfolios. If you scan Figure 2.8, you will see that dividend yields vary widely across companies.

The P/E ratio, or price-to-earnings ratio, is the ratio of the current stock price to last year's earnings. The P/E ratio tells us how much stock purchasers must pay per dollar of earnings the firm generates for each share. For GE, the ratio of price to earnings is 27.21. The P/E ratio also varies widely across firms. Where the dividend yield and P/E ratio are not reported in Figure 2.8, the firms have zero dividends, or zero or negative earnings. We shall have much to say about P/E ratios in Part Four. Finally, we see that GE's stock price has decreased by 7.59% since the beginning of the year.

Preferred Stock

Preferred stock has features similar to both equity and debt. Like a bond, it promises to pay a fixed stream of income each year. In this sense, preferred stock is similar to an infinite-maturity bond, that is, a perpetuity. It also resembles a bond in that it does not give the holder voting power regarding the firm's management.

preferred stock

Nonvoting shares in a corporation, usually paying a fixed stream of dividends.

Listing of stocks traded on the New York Stock Exchange

Source: *The Wall Street Journal Online*, May 5, 2017.

G	Symbol	Close	Net Chg	Vol	52-Week High	52-Week Low	Div	Yield	PE	YTD % Chg
Game Stop CIA	GME	23.57	−0.40	1,440,828	32.67	20.10	1.52	6.45	6.87	−6.69
Gannett	GCI	8.40	−0.45	824,448	16.48	7.30	0.64	7.62	23.33	−13.49
Gap	GPS	25.70	−0.41	3,705,292	30.74	17.00	0.92	3.58	15.21	14.53
GasLog Partners	GLOP	23.00	−0.65	310,485	25.20	17.26	2.00	8.70	9.75	11.92
GATX	GATX	59.19	−0.32	342,362	64.46	40.66	1.68	2.84	9.77	−3.88
GCP Applied Technologies	GCP	33.70	...	433,531	34.05	22.06	...	...	33.37	25.98
Genco Shipping & Trading	GNK	9.71	−0.64	200,018	14.99	3.62	...	...	...dd	31.57
General Cable	BGC	18.55	0.90	745,461	20.80	11.65	0.72	3.88	...dd	−2.62
General Dynamics	GD	194.55	0.37	1,085,423	196.97	132.68	3.36	1.73	20.03	12.68
General Electric	GE	29.20	−0.03	19,159,156	33.00	28.19	0.96	3.29	27.21	−7.59

Preferred stock is an equity investment, however. The firm retains discretion to make the dividend payments to the preferred stockholders: It has no contractual obligation to pay those dividends. Instead, preferred dividends are usually *cumulative;* that is, unpaid dividends cumulate and must be paid in full before any dividends may be paid to holders of common stock. In contrast, the firm does have a contractual obligation to make timely interest payments on the debt. Failure to make these payments sets off corporate bankruptcy proceedings.

Preferred stock also differs from bonds in terms of its tax treatment for the firm. Because preferred stock payments are treated as dividends rather than as interest on debt, they are not tax-deductible expenses for the firm. This disadvantage is offset to some extent by the fact that corporations may exclude 50% of dividends received from domestic corporations in the computation of their taxable income. (Until 2018, the dividend exclusion was 70%.) Preferred stocks, therefore, make desirable fixed-income investments for some corporations.

Even though preferred stock ranks after bonds in terms of the priority of its claim to the assets of the firm in the event of corporate bankruptcy, it often sells at lower yields than corporate bonds. Presumably this reflects the value of the dividend exclusion, because the higher risk of preferred stock would tend to result in higher yields than those offered by bonds. Individual investors, who cannot use the exclusion, generally will find preferred stock yields unattractive relative to those on other available assets.

Corporations issue preferred stock in variations similar to those of corporate bonds. Preferred stock can be callable by the issuing firm, in which case it is said to be *redeemable.* It also can be convertible into common stock at some specified conversion ratio. A relatively recent innovation is adjustable-rate preferred stock, which, like adjustable-rate bonds, ties the dividend rate to current market interest rates.

Depositary Receipts

American Depositary Receipts (ADRs) are certificates traded in U.S. markets that represent ownership in shares of a foreign company. Each ADR may correspond to ownership of a fraction of a foreign share, one share, or several shares of the foreign corporation. ADRs were created to make it easier for foreign firms to satisfy U.S. security registration requirements. They are the most common way for U.S. investors to directly invest in and trade the shares of foreign corporations.

2.4 STOCK AND BOND MARKET INDEXES

Stock Market Indexes

The daily performance of the Dow Jones Industrial Average is a staple portion of the evening news report. While the Dow is the best-known measure of the performance of the stock market, it is only one of several indicators. Other more broadly based indexes are computed and published daily. In addition, several indexes of bond market performance are widely available.

The ever-increasing role of international trade and investments has made indexes of foreign financial markets part of the general news. Thus, foreign stock exchange indexes such as the Nikkei Average of Tokyo or the *Financial Times* index of London have become household names.

The Dow Jones Industrial Average

The Dow Jones Industrial Average (DJIA) of 30 large, "blue-chip" corporations has been computed since 1896. Its long history probably accounts for its preeminence in the public mind. (The average covered only 20 stocks until 1928.)

Originally, the DJIA was calculated as the average price of the stocks included in the index. So, if there were 30 stocks in the index, one would add up the prices of the 30 stocks and divide by 30. The percentage change in the DJIA would then be the percentage change in the average price of the 30 shares.

This procedure means that the percentage change in the DJIA measures the return (excluding any dividends paid) on a portfolio that invests one share in each of the 30 stocks in the index. The value of such a portfolio (holding one share of each stock in the index) is the sum of the 30 prices. Because the percentage change in the *average* of the 30 prices is the same as the percentage change in the *sum* of the 30 prices, the index and the portfolio have the same percentage change each day.

The Dow measures the return (excluding dividends) on a portfolio that holds one share of each stock. The amount of money invested in each company in that portfolio is therefore proportional to the company's share price, so the Dow is called a **price-weighted average.**

price-weighted average

An average computed by adding the prices of the stocks and dividing by a "divisor."

Consider the data in Table 2.3 for a hypothetical two-stock version of the Dow Jones Average. Let's compare the changes in the value of the portfolio holding one share of each firm and the price-weighted index. Stock ABC starts at $25 a share and increases to $30. Stock XYZ starts at $100, but falls to $90.

Portfolio:	Initial value = $25 + $100 = $125
	Final value = $30 + $90 = $120
	Percentage change in portfolio value = −5/125 = −.04 = −4%
Index:	Initial index value = (25 + 100)/2 = 62.5
	Final index value = (30 + 90)/2 = 60
	Percentage change in index = −2.5/62.5 = −.04 = −4%

The portfolio and the index have identical 4% declines in value.

Notice that price-weighted averages give higher-priced shares more weight in determining the performance of the index. For example, although ABC increased by 20% while XYZ fell by only 10%, the index dropped in value. This is because the 20% increase in ABC represented a smaller dollar price gain ($5 per share) than the 10% decrease in XYZ ($10 per share). The "Dow portfolio" has four times as much invested in XYZ as in ABC because XYZ's price is four times that of ABC. Therefore, XYZ dominates the average. We conclude that a high-price stock can dominate a price-weighted average.

EXAMPLE 2.2

Price-Weighted Average

TABLE 2.3   Data to construct stock price indexes

Stock	Initial Price	Final Price	Shares (millions)	Initial Value of Outstanding Stock ($ million)	Final Value of Outstanding Stock ($ million)
ABC	$ 25	$30	20	$500	$600
XYZ	100	90	1	100	90
Total				$600	$690

TABLE 2.4   Data to construct stock price indexes after stock split

Stock	Initial Price	Final Price	Shares (millions)	Initial Value of Outstanding Stock ($ million)	Final Value of Outstanding Stock ($ million)
ABC	$25	$30	20	$500	$600
XYZ	50	45	2	100	90
Total				$600	$690

You might wonder why the DJIA is (in early 2018) at a level of about 25,000 if it is supposed to be the average price of the 30 stocks in the index. The DJIA no longer equals the average price of the 30 stocks because the averaging procedure is adjusted whenever a stock splits or pays a stock dividend of more than 10% or when one company in the group of 30 industrial firms is replaced by another. When these events occur, the divisor used to compute the "average price" is adjusted so as to leave the index unaffected by the event.

EXAMPLE 2.3

Splits and Price-Weighted Averages

Suppose firm XYZ from Example 2.2 splits two for one so that its share price falls to $50. We would not want the average to fall, as that would incorrectly indicate a fall in the general level of market prices. Following a split, the divisor must be reduced to a value that leaves the average unaffected. Table 2.4 illustrates this point. The initial share price of XYZ, which was $100 in Table 2.3, falls to $50 if the stock splits at the beginning of the period. Notice that the number of shares outstanding doubles, leaving the market value of the total shares unaffected.

We find the new divisor as follows: The index value before the stock split was 125/2 = 62.5. We must find a new divisor, d, that leaves the index unchanged after XYZ splits and its price falls to $50. Therefore we solve for d in the following equation:

$$\frac{\text{Price of ABC} + \text{Price of XYZ}}{d} = \frac{25 + 50}{d} = 62.5$$

which implies that the divisor must fall from its original value of 2.0 to a new value of 1.20.

Because the split changes the price of stock XYZ, it also changes the relative weights of the two stocks in the price-weighted average. Therefore, the return of the index is affected by the split.

At period-end, ABC will sell for $30, while XYZ will sell for $45, representing the same negative 10% return it was assumed to earn in Table 2.3. The new value of the price-weighted average will be (30 + 45)/1.20 = 62.5. The index is unchanged, so the rate of return is zero, greater than the −4% return that would have resulted in the absence of a split. The relative weight of XYZ, which is the poorer-performing stock, is reduced by a split because its price is lower, so the performance of the average is higher. This example illustrates that the implicit weighting scheme of a price-weighted average is somewhat arbitrary, being determined by the prices rather than by the outstanding market values (price per share times number of shares) of the shares in the average.

In the same way that the divisor is updated for stock splits, if one firm is dropped from the average and another firm with a different price is added, the divisor has to be updated to leave the average unchanged by the substitution. By 2018, the divisor for the Dow Jones Industrial Average had fallen to a value of about .145.

Because the Dow Jones averages are based on small numbers of firms, care must be taken to ensure that they are representative of the broad market. As a result, the composition of the

TABLE 2.5	Companies included in the Dow Jones Industrial Average: 1928 and 2018			
Dow Industrials in 1928	**Current Dow Companies**	**Ticker Symbol**	**Industry**	**Year Added to Index**
Wright Aeronautical	3M	MMM	Diversified industrials	1976
Allied Chemical	American Express	AXP	Consumer finance	1982
North American	Apple	AAPL	Electronic equipment	2015
Victor Talking Machine	Boeing	BA	Aerospace and defense	1987
International Nickel	Caterpillar	CAT	Construction	1991
International Harvester	Chevron	CVX	Oil and gas	2008
Westinghouse	Cisco Systems	CSCO	Computer equipment	2009
Texas Gulf Sulphur	Coca-Cola	KO	Beverages	1987
Texas Corp	DuPont	DD	Chemicals	1935
Standard Oil (NJ)	ExxonMobil	XOM	Oil and gas	1928
General Electric	General Electric	GE	Diversified industrials	1907
American Tobacco	Goldman Sachs	GS	Investment banking	2013
Sears Roebuck	Home Depot	HD	Home improvement retailers	1999
General Motors	Intel	INTC	Semiconductors	1999
Chrysler	IBM	IBM	Computer services	1979
Atlantic Refining	Johnson & Johnson	JNJ	Pharmaceuticals	1997
Paramount Publix	JPMorgan Chase	JPM	Banking	1991
Bethlehem Steel	McDonald's	MCD	Restaurants	1985
General Railway Signal	Merck	MRK	Pharmaceuticals	1979
Mack Trucks	Microsoft	MSFT	Software	1999
Union Carbide	Nike	NKE	Apparel	2013
American Smelting	Pfizer	PFE	Pharmaceuticals	2004
American Can	Procter & Gamble	PG	Household products	1932
Postum Inc	Travelers	TRV	Insurance	2009
Nash Motors	UnitedHealth Group	UNH	Health insurance	2012
American Sugar	United Technologies	UTX	Aerospace	1939
Goodrich	Verizon	VZ	Telecommunications	2004
Radio Corp	Visa	V	Electronic payments	2013
Woolworth	Walmart	WMT	Retailers	1997
U.S. Steel	Walt Disney	DIS	Broadcasting and entertainment	1991

average is changed every so often to reflect changes in the economy. Table 2.5 presents the composition of the Dow industrials in 1928 as well as its composition in 2018. The table presents striking evidence of the changes in the U.S. economy in the last century. Many of the "bluest of the blue chip" companies in 1928 no longer exist, and the industries that were the backbone of the economy in 1928 have given way to ones that could not have been imagined at the time.

Suppose XYZ's final price in Table 2.3 increases to $110, while ABC falls to $20. Find the percentage change in the price-weighted average of these two stocks. Compare that to the percentage return of a portfolio that holds one share in each company.

CONCEPT check **2.4**

The Standard & Poor's 500 Index

The Standard & Poor's Composite 500 (S&P 500) stock index represents an improvement over the Dow Jones averages in two ways. First, it is a more broadly based index of 500 firms. Second, it is a **market value–weighted index.** In the case of the firms XYZ and ABC in Example 2.2, the S&P 500 would give ABC five times the weight given to XYZ because the market value of its outstanding equity is five times larger, $500 million versus $100 million.

market value–weighted index

Index return equals the weighted average of the returns of each component security, with weights proportional to outstanding market value.

The S&P 500 is computed by calculating the total market value of the 500 firms in the index and the total market value of those firms on the previous day of trading.[5] The percentage increase in the total market value from one day to the next represents the increase in the index. The rate of return of the index equals the rate of return that would be earned by an investor holding a portfolio of all 500 firms in the index in proportion to their market value, except that the index does not reflect cash dividends paid by those firms.

EXAMPLE 2.4	To illustrate how value-weighted indexes are computed, look again at Table 2.3. The final value of all outstanding stock in our two-stock universe is $690 million. The initial value was $600 million.
Value-Weighted Indexes	Therefore, if the initial level of a market value–weighted index of stocks ABC and XYZ were set equal to an arbitrarily chosen starting value such as 100, the index value at year-end would be $100 \times (690/600) = 115$. The increase in the index would reflect the 15% return earned on a portfolio consisting of those two stocks held in proportion to outstanding market values.

Unlike the price-weighted index, the value-weighted index gives more weight to ABC. Whereas the price-weighted index fell because it was dominated by higher-priced XYZ, the value-weighted index rose because it gave more weight to ABC, the stock with the higher total market value.

Note also from Tables 2.3 and 2.4 that market value–weighted indexes are unaffected by stock splits. The total market value of the outstanding XYZ stock increases from $100 million to $110 million regardless of the stock split, thereby rendering the split irrelevant to the performance of the index.

A nice feature of both market value–weighted and price-weighted indexes is that they reflect the returns to straightforward portfolio strategies. If one were to buy each share in the index in proportion to its outstanding market value, the value-weighted index would perfectly track capital gains on the underlying portfolio. Similarly, a price-weighted index tracks the returns on a portfolio composed of equal shares of each firm.

Investors today can easily buy market indexes for their portfolios. One way is to purchase shares in mutual funds that hold shares in proportion to their representation in the S&P 500 as well as other stock indexes. These *index funds* yield a return equal to that of the particular index and so provide a low-cost passive investment strategy for equity investors. Another approach is to purchase an *exchange-traded fund,* or ETF, which is a portfolio of shares that can be bought or sold as a unit, just as a single share would be traded. Available ETFs range from portfolios that track extremely broad global market indexes all the way to narrow industry indexes. We discuss both mutual funds and ETFs in detail in Chapter 4.

CONCEPT check	2.5	Reconsider companies XYZ and ABC from Concept Check Question 2.4. Calculate the percentage change in the market value–weighted index. Compare that to the rate of return of a portfolio that holds $500 of ABC stock for every $100 of XYZ stock (i.e., an index portfolio).

Other U.S. Market Value Indexes

The New York Stock Exchange publishes a market-value-weighted composite index of all NYSE-listed stocks, in addition to subindexes for industrial, utility, transportation, and financial stocks. NASDAQ computes a Composite index of more than 3,000 firms traded on the NASDAQ market. The NASDAQ 100 is a subset of the larger firms in the Composite Index, but it accounts for a large fraction of its total market capitalization.

The most inclusive U.S. equity index is the Wilshire 5000 index of the market value of essentially all actively traded stocks in the U.S. At one point, it included more than 5,000 stocks, but today, there are fewer than 4,000 stocks traded in the U.S. A similar comprehensive index is published by CRSP (the Center for Research in Security Prices at the University of Chicago).

---

[5]Actually, most indexes today use a modified version of market value weights. Rather than weighting by total market value, they weight by the market value of "free float," that is, by the value of shares that are freely tradable among investors. For example, this procedure does not count shares held by founding families or governments, which are effectively not available for investors to purchase. The distinction is more important in Japan and Europe, where a higher fraction of shares are held in such nontraded portfolios.

Equally Weighted Indexes

Market performance is sometimes measured by an equally weighted average of the returns of each stock in an index. Such an averaging technique, by placing equal weight on each return, corresponds to a portfolio strategy that places equal dollar values in each stock. This is in contrast to both price weighting, which requires equal numbers of shares of each stock, and market value weighting, which requires investments in proportion to outstanding value.

Unlike price- or market value–weighted indexes, **equally weighted indexes** do not correspond to buy-and-hold portfolio strategies. Suppose you start with equal dollar investments in the two stocks of Table 2.3, ABC and XYZ. Because ABC increases in value by 20% over the year, while XYZ decreases by 10%, your portfolio is no longer equally weighted but is now more heavily invested in ABC. To reset the portfolio to equal weights, you would need to rebalance: Sell some ABC stock and/or purchase more XYZ stock. Such rebalancing would be necessary to align the return on your portfolio with that on the equally weighted index.

equally weighted index
An index computed from a simple average of returns.

Foreign and International Stock Market Indexes

Development in financial markets worldwide includes the construction of indexes for these markets. Among these are the Nikkei (Japan), FTSE (U.K., pronounced "footsie"), DAX (Germany), Hang Seng (Hong Kong), and TSX (Toronto). A leader in the construction of international indexes has been MSCI (Morgan Stanley Capital International), which computes dozens of country indexes and several regional indexes. Table 2.6 presents many of the indexes computed by MSCI.

TABLE 2.6 Sample of MSCI stock indexes

Regional Indexes		Countries	
Developed Markets	**Emerging Markets**	**Developed Markets**	**Emerging Markets**
EAFE (Europe, Australasia, Far East)	Emerging Markets (EM)	Australia	Brazil
Europe	EM Asia	Austria	Chile
EMU	EM Far East	Belgium	China
Far East	EM Latin America	Canada	Colombia
Kokusai (World excluding Japan)	EM Eastern Europe	Denmark	Czech Republic
Nordic Countries	EM Europe	Finland	Egypt
North America	EM Europe and Middle East	France	Greece
World		Germany	Hungary
Indonesia		Hong Kong	India
World excluding U.S.		Ireland	Korea
		Israel	Malaysia
		Italy	Mexico
		Japan	Peru
		Netherlands	Peru
		New Zealand	Philippines
		Norway	Poland
		Portugal	Russia
		Singapore	South Africa
		Spain	Taiwan
		Sweden	Thailand
		Switzerland	Turkey
		U.K.	
		U.S.	

Source: MSCI, **www.msci.com.**

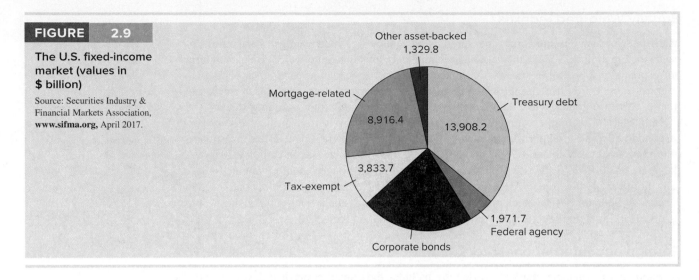

FIGURE   2.9

The U.S. fixed-income market (values in $ billion)

Source: Securities Industry & Financial Markets Association, **www.sifma.org,** April 2017.

Other asset-backed
1,329.8

Mortgage-related

Treasury debt

8,916.4

13,908.2

3,833.7

Tax-exempt

1,971.7
Federal agency

Corporate bonds

Bond Market Indicators

Just as stock market indexes provide guidance concerning the performance of the overall stock market, several bond market indicators measure the performance of various categories of bonds. The most well-known indexes are those of Merrill Lynch, Barclays, and the Citi Broad Investment Grade Bond Index. Figure 2.9 presents the components of the U.S. fixed income market in 2017.

The major problem with these indexes is that true rates of return on many bonds are difficult to compute because bonds trade infrequently, which makes it hard to get reliable, up-to-date prices. In practice, some prices must be estimated from bond-valuation models. These so-called "matrix prices" may differ from true market values.

2.5 DERIVATIVE MARKETS

Futures, options, and related derivative contracts provide payoffs that depend on the values of other variables, such as commodity prices, bond and stock prices, interest rates, or market index values. For this reason, these instruments sometimes are called **derivative assets:** Their values *derive from* the values of other assets. We discuss derivative assets in detail in Part Five.

derivative asset

A security with a payoff that depends on the prices of other securities.

Options

A **call option** gives its holder the right to purchase an asset for a specified price, called the *exercise* or *strike price,* on or before some specified expiration date. A May call option on Apple stock with exercise price $140, for example, entitles its owner to purchase Apple stock for a price of $140 at any time up to and including the option's expiration date in May. Each option contract is for the purchase of 100 shares, with quotations made on a per share basis. The holder of the call need not exercise the option; it will make sense to exercise only if the market value of the asset exceeds the exercise price.

When the market price exceeds the exercise price, the option holder may "call away" the asset for the exercise price and reap a benefit equal to the difference between the stock price and the exercise price. Otherwise, the option will be left unexercised. If not exercised before the expiration date, the option expires and no longer has value. Calls, therefore, provide greater profits when stock prices increase and so represent bullish investment vehicles.

In contrast, a **put option** gives its holder the right to sell an asset for a specified exercise price on or before a specified expiration date. A May put on Apple with exercise price $140 entitles its owner to sell Apple stock to the put writer at a price of $140 at any time before expiration in May even if the market price of Apple is lower than $140. Whereas profits on

call option

The right to buy an asset at a specified exercise price on or before a specified expiration date.

put option

The right to sell an asset at a specified exercise price on or before a specified expiration date.

FIGURE 2.10

Option prices on Apple (AAPL), April 18, 2017

Note: Apple stock price on April 18, 2017 was $141.20.

Source: Compiled from data downloaded from Nasdaq, **www.nasdaq.com**.

Expiration	Strike	Call	Put
May 12, 2017	135	7.63	1.17
May 12, 2017	140	3.80	2.71
May 12, 2017	145	1.61	5.60
June 16, 2017	135	8.05	2.07
June 16, 2017	140	4.80	3.90
June 16, 2017	145	2.50	6.65

call options increase when the asset increases in value, profits on put options increase when the asset value falls. The put is exercised only if its holder can deliver an asset worth less than the exercise price in return for the exercise price.

Figure 2.10 is an excerpt of options quotations for Apple. The price of Apple shares on this date was $141.20. The first two columns give the expiration date and exercise (or strike) price for each option. We have included listings for call and put options with exercise prices $135 through $145 per share and with expiration dates in May and June 2017.

The next columns provide the prices of each option. For example, the June 2017 expiration call with an exercise price of $140 sold for $4.80. Each option *contract* (on 100 shares) therefore cost $480.

Notice that the prices of call options decrease as the exercise price increases. For example, the June expiration call with exercise price $145 cost only $2.50. This makes sense, because the right to purchase a share at a higher price is less valuable. Conversely, put prices increase with the exercise price. The right to sell Apple at a price of $140 in June costs $3.90 while the right to sell at $145 cost $6.65.

Option prices also increase with time until expiration. Clearly, one would rather have the right to buy Apple for $140 at any time until June rather than at any time until May. Not surprisingly, this shows up in a higher price for the June expiration options. For example, the call with exercise price $140 expiring in May sold for only $3.80 compared to $4.80 for the June call.

CONCEPT check 2.6

What would be the profit or loss per share of stock to an investor who bought the June expiration Apple call option with exercise price $140, if the stock price at the expiration of the option is $150? What about a purchaser of the put option with the same exercise price and expiration?

Futures Contracts

A **futures contract** calls for delivery of an asset (or, in some cases, its cash value) at a specified delivery or maturity date, for an agreed-upon price, called the *futures price,* to be paid at contract maturity. The long position is held by the trader who commits to purchasing the commodity on the delivery date. The trader who takes the short position commits to delivering the commodity at contract maturity.

Figure 2.11 illustrates the listing of the corn futures contract on the Chicago Board of Trade for April 18, 2017. Each contract calls for delivery of 5,000 bushels of corn. Each row details prices for contracts expiring on various dates. The first row is for the nearest term or "front" contract, with maturity in May 2017. The most recent price was $3.6125 per bushel.

The long side of the contract profits from price increases. Suppose that at expiration, corn is selling for $3.8125 per bushel. The long trader who entered the contract at the futures price of $3.6125 on April 18 would pay that previously agreed-upon price for each bushel of corn, which at contract maturity would be worth $3.8125.

Because each contract calls for delivery of 5,000 bushels, the profit to the long position, ignoring brokerage fees, would equal $5,000 \times (\$3.8125 - \$3.6125) = \$1,000$. Conversely, the

futures contract

Obliges traders to purchase or sell an asset at an agreed-upon price at a specified future date.

FIGURE 2.11

Corn futures prices on the Chicago Mercantile Exchange, April 18, 2017

Source: www.cmegroup.com, April 18, 2017.

MATURITY	LAST	CHG	HIGH	LOW
May '17	3.6125	−0.0525	3.6800	3.6075
Jul '17	3.6775	−0.0550	3.7450	3.6725
Sep '17	3.7525	−0.0475	3.8125	3.7475
Dec '17	3.8575	−0.0450	3.9150	3.8525
Mar '18	3.9575	−0.0400	4.0025	3.9475

short position must deliver 5,000 bushels for the previously agreed-upon futures price. The short position's loss equals the long position's profit.

The *right* to purchase an asset at an agreed-upon price versus the *obligation* to purchase it distinguishes a call option from a long position in a futures contract. A futures contract *obliges* the long position to purchase the asset at the futures price; the call option merely *conveys the right* to purchase the asset at the exercise price. The purchase will be made only if the asset is ultimately worth more than the exercise price.

Clearly, the holder of a call has a better position than the holder of a long position on a futures contract with a futures price equal to the option's exercise price. This advantage, of course, comes only at a price. Call options must be purchased; futures investments are entered into without cost. The purchase price of an option is called the *premium*. It represents the compensation the purchaser of the call must pay for the ability to exercise the option only when it is advantageous to do so. Similarly, the difference between a put option and a short futures position is the right, as opposed to the obligation, to sell an asset at an agreed-upon price.

SUMMARY

- Money market securities are very short-term debt obligations. They are usually highly marketable and have relatively low credit risk. Their low maturities and low credit risk ensure minimal capital gains or losses. These securities often trade in large denominations, but they may be purchased indirectly through money market funds.

- Much of U.S. government borrowing is in the form of Treasury bonds and notes. These are coupon-paying bonds usually issued at or near par value. Treasury bonds are similar in design to coupon-paying corporate bonds.

- Municipal bonds are distinguished largely by their tax-exempt status. Interest payments (but not capital gains) on these securities are exempt from income taxes. The equivalent taxable yield offered by a municipal bond equals $r_{muni}/(1 - t)$, where r_{muni} is the municipal yield and t is the investor's tax bracket.

- Mortgage pass-through securities are pools of mortgages sold in one package. Owners of pass-throughs receive all principal and interest payments made by the borrower. The firm that originally issued the mortgage merely services it, simply "passing through" the payments to the purchasers of the mortgage. Payments of interest and principal on government agency pass-through securities are guaranteed, but payments on private-label mortgage pools are not.

- Common stock is an ownership share in a corporation. Each share entitles its owner to one vote on matters of corporate governance and to a prorated share of the dividends paid to shareholders. Stock (equivalently, equity) owners are the residual claimants on the income earned by the firm.

- Preferred stock usually pays a fixed stream of dividends for the life of the firm: It is a perpetuity. A firm's failure to pay the dividend due on preferred stock, however, does not set off corporate bankruptcy. Instead, unpaid dividends simply cumulate. Adjustable-rate preferred stock pays a dividend that is indexed to a short-term interest rate.

- Many stock market indexes measure the performance of the overall market. The Dow Jones averages, the oldest and best-known indicators, are price-weighted indexes. Today, many broad-based, market value–weighted indexes are computed daily. These include the

Standard & Poor's Composite 500 stock index, the NASDAQ index, the Wilshire 5000 Index, and several international indexes, including the Nikkei, FTSE, and DAX.
- A call option is a right to purchase an asset at a stipulated exercise price on or before an expiration date. A put option is the right to sell an asset at some exercise price. Calls increase in value, while puts decrease in value, as the price of the underlying asset increases.
- A futures contract is an obligation to buy or sell an asset at a stipulated futures price on a maturity date. The long position, which commits to purchasing, gains if the asset value increases, while the short position, which commits to delivering the asset, loses.

KEY TERMS

banker's acceptance, 29	Eurodollars, 29	municipal bonds, 34
call option, 46	Federal funds, 29	preferred stock, 39
certificate of deposit, 28	futures contract, 47	price-weighted average, 41
commercial paper, 28	London Interbank Offer	put option, 46
common stocks, 38	Rate (LIBOR), 30	repurchase agreements
corporate bonds, 36	market value–weighted	(repos), 29
derivative asset, 46	index, 43	Treasury bills, 27
equally weighted index, 45	money markets, 27	Treasury bonds, 32
		Treasury notes, 32

KEY FORMULAS

Equivalent taxable yield: $\dfrac{r_{muni}}{1-t}$ where r_{muni} is the rate on tax-free municipal debt and t is the combined federal plus state tax rate.

Cutoff tax bracket (for indifference to taxable versus tax-free bonds): $1 - \dfrac{r_{muni}}{r_{taxable}}$

PROBLEM SETS

 Select problems are available in McGraw-Hill's *Connect*. Please see the Supplements section of the book's frontmatter for more information.

1. What are the key differences between common stock, preferred stock, and corporate bonds? *(LO 2-1)*
2. Why do most professionals consider the Wilshire 5000 a better index of the performance of the broad stock market than the Dow Jones Industrial Average? *(LO 2-2)*
3. What features of money market securities distinguish them from other fixed-income securities? *(LO 2-1)*
4. What are the major components of the money market? *(LO 2-1)*
5. Describe alternative ways that an investor may add positions in international equity to his or her portfolio. *(LO 2-1)*
6. Why are high-tax-bracket investors more inclined to invest in municipal bonds than are low-bracket investors? *(LO 2-1)*
7. What is the LIBOR rate? The Federal funds rate? *(LO 2-1)*
8. How does a municipal revenue bond differ from a general obligation bond? Which would you expect to have a lower yield to maturity? *(LO 2-1)*
9. Why are corporations more apt to hold preferred stock than other potential investors? *(LO 2-1)*
10. What is meant by limited liability? *(LO 2-1)*
11. Which of the following *correctly* describes a repurchase agreement? *(LO 2-1)*
    a. The sale of a security with a commitment to repurchase the same security at a specified future date and a designated price.
    b. The sale of a security with a commitment to repurchase the same security at a future date left unspecified, at a designated price.
    c. The purchase of a security with a commitment to purchase more of the same security at a specified future date.

SCHWESER

12. Why are money market securities sometimes referred to as "cash equivalents"? *(LO 2-1)*

13. A municipal bond carries a coupon rate of 4.25% and is trading at par. What would be the equivalent taxable yield of this bond to a taxpayer in a 35% combined tax bracket? *(LO 2-1)*

14. Suppose that short-term municipal bonds currently offer yields of 4%, while comparable taxable bonds pay 5%. Which gives you the higher after-tax yield if your combined tax bracket is: *(LO 2-1)*
    a. Zero
    b. 10%
    c. 20%
    d. 30%

15. An investor is in a 30% combined federal plus state tax bracket. If corporate bonds offer 9% yields, what yield must municipals offer for the investor to prefer them to corporate bonds? *(LO 2-1)*

16. Find the equivalent taxable yield of the municipal bond in Problem 14 for tax brackets of: *(LO 2-1)*
    a. Zero
    b. 10%
    c. 20%
    d. 30%

17. Turn back to Figure 2.3 and look at the Treasury bond maturing in February 2043. *(LO 2-1)*
    a. How much would you have to pay to purchase one of these bonds?
    b. What is its coupon rate?
    c. What is the current yield (i.e., coupon income as a fraction of bond price) of the bond?

18. Turn to Figure 2.8 and look at the listing for General Dynamics. *(LO 2-1)*
    a. What was the firm's closing price yesterday?
    b. How many shares could you buy for $5,000?
    c. What would be your annual dividend income from those shares?
    d. What must be General Dynamics' earnings per share?

19. Consider the three stocks in the following table. P_t represents price at time t, and Q_t represents shares outstanding at time t. Stock C splits two-for-one in the last period. *(LO 2-2)*

	P_0	Q_0	P_1	Q_1	P_2	Q_2
A	90	100	95	100	95	100
B	50	200	45	200	45	200
C	100	200	110	200	55	400

    a. Calculate the rate of return on a price-weighted index of the three stocks for the first period ($t = 0$ to $t = 1$).
    b. What must happen to the divisor for the price-weighted index in year 2?
    c. Calculate the rate of return of the price-weighted index for the second period ($t = 1$ to $t = 2$).

20. Using the data in the previous problem, calculate the first-period rates of return on the following indexes of the three stocks: *(LO 2-2)*
    a. A market value–weighted index
    b. An equally weighted index

21. What problems would confront a mutual fund trying to create an index fund tied to an equally weighted index of a broad stock market? *(LO 2-2)*

22. What would happen to the divisor of the Dow Jones Industrial Average if FedEx, with a current price of around $210 per share, replaced Intel (with a current value of about $40 per share)? *(LO 2-2)*

23. A T-bill with face value $10,000 and 87 days to maturity is selling at a bank discount ask yield of 3.4%. *(LO 2-1)*
    a. What is the price of the bill?
    b. What is its bond equivalent yield?

24. Which security should sell at a greater price? *(LO 2-3)*
    a. A 10-year Treasury bond with a 5% coupon rate or a 10-year T-bond with a 6% coupon.
    b. A three-month expiration call option with an exercise price of $40 or a three-month call on the same stock with an exercise price of $35.
    c. A put option on a stock selling at $50 or a put option on another stock selling at $60. (All other relevant features of the stocks and options are assumed to be identical.)

25. Look at the futures listings for corn in Figure 2.11. Suppose you buy one contract for December 2017 delivery. If the contract closes in December at a price of $3.95 per bushel, what will be your profit or loss? (Each contract calls for delivery of 5,000 bushels.) *(LO 2-3)*

26. Turn back to Figure 2.10 and look at the Apple options. Suppose you buy a June expiration call option with exercise price $140. *(LO 2-3)*
    a. If the stock price in June is $144, will you exercise your call? What is the profit on your position?
    b. What if you had bought the June call with exercise price $135?
    c. What if you had bought the June put with exercise price $140?

27. What options position is associated with: *(LO 2-3)*
    a. The right to buy an asset at a specified price?
    b. The right to sell an asset at a specified price?
    c. The obligation to buy an asset at a specified price?
    d. The obligation to sell an asset at a specified price?

28. Why do call options with exercise prices higher than the price of the underlying stock sell for positive prices? *(LO 2-3)*

29. Both a call and a put currently are traded on stock XYZ; both have strike prices of $50 and maturities of six months. *(LO 2-3)*
    a. What will be the profit to an investor who buys the call for $4 in the following scenarios for stock prices in six months? (*i*) $40; (*ii*) $45; (*iii*) $50; (*iv*) $55; (*v*) $60.
    b. What will be the profit in each scenario to an investor who buys the put for $6?

30. What would you expect to happen to the spread between yields on commercial paper and Treasury bills if the economy were to enter a steep recession? *(LO 2-1)*

31. Examine the stocks listed in Figure 2.8. For what fraction of these stocks is the 52-week high price at least 50% greater than the 52-week low price? What do you conclude about the volatility of prices on individual stocks? *(LO 2-1)*

32. Find the after-tax return to a corporation that buys a share of preferred stock at $40, sells it at year-end at $40, and receives a $4 year-end dividend. The firm is in the 30% tax bracket. *(LO 2-1)*

Challenge

33. What is the difference between a put option and a short position in a futures contract? *(LO 2-3)*

34. What is the difference between a call option and a long position in a futures contract? *(LO 2-3)*

CFA Problem

1. Preferred stock yields often are lower than yields on bonds of the same quality because of: *(LO 2-1)*
   a. Marketability
   b. Risk
   c. Taxation
   d. Call protection

WEB *master*

1. Go to the website for The Walt Disney Co (DIS) and download its most recent annual report (its 10-K). Locate the company's Consolidated Balance Sheets and answer these questions:
   a. How much preferred stock is Disney authorized to issue? How much has been issued?
   b. How much common stock is Disney authorized to issue? How many shares are currently outstanding?
   c. Search for the term "Financing Activities." What is the total amount of borrowing listed for Disney? How much of this is medium-term notes?
   d. What other types of debt does Disney have outstanding?

2. Not all stock market indexes are created equal. Different methods are used to calculate various indexes, and different indexes will yield different assessments of "market performance." Using one of the following data sources, retrieve the stock price for five different firms on the first and last trading days of the previous month.

   www.nasdaq.com—Get a quote; then select *Charts* and specify one month. When the chart appears, click on a data point to display the underlying data.

   www.bloomberg.com—Get a quote; then plot the chart; next, use the moving line to see the closing price today and one month ago.

   finance.yahoo.com—Get a quote; then click on *Historical Data* and specify a date range.

   a. Compute the monthly return on a price-weighted index of the five stocks.
   b. Compute the monthly return on a value-weighted index of the five stocks.
   c. Compare the two returns and explain their differences. Explain how you would interpret each measure.

2.1 The bid price of the bond is 100.6797% of par, or $1,006.797. The asked price is 100.6953 or $1,006.953. This asked price corresponds to a yield of 1.732%. The ask price increased .3750 from its level yesterday, so the ask price then must have been 100.3203, or $1,003.203.

2.2 A 6% taxable return is equivalent to an after-tax return of 6%(1 − .30) = 4.3%. Therefore, you would be better off in the taxable bond. The equivalent taxable yield of the tax-free bond is 4%/(1 − .3) = 5.71%. So a taxable bond would have to pay a 5.71% yield to provide the same after-tax return as a tax-free bond offering a 4% yield.

2.3 a. You are entitled to a prorated share of GE's dividend payments and to vote in any of its stockholder meetings.
   b. Your potential gain is unlimited because GE's stock price has no upper bound.
   c. Your outlay was $30 × 100 = $3,000. Because of limited liability, this is the most you can lose.

2.4 The price-weighted index increases from 62.50 [=(100 + 25)/2] to 65 [=(110 + 20)/2], a gain of 4%. An investment of one share in each company requires an outlay of $125 that would increase in value to $130, for a return of 4% (=5/125), which equals the return to the price-weighted index.

2.5 The market value–weighted index return is calculated by computing the increase in the value of the stock portfolio. The portfolio of the two stocks starts with an initial value of $100 million + $500 million = $600 million and falls in value to $110 million + $400 million = $510 million, a loss of 90/600 = .15, or 15%. The index portfolio return is a weighted average of the returns on each stock with weights of ⅙ on XYZ and ⅚ on ABC (weights proportional to relative investments). Because the return on XYZ is 10%, while that on ABC is −20%, the index portfolio return is (⅙) 10 + (⅚)(−20) = −15%, equal to the return on the market value–weighted index.

2.6 The payoff to the call option is $150 − $140 = $10. The call cost $4.80. The profit is $10 − $4.80 = $5.20 per share. The put will pay off zero—it expires worthless since the stock price exceeds the exercise price. The loss is the cost of the put, $3.90.

Securities Markets

Learning Objectives

LO 3-1 Describe how firms issue securities to the public.

LO 3-2 Identify various types of orders investors can submit to their brokers.

LO 3-3 Describe trading practices in dealer markets, specialist-directed stock exchanges, and electronic communication networks.

LO 3-4 Compare the mechanics and investment implications of buying on margin and short-selling.

This chapter will provide you with a broad introduction to the many venues and procedures available for trading securities. We will see that trading mechanisms range from direct negotiation among market participants to fully automated computer crossing of trade orders.

The first time a security trades is when it is issued to the public. Therefore, we begin with a look at how securities are first marketed to the public by investment bankers, the midwives of securities. We turn next to a broad survey of how already-issued securities may be traded among investors, focusing on the differences between dealer markets, electronic markets, and specialist markets. With this background, we then turn to specific trading arenas such as the New York Stock Exchange, NASDAQ, and several all-electronic markets. We compare the mechanics of trade execution and the impact of cross-market integration of trading.

We then turn to the essentials of some specific types of transactions, such as buying on margin and short-selling stocks. We close the chapter with a look at some important aspects of the regulations governing security trading, including insider trading laws, circuit breakers, and the role of security markets as self-regulating organizations.

3.1 HOW FIRMS ISSUE SECURITIES

Firms regularly need to raise new capital to help pay for their many investment projects. Broadly speaking, they can raise funds either by borrowing money or by selling shares in the firm. Investment bankers are generally hired to manage the sale of these securities in what is called a **primary market** for newly issued securities. Once these securities are issued, however, investors might well wish to trade them among themselves. For example, you may decide to raise cash by selling some of your shares in Apple to another investor. This transaction would have no impact on the total outstanding number of Apple shares. Trades in existing securities take place in the so-called **secondary market.**

Shares of *publicly listed* firms trade continually on well-known markets such as the New York Stock Exchange or the NASDAQ stock market. There, any investor can choose to buy shares for his or her portfolio. These companies are also called *publicly traded, publicly owned,* or just *public companies.* Other firms, however, are *private corporations,* whose shares are held by small numbers of managers and investors. While ownership stakes in the firm are still determined in proportion to share ownership, those shares do not trade in public exchanges. Some private firms are relatively young companies that have not yet chosen to make their shares generally available to the public, others may be more established firms that are still largely owned by the company's founders or families, and others may simply have decided that private organization is preferable.

primary market
Market for new issues of securities.

secondary market
Market for already-existing securities.

Privately Held Firms

A privately held company is owned by a relatively small number of shareholders. Privately held firms have fewer obligations to release financial statements and other information to the public. This saves money and frees the firm from disclosing information that might be helpful to its competitors. Some firms also believe that eliminating requirements for quarterly earnings announcements gives them more flexibility to pursue long-term goals free of shareholder pressure.

When private firms wish to raise funds, they sell shares directly to a small number of institutional or wealthy investors in a **private placement.** Rule 144A of the SEC allows them to make these placements without preparing the extensive and costly registration statements required of a public company. While this is attractive, shares in privately held firms do not trade in secondary markets such as a stock exchange, and this greatly reduces their liquidity and presumably reduces the prices that investors will pay for them. *Liquidity* has many specific meanings, but generally speaking, it refers to the ability to trade an asset at a fair price on short notice. Investors demand price concessions to buy illiquid securities.

private placement
Primary offerings in which shares are sold directly to a small group of institutional or wealthy investors.

Until recently, privately held firms were allowed to have only up to 499 shareholders. This limited their ability to raise large amounts of capital from a wide base of investors. Thus, almost all of the largest companies in the U.S. have been public corporations.

As firms increasingly chafed against the informational requirements of going public, federal regulators came under pressure to loosen the constraints entailed by private ownership. The JOBS (Jumpstart Our Business Startups) Act, which was signed into law in 2012, increased the number of shareholders that a company may have before being required to register its common stock with the SEC and file public reports from 500 to 2,000. It also loosened rules limiting the degree to which private firms could market their shares to the public. For example, to make it easier for companies to engage in crowd funding, small public offerings may be exempt from the obligation to register with the SEC.

Trading in private corporations also evolved in recent years. To get around the maximum-investor restriction, middlemen formed partnerships to buy shares in private companies; the partnership counts as only one investor, even though many individuals may participate in it.

More recently, some firms have set up computer networks to enable holders of private-company stock to trade among themselves. However, unlike the public stock markets regulated by the SEC, these networks require little disclosure of financial information and provide correspondingly little oversight of the operations of the market. Skeptics worry that investors in these markets cannot obtain a clear view of the firm, the interest among other investors in the firm, or the process by which trades in the firm's shares are executed.

Publicly Traded Companies

initial public offering (IPO)

First public sale of stock by a formerly private company.

When a private firm decides that it wishes to raise capital from a wide range of investors, it may decide to *go public*. This means that it will sell its securities to the general public and allow those investors to freely trade those shares in established securities markets. This first issue of shares to the general public is called the firm's **initial public offering (IPO).** Later, the firm may go back to the public and issue additional shares. A *seasoned equity offering* is the sale of additional shares in firms that already are publicly traded. For example, a sale by Apple of new shares of stock would be considered a seasoned new issue.

Public offerings of both stocks and bonds typically are marketed by investment bankers who in this role are called **underwriters.** More than one investment banker usually markets the securities. A lead firm forms an underwriting syndicate of other investment bankers to share the responsibility for the stock issue.

underwriters

Underwriters purchase securities from the issuing company and resell them to the public.

Investment bankers advise the firm regarding the terms on which it should attempt to sell the securities. A preliminary registration statement must be filed with the Securities and Exchange Commission (SEC), describing the issue and the prospects of the company. When the statement is in final form and approved by the SEC, it is called the **prospectus.** At this point, the price at which the securities will be offered to the public is announced.

prospectus

A description of the firm and the security it is issuing.

In a typical underwriting arrangement, the investment bankers purchase the securities from the issuing company and then resell them to the public. The issuing firm sells the securities to the underwriting syndicate for the public offering price less a spread that serves as compensation to the underwriters. This procedure is called a *firm commitment*. In addition to the spread, the investment banker also may receive shares of common stock or other securities of the firm. Figure 3.1 depicts the relationships among the firm issuing the security, the lead underwriter, the underwriting syndicate, and the public.

Shelf Registration

An important innovation in the issuing of securities was introduced in 1982 when the SEC approved Rule 415, which allows firms to register securities and gradually sell them to the public for two years following the initial registration. Because the securities are already registered, they can be sold on short notice, with little additional paperwork. Moreover, they can be sold in small amounts without incurring substantial flotation costs. The securities are "on the shelf," ready to be issued, which has given rise to the term *shelf registration.*

CONCEPT check   **3.1**   Why does it make sense for shelf registration to be limited in time?

FIGURE 3.1

Relationship among a firm issuing securities, the underwriters, and the public

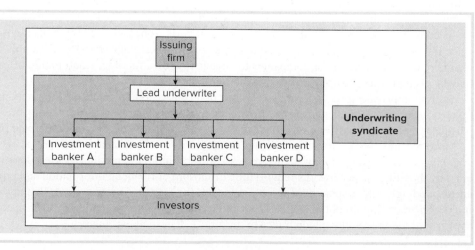

Initial Public Offerings

Investment bankers manage the issuance of new securities to the public. Once the SEC has commented on the registration statement and a preliminary prospectus has been distributed to interested investors, the investment bankers organize *road shows* in which they travel around the country to publicize the imminent offering. These road shows serve two purposes. First, they generate interest among potential investors and provide information about the offering. Second, they provide information to the issuing firm and its underwriters about the price at which they will be able to market the securities. Large investors communicate their interest in purchasing shares of the IPO to the underwriters; these indications of interest are called a *book* and the process of polling potential investors is called *bookbuilding*. The book provides valuable information to the issuing firm because institutional investors often will have useful insights about both the market demand for the security as well as the prospects of the firm and its competitors. It is common for investment bankers to revise both their initial estimates of the offering price of a security and the number of shares offered based on feedback from the investing community.

Why do investors truthfully reveal their interest in an offering to the investment banker? Might they be better off expressing little interest, in the hope that this will drive down the offering price? Truth is the better policy in this case because truth telling is rewarded. Shares of IPOs are allocated across investors in part based on the strength of each investor's expressed interest in the offering. If a firm wishes to get a large allocation when it is optimistic about the security, it needs to reveal its optimism. In turn, the underwriter needs to offer the security at a bargain price to these investors to induce them to participate in bookbuilding and share their information. Thus, IPOs commonly are underpriced compared to the price at which they could be marketed. Such underpricing is reflected in price jumps that occur on the date when the shares are first traded in public security markets. The 2017 IPO of Snap Inc., parent company of Snapchat, was a typical example of underpricing. The company issued about 200 million shares to the public at a price of $17. The stock price closed that day at $24.48, a bit more than 44% above the offering price.

While the explicit costs of an IPO tend to be around 7% of the funds raised, underpricing should be viewed as another cost of the issue. For example, if Snap had sold its shares for the $24.48 that investors obviously were willing to pay for them, its IPO would have raised 44% more money than it actually did. The money "left on the table" in this case far exceeded the explicit cost of the stock issue. Nevertheless, underpricing seems to be a universal phenomenon. For example, Figure 3.2 presents average first-day returns on IPOs of stocks across the world. The results consistently indicate that IPOs are marketed to investors at attractive prices.

Pricing of IPOs is not trivial and not all IPOs turn out to be underpriced. Some do poorly after issue. Facebook's 2012 IPO was a notable disappointment. Within a week of its IPO, Facebook's share price was 15% below the $38 offer price, and five months later, its shares were selling at about half the offer price. (In the end, however, those who held onto their shares profited; by early 2018, the share price was around $180.)

Interestingly, despite their typically attractive first-day returns, IPOs have been poor long-term investments. Ritter calculates the returns to a hypothetical investor who bought equal amounts of each U.S. IPO between 1980 and 2015 and held each position for five years. That portfolio would have underperformed "style-matched" portfolios of firms with comparable size and ratio of book value to market value by an average of about 7.16% per year.[1]

Other IPOs cannot even be fully sold to the market. Underwriters left with unmarketable securities are forced to sell them at a loss on the secondary market. Therefore, the investment banker bears the price risk of an underwritten issue.

3.2 HOW SECURITIES ARE TRADED

Financial markets develop to meet the needs of particular traders. Consider what would happen if organized markets did not exist. Any household wishing to invest in some type of financial asset would have to find others wishing to sell. Soon, venues where interested traders could

---

[1]Professor Jay Ritter's website contains a wealth of information and data about IPOs: **http://bear.warrington.ufl .edu/ritter/ipodata.htm.**

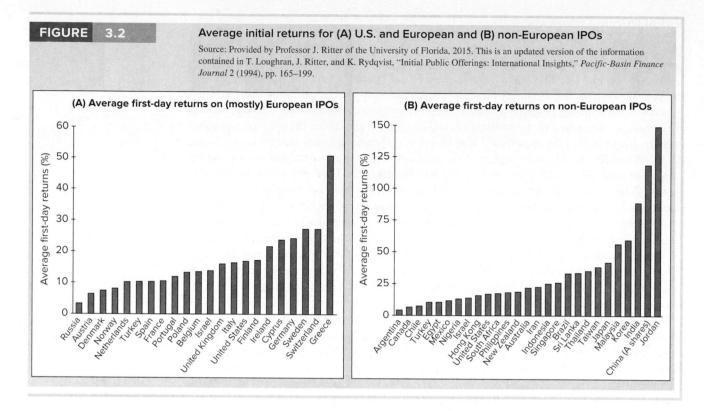

FIGURE   3.2   **Average initial returns for (A) U.S. and European and (B) non-European IPOs**

Source: Provided by Professor J. Ritter of the University of Florida, 2015. This is an updated version of the information contained in T. Loughran, J. Ritter, and K. Rydqvist, "Initial Public Offerings: International Insights," *Pacific-Basin Finance Journal* 2 (1994), pp. 165–199.

meet would become popular. Eventually, financial markets would emerge from these meeting places. Thus, a pub in old London called Lloyd's launched the maritime insurance industry. A Manhattan curb on Wall Street became synonymous with the financial world.

Types of Markets

We can differentiate four types of markets: direct search markets, brokered markets, dealer markets, and auction markets.

DIRECT SEARCH MARKETS   A *direct search market* is the least organized market. Buyers and sellers must seek each other out directly. An example of a transaction in such a market is the sale of a used television where the seller advertises for buyers on Craigslist. Such markets are characterized by sporadic participation and nonstandard goods. It would not pay for most people or firms to specialize in such markets.

BROKERED MARKETS   The next level of organization is a *brokered market.* In markets where trading in a good is active, brokers find it profitable to offer search services to buyers and sellers. A good example is the real estate market, where economies of scale in searches for available homes and for prospective buyers make it worthwhile for participants to pay brokers to organize the searches. Brokers in particular markets develop specialized knowledge on valuing assets traded in that market.

The *primary market,* where new issues of securities are offered to the public, is another example of a brokered market. In the primary market, investment bankers who market a firm's securities to the public act as brokers; they seek investors to purchase securities directly from the issuing corporation.

dealer markets

Markets in which traders specializing in particular assets buy and sell for their own accounts.

DEALER MARKETS   When trading activity in a particular type of asset increases, **dealer markets** arise. Dealers specialize in various assets, purchase these assets for their own accounts, and later sell them for a profit from their inventory. The spreads between dealers' buy (or "bid") prices and sell (or "asked") prices are a source of profit. Dealer markets save traders on search costs because market participants can easily look up the prices at which they can buy from or sell to dealers. A fair amount of market activity is required before dealing in a market is an attractive source of income. Most bonds trade in over-the-counter dealer markets.

AUCTION MARKETS   The most integrated market is an **auction market,** in which all traders converge at one place (either physically or "electronically") to buy or sell an asset. The New York Stock Exchange (NYSE) is an example of an auction market. An advantage of auction markets over dealer markets is that one need not search across dealers to find the best price for a good. If all participants converge, they can arrive at mutually agreeable prices and save the bid–ask spread.

auction market
An exchange or electronic platform where all traders can convene to buy or sell an asset.

Notice that both over-the-counter dealer markets and stock exchanges are secondary markets. They are organized for investors to trade existing securities among themselves.

Many assets trade in more than one type of market. What types of markets do the following trade in?
  a. Used cars
  b. Paintings
  c. Rare coins

CONCEPT **3.2**
c h e c k

Types of Orders

Before comparing alternative trading practices and competing security markets, it is helpful to begin with an overview of the types of trades an investor might wish to have executed in these markets. Broadly speaking, there are two types of orders: market orders and orders contingent on price.

MARKET ORDERS   Market orders are buy or sell orders that are to be executed immediately at current market prices. For example, our investor might call her broker and ask for the market price of Facebook. The broker might report back that the best **bid price** is $149.75 and the best **ask price** is $149.76, meaning that the investor would need to pay $149.76 to purchase a share and could receive $149.75 a share if she wished to sell some of her own holdings of Facebook. The **bid–ask spread** in this case is $0.01. So an order to buy 100 shares "at market" would result in purchase at $149.76, and an order to "sell at market" would be executed at $149.75.

bid price
The price at which a dealer or other trader is willing to purchase a security.

ask (or asked) price
The price at which a dealer or other trader will sell a security.

This simple scenario is subject to a few potential complications. First, posted price quotes actually represent commitments to trade up to a specified number of shares. If the market order is for more than this number of shares, the order may be filled at multiple prices. For example, if the asked price is good for orders up to 1,000 shares, and the investor wishes to purchase 1,500 shares, it may be necessary to pay a higher price for the last 500 shares. Figure 3.3 shows average *depth* for shares of stock (i.e., the total number of shares offered for trading at the best bid and ask prices). Notice that depth is considerably higher for the large stocks in the S&P 500 than for the smaller stocks that constitute the Russell 2000 index. Depth is considered another component of liquidity. Second, another trader may beat our investor to the quote, meaning that her order would then be executed at a worse price. Finally, the best price quote may change before her order arrives, again causing execution at a different price from the one at the moment of the order.

bid–ask spread
The difference between the bid and asked prices.

PRICE-CONTINGENT ORDERS   Investors also may place orders specifying prices at which they are willing to buy or sell a security. A **limit buy order** may instruct the broker to buy some number of shares if and when they may be obtained at or below a stipulated price. Conversely, a **limit sell** instructs the broker to sell if and when the stock price rises *above* a specified limit. A collection of limit orders waiting to be executed is called a *limit order book.*

limit buy (sell) order
An order specifying a price at which an investor is willing to buy or sell a security.

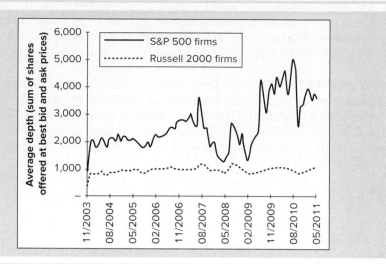

FIGURE   3.4

A portion of the limit
order book for Facebook
on the BATS market,
May 16, 2017

Source: www.bats.com

Facebook, Inc. (FB)

149.73 ↓0.56 (0.38%) 3:05 EDT

Bid		Ask	
Price	**Size**	**Price**	**Size**
147.75	50	149.76	500
149.74	70.1	149.77	308
149.73	150	149.78	300
149.72	400	149.79	500
149.71	400	149.80	884

Figure 3.4 is a portion of the limit order book for shares in Facebook taken from the BATS exchange (one of several electronic exchanges; more on these shortly). Notice that the best orders are at the top of the list: the offers to buy at the highest price and to sell at the lowest price. The buy and sell orders at the top of the list—$149.75 and $149.76—are called the *inside quotes;* they are the highest buy and lowest sell orders. For Facebook, the inside spread at this time was only 1 cent. However, order sizes at the inside quotes can be fairly small. Therefore, investors interested in larger trades face an *effective* spread greater than the nominal one since they cannot execute their entire trades at the inside price quotes.

CONCEPT   3.3
c h e c k

What type of trading order might you give to your broker in each of the following circumstances?

a. You want to buy shares of Intel to diversify your portfolio. You believe the share price is approximately at the "fair" value, and you want the trade done quickly and cheaply.

b. You want to buy shares of Intel but believe that the current stock price is too high given the firm's prospects. If the shares could be obtained at a price 5% lower than the current value, you would like to purchase shares for your portfolio.

c. You believe your shares of FedEx may be priced generously, and are thinking about them. But there is a chance that price fluctuations might result in a short-lived increase of a few dollars per share. If the share price rises by $2 you would be fully convinced they are overpriced and would want to sell them immediately.

Trading Mechanisms

An investor who wishes to buy or sell shares will place an order with a brokerage firm. The broker charges a commission for arranging the trade on the client's behalf. Brokers have several avenues by which they can execute that trade, that is, find a buyer or seller and arrange for the shares to be exchanged.

Broadly speaking, there are three trading systems employed in the United States: over-the-counter dealer markets, electronic communication networks, and specialist markets. Electronic trading is by far most prevalent, but the best-known markets such as NASDAQ or the New York Stock Exchange actually use a variety of trading procedures, so before delving into these markets, it is useful to understand the basic operation of each type of trading system.

DEALER MARKETS Roughly 35,000 securities trade on the **over-the-counter (OTC) market.** Thousands of brokers register with the SEC as security dealers. Dealers quote prices at which they are willing to buy or sell securities. A broker then executes a trade by contacting a dealer listing an attractive quote.

Before 1971, all OTC quotations were recorded manually and published daily on so-called pink sheets. In 1971, the National Association of Securities Dealers introduced its Automatic Quotations System, or NASDAQ, to link brokers and dealers in a computer network where price quotes could be displayed and revised. Dealers could use the network to display the bid price at which they were willing to purchase a security and the asked price at which they were willing to sell. The difference in these prices, the bid–ask spread, was the source of the dealer's profit. Brokers representing clients could examine quotes over the computer network, contact the dealer with the best quote, and execute a trade.

As originally organized, NASDAQ was more of a price quotation system than a trading system. While brokers could survey bid and ask prices across the network of dealers in the search for the best trading opportunity, actual trades required direct negotiation (often over the phone) between the investor's broker and the dealer in the security. However, as we will see, NASDAQ has progressed far beyond a pure price quotation system. While dealers still post bid and asked prices over the network, what is now called the **NASDAQ Stock Market** allows for electronic execution of trades at quoted prices without the need for direct negotiation, and the vast majority of trades are executed electronically.

ELECTRONIC COMMUNICATION NETWORKS (ECNS) **Electronic communication networks** allow participants to post market and limit orders over computer networks. The limit order book is available to all participants. An example of such an order book from BATS, one of the leading ECNs, appears in Figure 3.4. Orders that can be "crossed," that is, matched against another order, are executed automatically without requiring the intervention of a broker. For example, an order to buy a share at a price of $149.75 or lower will be immediately executed if there is an outstanding asked price of $149.75. Therefore, ECNs are true trading systems, not merely price quotation systems.

ECNs offer several advantages. Direct crossing of trades without using a broker-dealer system eliminates the bid–ask spread that otherwise would be incurred. Instead, trades are automatically crossed at a modest cost, typically less than a penny per share. ECNs are attractive as well because of the speed with which a trade can be executed. Finally, these systems offer investors considerable anonymity.

SPECIALIST MARKETS Specialist systems have been largely replaced by electronic communication networks, but as recently as two decades ago, they were still one of the important means by which stocks were traded. In these systems, exchanges such as the NYSE assign responsibility for managing the trading in each security to a **specialist.** Brokers wishing to buy or sell shares for their clients direct the trade to the specialist's post on the floor of the exchange. While each security is assigned to only one specialist, each specialist firm makes a market in many securities. The specialist maintains the limit order book of all outstanding unexecuted limit orders. When orders can be executed at market prices, the specialist executes or "crosses" the trade. The highest outstanding bid price and the lowest outstanding ask price "win" the trade.

over-the-counter (OTC) market
An informal network of brokers and dealers who negotiate sales of securities.

NASDAQ Stock Market
The computer-linked price quotation and trade execution system.

electronic communication networks (ECNs)
Computer networks that allow direct trading without the need for market makers.

specialist
A company that makes a market in the shares of one or more firms and that maintains a "fair and orderly market" by trading for its own inventory of shares.

Specialists are also mandated to maintain a "fair and orderly" market when the book of limit buy and sell orders is so thin that the spread between the highest bid price and lowest ask price becomes too wide. In this case, the specialist firm would be expected to offer to buy and sell shares from its own inventory at a narrower bid–ask spread. In this role, the specialist serves as a dealer in the stock and provides liquidity to other traders. In this context, liquidity providers are those who stand willing to buy securities from or sell securities to other traders.

3.3   THE RISE OF ELECTRONIC TRADING

When first established, NASDAQ was primarily an over-the-counter dealer market and the NYSE was a specialist market. But today both are primarily electronic markets. These changes were driven by an interaction of new technologies and new regulations. New regulations allowed brokers to compete for business, broke the hold that dealers once had on information about best-available bid and ask prices, forced integration of markets, and allowed securities to trade in ever-smaller price increments (called *tick sizes*). Technology made it possible for traders to rapidly compare prices across markets and direct their trades to the markets with the best prices. The resulting competition drove down the cost of trade execution to a tiny fraction of its value just a few decades ago.

In 1975, fixed commissions on the NYSE were eliminated, which freed brokers to compete for business by lowering their fees. In that year also, Congress amended the Securities Exchange Act to create the National Market System to at least partially centralize trading across exchanges and enhance competition among different market makers. The idea was to implement centralized reporting of transactions as well as a centralized price quotation system to give traders a broader view of trading opportunities across markets.

The aftermath of a 1994 scandal at NASDAQ turned out to be a major impetus in the further evolution and integration of markets. NASDAQ dealers were found to be colluding to maintain wide bid–ask spreads. For example, if a stock was listed at $30 bid–$30½ ask, a retail client who wished to buy shares from a dealer would pay $30½ while a client who wished to sell shares would receive only $30. The dealer would pocket the ½-point spread as profit. Other traders may have been willing to step in with better prices (e.g., they may have been willing to buy shares for $30⅛ or sell them for $30⅜), but those better quotes were not made available to the public, enabling dealers to profit from artificially wide spreads at the public's expense. When these practices came to light, an antitrust lawsuit was brought against NASDAQ.

In response to the scandal, the SEC instituted new order-handling rules. Published dealer quotes now had to reflect limit orders of customers, allowing them to effectively compete with dealers to capture trades. As part of the antitrust settlement, NASDAQ agreed to integrate quotes from ECNs into its public display, enabling the electronic exchanges to also compete for trades. Shortly after this settlement, the SEC adopted Regulation ATS (Alternative Trading Systems), giving ECNs the right to register as stock exchanges. Not surprisingly, they captured an ever-larger market share, and in the wake of this new competition, bid–ask spreads narrowed.

Even more dramatic narrowing of trading costs came in 1997, when the SEC allowed the minimum tick size to fall from one-eighth of a dollar to one-sixteenth. Not long after, in 2001, "decimalization" allowed the tick size to fall to 1 cent. Bid–ask spreads again fell dramatically. Figure 3.5 shows estimates of the "effective spread" (the cost of a transaction) during three distinct time periods defined by the minimum tick size. Notice how dramatically effective spread falls along with the minimum tick size.

Technology was also changing trading practices. The first ECN, Instinet, was established in 1969. By the 1990s, exchanges around the world were rapidly adopting fully electronic trading systems. Europe led the way in this evolution, but eventually U.S. exchanges followed suit. The National Association of Securities Dealers (NASD) spun off the NASDAQ Stock Market as a separate entity in 2000, which quickly evolved into a centralized limit-order matching system—effectively a large ECN. The NYSE acquired the electronic Archipelago Exchange in 2006 and renamed it NYSE Arca.

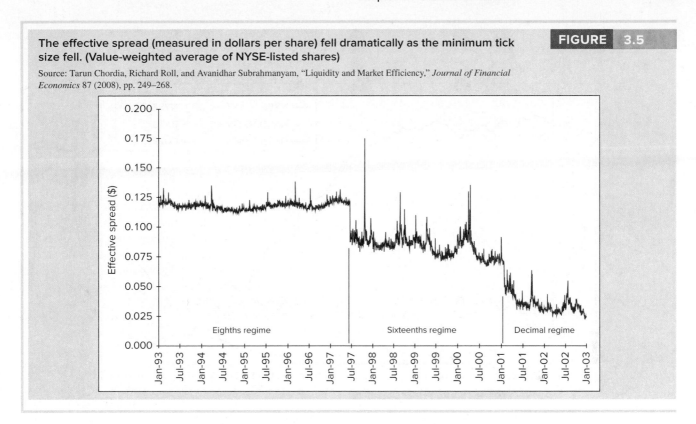

The effective spread (measured in dollars per share) fell dramatically as the minimum tick size fell. (Value-weighted average of NYSE-listed shares)

Source: Tarun Chordia, Richard Roll, and Avanidhar Subrahmanyam, "Liquidity and Market Efficiency," *Journal of Financial Economics* 87 (2008), pp. 249–268.

FIGURE 3.5

In 2005, the SEC adopted Regulation NMS (National Market System), which was fully implemented in 2007. The goal was to link exchanges electronically, thereby creating in effect one integrated electronic market. The regulation required exchanges to honor quotes of other exchanges when they could be executed automatically. An exchange that could not handle a quote electronically would be labeled a "slow market" under Reg NMS and could be ignored by other market participants. The NYSE, which was still devoted to the specialist system, was particularly at risk of being passed over, and in response to this pressure, it moved aggressively toward automated execution of trades. Electronic trading networks and the integration of markets in the wake of Reg NMS made it much easier for exchanges around the world to compete; the NYSE lost its effective monopoly in trading its own listed stocks, and by the end of the decade, its share in the trading of NYSE-listed stocks fell from about 75% to 25%.

Trading today is overwhelmingly electronic, at least for stocks. Bonds are still traded primarily in more traditional dealer markets.

3.4 U.S. MARKETS

The NYSE and the NASDAQ Stock Market remain the best-known U.S. stock markets. But electronic communication networks have steadily increased their market share. Figure 3.6 shows the comparative trading volume of NYSE-listed shares on the NYSE and NASDAQ as well as on the major ECNs, namely, BATS, NYSE Arca, and Direct Edge. Since this study was published, BATS and Direct Edge merged, creating one of the world's largest stock exchanges, called BATS Global Markets. The "Other" category, which now exceeds 30%, includes so-called dark pools, which we will discuss shortly.

NASDAQ

The NASDAQ Stock Market lists around 3,000 firms. It has steadily introduced ever-more sophisticated trading platforms, which today handle the great majority of its trades. The

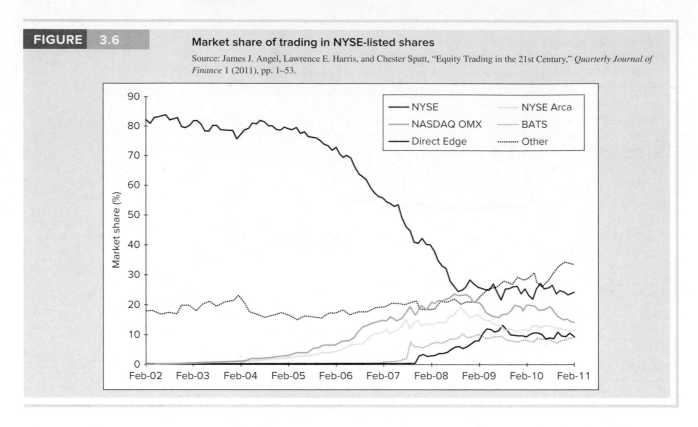

FIGURE   **3.6**

Market share of trading in NYSE-listed shares

Source: James J. Angel, Lawrence E. Harris, and Chester Spatt, "Equity Trading in the 21st Century," *Quarterly Journal of Finance* 1 (2011), pp. 1–53.

current version, called the NASDAQ Market Center, consolidates NASDAQ's previous electronic markets into one integrated system. NASDAQ merged in 2007 with OMX, a Swedish-Finnish company that controls seven Nordic and Baltic stock exchanges, to form NASDAQ OMX Group. In addition to maintaining the NASDAQ Stock Market, it also maintains several stock markets in Europe as well as an options and futures exchange in the U.S.

NASDAQ has three levels of subscribers. The highest, level 3 subscribers, are registered market makers. These are firms that make a market in securities, maintain inventories of securities, and post bid and ask prices at which they are willing to buy or sell shares. Level 3 subscribers can enter and change bid–ask quotes continually and have the fastest execution of trades. They profit from the spread between bid and ask prices.

Level 2 subscribers receive all bid and ask quotes but cannot enter their own quotes. They can see which market makers are offering the best prices. These subscribers tend to be brokerage firms that execute trades for clients but do not actively deal in stocks for their own account.

Level 1 subscribers receive only inside quotes (i.e., the best bid and ask prices) but do not see how many shares are being offered. These subscribers tend to be investors who are not actively buying or selling but want information on current prices.

The New York Stock Exchange

stock exchanges

Secondary markets where already-issued securities are bought and sold by members.

The NYSE is the largest U.S. **stock exchange** as measured by the market value of listed firms. In 2006, the NYSE merged with the Archipelago Exchange to form a publicly held company called the NYSE Group, and then in 2007, it merged with the European exchange Euronext to form NYSE Euronext. The firm acquired the American Stock Exchange in 2008, which was renamed NYSE Amex and focuses on small firms. A billion shares trade on the NYSE on a typical day. NYSE Arca is the firm's electronic communications network. In 2013, NYSE Euronext was acquired by Intercontinental Exchange (ICE), whose main business to date had been energy-futures trading. ICE has retained the NYSE Euronext name.

The NYSE was long committed to its specialist trading system, which relied heavily on human participation in trade execution. It began its transition to electronic trading for smaller trades in 1976 with the introduction of its DOT (Designated Order Turnaround) and later SuperDOT systems, which could route orders directly to the specialist. In 2000, the exchange launched Direct+, which could automatically cross smaller trades (up to 1,099 shares) without human intervention, and in 2004, it began eliminating the size restrictions on Direct+ trades. The change of emphasis dramatically accelerated in 2006 with the introduction of the NYSE Hybrid Market, which allowed brokers to send orders either for immediate electronic execution or to the specialist, who could seek price improvement from another trader. The Hybrid system allowed the NYSE to qualify as a fast market for the purposes of Regulation NMS but still offer the advantages of human intervention for more complicated trades. In contrast, NYSE's Arca marketplace is fully electronic.

ECNs

Over time, more fully automated markets have gained market share at the expense of less automated ones, in particular, the NYSE. Some of the biggest ECNs today are NASDAQ, BATS, and NYSE Arca. Brokers that have an affiliation with an ECN have computer access and can enter orders in the limit order book. As orders are received, the system determines whether there is a matching order, and if so, the trade is immediately crossed.

Originally, ECNs were open only to other traders using the same system. But following the implementation of Reg NMS, ECNs began listing limit orders on other networks. Traders could use their computer systems to sift through the limit order books of many ECNs and instantaneously route orders to the market with the best prices. Those cross-market links have become the impetus for one of the more popular strategies of so-called high-frequency traders, which seek to profit from even small, transitory discrepancies in prices across markets. Speed is obviously of the essence here, and ECNs compete in terms of the speed they can offer. **Latency** refers to the time it takes to accept, process, and deliver a trading order. BATS, for example, advertises (in 2017) average latency times of about 100 microseconds, that is, 0.0001 second.

latency
The time it takes to accept, process, and deliver a trading order.

3.5 NEW TRADING STRATEGIES

The marriage of electronic trading mechanisms with computer technology has had far-ranging impacts on trading strategies and tools. *Algorithmic trading* delegates trading decisions to computer programs. *High-frequency trading* is a special class of algorithmic trading in which computer programs initiate orders in tiny fractions of a second, far faster than any human could process the information driving the trade. Much of the market liquidity that once was provided by brokers making a market in a security has been displaced by these high-frequency traders. But when high-frequency traders abandon the market, as in the so-called flash crash of 2010, liquidity can likewise evaporate in a flash. *Dark pools* are trading venues that preserve anonymity but also affect market liquidity. We will address these emerging issues later in this section.

Algorithmic Trading

Algorithmic trading is the use of computer programs to make trading decisions. Well more than half of all equity volume in the U.S. is believed to be initiated by computer algorithms. Many of these trades exploit very small discrepancies in security prices and entail numerous and rapid cross-market price comparisons that are well suited to computer analysis. These strategies would not have been feasible before decimalization of the minimum tick size.

algorithmic trading
The use of computer programs to make rapid trading decisions.

Some algorithmic trades attempt to exploit very short-term trends (as short as a few seconds) as new information about a firm or, more controversially, about the intentions of other traders, becomes available. Others use versions of *pairs trading* in which normal price relations between pairs (or larger groups) of stocks seem temporarily disrupted and offer small profit opportunities as they move back into alignment. Still others attempt to exploit discrepancies between stock prices and prices of stock-index futures contracts.

Some algorithmic trading involves activities akin to traditional market making. The traders seek to profit from the bid–ask spread by buying a stock at the bid price and rapidly selling it at the ask price before the price can change. While this mimics the role of a market maker who provides liquidity to other traders in the stock, these algorithmic traders are not registered market makers and so do not have an affirmative obligation to maintain both bid and ask quotes. If they abandon a market during a period of turbulence, the shock to market liquidity can be disruptive. This seems to have been a problem during the flash crash of May 6, 2010, when the stock market encountered extreme volatility, with the Dow Jones average falling by 1,000 points before recovering around 600 points in intraday trading. The nearby box discusses this amazing and troubling episode.

High-Frequency Trading

high-frequency trading

A subset of algorithmic trading that relies on computer programs to make very rapid trading decisions.

It is easy to see that many algorithmic trading strategies require extremely rapid trade initiation and execution. **High-frequency trading** is a subset of algorithmic trading that relies on computer programs to make extremely rapid decisions. High-frequency traders compete for trades that offer very small profits. But if those opportunities are numerous enough, they can accumulate to big money.

We pointed out that one high-frequency strategy entails a sort of market making, attempting to profit from the bid–ask spread. Another relies on cross-market arbitrage, in which even tiny price discrepancies across markets allow the firm to buy a security at one price and simultaneously sell it at a slightly higher price. The competitive advantage in these strategies lies with the firms that are quickest to identify and execute these profit opportunities. There is a tremendous premium on being the first to "hit" a bid or asked price.

Trade execution times for high-frequency traders are now measured in milliseconds, even microseconds. This has induced trading firms to "co-locate" their trading centers next to the computer systems of the electronic exchanges. When execution or latency periods are less than a millisecond, the extra time it takes for a trade order to travel from a remote location to a New York exchange would be enough to make it nearly impossible to win the trade.

To understand why co-location has become a key issue, consider this calculation: Even light can travel only 186 miles in one millisecond, so an order originating in Chicago transmitted at the speed of light would take almost five milliseconds to reach New York. That order could not possibly compete with one launched from a co-located facility.

In some ways, co-location is a new version of an old phenomenon. Think about why, even before the advent of the telephone, so many brokerage firms originally located their headquarters in New York: They were "co-locating" with the NYSE so that their brokers could bring trades (on foot!) to the exchange quickly and efficiently. Today, trades are transmitted electronically, but competition among traders for fast execution means that the need to be near the market (now embodied in computer servers) remains.

Dark Pools

blocks

Large transactions in which at least 10,000 shares of stock are bought or sold.

Many large traders seek anonymity. They fear that if others see them executing a buy or a sell program, their intentions will become public and prices will move against them. Very large trades (called **blocks,** usually defined as a trade of more than 10,000 shares) were traditionally brought to "block houses," brokerage firms specializing in matching block buyers and sellers. Part of the expertise of block brokers was in identifying traders who might be interested in a large purchase or sale if given an offer. These brokers discreetly arranged large trades out of the public eye, and so avoided moving prices against their clients.

dark pools

Electronic trading networks where participants can anonymously buy or sell large blocks of securities.

Block trading today has largely been displaced by **dark pools,** trading systems in which participants can buy or sell large blocks of securities without showing their hand. Limit orders are not visible to the general public as they would be on a conventional exchange, and traders' identities can also be kept private. Trades are not reported until after they are crossed, which limits the vulnerability to other traders anticipating one's trading program.

THE FLASH CRASH OF MAY 2010

At 2:42 New York time on May 6, 2010, the Dow Jones Industrial Average was already down about 300 points for the day. The market was demonstrating concerns about the European debt crisis, and nerves were on edge. Then, in the next five minutes, the Dow dropped an *additional* 600 points. And only 20 minutes after that, it had recovered most of those 600 points. Besides the staggering intraday volatility of the broad market, trading in individual shares and ETFs was even more disrupted. The iShares Russell 1000 Value Fund temporarily fell from $59 a share to 8 cents. Shares in the large consulting company Accenture, which had just sold for $38, traded at 1 cent only a minute or two later. At the other extreme, price quotes for Apple and Hewlett-Packard momentarily increased to over $100,000. These markets were clearly broken.

The causes of the flash crash are still debated. An SEC report issued after the trade pointed to a $4 billion sale of market index futures contracts by a mutual fund (believed to be Waddell & Reed Financial). As market prices began to tumble, many algorithmic trading programs withdrew from the markets, and those that remained became net sellers, further pushing down equity prices. As more and more of these algorithmic traders shut down, liquidity in these markets evaporated: Buyers for many stocks simply disappeared.

Finally, trading was halted for a short period. When it resumed, buyers decided to take advantage of many severely depressed stock prices, and the market rebounded almost as quickly as it had crashed. Given the intraday turbulence and the clearly distorted prices at which some trades had been executed, the NYSE and NASDAQ decided to cancel all trades that were executed more than 60% away from a "reference price" close to the opening price of the day. Almost 70% of those canceled trades involved ETFs.

The SEC has since approved experimentation with new circuit breakers to halt trading for five minutes in large stocks that rise or fall by more than 10% in a five-minute period. The idea is to prevent trading algorithms from moving share prices quickly before human traders have a chance to determine whether those prices are moving in response to fundamental information.

The flash crash highlighted the fragility of markets in the face of huge variation in trading volume created by algorithmic traders. The potential for these high-frequency traders to withdraw from markets in periods of turbulence remains a concern, and many observers are not convinced that we are protected from future flash crashes.

Many large traders gravitate toward dark pools because it makes them less vulnerable to high-frequency traders. They want a trading venue where other traders find it more difficult to infer their trading intentions and trade in front of them. However, this ideal has not always been realized. In 2011, Pipeline LLC, which operated a dark pool, was accused of enabling high-frequency traders to participate in its market and to gauge the intentions of other participants in the pool. Similarly, in 2014, Barclays was accused of misrepresenting the level of high-frequency trading in a dark pool that it operated. There are lingering concerns regarding the extent to which dark pools provide the protections from other traders that they are purportedly designed to offer.

Dark pools are somewhat controversial because they contribute to the fragmentation of markets. When many orders are removed from the consolidated limit order book, there are fewer orders left to absorb fluctuations in demand for the security, and the public price may no longer be "fair" in the sense that it reflects all the potentially available information about security demand.

Another approach to dealing with large trades is to split them into many small trades, each of which can be executed on electronic markets, attempting to hide the fact that the total number of shares ultimately to be bought or sold is large. This trend has led to rapid decline in average trade size, which today is less than 300 shares.

Bond Trading

In 2006, the NYSE obtained regulatory approval to expand its bond trading system to include the debt issues of any NYSE-listed firm. In the past, each bond needed to be registered before listing; such a requirement was too onerous to justify listing most bonds. In conjunction with these new listings, the NYSE has expanded its electronic bond-trading platform, which is now called NYSE Bonds.

Nevertheless, the vast majority of bond trading occurs in the OTC market among bond dealers, even for bonds that are actually listed on the NYSE. This market is a network of bond dealers such as Merrill Lynch (now part of Bank of America), Salomon Smith Barney (a division of Citigroup), and Goldman Sachs that is linked by a computer quotation system.

Because dealers do not carry extensive inventories of the wide range of bonds that have been issued to the public, they cannot necessarily offer to sell bonds from their inventory to clients or even buy bonds for their own inventory. New electronic trading platforms, for example, MarketAxess, now exist to directly connect buyers and sellers. But these platforms have not yet displaced the traditional dealer market. One of the impediments to heavy electronic trading is lack of standardization in the bond market. A single company may have outstanding dozens of different bond issues, differing by coupon, maturity, and seniority. Any one of these outstanding bonds may trade only a few times a year. Given the great diversity of bond issues and the often sporadic trading activity of bond investors, even these electronic platforms rely for liquidity on participation by investment banks that are willing to act as dealers, maintaining inventories to be matched against investor orders. In the aftermath of the financial crisis and reduced capacity for risk taking, however, the banks have pulled back from this role.

In practice, therefore, the corporate bond market often is quite "thin," in that there may be few investors interested in trading a bond at any particular time. As a result, the bond market is subject to a type of liquidity risk, as it can be difficult to sell one's holdings quickly if the need arises.

3.6 GLOBALIZATION OF STOCK MARKETS

Figure 3.7 shows the market capitalization of firms listed on major stock exchanges around the world. By this measure, the NYSE Euronext is by far the largest equity market. All major stock markets today are effectively electronic.

Securities markets have come under increasing pressure in recent years to make international alliances or mergers. Much of this pressure is due to the impact of electronic trading. To a growing extent, traders view stock markets as networks that link them to other traders, and there are increasingly fewer limits on the securities around the world that they can trade. Against this background, it becomes more important for exchanges to provide the cheapest and most efficient mechanism by which trades can be executed and cleared. This argues for global alliances that can facilitate the nuts and bolts of cross-border trading and can benefit from economies of

Market capitalization of major world stock exchanges, 2016

Source: World Federation of Exchanges.

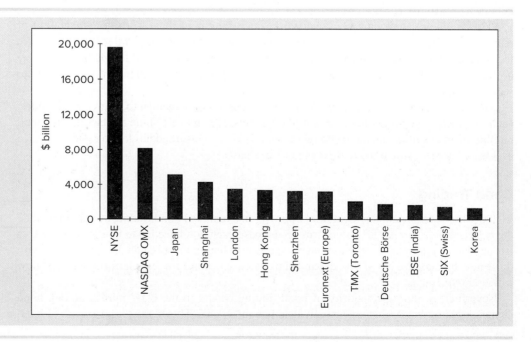

scale. Exchanges feel that they eventually need to offer 24-hour global markets. Finally, companies want to be able to go beyond national borders when they wish to raise capital.

These pressures have resulted in a broad trend toward market consolidation. After a wave of mergers in the last two decades, the industry now has a few giant security exchanges: ICE (Intercontinental Exchange, operating NYSE-Euronext, and several commodity futures and options markets), NASDAQ, the LSE (London Stock Exchange Group), Deutsche Boerse, the CME Group (largely options and futures trading), TSE (Tokyo Stock Exchange), and HKEX (Hong Kong Stock Exchange). Other mergers were attempted but blocked by opposition of antitrust regulators. Two of these failed deals were the proposed mergers between Deutsche Boerse and NYSE-Euronext in 2011 and between the LSE and Deutsche Boerse in 2017. Still, the attempts at these mergers indicates the pressure exchanges feel to combine.

3.7   TRADING COSTS

Part of the cost of trading a security is obvious and explicit. Your broker must be paid a commission. Individuals may choose from two kinds of brokers: full-service or discount brokers. Full-service brokers who provide a variety of services often are referred to as account executives or financial consultants.

Besides carrying out the basic services of executing orders, holding securities for safekeeping, extending margin loans, and facilitating short sales, brokers routinely provide information and advice relating to investment alternatives.

Full-service brokers usually depend on a research staff that prepares analyses and forecasts of general economic as well as industry and company conditions and often makes specific buy or sell recommendations. Some customers take the ultimate leap of faith and allow a full-service broker to make buy and sell decisions for them by establishing a *discretionary account,* which allows the broker to trade securities whenever deemed fit. (The broker cannot withdraw any funds, though.) This action requires an unusual degree of trust on the part of the customer, for an unscrupulous broker can "churn" an account, that is, trade securities excessively with the sole purpose of generating commissions.

Discount brokers, on the other hand, provide "no-frills" services. They buy and sell securities, hold them for safekeeping, offer margin loans, facilitate short sales, and that is all. The only information they provide about the securities they handle is price quotations. Discount brokerage services have become increasingly available in recent years. Many banks, thrift institutions, and mutual fund management companies now offer such services to the investing public as part of a general trend toward the creation of one-stop "financial supermarkets." Stock trading fees have fallen steadily over the last decade, and discount brokerage firms such as Schwab, E*Trade, or Ameritrade, not to mention mutual fund companies such as Fidelity, now offer commissions well below $10.

In addition to the explicit part of trading costs—the broker's commission—there is an implicit part—the dealer's bid–ask spread. Sometimes the broker is a dealer in the security being traded and charges no commission but instead collects the fee entirely in the form of the bid–ask spread. Another implicit cost of trading that some observers would distinguish is the price concession an investor may be forced to make for trading in quantities greater than those associated with the posted bid or asked prices.

3.8   BUYING ON MARGIN

When purchasing securities, investors have easy access to a source of debt financing called *broker's call loans.* Taking advantage of these loans is called *buying on margin.*

Purchasing stocks on margin means the investor borrows part of the purchase price of the stock. The **margin** in the account is the portion of the purchase price contributed by the investor; the remainder is borrowed from the broker. The brokers in turn borrow money from banks at the call money rate to finance these purchases; they then charge their clients that

margin
Describes securities purchased with money borrowed in part from a broker. The margin is the net worth of the investor's account.

rate (defined in Chapter 2) plus a service charge. All securities purchased on margin must be maintained with the brokerage firm in street name, for the securities are collateral for the loan.

The Board of Governors of the Federal Reserve System limits the extent to which stock purchases can be financed using margin loans. The current initial margin requirement is 50%, meaning that at least 50% of the purchase price must be paid for in cash, with the rest borrowed.

EXAMPLE 3.1

Margin

The percentage margin is defined as the ratio of the net worth, or the "equity value," of the account to the market value of the securities. To demonstrate, suppose an investor initially pays $6,000 toward the purchase of $10,000 worth of stock (100 shares at $100 per share), borrowing the remaining $4,000 from a broker. The initial balance sheet looks like this:

Assets		Liabilities and Owners' Equity	
Value of stock	$10,000	Loan from broker	$4,000
		Equity	$6,000

The initial percentage margin is

$$\text{Margin} = \frac{\text{Equity in account}}{\text{Value of stock}} = \frac{\$6,000}{\$10,000} = .60, \text{ or } 60\%$$

If the price declines to $70 per share, the account balance becomes:

Assets		Liabilities and Owners' Equity	
Value of stock	$7,000	Loan from broker	$4,000
		Equity	$3,000

The assets in the account fall by the full decrease in the stock value, as does the equity. The percentage margin is now

$$\text{Margin} = \frac{\text{Equity in account}}{\text{Value of stock}} = \frac{\$3,000}{\$7,000} = .43, \text{ or } 43\%$$

If the stock value in Example 3.1 were to fall below $4,000, owners' equity would become negative, meaning the value of the stock is no longer sufficient collateral to cover the loan from the broker. To guard against this possibility, the broker sets a *maintenance margin.* If the percentage margin falls below the maintenance level, the broker will issue a *margin call,* which requires the investor to add new cash or securities to the margin account. If the investor does not act, the broker may sell securities from the account to pay off enough of the loan to restore the percentage margin to an acceptable level.

EXAMPLE 3.2

Maintenance Margin

Suppose the maintenance margin is 30%. How far could the stock price fall before the investor would get a margin call?

Let P be the price of the stock. The value of the investor's 100 shares is then $100P$, and the equity in the account is $100P - \$4,000$. The percentage margin is $(100P - \$4,000)/100P$. The price at which the percentage margin equals the maintenance margin of .3 is found by solving the equation

$$\frac{100P - 4,000}{100P} = .3$$

which implies that $P = \$57.14$. If the price of the stock were to fall below $57.14 per share, the investor would get a margin call.

CONCEPT check **3.4**

Suppose the maintenance margin in Example 3.2 is 40%. How far can the stock price fall before the investor gets a margin call?

Why do investors buy securities on margin? They do so when they wish to invest an amount greater than their own money allows. Thus, they can achieve greater upside potential, but they also expose themselves to greater downside risk.

To see how, let's suppose an investor is bullish on Fincorp stock, which is selling for $100 per share. An investor with $10,000 to invest expects the share price to rise by 30% during the next year. Ignoring dividends, the expected rate of return would be 30% if the investor invested $10,000 to buy 100 shares.

But now assume the investor borrows another $10,000 from the broker and invests it in Fincorp, too. The total investment would be $20,000 (for 200 shares). Assuming an interest rate on the margin loan of 9% per year, what will the investor's rate of return be now (again ignoring dividends) if the stock goes up 30% by year's end?

The 200 shares will be worth $26,000. Paying off $10,900 of principal and interest on the margin loan leaves $15,100 (i.e., $26,000 – $10,900). The rate of return in this case will be

$$\frac{\$15,100 - \$10,000}{\$10,000} = 51\%$$

The investor has parlayed a 30% rise in the stock's price into a 51% rate of return on the $10,000 investment.

Doing so, however, magnifies the downside risk. Suppose that, instead of going up by 30%, the stock price drops by 30% to $70 per share. In that case, the 200 shares will be worth $14,000, and the investor is left with $3,100 after paying off the $10,900 of principal and interest on the loan. The result is a disastrous return of

$$\frac{\$3,100 - \$10,000}{\$10,000} = -69\%$$

Table 3.1 summarizes the possible results of these hypothetical transactions. If there is no change in the stock price, the investor loses 9%, the cost of the loan.

TABLE 3.1 Illustration of buying stock on margin

Change in Stock Price	End-of-Year Value of Shares	Repayment of Principal and Interest*	Investor's Rate of Return
30% increase	$26,000	$10,900	51%
No change	20,000	10,900	−9
30% decrease	14,000	10,900	−69

*Assuming the investor buys $20,000 worth of stock by borrowing $10,000 at an interest rate of 9% per year.

CONCEPT check **3.5**

Suppose that in the Fincorp example above, the investor borrows only $5,000 at the same interest rate of 9% per year. What will the rate of return be if the stock price increases by 30%? If it falls by 30%? If it remains unchanged?

Buying on Margin

The Excel spreadsheet model below makes it easy to analyze the impacts of different margin levels and the volatility of stock prices. It also allows you to compare return on investment for a margin trade with a trade using no borrowed funds.

	A	B	C	D	E	F	G	H
1								
2			Action or Formula	Ending	Return on		Ending	Return with
3			for Column B	St Price	Investment		St Price	No Margin
4	Initial Equity Investment	$10,000.00	Enter data		−42.00%			−19.00%
5	Amount Borrowed	$10,000.00	(B4/B10)−B4	$20.00	−122.00%		$20.00	−59.00%
6	Initial Stock Price	$50.00	Enter data	25.00	−102.00%		25.00	−49.00%
7	Shares Purchased	400	(B4/B10)/B6	30.00	−82.00%		30.00	−39.00%
8	Ending Stock Price	$40.00	Enter data	35.00	−62.00%		35.00	−29.00%
9	Cash Dividends During Hold Per.	$0.50	Enter data	40.00	−42.00%		40.00	−19.00%
10	Initial Margin Percentage	50.00%	Enter data	45.00	−22.00%		45.00	−9.00%
11	Maintenance Margin Percentage	30.00%	Enter data	50.00	−2.00%		50.00	1.00%
12				55.00	18.00%		55.00	11.00%
13	Rate on Margin Loan	8.00%	Enter data	60.00	38.00%		60.00	21.00%
14	Holding Period in Months	6	Enter data	65.00	58.00%		65.00	31.00%
15				70.00	78.00%		70.00	41.00%
16	**Return on Investment**			75.00	98.00%		75.00	51.00%
17	Capital Gain on Stock	−$4,000.00	B7*(B8−B6)	80.00	118.00%		80.00	61.00%
18	Dividends	$200.00	B7*B9					
19	Interest on Margin Loan	$400.00	B5*(B14/12)*B13					
20	Net Income	−$4,200.00	B17+B18−B19			LEGEND:		
21	Initial Investment	$10,000.00	B4			Enter data		
22	Return on Investment	−42.00%	B20/B21			Value calculated		

Excel Questions

1. Suppose you buy 100 shares of stock initially selling for $50, borrowing 25% of the necessary funds from your broker; that is, the initial margin on your purchase is 25%. You pay an interest rate of 8% on margin loans.

    a. How much of your own money do you invest? How much do you borrow from your broker?

    b. What will be your rate of return for the following stock prices at the end of a one-year holding period? (i) $40; (ii) $50; (iii) $60.

2. Repeat Question 1 assuming your initial margin was 50%. How does margin affect the risk and return of your position?

SHORT SALES

short sale

The sale of shares not owned by the investor but borrowed through a broker and later purchased to replace the loan.

An investor who is bullish on a firm would buy shares and later sell them, hopefully at a higher price. A bearish investor who wants to bet against a company can enter a **short sale,** which will profit from a *decline* in a security's price.

In a short sale, first you sell and then you buy the shares. The short-seller first borrows a share of stock from a broker and sells it. Later, the investor must purchase a share of the same stock in order to replace the share that was borrowed.[2] This is called *covering the short position.* Table 3.2 compares stock purchases to short sales.

The short-seller anticipates the stock price will fall, so that the share can be purchased later at a lower price than it initially sold for; if so, the short-sale will provide a profit. Short-sellers must not only replace the shares but also pay the lender of the security any dividends paid during the short sale.

---

[2]*Naked short-selling* is a variant on conventional short-selling. In a naked short, a trader sells shares that have not yet been borrowed, assuming that the shares can be acquired and delivered whenever the short sale needs to be closed out.

APPLICATIONS: Short Sale

This Excel spreadsheet model was built using Example 3.3 for Dot Bomb. The model allows you to analyze the effects of returns, margin calls, and different levels of initial and maintenance margins. The model also includes a sensitivity analysis for ending stock price and return on investment.

This spreadsheet is available in Connect

	A	B	C	D	E
1					
2			**Action or Formula**	**Ending**	**Return on**
3			**for Column B**	**St Price**	**Investment**
4	Initial Investment	$50,000.00	Enter data		60.00%
5	Initial Stock Price	$100.00	Enter data	$170.00	−140.00%
6	Number of Shares Sold Short	1,000	(B4/B9)/B5	160.00	−120.00%
7	Ending Stock Price	$70.00	Enter data	150.00	−100.00%
8	Cash Dividends Per Share	$0.00	Enter data	140.00	−80.00%
9	Initial Margin Percentage	50.00%	Enter data	130.00	−60.00%
10	Maintenance Margin Percentage	30.00%	Enter data	120.00	−40.00%
11				110.00	−20.00%
12	**Return on Short Sale**			100.00	0.00%
13	Capital Gain on Stock	$30,000.00	B6*(B5−B7)	90.00	20.00%
14	Dividends Paid	$0.00	B8*B6	80.00	40.00%
15	Net Income	$30,000.00	B13−B14	70.00	60.00%
16	Initial Investment	$50,000.00	B4	60.00	80.00%
17	Return on Investment	60.00%	B15/B16	50.00	100.00%
18				40.00	120.00%
19	**Margin Positions**			30.00	140.00%
20	Margin Based on Ending Price	114.29%	(B4+(B5*B6)−B14−(B6*B7))/(B6*B7)	20.00	160.00%
21				10.00	180.00%
22	Price for Margin Call	$115.38	(B4+(B5*B6)−B14)/(B6*(1+B10))		
23					**LEGEND:**
24					Enter data
25					Value calculated

Excel Questions

1. Suppose you sell short 100 shares of stock initially selling for $100 a share. Your initial margin requirement is 50% of the value of the stock sold. You receive no interest on the funds placed in your margin account.

   a. How much do you need to contribute to your margin account?

   b. What will be your rate of return for the following stock prices at the end of a one-year holding period (assume the stock pays no dividends)? (i) $90; (ii) $100; (iii) $110.

2. Repeat Question 1 (b) but now assume that the stock pays dividends of $2 per share at year-end. What is the relationship between the total rate of return on the stock and the return to your short position?

TABLE 3.2	Cash flows from purchasing versus short-selling shares of stock

Purchase of Stock

Time	Action	Cash Flow*
0	Buy share	−Initial price
1	Receive dividend, sell share	Ending price + Dividend

Profit = (Ending price + Dividend) − Initial price

Short Sale of Stock

Time	Action	Cash Flow*
0	Borrow share; sell it	+Initial price
1	Repay dividend and buy share to replace the share originally borrowed	−(Ending price + Dividend)

Profit = Initial price − (Ending price + Dividend)

*Note: A negative cash flow implies a cash *outflow*.

In practice, the shares loaned out for a short sale are typically provided by the short-seller's brokerage firm, which holds a wide variety of securities of its other investors in street name (i.e., the broker holds the shares registered in its own name on behalf of the client). The owner of the shares need not know that the shares have been lent to the short-seller. If the owner wishes to sell the shares, the brokerage firm will simply borrow shares from another investor. Therefore, the short sale may have an indefinite term. However, if the brokerage firm cannot locate new shares to replace the ones sold, the short-seller will need to repay the loan immediately by purchasing shares in the market and turning them over to the brokerage house to close out the loan.

Finally, exchange rules require that proceeds from a short sale must be kept on account with the broker. The short-seller cannot invest these funds to generate income, although large or institutional investors typically will receive some income from the proceeds of a short sale being held with the broker. Short-sellers also are required to post margin (cash or collateral) with the broker to cover losses should the stock price rise during the short sale.

EXAMPLE 3.3	
Short Sales	

To illustrate the mechanics of short-selling, suppose you are bearish (pessimistic) on Dot Bomb stock, and its market price is $100 per share. You tell your broker to sell short 1,000 shares. The broker borrows 1,000 shares either from another customer's account or from another broker.

The $100,000 cash proceeds from the short sale are credited to your account. Suppose the broker has a 50% margin requirement on short sales. This means you must have other cash or securities in your account worth at least $50,000 that can serve as margin on the short sale.

Let's say that you have $50,000 in Treasury bills. Your account with the broker after the short sale will then be:

Assets		Liabilities and Owners' Equity	
Cash	$100,000	Short position in Dot Bomb stock (1,000 shares owed)	$100,000
T-bills	50,000	Equity	50,000

Your initial percentage margin is the ratio of the equity in the account, $50,000, to the current value of the shares you have borrowed and eventually must return, $100,000:

$$\text{Percentage margin} = \frac{\text{Equity}}{\text{Value of stock owed}} = \frac{\$50,000}{\$100,000} = .50$$

Suppose you are right and Dot Bomb falls to $70 per share. You can now close out your position at a profit. To cover the short sale, you buy 1,000 shares to replace the ones you borrowed. Because the shares now sell for $70, the purchase costs only $70,000.[3] Because your account was credited for $100,000 when the shares were borrowed and sold, your profit is $30,000: The profit equals the decline in the share price times the number of shares sold short.

Like investors who purchase stock on margin, a short-seller must be concerned about margin calls. If the stock price rises, the margin in the account will fall; if margin falls to the maintenance level, the short-seller will receive a margin call.

---

[3]Notice that when buying on margin, you borrow a given amount of dollars from your broker, so the amount of the loan is independent of the share price. In contrast, when short-selling, you borrow a given number of *shares*, which must be returned. Therefore, when the price of the shares changes, the value of the loan also changes.

EXAMPLE 3.4

Margin Calls on Short Positions

Suppose the broker has a maintenance margin of 30% on short sales. This means the equity in your account must be at least 30% of the value of your short position at all times. How much can the price of Dot Bomb stock rise before you get a margin call?

Let P be the price of Dot Bomb stock. Then the value of the shares you must pay back is $1,000P$, and the equity in your account is $\$150,000 - 1,000P$. Your short position margin ratio is equity/value of stock $= (150,000 - 1,000P)/1,000P$. The critical value of P is thus

$$\frac{\text{Equity}}{\text{Value of shares owed}} = \frac{150,000 - 1,000P}{1,000P} = .3$$

which implies that $P = \$115.38$ per share. If Dot Bomb stock should *rise* above $\$115.38$ per share, you will get a margin call, and you will either have to put up additional cash or cover your short position by buying shares to replace the ones borrowed.

---

a. Construct the balance sheet if Dot Bomb goes up to $\$110$.

b. If the short position maintenance margin in Example 3.4 is 40%, how far can the stock price rise before the investor gets a margin call?

CONCEPT check 3.6

Short-selling periodically comes under attack, particularly during times of financial stress when share prices fall. The last few years have been no exception to this rule, and the nearby box examines the controversy surrounding short sales in greater detail.

3.10 REGULATION OF SECURITIES MARKETS

Trading in securities markets in the United States is regulated by a myriad of laws. The major governing legislation includes the Securities Act of 1933 and the Securities Exchange Act of 1934. The 1933 act requires full disclosure of relevant information relating to the issue of new securities. This is the act that requires registration of new securities and issuance of a prospectus that details the financial prospects of the firm. SEC approval of a prospectus or financial report is not an endorsement of the security as a good investment. The SEC cares only that the relevant facts are disclosed; investors must make their own evaluation of the security's value.

The 1934 act established the Securities and Exchange Commission to administer the provisions of the 1933 act. It also extended the disclosure principle of the 1933 act by requiring periodic disclosure of relevant financial information by firms with already-issued securities on secondary exchanges.

The 1934 act also empowers the SEC to register and regulate securities exchanges, OTC trading, brokers, and dealers. While the SEC is the administrative agency responsible for broad oversight of the securities markets, it shares responsibility with other regulatory agencies. The Commodity Futures Trading Commission (CFTC) regulates trading in futures markets, while the Federal Reserve has broad responsibility for the health of the U.S. financial system. In this role, the Fed sets margin requirements on stocks and stock options and regulates bank lending to securities markets participants.

The Securities Investor Protection Act of 1970 established the Securities Investor Protection Corporation (SIPC) to protect investors from losses if their brokerage firms fail. Just as the Federal Deposit Insurance Corporation provides depositors with federal protection against bank failure, the SIPC ensures that investors will receive securities held for their account in street name by a failed brokerage firm up to a limit of $\$500,000$ per customer. The SIPC is financed by levying an "insurance premium" on its participating, or member, brokerage firms.

On the MARKET FRONT

SHORT-SELLING COMES UNDER FIRE—AGAIN

Short-selling has long been viewed with suspicion, if not outright hostility. England banned short sales for a good part of the eighteenth century. Napoleon called short-sellers enemies of the state. In the U.S., short-selling was widely viewed as contributing to the market crash of 1929, and in 2008, short-sellers were blamed for the collapse of the investment banks Bear Stearns and Lehman Brothers. With share prices of other financial firms tumbling in September 2008, the SEC instituted a temporary ban on short-selling for about 800 of those firms. Similarly, the Financial Services Authority, the financial regulator in the U.K., prohibited short sales on about 30 financial companies, and Australia banned shorting altogether.

The motivation for these bans is that short sales put downward pressure on share prices that in some cases may be unwarranted: Stories abound of investors who first put on a short sale and then spread negative rumors about the firm to drive down its price. More often, however, shorting is an innocent bet that a share price is too high and is due to fall. Nevertheless, during the market stresses of late 2008, the widespread feeling was that even if short positions were legitimate, regulators should do what they could to prop up the affected institutions.

Hostility to short-selling may stem from confusion between bad news and the bearer of that news. Short-selling allows investors whose analysis indicates a firm is overpriced to take action on that belief—and to profit if they are correct. Rather than *causing* the stock price to fall, shorts may simply be *anticipating* a decline in the stock price. Their sales simply force the market to reflect the deteriorating prospects of troubled firms sooner than it might have otherwise. In other words, short-selling is part of the process by which the full range of information and opinion—pessimistic as well as optimistic—is brought to bear on stock prices.

For example, short-sellers took large (negative) positions in firms such as WorldCom, Enron, and Tyco even before these firms were exposed by regulators. In fact, one might argue that these emerging short positions helped regulators identify the previously undetected scandals. And in the end, Lehman and Bear Stearns were brought down by their very real losses on their mortgage-related investments—not by unfounded rumors.

Academic research supports the conjecture that short sales contribute to efficient "price discovery." For example, the greater the demand for shorting a stock, the lower its future returns tend to be; moreover, firms that attack short-sellers with threats of legal action or bad publicity tend to have especially poor future returns.[4] Short-sale bans may in the end be nothing more than an understandable, but nevertheless misguided, impulse to "shoot the messenger."

Security trading is also subject to state laws, known generally as *blue sky laws* because they are intended to give investors a clearer view of investment prospects. State laws to outlaw fraud in security sales existed before the Securities Act of 1933. Varying state laws were somewhat unified when many states adopted portions of the Uniform Securities Act, which was enacted in 1956.

Self-Regulation

In addition to government regulation, there is considerable self-regulation of the securities market. The most important overseer in this regard is the Financial Industry Regulatory Authority (FINRA), which is the largest nongovernmental regulator of securities firms in the United States. FINRA was formed in 2007 through the consolidation of the National Association of Securities Dealers (NASD) with the self-regulatory arm of the New York Stock Exchange. It describes its broad mission as the fostering of investor protection and market integrity. It examines securities firms, writes and enforces rules concerning trading practices, and administers a dispute resolution forum for investors and registered firms.

There is also self-regulation among the community of investment professionals. For example, the CFA Institute has developed standards of professional conduct that govern the behavior of members with the Chartered Financial Analysts designation, commonly referred to as CFAs. The nearby box presents a brief outline of those principles.

---

[4]See, for example, C. Jones and O. A. Lamont, "Short Sale Constraints and Stock Returns," *Journal of Financial Economics,* November 2002, pp. 207–239, or O. A. Lamont, "Go Down Fighting: Short Sellers vs. Firms," *Review of Asset Pricing Studies* (2), 2012, pp. 1–30.

On the MARKET FRONT

EXCERPTS FROM CFA INSTITUTE STANDARDS OF PROFESSIONAL CONDUCT

I. Professionalism

- Knowledge of the law. Members and Candidates must understand and comply with all applicable laws, rules, and regulations (including the CFA Institute Code of Ethics and Standards of Professional Conduct).
- Independence and objectivity. Members and Candidates must use reasonable care and judgment to achieve and maintain independence and objectivity in their professional activities.
- Misrepresentation. Members and Candidates must not knowingly make any misrepresentations relating to investment analysis, recommendations, actions, or other professional activities.

II. Integrity of Capital Markets

- Material nonpublic information. Members and Candidates who possess material non-public information must not act or cause others to act on the information.
- Market manipulation. Members and Candidates must not engage in practices that distort prices or artificially inflate trading volume with the intent to mislead market participants.

III. Duties to Clients

- Loyalty, prudence, and care. Members and Candidates must place their clients' interests before their employer's or their own interests.
- Fair dealing. Members and Candidates must deal fairly and objectively with all clients when providing investment analysis.
- Suitability. When Members and Candidates are in an advisory relationship with a client, they must make a reasonable inquiry into a client's or prospective client's investment experience, risk and return objectives, and financial constraints.

- Performance presentation. When communicating investment performance information, Members and Candidates must make reasonable efforts to ensure that it is fair, accurate and complete.
- Confidentiality. Members and Candidates must keep information about current, former, and prospective clients confidential unless disclosure is required by law or the client or prospective client permits disclosure.

IV. Duties to Employers

- Loyalty. Members and Candidates must act for the benefit of their employer.
- Responsibilities of Supervisors. Members and Candidates must make reasonable efforts to ensure that anyone subject to their supervision or authority complies with applicable laws, rules, regulations, and the Code and Standards.

V. Investment Analysis and Recommendations

- Diligence and Reasonable Basis. Members and Candidates must have a reasonable and adequate basis, supported by appropriate research and investigation, for any investment analysis, recommendation, or action.
- Communication. Members and Candidates must distinguish between fact and opinion in the presentation of investment analysis.

VI. Conflicts of Interest

- Disclosure of conflicts. Members and Candidates must make full and fair disclosure of all matters that reasonably could be expected to impair their independence and objectivity.
- Priority of transactions. Investment transactions for clients and employers must have priority over investment transactions in which a Member or Candidate is the beneficial owner.

VII. Responsibilities as CFA Institute Member or CFA Candidate

- Conduct. Members and Candidates must not engage in any conduct that compromises the reputation or integrity of CFA Institute or the CFA designation.

SOURCE: Excerpts from "Code of Ethics and Standards of Professional Conduct," *Standards of Practice Handbook,* 11th Ed. (c) 2014, CFA Institute.

The Sarbanes-Oxley Act

The scandals of 2000 to 2002 centered largely on three broad practices: allocations of shares in initial public offerings, tainted securities research and recommendations put out to the public, and, probably most importantly, misleading financial statements and accounting practices. The Sarbanes-Oxley Act, often called SOX, was passed by Congress in 2002 in response to these problems. Among its key provisions are:

- Creation of the Public Company Accounting Oversight Board to oversee the auditing of public companies.
- Rules requiring independent financial experts to serve on audit committees of a firm's board of directors.
- CEOs and CFOs must now personally certify that their firms' financial reports "fairly represent, in all material respects, the operations and financial condition of the company,"

and are subject to personal penalties if those reports turn out to be misleading. Following the letter of GAAP (generally accepted accounting principles) may still be necessary, but it is no longer sufficient accounting practice.

- Auditors may no longer provide several other services to their clients. This is intended to prevent potential profits on consulting work from influencing the quality of their audit.
- The board of directors must be composed of independent directors and hold regular meetings of directors in which company management is not present (and therefore cannot impede or influence the discussion).

More recently, there has been a fair amount of push-back on Sarbanes-Oxley. Many observers believe that the compliance costs associated with the law are too onerous, especially for smaller firms, and that heavy-handed regulatory oversight is giving foreign locales an undue advantage over the United States when firms decide where to list their securities. Moreover, the efficacy of single-country regulation is being tested in the face of increasing globalization and the ease with which funds can move across national borders.

One of the most contentious issues in regulation has to do with "rules" versus "principles." Rules-based regulation attempts to lay out specifically what practices are or are not allowed. This has generally been the approach in the U.S., particularly at the SEC. In contrast, principles-based regulation relies on a less explicitly defined set of understandings about risk taking, the goals of regulation, and the sorts of financial practices considered allowable. This has become the more popular model throughout the world.

Insider Trading

inside information

Nonpublic knowledge about a corporation possessed by corporate officers, major owners, or other individuals with privileged access to information about the firm.

Regulations also prohibit insider trading. It is illegal for anyone to transact in securities to profit from **inside information,** that is, private information held by officers, directors, or major stockholders that has not yet been divulged to the public. But the definition of insiders can be ambiguous. While it is obvious that the chief financial officer of a firm is an insider, it is less clear whether the firm's biggest supplier can be considered an insider. Yet a supplier may deduce the firm's near-term prospects from significant changes in orders. This gives the supplier a unique form of private information, yet the supplier is not technically an insider. These ambiguities plague security analysts, whose job is to uncover as much information as possible concerning the firm's expected prospects. The distinction between legal private information and illegal inside information can be fuzzy. (We return to this issue in Chapter 8.)

The SEC requires officers, directors, and major stockholders to report all transactions in their firm's stock. The SEC then puts out a compendium of insider trades. The idea is to inform the public of any implicit vote of confidence or no confidence made by insiders.

Insiders *do* exploit their knowledge. Three forms of evidence support this conclusion. First, there have been well-publicized convictions of principals in insider trading schemes.

Second, there is considerable evidence of "leakage" of useful information to some traders before any public announcement of that information. For example, share prices of firms announcing dividend increases (which the market interprets as good news concerning the firm's prospects) commonly increase in value a few days *before* the public announcement of the increase. Clearly, some investors are acting on the good news before it is released to the public. Share prices still rise substantially on the day of the public release of good news, however, indicating that insiders, or their associates, have not fully bid up the price of the stock to the level commensurate with the news.

A third form of evidence on insider trading has to do with returns earned on trades by insiders. Researchers have examined the SEC's summary of insider trading to measure the performance of insiders. In one of the best known of these studies, Jaffe (1974) examined the abnormal return of stocks over the months following purchases or sales by insiders. For months in which insider purchasers of a stock exceeded insider sellers of the stock by three or more, the stock had an abnormal return in the following eight months of about 5%. Moreover, when insider sellers exceeded insider buyers, the stock tended to perform poorly.

SUMMARY

- Firms issue securities to raise the capital necessary to finance their investments. Investment bankers market these securities to the public on the primary market. Investment bankers generally act as underwriters who purchase the securities from the firm and resell them to the public at a markup. Before the securities may be sold to the public, the firm must publish an SEC-approved prospectus that provides information on the firm's prospects.

- Already-issued securities are traded on the secondary market, that is, in organized stock markets, or, primarily for bonds, on the over-the-counter market. Brokerage firms that have access to exchanges sell their services to individuals, charging commissions for executing trades on their behalf.

- Trading may take place in dealer markets, via electronic communication networks, or in specialist markets. In dealer markets, security dealers post bid and ask prices at which they are willing to trade. Brokers execute trades for their clients at the best available prices. In electronic markets, the existing book of limit orders provides the terms at which trades can be executed. Mutually agreeable offers to buy or sell securities are automatically crossed by the computer system operating the market.

- NASDAQ was traditionally a dealer market in which a network of dealers negotiated directly over sales of securities. The NYSE was traditionally a specialist market. Today, however, the overwhelming majority of trades on both exchanges are electronic.

- Buying on margin means borrowing money from a broker in order to buy more securities than can be purchased with one's own money alone. By buying securities on a margin, an investor magnifies both the upside potential and the downside risk. If the equity in a margin account falls below the required maintenance level, the investor will get a margin call from the broker.

- Short-selling is the practice of selling securities that the seller does not own. The short-seller borrows the securities from a broker, sells them, and may be required to cover the short position by returning the shares at any time on demand. The cash proceeds of a short sale are kept in escrow by the broker, and the broker usually requires that the short-seller deposit additional cash or securities to serve as margin (collateral) for the short sale.

- Securities trading is regulated by the Securities and Exchange Commission, by other government agencies, and through self-regulation of the exchanges. Many of the important regulations have to do with full disclosure of relevant information concerning the securities in question. Insider trading rules also prohibit traders from attempting to profit from inside information.

KEY TERMS

algorithmic trading, 65	high-frequency trading, 66	primary market, 55
ask price, 59	initial public offering	private placement, 55
auction market, 59	(IPO), 56	prospectus, 56
bid–ask spread, 59	inside information, 78	secondary market, 55
bid price, 59	latency, 65	short sale, 72
blocks, 66	limit buy (sell) order, 59	specialist, 61
dark pools, 66	margin, 69	stock exchanges, 64
dealer markets, 58	NASDAQ Stock Market, 61	underwriters, 56
electronic communication	over-the-counter (OTC)	
networks (ECNs), 61	market, 61	

PROBLEM SETS

Select problems are available in McGraw-Hill's *Connect*. Please see the Supplements section of the book's frontmatter for more information.

1. What is the difference between an IPO (initial public offering) and an SEO (seasoned equity offering)? *(LO 3-1)*

2. What are some different components of the effective costs of buying or selling shares of stock? *(LO 3-3)*

3. What is the difference between a primary and a secondary market?   *(LO 3-3)*

4. How do security dealers earn their profits?   *(LO 3-3)*

5. In what circumstances are private placements more likely to be used than public offerings?   *(LO 3-1)*

6. What are the differences between a limit order and a market order?   *(LO 3-3)*

7. Why have average trade sizes declined in recent years?   *(LO 3-3)*

8. What is the role of an underwriter? A prospectus?   *(LO 3-1)*

9. How do margin trades magnify both the upside potential and downside risk of an investment portfolio?   *(LO 3-4)*

10. A market order has: *(LO 3-2)*
    a. Price uncertainty but not execution uncertainty.
    b. Both price uncertainty and execution uncertainty.
    c. Execution uncertainty but not price uncertainty.

11. Where would an illiquid security in a developing country *most likely* trade?   *(LO 3-3)*
    a. Broker markets.
    b. Electronic crossing networks.
    c. Electronic limit-order markets.

12. Are the following statements true or false? If false, correct them.   *(LO 3-4)*
    a. An investor who wishes to sell shares immediately should ask his or her broker to enter a limit order.
    b. The ask price is less than the bid price.
    c. An issue of additional shares of stock to the public by Microsoft would be called an IPO.
    d. An ECN (Electronic Communications Network) is a computer link used by security dealers primarily to advertise prices at which they are willing to buy or sell shares.

13. Call one full-service broker and one discount broker and find out the transaction costs of implementing the following strategies: *(LO 3-3)*
    a. Buying 100 shares of IBM now and selling them six months from now.
    b. Investing an equivalent amount in six-month at-the-money call options on IBM stock now and selling them six months from now.

14. DRK, Inc., has just sold 100,000 shares in an initial public offering. The underwriter's explicit fees were $60,000. The offering price for the shares was $40, but immediately upon issue, the share price jumped to $44.   *(LO 3-1)*
    a. What is your best guess as to the total cost to DRK of the equity issue?
    b. Is the entire cost of the underwriting a source of profit to the underwriters?

15. Dée Trader opens a brokerage account and purchases 300 shares of Internet Dreams at $40 per share. She borrows $4,000 from her broker to help pay for the purchase. The interest rate on the loan is 8%.   *(LO 3-4)*
    a. What is the margin in Dée's account when she first purchases the stock?
    b. If the share price falls to $30 per share by the end of the year, what is the remaining margin in her account?
    c. If the maintenance margin requirement is 30%, will she receive a margin call?
    d. What is the rate of return on her investment?

16. Old Economy Traders opened an account to short-sell 1,000 shares of Internet Dreams from the previous question. The initial margin requirement was 50%. (The margin account pays no interest.) A year later, the price of Internet Dreams has risen from $40 to $50, and the stock has paid a dividend of $2 per share.   *(LO 3-4)*
    a. What is the remaining margin in the account?
    b. If the maintenance margin requirement is 30%, will Old Economy receive a margin call?
    c. What is the rate of return on the investment?

17. Consider the following limit order book for a share of stock. The last trade in the stock occurred at a price of $50.   *(LO 3-3)*

Limit Buy Orders		Limit Sell Orders	
Price	Shares	Price	Shares
$49.75	500	$49.80	100
49.70	900	49.85	100
49.65	700	49.90	300
49.60	400	49.95	100
48.65	600		

a. If a market buy order for 100 shares comes in, at what price will it be filled?

b. At what price would the following market buy order be filled?

c. If you were a security dealer, would you want to increase or decrease your inventory of this stock?

18. You are bullish on Telecom stock. The current market price is $50 per share, and you have $5,000 of your own to invest. You borrow an additional $5,000 from your broker at an interest rate of 8% per year and invest $10,000 in the stock. **(LO 3-4)**

a. What will be your rate of return if the price of Telecom stock goes up by 10% during the next year? (Ignore the expected dividend.)

b. How far does the price of Telecom stock have to fall for you to get a margin call if the maintenance margin is 30%? Assume the price fall happens immediately.

Templates and spreadsheets are available in Connect

19. You are bearish on Telecom and decide to sell short 100 shares at the current market price of $50 per share. **(LO 3-4)**

a. How much in cash or securities must you put into your brokerage account if the broker's initial margin requirement is 50% of the value of the short position?

b. How high can the price of the stock go before you get a margin call if the maintenance margin is 30% of the value of the short position?

Templates and spreadsheets are available in Connect

20. Here is some price information on Marabel, Inc.:

	Bid	Asked
Marabel	$67.95	$68.05

You have placed a limit order to sell at $68. What are you telling your broker? Given market prices, will your order be executed? **(LO 3-2)**

21. Here is some price information on Fincorp stock. Suppose first that Fincorp trades in a dealer market. **(LO 3-2)**

Bid	Asked
55.25	55.50

a. Suppose you have submitted an order to your broker to buy at market. At what price will your trade be executed?

b. Suppose you have submitted an order to sell at market. At what price will your trade be executed?

c. Suppose you have submitted a limit order to sell at $55.62. What will happen?

d. Suppose you have submitted a limit order to buy at $55.37. What will happen?

22. You've borrowed $20,000 on margin to buy shares in Ixnay, which is now selling at $40 per share. Your account starts at the initial margin requirement of 50%. The maintenance margin is 35%. Two days later, the stock price falls to $35 per share. **(LO 3-4)**

a. Will you receive a margin call?

b. How low can the price of Ixnay shares fall before you receive a margin call?

23. On January 1, you sold short one round lot (that is, 100 shares) of Snow's stock at $21 per share. On March 1, a dividend of $3 per share was paid. On April 1, you

covered the short sale by buying the stock at a price of $15 per share. You paid 50 cents per share in commissions for each transaction. What is the value of your account on April 1?   *(LO 3-4)*

Challenge

24. Suppose that XTel currently is selling at $40 per share. You buy 500 shares using $15,000 of your own money, borrowing the remainder of the purchase price from your broker. The rate on the margin loan is 8%.   *(LO 3-4)*

    a. What is the percentage increase in the net worth of your brokerage account if the price of XTel *immediately* changes to (i) $44; (ii) $40; (iii) $36? What is the relationship between your percentage return and the percentage change in the price of XTel?

    b. If the maintenance margin is 25%, how low can XTel's price fall before you get a margin call?

    c. How would your answer to (*b*) change if you had financed the initial purchase with only $10,000 of your own money?

    d. What is the rate of return on your margined position (assuming again that you invest $15,000 of your own money) if XTel is selling *after one year* at (i) $44; (ii) $40; (iii) $36? What is the relationship between your percentage return and the percentage change in the price of XTel? Assume that XTel pays no dividends.

    e. Continue to assume that a year has passed. How low can XTel's price fall before you get a margin call?

25. Suppose that you sell short 500 shares of XTel, currently selling for $40 per share, and give your broker $15,000 to establish your margin account.   *(LO 3-4)*

    a. If you earn no interest on the funds in your margin account, what will be your rate of return after one year if XTel stock is selling at (i) $44; (ii) $40; (iii) $36? Assume that XTel pays no dividends.

    b. If the maintenance margin is 25%, how high can XTel's price rise before you get a margin call?

    c. Redo parts (*a*) and (*b*), but now assume that XTel also has paid a year-end dividend of $1 per share. The prices in part (*a*) should be interpreted as ex-dividend, that is, prices after the dividend has been paid.

WEB master

Several factors must be considered when selecting a brokerage firm. There are also a wide range of services that claim to objectively evaluate these firms. However, many are actually sponsored by the brokerage firms themselves.

Search for Barron's annual review of online brokers. Its 2017 review is available at **http://www.barrons.com/articles/barrons-2017-best-online-broker-ranking-1489811850,** but you can search for a more recent version. The survey provides general information as well as specific data on issues such as offerings, trading costs and so on.

1. Are all of the brokerage firms suitable if you want to open a cash account? Are they all suitable if you want a margin account?

2. Choose two of the firms listed. Assume that you want to buy 200 shares of LLY stock using a market order. If the order is filled at $82 per share, how much will the commission be for the two firms if you place an online order?

3. Are there any maintenance fees associated with the account at either brokerage firm?

4. Now assume that you have $10,000 to invest and will borrow the rest of the necessary investment through a margin account. What interest rate would you pay if you borrowed money to buy stock?

3.1 Limited-time shelf registration was introduced as a compromise between saving issue costs versus providing disclosure. Allowing unlimited shelf registration would circumvent "blue sky" laws that ensure proper disclosure as the financial circumstances of the firm change over time.

3.2 *a.* Used cars trade in dealer markets (used-car lots or auto dealerships) and in direct search markets when individuals advertise on websites.

    b. Paintings trade in broker markets when clients commission brokers to buy or sell art for them, in dealer markets at art galleries, and in auction markets.

    c. Rare coins trade in dealer markets, for example, in coin shops or shows, but they also trade in auctions and in direct search markets when individuals advertise they want to buy or sell coins.

3.3 *a.* You should give your broker a market order. It will be executed immediately and is the cheapest type of order in terms of brokerage fees.

    b. You should give your broker a limit order to buy, which will be executed only if the shares can be obtained at a price about 5% below the current price.

    c. You should give your broker a limit-sell order, which will be executed if the share price rises above the level at which you are convinced that the firm is overvalued.

3.4 Solving

$$\frac{100P - \$4,000}{100P} = .4$$

implies $P = \$66.67$ per share.

3.5 The investor will purchase 150 shares, with a rate of return as follows:

Year-End Change in Price	Year-End Value of Shares	Repayment of Principal and Interest	Investor's Rate of Return
30%	$19,500	$5,450	40.5%
No change	15,000	5,450	−4.5
−30%	10,500	5,450	−49.5

3.6 *a.* Once Dot Bomb stock goes up to $110, your balance sheet will be:

Assets		Liabilities and Owners' Equity	
Cash	$100,000	Short position in Dot Bomb	$110,000
T-bills	50,000	Equity	40,000

    b. Solving

$$\frac{\$150,000 - 1,000P}{1,000P} = .4$$

implies $P = \$107.14$ per share.

Mutual Funds and Other Investment Companies

Learning Objectives

LO 4-1 Cite advantages and disadvantages of investing with an investment company rather than buying securities directly.

LO 4-2 Contrast open-end mutual funds with closed-end funds, unit investment trusts, hedge funds, and exchange-traded funds.

LO 4-3 Define *net asset value* and measure the rate of return on a mutual fund.

LO 4-4 Classify mutual funds according to investment style.

LO 4-5 Demonstrate the impact of expenses and turnover on mutual fund investment performance.

C hapter 3 provided an introduction to the mechanics of trading securities and the structure of the markets in which securities trade. Very commonly, however, individual investors choose not to trade securities directly for their own accounts. Instead, they direct their funds to investment companies that purchase securities on their behalf. The most important of these financial intermediaries are mutual funds, which are currently owned by about one-half of U.S. households. Other types of investment companies, such as unit investment trusts and closed-end funds, also merit distinction.

We begin the chapter by describing and comparing the various types of investment companies—unit investment trusts, closed-end investment companies, and open-end investment companies, more commonly known as mutual funds. We devote most of our attention to mutual funds, examining the functions of such funds, their investment styles and policies, and the costs of investing in them.

Next, we take a first look at the investment performance of these funds. We consider the impact of expenses and turnover on net performance and examine the extent to which performance is consistent from one period to the next. In other words, will the mutual funds that were the best past performers be the best *future* performers? Finally, we discuss sources of information on mutual funds and consider in detail Morningstar's reports, one of the leading purveyors of such information.

4.1 INVESTMENT COMPANIES

Investment companies are financial intermediaries that collect funds from individual investors and invest those funds in a potentially wide range of securities or other assets. Pooling of assets is the key idea behind investment companies. Each investor has a claim to the portfolio established by the investment company in proportion to the amount invested. These companies thus provide a mechanism for small investors to "team up" to obtain the benefits of large-scale investing.

Investment companies perform several important functions for their investors:

1. *Record keeping and administration.* Investment companies issue periodic status reports, keeping track of capital gains distributions, dividends, investments, and redemptions, and they may reinvest dividend and interest income for shareholders.

2. *Diversification and divisibility.* By pooling their money, investment companies enable investors to hold fractional shares of many different securities. They can act as large investors even if any individual shareholder cannot.

3. *Professional management.* Investment companies can support full-time staffs of security analysts and portfolio managers who attempt to achieve superior investment results for their investors.

4. *Lower transaction costs.* Because they trade large blocks of securities, investment companies can achieve substantial savings on brokerage fees and commissions.

While all investment companies pool the assets of individual investors, they also need to divide claims to those assets among those investors. Investors buy shares in investment companies, and ownership is proportional to the number of shares purchased. The value of each share is called the **net asset value (NAV)**. Net asset value equals assets minus liabilities expressed on a per-share basis:

$$\text{Net asset value} = \frac{\text{Market value of assets minus liabilities}}{\text{Shares outstanding}}$$

Consider a mutual fund that manages a portfolio of securities worth $120 million. Suppose the fund owes $4 million to its investment advisers and owes another $1 million for rent, wages due, and miscellaneous expenses. The fund has 5 million shares. Then

$$\text{Net asset value} = \frac{\$120\ \text{million} - \$5\ \text{million}}{5\ \text{million shares}} = \$23\ \text{per share}$$

> **investment companies**
> Financial intermediaries that invest the funds of individual investors in securities or other assets.

> **net asset value (NAV)**
> Assets minus liabilities expressed on a per-share basis.

Consider these data from the 2016 year-end annual report of Fidelity's Value Fund. (All values are in millions.) What was the net asset value of the portfolio?

Assets:	$6,897.2
Liabilities:	$ 156.3
Shares:	65.45

CONCEPT **4.1**
check

4.2 TYPES OF INVESTMENT COMPANIES

In the United States, investment companies are classified by the Investment Company Act of 1940 as either unit investment trusts or managed investment companies. The portfolios of unit investment trusts are essentially fixed and thus are called "unmanaged." In contrast, managed companies are so named because securities in their investment portfolios continually are bought and sold: The portfolios are managed. Managed companies are further classified as either closed-end or open-end. Open-end companies are what we commonly call *mutual funds.*

Unit Investment Trusts

unit investment trusts

Money pooled from many investors that is invested in a portfolio fixed for the life of the fund.

Unit investment trusts are pools of money invested in a portfolio that is fixed for the life of the fund. To form a unit investment trust, a sponsor, typically a brokerage firm, buys a portfolio of securities which are deposited into a trust. It then sells to the public shares, or "units," in the trust, called *redeemable trust certificates.* All income and payments of principal from the portfolio are paid out by the fund's trustees (a bank or trust company) to the shareholders.

There is little active management of a unit investment trust because once established, the portfolio composition is fixed; hence these trusts are referred to as *unmanaged.* Trusts tend to invest in relatively uniform types of assets; for example, one trust may invest in municipal bonds, another in corporate bonds. The uniformity of the portfolio is consistent with the lack of active management. The trusts provide investors a vehicle to purchase a pool of one particular type of asset, which can be included in an overall portfolio as desired. Because portfolio composition is so stable, management fees can be lower than those of managed funds.

Sponsors of unit investment trusts earn their profit by selling shares in the trust at a premium to the cost of acquiring the underlying assets. For example, a trust that has purchased $5 million of assets may sell 5,000 shares to the public at a price of $1,030 per share, which (assuming the trust has no liabilities) represents a 3% premium over the net asset value of the securities held by the trust. The 3% premium is the trustee's fee for establishing the trust.

Investors who wish to liquidate their holdings of a unit investment trust may sell the shares back to the trustee for net asset value. The trustees can either sell enough securities from the asset portfolio to obtain the cash necessary to pay the investor, or may instead sell the shares to a new investor (again at a slight premium to net asset value).

Unit investment trusts have steadily lost market share to mutual funds in recent years. While mutual fund assets have soared, assets in such trusts declined from $105 billion in 1990 to only $85 billion in 2016.

Managed Investment Companies

There are two types of managed companies: closed-end and open-end. In both cases, the fund's board of directors, which is elected by shareholders, hires a management company to manage the portfolio for an annual fee that typically ranges from 0.2% to 1.5% of assets. In many cases the management company is the firm that organized the fund. For example, Fidelity Management and Research Corporation sponsors many Fidelity mutual funds and is responsible for managing the portfolios. It assesses a management fee on each Fidelity fund. In other cases, a mutual fund will hire an outside portfolio manager. For example, Vanguard has hired Wellington Management as the investment adviser for its Wellington Fund. Most management companies have contracts to manage several funds.

open-end fund

A fund that issues or redeems its shares at net asset value.

closed-end fund

Shares may not be redeemed, but instead are traded at prices that can differ from net asset value.

Open-end funds stand ready to redeem or issue shares at their net asset value (although both purchases and redemptions may involve sales charges). When investors in open-end funds wish to "cash out" their shares, they sell them back to the fund at NAV. In contrast, **closed-end funds** do not redeem or issue shares. Investors in closed-end funds who wish to cash out sell their shares to other investors. Shares of closed-end funds are traded on organized exchanges and can be purchased through brokers just like other common stock; their prices therefore can differ from NAV.

Figure 4.1 is a listing of closed-end funds from *The Wall Street Journal Online.* The first column gives the fund's name and ticker symbol. The next two columns give the fund's most recent net asset value and closing share price. The premium or discount is the percentage difference between price and NAV: (Price − NAV)/NAV. Discounts to NAV (indicated by negative differences) are more common than premiums; indeed, for the small sample in this figure, every fund is selling at a discount. Finally, the 52-week return based on the percentage change in share price plus dividend income is presented in the last column.

The common divergence of price from net asset value, often by wide margins, is a puzzle that has yet to be fully explained. To see why this is a puzzle, consider a closed-end fund that is selling at a discount from net asset value. If the fund were to sell all the assets in the portfolio, it would realize proceeds equal to net asset value. The difference between the market price of the fund and the fund's NAV would represent the per-share increase in the wealth of

FIGURE   4.1

Closed-end mutual funds

Source: *The Wall Street Journal Online,* May 18, 2017.

Fund (Ticker)	NAV	Mkt Price	Prem/ Disc %	52 Week Market Return %
Gabelli Div & Inc Tr (GDV)	22.52	21.08	−6.39	24.87
Gabelli Equity Trust (GAB)	6.07	6.00	−1.15	22.44
General Amer Investors (GAM)	39.86	33.51	−15.93	24.30
Guggenheim Enh Eq Inc (GPM)	8.55	8.16	−4.56	26.35
J Hancock Tx-Adv Div Inc (HTD)	26.03	25.09	−3.61	13.44
Liberty All-Star Equity (USA)	6.33	5.43	−14.22	25.01
Liberty All-Star Growth (ASG)	5.09	4.61	−9.43	29.62
Nuveen Tx-Adv TR Strat (JTA)	13.51	12.47	−7.70	22.27

the fund's investors. Despite this apparent profit opportunity, sizable discounts seem to persist for long periods of time.

Moreover, several studies have shown that, on average, fund premiums or discounts tend to dissipate over time, so funds selling at a discount receive a boost to their rate of return as the discount shrinks. Pontiff (1995) estimates that a fund selling at a 20% discount would have an expected 12-month return more than 6% greater than funds selling at net asset value.

Interestingly, while many closed-end funds sell at a discount from net asset value, the prices of these funds when originally issued are often above NAV. This is a further puzzle, as it is hard to explain why investors would purchase these newly issued funds at a premium to NAV when the shares tend to fall to a discount shortly after issue.

In contrast to closed-end funds, the price of open-end funds cannot fall below NAV, because these funds stand ready to redeem shares at NAV. The offering price will exceed NAV, however, if the fund carries a **load.** A load is, in effect, a sales charge. Load funds are sold by securities brokers and directly by mutual fund groups.

load

A sales commission charged on a mutual fund.

Unlike closed-end funds, open-end mutual funds do not trade on organized exchanges. Instead, investors simply buy shares from and liquidate through the investment company at net asset value. Thus, the number of outstanding shares of these funds changes daily. In early 2017, about $260 billion of assets were held in closed-end funds.

Other Investment Organizations

Some intermediaries are not formally organized or regulated as investment companies but nevertheless serve similar functions. Among the more important are commingled funds, real estate investment trusts, and hedge funds.

COMMINGLED FUNDS   Commingled funds are partnerships of investors that pool funds. The management firm that organizes the partnership, for example, a bank or insurance company, manages the funds for a fee. Typical partners in a commingled fund might be trust or retirement accounts that have portfolios much larger than those of most individual investors but are still too small to warrant managing on a separate basis.

Commingled funds are similar in form to open-end mutual funds. Instead of shares, though, the fund offers *units,* which are bought and sold at net asset value. A bank or insurance company may offer an array of different commingled funds, for example, a money market fund, a bond fund, and a common stock fund.

REAL ESTATE INVESTMENT TRUSTS (REITS)   A REIT is similar to a closed-end fund. REITs invest in real estate or loans secured by real estate. Besides issuing shares, they raise capital by borrowing from banks and issuing bonds or mortgages. Most of them are highly leveraged, with a typical debt ratio of 70%.

There are two principal kinds of REITs. *Equity trusts* invest in real estate directly, whereas *mortgage trusts* invest primarily in mortgage and construction loans. REITs generally are established by banks, insurance companies, or mortgage companies, which then serve as investment managers to earn a fee.

hedge fund

A private investment pool, open to wealthy or institutional investors, that is largely exempt from SEC regulation and therefore can pursue more speculative policies than mutual funds.

HEDGE FUNDS   Like mutual funds, **hedge funds** are vehicles that allow private investors to pool assets to be invested by a fund manager. Unlike mutual funds, however, hedge funds are commonly structured as private partnerships and thus are not subject to many SEC regulations. Typically they are open only to wealthy or institutional investors. Many require investors to agree to initial "lock-ups," that is, periods as long as several years in which investments cannot be withdrawn. Lock-ups allow hedge funds to invest in illiquid assets without worrying about meeting demands for redemption of funds. Moreover, because hedge funds are only lightly regulated, their managers can pursue other investment strategies that are not open to mutual fund managers, for example, heavy use of derivatives, short sales, and leverage.

Hedge funds by design are empowered to invest in a wide range of investments, with various funds focusing on derivatives, distressed firms, currency speculation, convertible bonds, emerging markets, merger arbitrage, and so on. Other funds may jump from one asset class to another as perceived investment opportunities shift.

Hedge funds enjoyed great growth in the last several years, with assets under management ballooning from about $50 billion in 1990 to about $4 trillion in 2017. We devote all of Chapter 20 to these funds.

4.3   MUTUAL FUNDS

Mutual fund is the common name for an open-end investment company. This is the dominant investment company in the U.S. today, accounting for about 88% of investment company assets. Assets under management in the U.S. mutual fund industry were over $16 trillion in early 2017. Roughly another $20 trillion was invested in mutual funds of non-U.S. sponsors.

Investment Policies

Each mutual fund has a specified investment policy, which is described in the fund's prospectus. For example, money market mutual funds hold the short-term, low-risk instruments of the money market (see Chapter 2 for a review of these securities), while bond funds hold fixed-income securities. Some funds have even more narrowly defined mandates. For example, some bond funds will hold primarily Treasury bonds, others primarily mortgage-backed securities.

Management companies manage a family, or "complex," of mutual funds. They organize an entire collection of funds and then collect a management fee for operating them. By managing many funds under one umbrella, these companies make it easy for investors to allocate assets across market sectors and to switch assets across funds while still benefiting from centralized record keeping. Some of the most well-known management companies are Fidelity, Vanguard, and T. Rowe Price. In 2017, there were about 8,000 mutual funds in the United States, which were offered by about 850 fund complexes.

Some of the more important fund types, classified by investment policy, are discussed next.

MONEY MARKET FUNDS   These funds invest in money market securities such as Treasury bills, commercial paper, repurchase agreements, or certificates of deposit. The average maturity of these assets tends to be a bit more than one month. They usually offer check-writing features, and net asset value is fixed at $1 per share,[1] so there are no tax implications such as capital gains or losses associated with redemption of shares.

---

[1] The box in Chapter 2 noted that money market funds are able to maintain NAV at $1 because they invest in short-maturity debt of the highest quality with minimal price risk. In rare circumstances, funds have experienced losses sufficient to drive NAV below $1. In September 2008, Reserve Primary Fund, the nation's oldest money market fund, "broke the buck" when it suffered losses on its holding of Lehman Brothers commercial paper, and its NAV fell to $0.97.

Money market funds are classified as *prime* versus *government*. As their name suggests, government funds hold short-term U.S. Treasury or agency securities and repurchase agreements collateralized by such securities. Prime funds also hold other money market instruments such as commercial paper or bank CDs. While these assets are certainly at the very safe end of the credit risk spectrum, they are nevertheless riskier than government securities and are more prone to suffer reduced liquidity in times of market stress. In the aftermath of the financial crisis, prime funds are now subject to "gates" that allow funds to temporarily halt redemptions during periods of severe disruption. Not surprisingly, there has been a large shift in demand from prime to government funds since the crisis.

Moreover, while both prime and government retail money market funds maintain net asset value at $1.00 per share, prime institutional funds now must calculate net asset value. While capital gains or losses will normally be very small, this "floating" of NAV has also contributed to a shift from prime to government funds.

EQUITY FUNDS Equity funds invest primarily in stock, although they may, at the portfolio manager's discretion, also hold fixed-income or other types of securities. Equity funds commonly will hold a small fraction of total assets in money market securities to provide the liquidity necessary to meet potential redemption of shares.

Stock funds are traditionally classified by their emphasis on capital appreciation versus current income. Thus, *income funds* tend to hold shares of firms with high dividend yields that provide high current income. *Growth funds* are willing to forgo current income, focusing instead on prospects for capital gains. While the classification of these funds is couched in terms of income versus capital gains, the more relevant distinction in practice concerns the level of risk these funds assume. Growth stocks—and therefore growth funds—are typically riskier and respond more dramatically to changes in economic conditions than do income funds.

SPECIALIZED SECTOR FUNDS Some equity funds, called *sector funds,* concentrate on a particular industry. For example, Fidelity markets dozens of "select funds," each of which invests in a specific industry such as biotechnology, utilities, energy, or telecommunications. Other funds specialize in securities of particular countries.

BOND FUNDS As the name suggests, these funds specialize in the fixed-income sector. Within that sector, however, there is considerable room for further specialization. For example, various funds will concentrate on corporate bonds, Treasury bonds, mortgage-backed securities, or municipal (tax-free) bonds. Indeed, some municipal bond funds invest only in bonds of a particular state in order to satisfy the investment desires of residents of that state who wish to avoid local as well as federal taxes on interest income. Many funds also specialize by maturity, ranging from short-term to intermediate to long-term, or by the credit risk of the issuer, ranging from very safe to high-yield or "junk" bonds.

INTERNATIONAL FUNDS Many funds have an international focus. *Global funds* invest in securities worldwide, including the United States. In contrast, *international funds* invest in securities of firms located outside the U.S. *Regional funds* concentrate on a particular part of the world, and *emerging market funds* invest in companies of developing nations.

BALANCED FUNDS Some funds are designed to be candidates for an individual's entire investment portfolio. These *balanced funds* hold both equities and fixed-income securities in relatively stable proportions. *Life-cycle funds* are balanced funds in which the asset mix can range from aggressive (primarily marketed to younger investors) to conservative (directed at older investors). Static allocation life-cycle funds maintain a stable mix across stocks and bonds, while *target-date funds* gradually become more conservative as the investor ages.

Many balanced funds are in fact **funds of funds.** These are mutual funds that primarily invest in shares of other mutual funds. Balanced funds of funds invest in equity and bond funds in proportions suited to their investment goals.

funds of funds

Mutual funds that primarily invest in shares of other mutual funds.

ASSET ALLOCATION AND FLEXIBLE FUNDS These funds are similar to balanced funds in that they hold both stocks and bonds. However, asset allocation funds may dramatically vary the proportions allocated to each market in accord with the portfolio manager's forecast of the relative performance of each sector. Hence, these funds are engaged in market timing and are not designed to be low-risk investment vehicles.

INDEX FUNDS An index fund tries to match the performance of a broad market index. The fund buys shares in securities included in a particular index in proportion to the security's representation in that index. For example, the Vanguard 500 Index Fund is a mutual fund that replicates the composition of the Standard & Poor's 500 stock price index. Because the S&P 500 is a value-weighted index, the fund buys shares in each S&P 500 company in proportion to the market value of that company's outstanding equity. Investment in an index fund is a low-cost and increasingly popular way for small investors to pursue a passive investment strategy—that is, to invest without engaging in security analysis. About 25% of assets held in equity funds in 2017 were in index funds. That fraction has grown considerably in recent years.

Of course, index funds can be tied to nonequity indexes as well. For example, Vanguard offers a bond index fund and a real estate index fund.

Table 4.1 breaks down the number of mutual funds by investment orientation. Sometimes the fund name describes its investment policy. For example, Vanguard's GNMA Fund invests in mortgage-backed securities, the Municipal Intermediate Fund invests in intermediate-term municipal bonds, and the High-Yield Corporate Bond Fund invests in large part in speculative grade, or "junk," bonds with high yields. However, names of common stock funds often reflect little or nothing about their investment policies. Examples are Vanguard's Windsor and Wellington funds.

TABLE 4.1	U.S. mutual funds by investment classification		
	Assets ($ billion)	**Percent of Total Assets**	**Number of Funds**
Equity funds			
Capital appreciation focus	$ 1,779	10.9%	1,315
World/international	2,163	13.2	1,518
Total return	4,635	28.4	1,919
Total equity funds	$ 8,577	52.5%	4,752
Bond funds			
Investment grade	$ 1,641	10.0%	625
High yield	373	2.3	245
World	420	2.6	370
Government	281	1.7	190
Multisector	320	2.0	171
Single-state municipal	161	1.0	319
National municipal	453	2.8	256
Total bond funds	3,650	22.3	2,176
Hybrid (bond/stock) funds	$ 1,389	8.5%	717
Money market funds			
Taxable	$ 2,598	15.9%	319
Tax-exempt	130	0.8	102
Total money market funds	2,728	16.7	421
Total	$16,344	100.0%	8,066

Note: Column sums subject to rounding error.

Source: 2017 *Investment Company Fact Book*, Investment Company Institute.

How Funds Are Sold

Mutual funds are generally marketed to the public either directly by the fund underwriter or indirectly through brokers acting on behalf of the underwriter. Direct-marketed funds are sold through the mail, various offices of the fund, over the phone, or on the Internet. Investors contact the fund directly to purchase shares. For example, if you look at the financial pages of your local newspaper, you will see several advertisements for funds, along with toll-free phone numbers or web addresses that you can use to receive a fund's prospectus and an application to open an account.

About half of fund sales today are distributed through a sales force. Brokers or financial advisers receive a commission for selling shares to investors. (Ultimately, the commission is paid by the investor. More on this shortly.) Investors who rely on their broker's advice to select their mutual funds should be aware that some brokers receive compensation for directing the sale to a particular fund; this arrangement creates a potential conflict of interest.

Many funds also are sold through "financial supermarkets" that can sell shares in funds of many complexes. These programs allow customers to buy funds from many different fund groups. Instead of charging customers a sales commission, the supermarket splits management fees with the mutual fund company. Another advantage is unified record keeping for all funds purchased from the supermarket, even if the funds are offered by different complexes. On the other hand, many contend that these supermarkets result in higher expense ratios because mutual funds pass along the costs of participating in these programs in the form of higher management fees.

4.4 COSTS OF INVESTING IN MUTUAL FUNDS

Fee Structure

An individual investor choosing a mutual fund should consider not only the fund's stated investment policy and past performance, but also its management fees and other expenses. Comparative data on virtually all important aspects of mutual funds are available in Morningstar's *Mutual Fund Sourcebook,* which can be found in many academic and public libraries. You should be aware of four general classes of fees.

OPERATING EXPENSES   Operating expenses are the costs incurred by the mutual fund in operating the portfolio, including administrative expenses and advisory fees paid to the investment manager. These expenses, usually expressed as a percentage of total assets under management, typically range from 0.2% to 1.5%. Shareholders do not receive an explicit bill for these operating expenses; however, the expenses periodically are deducted from the assets of the fund. Shareholders pay for these expenses through the reduced value of the portfolio.

The simple average of the expense ratio of all equity funds in the U.S. was 1.28% in 2016. But larger funds tend to have lower expense ratios (and investors place more of their assets in lower-cost funds), so the average expense ratio weighted by assets under management is considerably smaller, 0.63%. Not surprisingly, the average expense ratio of indexed funds (weighted by assets under management) is substantially lower, 0.09%, while that of actively managed funds is higher, 0.82%.

In addition to operating expenses, most funds assess fees to pay for marketing and distribution costs. These charges are used primarily to pay the brokers or financial advisers who sell the funds to the public. Investors can avoid these expenses by buying shares directly from the fund sponsor, but many investors are willing to incur these distribution fees in return for the advice they may receive from their broker.

FRONT-END LOAD   A front-end load is a commission or sales charge paid when you purchase the shares. These charges, which are used primarily to pay the brokers who sell the funds, may not exceed 8.5%, but in practice they are rarely higher than 6%. *Low-load funds* have loads that range up to 3% of invested funds. *No-load funds* have no front-end sales charges. About half of all funds today (measured by assets) are no load. Loads effectively reduce the amount of money invested. For example, each $1,000 paid for a fund with a 6% load results in a sales charge of $60 and fund investment of only $940. You need cumulative returns of 6.4% of your net investment (60/940 = 0.064) just to break even.

BACK-END LOAD   A back-end load is a redemption, or "exit," fee incurred when you sell your shares. Typically, funds that impose back-end loads start them at 5% or 6% and reduce them by one percentage point for every year the funds are left invested. Thus, an exit fee that starts at 6% would fall to 4% by the start of your third year. These charges are known more formally as "contingent deferred sales loads."

12B-1 CHARGES   The Securities and Exchange Commission allows the managers of so-called 12b-1 funds to use fund assets to pay for distribution costs such as advertising, promotional literature including annual reports and prospectuses, and, most important, commissions paid to brokers who sell the fund to investors. These **12b-1 fees** are named after the SEC rule that permits use of these plans. Funds may use annual 12b-1 charges instead of, or in addition to, front-end loads to generate the fees with which to pay brokers. As with operating expenses, investors are not explicitly billed for 12b-1 charges. Instead, the fees are deducted from the assets of the fund. Therefore, 12b-1 fees (if any) must be added to operating expenses to obtain the true annual expense ratio of the fund. The SEC requires all funds to include in the prospectus a consolidated expense table that summarizes all relevant fees. The 12b-1 fees are limited to 1% of a fund's average net assets per year.[2]

> **12b-1 fees**
>
> Annual fees charged by a mutual fund to pay for marketing and distribution costs.

Many funds offer "classes," which represent ownership in the same portfolio of securities, but with different combinations of fees. Typical Class A shares have front-end loads and a small 12b-1 fee, often around 0.25%. Class C shares rely more on 12b-1 fees. Class I shares are sold to institutional investors. These are sometimes called Class Y shares and carry no loads or 12b-1 fees.[3]

EXAMPLE 4.1

Fees for Various Classes (Dreyfus High Yield Fund)

Here are fees for different classes of the Dreyfus High Yield Fund in 2017. Notice the trade-off between front-end loads and 12b-1 charges in Class A versus Class C.

	Class A	Class C	Class I
Front-end load	4.50%[a]	0	0
Back-end load	0	1%[b]	0
12b-1 fees	0.25%	1.0[c]	0
Expense ratio	0.7%	0.7%	0.7%

Notes:

[a]Depending on size of investment. Load is lower for investments above $50,000.

[b]Depending on years until holdings are sold.

[c]Including annual service fee of 0.25%.

Each investor must choose the best combination of fees. Obviously, pure no-load no-fee funds distributed directly by the mutual fund group are the cheapest alternative, and these will often make the most sense for knowledgeable investors. But as we noted earlier, many investors are willing to pay for financial advice, and the commissions paid to advisers who sell these funds are the most common form of payment. Alternatively, investors may choose to hire a fee-only financial manager who charges directly for services instead of collecting commissions. These advisers can help investors select portfolios of low- or no-load funds (as well as provide other financial advice). Independent financial planners have become increasingly important distribution channels for funds in recent years.

---

[2]The maximum 12b-1 charge for the sale of the fund is 0.75%. However, an additional service fee of 0.25% of the fund's assets also is allowed for personal service and/or maintenance of shareholder accounts.

[3]Many funds used to market Class B shares as well. These relied on 12b-1 fees as well as a modest back-end load. If an investor held Class B shares for a long enough duration, typically 6–8 years, the shares would convert into Class A shares. However, Class B shares have become increasingly less common in recent years.

If you do buy a fund through a broker, the choice between paying a load and paying 12b-1 fees will depend primarily on your expected time horizon. Loads are paid only once for each purchase, whereas 12b-1 fees are paid annually. Thus, if you plan to hold your fund for a long time, a one-time load may be preferable to recurring 12b-1 charges.

Fees and Mutual Fund Returns

The rate of return on an investment in a mutual fund is measured as the increase or decrease in net asset value plus income distributions such as dividends or distributions of capital gains expressed as a fraction of net asset value at the beginning of the investment period. If we denote the net asset value at the start and end of the period as NAV_0 and NAV_1, respectively, then

$$\text{Rate of return} = \frac{NAV_1 - NAV_0 + \text{Income and capital gain distributions}}{NAV_0}$$

For example, if a fund has an initial NAV of $20 at the start of the month, makes income distributions of $0.15 and capital gain distributions of $0.05, and ends the month with NAV of $20.10, the monthly rate of return is computed as

$$\text{Rate of return} = \frac{\$20.10 - \$20.00 + \$0.15 + \$0.05}{\$20.00}$$
$$= 0.015, \text{ or } 1.5\%$$

Notice that this measure of the rate of return ignores any commissions such as front-end loads paid to purchase the fund.

On the other hand, the rate of return is affected by the fund's expenses and 12b-1 fees. This is because such charges are periodically deducted from the portfolio, which reduces net asset value. Thus the investor's rate of return on the fund equals the gross return on the underlying portfolio minus the total expense ratio.

EXAMPLE 4.2

Expenses and Rates of Return

To see how expenses can affect rate of return, consider a fund with $100 million in assets at the start of the year and with 10 million shares outstanding. The fund invests in a portfolio of stocks that provides no income but increases in value by 10%. The expense ratio, including 12b-1 fees, is 1%. What is the rate of return for an investor in the fund?

The initial NAV equals $100 million/10 million shares = $10 per share. In the absence of expenses, fund assets would grow to $110 million and NAV would grow to $11 per share, for a 10% rate of return. However, the expense ratio of the fund is 1%. Therefore, $1 million will be deducted from the fund to pay these fees, leaving the portfolio worth only $109 million, and NAV equal to $10.90. The rate of return on the fund is only 9%, which equals the gross return on the underlying portfolio minus the total expense ratio.

Fees can have a big effect on performance. Table 4.2 considers an investor who starts with $10,000 and can choose between three funds that all earn an annual 12% return on investment before fees but have different fee structures. The table shows the cumulative amount in each fund after several investment horizons. Fund A has total operating expenses of 0.5%, no load, and no 12b-1 charges. This might represent a low-cost producer such as Vanguard. Fund B has no load but has 1% management expenses and 0.5% in 12b-1 fees. This level of charges is toward the high end of actively managed equity funds. Finally, Fund C has 1% in management expenses, has no 12b-1 charges, but assesses an 8% front-end load on purchases.

Note the substantial return advantage of low-cost Fund A. Moreover, that differential is greater for longer investment horizons.

CONCEPT check 4.2

The Equity Fund sells Class A shares with a front-end load of 4% and Class B shares with 12b-1 fees of 0.5% annually as well as back-end load fees that start at 5% and fall by 1% for each full year the investor holds the portfolio (until the fifth year). Assume the rate of return on the fund portfolio net of operating expenses is 10% annually. What will be the value of a $10,000 investment in Class A and Class B shares if the shares are sold after (*a*) 1 year, (*b*) 4 years, (*c*) 10 years? Which fee structure provides higher net proceeds at the end of each investment horizon?

TABLE 4.2	Impact of costs on investment performance		
	Cumulative Proceeds (all dividends reinvested)		
	Fund A	**Fund B**	**Fund C**
Initial investment*	$10,000	$10,000	$ 9,200
5 years	17,234	16,474	15,502
10 years	29,699	27,141	26,123
15 years	51,183	44,713	44,018
20 years	88,206	73,662	74,173

Notes: Fund A is no load with 0.5% expense ratio, Fund B is no load with 1.5% total expense ratio, and Fund C has an 8% load on purchases and a 1% expense ratio. Gross return on all funds is 12% per year before expenses.

*After front-end load, if any.

Although expenses can have a big impact on net investment performance, it is sometimes difficult for the investor in a mutual fund to measure true expenses accurately. This is because of the common practice of paying for some expenses in **soft dollars.** A portfolio manager earns soft-dollar credits with a brokerage firm by directing the fund's trades to that broker. Based on those credits, the broker will pay for some of the mutual fund's expenses, such as databases, computer hardware, or stock-quotation systems. The soft-dollar arrangement means that the stockbroker effectively returns part of the trading commission to the fund. Purchases made with soft dollars are not included in the fund's expenses, so funds with extensive soft-dollar arrangements may report artificially low expense ratios to the public. However, the fund will have paid its brokers needlessly high commissions to obtain its soft-dollar "rebates." The impact of the higher trading commissions shows up in net investment performance rather than the reported expense ratio.

soft dollars

The value of research services that brokerage houses provide "free of charge" in exchange for the investment manager's business.

4.5 TAXATION OF MUTUAL FUND INCOME

Investment returns of mutual funds are granted "pass-through status" under the U.S. tax code, meaning that taxes are paid only by the investor in the mutual fund, not by the fund itself. The income is treated as passed through to the investor as long as the fund meets several requirements, most notably that the fund be sufficiently diversified and that virtually all income is distributed to shareholders.

A fund's short-term capital gains, long-term capital gains, and dividends are passed through to investors as though the investor earned the income directly. The pass-through of investment income has one important disadvantage for individual investors. If you manage your own portfolio, you decide when to realize capital gains and losses on any security; therefore, you can time those realizations to efficiently manage your tax liabilities. When you invest through a mutual fund, however, the timing of the sale of securities from the portfolio is out of your control, which reduces your ability to engage in tax management.[4]

A fund with a high portfolio turnover rate can be particularly "tax inefficient." **Turnover** is the ratio of the trading activity of a portfolio to the assets of the portfolio. It measures the fraction of the portfolio that is "replaced" each year. For example, a $100 million portfolio with $50 million in sales of some securities and purchases of other securities would have a turnover rate of 50%. High turnover means that capital gains or losses are being realized

turnover

The ratio of the trading activity of a portfolio to the assets of the portfolio.

---

[4] An interesting problem that an investor needs to be aware of derives from the fact that capital gains and dividends on mutual funds are typically paid out to shareholders once or twice a year. This means that an investor who has just purchased shares in a mutual fund can receive a capital gain distribution (and be taxed on that distribution) on transactions that occurred long before he or she purchased shares in the fund. This is particularly a concern late in the year when such distributions typically are made.

constantly, and therefore that the investor cannot time the realizations to manage his or her overall tax obligation. Until recently, turnover rates in equity funds have typically been around 60% when weighted by assets under management. By contrast, a low-turnover fund such as an index fund may have turnover as low as 2%, which is both tax-efficient and economical with respect to trading costs. In the last few years, asset-weighted average turnover has dropped considerably, falling to 34% in 2016. Part of this decline probably reflects the shift from actively managed to indexed funds.

SEC rules require funds to disclose the tax impact of portfolio turnover. Funds must include in their prospectus after-tax returns for the past 1-, 5-, and 10-year periods. Marketing literature that includes performance data also must include after-tax results. The after-tax returns are computed accounting for the impact of the taxable distributions of income and capital gains passed through to the investor, assuming the investor is in the maximum federal tax bracket.

An investor's portfolio currently is worth $1 million. During the year, the investor sells 1,000 shares of FedEx at a price of $150 per share and 10,000 shares of Cisco Systems at a price of $25 per share. The proceeds are used to buy 2,500 shares of IBM at $160 per share.

  a. What was the portfolio turnover rate?
  b. If the shares in FedEx originally were purchased for $140 each and those in Cisco were purchased for $20, and if the investor's tax rate on capital gains income is 15%, how much extra will the investor owe on this year's taxes as a result of these transactions?

4.6 EXCHANGE-TRADED FUNDS

Exchange-traded funds (ETFs) are offshoots of mutual funds first introduced in 1993 that allow investors to trade index portfolios just as they do shares of stock. The first ETF was the "Spider," a nickname for SPDR or Standard & Poor's Depository Receipt; the ETF maintains a portfolio matching the S&P 500 Index. Unlike mutual funds, which can be bought or redeemed only at the end of the day when NAV is calculated, investors could trade Spiders throughout the day, just like any other share of stock. Spiders gave rise to many similar products such as "Diamonds" (based on the Dow Jones Industrial Average, ticker DIA), Qubes (pronounced "cubes," based on the NASDAQ 100 Index, ticker QQQ), and WEBS (World Equity Benchmark Shares, which are shares in portfolios of foreign stock market indexes). By early 2017, about $2.5 trillion was invested in about 1,700 ETFs in five general classes: broad U.S. market indexes, narrow industry or "sector" portfolios, international indexes, commodities, and bond portfolios. Table 4.3, Panel A, presents some of the sponsors of ETFs; Panel B is a small sample of ETFs, which we include to give you a flavor of the sort of products available.

exchange-traded funds
Offshoots of mutual funds that allow investors to trade entire portfolios much like shares of stock.

Figure 4.2 shows the rapid growth in the ETF market since 1998. Until 2008, most ETFs were designed to track specified indexes, and ETFs tracking broad indexes still dominate the industry. However, there are dozens of industry-sector ETFs as well as funds that track particular characteristics such as value, growth, or dividends, and as Figure 4.2 makes clear, several commodity, bond, and international ETFs. Figure 4.3 shows that ETFs have captured a significant portion of the assets under management in the investment company universe.

The leader in the ETF market is BlackRock, which uses the product name iShares. The firm sponsors ETFs for several dozen equity index funds, including many broad U.S. equity indexes, broad international and single-country funds, and U.S. and global industry sector funds. BlackRock also offers several bond ETFs and a few commodity funds such as ones for gold and silver. For more information on these funds, go to **www.iShares.com.**

More recently, a variety of new ETF products have been devised. Among these are leveraged ETFs, with daily returns that are a targeted *multiple* of the returns on an index, and inverse ETFs, which move in the opposite direction to an index. A more recent innovation is actively managed ETFs that, like actively managed mutual funds, attempt to outperform

TABLE 4.3 ETF sponsors and products

A. ETF Sponsors

Sponsor	Product Name
BlackRock	iShares
Merrill Lynch	HOLDRS (Holding Company Depository Receipts: "Holders")
StateStreet	Select Sector SPDRs (S&P Depository Receipts: "Spiders")
Vanguard	Vanguard ETFs

B. Sample of ETF Products

Name	Ticker	Index Tracked
Broad U.S. indexes		
Spiders	SPY	S&P 500
Diamonds	DIA	Dow Jones Industrials
Qubes	QQQ	NASDAQ 100
iShares Russell 2000	IWM	Russell 2000
Total Stock Market (Vanguard)	VTI	Wilshire 5000
Industry indexes		
Energy Select Spider	XLE	S&P 500 energy companies
iShares Energy Sector	IYE	Dow Jones energy companies
Oil Service HOLDRS	OIH	Portfolio of oil service firms
Financial Sector Spider	XLF	S&P 500 financial companies
iShares Financial Sector	IYF	Dow Jones financial companies
Vanguard Financials ETF	VFH	MSCI financials index
International indexes		
WEBS United Kingdom	EWU	MCSI U.K. Index
WEBS France	EWQ	MCSI France Index
WEBS Japan	EWJ	MCSI Japan Index

passive indexes. However, until recently, these funds have had to report portfolio holdings on a daily basis, which makes it easy for competitors to take advantage of their buying and selling programs. This requirement has severely limited the growth of this segment of the market. In 2014, however, the SEC gave permission to Eaton Vance to offer an actively managed "nontransparent" ETF that is required to report its portfolio composition only once each quarter, the same frequency at which mutual funds disclose their portfolio holdings. Other companies such as BlackRock have also indicated interest in sponsoring nontransparent ETFs. At the end of 2016, there were 148 actively managed ETFs registered with the SEC with combined assets of nearly $29 billion.

Other even more exotic variations are so-called synthetic ETFs such as exchange-traded notes (ETNs) or exchange-traded vehicles (ETVs). These are nominally debt securities but with payoffs linked to the performance of an index. Often that index measures the performance of an illiquid and thinly traded asset class, so the ETF gives the investor the opportunity to add that asset class to his or her portfolio. However, rather than invest in those assets directly, the ETF achieves this exposure by entering a "total return swap" with an investment bank in which the bank agrees to pay the ETF the return on the index in exchange for a relatively fixed fee. These have become controversial, as the ETF is then exposed to risk that in a period of financial stress, the investment bank will be unable to fulfill its obligation, leaving investors without the returns they were promised.

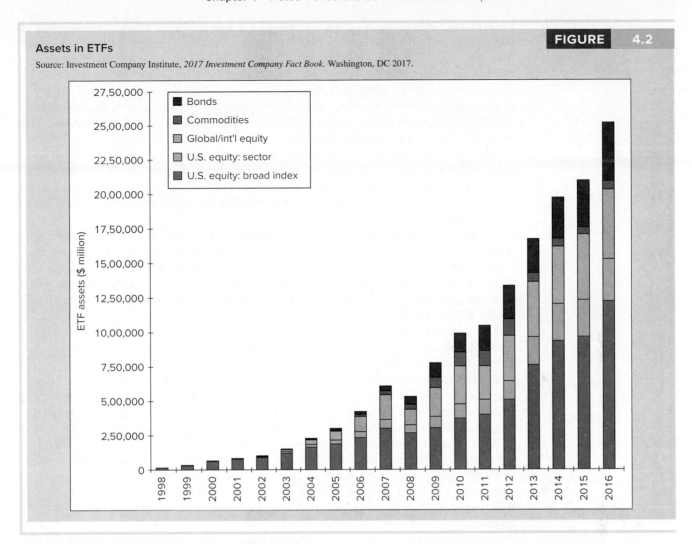

Assets in ETFs

Source: Investment Company Institute, *2017 Investment Company Fact Book*. Washington, DC 2017.

FIGURE 4.2

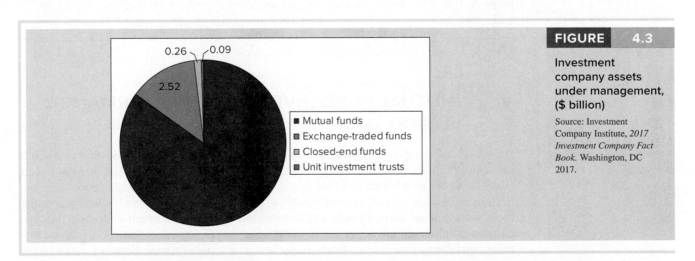

FIGURE 4.3

Investment company assets under management, ($ billion)

Source: Investment Company Institute, *2017 Investment Company Fact Book*. Washington, DC 2017.

ETFs offer several advantages over conventional mutual funds. First, as we just noted, a mutual fund's net asset value is quoted—and therefore, investors can buy or sell their shares in the fund—only once a day. In contrast, ETFs trade continuously. Moreover, like other shares, but unlike mutual funds, ETFs can be sold short or purchased on margin.

ETFs also offer a potential tax advantage over mutual funds. When large numbers of mutual fund investors redeem their shares, the fund must sell securities to meet the redemptions. The sale can trigger capital gains taxes, which are passed through to and must be paid by the remaining shareholders. In contrast, when small investors wish to redeem their position in an ETF they simply sell their shares to other traders, with no need for the fund to sell any of the underlying portfolio. Moreover, when large traders wish to redeem their position in the ETF, redemptions can be satisfied with shares of stock in the underlying portfolio. This redemption does not trigger a taxable event.

The ability of large investors to redeem ETFs for a portfolio of stocks constituting the index, or to exchange a portfolio of stocks for shares in the corresponding ETF, ensures that the price of an ETF cannot depart for long from the NAV of that portfolio. Any meaningful discrepancy would offer arbitrage trading opportunities for these large traders, which would quickly eliminate the disparity.

ETFs are also cheaper than mutual funds. Investors who buy ETFs do so through brokers, rather than buying directly from the fund. Therefore, the fund saves the cost of marketing itself directly to small investors. This reduction in expenses translates into lower management fees. For example, the expense ratio on Vanguard's Total Stock Market mutual fund, which tracks an index of the entire U.S. equity market, is 0.15%, whereas the ratio on its Total Stock Market ETF is only 0.04%.

There are some disadvantages to ETFs, however. First, while mutual funds can be bought for NAV with no expense from no-load funds, ETFs must be purchased from brokers for a fee. Investors also incur a bid–ask spread when purchasing an ETF.

In addition, because ETFs trade as securities, their prices can depart from NAV, at least for short periods, and these price discrepancies can easily swamp the cost advantage that ETFs otherwise offer. While those discrepancies typically are quite small, they can spike unpredictably when markets are stressed. Chapter 3 briefly discussed the so-called flash crash of May 6, 2010, when the Dow Jones Industrial Average fell by 583 points in *seven minutes,* leaving it down nearly 1,000 points for the day. Remarkably, the index recovered more than 600 points in the next 10 minutes. In the wake of this incredible volatility, the stock exchanges canceled many trades that had gone off at what were viewed as distorted prices. Around one-fifth of all ETFs changed hands on that day at prices less than one-half of their closing price, and ETFs accounted for about two-thirds of all canceled trades.

At least two problems were exposed in this episode. First, when markets are not working properly, it can be hard to measure the net asset value of the ETF portfolio, especially for ETFs that track less liquid assets. And, reinforcing this problem, some ETFs may be supported by only a very small number of dealers. If they drop out of the market during a period of turmoil, prices may swing wildly.

4.7 MUTUAL FUND INVESTMENT PERFORMANCE: A FIRST LOOK

We noted earlier that one of the benefits of mutual funds for the individual investor is the ability to delegate management of the portfolio to investment professionals. The investor retains control over the broad features of the overall portfolio through the asset allocation decision: Each individual chooses the percentages of the portfolio to invest in bond funds versus equity funds versus money market funds, and so forth, but can leave the specific security selection decisions within each investment class to the managers of each fund. Shareholders hope that these portfolio managers can achieve better investment performance than they could obtain on their own.

What is the investment record of the mutual fund industry? This seemingly straightforward question is deceptively difficult to answer because we need a standard against which to evaluate performance. For example, we clearly would not want to compare the investment performance of an equity fund to the rate of return available in the money market. The vast differences in the risk of these two markets dictate that year-by-year as well as average performance will differ considerably. We would expect to find that equity funds outperform money market funds (on average) as compensation to investors for the extra risk incurred in equity markets. How can we determine whether mutual fund portfolio managers are performing up to par *given* the level of risk they incur? In other words, what is the proper benchmark against which investment performance ought to be evaluated?

Measuring portfolio risk properly and using such measures to choose an appropriate benchmark is far from straightforward. We devote all of Parts Two and Three of the text to issues surrounding the proper measurement of portfolio risk and the trade-off between risk and return. In this chapter, therefore, we will satisfy ourselves with a first look at the question of fund performance by using only very simple performance benchmarks and ignoring the more subtle issues of risk differences across funds. However, we will return to this topic in Chapter 8, where we take a closer look at mutual fund performance after adjusting for differences in the exposure of portfolios to various sources of risk.

Here, we will use as a benchmark for the performance of equity fund managers the rate of return on the Wilshire 5000 Index. Recall from Chapter 2 that this is a value-weighted index of more than the roughly 3,600 stocks that trade on the NYSE, NASDAQ, and Amex stock markets.[5] It is the most inclusive index of the performance of U.S. equities. The performance of the Wilshire 5000 is a useful benchmark with which to evaluate professional managers because it corresponds to a simple passive investment strategy: Buy all the shares in the index in proportion to their outstanding market value. Moreover, this is a feasible strategy for even small investors, because the Vanguard Group offers an index fund (its Total Stock Market Index Fund) designed to replicate the performance of the Wilshire 5000. Using the Wilshire 5000 as a benchmark, we may pose the problem of evaluating the performance of mutual fund portfolio managers this way: How does the typical performance of actively managed equity mutual funds compare to the performance of a passively managed portfolio that simply replicates the composition of a broad index of the stock market?

Casual comparisons of the performance of the Wilshire 5000 Index versus that of professionally managed mutual fund portfolios show disappointing results for most fund managers. Figure 4.4 shows that the average return on diversified equity funds was below the return on the Wilshire 5000 Index in 28 of the 46 years from 1971 to 2016. The average return on the index was 12.1%, which was 1.0% greater than that of the average mutual fund.[6]

This result may seem surprising. After all, it would not seem unreasonable to expect that professional money managers should be able to outperform a very simple rule such as "hold an indexed portfolio." As it turns out, however, there may be good reasons to expect such a result. We will explore them in detail in Chapter 8, where we discuss the efficient market hypothesis.

Of course, one might argue that there are good managers and bad managers, and that good managers can, in fact, consistently outperform the index. To test this notion, we examine whether managers with good performance in one year are likely to repeat that performance in a following year. Is superior performance in any particular year due to luck, and therefore random, or due to skill, and therefore consistent from year to year?

To answer this question, we can examine the performance of a large sample of equity mutual fund portfolios, divide the funds into two groups based on total investment return, and ask: "Do funds with investment returns in the top half of the sample in one period continue to perform well in the subsequent period?"

Table 4.4 presents such an analysis from a study by Malkiel (1995). The table shows the fraction of "winners" (i.e., top-half performers) in each year that turn out to be winners or

---

[5] At one point, the Wilshire index comprised more than 5,000 stocks. But there are far fewer publicly traded firms today than two decades ago as many firms have either merged, failed, or gone private and delisted from the exchanges. These disappearing firms have not been replaced by newly public ones, as the number of IPOs also has dramatically declined in recent years.

[6] Actual funds incur trading costs while indexes do not, so a fair comparison between the returns on actively managed funds versus those on a passive index should first reduce the return on the Wilshire 5000 by an estimate of such costs. Vanguard's Total Stock Market Index portfolio, which tracks the Wilshire 5000, charges an expense ratio of about 0.15%, and, because it engages in little trading, incurs low trading costs. Therefore, it would be reasonable to reduce the returns on the index no more than 0.20%. This reduction would not erase the difference in average performance.

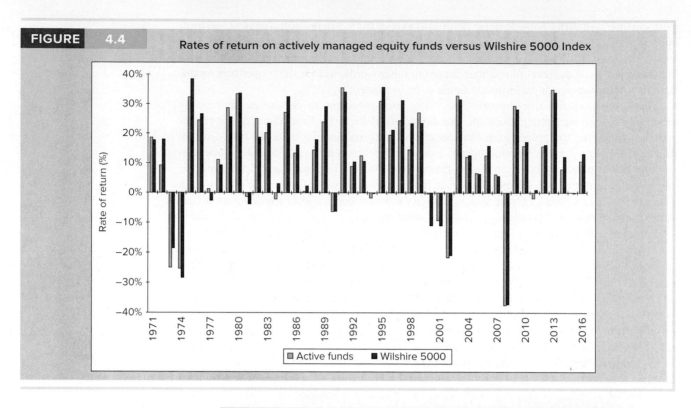

FIGURE 4.4 Rates of return on actively managed equity funds versus Wilshire 5000 Index

TABLE 4.4   Consistency of investment results

Initial Period Performance	Successive Period Performance	
	Top Half (%)	Bottom Half (%)
A. 1970s		
Top half	65.1%	34.9%
Bottom half	35.5	64.5
B. 1980s		
Top half	51.7	48.3
Bottom half	47.5	52.5

Source: Burton G. Malkiel, "Returns from Investing in Equity Mutual Funds 1971–1991," *Journal of Finance* 50 (June 1995), pp. 549–572.

losers in the following year. If performance were purely random from one period to the next, there would be entries of 50% in each cell of the table, as top- or bottom-half performers would be equally likely to perform in either the top or bottom half of the sample in the following period. On the other hand, if performance were due entirely to skill, with no randomness, we would expect to see entries of 100% on the diagonals and entries of 0% on the off-diagonals: Top-half performers would all remain in the top half while bottom-half performers similarly would all remain in the bottom half. In fact, Panel A shows that 65.1% of initial top-half performers in the 1970s fall in the top half of the sample in the following period, while 64.5% of initial bottom-half performers fall in the bottom half in the following period. This evidence is consistent with the notion that at least part of a fund's performance is a function of skill as opposed to luck, so that relative performance tends to persist from one period to the next.[7]

On the other hand, this relationship does not seem stable across different sample periods. While initial-year performance predicts subsequent-year performance in the 1970s (see Panel A), the pattern of persistence in performance virtually disappears in the 1980s (Panel B).

[7] Another possibility is that performance consistency is due to variation in fee structure across funds. We return to this possibility in Chapter 8.

A more recent analysis with similar results to those found by Malkiel was recently reported in *The Wall Street Journal*.[8] The study found that the best performing mutual funds in one period were no more likely than other funds to outperform in future periods. In fact, among U.S.-based domestic funds, top-performers (5-star funds) were more likely to fall into the *bottom* (1-star) rank than to maintain their position in the top tier. Past success was far from a predictor of future success.

Other studies also suggest that there is little performance persistence among professional managers, and if anything, bad performance is more likely to persist than good performance.[9] This makes some sense: It is easy to identify fund characteristics that will predictably lead to consistently poor investment performance, notably, high expense ratios and high turnover ratios with associated trading costs. It is far harder to identify the secrets of successful stock picking. (If it were easy, we would all be rich!) Thus, the consistency we do observe in fund performance may be due in large part to the poor performers. This suggests that the real value of past performance data is to avoid truly poor funds, even if identifying the future top performers is still a daunting task.

Suppose you observe the investment performance of 400 portfolio managers and rank them by investment returns during the year. Twenty percent of all managers are truly skilled, and therefore always fall in the top half, but the others fall in the top half purely because of good luck. What fraction of these top-half managers would you expect to be top-half performers next year? Assume skilled managers always are top-half performers.	**CONCEPT** c h e c k **4.4**

4.8   INFORMATION ON MUTUAL FUNDS

The first place to find information on a mutual fund is in its prospectus. The Securities and Exchange Commission requires that the prospectus describe the fund's investment objectives and policies in a concise "Statement of Investment Objectives" as well as in lengthy discussions of investment policies and risks. The fund's investment adviser and its portfolio manager also are described. The prospectus also presents the costs associated with purchasing shares in the fund in a fee table. Sales charges such as front-end and back-end loads as well as annual operating expenses such as management fees and 12b-1 fees are detailed in the fee table.

Funds provide information about themselves in two other sources. The Statement of Additional Information (SAI), also known as Part B of the prospectus, includes a list of the securities in the portfolio at the end of the fiscal year, audited financial statements, a list of the directors and officers of the fund as well as their personal investments in the fund, and data on brokerage commissions paid by the fund. Unlike the fund prospectus, however, investors do not receive the SAI unless they specifically request it; one industry joke is that SAI stands for "something always ignored." The fund's annual report also includes portfolio composition and financial statements, as well as a discussion of the factors that influenced fund performance over the last reporting period.

With more than 8,000 mutual funds to choose from, it can be difficult to find and select the fund that is best suited for a particular need. Several publications now offer "encyclopedias" of mutual fund information to help in the search process. One prominent source is Morningstar, which publishes a wealth of information about funds on its website, **www.morningstar.com.** Yahoo!'s site, **finance.yahoo.com/mutualfunds,** is a good source of information on recent performance and also provides some useful fund screening capability. The Investment Company Institute—the national association of mutual funds, closed-end funds, and unit investment trusts—publishes an annual *Directory of Mutual Funds* that includes information on fees as well as phone numbers to contact funds. To illustrate the range of information available about funds, we consider Morningstar's report on Fidelity's Magellan Fund, reproduced in Figure 4.5.

---

[8] The Morningstar Mirage, *The Wall Street Journal,* October 25, 2017.

[9] See, for example, Mark M. Carhart, "On Persistence in Mutual Fund Performance," *Journal of Finance* 52 (1997), 57–82. Carhart's study also addresses survivorship bias, the tendency for better-performing funds to stay in business and thus remain in the sample. We return to his study in Chapter 8.

FIGURE 4.5   Morningstar report

Source: Morningstar Mutual Funds, March 31, 2017, © 2017 Morningstar, Inc.

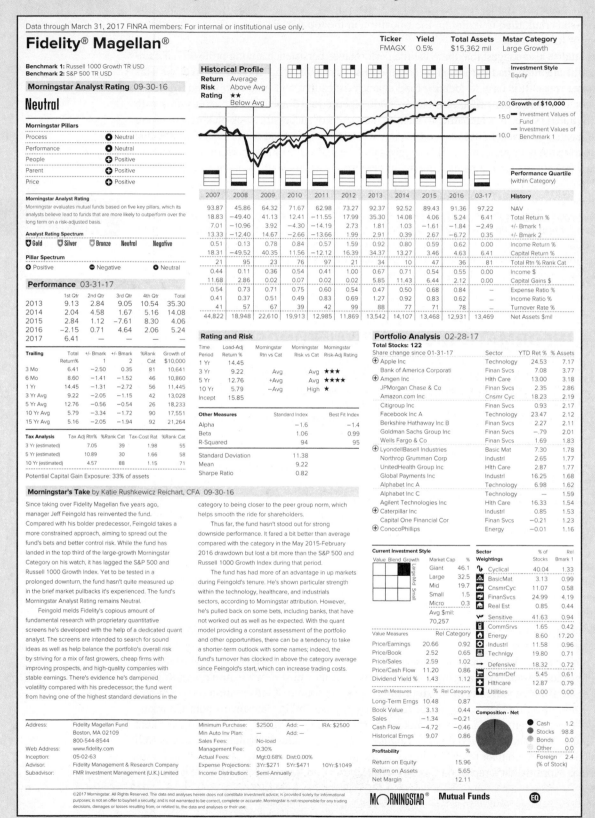

Data through March 31, 2017 FINRA members: For internal or institutional use only.

Fidelity® Magellan®

	Ticker	Yield	Total Assets	Mstar Category
	FMAGX	0.5%	$15,362 mil	Large Growth

Benchmark 1: Russell 1000 Growth TR USD
Benchmark 2: S&P 500 TR USD

Morningstar Analyst Rating 09-30-16

Neutral

Historical Profile
Return   Average
Risk   Above Avg
Rating   ★★ Below Avg

Investment Style
Equity

20.0 Growth of $10,000
15.0 — Investment Values of Fund
10.0 — Investment Values of Benchmark 1

Performance Quartile (within Category)

Morningstar Pillars

Process	● Neutral
Performance	● Neutral
People	⊕ Positive
Parent	⊕ Positive
Price	⊕ Positive

Morningstar Analyst Rating
Morningstar evaluates mutual funds based on five key pillars, which its analysts believe lead to funds that are more likely to outperform over the long term on a risk-adjusted basis.

Analyst Rating Spectrum
🏅 Gold   🏅 Silver   🏅 Bronze   Neutral   Negative

Pillar Spectrum
⊕ Positive   ● Negative   ● Neutral

	2007	2008	2009	2010	2011	2012	2013	2014	2015	2016	03-17	History
	93.87	45.86	64.32	71.67	62.98	73.27	92.37	92.52	89.43	91.36	97.22	NAV
	18.83	−49.40	41.13	12.41	−11.55	17.99	35.30	14.08	4.06	5.24	6.41	Total Return %
	7.01	−10.96	3.92	−4.30	−14.19	2.73	1.81	1.03	−1.61	−1.84	−2.49	+/- Bmark 1
	13.33	−12.40	14.67	−2.66	−13.66	1.99	2.91	0.39	2.67	−6.72	0.35	+/- Bmark 2
	0.51	0.13	0.78	0.84	0.57	1.59	0.92	0.80	0.59	0.62	0.00	Income Return %
	18.31	−49.52	40.35	11.56	−12.12	16.39	34.37	13.27	3.46	4.63	6.41	Capital Return %
	21	95	23	76	97	21	34	10	47	36	81	Total Rtn % Rank Cat
	0.44	0.11	0.36	0.54	0.41	1.00	0.67	0.71	0.54	0.55	0.00	Income $
	11.68	2.86	0.00	0.07	0.02	0.02	5.85	11.43	6.44	2.12	0.00	Capital Gains $
	0.54	0.73	0.71	0.75	0.60	0.54	0.47	0.50	0.68	0.84	—	Expense Ratio %
	0.41	0.37	0.51	0.49	0.83	0.69	1.27	0.92	0.83	0.62	—	Income Ratio %
	41	57	67	39	42	99	88	77	71	78	—	Turnover Rate %
	44,822	18,948	22,610	19,913	12,985	11,869	13,542	14,107	13,468	12,931	13,469	Net Assets $mil

Performance 03-31-17

	1st Qtr	2nd Qtr	3rd Qtr	4th Qtr	Total
2013	9.13	2.84	9.05	10.54	35.30
2014	2.04	4.58	1.67	5.16	14.08
2015	2.84	1.12	−7.61	8.30	4.06
2016	−2.15	0.71	4.64	2.06	5.24
2017	6.41	—	—	—	—

Trailing	Total Return%	+/- Bmark 1	+/- Bmark 2	%Rank Cat	Growth of $10,000
3 Mo	6.41	−2.50	0.35	81	10,641
6 Mo	8.60	−1.41	−1.52	46	10,860
1 Yr	14.45	−1.31	−2.72	56	11,445
3 Yr Avg	9.22	−2.05	−1.15	42	13,028
5 Yr Avg	12.76	−0.56	−0.54	26	18,233
10 Yr Avg	5.79	−3.34	−1.72	90	17,551
15 Yr Avg	5.16	−2.05	−1.94	92	21,264

Tax Analysis	Tax Adj Rtn%	%Rank Cat	Tax-Cost Rat	%Rank Cat
3 Yr (estimated)	7.05	39	1.98	55
5 Yr (estimated)	10.89	30	1.66	58
10 Yr (estimated)	4.57	88	1.15	71

Potential Capital Gain Exposure: 33% of assets

Rating and Risk

Time Period	Load-Adj Return %	Morningstar Rtn vs Cat	Morningstar Risk vs Cat	Morningstar Risk-Adj Rating
1 Yr	14.45			
3 Yr	9.22	Avg	Avg	★★★
5 Yr	12.76	+Avg	Avg	★★★★
10 Yr	5.79	−Avg	High	★
Incept	15.85			

Other Measures	Standard Index	Best Fit Index
Alpha	−1.6	−1.4
Beta	1.06	0.99
R-Squared	94	95
Standard Deviation	11.38	
Mean	9.22	
Sharpe Ratio	0.82	

Portfolio Analysis 02-28-17

Total Stocks: 122

Share change since 01-31-17	Sector	YTD Ret %	% Assets
⊕ Apple Inc	Technology	24.53	7.17
Bank of America Corporati	Finan Svcs	7.08	3.77
⊕ Amgen Inc	Hlth Care	13.00	3.18
JPMorgan Chase & Co	Finan Svcs	2.35	2.86
Amazon.com Inc	Cnsmr Cyc	18.23	2.19
Citigroup Inc	Finan Svcs	0.93	2.17
Facebook Inc A	Technology	23.47	2.12
Berkshire Hathaway Inc B	Finan Svcs	2.27	2.11
Goldman Sachs Group Inc	Finan Svcs	−.79	2.01
Wells Fargo & Co	Finan Svcs	1.69	1.83
⊕ LyondellBasell Industries	Basic Mat	7.30	1.78
Northrop Grumman Corp	Industrl	2.65	1.77
UnitedHealth Group Inc	Hlth Care	2.87	1.77
Global Payments Inc	Industrl	16.25	1.68
Alphabet Inc A	Technology	6.98	1.62
Alphabet Inc C	Technology	—	1.59
Agilent Technologies Inc	Hlth Care	16.33	1.54
⊕ Caterpillar Inc	Industrl	0.85	1.53
Capital One Financial Cor	Finan Svcs	−0.21	1.23
⊕ ConocoPhillips	Energy	−0.01	1.16

Current Investment Style

Value Blend Growth — Large Mid Small

Market Cap	%
Giant	46.1
Large	32.5
Mid	19.7
Small	1.5
Micro	0.3

Avg $mil: 70,257

Value Measures		Rel Category
Price/Earnings	20.66	0.92
Price/Book	2.52	0.65
Price/Sales	2.59	1.02
Price/Cash Flow	11.20	0.86
Dividend Yield %	1.43	1.12

Growth Measures	%	Rel Category
Long-Term Erngs	10.48	0.87
Book Value	3.13	0.44
Sales	−1.34	−0.21
Cash Flow	−4.72	−0.46
Historical Erngs	9.07	0.86

Profitability	%
Return on Equity	15.96
Return on Assets	5.65
Net Margin	12.11

Sector Weightings	% of Stocks	Rel Bmark 1
↻ Cyclical	40.04	1.33
🔧 BasicMat	3.13	0.99
🛒 CnsmrCyc	11.07	0.58
💲 FinanSvcs	24.99	4.19
🏠 Real Est	0.85	0.44
⚡ Sensitive	41.63	0.94
📶 CommSrvs	1.65	0.42
🔋 Energy	8.60	17.20
⚙ Industrl	11.58	0.96
💻 Technlgy	19.80	0.71
→ Defensive	18.32	0.72
CnsmrDef	5.45	0.61
Hlthcare	12.87	0.79
Utilities	0.00	0.00

Composition - Net

● Cash	1.2
● Stocks	98.8
● Bonds	0.0
● Other	0.0
Foreign	2.4
(% of Stock)	

Morningstar's Take by Katie Rushkewicz Reichart, CFA 09-30-16

Since taking over Fidelity Magellan five years ago, manager Jeff Feingold has reinvented the fund. Compared with his bolder predecessor, Feingold takes a more constrained approach, aiming to spread out the fund's bets and better control risk. While the fund has landed in the top third of the large-growth Morningstar Category on his watch, it has lagged the S&P 500 and Russell 1000 Growth Index. Yet to be tested in a prolonged downturn, the fund hasn't quite measured up in the brief market pullbacks it's experienced. The fund's Morningstar Analyst Rating remains Neutral.

Feingold melds Fidelity's copious amount of fundamental research with proprietary quantitative screens he's developed with the help of a dedicated quant analyst. The screens are intended to search for sound ideas as well as help balance the portfolio's overall risk by striving for a mix of fast growers, cheap firms with improving prospects, and high-quality companies with stable earnings. There's evidence he's dampened volatility compared with his predecessor; the fund went from having one of the highest standard deviations in the category to being closer to the peer group norm, which helps smooth the ride for shareholders.

Thus far, the fund hasn't stood out for strong downside performance. It fared a bit better than average compared with the category in the May 2015-February 2016 drawdown but lost a bit more than the S&P 500 and Russell 1000 Growth Index during that period.

The fund has had more of an advantage in up markets during Feingold's tenure. He's shown particular strength within the technology, healthcare, and industrials sectors, according to Morningstar attribution. However, he's pulled back on some bets, including banks, that have not worked out as well as he expected. With the quant model providing a constant assessment of the portfolio and other opportunities, there can be a tendency to take a shorter-term outlook with some names; indeed, the fund's turnover has clocked in above the category average since Feingold's start, which can increase trading costs.

Address:	Fidelity Magellan Fund	Minimum Purchase:	$2500	Add: —	IRA: $2500
	Boston, MA 02109	Min Auto Inv Plan:	—	Add: —	
	800-544-8544	Sales Fees:	No-load		
Web Address:	www.fidelity.com	Management Fee:	0.30%		
Inception:	05-02-63	Actual Fees:	Mgt:0.68% Dist:0.00%		
Advisor:	Fidelity Management & Research Company	Expense Projections:	3Yr:$271 5Yr:$471	10Yr:$1049	
Subadvisor:	FMR Investment Management (U.K.) Limited	Income Distribution:	Semi-Annually		

MORNINGSTAR®   Mutual Funds   ⓔⓠ

The table on the left labeled "Performance" first shows the fund's quarterly returns in the last few years, and just below that, returns over longer periods. You can compare returns to two benchmarks (the Russell 1000 and the S&P 500) in the rows labeled +/− Bmark, as well as its percentile rank within its comparison (or "Mstar category") group (funds with a large growth stock orientation). The table toward the top right of the page provides information on return history as well as expenses. The Rating and Risk table provides several measures of the fund's risk and return characteristics. (We will discuss these measures in Part Two of the text.) The fund has provided good returns compared to risk in the last five years, earning it a four-star rating, but its 10-year performance has been disappointing. Of course, we are all accustomed to the disclaimer that "past performance is not a reliable measure of future results," and this is presumably true as well of Morningstar's star ratings. Consistent with this disclaimer, past results have had little predictive power for future performance, as we saw in the previous section.

More data on the performance of the fund are provided in the graph near the top of the page. The line graph compares the growth of $10,000 invested in the fund versus its first benchmark over the last 10 years. Below the line graph are boxes for each year that depict the relative performance of the fund for that year. The shaded area on the box shows the quartile in which the fund's performance falls relative to other funds with the same objective. If the shaded band is at the top of the box, the firm was a top quartile performer in that period, and so on. The table below the bar charts presents historical data on the year-by-year performance of the fund.

Below the table, the "Portfolio Analysis" table shows the asset allocation of the fund, and then Morningstar's well-known style box. In this box, Morningstar evaluates style along two dimensions: One dimension is the size of the firms held in the portfolio as measured by the market value of outstanding equity; the other dimension is a value/growth measure. Morningstar defines *value stocks* as those with low ratios of market price per share to various measures of value. It puts stocks on a growth-value continuum based on the ratios of stock price to the firm's earnings, book value, sales, cash flow, and dividends. Value stocks are those with a low price relative to these measures of value. In contrast, *growth stocks* have high ratios, suggesting that investors in these firms must believe that the firm will experience rapid growth to justify the prices at which the stocks sell. In Figure 4.5, the shaded box shows that the Magellan Fund tends to hold larger firms (top row) and growth stocks (right column).

Finally, the tables in the right column provide information on the current composition of the portfolio. You can find the fund's 20 "Top Holdings" there as well as the weighting of the portfolio across various sectors of the economy.

SUMMARY

- Unit investment trusts, closed-end management companies, and open-end management companies are all classified and regulated as investment companies. Unit investment trusts are essentially unmanaged in the sense that the portfolio, once established, is fixed. Managed investment companies, in contrast, may change the composition of the portfolio as deemed fit by the portfolio manager. Closed-end funds are traded like other securities; they do not redeem shares for their investors. Open-end funds will redeem shares for net asset value at the request of the investor.
- Net asset value equals the market value of assets held by a fund minus the liabilities of the fund divided by the shares outstanding.
- Mutual funds free the individual from many of the administrative burdens of owning individual securities and offer professional management of the portfolio. They also offer advantages that are available only to large-scale investors, such as lower trading costs. On the other hand, funds are assessed management fees and incur other expenses, which reduce the investor's rate of return. Funds also eliminate some of the individual's control over the timing of capital gains realizations.

- Mutual funds often are categorized by investment policy. Major policy groups include money market funds; equity funds, which are further grouped according to emphasis on income versus growth; fixed-income funds; balanced and income funds; asset allocation funds; index funds; and specialized sector funds.
- Costs of investing in mutual funds include front-end loads, which are sales charges; back-end loads, which are redemption fees or, more formally, contingent-deferred sales charges; operating expenses; and 12b-1 charges, which are recurring fees used to pay for the expenses of marketing the fund to the public.
- Income earned on mutual fund portfolios is not taxed at the level of the fund. Instead, as long as the fund meets certain requirements for pass-through status, the income is treated as being earned by the investors in the fund.
- The average rate of return of the average equity mutual fund in the last 46 years has been below that of a passive index fund holding a portfolio to replicate a broad-based index like the S&P 500 or Wilshire 5000. Some of the reasons for this disappointing record are the costs incurred by actively managed funds, such as the expense of conducting the research to guide stock-picking activities, and trading costs due to higher portfolio turnover. The record on the consistency of fund performance is mixed. In some sample periods, the better-performing funds continue to perform well in the following periods; in other sample periods they do not.

KEY TERMS

closed-end fund, 86	investment companies, 85	soft dollars, 94
exchange-traded funds, 95	load, 87	turnover, 94
funds of funds, 89	net asset value (NAV), 85	12b-1 fees, 92
hedge fund, 88	open-end fund, 86	unit investment trust, 86

PROBLEM SETS

 **Select problems are available in McGraw-Hill's** *Connect.* **Please see the Supplements section of the book's frontmatter for more information.**

1. What are the benefits to small investors of investing via mutual funds? What are the disadvantages? *(LO 4-1)*

2. Why can closed-end funds sell at prices that differ from net value while open-end funds do not? *(LO 4-2)*

3. What is a 12b-1 fee? *(LO 4-1)*

4. What are some differences between a unit investment trust and a closed-end fund? *(LO 4-2)*

5. What are the advantages and disadvantages of exchange-traded funds versus mutual funds? *(LO 4-2)*

6. What are some differences between hedge funds and mutual funds? *(LO 4-2)*

7. Would you expect a typical open-end fixed-income mutual fund to have higher or lower operating expenses than a fixed-income unit investment trust? Why? *(LO 4-2)*

8. Balanced funds and asset allocation funds each invest in both the stock and bond markets. What is the difference between these types of funds? *(LO 4-4)*

9. What are some comparative advantages of investing your assets in the following: *(LO 4-2)*
   a. Unit investment trusts.
   b. Open-end mutual funds.
   c. Individual stocks and bonds that you choose for yourself.

10. Open-end equity mutual funds find it necessary to keep a small fraction of total invest-
    ments, typically around 5% of the portfolio, in very liquid money market assets. Closed-
    end funds do not have to maintain such a position in "cash-equivalent" securities. What
    difference between open-end and closed-end funds might account for their differing
    policies? *(LO 4-2)*

11. An open-end fund has a net asset value of $10.70 per share. It is sold with a front-end
    load of 6%. What is the offering price?   *(LO 4-3)*

12. If the offering price of an open-end fund is $12.30 per share and the fund is sold with a
    front-end load of 5%, what is its net asset value?   *(LO 4-3)*

13. The composition of the Fingroup Fund portfolio is as follows:

Stock	Shares	Price
A	200,000	$35
B	300,000	40
C	400,000	20
D	600,000	25

    The fund has not borrowed any funds, but its accrued management fee with the portfolio
    manager currently totals $30,000. There are 4 million shares outstanding. What is the
    net asset value of the fund?   *(LO 4-3)*

14. Reconsider the Fingroup Fund in the previous problem. If during the year the portfolio
    manager sells all of the holdings of stock D and replaces it with 200,000 shares of stock
    E at $50 per share and 200,000 shares of stock F at $25 per share, what is the portfolio
    turnover rate?   *(LO 4-5)*

15. The Closed Fund is a closed-end investment company with a portfolio currently worth
    $200 million. It has liabilities of $3 million and 5 million shares outstanding.   *(LO 4-3)*
    a. What is the NAV of the fund?
    b. If the fund sells for $36 per share, what is its premium or discount as a percent of
       NAV?

16. Corporate Fund started the year with a net asset value of $12.50. By year-end, its NAV
    equaled $12.10. The fund paid year-end distributions of income and capital gains of
    $1.50. What was the rate of return to an investor in the fund?   *(LO 4-3)*

17. A closed-end fund starts the year with a net asset value of $12. By year-end, NAV equals
    $12.10. At the beginning of the year, the fund is selling at a 2% premium to NAV. By
    the end of the year, the fund is selling at a 7% discount to NAV. The fund paid year-end
    distributions of income and capital gains of $1.50.   *(LO 4-3)*
    a. What is the rate of return to an investor in the fund during the year?
    b. What would have been the rate of return to an investor who held the same securities
       as the fund manager during the year?

18. Loaded-Up Fund charges a 12b-1 fee of 1% and maintains an expense ratio of .75%.
    Economy Fund charges a front-end load of 2%, but has no 12b-1 fee and an expense
    ratio of .25%. Assume the rate of return on both funds' portfolios (before any fees) is
    6% per year. How much will an investment in each fund grow to after: *(LO 4-5)*
    a. 1 year?
    b. 3 years?
    c. 10 years?

19. City Street Fund has a portfolio of $450 million and liabilities of $10 million.   *(LO 4-3)*
    a. If there are 44 million shares outstanding, what is the net asset value?
    b. If a large investor redeems 1 million shares, what happens to the portfolio value, to
       shares outstanding, and to NAV?

20. *a.* Impressive Fund had excellent investment performance last year, with portfolio returns that placed it in the top 10% of all funds with the same investment policy. Do you expect it to be a top performer next year? Why or why not?
    b. Suppose instead that the fund was among the poorest performers in its comparison group. Would you be more or less likely to believe its relative performance will persist into the following year? Why? *(LO 4-5)*

21. Consider a mutual fund with $200 million in assets at the start of the year and with 10 million shares outstanding. The fund invests in a portfolio of stocks that provides dividend income at the end of the year of $2 million. The stocks included in the fund's portfolio increase in price by 8%, but no securities are sold, and there are no capital gains distributions. The fund charges 12b-1 fees of 1%, which are deducted from portfolio assets at year-end. *(LO 4-3)*
    a. What is the net asset value at the start and end of the year?
    b. What is the rate of return for an investor in the fund?

22. The New Fund had average daily assets of $2.2 billion in the past year. The fund sold $400 million and purchased $500 million worth of stock during the year. What was its turnover ratio? *(LO 4-5)*

23. The New Fund (from Problem 22) had an expense ratio of 1.1%, and its management fee was 0.7%. *(LO 4-5)*
    a. What were the total fees paid to the fund's investment managers during the year?
    b. What were the other administrative expenses?

24. You purchased 1,000 shares of the New Fund at a price of $20 per share at the beginning of the year. You paid a front-end load of 4%. The securities in which the fund invests increase in value by 12% during the year. The fund's expense ratio is 1.2%. What is your rate of return on the fund if you sell your shares at the end of the year? *(LO 4-5)*

25. The Investments Fund sells Class A shares with a front-end load of 6% and Class B shares with 12b-1 fees of 0.5% annually as well as back-end load fees that start at 5% and fall by 1% for each full year the investor holds the portfolio (until the fifth year). Assume the portfolio rate of return net of operating expenses is 10% annually. *(LO 4-5)*
    a. If you plan to sell the fund after four years, are Class A or Class B shares the better choice for you?
    b. What if you plan to sell after 15 years?

26. You are considering an investment in a mutual fund with a 4% load and an expense ratio of 0.5%. You can invest instead in a bank CD paying 6% interest. *(LO 4-5)*
    a. If you plan to invest for two years, what annual rate of return must the fund portfolio earn for you to be better off in the fund than in the CD? Assume annual compounding of returns.
    b. How does your answer change if you plan to invest for six years? Why does your answer change?
    c. Now suppose that instead of a front-end load the fund assesses a 12b-1 fee of .75% per year.
        i. What annual rate of return must the fund portfolio earn for you to be better off in the fund than in the CD?
        ii. Does your answer in this case depend on your time horizon?

27. Suppose that every time a fund manager trades stock, transaction costs such as commissions and bid–ask spreads amount to 0.4% of the value of the trade. If the portfolio turnover rate is 50%, by how much is the total return of the portfolio reduced by trading costs? *(LO 4-5)*

28. You expect a tax-free municipal bond portfolio to provide a rate of return of 4%. Management fees of the fund are 0.6%. *(LO 4-4)*
    a. What fraction of portfolio income is given up to fees?
    b. If the management fees for an equity fund also are 0.6%, but you expect a portfolio return of 12%, what fraction of portfolio income is given up to fees?

c. Why might management fees be a bigger factor in your investment decision for bond funds than for stock funds? Can your conclusion help explain why unmanaged unit investment trusts tend to focus on the fixed-income market?

29. Why would it be challenging to properly compare the performance of an equity fund to a fixed-income mutual fund? *(LO 4-4)*

Challenge

30. Suppose you observe the investment performance of 350 portfolio managers for five years and rank them by investment returns during each year. After five years, you find that 11 of the funds have investment returns that place the fund in the top half of the sample in each and every year of your sample. Such consistency of performance indicates to you that these must be the funds whose managers are in fact skilled, and you invest your money in these funds. Is your conclusion warranted? *(LO 4-5)*

Go to **www.morningstar.com.** In the Morningstar Tools section, click on the link for the *Mutual Fund Screener.* Set the criteria you desire, then click on the *Show Results* tab. If you get no funds that meet all of your criteria, choose the criterion that is least important to you and relax that constraint. Continue the process until you have several funds to compare.

WEB *master*

1. Examine all of the views available in the drop-down box menu (*Snapshot, Performance, Portfolio,* and *Nuts and Bolts*) to answer the following questions:
   - Which fund has the best expense ratio?
   - Which funds have the lowest Morningstar Risk rating?
   - Which fund has the best 3-year return? Which has the best 10-year return?
   - Which fund has the lowest turnover ratio? Which has the highest?
   - Which fund has the longest manager tenure? Which has the shortest?
   - Do you need to eliminate any of the funds from consideration due to a minimum initial investment that is higher than you are capable of making?

2. Based on what you know about the funds, which one do you think would be the best one for your investment?

3. Select up to five funds that are of the most interest to you. Click on the button that says *Score These Results.* Customize the criteria listed by indicating their importance to you. Examine the score results. Does the fund with the highest score match the choice you made in part 2?

4.1 NAV = ($6,897.2 − $156.3)/65.45 = $102.99

SOLUTIONS TO CONCEPT *checks*

4.2 The net investment in the Class A shares after the 4% commission is $9,600. If the fund earns a 10% return, the investment will grow after n years to $9,600 $\times$ $(1.10)^n$. The Class B shares have no front-end load. However, the net return to the investor after 12b-1 fees will be only 9.5%. In addition, there is a back-end load that reduces the sales proceeds by a percentage equal to (5 − years until sale) until the fifth year, when the back-end load expires.

Horizon	Class A Shares $9,600 $\times$ $(1.10)^n$	Class B Shares $10,000 $\times$ $(1.095)^n$ $\times$ (1 − percentage exit fee)	
1 year	$10,560.00	$10,000 $\times$ (1.095) $\times$ (1 − .04)	= $10,512.00
4 years	$14,055.36	$10,000 $\times$ $(1.095)^4$ $\times$ (1 − .01)	= $14,232.89
10 years	$24,899.93	$10,000 $\times$ $(1.095)^{10}$	= $24,782.28

For a very short horizon such as one year, the Class A shares are the better choice. The front-end and back-end loads are equal, but the Class A shares don't have to pay the 12b-1 fees. For moderate horizons such as four years, the Class B shares dominate because the front-end load of the Class A shares is more costly than the 12b-1 fees and the now-smaller exit fee. For long horizons of 10 years or more, Class A again dominates. In this case, the one-time front-end load is less expensive than the continuing 12b-1 fees.

4.3 *a.* Turnover = $400,000 in trades per $1 million of portfolio value = 40%.

   b. Realized capital gains are $10 × 1,000 = $10,000 on FedEx and $5 × 10,000 = $50,000 on Cisco. The tax owed on the capital gains is therefore .15 × $60,000 = $9,000.

4.4 Twenty percent of the managers are skilled, which accounts for .2 × 400 = 80 of those managers who appear in the top half. There are 120 slots left in the top half, and 320 other managers, so the probability of an unskilled manager "lucking into" the top half in any year is 120/320, or .375. Therefore, of the 120 lucky managers in the first year, we would expect .375 × 120 = 45 to repeat as top-half performers next year. Thus, we should expect a total of 80 + 45 = 125, or 62.5%, of the better initial performers to repeat their top-half performance.

Portfolio Theory

The last 90 years witnessed the Great Depression, seven additional recessions of varying severity, and the deep recession that began in 2007. Yet even with these downturns, a dollar invested in a broad portfolio of stocks grew over this period to a value more than 250 times that of a dollar invested in safe assets such as Treasury bills. Why then would anyone invest in a safe asset? Because investors are risk averse, and risk is as important to them as the expected value of returns. Chapter 5, the first of five in Part Two, provides the tools needed to interpret the history of rates of return, and the lessons that history offers for how investors might go about constructing portfolios using both safe and risky assets.

The proportion of wealth that an investor will choose to put at risk depends on the trade-off between risk and return that is offered by risky assets. Chapter 6 lays out modern portfolio theory (MPT), which involves the construction and properties of an optimal risky portfolio. It aims to accomplish efficient diversification across asset classes like bonds and stocks and across individual securities within these asset classes.

This analysis quickly raises other questions. For example, how should one measure the risk of an individual asset held as part of a diversified portfolio? You may be surprised at the answer. Once we have an acceptable measure of risk, what precisely should be the relation between risk and return? And what is the minimally acceptable rate of return for an investment to be considered attractive? These questions also are addressed in this part of the text. Chapter 7 introduces the Capital Asset Pricing Model (CAPM) and Arbitrage Pricing Theory (APT), as well as index and multi-index models, all mainstays of applied financial economics. These models link risk with the return investors can reasonably expect on various securities.

Next, we come to one of the most controversial topics in investment management, the question of whether portfolio managers—amateur or professional—can outperform simple investment strategies such as "buy a market index fund." The evidence in Chapter 8 will at least make you pause before pursuing active strategies. You will come to appreciate how good active managers must be to outperform passive strategies. Finally, Chapter 9 on behavioral finance is concerned with documented irrationality in investor behavior that might lead to observed anomalies in patterns of asset returns.

Chapters in This Part

Risk, Return, and the Historical Record

Learning Objectives

LO 5-1 Compute various measures of return on multiyear investments.

LO 5-2 Use either historical data on the past performance of stocks and bonds or forward-looking scenario analysis to characterize the risk and return features of these investments.

LO 5-3 Determine the expected return and risk of portfolios that are constructed by combining risky assets with risk-free investments in Treasury bills.

LO 5-4 Use the Sharpe ratio to evaluate the performance of a portfolio and provide a guide for capital allocation.

Investors today have access to a vast array of assets and can easily construct portfolios that include foreign stocks and bonds, real estate, precious metals, and collectibles. Even more complex strategies may include futures, options, and other derivatives to insure portfolios against specified risks. What constitutes a satisfactory investment portfolio constructed from these many assets?

Clearly, every individual security must be judged on its contributions to both the expected return and the risk of the entire portfolio. We begin with an examination of various conventions for measuring and reporting rates of return. Next, we turn to the historical performance of several broadly diversified portfolios.

We then consider the simplest form of risk control, capital allocation: choosing the fraction of the portfolio invested in virtually risk-free versus risky securities. We show how to calculate the performance one may expect from various allocations and contemplate the mix that would best suit different investors. With this background, we can evaluate a passive strategy that will serve as a benchmark for the active strategies considered in the next chapter.

5.1 RATES OF RETURN

The **holding-period return (HPR)** on a share of stock reflects both the increase (or decrease) in the price of the share over the investment period as well as any dividend income the share has provided. It is defined as dollars earned (price appreciation plus dividends) per dollar invested:

holding-period return (HPR)

Rate of return over a given investment period.

$$\text{HPR} = \frac{\text{Ending price} - \text{Beginning price} + \text{Cash dividend}}{\text{Beginning price}} \qquad (5.1)$$

This definition assumes that the dividend is paid at the end of the holding period. When dividends are received earlier, you also need to account for reinvestment income between the receipt of the dividend and the end of the holding period. The percentage return from dividends, cash dividends/beginning price, is called the *dividend yield,* and the percentage price increase is called the *capital gains yield.* Therefore the dividend yield plus the capital gains yield equals the HPR.

The price of a share of a stock is currently $100, and your time horizon is one year. You expect the cash dividend during the year to be $4, so your expected dividend yield is 4%.

Your HPR will depend on the price one year from now. Suppose your best guess is that it will be $110 per share. If you are right, the HPR will be

$$\text{HPR} = \frac{\$110 - \$100 + \$4}{\$100} = .14, \text{ or } 14\%$$

Your predicted capital gain is $10, which implies a capital gains yield of $10/$100 = .10, or 10%. The HPR is the sum of the dividend yield plus the capital gains yield, 4% + 10% = 14%.

EXAMPLE 5.1

Holding-Period Return

Our definition of holding-period return is easy to modify for other types of investments. For example, the HPR on a bond would use the same formula, with interest or coupon payments taking the place of dividends.

Measuring Investment Returns over Multiple Periods

The HPR is a simple and unambiguous measure of investment return over a single period. But often you will be interested in average returns over longer periods of time. For example, you might want to measure how well a mutual fund has performed over the preceding five-year period. In this case, return measurement becomes ambiguous.

Consider a fund that starts with $1 million under management. It receives additional funds from new and existing shareholders and also redeems shares of existing shareholders so that net cash inflow can be positive or negative. The fund's annual results are given in Table 5.1, with negative numbers in parentheses.

The numbers indicate that when the firm does well (i.e., achieves a high HPR), it attracts new funds; otherwise it may suffer a net outflow. For example, the 10% return in the first year by itself increased assets under management by .10 × $1 million = $100,000; it also elicited new investments of $100,000, thus bringing assets under management to $1.2 million by the end of the year. An even better HPR of 25% in the second year elicited a larger net inflow, and the second year ended with $2 million under management. However, HPR in the third year was negative, and net inflows were negative.

How would we characterize fund performance over the entire period, given that the fund experienced both cash inflows and outflows? There are several alternative measures of performance, each with its own advantages and shortcomings: the *arithmetic average, geometric average,* and *dollar-weighted return.* These measures may vary considerably, so it is important to understand their differences.

TABLE 5.1	Annual cash flows and rates of return of a mutual fund			
	1st Year	**2nd Year**	**3rd Year**	**4th Year**
Assets under management at start of year ($ million)	1.0	1.2	2.0	0.8
Holding-period return (%)	10.0	25.0	(20.0)	20.0
Total assets before net inflows	1.1	1.5	1.6 ·	0.96
Net inflow ($ million)*	0.1	0.5	(0.8)	0.6
Assets under management at end of year ($ million)	1.2	2.0	0.8	1.56

*New investment less redemptions and distributions, all assumed to occur at the end of each year.

arithmetic average

The sum of returns in each period divided by the number of periods.

geometric average

The single per-period return that gives the same cumulative performance as the sequence of actual returns.

ARITHMETIC AVERAGE   The **arithmetic average** of the annual returns is just the sum of the returns divided by the number of years: $(10 + 25 - 20 + 20)/4 = 8.75\%$. The arithmetic average of past returns is a common forecast of performance for future periods.

GEOMETRIC AVERAGE   The **geometric average** of the quarterly returns is equal to the single per-period return that would give the same cumulative performance as the sequence of actual returns. We calculate the geometric average by compounding the actual period-by-period returns and then finding the single per-period rate that will compound to the same final value. In our example, the geometric average return, r_G, is defined by:

$$(1 + .10) \times (1 + .25) \times (1 - .20) \times (1 + .20) = (1 + r_G)^4$$

The left-hand side of this equation is the compounded final value of a $1 investment earning the four annual returns. The right-hand side is the compounded value of a $1 investment earning r_G *each* year. We solve for r_G:

$$r_G = [(1 + .10) \times (1 + .25) \times (1 - .20) \times (1 + .20)]^{1/4} - 1 = .0719, \text{ or } 7.19\% \qquad \textbf{(5.2)}$$

The geometric return is also called a *time-weighted average return* because it ignores the year-by-year variation in funds under management. In fact, cumulative returns will be larger if high returns are earned in periods when larger sums have been invested and low returns are earned when less money is at risk. In Table 5.1, the higher returns (25% and 20%) were achieved in years 2 and 4, when the fund managed $1,200,000 and $800,000, respectively. The lower returns (–20% and 10%) occurred when the fund managed $2,000,000 and $1,000,000, respectively. In this case, better returns were earned when *less* money was under management—an unfavorable combination.

Published data on past returns earned by mutual funds actually are *required* to be time-weighted returns. The rationale for this practice is that since the fund manager does not have full control over the amount of assets under management, we should not weight returns in one period more heavily than those in other periods when assessing "typical" past performance.

DOLLAR-WEIGHTED RETURN   To account for varying amounts under management, we treat the fund cash flows as we would a capital budgeting problem in corporate finance and compute the portfolio manager's internal rate of return (IRR). The initial value of $1 million and the net cash inflows are treated as the cash flows associated with an investment "project." The year-4 "liquidation value" of the portfolio is the final cash flow of the project. In our example, the investor's net cash flows are as follows:

	Year				
	0	**1**	**2**	**3**	**4**
Net cash flow ($ million)	−1.0	−.1	−.5	.8	−.6 + 1.56 = .96

The entry for year 0 reflects the starting contribution of $1 million; the negative entries for years 1 and 2 are additional net inflows in those years, whereas the positive value for year 3 signifies a withdrawal of funds. Finally, the entry for year 4 represents the sum of the final (negative) cash inflow plus the value of the portfolio at the end of the fourth year. The latter is the value for which the portfolio could have been liquidated at the end of that year.

The **dollar-weighted average return** is the internal rate of return of the project. The IRR is the interest rate that sets the present value of the cash flows realized on the portfolio (including the $1.56 million for which the portfolio can be liquidated at the end of the fourth year) equal to the initial cost of establishing the portfolio. It therefore is the interest rate that satisfies the following equation:

dollar-weighted average return

The internal rate of return on an investment.

$$0 = -1.0 + \frac{-.1}{1 + IRR} + \frac{-.5}{(1 + IRR)^2} + \frac{.8}{(1 + IRR)^3} + \frac{.96}{(1 + IRR)^4} \qquad \textbf{(5.3)}$$

The solution to Equation 5.3 is IRR = 0.0338 = 3.38%. The dollar-weighted return in this example is smaller than the time-weighted return of 7.19% because, as we noted, the portfolio returns were higher when less money was under management. The difference between the dollar- and time-weighted average return in this case is quite large.

A fund begins with $10 million and reports the following monthly results (with negative figures in parentheses):

CONCEPT check 5.1

	Month		
	1	**2**	**3**
Net inflows (end of month, $ million)	3	5	0
HPR (%)	2	8	(4)

Compute the arithmetic, time-weighted, and dollar-weighted average monthly returns.

Conventions for Annualizing Rates of Return

There are several ways to annualize rates of return, i.e., express them as return per year. Returns on assets with regular intra-year cash flows, such as mortgages (with monthly payments) and bonds (with semiannual coupons), usually are quoted as annual percentage rates (APRs), which annualize per-period rates using a simple interest approach, ignoring compound interest:

$$APR = \text{Per-period rate} \times \text{Periods per year}$$

However, because it ignores compounding, the APR does not equal the rate at which your invested funds actually grow. The latter is called the *effective annual rate* (EAR). When there are n compounding periods in the year, we first recover the rate per period as APR/n and then compound that rate for the number of periods in a year. For example, $n = 12$ for monthly payment mortgages and $n = 2$ for bonds making payments semiannually.

$$1 + \text{EAR} = (1 + \text{Rate per period})^n = \left(1 + \frac{\text{APR}}{n}\right)^n \tag{5.4}$$

Because the rate earned each period is APR/n, after one year (when n periods have passed), your cumulative return is $(1 + \text{APR}/n)^n$. Note that one needs to know the holding period when given an APR in order to convert it to an effective rate.

Rearranging Equation 5.4, we can also find APR given EAR:[1]

$$\text{APR} = [(1 + \text{EAR})^{1/n} - 1] \times n$$

EXAMPLE 5.2	Suppose you buy a $10,000 face value Treasury bill maturing in six months for $9,900. On the bill's maturity date you collect the face value. Because there are no other interest payments, the holding-period return for this six-month investment is

Annualizing Treasury-Bill Returns

$$\text{HPR} = \frac{\text{Cash income} + \text{Price change}}{\text{Initial price}} = \frac{0 + \$100}{\$9,900} = .0101 = 1.01\%$$

The APR on this investment is therefore 1.01% × 2 = 2.02%. The effective annual rate is a bit higher:

$$1 + \text{EAR} = (1.0101)^2 = 1.0203$$

which implies that EAR = .0203 = 2.03%.

EAR diverges from APR by greater amounts as n becomes larger (we compound cash flows more frequently). In the limit, we can envision continuous compounding when n becomes extremely large in Equation 5.4. With continuous compounding, the APR is related to EAR by

$$1 + \text{EAR} = e^{\text{APR}} \tag{5.5A}$$

or, equivalently,

$$\text{APR} = ln(1 + \text{EAR}) = r_{cc} \tag{5.5B}$$

As Equation 5.5B shows, we will use the notation r_{cc} when we want to highlight that we are using continuously compounded rates.

The difficulties in interpreting rates of return over time do not end here. Two thorny issues remain: the uncertainty surrounding the investment in question and the effect of inflation.

5.2 INFLATION AND THE REAL RATE OF INTEREST

nominal interest rate

The interest rate in terms of nominal (not adjusted for purchasing power) dollars.

When prices of goods and services change, we need to distinguish between *nominal* and *real* rates of return. When you invest money in a bank account, for example, you are typically quoted a **nominal interest rate.** This is the rate at which the *dollar value* of your account grows. In contrast, the **real interest rate** is the rate at which the goods you can buy with your funds grows.

real interest rate

The growth rate of purchasing power derived from an investment.

To illustrate, suppose that one year ago you deposited $1,000 in a 1-year bank deposit guaranteeing a rate of interest of 10%. This is your nominal rate of return. You are about to collect $1,100 in cash. What is the real return on your investment? That depends on what your

---

[1]The Excel function "EFFECT" will convert APR to EAR, while "NOMINAL" will do the reverse.

money can buy today relative to what you *could* buy a year ago. The consumer price index (CPI) measures purchasing power by averaging the prices of goods and services in the consumption basket of an average urban family of four.

Suppose the **inflation rate** (the percent change in the CPI, denoted by i) is running at $i = 6\%$. So a loaf of bread that cost \$1 last year might cost \$1.06 this year. Last year you could buy 1,000 loaves with your funds. After investing for a year, you can buy \$1,100/\$1.06 = 1,038 loaves. The rate at which your purchasing power has increased is therefore 3.8%. This is your real rate of return.

inflation rate

The rate at which prices are rising, measured as the rate of increase of the CPI.

Part of your interest earnings have been offset by the reduction in the purchasing power of the dollars you will receive at the end of the year. With a 10% interest rate, after you net out the 6% reduction in the purchasing power of money, you are left with a net increase in purchasing power of almost 4%.

Your purchasing power increases in proportion to the growth of invested funds but falls with the growth of prices. In our example, when you earned a 10% nominal return in your bank deposit, but bread prices increased by 6%, the number of loaves you could buy increased by a multiple of 1.10/1.06 = 1.038. In general, if we call r_{nom} the nominal interest rate, r_{real} the real rate, and i the inflation rate, then we conclude

$$1 + r_{real} = \frac{1 + r_{nom}}{1 + i} \tag{5.6}$$

Equation 5.6 can be rearranged to solve for the real rate as:

$$r_{real} = \frac{r_{nom} - i}{1 + i} \tag{5.7}$$

A common approximation to Equation 5.7 is

$$r_{real} \approx r_{nom} - i \tag{5.8}$$

In words, the real rate of interest is approximately the nominal rate reduced by the rate of inflation. The approximation rule, Equation 5.8, overstates the real rate by the factor $1 + i$.

If the interest rate on a one-year CD is 8%, and you expect inflation to be 5% over the coming year, then using the approximation given in Equation 5.8, you expect the real rate to be $r_{real} = 8\% - 5\% = 3\%$. Using the exact formula given in Equation 5.7, the real rate is $r_{real} = \frac{.08 - .05}{1 + .05} = .0286$, or 2.86%. Therefore, the approximation rule overstates the expected real rate by only .14 percentage points. The approximation rule is more accurate for small inflation rates and is perfectly exact for continuously compounded rates.[2]

EXAMPLE 5.3

Real versus Nominal Rates

The Equilibrium Nominal Rate of Interest

We've seen that the real rate of return is approximately the nominal rate minus the inflation rate. Because investors should be concerned with real returns—the increase in their purchasing power—they will demand higher nominal rates of return when expected inflation is higher.

Irving Fisher (1930) argued that the nominal rate ought to increase one-for-one with increases in the expected inflation rate. Such an increase would be needed to preserve investors' real rate of return. Using $E(i)$ to denote the current expected inflation over the coming period, the *Fisher equation* is

$$r_{nom} = r_{real} + E(i) \tag{5.9}$$

---

[2]Notice that for continuously compounded rates, Equation 5.8 is perfectly accurate. Because $\ln(x/y) = \ln(x) - \ln(y)$, the continuously compounded real rate of return, $r_{cc}(real)$, can be derived from the effective annual rates as

$$r_{cc}(real) = \ln(1 + r_{real}) = \ln\left(\frac{1 + r_{nom}}{1 + i}\right) = \ln(1 + r_{nom}) - \ln(1 + i) = r_{cc}(nom) - i_{cc}$$

Suppose the real rate of interest is 2%, and expected inflation is 4%, so that the nominal interest rate is about 6%. If expected inflation rises to 5%, the nominal interest rate should climb to roughly 7%. The increase in the nominal rate offsets the increase in expected inflation, giving investors an unchanged growth rate of purchasing power of 2%.

CONCEPT check	5.2	
		a. Suppose the real interest rate is 3% per year, and the expected inflation rate is 8%. What is the nominal interest rate?
		b. Suppose the expected inflation rate rises to 10%, but the real rate is unchanged. What must happen to the nominal interest rate?

Equation 5.9 relates to expected inflation, but all we can observe is actual inflation. So the empirical validity of the Fisher equation will depend in large part on how well market participants can predict inflation over their investment horizons.

Table 5.2 summarizes the history of returns on 1-month U.S. Treasury bills, the inflation rate, and the resultant real rate. You can find the entire post-1926 history of the monthly rates of these series in Connect (**http://mhhe.com/bodie11e**).

The first set of columns of Table 5.2 lists average annual rates for three periods. Over the full sample, the average nominal rate on T-bills was 3.42%. However, the average inflation rate of 2.99% meant that the average real return on bills was only 0.53%. But the variation within this period was considerable.

The average nominal interest rate over the more recent portion of our history, 1952–2016 (essentially the postwar period), 4.38%, was noticeably higher than in the earlier portion, 1.04%. The reason is inflation, which also had a noticeably higher average value, 3.51%, in the later portion of the sample than in the earlier period, 1.68%. Nevertheless, nominal interest rates in the recent period were still high enough to leave a higher average real rate, 0.86%, compared with a negative 29 basis points (–0.29%) for the earlier period.

Figure 5.1 shows why we divide the sample period at 1952. After that year, inflation is far less volatile, and, probably as a result, the nominal interest rate tracks the inflation rate far more reliably, resulting in a far more stable real interest rate. This shows up as the dramatic reduction in the standard deviation of the real rate documented in the last column of Table 5.2. Whereas the standard deviation is 6.27% in the early part of the sample, it is only 2.14% in the later portion. The lower standard deviation of the real rate in the post-1952 period reflects a similar decline in the standard deviation of the inflation rate. We conclude that the Fisher relation appears to work far better when inflation is itself more predictable and investors can more accurately gauge the nominal interest rate they require to provide an acceptable real rate of return.

5.3   RISK AND RISK PREMIUMS

Any investment involves some degree of uncertainty about future holding-period returns, and in many cases that uncertainty is considerable. Sources of investment risk range from macroeconomic fluctuations, to the changing fortunes of various industries, to firm-specific unexpected developments.

TABLE 5.2   Statistics for T-bill rates, inflation rates, and real rates, 1926–2016

	Average Annual Rates			Standard Deviation		
	T-bills	**Inflation**	**Real T-bill**	**T-bills**	**Inflation**	**Real T-bill**
Full sample	3.42	2.99	0.53	3.12	4.05	3.80
1926–1951	1.04	1.68	–0.29	1.29	5.95	6.27
1952–2016	4.38	3.51	0.86	3.13	2.87	2.14

The real rate in each year is computed as $(1 + r_{nom})/(1 + i) - 1$. The table provides the average value of each year's real rate. This average differs somewhat from the real rate one would compute by using the sample average values of r_{nom} and i in Equation 5.6.

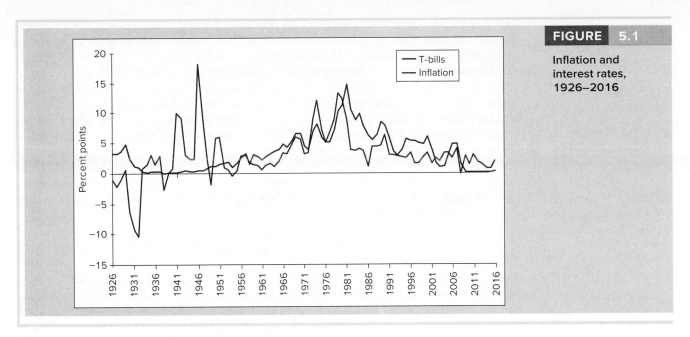

FIGURE 5.1

Inflation and interest rates, 1926–2016

Scenario Analysis and Probability Distributions

When we attempt to measure risk, we begin with the question: What holding-period returns (HPRs) are possible, and how likely are they? A good way to approach this question is to devise a list of possible economic outcomes, or *scenarios,* and specify both the probability of each scenario and the HPR the asset will realize in that scenario. Therefore, this approach is called **scenario analysis.** The list of possible HPRs with associated probabilities is the **probability distribution** of HPRs. Consider an investment in a broad portfolio of stocks, say, a stock index fund. A very simple scenario analysis for the index fund (assuming only four possible scenarios) is illustrated in Spreadsheet 5.1.

The probability distribution lets us derive measurements for both the reward and the risk of the investment. The reward from the investment is its **expected return,** which you can think of as the average HPR you would earn if you were to repeat an investment in the asset many times. The expected return also is called the *mean of the distribution* of HPRs and often is referred to as the *mean return.*

To compute the expected return from the data provided, we label scenarios by s and denote the HPR in each scenario as $r(s)$, with probability $p(s)$. The expected return, denoted $E(r)$, is then the weighted average of returns in all possible scenarios, $s = 1, \ldots, S$, with weights equal to the probability of that particular scenario.

$$E(r) = \sum_{s=1}^{S} p(s)r(s) \qquad \textbf{(5.10)}$$

scenario analysis

Process of devising a list of possible economic scenarios and specifying the likelihood of each one, as well as the HPR that will be realized in each case.

probability distribution

List of possible outcomes with associated probabilities.

expected return

The mean value of the distribution of HPR.

	A	B	C	D	E	F	G
1				Column B x	Deviation from	Squared deviation	Column B x
2	**Scenario**	**Probability**	**HPR (%)**	Column C	mean return	from mean return	Column F
3	1. Severe recession	0.05	−37	−1.85	−47.0	2209.0	110.45
4	2. Mild recession	0.25	−11	−2.75	−21.0	441.0	110.25
5	3. Normal growth	0.40	14	5.60	4.0	16.0	6.40
6	4. Boom	0.30	30	9.00	20.0	400.0	120.00
7	**Column sums:**		Mean return:	10.00		Variance:	347.10
8						Standard deviation (%):	18.63

This spreadsheet is available in Connect

Each entry in column D of Spreadsheet 5.1 corresponds to one of the products in the summation in Equation 5.10. The value in cell D7, which is the sum of these products, is therefore the expected return. Therefore, $E(r) = 10\%$.

Because there is risk to the investment, the actual return may be (a lot) more or less than 10%. If a "boom" materializes, the return will be better, 30%, but in a severe recession the return will be a disappointing –37%. How can we quantify this uncertainty?

The "surprise" return in any scenario is the difference between the actual return and the expected return. For example, in a boom (scenario 4) the surprise is $r(4) - E(r) = 30\% - 10\% = 20\%$. In a severe recession (scenario 1), the surprise is $r(1) - E(r) = -37\% - 10\% = -47\%$.

Uncertainty surrounding the investment is a function of both the magnitudes and the probabilities of the possible surprises. To summarize uncertainty with a single number, we define the **variance** as the expected value of the *squared* deviation from the mean (the expected squared "surprise" across scenarios).

variance

The expected value of the squared deviation from the mean.

$$\text{Var}(r) \equiv \sigma^2 = \sum_{s=1}^{S} p(s)\,[r(s) - E(r)]^2 \tag{5.11}$$

We square the deviations because otherwise, negative deviations would offset positive deviations with the result that the expected deviation from the mean return would necessarily be zero. Squared deviations are necessarily positive. Squaring exaggerates large (positive or negative) deviations and deemphasizes small deviations.

Another result of squaring deviations is that the variance has a dimension of percent squared. To give the measure of risk the same dimension as expected return (%), we use the **standard deviation,** defined as the square root of the variance:

standard deviation

The square root of the variance.

$$SD(r) \equiv \sigma = \sqrt{\text{Var}(r)} \tag{5.12}$$

EXAMPLE 5.4

Expected Return and Standard Deviation

Applying Equation 5.10 to the data in Spreadsheet 5.1, we find that the expected rate of return on the stock index fund is

$$E(r) = .05 \times (-37) + .25 \times (-11) + .40 \times 14 + .30 \times 30 = 10\%$$

We use Equation 5.11 to find the variance. First we take the difference between the holding-period return in each scenario and the mean return, then we square that difference, and finally we multiply by the probability of each scenario. The sum of the probability-weighted squared deviations is the variance.

$$\sigma^2 = .05(-37 - 10)^2 + .25(-11 - 10)^2 + .40(14 - 10)^2 + .30(30 - 10)^2$$

and so the standard deviation is

$$\sigma = \sqrt{347.10} = 18.63\%$$

Column G of Spreadsheet 5.1 replicates these calculations. Each entry in that column is the squared deviation from the mean multiplied by the probability of that scenario. The sum of the probability-weighted squared deviations that appears in cell G7 is the variance, and the square root of that value is the standard deviation (in cell G8).[3]

---

[3]The Excel function SUMPRODUCT provides a convenient way to calculate both mean and variance. For example, SUMPRODUCT(B3:B6,C3:C6) will multiply each element of the first column specified (column B) by the corresponding element of the second column (column C), and then add up each of those products. In Spreadsheet 5.1, each of these products would be the probability of each scenario times the holding period return in that scenario. The sum of those products is the expected return (see Equation 5.10). Similarly, SUMPRODUCT(B3:B6,F3:F6) will multiply the probability of each scenario by the squared deviation from the mean in that scenario (column F), add up those terms, and thus provide the variance of returns (Equation 5.11).

The current value of a stock portfolio is $23 million. A financial analyst summarizes the uncertainty about next year's holding-period return using the scenario analysis in the following spreadsheet. What are the holding-period returns of the portfolio in each scenario? Calculate the expected holding-period return and the standard deviation of returns.

	A	B	C	D	E
1	Business conditions	Scenario, s	Probability, p	End-of-year value ($ million)	Annual dividend ($ million)
2	High growth	1	0.30	35	4.40
3	Normal growth	2	0.45	27	4.00
4	No growth	3	0.20	15	4.00
5	Recession	4	0.05	8	2.00

The Normal Distribution

The normal distribution is central to the theory *and* practice of investments. Its familiar bell-shaped plot is symmetric, with identical values for all three standard measures of "typical" results: the mean (the expected value discussed earlier), the median (the value above and below which we expect 50% of the observations), and the mode (the most likely value).

Figure 5.2 illustrates a normal distribution with a mean of 10% and standard deviation (SD) of 20%. Notice that the probabilities are highest for outcomes near the mean and are significantly lower for outcomes far from the mean.

But what do we mean by an outcome "far" from the mean? A return 15% below the mean would hardly be noteworthy if typical volatility were high, for example, if the standard deviation of returns were 20%, but that same outcome would be highly unusual if the standard deviation were only 5%. For this reason, it is often useful to think about deviations from the mean in terms of how many standard deviations they represent. If the standard deviation is 20%, that 15% negative surprise would be only three-fourths of a standard deviation, unfortunate perhaps, but not uncommon. But if the standard deviation were only 5%, a 15% deviation would be a "three-sigma event," and quite rare.

We can transform any normally distributed return, r_i, into a "standard deviation score," by first subtracting the mean return (to obtain the distance from the mean or the return "surprise") and then dividing by the standard deviation (which enables us to measure distance from the mean in units of standard deviations).

$$r_i^{std} = \frac{r_i - E(r_i)}{\sigma_i} \qquad (5.13A)$$

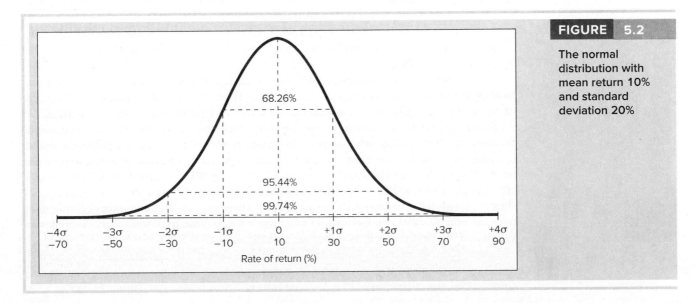

FIGURE 5.2

The normal distribution with mean return 10% and standard deviation 20%

The standardized return, which we denote using the superscript std, is normally distributed with a mean of zero and a standard deviation of 1.

Conversely, we can start with a standardized return and recover the original return by multiplying the standardized return by the standard deviation and adding back the mean:

$$r_i = E(r_i) + r_i^{std} \times \sigma_i \qquad \text{(5.13B)}$$

In fact, this is how we drew Figure 5.2. Start with a standard normal (mean = 0 and SD = 1); next, multiply the distance from the mean by the assumed standard deviation of 20%; finally, recenter the mean away from zero by adding 10%. This gives us a normal variable with mean 10% and standard deviation 20%.

Figure 5.2 shows that when returns are normally distributed, roughly two-thirds (more precisely, 68.26%) of the observations fall within one standard deviation of the mean, that is, the probability that any observation in a sample of returns would be no more than one standard deviation away from the mean is 68.26%. Deviations from the mean of more than two SDs are even rarer: 95.44% of the observations are expected to lie within this range. Finally, only 2.6 out of 1,000 observations are expected to deviate from the mean by three or more SDs.

Two special properties of the normal distribution lead to critical simplifications of investment management when returns are normally distributed:

1. The return on a portfolio comprising two or more assets whose returns are normally distributed also will be normally distributed.

2. The normal distribution is completely described by its mean and standard deviation. No other statistic is needed to learn about the behavior of normally distributed returns.

   These two properties in turn imply this far-reaching conclusion:

3. The standard deviation is the appropriate measure of risk for a portfolio of assets with normally distributed returns. In this case, no other statistic can improve the risk assessment conveyed by the standard deviation of a portfolio.

Normality and the Investment Horizon

The fact that portfolios of normally distributed assets also are normally distributed greatly simplifies analysis of risk because standard deviation, an easy-to-calculate number, is the appropriate risk measure for normally distributed portfolios.

But even if returns are normal for any particular time period, will they also be normal for other holding periods? Suppose that monthly rates are normally distributed with a mean of 1%. The expected annual rate of return is then $1.01^{12} - 1$. Can this annual rate, which is a nonlinear function of the monthly return, also be normally distributed? Unfortunately, the answer is no. Similarly, if daily returns are normally distributed, then monthly rates, which equal $(1 + \text{daily rate})^{30} - 1$, would not be. So, do we really get to enjoy the simplifications offered by the normal distribution?

Despite these potential complications, when returns over very short time periods (e.g., an hour or even a day) are normally distributed, then HPRs up to holding periods as long as a month will be *nearly* normal, so in practice we often can treat them as if they are normal.

To see why relatively short-term rates are still nearly normal, consider these calculations: Suppose that the continuously compounded return is normal and that in a particular month it equals .01 (i.e., 1%; we must work with decimals when using continuously compounded rates). This implies an effective monthly rate of $e^{.01} - 1 = .01005$. The difference between the effective and continuously compounded rates here is trivial, only one-half of a basis point. For shorter periods the difference will be smaller still. Therefore, when continuously compounded rates are normal, rates over periods up to a month are so close to continuously compounded values that we can treat them as if they are actually normal.

Longer-term, for example, annual HPRs will indeed deviate more substantially from normality. Using our numbers, with a continuously compounded rate of 1% per month, the continuously compounded annual rate would be 12%, and the effective annual rate (using Equation 5.5A) would be $e^{.12} - 1 = .1275$. At this horizon, the difference between the effective annual rate and the continuously compounded rate is meaningful, .75%. But even here, if we express HPRs as continuously compounded rates, they will remain normally distributed. The practical implication is this: Use continuously compounded rates when normality plays a crucial role.

Another important aspect of (normal) continuously compounded rates over time is this: Just as the total continuously compounded rate grows in direct proportion to the length of the investment period, so does the variance (*not* the standard deviation) of the total continuously compounded return. Hence, for an asset with annual continuously compounded SD of .20 (20%), the annual variance is $.20^2 = .04$, and the quarterly variance is .01, implying a quarterly standard deviation of .10, or 10%. Because variance grows in direct proportion to time, the standard deviation grows in proportion to the square root of time.

Deviation from Normality and Tail Risk

Standard deviation measures the dispersion of possible asset returns. But suppose you are worried more specifically about large investment losses in worst-case scenarios for your portfolio. You might ask: "How much would I lose in a fairly extreme outcome, for example, if my return were in the fifth percentile of the distribution?" You can expect your investment experience to be worse than this value only 5% of the time and better 95% of the time. In investments parlance, this cutoff is called the **value at risk** (denoted by **VaR,** to distinguish it from Var, the common notation for variance). A loss-averse investor might desire to limit portfolio VaR, that is, limit the loss corresponding to a particular threshold probability such as 5%. The most common probability thresholds used for VaR analysis are 5% and 1%.

For normally distributed returns, the precise value of the VaR can be derived from the mean and standard deviation of the distribution. We can calculate the 5% VaR using Excel's standard normal function = NORMSINV(0.05). This function computes the fifth percentile of a normal distribution with a mean of zero and a variance of 1, which turns out to be −1.64485. In other words, a value that is 1.64485 standard deviations below the mean would be in the fifth percentile of the distribution and, therefore, correspond to a VaR of 5%.

$$\text{VaR}(5\%) = E(r) + (-1.64485)\sigma \tag{5.14}$$

We can also obtain this value directly from Excel's *nonstandard* normal distribution function = NORMINV(.05, $E(r)$, σ).

When returns are *not* normal, the VaR conveys important additional information beyond mean and standard deviation, specifically, the exposure to severe losses arising from deviations from normality. Faced with a distribution of actual returns that may not be normally distributed, we must estimate the VaR directly. The 5% VaR is the fifth-percentile rate of return. If the probability distribution stipulated in your scenario analysis does not specify a return exactly corresponding to a fifth-percentile value, you will need to use interpolation to find the 5% VaR.

In practice, analysts sometimes compare the historical VaR to the VaR implied by a normal distribution with the same mean and SD as the sample rates. The difference between these VaR values is one measure of the departure of the observed rates from normality.

value at risk (VaR)

Measure of downside risk. The worst loss that will be suffered with a given probability, often 1% or 5%.

---

a. Return to Concept Check 5.3. What is the 5% VaR of the portfolio?
b. What is the VaR of a portfolio with normally distributed returns with the same mean and standard deviation as this portfolio?

CONCEPT check **5.4**

Because risk is highly sensitive to extreme negative returns, three additional statistics are used to indicate whether a portfolio's probability distribution differs significantly from normality with respect to potential extreme values. The first is **kurtosis,** which compares the frequency of extreme values (good or bad) to that of the normal distribution. The kurtosis of

kurtosis

Measure of the fatness of the tails of a probability distribution relative to that of a normal distribution. Indicates likelihood of extreme outcomes.

the normal distribution is zero, so positive values indicate higher frequency of extreme values than this benchmark. Kurtosis sometimes is called a measure of "fat tails," as plots of probability distributions with higher likelihood of extreme events will be higher than the normal distribution at both ends or "tails" of the distribution. Likewise, exposure to extreme events is often called *tail risk,* because these are outcomes in the far reaches or tails of the probability distribution.

Just as variance is the average value of *squared* deviations from the average, kurtosis is calculated from the average value of deviations raised to the *fourth* power (expressed as a multiple of the fourth power of standard deviation). Because the deviations are raised to the fourth power while they are raised only to the second power when calculating variance, kurtosis is much more sensitive to extreme outcomes and therefore is a natural measure of tail risk.

skew

Measure of the asymmetry of a probability distribution.

The second statistic is the **skew,** which measures the asymmetry of the distribution. Skew is the average value of deviations from the mean raised to the *third* power (expressed as a multiple of the third power of standard deviation). When negative deviations are raised to an odd power, the result remains negative. Therefore, negative values of skew indicate that extreme *bad* outcomes are more frequent than extreme positive ones while positive skew implies that extreme positive outcomes are more frequent. In contrast, because kurtosis takes deviations to an even power, all outcomes are positive, so kurtosis measures the tendency to observe outcomes in *either* end of the probability distribution, positive or negative.

Finally, a third common measure of tail risk is the relative frequency of large, negative returns compared with those frequencies in a normal distribution with the same mean and standard deviation. Extreme returns are often called *jumps,* as the stock price makes a big sudden movement. A rough measure of downside risk compares the fraction of observations with returns 3 or more standard deviations below the mean to the relative frequency of negative 3-sigma returns in the normal distribution, which is only 0.13%, that is, 1.3 observations per 1,000. Thus, these returns are rare, but when they occur, they have a large impact on investment performance.

Risk Premiums and Risk Aversion

How much, if anything, would you invest in the index stock fund described in Spreadsheet 5.1? First, you must ask how much of an expected reward is offered to compensate for the risk of the portfolio.

risk-free rate

The rate of return that can be earned with certainty, often measured by the rate on Treasury bills.

We measure "reward" as the difference between the expected HPR on the index fund and the **risk-free rate,** the rate you can earn on Treasury bills. We call this difference the **risk premium.** If the risk-free rate in the example is 4% per year, and the expected index fund return is 10%, then the risk premium is 6% per year.

The rate of return on Treasury bills also varies over time. However, we know the rate of return on T-bills *at the beginning* of the holding period, while we can't know the return we will earn on risky assets until the end of the holding period. Therefore, to study the risk premium on risky assets we compile a series of **excess returns,** that is, returns in excess of the T-bill rate in each period. A reasonable forecast of an asset's risk premium is the average of its historical excess returns.

risk premium

An expected return in excess of that on risk-free securities.

excess return

Rate of return in excess of the risk-free rate.

The degree to which investors are willing to commit funds to stocks depends in part on their **risk aversion.** It seems obvious that investors are risk averse in the sense that, without a positive risk premium, they would not be willing to invest in stocks. In theory then, there must always be a positive risk premium on risky assets in order to induce risk-averse investors to hold the existing supply of these assets.

risk aversion

Reluctance to accept risk.

A positive risk premium distinguishes speculation from gambling. Investors taking on risk to earn a risk premium are speculating. Speculation is undertaken *despite* the risk because of a favorable risk-return trade-off. In contrast, gambling is the assumption of risk for no purpose beyond the enjoyment of the risk itself. Gamblers take on risk even without a risk premium.

To determine an investor's optimal portfolio strategy, we need to quantify his degree of risk aversion. To do so, we look at how willing he is to trade off risk against expected return. An obvious benchmark is the risk-free asset, which has neither volatility nor a risk premium: It pays a certain rate of return, r_f. Risk-averse investors will not hold risky assets without the prospect of earning some premium above the risk-free rate. Thus, a natural way to estimate risk aversion is to look at the risk-return trade-off of portfolios in which individuals have been willing to invest. We infer higher risk aversion if they have demanded higher risk premiums for any given level of risk.

More specifically, an individual's degree of risk aversion can be inferred by contrasting the risk premium on the investor's entire wealth (his complete portfolio, C), $E(r_C) - r_f$, against the variance of the portfolio return, σ_C^2. The risk premium and volatility of the *individual* assets in the complete wealth portfolio do not concern the investor here. All that counts is the bottom line: *complete portfolio* risk premium versus *complete portfolio* risk.

The ratio of risk premium to variance measures the "reward" demanded per unit of volatility. For example if we observed an investor whose entire wealth has been invested in portfolio Q with annual risk premium of .10 (10%) and variance of .0256 (SD = .16, or 16%), we would infer this investor's degree of risk aversion as:

$$A = \frac{E(r_Q) - r_f}{\sigma_Q^2} = \frac{0.10}{0.0256} = 3.91 \qquad (5.15)$$

We call the ratio of a portfolio's risk premium to its variance the **price of risk**.[4] Later in the section, we turn the question around and ask how an investor with a given degree of risk aversion, say, $A = 3.91$, should allocate wealth between the risky and risk-free assets.

To get an idea of the risk aversion exhibited by investors in U.S. capital markets, we can look at a representative portfolio held by these investors. Assume that all short-term borrowing offsets lending; that is, average net borrowing and lending are zero. In that case, the average investor holds a complete portfolio represented by a stock market index such as the S&P 500; call it M. Using a long-term series of historical returns on the S&P 500 to estimate investors' expectations about mean and variance, we can recast Equation 5.15 with these stock market data to obtain an estimate of average risk aversion. Roughly speaking, the average excess return on the market has been .08, and variance has been nearly .04. Therefore, we infer average risk aversion as:

$$\overline{A} = \frac{\text{Average}(r_M) - r_f}{\text{Sample } \sigma_M^2} \approx \frac{0.08}{0.04} = 2 \qquad (5.16)$$

The price of risk of the market index portfolio, which reflects the risk aversion of the average investor, is sometimes called the *market price of risk*. Conventional wisdom holds that plausible estimates for the value of A lie in the range of $1.5 - 4$.

The Sharpe Ratio

Risk aversion implies that investors will demand a higher reward (as measured by their portfolio risk premium) to accept higher portfolio volatility. A statistic commonly used to rank portfolios in terms of this risk-return trade-off is the **Sharpe ratio,** defined as

$$S = \frac{\text{Portfolio risk premium}}{\text{Standard deviation of portfolio excess return}} = \frac{E(r_P) - r_f}{\sigma_P} \qquad (5.17)$$

A risk-free asset would have a risk premium of zero and a standard deviation of zero. Therefore, the Sharpe ratio of a risky portfolio quantifies the incremental reward (the increase in risk premium) for each increase of 1% in the portfolio standard deviation (SD). For example, the Sharpe ratio of a portfolio with an annual risk premium of 8% and standard deviation of 20% is 8/20 = 0.4. A higher Sharpe ratio indicates a better reward per unit of SD, in other words, a more efficient portfolio. Portfolio analysis in terms of mean and standard deviation (or variance) of excess returns is called **mean-variance analysis.**

price of risk

The ratio of portfolio risk premium to variance.

Sharpe ratio

Ratio of portfolio risk premium to standard deviation.

mean-variance analysis

Evaluating portfolios according to their expected returns and standard deviations (or variances).

---

[4]Notice that when we use variance rather than SD, the price of risk of a portfolio does not depend on the holding period. The reason is that variance is proportional to the holding period. Since portfolio return and risk premium also are proportional to the holding period, the portfolio pays the same price of risk for any holding period.

A warning: We will see in the next chapter that while standard deviation is a useful risk measure for diversified portfolios, it is not a useful way to think about the risk of individual securities. Therefore, the Sharpe ratio is a valid statistic only for ranking *portfolios;* it is *not* appropriate for comparing individual assets. We will examine the historical Sharpe ratios of broadly diversified portfolios that reflect the performance of some important asset classes.

CONCEPT
check   **5.5**

a. A respected analyst forecasts that the return of the market index over the coming year will be 10%. The one-year T-bill rate is 5%. Examination of recent returns of the S&P 500 Index suggests that the standard deviation of returns will be 18%. What does this information suggest about the degree of risk aversion of the average investor, assuming that the average portfolio resembles the market index?

b. What is the Sharpe ratio of the index portfolio in (*a*)?

5.4 THE HISTORICAL RECORD

Using Time Series of Returns

Scenario analysis begins with a probability distribution of future returns. But where do the probabilities and rates of return come from? In large part, they are estimated from a sample of historical returns. Suppose we observe a 10-year time series of monthly returns on a diversified portfolio of stocks. We can interpret each of the 120 observations as one potential "scenario" offered to us by history. From this history, we can develop a scenario analysis of future returns.

As a first step, we estimate the expected return and standard deviation for the historical sample. We assume that each of the 120 returns represents one independent draw from the historical probability distribution. Hence, each return is assigned an equal probability of $1/120 = .0083$. When you use such equal probabilities in Equation 5.10, you obtain the arithmetic average of the observations, often used to estimate the mean return.

The same approach can be applied to VaR. We sort the returns from highest to lowest. The bottom six observations in a sample of 120 returns comprise the lower 5% of the distribution. The seventh observation from the bottom is just at the fifth percentile (it exceeds exactly 5% of the sample observations), and so it would be the 5% VaR for the historical sample.

Estimating variance from Equation 5.11 requires a minor modification. Remember that variance is the expected value of squared deviations from the mean return. But the true mean is not observable; when using historical data, we *estimate* it using the sample average. If we compute variance as the average of squared deviations from the sample average, we will slightly underestimate it because this procedure ignores the fact that the sample average necessarily includes some estimation error. The necessary correction turns out to be simple: With a sample of n observations, we divide the sum of the squared deviations from the sample average by $n - 1$ instead of n. This modification is sometimes called a correction for degrees of freedom bias. Thus, the estimates of variance and standard deviation from a time series of returns, r_t, are

$$\bar{r}_t = \frac{1}{n}\sum r_t; \ \text{Var}(r_t) = \frac{1}{n-1}\sum(r_t - \bar{r}_t)^2; \ \text{SD}(r_t) = \sqrt{\text{Var}(r_t)} \tag{5.18}$$

EXAMPLE 5.5

Estimating Mean and Standard Deviation from Historical Data

To illustrate how to calculate average returns and standard deviations from historical data, let's compute these statistics for the returns on a hypothetical stock index fund using five years of data from the following table. The average return over this period is 16.7%, computed by dividing the sum of column (1), below, by the number of observations. In column (2), we take the deviation of each year's

(continued)

return from the 16.7% average return. In column (3), we calculate the squared deviation. The variance is, from Equation 5.18, the sum of the five squared deviations divided by (5 − 1). The standard deviation is the square root of the variance. If you input the column of rates into an Excel spreadsheet, the AVERAGE and STDEV.S functions will give you the statistics directly.

EXAMPLE 5.5

Estimating Mean and Standard Deviation from Historical Data (concluded)

Year	(1) Rate of Return(%)	(2) Deviation from Average Return(%)	(3) Squared Deviation
1	16.9	0.2	0.0
2	31.3	14.6	213.2
3	−3.2	−19.9	396.0
4	30.7	14.0	196.0
5	7.7	−9.0	81.0
Total	83.4		886.2

Average rate of return = 83.4/5 = 16.7%

Variance = 886.2/(5 − 1) = 221.55

Standard deviation = $\sqrt{221.55}$ = 14.9%

Risk and Return: A First Look

We begin our empirical examination of risk and return by comparing the performance of Treasury bills, long-term (specifically, 10-year maturity) Treasury bonds, and a diversified portfolio of U.S. stocks. T-bills are widely considered the least risky of all assets. There is essentially no risk that the U.S. government will fail to honor its commitments to these investors, and their short maturities mean that their prices are stable. Long-term U.S. Treasury bonds are also certain to be repaid, but the prices of these bonds fluctuate as interest rates vary, so they impose meaningful risk. Finally, common stocks are the riskiest of the three groups of securities. As a part-owner of the corporation, your return will depend on the success or failure of the firm.

Our stock portfolio is the broadest possible U.S. equity portfolio, including all stocks listed on the NYSE, AMEX, and NASDAQ. We denote this as "the U.S. market index." Because larger firms play a greater role in the economy, this index is a value-weighted portfolio and therefore dominated by the large-firm corporate sector. The monthly data series include returns on these stocks from July 1926 to March 2017, a sample period spanning about 90 years. The annual return series comprise full-year returns from 1927–2016.

Figure 5.3 is a frequency distribution of annual returns on these three portfolios. The greater volatility of stock returns compared to T-bill or T-bond returns is immediately apparent. Compared to stock returns, the distribution of T-bond returns is far more concentrated in the middle of the distribution, with far fewer outliers. The distribution of T-bill returns is even tighter. More to the point, the spread of the T-bill distribution does not reflect risk but rather changes in the risk-free rate over time.[5]

While the frequency distribution is a handy visual representation of investment risk, we also need a way to quantify that volatility; this is provided by the standard deviation of returns.

---

[5]You may wonder about the negative T-bill rates that show up in the frequency distribution in Panel A of Figure 5.3. The federal government did not issue T-bills until the 1940s. For earlier dates, we use commercial paper as the closest approximation to a short-term risk-free asset. In a few instances, they were issued slightly above par value and thus yielded slightly negative rates. Anyone buying a T-bill knows exactly what the (nominal) return will be when the bill matures, so variation in the return is not a reflection of risk over that short holding period.

FIGURE 5.3

Frequency distribution of annual returns on U.S. Treasury bills, Treasury bonds, and common stocks, 1927–2016

(A) Treasury bills

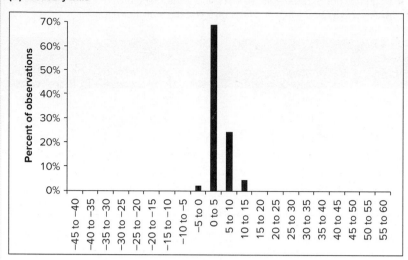

(B) 10-year Treasury bonds

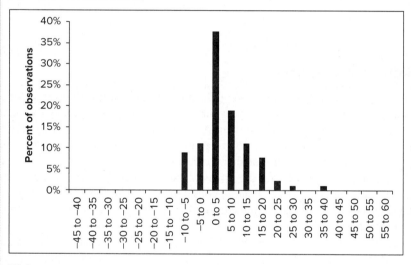

(C) Common stocks

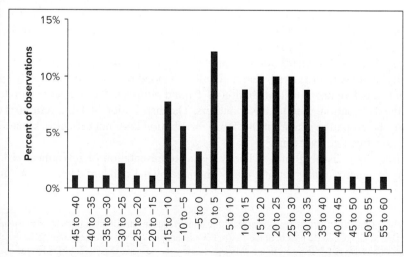

TABLE 5.3	Risk and return of investments in major asset classes, 1927–2016		
	T-bills	**T-bonds**	**Stocks**
Arithmetic average	3.42	5.51	11.91
Risk premium	N/A	2.08	8.48
Standard deviation	3.14	8.14	19.99
max	14.71	38.07	56.38
min	−0.02	−8.47	−43.73

Table 5.3 shows that the standard deviation of the return on stocks over this period, 19.99%, was more than double that of T-bonds, 8.14%, and more than six times that of T-bills. Of course, that greater risk brought with it greater reward. The excess return on stocks (i.e., the return in excess of the T-bill rate) averaged 8.48% per year, providing a generous risk premium to equity investors.

Table 5.3 uses a fairly long sample period to estimate the average level of risk and reward. While averages may well be useful indications of what we might expect going forward, we nevertheless should expect both risk and expected return to fluctuate over time. Figure 5.4 plots the standard deviation of the market's excess return in each year calculated from the 12 most recent monthly returns. While market risk clearly ebbs and flows, aside from its abnormally high values during the Great Depression, there does not seem to be any obvious trend in its level. This gives us more confidence that historical risk estimates provide useful guidance about the future.

Of course, as we emphasized in the previous sections, unless returns are normally distributed, standard deviation is not sufficient to measure risk. We also need to think about "tail risk," that is, our exposure to unlikely but very large outcomes in the left tail of the probability

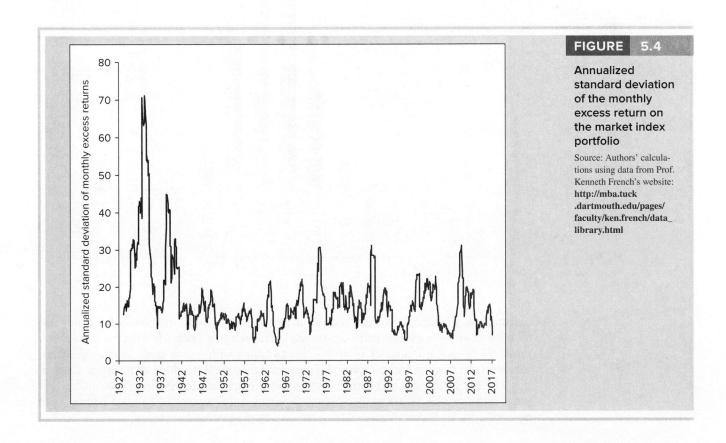

FIGURE 5.4

Annualized standard deviation of the monthly excess return on the market index portfolio

Source: Authors' calculations using data from Prof. Kenneth French's website: **http://mba.tuck .dartmouth.edu/pages/ faculty/ken.french/data_ library.html**

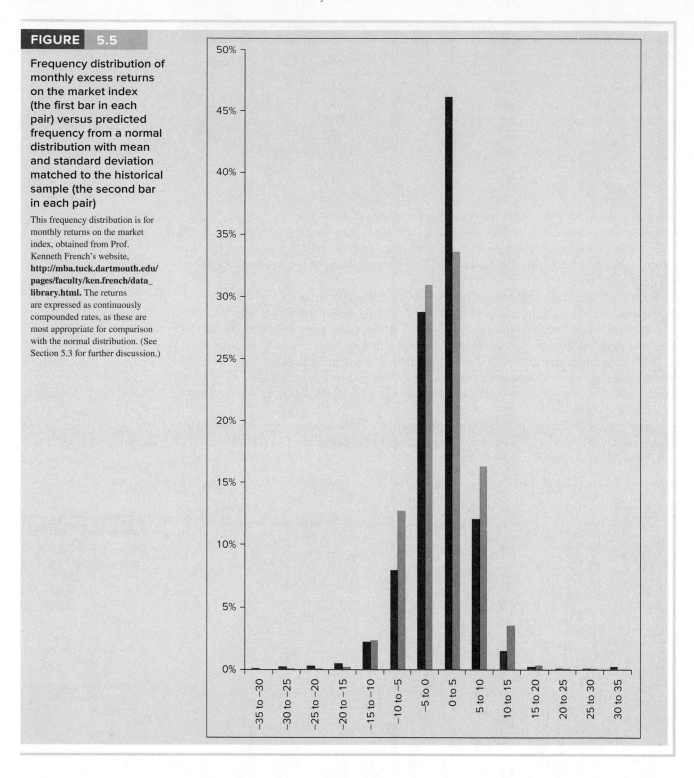

Frequency distribution of monthly excess returns on the market index (the first bar in each pair) versus predicted frequency from a normal distribution with mean and standard deviation matched to the historical sample (the second bar in each pair)

This frequency distribution is for monthly returns on the market index, obtained from Prof. Kenneth French's website, **http://mba.tuck.dartmouth.edu/ pages/faculty/ken.french/data_ library.html.** The returns are expressed as continuously compounded rates, as these are most appropriate for comparison with the normal distribution. (See Section 5.3 for further discussion.)

distributions. Figure 5.5 provides some evidence of this exposure. It shows a frequency distribution of *monthly* excess returns on the market index since 1926. The first bar in each pair shows the historical frequency of excess returns falling within each range, while the second bar shows the frequencies that we *would* observe if these returns followed a normal distribution with the same mean and variance as the actual empirical distribution. You can see here some evidence of a fat-tailed distribution: The actual frequencies of extreme returns, both high and low, are higher than would be predicted by the normal distribution.

Further evidence on the distribution of excess equity returns is given in Table 5.4. Here, we use monthly data on both the market index and, for comparison, several "style" portfolios. You may remember from Chapter 4, Figure 4.5, that the performance of mutual funds is routinely evaluated relative to other funds with similar investment styles. (See the Morningstar style box in Figure 4.5.) Style is commonly defined along two dimensions: size (do the funds invest in large cap or small cap firms?) and value versus growth. Firms with high ratios of market value to book value are viewed as "growth firms" because, to justify their high prices relative to current book values, the market must anticipate rapid growth.

The use of style portfolios as a benchmark for performance evaluation traces back to influential papers by Eugene Fama and Kenneth French, who extensively documented that firm size and the book value-to-market value ratio predict average returns; these patterns have since been corroborated in stock exchanges around the world.[6] A high book-to-market (B/M) ratio is interpreted as an indication that the value of the firm is driven primarily by assets already in place, rather than the prospect of high future growth. These are called "value" firms. In contrast, a low book-to-market ratio is typical of firms whose market value derives mostly from ample growth opportunities. Realized average returns, other things equal, historically have been higher for value firms than for growth firms and for small firms than for large ones. The Fama-French database includes returns on portfolios of U.S. stocks sorted by size (Big; Small) and by B/M ratios (High; Medium; Low).[7]

Following the Fama-French classifications, we classify firms in the top 30% of B/M ratio as "value firms" and firms ranked in the bottom 30% as "growth firms." We also split firms into above and below median levels of market capitalization to establish subsamples of small versus large firms. We thus obtain four comparison portfolios: Big/Growth, Big/Value, Small/Growth, and Small/Value.

TABLE 5.4	Statistics for monthly excess returns on the market index and four "style" portfolios				
	Market index	Big/ Growth	Big/ Value	Small/ Growth	Small/ Value
A. July 1926–March 2017					
Mean excess return (annualized)	8.41	8.10	11.96	8.75	15.57
Standard deviation (annualized)	18.58	18.40	24.82	26.15	28.32
Sharpe ratio	0.45	0.44	0.48	0.33	0.55
Skew	0.19	−0.10	1.63	0.69	2.18
Kurtosis	7.82	5.63	18.25	7.83	22.15
VaR (1%) actual (monthly) returns	−13.81	−14.50	−19.48	−20.56	−20.42
VaR (1%) normal distribution	−11.82	−11.73	−15.75	−16.87	−17.82
% of monthly returns more than 3 SD below mean	0.94%	0.75%	0.85%	0.85%	0.57%
B. January 1952–March 2017					
Mean excess return (annualized)	7.68	7.36	10.35	7.23	13.65
Standard deviation (annualized)	14.83	15.42	16.50	22.28	18.47
Sharpe ratio	0.52	0.48	0.63	0.32	0.74
Skew	−0.53	−0.37	−0.32	−0.38	−0.34
Kurtosis	1.93	1.84	2.26	2.15	3.42
VaR (1%) actual (monthly) returns	−10.77	−10.97	−12.49	−17.08	−15.15
VaR (1%) normal distribution	−9.32	−9.74	−10.22	−14.36	−11.27
% of monthly returns more than 3 SD below mean	0.47%	0.47%	0.75%	0.66%	0.85%

Source: Authors' calculations using data from Prof. Kenneth French's website: **http://mba.tuck.dartmouth.edu/pages/faculty/ken.french/data_library.html.**

[6]This literature began in earnest with their publication, "The Cross Section of Expected Stock Returns," *Journal of Finance* 47, pp. 427–465.

[7]We use the Fama-French data to construct Figures 5.3 to 5.5 and Tables 5.3 and 5.4. The database is available at: **http://mba.tuck.dartmouth.edu/pages/faculty/ken.french/data_library.html.**

Table 5.4, Panel A, presents results using monthly data for the full sample period, July 1926–March 2017. The top two lines show the annualized average excess return and standard deviation of each portfolio. The broad market index outperformed T-bills by an average of 8.41% per year, with a standard deviation of 18.58%, resulting in a Sharpe ratio (third line) of 8.41/18.58 = .45. In line with the Fama-French analysis, small/value firms had the highest average excess return and the best risk–return trade-off with a Sharpe ratio of .55. However, Figure 5.5 shows that the distribution of stock returns appears to exhibit tails that are fatter than the normal distribution, so we need to consider risk measures beyond just the standard deviation. The table therefore also presents several measures of tail risk.

Some of these other risk measures actually do not show meaningful departures from the symmetric normal distribution. Skew is generally near zero; if downside risk were substantially greater than upside potential, we would expect skew to be negative, but in fact, it actually tends to be positive. In addition, while the actual 1% VaR of these portfolios are uniformly higher than the 1% VaR that would be predicted from normal distributions with means and standard deviations matched to the historical sample, the differences between the empirical and predicted VaR statistics are not large. By this metric as well, the normal appears to be a decent approximation to the actual return distribution.

However, there is other evidence suggesting fat tails in the return distributions of these portfolios. To begin, note that kurtosis (the measure of the "fatness" of both tails of the distribution) is uniformly high. Investors are, of course, concerned with the lower (left) tail of the distribution; they do not lose sleep over their exposure to extreme good returns! Unfortunately, the table suggests that the left tail of the return distribution is overrepresented compared to the normal distribution. If excess returns were normally distributed, then only .13% of them would fall more than 3 standard deviations below the mean. In fact, the bottom line of the panel shows that actual incidence of excess returns below that cutoff are at least a few multiples of .13% for each portfolio.

Figure 5.1 showed us that the postwar years (more accurately, the years after 1951) have been far more predictable, at least with respect to inflation and interest rates. This suggests that it may be instructive to examine stock returns in the post-1951 period as well to see if risk and return characteristics for equity investments have changed meaningfully in the more recent period. The relevant statistics are given in Panel B of Table 5.4. Perhaps not surprisingly in light of the history of inflation and interest rates, the more recent period is in fact less volatile. Standard deviations for all five portfolios are noticeably lower in recent years, and kurtosis, our measure of fat tails, drops dramatically. VaR also falls. While the percentage of excess returns that are more than 3 SD below the mean changes inconsistently across portfolios, because SD is lower in this period, those negative returns are also less dramatic.

To summarize, the frequency distribution in Figure 5.5 and the statistics in Table 5.4 for the market index as well as the style portfolios provide some, admittedly inconsistent, evidence of fat tails, so investors should not take normality for granted. On the other hand, extreme returns are in fact quite uncommon, especially in more recent years. The incidence of returns on the market index in the post-1951 period that are worse than 3 standard deviations below the mean is .47%, compared to a prediction of .13% for the normal distribution. The "excess" rate of extreme bad outcomes is thus only .34%, or about once in 294 months (24½ years). So it is not unreasonable to accept the simplification offered by normality as an acceptable approximation as we think about constructing and evaluating our portfolios.

5.5 ASSET ALLOCATION ACROSS RISKY AND RISK-FREE PORTFOLIOS

History shows that long-term bonds have been riskier investments than investments in Treasury bills and that stock investments have been riskier still. At the same time, the riskier investments have offered higher average returns. But investors do not make all-or-nothing choices from these investment classes. They normally include securities from all asset classes in their portfolios.

A simple strategy to control portfolio risk is to specify the fraction of the portfolio invested in broad asset classes such as stocks, bonds, and safe assets. This aspect of portfolio management is called **asset allocation** and plays an important role in the determination of portfolio performance. Consider this statement by John Bogle, made when he was the chairman of the Vanguard Group of Investment Companies:

> The most fundamental decision of investing is the allocation of your assets: How much should you own in stock? How much should you own in bonds? How much should you own in cash reserves? . . . That decision [has been shown to account] for an astonishing 94% of the differences in total returns achieved by institutionally managed pension funds. . . . There is no reason to believe that the same relationship does not also hold true for individual investors.[8]

The most basic form of asset allocation classifies assets as either risky or risk free. The fraction of the portfolio placed in risky assets is called the **capital allocation to risky assets** and speaks directly to investor risk aversion.

To focus on the capital allocation decision, we think about an investor who allocates funds between T-bills and a portfolio of risky assets. We can envision the risky portfolio, *P*, as a mutual fund or ETF (exchange-traded fund) that includes a bundle of risky assets in desired, fixed proportions. Thus, when we shift wealth into and out of *P*, we do not change the relative proportion of the various securities within the risky portfolio. We put off until the next chapter the question of how to best construct the risky portfolio. We call the overall portfolio composed of the risk-free asset and the risky portfolio the **complete portfolio** that includes the investor's entire wealth.

The Risk-Free Asset

The power to tax and to control the money supply lets the government, and only the government, issue default-free (Treasury) bonds and bills. The default-free guarantee by itself is not sufficient to make the bonds risk-free in real terms, since inflation affects purchasing power. The only risk-free asset in real terms would be a price-indexed government bond such as TIPS. Even then, a default-free, perfectly indexed bond offers a guaranteed real return to an investor only if the maturity of the bond is identical to the investor's desired holding period. These qualifications notwithstanding, it is common to view Treasury bills as *the* risk-free asset. Any inflation uncertainty over the course of a few weeks, or even months, is negligible compared to the uncertainty of stock market returns.

In practice, most investors treat a broader range of money market instruments as effectively risk-free assets. All the money market instruments are virtually immune to interest rate risk (unexpected fluctuations in the price of a bond due to changes in market interest rates) because of their short maturities, and all are fairly safe in terms of default or credit risk.

Money market mutual funds hold, for the most part, three types of securities: Treasury bills, other short-term Treasury and U.S. agency securities, and repurchase agreements. They also hold bank certificates of deposit (CDs) and commercial paper. These instruments do carry some default risk and therefore offer higher promised yields than Treasury bills. A history of the yield spread between 90-day CDs and T-bills appeared in Figure 2.2 in Chapter 2. Nevertheless, the risk of any of these money market instruments is trivial compared to that of long-term bonds. Hence, we treat money market funds, as well as T-bills, as representing the most easily accessible risk-free asset for most investors.

Portfolio Expected Return and Risk

Consider the hierarchy of decisions an investor must make in a capital allocation framework. The properties of the risky portfolio are summarized by expected return and risk, as measured by standard deviation. The risk-free asset has a standard deviation of zero: Its rate of return is

asset allocation
Portfolio choice among broad investment classes.

capital allocation to risky assets
The choice between risky and risk-free assets.

complete portfolio
The entire portfolio including risky and risk-free assets.

[8]John C. Bogle, *Bogle on Mutual Funds* (Burr Ridge, IL: Irwin Professional Publishing, 1994), p. 235.

known. The investor must decide on the fraction of the *complete* portfolio that will be allocated to the risky portfolio. To make this choice, one must first determine the expected return and risk corresponding to any possible allocation. This is the technical part of the allocation decision.

Given the available trade-off between risk and return, which is common to all investors, each individual can choose his or her preferred allocation between the risky portfolio and the risk-free asset. This choice depends on personal preferences, specifically risk aversion. We begin with the risk-return trade-off.

Because the composition of the risky portfolio, *P*, already has been determined, the only concern here is with the proportion of the investment budget (*y*) to be allocated to it. The remaining proportion (1 − *y*) is to be invested in the risk-free asset, which has a rate of return denoted r_f.

We denote the *actual* risky rate of return on *P* by r_P, the *expected* rate of return by $E(r_P)$, and its standard deviation by σ_P. In our numerical example, we assume $E(r_P) = 15\%$, $\sigma_P = 22\%$, and $r_f = 7\%$. Thus, the risk premium on the risky asset is $E(r_P) - r_f = 8\%$.

Let's start with two extreme cases. If you invest all of your funds in the risky asset, that is, $y = 1$, the expected return on your complete portfolio will be 15% and the standard deviation will be 22%. This combination of risk and return is plotted as point *P* in Figure 5.6. At the other extreme, you might put all of your funds into the risk-free asset, that is, $y = 0$. In this case, you would earn a riskless return of 7%. (This choice is plotted as point *F* in Figure 5.6.)

Now consider more moderate choices. For example, if you allocate equal amounts of your complete portfolio, *C*, to the risky and risk-free assets, that is, you choose $y = .5$, the expected return on the complete portfolio will be the average of $E(r_P)$ and r_f. Therefore, $E(r_C) = .5 \times 7\% + .5 \times 15\% = 11\%$. The risk premium of the complete portfolio is therefore 11% − 7% = 4%, which is half of the risk premium of *P*. The standard deviation of the portfolio also is one-half of *P*'s, that is, 11%. When you reduce the fraction of the complete portfolio allocated to the risky asset by half, you reduce both the risk and risk premium by half.

To generalize, the risk premium of the complete portfolio, *C*, equals the risk premium of the risky asset times the fraction of the portfolio invested in the risky asset:

$$E(r_C) - r_f = y[E(r_P) - r_f]$$

(5.19)

The standard deviation of the complete portfolio equals the standard deviation of the risky asset times the fraction of the portfolio invested in the risky asset:

$$\sigma_C = y\sigma_P$$

(5.20)

In sum, both the risk premium and the standard deviation of the complete portfolio increase in proportion to the investment in the risky portfolio. Therefore, the points that describe the

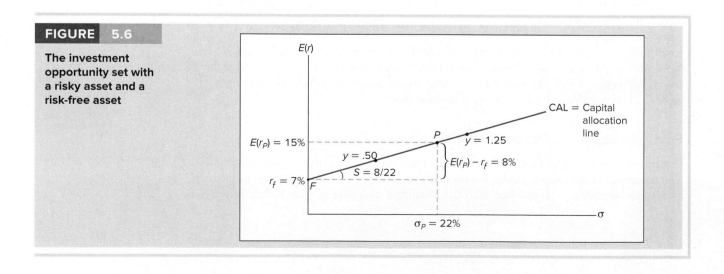

FIGURE 5.6

The investment opportunity set with a risky asset and a risk-free asset

risk and return of the complete portfolio for various capital allocations, y, all plot on the straight line connecting F and P, as shown in Figure 5.6, with an intercept of r_f and slope (rise/run) equal to the Sharpe ratio of P:

$$S = \frac{E(r_P) - r_f}{\sigma_P} = \frac{15 - 7}{22} = .36 \qquad \qquad \textbf{(5.21)}$$

CONCEPT
check   **5.6**

What are the expected return, risk premium, standard deviation, and ratio of risk premium to standard deviation for a complete portfolio with $y = .75$?

The Capital Allocation Line

The line plotted in Figure 5.6 depicts the risk-return combinations available by varying capital allocation, that is, by choosing different values of y. For this reason it is called the **capital allocation line (CAL).** The slope, S, of the CAL equals the increase in expected return that an investor can obtain per unit of additional standard deviation, or equivalently, extra return per extra risk. This is the Sharpe ratio, after William Sharpe who first suggested its use. It is obvious why the Sharpe ratio is sometimes called the *reward-to-volatility ratio.*

Notice that the Sharpe ratio is the same for risky portfolio P and the complete portfolio C that places equal weights in P and the risk-free asset:

capital allocation line (CAL) Plot of risk-return combinations available by varying portfolio allocation between a risk-free asset and a risky portfolio.

	Expected Return	Risk Premium	Standard Deviation	Sharpe Ratio
Portfolio P:	15%	8%	22%	$\frac{8}{22} = 0.36$
Portfolio C:	11%	4%	11%	$\frac{4}{11} = 0.36$

In fact, the Sharpe ratio is the same for all complete portfolios that plot on the capital allocation line. While the risk-return combinations differ according to the investor's choice of y, the *ratio* of reward to risk is constant.

What about points on the CAL to the right of portfolio P in the investment opportunity set? You can construct complete portfolios to the right of point P by borrowing, that is, by choosing $y > 1$. This means that you borrow a proportion of $y - 1$ and invest both the borrowed funds and your own wealth in the risky portfolio P. If you can borrow at the risk-free rate, $r_f = 7\%$, then your rate of return will be $r_C = (1 - y)r_f + yr_P = r_f + y(r_P - r_f)$. This complete portfolio has risk premium of $y[E(r_P) - r_f]$ and SD $= y\sigma_P$. Verify that your Sharpe ratio equals that of any other portfolio on the same CAL.

Suppose the investment budget is $300,000, and an investor borrows an additional $120,000, investing the $420,000 in the risky asset. This is a levered position in the risky asset, which is financed in part by borrowing. In that case

EXAMPLE 5.7

Levered Complete Portfolios

$$y = \frac{420,000}{300,000} = 1.4$$

and $1 - y = 1 - 1.4 = -.4$, reflecting a short position in the risk-free asset, or a borrowing position. Rather than lending at a 7% interest rate, the investor borrows at 7%. With weights of $-.4$ in the risk-free asset and 1.4 in the risky portfolio, the portfolio rate of return is

$$E(r_C) = (-.4) \times 7\% + 1.4 \times 15\% = 18.2\%$$

(continued)

Another way to find this portfolio rate of return is as follows: You expect to earn $63,000 (15% of $420,000) on your investment in P and pay $8,400 (7% of $120,000) in interest on the loan. Simple subtraction yields an expected profit of $54,600, which is 18.2% of your investment budget of $300,000. Therefore, $E(r_C) = 18.2\%$.

Your portfolio still exhibits the same reward-to-volatility or Sharpe ratio:

$$\sigma_C = 1.4 \times 22\% = 30.8\%$$

$$S = \frac{E(r_C) - r_f}{\sigma_C} = \frac{11.2\%}{30.8\%} = .36$$

As you might have expected, the levered portfolio has both a higher expected return and a higher standard deviation than an unlevered position in the risky asset.

Risk Aversion and Capital Allocation

We have developed the CAL, the graph of all feasible risk-return combinations available from allocating the complete portfolio between a risky portfolio and a risk-free asset. The investor confronting the CAL now must choose one optimal combination from the set of feasible choices. This choice entails a trade-off between risk and return. Individual investors with different levels of risk aversion, given an identical capital allocation line, will choose different positions in the risky asset. Specifically, the more risk-averse investors will choose to hold *less* of the risky asset and *more* of the risk-free asset.

How can we find the best allocation between the risky portfolio and risk-free asset? Recall from Equation 5.16 that a particular investor's degree of risk aversion (A) measures the price of risk she demands from the complete portfolio in which her entire wealth is invested. The compensation for risk demanded by the investor must be compared to the price of risk offered by the risky portfolio, P. It turns out that we can find the investor's preferred capital allocation, y, by dividing the risky portfolio's price of risk by the investor's risk aversion, her *required* price of risk:

$$y = \frac{\text{Available risk premium to variance ratio}}{\text{Required risk premium to variance ratio}} = \frac{\left[E(r_P) - r_f\right]/\sigma_P^2}{A} = \frac{E(r_P) - r_f}{A\,\sigma_P^2} \quad \textbf{(5.22)}$$

Equation 5.22 has the intuitive implication that the optimal allocation to the risky portfolio is directly proportional to its price of risk and inversely proportional to the investor's risk aversion.

What would the investor of Equation 5.15 (with $A = 3.91$) do when faced with the market index portfolio of Equation 5.16 (with price of risk $= 2$)? Equation 5.22 tells us that this investor would invest $y = 2/3.91 = 0.51$ (51%) in the market index portfolio and a proportion $1 - y = 0.49$ in the risk-free asset.

Graphically, more risk-averse investors will choose portfolios near point F on the capital allocation line plotted in Figure 5.6. More risk-tolerant investors will choose points closer to P, with higher expected return and higher risk. The most risk-tolerant investors will choose portfolios to the right of point P. These levered portfolios provide even higher expected returns, but even greater risk.

The investor's asset allocation choice also will depend on the trade-off between risk and return. When the Sharpe ratio is higher, investors will take on riskier positions. Suppose an investor reevaluates the probability distribution of the risky portfolio and now perceives a greater expected return without an accompanying increase in the standard deviation. This amounts to an increase in the Sharpe ratio or, equivalently, an increase in the slope of the CAL. As a result, this investor will choose a higher y, that is, a greater position in the risky portfolio.

One role of a professional financial adviser is to present investment opportunity alternatives to clients, obtain an assessment of the client's risk tolerance, and help determine the appropriate complete portfolio.[9]

5.6   PASSIVE STRATEGIES AND THE CAPITAL MARKET LINE

A **passive strategy** is based on the premise that securities are fairly priced, and it avoids the costs involved in undertaking security analysis. Such a strategy might at first blush appear to be naive. However, we will see in Chapter 8 that intense competition among professional money managers might indeed force security prices to levels at which further security analysis is unlikely to turn up significant profit opportunities. Passive investment strategies may make sense for many investors.

passive strategy
Investment policy that avoids security analysis. Often entails indexing.

To avoid the costs of acquiring information on any individual stock or group of stocks, we may follow a "neutral" diversification approach. Select a diversified portfolio of common stocks that mirrors the corporate sector of the broad economy. This results in a value-weighted portfolio, which, for example, invests a proportion in GE stock that equals the ratio of GE's market value to the market value of all listed stocks.

Such strategies are called *indexing*. The investor chooses a portfolio of all the stocks in a broad market index such as the S&P 500. The rate of return on the portfolio then replicates the return on the index. Indexing has become a popular strategy for passive investors. We call the capital allocation line provided by one-month T-bills and a broad index of common stocks the **capital market line (CML).** That is, a passive strategy using the broad stock market index as the risky portfolio generates an investment opportunity set that is represented by the CML.

capital market line (CML)
The capital allocation line using the market index portfolio as the risky asset.

Historical Evidence on the Capital Market Line

Table 5.5[10] presents data on the historical performance of the S&P 500 index for the period 1927–2016 as well as for three subperiods. The Sharpe ratio for the overall period, 1927–2016, was .42. In other words, investors enjoyed a .42% average excess return over the T-bill rate for every 1% of standard deviation.

But the risk-reward trade-off we infer from the historical data is far from precise. This is because the excess return on the market index is so variable, with an annual standard deviation of 20.29%. With such high year-by-year volatility, it is no surprise that that reward-to-risk trade-off was also highly variable. Sharpe ratios across subperiods vary dramatically, ranging from 0.31 to 0.50. The lesson here is that we should be very humble when we use historical data to forecast future performance. Returns and the risk-return trade-off are extremely difficult to predict, and we can have only a loose sense of what that trade-off will be in coming periods.

TABLE 5.5	Excess returns statistics for the market index		
	Average	**Std Dev**	**Sharpe Ratio**
1926–1927	8.48	20.29	0.42
1927–1956	11.22	24.75	0.45
1957–1987	5.46	17.91	0.31
1988–2016	8.88	17.69	0.50

[9]"Risk tolerance" is simply the flip side of "risk aversion." Either term is a reasonable way to describe attitudes toward risk. We generally find it easier to talk about risk *aversion,* but practitioners often focus on risk *tolerance.*

[10] Table 5.5 is constructed using annual data from 1927 through 2016.

TRIUMPH OF THE OPTIMISTS

As a whole, the last nine decades have been very kind to U.S. equity investors. Even accounting for miserable returns during the financial crisis, stock investments have outperformed investments in safe Treasury bills by about 8% per year. The real rate of return averaged more than 6%, implying an expected doubling of the real value of the investment portfolio about every 12 years!

Is this experience representative? A book by three professors at the London Business School, Elroy Dimson, Paul Marsh, and Mike Staunton, extends the U.S. evidence to other countries and to longer time periods. Their conclusion is given in the book's title, *Triumph of the Optimists*:[11] In every country in their study (which included markets in North America, Europe, Asia, and Africa), the investment optimists—those who bet on the economy by investing in stocks rather than bonds or bills—were vindicated. Over the long haul, stocks beat bonds everywhere.

On the other hand, the equity risk premium is probably not as large as the post-1926 evidence from Table 5.5 would seem to indicate. First, results from the first 25 years of the last century (which included the first World War) were less favorable to stocks. Second, U.S. returns have been better than those of most other countries, and so a more representative value for the historical risk premium may be lower than the U.S. experience. Finally, the sample that is amenable to historical analysis suffers from a self-selection problem. Only those markets that have survived to be studied can be included in the analysis. This leaves out countries such as Russia or China, whose markets were shut down during communist rule, and whose results if included would surely bring down the average historical performance of equity investments. Nevertheless, there is powerful evidence of a risk premium that shows its force everywhere the authors looked.

In fact, there has been considerable debate among financial economists about the "true" equity risk premium, with an emerging consensus that the historical average may be an unrealistically high estimate of the future risk premium. This argument is based on several factors: the use of longer time periods in which equity returns are examined; a broad range of countries rather than just the U.S. in which excess returns are computed (Dimson, Marsh, and Staunton, 2001); direct surveys of financial executives about their expectations for stock market returns (Graham and Harvey, 2001); and inferences from stock market data about investor expectations (Jagannathan, McGrattan, and Scherbina, 2000; Fama and French, 2002). The nearby box discusses some of this evidence.

Costs and Benefits of Passive Investing

The fact that an individual's capital allocation decision is hard does not imply that its implementation needs to be complex. A passive strategy is simple and inexpensive to implement: Choose a broad index fund or ETF and divide your savings between it and a money market fund. To justify spending your own time and effort or paying a professional to pursue an active strategy requires some evidence that those activities are likely to be profitable. As we shall see later in the text, this is much harder to come by than you might expect!

To choose an active strategy, an investor must be convinced that the benefits outweigh the cost, and the cost can be quite large. As a benchmark, annual expense ratios for index funds are around 10 and 40 basis points for U.S. and international stocks, respectively. The cost of utilizing a money market fund is smaller, and T-bills can be purchased at no cost.

Here is a very cursory idea of the cost of active strategies: The annual expense ratio of an active stock mutual fund averages around .8% of invested assets, and mutual funds that invest in more exotic assets such as real estate or precious metals can be more expensive still. A typical hedge fund will cost you 1% to 2% of invested assets plus around 20% of any returns above the risk-free rate.

Because of the power of compounding, an extra 1% of annual costs can have large consequences for the future value of your portfolio. With a risk-free rate of 2% and a risk premium

---

[11]Elroy Dimson, Paul Marsh, and Mike Staunton, *Triumph of the Optimists: 101 Years of Global Investment Returns* (Princeton, NJ: Princeton University Press, 2002).

of 8%, you might expect your wealth to grow by a multiple of $1.10^{30} = 17.45$ over a 30-year investment horizon. If fees are 1%, then your net return is reduced to 9%, and your wealth grows by a multiple of only $1.09^{30} = 13.26$ over that same horizon. That seemingly small management fee reduces your final wealth by about one-quarter.

The potential benefits of active strategies are discussed in detail in Chapter 8. The news is generally not that good for active investors. However, the factors that keep the active management industry going are (1) the large potential of enrichment from successful investments—the same power of compounding works in your favor if you can add even a few basis points to total return, (2) the difficulty in assessing performance (discussed in Chapter 18), and (3) uninformed investors who are willing to pay for professional money management. While some money managers may be able to outperform passive strategies, the questions to resolve are (1) how to identify them and (2) if their fees outstrip their potential. Whatever choice one makes, one thing is clear: The CML using the passive market index is not obviously inferior.

SUMMARY

- The real interest rate approximately equals the nominal rate minus the inflation rate. The nominal rate tends to rise when inflation rises, making the real rate more stable than the nominal rate.
- U.S. T-bills provide a perfectly risk-free asset in nominal terms only. Nevertheless, the standard deviation of rates on short-term T-bills is small compared to that of assets such as long-term bonds and common stocks, so for the purpose of our analysis, we consider T-bills the risk-free asset. Besides T-bills, money market funds hold short-term, safe obligations such as repurchase agreements and commercial paper. These entail some default risk but relatively little compared to most other risky assets. For convenience, we also may refer to money market funds as risk-free assets.
- The expected rate of return is the weighted average of returns in all possible scenarios with weights equal to the probability of each scenario. The variance is the probability-weighted average of all possible squared deviations from the mean return. Standard deviation is the square root of variance.
- When returns are normally distributed, the mean and standard deviation fully describe the probability distribution of returns. However, historical returns on stocks exhibit somewhat more frequent, large negative deviations from the mean than would be predicted from a normal distribution. The value at risk, skew, and kurtosis of the actual distribution quantify the deviation from normality and the implied tail risk of these investments.
- Investors face a trade-off between risk and expected return. Historical data confirm our intuition that assets with low degrees of risk should provide lower returns on average than do those of higher risk.
- Shifting funds from the risky portfolio to the risk-free asset is the simplest way to reduce risk. Another method involves diversification of the risky portfolio. We take up diversification in later chapters.
- A risky investment portfolio can be characterized by its Sharpe, or reward-to-volatility, ratio. This ratio is the slope of the capital allocation line (CAL), the line connecting the risk-free asset to the risky asset. All combinations of the risky and risk-free asset lie on this line. Investors would prefer a steeper-sloping CAL, because that means higher expected returns for any level of risk.
- An investor's preferred choice among the portfolios on the capital allocation line will depend on risk aversion. Risk-averse investors will weight their complete portfolios more heavily toward Treasury bills. Risk-tolerant investors will hold higher proportions of their complete portfolios in the risky asset.
- The capital market line is the capital allocation line that results from using a passive investment strategy that treats a market index portfolio, such as the Standard & Poor's 500, as the risky asset. Passive strategies are low-cost ways of obtaining well-diversified portfolios with performance that will reflect that of the broad stock market.

KEY TERMS

arithmetic average, 112
asset allocation, 131
capital allocation to risky
   assets, 131
capital allocation line
   (CAL), 133
capital market line (CML), 135
complete portfolio, 131
dollar-weighted average
   return, 113
excess return, 122

expected return, 117
geometric average, 112
holding-period return
   (HPR), 111
inflation rate, 115
kurtosis, 121
mean-variance analysis, 123
nominal interest rate, 114
passive strategy, 135
price of risk, 123
probability distribution, 117

real interest rate, 114
risk aversion, 122
risk-free rate, 122
risk premium, 122
scenario analysis, 117
Sharpe ratio, 123
skew, 122
standard deviation, 118
value at risk (VaR), 121
variance, 118

KEY FORMULAS

Arithmetic average of n returns: $(r_1 + r_2 + \cdots + r_n)/n$

Geometric average of n returns: $[(1 + r_1)(1 + r_2) \cdots (1 + r_n)]^{1/n} - 1$

Continuously compounded rate of return, r_{cc}: $\ln(1 + \text{Effective annual rate})$

Real rate of return: $\dfrac{1 + \text{Nominal return}}{1 + \text{Inflation rate}} - 1$

Real rate of return (continuous compounding): $r_{\text{nominal}} - \text{Inflation rate}$

Expected return: $\Sigma\,[\text{prob(Scenario)} \times \text{Return in scenario}]$

Variance: $\Sigma\,[\text{prob(Scenario)} \times (\text{Deviation from mean in scenario})^2]$

Standard deviation: $\sqrt{\text{Variance}}$

Sharpe ratio: $\dfrac{\text{Portfolio risk premium}}{\text{Standard deviation of excess return}} = \dfrac{E(r_P) - r_f}{\sigma_P}$

Optimal capital allocation to the risky asset, y: $\dfrac{E(r_P) - r_f}{A\sigma_P^2}$

PROBLEM SETS

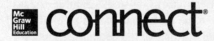

Select problems are available in McGraw-Hill's *Connect*. Please see the Supplements section of the book's frontmatter for more information.

1. Suppose you've estimated that the fifth-percentile value at risk of a portfolio is −30%. Now you wish to estimate the portfolio's first-percentile VaR (the value below which lie 1% of the returns). Will the 1% VaR be greater or less than −30%?   *(LO 5-2)*

2. The real interest rate approximately equals the nominal rate minus the inflation rate. Suppose the inflation rate increases from 3% to 5%. Does the Fisher equation imply that this increase will result in a fall in the real rate of interest? Explain.   *(LO 5-4)*

3. When estimating a Sharpe ratio, would it make sense to use the average excess real return that accounts for inflation?   *(LO 5-4)*

4. You've just decided upon your capital allocation for the next year, when you realize that you've underestimated both the expected return and the standard deviation of your risky portfolio by a multiple of 1.05. Will you increase, decrease, or leave unchanged your allocation to risk-free T-bills?   *(LO 5-4)*

5. Suppose your expectations regarding the stock market are as follows:

State of the Economy	Probability	HPR
Boom	0.3	44%
Normal growth	0.4	14
Recession	0.3	−16

Use Equations 5.10–5.12 to compute the mean and standard deviation of the HPR on stocks.   *(LO 5-4)*

6. The stock of Business Adventures sells for $40 a share. Its likely dividend payout and end-of-year price depend on the state of the economy by the end of the year as follows: *(LO 5-2)*

	Dividend	Stock Price
Boom	$2.00	$50
Normal economy	1.00	43
Recession	0.50	34

   a. Calculate the expected holding-period return and standard deviation of the holding-period return. All three scenarios are equally likely.

   b. Calculate the expected return and standard deviation of a portfolio invested half in Business Adventures and half in Treasury bills. The return on bills is 4%.

7. XYZ stock price and dividend history are as follows:

Year	Beginning-of-Year Price	Dividend Paid at Year-End
2015	$100	$4
2016	110	4
2017	90	4
2018	95	4

   An investor buys three shares of XYZ at the beginning of 2015, buys another two shares at the beginning of 2016, sells one share at the beginning of 2017, and sells all four remaining shares at the beginning of 2018.   *(LO 5-1)*

   a. What are the arithmetic and geometric average time-weighted rates of return for the investor?

   b. What is the dollar-weighted rate of return? (*Hint:* Carefully prepare a chart of cash flows for the *four* dates corresponding to the turns of the year for January 1, 2015, to January 1, 2018. If your calculator cannot calculate internal rate of return, you will have to use a spreadsheet or trial and error.)

8. *a.* Suppose you forecast that the standard deviation of the market return will be 20% in the coming year. If the measure of risk aversion in Equation 5.16 is $A = 4$, what would be a reasonable guess for the expected market risk premium?

   b. What value of A is consistent with a risk premium of 9%?

   c. What will happen to the risk premium if investors become more risk tolerant?   *(LO 5-4)*

9. Using the historical risk premiums as your guide, what is your estimate of the expected annual HPR on the market index stock portfolio if the current risk-free interest rate is 3%?   *(LO 5-3)*

10. What has been the historical average *real* rate of return on stocks, Treasury bonds, and Treasury bills?   *(LO 5-2)*

11. Consider a risky portfolio. The end-of-year cash flow derived from the portfolio will be either $50,000 or $150,000, with equal probabilities of 0.5. The alternative riskless investment in T-bills pays 5%.   *(LO 5-3)*

   a. If you require a risk premium of 10%, how much will you be willing to pay for the portfolio?

   b. Suppose the portfolio can be purchased for the amount you found in (*a*). What will the expected rate of return on the portfolio be?

   c. Now suppose you require a risk premium of 15%. What is the price you will be willing to pay now?

   d. Comparing your answers to (*a*) and (*c*), what do you conclude about the relationship between the required risk premium on a portfolio and the price at which the portfolio will sell?

For Problems 12–16, assume that you manage a risky portfolio with an expected rate of return of 17% and a standard deviation of 27%. The T-bill rate is 7%.

12. Your client chooses to invest 70% of a portfolio in your fund and 30% in a T-bill money market fund.   *(LO 5-3)*

    a. What is the expected return and standard deviation of your client's portfolio?

    b. Suppose your risky portfolio includes the following investments in the given proportions:

Stock A	27%
Stock B	33
Stock C	40

    What are the investment proportions of each stock in your client's overall portfolio, including the position in T-bills?

    c. What is the Sharpe ratio (S) of your risky portfolio and your client's overall portfolio?

    d. Draw the CAL of your portfolio on an expected return/standard deviation diagram. What is the slope of the CAL? Show the position of your client on your fund's CAL.

13. Suppose the same client in the previous problem decides to invest in your risky portfolio a proportion (y) of his total investment budget so that his overall portfolio will have an expected rate of return of 15%.   *(LO 5-3)*

    a. What is the proportion y?

    b. What are your client's investment proportions in your three stocks and in T-bills?

    c. What is the standard deviation of the rate of return on your client's portfolio?

14. Suppose the same client as in the previous problem prefers to invest in your portfolio a proportion (y) that maximizes the expected return on the overall portfolio subject to the constraint that the overall portfolio's standard deviation will not exceed 20%.   *(LO 5-3)*

    a. What is the investment proportion, y?

    b. What is the expected rate of return on the overall portfolio?

15. You estimate that a passive portfolio invested to mimic the S&P 500 stock index provides an expected rate of return of 13% with a standard deviation of 25%. Draw the CML and your fund's CAL on an expected return/standard deviation diagram.   *(LO 5-4)*

    a. What is the slope of the CML?

    b. Characterize in one short paragraph the advantage of your fund over the index fund.

16. Your client (see previous problem) wonders whether to switch the 70% that is invested in your fund to the index portfolio.   *(LO 5-4)*

    a. Explain to your client the disadvantage of the switch.

    b. Show your client the maximum fee you could charge (as a percent of the investment in your fund, deducted at the end of the year) that would still leave him at least as well off investing in your fund as in the passive one. (*Hint:* The fee will lower the slope of your client's CAL by reducing the expected return net of the fee.)

17. What do you think would happen to the expected return on stocks if investors perceived an increase in the volatility of stocks?   *(LO 5-4)*

18. You manage an equity fund with an expected risk premium of 10% and a standard deviation of 14%. The rate on Treasury bills is 6%. Your client chooses to invest $60,000 of her portfolio in your equity fund and $40,000 in a T-bill money market fund. What is the expected return and standard deviation of your client's portfolio?   *(LO 5-3)*

19. What is the reward-to-volatility (Sharpe) ratio for the *equity fund* in the previous problem?   *(LO 5-4)*

For Problems 20–22, download the spreadsheet containing the data used to prepare Table 5.3, "Rates of return, 1927–2016," from Connect.

Templates and spreadsheets are available in Connect

20. Calculate the means and standard deviations of small stock returns as Table 5.3 of the text provides for large stocks. *(LO 5-2)*

    a. Have small stocks provided better reward-to-volatility (Sharpe) ratios than large stocks?

    b. Do small stocks show a similar higher standard deviation in the earliest subperiod as Table 5.5 documents for large stocks?

21. Convert the nominal returns on large stocks to real rates. Reproduce Table 5.3 using real rates instead of excess returns. Compare the results to those of Table 5.3. Are real or nominal returns more volatile in this sample period? *(LO 5-1)*

22. Repeat the previous problem for small stocks and compare the results for real versus nominal returns. *(LO 5-1)*

Challenge

23. Download the annual returns for the years 1927–2016 on the combined market index (of the NYSE/NASDAQ/AMEX markets) as well as the S&P 500 from Connect. For both indexes, calculate: *(LO 5-2)*

    a. Average return.

    b. Standard deviation of return.

    c. Skew of return.

    d. Kurtosis of return.

    e. The 5% value at risk.

    f. Based on your answers to parts *(b)*–*(e)*, compare the risk of the two indexes.

Templates and spreadsheets are available in Connect

CFA PROBLEMS

1. A portfolio of nondividend-paying stocks earned a geometric mean return of 5% between January 1, 2010, and December 31, 2016. The arithmetic mean return for the same period was 6%. If the market value of the portfolio at the beginning of 2010 was $100,000, what was the market value of the portfolio at the end of 2016? *(LO 5-1)*

2. Which of the following statements about the standard deviation is/are *true*? A standard deviation: *(LO 5-2)*

    a. Is the square root of the variance.

    b. Is denominated in the same units as the original data.

    c. Can be a positive or a negative number.

3. Which of the following statements reflects the importance of the asset allocation decision to the investment process? The asset allocation decision: *(LO 5-3)*

    a. Helps the investor decide on realistic investment goals.

    b. Identifies the specific securities to include in a portfolio.

    c. Determines most of the portfolio's returns and volatility over time.

    d. Creates a standard by which to establish an appropriate investment time horizon.

Use the following data in answering CFA Questions 4–6.

Investment	Expected Return, $E(r)$	Standard Deviation, σ
1	0.12	0.30
2	0.15	0.50
3	0.21	0.16
4	0.24	0.21

Suppose investor "satisfaction" with a portfolio increases with expected return and decreases with variance according to the following "utility" formula: $U = E(r) - \frac{1}{2} A\sigma^2$ where A denotes the investor's risk aversion.

4. Based on the formula for investor satisfaction or "utility," which investment would you select if you were risk averse with $A = 4$?   *(LO 5-4)*

5. Based on the formula above, which investment would you select if you were risk neutral, with $A = 0$?   *(LO 5-4)*

6. The variable (A) in the utility formula represents the: *(LO 5-4)*
   a. Investor's return requirement.
   b. Is higher when the investor demands a greater risk premium as compensation for a given increase in the variance of returns.
   c. Preference for one unit of return per four units of risk.

Use the following scenario analysis for stocks X and Y to answer CFA Questions 7 through 9.

	Bear Market	Normal Market	Bull Market
Probability	0.2	0.5	0.3
Stock X	−20%	18%	50%
Stock Y	−15%	20%	10%

7. What are the expected returns for stocks X and Y?   *(LO 5-2)*

8. What are the standard deviations of returns on stocks X and Y?   *(LO 5-2)*

9. Assume that of your $10,000 portfolio, you invest $9,000 in stock X and $1,000 in stock Y. What is the expected return on your portfolio?   *(LO 5-3)*

10. Probabilities for three states of the economy and probabilities for the returns on a particular stock in each state are shown in the table below.

State of Economy	Probability of Economic State	Stock Performance	Probability of Stock Performance in Given Economic State
Good	0.3	Good	0.6
		Neutral	0.3
		Poor	0.1
Neutral	0.5	Good	0.4
		Neutral	0.3
		Poor	0.3
Poor	0.2	Good	0.2
		Neutral	0.3
		Poor	0.5

What is the probability that the economy will be neutral *and* the stock will experience poor performance?   *(LO 5-2)*

11. An analyst estimates that a stock has the following probabilities of return depending on the state of the economy. What is the expected return of the stock?   *(LO 5-2)*

State of Economy	Probability	Return
Good	0.1	15%
Normal	0.6	13
Poor	0.3	7

1. Use data from **finance.yahoo.com** to answer the following questions.
   a. Select the Company tab and enter the ticker symbol for Adobe, ADBE. Click on the *Profile* tab to see an overview of the company.
   b. What is the latest price reported in the *Summary* section? What is the 12-month target price? Calculate the expected holding-period return based on these prices.
   c. Use the *Historical Data* section to answer the question "How much would I have today if I invested $10,000 in ADBE five years ago?" Using this information, calculate the five-year holding-period return on Adobe's stock.

2. From the *Historical Data* tab, download Adobe's dividend-adjusted stock price for the last 24 months into an Excel spreadsheet. Calculate the monthly rate of return for each month, the average return, and the standard deviation of returns over that period.

3. Calculating the real rate of return is an important part of evaluating an investment's performance. To do this, you need to know the nominal return on your investment and the rate of inflation during the corresponding period. To estimate the expected real rate of return before you make an investment, you can use the expected nominal return and the expected inflation rate.
   a. Go to **www.bankrate.com** and click on the *CD Rates* tab. Select a term of one year and obtain a sample of CD rate from banks across the nation (these will be nominal rates).
   b. Use the St. Louis Federal Reserve's website at **https://fred.stlouisfed.org/** as a source for data about expected inflation. Search for "MICH inflation," which will provide you with the University of Michigan Inflation Expectation data series (MICH). What is the expected inflation rate for the next year?
   c. On the basis of your answers to parts (*a*) and (*b*), calculate the expected real rate of return on a one-year CD investment.
   d. What does the result tell you about real interest rates? Are they positive or negative, and what does this mean?

5.1 a. The arithmetic average is $(2 + 8 - 4)/3 = 2\%$ per month.
   b. The time-weighted (geometric) average is
      $[(1 + .02) \times (1 + .08) \times (1 - .04)]^{1/3} - 1 = .0188 = 1.88\%$ per month.
   c. We compute the dollar-weighted average (IRR) from the cash flow sequence (in $ millions):

	Month		
	1	**2**	**3**
Assets under management at beginning of month	10.0	13.2	19.256
Investment profits ($ million) during month (HPR × Assets)	0.2	1.056	(0.77)
Net inflows during month	3.0	5.0	0.0
Assets under management at end of month	13.2	19.256	18.486

		Time		
	0	**1**	**2**	**3**
Net cash flow*	−10	−3.0	−5.0	+18.486

* Time 0 is today. Time 1 is the end of the first month. Time 3 is the end of the third month, when net cash flow equals the ending value (potential liquidation value) of the portfolio.

The IRR of the sequence of net cash flows is 1.17% per month.

The dollar-weighted average is less than the time-weighted average because the negative return was realized when the fund had the most money under management.

5.2 *a.* Solving:

$$1 + r_{nom} = (1 + r_{real})(1 + i) = (1.03)(1.08) = 1.1124$$

$$r_{nom} = 11.24\%$$

b. Solving:

$$1 + r_{nom} = (1.03)(1.10) = 1.133$$

$$r_{nom} = 13.3\%$$

5.3 Computing the HPR for each scenario, we convert the price and dividend data to rate-of-return data:

Scenario	Prob	Ending Value ($ million)	Dividend ($ million)	HPR	HPR × Prob	Deviation: HPR-mean	Prob × Dev'n Squared
1	0.30	$35	$4.40	0.713	0.214	0.406	0.049
2	0.45	27	4.00	0.348	0.157	0.040	0.001
3	0.20	15	4.00	−0.174	−0.035	−0.481	0.046
4	0.05	8	2.00	−0.565	−0.028	−0.873	0.038
Sum:					0.307		0.135

Expected HPR = .307 = 30.7%

Variance = .135

Standard deviation = $\sqrt{.135}$ = .367 = 36.7%

5.4 *a.* VaR = −56.5%. this is the return that characterizes the bottom 5% of the probability distribution.

b. The fifth percentile of the normal distribution occurs at a value that is 1.64485 standard deviations below the mean (see Equation 5.14). For this portfolio, that corresponds to a return of 30.7% − 1.64485 × 36.7% = −29.67%. The actual VaR for this portfolio is considerably worse than the prediction of the normal distribution, which implies meaningful tail risk.

5.5 *a.* If the average investor chooses the market index, then the implied degree of risk aversion is given by Equation 5.17:

$$A = \frac{.10 - .05}{.18^2} = 1.54$$

b. $S = \dfrac{10 - 5}{18} = .28$

5.6 $E(r) = 7 + .75 \times 8\% = 13\%$

$\sigma = .75 \times 22\% = 16.5\%$

Risk premium = 13 − 7 = 6%

$$S = \frac{\text{Risk premium}}{\text{Standard deviation}} = \frac{13 - 7}{16.5} = .36$$

Efficient Diversification

Learning Objectives

LO 6-1 Show how covariance and correlation affect the power of diversification to reduce portfolio risk.

LO 6-2 Calculate mean, variance, and covariance using either historical data or scenario analysis.

LO 6-3 Construct efficient portfolios and use the Sharpe ratio to evaluate portfolio efficiency.

LO 6-4 Calculate the composition of the optimal risky portfolio.

LO 6-5 Use index models to analyze the risk and return characteristics of securities and portfolios.

LO 6-6 Understand the effect of investment horizon on portfolio risk.

I n this chapter we describe how investors can construct the best possible risky portfolio. The key concept is efficient diversification.

The notion of diversification is age-old. The adage "Don't put all your eggs in one basket" obviously predates formal economic theory. However, a rigorous model showing how to make the most of the power of diversification was not devised until 1952, a feat for which Harry Markowitz won the Nobel Prize in Economics. This chapter is largely developed from his work, as well as from later insights that built on his work.

We start with a bird's-eye view of how diversification reduces the variability of portfolio returns. We then turn to the construction of optimal risky portfolios. We follow a top-down approach, starting with asset allocation across a small set of broad asset classes, such as stocks, bonds, and money market securities. Then we show how the principles of optimal asset allocation can be generalized to the problem of security selection among many risky assets. We discuss the efficient set of risky portfolios and show how it leads to the best capital allocation. Finally, we show how index models of security returns can simplify the search for efficient portfolios and the interpretation of the risk characteristics of individual securities.

The last section examines the common fallacy that long-term investment horizons mitigate the impact of asset risk. We show that the common belief in "time diversification" is in fact an illusion.

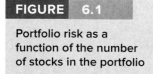

6.1   DIVERSIFICATION AND PORTFOLIO RISK

Suppose your risky portfolio comprises only one stock, say, Digital Computer Corporation. What are the sources of risk affecting this "portfolio"?

We can identify two broad sources of uncertainty. The first is the risk from general economic conditions, such as business cycles, inflation, interest rates, exchange rates, and so forth. None of these macroeconomic factors can be predicted with certainty, and all affect Digital stock. Then you must add firm-specific influences, such as Digital's success in R&D, its management style and philosophy, and so on. *Firm-specific* factors are those that affect Digital without noticeably affecting other firms.

Now consider adding another security to the risky portfolio. If you invest half of your risky portfolio in ExxonMobil, leaving the other half in Digital, what happens to portfolio risk? Because the firm-specific influences on the two stocks are unrelated (statistically speaking, the influences are uncorrelated), this strategy should reduce portfolio risk. For example, when oil prices fall, hurting ExxonMobil, computer prices might rise, helping Digital. The two effects are offsetting, which stabilizes portfolio return.

But why stop at only two stocks? Diversifying into many more securities continues to reduce exposure to firm-specific factors, so portfolio volatility should continue to fall. Ultimately, however, there is no way to avoid all risk. To the extent that virtually all securities are affected by common macroeconomic factors, we cannot eliminate exposure to general economic risk, no matter how many stocks we hold.

Figure 6.1 illustrates these concepts. When all risk is firm-specific, as in Figure 6.1A, diversification can reduce risk to arbitrarily low levels. With all risk sources independent, and with investment spread across many securities, exposure to any particular source of risk is negligible. This is an application of the law of large numbers. Risk reduction by spreading exposure across many independent risk sources is called the *insurance principle*.

market risk, systematic risk, nondiversifiable risk

Risk factors common to the whole economy.

unique risk, firm-specific risk, nonsystematic risk, diversifiable risk

Risk that can be eliminated by diversification.

When a common source of risk affects all firms, however, even extensive diversification cannot eliminate all risk. In Figure 6.1B, portfolio standard deviation falls as the number of securities increases, but it is not reduced to zero. The risk that remains even after diversification is called **market risk,** risk that is attributable to marketwide risk sources. Equivalent terms are **systematic risk** or **nondiversifiable risk.** The risk that *can* be eliminated by diversification is called **unique risk, firm-specific risk, nonsystematic risk,** or **diversifiable risk.**

This analysis is borne out by empirical studies. Figure 6.2 shows the effect of portfolio diversification, using data on NYSE stocks. The figure shows the average standard deviations of equally weighted portfolios constructed by selecting stocks at random as a function of the number of stocks in the portfolio. On average, portfolio risk does fall with diversification, but

FIGURE 6.1

Portfolio risk as a function of the number of stocks in the portfolio

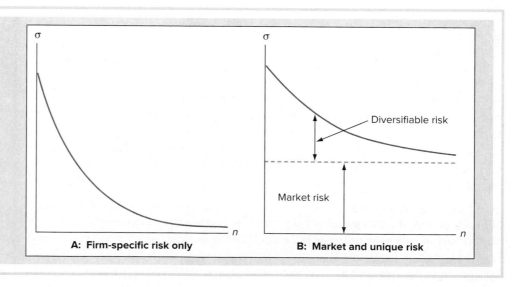

On the MARKET FRONT

DANGEROUS 401(K) PLANS

For many individuals, the 401(k) plan is the major source of retirement savings. The employee puts aside a given percentage of wages, in the process sheltering income from current taxation. In addition, the employer commonly matches some fraction of that contribution. So if the employee places, let's say, 8% of his or her salary in the 401(k) plan, the employer might contribute an additional 4% of salary. In many plans, the savings are invested in shares of the company stock. As part owners of the firm, employees might be encouraged to work smarter and harder, making everyone better off. It sounds like a win-win arrangement; what could go wrong? Plenty, it turns out.

The problem is that once you start concentrating your portfolio in your company stock, you increase risk in two ways.

First, focusing your investments in any single company rather than a diversified portfolio almost never makes sense. A single stock typically has more than double the volatility of a diversified portfolio. So when you load up your 401(k) plan with the stock of one company, you are taking on much greater volatility than is necessary, and much of that volatility does not even translate to higher average returns.

Second, when you invest in your own company, you are doubling down on your exposure to that single firm. If your company implodes, you can lose your source of income at the same time that your investment portfolio is decimated. Just ask the employees of Lehman Brothers, whose 401(k) plans entailed massive positions in the company stock; when the company failed, the employees' 401(k) plans were wiped out along with their jobs.

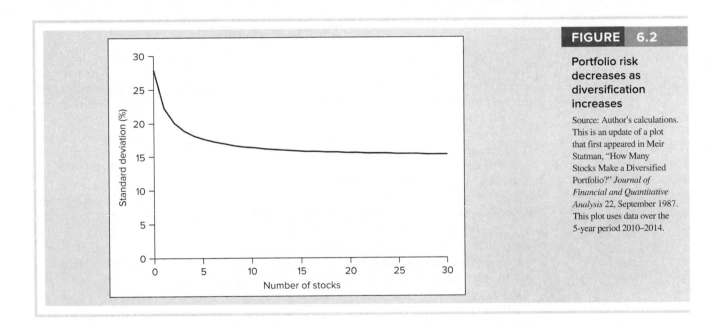

FIGURE 6.2

Portfolio risk decreases as diversification increases

Source: Author's calculations. This is an update of a plot that first appeared in Meir Statman, "How Many Stocks Make a Diversified Portfolio?" *Journal of Financial and Quantitative Analysis* 22, September 1987. This plot uses data over the 5-year period 2010–2014.

the power of diversification to reduce risk is limited by common sources of risk. The nearby box highlights the dangers of neglecting diversification.

In light of this discussion, it is worth pointing out that general macroeconomic conditions in the United States do not move in lockstep with those in other countries. International diversification may further reduce portfolio risk, but here too, global economic and political factors affecting all countries to various degrees will limit the extent of risk reduction.

6.2 ASSET ALLOCATION WITH TWO RISKY ASSETS

In the last section we considered naïve diversification using equally weighted portfolios of several securities. It is time now to study *efficient* diversification, whereby we construct portfolios that provide the lowest possible risk for any given level of expected return.

Portfolios of two risky assets are relatively easy to analyze, and they illustrate the principles and considerations that apply to portfolios of many assets. So we will begin with a two-asset risky portfolio, where we assume the two assets are a bond fund and a stock fund.

Spreadsheets are
available in Connect

	A	B	C	D	E	F
1			**Stock Fund**		**Bond Fund**	
2	Scenario	Probability	Rate of Return	Col B × Col C	Rate of Return	Col B × Col E
3	Severe recession	0.05	−37	−1.9	−9	−0.45
4	Mild recession	0.25	−11	−2.8	15	3.8
5	Normal growth	0.40	14	5.6	8	3.2
6	Boom	0.30	30	9.0	−5	−1.5
7	Expected or Mean Return:			SUM: 10.0		SUM: 5.0

Once we understand the portfolios of two risky assets, we will reintroduce the choice of the risk-free asset. This will complete the asset allocation problem across the three key asset classes: stocks, bonds, and T-bills. Constructing efficient portfolios of many risky securities is a straightforward extension of this stripped-down asset allocation exercise.

Covariance and Correlation

To optimally construct a portfolio from risky assets, we need to understand how the uncertainties of asset returns interact. A key determinant of portfolio risk is the extent to which the returns on the two assets vary either in tandem or in opposition. Portfolio risk depends on the *covariance* between the returns of the assets in the portfolio. We can see why using a simple scenario analysis.

The scenario analysis in Spreadsheet 6.1 posits four possible scenarios for the economy: a severe recession, a mild recession, normal growth, and a boom. The performance of stocks follows the broad economy, returning, respectively, −37%, −11%, 14%, and 30% in the four scenarios. In contrast, we assume bonds perform best in a mild recession, returning 15% (since falling interest rates result in capital gains), and in the normal growth scenario, where their return is 8%. They suffer from defaults in severe recession, resulting in a negative return, −9%, and from inflation (which leads to higher nominal interest rates) in the boom scenario, where their return is −5%. Notice that bonds outperform stocks in both the mild and severe recession scenarios. In both normal growth and boom scenarios, stocks outperform bonds.

The expected return on each fund equals the probability-weighted average of the outcomes in the four scenarios. The last row of Spreadsheet 6.1 shows that the expected return of the stock fund is 10% and that of the bond fund is 5%. As we saw in Chapter 5, the variance is the probability-weighted average of the squared deviations of actual returns from the expected return; the standard deviation is the square root of the variance. These values are computed in Spreadsheet 6.2.

Spreadsheets are
available in Connect

	A	B	C	D	E	F	G	H	I	J
1				**Stock Fund**				**Bond Fund**		
2				Deviation				Deviation		
3			Rate	from		Column B	Rate	from		Column B
4			of	Expected	Squared	×	of	Expected	Squared	×
5	Scenario	Prob.	Return	Return	Deviation	Column E	Return	Return	Deviation	Column I
6	Severe recession	0.05	−37	−47	2209	110.45	−9	−14	196	9.80
7	Mild recession	0.25	−11	−21	441	110.25	15	10	100	25.00
8	Normal growth	0.40	14	4	16	6.40	8	3	9	3.60
9	Boom	0.30	30	20	400	120.00	−5	−10	100	30.00
10					Variance = SUM	347.10			Variance:	68.40
11				Standard deviation = SQRT(Variance)		18.63			Std. Dev.:	8.27

SPREADSHEET 6.3

Performance of a portfolio invested in the stock and bond funds

	A	B	C	D	E	F	G
1			Portfolio invested 40% in stock fund and 60% in bond fund				
2			Rate	Column B	Deviation from		Column B
3			of	×	Expected	Squared	×
4	Scenario	Probability	Return	Column C	Return	Deviation	Column F
5	Severe recession	0.05	−20.2	−1.01	−27.2	739.84	36.99
6	Mild recession	0.25	4.6	1.15	−2.4	5.76	1.44
7	Normal growth	0.40	10.4	4.16	3.4	11.56	4.62
8	Boom	0.30	9.0	2.70	2.0	4.00	1.20
9		Expected return:		7.00		Variance:	44.26
10						Standard deviation:	6.65

Spreadsheets are available in Connect

What about the risk and return characteristics of a portfolio made up from the stock and bond funds? Consider a portfolio with 40% in stocks and 60% in bonds. The portfolio return is the weighted average of the returns on each fund with weights equal to the proportion of the portfolio invested in each fund. For example,

$$\text{Portfolio return in mild recession} = .40 \times (-11\%) + .60 \times 15\% = 4.6\%,$$

which appears in cell C6 of Spreadsheet 6.3.

Spreadsheet 6.3 shows the rate of return of the portfolio in each scenario. Notice that while the portfolio's expected return is just the weighted average of the expected return of the two assets, *portfolio volatility is actually lower than that of either component fund:* The standard deviation of the diversified portfolio, 6.65%, is considerably smaller than that of stocks, 18.63%, and even smaller than that of bonds, 8.27%.

The low risk of the portfolio is due to the inverse relationship between the performances of the stock and bond funds. In a mild recession, stocks fare poorly, but this is offset by the large positive return of the bond fund. Conversely, in the boom scenario, bond prices fall, but stocks do very well. Portfolio risk is reduced because variations in the returns of the two assets are generally offsetting.

The natural question investors should ask, therefore, is how one can measure the tendency of the returns on two assets to vary either in tandem or in opposition to each other. The statistics that provide this measure are the covariance and the correlation coefficient.

The covariance is calculated in a manner similar to the variance. Instead of multiplying the difference of an asset return from its expected value by itself (i.e., squaring it), we multiply it by the deviation of the *other* asset return from *its* expectation. The sign and magnitude of this product are determined by whether deviations from the mean move together (i.e., are both positive or both negative in the same scenarios) and whether they are small or large at the same time.

We start in Spreadsheet 6.4 with the deviation of the return on each fund from its expected value (columns C and D). In column E, we multiply the stock fund's deviation from its mean by the bond fund's deviation. The product will be positive if both asset returns exceed their respective means or if both fall short of their respective means. The product will be negative if one asset exceeds its mean return when the other falls short. Row 4 shows that in a mild recession, the stock fund return falls short of its expected value by 21%, while the bond fund return exceeds its mean by 10%. Therefore, the product of the two deviations is $-21 \times 10 = -210$, as reported in column E. The product of deviations is negative because one asset (stocks) performs poorly while the other (bonds) performs well.

The probability-weighted average of the products is called *covariance* and measures the *average* tendency of the asset returns to vary in tandem, that is, to co-vary. The formula for the

SPREADSHEET   6.4

Covariance between the returns of the stock and bond funds

Spreadsheets are
available in Connect

	A	B	C	D	E	F
1			Deviation from Mean Return		Covariance	
2	Scenario	Probability	Stock Fund	Bond Fund	Product of Dev	Col B × Col E
3	Severe recession	0.05	−47	−14	658	32.9
4	Mild recession	0.25	−21	10	−210	−52.5
5	Normal growth	0.40	4	3	12	4.8
6	Boom	0.30	20	−10	−200	−60.0
7				Covariance =	SUM:	−74.8
8	Correlation coefficient = Covariance/(StdDev(stocks)*StdDev(bonds)) =					−0.49

covariance of the returns on the stock and bond funds is given in Equation 6.1. Each particular scenario in this equation is labeled or "indexed" by i. In general, i ranges from scenario 1 to n (the total number of scenarios; here, $n = 4$). The probability of each scenario is denoted $p(i)$.

$$\text{Cov}(r_S, r_B) = \sum_{i=1}^{n} p(i)\left[r_S(i) - E(r_S)\right]\left[r_B(i) - E(r_B)\right] \tag{6.1}$$

The covariance of the stock and bond funds is computed from Equation 6.1 in cell F7 of Spreadsheet 6.4. The negative value for the covariance indicates that the two assets, on average, vary inversely; when one performs well, the other tends to perform poorly.

Like variance, the unit of covariance is percent square, which is why it is difficult to interpret its magnitude. For instance, does the covariance of −74.8 in cell F7 indicate that the inverse relationship between the returns on stock and bond funds is strong? It's hard to say. An easier statistic to interpret is the *correlation coefficient,* which is the covariance divided by the product of the standard deviations of the returns on each fund. We denote the correlation coefficient by the Greek letter rho, ρ.

$$\text{Correlation coefficient} = \rho_{SB} = \frac{\text{Cov}(r_S, r_B)}{\sigma_S \sigma_B} = \frac{-74.8}{18.63 \times 8.27} = -.49 \tag{6.2}$$

Correlation is a pure number and can range from −1 to +1. A correlation of −1 indicates that one asset's return varies perfectly inversely with the other's. With a correlation of −1, you could predict 100% of the variability of one asset's return if you knew the return on the other asset. Conversely, a correlation of +1 would indicate perfect positive correlation. A correlation of zero indicates that the returns on the two assets are unrelated. The correlation coefficient of $\rho_{SB} = -.49$ in Equation 6.2 confirms the tendency of the returns on the stock and bond funds to vary inversely.

Equation 6.2 shows that whenever the covariance is called for in a calculation we can replace it with the following expression using the correlation coefficient:

$$\text{Cov}(r_S, r_B) = \rho_{SB}\sigma_S \sigma_B \tag{6.3}$$

We are now ready to derive the risk and return features of portfolios of risky assets.

CONCEPT
check   **6.1**

Suppose the rates of return of the bond portfolio in the four scenarios of Spreadsheet 6.1 are −10% in a severe recession, 10% in a mild recession, 7% in a normal period, and 2% in a boom. The stock returns in the four scenarios are −37%, −11%, 14%, and 30%. What are the covariance and correlation coefficient between the rates of return on the two portfolios?

Using Historical Data

We've seen that portfolio risk and return depend on the means and variances of the component securities, as well as on the covariance between their returns. One way to obtain these inputs is a scenario analysis as in Spreadsheets 6.1–6.4. A common alternative approach to produce these inputs is to make use of historical data. The idea is that variability and covariability change slowly over time. Thus, if we estimate these statistics from recent data, our estimates will provide useful predictions for the near future.

We begin by using realized returns to estimate variances and covariances. The estimate of variance is the average value of the squared deviations around the sample average; the estimate of the covariance is the average value of the cross-product of deviations. Notice that, as in scenario analysis, the focus for risk is on deviations of returns from their average value. Instead of using mean returns based on the scenario analysis, however, we use average returns during the sample period. We can illustrate with an example.

Consider the 10 annual returns for the two mutual funds presented in the following spreadsheet. Although this sample period is far shorter than most analysts would use, for the sake of illustration we will pretend that it is adequate to estimate mean returns and relevant risk statistics with acceptable precision. In practice, analysts would use higher-frequency data (e.g., monthly or even daily data) to estimate risk coefficients and would, as well, supplement historical data with fundamental analysis to forecast future returns.

The spreadsheet starts with the raw return data in columns B and C. We use standard Excel functions to obtain average returns, standard deviation, covariance, and correlation (see rows 18–21). We also confirm (in cell F14) that covariance is the average value of the product of each asset's deviation from its mean return.

The average returns and standard deviations in this spreadsheet are similar to those of our previous scenario analysis. However, the correlation between stock and bond returns in this example is low but positive, which is more consistent with historical experience than the strongly negative correlation of −.49 implied by our scenario analysis.

EXAMPLE 6.1

Using Historical Data to Estimate Means, Standard Deviations, Covariance, and Correlation

	A	B	C	D	E	F
1		**Rates of Return**		**Deviations from Average Returns**		Products of
2	Year	Stock Fund	Bond Fund	Stock Fund	Bond Fund	Deviations
3	2009	30.17	5.08	20.17	0.08	1.53
4	2010	32.97	7.52	22.97	2.52	57.78
5	2011	21.04	−8.82	11.04	−13.82	−152.56
6	2012	−8.10	5.27	−18.10	0.27	−4.82
7	2013	−12.89	12.20	−22.89	7.20	−164.75
8	2014	−28.53	−7.79	−38.53	−12.79	493.00
9	2015	22.49	6.38	12.49	1.38	17.18
10	2016	12.58	12.40	2.58	7.40	19.05
11	2017	14.81	17.29	4.81	12.29	59.05
12	2018	15.50	0.51	5.50	−4.49	−24.70
13						
14	Average	10.00	5.00	Covariance = Average product of deviations:		30.08
15	SD	19.00	8.00	Correlation = Covariance/(SD stocks*SD bonds):		0.20
16						
17	**Excel formulas**					
18	Average	=AVERAGE(B3:B12)				
19	Std deviation	=STDEV.P(B3:B12)				
20	Covariance	=COVAR(B3:B12,C3:C12)				
21	Correlation	=CORREL(B3:B12,C3:C12)				
22						
23						

Two comments on Example 6.1 are in order. First, you may recall from a statistics class and from Chapter 5 that when variance is estimated from a sample of n observed returns, it is common to divide the squared deviations by $n - 1$ rather than by n. This is because we take deviations from an estimated average return rather than the true (but unknown) expected return; this procedure is said to adjust for a "lost degree of freedom." In Excel, the function STDEV.P computes standard deviation dividing by n, while the function STDEV.S uses $n - 1$.

Excel's covariance and correlation functions both use n. In Example 6.1, we ignored this fine point, and divided by n throughout. In any event, the correction for the lost degree of freedom is negligible when there are plentiful observations. For example, with 60 returns (e.g., five years of monthly data), the difference between dividing by 60 or 59 will affect variance or covariance by a multiple of only 1.017.

Second, we offer a warning about the statistical reliability of historical estimates. Estimates of variance and covariance from past data are generally reliable forecasts (at least for the short term). However, averages of past returns typically provide highly noisy (i.e., imprecise) forecasts of future expected returns. In this example, we use past averages from small samples because our objective is to demonstrate the methodology. In practice, professional investors spend most of their resources on macroeconomic and security analysis to improve their estimates of mean returns.

<table>
<tr><td>

CONCEPT
check

6.2
</td><td>

The following tables present returns on various pairs of stocks in several periods. In part A, we show you a scatter diagram of the returns on the first pair of stocks. Draw (or prepare in Excel) similar scatter diagrams for cases B through E. Match up your diagrams (A–E) to the following list of correlation coefficients by choosing the correlation that best describes the relationship between the returns on the two stocks: $\rho = -1, 0, .2, .5, 1.0$.
</td></tr>
</table>

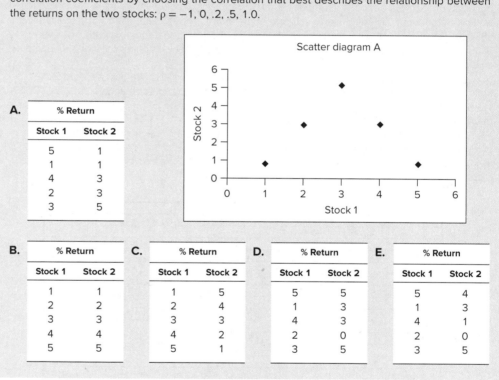

A.

% Return	
Stock 1	**Stock 2**
5	1
1	1
4	3
2	3
3	5

B.

% Return	
Stock 1	**Stock 2**
1	1
2	2
3	3
4	4
5	5

C.

% Return	
Stock 1	**Stock 2**
1	5
2	4
3	3
4	2
5	1

D.

% Return	
Stock 1	**Stock 2**
5	5
1	3
4	3
2	0
3	5

E.

% Return	
Stock 1	**Stock 2**
5	4
1	3
4	1
2	0
3	5

The Three Rules of Two-Risky-Asset Portfolios

Suppose a proportion denoted by w_B is invested in the bond fund and the remainder, $1 - w_B$, denoted by w_S, is invested in the stock fund. The properties of the portfolio are determined by the following three rules governing combinations of random variables:

Rule 1: The rate of return on a portfolio is the weighted average of returns on the component securities, with the portfolio proportions as weights.

$$r_P = w_B r_B + w_S r_S \qquad \text{(6.4)}$$

Rule 2: The expected *rate of return on a portfolio is the weighted average of the* expected *returns on the component securities, with the portfolio proportions as weights.*

$$E(r_P) = w_B E(r_B) + w_S E(r_S) \qquad \text{(6.5)}$$

Rules 1 and 2 say that a portfolio's actual return and its mean return are linear functions of the component security returns and portfolio weights. This is not so for portfolio variance, as the third rule shows.

Rule 3: The variance of the rate of return on a two-risky-asset portfolio is

$$\sigma_P^2 = (w_B\sigma_B)^2 + (w_S\sigma_S)^2 + 2(w_B\sigma_B)(w_S\sigma_S)\rho_{BS} \tag{6.6}$$

where ρ_{BS} is the correlation coefficient between the returns on the stock and bond funds. Notice that Equation 6.3 implies that we may replace the last term in Equation 6.6 with $2w_Bw_SCov(r_B, r_S)$.

The variance of a portfolio is the *sum* of the contributions of the component security variances *plus* a term that involves the correlation coefficient (and hence, covariance) between the returns on the component securities. We know from the last section why this last term arises. When the correlation between the component securities is small or negative, there will be a greater tendency for returns on the two assets to offset each other. This will reduce portfolio risk. Equation 6.6 tells us that portfolio variance is lower when the correlation coefficient is lower.

The formula describing portfolio variance is more complicated than that describing portfolio return. This complication has a virtue, however: a tremendous potential for gains from diversification.

The Risk-Return Trade-Off with Two-Risky-Assets Portfolios

We can assess the benefit from diversification by using Rules 2 and 3 to compare the risk and expected return of a better-diversified portfolio to a less-diversified benchmark. Suppose an investor estimates the following input data:

$$E(r_B) = 5\%;\ \sigma_B = 8\%;\ E(r_S) = 10\%;\ \sigma_S = 19\%;\ \rho_{BS} = .2$$

Currently, all funds are invested in the bond fund, but the invester ponders a portfolio invested 40% in stock and 60% in bonds. Using Rule 2, the expected return of this portfolio is

$$E(r_P) = .4 \times 10\% + .6 \times 5\% = 7\%,$$

which represents an increase of 2% compared to a bond-only investment. Using Rule 3, the portfolio standard deviation is

$$\sigma_P = \sqrt{(.4 \times 19)^2 + (.6 \times 8)^2 + 2(.4 \times 19) \times (.6 \times 8) \times .2} = 9.76\%,$$

which is less than the weighted average of the component standard deviations: $.4 \times 19 + .6 \times 8 = 12.40\%$. The difference of 2.64% reflects the benefits of diversification. This benefit is cost-free in the sense that diversification allows us to experience the full contribution of the stock's higher expected return, while keeping the portfolio standard deviation below the average of the component standard deviations.

Suppose we invest 85% in bonds and only 15% in stocks. This portfolio has an expected return *greater* than bonds [notice that $(.85 \times 5) + (.15 \times 10) = 5.75\%$], and, at the same time, a standard deviation *less* than bonds. Using Equation 6.6 again, we find that the portfolio variance is

$$(.85 \times 8)^2 + (.15 \times 19)^2 + 2(.85 \times 8)(.15 \times 19) \times .2 = 62.1$$

and, accordingly, the portfolio standard deviation is $\sqrt{62.1} = 7.88\%$, which is less than the standard deviation of either bonds or stocks alone. Taking on a more volatile asset (stocks) actually reduces portfolio risk! Such is the power of diversification.

EXAMPLE 6.2

Benefits from Diversification

We can find investment proportions that will reduce portfolio risk even further. The risk-minimizing proportions are 90.8% in bonds and 9.2% in stocks.[1] With these proportions, the portfolio standard deviation will be 7.80%, and the portfolio's expected return will be 5.46%.

Is this portfolio preferable to the one considered in Example 6.2, with 15% in the stock fund? That depends on how the investor trades off risk against return, because the portfolio with the lower variance also has a lower expected return.

investment opportunity set

Set of available portfolio risk-return combinations.

What the analyst can and must do is show investors the entire **investment opportunity set.** This is the set of all attainable combinations of risk and return offered by portfolios formed using the available assets in differing proportions. We find the investment opportunity set using Spreadsheet 6.5. Columns A and B set out several different proportions for investments in the stock and bond funds. The next columns present the portfolio expected return and standard deviation corresponding to each allocation. These risk-return combinations are plotted in Figure 6.3.

SPREADSHEET 6.5

The investment opportunity set with the stock and bond funds

X

Spreadsheets are available in Connect

	A	B	C	D	E
1			**Input Data**		
2	$E(r_S)$	$E(r_B)$	σ_S	σ_B	ρ_{BS}
3	10	5	19	8	0.2
4	Portfolio Weights		Expected Return, $E(r_p)$		Std Dev
5	$w_S = 1 - w_B$	w_B	Col A*A3 + Col B*B3		(Equation 6.6)
6	−0.2	1.2	4.0		9.59
7	−0.1	1.1	4.5		8.62
8	0.0	1.0	5.0		8.00
9	0.092	0.908	5.46		7.804
10	0.1	0.9	5.5		7.81
11	0.2	0.8	6.0		8.07
12	0.3	0.7	6.5		8.75
13	0.4	0.6	7.0		9.77
14	0.5	0.5	7.5		11.02
15	0.6	0.4	8.0		12.44
16	0.7	0.3	8.5		13.98
17	0.8	0.2	9.0		15.60
18	0.9	0.1	9.5		17.28
19	1.0	0.0	10.0		19.00
20	1.1	−0.1	10.5		20.75
21	1.2	−0.2	11.0		22.53
22	Notes:				
23	1. Negative weights indicate short positions.				
24	2. The weights of the minimum-variance portfolio are computed using the formula in Footnote 1.				
25	3. The highlighted row is the minimum-variance portfolio.				

The Mean-Variance Criterion

Investors desire portfolios that lie to the "northwest" in Figure 6.3. These are portfolios with high expected returns (toward the "north" of the figure) and low volatility (to the "west"). These preferences mean that we can compare portfolios using a *mean-variance criterion* in the following way: Portfolio *A* is said to dominate portfolio *B* if all investors prefer *A* over *B*. This will be the case if it has higher mean return and lower variance or standard deviation:

$$E(r_A) \geq E(r_B) \text{ and } \sigma_A \leq \sigma_B$$

---

[1] The formula for the weight in bonds in the minimum-variance (and hence minimum-standard deviation) portfolio is $w_B = \dfrac{\sigma_S^2 - \sigma_B \sigma_S \rho_{BS}}{\sigma_S^2 + \sigma_B^2 - 2\sigma_B \sigma_S \rho_{BS}}$, and the weight in stocks is $w_S = 1 - w_B$. When the correlation is zero, the variance-minimizing weight simplifies to the ratio of stock variance to the sum of the variances of stocks and bonds: $w_B = \dfrac{\sigma_S^2}{\sigma_S^2 + \sigma_B^2}$.

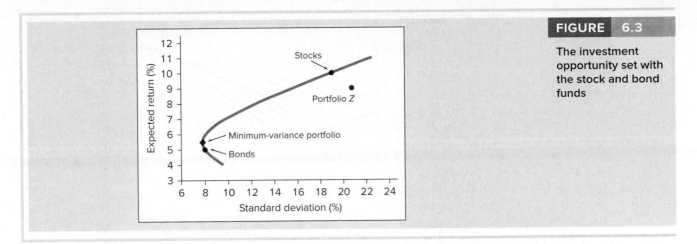

FIGURE 6.3

The investment opportunity set with the stock and bond funds

Graphically, when we plot the expected return and standard deviation of each portfolio in Figure 6.3, portfolio A will lie to the northwest of B. Given a choice between portfolios A and B, *all* investors would choose A. For example, the stock fund in Figure 6.3 dominates portfolio Z; the stock fund has higher expected return and lower volatility.

Portfolios that lie below the minimum-variance portfolio in the figure can therefore be rejected out of hand as inefficient. Any portfolio on the downward-sloping portion of the curve (including the bond fund) is "dominated" by the portfolio that lies directly above it on the upward-sloping portion of the curve since that portfolio has higher expected return and equal standard deviation. The best choice among the portfolios on the upward-sloping portion of the curve is not as obvious, because in this region higher expected return is accompanied by greater risk. We will discuss the best choice when we introduce the risk-free asset to the portfolio decision.

So far we have assumed a correlation of 0.2 between stock and bond returns. We know that low correlation aids diversification and that a higher correlation coefficient reduces the effect of diversification. What are the implications of perfect positive correlation between bonds and stocks?

A correlation coefficient of 1 simplifies Equation 6.6 for portfolio variance. Looking at it again, you will see that substitution of $\rho_{BS} = 1$ allows us to "complete the square" of the quantities $w_B\sigma_B$ and $w_S\sigma_S$ to obtain

$$\sigma_P^2 = w_B^2\sigma_B^2 + w_S^2\sigma_S^2 + 2w_B\sigma_B w_S\sigma_S = (w_B\sigma_B + w_S\sigma_S)^2$$
$$\sigma_P = w_B\sigma_B + w_S\sigma_S$$

In this special case, with perfect positive correlation, the portfolio standard deviation is a weighted average of the component security standard deviations. In this (and only this) circumstance, there are no gains to be had from diversification. Both the portfolio mean and the standard deviation are simple weighted averages. Figure 6.4 shows the opportunity set with perfect positive correlation—a straight line through the component securities. No portfolio can be discarded as inefficient in this case, and the choice among portfolios depends only on risk aversion. Diversification in the case of perfect positive correlation is not effective.

Perfect positive correlation is the *only* case in which there is no benefit from diversification. Whenever $\rho < 1$, the portfolio standard deviation is less than the weighted average of the standard deviations of the component securities. Therefore, *there are benefits to diversification whenever asset returns are less than perfectly positively correlated.*

Our analysis has ranged from very attractive diversification benefits ($\rho_{BS} < 0$) to no benefits at all ($\rho_{BS} = 1$). For ρ_{BS} within this range, the benefits will be somewhere in between.

Investment opportunity sets for bonds and stocks with various correlation coefficients

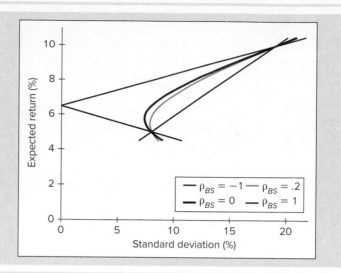

A realistic correlation coefficient between stocks and bonds based on historical experience is actually around 0.20, which is why we include a graph for $\rho_{BS} = .2$ in Figure 6.4. Spreadsheet 6.6 enumerates some of the points on the various opportunity sets in Figure 6.4. As the figure illustrates, $\rho_{BS} = .2$ is a lot better for diversification than perfect positive correlation and a bit worse than zero correlation.

Investment opportunity set for stocks and bonds with various correlation coefficients

	A	B	C	D	E	F	G
1			**Input Data**				
2	$E(r_S)$	$E(r_B)$	σ_S	σ_B			
3	10	5	19	8			
4							
5	Weights in Stocks	Portfolio Expected Return	Portfolio Standard Deviation[1] for Given Correlation, ρ				
6	w_S	$E(r_P) = $ Col A*A3 + (1 − Col A)*B3	−1	0	0.2	0.5	1
7	−0.1	4.5	10.70	9.00	8.62	8.02	6.90
8	0.0	5.0	8.00	8.00	8.00	8.00	8.00
9	0.1	5.5	5.30	7.45	7.81	8.31	9.10
10	0.2	6.0	2.60	7.44	8.07	8.93	10.20
11	0.3	6.5	0.10	7.99	8.75	9.79	11.30
12	0.4	7.0	2.80	8.99	9.77	10.83	12.40
13	0.6	8.0	8.20	11.84	12.44	13.29	14.60
14	0.8	9.0	13.60	15.28	15.60	16.06	16.80
15	1.0	10.0	19.00	19.00	19.00	19.00	19.00
16	1.1	10.5	21.70	20.92	20.75	20.51	20.10
17			Minimum-Variance Portfolio[2,3,4,5]				
18	$w_S(min) = (\sigma_B{}^2 − \sigma_B\sigma_S\rho)/(\sigma_S{}^2 + \sigma_B{}^2 − 2^*\sigma_B\sigma_S\rho) = $		0.2963	0.1506	0.0923	−0.0440	−0.7273
19	$E(r_P) − w_S(min)^*A3 + (1 − w_S(min))^*B3 = $		6.48	5.75	5.46	4.78	1.36
20		$\sigma_P = $	0.00	7.37	7.80	7.97	0.00

Spreadsheets are available in Connect

Notes:

1. $\sigma_P = $ SQRT[(Col A*C3)^2 + ((1 − Col A)*D3)^2 + 2*Col A*C3*(1 − Col A)*D3*ρ]

2. The standard deviation is calculated from Equation 6.6 using the weights of the minimum-variance portfolio:

   $$\sigma_P = \text{SQRT}[(w_S(min)^*C3)^2 + ((1 − w_S(min))^*D3)^2 + 2^*w_S(min)^*C3^*(1 − w_S(min))^*D3^*\rho]$$

3. As the correlation coefficient grows, the minimum-variance portfolio requires a smaller position in stocks (even a negative position for higher correlations), and the performance of this portfolio becomes less attractive.

4. Notice that with correlation of .5 or higher, minimum variance is achieved with a short position in stocks. The standard deviation is lower than that of bonds, but the mean is lower as well.

5. With perfect positive correlation (column G), you can drive the standard deviation to zero by taking a large, short position in stocks. The mean return is then as low as 1.36%.

Negative correlation between a pair of assets is also possible. When correlation is negative, there will be even greater diversification benefits. Again, let us start with the extreme. With perfect negative correlation, we substitute $\rho_{BS} = -1$ in Equation 6.6 and simplify it by completing the square:

$$\sigma_P^2 = (w_B\sigma_B - w_S\sigma_S)^2$$

and, therefore,

$$\sigma_P = \text{ABS}[w_B\sigma_B - w_S\sigma_S] \tag{6.7}$$

The right-hand side of Equation 6.7 denotes the absolute value of $w_B\sigma_B - w_S\sigma_S$. The solution involves the absolute value because standard deviation cannot be negative.

With perfect negative correlation, the benefits from diversification stretch to the limit. Equation 6.7 yields the proportions that will reduce the portfolio standard deviation all the way to zero.[2] With our data, this will happen when $w_B = 70.37\%$. While exposing us to zero risk, investing 29.63% in stocks (rather than placing all funds in bonds) will still increase the portfolio expected return from 5% to 6.48%. Of course, we can hardly expect results this attractive in reality.

Suppose that for some reason you are *required* to invest 50% of your portfolio in bonds and 50% in stocks. Use the assumed values for mean returns and standard deviations in Spreadsheet 6.5 to answer the following questions.

a. If the standard deviation of your portfolio is 10%, what must be the correlation coefficient between stock and bond returns?

b. What is the expected rate of return on your portfolio?

c. Now suppose that the correlation between stock and bond returns is 0.22 instead of the value you found in part (*a*) but that you are free to choose whatever portfolio proportions you desire. Are you likely to be better or worse off than you were in part (*a*)?

CONCEPT check 6.3

6.3 THE OPTIMAL RISKY PORTFOLIO WITH A RISK-FREE ASSET

Now we expand the asset allocation problem to include a risk-free asset. When choosing their capital allocation between risky and risk-free portfolios, investors naturally will want to work with the risky portfolio that offers the greatest reward for assuming risk. We will see that this is the portfolio with highest reward-to-volatility or Sharpe ratio. The higher the Sharpe ratio, the greater is the expected return corresponding to any level of volatility. Therefore, our next step will be the construction of a risky portfolio combining the major asset classes (here a bond and a stock fund) that provides the highest possible Sharpe ratio.

We will continue to use the input data from Spreadsheet 6.5. Suppose then that we are still confined to the risky bond and stock funds but now can also invest in T-bills yielding 3%. When we add the risk-free asset to a risky portfolio constructed from stocks and bonds, the resulting opportunity set is the straight line that we called the CAL (capital allocation line) in Chapter 5. We now consider various CALs constructed from risk-free bills and a variety of possible risky portfolios, each formed by combining the stock and bond funds in alternative proportions.

We start in Figure 6.5 with the opportunity set of risky assets constructed only from the bond and stock funds. The lowest-variance risky portfolio is labeled MIN (denoting the

---

[2]The proportion in bonds that will drive the standard deviation to zero when $\rho = -1$ is

$$w_B = \frac{\sigma_S}{\sigma_B + \sigma_S}$$

Compare this formula to the formula in footnote 1 for the variance-minimizing proportions when $\rho = 0$.

FIGURE   6.5

The opportunity set of
stocks, bonds, and a
risk-free asset with two
capital allocation lines

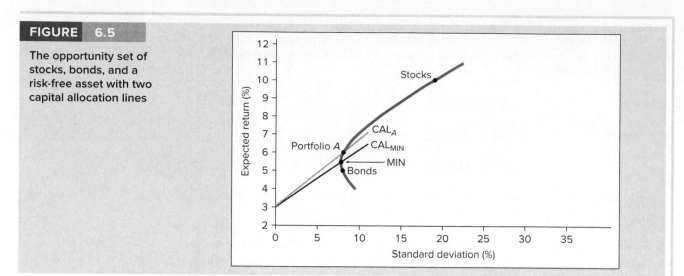

minimum-variance portfolio). CAL$_{MIN}$ is drawn through it and shows the risk-return trade-off
with various positions in T-bills and portfolio MIN. It is immediately evident from the figure
that we could do better (i.e., obtain a higher Sharpe ratio) by using portfolio *A* instead of MIN
as the risky portfolio. CAL$_A$ dominates CAL$_{MIN}$ in the sense that it offers a higher expected
return for any level of volatility.

The slope of the CAL corresponding to a risky portfolio, *P,* is the Sharpe ratio of that portfolio, that is, the ratio of its expected excess return to its standard deviation:

$$S_P = \frac{E(r_P) - r_f}{\sigma_P} \qquad \textbf{(6.8)}$$

With a T-bill rate of 3%, we can find and compare the Sharpe ratios of portfolios *A* and
MIN. Portfolio *A,* with a weight in the stock fund of 0.2, offers an expected return of 6% with
an SD of 8.07% (see row 10 of Spreadsheet 6.6). Therefore, the Sharpe ratios of these two
portfolios are:

$$S_{MIN} = \frac{5.46 - 3}{7.80} = .32 \quad S_A = \frac{6 - 3}{8.07} = .37 \qquad \textbf{(6.9)}$$

The higher ratio for portfolio *A* compared to MIN measures the improvement it offers in the
risk-return trade-off.

But why stop at portfolio *A*? We can continue to ratchet the CAL upward until it reaches
the ultimate point of tangency with the investment opportunity set. This produces the CAL
with the highest feasible Sharpe ratio. Therefore, the tangency portfolio in Figure 6.6 is the
optimal risky portfolio (denoted portfolio *O*) to mix with T-bills; in general, the optimal
portfolio is defined as the risky portfolio that generates the steepest CAL.

To find the composition of the optimal risky portfolio, *O,* we search for weights in the
stock and bond funds that maximize the portfolio's Sharpe ratio. With only two risky assets,
we can solve for the optimal portfolio weights using the following formula:[3]

optimal risky portfolio

The best combination of risky
assets to be mixed with safe
assets when forming the complete portfolio.

$$w_B = \frac{[E(r_B) - r_f]\sigma_S^2 - [E(r_S) - r_f]\sigma_B\sigma_S\rho_{BS}}{[E(r_B) - r_f]\sigma_S^2 + [E(r_S) - r_f]\sigma_B^2 - [E(r_B) - r_f + E(r_S) - r_f]\sigma_B\sigma_S\rho_{BS}} \qquad \textbf{(6.10)}$$

$$w_S = 1 - w_B$$

[3] Equation 6.10, providing the weights that maximize the Sharpe ratio, can be obtained using calculus: Write the
Sharpe ratio of a portfolio formed from the stock and bond funds as a function of w_B and $w_S = 1 - w_B$, as well as
the expected returns, standard deviations, and correlation coefficient of the two funds. Setting the derivative of the
Sharpe ratio with respect to w_B equal to zero produces an equation that can be solved for the optimal w_B.

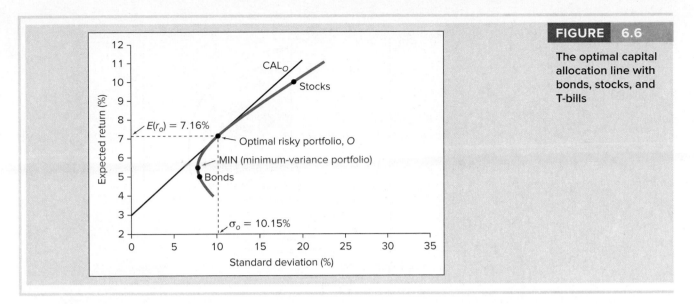

FIGURE 6.6

The optimal capital allocation line with bonds, stocks, and T-bills

Using the risk premiums (expected excess return over the risk-free rate) of the stock and bond funds, their standard deviations, and the correlation between their returns in Equation 6.10, we find that the weights of the optimal portfolio are $w_B(O) = .568$ and $w_S(O) = .432$. Using these weights, Equations 6.5, 6.6, and 6.8 imply that $E(r_O) = 7.16\%$, $\sigma_O = 10.15\%$, and therefore the Sharpe ratio of the optimal portfolio (the slope of its CAL) is

$$S_O = \frac{E(r_O) - r_f}{\sigma_O} = \frac{7.16 - 3}{10.15} = .41$$

This Sharpe ratio is significantly higher than those provided by either the bond or stock portfolios alone.

In the last chapter we saw that the preferred *complete* portfolio formed from a risky portfolio and a risk-free asset depends on risk aversion. More risk-averse investors prefer low-risk portfolios despite the lower expected return, while more risk-tolerant investors choose higher-risk, higher-return portfolios. Both types of investors, however, will choose portfolio O as their risky portfolio as it provides the highest return *per unit* of risk, that is, the steepest capital allocation line. Investors will differ only in their allocation of investment funds between portfolio O and the risk-free asset.

Figure 6.7 shows one possible choice for the preferred complete portfolio, C. The investor places 55% of wealth in portfolio O and 45% in Treasury bills. The rate of return and volatility of the portfolio are

$$E(r_C) = 3\% \times .45 + 7.16\% \times .55 = 5.29\%$$
$$\sigma_C = .55 \times 10.15\% = 5.58\%$$

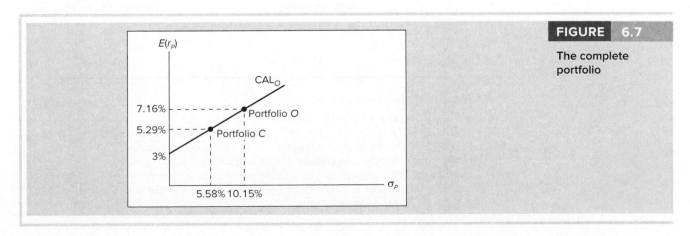

FIGURE 6.7

The complete portfolio

FIGURE   **6.8**

FIGURE   **6.8**

The composition of the
complete portfolio: The
solution to the asset
allocation problem

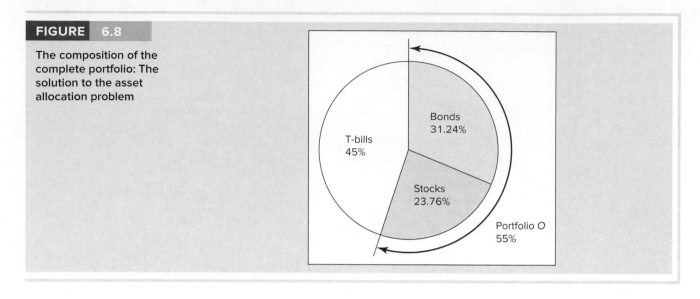

Because portfolio O is a mix of the bond fund and stock fund with weights of 56.8% and 43.2%, the overall asset allocation of the *complete* portfolio is as follows:

Weight in risk-free asset		45.00%
Weight in bond fund	0.568 × 55% =	31.24
Weight in stock fund	0.432 × 55% =	23.76
Total		100.00%

Figure 6.8 depicts the overall asset allocation. The allocation reflects considerations of both efficient diversification (the construction of the optimal risky portfolio, O) and risk aversion (the allocation of funds between the risk-free asset and the risky portfolio O to form the complete portfolio, C).

CONCEPT
check   **6.4**

A universe of securities includes a risky stock (X), a stock-index fund (M), and T-bills. The data for the universe are:

	Expected Return	Standard Deviation
X	15%	50%
M	10	20
T-bills	5	0

The correlation coefficient between X and M is −.2.

  a. Draw the opportunity set of securities X and M.
  b. Find the optimal risky portfolio (O), its expected return, standard deviation, and Sharpe ratio. Compare with the Sharpe ratios of X and M, each taken individually.
  c. Find the slope of the CAL generated by T-bills and portfolio O.
  d. Suppose an investor places 2/9 (i.e., 22.22%) of the complete portfolio in the risky portfolio O and the remainder in T-bills. Calculate the composition of the complete portfolio, its expected return, SD, and Sharpe ratio.

| 6.4 | **EFFICIENT DIVERSIFICATION WITH MANY RISKY ASSETS** |

We extend the two-risky-assets portfolio methodology to many risky assets in three steps. First, we generalize the two-risky-asset opportunity set to allow for many assets. Next we determine the optimal risky portfolio that supports the steepest CAL, that is, maximizes the Sharpe ratio. Finally, we choose a complete portfolio on CAL_O based on risk aversion by mixing the risk-free asset with the optimal risky portfolio.

The Efficient Frontier of Risky Assets

To get a sense of how additional risky assets can improve investment opportunities, look at Figure 6.9. Points *A, B,* and *C* represent the expected returns and standard deviations of three stocks. The curve passing through *A* and *B* shows the risk-return combinations of portfolios formed from those two stocks. Similarly, the curve passing through *B* and *C* shows portfolios formed from those two stocks. Now observe point *E* on the *AB* curve and point *F* on the *BC* curve. These points represent two portfolios chosen from the set of *AB* and *BC* combinations. The curve that passes through *E* and *F* in turn represents portfolios constructed from portfolios *E* and *F*. Since *E* and *F* are themselves constructed from *A, B,* and *C,* this curve shows some of the portfolios constructed from these *three* stocks. Notice that curve *EF* extends the investment opportunity set to the northwest, which is the desired direction.

Now we can continue to take other points (each representing portfolios) from these three curves and further combine them into new portfolios, thus shifting the opportunity set even farther to the northwest. You can see that this process would work even better with more stocks. Moreover, the boundary or "envelope" of all the curves thus developed will lie quite away from the individual stocks in the northwesterly direction, as shown in Figure 6.10.

The analytical technique to derive the efficient set of risky assets was developed by Harry Markowitz, and is often referred to as the *Markowitz model.* We sketch his approach here.

First, we determine the risk-return opportunity set. The aim is to construct from the universe of available securities the northwestern-most portfolios in terms of expected return and standard deviation. The input data are the expected returns and standard deviations of each asset in the universe, along with the correlation coefficients between each pair of assets. The graph that connects all the northwestern-most portfolios is called the **efficient frontier** of risky assets. It represents the set of portfolios that offers the highest possible expected rate of return for each level of portfolio standard deviation. These portfolios may be viewed as efficiently diversified. One such frontier is shown in Panel A of Figure 6.10.

efficient frontier
Graph representing a set of portfolios that maximizes expected return at each level of portfolio volatility.

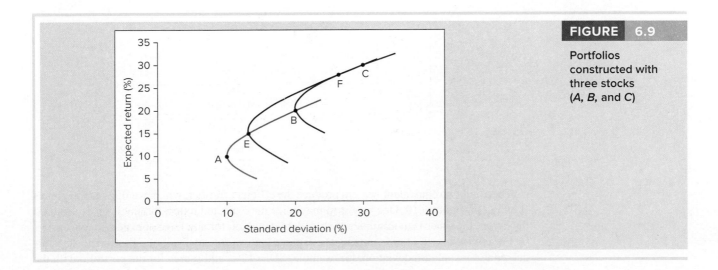

FIGURE 6.9

Portfolios constructed with three stocks (*A, B,* and *C*)

FIGURE   6.10

The efficient frontier of risky assets and individual assets. In Panel B, we maximize $E(r)$ for any choice of standard deviation. In Panel C, we minimize standard deviation for each choice of $E(r)$.

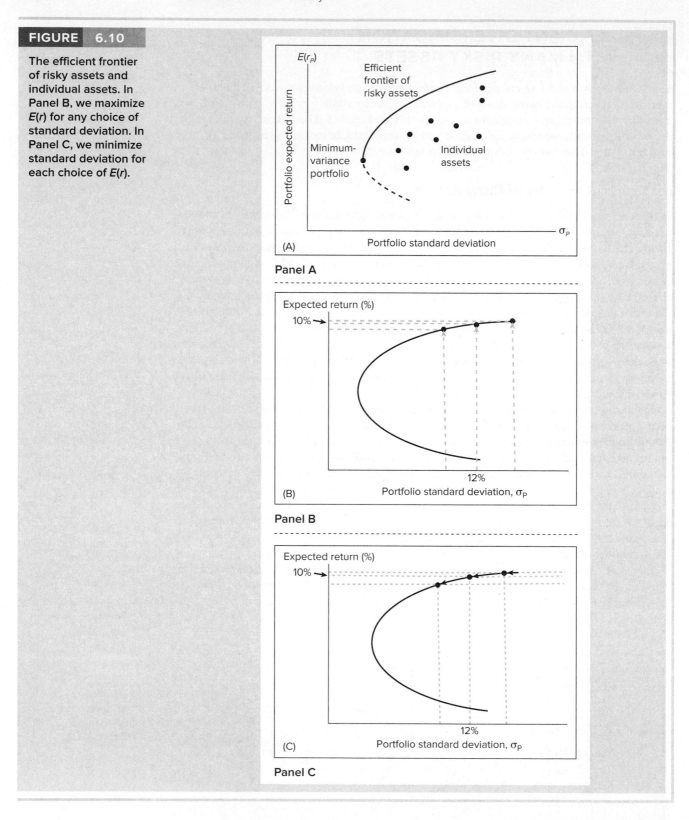

Panel A

Panel B

Panel C

There are two equivalent ways to produce the efficient frontier, which we illustrate in Panels B and C of Figure 6.10. One way is to maximize the expected return for any level of standard deviation; the other is to minimize the standard deviation for any level of expected return.

For the first method, maximizing the expected return for any level of risk, we choose a target value for standard deviation, for example, SD = 12%, and search for the portfolio with the highest possible expected return consistent with this level of volatility. So we give our optimization software an assignment to maximize expected return subject to two constraints: (*i*) The portfolio weights must sum to 1 (this is called the *feasibility* constraint, since any legitimate portfolio must have weights that sum to 100%), and (*ii*) the portfolio SD must match the targeted value, $\sigma = 12\%$. The optimization software searches over all portfolios with $\sigma = 12\%$ and finds the highest feasible portfolio on the vertical line drawn at $\sigma = 12\%$; this is the portfolio with the highest expected return. That portfolio is located at the top of the vertical arrow that rises from SD = 12%. The horizontal tracer line from this point to the vertical axis indicates that for this portfolio, $E(r) = 10\%$. You now have one point on the efficient frontier. Repeat for other target levels of volatility and you will find other points on the frontier. When you "connect the dots" as we have done in Panel B, you will have drawn a frontier like that in Figure 6.10.

The second method is to minimize volatility for any level of expected return. Here, you need to draw a few *horizontal* lines above the global minimum-variance portfolio *G* (portfolios lying below *G* are inefficient because they offer a *lower* risk premium and *higher* variance than *G*). In Panel C, we have drawn the first horizontal line at an expected return of 10%. Now the software's assignment is to minimize the SD subject to the feasibility constraint. But in this method, we replace the constraint on SD with one on the portfolio's expected return, that is, we require that $E(r) = 10\%$. So we seek the portfolio that is farthest to the left along the horizontal line drawn at a level of 10% —this is the portfolio with the lowest SD consistent with an expected return of 10%. You already know from Panel B that this portfolio must be at $\sigma = 12\%$. Repeat this approach using other expected returns, and you will find other points along the efficient frontier. Again, connect the dots as we have done in Panel C, and you will have the frontier of Figure 6.10.

In practice, various constraints may preclude a particular investor from choosing portfolios on the efficient frontier. If an institution is prohibited from taking short positions in any asset, the portfolio manager must add constraints to the optimization program that rule out negative (short) positions. To impose a short-sale restriction, the additional constraints in the optimization program are that all asset weights in the optimal portfolio must be greater than or equal to zero.

Some clients may want to ensure a minimum level of expected dividend yield. In this case, input data must include a set of expected dividend yields, and the optimization program is given the constraint that the expected *portfolio* dividend yield will equal or exceed the desired level. Another common constraint forbids investments in companies engaged in "undesirable social activity." This constraint implies that portfolio weights in these companies must equal zero.

In principle, portfolio managers can tailor an efficient frontier to meet any particular objective. Of course, any constraint carries a price tag in the sense that an efficient frontier subject to additional constraints will offer a lower Sharpe ratio.

Deriving the efficient frontier and graphing it with any number of assets and any set of constraints is quite straightforward. For a not-too-large number of assets, the efficient frontier can be computed and graphed even with a spreadsheet program.

Choosing the Optimal Risky Portfolio

The second step of the optimization plan involves the risk-free asset. Using the risk-free rate, we search for the capital allocation line with the highest Sharpe ratio (the steepest slope), just as we did in Figures 6.5 and 6.6.

The CAL formed from the optimal risky portfolio (*O*) will be tangent to the efficient frontier of risky assets discussed above. Because this CAL lies above all other feasible CALs, Portfolio *O* is the optimal risky portfolio.

There is yet another way to find the best risky portfolio. Because we know that the optimal portfolio is the one that maximizes the Sharpe ratio, rather than solving for the entire efficient frontier, we can proceed directly to determining the optimal portfolio. We ask our optimization program to maximize the Sharpe ratio subject only to the feasibility constraint (that portfolio weights sum to 1). The portfolio providing the highest possible Sharpe ratio is the optimal portfolio O. While this last approach does not produce the entire minimum-variance frontier, in many applications, only the optimal risky portfolio is necessary.

The Preferred Complete Portfolio and a Separation Property

Finally, each investor chooses the appropriate mix between the optimal risky portfolio (O) and T-bills, exactly as in Figure 6.7.

A portfolio manager will offer the same risky portfolio (O) to all clients, no matter what their degrees of risk aversion. Risk aversion comes into play only when clients select their desired point on the CAL. Regardless of risk aversion, all clients will use portfolio O as the optimal risky investment vehicle.

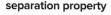

separation property

The property that implies portfolio choice can be separated into two independent tasks: (1) determination of the optimal risky portfolio, which is a purely technical problem, and (2) the personal choice of the best mix of the risky portfolio and the risk-free asset.

This result is called a **separation property,** introduced by James Tobin (1958). Its name reflects the fact that portfolio choice can be separated into two independent tasks. The first task, to determine the optimal risky portfolio (O), is purely technical. Given the input data, the best risky portfolio is the same for all clients regardless of risk aversion. The second task, construction of the complete portfolio from bills and portfolio O, is personal and depends on risk aversion. Here the client is the decision maker.

In practice, optimal risky portfolios for different clients may vary because of constraints on short sales, dividend yield, tax considerations, or other client preferences. Our analysis, though, suggests that a few portfolios may be sufficient to serve the demands of a wide range of investors. We see here the theoretical basis of the mutual fund industry.

The (computerized) optimization technique is the easiest part of portfolio construction. When different managers use different input data, they will develop different efficient frontiers and offer different "optimal" portfolios. Therefore, the real arena of the competition among portfolio managers is in the sophisticated security analysis that produces the input estimates. The rule of GIGO (garbage in–garbage out) applies fully to portfolio selection. If the quality of security analysis is poor, a passive portfolio such as a market-index fund will yield better results than an active portfolio tilted toward *seemingly* favorable securities.

CONCEPT
c h e c k   **6.5**

Two portfolio managers work for competing investment management houses. Each employs security analysts to prepare input data for the construction of the optimal portfolio. When all is completed, the efficient frontier obtained by manager A dominates that of manager B in that A's optimal risky portfolio lies northwest of B's. Is the more attractive efficient frontier asserted by manager A evidence that she really employs better security analysts?

Constructing the Optimal Risky Portfolio: An Illustration

To illustrate how the optimal risky portfolio might be constructed, suppose an analyst wished to construct an efficiently diversified global portfolio using the stock market indices of six countries. Panel A of Table 6.1 shows the input list. The values for standard deviations and the correlation matrix are estimated from historical data, while forecasts of risk premiums are generated from fundamental analysis. Examination of the table shows the U.S. index portfolio has the highest Sharpe ratio. Given the high Sharpe ratio for the U.S. in this period, one might be tempted to conclude that U.S. investors would not have benefited much from international diversification. But even in this sample period, we will see that diversification is beneficial.

Panel B shows the efficient frontier developed as follows: First we generate the global minimum-variance portfolio G by minimizing the SD with just the feasibility constraint, and then we find portfolio O by maximizing the Sharpe ratio subject only to the same constraint. To fill out the curve, we choose more risk premiums; for each, we minimize portfolio volatility. In all, we have 13 points to draw the graph in Figure 6.11, one of which is the maximum-Sharpe-ratio portfolio, O.

The results are striking. Observe that the SD of the global minimum-variance portfolio, 10.94%, is far lower than that of the lowest-variance country (the U.K.), which has an SD of 14.93%. G is formed by taking short positions in Germany and France, as well as a large

TABLE 6.1 Efficient frontiers for international diversification with and without short sales and CAL with short sales

A. Input List

Excess Returns

	Mean	SD	Sharpe Ratio	INPUT LIST
U.S.	0.0600	0.1495	0.4013	Expected excess returns from fundamental analysis.
U.K.	0.0530	0.1493	0.3551	Standard deviations and correlation matrix constructed
FRANCE	0.0680	0.2008	0.3386	from historical returns.
GERMANY	0.0800	0.2270	0.3525	
JAPAN	0.0450	0.1878	0.2397	
CHINA	0.0730	0.3004	0.2430	

Correlation Matrix

	U.S.	U.K.	France	Germany	Japan	China
U.S.	1					
U.K.	0.83	1				
FRANCE	0.83	0.92	1			
GERMANY	0.85	0.88	0.96	1		
JAPAN	0.43	0.44	0.47	0.43	1	
CHINA	0.16	0.28	0.26	0.29	0.14	1

B. Efficient Frontier: Short Sales Allowed

Portfolio:	(1)	(2)	G	(4)	(5)	(6)	(7)	O	(9)	(10)	(11)	(12)	(13)
Risk premium	0.0325	0.0375	0.0410	0.0425	0.0450	0.0500	0.0550	0.058474	0.0600	0.0650	0.0700	0.0800	0.0850
SD	0.1147	0.1103	0.1094	0.1095	0.1106	0.1154	0.1234	0.130601	0.1341	0.1469	0.1612	0.1933	0.2104
Slope (Sharpe)	0.2832	0.3400	0.3749	0.3880	0.4070	0.4334	0.4457	0.447733	0.4474	0.4425	0.4341	0.4140	0.4040
Portfolio weights													
U.S.	0.5948	0.6268	0.6476	0.6569	0.6724	0.7033	0.7342	0.755643	0.7651	0.7960	0.8269	0.8887	0.9196
U.K.	1.0667	0.8878	0.7681	0.7155	0.6279	0.4527	0.2775	0.155808	0.1023	−0.0728	−0.2480	−0.5984	−0.7736
FRANCE	−0.1014	−0.1308	−0.1618	−0.1727	−0.1908	−0.2272	−0.2635	−0.28880	−0.2999	−0.3362	−0.3725	−0.4452	−0.4816
GERMANY	−0.8424	−0.6702	−0.5431	−0.4901	−0.4019	−0.2253	−0.0487	−0.07400	0.1278	0.3044	0.4810	0.8341	1.0107
JAPAN	0.2158	0.1985	0.1866	0.1815	0.1729	0.1558	0.1386	0.126709	0.1215	0.1043	0.0872	0.0529	0.0357
CHINA	0.0664	0.0879	0.1025	0.1089	0.1195	0.1407	0.1619	0.176649	0.1831	0.2043	0.2256	0.2680	0.2892

C. Capital Allocation Line (CAL) with Short Sales

Risk premium	0.0000	0.0494	0.0490	0.0490	0.0495	0.0517	0.0553	0.0585	0.0600	0.0658	0.0722	0.0865	0.1343
SD	0.0000	0.1103	0.1094	0.1095	0.1106	0.1154	0.1234	0.1306	0.1341	0.1469	0.1612	0.1933	0.3000

D. Efficient Frontier: No Short Sales

Portfolio	(1)	(2)	(3)	(4)	(5)	Min Var	(7)	(8)	Optimum	(10)	(11)	(12)	(13)
Risk premium	0.0450	0.0475	0.0490	0.0510	0.0535	0.0560	0.0573	0.0590	0.0607	0.0650	0.07	0.0750	0.0800
SD	0.1878	0.1555	0.1435	0.1372	0.1330	0.131648	0.1321	0.1337	0.1367	0.1493	0.1675332	0.1893	0.2270
Slope (Sharpe)	0.2397	0.3055	0.3414	0.3718	0.4022	0.425089	0.4339	0.4411	0.4439	0.4353	0.4178277	0.3963	0.3525
Portfolio weights													
U.S.	0.0000	0.0000	0.0000	0.0671	0.2375	0.4052	0.4964	0.6122	0.7067	0.6367	0.4223	0.1680	0.0000
U.K.	0.0000	0.3125	0.5000	0.5465	0.3967	0.2491	0.1689	0.0670	0.0000	0.0000	0.0000	0.0000	0.0000
FRANCE	0.0000	0.0000	0.0000	0.0000	0.0000	0.0000	0.0000	0.0000	0.0000	0.0000	0.0000	0.0000	0.0000
GERMANY	0.0000	0.0000	0.0000	0.0000	0.0000	0.0000	0.0000	0.0000	0.0000	0.1324	0.3558	0.5976	1.0000
JAPAN	1.0000	0.6875	0.5000	0.3642	0.3029	0.2424	0.2096	0.1679	0.1114	0.0232	0.0000	0.0000	0.0000
CHINA	0.0000	0.0000	0.0000	0.0222	0.0630	0.1032	0.1251	0.1529	0.1819	0.2077	0.2219	0.2343	0.0000

FIGURE 6.11

Efficient frontiers and CAL from Table 6.1

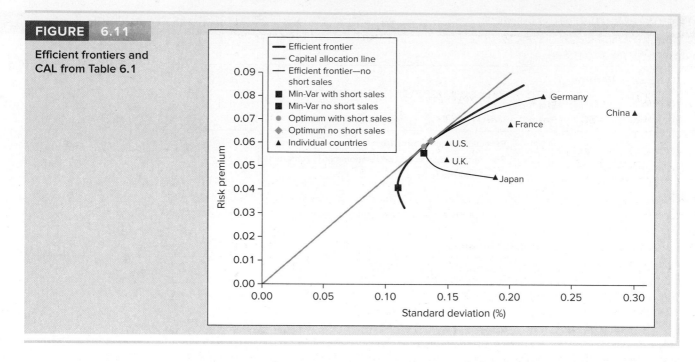

position in the relatively low-risk U.K. Moreover, the Sharpe ratio of this portfolio is higher than that of all countries but the U.S! Still, even this portfolio will be rejected in favor of the highest Sharpe-ratio portfolio.

Portfolio O attains a Sharpe ratio of .4477, compared to the U.S. ratio of .4013, a significant improvement that can be verified from the CAL shown in Panel C. The points in Panel C are selected to have the same SD as those of the efficient frontier portfolios, so the risk premium for each equals the SD times the Sharpe ratio of portfolio O.[4] Notice that portfolio (9) on the CAL has the same risk premium as the U.S., 6%, but an SD of 13.41%, fully 1.5% less than the 14.95% SD of the U.S. All this is achieved while still investing 76.51% of the portfolio in the U.S., although it does require a large short position in France (−29.99%).

Many institutional investors are prohibited from taking short positions, and individuals may be averse to large short positions because the unlimited upward potential of stock prices implies unlimited potential losses on short sales. Panel D shows the efficient frontier when an additional constraint is applied to each portfolio, namely, that all weights must be nonnegative.

Take a look at the two frontiers in Figure 6.11. The no-short-sale frontier is clearly inferior on both ends. This is because both very low-return and very high-return frontier portfolios will typically entail short positions. At the low-return/low-volatility end of the frontier, efficient portfolios take short positions in stocks with a high correlation and low-risk premium that can reduce variance with low impact on expected return. At the other (high expected return) end of the frontier, we find short positions in low-risk-premium stocks in favor of larger positions in high-risk-premium stocks. Therefore, the short-sale constrained efficient frontier diverges further from the unconstrained frontier for extreme-risk premiums.

6.5	**A SINGLE-INDEX STOCK MARKET**

index model

Model that relates stock returns to returns on both a broad market index and firm-specific factors.

We started this chapter with the distinction between systematic and firm-specific risk. Systematic risk is macroeconomic, affecting all securities, while firm-specific risk factors affect only one particular firm or, at most, a cluster of firms. **Index models** are statistical models designed to estimate these two components of risk for a particular security or portfolio. The

---

[4] Since the Sharpe ratio is S = risk premium/SD, we can rearrange to show that SD = risk premium/S_O. The CAL has the same slope everywhere, equal to the Sharpe ratio of portfolio O that supports it.

first to use an index model to explain the benefits of diversification was another Nobel Prize winner, William F. Sharpe (1963). We will introduce his major work (the capital asset pricing model) in the next chapter.

The popularity of index models is due to their practicality. To construct the efficient frontier from a universe of 100 securities, we would need to estimate 100 expected returns, 100 variances, and $100 \times 99/2 = 4,950$ covariances. And a universe of 100 securities is actually quite small. A universe of 1,000 securities would require estimates of $1,000 \times 999/2 = 499,500$ covariances, as well as 1,000 expected returns and variances. The index model asserts that one common systematic factor is responsible for all the covariability of stock returns, with all other variability due to firm-specific factors. This assumption dramatically simplifies the analysis.

The intuition that motivates the index model can be seen in Figure 6.12. We begin with a historical sample of paired observations of excess returns on the market index and a particular security, let's say shares in Ford. In Figure 6.12, we have 60 pairs of monthly excess returns, one for each month in a five-year sample. Each dot represents the pair of returns in one particular month. For example, in January 2012, Ford's excess return was 15.9% while the market's was 5.4%.

To describe the *typical* relation between the return on Ford and the return on the market index, we fit a straight line through the *scatter diagram* in Figure 6.12. It is clear from this "line of best fit" that there is a positive relation between Ford's return and the market's. This is evidence for the importance of broad market conditions on the performance of Ford's stock. The slope of the line reflects the sensitivity of Ford's return to market conditions: A steeper line would imply that Ford's rate of return is more responsive to the market return. On the other hand, the scatter diagram also shows that market conditions are not the entire story: If returns *perfectly* tracked those of the market, then all return pairs would lie exactly on the line. The scatter of points *around* the line is evidence that firm-specific events also have a significant impact on Ford's return.

How might we determine the line of best fit? We use R_i to denote an **excess return,** so the market index, M, has an excess return of $R_M = r_M - r_f$, and Ford's excess return is $R_{\text{Ford}} = r_{\text{Ford}} - r_f$. We estimate the line using a single-variable linear regression. Specifically, we regress Ford's excess return on the excess return of the index, R_M. More generally, for

excess return

Rate of return in excess of the risk-free rate.

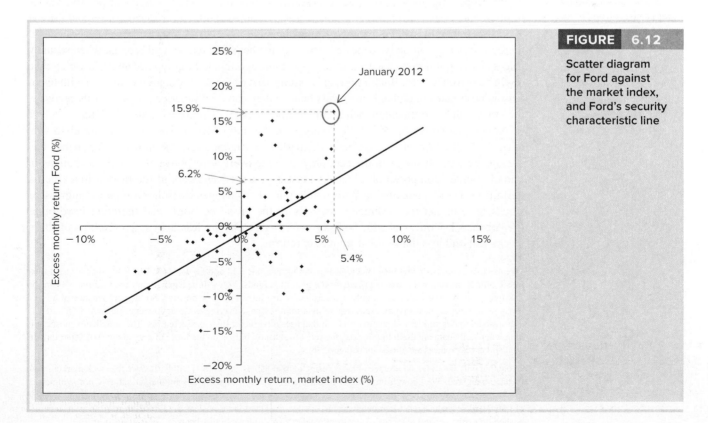

FIGURE 6.12

Scatter diagram for Ford against the market index, and Ford's security characteristic line

any stock *i,* denote the excess return in month *t* by $R_i(t)$ and the market index excess return by $R_M(t)$. Then the index model can be written as the following *regression equation:*

$$R_i(t) = \alpha_i + \beta_i R_M(t) + e_i(t) \tag{6.11}$$

alpha

A stock's expected return beyond that consistent with its beta and the market's excess return.

beta

The sensitivity of a security's return to the return on the market index.

systematic risk

The portion of risk common to the entire economy, also known as market risk or nondiversifiable risk.

firm-specific or residual risk

Component of return variance that is independent of the market factor.

security characteristic line (SCL)

Plot of a security's *predicted excess* return given the excess return of the market.

The intercept of this equation is security *i*'s **alpha** (denoted by the Greek letter α_i), the security's expected excess return when the market excess return is zero. It is the vertical intercept in Figure 6.12. It also can be thought of as the expected return on the stock in excess of the T-bill rate beyond any return induced by movements in the broad market.[5]

The slope of the line in Figure 6.12 is called the security's beta coefficient, β_i. **Beta** is the amount by which the security return tends to increase or decrease for every 1% increase or decrease in the return on the index, and therefore measures the security's sensitivity to market-wide economic shocks. Therefore, beta is a natural measure of **systematic risk.** The term $e_i(t)$ is the zero-mean, firm-specific surprise in the security return in month *t,* and is often called the *residual.* The greater the residuals (positive or negative), the wider is the scatter of returns around the straight line in Figure 6.12. This scatter reflects the impact of **firm-specific** or equivalently **residual risk.** Both residual risk and systematic risk contribute to the total volatility of returns.

It turns out that when we estimate the regression line for the scatter diagram in Figure 6.12, we obtain the following estimates:

$$R_{\text{Ford}}(t) = -.98\% + 1.32 R_M(t) + e_i(t) \tag{6.12}$$

This regression line "best fits" the data in the scatter diagram (Figure 6.12). We call this line Ford's **security characteristic line (SCL).**

The SCL tells us that on average, Ford's stock rose an additional 1.32% for every additional 1% return in the stock market index. The average value of the residual is zero, so for this sample period, in a month where the market was "flat," with an excess return of zero, Ford's excess return would be predicted to be −.98%.

Investors naturally will be attracted to stocks with positive values of alpha, as positive values imply higher average excess returns (i.e., risk premiums) without the "cost" of any additional exposure to market risk. For example, α may be large if you think a security is underpriced and therefore offers an attractive expected return. In the next chapter, we will see that when security prices are in equilibrium, such attractive opportunities ought to be competed away, in which case α will be driven to zero. But for now, let's assume that each security analyst comes up with his or her own estimates of alpha. If managers believe they can do a superior job of security analysis, then they will be confident in their ability to find stocks with nonzero values of alpha.

Notice that so far, there is little "theory" in the index model. The model is merely a way to *describe* the typical relation between market returns and returns on particular firms. The average beta of all stocks in the economy is 1; the average response of a stock to changes in a market index composed of all stocks must be 1-for-1.[6] The beta of the market index is, by definition, 1; the index obviously responds 1-for-1 to changes in itself. *Cyclical* or aggressive stocks have higher-than-average sensitivity to the broad economy and therefore have betas greater than 1. Conversely, the betas of *defensive* stocks are less than 1. The returns of these stocks respond less than 1-for-1 to market returns.

[5] We use excess returns rather than total returns in both Equations 6.11 and Figure 6.12. This is because we treat risk-free T-bills as an alternative parking place for the investor's funds. You will be happy to have moved funds from the risk-free asset to a risky alternative only if the *excess* return turns out to be positive. So the performance of a risky investment is better measured by excess rather than total return. Nevertheless, practitioners often use a "modified" index model that is similar to Equation 6.11 but that uses total rather than excess returns. This practice is most common when daily data are used. In this case, the rate of return on bills is on the order of only about 0.01% per day, so total and excess returns are almost indistinguishable.

[6] Note that only the *weighted* average of betas (using market values as weights) will be 1, since the stock market index is value-weighted. We know from Chapter 5 that the distribution of securities by market value is not symmetric: There are relatively few large corporations and many more smaller ones. As a result, the simple average of the betas of individual securities, when computed against a value-weighted index such as the S&P 500, will be greater than 1, pushed up by the general tendency of stocks of smaller firms to have higher betas.

While the index model is mostly descriptive, it nevertheless will help us address these two important theoretical questions: (1) What relation might we expect to observe between a stock's beta and its expected return? and (2) What value for alpha should we expect to observe when markets are in equilibrium? We will have much to say on these topics below.

In sum, the index model separates the realized rate of return on a security into macro (systematic) and micro (firm-specific) components. The excess rate of return on each security is the sum of three components:

	Symbol
1. The component of excess return due to movements in the overall market (as represented by the index R_M); β_i is the security's responsiveness to the market.	$\beta_i R_M$
2. The component attributable to unexpected events that are relevant only to this security (firm-specific).	e_i
3. The stock's expected excess return if the market factor is neutral, that is, if the market-index excess return is zero.	α_i

Because the firm-specific component of the stock return is uncorrelated with the market return, we can write the variance of the excess return of the stock as[7]

$$
\begin{aligned}
\text{Variance }(R_i) &= \text{Variance }(\alpha_i + \beta_i R_M + e_i) \\
&= \text{Variance }(\beta_i R_M) + \text{Variance }(e_i) \\
&= \beta_i^2 \sigma_M^2 \qquad\qquad\quad + \sigma^2(e_i) \\
&= \text{Systematic risk } + \text{Firm-specific risk}
\end{aligned}
\tag{6.13}
$$

Therefore, the total variance of the rate of return of each security is a sum of two components:

1. The variance attributable to the uncertainty of the entire market. This variance depends on both the variance of R_M, denoted σ_M^2, *and* the beta of the stock.
2. The variance of the firm-specific return, e_i, which is independent of market performance.

Statistical Interpretation of the Single-Index Model

We pointed out that Equation 6.11 may be interpreted as a single-variable *regression equation* of R_i on the market excess return R_M. The excess return on the security (R_i) is the dependent variable that is to be explained by the regression. On the right-hand side of the equation are the intercept α_i; the regression (slope) coefficient beta, β_i, multiplying the independent (explanatory) variable R_M; and the residual (unexplained) return, e_i.

However, the regression line does not represent *actual* returns; points on the scatter diagram almost never lie exactly on the regression line. Rather, the line represents average tendencies; it shows the *expectation* of R_{Ford} given the market excess return, R_M. The algebraic representation of the regression line is

$$
E(R_{\text{Ford}}|R_M) = \alpha_{\text{Ford}} + \beta_{\text{Ford}} R_M
\tag{6.14}
$$

which reads: The expectation of R_{Ford} given a value of R_M equals the intercept plus the slope coefficient times the value of R_M.

Because the regression line represents expectations and these expectations may not be realized (as Figure 6.12 shows), the *actual* returns also include a residual, e_i, reflecting the firm-specific component of return. This surprise is measured by the vertical distance between the point of the scatter diagram and the regression line. For example, in January 2012, when the market excess return was 5.4%, we would have predicted Ford's excess return to be $-.98\% + 1.32 \times 5.4\% = 6.2\%$. In fact, its actual excess return was 15.9%, resulting in a large positive *residual* of 9.7%, as shown in Figure 6.12. Ford must have had very good firm-specific news in that month.

---

[7] The covariance between R_M and e is zero. Also, because α_i is not random, it has no bearing on the variance of R_i.

The dispersion of the scatter of actual returns about the regression line is measured by the variance of the residuals, $\sigma^2(e)$. The magnitude of this firm-specific risk varies across securities. One way to measure the relative importance of systematic risk is to measure the ratio of systematic variance to total variance. This is called the R-square of the regression line:

$$\text{R-square} = \frac{\text{Systematic (or explained) variance}}{\text{Total variance}}$$

$$= \frac{\beta_{\text{Ford}}^2 \sigma_M^2}{\sigma_{\text{Ford}}^2} = \frac{\beta_{\text{Ford}}^2 \sigma_M^2}{\beta_{\text{Ford}}^2 \sigma_M^2 + \sigma^2(e_{\text{Ford}})} \tag{6.15}$$

R-square is the ratio of explained variance to total variance, that is, the proportion of total variance that can be attributed to market fluctuations. When residual variance is lower, R-square will be higher. In the limit, if $\sigma^2(e)$ were zero, then R-square would be 1.0. In this case, with no firm-specific risk at all, the market index excess return would fully explain the excess return on the stock. In general, the R-square is the square of the correlation coefficient between the market and stock returns.

If beta is negative, then when the market goes up, the stock is more likely to go down. Their excess returns will have a negative correlation. Nevertheless, knowing the market return conveys information about the stock's return, so the R-square will still be above zero. At either extreme, for a correlation coefficient of either 1 or −1, the return on the security is fully determined by the return on the market index, R-square will be 1, and all points of the scatter diagram will lie exactly on the line of best fit.

In general, therefore, a high R-square (equivalently, a correlation coefficient with high absolute value), tells us that systematic factors dominate firm-specific factors in determining the return on the stock. In contrast, low R-squares imply that the market plays a relatively unimportant part in explaining the variance of the stock's return; in this case, firm-specific factors dominate.

CONCEPT check 6.6

Interpret the eight scatter diagrams of Figure 6.13 in terms of systematic risk, diversifiable risk, and the intercept.

FIGURE 6.13

Various scatter diagrams

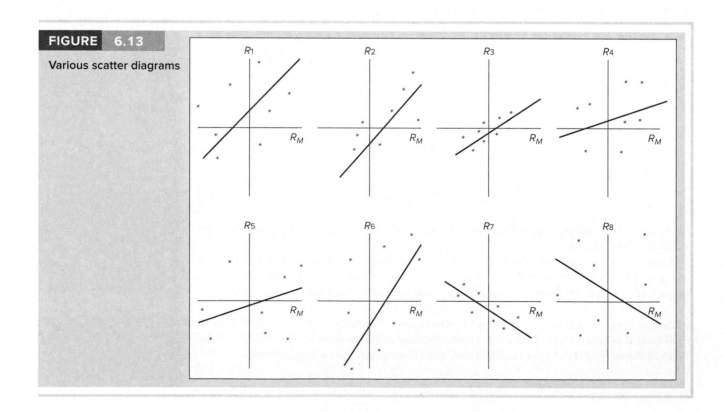

Example 6.3 illustrates how you can use a spreadsheet to estimate the single-index model from historical data.

EXAMPLE 6.3

Estimating the Index Model Using Historical Data

The following spreadsheet illustrates how to set up a regression analysis to estimate the parameters of the index model regression. We enter 12 months of hypothetical returns for two stocks and the market index, as well as the risk-free rate, and calculate excess rates of return in columns G through I. Then we go to the *Data* tab, click on *Data Analysis,* and choose the *Regression* tool. The tool will ask you to input the range for the left-hand side variable (the Y range), the right-hand side variable (the X range), and the location where you would like the regression output. For stock ABC, the Y range is H4:H15 and the X range is G4:G15.

The regression output includes R-square (cell D22), the standard deviation of the regression residuals (called standard error, cell D24), the estimated alpha and beta of the stock for this (very short) sample period (cells D29 and D30), and measures of the precision of those estimates in the columns for standard error of regression coefficients, *t*-statistic, and *p*-value.

ABC has low systematic risk, with a beta of only .525. Its R-square is .252, indicating that only 25.2% of the variance in its returns was driven by movements in the market index.

	A	B	C	D	E	F	G	H	I
1		Risk-Free	Rate of Return				Excess rate of Return		
2	Month	rate	Market Index	Stock ABC	Stock XYZ		Market Index	Stock ABC	Stock XYZ
3									
4	1	1.02%	3.71%	2.81%	4.23%		2.69%	1.79%	3.21%
5	2	1.06%	0.28%	−1.89%	−0.78%		−0.78%	−2.95%	−1.84%
6	3	1.11%	2.84%	1.85%	3.02%		1.73%	0.74%	1.91%
7	4	1.04%	−1.51%	−1.36%	−2.98%		−2.55%	−2.40%	−4.02%
8	5	0.98%	−1.86%	−3.31%	−2.34%		−2.84%	−4.29%	−3.32%
9	6	1.03%	−2.29%	9.72%	2.03%		−3.32%	8.69%	1.00%
10	7	1.06%	−1.77%	0.91%	−0.56%		−2.83%	−0.15%	−1.62%
11	8	1.05%	−8.49%	−5.09%	−6.45%		−9.54%	−6.14%	−7.50%
12	9	1.05%	4.39%	3.63%	6.85%		3.34%	2.58%	5.80%
13	10	1.07%	−2.63%	−3.21%	−3.09%		−3.70%	−4.28%	−4.16%
14	11	1.04%	1.37%	2.81%	2.63%		0.33%	1.77%	1.59%
15	12	1.01%	5.39%	2.82%	6.95%		4.38%	1.81%	5.94%
16									
17									
18			**REGRESSION OUTPUT FOR STOCK ABC**						
19									
20			*Regression Statistics*						
21			Multiple R	0.502					
22			R Square	0.252					
23			Adjusted R Square	0.177					
24			Standard Error	0.037					
25			Observations	12					
26									
27									
28				Coefficients	Standard Error		t-Statistic	p-value	
29			Intercept (alpha)	0.34%	1.11%		0.306	0.766	
30			Market index	0.525	0.286		1.836	0.096	

CONCEPT check 6.7

a. What is the regression line of XYZ in Example 6.3?
b. Does ABC or XYZ have greater systematic risk?
c. What proportion of the variance of XYZ is firm-specific risk?

Learning from the Index Model

In Example 6.3, we showed how to estimate index model regressions in Excel. We started by collecting a sample of monthly observations of excess returns on each firm and the market index. We then fit the "best" straight line through the scatter to describe the typical relation between the return on the stock and that on the market index. This is exactly how we estimated the regression line for Ford in Figure 6.2. The slope of the line is the estimate of Ford's beta,

The following is an excerpt from a spreadsheet that contains monthly returns for three stocks over the three-year period 2007–2009, which spans the financial crisis.

	A	B	C	D	E	F
1	Total monthly rates of return (decimal)					
2	Month	Ford	Walmart	Bank of America	Market Index	T-bill rate
3	Jan-07	0.0826	0.0327	-0.0152	0.0194	0.0042
4	Feb-07	-0.0271	0.0130	-0.0226	-0.0140	0.0042
5	Mar-07	-0.0025	-0.0236	0.0037	0.0129	0.0041
6	Apr-07	0.0190	0.0207	-0.0024	0.0398	0.0041
7	May-07	0.0373	-0.0021	0.0073	0.0389	0.0039
8	Jun-07	0.1295	0.0107	-0.0359	-0.0148	0.0038
9	Jul-07	-0.0966	-0.0449	-0.0301	-0.0318	0.0040
10	Aug-07	-0.0823	-0.0457	0.0687	0.0116	0.0035

Excel Questions

1. What were the betas of each of these firms?

2. In light of each firm's exposure to the financial crisis, do the relative sizes of the betas you find for each firm make intuitive make sense to you?

the intercept, its alpha, and the scatter of residuals around the regression line reflected the standard deviation of the firm-specific or residual risk of Ford's returns.

Table 6.2 shows index model regressions for a sample of almost 20 large companies. Notice that the average beta of the firms is 0.915, not so far from the expected value of 1.0. The model seems to provide reasonable estimates of systematic risk. As one would expect, firms with high exposure to the state of the macroeconomy (e.g., U.S. Steel, Ford, and Disney) have betas greater than 1. Firms whose business is less sensitive to the macroeconomy (e.g., Walmart, McDonald's, and Coca-Cola) have betas less than 1. In almost all cases, the regression beta is far greater than twice its standard error. This tells us that the *t*-statistic for beta is far above 2, so we can easily reject the hypothesis that the true beta is zero. In other words, there is strong evidence that returns on these stocks are driven in part by the performance of the broad market.

While alpha for this sample of firms ranged from −3.9% per month to 1.8% per month, the average alpha in this sample was almost precisely zero. Because this non-market risk premium averaged zero, we conclude that these firms, on average, were neither underpriced nor overpriced. Some did better than was expected at the beginning of the 5-year period, and others did worse, but there was no obvious systematic tendency to out- or underperform initial expectations. Moreover, these estimates of alpha were generally small compared to the statistical uncertainty surrounding their true values. There are only two firms in the entire sample for which the estimate of alpha was more than twice its standard error. In other words, the alpha estimates, by and large, are not statistically significant. As a general rule, one would not be able to reject the hypothesis that the true values were zero.

The index model regressions also tell us a lot about firm-specific risk. The column titled Residual Standard Deviation is the standard deviation of the residual terms, *e,* and is our measure of firm-specific risk. Notice how high that risk is, averaging 5.5% per month. This reminds us again of the importance of diversification. Anyone who concentrates a portfolio in just one or a few securities is bearing an enormous amount of volatility that can easily be diversified.

The high levels of firm-specific risk are reflected as well in the R-square of these regressions. For this sample of stocks, only 28.1% of return variance is due to the market, implying

TABLE 6.2 Index model estimates: Regressions of excess stock returns on the excess return of the broad market index over 60 months, 2011–2015

Ticker	Company	Beta	Alpha	R-Square	Residual Std Dev	Standard Error Beta	Standard Error Alpha	Adjusted Beta
MSFT	Microsoft	0.856	0.008	0.224	0.056	0.209	0.007	0.904
KO	Coca-Cola	0.406	0.004	0.129	0.037	0.138	0.005	0.604
XOM	ExxonMobil	0.876	−0.003	0.460	0.033	0.125	0.004	0.917
GE	General Electric	1.093	0.004	0.467	0.041	0.153	0.005	1.062
BA	Boeing	0.944	0.009	0.350	0.045	0.169	0.006	0.963
NEM	Newmont Mining	0.316	−0.016	0.011	0.107	0.400	0.014	0.544
PFE	Pfizer	0.837	0.007	0.432	0.034	0.126	0.004	0.891
F	Ford	1.326	−0.010	0.394	0.058	0.216	0.008	1.217
DIS	Walt Disney	1.352	0.009	0.617	0.037	0.140	0.005	1.235
BP	BP	1.533	−0.012	0.584	0.045	0.170	0.006	1.355
MCD	McDonald's	0.455	0.006	0.186	0.033	0.125	0.004	0.637
WMT	Walmart	0.209	0.003	0.023	0.048	0.179	0.006	0.473
INTC	Intel	0.831	0.006	0.221	0.055	0.205	0.007	0.887
BAC	Bank of America	1.681	−0.005	0.361	0.078	0.294	0.010	1.454
VZ	Verizon	0.237	0.007	0.037	0.042	0.158	0.006	0.492
X	U.S. Steel	1.844	−0.039	0.255	0.111	0.414	0.015	1.563
AMZN	Amazon	0.866	0.018	0.142	0.075	0.279	0.010	0.911
GOOG	Alphabet (Google)	0.799	0.011	0.166	0.063	0.235	0.008	0.866
	AVERAGE	0.915	0.000	0.281	0.055	0.207	0.007	0.943
	STD DEVIATION	0.488	0.013	0.186	0.024	0.088	0.003	0.325

that 71.9% is due to firm-specific factors. Of course, diversified portfolios will have far lower residual standard deviations and far higher R-squares. We will return to this point in the next chapter.

PREDICTING BETAS   As an empirical rule, it appears that betas exhibit a statistical property called *mean reversion*. This suggests that high-β (that is, $\beta > 1$) securities tend to exhibit a lower β in the future, while low-β (that is, $\beta < 1$) securities exhibit a higher β in future periods. Researchers who desire predictions of future betas often adjust beta estimates from historical data to account for regression toward 1.

A simple way to account for mean reversion is to forecast beta as a weighted average of the sample estimate and the average beta, which must be 1. A common back-of-the-envelope weighting scheme is $2/3$ on the sample estimate and $1/3$ on the value 1. For example, suppose that past data yield a beta estimate of 0.65. Thus, the adjusted forecast of beta will be

$$\text{Adjusted beta} = 2/3 \times .65 + 1/3 \times 1 = .77$$

The final forecast of beta is in fact closer to 1 than the sample estimate. If you look at the last column of Table 6.2, you will see the adjusted beta for each firm in the sample.

A more sophisticated adjustment technique would base the weight assigned to the sample beta on its statistical quality. A more precise estimate of beta would get a higher weight. However, as Table 6.2 shows, statistical estimates of beta from past data are generally not precise, because there is a lot of "noise" in the data due to firm-specific events. The problem is less severe with portfolios because diversification reduces firm-specific variance.

One might hope that more precise estimates of beta could be obtained by using longer time series of returns. Unfortunately, this is not a solution because betas change over time and old data can provide a misleading guide to current betas.

Using Security Analysis with the Index Model

Imagine that you are a portfolio manager in charge of the endowment of a small charity. Absent the resources to engage in security analysis, you would choose a passive portfolio comprising index funds and T-bills. Denote this portfolio as M. You estimate its standard deviation as σ_M and acquire a forecast of its risk premium as R_M. Now you find that you have sufficient resources to perform fundamental analysis on just one stock, say Google. You forecast Google's risk premium as R_G and estimate its beta (β_G) and residual SD, $\sigma(e_G)$. How should you proceed?

Treynor and Black (1973) proposed an elegant solution to this problem using estimates from the index model. We will only sketch out their argument and provide some intuition for the portfolio guidance that emerges from their approach.

Treynor and Black would view the investor in our example as mixing two risky securities: the passive market index, M, and the single analyzed stock, Google. With this limitation, the goal is to find the optimal mix of these two assets, specifically, the mix that results in a portfolio with the highest possible Sharpe ratio. Equation 6.10 already gives us an expression for the optimal portfolio weights, but it turns out that the index model allows us to simplify this expression.

Notice that your forecast of R_G implies that Google's alpha is $\alpha_G = R_G - \beta_G R_M$. We use two key statistics, $\alpha_G/\sigma^2(e_G)$ and R_M/σ_M^2, to find the position of Google in the optimal risky portfolio in two steps. In step 1, we compute

$$w_G^0 = \frac{\alpha_G/\sigma^2(e_G)}{R_M/\sigma_M^2} \tag{6.16}$$

In step 2, we adjust the value from Equation 6.16 for the beta of Google:

$$w_G^* = \frac{w_G^0}{1 + w_G^0(1 - \beta_G)}; \quad w_M^* = 1 - w_G^* \tag{6.17}$$

The Sharpe ratio of this portfolio exceeds that of the passive portfolio M, S_M, according to

$$S_O^2 - S_M^2 = \left(\frac{\alpha_G}{\sigma(e_G)}\right)^2 \tag{6.18}$$

Equation 6.16 tells us that the optimal position in Google entails a trade-off between alpha and potentially diversifiable risk. If Google seems underpriced, offering a positive alpha, it becomes attractive to add it to the portfolio. But by concentrating the portfolio in Google, the investor incurs a higher-than-necessary level of otherwise diversifiable risk. The higher the ratio of alpha to residual risk, the more Google the investor will be willing to hold in the portfolio. Similarly, Equation 6.18 tells us that the improvement to the risky portfolio's Sharpe ratio compared to the purely passive market index portfolio will be a function of the ratio $\alpha_G/\sigma(e_G)$, which is called Google's **information ratio**.[8]

information ratio

Ratio of alpha to the standard deviation of the residual.

active portfolio

The portfolio formed by optimally combining analyzed stocks.

The value of the Treynor-Black model can be dramatic when you analyze more than one stock. You can view Google in the previous example as comprising your entire **active portfolio.** If instead of Google alone you analyze several stocks, a portfolio of these stocks would make up your active portfolio, which then would be mixed with the passive index. You would use the alpha, beta, and residual SD of the active portfolio in Equations 6.16–6.18 to obtain the weights of the optimal portfolio, O, and its Sharpe ratio. Thus, the only remaining task is to determine the exact composition of the active portfolio, as well as its alpha, beta, and residual standard deviation.

Suppose that in addition to analyzing Google, you analyze Digital's stock (D) and estimate its alpha, beta, and residual variance. You estimate the ratio for Google, $\alpha_G/\sigma^2(e_G)$, the

---

[8] Some writers define the information ratio as *excess return* per unit of nonsystematic standard deviation, and use *appraisal ratio* to refer to the ratio of *alpha* to nonsystematic risk. We will consistently define the information ratio as the ratio of alpha to the standard deviation of residual returns. But we warn you that usage does vary.

corresponding ratio for Digital, and the sum of these ratios for all stocks in the active portfolio. Using Google and Digital,

$$\sum_i \alpha_i/\sigma^2(e_i) = \alpha_G/\sigma^2(e_G) + \alpha_D/\sigma^2(e_D) \tag{6.19}$$

Treynor and Black showed that the optimal weights of Google and Digital in the active portfolio, A, are

$$w_{GA} = \frac{\alpha_G/\sigma^2(e_G)}{\sum_i \alpha_i/\sigma^2(e_i)}; \quad w_{DA} = \frac{\alpha_D/\sigma^2(e_D)}{\sum_i \alpha_i/\sigma^2(e_i)} \tag{6.20}$$

Here again, the active portfolio entails two offsetting considerations. On the one hand, a stock with a higher alpha value calls for a high weight to take advantage of its attractive expected return. On the other hand, a high residual variance leads us to temper our position in the stock to avoid bearing firm-specific risk.

The alpha and beta of the active portfolio are weighted averages of each component stock's alpha and beta, and the residual variance is the weighted sum of each stock's residual variance, using the squared portfolio weights:

$$\alpha_A = w_{GA}\alpha_{GA} + w_{DA}\alpha_{DA}; \quad \beta_A = w_{GA}\beta_{GA} + w_{DA}\beta_{DA}$$
$$\sigma^2(e_A) = w_{GA}^2\sigma^2(e_G) + w_{DA}^2\sigma^2(e_D) \tag{6.21}$$

Given these parameters, we can now use Equations 6.16–6.18 to determine the weight of the active portfolio in the optimal portfolio and the Sharpe ratio it achieves.

EXAMPLE 6.4

The Treynor-Black Model

Suppose your benchmark passive position is the S&P 500 Index. The input list in Panel A of Table 6.3 includes the data for the passive index as well as the two stocks, Google and Digital. Both stocks have positive alpha values, so you would expect the optimal portfolio to be tilted toward these stocks. However, the tilt will be limited to avoid excessive exposure to otherwise-diversifiable firm-specific risk. The optimal trade-off maximizes the Sharpe ratio. We use the Treynor-Black model to accomplish this task.

We begin in Panel B assuming that the *active portfolio* solely comprises Google, which has an information ratio of 1.04/9.01 = .115. This "portfolio" is then combined with the passive index to form the optimal risky portfolio as in Equations 6.16–6.18. The calculations in Table 6.2 show that the optimal portfolio achieves a Sharpe ratio of 0.20, compared with 0.16 for the passive index. This optimal portfolio is invested 43.64% in Google and 56.36% in the S&P 500.

In Panel C, we add Digital to the list of actively analyzed stocks. The optimal weights of each stock in the active portfolio are 55.53% in Google and 44.47% in Digital. This gives the active portfolio an information ratio of 0.14, which improves the Sharpe ratio of the optimal portfolio to 0.24. The optimal portfolio invests 91.73% in the active portfolio and 8.27% in the index. This large tilt is acceptable because the residual standard deviation of the active portfolio (6.28%) is far less than that of either stock. Finally, the optimal portfolio weight in Google is 50.94% and 40.79% in Digital. Notice that the weight in Google is now *larger* than its weight without Digital! This, too, is a result of diversification within the active position that allows a larger tilt toward Google's large alpha.

6.6 RISK POOLING, RISK SHARING, AND TIME DIVERSIFICATION

So far, we have envisioned portfolio investment for "one period," but have been silent on how long that period may be. It might seem that we can take it to be of any length, so that our analysis would apply equally to short-term as well as long-term investments. Yet many contend that investing over long periods of time provides "time diversification," that is, even though the market index may underperform bills in any particular year, the law of averages

TABLE 6.3 | Construction of optimal portfolios using the index model

Input List

		Active Portfolio	
	Passive Portfolio (S&P 500)	**Google**	**Digital**
A. Input Data			
Risk premium	0.7	2.20	1.74
Standard deviation	4.31	11.39	10.49
Sharpe ratio	0.16	not applicable	
Alpha		1.04	0.75
Beta		1.65	1.41
Residual standard deviation		9.01	8.55
Information ratio = alpha/residual SD		0.1154	0.0877
Alpha/residual variance		0.0128	0.0103

Portfolio Construction

B. Optimal Portfolio with Google Only in Active Portfolio

Performance data

Sharpe ratio = SQRT (index Sharpe^2 + Google information ratio^2)	0.20		
Composition of optimal portfolio			
w^0 = (alpha/residual variance)/(index risk premium/index variance)		0.3400	
w^* = w^0/(1 + w^0(1 − beta))	0.5636	0.4364	

C. Optimal Portfolio with Google and Digital in the Active Portfolio

				Active Portfolio (sum)
Composition of the active portfolio				
w^0 of stock (Equation 6.15)		0.3400	0.2723	0.6122
w^0/Sum w^0 of analyzed stocks		0.5553	0.4447	1.0000
Performance of the active portfolio				
alpha = weight in active portfolio × stock alpha		0.58	0.33	0.91
beta = weight in active portfolio × stock beta		0.92	0.63	1.54
Residual variance = square weight × stock residual variance		25.03	14.46	39.49
Residual SD = SQRT (active portfolio residual variance)				6.28
Information ratio = active portfolio alpha/residual SD				0.14
Performance of the optimal portfolio				
Sharpe ratio	0.24			

	Index	**Active**	
Composition of optimal portfolio			
w^0		0.6122	
w^*	0.0827	0.9173	

		Google	**Digital**
Weight of active portfolio × weight of stock in active portfolio		0.5094	0.4079

Spreadsheets are available in Connect

implies that because of its positive risk premium, the market will surely outperform bills over long investment periods. Therefore, they argue, longer-horizon investors can prudently allocate higher proportions of their portfolios to the market.

Is this a valid argument? It is not, but the question brings up subtle questions about how diversification works. In this last section, therefore, we reconsider the arguments underlying how diversification brings about risk reduction and then show why the notion of time diversification is based on a misinterpretation of the theory of portfolio diversification.

Consider an insurance company selling many identical fire insurance policies. The payoff on any particular policy is a random amount, x, where the variance of x is σ^2. The company's total payout equals the sum of the payout on each individual policy, $\sum_{i=1}^{n} x_i$. In the context of diversification, one might think that if the firm sold n uncorrelated policies, it would diversify away practically all risk. But this argument is not quite right.

When the risk of a fire across different policyholders is uncorrelated, the variance of total payouts is just the sum of the individual policy variances (because we don't have to worry about covariance terms). Therefore,

$$\text{Var}\left(\sum_{i=1}^{n} x_i\right) = n\sigma^2 \qquad\qquad\qquad \textbf{(6.22)}$$

In contrast, the variance of the *average* payoff across policies is

$$\text{Var}\left(\frac{1}{n}\sum_{i=1}^{n} x_i\right) = \frac{1}{n^2} \times n\sigma^2 = \frac{\sigma^2}{n} \qquad\qquad\qquad \textbf{(6.23)}$$

The standard deviation of the average payoff is $\sigma/\sqrt{n}$. As the firm writes more and more policies, n increases and the uncertainty in the average payoff becomes progressively smaller, eventually approaching zero.

But is the insurance company's profit really getting safer? A few seconds of thought should convince you that this cannot possibly be the case. How can assuming exposure to an additional uncorrelated risky policy reduce risk? That would be like saying that a gambler who returns to the roulette table for one more spin is reducing his risk by diversifying across his many bets. His *average* payoff per bet may become more predictable, but the *total amount* won or lost will necessarily be more uncertain. Likewise, while the variance of the *average* insurance policy payoff decreases with the number of policies (Equation 6.23), the variance of the total payoff actually becomes more uncertain (Equation 6.22).

Thus, *risk pooling*, that is, pooling together many independent sources of risk, is only part of the business model of the insurance industry. An additional, essential part of the strategy is *risk sharing*. Suppose that the insurance company sells n policies. Now the firm goes public and sell shares to investors. Let's say n investors each purchase one share of the company so that each owns $1/n$ of the firm. As n increases, each investor's investment is unchanged: While there are more policies, that larger risk pool is dispersed across additional shareholders. With total payouts of $\sum_{i=1}^{n} x_i$, and an ownership share of $1/n$, the variance of each investor's exposure is $\text{Var}\left(\frac{1}{n}\sum_{i=1}^{n} x_i\right) = \frac{1}{n^2} \times n\sigma^2 = \frac{\sigma^2}{n}$, which does approach zero as n increases.

This calculation shows us that risk sharing is the key complement to risk pooling. As more and more policies are pooled together, they are shared by ever-more investors, thus preventing any individual's total risk from growing with the number of policies. As more policies are added to the insured pool, each investor's exposure to any single policy shrinks. The law of averages does work—but you must make sure not to inadvertently scale up your bet as you "diversify" across many sources of risk.

This argument is also crucial for our understanding of diversification of stock portfolios. Diversifying a portfolio means dividing a *fixed* investment budget across many assets. We used this assumption throughout the chapter when we specified a (fixed) size of investor wealth and focused only on how to apportion that wealth across different assets. If a portfolio of \$100,000 exclusively invested in Microsoft is to be diversified, that fixed \$100,000 must be divided between shares of Microsoft and shares of (let's say) Amazon as well as many other firms. An investor who currently has \$100,000 invested in Microsoft would *not* reduce total risk by adding another \$100,000 investment in Amazon. That would put more money at risk, just as selling more policies without spreading the exposure across more investors would increase, not decrease, the variance of insurance company returns. True diversification requires that a given investment budget be allocated across a large number of different assets, thus limiting the exposure to any one security.

Time Diversification

What does this analysis imply about time diversification and the risk of long-term investments? Think about a one-year investment in a stock index as analogous to a firm that sells one insurance policy. Extending your horizon to a second year is like selling a second policy. What does this do to your risk? Your average return per year may be more predictable, but by putting your money at risk for an additional year, the uncertainty of your cumulative return surely increases. This is like an insurance company that engages in risk pooling, but not risk sharing. As it piles on more bets, risk must increase. It should be clear that longer horizons alone do not reduce risk.

True diversification means holding fixed the total funds put at risk, and then spreading exposure across multiple sources of uncertainty. In the context of extending the time horizon, this would require that a two-year investor who puts her funds at risk for two years instead of one would place only half as much in the stock market each year as a one-year investor. This halves the exposure to each year's uncertain events, just as risk sharing with another investor would reduce each investor's exposure to each policy by half.

To illustrate the fallacy of time diversification, let's work through a concrete example. We will assume that market returns are independent from year to year, with a mean annual return of 5% and standard deviation 30%. To simplify a bit, let's also assume the risk-free rate is zero, so the question of whether stocks outperform bills is equivalent to the question of whether the stock return is positive.

It also is helpful to use continuously compounded returns, which means that the total or cumulative return after n years is just the sum of the year-by-year continuously compounded returns, the variance of the cumulative return is n times the annual variance, and therefore, the standard deviation is $\sqrt{n}$ times the one-year standard deviation. On the other hand, the standard deviation of the *average* return is $1/\sqrt{n}$ times the one-year standard deviation. These are effectively the same relations that we found in Equations 6.22 and 6.23.

Table 6.4 shows the impact of investment horizon on risk. The mean return per year is 0.05 (line 1) so the expected total or cumulative return is 0.05 times the time horizon (line 2).

TABLE 6.4   Investment risk for different horizons

| | Investment Horizon (years) | | | |
	1	10	30	Comment
1. Mean of average return	0.050	0.050	0.050	=.05
2. Mean of total return	0.050	0.500	1.500	=.05*T
3. Std Dev of total return	0.300	0.949	1.643	=.30√T
4. Std Dev of average return	0.300	0.095	0.055	=.30√T
5. Prob(return > 0)	0.566	0.701	0.819	From normal distribution
6. 1% VaR total return	−0.648	−1.707	−2.323	Continuously compounded cumulative return
7. Cumulative loss at 1% VaR	0.477	0.819	0.902	= 1 − exp(cumulative return from line 6)
8. 0.1% VaR total return	−0.877	−2.432	−3.578	Continuously compounded return
9. Cumulative loss at 0.1% VaR	0.584	0.912	0.972	= 1 − exp(cumulative return from line 7

The standard deviation of cumulative returns increases in proportion to the square root of the investment horizon while the standard deviation of the average return *falls* with the square root of the horizon (lines 3 and 4). Because expected return is positive while the standard deviation falls with the investment horizon, the probability that the average return will be positive increases as the time horizon extends. If we assume returns are normally distributed, we can calculate that probability exactly (line 5). The probability of a positive return approaches 100% as the investor's time horizon gets ever longer. This is the essence of the argument that time diversification reduces risk.

But probabilities do not tell the entire story. We also need to ask how bad performance can be in the event that it falls in the left tail of the distribution. Because the standard deviation of the total return increases with investment horizon (line 3), the magnitude of underperformance in the event of underperformance will be progressively worse. For example, the 1% VaR (value at risk) for the one-year horizon entails a loss of 47.7% of invested funds, while the 1% VaR at a 30-year horizon is a catastrophic cumulative loss of 90.2% (line 7). Performance is even more extreme for the 0.1% VaR. Clearly, investment returns are not safer at long horizons, and time diversification is only an illusion.

SUMMARY

- The expected rate of return of a portfolio is the weighted average of the component asset expected returns with the investment proportions as weights.
- The variance of a portfolio is a sum of the contributions of the component-security variances *plus* terms involving the covariance among assets.
- Even if correlations are positive, the portfolio standard deviation will be less than the weighted average of the component standard deviations, as long as the assets are not *perfectly* positively correlated. Thus, portfolio diversification reduces risk as long as assets are less than perfectly correlated.
- The contribution of an asset to portfolio variance depends on its correlation with the other assets in the portfolio as well as on its own variance. An asset that is perfectly negatively correlated with a portfolio can be used to reduce the portfolio variance to zero. Thus, it can serve as a perfect hedge.
- The efficient frontier of risky assets is the graphical representation of the set of portfolios that maximizes portfolio expected return for a given level of portfolio standard deviation. Rational investors will choose a portfolio on the efficient frontier.
- A portfolio manager identifies the efficient frontier by first establishing estimates for the expected returns and standard deviations and determining the correlations among them. The input data are then fed into an optimization program that produces the investment proportions, expected returns, and standard deviations of the portfolios on the efficient frontier.
- In practice, portfolio managers will identify different efficient portfolios because of differences in the methods and quality of security analysis. Managers compete on the quality of their security analysis relative to their management fees.
- If a risk-free asset is available and input data are identical, all investors will choose the same portfolio on the efficient frontier, the one that is tangent to the CAL. This is the risky portfolio with the highest Sharpe ratio. All investors with identical input data will hold the identical risky portfolio, differing only in how much each allocates to this optimal portfolio versus to the risk-free asset. This result is characterized as the separation principle of portfolio selection.
- The single-index model expresses the excess return on a security as a function of the market excess return: $R_i = \alpha_i + \beta_i R_M + e_i$. This equation also can be interpreted as a regression of the security excess return on the market-index excess return. The regression line has intercept α_i and slope β_i and is called the security characteristic line.

- In a single-index model, the variance of the rate of return on a security or portfolio can be decomposed into systematic and firm-specific risk. The systematic component of variance equals β^2 times the variance of the market excess return. The firm-specific component is the variance of the residual term in the index-model equation.
- The information ratio is the ratio of alpha to the standard deviation of firm-specific risk. Shares with higher alphas are more attractive, as they provide a higher expected return for any level of systematic risk. But tilting portfolios toward individual firms exposes the investor to higher levels of residual (firm-specific) risk that could be diversified. A share with a higher information ratio offers a better risk-return trade-off and calls for a larger weight in an active portfolio. The Treynor-Black model uses the index model to form optimal active positions.
- Time diversification is the notion that longer time horizons provide diversification across different investment periods and therefore reduce risk. This notion is based on a misinterpretation of how diversification works. Longer horizons make cumulative investment results more, not less, risky.

KEY TERMS

active portfolio, 174	index model, 166	optimal risky portfolio, 158
alpha, 168	information ratio, 174	residual risk, 168
beta, 168	investment opportunity	security characteristic
diversifiable risk, 146	set, 154	line, 168
efficient frontier, 161	market risk, 146	separation property, 164
excess return, 167	nondiversifiable risk, 146	systematic risk, 146, 168
firm-specific risk, 146, 168	nonsystematic risk, 146	unique risk, 146

KEY FORMULAS

The expected rate of return on a portfolio: $E(r_P) = w_B E(r_B) + w_S E(r_S)$

The variance of the return on a portfolio: $\sigma_P^2 = (w_B \sigma_B)^2 + (w_S \sigma_S)^2 + 2(w_B \sigma_B)(w_S \sigma_S)\rho_{BS}$

The Sharpe ratio of a portfolio: $S_P = \dfrac{E(r_P) - r_f}{\sigma_P}$

Portfolio weights that maximize the Sharpe ratio of a portfolio constructed from two risky assets (B and S) and a risk-free asset:

$$w_B = \frac{[E(r_B) - r_f]\sigma_S^2 - [E(r_S) - r_f]\sigma_B\sigma_S\rho_{BS}}{[E(r_B) - r_f]\sigma_S^2 + [E(r_S) - r_f]\sigma_B^2 - [E(r_B) - r_f + E(r_S) - r_f]\sigma_B\sigma_S\rho_{BS}}$$

$$w_S = 1 - w_B$$

The index-model equation: $R_i = \alpha_i + \beta_i R_M + e_i$

Decomposition of variance based on the index-model equation:

$$\text{Variance}(R_i) = \beta_i^2 \sigma_M^2 + \sigma^2(e_i)$$

Percent of security variance explained by the index return:

$$R\text{-square} = \frac{\text{Systematic (or explained) variance}}{\text{Total variance}}$$
$$= \frac{\beta_i^2 \sigma_M^2}{\sigma_i^2} = \frac{\beta_i^2 \sigma_M^2}{\beta_i^2 \sigma_M^2 + \sigma^2(e_i)}$$

Optimal position in the active portfolio, A:

$$w_A^* = \frac{w_A^0}{1 + w_A^0(1 - \beta_A)}; \quad w_M^* = 1 - w_A^*$$

$$w_A^0 = \frac{\alpha_A/\sigma^2(e_A)}{R_M/\sigma_M^2}$$

Optimal weight of a security, G, in the active portfolio, A: $w_{GA} = \dfrac{\alpha_G/\sigma^2(e_G)}{\sum_i \alpha_i/\sigma^2(e_i)}$

 Select problems are available in McGraw-Hill's *Connect*. Please see the Supplements section of the book's frontmatter for more information.

PROBLEM SETS

1. In forming a portfolio of two risky assets, what must be true of the correlation coefficient between their returns if there are to be gains from diversification? Explain. *(LO 6-1)*

2. When adding a risky asset to a portfolio of many risky assets, which property of the asset has a greater influence on risk: its standard deviation or its covariance with the other assets? Explain. *(LO 6-1)*

3. A portfolio's expected return is 12%, its standard deviation is 20%, and the risk-free rate is 4%. Which of the following would make for the greatest increase in the portfolio's Sharpe ratio? *(LO 6-3)*
   a. An increase of 1% in expected return.
   b. A decrease of 1% in the risk-free rate.
   c. A decrease of 1% in its standard deviation.

4. An investor ponders various allocations to the optimal risky portfolio and risk-free T-bills to construct his complete portfolio. How would the Sharpe ratio of the complete portfolio be affected by this choice? *(LO 6-3)*

5. The standard deviation of the market-index portfolio is 20%. Stock A has a beta of 1.5 and a residual standard deviation of 30%. *(LO 6-5)*
   a. What would make for a larger increase in the stock's variance: an increase of 0.15 in its beta or an increase of 3% (from 30% to 33%) in its residual standard deviation?
   b. An investor who currently holds the market-index portfolio decides to reduce the portfolio allocation to the market index to 90% and to invest 10% in stock A. Which of the changes in (a) will have a greater impact on the portfolio's standard deviation?

6. Suppose that the returns on the stock fund presented in Spreadsheet 6.1 were –40%, –14%, 17%, and 33% in the four scenarios. *(LO 6-2)*
   a. Would you expect the mean return and variance of the stock fund to be more than, less than, or equal to the values computed in Spreadsheet 6.2? Why?
   b. Calculate the new values of mean return and variance for the stock fund using a format similar to Spreadsheet 6.2. Confirm your intuition from part (a).
   c. Calculate the new value of the covariance between the stock and bond funds using a format similar to Spreadsheet 6.4. Explain intuitively the change in the covariance.

7. Use the rate-of-return data for the stock and bond funds presented in Spreadsheet 6.1, but now assume that the probability of each scenario is as follows: severe recession: .10; mild recession: .20; normal growth: .35; boom: .35. *(LO 6-2)*
   a. Would you expect the variance of the stock fund to be more than, less than, or equal to the values computed in Spreadsheet 6.2? Why?
   b. Calculate the new value of variance for the stock fund using a format similar to Spreadsheet 6.2. Confirm your intuition from part (a).
   c. Calculate the new value of the covariance between the stock and bond funds using a format similar to Spreadsheet 6.4. Explain intuitively why the absolute value of the covariance has changed.

The following data apply to Problems 8–12.

A pension fund manager is considering three mutual funds. The first is a stock fund, the second is a long-term government and corporate bond fund, and the third is a T-bill money market fund that yields a sure rate of 5.5%. The probability distributions of the risky funds are:

	Expected Return	Standard Deviation
Stock fund (S)	15%	32%
Bond fund (B)	9	23

The correlation between the fund returns is 0.15.

8. Tabulate and draw the investment opportunity set of the two risky funds. Use investment proportions for the stock fund of 0% to 100% in increments of 20%. What expected return and standard deviation does your graph show for the minimum-variance portfolio? *(LO 6-2)*

9. Draw a tangent from the risk-free rate to the opportunity set. What does your graph show for the expected return and standard deviation of the optimal risky portfolio? *(LO 6-3)*

10. What is the Sharpe ratio of the best feasible CAL?   *(LO 6-3)*

11. Suppose now that your portfolio must yield an expected return of 12% and be efficient, that is, on the best feasible CAL.   *(LO 6-4)*
    a. What is the standard deviation of your portfolio?
    b. What is the proportion invested in the T-bill fund and each of the two risky funds?

12. *a.* If you were to use only the two risky funds and still require an expected return of 12%, what would be the investment proportions of your portfolio?
    b. Compare its standard deviation to that of the optimal portfolio in the previous problem. What do you conclude?   *(LO 6-4)*

13. Stocks offer an expected rate of return of 10% with a standard deviation of 20%, and gold offers an expected return of 5% with a standard deviation of 25%.   *(LO 6-3)*
    a. In light of the apparent inferiority of gold to stocks with respect to both mean return and volatility, would anyone hold gold? If so, demonstrate graphically why one would do so.
    b. How would you answer (*a*) if the correlation coefficient between gold and stocks were 1? Draw a graph illustrating why one would or would not hold gold.
    c. Could these expected returns, standard deviations, and correlation represent an equilibrium for the security market?

14. Suppose that many stocks are traded in the market and that it is possible to borrow at the risk-free rate, r_f. The characteristics of two of the stocks are as follows:

Stock	Expected Return	Standard Deviation
A	8%	40%
B	13	60
Correlation = −1		

Could the equilibrium r_f be greater than 10%? (*Hint:* Can a particular stock portfolio be substituted for the risk-free asset?)   *(LO 6-3)*

15. You can find a spreadsheet containing annual returns on stocks and Treasury bonds in Connect. Copy the data for the last 20 years into a new spreadsheet. Analyze the risk-return trade-off that would have characterized portfolios constructed from large stocks and long-term Treasury bonds over the last 20 years.
    a. What was the average rate of return and standard deviation of each asset?
    b. What was the correlation coefficient of their annual returns?

Χ

Templates and
spreadsheets are available
in Connect

    c. What would have been the average return and standard deviation of portfolios with differing weights in the two assets? For example, consider weights in stocks starting at zero and incrementing by .10 up to a weight of 1.

    d. What was the average return and standard deviation of the minimum-variance combination of stocks and bonds? *(LO 6-2)*

16. Assume expected returns and standard deviations for all securities, as well as the risk-free rate for lending and borrowing, are known. Will investors arrive at the same optimal risky portfolio? Explain. *(LO 6-4)*

17. Your assistant gives you the following diagram as the efficient frontier of the group of stocks you asked him to analyze. The diagram looks a bit odd, but your assistant insists he double-checked his analysis. Would you trust him? Is it possible to get such a diagram? *(LO 6-4)*

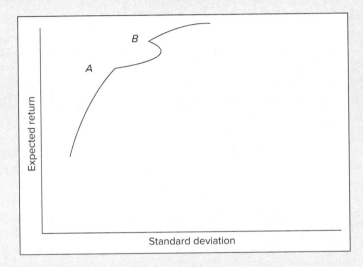

18. What is the relationship of the portfolio standard deviation to the weighted average of the standard deviations of the component assets? *(LO 6-1)*

19. A project has a 0.7 chance of doubling your investment in a year and a 0.3 chance of halving your investment in a year. What is the standard deviation of the rate of return on this investment? *(LO 6-2)*

20. Investors expect the market rate of return this year to be 10%. The expected rate of return on a stock with a beta of 1.2 is currently 12%. If the market return this year turns out to be 8%, how would you revise your expectation of the rate of return on the stock? *(LO 6-5)*

21. The following figure shows plots of monthly rates of return and the stock market for two stocks. *(LO 6-5)*

    a. Which stock is riskier to an investor currently holding a diversified portfolio of common stock?

    b. Which stock is riskier to an undiversified investor who puts all of his funds in only one of these stocks?

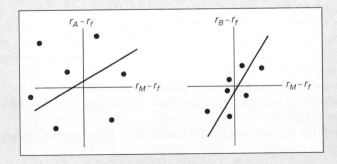

22. Log in to Connect and link to the material for Chapter 6, where you will find a spreadsheet containing monthly rates of return for Apple, the S&P 500, and T-bills over a recent five-year period. Set up a spreadsheet just like that of Example 6.3 and find the beta of Apple.   **(LO 6-5)**

23. Here are rates of return for six months for Generic Risk, Inc. What is Generic's beta? (*Hint:* Find the answer by plotting the scatter diagram.)   **(LO 6-5)**

Month	Market Return	Generic Return
1	0%	+2%
2	0	0
3	−1	0
4	−1	−2
5	+1	+4
6	+1	+2

Challenge

24. Log in to Connect to find rate-of-return data over a 60-month period for Alphabet, the parent company of Google, the T-bill rate, and the S&P 500, which we will use as the market-index portfolio.   **(LO 6-4)**

    a. Use these data and Excel's regression function to compute Google's excess return in each month as well as its alpha, beta, and residual standard deviation, $\sigma(e)$, over the entire period.

    b. What was the Sharpe ratio of the S&P 500 over this period?

    c. What was Google's information ratio over this period?

    d. If someone whose risky portfolio is currently invested in an index portfolio such as the S&P 500 wishes to take a position in Google based on the estimates from parts (a)–(c), what would be the optimal fraction of the risky portfolio to invest in Google? Use Equations 6.16 and 6.17.

    e. Based on Equation 6.18 and your answer to part (d), by how much would the Sharpe ratio of the optimal risky portfolio increase given the incremental position in Google?

25. Neighborhood Insurance sells fire insurance policies to local homeowners. The premium is $110, the probability of a fire is .001, and in the event of a fire, the insured damages (the payout on the policy) will be $100,000.   **(LO 6-6)**

    a. Make a table of the two possible payouts on each policy with the probability of each.

    b. Suppose you own the entire firm, and the company issues only one policy. What are the expected value and variance of your profit?

    c. Now suppose your company issues two policies. The risk of fire is independent across the two policies. Make a table of the *three* possible payouts along with their associated probabilities.

    d. What are the expected value and variance of your profit?

    e. Compare your answers to (b) and (d). Did risk pooling increase or decrease the variance of your profit?

    f. Continue to assume the company has issued two policies, but now assume you take on a partner, so that you each own one-half of the firm. Make a table of *your share* of the possible payouts the company may have to make on the two policies, along with their associated probabilities.

    g. What are the expected value and variance of your profit?

    h. Compare your answers to (b) and (g). What has happened to your risk? What about your expected profit?

    i. Comparing the answers to (e) and (h), what do you conclude about risk sharing versus risk pooling?

CFA Problems

1. A three-asset portfolio has the following characteristics:

Asset	Expected Return	Standard Deviation	Weight
X	15%	22%	0.50
Y	10	8	0.40
Z	6	3	0.10

   What is the expected return on this three-asset portfolio? *(LO 6-1)*

2. George Stephenson's current portfolio of $2 million is invested as follows:

Summary of Stephenson's Current Portfolio				
	Value	Percent of Total	Expected Annual Return	Annual Standard Deviation
Short-term bonds	$ 200,000	10%	4.6%	1.6%
Domestic large-cap equities	600,000	30	12.4	19.5
Domestic small-cap equities	1,200,000	60	16.0	29.9
Total portfolio	$2,000,000	100%	13.8%	23.1%

   Stephenson soon expects to receive an additional $2 million and plans to invest the entire amount in an index fund that best complements the current portfolio. Stephanie Coppa, CFA, is evaluating the four index funds shown in the following table for their ability to produce a portfolio that will meet two criteria relative to the current portfolio: (1) maintain or enhance expected return and (2) maintain or reduce volatility.

   Each fund is invested in an asset class that is not substantially represented in the current portfolio.

Index Fund Characteristics			
Index Fund	Expected Annual Return	Expected Annual Standard Deviation	Correlation of Returns with Current Portfolio
Fund A	15%	25%	+0.80
Fund B	11	22	+0.60
Fund C	16	25	+0.90
Fund D	14	22	+0.65

   State which fund Coppa should recommend to Stephenson. Justify your choice by describing how your chosen fund *best* meets both of Stephenson's criteria. No calculations are required. *(LO 6-4)*

3. Abigail Grace has a $900,000 fully diversified portfolio. She subsequently inherits ABC Company common stock worth $100,000. Her financial adviser provided her with the following estimates: *(LO 6-5)*

Risk and Return Characteristics		
	Expected Monthly Returns	Standard Deviation of Monthly Returns
Original Portfolio	0.67%	2.37%
ABC Company	1.25	2.95

The correlation coefficient of ABC stock returns with the original portfolio returns is .40.

a. The inheritance changes Grace's overall portfolio and she is deciding whether to keep the ABC stock. Assuming Grace keeps the ABC stock, calculate the:

    i. Expected return of her new portfolio which includes the ABC stock.

    ii. Covariance of ABC stock returns with the original portfolio returns.

    iii. Standard deviation of her new portfolio which includes the ABC stock.

b. If Grace sells the ABC stock, she will invest the proceeds in risk-free government securities yielding 0.42% monthly. Assuming Grace sells the ABC stock and replaces it with the government securities, calculate the:

    i. Expected return of her new portfolio which includes the government securities.

    ii. Covariance of the government security returns with the original portfolio returns.

    iii. Standard deviation of her new portfolio which includes the government securities.

c. Determine whether the beta of her new portfolio, which includes the government securities, will be higher or lower than the beta of her original portfolio.

d. Based on conversations with her husband, Grace is considering selling the $100,000 of ABC stock and acquiring $100,000 of XYZ Company common stock instead. XYZ stock has the same expected return and standard deviation as ABC stock. Her husband comments, "It doesn't matter whether you keep all of the ABC stock or replace it with $100,000 of XYZ stock." State whether her husband's comment is correct or incorrect. Justify your response.

e. In a recent discussion with her financial adviser, Grace commented, "If I just don't lose money in my portfolio, I will be satisfied." She went on to say, "I am more afraid of losing money than I am concerned about achieving high returns." Describe *one* weakness of using standard deviation of returns as a risk measure for Grace.

The following data apply to CFA Problems 4–6:

Hennessy & Associates manages a $30 million equity portfolio for the multimanager Wilstead Pension Fund. Jason Jones, financial vice president of Wilstead, noted that Hennessy had rather consistently achieved the best record among the Wilstead's six equity managers. Performance of the Hennessy portfolio had been clearly superior to that of the S&P 500 in four of the past five years. In the one less favorable year, the shortfall was trivial.

Hennessy is a "bottom-up" manager. The firm largely avoids any attempt to "time the market." It also focuses on selection of individual stocks, rather than the weighting of favored industries.

There is no apparent conformity of style among the six equity managers. The five managers, other than Hennessy, manage portfolios aggregating $250 million, made up of more than 150 individual issues.

Jones is convinced that Hennessy is able to apply superior skill to stock selection, but the favorable results are limited by the high degree of diversification in the portfolio. Over the years, the portfolio generally held 40–50 stocks, with about 2% to 3% of total funds committed to each issue. The reason Hennessy seemed to do well most years was that the firm was able to identify each year 10 or 12 issues that registered particularly large gains.

Based on this overview, Jones outlined the following plan to the Wilstead pension committee:

Let's tell Hennessy to limit the portfolio to no more than 20 stocks. Hennessy will double the commitments to the stocks that it really favors and eliminate the remainder. Except for this one new restriction, Hennessy should be free to manage the portfolio exactly as before.

All the members of the pension committee generally supported Jones's proposal, because all agreed that Hennessy had seemed to demonstrate superior skill in selecting stocks. Yet the proposal was a considerable departure from previous practice, and several committee members raised questions.

4. Answer the following: *(LO 6-1)*

a. Will the limitation of 20 stocks likely increase or decrease the risk of the portfolio? Explain.

b. Is there any way Hennessy could reduce the number of issues from 40 to 20 without significantly affecting risk? Explain.

5. One committee member was particularly enthusiastic concerning Jones's proposal. He suggested that Hennessy's performance might benefit further from reduction in the number of issues to 10. If the reduction to 20 could be expected to be advantageous, explain why reduction to 10 might be less likely to be advantageous. (Assume that

Wilstead will evaluate the Hennessy portfolio independently of the other portfolios in the fund.) *(LO 6-1)*

6. Another committee member suggested that, rather than evaluate each managed portfolio independently of other portfolios, it might be better to consider the effects of a change in the Hennessy portfolio on the total fund. Explain how this broader point of view could affect the committee decision to limit the holdings in the Hennessy portfolio to either 10 or 20 issues. *(LO 6-1)*

7. Dudley Trudy, CFA, recently met with one of his clients. Trudy typically invests in a master list of 30 equities drawn from several industries. As the meeting concluded, the client made the following statement: "I trust your stock-picking ability and believe that you should invest my funds in your five best ideas. Why invest in 30 companies when you obviously have stronger opinions on a few of them?" Trudy plans to respond to his client within the context of Modern Portfolio Theory. *(LO 6-1)*

   a. Contrast the concepts of systematic risk and firm-specific risk, and give an example of each type of risk.

   b. Critique the client's suggestion. Discuss how both systematic and firm-specific risk change as the number of securities in a portfolio is increased.

---

1. Go to **finance.yahoo.com** and download five years of monthly closing prices for Eli Lilly (ticker = LLY), Alcoa (AA), and the S&P 500 Index (^GSPC). Download the data into an Excel file and use the Adjusted-Close prices, which adjust for dividend payments, to calculate the monthly rate of return for each price series. Use an XY scatter plot chart with no line joining the points to plot Alcoa's returns against the S&P 500. Now select one of the data points, and right-click to obtain a shortcut menu allowing you to enter a trend line. This is Alcoa's characteristic line, and the slope is Alcoa's beta. Repeat this process for Lilly. What conclusions can you draw from each company's characteristic line?

WEB *master*

2. Following the procedures in the previous question, find five years of monthly returns for Target. Using the first two years of data, what is Target's beta? What is the beta using the latest two years of data? How stable is the beta estimate? If you use all five years of data, how close is your estimate of beta to the estimate reported in Yahoo's *Key Statistics* section?

3. Following the procedures in the previous questions, find five years of monthly returns for the following firms: Genzyme Corporation, Sony, Cardinal Health, Inc., Black & Decker Corporation, and Kellogg Company. Copy the returns from these five firms into a single Excel workbook, with the returns for each company properly aligned. Use the full range of available data. Then do the following:

   a. Using the Excel functions for average (AVERAGE) and sample standard deviation (STDEV.S), calculate the average and the standard deviation of the returns for each of the firms.

   b. Using Excel's correlation function (CORREL), construct the correlation matrix for the five stocks based on their monthly returns for the entire period. What are the lowest and the highest individual pairs of correlation coefficients? (*Alternative:* You may use Excel's Data Analysis Tool to generate the correlation matrix.)

4. Several online tools will calculate the efficient frontier. One is **www.portfoliovisualizer .com**. Select its *Portfolio Optimization* tool and choose the option for *Historical Efficient Frontier*. The site allows you to construct portfolios from either specific stocks or general asset classes. The default is to restrict portfolio weights to be between 0% and 100%, but you can override this feature. Choose at least four asset classes from the drop-down menu using data for the most recent 10-year period. Select a diverse range of asset classes, including for example, equity, fixed-income, and international assets.

   a. Find the efficient frontier in the absence of short sales.

   b. Now find the efficient frontier allowing the minimum weight in any asset class to be −100%. Does loosening the short-sale constraint substantially shift the efficient frontier to the northwest?

   c. Now try the *Forecasted Efficient Frontier* tool, where you can input your own estimates of expected return and volatility. How sensitive are portfolio weights to assumed expected return?

6.1 Recalculation of Spreadsheets 6.1 and 6.4 shows that the covariance is now −5.80 and the correlation coefficient is −0.07.

	A	B	C	D	E	F
1				Stock Fund		Bond Fund
2	Scenario	Probability	Rate of Return	Col B × Col C	Rate of Return	Col B × Col E
3	Severe recession	0.05	−37.0	−1.9	−10	−0.5
4	Mild recession	0.25	−11.0	−2.8	10	2.5
5	Normal growth	0.40	14.0	5.6	7	2.8
6	Boom	0.30	30.0	9.0	2	0.6
7	Expected or Mean Return:			SUM: 10.0		SUM: 5.4
8						
9				Deviation from Mean Return		Covariance
10	Scenario	Probability	Stock Fund	Bond Fund	Product of Dev	Col B × Col E
11	Severe recession	0.05	−47.0	−15.4	723.8	36.19
12	Mild recession	0.25	−21.0	4.6	−96.6	−24.15
13	Normal growth	0.40	4.0	1.6	6.4	2.56
14	Boom	0.30	20.0	−3.4	−68.0	−20.40
15		SD =	18.63	4.65	Covariance =	−5.80
16	Correlation coefficient = Covariance/(StdDev(stocks)*StdDev(bonds)) =					−0.07

6.2 The scatter diagrams for pairs B–E are shown below. Scatter diagram A (presented with the Concept Check) shows an exact mirror image between the pattern of points 1,2,3 versus 3,4,5. Therefore, the correlation coefficient is zero. Scatter diagram B shows perfect positive correlation (1). Similarly, C shows perfect negative correlation (−1). Now compare the scatters of D and E. Both show a general positive correlation, but scatter D is tighter. Therefore, D is associated with a correlation of about 0.5 (use a spreadsheet to show that the exact correlation is .54), and E is associated with a correlation of about 0.2 (show that the exact correlation coefficient is .23).

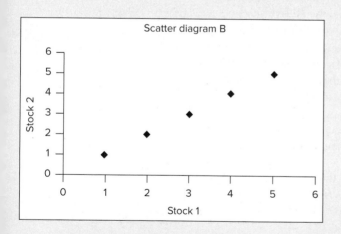

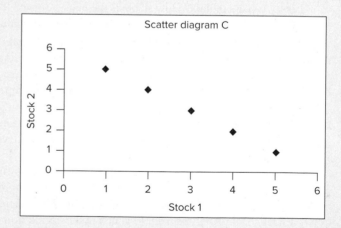

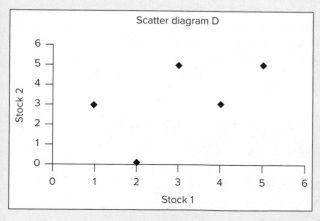

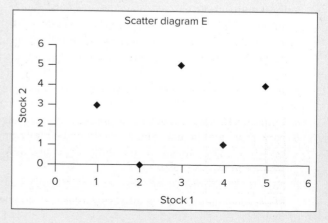

6.3 *a.* Using Equation 6.6 with the data $\sigma_B = 8$; $\sigma_S = 19$; $w_B = .5$; and $w_S = 1 - w_B = .5$, we obtain the equation

$$\sigma_P^2 = 10^2 = (w_B\sigma_B)^2 + (w_S\sigma_S)^2 + 2(w_B\sigma_B)(w_S\sigma_S)\rho_{BS}$$
$$= (.5 \times 8)^2 + (.5 \times 19)^2 + 2(.5 \times 8)(.5 \times 19)\rho_{BS}$$

which yields $\rho = -.0822$.

b. Using Equation 6.5 and the additional data $E(r_B) = 5\%$; $E(r_S) = 10\%$, we obtain

$$E(r_P) = w_B E(r_B) + w_S E(r_S) = (.5 \times 5) + (.5 \times 10) = 7.5\%$$

c. On the one hand, you should be happier with a correlation of 0.17 than with 0.22 since the lower correlation implies greater benefits from diversification and means that, for any level of expected return, there will be lower risk. On the other hand, the constraint that you must hold 50% of the portfolio in bonds represents a cost to you as it prevents you from choosing the risk-return trade-off most suited to your tastes. Unless you would choose to hold about 50% of the portfolio in bonds anyway, you are better off with the slightly higher correlation but with the ability to choose your own portfolio weights.

6.4 *a.* Implementing Equations 6.5 and 6.6, we generate data for the graph. See Spreadsheet 6.7 and Figure 6.14.

SPREADSHEET 6.7

For Concept Check 4. Mean and standard deviation for various portfolio applications

	A	B	C	D	E	F	G
5		Data	X	M	T-Bills		
6		Mean (%)	15	10	5		
7		Std. Dev. (%)	50	20	0		
8		Corr. Coeff. X and S		-0.20			
9		Portfolio Opportunity set					
10		Weight in X	Weight in S	Pf Mean (%)	Pf Std Dev (%)		
11		-1.00	2.00	5.00	70.00		
12		-0.90	1.90	5.50	64.44		
13		-0.80	1.80	6.00	58.92	=B13*$C$6+C13*$D$6	
14		-0.70	1.70	6.50	53.45		
15		-0.60	1.60	7.00	48.04		
16		-0.50	1.50	7.50	42.72		
17		-0.40	1.40	8.00	37.52		
18		-0.30	1.30	8.50	32.51	=(B15^2*$C$7^2	
19		-0.20	1.20	9.00	27.78	+C15^2*$D$7^2	
20		-0.10	1.10	9.50	23.52	+2*B15*C15	
21		0.00	1.00	10.00	20.00	*$C$7*$D$7*$D$8)^0.5	
22		0.10	0.90	10.50	17.69		
23		0.20	0.80	11.00	17.09		
24		0.30	0.70	11.50	18.36		
25		0.40	0.60	12.00	21.17		
26		0.50	0.50	12.50	25.00		
27		0.60	0.40	13.00	29.46		
28		0.70	0.30	13.50	34.31		
29		0.80	0.20	14.00	39.40		
30		0.90	0.10	14.50	44.64		
31		1.00	0.00	15.00	50.00		
32		1.10	-0.10	15.50	55.43		
33		1.20	-0.20	16.00	60.93		
34		1.30	-0.30	16.50	66.46		
35		1.40	-0.40	17.00	72.03		
36		1.50	-0.50	17.50	77.62		
37		1.60	-0.60	18.00	83.23		
38		1.70	-0.70	18.50	88.87		
39		1.80	-0.80	19.00	94.51		
40		1.90	-0.90	19.50	100.16		
41		2.00	-1.00	20.00	105.83		
42	Min. Var Pf	0.18	0.82	10.91	17.06		
43	Optimal Pf	0.26	0.74	11.28	17.59		
44							
45							
46		=((C6-E6)*D7^2-(D6-E6)*C7*D7*D8)/					
47		((C6-E6)*D7^2+(D6-E6)*C7^2-(C6-E6+D6-E6)*C7*D7*D8)					
48							
49							

FIGURE 6.14

FIGURE 6.14

For Concept Check 6.4. Plot of mean return versus standard deviation using data from spreadsheet.

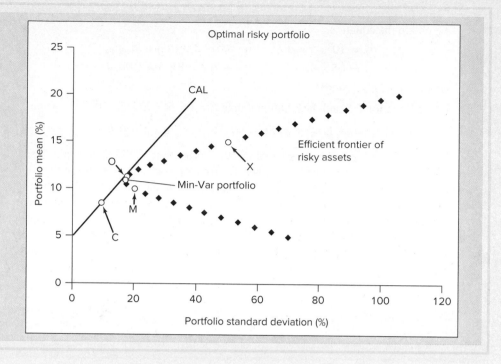

b. Implementing the formulas indicated in Spreadsheet 6.6, we generate the optimal risky portfolio (*O*) and the minimum-variance portfolio.

c. The slope of the CAL is equal to the risk premium of the optimal risky portfolio divided by its standard deviation $(11.28 - 5)/17.59 = .357$.

d. The mean of the complete portfolio is $.2222 \times 11.28 + .7778 \times 5 = 6.395\%$, and its standard deviation is $.2222 \times 17.58 = 3.91\%$. Sharpe ratio $= (6.395 - 5)/3.91 = .357$.

The composition of the complete portfolio is
$.2222 \times .26 = .06$ (i.e., 6%) in *X*
$.2222 \times .74 = .16$ (i.e., 16%) in *M*
and 78% in T-bills.

6.5 Efficient frontiers derived by portfolio managers depend on forecasts of the rates of return on various securities and estimates of risk, that is, standard deviations and correlation coefficients. The forecasts themselves do not control outcomes. Thus, to prefer a manager with a rosier forecast (northwesterly frontier) is tantamount to rewarding the bearers of good news and punishing the bearers of bad news. What the investor wants is to reward bearers of *accurate* news. Investors should monitor forecasts of portfolio managers on a regular basis to develop a track record of their forecasting accuracy. Portfolio choices of the more accurate forecasters will, in the long run, outperform the field.

6.6 a. Beta, the slope coefficient of the security on the factor: Securities $R_1 - R_6$ have a positive beta. These securities move, on average, in the same direction as the market (R_M). R_1, R_2, R_6 have large betas, so they are "aggressive" in that they carry more systematic risk than R_3, R_4, R_5, which are "defensive." R_7 and R_8 have a negative beta. These are hedge assets that carry negative systematic risk.

b. Intercept, the expected return when the market is neutral: The estimates show that R_1, R_4, R_8 have a positive intercept, while R_2, R_3, R_5, R_6, R_7 have negative intercepts. To the extent that one believes these intercepts will persist, a positive value is preferred.

c. Residual variance, the nonsystematic risk: R_2, R_3, R_7 have a relatively low residual variance. With sufficient diversification, residual risk eventually will be eliminated, and, hence, the difference in the residual variance is of little economic significance.

    d. Total variance, the sum of systematic and nonsystematic risk: R_3 has a low beta and low residual variance, so its total variance will be low. R_1, R_6 have high betas and high residual variance, so their total variance will be high. But R_4 has a low beta and high residual variance, while R_2 has a high beta with a low residual variance. In sum, total variance often will misrepresent systematic risk, which is the part that matters.

6.7 *a.* To obtain the characteristic line of XYZ, we continue the spreadsheet of Example 6.3 and run a regression of the excess return of XYZ on the excess return of the market-index fund.

      The regression output shows that the slope coefficient of XYZ is 0.992 and the intercept is 0.83%; hence the characteristic line is $R_{XYZ} = .83 + .992R_{Market}$.

    b. The beta coefficient of ABC is 0.525, less than XYZ's 0.992, implying that ABC has less systematic risk.

    c. The regression of XYZ on the market index shows an R-square of 0.845. Hence the proportion of firm-specific variance (nonsystematic risk) is 0.155, or 15.5%.

Summary Output	
Regression Statistics	
Multiple R	0.919
R-square	0.845
Adjusted R-square	0.829
Standard error	0.017
Observations	12

	Coefficients	Standard Error	*t*-Stat	*p*-Value	Lower 95%	Upper 95%
Intercept (alpha)	0.83%	0.52%	1.600	0.141	−30.62	38.48
Market	0.992	0.134	7.379	0.000	−0.635	1.798

Capital Asset Pricing and Arbitrage Pricing Theory

Learning Objectives

LO 7-1 Use the implications of capital market theory to estimate security risk premiums.

LO 7-2 Construct and use the security market line.

LO 7-3 Specify and use a multifactor security market line.

LO 7-4 Take advantage of an arbitrage opportunity with a portfolio that includes mispriced securities.

LO 7-5 Use arbitrage pricing theory with more than one factor to identify mispriced securities.

The capital asset pricing model, almost always referred to as the CAPM, is a centerpiece of modern financial economics. The model predicts the relationship we should observe between the risk of an asset and its expected return. This relationship serves two vital functions.

First, it provides a benchmark rate of return for evaluating possible investments. For example, a security analyst might want to know whether the expected return she forecasts for a stock is more or less than its "fair" return given its risk. Second, the model helps us make an educated guess as to the expected return on assets that have not yet been traded in the marketplace. For example, how do we price an initial public offering of stock? How will a major new investment project affect the return investors require on a company's stock?

Although the CAPM does not fully withstand empirical tests, it is widely used because of the insight it offers. All generalizations of the model retain its central conclusion that only systematic risk will be rewarded with a risk premium. While the best way to measure that systematic risk can be subtle, all the more complex cousins of the basic CAPM can be viewed as variations on this crucial theme.

The intuition behind the CAPM allows for multiple sources of risk. Therefore, we also discuss multifactor models of risk and return, and we show how these result in richer descriptions of the risk-return relationship.

Finally, we consider an alternative derivation of the risk-return relationship known as arbitrage pricing theory (APT). Arbitrage is the exploitation of security mispricing to earn risk-free economic profits. The most basic principle of capital market theory is that prices ought to be aligned to eliminate risk-free profit opportunities. If actual prices allowed for such arbitrage, the resulting opportunities for profitable trading would lead to strong pressure on security prices that would persist until equilibrium is restored and the opportunities eliminated. We will see that this no-arbitrage principle leads to a risk-return relationship like that of the CAPM. Like the generalized version of the CAPM, the simple APT is easily extended to accommodate multiple sources of systematic risk.

7.1 THE CAPITAL ASSET PRICING MODEL

Historically, the CAPM was developed prior to the index model introduced in the previous chapter (Equation 6.11). The index model was widely adopted as a natural description of the stock market immediately on the heels of the CAPM because the CAPM implications so neatly match the intuition underlying the model. So it makes sense to use the index model to help understand the lessons of the CAPM.

As we saw in the last chapter, the index model describes an empirical relationship between the excess return on an individual stock, R_i, and that of a broad market-index portfolio, R_M: $R_i = \alpha_i + \beta_i R_M + e_i$, where e_i is zero-mean "noise," or firm-specific risk. Therefore, the expected excess return on a stock, given the market's excess return, R_M, is $E(R_i|R_M) = \beta_i R_M + \alpha_i$.

According to this equation, there are two paths to a positive risk premium. First, if a stock has a positive beta it will "inherit" some of the market's risk premium. However, there is a cost to this benefit: that positive beta also means that the stock is exposed to systematic risk. Higher betas therefore imply higher risk premiums, but higher market risk. In the end, this trade-off is "neutral," in the sense that the higher reward that accompanies higher beta is exactly the same as one would realize by moving along the capital market line, shifting from bills into the market index. In other words, the trade-off is neither better nor worse than that offered by a passive indexing strategy. However, the second potential path to a higher risk premium, investing in stocks with positive alphas, would be a cost-free benefit. Higher alphas would imply higher expected returns *without* a corresponding increase in risk.

What does this mean to portfolio managers? Hunt for positive-alpha stocks, don't invest in negative-alpha stocks, and, better yet, sell short negative-alpha stocks if short sales are feasible. Investor demand for a positive-alpha stock will increase its price. As the price of a stock rises, other things being equal, its expected return falls, reducing and ultimately eliminating the very alpha that first created the excess demand. Conversely, the drop in demand for a negative-alpha stock will reduce its price, pushing its alpha back toward zero. In the end, such buying or selling pressure will leave most securities with zero alpha values most of the time. Put another way, unless and until your own analysis of a stock tells you otherwise, you should assume alpha is zero.

When alpha is zero, there is no reward from bearing firm-specific risk; the only way to earn a higher expected return than the T-bill rate is by bearing systematic risk. In other words, the equilibrium risk premium will be determined solely by systematic risk, as measured by beta. With no reward to bearing diversifiable risk, the best portfolio is the one that completely eliminates it, and that is an indexed portfolio that mimics the broad market. These are the conclusions of the CAPM. Now let's examine the model and its implications more carefully.

The Model: Assumptions and Implications

The **capital asset pricing model (CAPM)** is based on two sets of assumptions, listed in Table 7.1. The first set pertains to investor behavior, and allows us to assume that investors are alike in most important ways, specifically that they are all mean-variance optimizers with a common time horizon and a common set of information reflected in their use of an identical input list. The second set pertains to market structure, asserting that markets are well-functioning with few impediments to trading. Even a cursory consideration of these assumptions reveals that they are fairly strong, and one may justifiably wonder whether a

capital asset pricing model (CAPM)

A model that relates the required rate of return on a security to its systematic risk as measured by beta.

TABLE 7.1   The assumptions of the CAPM

1. **Investor behavior**

   a. Investors are rational, mean-variance optimizers.

   b. Their common planning horizon is a single period.

   c. Investors all use identical input lists, an assumption often termed **homogeneous expectations.** Homogeneous expectations are consistent with the assumption that all relevant information is publicly available.

2. **Market structure**

   a. All assets are publicly held and trade on public exchanges.

   b. Investors can borrow or lend at a common risk-free rate, and they can take short positions on traded securities.

   c. No taxes.

   d. No transaction costs.

theory derived from them will withstand empirical tests. Therefore, later in the chapter, we will turn to some generalizations of the model.

Still, the simple version of the CAPM is a good place to start. While the appropriate quantification of risk and the prediction for the exact risk-return trade-off may differ across more sophisticated variants of the model, its central implication, that risk premia will be proportional to systematic risk and independent of firm-specific risk, remains valid in all of its extensions. In part because of this commonality, the simple CAPM remains in wide use despite its empirical shortcomings.

We start by summarizing the equilibrium that will prevail in this economy. We elaborate on these implications in the following sections.

market portfolio (M)

The portfolio for which each security is held in proportion to its total market value.

1. All investors will choose to hold the **market portfolio (M),** which includes all assets in the investable universe. For simplicity, we shall refer to all assets as stocks. The proportion of each stock in the market portfolio equals the market value of the stock (price per share times the number of shares outstanding) divided by the total market value of all stocks.

2. The market portfolio will be on the efficient frontier. Moreover, it will be the optimal risky portfolio, the tangency point of the capital allocation line (CAL) to the efficient frontier. As a result, the capital market line (CML), the line from the risk-free rate through the market portfolio, M, is also the best attainable capital allocation line. All investors hold M as their optimal risky portfolio, differing only in the amount invested in it versus in the risk-free asset.

3. The risk premium on the market portfolio will be proportional to the variance of the market portfolio and investors' typical degree of risk aversion. Mathematically,

$$E(r_M) - r_f = \overline{A}\sigma_M^2 \qquad (7.1)$$

where σ_M is the standard deviation of the return on the market portfolio and $\overline{A}$ represents the degree of risk aversion of the average investor.

4. The risk premium on individual assets will equal the product of the risk premium on the market portfolio (M) and the *beta coefficient* of the security on the market portfolio. Beta measures the extent to which returns respond to the market portfolio. In the index model, beta is the regression (slope) coefficient of the security return on the market return, representing sensitivity to fluctuations in the overall security market.

Why All Investors Would Hold the Market Portfolio

We begin by assuming that all investors optimize their portfolios using the Markowitz model of efficient diversification. That is, each investor uses an input list (specifying expected returns, variances, and covariances) to draw an efficient frontier employing all available risky assets and identifies the efficient risky portfolio, P, by drawing the tangent CAL (capital allocation line) to the frontier as in Figure 7.1. Notice that this framework employs Assumptions 1(a) (investors are all mean-variance optimizers), 2(a) (all assets trade and therefore can be held in investors' portfolios), and 2(b) (investors can borrow or lend at the risk-free rate and therefore can select portfolios along the capital allocation line of the tangency portfolio).

The CAPM asks what would happen if all investors shared an identical investable universe and used the same input list to draw their efficient frontiers. The use of a common input list obviously requires Assumption 1(c), but notice that it also relies on Assumption 1(b), that each investor is optimizing for a common investment horizon. It also implicitly assumes that investor choices will not be affected by differences in tax rates or trading costs that could affect net rates of return (Assumptions 2[c] and 2[d]).

Not surprisingly in light of our assumptions, investors would derive identical efficient frontiers of risky assets. Facing the same risk-free rate (Assumption 2[b]), they would then draw an identical tangent CAL and naturally all would arrive at the same risky portfolio, P. All investors therefore would choose the same set of weights for each risky asset. What must be these weights?

A key insight of the CAPM is this: Because the market portfolio is the aggregation of all of these *identical* risky portfolios, it too must have the same weights. (Notice that this conclusion relies on Assumption 2[a] because it requires that *all* assets can be traded and included in investors' portfolios.) Therefore, if all investors choose the same risky portfolio, it must be the *market* portfolio, that is, the value-weighted portfolio of all assets in the investable universe. We conclude that the capital allocation line based on each investor's optimal risky portfolio will in fact also be the capital *market* line, as depicted in Figure 7.1. This implication will allow us to say much about the risk–return trade-off.

The Passive Strategy Is Efficient

The CAPM implies that a passive strategy, using the CML as the optimal CAL, is a powerful alternative to an active strategy. The market portfolio proportions are a result of investors' buy and sell orders that cease only when there is no more profit to be made. In the simple world of the CAPM, active investors use precious resources to conduct their security analysis. A passive investor receives a "free ride" by simply investing in the market portfolio and benefiting from the efficiency of that portfolio. In fact, in the absence of private information (Assumption 1[c]), an investor whose risky portfolio is anything other than the market will end on a CAL that is inferior to the CML used by passive investors.

We sometimes call this result a **mutual fund theorem** because it implies that only one mutual fund of risky assets—the market index fund—is sufficient to satisfy the investment demands of all investors. The mutual fund theorem is another incarnation of the separation property discussed in Chapter 6. Assuming all investors choose to hold a market-index mutual fund, we can separate portfolio selection into two components: (1) a technical side, in which

mutual fund theorem

States that all investors desire the same portfolio of risky assets and can be satisfied by a single mutual fund composed of that portfolio.

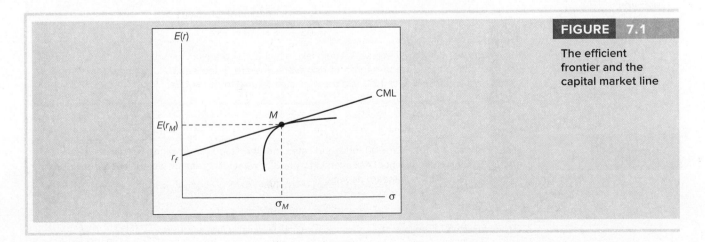

FIGURE 7.1

The efficient frontier and the capital market line

an efficient mutual fund is created by professional managers; and (2) a personal side, in which an investor's risk aversion determines the allocation of the complete portfolio between the mutual fund and the risk-free asset. Here, all investors agree that the mutual fund they would like to hold is invested in the market portfolio.

While investment managers in the real world generally construct risky portfolios that differ from the market index, we attribute this to the differences in their estimates of risk and expected return (in violation of Assumption 1[c]). Nevertheless, a passive investor who does not engage in security analysis may view the market index as a reasonable first approximation to an efficient risky portfolio.

CONCEPT check	7.1	If only some investors perform security analysis while all others hold the market portfolio (*M*), would the CML still be the efficient CAL for investors who do not engage in security analysis? Explain.

The Risk Premium of the Market Portfolio

In Chapter 5 we showed how individual investors decide how much to invest in the risky portfolio when they also have access to risk-free assets. Returning now to the decision of how much to invest in the market portfolio *M* and how much in the risk-free asset, what can we deduce about the equilibrium risk premium of portfolio *M*?

Equation 7.1 states that the equilibrium risk premium of the market portfolio, $E(r_M) - r_f$, will be proportional to the degree of risk aversion of the average investor and to the risk of the market portfolio, σ_M^2. Now we can explain this result.

When investors purchase stocks, their demand drives up prices, thereby lowering expected rates of return and risk premiums. But when risk premiums fall, investors will move some of their funds from the risky market portfolio into the risk-free asset. In equilibrium, the risk premium on the market portfolio must be just high enough to induce investors to hold the available supply of stocks. If the risk premium is too high, there will be excess demand for securities, and prices will rise; if it is too low, investors will not hold enough stock to absorb the supply, and prices will fall. The *equilibrium* risk premium of the market portfolio is therefore proportional both to the risk of the market, as measured by the variance of its returns, and to the degree of risk aversion of the average investor, denoted by $\overline{A}$ in Equation 7.1.

EXAMPLE 7.1	Suppose the risk-free rate is 5%, the average investor has a risk-aversion coefficient of $\overline{A} = 2$, and the standard deviation of the market portfolio is 20%. According to Equation 7.1, we can estimate the equilibrium value of the market risk premium[1] as $2 \times .20^2 = .08$. So the expected rate of return on the market must be
Market Risk, the Risk Premium, and Risk Aversion	

$$E(r_M) = r_f + \text{Equilibrium risk premium}$$
$$= .05 + .08 = .13 = 13\%$$

If investors were more risk averse, it would take a higher risk premium to induce them to hold shares. For example, if the average degree of risk aversion were 3, the equilibrium market risk premium would be $3 \times .20^2 = .12$, or 12%, and the expected return would be 17%.

CONCEPT check	7.2	Historical data for the S&P 500 Index indicates that the standard deviation of returns has been about 20%. If the coefficient of risk aversion were 3.5, what risk premium would have been consistent with this historical standard deviation?

---

[1]To use Equation 7.1, we must express returns in decimal form rather than as percentages.

Expected Returns on Individual Securities

We saw in Section 6.5, Equation 6.13, that the contribution of a single security to the systematic risk of a portfolio depends on its beta. Beta tells us how strongly the security responds to market-wide shocks. Aggressive stocks, with betas greater than 1, exaggerate the response of the portfolio to broad market movements, while defensive stocks, with betas below 1, dampen the response.

As investors diversify, their exposure to the firm-specific risk of any individual security steadily diminishes, but their exposure to market-wide movements remains. This was the lesson of Figure 6.1 in the last chapter. As a result, what will matter to diversified investors is the *systematic* risk of the portfolio and the contribution each stock makes to that risk. Investors will naturally look for stocks with the best incremental reward (risk premium) compared to incremental systematic risk. In equilibrium, the ratio of reward to risk should be equalized across all stocks. For example, if we focus on one particular stock, say Digital Computer, and compare it to the market index (with a beta of 1) we should find that

$$\frac{E(r_M) - r_f}{1} = \frac{E(r_D) - r_f}{\beta_D}$$

Rearranging results in the CAPM's **expected return–beta relationship:**

$$E(r_D) = r_f + \beta_D[E(r_M) - r_f] \tag{7.2}$$

In words, an asset's risk premium equals the asset's systematic risk measure (its beta) times the risk premium of the (benchmark) market portfolio. This expected return (equivalently, mean return)–beta relationship is the most familiar expression of the CAPM.

Equation 7.2 tells us that the total expected rate of return is the sum of the risk-free rate (compensation for "waiting," i.e., the time value of money) plus a risk premium (compensation for "worrying" about investment returns). Moreover, it makes a very specific prediction about the size of the risk premium, that it is the product of a benchmark risk premium (that of the broad market portfolio) and the relative risk of the particular asset as measured by its beta.

Notice what the risk premium does *not* depend on: the total volatility of the stock. So, for example, the stock market performance of a firm developing a new drug that may be a great success or a total failure may have extremely high variance, but investors in those shares will not for that reason demand a high expected return. They recognize that because the success of the firm is largely independent of macroeconomic risk and the return on the rest of their portfolio, its contribution to overall portfolio risk is low, and therefore does not warrant a large risk premium. The CAPM predicts that only systematic risk should be "priced," that is, command a risk premium; firm-specific risk should not be priced.

expected return–beta relationship

Implication of the CAPM that security risk premiums should be proportional to beta

---

Suppose the risk premium of the market portfolio is 8%, and we estimate the beta of Digital as $\beta_D = 1.2$. The risk premium predicted for the stock is therefore 1.2 times the market risk premium, or $1.2 \times 8\% = 9.6\%$. The expected rate of return on Digital is the risk-free rate plus the risk premium. For example, if the T-bill rate were 3%, the expected rate of return would be $3\% + 9.6\% = 12.6\%$, or, using Equation 7.2 directly,

$$E(r_D) = r_f + \beta_D[\text{Market risk premium}]$$
$$= 3\% + 1.2 \times 8\% = 12.6\%$$

If the estimate of Digital's beta were only 1.1, its required risk premium would fall to 8.8%. Similarly, if the market risk premium were only 6% and $\beta_D = 1.2$, Digital's risk premium would be only 7.2%.

EXAMPLE 7.2

Expected Returns and Risk Premiums

The fact that many investors hold active portfolios that differ from the market portfolio does not necessarily invalidate the CAPM. Any highly diversified portfolio can shed almost all firm-specific risk and will be subject only to systematic risk. Even if one does not hold the precise market portfolio, a well-diversified portfolio will be so highly correlated with the market that a stock's beta relative to the market still will be a useful risk measure.

In fact, several researchers have shown that modified versions of the CAPM will hold despite differences among individuals that may cause them to hold different portfolios. A study by Brennan (1970) examines the impact of differences in investors' personal tax rates on market equilibrium. Another study by Mayers (1972) looks at the impact of nontraded assets such as human capital (earning power). Both find that while the market portfolio is no longer each investor's optimal risky portfolio, a modified version of the mean–beta relationship still holds.

If the mean–beta relationship holds for each individual asset, it must hold for any combination of assets. The beta of a portfolio is simply the weighted average of the betas of the stocks in the portfolio, using as weights the portfolio proportions. Thus, beta also predicts a portfolio's risk premium in accordance with Equation 7.2.

EXAMPLE 7.3	Consider the following portfolio:

Portfolio Beta and Risk Premium

Asset	Beta	Risk Premium	Portfolio Weight
Microsoft	1.2	9.0%	0.5
American Electric Power	0.8	6.0	0.3
Gold	0.0	0.0	0.2
Portfolio	0.84	?	1.0

If the market risk premium is 7.5%, the CAPM predicts that the risk premium on each stock is its beta times 7.5%, and the risk premium on the portfolio is .84 × 7.5% = 6.3%. This is the same result that is obtained by taking the weighted average of the risk premiums of the individual stocks. (Verify this for yourself.)

A word of caution: We often hear that a well-managed firm will provide a high rate of return. This is true when referring to the *firm's* accounting return on investments in plant and equipment. The CAPM, however, predicts returns on investments in the *securities* of the firm that trade in capital markets.

Say everyone knows a firm is well run. Its stock price will be bid up, and returns to stockholders at those high prices will not be extreme. Security prices reflect public information about a firm's prospects, but only the risk of the company (as measured by beta) should affect *expected returns*. In a rational market, investors receive high expected returns only if they bear systematic risk.

CONCEPT check **7.3**	Suppose the risk premium on the market portfolio is estimated at 8% with a standard deviation of 22%. What is the risk premium on a portfolio invested 25% in GE with a beta of 0.8 and 75% in Digital with a beta of 1.2?

The Security Market Line

The expected return–beta relationship or equivalently, the mean-beta relationship, is a reward-risk equation. The beta of a security is the appropriate measure of its risk because beta determines the security's contribution to the variance of the efficiently diversified optimal risky portfolio.

security market line (SML)

Graphical representation of the expected return-beta relationship of the CAPM.

The mean–beta relationship is represented by the **security market line (SML)** in Figure 7.2. Its slope is the risk premium of the market portfolio. At the point where $\beta = 1$ (the beta of the market portfolio), we can read off the vertical axis the expected return on the market portfolio.

It is useful to compare the SML to the capital market line. The CML graphs the risk premiums of efficient complete portfolios (made up of the market portfolio and the risk-free asset) as a function of portfolio standard deviation. This is appropriate because standard deviation is a valid measure of risk for portfolios that are candidates for an investor's complete portfolio.

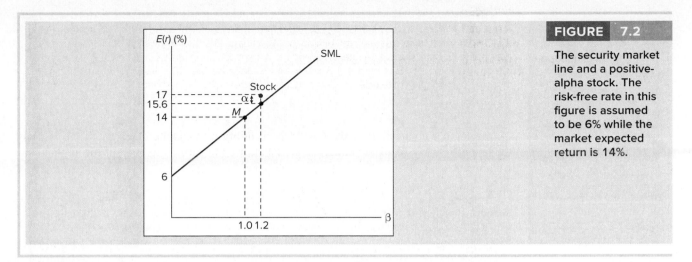

FIGURE 7.2

The security market line and a positive-alpha stock. The risk-free rate in this figure is assumed to be 6% while the market expected return is 14%.

The SML, in contrast, graphs *individual-asset* risk premiums as a function of asset risk. The relevant measure of risk for an individual asset (which is held as part of a diversified portfolio) is not the asset standard deviation but rather the asset beta. The SML is valid both for individual assets and portfolios.

The security market line provides a benchmark for evaluation of investment performance. The SML provides the required rate of return that will compensate investors for the beta risk of that investment, as well as for the time value of money.

Because the SML is the graphical representation of the mean–beta relationship, "fairly priced" assets plot exactly on the SML. The expected returns of such assets are commensurate with their risk. Whenever the CAPM holds, all securities must lie on the SML. Underpriced stocks would plot above the SML: Given beta, their expected returns are greater than is indicated by the CAPM. Overpriced stocks would plot below the SML. The difference between the fair (i.e., equilibrium) and the actual expected rate of return on a stock is the **alpha,** denoted α. The expected return on a mispriced security (one with a nonzero value of alpha) is given by $E(r) = \alpha + r_f + \beta[E(r_M) - r_f]$.

alpha

The abnormal rate of return on a security in excess of what would be predicted by an equilibrium model such as the CAPM.

Suppose the return on the market is expected to be 14%, a stock has a beta of 1.2, and the T-bill rate is 6%. The SML would predict an expected return on the stock of

$$E(r) = r_f + \beta[E(r_M) - r_f]$$
$$= 6 + 1.2(14 - 6) = 15.6\%$$

If one believes the stock will provide instead a return of 17%, its implied alpha would be 1.4%, as shown in Figure 7.2. If instead the expected return were only 15%, the stock alpha would be negative, −0.6%.

EXAMPLE 7.4

The Alpha of a Security

Applications of the CAPM

One place the CAPM may be used is in the investment management industry. The SML provides a benchmark to assess the expected return that is commensurate with an asset's risk. Then an analyst calculates the return she actually expects. Notice that we depart here from the simple CAPM world in that active investors apply their own analysis to derive a private "input list." If a stock is perceived to be a good buy, or underpriced, it will provide a positive alpha, that is, an expected return in excess of the fair return stipulated by the SML.

The CAPM is also useful in capital budgeting decisions. When a firm is considering a new project, the SML provides the required return demanded of the project. This is the cutoff internal rate of return (IRR) or "hurdle rate" for the project.

EXAMPLE 7.5

The CAPM and Capital Budgeting

Suppose Silverado Springs Inc. is considering a new spring-water bottling plant. The business plan forecasts an internal rate of return of 14% on the investment. Research shows the beta of similar products is 1.3. Thus, if the risk-free rate is 4%, and the market risk premium is estimated at 8%, the hurdle rate for the project should be $4 + 1.3 \times 8 = 14.4\%$. Because the IRR is less than the risk-adjusted discount or hurdle rate, the project has a negative net present value and ought to be rejected.

Yet another application of the CAPM is in utility rate-making cases. Here the issue is the rate of return a regulated utility should be allowed to earn on its investment in plant and equipment.

EXAMPLE 7.6

The CAPM and Regulation

Suppose shareholder equity invested in a utility is $100 million, and the equity beta is 0.6. If the T-bill rate is 6%, and the market risk premium is 8%, then a fair annual profit will be $6 + (.6 \times 8) = 10.8\%$ of $100 million, or $10.8 million. Because regulators accept the CAPM, they will allow the utility to set prices at a level expected to generate these profits.

CONCEPT check   7.4

a. Stock XYZ has an expected return of 12% and $\beta = 1$. Stock ABC is expected to return 13% with a beta of 1.5. The market's expected return is 11% and $r_f = 5\%$. According to the CAPM, which stock is a better buy? What is the alpha of each stock? Plot the SML and the two stocks. Show the alphas of each on the graph.

b. The risk-free rate is 8% and the expected return on the market portfolio is 16%. A firm considers a project with an estimated beta of 1.3. What is the required rate of return on the project? If the IRR of the project is 19%, what is the project alpha?

7.2 THE CAPM AND INDEX MODELS

The CAPM has two limitations: It relies on the theoretical market portfolio, which includes *all* assets (including real estate, human capital, foreign stocks, etc.), and it applies to *expected* as opposed to actual returns. To implement and test the CAPM, we cast it in the form of an *index model* and use realized, not expected, returns.

The index model replaces the theoretical all-inclusive portfolio with an index such as the S&P 500 or the more inclusive market index introduced in Chapter 5. The composition and rate of return of these broad indexes are unambiguous and widely published, and therefore provide a clear benchmark for performance evaluation.

We can start with the central prediction of the CAPM: The market portfolio is mean-variance efficient. An index model can be used to test this hypothesis by verifying that an index designed to represent the full market is mean-variance efficient. To test mean-variance efficiency of an index, we must show that its Sharpe ratio is not surpassed by any other portfolio. We will examine tests of this question in the next chapter.

The security market line is the most common way to pose the implications of the CAPM, that is, that a stock's risk premium is the product of its beta and the market risk premium. This can also be tested using the index model from the last chapter.

The index model asserts that security excess returns can be described by Equation 6.11, which is restated here as Equation 7.3:

$$r_{it} - r_{ft} = \alpha_i + \beta_i(r_{Mt} - r_{ft}) + e_{it} \qquad (7.3)$$

where r_{it} is the holding-period return (HPR) on asset i in period t and α_i and β_i are the intercept and slope of the security characteristic line that relates asset i's realized excess return to the realized excess return of the index. We denote the index return in period t by r_{Mt} to emphasize that the index is proxying for the market portfolio. Equation 7.3 states that the realized excess return on any stock is the sum of the realized excess return due to market-wide factors, $\beta_i(r_{Mt} - r_{ft})$, a nonmarket risk premium, α_i, and a firm-specific outcome for that period summarized by e_{it}. Because the expectation of the firm-specific residual is zero, the *expected* excess return, equivalently the risk premium, of stock i would be given by Equation 7.4:

$$E(r_{it}) - r_{ft} = \alpha_i + \beta_i \left[E(r_{Mt}) - r_{ft} \right] \tag{7.4}$$

The expected return-beta relationship of the CAPM, which we rearrange very slightly from Equation 7.2, states that in any period,

$$E(r_{it}) - r_f = \beta_i \left[E(r_{Mt}) - r_{ft} \right] \tag{7.5}$$

Comparing Equation 7.4 to Equation 7.5 we see that the prediction of the CAPM is that for every stock, $\alpha_i = 0$.

The logic of the CAPM is that the only reason for a stock to offer an expected return greater than the risk-free rate is that the stock imposes systematic risk for which the investor must be compensated. However, a positive alpha promises reward without risk. Investors will relentlessly pursue positive-alpha stocks and bid up their prices; at those higher prices, expected rates of return will be lower. Symmetrically, investors will shun or short-sell negative-alpha stocks, driving down their prices and driving up their expected returns. This portfolio rebalancing will continue until all alpha values are driven to zero. At this point, investors will be content to fully diversify and eliminate unique risk, that is, to hold the broadest possible market portfolio. When all stocks have zero alphas, the market portfolio is the optimal risky portfolio.

Thus, one implication of the CAPM is that if one estimates the index model regression with a market index that adequately represents the full market portfolio, estimated values of alpha for any group of stocks should cluster around zero. In any sample period, some firms will do better than expected and their alphas will positive. Other firms will do worse, and theirs will be negative. On average, however, alphas should be zero. We will turn to some of the empirical evidence on this prediction in Chapter 8.

Operationalizing the CAPM in the form of an index model has a drawback, however. If intercepts of regressions of returns on an index differ substantially from zero, you will not be able to tell whether it is because you have chosen a bad index to proxy for the market or because the theory is not useful. This problem was first pointed out by Richard Roll (1977) and is called *Roll's critique*, which we discuss in the next section.

In actuality, some instances of persistent, positive significant CAPM alpha values have been identified; these will be discussed in Chapter 8. Among these are (1) small versus large stocks; (2) stocks of companies that have recently announced unexpectedly good earnings; (3) stocks with high ratios of book value to market value; and (4) stocks with "momentum" that have experienced recent advances in price. These results pose meaningful challenges to the model.

7.3   HOW WELL DOES THE CAPM PREDICT RISK PREMIUMS?

In many ways, portfolio theory and the CAPM have become accepted tools in the practitioner community. Many investment professionals think about the distinction between firm-specific and systematic risk and are comfortable with the use of beta to measure systematic risk. One extensive survey found that about three-quarters of financial managers use the CAPM when estimating the cost of capital.[2] In the asset management industry, alpha is regularly computed. On the other hand, compensation of portfolio managers is rarely based on alpha or other theoretically appropriate risk-adjusted measures such as those addressed later in the text (see Chapter 18). What can we make of this?

---

[2] See J. R. Graham and C. R. Harvey, "The Theory and Practice of Corporate Finance: Evidence from the Field," *Journal of Financial Economics* 61 (2001), pp. 187–243.

Part of the problem clearly derives from the mixed success of the CAPM in explaining variation in rates of return across assets. Let's review some of the evidence on this score.

The CAPM was first published by Sharpe in 1964 and took the world of finance by storm. Early tests by Black, Jensen, and Scholes (1972) and Fama and MacBeth (1973) were partially supportive of the CAPM: Average returns were higher for higher-beta portfolios, but the reward for beta risk was less than predicted by the simple version of the CAPM.

While this sort of evidence against the CAPM remained largely within the ivory towers of academia, Roll's (1977) paper "A Critique of Capital Asset Pricing Tests" shook the practitioner world as well. Roll pointed out that the true market portfolio can never be observed. The usual stock market indexes used as proxies for the market portfolio actually exclude the majority of investor wealth, for example, real estate, fixed income securities, foreign investments, and not least, the value of human capital. Without a good measure of the return on a broad measure of investor assets, the theory is *necessarily* untestable.

The publicity given the now classic "Roll's critique" resulted in popular articles such as "Is Beta Dead?"[3] Although Roll is absolutely correct on theoretical grounds, more recent research suggests that the error introduced by using a broad market index as proxy for the true, unobserved market portfolio is perhaps not even the greatest problem of the CAPM. For example, Fama and French (1992) published a study that dealt the CAPM an even harsher blow. They found that in contradiction to the CAPM, certain characteristics of the firm, namely, size and the ratio of market to book value, were far more useful in predicting future returns than beta.

Fama and French and many others have published follow-up studies on this topic. It seems clear from these studies (to which we will return in more detail later in the chapter) that beta does not tell the whole story of risk. There seem to be risk factors that affect security returns beyond beta's one-dimensional measurement of market sensitivity. In the next section, we introduce a theory of risk premiums that explicitly allows for multiple risk factors.

Liquidity, a different kind of risk factor, also was ignored for a long time. Although first analyzed by Amihud and Mendelson as early as 1986, it is difficult to accurately measure and incorporate in portfolio management. Nevertheless, there is now ample evidence that trading mechanisms on stock exchanges affect the liquidity of assets traded on these exchanges and significantly affect their market value.

Despite all these issues, beta is not dead. Research shows that when we use a more inclusive proxy for the market portfolio than the S&P 500 (specifically, an index that includes human capital) and allow for the fact that beta changes over time, the performance of beta in explaining security returns improves (Jagannathan and Wang, 1996). We know that the CAPM is not a perfect model and that it will continue to be refined. Still, the logic of the model is compelling and captures the two key points made by all of its more sophisticated variants: first, the crucial distinction between diversifiable risk and systematic risk that cannot be avoided by diversification, and second, the fact that investors will demand a premium for bearing nondiversifiable risk. The CAPM therefore provides a useful framework for thinking rigorously about the relationship between security risk and return.

7.4   MULTIFACTOR MODELS AND THE CAPM

The index model allows us to decompose stock variance into systematic risk and firm-specific risk that can be diversified in large portfolios. In the index model, the return on the market portfolio summarized the aggregate impact of macroeconomic factors. In reality, however, systematic risk is not due to one source but instead derives from uncertainty in a number of economywide factors such as business-cycle risk, interest or inflation rate risk, energy price risk, and so on. It stands to reason that a more explicit representation of systematic risk, allowing stocks to exhibit different sensitivities to its various facets, would constitute a useful refinement of the single-factor model. Merton (1973) was the first to show how the CAPM could be extended to allow for multiple sources of systematic risk.

---

[3] A. Wallace, "Is Beta Dead?" *Institutional Investor* 14 (July 1980), pp. 22–30.

We would expect that models that allow for several systematic factors—**multifactor models**—can provide better descriptions of security returns. Merton's model results in a multifactor security market line in which extra-market risk factors capture the impact of the important dimensions of systematic risk that investors wish to hedge.

Let's illustrate with a two-factor model. Suppose the two most important macroeconomic sources of risk are the state of the business cycle, reflected in returns on a broad market index, and unanticipated changes in interest rates, captured by returns on a Treasury-bond portfolio. The return on any stock will respond both to sources of macro risk and to its own firm-specific influences. Therefore, we can expand the single-index model, Equation 7.3 as follows, using upper case R to denote excess returns:

$$R_{it} = \alpha_i + \beta_{iM} R_{Mt} + \beta_{iTB} R_{TBt} + e_{it} \tag{7.6}$$

where β_{iTB} is the sensitivity of stock i's excess return to that of the T-bond portfolio and R_{TBt} is the excess return of the T-bond portfolio in month t.

How must the security market line of the CAPM be modified to reflect multiple sources of systematic risk? Not surprisingly, a multifactor index model gives rise to a multifactor security market line in which the risk premium is determined by the exposure to *each* systematic risk factor and by a risk premium associated with each of those factors.

In the two-factor economy of Equation 7.6, the expected rate of return on a security would be the sum of three terms:

1. The risk-free rate of return.
2. The security's sensitivity to the market index (i.e., its market beta, β_{iM}) times the risk premium of the index, $[E(r_M) - r_f]$.
3. The security's sensitivity to interest rate risk (i.e., its T-bond beta, β_{iTB}) times the risk premium of the T-bond portfolio, $[E(r_{TB}) - r_f]$.

This conclusion is expressed mathematically as a two-factor security market line for security i:

$$E(r_i) = r_f + \beta_{iM}\big[E(r_M) - r_f\big] + \beta_{iTB}\big[E(r_{TB}) - r_f\big] \tag{7.7}$$

Equation 7.7 is an expansion of the simple security market line. Once we generalize the single-index SML to multiple risk sources, each with its own risk premium, the insights are similar.

multifactor models

Models of security markets positing that returns respond to several systematic factors.

Northeast Airlines has a market beta of 1.2 and a T-bond beta of 0.7. Suppose the risk premium of the market index is 6%, while that of the T-bond portfolio is 3%. Then the overall risk premium on Northeast stock is the sum of the risk premiums required as compensation for each source of systematic risk.

The portion of the risk premium attributable to market risk is the stock's exposure to that risk, 1.2, multiplied by the corresponding risk premium, 6%, or 1.2 × 6% = 7.2%. Similarly, the risk premium attributable to interest rate risk is .7 × 3% = 2.1%. The total risk premium is 7.2 + 2.1 = 9.3%. Therefore, if the risk-free rate is 4%, the expected return on the portfolio should be

4.0%	Risk-free rate
+ 7.2	+ Risk premium for exposure to market risk
+ 2.1	+ Risk premium for exposure to interest rate risk
13.3%	Total expected return

More concisely,

$$E(r) = 4\% + 1.2 \times 6\% + .7 \times 3\% = 13.3\%$$

EXAMPLE 7.7

A Two-Factor SML

The multifactor model clearly gives us a richer way to think about risk exposures and compensation for those exposures than the single-index model or the CAPM. But what are the relevant additional systematic factors?

Economic theory suggests factors that affect investor welfare in three possible ways: (1) factors that are correlated with prices of important consumption goods, such as housing or energy; (2) factors that are correlated with future investment opportunities, such as interest rates, return volatility, or risk premiums; and (3) factors that correlate with the general state of the economy, such as industrial production and employment. Alas, multifactor equations employing likely candidates for these theoretically plausible factors have not produced sufficient improvement over the explanatory power of the single-factor model. Instead, the most common approach to multifactor models today follows from work by Eugene Fama and Kenneth French (1992), who proposed extra-market factors based on empirical success in predicting excess returns. We turn next to their approach.

The Fama-French Three-Factor Model

Fama and French proposed a three-factor model that has become a standard tool for empirical studies of asset returns. They add to the market-index portfolios formed on the basis of firm size and book-to-market ratio to explain average returns. These additional factors are motivated by the observations that average returns on stocks of small firms and firms with high ratios of book value of equity to market value of equity have been higher than predicted by the CAPM.

Firms with a high book-to-market ratio disproportionately include relatively mature firms. These firms derive a larger share of their market value from assets already in place, rather than growth opportunities. This group often is called *value stocks*. In contrast, low-B/M companies are viewed as *growth firms* whose market values derive from anticipated growth in future cash flows, rather than from assets already in place. Considerable evidence (which we will review in the following chapter) suggests that value stocks have offered a higher average rate of return than growth stocks; the differential is known as the *value premium*.

Fama and French do not view firm size or the book-to-market ratio as directly dictating a firm's risk premium. Instead, they view these factors as proxies for more fundamental sources of risk that are not fully captured by the security's CAPM beta. These extra-market factors therefore may be interpreted as portfolios that provide exposure to fundamental risk factors, whatever they may be.

One mechanism by which a high book-to-market ratio may capture aspects of systematic risk is through the impact of large fixed assets. When the economy tanks, these assets cannot be used at full capacity, and a large share of their value may be lost. Therefore, a high B/M ratio, which can result from large investments in fixed assets, may imply higher systematic risk than indicated by historically estimated beta.

Firm size may also predict some aspects of risk. Shares of large firms may be less risky than those of small firms, other things being equal, because they are covered by more analysts, and there is more accurate information about them. With better-informed investors, prices will more accurately reflect true value and be less susceptible to systematic as well as firm-specific fluctuations. With deeper pockets and greater debt capacity, large firms also can better withstand economic downturns. On both counts, stock in small firms will command higher risk premiums than indicated by beta alone.

Estimating a Three-Factor SML

Fama and French propose measuring the size factor as the difference in returns in firms with low market values (low capitalization firms) versus those with high market values ("high cap" firms). They denote the size factor by SMB (small minus big). Their proxy for the

TABLE 7.2	Estimates of single-index and three-factor Fama-French regressions for Ford, monthly data, January 2011–December 2015	

	Single factor model	**Three-factor model**
Intercept	−.978% (−1.277)	−.742% (−.958)
$r_M - r_f$	1.326 (6.145)	1.235 (5.430)
SMB		.246 (0.667)
HML		.692 (1.612)
R-square	.394	.426
Residual std dev	5.77%	5.72%

Source: Authors' calculations.

value-versus-growth factor is the difference in returns in stocks with high versus low ratios of book-to-market value, which they denote by HML (high minus low).

Taking the difference in returns between two portfolios has an economic interpretation. The SMB return, for example, equals the return from a long position in small stocks, financed with a short position in the large stocks. Note that this is a portfolio that entails no *net* investment.[4]

In the previous chapter, we estimated the single-index model for Ford. Now we are ready to estimate Ford's three-factor model. To do so, we need to estimate Ford's beta on each factor. Therefore, we generalize regression Equation 7.3 of the single index model and fit the following multiple regression equation:

$$r_{\text{Ford},t} - r_{ft} = \alpha_{\text{Ford}} + \beta_M(r_{M,t} - r_{ft}) + \beta_{\text{HML}}\, r_{\text{HML},t} + \beta_{\text{SMB}}\, r_{\text{SMB},t} + e_{\text{Ford},t} \qquad \textbf{(7.8)}$$

The three betas on the right-hand side of Equation 7.8 denote Ford's beta against the three hypothesized sources of systematic risk: the market (M), the value-versus-growth factor (HML), and the size factor (SMB).

Table 7.2 shows estimates of the single factor and three-factor index model for Ford. The intercept in each regression is the estimate of (monthly) alpha over the sample period. The coefficient on the excess market index return, $r_M - r_f$ is the estimate of the conventional beta, while the coefficients on SMB and HML are estimates of the betas against the two extra-market risk factors. The terms in parentheses are the t-statistics associated with each parameter estimate.

As it turns out, the extra-market risk factors do not add much to Ford's risk profile. While the betas on both SMB and HML are positive, indicating some tendency for Ford's return to be higher when small firms outperform large ones and when high book-to-market firms outperform low ones, neither estimate is statistically significant; both t-statistics are below the conventional cutoff of 2. Adding the two factors neither increases the R-square of the regression meaningfully, nor reduces the standard deviation of the unexplained residuals. Thus, we conclude that for Ford, the standard market beta is the primary determinant of risk. Other firms, of course, will have their own unique configuration of exposures to the various risk factors.

Using the three-factor model to estimate expected returns requires forecasts of the premiums on the two extra-market risk premium as well as that on the market index. Suppose the risk-free rate is $r_f = 1\%$, the market risk premium is $E(r_M) - r_f = 6\%$, the risk premium on

[4] Interpreting the returns on the SMB and HML portfolios is a bit subtle because both portfolios are zero net investments, and therefore one cannot compute profit per dollar invested. For example, in the SMB portfolio, for every dollar held in small capitalization stocks, there is an offsetting short position in large capitalization stocks. The "return" for this portfolio is actually the profit on the overall position per dollar invested in the small-cap firms (or equivalently, per dollar shorted in the large-cap firms).

SMB is 2%, and the risk premium on HML is 3%. Then the expected return on Ford would be calculated using these benchmark risk premiums and the betas estimated in Table 7.2:[5]

$$E(r_{\text{Ford}}) = r_f + \beta_{\text{Ford},M}\left[E(r_M) - r_f\right] + \beta_{\text{Ford,SMB}}\, E(r_{\text{SMB}}) + \beta_{\text{Ford,HML}}\, E(r_{\text{HML}})$$
$$1\% + (1.235 \times 6\%) + (.246 \times 2\%) + (.692 \times 3\%) = 10.978\%$$

If instead, we used the beta estimate from the single-index model, we would obtain an expected return of

$$r_f + \beta\left[E(r_M) - r_f\right] = 1\% + 1.326 \times 6\% = 8.956\%$$

Ford's positive betas on the SMB and HML factors mean that the inferred expected return from the three-factor model is higher than from the single-index model.

Notice that in neither case do we add the regression estimate of alpha to the forecast of expected return. Equilibrium expected returns depend only on risk; the expectation of alpha in market equilibrium must be zero. While a security may have outperformed its benchmark return in a particular sample period (as reflected in a positive alpha), we would not expect that performance to continue into the future. In fact, as an empirical matter, individual firm alphas show virtually no persistence over time.

Multifactor Models and the Validity of the CAPM

The single-index CAPM fails empirical tests because its empirical representation, the single-index model, inadequately explains returns on too many securities. In short, too many statistically significant values of alpha (which the CAPM says should be zero) show up in single-index regressions. Despite this failure, it is still widely used in the industry.

Multifactor models such as the FF model may also be tested by the prevalence of significant alpha values. The three-factor model shows a material improvement over the single-index model in that regard. But the use of multi-index models comes at a price: They require forecasts of the additional factor returns. If forecasts of those additional factors are themselves subject to forecast error, these models will be less accurate than the theoretically inferior single-index model. Nevertheless, multifactor models have a definite appeal because it is clear that real-world risk is multifaceted.

The original FF model has spawned a cottage industry generating new factor portfolios, including, but not limited to, momentum or liquidity factors. One expects that the incremental contributions of these additional factors will be smaller than those of the first two, SMB and HML. Still, the search for the ultimate version of the expected return-risk relationship is far from over.

7.5   ARBITRAGE PRICING THEORY

One reason for skepticism about the validity of the CAPM is the unrealistic nature of the assumptions needed to derive it. Most unappealing are Assumptions 1(a)–1(c), namely, that all investors are identical in every way but wealth and risk aversion. For this reason, as well as for its economic insights, an alternative approach to asset pricing called the arbitrage pricing theory is of great interest. To understand this theory we begin with the concept of *arbitrage*.

arbitrage

Creation of riskless profits made possible by relative mispricing among securities.

Arbitrage is the act of exploiting mispricing of two or more securities to achieve risk-free profits. As a trivial example, consider a security that is priced differently in two markets. A long position in the cheaper market financed by a short position in the expensive market will lead to a sure profit. As investors avidly pursue this strategy, prices are forced back into alignment, so arbitrage opportunities vanish almost as quickly as they materialize.

---

[5] When we estimate Equation 7.8, we must subtract the risk-free return from the market return but not from the returns on the SMB or HML portfolios. This is because the SMB and HML factors are *already* risk premiums, for size or book-to-market, respectively. We subtract the risk-free rate from the market index return to similarly cast it as a risk premium. The data for the factor portfolios are available from Kenneth French's website: **mba.tuck.dartmouth .edu/pages/faculty/ken.french/data_library.html**.

The first to apply this concept to equilibrium security returns was Ross (1976), who developed the **arbitrage pricing theory (APT).** The APT depends on the observation that well-functioning capital markets preclude arbitrage opportunities. A violation of the APT's pricing relationships will cause extremely strong pressure to restore them even if only a limited number of investors become aware of the discrepancy. Ross's accomplishment is to derive the equilibrium rates of return that would prevail in a market where prices are aligned to obey the "no-arbitrage rule."

arbitrage pricing theory (APT)

A theory of risk-return relationships derived from no-arbitrage considerations in large capital markets.

Diversification in a Single-Index Security Market

Imagine a portfolio formed from securities whose returns follow the single-index model (see Equation 7.3). What are the systematic and nonsystematic variances of this portfolio?

The beta of the portfolio is a simple average of the individual security betas; call that average beta, β. The systematic variance equals $\beta^2 \sigma_M^2$. This is the level of market risk in Figure 6.1B. The market variance (σ_M^2) and the beta of the portfolio determine its market risk.

The systematic component of each security's return, $\beta_i R_M$, is determined completely by the market factor and therefore is perfectly correlated with the systematic part of any other security's return. Hence, there are no diversification effects on systematic risk no matter how many securities are involved. A single security has the same *systematic* risk as a diversified portfolio with the same beta. The number of securities makes no difference.

It is quite different with firm-specific risk. Consider a portfolio of n securities with weights w_i in each. The nonsystematic portion of the portfolio return is

$$e_P = \sum_{i=1}^{n} w_i e_i$$

Because the firm-specific terms, e_i, are uncorrelated, the portfolio nonsystematic variance is the weighted sum of the individual firm-specific variances:[6]

$$\sigma^2(e_P) = \sum_{i=1}^{n} w_i^2 \sigma^2(e_i) \qquad \textbf{(7.9)}$$

Each individual nonsystematic variance is multiplied by the *square* of the portfolio weight. With diversified portfolios, the squared weights are very small. For example, if $w_i = .01$ (think of a portfolio with 100 securities), then $w_i^2 = .0001$. The sum in Equation 7.9 is therefore far less than the average firm-specific variance of the stocks in the portfolio. We conclude that the impact of nonsystematic risk becomes ever smaller as the number of securities grows and the portfolio becomes more diversified.

We see this effect dramatically in the scatter diagrams of Figure 7.3. The colored dots are the monthly returns over a five-year period for a single stock, Union Pacific Railroad, versus the return on the market index. The black dots are for a diversified stock mutual fund, Vanguard's Growth & Income Fund. During the period, both the stock and the fund had virtually identical betas. But their nonsystematic risk differed considerably: The scatter of Union Pacific's returns fall considerably further from the regression line than do the mutual fund's, for which diversification has virtually eliminated residual risk.

In sum, the number of securities in the portfolio has no bearing on systematic risk. Only average beta matters. In contrast, firm-specific risk becomes increasingly irrelevant as the portfolio becomes more diversified. This is a crucial insight when we think about the risk-return relationship. One would not expect investors to be rewarded for bearing risk that can be easily eliminated through diversification. Moreover, diversified investors who have eliminated their exposure to firm-specific risk will be exposed only to systematic risk and therefore will treat beta as the relevant risk measure. Therefore, risk premiums should depend on the security's beta, not on its firm-specific risk. This is the basis of the APT's security market line that we are now ready to derive.

---

[6] We use the result from statistics that when we multiply a random variable (in this case, e_i) by a constant (in this case, w_i), the variance is multiplied by the *square* of the constant. The variance of the sum in Equation 7.9 equals the sum of the variances because in this case (by assumption in the index model) all covariances are zero.

FIGURE 7.3

Scatter diagram for Union Pacific Railroad (colored dots) and the Vanguard Growth & Income fund (black dots). Both have betas almost precisely equal to 1, but the single stock has far greater diversifiable risk.

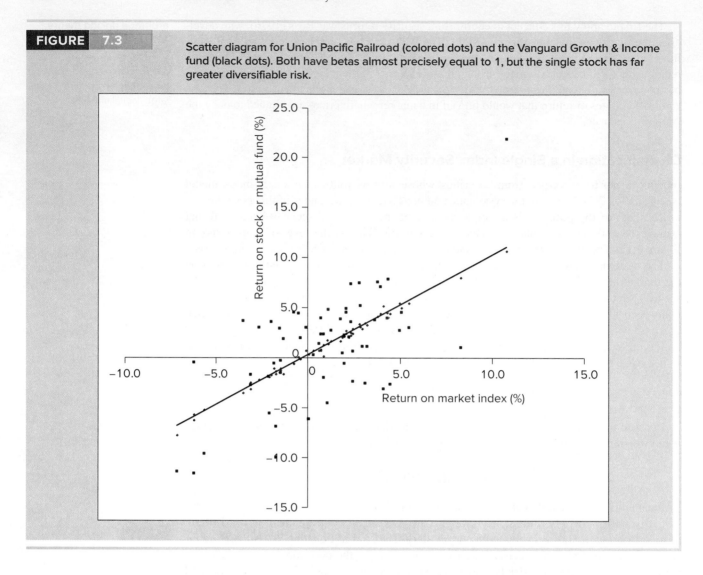

Well-Diversified Portfolios

well-diversified portfolio

A portfolio sufficiently diversified that nonsystematic risk is negligible.

Equation 7.9 tells us that as diversification progresses, that is, as the weight in each security approaches zero, the nonsystematic variance of the portfolio approaches zero. We will define a **well-diversified portfolio** as one for which each weight, w_i, is small enough that for practical purposes the nonsystematic variance, $\sigma^2(e_P)$, is negligible.

Because the expected value of e_P for any well-diversified portfolio is zero, and its variance also is effectively zero, any realized value of e_P will be virtually zero. Therefore, for a well-diversified portfolio, P, for all practical purposes, we can drop the residual term from the index model equation, which therefore becomes

$$r_P - r_f = \alpha_P + \beta_P(r_M - r_f) \tag{7.10}$$

The solid line in Figure 7.4, Panel A, plots the excess return of a well-diversified portfolio P with $E(r_P) - r_f = E(R_P) = 10\%$ and $\beta_P = 1$ for various realizations of the market excess return. Compare Panel A with Panel B, which is a similar graph for a single stock (S) with $\beta_S = 1$. The undiversified stock is subject to nonsystematic risk, which is seen in a scatter of points around the line. The well-diversified portfolio's return, in contrast, is determined completely by the systematic factor.

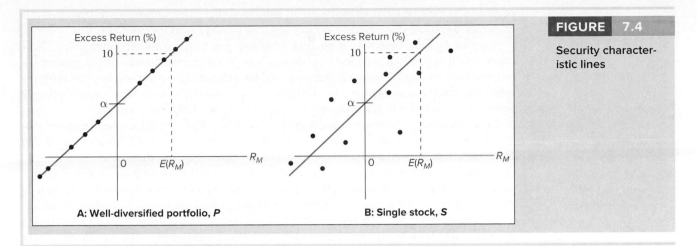

FIGURE 7.4

Security character-
istic lines

A: Well-diversified portfolio, *P*

B: Single stock, *S*

The Security Market Line of the APT

Suppose you form a well-diversified portfolio, let's say with a beta of 0.7. According to Equation 7.10, its return in any period would be $r_P = r_f + \alpha_P + .7(r_M - r_f)$. Now consider another portfolio constructed by mixing the market index and T-bills with weights of 0.7 and 0.3. We call this a *mimicking portfolio* because it duplicates the systematic exposure of portfolio *P*. The return on the mimicking portfolio would be $.3r_f + .7r_M$, which can be rewritten as $r_f + .7(r_M - r_f)$. Now suppose you buy \$1 of portfolio *P* and sell \$1 worth of the mimicking portfolio. Your net investment would be zero, and your proceeds would be *riskless:*

Long \$1 in portfolio *P*	$\$1 \times [r_f + \alpha_P + .7(r_M - r_f)]$
Short \$1 in mimicking portfolio	$-\$1 \times [r_f + .7(r_M - r_f)]$
Net profit	$\$1 \times \alpha_P$

If α_P were positive, investors would pursue this strategy (which is riskless and requires zero net investment) at an infinitely large scale and make an infinitely large profit. If α_P were negative, investors would do the reverse, selling \$1 of *P* and buying \$1 of the mimicking portfolio, again clearing an infinite profit. These large-scale investments would continue indefinitely until alpha was driven to zero. No matter what the beta of portfolio *P*, we could pursue this same strategy. We conclude that α_P in Equation 7.10 must be zero if capital markets are to rule out easy arbitrage opportunities.

Therefore, set $\alpha_P = 0$ and take expectations in Equation 7.10 to find the expected return on the portfolio:

$$E(r_P) = r_f + \beta_P [E(r_M) - r_f] \qquad \textbf{(7.11)}$$

But this is the familiar expected return-beta relation of the CAPM! Its message—that beta and not firm-specific risk should drive asset risk premiums—should not be surprising in light of our earlier conclusion that firm-specific risk can be eliminated through diversification. Equation 7.11 establishes that the SML of the CAPM must also apply to well-diversified portfolios simply by virtue of the no-arbitrage requirement of the APT.

Individual Assets and the APT

We have demonstrated that if arbitrage opportunities are to be ruled out, each well-diversified portfolio's expected return must satisfy the SML predicted by the CAPM. The natural question is whether this relationship tells us anything about the expected returns on the component stocks. The answer is that if this relationship is to be satisfied by *all* well-diversified portfolios, it must be satisfied by *almost* all individual securities, although a full proof of this proposition is somewhat difficult. We can illustrate the argument less formally.

Suppose that the expected return–beta relationship is violated for all single assets. Now create a well-diversified portfolio from these assets. What are the chances that in spite of the fact that the relationship generally does *not* hold for individual assets, it *will* hold for the portfolio? The chances are small, but it is perhaps possible that the relationships among the single securities are violated in offsetting ways so that somehow it holds for portfolio.

Now construct yet another well-diversified portfolio. What are the chances that the violations of the relationships for single securities are such that this portfolio also will fulfill the no-arbitrage expected return–beta relationship? Obviously, the chances are smaller still. Continue with other well-diversified portfolio, and so on. If the no-arbitrage expected return–beta relationship has to hold for each of these different, well-diversified portfolios, it must be virtually certain that the relationship holds for all but a small number of individual securities.

We use the term *virtually certain* advisedly because we must distinguish this conclusion from the statement that all securities surely fulfill this relationship. The reason we cannot make the latter statement has to do with a property of well-diversified portfolios.

Recall that to qualify as well diversified, a portfolio must have very small positions in all securities. If, for example, only one security violates the expected return–beta relationship, then the effect of this violation on a well-diversified portfolio will be too small to be of importance for any practical purpose, and meaningful arbitrage opportunities will not arise. But if many securities violate the expected return–beta relationship, the relationship will no longer hold for well-diversified portfolios, and arbitrage opportunities will be available. Consequently, we conclude that the no-arbitrage condition in a single-index security market implies the expected return–beta relationship for all well-diversified portfolios and for all but possibly a *small* number of individual securities.

Well-Diversified Portfolios in Practice

What is the effect of diversification on portfolio standard deviation *in practice,* where portfolio size is not unlimited? To illustrate, consider the residual standard deviation of a 1,000-stock portfolio with equal weights on each component stock. If the annualized residual standard deviation for each stock is $\sigma(e_i) = 40\%$, then the portfolio achieves a small but still not negligible standard deviation of $40/\sqrt{1,000} = 1.26\%$.

What is a "large" portfolio? Many widely held ETFs or mutual funds hold hundreds of different shares, but few hold more than 1,000. Therefore, for plausible portfolios, even broad diversification is not likely to achieve the risk reduction of the APT's "well-diversified" ideal. This is a shortcoming in the model. On the other hand, even the levels of residual risk attainable in practice should make the APT's security market line at the very least a good approximation to the risk-return relation. We address the comparative strengths of the APT and the CAPM as models of risk and return in the next section.

The APT and the CAPM

The APT serves many of the same functions as the CAPM. It gives us a benchmark for rates of return that can be used in capital budgeting, security valuation, or investment performance evaluation. Moreover, the APT highlights the crucial distinction between nondiversifiable risk, which requires a reward in the form of a risk premium, and diversifiable risk, which does not.

In many ways, the APT is an extremely appealing model. Whereas the CAPM relies on marginal trade-offs between risk and return in the mean-variance efficient portfolio, the APT appeals to a more compelling arbitrage strategy. It does not require that almost all investors be mean-variance optimizers. Instead, it is built on the highly plausible assumption that a rational capital market will preclude arbitrage opportunities. A violation of the APT's pricing relationships will cause extremely strong pressure to restore them. Moreover, the APT provides an expected return–beta relationship using as a benchmark a well-diversified index portfolio rather than the elusive and impossible-to-observe market portfolio of *all* assets that underpins the CAPM. When we replace the unobserved market portfolio of the CAPM with a broad, but observable, index portfolio, we can no longer be sure that this portfolio will be an adequate benchmark for the CAPM's security market line.

In spite of these apparent advantages, the APT does not fully dominate the CAPM. The CAPM provides an unequivocal statement on the expected return–beta relationship for all securities, whereas the APT implies that this relationship holds for all but perhaps a small number of securities. Because the APT is built on the foundation of well-diversified portfolios, it cannot rule out a violation of the expected return–beta relationship for any particular asset. Moreover, we've seen that even large portfolios may have nonnegligible residual risk.

In the end, however, it is noteworthy and comforting that despite the different paths they take to get there, both models arrive at the same security market line. Most important, they both highlight the distinction between firm-specific and systematic risk, which is at the heart of all modern models of risk and return.

Multifactor Generalization of the APT

So far, we've examined the APT in a one-factor world. In reality, as we pointed out above, there are several sources of systematic risk such as uncertainty in the business cycle, interest rates, energy prices, and so on. Presumably, exposure to any of these factors will affect a stock's appropriate expected return. The APT can be generalized to accommodate these multiple sources of risk in a manner much like the multifactor CAPM.

Expanding the single-index model of Equation 7.3 to a two-index model:

$$r_i - r_f = \beta_{i1}(r_{M1} - r_f) + \beta_{i2}(r_{M2} - r_f) + \alpha_i + e_i \qquad (7.12)$$

where $r_{M1} - r_f$ and $r_{M2} - r_f$ are the excess returns on "factor portfolios" designed to track the two systematic factors. Factor 1 might be, for example, unanticipated changes in industrial production, while factor 2 might represent unanticipated changes in short-term interest rates. We assume again that there are many securities available with any combination of betas. This implies that we can form well-diversified **factor portfolios** with a beta of 1 on one factor and 0 on all others. Thus, a factor portfolio with a beta of 1 on the first factor will have a rate of return of r_{M1}; a factor portfolio with a beta of 1 on the second factor will have a rate of return of r_{M2}; and so on. Factor portfolios serve as the benchmark portfolios for a multifactor generalization of the security market line relationship.

factor portfolio

A well-diversified portfolio constructed to have a beta of 1 on one factor and a beta of 0 on any other factor.

Suppose the two factor portfolios, here called portfolios 1 and 2, have expected returns $E(r_1) = 10\%$ and $E(r_2) = 12\%$. Suppose further that the risk-free rate is 4%. The risk premium on the first factor portfolio is therefore 6%, while that on the second factor portfolio is 8%.

Now consider an arbitrary well-diversified portfolio (P), with beta on the first factor, $\beta_{P1} = .5$, and on the second factor, $\beta_{P2} = .75$. Like the multifactor CAPM, the multifactor APT states that the portfolio risk premium must equal the sum of the risk premiums required as compensation for each source of systematic risk. The risk premium attributable to risk factor 1 is the portfolio's exposure to factor 1, β_{P1}, times the risk premium earned on the first factor portfolio, $E(r_1) - r_f$. Therefore, the portion of portfolio P's risk premium that is compensation for its exposure to the first risk factor is $\beta_{P1}[E(r_1) - r_f] = .5(10\% - 4\%) = 3\%$, while the risk premium attributable to risk factor 2 is $\beta_{P2}[E(r_2) - r_f] = .75(12\% - 4\%) = 6\%$. The total risk premium on the portfolio, therefore, should be $3 + 6 = 9\%$, and the total return on the portfolio should be 13%.

4%	Risk-free rate
+ 3%	Risk premium for exposure to factor 1
+ 6%	Risk premium for exposure to factor 2
13%	Total expected return

EXAMPLE 7.8

Multifactor SML

If the actual expected return on portfolio P in Example 7.8 were not 13%, there would be an arbitrage opportunity. To illustrate, suppose portfolio P actually has an expected return of 15%, and therefore a positive alpha of 2%.

As before, the idea is to create a mimicking portfolio that duplicates P's systematic risk. So if β_{P1} is the beta of portfolio P against the first factor portfolio and β_{P2} is its beta against the second factor portfolio, we would form the mimicking portfolio as follows: The weight of the mimicking portfolio in factor portfolio 1 should be β_{P1}, the weight in factor portfolio 2 should be β_{P2}, and the remainder of the mimicking portfolio should be placed in T-bills, which therefore will have a weight of $(1 - \beta_{P1} - \beta_{P2})$. The rate of return on the mimicking portfolio is therefore

$$\beta_{P1} r_{M1} + \beta_{P2} r_{M2} + (1 - \beta_{P1} - \beta_{P2}) r_f = r_f + \beta_{P1}(r_{M1} - r_f) + \beta_{P2}(r_{M2} - r_f) \qquad \textbf{(7.13)}$$

There is no residual risk term in Equation 7.13 because the mimicking portfolio is composed of well-diversified factor portfolios. Its expected return is $4\% + .5(10 - 4) + .75(12 - 4) = 13\%$. Thus, the mimicking portfolio has exactly the same factor exposures as portfolio P, but its expected return is 13% rather than 15%. This is another way to see that $\alpha_P = 2\%$.

Given its higher return and identical factor exposure, arbitrageurs will buy large amounts of portfolio P and sell equal amounts of the mimicking portfolio. Their net investments are zero and their positions are risk-free because the factor exposures on portfolio P and the mimicking portfolio cancel out. This arbitrage activity will push up the price of portfolio P and drive down its expected rate of return until α_P is forced to zero. We conclude that in the absence of arbitrage opportunities, the multifactor SML must prevail.

With two sources of systematic risk, two factor portfolios, $M1$ and $M2$, and betas of β_1 and β_2, respectively, on those portfolios, we can express the two-factor SML for security i as:

$$E(r_i) = r_f + \beta_1 \left[E(r_{M1}) - r_f \right] + \beta_2 \left[E(r_{M2}) - r_f \right] \qquad \textbf{(7.14)}$$

Just as the single-factor APT and CAPM give rise to the same SML, the multifactor extensions of the two models also produce identical SMLs.

CONCEPT check **7.6** Using the factor portfolios of Example 7.8, find the fair rate of return on a security with $\beta_1 = .2$ and $\beta_2 = 1.4$.

Smart Betas and Multifactor Models

We've seen that both the CAPM and the APT have multifactor generalizations. There are at least two important implications of these generalizations. First, investors should be aware that their portfolios are subject to more than one systematic source of risk, and that they need to think about how much exposure they wish to establish to each systematic factor. Second, when they evaluate investment performance, they should be aware that risk premiums come from exposure to several risk factors, and that alpha needs to be computed controlling for each of them.

A new product called *smart-beta ETFs* has important implications for both of these issues. They are analogous to index ETFs, but instead of tracking a broad market index using market capitalization weights, they are funds designed to provide exposure to specific characteristics such as value, growth, or volatility. Among the more prominent themes are the extra-market factors of the Fama-French three-factor model: size (SMB) and value (HML). Another common factor is momentum (WML, for winners-minus-losers), which is the return on a portfolio that buys recent well-performing stocks and sells poorly performing ones. Other recently considered factors are based on volatility, as measured by the standard deviation of stock returns; quality, the difference in returns of firms with high versus low return on assets or similar measures of profitability; investment, the difference between returns on firms with high versus low rates of asset growth; and dividend yield.

Smart-beta ETFs allow investors to tailor portfolio exposures either toward or away from a range of extra-market risk factors using easy-to-trade index-like products. They are therefore well-suited to a multifactor environment. They also raise the question of appropriate performance evaluation. When investors can cheaply and effectively manage exposure to multidimensional sources of systematic risk, investment success is captured by a multifactor alpha, providing a clean measure of the success of security selection. This is the message of the multifactor SML presented in Equation 7.14.

In this regard, interesting preliminary research by Cao, Hsu, Xiao, and Zhan (2018) indicates that since smart-beta ETFs have been introduced, investors have increasingly shifted toward multifactor SMLs in assessing mutual fund performance. Their evidence is that since the advent of active trading in these ETFs, the flow of money into or out of mutual funds has more closely tracked multifactor alphas rather than traditional one-factor CAPM alphas.

SUMMARY

- The CAPM assumes investors are rational, single-period planners who agree on a common input list from security analysis and seek mean-variance optimal portfolios.
- The CAPM assumes ideal security markets in the sense that (*a*) there are no taxes, (*b*) there are no transaction costs, (*c*) all risky assets are publicly traded, and (*d*) any amount can be borrowed and lent at a fixed, risk-free rate. These assumptions mean that all investors will hold identical risky portfolios. The CAPM implies that, in equilibrium, the market portfolio is the unique mean-variance efficient tangency portfolio, which indicates that a passive strategy is efficient.
- The market portfolio is value-weighted. Each security is held in a proportion equal to its market value divided by the total market value of all securities. The risk premium on the market portfolio is proportional to its variance, σ_M^2, and to the risk aversion of the average investor.
- The CAPM implies that the risk premium on any individual asset or portfolio is the product of the risk premium of the market portfolio and the asset's beta. The security market line shows the return demanded by investors as a function of the beta of their investment. This expected return is a benchmark for evaluating investment performance.
- In a single-index security market, once an index is specified, a security beta can be estimated from a regression of the security's excess return on the index's excess return. This regression line is called the security characteristic line (SCL). The intercept of the SCL, called alpha, represents the average excess return on the security when the index excess return is zero. The CAPM implies that alphas should average zero.
- The CAPM and the security market line can be used to establish benchmarks for evaluation of investment performance or to determine appropriate discount rates for capital budgeting applications. They are also used in regulatory proceedings concerning the "fair" rate of return for regulated industries.
- The CAPM is usually implemented as a single-factor model, with all systematic risk summarized by the return on a broad market index. However, multifactor generalizations of the basic model may be specified to accommodate multiple sources of systematic risk. In such multifactor extensions of the CAPM, the risk premium of any security is determined by its sensitivity to each systematic risk factor as well as the risk premium associated with that source of risk.
- There are two general approaches to finding extra-market systematic risk factors. One looks for factors that are empirically associated with high average returns and so may be proxies for relevant measures of systematic risk. The other focuses on factors that are plausibly important sources of risk to wide segments of investors and may thus command risk premiums.
- An arbitrage opportunity arises when the disparity between two or more security prices enables investors to construct a zero net investment portfolio that will yield a sure profit. The presence of arbitrage opportunities and the resulting volume of trades will create pressure on security prices that will persist until prices reach levels that preclude arbitrage. Only a few investors need to become aware of arbitrage opportunities to trigger this process because of the large volume of trades in which they will engage.

- When securities are priced so that there are no arbitrage opportunities, the market satisfies the no-arbitrage condition. Price relationships that satisfy the no-arbitrage condition are important because we expect them to hold in real-world markets.
- Portfolios are called *well diversified* if they include a large number of securities in such proportions that the residual or diversifiable risk of the portfolio is negligible.
- In a single-factor security market, all well-diversified portfolios must satisfy the expected return–beta relationship of the SML in order to satisfy the no-arbitrage condition. If all well-diversified portfolios satisfy the expected return–beta relationship, then all but a small number of securities also must satisfy this relationship.
- The APT implies the same expected return–beta relationship as the CAPM yet does not require that all investors be mean-variance optimizers. The price of this generality is that the APT does not guarantee this relationship for all securities at all times.
- A multifactor APT generalizes the single-factor model to accommodate several sources of systematic risk.

KEY TERMS

alpha, 199
arbitrage, 206
arbitrage pricing theory (APT), 207
capital asset pricing model (CAPM), 193

expected return–beta relationship, 197
factor portfolio, 211
market portfolio (M), 194
multifactor models, 203
mutual fund theorem, 195

security market line (SML), 198
well-diversified portfolio, 208

KEY FORMULAS

Market portfolio risk premium is proportional to average risk aversion and market risk:

$$E(r_M) - r_f = \bar{A}\sigma_M^2$$

CAPM, SML: Expected return as a function of systematic risk:

$$E(r_i) = r_f + \beta_i[E(r_M) - r_f]$$

The index model in realized returns:

$$r_{it} - r_{ft} = \alpha_i + \beta_i(r_{Mt} - r_{ft}) + e_{it}$$

The two-index model for stock i in realized excess returns, where returns on portfolios $M1$ and $M2$ capture the two systematic factors:

$$R_{it} = \alpha_i + \beta_{i,M1}R_{M1,t} + \beta_{i,M2}R_{M2,t} + e_{it}$$

The two-factor SML (where $M1$ and $M2$ denote the two factor portfolios):

$$E(r_i) = r_f + \beta_{i,M1}[E(r_{M1}) - r_f] + \beta_{i,M2}[E(r_{M2}) - r_f]$$

The Fama-French three-factor model:

$$r_i - r_f = \alpha_i + \beta_M(r_M - r_f) + \beta_{HML}r_{HML} + \beta_{SMB}r_{SMB} + e_i$$

PROBLEM SETS

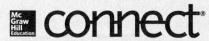

Select problems are available in McGraw-Hill's *Connect.* Please see the Supplements section of the book's frontmatter for more information.

1. Suppose investors believe that the standard deviation of the market-index portfolio has increased by 50%. What does the CAPM imply about the effect of this change on the required rate of return on Google's investment projects? *(LO 7-1)*

2. Consider the statement: "If we can identify a portfolio with a higher Sharpe ratio than the S&P 500 Index portfolio, then we should reject the single-index CAPM." Do you agree or disagree? Explain. *(LO 7-1)*

3. Are the following true or false? Explain. *(LO 7-5)*
   a. Stocks with a beta of zero offer an expected rate of return of zero.
   b. The CAPM implies that investors require a higher return to hold highly volatile securities.
   c. You can construct a portfolio with a beta of 0.75 by investing 0.75 of the investment budget in T-bills and the remainder in the market portfolio.

4. Here are data on two companies. The T-bill rate is 4% and the market risk premium is 6%.

Company	$1 Discount Store	Everything $5
Forecast return	12%	11%
Standard deviation of returns	8%	10%
Beta	1.5	1.0

   What should be the expected rate of return for each company, according to the capital asset pricing model (CAPM)? *(LO 7-1)*

5. Characterize each company in the previous problem as underpriced, overpriced, or properly priced. *(LO 7-2)*

6. What is the expected rate of return for a stock that has a beta of 1 if the expected return on the market is 15%? *(LO 7-2)*
   a. 15%.
   b. More than 15%.
   c. Cannot be determined without the risk-free rate.

7. Kaskin, Inc., stock has a beta of 1.2 and Quinn, Inc., stock has a beta of 0.6. Which of the following statements is *most* accurate? *(LO 7-1)*
   a. The equilibrium expected rate of return is higher for Kaskin than for Quinn.
   b. The stock of Kaskin has higher volatility than Quinn.
   c. The stock of Quinn has more systematic risk than that of Kaskin.

8. In a single-factor market, the SML relationship of both the CAPM and the APT states that the risk premium on any security is proportional to beta, or equivalently, that the security's expected return must be a linear function of beta. Suppose this is not the case, specifically, that expected return rises more than proportionately with beta as in the following figure. *(LO 7-1)*

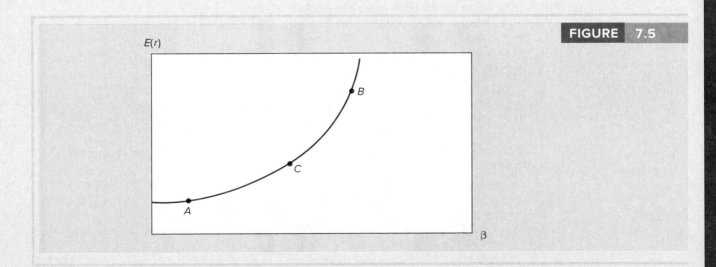

FIGURE 7.5

a. How could you construct a positive-alpha security in the context of the CAPM, or an arbitrage portfolio in the context of the APT?

b. Could this figure be an accurate depiction of the mean-beta relationship in market equilibrium? *Hint:* Consider the return on a combination of portfolios A and B constructed to match the beta of portfolio C.

c. Some researchers have examined the relationship between average returns on diversified portfolios and the β and β² of those portfolios. What should they have discovered about the effect of β² on portfolio return?

9. What must be the beta of a portfolio with $E(r_P) = 20\%$, if $r_f = 5\%$ and $E(r_M) = 15\%$? *(LO 7-2)*

10. The market price of a security is $40. Its expected rate of return is 13%. The risk-free rate is 7%, and the market risk premium is 8%. What will the market price of the security be if its beta doubles (and all other variables remain unchanged)? Assume the stock is expected to pay a constant dividend in perpetuity. *(LO 7-2)*

11. You are a consultant to a large manufacturing corporation considering a project with the following net after-tax cash flows (in millions of dollars):

Years from Now	After-Tax CF
0	−20
1–9	10
10	20

The project's beta is 1.7. Assuming $r_f = 9\%$ and $E(r_M) = 19\%$, what is the net present value of the project? What is the highest possible beta estimate for the project before its NPV becomes negative? *(LO 7-2)*

12. Consider the following table, which gives a security analyst's expected return on two stocks for two particular market returns: *(LO 7-2)*

Market Return	Aggressive Stock	Defensive Stock
5%	2%	3.5%
20	32	14

a. What are the betas of the two stocks?

b. What is the expected rate of return on each stock if the market return is equally likely to be 5% or 20%?

c. If the T-bill rate is 8%, and the market return is equally likely to be 5% or 20%, draw the SML for this economy.

d. Plot the two securities on the SML graph. What are the alphas of each?

e. What hurdle rate should be used by the management of the aggressive firm for a project with the risk characteristics of the defensive firm's stock?

If the simple CAPM is valid, which of the situations in Problems 13–19 below are possible? Explain. Consider each situation independently.

13.

Portfolio	Expected Return	Beta
A	20%	1.4
B	25	1.2

(LO 7-1)

14.

Portfolio	Expected Return	Standard Deviation
A	30%	35%
B	40	25

(LO 7-1)

15.

Portfolio	Expected Return	Standard Deviation
Risk-free	10%	0%
Market	18	24
A	16	12

(LO 7-1)

16.

Portfolio	Expected Return	Standard Deviation
Risk-free	10%	0%
Market	18	24
A	20	22

(LO 7-1)

17.

Portfolio	Expected Return	Beta
Risk-free	10%	0
Market	18	1.0
A	16	1.5

(LO 7-1)

18.

Portfolio	Expected Return	Beta
Risk-free	10%	0
Market	18	1.0
A	16	0.9

(LO 7-1)

19.

Portfolio	Expected Return	Standard Deviation
Risk-free	10%	0%
Market	18	24
A	16	22

(LO 7-1)

20. Go to Connect and link to Chapter 7 materials, where you will find a spreadsheet with monthly returns for GM, Ford, Toyota, the S&P 500, and Treasury bills.   *(LO 7-1)*
    a. Estimate the index model for each firm over the full five-year period. Compare the betas of each firm.
    b. Now estimate the betas for each firm using only the first two years of the sample and then using only the last two years. How stable are the beta estimates obtained from these shorter subperiods?

In Problems 21–23 below, assume the risk-free rate is 8% and the expected rate of return on the market is 18%. Use the SML of the simple (one-factor) CAPM to answer these questions.

21. A share of stock is now selling for $100. It will pay a dividend of $9 per share at the end of the year. Its beta is 1. What must investors expect the stock to sell for at the end of the year? *(LO 7-2)*

22. I am buying a firm with an expected perpetual cash flow of $1,000 but am unsure of its risk. If I think the beta of the firm is 0, when the beta is really 1, how much *more* will I offer for the firm than it is truly worth? *(LO 7-2)*

23. A stock has an expected return of 6%. What is its beta? *(LO 7-2)*

24. Two investment advisers are comparing performance. One averaged a 19% return and the other a 16% return. However, the beta of the first adviser was 1.5, while that of the second was 1. *(LO 7-2)*
    a. Can you tell which adviser was a better selector of individual stocks (aside from the issue of general movements in the market)?
    b. If the T-bill rate were 6% and the market return during the period were 14%, which adviser would be the superior stock selector?
    c. What if the T-bill rate were 3% and the market return 15%?

25. Suppose the yield on short-term government securities (perceived to be risk-free) is about 4%. Suppose also that the expected return required by the market for a portfolio with a beta of 1 is 12%. According to the capital asset pricing model: *(LO 7-2)*
    a. What is the expected return on the market portfolio?
    b. What would be the expected return on a zero-beta stock?
    c. Suppose you consider buying a share of stock at a price of $40. The stock is expected to pay a dividend of $3 next year and to sell then for $41. The stock risk has been evaluated at $\beta = -.5$. Is the stock overpriced or underpriced?

26. Based on current dividend yields and expected capital gains, the expected rates of return on portfolios A and B are 11% and 14%, respectively. The beta of A is .8 while that of B is 1.5. The T-bill rate is currently 6%, while the expected rate of return of the S&P 500 Index is 12%. The standard deviation of portfolio A is 10% annually, while that of B is 31%, and that of the index is 20%. *(LO 7-2)*
    a. If you currently hold a market-index portfolio, would you choose to add either of these portfolios to your holdings? Explain.
    b. If instead you could invest *only* in bills and one of these portfolios, which would you choose?

27. Consider the following data for a single-index economy. All portfolios are well diversified.

Portfolio	E(r)	Beta
A	10%	1.0
F	4	0

Suppose another portfolio E is well diversified with a beta of 2/3 and expected return of 9%. Would an arbitrage opportunity exist? If so, what would the arbitrage strategy be? *(LO 7-4)*

28. Assume both portfolios A and B are well diversified, that $E(r_A) = 14\%$ and $E(r_B) = 14.8\%$. If the economy has only one factor, and $\beta_A = 1$ while $\beta_B = 1.1$, what must be the risk-free rate? *(LO 7-4)*

29. Assume the return on a market index represents the common factor and all stocks in the economy have a beta of 1. Firm-specific returns all have a standard deviation of 30%.

Suppose an analyst studies 20 stocks and finds that one-half have an alpha of 3%, and one-half have an alpha of −3%. The analyst then buys $1 million of an equally weighted portfolio of the positive-alpha stocks and sells short $1 million of an equally weighted portfolio of the negative-alpha stocks.   *(LO 7-4)*

   a. What is the expected profit (in dollars), and what is the standard deviation of the analyst's profit?

   b. How does your answer change if the analyst examines 50 stocks instead of 20? 100 stocks?

30. If the APT is to be a useful theory, the number of systematic factors in the economy must be small. Why?   *(LO 7-4)*

31. The APT itself does not provide information on the factors that one might expect to determine risk premiums. How should researchers decide which factors to investigate? Is industrial production a reasonable factor to test for a risk premium? Why or why not?   *(LO 7-3)*

32. Suppose two factors are identified for the U.S. economy: the growth rate of industrial production, IP, and the inflation rate, IR. IP is expected to be 4% and IR 6%. A stock with a beta of 1 on IP and 0.4 on IR currently is expected to provide a rate of return of 14%. If industrial production actually grows by 5%, while the inflation rate turns out to be 7%, what is your best guess for the rate of return on the stock?   *(LO 7-3)*

33. Suppose there are two independent economic factors, M_1 and M_2. The risk-free rate is 7%, and all stocks have independent firm-specific components with a standard deviation of 50%. Portfolios A and B are both well diversified.

Portfolio	Beta on M_1	Beta on M_2	Expected Return (%)
A	1.8	2.1	40
B	2.0	−0.5	10

What is the expected return–beta relationship in this economy?   *(LO 7-5)*

Challenge

34. As a finance intern at Pork Products, Jennifer Wainwright's assignment is to come up with fresh insights concerning the firm's cost of capital. She decides that this would be a good opportunity to try out the new material on the APT that she learned last semester. As such, she decides that three promising factors would be (i) the return on a broad-based index such as the S&P 500; (ii) the level of interest rates, as represented by the yield to maturity on 10-year Treasury bonds; and (iii) the price of hogs, which are particularly important to her firm. Her plan is to find the beta of Pork Products against each of these factors and to estimate the risk premium associated with exposure to each factor. Comment on Jennifer's choice of factors. Which are most promising with respect to the likely impact on her firm's cost of capital? Can you suggest improvements to her specification?   *(LO 7-3)*

35. Suppose the market can be described by the following three sources of systematic risk. Each factor in the following table has a mean value of zero (so factor values represent realized surprises relative to prior expectations), and the risk premiums associated with each source of systematic risk are given in the last column.

Systematic Factor	Risk Premium
Industrial production, IP	6%
Interest rates, INT	2
Credit risk, CRED	4

The excess return, R, on a particular stock is described by the following equation that relates realized returns to surprises in the three systematic factors:

$$R = 6\% + 1.0 \text{ IP} + .5 \text{ INT} + .75 \text{ CRED} + e$$

Find the equilibrium expected excess return on this stock using the APT. Is the stock overpriced or underpriced?   *(LO 7-3)*

CFA Problems

1. Which of the following statements about the security market line (SML) are *true*?   *(LO 7-2)*
   a. The SML provides a benchmark for evaluating expected investment performance.
   b. The SML leads all investors to invest in the same portfolio of risky assets.
   c. The SML is a graphic representation of the relationship between expected return and beta.
   d. Properly valued assets plot exactly on the SML.

2. Karen Kay, a portfolio manager at Collins Asset Management, is using the capital asset pricing model for making recommendations to her clients. Her research department has developed the information shown in the following exhibit.   *(LO 7-2)*

Forecasted Returns, Standard Deviations, and Betas			
	Forecasted Return	Standard Deviation	Beta
Stock X	14.0%	36%	0.8
Stock Y	17.0	25	1.5
Market index	14.0	15	1.0
Risk-free rate	5.0		

   a. Calculate expected return and alpha for each stock.
   b. Identify and justify which stock would be more appropriate for an investor who wants to:
      i. Add this stock to a well-diversified equity portfolio.
      ii. Hold this stock as a single-stock portfolio.

3. Joan McKay is a portfolio manager for a bank trust department. McKay meets with two clients, Kevin Murray and Lisa York, to review their investment objectives. Each client expresses an interest in changing his or her individual investment objectives. Both clients currently hold well-diversified portfolios of risky assets.   *(LO 7-1)*
   a. Murray wants to increase the expected return of his portfolio. State what action McKay should take to achieve Murray's objective. Justify your response in the context of the capital market line.
   b. York wants to reduce the risk exposure of her portfolio but does not want to engage in borrowing or lending activities to do so. State what action McKay should take to achieve York's objective. Justify your response in the context of the security market line.

4. Jeffrey Bruner, CFA, uses the capital asset pricing model (CAPM) to help identify mispriced securities. A consultant suggests Bruner use arbitrage pricing theory (APT) instead. In comparing CAPM and APT, the consultant made the following arguments:
   a. Both the CAPM and APT require a mean-variance efficient market portfolio.
   b. The CAPM assumes that one specific factor explains security returns but APT does not.

   State whether each of the consultant's arguments is correct or incorrect. Indicate, for each incorrect argument, why the argument is incorrect.   *(LO 7-5)*

5. The security market line depicts: *(LO 7-2)*
   a. A security's expected return as a function of its systematic risk.
   b. The market portfolio as the optimal portfolio of risky securities.
   c. The relationship between a security's return and the return on an index.
   d. The complete portfolio as a combination of the market portfolio and the risk-free asset.

6. According to CAPM, the expected rate of return of a portfolio with a beta of 1 and an alpha of 0 is: *(LO 7-2)*
   a. Between r_M and r_f.
   b. The risk-free rate, r_f.
   c. $\beta (r_M - r_f)$.
   d. The expected return on the market, r_M.

The following table (for CFA Problems 7 and 8) shows risk and return measures for two portfolios.

Portfolio	Average Annual Rate of Return	Standard Deviation	Beta
R	11%	10%	0.5
S&P 500	14	12	1.0

7. When plotting portfolio R on the preceding table relative to the SML, portfolio R lies: *(LO 7-2)*
   a. On the SML.
   b. Below the SML.
   c. Above the SML.
   d. Insufficient data given.

8. When plotting portfolio R relative to the capital market line, portfolio R lies: *(LO 7-2)*
   a. On the CML.
   b. Below the CML.
   c. Above the CML.
   d. Insufficient data given.

9. Briefly explain whether investors should expect a higher return from holding portfolio A versus portfolio B under capital asset pricing theory (CAPM). Assume that both portfolios are fully diversified. *(LO 7-2)*

	Portfolio A	Portfolio B
Systematic risk (beta)	1.0	1.0
Specific risk for each individual security	High	Low

10. Assume that both X and Y are well-diversified portfolios and the risk-free rate is 8%.

Portfolio	Expected Return	Beta
X	16%	1.00
Y	12	0.25

In this situation you could conclude that portfolios X and Y: *(LO 7-4)*
   a. Are in equilibrium.
   b. Offer an arbitrage opportunity.
   c. Are both underpriced.
   d. Are both fairly priced.

11. According to the theory of arbitrage: *(LO 7-4)*
    a. High-beta stocks are consistently overpriced.
    b. Low-beta stocks are consistently overpriced.
    c. Positive-alpha investment opportunities will quickly disappear.
    d. Rational investors will pursue arbitrage consistent with their risk tolerance.

12. A zero-investment, well-diversified portfolio with a positive alpha could arise if: *(LO 7-5)*
    a. The expected return of the portfolio equals zero.
    b. The capital market line is tangent to the opportunity set.
    c. The law of one price remains unviolated.
    d. A risk-free arbitrage opportunity exists.

13. An investor takes as large a position as possible when an equilibrium price relationship is violated. This is an example of: *(LO 7-4)*
    a. A dominance argument.
    b. The mean-variance efficient frontier.
    c. Arbitrage activity.
    d. The capital asset pricing model.

14. In contrast to the capital asset pricing model, arbitrage pricing theory: *(LO 7-4)*
    a. Requires that markets be in equilibrium.
    b. Uses risk premiums based on micro variables.
    c. Specifies the number and identifies specific factors that determine expected returns.
    d. Does not require the restrictive assumptions concerning the market portfolio.

WEB *master*

1. A firm's beta can be estimated from the slope of the security characteristic line (SCL) The first step is to plot the return on the firm's stock (*y*-axis) versus the return on a broad market index (*x*-axis). Next, a regression line is estimated to find the slope.
    a. Go to **finance.yahoo.com,** enter the ticker symbol for Alcoa (AA), and click on *Historical Data.* Choose *Monthly Frequency* and enter starting and ending dates that correspond to the most recent five years. Download the data to a spreadsheet.
    b. Repeat the process to get comparable data for the S&P 500 Index (ticker ^GSPC). Download the data and copy it into the same spreadsheet as Alcoa with dates aligned.
    c. Calculate the excess return on the stock and the return on the index for each month using the adjusted closing prices, which include dividend income. (You can find monthly T-bill rates at the St. Louis Fed's website **fred.stlouisfed.org**. Search for T-bill rates.)
    d. Prepare an *xy* scatter plot with no line inserted. Be sure that the firm's excess returns represent the *y*-variable and the market's excess returns represent the *x*-variable.
    e. Select one of the data points by pointing to it and clicking the left mouse button. After the point is selected, right-click to pull up a shortcut menu. Select *Add Trend-line,* choose the linear type, then click on the *Options* tab and select *Display Equation on Chart.* When you click on OK, the trendline and the equation appear. The trend-line represents the regression equation. What are Alcoa's alpha and beta?

2. In the previous question, you used 60 months of data to calculate the SCL for Alcoa. Now compute it for two consecutive periods. Estimate the index-model regression using the first 30 months of data, and then repeat the process using the second half of the sample. This will give you the alpha (intercept) and beta (slope) estimates for two consecutive time periods. How do the two alphas compare to each other? Select 11 other firms and repeat the regressions to find both alphas and betas for the first period and the second period.

3. Given your results for Question 2, investigate the extent to which beta in one period predicts beta in future periods and whether alpha in one period predicts alpha in future periods. Regress the beta of each firm in the second period (*y*-variable) against the

beta in the first period (*x*-variable). (If you estimated regressions for a dozen firms in Question 2, you will have 12 observations in this regression.) Do the same for the alphas of each firm. Our expectation is that beta in the first period predicts beta in the next period but that alpha in the first period has no power to predict alpha in the next period. (In other words, the regression coefficient on first-period beta will be statistically significant in explaining second-period beta, but the coefficient on alpha will not be.) Why does our prediction make sense? Is it borne out by the data?

4. *a.* Which of the stocks would you classify as defensive? Which would be classified as aggressive?

   b. Do the beta coefficients for the low-beta firms make sense given the industries in which these firms operate? Briefly explain.

7.1 The CML would still represent efficient investments. We can characterize the entire population by two representative investors. One is the "uninformed" investor, who does not engage in security analysis and holds the market portfolio, while the other optimizes using the Markowitz algorithm with input from security analysis. The uninformed investor does not know what input the informed investor uses to make portfolio purchases. The uninformed investor knows, however, that if the other investor is informed, the market portfolio proportions will be optimal. Therefore, to depart from these proportions would constitute an uninformed bet, which will, on average, reduce the efficiency of diversification with no compensating improvement in expected returns.

7.2 Equation 7.1 tells us that for the historical standard deviation and a coefficient of risk aversion of 3.5, the risk premium would be

$$E(r_M) - r_f = \bar{A}\sigma_M^2 = 3.5 \times .20^2 = .14 = 14\%$$

7.3 $\beta_{Digital} = 1.2$, $\beta_{GE} = .8$. Therefore, given the investment proportions, the portfolio beta is

$$\beta_P = w_{Digital}\beta_{Digital} + w_{GE}\beta_{GE} = (.75 \times 1.2) + (.25 \times 8) = 1.1$$

and the risk premium of the portfolio will be

$$E(r_P) - r_f = \beta_P[E(r_M) - r_f] = 1.1 \times 8\% = 8.8\%$$

7.4 *a.* The alpha of a stock is its expected return in excess of that required by the CAPM.

$$\alpha = E(r) - \{r_f + \beta[E(r_M) - r_f]\}$$
$$\alpha_{XYZ} = 12 - [5 + 1.0(11 - 5)] = 1$$
$$\alpha_{ABC} = 13 - [5 + 1.5(11 - 5)] = -1\%$$

   b. The project-specific required rate of return is determined by the project beta coupled with the market risk premium and the risk-free rate. The CAPM tells us that an acceptable expected rate of return for the project is

$$r_f + \beta[E(r_M) - r_f] = 8 + 1.3(16 - 8) = 18.4\%$$

   which becomes the project's hurdle rate. If the IRR of the project is 19%, then it is desirable. Any project (of similar beta) with an IRR less than 18.4% should be rejected.

7.5 Use Equation 7.7 to find that $E(r) = 4\% + 1.2 \times 4\% + .7 \times 2\% = 10.2\%$

7.6 Using Equation 7.14, the expected return is

$$4\% + (0.2 \times 6\%) + (1.4 \times 8\%) = 16.4\%$$

The Efficient Market Hypothesis

Learning Objectives

LO 8-1 Demonstrate why security price changes should be essentially unpredictable in an efficient market.

LO 8-2 Cite evidence that supports and contradicts the efficient market hypothesis.

LO 8-3 Provide interpretations of various stock market "anomalies."

LO 8-4 Formulate investment strategies that make sense in informationally efficient markets.

One of the early applications of computers in economics in the 1950s was to analyze economic time series. Business-cycle theorists felt that tracing the evolution of several economic variables over time would clarify and predict the progress of the economy through boom and bust periods. A natural candidate for analysis was the behavior of stock market prices over time. On the assumption that stock prices reflect the prospects of the firm, recurrent patterns of peaks and troughs in economic performance ought to show up in those prices.

When Maurice Kendall (1953) examined this proposition, however, he found to his great surprise that he could identify no predictable patterns in stock prices. Prices seemed to evolve randomly. They were as likely to go up as they were to go down on any particular day, regardless of past performance.

At first blush, Kendall's results were disturbing to some financial economists. They seemed to imply that the stock market is dominated by erratic market psychology, or "animal spirits"—that it follows no logical rules. In short, the results appeared to confirm the irrationality of the market. On further reflection, however, economists came to reverse their interpretation of Kendall's study.

It soon became apparent that random price movements indicated a well-functioning or efficient market, not an irrational one. In this chapter we explore the reasoning behind what may seem a surprising conclusion. We show how competition among analysts leads naturally to market efficiency, and we examine the implications of the efficient market hypothesis for investment policy. We also consider empirical evidence that supports and contradicts the notion of market efficiency.

8.1   RANDOM WALKS AND EFFICIENT MARKETS

Suppose Kendall had discovered that changes in stock prices can be reliably predicted. What a gold mine this would have been. If they could predict stock prices, investors would reap unending profits simply by purchasing stocks that the computer model implied were about to increase in price and selling those about to fall.

A moment's reflection should be enough to convince yourself that this situation could not persist for long. For example, suppose the model predicts with great confidence that XYZ stock price, currently at $100 per share, will rise dramatically in three days to $110. What would all investors with access to the model's prediction do today? Obviously, they would place a great wave of buy orders to cash in on the forthcoming increase in stock price. No one holding XYZ, however, would be willing to sell. The net effect is therefore an *immediate* jump in the stock price to $110 as the market digests and reflects the "good news" implicit in the model's forecast.

This simple example illustrates why Kendall's attempt to find recurrent patterns in stock price movements was likely to fail. A forecast about favorable *future* performance leads instead to favorable *current* performance, as market participants all try to get in on the action before the price increase.

More generally, one might say that any information that could be used to predict stock performance should already be reflected in stock prices. As soon as there is any information indicating that a stock is underpriced, investors flock to buy the stock and immediately bid up its price to a fair level, where only ordinary rates of return can be expected. These "ordinary rates" are simply rates of return commensurate with the risk of the stock.

However, if prices are bid immediately to fair levels, given all available information, it must be that they increase or decrease only in response to new information. New information, by definition, must be unpredictable; if it could be predicted, then the prediction would be part of today's information. Thus, stock prices that change in response to new (that is, previously unpredicted) information also must move unpredictably.

This is the essence of the argument that stock prices should follow a **random walk,** that is, that price changes should be random and unpredictable. Far from a proof of market irrationality, randomly evolving stock prices would be the necessary consequence of intelligent investors competing to discover relevant information on which to buy or sell stocks before the rest of the market becomes aware of that information.

random walk

The notion that stock price changes are random and unpredictable.

Don't confuse randomness in price *changes* with irrationality in the *level* of prices. If prices are determined rationally, then only new information will cause them to change. Therefore, a random walk would be the natural result of prices that always reflect all current knowledge. Indeed, if stock price movements were predictable, that would be damning evidence of stock market inefficiency, because the ability to predict prices would indicate that all available information was not already reflected in stock prices. Therefore, the notion that stocks already reflect all available information is referred to as the **efficient market hypothesis (EMH).**[1]

efficient market hypothesis (EMH)

The hypothesis that prices of securities fully reflect available information about securities.

Figure 8.1 illustrates the response of stock prices to new information in an efficient market. The graph plots the cumulative firm-specific return of a sample of companies that were targets of takeover attempts. In most takeovers, the acquiring firm pays a substantial premium over current market prices. Therefore, an announcement of a takeover attempt should cause the stock price to jump. The figure shows that stock prices jump dramatically on the day the news becomes public. However, there is no further drift in prices *after* the announcement date, suggesting that prices reflect the new information, including the likely magnitude of the takeover premium, by the end of the trading day.

Even more dramatic evidence of rapid response to new information may be found in intraday prices. For example, Patel and Wolfson (1984) show that most of the stock price response to corporate dividend or earnings announcements occurs within 10 minutes of the

---

[1]Market efficiency should not be confused with the idea of efficient portfolios introduced in Chapter 6. An informationally efficient *market* is one in which information is rapidly disseminated and reflected in prices. An efficient *portfolio* is one with the highest expected return for a given level of risk.

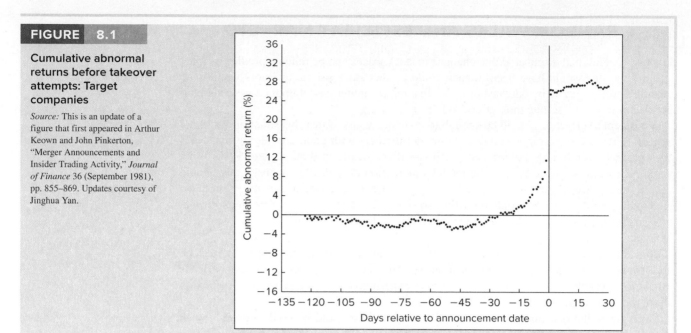

Cumulative abnormal returns before takeover attempts: Target companies

Source: This is an update of a figure that first appeared in Arthur Keown and John Pinkerton, "Merger Announcements and Insider Trading Activity," *Journal of Finance* 36 (September 1981), pp. 855–869. Updates courtesy of Jinghua Yan.

announcement. A nice illustration of such rapid adjustment is provided in a study by Busse and Green (2002), who track minute-by-minute stock prices of firms featured on CNBC's "Morning" or "Midday Call" segments.[2] Minute 0 in Figure 8.2 is the time at which the stock is mentioned on the midday show. The top line is the average price movement of stocks that receive positive reports, while the bottom line reports returns on stocks with negative reports. Notice that the top line levels off, indicating that the market has fully digested the news within 5 minutes of the report. The bottom line levels off within about 12 minutes.

Competition as the Source of Efficiency

Why should we expect stock prices to reflect "all available information"? After all, if you are willing to spend time and money on gathering information, it might seem reasonable that you could turn up something that has been overlooked by the rest of the investment community.

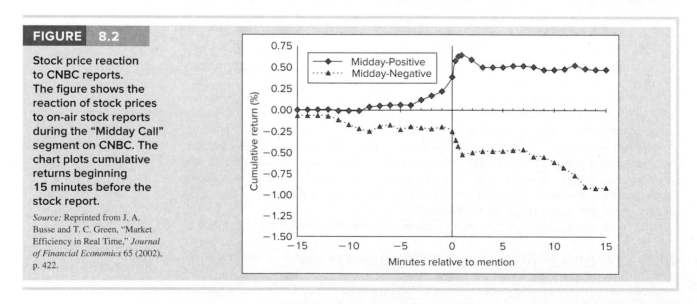

Stock price reaction to CNBC reports. The figure shows the reaction of stock prices to on-air stock reports during the "Midday Call" segment on CNBC. The chart plots cumulative returns beginning 15 minutes before the stock report.

Source: Reprinted from J. A. Busse and T. C. Green, "Market Efficiency in Real Time," *Journal of Financial Economics* 65 (2002), p. 422.

[2]You can find an intraday movie version of this figure at **www.bus.emory.edu/cgreen/cnbc.htm.**

When information is costly to uncover and analyze, one would expect investment analysis calling for such expenditures to result in an increased expected return.

This point has been stressed by Grossman and Stiglitz (1980). They argued that investors will have an incentive to spend time and resources to analyze and uncover new information only if such activity is likely to generate higher investment returns. Thus, in market equilibrium, efficient information-gathering activity should be fruitful. Moreover, it would not be surprising to find that the degree of efficiency differs across various markets. For example, emerging markets that are less intensively analyzed than U.S. markets or in which accounting disclosure requirements are less rigorous may be less efficient than U.S. markets. Small stocks that receive relatively little coverage by Wall Street analysts may be less efficiently priced than large ones. Therefore, while we would not go so far as to say that you absolutely cannot come up with new insights, it makes sense to consider and respect your competition.

Consider an investment management fund currently managing a $5 billion portfolio. Suppose that the fund manager can devise a research program that could increase the portfolio rate of return by one-tenth of 1% per year, a seemingly modest amount. This program would increase the dollar return to the portfolio by $5 billion × .001, or $5 million. Therefore, the fund should be willing to spend up to $5 million per year on research to increase stock returns by a mere tenth of 1% per year. With such large rewards for such small increases in investment performance, it should not be surprising that professional portfolio managers are willing to spend large sums on industry analysts, technical support, and research effort, and therefore that price changes are, generally speaking, difficult to predict.

With so many well-backed analysts willing to spend considerable resources on research, easy pickings in the market will be rare. Moreover, the incremental rates of return on research activity may be so small that only managers of the largest portfolios will find them worth pursuing.

EXAMPLE 8.1

Rewards for Incremental Performance

Although it may not literally be true that "all" relevant information will be uncovered, it is likely that there are many investigators hot on the trail of most leads that seem able to improve investment performance. Competition among these many well-backed, highly paid, aggressive analysts ensures that, as a general rule, stock prices ought to reflect available information regarding their proper levels.

It is often said that the most precious commodity on Wall Street is information, and the competition for it is intense. Consider the industry of so-called alternative data firms that has emerged to uncover and sell to large investors information that might shed light on corporate prospects. For example, these firms use satellite imagery to estimate the number of cars parked outside big retailers such as Walmart, thereby getting a sense of daily sales. Other firms use satellite imagery to estimate the height of oil tanks and thus the size of oil stocks. Some firms employ large computer networks and machine learning to keep tabs on social media in the hopes of stumbling on relevant information before it becomes common knowledge.[3]

Sometimes the quest for a competitive advantage can tip over into a search for illegal inside information. Recent years have witnessed several major insider trading cases. For example, in 2011, Raj Rajaratnam, the head of the Galleon Group hedge fund, which once managed $6.5 billion, was convicted for soliciting tips from a network of corporate insiders and traders. In 2014, another successful hedge fund, SAC Capital Advisors, paid $1.8 billion to settle an insider trading probe. While these firms crossed the line separating legitimate and prohibited means to acquire information, that line is often murky. For example, *expert-network* firms connect (for a fee) investors to industry experts who can provide a unique perspective on a company. As the nearby box discusses, this sort of arrangement can ease the path to insider trading and, in fact, was a key component of the case against SAC Capital.

---

[3]For other interesting examples, see "The Watchers," *The Economist*, August 20, 2016, p. 56.

MATCHMAKERS FOR THE INFORMATION AGE

The most precious commodity on Wall Street is information, and informed players can charge handsomely for providing it. An industry of so-called *expert-network providers* has emerged to sell access to experts with unique insights about a wide variety of firms and industries to investors who need that information to make decisions. These firms have been dubbed "matchmakers for the information age." Experts can range from doctors who help predict the release of blockbuster drugs to meteorologists who forecast weather that can affect commodity prices to business executives who can provide specialized insight about companies and industries.

But some of those experts have peddled prohibited inside information. In 2011, a consultant for Primary Global Research was convicted of selling information to the hedge fund SAC Capital Advisors. Several other employees of Primary Global also were charged with insider trading.

Expert firms are supposed to provide only public information, along with the expert's insights and perspective. But the temptation to hire experts with inside information and charge handsomely for access to them is obvious. The SEC has raised concerns about the boundary between legitimate and illegal services.

In the wake of increased scrutiny, compliance efforts of both buyers and sellers of expert information have mushroomed. The largest network firm is Gerson Lehrman Group, with a stable of 300,000 experts. It now maintains down-to-the-minute records of which of its experts talks to whom and the topics they have discussed.[4] These records could be turned over to authorities in the event of an insider trading investigation. And for their part, some hedge funds have simply ceased working with expert-network firms or have promulgated clearer rules for when their employees may talk with consultants.

Even with these safeguards, however, there remains room for trouble. For example, an investor may meet an expert through a legitimate network, and then the two may establish a consulting relationship on their own. The legal matchmaking becomes the precursor to the illegal selling of insider tips. Where there is a will to cheat, there usually will be a way.

Versions of the Efficient Market Hypothesis

It is common to distinguish among three versions of the EMH: the weak, semistrong, and strong forms of the hypothesis. These versions differ by their notions of what is meant by the term "all available information."

weak-form EMH

The assertion that stock prices already reflect all information contained in the history of past trading.

The **weak-form** hypothesis asserts that stock prices already reflect all information that can be derived by examining market trading data such as the history of past prices, trading volume, or short interest. This version of the hypothesis implies that trend analysis is fruitless. Past stock price data are publicly available and virtually costless to obtain. The weak-form hypothesis holds that if such data ever conveyed reliable signals about future performance, all investors already would have learned to exploit them. Ultimately, the signals lose their value as they become widely known because a buy signal, for instance, would result in an immediate price increase.

semistrong-form EMH

The assertion that stock prices already reflect all publicly available information.

The **semistrong-form** hypothesis states that all publicly available information regarding the prospects of a firm already must be reflected in the stock price. Such information includes, in addition to past prices, fundamental data on the firm's product line, quality of management, balance sheet composition, patents held, earning forecasts, and accounting practices. Again, if investors have access to such information from publicly available sources, one would expect it to be reflected in stock prices.

strong-form EMH

The assertion that stock prices reflect all relevant information, including inside information.

Finally, the **strong-form** version of the efficient market hypothesis states that stock prices reflect all relevant information, even including information available only to company insiders. This version of the hypothesis is quite extreme. Few would argue with the proposition that corporate officers have access to pertinent information long enough before public release to enable them to profit from trading on it. Indeed, much of the activity of the Securities and Exchange Commission is directed toward preventing insiders from profiting by exploiting their privileged position. Rule 10b-5 of the Security Exchange Act of 1934 sets limits on trading by corporate officers, directors, and substantial owners, requiring them to report trades to

---

[4]"Expert Networks Are the Matchmakers for the Information Age," *The Economist,* June 16, 2011.

the SEC. These insiders, their relatives, and any associates who trade on information supplied by insiders are considered in violation of the law.

Defining insider trading is not always easy, however. After all, stock analysts are in the business of uncovering information not already widely known to market participants. As we saw in Chapter 3 and in the nearby box, the distinction between private and inside information is sometimes murky.

Notice one thing that all versions of the EMH have in common: They all assert that prices should reflect *available* information. We do not expect traders to be superhuman or market prices to always be right. We will always like more information about a company's prospects than will be available. Sometimes market prices will turn out in retrospect to have been outrageously high; at other times, absurdly low. The EMH asserts only that at the given time, using current information, we cannot be sure if today's prices will ultimately prove themselves to have been too high or too low. If markets are rational, however, we can expect them to be correct on average.

a. Suppose you observed that high-level managers make superior returns on investments in their company's stock. Would this be a violation of weak-form market efficiency? Would it be a violation of strong-form market efficiency? *b.* If the weak form of the efficient market hypothesis is valid, must the strong form also hold? Conversely, does strong-form efficiency imply weak-form efficiency?	**CONCEPT** check **8.1**

8.2   IMPLICATIONS OF THE EMH

Technical Analysis

Technical analysis is essentially the search for recurrent and predictable patterns in stock prices. Although technicians recognize the value of information regarding future economic prospects of the firm, they believe that such information is not necessary for a successful trading strategy. This is because whatever the fundamental reason for a change in stock price, if the price responds slowly enough, the analyst will be able to identify a trend that can be exploited during the adjustment period. The key to successful technical analysis is a sluggish response of stock prices to fundamental supply-and-demand factors. This prerequisite, of course, is diametrically opposed to the notion of an efficient market.

Technical analysts are sometimes called *chartists* because they study records or charts of past stock prices, hoping to find patterns they can exploit to make a profit. As an example of technical analysis, consider the *relative strength* approach. The chartist compares stock performance over a recent period to performance of the market or other stocks in the same industry. A simple version of relative strength takes the ratio of the stock price to a market indicator such as the S&P 500 Index. If the ratio increases over time, the stock is said to exhibit relative strength because its price performance is better than that of the broad market. Such strength presumably may continue for a long enough period of time to offer profit opportunities.

One of the most commonly heard components of technical analysis is the notion of **resistance levels** or **support levels.** These values are said to be price levels above which it is difficult for stock prices to rise or below which it is unlikely for them to fall, and they are believed to be levels determined by market psychology.

technical analysis
Research on recurrent and predictable stock price patterns and on proxies for buy or sell pressure in the market.

resistance level
A price level above which it is supposedly unlikely for a stock or stock index to rise.

support level
A price level below which it is supposedly unlikely for a stock or stock index to fall.

Consider stock XYZ, which traded for several months at a price of $72 and then declined to $65. If the stock price eventually begins to increase, $72 is considered a resistance level (according to this theory) because investors who bought originally at $72 will be eager to sell their shares as soon as they can break even on their investment. Therefore, at prices near $72 a wave of selling pressure would exist. Such activity imparts a type of "memory" to the market that allows past price history to influence current prospects.	**EXAMPLE 8.2** *Resistance Levels*

The efficient market hypothesis implies that technical analysis should be fruitless. The past history of prices and trading volume is publicly available at minimal cost. Therefore, any information that was ever available from analyzing past trading has already been reflected in stock prices. As investors compete to exploit their common knowledge of a stock's price history, they necessarily drive stock prices to levels where expected rates of return are exactly commensurate with risk. At those levels one cannot expect abnormal returns.

As an example of how this process works, consider what would happen if the market believed that a level of $72 truly were a resistance level in Example 8.2. No one would be willing to purchase the stock at a price of $71.50, because it would have almost no room to increase in price but ample room to fall. However, if no one would buy it at $71.50, then $71.50 would become a resistance level. But then, using a similar analysis, no one would buy it at $71, or $70, and so on. The notion of a resistance level poses a logical conundrum. Its simple resolution is the recognition that if the stock is ever to sell at $71.50, investors *must* believe that the price can as easily increase as fall. The fact that investors are willing to purchase (or even hold) the stock at $71.50 is evidence of their belief that they can earn a fair expected rate of return at that price.

CONCEPT check   8.2   If everyone in the market believes in resistance levels, why do these beliefs not become self-fulfilling prophecies?

An interesting question is whether a technical rule that seems to work will continue to work once it becomes widely recognized. A clever analyst may occasionally uncover a profitable trading rule; the real test of efficient markets is whether the rule itself becomes reflected in stock prices once its efficacy is discovered. As many traders attempt to exploit a useful trading technique and prices begin to reflect their activity, the approach should become less and less profitable. In this sense, price patterns ought to be *self-destructing*.

Thus, the market dynamic is one of a continual search for profitable trading rules, followed by destruction by overuse of those rules found to be successful, followed by more search for yet-undiscovered rules. We return to the rationale for technical analysis as well as some of its methods in the next chapter.

Fundamental Analysis

fundamental analysis

Research on determinants of stock value, such as earnings and dividend prospects, expectations for future interest rates, and risk of the firm.

Fundamental analysis uses earnings and dividend prospects of the firm, expectations of future interest rates, and risk evaluation of the firm to determine proper stock prices. Ultimately, it represents an attempt to determine the present value of all the payments a stockholder will receive from each share of stock. If that value exceeds the stock price, the fundamental analyst would recommend purchasing the stock.

Fundamental analysts usually start with a study of past earnings and an examination of company financial statements. They supplement this analysis with further detailed economic analysis, ordinarily including an evaluation of the quality of the firm's management, the firm's standing within its industry, and the prospects for the industry as a whole. The hope is to attain insight into future performance of the firm that is not yet recognized by the rest of the market. Chapters 12 through 14 provide a detailed discussion of the types of analyses that underlie fundamental analysis.

Once again, the efficient market hypothesis predicts that *most* fundamental analysis also is doomed to failure. If the analyst relies on publicly available earnings and industry information, his or her evaluation of the firm's prospects is not likely to be significantly more accurate than those of rival analysts. There are many well-informed, well-financed firms conducting such market research, and in the face of such competition it will be difficult to uncover data not also available to other analysts. Only analysts with a unique insight will be rewarded.

Fundamental analysis is more difficult than merely identifying well-run firms with good prospects. Discovery of good firms does an investor no good in and of itself if the rest of the market also knows those firms are good. If the knowledge is already public, the investor will be forced to pay a high price for those firms and will not realize a superior return.

The trick is not to identify firms that are good but to find firms that are *better* than everyone else's estimate. Similarly, troubled firms can be great bargains if their prospects are not quite as bad as their stock prices suggest.

This is why fundamental analysis is difficult. It is not enough to do a good analysis of a firm; you can make money only if your analysis is better than that of your competitors because the market price will already reflect all commonly recognized information.

Active versus Passive Portfolio Management

By now it is apparent that casual efforts to pick stocks are not likely to pay off. Competition among investors ensures that any easily implemented stock evaluation technique will be used widely enough that any insights derived will be reflected in stock prices. Only serious analysis and uncommon techniques are likely to generate the *differential* insight necessary to yield trading profits.

Moreover, these techniques are economically feasible only for managers of large portfolios. If you have only $100,000 to invest, even a 1%-per-year improvement in performance generates only $1,000 per year, hardly enough to justify herculean efforts. The billion-dollar manager, however, reaps extra income of $10 million annually from the same 1% increment.

If small investors are at a disadvantage in active portfolio management, what are their choices? They are better off investing in mutual funds or exchange-traded funds (ETFs). By pooling resources in this way, they can gain from economies of scale.

More difficult decisions remain, though. Can investors be sure that even large funds have the ability or resources to uncover mispriced stocks? Furthermore, will any mispricing be sufficiently large to repay the costs entailed in active portfolio management?

Proponents of the efficient market hypothesis believe that active management is largely wasted effort and unlikely to justify the expenses incurred. Therefore, they advocate a **passive investment strategy** that makes no attempt to outsmart the market. A passive strategy aims only at establishing a well-diversified portfolio of securities without attempting to find under- or overvalued stocks. Passive management is usually characterized by a buy-and-hold strategy. When stock prices are at fair levels, it makes no sense to buy and sell frequently, which generates trading costs without increasing expected performance.

One common strategy for passive management is to create an **index fund,** which is a portfolio designed to replicate the performance of a broad-based index of stocks. For example, Vanguard's 500 Index Fund holds stocks in direct proportion to their weight in the Standard & Poor's 500 stock price index. Investors in this fund obtain broad diversification with relatively low management fees. The fees can be kept to a minimum because Vanguard does not need to pay analysts to assess stock prospects and does not incur transaction costs from high portfolio turnover. Indeed, while the typical annual expense ratio for an actively managed equity fund is almost 1% of assets, the expense ratio of the 500 Index Fund is only 0.14% and falls to 0.04% for larger investors. Today, Vanguard's 500 Index Fund is among the largest equity mutual funds, with over $400 billion of assets in early 2018. The share of equity mutual funds held in indexed portfolios has risen dramatically, from only 10% in 2001 to around 25% in 2018. ETFs, which represent a further 10% of total stock investments, are also primarily indexed products.

Indexing need not be limited to the S&P 500, however. For example, some of the funds offered by the Vanguard Group track the broader-based CRSP[5] index of the total U.S. equity market, the Barclays Capital U.S. Aggregate Bond Index, the CRSP index of small-capitalization U.S. companies, and the *Financial Times* indexes of the European and Pacific Basin equity markets. Several other mutual fund complexes offer indexed portfolios, but Vanguard dominates the retail market for indexed mutual funds. In 2015, Vanguard's bond index fund became the largest fixed-income mutual fund.

ETFs are a close (and usually lower-expense) alternative to indexed mutual funds. As described in Chapter 4, these are shares in diversified portfolios that can be bought or sold

passive investment strategy

Buying a well-diversified portfolio without attempting to search out mispriced securities.

index fund

A mutual fund holding shares in proportion to their representation in a market index such as the S&P 500.

---

[5]CRSP is the Center for Research in Security Prices at the University of Chicago.

just like shares of individual stock. ETFs matching several broad stock market indexes such as the S&P 500 or CRSP indexes and dozens of international and industry stock indexes are available to investors who want to hold a diversified sector of a market without attempting active security selection.

CONCEPT check 8.3

What would happen to market efficiency if *all* investors attempted to follow a passive strategy?

The Role of Portfolio Management in an Efficient Market

If the market is efficient, why not throw darts at *The Wall Street Journal* instead of trying rationally to choose a stock portfolio? This is a tempting conclusion to draw from the notion that security prices are fairly set, but it is far too facile. There is a role for rational portfolio management, even in perfectly efficient markets.

You have learned that a basic principle in portfolio selection is diversification. Even if all stocks are priced fairly, each still poses firm-specific risk that can be eliminated through diversification. Therefore, rational security selection, even in an efficient market, calls for the selection of a well-diversified portfolio providing the systematic risk level that the investor wants.

Rational investment policy also requires that tax considerations be reflected in security choice. High-tax-bracket investors generally will not want the same securities that low-bracket investors find favorable. At an obvious level, high-bracket investors find it advantageous to buy tax-exempt municipal bonds despite their relatively low pretax yields, whereas those same bonds are unattractive to low-tax-bracket investors. At a more subtle level, high-bracket investors might want to tilt their portfolios in the direction of capital gains as opposed to interest income, because capital gains are taxed less heavily and because the option to defer the realization of capital gains income is more valuable the higher the current tax bracket. They also will be more attracted to investment opportunities for which returns are sensitive to tax benefits, such as real estate ventures.

A third argument for rational portfolio management relates to the particular risk profile of the investor. For example, a Toyota executive whose annual bonus depends on Toyota's profits generally should not invest additional amounts in auto stocks. To the extent that his or her compensation already depends on Toyota's well-being, the executive is already overinvested in Toyota and should not exacerbate the lack of diversification. This lesson was learned with considerable pain in September 2008 by Lehman Brothers employees who were famously invested in their own firm when the company failed. Roughly 30% of the shares in the firm were owned by its 24,000 employees, and their losses on those shares were around $10 billion.

Investors of varying ages also might warrant different portfolio policies with regard to risk bearing. For example, older investors who are essentially living off savings might choose to avoid long-term bonds whose market values fluctuate dramatically with changes in interest rates (discussed in Part Four). Because these investors are living off accumulated savings, they require conservation of principal. In contrast, younger investors might be more inclined toward long-term inflation-indexed bonds. The steady flow of real income over long periods of time that is locked in with these bonds can be more important than preservation of principal to those with long life expectancies.

In conclusion, there is a role for portfolio management even in an efficient market. Investors' optimal positions will vary according to factors such as age, tax bracket, risk aversion, and employment. The role of the portfolio manager in an efficient market is to tailor the portfolio to these needs, rather than to beat the market.

Resource Allocation

We've focused so far on the investments implications of the efficient market hypothesis. Deviations from efficiency may offer profit opportunities to better-informed traders at the expense of less-informed traders.

However, deviations from informational efficiency would also result in a large cost that will be borne by all citizens, namely, inefficient resource allocation. Recall that in a capitalist economy, investments in *real* assets such as plant, equipment, and know-how are guided in large part by the prices of financial assets. For example, if the value of telecommunication capacity reflected in stock market prices exceeds the cost of installing such capacity, managers might justifiably conclude that telecom investments seem to have positive net present value. In this manner, capital market prices guide allocation of real resources.

If markets were inefficient and securities commonly mispriced, then resources would be systematically misallocated. Corporations with overpriced securities will be able to obtain capital too cheaply, and corporations with undervalued securities might forgo investment opportunities because the cost of raising capital will be too high. Therefore, inefficient capital markets would diminish one of the most potent benefits of a market economy. As an example of what can go wrong, consider the dot-com bubble of the late 1990s, which sent a strong but, as it turned out, wildly overoptimistic signal about prospects in Internet and telecommunication firms and ultimately led to substantial overinvestment in those industries.

Before writing off markets as a means to guide resource allocation, however, one has to be reasonable about what can be expected from market forecasts. In particular, you shouldn't confuse an efficient market, where all available information is reflected in prices, with a perfect-foresight market. As we said earlier, "all available information" is still far from complete information, and generally rational market forecasts will sometimes be wrong; sometimes, in fact, they will be very wrong.

8.3   ARE MARKETS EFFICIENT?

The Issues

Not surprisingly, the efficient market hypothesis does not exactly arouse enthusiasm in the community of professional portfolio managers. It implies that a great deal of the activity of these managers—the search for undervalued securities—is at best wasted effort, and quite probably harmful to clients because it costs money and leads to imperfectly diversified portfolios. Consequently, the EMH has never been widely accepted on Wall Street, and debate continues on the degree to which security analysis can improve investment performance. However, the following issues imply that the debate probably never will be settled: the *magnitude issue,* the *selection bias issue,* and the *lucky event issue.*

THE MAGNITUDE ISSUE   We noted that an investment manager overseeing a $5 billion portfolio who can improve performance by only 0.1% per year will increase investment earnings by .001 × $5 billion = $5 million annually. This manager clearly would be worth her salary! Yet can we, as observers, statistically measure her contribution? Probably not: A 0.1% annual contribution would be swamped by the volatility of the market. Remember, the annual standard deviation of the well-diversified S&P 500 Index has been around 20%. Against these fluctuations a small increase in performance would be hard to detect.

All might agree that stock prices are very close to fair values and that only managers of large portfolios can earn enough trading profits to make the exploitation of minor mispricing worth the effort. According to this view, the actions of intelligent investment managers are the driving force behind the constant evolution of market prices to fair levels. Rather than ask the qualitative question, "Are markets efficient?" we should instead ask a more quantitative question: "How efficient are markets?"

THE SELECTION BIAS ISSUE   Suppose you discover an investment scheme that could really make money. You have two choices: either publish your technique in *The Wall Street Journal* to win fleeting fame, or keep your technique secret and use it to earn millions of dollars. Most investors would choose the latter option, which presents us with a conundrum. Only investors who find that an investment scheme cannot generate abnormal returns will be willing to report their findings to the whole world. Hence, opponents of the efficient markets'

On the MARKET FRONT

HOW TO GUARANTEE A SUCCESSFUL MARKET NEWSLETTER

Suppose you want to make your fortune publishing a market newsletter. You need first to convince potential subscribers that you have talent worth paying for. But what if you have no talent? The solution is simple: Start eight newsletters.

In year 1, let four of your newsletters predict an up-market and four a down-market. In year 2, let half of the originally optimistic group of newsletters continue to predict an up-market and the other half a down-market. Do the same for the originally pessimistic group. Continue in this manner to obtain the pattern of predictions shown in the table (U = prediction of an up-market, D = prediction of a down-market).

After three years, no matter what has happened to the market, one of the newsletters would have had a perfect prediction record. This is because after three years there are $2^3 = 8$ outcomes for the market, and we have covered all eight possibilities with the eight newsletters. Now, we simply slough off the seven unsuccessful newsletters, and market the eighth newsletter based on its perfect track record. If we want to establish a newsletter with a perfect track record over a four-year period, we need $2^4 = 16$ newsletters. A five-year period requires 32 newsletters, and so on.

After the fact, the one newsletter that was always right will attract attention for your uncanny foresight and investors will rush to pay large fees for its advice. Your fortune is made, and you have never even researched the market!

WARNING: This scheme is illegal! The point, however, is that with hundreds of market newsletters, you can find one that has stumbled onto an apparently remarkable string of successful predictions without any real degree of skill. After the fact, *someone's* prediction history can seem to imply great forecasting skill. This person is the one we will read about in *The Wall Street Journal;* the others will be forgotten.

Newsletter Predictions								
Year	1	2	3	4	5	6	7	8
1	U	U	U	U	D	D	D	D
2	U	U	D	D	U	U	D	D
3	U	D	U	D	U	D	U	D

view of the world always can disregard evidence that various techniques do not provide investment rewards, and argue that the techniques that do work simply are not being reported to the public. This is a problem in *selection bias;* the outcomes we are able to observe have been preselected in favor of failed attempts. Therefore, we cannot fairly evaluate the true ability of portfolio managers to generate winning stock market strategies.

THE LUCKY EVENT ISSUE   In virtually any month it seems we read an article about some investor or investment company with a fantastic investment performance over the recent past. Surely the superior records of such investors disprove the efficient market hypothesis.

Yet this conclusion is far from obvious. As an analogy to the investment game, consider a contest to flip the most number of heads out of 50 trials using a fair coin. The expected outcome for any person is, of course, 50% heads and 50% tails. If 10,000 people, however, compete in this contest, it would not be surprising if at least one or two contestants flipped more than 75% heads. In fact, elementary statistics tells us that the expected number of contestants flipping 75% or more heads would be two. It would be silly, though, to crown these people the "head-flipping champions of the world." Obviously, they are simply the contestants who happened to get lucky on the day of the event. (See *On the Market Front—How to Guarantee a Successful Market Newsletter.*)

The analogy to efficient markets is clear. If any stock is fairly priced given all available information, any bet on a stock is simply a coin toss with equal likelihood of winning or losing the bet. However, if many investors using a variety of schemes make fair bets, statistically speaking, *some* of those investors will be lucky and win a great majority of the bets. For every big winner, there may be many big losers, but we never hear of them. The winners, though, turn up in *The Wall Street Journal* as the latest stock market gurus; then they can make a fortune publishing market newsletters.

Our point is that after the fact there will have been at least one successful investment scheme. A doubter will call the results luck; the successful investor will call it skill. The proper test would be to see whether the successful investors can repeat their performance in another period, yet this approach is rarely taken.

Legg Mason's Value Trust, managed by Bill Miller, outperformed the S&P 500 in each of the 15 years ending in 2005. Is Miller's performance sufficient to dissuade you from a belief in efficient markets? If not, would *any* performance record be sufficient to dissuade you? Now consider that in the next 3 years, the fund dramatically underperformed the S&P 500; by the end of 2008, its cumulative 18-year performance was barely different from the index. Does this affect your opinion?

CONCEPT
check   **8.4**

With these caveats in mind, we turn now to some of the empirical tests of the efficient market hypothesis.

Weak-Form Tests: Patterns in Stock Returns

RETURNS OVER SHORT HORIZONS   Early tests of efficient markets were tests of the weak form. Could speculators find trends in past prices that would enable them to earn abnormal profits? This is essentially a test of the efficacy of technical analysis.

One way of discerning trends in stock prices is by measuring the *serial correlation* of stock market returns. Serial correlation refers to the tendency for stock returns to be related to past returns. Positive serial correlation means that positive returns tend to follow positive returns (a momentum type of property). Negative serial correlation means that positive returns tend to be followed by negative returns (a reversal or "correction" property). Both Conrad and Kaul (1988) and Lo and MacKinlay (1988) examine weekly returns of NYSE stocks and find positive serial correlation over short horizons. However, the correlation coefficients of weekly returns tend to be fairly small, at least for large stocks for which price data are the most reliably up to date. Thus, while these studies demonstrate weak price trends over short periods,[6] the evidence does not clearly suggest the existence of trading opportunities.

While broad market indexes demonstrate only weak serial correlation, there appears to be stronger momentum in performance across market sectors exhibiting the best and worst recent returns. In an investigation of intermediate-horizon stock price behavior (using 3- to 12-month holding periods), Jegadeesh and Titman (1993) found a **momentum effect** in which good or bad recent performance of particular stocks continues over time. They conclude that while the performance of individual stocks is highly unpredictable, *portfolios* of the best-performing stocks in the recent past appear to outperform other stocks with enough reliability to offer profit opportunities. Thus, it appears that there is evidence of short- to intermediate-horizon price momentum in both the aggregate market and cross-sectionally (i.e., across particular stocks).

momentum effect
The tendency of poorly performing stocks and well-performing stocks in one period to continue that abnormal performance in following periods.

RETURNS OVER LONG HORIZONS   Although short- to intermediate-horizon returns suggest momentum in stock market prices, studies of long-horizon returns (i.e., returns over multiyear periods) by Fama and French (1988) and Poterba and Summers (1988) indicate pronounced *negative* long-term serial correlation in the performance of the aggregate market. The latter result has given rise to a "fads hypothesis," which asserts that the stock market might overreact to relevant news. Such overreaction leads to positive serial correlation (momentum) over short time horizons. Subsequent correction of the overreaction leads to poor performance following good performance and vice versa. The corrections mean that a run of positive returns eventually will tend to be followed by negative returns, leading to negative serial correlation over longer horizons. These episodes of apparent overshooting followed by correction give the stock market the appearance of fluctuating around its fair value.

These long-horizon results are dramatic but still not conclusive. First, the study results need not be interpreted as evidence for stock market fads. An alternative interpretation of these results holds that they indicate only that the market risk premium varies over time. For

---

[6]On the other hand, there is evidence that share prices of individual securities (as opposed to broad market indexes) are more prone to reversals than continuations at very short horizons. See, for example, B. Lehmann, "Fads, Martingales and Market Efficiency," *Quarterly Journal of Economics* 105 (February 1990), pp. 1–28; and N. Jegadeesh, "Evidence of Predictable Behavior of Security Returns," *Journal of Finance* 45 (September 1990), pp. 881–898. However, as Lehmann notes, this is probably best interpreted as due to liquidity problems after big movements in stock prices as market makers adjust their positions in the stock.

example, when the risk premium and the required return on the market rise, stock prices will fall. When the market then rises (on average) at this higher rate of return, the data convey the impression of a stock price recovery. In this view, the apparent overshooting and correction are in fact no more than a rational response of market prices to changes in discount rates.

In addition to studies suggestive of overreaction in overall stock market returns over long horizons, many other studies suggest that over long horizons, extreme performance in particular securities also tends to reverse itself: The stocks that have performed best in the recent past seem to underperform the rest of the market in following periods, while the worst past performers tend to offer above-average future performance. De Bondt and Thaler (1985) and Chopra, Lakonishok, and Ritter (1992) find strong tendencies for poorly performing stocks in one period to experience sizable reversals over the subsequent period, while the best-performing stocks in a given period tend to follow with poor performance in the following period.

For example, the De Bondt and Thaler study found that if one were to rank-order the performance of stocks over a five-year period and then group stocks into portfolios based on investment performance, the base-period "loser" portfolio (defined as the 35 stocks with the worst investment performance) outperformed the "winner" portfolio (the top 35 stocks) by an average of 25% (cumulative return) in the following three-year period. This **reversal effect,** in which losers rebound and winners fade back, suggests that the stock market overreacts to relevant news. After the overreaction is recognized, extreme investment performance is reversed. This phenomenon would imply that a *contrarian* investment strategy—investing in recent losers and avoiding recent winners—should be profitable. Moreover, these returns seem pronounced enough to be exploited profitably.

Thus, it appears that there may be short-run momentum but long-run reversal patterns in price behavior both for the market as a whole and across sectors of the market. One interpretation of this pattern is that short-run overreaction (which causes momentum in prices) may lead to long-term reversals (when the market recognizes its past error).

reversal effect

The tendency of poorly performing stocks and well-performing stocks in one period to experience reversals in the following period.

Predictors of Broad Market Returns

Several studies have documented the ability of easily observed variables to predict market returns. For example, Fama and French (1988) showed that the return on the aggregate stock market tends to be higher when the dividend/price ratio, the dividend yield, is high. Campbell and Shiller (1988) found that the earnings yield can predict market returns. Keim and Stambaugh (1986) showed that bond market data such as the spread between yields on high- and low-grade corporate bonds also help predict broad market returns.

Again, the interpretation of these results is difficult. On the one hand, they may imply that abnormal stock returns can be predicted, in violation of the efficient market hypothesis. More probably, however, these variables are proxying for variation in the market risk premium. For example, given a level of dividends or earnings, stock prices will be lower and dividend and earnings yields will be higher when the risk premium (and therefore the expected market return) is higher. Thus, a high dividend or earnings yield will be associated with higher market returns. But rather than a violation of market efficiency, the predictability of market returns is due to predictability in the risk premium.

Fama and French (1989) showed that the yield spread between high- and low-grade bonds has greater predictive power for returns on low-grade bonds than high-grade bonds, and greater predictive power for stock rather than bond returns, suggesting that the predictability in returns is in fact a risk premium rather than evidence of market inefficiency. Similarly, the fact that the dividend yield on stocks helps to predict bond market returns suggests that the yield captures a risk premium common to both markets rather than mispricing in the equity market.

Semistrong Tests: Market Anomalies

Fundamental analysis uses a much wider range of information to create portfolios than does technical analysis. Investigations of the efficacy of fundamental analysis ask whether publicly available information beyond the trading history of a security can be used to improve investment performance, and therefore they are tests of semistrong-form market efficiency. Surprisingly, several easily accessible statistics, for example, a stock's price–earnings ratio or its market capitalization, seem to predict abnormal risk-adjusted returns. Findings such as these, which we will review in the following pages, are difficult to reconcile with the efficient market hypothesis and therefore are often referred to as efficient market **anomalies.**

anomalies

Patterns of returns that seem to contradict the efficient market hypothesis.

A difficulty in interpreting these tests is that we usually need to adjust for portfolio risk before evaluating the success of an investment strategy. Many tests, for example, have used the CAPM to adjust for risk. However, we know that even if beta is a relevant descriptor of stock risk, the empirically measured quantitative trade-off between risk as measured by beta and expected return differs from the predictions of the CAPM. If we use the CAPM to adjust portfolio returns for risk, inappropriate adjustments may lead to the conclusion that various portfolio strategies can generate superior returns, when in fact it simply is the risk adjustment procedure that has failed.

Another way to put this is to note that tests of risk-adjusted returns are *joint tests* of the efficient market hypothesis *and* the risk adjustment procedure. If it appears that a portfolio strategy can generate superior returns, we must then choose between rejecting the EMH and rejecting the risk adjustment technique. Usually, the risk adjustment technique is based on more-questionable assumptions than is the EMH; by opting to reject the procedure, we are left with no conclusion about market efficiency.

An example of this issue is the discovery by Basu (1977, 1983) that portfolios of low price–earnings (P/E) ratio stocks have higher returns than do high P/E portfolios. The **P/E effect** holds up even if returns are adjusted for portfolio beta. Is this a confirmation that the market systematically misprices stocks according to P/E ratio? This would be an extremely surprising and, to us, disturbing conclusion, because P/E ratios are so simple to observe. Although it may be possible to earn superior returns through unusual insight, it hardly seems plausible that such a simplistic technique is enough to generate abnormal returns.

P/E effect

Portfolios of low P/E stocks have exhibited higher average risk-adjusted returns than high P/E stocks.

Another interpretation of these results is that returns are not properly adjusted for risk. If two firms have the same expected earnings, the riskier stock will sell at a lower price and lower P/E ratio. Because of its higher risk, the low P/E stock also will have higher expected returns. Therefore, unless the CAPM beta fully adjusts for risk, P/E will act as a useful additional indicator of risk and will be associated with abnormal returns if the CAPM is used to establish benchmark performance.

THE SMALL-FIRM EFFECT   The so-called size or **small-firm effect,** originally documented by Banz (1981), is illustrated in Figure 8.3. It shows the historical performance of portfolios formed by dividing the NYSE stocks into 10 portfolios each year according to firm size (i.e., the total value of outstanding equity). Average annual returns between 1926 and 2016 are consistently higher on the small-firm portfolios. The difference in average annual return between portfolio 10 (with the largest firms) and portfolio 1 (with the smallest firms) is 7.6%. Of course, the smaller-firm portfolios tend to be riskier. But even when returns are adjusted for risk using the CAPM, there is still a consistent premium for the smaller-sized portfolios.

small-firm effect

Stocks of small firms have earned abnormal returns, primarily in the month of January.

Imagine earning a premium of this size on a billion-dollar portfolio. Yet it is remarkable that following a simple (even simplistic) rule such as "invest in low-capitalization stocks" should enable an investor to earn excess returns. After all, any investor can measure firm size at little cost. One would not expect such minimal effort to yield such large rewards.

THE NEGLECTED-FIRM AND LIQUIDITY EFFECTS   Arbel and Strebel (1983) gave another interpretation of the small-firm effect. Because they tend to be neglected by large institutional traders, information about smaller firms is less available. This information deficiency makes smaller firms riskier investments that command higher returns. "Brand-name" firms, after all, are subject to considerable monitoring from institutional investors, which promises high-quality information, and presumably investors do not purchase "generic" stocks without the prospect of greater returns.

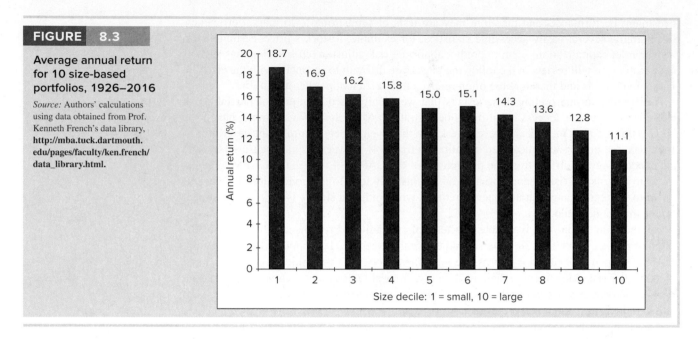

FIGURE 8.3

Average annual return for 10 size-based portfolios, 1926–2016

Source: Authors' calculations using data obtained from Prof. Kenneth French's data library, **http://mba.tuck.dartmouth. edu/pages/faculty/ken.french/ data_library.html.**

neglected-firm effect

The tendency of investments in stock of less well-known firms to generate abnormal returns.

Merton (1987) provides a rationale for the **neglected-firm effect.** He shows that neglected firms might be expected to earn higher equilibrium returns as compensation for the risk associated with limited information. In this sense the neglected-firm premium is not strictly a market inefficiency but is a type of risk premium.

Work by Amihud and Mendelson (1986, 1991) on the effect of liquidity on stock returns might be related to both the small-firm and neglected-firm effects. They argue that investors will demand a rate-of-return premium to invest in less liquid stocks that entail higher trading costs. In accord with their hypothesis, Amihud and Mendelson showed that these stocks show a strong tendency to exhibit abnormally high risk-adjusted rates of return. Because small and less-analyzed stocks as a rule are less liquid, the liquidity effect might be a partial explanation of their abnormal returns. However, exploiting these effects can be more difficult than it would appear. The high trading costs on small stocks can easily wipe out any apparent abnormal profit opportunity.

BOOK-TO-MARKET RATIOS Fama and French (1992) showed that a powerful predictor of returns across securities is the ratio of the book value of the firm's equity to the market value of equity. Fama and French stratified firms into 10 groups according to book-to-market ratios and examined the average rate of return of each of the 10 groups. Figure 8.4 is an updated version of their results. The decile with the highest book-to-market ratio had an average annual return of 17.0%, while the lowest-ratio decile averaged only 10.9%. The dramatic dependence of returns on book-to-market ratio is independent of beta, suggesting either that high book-to-market ratio firms are relatively underpriced or that the book-to-market ratio is serving as a proxy for a risk factor that affects equilibrium expected returns.

book-to-market effect

The tendency for investments in shares of firms with high ratios of book value to market value to generate abnormal returns.

In fact, Fama and French found that after controlling for the size and **book-to-market effects,** beta seemed to have no power to explain average security returns. This finding is an important challenge to the notion of rational markets because it seems to imply that a factor that should affect returns—systematic risk—seems not to matter, while a factor that should not matter—the book-to-market ratio—seems capable of predicting future returns.

POST-EARNINGS-ANNOUNCEMENT PRICE DRIFT A fundamental principle of efficient markets is that any new information ought to be reflected in stock prices very rapidly. A puzzling anomaly, therefore, is the apparently sluggish response of stock prices to firms'

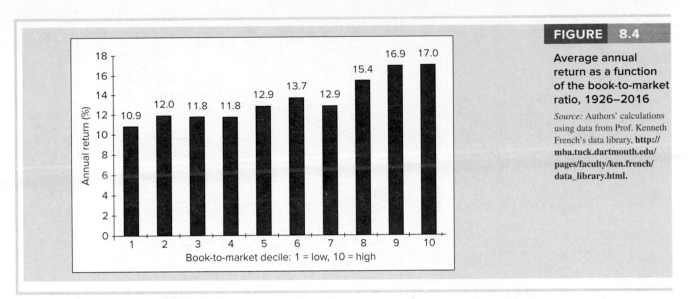

FIGURE 8.4

Average annual return as a function of the book-to-market ratio, 1926–2016

Source: Authors' calculations using data from Prof. Kenneth French's data library, **http://mba.tuck.dartmouth.edu/pages/faculty/ken.french/data_library.html.**

earnings announcements, as uncovered by Ball and Brown (1968). Their results were later confirmed and extended in many other papers.[7]

The "news content" of an earnings announcement can be evaluated by comparing the announcement of actual earnings to the value previously expected by market participants. The difference is the "earnings surprise." (Market expectations of earnings can be roughly measured by averaging the published earnings forecasts of Wall Street analysts or by applying trend analysis to past earnings.) Rendleman, Jones, and Latané (1982) provide an influential study of sluggish price response to earnings announcements. They calculate earnings surprises for a large sample of firms, rank the magnitude of the surprise, divide firms into 10 deciles based on the size of the surprise, and calculate abnormal returns for each decile. The abnormal return of each portfolio is the return adjusting for both the market return in that period and the portfolio beta. It measures return over and above what would be expected given market conditions in that period. Figure 8.5 plots cumulative abnormal returns by decile.

Their results are dramatic. The correlation between ranking by earnings surprise and abnormal returns across deciles is as expected. There is a large abnormal return (a jump in cumulative abnormal return) on the earnings announcement day (time 0). The abnormal return is positive for positive-surprise firms and negative for negative-surprise firms.

The more remarkable, and interesting, result of the study concerns stock price movement *after* the announcement date. The cumulative abnormal returns of positive-surprise stocks continue to rise—in other words, exhibit momentum—even after the earnings information becomes public, while the negative-surprise firms continue to suffer negative abnormal returns. The market appears to adjust to the earnings information only gradually, resulting in a sustained period of abnormal returns.

Evidently, one could have earned abnormal profits simply by waiting for earnings announcements and purchasing a stock portfolio of positive-earnings-surprise companies. These are precisely the types of predictable continuing trends that ought to be impossible in an efficient market.

---

[7]There is a voluminous literature on this phenomenon, often referred to as post-earnings-announcement price drift. See, for example, V. Bernard and J. Thomas, "Evidence That Stock Prices Do Not Fully Reflect the Implications of Current Earnings for Future Earnings," *Journal of Accounting and Economics* 13 (1990), pp. 305–340, or R. H. Battalio and R. Mendenhall, "Earnings Expectation, Investor Trade Size, and Anomalous Returns around Earnings Announcements," *Journal of Financial Economics* 77 (2005), pp. 289–319.

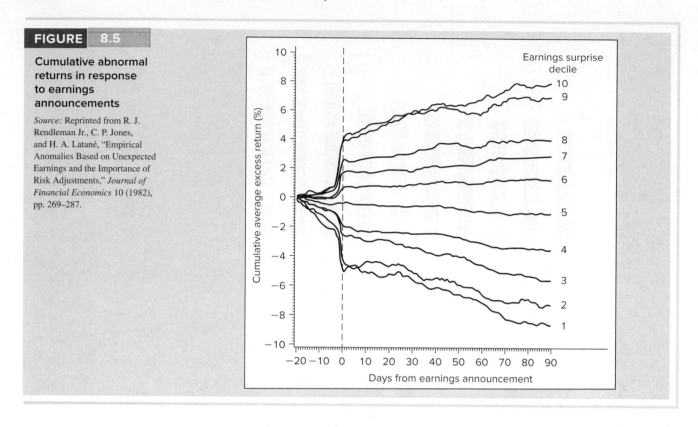

FIGURE 8.5

Cumulative abnormal returns in response to earnings announcements

Source: Reprinted from R. J. Rendleman Jr., C. P. Jones, and H. A. Latané, "Empirical Anomalies Based on Unexpected Earnings and the Importance of Risk Adjustments," *Journal of Financial Economics* 10 (1982), pp. 269–287.

BUBBLES AND MARKET EFFICIENCY   Every so often, it seems (at least in retrospect) that asset prices lose their grounding in reality. For example, in the tulip mania in seventeenth-century Holland, tulip prices peaked at several times the annual income of a skilled worker. This episode has become the symbol of a speculative "bubble" in which prices appear to depart from any semblance of intrinsic value. Less than a century later, the South Sea bubble in England became almost as famous. In this episode, the share price of the South Sea Company rose from £128 in January 1720 to £550 in May and peaked at around £1,000 in August—just before the bubble burst and the share price collapsed to £150 in September, leading to widespread bankruptcies among those who had borrowed to buy shares on credit. In fact, the company was a major lender of money to investors willing to buy (and thus bid up) its shares. This sequence may sound familiar to anyone who lived through the dot-com boom and bust of 1995–2002[8] or, more recently, the financial turmoil of 2008, with origins widely attributed to a collapsing housing price bubble (see Chapter 1).

It is hard to defend the position that security prices in these instances represented rational, unbiased assessments of intrinsic value. And, in fact, some economists, most notably Hyman Minsky, have suggested that bubbles arise naturally. During periods of stability and rising prices, investors extrapolate that stability into the future and become more willing to take on risk. Risk premiums shrink, leading to further increases in asset prices, and expectations become even more optimistic in a self-fulfilling cycle. But, in the end, pricing and risk taking become excessive and the bubble bursts. Ironically, the initial period of stability fosters the complacency about risk that ultimately results in instability.

But beware of jumping to the conclusion that asset prices may generally be thought of as arbitrary and obvious trading opportunities abundant. First, most bubbles become "obvious" only *after* they have burst. At the time, there is often a seemingly defensible rationale for the

---

[8]The dot-com boom gave rise to the term *irrational exuberance*. In this vein, consider that one company, going public in the investment boom of 1720, described itself simply as "a company for carrying out an undertaking of great advantage, but nobody to know what it is."

price run-up. In the dot-com boom, for example, many contemporary observers rationalized stock price gains as justified by the prospect of a new and more profitable economy, driven by technological advances. Even the irrationality of the tulip mania may have been overblown in its later retelling.[9] In addition, security valuation is intrinsically difficult and entails considerable imprecision.

Moreover, even if you suspect that prices are in fact "wrong," it can be difficult to take advantage of them. We explore these issues in more detail in the following chapter. For now, we can simply point out some impediments to making aggressive bets against an asset: the costs of short-selling overpriced securities as well as potential problems obtaining the securities to sell short and the possibility that, even if you are ultimately correct, the market may disagree and prices still can move dramatically against you in the short term, thus wiping out your portfolio.

Strong-Form Tests: Inside Information

It would not be surprising if insiders were able to make superior profits trading in their firm's stock. In other words, we do not expect markets to be strong-form efficient; we regulate and limit trades based on inside information. The ability of insiders to trade profitably in their own stock has been documented in studies by Jaffe (1974), Seyhun (1986), Givoly and Palmon (1985), and others. Jaffe's was one of the first studies to document the tendency for stock prices to rise after insiders intensively bought shares and to fall after intensive insider sales.

Can other investors benefit by following insiders' trades? The Securities and Exchange Commission requires all insiders to register their trading activity, and these trades become public. If markets are efficient, fully and immediately processing that information, investors should no longer be able to profit from following those trades. Several Internet sites contain information on insider trading.

The study by Seyhun found that following insider transactions would be to no avail. Although there was some tendency for stock prices to increase even after the report of insider buying, the abnormal returns were not large enough to overcome transaction costs.

Interpreting the Anomalies

How should we interpret the ever-growing anomalies literature? Does it imply that markets are grossly inefficient, allowing for simplistic trading rules to offer large profit opportunities? Or are there other, more-subtle interpretations?

RISK PREMIUMS OR INEFFICIENCIES?   The small-firm, market-to-book, momentum, and long-term reversal effects are currently among the most puzzling phenomena in empirical finance. There are several interpretations of these effects. First note that to some extent, some of these phenomena may be related. The feature that small firms, high-book-to-market firms, and recent "losers" seem to have in common is a stock price that has fallen considerably in recent months or years. Indeed, a firm can become a small firm or a low-market-to-book firm by suffering a sharp drop in price. These groups therefore may contain a relatively high proportion of distressed firms that have suffered recent difficulties.

Fama and French (1993) argue that these effects can be explained as manifestations of risk premiums. Using their three-factor model, they show that stocks with higher "betas" (also known in this context as factor loadings) on size or book-to-market factors have higher average returns; they interpret these returns as evidence of a risk premium associated with the factor. This model does a much better job than the one-factor CAPM in explaining security returns. While size or book-to-market ratios per se are obviously not risk factors, they perhaps might act as proxies for more fundamental determinants of risk. In this regard, it is

---

[9]For interesting discussions of this possibility, see Peter Garber, *Famous First Bubbles: The Fundamentals of Early Manias* (Cambridge: MIT Press, 2000), and Anne Goldgar, *Tulipmania: Money, Honor, and Knowledge in the Dutch Golden Age* (Chicago: University of Chicago Press, 2007).

FIGURE   8.6

Return to style portfolio as a predictor of GDP growth. Average difference in the return on the style portfolio in years before good GDP growth versus in years before bad GDP growth. Positive value means the style portfolio does better in years prior to good macroeconomic performance. HML = high-minus-low portfolio, sorted on ratio of book-to-market value. SMB = small-minus-big portfolio, sorted on firm size.

Source: Reprinted from J. Liew and M. Vassalou, "Can Book-to-Market, Size, and Momentum Be Risk Factors That Predict Economic Growth?" *Journal of Financial Economics* 57 (2000), pp. 221–245.

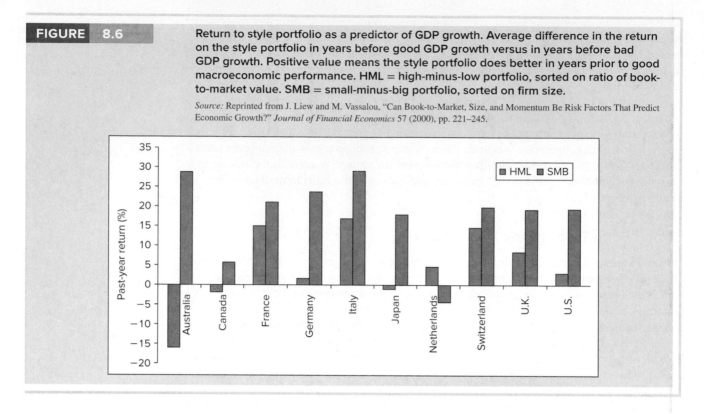

noteworthy that returns to "style portfolios," for example, returns on the Fama-French high-minus-low book-to-market portfolio, or small-minus-big size portfolio, do indeed seem to predict business cycles in many countries. Figure 8.6 shows that returns on these portfolios tend to have positive returns in years prior to rapid growth in gross domestic product.

The opposite interpretation is offered by Lakonishok, Shleifer, and Vishny (1995), who argue that these phenomena are evidence of inefficient markets, more specifically, of systematic errors in the forecasts of stock analysts. They believe that analysts extrapolate past performance too far into the future and therefore overprice firms with recent good performance and underprice firms with recent poor performance. Ultimately, when market participants recognize their errors, prices reverse. This explanation is consistent with the reversal effect and also, to a degree, with the small-firm and book-to-market effects because firms with sharp price drops may tend to be small or have high book-to-market ratios.

If Lakonishok, Shleifer, and Vishny are correct, we ought to find that analysts systematically err when forecasting returns of recent "winner" versus "loser" firms. A study by La Porta (1996) is consistent with this pattern. He finds that shares of firms for which analysts predict low growth rates of earnings actually perform better than those with high expected earnings growth. Analysts seem overly pessimistic about firms with low growth prospects and overly optimistic about firms with high growth prospects. When these too-extreme expectations are "corrected," the low-expected-growth firms outperform high-expected-growth firms.

ANOMALIES OR DATA MINING?

We have covered many of the so-called anomalies cited in the literature, but our list could go on and on. Some wonder whether these anomalies are really unexplained puzzles or whether they instead are an artifact of data mining. After all, if one reruns the database of past returns over and over and examines stock returns along enough dimensions, simple chance will cause some criteria to *appear* to predict returns.

Still, even acknowledging the potential for data mining, a common thread seems to run through many of these anomalies, lending support to the notion that there is a real puzzle to explain. Value stocks—defined by low P/E ratio, high book-to-market ratio, or depressed prices relative to historic levels—seem to have provided higher average returns than "glamour" or growth stocks.

One way to address the problem of data mining is to find a data set that has not already been researched and see whether the relationship in question shows up in the new data. Such studies have revealed size, momentum, and book-to-market effects in security markets around the world. While these phenomena may be a manifestation of a systematic risk premium, the precise nature of that risk is not fully understood.

ANOMALIES OVER TIME We pointed out previously that while no market can be perfectly efficient, in well-functioning markets, anomalies ought to be self-destructing. As market participants learn of profitable trading strategies, their attempts to exploit them should move prices to levels at which abnormal profits are no longer available.

McLean and Pontiff (2016) test this dynamic. They identify 97 characteristics identified in the academic literature as associated with abnormal returns and track the publication date of each finding. This allows them to break the sample for each anomaly at dates corresponding to when that particular finding became public. They conclude that the post-publication decay in abnormal return is about 60% (e.g., a 5% abnormal return pre-publication falls on average to 2% after publication).[10] They show that trading volume and variance in stocks identified with anomalies increase, as does short interest in "overpriced" stocks. These patterns are consistent with informed participants attempting to exploit newly recognized mispricing. Moreover, the decay in alpha is most pronounced for stocks that are larger, more liquid, and with low idiosyncratic risk. These are precisely the stocks for which trading activity in pursuit of reliable abnormal returns is most feasible. Thus, while abnormal returns do not fully disappear, these results are consistent with a market groping its way toward greater efficiency over time.

Chordia, Subrahmanyam, and Tong (2012) find evidence that liquidity and low trading costs facilitate efficient price discovery. They focus on abnormal returns associated with several characteristics including size, book-to-market ratio, momentum, and turnover (which may be inversely related to the neglected firm effect). They break their sample at 1993, shortly before tick sizes began their rapid decline in U.S. markets, and show that the abnormal returns associated with many of these characteristics in the pre-1993 period largely disappear in the post-1993 period. Their interpretation is that the market became more efficient as the costs of taking advantage of anomalies declined.

8.4 MUTUAL FUND AND ANALYST PERFORMANCE

We have documented some of the apparent chinks in the armor of efficient market proponents. For investors, the issue of market efficiency boils down to whether skilled investors can make consistent abnormal trading profits. So we will compare the performance of market professionals to that of a passive index fund. We will look at two facets of professional performance: that of stock market analysts who recommend investment positions and that of mutual fund managers who actually manage portfolios.

Stock Market Analysts

Stock market analysts historically have worked for brokerage firms, which presents an immediate problem in interpreting the value of their advice: Analysts have tended to be overwhelmingly positive in their assessment of the prospects of firms.[11] For example, Barber, Lehavy, McNichols, and Trueman (2001) find that on a scale of 1 (strong buy) to 5 (strong

---

[10]About 26% of that decay occurs between the final date of the sample and the publication date, which the authors note may reflect the portion of apparent abnormal returns that actually are due to data mining. The remaining decay would then be attributable to the actions of sophisticated investors whose trades move anomalous prices back toward intrinsic value.

[11]This problem may be less severe in the future; as noted in Chapter 3, one recent reform intended to mitigate the conflict of interest in having brokerage firms that sell stocks also provide investment advice is to separate analyst coverage from the other activities of the firm.

sell), the average recommendation for 5,628 covered firms in 1996 was 2.04. As a result, one cannot take positive recommendations (e.g., to buy) at face value. Instead, we must look at either the relative enthusiasm of analyst recommendations compared to those for other firms or at the change in consensus recommendations.

Womack (1996) focuses on changes in analysts' recommendations and finds that positive changes are associated with increased stock prices of about 5% and negative changes result in average price decreases of 11%. One might wonder whether these price changes reflect the market's recognition of analysts' superior information or insight about firms or, instead, simply result from new buy or sell pressure brought on by the recommendations themselves. Womack argues that price impact seems to be permanent and, therefore, consistent with the hypothesis that analysts do in fact reveal new information. Jegadeesh, Kim, Krische, and Lee (2004) also find that changes in recommendations are reliably associated with price changes, but that *levels* of consensus recommendations are not.

Barber, Lehavy, McNichols, and Trueman (2001) focus on the level of consensus recommendations and show that firms with the most favorable recommendations outperform those with the least favorable recommendations. However, the authors note that portfolio strategies based on analyst recommendations would result in extremely heavy trading activity with associated costs that probably would wipe out the potential profits from the strategy.

In sum, the literature suggests that some value is added by analysts, but ambiguity remains. Are superior returns following analyst upgrades due to revelation of new information or due to changes in investor demand in response to the changed outlook? Also, are these results exploitable by investors who necessarily incur trading costs?

Mutual Fund Managers

As we pointed out in Chapter 4, casual evidence does not support the claim that professionally managed portfolios can consistently beat the market. Figure 4.4 demonstrated that between 1972 and 2016 the returns of a passive portfolio indexed to the Wilshire 5000 typically would have been better than those of the average equity fund. On the other hand, there was some (admittedly inconsistent) evidence of minor persistence in performance, meaning that the better managers in one period tended to be better managers in following periods. Such consistency would not be possible if market prices already reflect all relevant information.

However, the analyses cited in Chapter 4 were based on total returns without adjustment for exposure to systematic risk factors. In this section we revisit the question of mutual fund performance, paying more attention to the benchmark against which performance ought to be evaluated.

As a first pass, we can examine the risk-adjusted returns (i.e., the CAPM alpha, or return in excess of required return based on beta and the market return in each period) of a large sample of mutual funds. But the market index may not be an adequate benchmark against which to evaluate mutual fund returns. Because mutual funds tend to maintain considerable holdings in equity of small firms, whereas the S&P 500 exclusively comprises large firms, mutual funds as a whole will tend to outperform the S&P when small firms outperform large ones and underperform when small firms fare worse.

The importance of the benchmark can be illustrated by examining the returns on small stocks in various subperiods.[12] In the 20-year period between 1945 and 1964, for example, a small-stock index underperformed the S&P 500 by about 4% per year (i.e., the alpha of the small-stock index after adjusting for systematic risk was −4%). In the following 20-year period, between 1965 and 1984, small stocks outperformed the S&P 500 Index by 10%. Thus, if one were to examine mutual fund returns in the earlier period, they would tend to look poor, not necessarily because fund managers were poor stock pickers but simply because mutual funds as a group tended to hold more small stocks than were represented in the S&P 500. In

---

[12]This illustration and the statistics cited are based on E. J. Elton, M. J. Gruber, S. Das, and M. Hlavka, "Efficiency with Costly Information: A Reinterpretation of Evidence from Managed Portfolios," *Review of Financial Studies* 6 (1993), pp. 1–22.

the later period, funds would look better on a risk-adjusted basis relative to the S&P 500 because small stocks performed better. The "style choice," that is, the exposure to small stocks (which is an asset allocation decision) would dominate the evaluation of performance even though it has little to do with managers' stock-picking ability.[13]

The conventional performance benchmark today is a four-factor model, which employs the three Fama-French factors (the return on the market index, and returns to portfolios based on size and book-to-market ratio) augmented by a momentum factor (a portfolio constructed based on prior-year stock return). Alphas constructed from a multifactor index model using these four factors control for a wide range of style choices that may affect returns, for example, an inclination to growth versus value or small- versus large-capitalization stocks. Figure 8.7 shows a frequency distribution of four-factor alphas for U.S. domestic equity funds.[14] The results show that the distribution of alpha is roughly bell-shaped, with a slightly negative mean. On average, it does not appear that these funds outperform their style-matched benchmarks.

Consistent with Figure 8.7, Fama and French (2010) use the four-factor model to assess the performance of equity mutual funds and show that while they may exhibit positive alphas *before* fees, after the fees charged to their customers, alphas were negative. Likewise, Wermers (2000), who uses both style portfolios as well as the characteristics of the stocks held by mutual funds to control for performance, also finds positive gross alphas but negative net alphas after controlling for fees and risk.

Carhart (1997) reexamines the issue of consistency in mutual fund performance to see whether better performers in one period continue to outperform in later periods. He uses the four-factor benchmark and finds that after controlling for these factors, there is only minor persistence in relative performance across managers. Moreover, much of that persistence seems due to expenses and transactions costs rather than gross investment returns.

Even allowing for expenses and turnover, some amount of performance persistence seems to be due to differences in investment strategy. Carhart finds, however, that the evidence

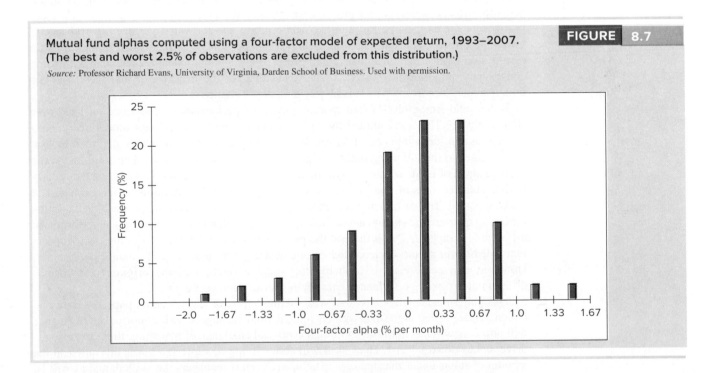

FIGURE 8.7

Mutual fund alphas computed using a four-factor model of expected return, 1993–2007. (The best and worst 2.5% of observations are excluded from this distribution.)

Source: Professor Richard Evans, University of Virginia, Darden School of Business. Used with permission.

---

[13]Remember that the asset allocation decision is usually in the hands of the individual investor. Investors allocate their investment portfolios to funds in asset classes they desire to hold, and they can reasonably expect only that mutual fund portfolio managers will choose stocks advantageously *within* those asset classes.

[14]We are grateful to Professor Richard Evans for these data.

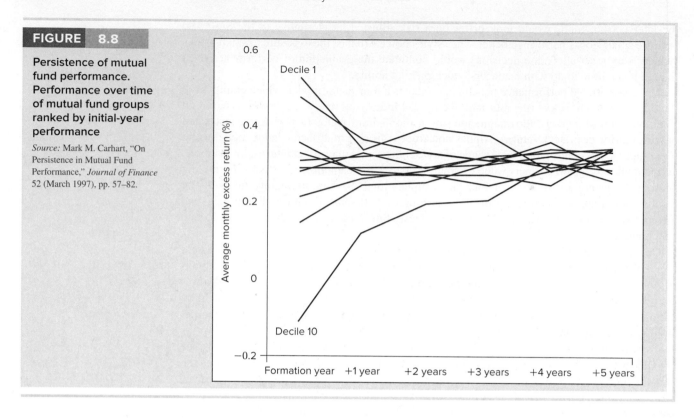

FIGURE 8.8

Persistence of mutual fund performance. Performance over time of mutual fund groups ranked by initial-year performance

Source: Mark M. Carhart, "On Persistence in Mutual Fund Performance," *Journal of Finance* 52 (March 1997), pp. 57–82.

of persistence is concentrated at the two extremes. Figure 8.8, from his study, documents performance persistence. Equity funds are ranked into 1 of 10 groups by performance in the formation year, and the performance of each group in the following years is plotted. It is clear that except for the best-performing top-decile group and the worst-performing 10th-decile group, performance in future periods is almost independent of earlier-year returns. Carhart's results suggest that there may be a small group of exceptional managers who can with some consistency outperform a passive strategy, but that for the majority of managers over- or underperformance in any period is largely a matter of chance.

Bollen and Busse (2004) find more evidence of performance persistence, at least over short horizons. They rank mutual fund performance using the four-factor model over a base quarter, assign funds into one of 10 deciles according to base-period alpha, and then look at performance in the following quarter. Figure 8.9 illustrates their results. The solid line is the average alpha of funds within each of the deciles in the base period (expressed on a quarterly basis). The steepness of that line reflects the considerable dispersion in performance in the ranking period. The dashed line is the average performance of the funds in each decile in the following quarter. The shallowness of this line indicates that most of the original performance differential disappears. Nevertheless, the plot is still clearly downward-sloping, so it appears that at least over a short horizon such as one quarter, there is some performance consistency. However, that persistence is probably too small a fraction of the original performance differential to justify performance chasing by mutual fund customers.

This pattern is actually consistent with the prediction of an influential paper by Berk and Green (2004). They argue that skilled mutual fund managers with abnormal performance will attract new funds until the additional costs and challenge of managing those extra funds drive alphas down to zero. Thus, skill will show up not in superior returns but rather in the amount of funds under management. Therefore, even if managers are skilled, alphas will be short-lived, as they seem to be in Figure 8.9.

Del Guercio and Reuter (2014) offer a finer interpretation of mutual fund performance. They split mutual fund investors into those who buy funds directly for themselves versus those who purchase funds through brokers, reasoning that the direct-sold segment may be

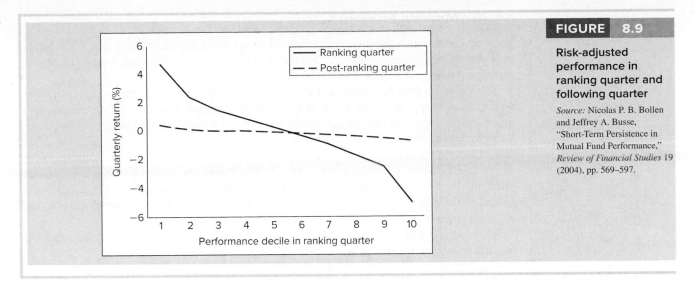

FIGURE   8.9

Risk-adjusted performance in ranking quarter and following quarter

Source: Nicolas P. B. Bollen and Jeffrey A. Busse, "Short-Term Persistence in Mutual Fund Performance," *Review of Financial Studies* 19 (2004), pp. 569–597.

more financially literate while the broker-sold segment is less comfortable making financial decisions without professional advice. Consistent with this hypothesis, they show that direct-sold investors direct their assets to funds with positive alphas (consistent with the Berk-Green model), but broker-sold investors generally do not. This provides an incentive for direct-sold funds to invest relatively more in alpha-generating inputs such as talented portfolio managers or analysts than broker-sold funds. Moreover, they show that the after-fee performance of direct-sold funds is as good as that of index funds (again, consistent with Berk-Green), while the performance of broker-sold funds is considerably worse. It thus appears that the average underperformance of actively managed mutual funds is driven largely by broker-sold funds, and that this underperformance may be interpreted as an implicit cost that less informed investors pay for the advice they get from their brokers.

In contrast to the extensive studies of equity fund managers, there have been few studies of the performance of bond fund managers. Blake, Elton, and Gruber (1993) examined the performance of fixed-income mutual funds. They found that, on average, bond funds underperform passive fixed-income indexes by an amount roughly equal to expenses and that there is no evidence that past performance can predict future performance. More recently, Chen, Ferson, and Peters (2010) find that, on average, bond mutual funds outperform passive bond indexes in terms of gross returns but underperform once the fees they charge their investors are subtracted, a result similar to those others have found for equity funds.

Thus, the evidence on the risk-adjusted performance of professional managers is mixed at best. We conclude that the performance of professional managers is broadly consistent with market efficiency. The amounts by which professional managers as a group beat or are beaten by the market fall within the margin of statistical uncertainty. In any event, it is quite clear that performance superior to passive strategies is far from routine. Studies show either that most managers cannot outperform passive strategies or that if there is a margin of superiority, it is small.

On the other hand, a small number of investment superstars—Peter Lynch (formerly of Fidelity's Magellan Fund), Warren Buffett (of Berkshire Hathaway), John Templeton (formerly of the Templeton Funds), and Mario Gabelli (of GAMCO), among them—have compiled career records that show a consistency of superior performance hard to reconcile with absolutely efficient markets. In a careful statistical analysis of mutual fund "stars," Kosowski, Timmerman, Wermers, and White (2006) conclude that the stock-picking ability of a minority of managers is sufficient to cover their costs and that their superior performance tends to persist over time. However, Nobel Prize–winner Paul Samuelson (1989) points out that the records of the vast majority of professional money managers offer convincing evidence that there are no easy strategies to guarantee success in the securities markets.

So, Are Markets Efficient?

There is a telling joke about two economists walking down the street. They spot a $20 bill on the sidewalk. One starts to pick it up, but the other one says, "Don't bother; if the bill were real someone would have picked it up already."

The lesson is clear. An overly doctrinaire belief in efficient markets can paralyze the investor and make it appear that no research effort can be justified. This extreme view is probably unwarranted. There are enough anomalies in the empirical evidence to justify the search for underpriced securities that clearly goes on.

The bulk of the evidence, however, suggests that any supposedly superior investment strategy should be taken with many grains of salt. The market is competitive *enough* that only differentially superior information or insight will earn money; the easy pickings have been picked. In the end it is likely that the margin of superiority that any professional manager can add is so slight that the statistician will not easily be able to detect it.

We conclude that markets are very efficient, but that rewards to the especially diligent, intelligent, or creative may in fact be waiting.

SUMMARY

- Statistical research has shown that to a close approximation stock prices seem to follow a random walk with no discernible predictable patterns that investors can exploit. Such findings are now taken to be evidence of market efficiency, that is, evidence that market prices reflect all currently available information. Only new information will move stock prices, and this information is equally likely to be good news or bad news.

- Market participants distinguish among three forms of the efficient market hypothesis. The weak form asserts that all information to be derived from past trading data already is reflected in stock prices. The semistrong form claims that all publicly available information is already reflected. The strong form, which generally is acknowledged to be extreme, asserts that all information, including insider information, is reflected in prices.

- Technical analysis focuses on stock price patterns and on proxies for buy or sell pressure in the market. Fundamental analysis focuses on the determinants of the underlying value of the firm, such as profitability and growth prospects. Because both types of analysis are based on public information, neither should generate excess profits if markets are operating efficiently.

- Proponents of the efficient market hypothesis often advocate passive as opposed to active investment strategies. The policy of passive investors is to buy and hold a broad-based market index. They expend resources neither on market research nor on frequent purchase and sale of stocks. Passive strategies may be tailored to meet individual investor circumstances.

- Empirical studies of technical analysis do not generally support the hypothesis that such analysis can generate superior trading profits. One notable exception to this conclusion is the apparent success of momentum-based strategies over intermediate-term horizons.

- Several anomalies regarding fundamental analysis have been uncovered. These include the value versus growth (book-to-market) effect, the small-firm effect, the momentum effect, the neglected-firm effect, and post-earnings-announcement price drift. Whether these anomalies represent market inefficiency or poorly understood risk premiums is still a matter of debate.

- By and large, the performance record of professionally managed funds lends little credence to claims that most professionals can consistently beat the market.

KEY TERMS

PROBLEM SETS

connect Select problems are available in McGraw-Hill's Connect. Please see the Supplements section of the book's frontmatter for more information.

1. If markets are efficient, what should be the correlation coefficient between stock returns for two nonoverlapping time periods? *(LO 8-1)*

2. "If all securities are fairly priced, all must offer equal expected rates of return." Comment. *(LO 8-1)*

3. If prices are as likely to increase as decrease, why do investors earn positive returns from the market on average? *(LO 8-1)*

4. A successful firm like Microsoft has consistently generated large profits for years. Is this a violation of the EMH? *(LO 8-2)*

5. At a cocktail party, your co-worker tells you that he has beaten the market for each of the last three years. Suppose you believe him. Does this shake your belief in efficient markets? *(LO 8-2)*

6. Which of the following statements are *true* if the efficient market hypothesis holds? *(LO 8-1)*
   a. It implies that future events can be forecast with perfect accuracy.
   b. It implies that prices reflect all available information.
   c. It implies that security prices change for no discernible reason.
   d. It implies that prices do not fluctuate.

7. In an efficient market, professional portfolio management can offer all of the following benefits *except* which of the following? *(LO 8-4)*
   a. Low-cost diversification.
   b. A targeted risk level.
   c. Low-cost record keeping.
   d. A superior risk-return trade-off.

8. Which version of the efficient market hypothesis (weak, semistrong, or strong-form) focuses on the most inclusive set of information? *(LO 8-1)*

9. "Constantly fluctuating stock prices suggest that the market does not know how to price stocks." Respond. *(LO 8-1)*

10. Which of the following sources of market inefficiency would be most easily exploited? *(LO 8-4)*
    a. A stock price drops suddenly due to a large block sale by an institution.
    b. A stock is overpriced because traders are restricted from short sales.
    c. Stocks are overvalued because investors are exuberant over increased productivity in the economy.

11. Which of the following would most appear to contradict the proposition that the stock market is *weakly* efficient? Explain. *(LO 8-3)*
    a. Over 25% of mutual funds outperform the market on average.
    b. Insiders earn abnormal trading profits.
    c. Every January, the stock market earns abnormal returns.

12. Suppose that, after conducting an analysis of past stock prices, you come up with the following observations. Which would appear to contradict the *weak form* of the efficient market hypothesis? Explain. *(LO 8-3)*

    a. The average rate of return is significantly greater than zero.

    b. The correlation between the return during a given week and the return during the following week is zero.

    c. One could have made superior returns by buying stock after a 10% rise in price and selling after a 10% fall.

    d. One could have made higher-than-average capital gains by holding stocks with low dividend yields.

13. Which of the following observations would provide evidence *against* the *semistrong form* of the efficient market theory? Explain. *(LO 8-3)*

    a. Mutual fund managers do not on average make superior returns.

    b. You cannot make superior profits by buying (or selling) stocks after the announcement of an abnormal rise in dividends.

    c. Low P/E stocks tend to have positive abnormal returns.

    d. In any year approximately 50% of mutual funds outperform the market.

14. Steady Growth Industries has never missed a dividend payment in its 94-year history. Does this make it more attractive to you as a possible purchase for your stock portfolio? *(LO 8-4)*

15. Suppose you find that before large dividend increases, stocks show on average consistently positive abnormal returns. Is this a violation of the EMH? *(LO 8-3)*

16. "If the business cycle is predictable, and a stock has a positive beta, the stock's returns also must be predictable." Respond. *(LO 8-1)*

17. Which of the following phenomena would be either consistent with or a violation of the efficient market hypothesis? Explain briefly. *(LO 8-3)*

    a. Nearly half of all professionally managed mutual funds are able to outperform the S&P 500 in a typical year.

    b. Money managers who outperform the market (on a risk-adjusted basis) in one year are likely to outperform in the following year.

    c. Stock prices tend to be predictably more volatile in January than in other months.

    d. Stock prices of companies that announce increased earnings in January tend to outperform the market in February.

    e. Stocks that perform well in one week perform poorly in the following week.

18. Why are the following "effects" considered efficient market anomalies? Are there rational explanations for these effects? *(LO 8-2)*

    a. P/E effect.

    b. Book-to-market effect.

    c. Momentum effect.

    d. Small-firm effect.

19. Dollar-cost averaging means that you buy equal dollar amounts of a stock every period, for example, $500 per month. The strategy is based on the idea that when the stock price is low, your fixed monthly purchase will buy more shares, and when the price is high, fewer shares. Averaging over time, you will end up buying more shares when the stock is cheaper and fewer when it is relatively expensive. Therefore, by design, you will exhibit good market timing. Evaluate this strategy. *(LO 8-4)*

20. We know that the market should respond positively to good news and that good-news events such as the coming end of a recession can be predicted with at least some accuracy. Why, then, can we not predict that the market will go up as the economy recovers? *(LO 8-1)*

21. You know that firm XYZ is very poorly run. On a scale of 1 (worst) to 10 (best), you would give it a score of 3. The market consensus evaluation is that the management score is only 2. Should you buy or sell the stock? *(LO 8-4)*

22. Good News, Inc., just announced an increase in its annual earnings, yet its stock price fell. Is there a rational explanation for this phenomenon? *(LO 8-1)*

23. Shares of small firms with thinly traded stocks tend to show positive CAPM alphas. Is this a violation of the efficient market hypothesis?   *(LO 8-3)*

Challenge

24. Examine the accompanying figure, which presents cumulative abnormal returns (CARs) both before and after dates on which insiders buy or sell shares in their firms. How do you interpret this figure? What are we to make of the pattern of CARs before and after the event date?   *(LO 8-3)*

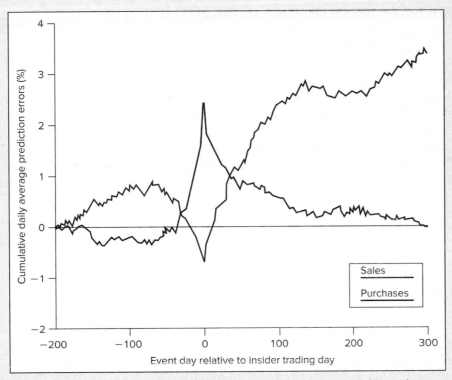

Source: Nejat H. Seyhun, "Insiders, Profits, Costs of Trading and Market Efficiency," *Journal of Financial Economics* 16 (1986), pp. 189–212.

25. Suppose that as the economy moves through a business cycle, risk premiums also change. For example, in a recession when people are concerned about their jobs, risk aversion and therefore risk premiums might be higher. In a booming economy, tolerance for risk might be higher and risk premiums lower.   *(LO 8-3)*
    a. Would a predictably shifting risk premium such as described here be a violation of the efficient market hypothesis?
    b. How might a cycle of increasing and decreasing risk premiums create an appearance that stock prices "overreact," first falling excessively and then seeming to recover?

CFA PROBLEMS

1. The semistrong form of the efficient market hypothesis asserts that stock prices: *(LO 8-1)*
    a. Fully reflect all historical price information.
    b. Fully reflect all publicly available information.
    c. Fully reflect all relevant information including insider information.
    d. May be predictable.

2. Assume that a company announces an unexpectedly large cash dividend to its shareholders. In an efficient market *without* information leakage, one might expect: *(LO 8-1)*
    a. An abnormal price change at the announcement.
    b. An abnormal price increase before the announcement.
    c. An abnormal price decrease after the announcement.
    d. No abnormal price change before or after the announcement.

3. Which one of the following would provide evidence *against* the *semistrong form* of the efficient market theory?   *(LO 8-3)*
    a. About 50% of pension funds outperform the market in any year.
    b. You cannot make abnormal profits by buying stocks after an announcement of strong earnings.
    c. Trend analysis is worthless in forecasting stock prices.
    d. Low P/E stocks tend to have positive abnormal returns over the long run.

4. According to the efficient market hypothesis: *(LO 8-3)*
    a. High-beta stocks are consistently overpriced.
    b. Low-beta stocks are consistently overpriced.
    c. Positive alphas on stocks will quickly disappear.
    d. Negative-alpha stocks consistently yield low returns for arbitrageurs.

5. A "random walk" occurs when: *(LO 8-1)*
    a. Stock price changes are random but predictable.
    b. Stock prices respond slowly to both new and old information.
    c. Future price changes are uncorrelated with past price changes.
    d. Past information is useful in predicting future prices.

6. A market anomaly refers to: *(LO 8-3)*
    a. An exogenous shock to the market that is sharp but not persistent.
    b. A price or volume event that is inconsistent with historical price or volume trends.
    c. A trading or pricing structure that interferes with efficient buying and selling of securities.
    d. Price behavior that differs from the behavior predicted by the efficient market hypothesis.

7. Some scholars contend that professional managers are incapable of outperforming the market. Others come to an opposite conclusion. Compare and contrast the assumptions about the stock market that support (*a*) passive portfolio management and (*b*) active portfolio management.   *(LO 8-2)*

8. You are a portfolio manager meeting a client. During the conversation that follows your formal review of her account, your client asks the following question: *(LO 8-2)*

    My grandson, who is studying investments, tells me that one of the best ways to make money in the stock market is to buy the stocks of small-capitalization firms as well as stocks with high ratios of book value to market value. What is he talking about?
    a. Identify the apparent market anomalies that would justify the proposed strategy.
    b. Explain why you believe such a strategy might or might not work in the future.

9. a. Briefly explain the concept of the efficient market hypothesis (EMH) and each of its three forms—weak, semistrong, and strong—and briefly discuss the degree to which existing empirical evidence supports each of the three forms of the EMH.   *(LO 8-2)*
    b. Briefly discuss the implications of the efficient market hypothesis for investment policy as it applies to: *(LO 8-4)*
        i. Technical analysis in the form of charting.
        ii. Fundamental analysis.
    c. Briefly explain the roles or responsibilities of portfolio managers in an efficient market environment.   *(LO 8-4)*

10. Growth and value can be defined in several ways. *Growth* usually conveys the idea of a portfolio emphasizing or including only companies believed to possess above-average future rates of per-share earnings growth. Low current yield, high price-to-book ratios, and high price-to-earnings ratios are typical characteristics of such portfolios. *Value* usually conveys the idea of portfolios emphasizing or including only issues currently showing low price-to-book ratios, low price-to-earnings ratios, above-average levels of dividend yield, and market prices believed to be below the issues' intrinsic values.   *(LO 8-3)*
    a. Identify and provide reasons why, over an extended period of time, value-stock investing might outperform growth-stock investing.
    b. Explain why the outcome suggested in (*a*) should not be possible in a market widely regarded as being highly efficient.

11. Your investment client asks for information concerning the benefits of active portfolio management. She is particularly interested in the question of whether active managers can be expected to consistently exploit inefficiencies in the capital markets to produce above-average returns without assuming higher risk.

    The semistrong form of the efficient market hypothesis asserts that all publicly available information is rapidly and correctly reflected in securities prices. This implies that investors cannot expect to derive above-average profits from purchases made after information has become public because security prices already reflect the information's full effects. *(LO 8-2)*

    a. Identify and explain two examples of empirical evidence that tend to support the EMH implication stated above.

    b. Identify and explain two examples of empirical evidence that tend to refute the EMH implication stated above.

    c. Discuss reasons why an investor might choose not to index even if the markets were, in fact, semistrong-form efficient.

---

1. Use data from **finance.yahoo.com** to answer the following questions.
    a. Collect the following data for 25 firms of your choosing.
        i. Book-to-market (equivalently, price-to-book) ratio.
        ii. Price–earnings ratio.
        iii. Market capitalization (size).
        iv. PEG ratio (i.e., the *P/E* ratio divided by expected growth rate).
        v. Another criterion that interests you.

        You can find this information by choosing a company and then clicking on *Statistics*. Rank the firms based on each of the criteria separately, and divide the firms into five groups based on their ranking for each criterion. Calculate the average rate of return for each group of firms.

        Do you confirm or reject any of the anomalies cited in this chapter? Can you uncover a new anomaly? Note: For your test to be valid, you must form your portfolios based on criteria observed at the *beginning* of the period when you form the stock groups. Why?

    b. From either the *Summary* or *Statistics* tab, find the beta of each of the firms in part (*a*). Use this beta, the T-bill rate, and the return on the S&P 500 to calculate the risk-adjusted abnormal return of each stock group. Does any anomaly uncovered in the previous question persist after controlling for risk?

    c. Now form stock groups that use two criteria simultaneously. For example, form a portfolio of stocks that are both in the lowest quintile of price–earnings ratio and in the highest quintile of book-to-market ratio. Does selecting stocks based on more than one characteristic improve your ability to devise portfolios with abnormal returns? Repeat the analysis by forming groups that meet three criteria simultaneously. Does this yield any further improvement in abnormal returns?

8.1 a. A high-level manager might well have private information about the firm. Her ability to trade profitably on that information is not surprising. This ability does not violate weak-form efficiency: The abnormal profits are not derived from an analysis of past price and trading data. If they were, this would indicate that there is valuable information that can be gleaned from such analysis. But this ability does violate strong-form efficiency. Apparently, there is some private information that is not already reflected in stock prices.

b. The information sets that pertain to the weak, semistrong, and strong form of the EMH can be described by the following illustration:

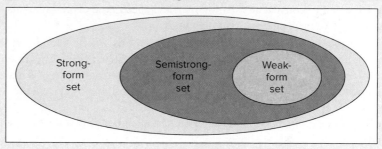

The weak-form information set includes only the history of prices and volumes. The semistrong-form set includes the weak-form set *plus* all other publicly available information. In turn, the strong-form set includes the semistrong set *plus* insiders' information. It is illegal to act on this incremental information (insiders' private information). The direction of *valid* implication is

Strong-form EMH $\Rightarrow$ Semistrong-form EMH $\Rightarrow$ Weak-form EMH

The reverse direction implication is *not* valid. For example, stock prices may reflect all past price data (weak-form efficiency) but may not reflect relevant fundamental data (semistrong-form inefficiency).

8.2 The point we made in the preceding discussion is that the very fact we observe stock prices near so-called resistance levels belies the assumption that the price can be a resistance level. If a stock is observed to sell *at any price,* then investors must believe a fair rate of return can be earned if the stock is purchased at that price. It is logically impossible for a stock to have a resistance level *and* offer a fair rate of return at prices just below the resistance level. If we accept that prices are appropriate, we must reject any presumption concerning resistance levels.

8.3 If *everyone* follows a passive strategy, sooner or later prices will fail to reflect new information. At this point there are profit opportunities for active investors who uncover mispriced securities. As they buy and sell these assets, prices again will be driven to fair levels.

8.4 The answer depends on your prior beliefs about market efficiency. Miller's initial record was incredibly strong. On the other hand, with so many funds in existence, it is less surprising that *some* fund would appear to be consistently superior after the fact. Exceptional past performance of a small number of managers is possible by chance even in an efficient market. A better test is provided in "continuation studies." Are better performers in one period more likely to repeat that performance in later periods? Miller's record in the last three years fails the continuation or consistency criterion.

Behavioral Finance and Technical Analysis

Learning Objectives

LO 9-1 Describe several behavioral biases, and explain how they could lead to anomalies in stock market prices and returns.

LO 9-2 Explain why limits to arbitrage might allow anomalies due to behavioral biases to persist over time.

LO 9-3 Identify reasons why technical analysis may be profitable.

LO 9-4 Use indicators such as volume, put/call ratios, breadth, short interest, or confidence indexes to measure the "technical conditions" of the market.

The efficient market hypothesis makes two important predictions. First, it implies that security prices properly reflect whatever information is available to investors. A second implication follows immediately: Active traders will find it difficult to outperform passive strategies such as holding market indexes. To do so would require differential insight; this in a highly competitive market is very hard to come by.

Unfortunately, it is hard to devise measures of the "true" or intrinsic value of a security, and correspondingly difficult to test directly whether prices match those values. Therefore, most tests of market efficiency have focused on the performance of active trading strategies. These tests have been of two kinds. The anomalies literature has examined strategies that apparently *would* have provided superior risk-adjusted returns (e.g., investing in stocks with momentum or in value rather than glamour stocks). Other tests have looked at the results of *actual* investments by asking whether professional managers have been able to beat the market.

Neither class of tests has proven fully conclusive. The anomalies literature suggests that several strategies would have provided superior returns. But there are questions as to whether some of these apparent anomalies reflect risk premiums not captured by simple models of risk and return, or even if they merely reflect data mining. Moreover, the apparent inability of the typical money manager to turn these anomalies into superior returns on actual portfolios casts additional doubt on their "reality."

A relatively new school of thought dubbed *behavioral finance* argues that the sprawling literature on trading strategies has missed a larger and more important point by overlooking the first implication of efficient markets—the correctness of security prices. This may be the more important implication because market economies rely on prices to allocate resources efficiently. The behavioral school argues that even if security prices are wrong, it still can be difficult to exploit them, and, therefore, that the failure to uncover obviously successful trading rules or traders cannot be taken as proof of market efficiency.

Whereas conventional theories presume that investors are rational, behavioral finance starts with the assumption that they are not. We will examine some of the information-processing and behavioral irrationalities uncovered by psychologists in other contexts and show how these tendencies applied to financial markets might result in some of the anomalies discussed in the previous chapter. We then consider the limitations of strategies designed to take advantage of behaviorally induced mispricing. If the limits to such arbitrage activity are severe, mispricing can survive even if some rational investors attempt to exploit it. We turn next to technical analysis and show how behavioral models give some support to techniques that clearly would be useless in efficient markets. We close the chapter with a brief survey of some of these technical strategies.

9.1　THE BEHAVIORAL CRITIQUE

behavioral finance

Models of financial markets that emphasize potential implications of psychological factors affecting investor behavior.

The premise of **behavioral finance** is that conventional financial theory ignores how real people make decisions and that people make a difference.[1] A growing number of economists have come to interpret the anomalies literature as consistent with several "irrationalities" that seem to characterize individuals making complicated decisions. These irrationalities fall into two broad categories: first, that investors do not always process information correctly and therefore infer incorrect probability distributions about future rates of return; and second, that even given a probability distribution of returns, they often make inconsistent or systematically suboptimal decisions.

Of course, the existence of irrational investors would not by itself be sufficient to render capital markets inefficient. If such irrationalities did affect prices, then sharp-eyed arbitrageurs taking advantage of profit opportunities might be expected to push prices back to their proper values. Thus, the second leg of the behavioral critique is that in practice the actions of such arbitrageurs are limited and therefore insufficient to force prices to match intrinsic value.

This leg of the argument is important. Virtually everyone agrees that if prices are right (i.e., price = intrinsic value), then there are no easy profit opportunities. But the converse is not necessarily true. If behaviorists are correct about limits to arbitrage activity, then the absence of profit opportunities does not necessarily imply that markets are efficient. We've noted that most tests of the efficient market hypothesis have focused on the existence of profit opportunities, often as reflected in the performance of money managers. But their failure to systematically outperform passive investment strategies need not imply that markets are in fact efficient.

We will start our summary of the behavioral critique with the first leg of the argument, surveying a sample of the informational processing errors uncovered by psychologists in other areas. We next examine a few of the behavioral irrationalities that seem to characterize decision makers. Finally, we look at limits to arbitrage activity and conclude with a tentative assessment of the import of the behavioral debate.

---

[1]The discussion in this section is based on an excellent survey article: Nicholas Barberis and Richard Thaler, "A Survey of Behavioral Finance," in the *Handbook of the Economics of Finance,* eds. G. M. Constantinides, M. Harris, and R. Stulz (Amsterdam: Elsevier, 2003).

Information Processing

Errors in information processing can lead investors to misestimate the true probabilities of possible events or associated rates of return. Several such biases have been uncovered. Here are four of the more important ones.

FORECASTING ERRORS Several experiments by Kahneman and Tversky (1972, 1973) indicate that people give too much weight to recent experience compared to prior beliefs when making forecasts (sometimes dubbed a *memory bias*) and tend to make forecasts that are too extreme given the uncertainty inherent in their information. De Bondt and Thaler (1990) argue that the P/E effect can be explained by earnings expectations that are too extreme. In this view, when forecasts of a firm's future earnings are high, perhaps due to favorable recent performance, they tend to be *too* high relative to the objective prospects of the firm. This results in a high initial P/E (due to the optimism built into the stock price) and poor subsequent performance when investors recognize their error. Thus, high P/E firms tend to be poor investments.

OVERCONFIDENCE People tend to overestimate the precision of their beliefs or forecasts, and they tend to overestimate their abilities. In one famous survey, 90% of drivers in Sweden ranked themselves as better-than-average drivers. Such overconfidence may be responsible for the prevalence of active versus passive investment management—itself an anomaly to adherents of the efficient market hypothesis. Despite the growing popularity of indexing, only about 25% of the equity in the mutual fund industry is held in indexed accounts. The dominance of active management in the face of the typical underperformance of such strategies (consider the generally disappointing performance of actively managed mutual funds reviewed in Chapter 4 as well as in the previous chapter) is consistent with a tendency to overestimate ability.

An interesting example of overconfidence in financial markets is provided by Barber and Odean (2001), who compare trading activity and average returns in brokerage accounts of men and women. They find that men (in particular, single men) trade far more actively than women, consistent with the generally greater overconfidence among men documented in the psychology literature. They also find that trading activity is highly predictive of poor investment performance. The top 20% of accounts ranked by portfolio turnover had average returns seven percentage points lower than the 20% of the accounts with the lowest turnover rates. As they conclude, "Trading [and by implication, overconfidence] is hazardous to your wealth."

Overconfidence appears to be a widespread phenomenon, also showing up in many corporate finance contexts. For example, overconfident CEOs are more likely to overpay for target firms when making corporate acquisitions (Malmendier and Tate, 2008). Just as overconfidence can degrade portfolio investments, it also can lead such firms to make poor investments in real assets.

CONSERVATISM A **conservatism bias** means that investors are too slow (too conservative) in updating their beliefs in response to new evidence. This means that they might initially underreact to news about a firm, so that prices will fully reflect new information only gradually. Such a bias would give rise to momentum in stock market returns.

conservatism bias

Investors are too slow (too conservative) in updating their beliefs in response to recent evidence.

SAMPLE-SIZE NEGLECT AND REPRESENTATIVENESS The notion of **representativeness bias** holds that people commonly do not take into account the size of a sample, acting as if a small sample is just as representative of a population as a large one. They may therefore infer a pattern too quickly based on a small sample and extrapolate apparent trends too far into the future. It is easy to see how such a pattern would be consistent with overreaction and correction anomalies. A short-lived run of good earnings reports or high stock returns would lead such investors to revise their assessments of likely future performance and thus generate buying pressure that exaggerates the price run-up. Eventually, the gap between price and intrinsic value becomes glaring and the market corrects its initial error.

representativeness bias

People are too prone to believe that a small sample is representative of a broad population and infer patterns too quickly.

Interestingly, stocks with the best recent performance suffer reversals precisely in the few days surrounding management earnings forecasts or actual earnings announcements, suggesting that the correction occurs just as investors learn that their initial beliefs were too extreme (Chopra, Lakonishok, and Ritter, 1992).

CONCEPT
check **9.1**

We saw in the previous chapter that stocks seem to exhibit a pattern of short- to middle-term momentum, along with long-term reversals. How might this pattern arise from an interplay between the conservatism and representativeness biases?

Behavioral Biases

Even if information processing were perfect, many studies conclude that individuals would tend to make less-than-fully rational decisions using that information. These behavioral biases largely affect how investors frame questions of risk versus return, and therefore make risk-return trade-offs.

framing

Decisions are affected by how choices are posed, for example, as gains relative to a low baseline level or losses relative to a higher baseline.

FRAMING Decisions seem to be affected by how choices are **framed.** For example, an individual may reject a bet when it is posed in terms of the risk surrounding possible gains but may accept that same bet when described in terms of the risk surrounding potential losses. In other words, individuals may act risk averse in terms of gains but risk seeking in terms of losses. But in many cases, the choice of how to frame a risky venture—as involving gains or losses—can be arbitrary.

EXAMPLE 9.1

Framing

Consider a coin toss with a payoff of $50 for tails. Now consider a gift of $50 that is bundled with a bet that imposes a loss of $50 if that coin toss comes up heads. In both cases, you end up with zero for heads and $50 for tails. But the former description frames the coin toss as posing a risky gain while the latter frames the coin toss in terms of risky losses. The difference in framing can lead to different attitudes toward the risky payoff.

---

mental accounting

A specific form of framing in which people segregate certain decisions.

MENTAL ACCOUNTING **Mental accounting** is a specific form of framing in which people segregate certain decisions. For example, an investor may take a lot of risk with one investment account but establish a very conservative position with another account that is dedicated to her child's education. Rationally, it might be better to view both accounts as part of the investor's overall portfolio with the risk-return profiles of each integrated into a unified framework. Nevertheless, Shefrin and Statman (2000) point out that a central distinction between conventional and behavioral finance theory is that the behavioral approach views investors as building their portfolios in "distinct mental account layers in a pyramid of assets," where each layer may be tied to particular goals and elicit different levels of risk aversion.

In another paper, Shefrin and Statman (1984) argue that behavioral motives are consistent with some investors' irrational preference for stocks with high cash dividends (they feel free to spend dividend income, but would not "dip into capital" by selling a few shares of another stock with the same total rate of return) and with a tendency to ride losing stock positions for too long (because "behavioral investors" are reluctant to realize losses). In fact, investors are more likely to sell stocks with gains than those with losses, precisely contrary to a tax-minimization strategy (Shefrin and Statman, 1985; Odean, 1998). This reluctance to realize losses is known as the **disposition effect.**

disposition effect

The reluctance of investors to sell shares in investments that have fallen in price.

Mental accounting effects also can help explain momentum in stock prices. The *house money effect* refers to gamblers' greater willingness to accept new bets if they currently are ahead. They think of (i.e., frame) the bet as being made with their "winnings account," that is, with the casino's and not with their own money, and thus are more willing to accept risk. Analogously, after a stock market run-up, individuals may view investments as largely funded out of a "capital gains account," become more tolerant of risk, discount future cash flows at a lower rate, and thus further push up prices.

REGRET AVOIDANCE Psychologists have found that individuals who make decisions that turn out badly have more regret (blame themselves more) when that decision was more unconventional. For example, buying a blue-chip portfolio that turns down is not as painful as experiencing the same losses on an unknown start-up firm. Any losses on the blue-chip stocks can be more easily attributed to bad luck rather than bad decision making and cause less regret. De Bondt and Thaler (1987) argue that such **regret avoidance** is consistent with both the size and book-to-market effect. Higher-book-to-market firms tend to have depressed stock prices. These firms are "out of favor" and more likely to be in a financially precarious position. Similarly, smaller, less well-known firms are also less conventional investments. Such firms require more "courage" on the part of the investor, which increases the required rate of return. Mental accounting can add to this effect. If investors focus on the gains or losses of individual stocks, rather than on broad portfolios, they can become more risk averse concerning stocks with recent poor performance, discount their cash flows at a higher rate, and thereby create a value-stock risk premium.

regret avoidance
People blame themselves more for unconventional choices that turn out badly so they avoid regret by making conventional decisions.

> How might the P/E effect (discussed in the previous chapter) also be explained as a consequence of regret avoidance?

CONCEPT check **9.2**

AFFECT Conventional models of portfolio choice focus on asset risk and return. But behavioral finance focuses as well on *affect,* which is a feeling of "good" or "bad" that consumers may attach to a potential purchase or investors to a stock. For example, firms with reputations for socially responsible policies or attractive working conditions, or those producing popular products, may generate higher affect in public perception. If investors favor stocks with good affect, that might drive up prices and drive down average rates of return. Statman, Fisher, and Anginer (2008) look for evidence that affect influences security pricing. They find that stocks ranked high in *Fortune*'s survey of most admired companies (i.e., with high affect) tended to have lower average risk-adjusted returns than the least admired firms, suggesting that their prices have been bid up relative to their underlying profitability and, therefore, that their expected future returns are lower.

PROSPECT THEORY **Prospect theory** modifies the analytic description of rational risk-averse investors found in standard financial theory.[2] Figure 9.1, Panel A, illustrates the conventional description of a risk-averse investor. Higher wealth provides higher satisfaction or "utility," but at a diminishing rate (the curve flattens as the individual becomes wealthier). This gives rise to risk aversion: A gain of $1,000 increases utility by less than a loss of $1,000 reduces it; therefore, investors will reject risky prospects that don't offer a risk premium.

prospect theory
Behavioral theory that investor utility depends on gains or losses from investors' starting position, rather than on their levels of wealth.

Figure 9.1, Panel B, shows a competing description of preferences characterized by "loss aversion." Utility depends not on the *level* of wealth, as in Panel A, but on *changes* in wealth from current levels. Moreover, to the left of zero (zero denotes no change from current wealth), the curve is convex rather than concave. This has several implications. Whereas many conventional utility functions imply that investors may become less risk averse as wealth increases, the function in Panel B always recenters on current wealth, thereby ruling out such decreases in risk aversion and possibly helping to explain high average historical equity risk premiums. Moreover, the convex curvature to the left of the origin in Panel B will induce investors to be risk seeking rather than risk averse when it comes to losses. Consistent with loss aversion, traders in the T-bond futures contract have been observed to assume significantly greater risk in afternoon sessions following morning sessions in which they have lost money (Coval and Shumway, 2005).

These are only a sample of many behavioral biases uncovered in the literature. Many have implications for investor behavior.

---

[2] Prospect theory originated with a highly influential paper about decision making under uncertainty by D. Kahneman and A. Tversky, "Prospect Theory: An Analysis of Decision under Risk," *Econometrica* 47 (1979), pp. 263–291.

Prospect theory
Panel A: A conventional utility function is defined in terms of wealth and is concave, resulting in risk aversion. Panel B: Under loss aversion, the utility function is defined in terms of changes from current wealth. It is also convex to the left of the origin, giving rise to risk-seeking behavior in terms of losses.

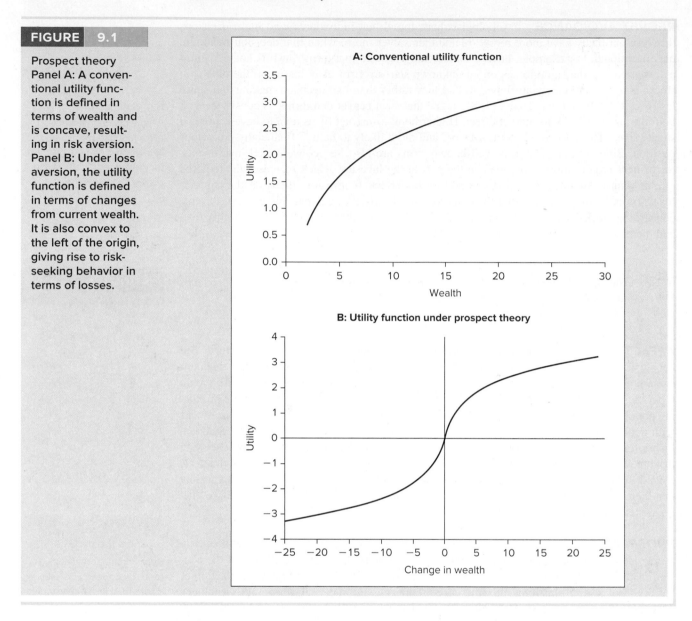

A: Conventional utility function

B: Utility function under prospect theory

Limits to Arbitrage

Behavioral biases would not matter for stock pricing if rational arbitrageurs could fully exploit the mistakes of behavioral investors. Trades of profit-seeking investors would correct any misalignment of prices. However, behavioral advocates argue that in practice, several factors limit the ability to profit from mispricing.[3]

FUNDAMENTAL RISK Suppose that a share of IBM is underpriced. Buying it may present a profit opportunity, but it is hardly risk-free because the presumed market underpricing can get worse. While price eventually should converge to intrinsic value, this may not happen until after the trader's investment horizon. For example, the investor may be a mutual fund manager who may lose clients (not to mention a job!) if short-term performance is poor or a trader who may run through her capital if the market turns against her, even temporarily.

[3] Some of the more influential references on limits to arbitrage are J. B. DeLong, A. Schleifer, L. Summers, and R. Waldmann, "Noise Trader Risk in Financial Markets," *Journal of Political Economy* 98 (August 1990), pp. 704–738; and A. Schleifer and R. Vishny, "The Limits of Arbitrage," *Journal of Finance* 52 (March 1997), pp. 35–55.

A comment often attributed to the famous economist John Maynard Keynes is that "markets can remain irrational longer than you can remain solvent." The *fundamental risk* incurred in exploiting apparent profit opportunities presumably will limit the activity of traders.

For most of 2010, the NASDAQ index fluctuated at a level around 2,300. From that perspective, the value the index had reached only 10 years earlier, around 5,000, seemed obviously crazy. Surely some investors living through the Internet "bubble" of the late 1990s must have identified the index as grossly overvalued, suggesting a good selling opportunity. But this hardly would have been a riskless arbitrage opportunity. Consider that NASDAQ may also have been overvalued in 1999 when it first crossed above 3,500. An investor in 1999 who believed that NASDAQ was overvalued at 3,500 and decided to sell it short would have suffered enormous losses as the index increased by another 1,500 points before finally peaking at 5,000. NASDAQ did finally crash, falling below 1,200 in late 2002. While the investor might have derived considerable satisfaction at eventually being proven right about the over-pricing, by entering a year before the market "corrected," he might also have gone broke.

EXAMPLE 9.2

Fundamental Risk

IMPLEMENTATION COSTS   Exploiting overpricing can be particularly difficult. Short-selling a security entails costs; short-sellers may have to return the borrowed security on little notice, rendering the horizon of the short sale uncertain; other investors such as many pension or mutual fund managers face strict limits on their discretion to short securities. This can limit the ability of arbitrage activity to force prices to fair value.

MODEL RISK   One always has to worry that an apparent profit opportunity is more apparent than real. Perhaps you are using a faulty model to value the security, and the price actually is right. Mispricing may make a position a good bet, but it is still a risky one, which limits the extent to which it will be pursued.

Limits to Arbitrage and the Law of One Price

Although one can debate the implications of much of the anomalies literature, surely the Law of One Price (positing that effectively identical assets should have identical prices) should be satisfied in rational markets. Yet there are several instances where the law seems to have been violated. These instances are good case studies of the limits to arbitrage.

"SIAMESE TWIN" COMPANIES[4]   In 1907, Royal Dutch Petroleum and Shell Transport merged their operations into one firm. The two original companies, which continued to trade separately, agreed to split all profits from the joint company on a 60/40 basis. Shareholders of Royal Dutch receive 60% of the cash flow, and those of Shell receive 40%. One would therefore expect that Royal Dutch should sell for exactly 60/40 = 1.5 times the price of Shell. But this is not the case. Figure 9.2 shows that the relative value of the two firms has departed considerably from this "parity" ratio for extended periods of time.

Doesn't this mispricing give rise to an arbitrage opportunity? If Royal Dutch sells for more than 1.5 times Shell, why not buy relatively underpriced Shell and short-sell overpriced Royal? This seems like a reasonable strategy, but if you had followed it in February 1993 when Royal sold for about 10% more than its parity value, Figure 9.2 shows that you would have lost a lot of money as the premium widened to about 17% before finally reversing after 1999. As in Example 9.2, this opportunity posed fundamental risk.

EQUITY CARVE-OUTS   Several equity carve-outs also have violated the Law of One Price.[5] To illustrate, consider the case of 3Com, which in 1999 decided to spin off its Palm division. It first sold 5% of its stake in Palm in an IPO, announcing that it would distribute the

---

[4]This discussion is based on K. A. Froot and E. M. Dabora, "How Are Stock Prices Affected by the Location of Trade?" *Journal of Financial Economics* 53 (1999), pp. 189–216.

[5]O. A. Lamont and R. H. Thaler, "Can the Market Add and Subtract? Mispricing in Tech Carve-Outs," *Journal of Political Economy* 111 (2003), pp. 227–268.

Pricing of Royal Dutch relative to Shell (*deviation from parity*)

Source: O. A. Lamont and R. H. Thaler, "Anomalies: The Law of One Price in Financial Markets," *Journal of Economic Perspectives* 17 (Fall 2003), pp. 191–202.

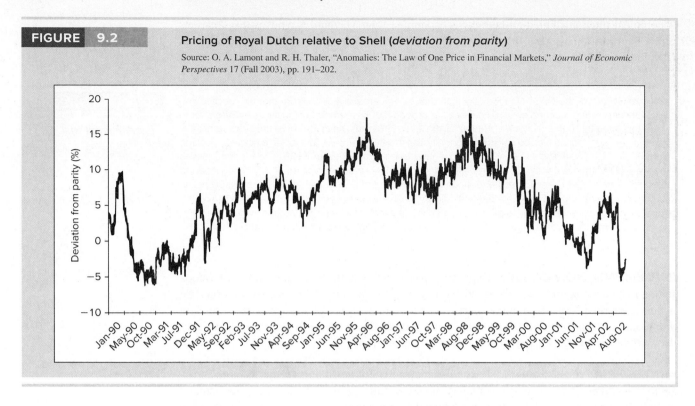

remaining 95% of its Palm shares to 3Com shareholders six months later in a spinoff. Each 3Com shareholder would receive 1.5 shares of Palm in the spinoff.

Once Palm shares began trading, but prior to the spinoff, the share price of 3Com should have been *at least* 1.5 times that of Palm. After all, each share of 3Com entitled its owner to 1.5 shares of Palm *plus* an ownership stake in a profitable company. Instead, Palm shares at the IPO actually sold for *more* than the 3Com shares. The *stub value* of 3Com (i.e., the value of each 3Com share net of the value of the claim to Palm represented by that share) could be computed as the price of 3Com minus 1.5 times the price of Palm. This calculation, however, implies that 3Com's stub value was negative, this despite the fact that it was a profitable company with cash assets alone of about $10 per share.

Again, an arbitrage strategy seems obvious. Why not buy 3Com and sell Palm? The limit to arbitrage in this case was the inability of investors to sell Palm short. Virtually all available shares in Palm were already borrowed and sold short, and the negative stub values persisted for more than two months.

CLOSED-END FUNDS   We noted in Chapter 4 that closed-end funds often sell for substantial discounts or premiums from net asset value. This is "nearly" a violation of the Law of One Price because one would expect the value of the fund to equal the value of the shares it holds. We say nearly, because in practice, there are a few wedges between the value of the closed-end fund and its underlying assets. One is expenses. The fund incurs expenses that ultimately are paid for by investors, and these will reduce share price. On the other hand, if managers can invest fund assets to generate positive risk-adjusted returns, share price might exceed net asset value.

Lee, Shleifer, and Thaler (1991) argue that the patterns of discounts and premiums on closed-end funds are driven by changes in investor sentiment. They note that discounts on various funds move together and are correlated with the return on small stocks, suggesting that all are affected by common variation in sentiment. One might consider buying funds selling at a discount from net asset value and selling those trading at a premium, but discounts and premiums can widen, subjecting this strategy too to fundamental risk. Pontiff (1996) demonstrates that deviations of price from net asset value in closed-end funds tend to be higher in funds that are more difficult to arbitrage, for example, those with more idiosyncratic volatility.

Fundamental risk may be limited by a "deadline" that forces a convergence between price and intrinsic value. What do you think would happen to a closed-end fund's discount if the fund announced that it plans to liquidate in six months, at which time it will distribute NAV to its shareholders?

However, closed-end fund discounts may also be examples of apparent anomalies that have alternative, rational explanations. Ross (2002) points out that they can be reconciled with rational investors even if expenses or fund abnormal returns are modest. He shows that if a fund has a dividend yield of δ, an alpha (risk-adjusted abnormal return) of α, and expense ratio of ε, then using the constant-growth dividend discount model (see Chapter 13), the premium of the fund over its net asset value will be

$$\frac{\text{Price} - \text{NAV}}{\text{NAV}} = \frac{\alpha - \varepsilon}{\delta + \varepsilon - \alpha}$$

If the fund manager's performance more than compensates for expenses (i.e., if $\alpha > \varepsilon$), the fund will sell at a premium to NAV; otherwise it will sell at a discount. For example, suppose $\alpha = .015$, the expense ratio is $\varepsilon = .0125$, and the dividend yield is $\delta = .02$. Then the premium will be 0.14, or 14%. But if the market turns sour on the manager and revises its estimate of α downward to 0.005, that premium quickly turns into a discount of 43%.

This analysis might explain why the public is willing to purchase closed-end funds at a premium; if investors do not expect α to exceed ε, they won't purchase shares in the fund. But the fact that most premiums eventually turn into discounts indicates how difficult it is for management to fulfill these expectations.[6]

Bubbles and Behavioral Economics

In Example 9.2, we pointed out that the stock market run-up of the late 1990s, and even more spectacularly, the run-up of the technology-heavy NASDAQ market, seems in retrospect to have been an obvious bubble. In a six-year period beginning in 1995, the NASDAQ index increased by a factor of more than 6. Former Fed chairman Alan Greenspan famously characterized the dot-com boom as an example of "irrational exuberance," and his assessment turned out to be correct: By October 2002, the index fell to less than one-fourth the peak value it had reached only two and a half years earlier. This episode seems to be a case in point for advocates of the behavioral school, exemplifying a market moved by irrational investor sentiment. Moreover, in accord with behavioral patterns, as the dot-com boom developed, it seemed to feed on itself, with investors increasingly confident of their investment prowess (overconfidence bias) and apparently willing to extrapolate short-term patterns into the distant future (representativeness bias).

Only five years later, another bubble, this time in housing prices, was under way. As in the dot-com bubble, expectations of continued price increases fueled speculative demand by purchasers. Shortly thereafter, of course, housing prices stalled and then fell. The bursting bubble set off the worst financial crisis in 75 years.

On the other hand, bubbles are a lot easier to identify as such once they are over. While they are going on, it is not as clear that prices are irrationally exuberant, and, indeed, many financial commentators at the time justified the dot-com boom as consistent with glowing forecasts for the "new economy." A simple example shows how hard it can be to tie down the fair value of stock investments.[7]

---

[6]We might ask why this logic of discounts and premiums does not apply to open-end mutual funds that incur similar expense ratios. Because investors in these funds can redeem shares for NAV, the shares cannot sell at a discount to NAV. Expenses in open-end funds reduce returns in each period rather than being capitalized into price and inducing a discount.

[7]The following example is taken from R. A. Brealey, S. C. Myers, and F. Allen, *Principles of Corporate Finance*, 9th ed. (Burr Ridge, IL: McGraw-Hill/Irwin, 2008).

EXAMPLE 9.3

A Stock Market Bubble?

In 2000, near the peak of the dot-com boom, the dividends paid by the firms included in the S&P 500 totaled $154.6 million. If the discount rate for the index was 9.2% and the expected dividend growth rate was 8%, the value of these shares according to the constant-growth dividend discount model (see Chapter 13 for more on this model) would be

$$\text{Value} = \frac{\text{Dividend}}{\text{Discount rate} - \text{Growth rate}} = \frac{\$154.6}{.092 - .08} = \$12{,}883 \text{ million}$$

This was quite close to the actual total value of those firms at the time. But the estimate is highly sensitive to the input values, and even a small reassessment of their prospects would result in a big revision of price. Suppose the expected dividend growth rate fell to 7.4%. This would reduce the value of the index to

$$\text{Value} = \frac{\text{Dividend}}{\text{Discount rate} - \text{Growth rate}} = \frac{\$154.6}{.092 - .074} = \$8{,}589 \text{ million}$$

which was about the value to which the S&P 500 firms had fallen by October 2002. In light of this example, the run-up and crash of the 1990s seem easier to reconcile with rational behavior.

Still, other evidence seems to tag the dot-com boom as at least partially irrational. Consider, for example, the results of a study by Rau, Dimitrov, and Cooper (2001) documenting that firms adding ".com" to the end of their names during this period enjoyed a meaningful stock price increase. That doesn't sound like rational valuation.

Evaluating the Behavioral Critique

As investors, we are concerned with the existence of profit opportunities. The behavioral explanations of efficient market anomalies do not give guidance as to how to exploit any irrationality.

However, as we have emphasized above, one of the important implications of the efficient market hypothesis is that security prices serve as reliable guides to the allocation of real assets. If prices are distorted, then capital markets will give misleading signals (and incentives) as to where the economy may best allocate resources. In this crucial dimension, the behavioral critique of the efficient market hypothesis is certainly important irrespective of any implication for investment strategies.

There is considerable debate among financial economists concerning the strength of the behavioral critique. Many believe that the behavioral approach is too unstructured, in effect allowing virtually any anomaly to be explained by some combination of irrationalities chosen from a laundry list of behavioral biases. While it is easy to "reverse engineer" a behavioral explanation for any particular anomaly, these critics would like to see a consistent or unified behavioral theory that can explain a *range* of anomalies.

More fundamentally, others are not convinced that the anomalies literature as a whole is a convincing indictment of the efficient market hypothesis. Fama (1998) reviews the anomalies literature and poses a challenge to the behavioral school. He notes that the anomalies are inconsistent in terms of their support for one type of irrationality versus another. For example, some papers document long-term corrections (consistent with overreaction), while others document long-term continuations of abnormal returns (consistent with underreaction). Moreover, the statistical significance of many of these results is hard to assess. Even small errors in choosing a benchmark against which to compare returns can cumulate to large apparent abnormalities in long-term returns.

The behavioral critique of full rationality in investor decision making is well taken, but the extent to which limited rationality affects asset pricing remains controversial. Whether or not investor irrationality affects asset prices, however, behavioral finance already makes important points about portfolio management. Investors who are aware of the potential pitfalls in information processing and decision making that seem to characterize their peers should be better able to avoid such errors. Ironically, the insights of behavioral finance may lead to some of the same policy conclusions embraced by efficient market advocates. For example, an easy way to avoid some behavioral minefields is to pursue passive, largely indexed portfolio strategies. It seems that only rare individuals can consistently beat passive strategies; this conclusion may hold true whether your fellow investors are behavioral or rational.

9.2 TECHNICAL ANALYSIS AND BEHAVIORAL FINANCE

Technical analysis attempts to exploit recurring and predictable patterns in stock prices to generate superior investment performance. Technicians do not deny the value of fundamental information but believe that prices only gradually close in on intrinsic value. As fundamentals shift, astute traders can exploit the adjustment to a new equilibrium.

For example, one of the best-documented behavioral tendencies is the *disposition effect,* which refers to the tendency of investors to hold on to losing investments. Behavioral investors seem reluctant to realize losses. Grinblatt and Han (2005) show that the disposition effect can lead to momentum in stock prices even if fundamental values follow a random walk. The fact that the demand of "disposition investors" for a company's shares depends on the price history of those shares means that prices close in on fundamental values only over time, consistent with the central motivation of technical analysis.

Hoffman and Shefrin (2014) find that investors who use technical analysis appear to exhibit similar behavioral traits as those linked to overconfidence and excessive optimism. Behavioral biases may also be consistent with technical analysts' use of volume data. An important behavioral trait noted above is overconfidence, a systematic tendency to overestimate one's abilities. As traders become overconfident, they may trade more, inducing an association between trading volume and market returns (Gervais and Odean, 2001). Technical analysis thus uses volume data as well as price history to direct trading strategy.

Finally, technicians believe that market fundamentals can be perturbed by irrational or behavioral factors, sometimes labeled "sentiment variables." More or less random price fluctuations will accompany any underlying price trend, creating opportunities to exploit corrections as these fluctuations dissipate.

Trends and Corrections

Much of technical analysis seeks to uncover trends in market prices. This is in effect a search for momentum. Momentum can be absolute, in which case one searches for upward price trends, or relative, in which case the analyst looks to invest in one sector over another (or even take on a long-short position in the two sectors). Relative strength statistics (discussed later in this chapter) are designed to uncover these cross-sector potential opportunities.

MOMENTUM AND MOVING AVERAGES While we all would like to buy shares in firms whose prices are trending upward, this begs the question of how to identify the underlying direction of prices, if in fact such trends actually exist. A primary tool for this purpose is the moving average.

The moving average of a stock price is the average price over a given interval, where that interval is updated as time passes. For example, a 50-day moving average traces the average price over the previous 50 days. The average is recomputed each day by dropping the oldest observation and adding the newest. Figure 9.3 is a moving-average chart for Intel. Notice that the moving average (the blue curve) is a "smoothed" version of the original data series (the jagged red curve).

After a period in which prices have been falling, the moving average will be above the current price (because the moving average continues to "average in" the older and higher prices until they leave the sample period). In contrast, when prices have been rising, the moving average will be below the current price.

Breaking through the moving average from below, as at point *A* in Figure 9.3, is taken as a bullish signal, because it signifies a shift from a falling trend (with prices below the moving average) to a rising trend (with prices above the moving average). Conversely, when prices drop below the moving average, as at point *B,* analysts might conclude that market momentum has become negative.

FIGURE **9.3** **Share price and 50-day moving average for Intel (INTC)**
Source: Yahoo! Finance, **finance.yahoo.com,** May 25, 2017.

Other techniques also are used to uncover potential momentum in stock prices. Two of the more famous ones are Elliott wave theory and Kondratieff waves. Both posit the existence of long-term trends in stock market prices that may be disturbed by shorter-term trends as well as daily fluctuations of little importance. Elliott wave theory superimposes long-term and short-term wave cycles in an attempt to describe the complicated pattern of actual price movements. Once the longer-term waves are identified, investors presumably can buy when the long-term direction of the market is positive. While there is considerable noise in the actual evolution of stock prices, by properly interpreting the wave cycles, one can, according to the theory, predict broad movements. Similarly, Kondratieff waves are named after a Russian economist who asserted that the macroeconomy (and therefore the stock market) moves in broad waves lasting between 48 and 60 years. Kondratieff's assertion is hard to evaluate empirically, however, because cycles that last about 50 years provide only two independent data points per century, which is hardly enough data to test the predictive power of the theory.

EXAMPLE 9.4

Moving Averages

Consider the price data in the following table. Each observation represents the closing level of the Dow Jones Industrial Average (DJIA) on the last trading day of the week. The five-week moving average for each week is the average of the DJIA over the previous five weeks. For example, the first entry, for week 5, is the average of the index value between weeks 1 and 5: 21,290, 21,380, 21,399, 21,379, and 21,450. The next entry is the average of the index values between weeks 2 and 6, and so on.

Figure 9.4 plots the level of the index and the five-week moving average. Notice that while the index itself moves up and down rather abruptly, the moving average is a relatively smooth series, because the impact of each week's price movement is averaged with that of the previous weeks. Week 16 is a bearish point according to the moving-average rule. The price series crosses from above the moving average to below it, signifying the beginning of a downward trend in stock prices.

(continued)

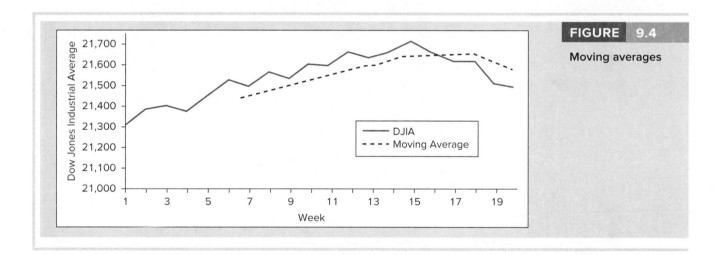

EXAMPLE 9.4

*Moving Averages
(concluded)*

Week	DJIA	5-Week Moving Average	Week	DJIA	5-Week Moving Average
1	21,290		11	21,590	21,555
2	21,380		12	21,652	21,586
3	21,399		13	21,625	21,598
4	21,379		14	21,657	21,624
5	21,450	21,380	15	21,699	21,645
6	21,513	21,424	16	21,647	21,656
7	21,500	21,448	17	21,610	21,648
8	21,565	21,481	18	21,595	21,642
9	21,524	21,510	19	21,499	21,610
10	21,597	21,540	20	21,466	21,563

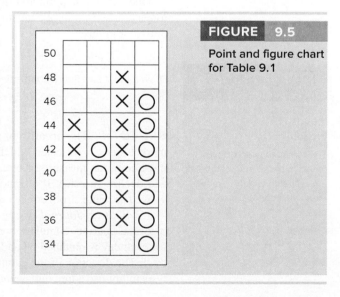

FIGURE   9.4

Moving averages

POINT AND FIGURE CHARTS   A variant on pure trend analysis is the *point and figure chart* depicted in Figure 9.5. This figure has no time dimension. It simply traces significant upward or downward movements in stock prices without regard to their timing. The data for Figure 9.5 come from Table 9.1.

Suppose, as in Table 9.1, that a stock's price is currently $40. If the price rises by at least $2, you put an X in the first column at $42 in Figure 9.5. Another increase of at least $2 calls for placement of another X in the first column, this time at the $44 level. If the stock then falls by at least $2, you start a new column and put an O next to $42. Each subsequent $2 price fall results in another O in the second column. When prices reverse yet again and head upward, you begin the third column with an X denoting each consecutive $2 price increase.

The single asterisks in Table 9.1 mark an event resulting in the placement of a new X or O in the chart. The daggers denote price movements that result in the start of a new column of Xs or Os.

FIGURE   9.5

Point and figure chart for Table 9.1

TABLE 9.1	Stock price history		
Date	**Price**	**Date**	**Price**
January 2	$40.00	February 1	$40.00*
January 3	40.50	February 2	41.00
January 4	41.00	February 5	40.50
January 5	42.00*	February 6	42.00*
January 8	41.50	February 7	45.00*
January 9	42.50	February 8	44.50
January 10	43.00	February 9	46.00*
January 11	43.75	February 12	47.00
January 12	44.00*	February 13	48.00*
January 15	45.00	February 14	47.50
January 16	44.00	February 15	46.00†
January 17	41.50†	February 16	45.00
January 18	41.00	February 19	44.00*
January 19	40.00*	February 20	42.00*
January 22	39.00	February 21	41.00
January 23	39.50	February 22	40.00*
January 24	39.75	February 23	41.00
January 25	38.00*	February 26	40.50
January 26	35.00*	February 27	38.00*
January 29	36.00†	February 28	39.00
January 30	37.00	March 1	36.00*
January 31	39.00*	March 2	34.00*

*Indicates an event that has resulted in a stock price increase or decrease of at least $2.

†Denotes a price movement that has resulted in either an upward or a downward reversal in the stock price.

Sell signals are generated when the stock price *penetrates* previous lows, and buy signals occur when previous high prices are penetrated. A *congestion area* is a horizontal band of Xs and Os created by several price reversals. These regions correspond to support and resistance levels and are indicated in Figure 9.6, which is an actual chart with congestion and resistance levels marked.

One can devise point and figure charts using price increments other than $2, but it is customary in setting up a chart to require reasonably substantial price changes before marking pluses or minuses.

CONCEPT
check   **9.4**   Draw a point and figure chart using the history in Table 9.1 with price increments of $3.

---

breadth

The extent to which movements in broad market indexes are reflected widely in movements of individual stock prices.

BREADTH   The **breadth** of the market is a measure of the extent to which movement in a market index is reflected widely in the price movements of all the stocks in the market. The most common measure of breadth is the spread between the number of stocks that advance and decline in price. If advances outnumber declines by a wide margin, then the market is viewed as being stronger because the rally is widespread. These numbers are reported daily in *The Wall Street Journal* (see Figure 9.7).

Some analysts cumulate breadth data each day as in Table 9.2. The cumulative breadth for each day is obtained by adding that day's net advances (or declines) to the previous day's total. The direction of the cumulated series is then used to discern broad market trends. Analysts might use a moving average of cumulative breadth to gauge broad trends.

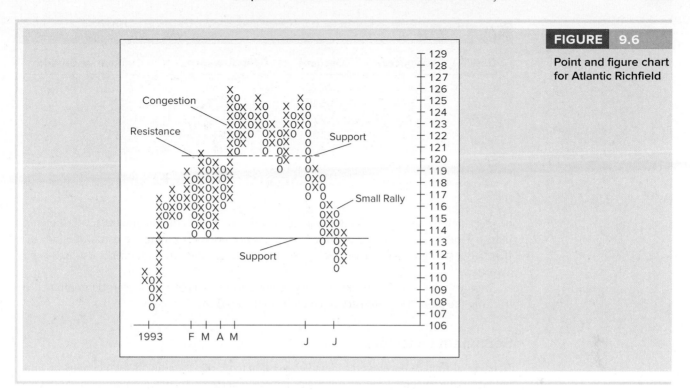

FIGURE 9.6

Point and figure chart for Atlantic Richfield

RELATIVE STRENGTH **Relative strength** measures the extent to which a security has outperformed or underperformed either the market as a whole or its particular industry. Relative strength is computed by calculating the ratio of the price of the security to a price index for the industry. For example, the relative strength of Toyota versus the auto industry would

relative strength

Recent performance of a given stock or industry compared to that of a broader market index.

Market diary

Source: *The Wall Street Journal Online*, May 25, 2017.

FIGURE 9.7

	4:06 PM EDT 5/25/2017		
Markets Diary **Issues**	**NYSE**	**NASDAQ**	**NYSE MKT**
Advancing	1,569	1,531	130
Declining	1,423	1,324	165
Unchanged	124	162	34
Total	3,116	3,017	329
Issues at			
New 52 Week High	238	222	6
New 52 Week Low	42	64	7
Share Volume			
Total	3,537,923,017	1,777,718,240	92,408,271
Advancing	1,513,206,869	1,135,738,916	37,411,984
Declining	1,999,419,305	610,544,842	47,595,937
Unchanged	25,296,843	31,434,482	7,400,350

See 4 p.m. Closing Diaries. Volume updates until 8 p.m.   Get Markets Diary by Email

TABLE 9.2	Breadth			
Day	Advances	Declines	Net Advances	Cumulative Breadth
1	1,802	1,748	54	54
2	1,917	1,640	277	331
3	1,703	1,772	−69	262
4	1,512	2,122	−610	−348
5	1,633	2,004	−371	−719

Note: The sum of advances plus declines varies across days because some stock prices are unchanged.

be measured by movements in the ratio of the price of Toyota divided by the level of an auto industry index. A rising ratio implies Toyota has been outperforming the rest of the industry. If relative strength can be assumed to persist over time, then this would be a signal to buy Toyota.

Similarly, the strength of an industry relative to the whole market can be computed by tracking the ratio of the industry price index to the market price index.

Sentiment Indicators

Behavioral finance devotes considerable attention to market "sentiment," which may be interpreted as the general level of optimism among investors. Technical analysts have devised several measures of sentiment; we review a few of them.

TRIN STATISTIC Market volume is sometimes used to measure the strength of a market rise or fall. Technicians consider market advances to be a more favorable omen of continued price increases when they are associated with increased trading volume. Similarly, market reversals are considered more bearish when associated with higher volume. The **trin statistic** is defined as

trin statistic
The ratio of average volume in declining issues to average volume in advancing issues.

$$\text{Trin} = \frac{\text{Volume declining/Number declining}}{\text{Volume advancing/Number advancing}}$$

Therefore, trin is the ratio of average trading volume in declining issues to average volume in advancing issues. Ratios above 1 are considered bearish because the falling stocks would then have higher average volume than the advancing stocks, indicating net selling pressure.

The Wall Street Journal Online provides the data necessary to compute trin in its Markets Diary section. Using the data in Figure 9.7, trin for the NYSE on this day was:

$$\text{Trin} = \frac{1,999,419,305/1,423}{1,513,206,869/1,569} = 1.457$$

Remember, however, that for every buyer, there must be a seller of stock. Rising volume in a rising market should not necessarily indicate a larger imbalance of buyers versus sellers. For example, a trin statistic above 1, which is considered bearish, could equally well be interpreted as indicating that there is more *buying* activity in declining issues.

CONFIDENCE INDEX *Barron's* computes a confidence index using data from the bond market. The presumption is that actions of bond traders reveal trends that will emerge soon in the stock market.

confidence index
Ratio of the yield of top-rated corporate bonds to the yield on intermediate-grade bonds.

The **confidence index** is the ratio of the average yield on 10 top-rated corporate bonds divided by the average yield on 10 intermediate-grade corporate bonds. The ratio will always be below 1 because higher-rated bonds will offer lower promised yields to maturity. When bond traders are optimistic about the economy, however, they might require smaller default premiums on lower-rated debt. Hence, the yield spread will narrow, and the confidence index will approach 1. Therefore, higher values of the confidence index are bullish signals.

SHORT INTEREST   **Short interest** is the total number of shares of stock currently sold short in the market. Some technicians interpret high levels of short interest as bullish, others as bearish. The bullish perspective is that, because all short sales must be covered (i.e., short-sellers eventually must purchase shares to return the ones they have borrowed), short interest represents latent future demand for the stocks. As short sales are covered, the demand created by the share purchase will force prices up.

The bearish interpretation of short interest is based on the fact that short-sellers tend to be larger, more sophisticated investors. Accordingly, increased short interest reflects bearish sentiment by the "smart money," which would be a negative signal of the market's prospects.

short interest
The total number of shares currently sold short in the market.

PUT/CALL RATIO   Call options give investors the right to buy a stock at a fixed "exercise" price and therefore are a way of betting on stock price increases. Put options give the right to sell a stock at a fixed price and therefore are a way of betting on stock price decreases.[8] The ratio of outstanding put options to outstanding call options is called the **put/call ratio.** Because put options do well in falling markets while call options do well in rising markets, a rising ratio is taken as a sign of broad investor pessimism and a coming market decline.

Contrarian investors, however, believe that a good time to buy is when the rest of the market is bearish because stock prices are then unduly depressed. Therefore, they would take an increase in the put/call ratio as a signal of a buy opportunity.

put/call ratio
Ratio of put options to call options outstanding on a stock.

A Warning

The search for patterns in stock market prices is nearly irresistible, and the ability of the human eye to discern apparent patterns is remarkable. Unfortunately, it is possible to perceive patterns that really don't exist. Consider Figure 9.8, which presents simulated and actual values of the Dow Jones Industrial Average during 1956 taken from a famous study by Harry Roberts (1959). In Figure 9.8, Panel B, it appears as though the market presents a classic head-and-shoulders pattern where the middle hump (the head) is flanked by two shoulders. When the price index "pierces the right shoulder"—a technical trigger point—it is believed to be heading lower, and it is time to sell your stocks. Figure 9.8, Panel A, also looks like a "typical" stock market pattern.

However, one of these panels was constructed from real data while one was generated using "returns" created by a random-number generator which *by construction* were patternless. Can you tell which is which?[9]

Figure 9.9 shows the weekly price *changes* behind the two panels in Figure 9.8. Here the randomness in both series—the stock price as well as the simulated sequence—is obvious.

A problem related to the tendency to perceive patterns where they don't exist is data mining. After the fact, you can always find patterns and trading rules that would have generated enormous profits. If you test enough rules, some will have worked in the past. Unfortunately, picking a theory that would have worked after the fact carries no guarantee of future success.

In evaluating trading rules, you should always ask whether the rule would have seemed reasonable *before* you looked at the data. If not, you might be buying into the one arbitrary rule among many that happened to have worked in that particular sample. The crucial question is whether there is reason to believe that what worked in the past should continue to work in the future.

---

[8]Puts and calls were defined in Chapter 2, Section 2.5. They are discussed more fully in Chapter 15.

[9]Panel A is based on the real data.

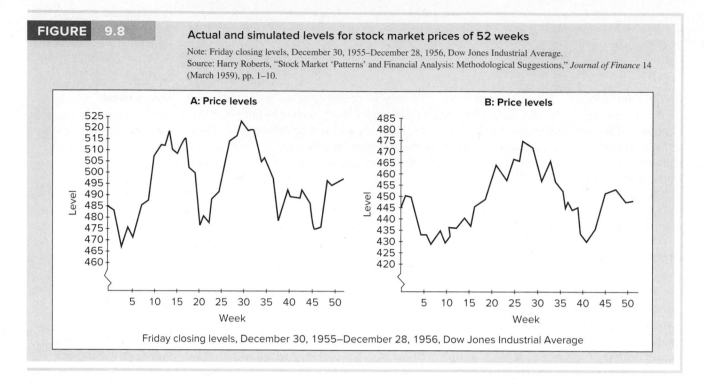

FIGURE   9.8

Actual and simulated levels for stock market prices of 52 weeks

Note: Friday closing levels, December 30, 1955–December 28, 1956, Dow Jones Industrial Average.
Source: Harry Roberts, "Stock Market 'Patterns' and Financial Analysis: Methodological Suggestions," *Journal of Finance* 14 (March 1959), pp. 1–10.

Friday closing levels, December 30, 1955–December 28, 1956, Dow Jones Industrial Average

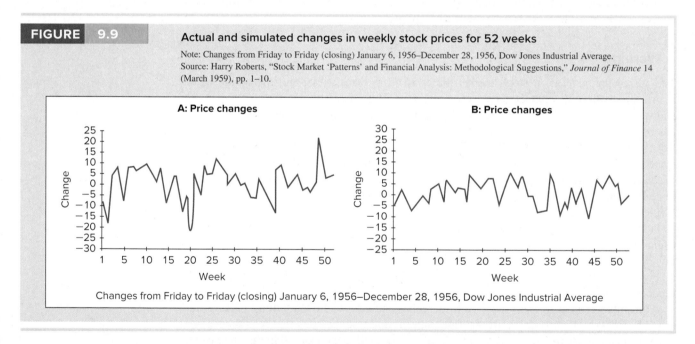

FIGURE   9.9

Actual and simulated changes in weekly stock prices for 52 weeks

Note: Changes from Friday to Friday (closing) January 6, 1956–December 28, 1956, Dow Jones Industrial Average.
Source: Harry Roberts, "Stock Market 'Patterns' and Financial Analysis: Methodological Suggestions," *Journal of Finance* 14 (March 1959), pp. 1–10.

Changes from Friday to Friday (closing) January 6, 1956–December 28, 1956, Dow Jones Industrial Average

SUMMARY

- Behavioral finance focuses on systematic irrationalities that characterize investor decision making. These "behavioral shortcomings" may be consistent with several efficient market anomalies.
- Among the information processing errors uncovered in the psychology literature are memory bias, overconfidence, conservatism, and representativeness. Behavioral tendencies include framing, mental accounting, regret avoidance, and loss aversion.
- Limits to arbitrage activity impede the ability of rational investors to exploit pricing errors induced by behavioral investors. For example, fundamental risk means that even

if a security is mispriced, it still can be risky to attempt to exploit the mispricing. This limits the actions of arbitrageurs who take positions in mispriced securities. Other limits to arbitrage are implementation costs, model risk, and costs to short-selling. Occasional failures of the Law of One Price suggest that limits to arbitrage are sometimes severe.

- The various limits to arbitrage mean that even if prices do not equal intrinsic value, it still may be difficult to exploit the mispricing. As a result, the failure of traders to beat the market may not be proof that markets are in fact efficient, with prices equal to intrinsic value.
- Technical analysis is the search for recurring and predictable patterns in stock prices. It is based on the premise that prices only gradually close in on intrinsic value. As fundamentals shift, astute traders can exploit the adjustment to a new equilibrium.
- Technical analysts look for trends in stock prices. Moving averages, relative strength, and breadth are used in various trend-based strategies. Technical analysts also uses volume data and sentiment indicators. These strategies are broadly consistent with several behavioral models of investor activity.
- Some sentiment indicators are the trin statistic, the confidence index, and the put/call ratio.

PROBLEM SETS

 Select problems are available in McGraw-Hill's *Connect*. Please see the Supplements section of the book's frontmatter for more information.

1. Match each example to one of the following behavioral characteristics.   *(LO 9-1)*

a. Investors are slow to update their beliefs when given new evidence.	i. Disposition effect
b. Investors are reluctant to bear losses due to their unconventional decisions.	ii. Representativeness bias
c. Investors exhibit less risk tolerance in their retirement accounts versus their other stock accounts.	iii. Regret avoidance
d. Investors are reluctant to sell stocks with "paper" losses.	iv. Conservatism bias
e. Investors disregard sample size when forming views about the future from the past.	v. Mental accounting

2. After reading about three successful investors in *The Wall Street Journal* you decide that active investing will also provide you with superior trading results. What sort of behavioral tendency are you exhibiting?   *(LO 9-1)*

3. What do we mean by fundamental risk, and why may such risk allow behavioral biases to persist for long periods of time?   *(LO 9-2)*

4. What are the strong points of the behavioral critique of the efficient market hypothesis? What are some problems with the critique?   *(LO 9-2)*

5. What are some possible investment implications of the behavioral critique?   *(LO 9-1)*

6. Jill Davis tells her broker that she does not want to sell her stocks that are below the price she paid for them. She believes that if she just holds on to them a little longer, they will recover, at which time she will sell them. What behavioral characteristic does Davis display?   *(LO 9-1)*
   a. Loss aversion
   b. Conservatism
   c. Disposition effect

7. After Polly Shrum sells a stock, she avoids following it in the media. She is afraid that it may subsequently increase in price. What behavioral characteristic does Shrum have as the basis for her decision making?   *(LO 9-1)*
   a. Fear of regret
   b. Representativeness
   c. Mental accounting

8. All of the following actions are consistent with feelings of regret *except:*   *(LO 9-1)*
   a. Selling losers quickly.
   b. Hiring a full-service broker.
   c. Holding on to losers too long.

9. Which one of the following would be a bullish signal to a technical analyst using moving average rules?   *(LO 9-4)*
   a. A stock price crosses above its 52-week moving average.
   b. A stock price crosses below its 52-week moving average.
   c. The stock's moving average is increasing.
   d. The stock's moving average is decreasing.

10. What is meant by data mining, and why must technical analysts be careful not to engage in it?   *(LO 9-3)*

11. Even if prices follow a random walk, they still may not be informationally efficient. Explain why this may be true, and why it matters for the efficient allocation of capital.   *(LO 9-2)*

12. What is meant by "limits to arbitrage"? Give some examples of such limits.   *(LO 9-2)*

13. Following a shock to a firm's intrinsic value, the share price will slowly but surely approach that new intrinsic value. Is this view characteristic of a technical analyst or a believer in efficient markets? Explain.   *(LO 9-3)*

14. Use the data from *The Wall Street Journal* in Figure 9.7 to calculate the trin ratio for NASDAQ. Is the trin ratio bullish or bearish?   *(LO 9-4)*

15. Calculate breadth for NASDAQ using the data in Figure 9.7. Is the signal bullish or bearish?   *(LO 9-4)*

16. Collect data on the DJIA for a period covering a few months. (You can download a historical sample from **finance.yahoo.com.**) Try to identify primary trends. Can you tell whether the market currently is in an upward or downward trend?   *(LO 9-4)*

17. Suppose Baa-rated bonds currently yield 6%, while Aa-rated bonds yield 4%. Now suppose that due to an increase in the expected inflation rate, the yields on both bonds increase by 1%.   *(LO 9-4)*
   a. What would happen to the confidence index?
   b. Would this be interpreted as bullish or bearish by a technical analyst?
   c. Does this make sense to you?

18. Table 9.3 presents price data for Computers, Inc., and a computer industry index. Does Computers, Inc., show relative strength over this period?   *(LO 9-4)*

19. Use the data in Table 9.3 to compute a five-day moving average for Computers, Inc. Can you identify any buy or sell signals?   *(LO 9-4)*

20. a. Construct a point and figure chart for Computers, Inc., using the data in Table 9.3. Use $2 increments for your chart.
    b. Do the buy or sell signals derived from your chart correspond to those derived from the moving-average rule (see the previous problem)?   *(LO 9-4)*

TABLE 9.3   Computers, Inc., stock price history

Trading Day	Computers, Inc.	Industry Index	Trading Day	Computers, Inc.	Industry Index
1	19.63	50.0	21	19.63	54.1
2	20.00	50.1	22	21.50	54.0
3	20.50	50.5	23	22.00	53.9
4	22.00	50.4	24	23.13	53.7
5	21.13	51.0	25	24.00	54.8
6	22.00	50.7	26	25.25	54.5
7	21.88	50.5	27	26.25	54.6
8	22.50	51.1	28	27.00	54.1
9	23.13	51.5	29	27.50	54.2
10	23.88	51.7	30	28.00	54.8
11	24.50	51.4	31	28.50	54.2
12	23.25	51.7	32	28.00	54.8
13	22.13	52.2	33	27.50	54.9
14	22.00	52.0	34	29.00	55.2
15	20.63	53.1	35	29.25	55.7
16	20.25	53.5	36	29.50	56.1
17	19.75	53.9	37	30.00	56.7
18	18.75	53.6	38	28.50	56.7
19	17.50	52.9	39	27.75	56.5
20	19.00	53.4	40	28.00	56.1

21. Yesterday, the Dow Jones industrials gained 54 points. However, 1,704 issues declined in price while 1,367 advanced. Why might a technical analyst be concerned even though the market index rose on this day?   *(LO 9-4)*

22. Table 9.4 contains data on market advances and declines. Calculate cumulative breadth and decide whether this technical signal is bullish or bearish.   *(LO 9-4)*

23. If the trading volume in advancing shares on day 1 in the previous problem was 1.1 billion shares, while the volume in declining issues was 0.9 billion shares, what was the trin statistic for that day? Was trin bullish or bearish?   *(LO 9-4)*

24. Using the following data on bond yields, calculate the change in the confidence index from last year to this year. What besides a change in confidence might explain the pattern of yield changes?   *(LO 9-4)*

	This Year	Last Year
Yield on top-rated corporate bonds	4%	7%
Yield on intermediate-grade corporate bonds	6%	9%

TABLE 9.4   Market advances and declines

Day	Advances	Declines	Day	Advances	Declines
1	906	704	6	970	702
2	653	986	7	1,002	609
3	721	789	8	903	722
4	503	968	9	850	748
5	497	1,095	10	766	766

25. Log in to Connect and link to the material for Chapter 9, where you will find five years of weekly returns for the S&P 500.   *(LO 9-4)*

   a. Set up a spreadsheet to calculate the 26-week moving average of the index. Set the value of the index at the beginning of the sample period equal to 100. The index value in each week is then updated by multiplying the previous week's level by (1 + rate of return over previous week).

   b. Identify every instance in which the index crosses through its moving average from below. In how many of the weeks following a cross-through does the index increase? Decrease?

   c. Identify every instance in which the index crosses through its moving average from above. In how many of the weeks following a cross-through does the index increase? Decrease?

   d. How well does the moving-average rule perform in identifying buy or sell opportunities?

26. Log in to Connect and link to the material for Chapter 9, where you will find five years of weekly returns for the S&P 500 and Fidelity's Select Banking Fund (ticker FSRBX).   *(LO 9-4)*

   a. Set up a spreadsheet to calculate the relative strength of the banking sector compared to the broad market. (*Hint:* As in the previous problem, set the initial value of the sector index and the S&P 500 Index equal to 100, and use each week's rate of return to update the level of each index.)

   b. Identify every instance in which the relative strength ratio increases by at least 5% from its value five weeks earlier. In how many of the weeks immediately following a substantial increase in relative strength does the banking sector outperform the S&P 500? In how many of those weeks does the banking sector underperform the S&P 500?

   c. Identify every instance in which the relative strength ratio decreases by at least 5% from its value five weeks earlier. In how many of the weeks immediately following a substantial decrease in relative strength does the banking sector underperform the S&P 500? In how many of those weeks does the banking sector outperform the S&P 500?

   d. How well does the relative strength rule perform in identifying buy or sell opportunities?

Challenge

27. One apparent violation of the Law of One Price is the pervasive discrepancy between the prices and net asset values of closed-end mutual funds. Would you expect to observe greater discrepancies on diversified or less diversified funds? Why?   *(LO 9-2)*

CFA Problems

1. Don Sampson begins a meeting with his financial adviser by outlining his investment philosophy as shown below:

Statement Number	Statement
1	Investments should offer strong return potential but with very limited risk. I prefer to be conservative and to minimize losses, even if I miss out on substantial growth opportunities.
2	All nongovernmental investments should be in industry-leading and financially strong companies.
3	Income needs should be met entirely through interest income and cash dividends. All equity securities held should pay cash dividends.

continued

Statement Number	Statement
4	Investment decisions should be based primarily on consensus forecasts of general economic conditions and company-specific growth.
5	If an investment falls below the purchase price, that security should be retained until it returns to its original cost. Conversely, I prefer to take quick profits on successful investments.
6	I will direct the purchase of investments, including derivative securities, periodically. These aggressive investments result from personal research and may not prove consistent with my investment policy. I have not kept records on the performance of similar past investments, but I have had some "big winners."

Select the statement from the table above that best illustrates each of the following behavioral finance concepts. Justify your selection. *(LO 9-1)*
   i. Mental accounting.
   ii. Overconfidence (illusion of control).
   iii. Disposition effect.

2. Monty Frost's tax-deferred retirement account is invested entirely in equity securities. Because the international portion of his portfolio has performed poorly in the past, he has reduced his international equity exposure to 2%. Frost's investment adviser has recommended an increased international equity exposure. Frost responds with the following comments:
   a. Based on past poor performance, I want to sell all my remaining international equity securities once their market prices rise to equal their original cost.
   b. Most diversified international portfolios have had disappointing results over the past five years. During that time, however, the market in country XYZ has outperformed all other markets, even our own. If I do increase my international equity exposure, I would prefer that the entire exposure consist of securities from country XYZ.
   c. International investments are inherently more risky. Therefore, I prefer to purchase any international equity securities in my "speculative" account, my best chance at becoming rich. I do not want them in my retirement account, which has to protect me from poverty in my old age.

   Frost's adviser is familiar with behavioral finance concepts but prefers a traditional or standard finance approach (modern portfolio theory) to investments.

   Indicate the behavioral finance concept that Frost most directly exhibits in each of his three comments. Explain how each of Frost's comments can be countered by using an argument from standard finance. *(LO 9-1)*

3. Louise and Christopher Maclin live in London, United Kingdom, and currently rent an apartment in the metropolitan area. During an initial discussion of the Maclins' financial plans, Christopher Maclin makes the following statements to the Maclins' financial adviser, Grant Webb:
   a. "I have used the Internet extensively to research the outlook for the housing market over the next five years, and I believe now is the best time to buy a house."
   b. "I do not want to sell any bond in my portfolio for a lower price than I paid for the bond."
   c. "I will not sell any of my company stock because I know my company and I believe it has excellent prospects for the future."

   For each statement (a)–(c) identify the behavioral finance concept most directly exhibited. Explain how each behavioral finance concept is affecting the Maclins' investment decision making. *(LO 9-1)*

4. During an interview with her investment adviser, a retired investor made the following two statements:
   a. "I have been very pleased with the returns I've earned on Petrie stock over the past two years, and I am certain that it will be a superior performer in the future."

    b. "I am pleased with the returns from the Petrie stock because I have specific uses for that money. For that reason, I certainly want my retirement fund to continue owning the Petrie stock."

Identify which principle of behavioral finance is most consistent with each of the investor's two statements.   *(LO 9-1)*

5. Claire Pierce comments on her life circumstances and investment outlook:

I must support my parents who live overseas on Pogo Island. The Pogo Island economy has grown rapidly over the past two years with minimal inflation, and consensus forecasts call for a continuation of these favorable trends for the foreseeable future. Economic growth has resulted from the export of a natural resource used in an exciting new technology application.

I want to invest 10% of my portfolio in Pogo Island government bonds. I plan to purchase long-term bonds because my parents are likely to live more than 10 years. Experts uniformly do not foresee a resurgence of inflation on Pogo Island, so I am certain that the total returns produced by the bonds will cover my parents' spending needs for many years to come. There should be no exchange rate risk because the bonds are denominated in local currency. I want to buy the Pogo Island bonds but am not willing to distort my portfolio's long-term asset allocation to do so. The overall mix of stocks, bonds, and other investments should not change. Therefore, I am considering selling one of my U.S. bond funds to raise cash to buy the Pogo Island bonds. One possibility is my High Yield Bond Fund, which has declined 5% in value year to date. I am not excited about this fund's prospects; in fact I think it is likely to decline more, but there is a small probability that it could recover very quickly. So I have decided instead to sell my Core Bond Fund that has appreciated 5% this year. I expect this investment to continue to deliver attractive returns, but there is a small chance this year's gains might disappear quickly.

Once that shift is accomplished, my investments will be in great shape. The sole exception is my Small Company Fund, which has performed poorly. I plan to sell this investment as soon as the price increases to my original cost.

Identify three behavioral finance concepts illustrated in Pierce's comments and describe each of the three concepts. Discuss how an investor practicing standard or traditional finance would challenge each of the three concepts.   *(LO 9-1)*

WEB *master*

1. Log on to **finance.yahoo.com** to find the monthly dividend-adjusted closing prices for the most recent four years for Abercrombie & Fitch (ANF). Also collect the closing level of the S&P 500 Index over the same period.
   a. Calculate the four-month moving average of both the stock and the S&P 500 over time. For each series, use Excel to plot the moving average against the actual level of the stock price or index. Examine the instances where the moving average and price series cross. Is the stock more or less likely to increase when the price crosses through the moving average? Does it matter whether the price crosses the moving average from above or below? How reliable would an investment rule based on moving averages be? Perform your analysis for both the stock price and the S&P 500.
   b. Calculate and plot the relative strength of the stock compared to the S&P 500 over the sample period. Find all instances in which relative strength of the stock increases by more than 10 percentage points (e.g., an increase in the relative strength index from 0.93 to 1.03) and all those instances in which relative strength of the stock decreases by more than 10 percentage points. Is the stock more or less likely to outperform the S&P in the following two months when relative strength has increased or to underperform when relative strength has decreased? In other words, does relative strength continue? How reliable would an investment rule based on relative strength be?
2. Yahoo! Finance provides considerable data that can be used for technical analysis. Short interest ratios are found in the *Statistics* table for each stock. You can also prepare charts

of moving averages for any company by clicking the price chart for the company and then clicking on *Indicators*. You can select the moving average option and specify the length of the moving average. Prepare charts of moving averages and obtain short interest ratios for GE and Amazon (AMZN). Prepare a one-year chart of the 25- and 50-day average price of GE, AMZN, and the S&P 500 Index.

a. Which, if either, of the companies is priced above its 25- and 50-day averages?

b. Would you consider their charts as bullish or bearish? Why?

c. What are the short interest ratios for the two companies?

9.1 Conservatism implies that investors will at first respond too slowly to new information, leading to trends in prices. Representativeness can lead them to extrapolate trends too far into the future and overshoot intrinsic value. Eventually, when the pricing error is corrected, we observe a reversal.

9.2 Out-of-favor stocks will exhibit low prices relative to various proxies for intrinsic value such as earnings. Because of regret avoidance, these stocks will need to offer a more attractive rate of return to induce investors to hold them. Thus, low P/E stocks might on average offer higher rates of return.

9.3 At liquidation, price will equal NAV. This puts a limit on fundamental risk. Investors need only carry the position for a few months to profit from the elimination of the discount. Moreover, as the liquidation date approaches, the discount should dissipate. This greatly limits the risk that the discount can move against the investor. At the announcement of impending liquidation, the discount should immediately disappear, or at least shrink considerably.

9.4

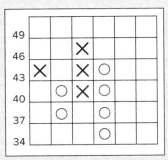

9.5 By the time the news of the recession affects bond yields, it also ought to affect stock prices. The market should fall *before* the confidence index signals that the time is ripe to sell.

Debt Securities

Bond markets used to be a sedate arena for risk-averse investors who wanted worry-free investments with modest but stable returns. They are no longer so quiet. The fixed-income market was at the center of the financial crisis of 2008–2009 as well as the sovereign debt crisis that began in 2009.

These markets are no longer free of risk. Interest rates in the last three decades have become more volatile than anyone in 1965 would have dreamed possible. Volatility means that investors have great opportunities for gain, but also for losses, and we have seen dramatic examples of both in recent years.

Long-Term Capital Management, at the time the world's most successful hedge fund, shocked Wall Street when it was felled by investment reversals in 1998, among them losses of more than $1 billion on its interest rate positions. But those losses seem almost quaint when compared to the devastation suffered in the market meltdown of 2008–2009. The beginning of that period was signaled by revelation of losses of $1 billion on mortgage bonds held by two Bear Stearns hedge funds in 2007. Over the course of the next two years, hundreds of billions were lost by investors in other mortgage-backed bonds and those who sold insurance on those securities. Of course, in many of these instances, there were traders on the other side of the transaction who did quite well. The bearish bets made by hedge fund manager John Paulson in 2007 made his funds more than $15 billion.

The chapters in Part Three provide an introduction to debt markets and securities. We will show you how to value such securities and why their values change with interest rates. We will see what features determine the sensitivity of bond prices to interest rates and how investors measure and manage interest rate risk.

Learning Objectives

LO 10-1 Explain the general terms of a bond contract and how bond prices are quoted in the financial press.

LO 10-2 Compute a bond's price given its yield to maturity, and compute its yield to maturity given its price.

LO 10-3 Calculate how bond prices will change over time for a given interest rate projection.

LO 10-4 Describe call, convertibility, and sinking fund provisions, and analyze how these provisions affect a bond's price and yield to maturity.

LO 10-5 Identify the determinants of bond safety and rating and how credit risk is reflected in bond yields and the prices of credit default swaps.

LO 10-6 Calculate several measures of bond return, and demonstrate how these measures may be affected by taxes.

LO 10-7 Analyze the factors likely to affect the shape of the yield curve at any time, and impute forward rates from the yield curve.

I n the previous chapters on risk and return relationships, we have treated securities at a high level of abstraction. We have assumed implicitly that a prior, detailed analysis of each security already has been performed and that its risk and return features have been assessed.

We turn now to specific analyses of particular security markets. We examine valuation principles, determinants of risk and return, and portfolio strategies commonly used within and across the various markets.

We begin by analyzing debt securities. A debt security is a claim on a specified periodic stream of income. Debt securities are often called *fixed-income securities,* because they promise either a fixed stream of income or one determined according to a specified formula. These securities have the advantage of being relatively easy to understand because the payment formulas are specified in advance. Uncertainty about their cash flows is minimal as long as the issuer of the security is sufficiently creditworthy. That makes these securities a convenient starting point for our analysis of the universe of potential investment vehicles.

The bond is the basic debt security, and this chapter starts with an overview of bond markets, including Treasury, corporate, and international bonds. We turn next to pricing, showing how bond prices are set in accordance with market interest rates and why they change with those rates. Given this background, we can compare myriad measures of bond returns such as yield to maturity, yield to call, holding-period return, and realized compound rate of return. We show how bond prices evolve over time, discuss certain tax rules that apply to debt securities, and show how to calculate after-tax returns. Next, we consider the impact of default or credit risk on bond pricing and look at the determinants of credit risk and the default premium built into bond yields. Finally, we turn to the term structure of interest rates, the relationship between yield to maturity and time to maturity.

10.1 BOND CHARACTERISTICS

A **bond** is a security that is issued in connection with a borrowing arrangement. The borrower issues (i.e., sells) a bond to the lender for some amount of cash; the bond is in effect the "IOU" of the borrower. The issuer agrees to make specified payments to the bondholder on specified dates. In a typical coupon, the issuer makes semiannual payments of interest for the life of the bond. These are called *coupon payments* because, in precomputer days, most bonds had coupons that investors would clip off and present to claim the interest payment. When the bond matures, the issuer retires the debt by paying the bond's **par value** (or equivalently, its **face value**). The **coupon rate** of the bond determines the interest payment: The annual payment equals the coupon rate times the bond's par value. The coupon rate, maturity date, and par value of the bond are part of the *bond indenture*, which is the contract between the issuer and the bondholder.

To illustrate, a bond with a par value of $1,000 and a coupon rate of 8% might be sold for $1,000. The issuer then pays the bondholder 8% of $1,000, or $80 per year, for the stated life of the bond, say, 30 years. The $80 payment typically comes in two semiannual installments of $40 each. At the end of the 30-year life of the bond, the issuer also pays the $1,000 par value to the bondholder.

Bonds usually are issued with coupon rates set just high enough to induce investors to pay par value to buy the bond. Sometimes, however, **zero-coupon bonds** are issued that make no coupon payments. In this case, investors receive par value at the maturity date but receive no interest payments until then: The bond has a coupon rate of zero. These bonds are issued at prices considerably below par value, and the investor's return comes solely from the difference between issue price and the payment of par value at maturity. We will return to these bonds below.

bond
A security that obligates the issuer to make specified payments to the holder over a period of time.

par value, face value
The payment to the bondholder at the maturity of the bond.

coupon rate
A bond's annual interest payment per dollar of par value.

zero-coupon bond
A bond paying no coupons that sells at a discount and provides only a payment of par value at maturity.

Treasury Bonds and Notes

Figure 10.1 is an excerpt from the listing of Treasury issues from the *The Wall Street Journal Online*. Treasury notes are issued with original maturities between 1 and 10 years, while Treasury bonds are issued with maturities ranging from 10 to 30 years. Both bonds and notes may be purchased directly from the Treasury in denominations of only $100, but denominations of $1,000 are far more common. Both make semiannual coupon payments.

The highlighted issue in Figure 10.1 matures on February 15, 2047. Its coupon rate is 3%. Par value is $1,000; thus, the bond pays interest of $30 per year in two semiannual payments of $15. Payments are made in February and August of each year. Although bonds are typically sold in denominations of $1,000 par value, the bid and ask prices[1] are quoted as a percentage

---

[1]Recall that the bid price is the price at which you can sell the bond to a dealer. The ask price, which is slightly higher, is the price at which you can buy the bond from a dealer.

FIGURE   10.1

Prices and yields of
U.S. Treasury bonds,
February 15, 2017

Source: *The Wall Street
Journal Online,* April 22,
2017.

Maturity	Coupon	Bid	Ask	Chg	Ask yield to maturity
15-Feb-2018	3.500	102.5000	102.5156	−0.0547	0.959
31-Dec-2020	1.750	99.7188	99.7344	−0.1406	1.821
15-Nov-2022	1.625	97.0938	97.1094	−0.2188	2.163
15-Feb-2026	1.625	92.9141	92.9297	−0.2734	2.508
15-Feb-2026	6.000	128.4922	128.5078	−0.3438	2.450
15-May-2030	6.250	140.5547	140.6172	−0.4453	2.604
15-Nov-2043	3.750	112.3984	112.4297	−0.7734	3.065
15-Feb-2047	3.000	98.2500	98.2813	−0.5703	3.088

of par value. Therefore, the ask price is 98.2813% of par value, or $982.813. The minimum price increment, or *tick size,* in *The Wall Street Journal* listing is 1/128, so this bond may also be viewed as selling for $98\frac{36}{128}\%$ of par value.[2]

The last column, labeled "Ask Yld," is the bond's yield to maturity based on the ask price. The yield to maturity is often interpreted as a measure of the average rate of return to an investor who purchases the bond for the asked price and holds it until its maturity date. We will have much to say about yield to maturity below.

ACCRUED INTEREST AND QUOTED BOND PRICES   The bond prices that you see quoted in the financial pages are not actually the prices that investors pay for the bond. This is because the quoted price does not include the interest that accrues between coupon payment dates.

If a bond is purchased between coupon payments, the buyer must pay the seller for accrued interest, the prorated share of the upcoming semiannual coupon. For example, if 30 days have passed since the last coupon payment, and there are 182 days in the semiannual coupon period, the seller is entitled to a payment of accrued interest of $\frac{30}{182}$ of the semiannual coupon. The sale, or *invoice price* of the bond, which is the amount the buyer actually pays, would equal the stated price plus the accrued interest.

In general, the formula for the amount of accrued interest between two dates is

$$\text{Accrued interest} = \frac{\text{Annual coupon payment}}{2} \times \frac{\text{Days since last coupon payment}}{\text{Days separating coupon payments}}$$

EXAMPLE 10.1

Accrued Interest

Suppose that the coupon rate is 8%. Then the semiannual coupon payment is $40. Because 30 days have passed since the last coupon payment, the accrued interest on the bond is $40 \times \frac{30}{182} = \$6.59$. If the quoted price of the bond is $990, then the invoice price will be $990 + $6.59 = $996.59.

The practice of quoting bond prices net of accrued interest explains why the price of a maturing bond is listed at $1,000 rather than $1,000 plus one coupon payment. A purchaser of an 8% coupon bond one day before the bond's maturity would receive $1,040 on the following day and so should be willing to pay $1,040. In fact, $40 of that total payment constitutes the

[2]Bonds traded on formal exchanges are subject to minimum tick sizes set by the exchange. For example, the minimum price increment, or tick size, on the two-year Treasury bond futures contract (traded on the Chicago Board of Trade) is 1/128, although longer-term T-bonds have larger tick sizes. Private traders can negotiate their own tick size. For example, you can find price quotes on Bloomberg screens with tick sizes as low as 1/256.

Listing of corporate bonds

Source: FINRA (Financial Industry Regulatory Authority), May 30, 2017.

Issuer Name	Symbol	Coupon	Maturity	Moody's®/ S&P	High	Low	Last	Change	Yield%
NORTHWESTERN UNIV	NWUA4062616	4.643%	12/01/2044	/AAA	118.50400	118.30400	118.50400	2.245000	3.579884
SANOFI S A	SNY3990861	1.250%	04/10/2018	A1/	99.94500	99.82800	99.91960	0.143600	1.344026
MORGAN STANLEY	MS4190343	1.875%	01/05/2018	A3/BBB+	100.38300	100.12700	100.30600	−0.060733	1.355591
WESTPAC BKG CORP	WBK4461873	2.150%	03/06/2020	Aa2/	100.38400	100.27000	100.38400	0.075000	2.005983
ROYAL BK CDA	RY4207609	1.875%	02/05/2020	Aaa/	99.89200	99.81200	99.81200	0.079000	1.946994
CREDIT SUISSE AG NEW YORK BRH MEDIUM TER	CS4237858	1.700%	04/27/2018	A1/A	100.09500	100.03600	100.07600	0.053000	1.614536
PACCAR FINL CORP MEDIUM TERM SR NTS BOOK	PCAR4361418	1.300%	05/10/2019	A1/A+	99.18213	99.05900	99.11600	0.050000	1.764976
HSBC USA INC	HBC4217868	2.350%	03/05/2020	A2/A	100.76200	100.56400	100.56400	−0.214000	2.137972

accrued interest for the preceding half-year period. The bond price is quoted net of accrued interest and thus appears as $1,000.[3]

Corporate Bonds

Like the government, corporations borrow money by issuing bonds. Figure 10.2 is a sample of corporate bond listings. Although some bonds trade electronically on the NYSE Bonds platform, and some electronic trading platforms now allow participants to trade bonds directly, most bonds still trade on a traditional over-the-counter market in a network of bond dealers linked by a computer quotation system. In part, this is due to the lack of uniformity of bond issues. While most public firms have issued only one class of common stock, they may have dozens of bonds differing by maturity, coupon rate, seniority, and so on. Therefore, the bond market can be quite "thin," in that there are few investors interested in trading a particular issue at any particular time.

The bond listings in Figure 10.2 include the coupon, maturity, price, and yield to maturity of each bond. The "Rating" column is the estimation of bond safety given by the three major bond rating agencies, Moody's, Standard & Poor's, and Fitch. Bonds with A ratings are safer than those rated B or below. As a general rule, safer bonds with higher ratings promise lower yields to maturity. We will return to this topic toward the end of the chapter.

CALL PROVISIONS ON CORPORATE BONDS   Some corporate bonds are issued with call provisions, allowing the issuer to repurchase the bond at a specified *call price* before the maturity date. For example, if a company issues a bond with a high coupon rate when market interest rates are high, and interest rates later fall, the firm might like to retire the high-coupon debt and issue new bonds at a lower coupon rate to reduce interest payments. The proceeds from the new bond issue are used to pay for the repurchase of the existing higher-coupon bonds at the call price. This is called *refunding*. **Callable bonds** typically come with a period of call protection, an initial time during which the bonds are not callable. Such bonds are referred to as *deferred* callable bonds.

The option to call the bond is valuable to the firm, allowing it to buy back the bonds and refinance at lower interest rates when market rates fall. Of course, the firm's benefit is the bondholder's burden. Holders of called bonds may be forced to forfeit their bonds for the call

callable bonds

Bonds that may be repurchased by the issuer at a specified call price during the call period.

---

[3]In contrast to bonds, stocks do not trade at flat prices with adjustments for "accrued dividends." Whoever owns the stock when it goes "ex-dividend" receives the entire dividend payment, and the stock price reflects the value of the upcoming dividend. The price therefore typically falls by about the amount of the dividend on the "ex day." There is no need to differentiate between reported and invoice prices for stocks.

price, thereby giving up the prospect of an attractive lending rate on their original investment. To compensate investors for this risk, callable bonds are issued with higher coupons and promised yields to maturity than noncallable bonds.

convertible bond

A bond with an option allowing the bondholder to exchange the bond for a specified number of shares of common stock in the firm.

CONVERTIBLE BONDS **Convertible bonds** give bondholders an option to exchange each bond for a specified number of shares of common stock of the firm. The *conversion ratio* gives the number of shares for which each bond may be exchanged. Suppose a convertible bond is issued at par value of $1,000 and is convertible into 40 shares of a firm's stock. The current stock price is $20 per share, so the option to convert is not profitable now. Should the stock price later rise to $30, however, each bond may be converted profitably into $1,200 worth of stock. The *market conversion value* is the current value of the shares for which the bonds may be exchanged. At the $20 stock price, for example, the bond's conversion value is $800. The *conversion premium* is the excess of the bond price over its conversion value. If the bond were selling currently for $950, its premium would be $150.

Convertible bondholders benefit from price appreciation of the company's stock. Not surprisingly, this benefit comes at a price; convertible bonds offer lower coupon rates and stated or promised yields to maturity than nonconvertible bonds. At the same time, the actual return on the convertible bond may exceed the stated yield to maturity if the option to convert becomes profitable.

We discuss convertible and callable bonds further in Chapter 15.

put bond

A bond that the holder may choose either to exchange for par value at some date or to extend for a given number of years.

PUTTABLE BONDS Whereas a callable bond gives the issuer the option to extend or retire the bond at the call date, an *extendable* or **put bond** gives this option to the bondholder. If the bond's coupon rate exceeds current market yields, for instance, the bondholder will choose to extend the bond's life. If the bond's coupon rate is too low, it will be optimal not to extend; the bondholder instead reclaims principal, which can be invested at current yields.

floating-rate bonds

Bonds with coupon rates periodically reset according to a specified market rate.

FLOATING-RATE BONDS **Floating-rate bonds** make interest payments that are tied to some measure of current market rates. For example, the rate might be adjusted annually to the current T-bill rate plus 2%. If the one-year T-bill rate at the adjustment date is 4%, the bond's coupon rate over the next year would then be 6%. This arrangement means that the bond always pays approximately current market rates.

The major risk involved in floaters has to do with changing credit conditions. The yield spread is fixed over the life of the security, which may be many years. If the financial health of the firm deteriorates, then investors will demand a greater yield premium than is offered by the security. In this case, the price of the bond will fall. While the coupon rate on floaters adjusts to changes in the general level of market interest rates, it does not adjust to changes in the financial condition of the firm.

Preferred Stock

Although preferred stock strictly speaking is considered to be equity, it often is included in the fixed-income universe. This is because, like bonds, preferred stock promises to pay a specified stream of income. However, unlike bonds, the failure to pay the promised dividend does not result in corporate bankruptcy. Instead, the dividends owed simply cumulate, and the common stockholders may not receive any dividends until the preferred stockholders have been paid in full. In the event of bankruptcy, the claim of preferred stockholders to the firm's assets has lower priority than that of bondholders but higher priority than that of common stockholders.

Preferred stock usually pays a fixed dividend. Therefore, it is in effect a perpetuity, providing a level cash flow indefinitely. In contrast, floating-rate preferred stock is much like floating-rate bonds. The dividend rate is linked to a measure of current market interest rates and is adjusted at regular intervals.

Unlike interest payments on bonds, dividends on preferred stock are not considered tax-deductible expenses to the firm. This reduces their attractiveness as a source of capital to issuing firms. On the other hand, there is an offsetting tax advantage to preferred stock. When one corporation buys the preferred stock of another, it pays taxes on only 50% of the dividends received. For example, if the firm's tax bracket is 21%, and it receives $10,000 in preferred-dividend payments, it pays taxes on only $5,000: Total taxes owed are .21 × $5,000 = $1,050. The firm's effective tax rate on preferred dividends is therefore only .50 × 21% = 10.5%. Given this tax rule, it is not surprising that most preferred stock is held by corporations.

Preferred stock rarely gives its holders full voting privileges in the firm. However, if the preferred dividend is skipped, the preferred stockholders will then be provided some voting power.

Other Domestic Issuers

There are, of course, several issuers of bonds in addition to the Treasury and private corporations. For example, state and local governments issue municipal bonds. Their outstanding feature is that Their interest payments are tax-free. We examined municipal bonds, the value of the tax exemption, and the equivalent taxable yield of these bonds in Chapter 2.

Government agencies, such as the Federal Home Loan Bank Board, the Farm Credit agencies, and the mortgage pass-through agencies Ginnie Mae, Fannie Mae, and Freddie Mac also issue considerable amounts of bonds. These too were reviewed in Chapter 2.

International Bonds

International bonds are commonly divided into two categories: *foreign bonds* and *Eurobonds*. Foreign bonds are issued by a borrower from a country other than the one in which the bond is sold. The bond is denominated in the currency of the country in which it is marketed. For example, a dollar-denominated bond issued in the U.S. by a German firm is considered a foreign bond. These bonds are given colorful names based on the countries in which they are marketed. For example, foreign bonds sold in the U.S. are called *Yankee bonds*. Yen-denominated bonds sold in Japan by non-Japanese issuers are called *Samurai bonds*. British-pound-denominated foreign bonds sold in the U.K. are called *bulldog bonds*.

In contrast to foreign bonds, Eurobonds are denominated in one currency, usually that of the issuer, but sold in other national markets. For example, the Eurodollar market refers to dollar-denominated bonds sold outside the U.S. (not just in Europe). Because the Eurodollar market falls outside U.S. jurisdiction, these bonds are not regulated by U.S. federal agencies. Similarly, Euroyen bonds are yen-denominated bonds selling outside Japan, Eurosterling bonds are pound-denominated bonds selling outside the U.K., and so on.

Innovation in the Bond Market

Issuers constantly develop innovative bonds with unusual features; these issues illustrate that bond design can be extremely flexible. Here are examples of some novel bonds. They should give you a sense of the potential variety in security design.

INVERSE FLOATERS   These are similar to the floating-rate bonds we described earlier, except that the coupon rate on these bonds *falls* when the general level of interest rates rises. Investors in these bonds suffer doubly when rates rise. Not only does the present value of each dollar of cash flow from the bond fall as the discount rate rises, but the level of those cash flows falls as well. (Of course, investors in these bonds benefit doubly when rates fall.)

ASSET-BACKED BONDS   Miramax has issued bonds with coupon rates tied to the financial performance of *Pulp Fiction* and other films. Solar City has issued bonds with payments backed by revenue generated by the rooftop solar panels it has installed throughout the country. "David Bowie bonds" have been issued with payments tied to royalties on some of his albums. These are examples of asset-backed securities. The income from a specified group of assets is used to service the debt. More conventional asset-backed securities are mortgage-backed securities or securities backed by auto or credit card loans, as we discussed in Chapter 2.

TABLE 10.1	Principal and interest payments for a Treasury Inflation Protected Security						
Time	Inflation in Year Just Ended	Par Value	Coupon Payment	+	Principal Repayment	=	Total Payment
0		$1,000.00					
1	2%	1,020.00	$40.80		0		$ 40.80
2	3	1,050.60	42.02		0		42.02
3	1	1,061.11	42.44		$1,061.11		1,103.55

PAY-IN-KIND BONDS   Issuers of pay-in-kind bonds may choose to pay interest either in cash or in additional bonds. If the issuer is short on cash, it will likely choose to pay with new bonds rather than scarce cash.

CATASTROPHE BONDS   Oriental Land Co., which manages Tokyo Disneyland, has issued bonds with a final payment that depends on whether there has been an earthquake near the park. FIFA (the Fédération Internationale de Football Association) once issued catastrophe bonds with payments that would have been halted if terrorism had forced the cancellation of the World Cup. In 2017, the World Bank issued "pandemic bonds" in which investors forfeit their principal if any of six deadly viruses such as Ebola reach a specified contagion level. The bonds raise money for the World Bank's efforts to fight potential pandemics, but they relieve the Bank of its payment burden if it is overwhelmed with expenses from disease outbreaks.

These bonds are a way to transfer "catastrophe risk" from insurance companies to the capital markets. Investors in these bonds receive compensation in the form of higher coupon rates for taking on the risk. But in the event of a catastrophe, the bondholders will lose all or part of their investments. "Disaster" can be defined either by total insured losses or by specific criteria such as wind speed in a hurricane, Richter level in an earthquake, or contagion level as in the pandemic bonds. Issuance of catastrophe bonds has grown in recent years as insurers have sought ways to spread their risks across a wider spectrum of the capital market. Approximately $30 billion of various catastrophe bonds were outstanding in 2017.

INDEXED BONDS   Indexed bonds make payments that are tied to a general price index or the price of a particular commodity. For example, Mexico has issued bonds with payments that depend on the price of oil. Some bonds are indexed to the general price level. The United States Treasury started issuing such inflation-indexed bonds in January 1997. They are called Treasury Inflation Protected Securities (TIPS). By tying the par value of the bond to the general level of prices, coupon payments, as well as the final repayment of par value, on these bonds increase in direct proportion to the consumer price index. Therefore, the interest rate on these bonds is a risk-free real rate.

To illustrate how TIPS work, consider a newly issued bond with a three-year maturity, par value of $1,000, and a coupon rate of 4%. For simplicity, we will assume the bond makes annual coupon payments. Assume that inflation turns out to be 2%, 3%, and 1% in the next three years. Table 10.1 shows how the bond cash flows will be calculated. The first payment comes at the end of the first year, at $t = 1$. Because inflation over the year was 2%, the par value of the bond increases from $1,000 to $1,020. The coupon payment is therefore .04 × $1,020 = $40.80. Notice that principal value increases by the inflation rate, and because the coupon payments are 4% of principal, they too increase in proportion to the general price level. Therefore, the cash flows paid by the bond are fixed in *real* terms. When the bond matures, the investor receives a final coupon payment of $42.44 plus the (price-level-indexed) repayment of principal, $1,061.11.[4]

---

[4]By the way, total nominal income (i.e., coupon plus that year's increase in principal) is treated as taxable income in each year.

The *nominal* rate of return on the bond in the first year is

$$\text{Nominal return} = \frac{\text{Interest} + \text{Price appreciation}}{\text{Initial price}} = \frac{40.80 + 20}{1,000} = 6.08\%$$

The real rate of return is precisely the 4% real yield on the bond:

$$\text{Real return} = \frac{1 + \text{Nominal return}}{1 + \text{Inflation}} - 1 = \frac{1.0608}{1.02} - 1 = .04, \text{ or } 4\%$$

One can show in a similar manner (see Problem 19 in the end-of-chapter questions) that the rate of return in each of the three years is 4% as long as the real yield on the bond remains constant. If real yields do change, then there will be capital gains or losses on the bond. In early 2018, the real yield on TIPS bonds with 30-year maturity was a shade below 1%.

10.2 BOND PRICING

A bond's coupon and principal repayments all occur months or years in the future. Therefore, the price an investor is willing to pay for them depends on the value of dollars to be received in the future compared to dollars in hand today. This "present value" calculation depends in turn on market interest rates. As we saw in Chapter 5, the nominal risk-free interest rate equals the sum of (1) a real risk-free rate of return and (2) a premium above the real rate to compensate for expected inflation. In addition, because most bonds are not riskless, the discount rate will embody an additional premium that reflects bond-specific characteristics such as default risk, liquidity, tax attributes, call risk, and so on.

We simplify for now by assuming there is one interest rate that is appropriate for discounting cash flows of any maturity, but we can relax this assumption easily. In practice, there may be different discount rates for cash flows accruing in different periods. For the time being, however, we ignore this refinement.

To value a security, we discount its expected cash flows by the appropriate discount rate. Bond cash flows consist of coupon payments until the maturity date plus the final payment of par value. Therefore

$$\text{Bond value} = \text{Present value of coupons} + \text{Present value of par value}$$

If we call the maturity date T and call the discount rate r, the bond value can be written as

$$\text{Bond value} = \sum_{t=1}^{T} \frac{\text{Coupon}}{(1+r)^t} + \frac{\text{Par value}}{(1+r)^T} \tag{10.1}$$

The summation sign in Equation 10.1 directs us to add the present value of each coupon payment; each coupon is discounted based on the time until it will be paid. The first term on the right-hand side of Equation 10.1 is the present value of an annuity. The second term is the present value of a single amount, the final payment of the bond's par value.

You may recall from an introductory finance class that the present value of a $1 annuity that lasts for T periods when the interest rate equals r is $\frac{1}{r}\left[1 - \frac{1}{(1+r)^T}\right]$. We call this expression the T-period *annuity factor* for an interest rate of r.[5] Similarly, we call $\frac{1}{(1+r)^T}$

---

[5]Here is a quick derivation of the formula for the present value of an annuity. An annuity lasting T periods can be viewed as an equivalent to a perpetuity whose first payment comes at the end of the current period *less* another perpetuity whose first payment doesn't come until the end of period $T+1$. The immediate perpetuity net of the delayed perpetuity provides exactly T payments. We know that the value of a $1 per period perpetuity is $1/r$. Therefore, the present value of the delayed perpetuity is $1/r$ discounted for T additional periods, or $\frac{1}{r} \times \frac{1}{(1+r)^T}$. The present value of the annuity is the present value of the first perpetuity minus the present value of the delayed perpetuity, or $\frac{1}{r}\left[1 - \frac{1}{(1+r)^T}\right]$.

the *PV factor*, that is, the present value of a single payment of $1 to be received in T periods. Therefore, we can write the price of the bond as

$$\text{Price} = \text{Coupon} \times \frac{1}{r}\left[1 - \frac{1}{(1+r)^T}\right] + \text{Par value} \times \frac{1}{(1+r)^T} \quad \text{(10.2)}$$

$$= \text{Coupon} \times \text{Annuity factor}(r, T) + \text{Par value} \times \text{PV factor}(r, T)$$

EXAMPLE 10.2

Bond Pricing

We discussed earlier an 8% coupon, 30-year maturity bond with par value of $1,000 paying 60 semi-annual coupon payments of $40 each. Suppose that the interest rate is 8% annually, or $r = 4\%$ per six-month period. Then the value of the bond can be written as

$$\text{Price} = \sum_{t=1}^{60} \frac{\$40}{(1.04)^t} + \frac{\$1,000}{(1.04)^{60}}$$

$$= \$40 \times \text{Annuity factor}(4\%, 60) + \$1,000 \times \text{PV factor}(4\%, 60)$$

It is easy to confirm that the present value of the bond's 60 semiannual coupon payments of $40 each is $904.94 and that the $1,000 final payment of par value has a present value of $95.06, for a total bond value of $1,000. You can calculate this value directly from Equation 10.2, perform these calculations on any financial calculator (see Example 10.3), use a spreadsheet (see Column F of Spreadsheet 10.1), or a set of present value tables.

In this example, the coupon rate equals the market interest rate, and the bond price equals par value. If the interest rate were not equal to the bond's coupon rate, the bond would not sell at par. For example, if the interest rate rises to 10% (5% per six months), the bond's price will fall by $189.29, to $810.71, as follows:

$$\$40 \times \text{Annuity factor}(5\%, 60) + \$1,000 \times \text{PV factor}(5\%, 60)$$
$$= \$757.17 + \$53.54 = \$810.71$$

At a higher interest rate, the present value of the payments is lower. Therefore, bond prices fall as market interest rates rise. This illustrates a crucial general rule in bond valuation.[6]

Bond prices are tedious to calculate without a spreadsheet or financial calculator, but they are easy to calculate with either. Financial calculators designed with present value and future value formulas already programmed can greatly simplify calculations of the sort we just encountered in Example 10.2. The basic financial calculator uses five keys that correspond to the inputs for time-value-of-money problems such as bond pricing:

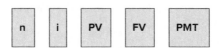

- *n* is the number of time periods. For a bond, *n* equals the number of periods until maturity. If the bond makes semiannual payments, *n* is the number of half-year periods or, equivalently, the number of semiannual coupon payments. For example, if the bond has 10 years until maturity, you would enter 20 for *n* because each payment period is one-half year.
- *i* is the interest rate per period, expressed as a percentage (not as a decimal, which is required by spreadsheet programs). For example, if the interest rate is 6%, you would enter 6, not .06.
- *PV* is the present value. Many calculators require that PV be entered as a negative number, because the purchase of the bond entails a cash *outflow*, while the receipt of coupon payments and face value are cash *inflows*.
- *FV* is the future value or face value of the bond. In general, FV is interpreted as a one-time future payment of a cash flow, which, for bonds, is the face (i.e., par) value.

---

[6]Here is a trap to avoid: You should not confuse the bond's *coupon* rate, which determines the interest paid to the bondholder, with the market interest rate. Once a bond is issued, its coupon rate is fixed. When the *market* interest rate increases, investors discount any fixed payments at a higher discount rate, which means present values, and bond prices fall.

- *PMT* is the amount of any recurring payment. For coupon bonds, PMT is the coupon payment; for zero-coupon bonds, PMT will be zero.

Given any four of these inputs, the calculator will solve for the fifth.

EXAMPLE 10.3

Bond Pricing on a Financial Calculator

We can illustrate how to use a financial calculator with the bond in Example 10.2. To find its price when the annual market interest rate is 8%, you would enter these inputs (in any order):

n	60	The bond has a maturity of 30 years, so it makes 60 semiannual payments.
i	4	The *semiannual* interest rate is 4%.
FV	1,000	The bond will provide a one-time cash flow of $1,000 when it matures.
PMT	40	Each semiannual coupon payment is $40.

On most calculators, you now punch the "compute" key (labeled "*COMP*" or "*CPT*") and then enter PV to obtain the bond price, that is, the present value today of the bond's cash flows. If you do this, you should find a value of −1,000. The negative sign signifies that while the investor receives cash flows from the bond, the price paid to *buy* the bond is a cash *out*flow, or a negative cash flow.

If you want to find the value of the bond when the interest rate is 10% (the second part of Example 10.2), just enter 5% for the semiannual interest rate (type "5" and then "*i*"), and then when you compute PV, you will find that it is −810.71.

Figure 10.3 shows the price of the 30-year, 8% coupon bond for a range of interest rates including 8%, at which the bond sells at par, and 10%, at which it sells for $810.71. The negative slope illustrates the inverse relationship between prices and yields. The shape of the curve in Figure 10.3 implies that an increase in the interest rate results in a price decline that is smaller than the price gain resulting from a decrease of equal magnitude in the interest rate. This property of bond prices is called *convexity* because of the convex shape of the bond price curve. This curvature reflects the fact that progressive increases in the interest rate result in progressively smaller reductions in the bond price.[7] Therefore, the price curve becomes flatter at higher interest rates. We will return to convexity in the next chapter.

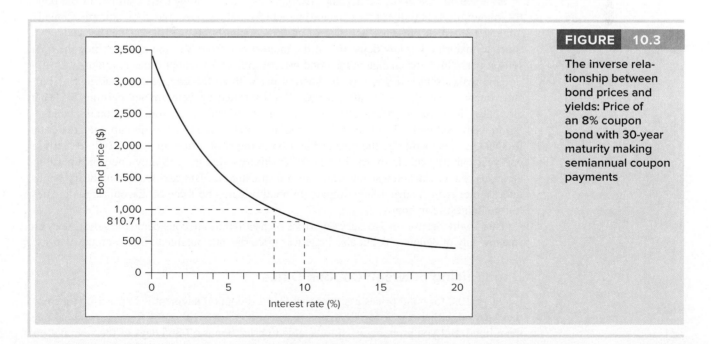

FIGURE 10.3

The inverse relationship between bond prices and yields: Price of an 8% coupon bond with 30-year maturity making semiannual coupon payments

[7]The progressively smaller impact of interest rate increases results largely from the fact that at higher rates the bond is worth less. Therefore, an additional increase in rates operates on a smaller initial base, resulting in a smaller price reduction.

TABLE 10.2   Bond prices at different interest rates (8% coupon bond, coupons paid semiannually)

Time to Maturity	Bond Price at Given Market Interest Rate				
	2%	4%	6%	8%	10%
1 year	$1,059.11	$1,038.83	$1,019.13	$1,000.00	$981.41
10 years	1,541.37	1,327.03	1,148.77	1,000.00	875.38
20 years	1,985.04	1,547.11	1,231.15	1,000.00	828.41
30 years	2,348.65	1,695.22	1,276.76	1,000.00	810.71

CONCEPT check 10.2

Calculate the price of the bond if the market interest rate falls from 4% to 3% per half-year. Compare the capital gains for the fall in the interest rate to the capital losses incurred when the rate increases from 4% to 5%.

Corporate bonds typically are issued at par value. This means the underwriters of the bond issue (the firms that market the bonds to the public for the issuing corporation) must choose a coupon rate that very closely approximates market yields. If the coupon rate is inadequate, investors will not pay par value for the bonds.

After the bonds are issued, bondholders may buy or sell bonds in secondary markets. In these markets, bond prices fluctuate inversely with the market interest rate.

The inverse relationship between price and yield is a central feature of fixed-income securities. Interest rate fluctuations represent the main source of risk in the bond market, and we devote considerable attention in the next chapter to assessing the sensitivity of bond prices to market yields. For now, however, we simply highlight one key factor that determines that sensitivity, namely, the maturity of the bond.

As a general rule, keeping all other factors the same, the longer the maturity of the bond, the greater the sensitivity of its price to fluctuations in the interest rate. For example, consider Table 10.2, which presents the price of an 8% coupon bond at different market yields and times to maturity. For any departure of the interest rate from 8% (the rate at which the bond sells at par value), the change in the bond price is greater for longer times to maturity.

This makes sense. If you buy the bond at par with an 8% coupon rate, and market rates subsequently rise, then you suffer a loss: You have tied up your money earning 8% when alternative investments offer higher returns. This is reflected in a capital loss on the bond—a fall in its market price. The longer the period for which your money is tied up, the greater the loss and, correspondingly, the greater the drop in the bond price. In Table 10.2, the row for one-year maturity bonds shows little price sensitivity—that is, with only one year's earnings at stake, changes in interest rates are not too threatening. But for 30-year maturity bonds, interest rate swings have a large impact on bond prices. The force of discounting is greatest for the longest-term bonds.

This is why short-term Treasury securities such as T-bills are considered the safest. They are free not only of default risk but also largely of price risk attributable to interest rate volatility.

Bond Pricing between Coupon Dates

Equation 10.2 for bond prices assumes that the next coupon payment is in precisely one payment period, either a year for an annual payment bond or six months for a semiannual payment bond. But you probably want to be able to price bonds all 365 days of the year, not just on the one or two dates each year that it makes a coupon payment!

In principle, the fact that the bond is between coupon dates does not affect the pricing problem. The procedure is always the same: Compute the present value of each remaining payment and sum up. But if you are between coupon dates, there will be fractional periods remaining until each payment, and this does complicate the arithmetic computations.

Fortunately, bond pricing functions are included in many financial calculators and spreadsheet programs such as Excel. The spreadsheets allow you to enter today's date as well as the maturity date of the bond and so can provide prices for bonds at any date.

As we pointed out earlier, bond prices are typically quoted net of accrued interest. These prices, which appear in the financial press, are called *flat prices*. The actual *invoice price* that a buyer pays for the bond includes accrued interest. Thus,

$$\text{Invoice price} = \text{Flat price} + \text{Accrued interest}$$

When a bond pays its coupon, flat price equals invoice price because at that moment accrued interest reverts to zero. However, this will be the exceptional case, not the rule.

Excel pricing functions provide the flat price of the bond. To find the invoice price, we need to add accrued interest. Excel also provides functions that count the days since the last coupon payment and thus can be used to compute accrued interest. Spreadsheet 10.1 illustrates how to use these functions. The spreadsheet provides examples using bonds that have just paid a coupon and so have zero accrued interest, as well as a bond that is between coupon dates.

Bond Pricing in Excel

Excel asks you to input both the date you buy the bond (called the *settlement date*) and the maturity date of the bond.

The Excel function for bond price is

= PRICE (settlement date, maturity date, annual coupon rate, yield to maturity, redemption value as percent of par value, number of coupon payments per year)

For the 3% coupon February 2047 maturity bond highlighted in Figure 10.1, we would enter the values in Spreadsheet 10.1, Column B. Alternatively, we could simply enter the following function in Excel:

= PRICE(DATE(2017,2,15), DATE(2047,2,15), .03, .03088, 100, 2)

The DATE function in Excel, which we use for both the settlement and maturity dates, uses the format DATE(year,month,day). The first date is February 15, 2017, when the bond is purchased, and the second is February 15, 2047, when it matures.

Notice that the coupon rate and yield to maturity in Excel must be expressed as decimals, not percentages (as they would be in financial calculators). In most cases, redemption value is 100 (i.e., 100% of par value), and the resulting price similarly is expressed as a percent of par

---

SPREADSHEET 10.1

Valuing Bonds Using a Spreadsheet

	A	B	C	D	E	F	G
1		3% coupon bond,		3.75% coupon bond,		8% coupon bond,	
2		maturing Feb 2047	Formula in column B	maturing November 2043		30-year maturity	
3							
4	Settlement date	2/15/2017	=DATE(2017,2,15)	2/15/2017		1/1/2000	
5	Maturity date	2/15/2047	=DATE(2047,2,15)	11/15/2043		1/1/2030	
6	Annual coupon rate	0.03		0.0375		0.08	
7	Yield to maturity	0.03088		0.03065		0.1	
8	Redemption value (% of face value)	100		100		100	
9	Coupon payments per year	2		2		2	
10							
11							
12	Flat price (% of par)	98.2867	=PRICE(B4,B5,B6,B7,B8,B9)	112.4398		81.0707	
13	Days since last coupon	0	=COUPDAYBS(B4,B5,2,1)	92		0	
14	Days in coupon period	181	=COUPDAYS(B4,B5,2,1)	181		182	
15	Accrued interest	0	=(B13/B14)*B6*100/2	0.953		0	
16	Invoice price	98.2867	=B12+B15	113.3928		81.0707	

X

Spreadsheets are available in Connect

value. Occasionally, however, you may encounter bonds that pay off at a premium or discount to par value. One example would be callable bonds, discussed shortly.

The value of the bond returned by the pricing function is 98.2867 (cell B12), which is within 1 cent of the price reported in *The Wall Street Journal*. (The yield to maturity is reported to only three decimal places, which induces some rounding error.) This bond has just paid a coupon. In other words, the settlement date is precisely at the beginning of the coupon period, so no adjustment for accrued interest is necessary.

To illustrate the procedure for bonds between coupon payments, let's apply the spreadsheet to the 3.75% coupon November 2043 bond which also appears in Figure 10.1. Using the entries in column D of the spreadsheet, we find in cell D12 that the (flat) price of the bond is 112.4398, which, except for minor rounding error, matches the price given in *The Wall Street Journal*.

What about the bond's invoice price? Rows 12 through 16 make the necessary adjustments. The function described in cell C13 counts the days since the last coupon. This day count is based on the bond's settlement date, maturity date, coupon period (1 = annual; 2 = semiannual), and day count convention (choice 1 uses actual days). The function described in cell C14 counts the total days in each coupon payment period. Therefore, the entries for accrued interest in row 15 are the semiannual coupon multiplied by the fraction of a coupon period that has elapsed since the last payment. Finally, the invoice prices in row 16 are the sum of flat price plus accrued interest.

As a final example, suppose you wish to find the price of the bond in Example 10.2. It is a 30-year maturity bond with a coupon rate of 8% (paid semiannually). The market interest rate given in the latter part of the example is 10%. However, you are not given a specific settlement or maturity date. You can still use the PRICE function to value the bond. Simply choose an *arbitrary* settlement date (January 1, 2000, is convenient) and let the maturity date be 30 years hence. The appropriate inputs appear in column F of the spreadsheet, with the resulting price, 81.071% of face value, appearing in cell F16.

10.3   BOND YIELDS

Most bonds do not sell for par value. But ultimately, barring default, they will mature to par value. Therefore, we would like a measure of rate of return that accounts for coupon income as well as the price increase or decrease over the bond's life. The yield to maturity is the standard measure of the total rate of return. However, it is far from perfect, and we will explore several variations of this measure.

Yield to Maturity

yield to maturity (YTM)

The discount rate that makes the present value of a bond's payments equal to its price.

In practice, investors considering the purchase of a bond are not quoted a promised rate of return. Instead, they must use the bond price, maturity date, and coupon payments to infer the return offered over the life of the bond. The **yield to maturity (YTM)** is defined as the discount rate that makes the present value of a bond's payments equal to its price. It is often viewed as a measure of the average rate of return that will be earned on a bond if it is bought now and held until maturity. To calculate the yield to maturity, we solve the bond price equation for the interest rate given the bond's price.

EXAMPLE 10.4

Yield to Maturity

Suppose an 8% coupon, 30-year bond is selling at $1,276.76. What average rate of return would be earned by an investor purchasing the bond at this price? We find the interest rate at which the present value of the remaining 60 semiannual payments equals the bond price. Therefore, we solve for r in the following equation:

$$\$1,276.76 = \sum_{t=1}^{60} \frac{\$40}{(1+r)^t} + \frac{\$1,000}{(1+r)^{60}}$$

(continued)

or, equivalently,

$$1{,}276.76 = 40 \times \text{Annuity factor}(r, 60) + 1{,}000 \times \text{PV factor}(r, 60)$$

These equations have only one unknown variable, the interest rate, r. You can use a financial calculator or spreadsheet to confirm that the solution is $r = .03$, or 3% per half-year.[8] This is the bond's yield to maturity.

The financial press reports yields on an annualized basis. It annualizes the bond's semiannual yield using simple interest techniques, resulting in an annual percentage rate or APR. Yields annualized using simple interest are also called *bond equivalent yields*. Therefore, this bond's semiannual yield would be doubled and reported in the newspaper as a bond equivalent yield of 6%.

The *effective* annual yield of the bond, however, accounts for compound interest. If one earns 3% interest every six months, then after one year, each dollar invested grows with interest to $1 \times (1.03)^2 = 1.0609$, and the effective annual interest rate on the bond is 6.09%.

EXAMPLE 10.4

Yield to Maturity (concluded)

In Example 10.4, we noted that a financial calculator or spreadsheet can be used to find the yield to maturity on the coupon bond. Here are two examples demonstrating how you can use these tools. Example 10.5 illustrates the use of financial calculators while Example 10.6 uses Excel.

Consider the yield to maturity problem in Example 10.4. On a financial calculator, we would enter the following inputs (in any order):

n	60	The bond has a maturity of 30 years, so it makes 60 semiannual payments.
PMT	40	Each semiannual coupon payment is $40.
PV	(−)1,276.76	The bond can be purchased for $1,276.76, which on some calculators must be entered as a negative number as it is a cash outflow.
FV	1,000	The bond will provide a one-time cash flow of $1,000 when it matures.

Given these inputs, you now use the calculator to find the interest rate at which $1,276.76 actually equals the present value of the 60 payments of $40 each plus the one-time payment of $1,000 at maturity. On some calculators, you first punch the "compute" key (labeled "*COMP*" or "*CPT*") and then enter i to have the interest rate computed. You should find that $i = 3$, or 3% semiannually, as we claimed. (Notice that just as the cash flows are paid semiannually, the computed interest rate is a rate per semiannual time period.) The bond equivalent yield will be reported in the financial press as 6%.

EXAMPLE 10.5

Finding Yield to Maturity Using a Financial Calculator

Excel also contains built-in functions to compute yield to maturity. The following example, along with Spreadsheet 10.2, illustrates.

Excel's function for yield to maturity is

=YIELD(settlement date, maturity date, annual coupon rate, bond price, redemption value as percent of par value, number of coupon payments per year)

The bond price used in the function should be the reported, or "flat," price, without accrued interest. For example, to find the yield to maturity of the bond in Example 10.5, we would use column B of Spreadsheet 10.2. If the coupons were paid only annually, we would change the entry for payments per year to 1 (see cell D8), and the yield would fall slightly to 5.99%.

EXAMPLE 10.6

Finding Yield to Maturity Using Excel

The yield to maturity is the internal rate of return on an investment in the bond. It can be interpreted as the compound rate of return over the life of the bond under the assumption that all bond coupons can be reinvested at that yield,[9] and is therefore widely accepted as a proxy for average return.

[8]Without a financial calculator or spreadsheet, you still could solve the equation, but you would need to use a trial-and-error approach.

[9]If the reinvestment rate does not equal the bond's yield to maturity, the compound rate of return will differ from YTM. This is demonstrated below in Example 10.8.

SPREADSHEET 10.2

Finding Yield to Maturity Using a Spreadsheet (30-year maturity bond, coupon rate = 8%, price = 100% of par)

Spreadsheets are
available in Connect

	A	B	C	D
1		Semiannual coupons		Annual coupons
2				
3	Settlement date	1/1/2000		1/1/2000
4	Maturity date	1/1/2030		1/1/2030
5	Annual coupon rate	0.08		0.08
6	Bond price (flat)	127.676		127.676
7	Redemption value (% of face value)	100		100
8	Coupon payments per year	2		1
9				
10	**Yield to maturity (decimal)**	0.0600		0.0599

The formula entered here is =YIELD(B3,B4,B5,B6,B7,B8)

current yield

Annual coupon divided by
bond price.

Yield to maturity differs from the **current yield** of a bond, which is the bond's annual coupon payment divided by its price. The current yield of the 8%, 30-year bond selling at $1,276.76 is $80/$1,276.76 = .0627, or 6.27% per year. In contrast, we just saw that the effective annual yield to maturity is 6.09%. For this bond, which is selling at a premium over par value ($1,276 rather than $1,000), the coupon rate (8%) exceeds the current yield (6.27%), which exceeds the yield to maturity (6.09%). The coupon rate exceeds current yield because the coupon rate divides the coupon payments by par value ($1,000), which is less than the bond price ($1,276). In turn, the current yield exceeds yield to maturity because the yield to maturity accounts for the built-in capital loss on the bond; the bond bought today for $1,276 will eventually fall in value to $1,000 at maturity.

premium bonds

Bonds selling above par value.

discount bonds

Bonds selling below par value.

This example illustrates a general rule: For **premium bonds** (bonds selling above par value), coupon rate is greater than current yield, which in turn is greater than yield to maturity. For **discount bonds** (bonds selling below par value), these relationships are reversed (see Concept Check 10.3).

It is common to hear people talking loosely about the yield on a bond. In these cases, they almost always are referring to the yield to maturity.

CONCEPT
check 10.3

What will be the relationship among coupon rate, current yield, and yield to maturity for bonds selling at discounts from par? Illustrate using the 30-year 8% (semiannual payment) coupon bond assuming it is selling at a yield to maturity of 10%.

Yield to Call

Yield to maturity is calculated on the assumption that the bond will be held until maturity. What if the bond is callable, however, and may be retired prior to the maturity date?

Figure 10.4 illustrates the risk of call to the bondholder. The colored line is the value of a "straight" (that is, noncallable) bond with par value of $1,000, an 8% coupon rate, and a 30-year time to maturity as a function of the market interest rate. If interest rates fall, the bond price, which equals the present value of the promised payments, can rise substantially. Now consider a bond that has the same coupon rate and maturity date but is callable at 110% of par value, or $1,100. When interest rates fall, the present value of the bond's *scheduled* payments rises, but the call provision allows the issuer to repurchase the bond at the call price. If the call price is less than the present value of the scheduled payments, the issuer can call the bond at the expense of the bondholder.

The dark line in Figure 10.4 is the value of the callable bond. At high market interest rates, the risk of call is negligible because the present value of scheduled payments is substantially less than the call price; therefore, the values of the straight and callable bonds converge. At lower rates, however, the values of the bonds begin to diverge, with the difference reflecting

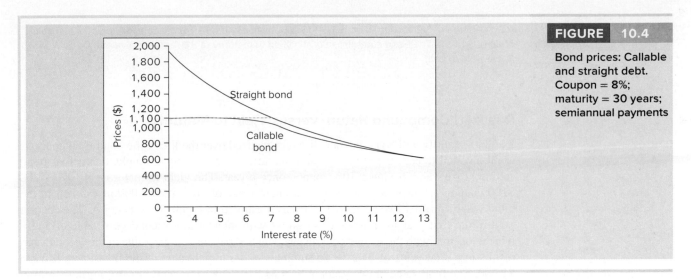

FIGURE 10.4

Bond prices: Callable
and straight debt.
Coupon = 8%;
maturity = 30 years;
semiannual payments

the value of the firm's option to reclaim the callable bond at the call price. At very low market
rates the present value of scheduled payments significantly exceeds the call price, so the bond
is called. Its value at this point is simply the call price, $1,100.

This analysis suggests that investors might be more interested in a bond's yield to call than
its yield to maturity, especially if the bond is likely to be called. The yield to call is calculated
just like the yield to maturity, except that the time until call replaces time until maturity and
the call price replaces the par value. This computation is sometimes called "yield to first call,"
as it assumes the issuer will call the bond as soon as it may do so.

Suppose the 8% coupon, 30-year maturity bond sells for $1,150 and is callable in 10 years at a call
price of $1,100. Its yield to maturity and yield to call would be calculated using the following inputs:

EXAMPLE 10.7

Yield to Call

	Yield to Call	Yield to Maturity
Coupon payment	$40	$40
Number of semiannual periods	20 periods	60 periods
Final payment	$1,100	$1,000
Price	$1,150	$1,150

Yield to call is then 6.64%. To confirm this on your calculator, input $n = 20$; PV = (−)1150; FV =
1100; PMT = 40; compute i as 3.32%, or 6.64% bond equivalent yield. In contrast, yield to maturity
is 6.82%. To confirm, input $n = 60$; PV = (−)1150; FV = 1000; PMT = 40; compute i as 3.41%, or
6.82% bond equivalent yield. In Excel, you can calculate yield to call as =YIELD(DATE(2000,1,1),
DATE(2010,1,1), .08, 115, 110, 2). Notice that redemption value is 110, that is, 110% of par value.

While most callable bonds are issued with an initial period of explicit call protection, an
additional implicit form of call protection operates for bonds selling at deep discounts from
their call prices. Even if interest rates fall a bit, deep-discount bonds still will sell below the
call price and thus will not be vulnerable to a call.

Premium bonds that might be selling near their call prices are especially apt to be called
if rates fall further. If interest rates fall, a callable premium bond is likely to provide a lower
return than could be earned on a discount bond whose potential price appreciation is not
limited by the likelihood of a call. This is why investors in premium bonds may be most interested in its yield to call.

A 20-year maturity 9% coupon bond paying coupons semiannually is callable in five years at a call price of $1,050. The bond currently sells at a yield to maturity of 8% (bond equivalent yield). What is the yield to call?

Realized Compound Return versus Yield to Maturity

Yield to maturity will equal the rate of return realized over the life of the bond if all coupons are reinvested to earn the bond's yield to maturity. Consider, for example, a two-year bond selling at par value paying a 10% coupon once a year. The yield to maturity is 10%. If the $100 coupon payment is reinvested at an interest rate of 10%, the $1,000 investment in the bond will grow after two years to $1,210, as illustrated in Figure 10.5, Panel A. The coupon paid in the first year is reinvested and grows with interest to a second-year value of $110, which, together with the second coupon payment and payment of par value in the second year, results in a total value of $1,210. To summarize, the initial value of the investment is $V_0 = \$1,000$. The final value in two years is $V_2 = \$1,210$. The compound rate of return, therefore, is calculated as follows.

$$V_0(1 + r)^2 = V_2$$
$$\$1,000(1 + r)^2 = \$1,210$$
$$r = .10 = 10\%$$

realized compound return

Compound rate of return on a bond with all coupons reinvested until maturity.

With a reinvestment rate equal to the 10% yield to maturity, the **realized compound return** also equals yield to maturity.

But what if the reinvestment rate is not 10%? If the coupon can be invested at more than 10%, funds will grow to more than $1,210, and the realized compound return will exceed 10%. If the reinvestment rate is less than 10%, so will be the realized compound return. Consider the following example.

EXAMPLE 10.8

Realized Compound Return

Suppose the interest rate at which the coupon can be invested is only 8%. The following calculations are illustrated in Panel B of Figure 10.5.

Future value of first coupon payment with interest earnings	$100 × 1.08 = $ 108
Cash payment in second year (final coupon plus par value)	1,100
Total value of investment with reinvested coupons	$1,208

The realized compound return is the compound rate of growth of invested funds, assuming that all coupon payments are reinvested. The investor purchased the bond for par at $1,000, and the investment grew to $1,208. So the realized compound yield is less than 10%:

$$\$1,000(1 + r)^2 = \$1,208$$
$$r = .0991 = 9.91\%$$

Example 10.8 highlights the problem with conventional yield to maturity when reinvestment rates can change over time. However, in an economy with future interest rate uncertainty, the rates at which interim coupons will be reinvested are not yet known. Therefore, while realized compound return can be computed *after* the investment period ends, it cannot be computed in advance without a forecast of future reinvestment rates. This reduces much of the attraction of the realized return measure.

horizon analysis

Analysis of bond returns over a multiyear horizon, based on forecasts of the bond's yield to maturity and the reinvestment rate of coupons.

We also can calculate realized compound yield over holding periods greater than one period. This is called **horizon analysis** and is similar to the procedure in Example 10.8. The forecast of total return depends on your forecasts of *both* the bond's yield to maturity when you sell it *and*

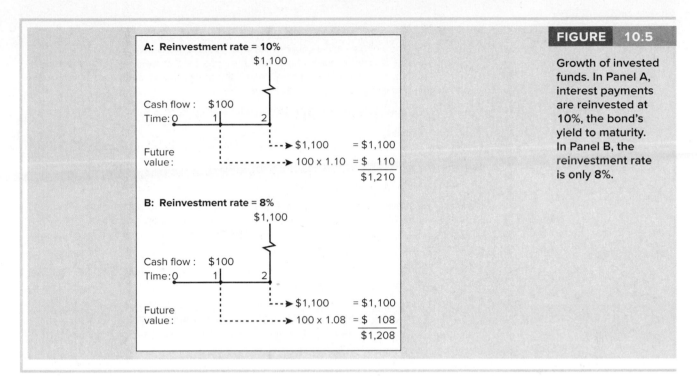

FIGURE 10.5

Growth of invested funds. In Panel A, interest payments are reinvested at 10%, the bond's yield to maturity. In Panel B, the reinvestment rate is only 8%.

the rate at which you are able to reinvest coupon income. With a longer investment horizon, however, reinvested coupons will be a larger component of final proceeds.

> Suppose you buy a 30-year, 7.5% (annual payment) coupon bond for $980 (when its yield to maturity is 7.67%) and you plan to hold it for 20 years. You forecast that the bond's yield to maturity will be 8% when it is sold and that the reinvestment rate on the coupons will be 6%. At the end of your investment horizon, the bond will have 10 years remaining until maturity, so the forecast sales price (using a yield to maturity of 8%) is $966.45. The 20 coupon payments will grow with compound interest to $2,758.92. (This is the future value of a 20-year $75 annuity with an interest rate of 6%.)
> Based on these forecasts, your $980 investment will grow in 20 years to $966.45 + $2,758.92 = $3,725.37. This corresponds to an annualized compound return of 6.90%:
>
> $$\$980(1+r)^{20} = \$3,725.37$$
> $$r = .0690 = 6.90\%$$

EXAMPLE 10.9

Horizon Analysis

Examples 10.8 and 10.9 demonstrate that as interest rates change, bond investors are subject to two offsetting sources of risk. On the one hand, when rates rise, bond prices fall, which reduces the value of the portfolio. On the other hand, reinvested coupon income will compound more rapidly at those higher rates. This **reinvestment rate risk** will offset price risk. In the next chapter, we will explore this trade-off in more detail and will discover that by carefully tailoring their bond portfolios, investors can precisely balance these two effects for any given investment horizon.

reinvestment rate risk
Uncertainty surrounding the cumulative future value of reinvested bond coupon payments.

10.4 BOND PRICES OVER TIME

A bond will sell at par value when its coupon rate equals the market interest rate. In these circumstances, the investor receives fair compensation for the time value of money in the form of the recurring coupon payments. No further capital gain is necessary to provide fair compensation.

When the coupon rate is lower than the market interest rate, the coupon payments alone will not provide bond investors as high a return as they could earn elsewhere. To receive a competitive return, they also need some price appreciation. The bonds, therefore, must sell below par value to provide a "built-in" capital gain on the investment.

EXAMPLE 10.10

Fair Holding-Period Return

To illustrate built-in capital gains or losses, suppose a bond was issued several years ago when the interest rate was 7%. The bond's annual coupon rate was thus set at 7%. (We suppose for simplicity that the bond pays its coupon annually.) Now, with three years left in the bond's life, the market interest rate is 8% per year. The bond's fair market price is the present value of the remaining annual coupons plus payment of par value. That present value is[10]

$$\$70 \times \text{Annuity factor}(8\%, 3) + \$1,000 \times \text{PV factor}(8\%, 3) = \$974.23$$

which is less than par value.

In another year, after the next coupon is paid and remaining maturity falls to two years, the bond will sell at

$$\$70 \times \text{Annuity factor}(8\%, 2) + \$1,000 \times \text{PV factor}(8\%, 2) = \$982.17$$

thereby providing a capital gain over the year of $7.94. If an investor had purchased the bond at $974.23, the total return over the year would equal the coupon payment plus capital gain, or $70 + $7.94 = $77.94. This represents a rate of return of $77.94/$974.23, or 8%, exactly the current rate of return available elsewhere in the market.

CONCEPT check 10.5

What will be the price of the bond in Example 10.10 in yet another year, when only one year remains until maturity? What is the rate of return to an investor who purchases the bond at $982.17 and sells it one year later?

When bond prices are set according to the present value formula, any discount from par value provides an anticipated capital gain that will augment a below-market coupon rate by just enough to provide a fair total rate of return. Conversely, if the coupon rate exceeds the market interest rate, the interest income by itself is greater than that available elsewhere in the market. Investors will bid up the bond price above par value. As the bond approaches maturity, its price will fall because fewer of these above-market coupon payments remain. The resulting capital loss offsets the large coupon payments so that the bondholder again receives only a competitive rate of return.

Problem 16 at the end of the chapter asks you to work through the case of the high-coupon bond. Figure 10.6 traces out the prices (net of accrued interest) of two bonds, a "premium bond" with a coupon above the yield to maturity and a "discount bond" with a coupon rate below yield to maturity. The low-coupon bond enjoys capital gains as price steadily approaches par value, while the high-coupon bond suffers capital losses.[11]

We use these examples to show that each bond offers investors the same total rate of return. Although the capital gains versus income components differ, the price of each bond is set to provide competitive rates, as we should expect in well-functioning capital markets. Security returns all should be comparable on an after-tax risk-adjusted basis. If they are not, investors will try to sell low-return securities, thereby driving down their prices until the total return at the now-lower price is competitive with other securities. Prices should continue to adjust until all securities are fairly priced in that expected returns are comparable (given appropriate risk and tax adjustments).

We see evidence of this price adjustment in Figure 10.1. Compare the two bonds maturing in February 2026. One has a coupon rate of 1.625%, while the other's coupon rate is much higher, 6%. But the higher coupon rate on that bond does not mean that it offers a higher return; instead, it sells at a higher price. The yields to maturity on the two bonds are nearly

[10]Using a calculator, enter $n = 3$, $i = 8$, PM$T = 70$, F$V = 1000$, and compute PV.

[11]We assume in the figure that the market interest rate is constant. If interest rates are volatile, the price path will be "jumpy," vibrating around the price path in Figure 10.6 and reflecting capital gains or losses as interest rates fluctuate. Ultimately, however, the price must reach par value at the maturity date, so, on average, the price of the premium bond will fall over time while that of the discount bond will rise.

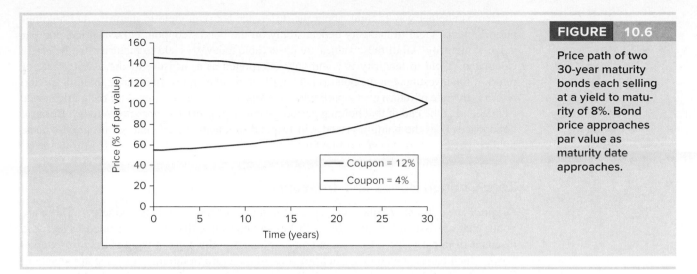

FIGURE 10.6

Price path of two 30-year maturity bonds each selling at a yield to maturity of 8%. Bond price approaches par value as maturity date approaches.

equal, both around 2.5%. This makes sense because investors should care about their total return, including both coupon income as well as price change. In the end, prices of similar-maturity bonds adjust until yields are pretty much equalized.

Of course, the yields across bonds in Figure 10.1 are not all precisely equal. Clearly, longer-term bonds at this time offered higher promised yields, a common pattern, and one that reflects the relative risks of the bonds. We will explore the relationship between yield and time to maturity later in the chapter.

Yield to Maturity versus Holding-Period Return

In Example 10.10, the holding-period return and the yield to maturity were equal. The bond yield started and ended the year at 8%, and the bond's holding-period return also equaled 8%. This turns out to be a general result. When the yield to maturity is unchanged over the period, the rate of return on the bond will equal that yield. As we noted, this should not be surprising: The bond must offer a rate of return competitive with those available on other securities.

However, when yields fluctuate, so will a bond's rate of return. Unanticipated changes in market rates will result in unanticipated changes in bond returns, and, after the fact, a bond's holding-period return can be better or worse than the yield at which it initially sells. An increase in the bond's yield to maturity acts to reduce its price, which means that the holding-period return will be less than the initial yield. Conversely, a decline in yield to maturity results in a holding-period return greater than the initial yield.

Consider a 30-year bond paying an annual coupon of $80 and selling at par value of $1,000. The bond's initial yield to maturity is 8%. If the yield remains at 8% over the year, the bond price will remain at par, so the holding-period return also will be 8%. But if the yield falls below 8%, the bond price will increase. Suppose the yield falls and the price increases to $1,050. Then the holding-period return is greater than 8%:

$$\text{Holding-period return} = \frac{\$80 + (\$1{,}050 - \$1{,}000)}{\$1{,}000} = .13 \text{ or } 13\%$$

EXAMPLE 10.11

Yield to Maturity versus Holding-Period Return

Show that if the yield to maturity increases, then holding-period return is *less* than that initial yield. For example, suppose in Example 10.11 that by the end of the first year, the bond's yield to maturity is 8.5%. Find the one-year holding-period return and compare it to the bond's initial 8% yield to maturity.

CONCEPT check 10.6

Here is another way to think about the difference between yield to maturity and holding-period return. Yield to maturity depends only on the bond's coupon, *current* price, and par value at maturity. All of these values are observable today, so yield to maturity can be easily calculated. Yield to maturity is commonly interpreted as a measure of the *average* rate of return if the investment in the bond is held until the bond matures. In contrast, holding-period return is the rate of return over a particular investment period and depends on the market price of the bond at the end of that holding period; of course this price is *not* known today. Because bond prices over the holding period will respond to unanticipated changes in interest rates, holding-period return can at most be forecast.

Zero-Coupon Bonds and Treasury STRIPS

Original-issue discount bonds are less common than coupon bonds issued at par. These are bonds that are issued intentionally with low coupon rates that cause the bond to sell at a discount from par value. The most common example of this type of bond is the *zero-coupon bond,* which carries no coupons and provides all its return in the form of price appreciation. Zeros provide only one cash flow to their owners, on the maturity date of the bond.

U.S. Treasury bills are examples of short-term zero-coupon instruments. If the bill has face value of $10,000, the Treasury issues or sells it for some amount less than $10,000, agreeing to repay $10,000 at maturity. All of the investor's return comes in the form of price appreciation.

Longer-term zero-coupon bonds are commonly created from coupon-bearing notes and bonds. A brokerage that purchases a Treasury coupon bond may ask the Treasury to separate the cash flows into a series of independent securities, where each security is a claim to one of the payments of the original bond. For example, a 10-year coupon bond would be "stripped" of its 20 semiannual coupons and each coupon payment would be treated as a stand-alone zero-coupon bond. The maturities of these bonds would thus range from six months to 10 years. The final payment of principal would be treated as another stand-alone zero-coupon security. Each of the payments would then be treated as an independent security and assigned its own CUSIP number, the security identifier that allows for electronic trading over the Fedwire system. The payments are still considered obligations of the U.S. Treasury. The Treasury program under which coupon stripping is performed is called STRIPS (Separate Trading of Registered Interest and Principal of Securities), and these zero-coupon securities are called *Treasury strips.*

What should happen to prices of zeros as time passes? On their maturity dates, zeros must sell for par value. Before maturity, however, they should sell at discounts from par, because of the time value of money. As time passes, price should approach par value. In fact, if the interest rate is constant, a zero's price will increase at exactly the rate of interest.

To illustrate, consider a zero with 30 years until maturity, and suppose the market interest rate is 10% per year. The price of the bond today is $1,000/(1.10)^{30} = \$57.31$. Next year, with only 29 years until maturity, if the yield to maturity is still 10%, the price will be $1,000/(1.10)^{29} = \$63.04$, a 10% increase over its previous-year value. Because the par value of the bond is now discounted for one less year, its price has increased by the one-year discount factor.

Figure 10.7 presents the price path of a 30-year zero-coupon bond for an annual market interest rate of 10%. The bond's price rises exponentially, not linearly, until its maturity.

After-Tax Returns

The tax authorities recognize that the "built-in" price appreciation on original-issue discount (OID) bonds such as zero-coupon bonds represents an implicit interest payment to the holder of the security. The Internal Revenue Service (IRS), therefore, calculates a price appreciation schedule to impute taxable interest income for the built-in appreciation during a tax year, even if the asset is not sold or does not mature until a future year. Any additional gains or losses

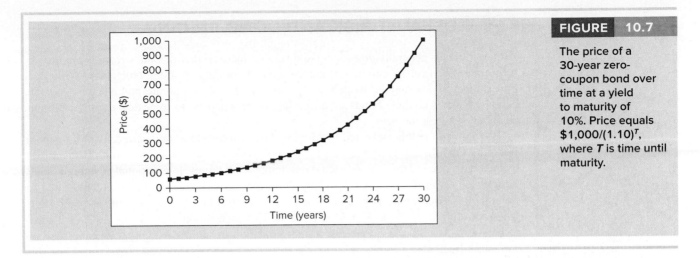

FIGURE 10.7

The price of a 30-year zero-coupon bond over time at a yield to maturity of 10%. Price equals $\$1{,}000/(1.10)^T$, where T is time until maturity.

that arise from changes in market interest rates are treated as capital gains or losses if the OID bond is sold during the tax year.

> If the interest rate originally is 10%, the 30-year zero would be issued at a price of $\$1{,}000/1.10^{30} =$ $57.31. The following year, the IRS calculates what the bond price would be if its yield were still 10%. This is $\$1{,}000/1.10^{29} = \$63.04$. Therefore, the IRS imputes interest income of $\$63.04 - \$57.31 =$ $5.73. This amount is subject to tax. Notice that the imputed interest income is based on a "constant yield method" that ignores any changes in market interest rates.
>
> If interest rates actually fall, let's say to 9.9%, the bond price will be $\$1{,}000/1.099^{29} = \$64.72$. If the bond is sold, then the difference between $64.72 and $63.04 will be treated as capital gains income and taxed at the capital gains tax rate. If the bond is not sold, then the price difference is an unrealized capital gain and does not result in taxes in that year. In either case, the investor must pay taxes on the $5.73 of imputed interest at whatever tax rate applies to interest income.

EXAMPLE 10.12

Taxation of Original-Issue Discount Bonds

The procedure illustrated in Example 10.12 applies as well to the taxation of other original-issue discount bonds, even if they are not zero-coupon bonds. Consider, as another example, a 30-year maturity bond that is issued with a coupon rate of 4% and a yield to maturity of 8%. For simplicity, we will assume that the bond pays coupons once annually. Because of the low coupon rate, the bond will be issued at a price far below par value, specifically at a price of $549.69. (Confirm this for yourself.) If the bond's yield to maturity is still 8%, then its price in one year will rise to $553.66. (Confirm this also.) The pretax holding-period return is exactly 8%:

$$\text{HPR} = \frac{\$40 + (\$553.66 - \$549.69)}{\$549.69} = .08$$

The increase in the bond price based on a constant yield, however, is treated as interest income, so the investor is required to pay taxes on imputed interest income of $553.66 − $549.69 = $3.97, as well as on the explicit coupon income of $40. If the bond's yield actually changes during the year, the difference between the bond's price and the "constant yield value" of $553.66 would be treated as capital gains income if the bond were sold at year-end.

> Suppose that the yield to maturity of the 4% coupon, 30-year maturity bond falls to 7% by the end of the first year and that the investor sells the bond after the first year. If the investor's federal plus state tax rate on interest income is 38% and the combined tax rate on capital gains is 20%, what is the investor's after-tax rate of return?

CONCEPT check 10.7

10.5   DEFAULT RISK AND BOND PRICING

Although bonds generally *promise* a fixed flow of income, that income stream is not guaranteed unless the investor can be sure the issuer will not default on the obligation. While U.S. government bonds may be treated as free of default risk, corporate bonds cannot be. The actual payments on these bonds are uncertain, for they depend to some degree on the ultimate financial status of the firm.

Bond default risk is measured by Moody's Investor Services, Standard & Poor's Corporation, and Fitch Investors Service, all of which provide financial information on firms as well as the credit risk of large corporate and municipal bond issues. International sovereign bonds, which also entail default risk, especially in emerging markets, also are commonly rated for default risk. Each rating firm assigns letter grades to reflect its assessment of bond safety. The top rating is AAA or Aaa. Moody's modifies each rating class with a 1, 2, or 3 suffix (e.g., Aaa1, Aaa2, Aaa3) to provide a finer gradation of ratings. The other agencies use a + or − modification.

Those rated BBB and above (S&P, Fitch) or Baa and above (Moody's) are considered **investment grade bonds,** while lower-rated bonds are classified as **speculative grade or junk bonds.** Certain regulated institutional investors such as insurance companies have not always been allowed to invest in speculative grade bonds.

Figure 10.8 provides definitions of each bond rating classification.

investment grade bond

A bond rated BBB and above by Standard & Poor's or Baa and above by Moody's.

speculative grade or junk bond

A bond rated BB or lower by Standard & Poor's, Ba or lower by Moody's, or unrated.

Junk Bonds

Junk bonds, also known as *high-yield bonds,* are nothing more than speculative grade (low-rated or unrated) bonds. Before 1977, almost all junk bonds were "fallen angels," that is, bonds issued by firms that originally had investment grade ratings but that had since been downgraded. In 1977, however, firms began to issue "original-issue junk."

Much of the credit for this innovation is given to Drexel Burnham Lambert, and especially its trader, Michael Milken. Drexel had long enjoyed a niche as a junk bond trader and had established a network of potential investors in junk bonds. Firms not able to muster an investment grade rating were happy to have Drexel (and other investment bankers) market their bonds directly to the public, as this opened up a new source of financing. Junk issues were a lower-cost financing alternative than borrowing from banks.

High-yield bonds gained considerable notoriety in the 1980s when they were used as financing vehicles in leveraged buyouts and hostile takeover attempts. Shortly thereafter, however, the legal difficulties of Drexel and Michael Milken in connection with Wall Street's insider trading scandals of the late 1980s tainted the junk bond market.

At the height of Drexel's difficulties, the high-yield bond market nearly dried up but eventually rebounded dramatically. However, the average credit quality of newly issued high-yield debt today is higher than the average quality in the boom years of the 1980s. Of course, junk bonds are more vulnerable to financial distress than investment grade bonds. During the financial crisis of 2008–2009, prices on these bonds fell dramatically, and their yields to maturity rose equally dramatically. The spread between yields on Treasury bonds and B-rated bonds widened from around 3% in early 2007 to an astonishing 19% by the start of 2009.

Determinants of Bond Safety

Bond rating agencies base their quality ratings largely on an analysis of the level and trend of some of the issuer's financial ratios. The key ratios used to evaluate safety are:

1. *Coverage ratio.* Ratio of company earnings to fixed costs. For example, the *times-interest-earned ratio* is the ratio of earnings before interest payments and taxes to interest obligations. The *fixed-charge coverage ratio* includes lease payments and sinking fund payments with interest obligations to arrive at the ratio of earnings to all fixed-cash obligations. Low or falling coverage ratios signal possible cash flow difficulties.

FIGURE 10.8

Definitions of each bond rating class

Sources: From Stephen A. Ross, Randolph W. Westerfield, and Jeffrey F. Jaffe, *Corporate Finance*, 9th ed. © 2010, McGraw-Hill Publishing. Data from various editions of *Standard & Poor's Bond Guide* and *Moody's Bond Guide*.

	Bond Ratings			
	Very High Quality	**High Quality**	**Speculative**	**Very Poor**
Standard & Poor's	AAA AA	A BBB	BB B	CCC D
Moody's	Aaa Aa	A Baa	Ba B	Caa C

At times both Moody's and Standard & Poor's use adjustments to these ratings. S&P uses plus and minus signs: A+ is the strongest A rating and A− the weakest. Moody's uses a 1, 2, or 3 designation, with 1 indicating the strongest.

Moody's	S&P	
Aaa	AAA	Debt rated Aaa and AAA has the highest rating. Capacity to pay interest and principal is extremely strong.
Aa	AA	Debt rated Aa and AA has a very strong capacity to pay interest and repay principal. Together with the highest rating, this group comprises the high-grade bond class.
A	A	Debt rated A has a strong capacity to pay interest and repay principal, although it is somewhat more susceptible to the adverse effects of changes in circumstances and economic conditions than debt in higher-rated categories.
Baa	BBB	Debt rated Baa and BBB is regarded as having an adequate capacity to pay interest and repay principal. Whereas it normally exhibits adequate protection parameters, adverse economic conditions or changing circumstances are more likely to lead to a weakened capacity to pay interest and repay principal for debt in this category than in higher-rated categories. These bonds are medium grade obligations.
Ba B Caa Ca	B CCC CC	Debt rated in these categories is regarded, on balance, as predominantly speculative with respect to capacity to pay interest and repay principal in accordance with the terms of the obligation. BB and Ba indicate the lowest degree of speculation, and CC and Ca the highest degree of speculation. Although such debt will likely have some quality and protective characteristics, these are outweighed by large uncertainties or major risk exposures to adverse conditions. Some issues may be in default.
C	C	This rating is reserved for income bonds on which no interest is being paid.
D	D	Debt rated D is in default, and payment of interest and/or repayment of principal is in arrears.

2. *Leverage ratio (debt-to-equity ratio).* A too-high leverage ratio indicates excessive indebtedness, raising the possibility the firm will be unable to earn enough to satisfy the obligations on its bonds.

3. *Liquidity ratios.* The two common liquidity ratios are the *current ratio* (current assets/current liabilities) and the *quick ratio* (current assets excluding inventories/current liabilities). These ratios measure the firm's ability to raise cash from its most liquid assets.

4. *Profitability ratios.* Measure of rates of return on assets or equity. The profitability ratio is an indicator of a firm's overall performance. The *return on assets* (earnings before interest and taxes divided by total assets) or *return on equity* (net income/equity) are the most

popular of these measures. Firms with higher return on assets or equity should be better able to raise money in security markets because they offer prospects for better returns on the firm's investments.

5. *Cash flow-to-debt ratio.* This is the ratio of total cash flow to outstanding debt.

Moody's periodically computes median values of selected ratios for firms in several rating classes, which we present in Table 10.3. Of course, ratios must be evaluated in the context of industry standards, and analysts differ in the weights they place on particular ratios. Nevertheless, Table 10.3 demonstrates the tendency of ratios to improve along with the firm's rating class.

Bond Indentures

indenture

The document defining the contract between the bond issuer and the bondholder.

In addition to specifying a payment schedule, the bond **indenture,** which is the contract between the issuer and the bondholder, also specifies a set of restrictions that protect the rights of the bondholders. Such restrictions include provisions relating to collateral, sinking funds, dividend policy, and further borrowing. The issuing firm agrees to these so-called protective covenants to market its bonds to investors concerned about the safety of the bond issue.

sinking fund

A bond indenture that calls for the issuer to periodically repurchase some proportion of the outstanding bonds prior to maturity.

SINKING FUNDS   Bonds call for the payment of par value at the end of the bond's life. This payment constitutes a large cash commitment for the issuer. To help ensure that the commitment does not create a cash flow crisis, the firm may agree to establish a **sinking fund** to spread the payment burden over several years. The fund may operate in one of two ways:

1. The firm may repurchase a fraction of the outstanding bonds in the open market each year.
2. The firm may purchase a fraction of outstanding bonds at a special call price associated with the sinking fund provision. The firm has an option to purchase the bonds at either the market price or the sinking fund price, whichever is lower. To allocate the burden of the sinking fund call fairly among bondholders, the bonds chosen for the call are selected at random based on serial number.[12]

The sinking fund call differs from a conventional call provision in two important ways. First, the firm can repurchase only a limited fraction of the bond issue at the sinking fund call

TABLE 10.3 Financial ratios by rating class

	Aaa	Aa	A	Baa	Ba	B	C
EBITA/Assets (%)	20.9%	15.6%	13.8%	10.9%	9.1%	7.1%	4.0%
Operating profit margin (%)	22.0%	17.1%	17.6%	14.1%	11.2%	8.9%	4.1%
EBITA to interest coverage (multiple)	28.9	15.1	9.7	5.9	3.5	1.7	0.6
Debt/EBITDA (multiple)	0.58	2.03	1.83	2.58	3.41	5.26	8.35
Debt/(Debt + Equity)	19.3%	50.2%	38.6%	46.2%	51.7%	72.0%	98.0%
Funds from operations/Total debt (multiple)	1.335	0.385	0.425	0.296	0.206	0.120	0.031
Retained cash flow/Net debt (multiple)	1.3	0.3	0.4	0.3	0.2	0.1	0.0

Note: EBITA is earnings before interest, taxes, and amortization.

Source: Moody's Financial Metrics, *Key Ratios by Rating and Industry for Global Non-Financial Corporations,* December 2013.

[12]While it is less common, the sinking fund provision also may call for periodic payments to a trustee, with the payments invested so that the accumulated sum can be used for retirement of the entire issue at maturity.

price. At most, some indentures allow firms to use a *doubling option,* which allows repurchase of double the required number of bonds at the sinking fund call price. Second, while callable bonds generally have call prices above par value, the sinking fund call price usually is set at the bond's par value.

Although sinking funds ostensibly protect bondholders by making principal repayment more likely, they can hurt the investor. The firm will choose to buy back discount bonds (selling below par) at their market price, while exercising its option to buy back premium bonds (selling above par) at par. Therefore, if interest rates fall and bond prices rise, a firm will benefit from the sinking fund provision that enables it to repurchase its bonds at below-market prices. In these circumstances, the firm's gain is the bondholder's loss.

One bond issue that does not require a sinking fund is a *serial bond* issue in which the firm sells bonds with staggered maturity dates. As bonds mature sequentially, the principal repayment burden is spread over time just as it is with a sinking fund. Unlike sinking fund bonds, serial bonds do not confront security holders with the risk that a particular bond may be called for the sinking fund. The disadvantage, however, is that the bonds of each maturity date are different bonds, which reduces the liquidity of the issue.

SUBORDINATION OF FURTHER DEBT   One of the factors determining bond safety is the total outstanding debt of the issuer. If you bought a bond today, you would be understandably distressed to see the firm tripling its outstanding debt tomorrow. Your bond would be riskier than it appeared when you bought it. To prevent firms from harming bondholders in this manner, **subordination clauses** restrict the amount of their additional borrowing. Additional debt might be required to be subordinated in priority to existing debt; that is, in the event of bankruptcy, *subordinated* or *junior* debtholders will not be paid unless and until the senior debt is fully paid off.

subordination clauses

Restrictions on additional borrowing that stipulate that senior bondholders will be paid first in the event of bankruptcy.

DIVIDEND RESTRICTIONS   Covenants limiting dividends protect bondholders because they force the firm to retain assets rather than pay them out to stockholders. A typical restriction disallows payments of dividends if cumulative dividends paid since the firm's inception exceed cumulative retained earnings plus proceeds from sales of stock.

COLLATERAL   Some bonds are issued with specific collateral behind them. **Collateral** is a particular asset that the bondholders receive if the firm defaults. If the collateral is property, the bond is called a *mortgage bond.* If the collateral takes the form of other securities held by the firm, the bond is a *collateral trust bond.* In the case of equipment, the bond is known as an *equipment obligation bond.* This last form of collateral is used most commonly by firms such as railroads, where the equipment is fairly standard and can be easily sold to another firm should the firm default.

collateral

A specific asset pledged against possible default on a bond.

Collateralized bonds generally are considered safer than general **debenture** bonds, which are unsecured, meaning they do not provide for specific collateral; credit risk of unsecured bonds depends on the general earning power of the firm. If the firm defaults, debenture owners become general creditors of the firm. Because they are safer, collateralized bonds generally offer lower yields than general debentures.

debenture

A bond not backed by specific collateral.

Figure 10.9 shows the terms of a large bond issue by Apple in 2015. We have added some explanatory notes alongside the terms of the issue.

Yield to Maturity and Default Risk

Because corporate bonds are subject to default risk, we must distinguish between the bond's promised yield to maturity and its expected yield. The promised or stated yield will be realized only if the firm meets the obligations of the bond issue. Therefore, the stated yield is the *maximum possible* yield to maturity of the bond. The expected yield to maturity must take into account the possibility of a default.

FIGURE   10.9

Callable bond issued by Apple

Comment	Description of Bond
1. Interest of 3.45% will be payable on February 9 and August 9 of each year. Thus every 6 months each note will pay interest of (.0345/2) × $1,000 = $17.25.	→ ISSUE: Apple Inc. 3.45% Notes
2. Investors will be repaid the $1,000 face value in 2045.	→ DUE: February 9, 2045
3. Moody's bond rating is Aa, the second-highest-quality rating.	→ RATING: Aa
4. A trustee is appointed to look after investors' interest.	→ TRUSTEE: Issued under an indenture between Apple and The Bank of New York Mellon Trust Company
5. The bonds are registered. The registrar keeps a record of who owns the bonds.	→ REGISTERED: Issued in registered, book - entry form
6. The company is not obliged to repay any of the bonds on a regular basis before maturity.	→ SINKING FUND: None
7. The company has the option to buy back the notes. The redemption price is the greater of $1,000 or a price that is determined by the value of an equivalent Treasury bond.	→ CALLABLE: In whole or in part at any time
8. The notes are senior debt, ranking equally with all Apple's other unsecured senior debt.	→ SENIORITY
9. The notes are not secured; that is, no assets have been set aside to protect the noteholders in the event of default. However, if Apple sets aside assets to protect any other bondholders, the notes will also be secured by these assets. This is termed *a negative pledge clause.*	→ SECURITY: The notes are unsecured. However, "if Apple shall incur, assume or guarantee any Debt, ... it will secure ... the debt securities then outstanding equally and ratably with ... such Debt."
10. The principal amount of the issue was $2 billion. The notes were sold at 99.11% of their principal value.	→ OFFERED: $2,000,000,000 at 99.11%
11. The book runners are the managing underwriters to the issue and maintain the book of securities sold.	→ JOINT BOOK - RUNNING MANAGERS: Goldman, Sachs; Deutsche Bank Securities

For example, at the height of the financial crisis in October 2008, as Ford Motor Company struggled, its 6.625% coupon bonds due in 2028 were rated CCC and were selling at about 33% of par value, resulting in a yield to maturity of about 20%. Investors did not really believe the expected rate of return on these bonds was 20%. They recognized the distinct possibility that bondholders would not receive all the payments promised in the bond contract and that the yield based on *expected* cash flows was far less than the yield based on *promised* cash flows. As it turned out, of course, Ford weathered the storm, and investors who purchased its bonds made a very nice profit: In 2017, the bonds were selling at prices about 20% *above* par value.

Example 10.13 suggests that when a bond becomes more subject to default risk, its price will fall, and therefore its promised yield to maturity will rise. Therefore, the default premium,

---

EXAMPLE 10.13

Expected versus Promised Yield

Suppose a firm issued a 9% coupon bond 20 years ago. The bond now has 10 years left until it matures, but the firm is having financial difficulties. Investors believe that the firm will be able to make good on the remaining interest payments but that at the maturity date, it will be forced into bankruptcy and bondholders will receive only 70% of par value. The bond is selling at $750. Yield to maturity (YTM) would then be calculated using the inputs shown in the following table.

	Expected YTM	Stated YTM
Coupon payment	$45	$45
Number of semiannual periods	20 periods	20 periods
Final payment	$700	$1,000
Price	$750	$750

The stated yield to maturity, which is based on promised payments, is 13.7%. Based on the expected payment of $700 at maturity, however, the yield would be only 11.6%. The stated yield to maturity is greater than the yield investors actually expect to earn.

the spread between the stated yield to maturity and that on otherwise comparable Treasury bonds, will rise. However, its expected yield to maturity, which ultimately is tied to the systematic risk of the bond, will be far less affected. Let's continue the example.

EXAMPLE 10.14

Default Risk and the Default Premium

Suppose that the condition of the firm in Example 10.13 deteriorates further, and investors now believe that the bond will pay off only 55% of face value at maturity. Because of the higher risk, investors now demand an expected yield to maturity of 12% (i.e., 6% semiannually), which is 0.4% higher than in Example 10.13. But the price of the bond will fall from $750 to $688 [($n = 20$; $i = 6$; FV = 550; PMT = $45)]. At this price, the stated yield to maturity based on promised cash flows is 15.2%. While the expected yield to maturity has increased by 0.4%, the drop in price has caused the promised yield to maturity (and the default premium) to rise by 1.5%.

To compensate for the possibility of default, corporate bonds must offer a **default premium.** The default premium is the difference between the promised yield on a corporate bond and the yield of an otherwise identical government bond that is riskless in terms of default. If the firm remains solvent and actually pays the investor all of the promised cash flows, the investor will realize a higher yield to maturity than would be realized from the government bond. If, however, the firm goes bankrupt, the corporate bond is likely to provide a lower return than the government bond. The corporate bond has the potential for both better and worse performance than the default-free Treasury bond. In other words, it is riskier.

default premium

The increment to promised yield that compensates the investor for default risk.

The pattern of default premiums offered on risky bonds is sometimes called the *risk structure of interest rates.* The greater the default risk, the higher the default premium. Figure 10.10 shows spreads between yields to maturity of bonds of different risk classes since 1997. You can see here clear evidence of default-risk premiums on promised yields. Notice, for example, the incredible run-up of credit spreads during the crisis of 2008–2009.

Credit Default Swaps

A **credit default swap (CDS)** is in effect an insurance policy on the default risk of a bond or loan. To illustrate, the annual premium in early 2010 on a five-year Greek Sovereign CDS was about 3%, meaning that the CDS buyer would pay the seller an annual "insurance premium" of $3 for each $100 of bond principal. The CDS seller collects these annual payments for the term of the contract, but must compensate the buyer for loss of bond value in the event of a default.[13]

credit default swap (CDS)

An insurance policy on the default risk of a corporate bond or loan.

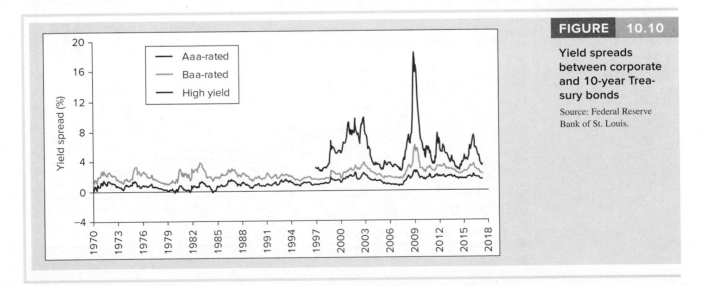

FIGURE 10.10

Yield spreads between corporate and 10-year Treasury bonds

Source: Federal Reserve Bank of St. Louis.

[13] Actually, credit default swaps may pay off even short of an actual default. The contract specifies which particular "credit events" will trigger a payment. For example, restructuring (rewriting the terms of a firm's outstanding debt as an alternative to formal bankruptcy proceedings) may be defined as a triggering credit event.

As originally envisioned, credit default swaps were designed to allow lenders to buy protection against losses on sizable loans. The natural buyers of CDSs would then be large bondholders or banks that had made large loans and wished to enhance the creditworthiness of those loans. Even if the bond issuer had shaky credit standing, the "insured" debt would be as safe as the issuer of the CDS. An investor holding a bond with a BB rating could, in principle, raise the effective quality of the debt to AAA by buying a CDS on the issuer.

This insight suggests how CDS contracts should be priced. If a BB-rated bond bundled with insurance via a CDS is effectively equivalent to an AAA-rated bond, then the fair price of the swap ought to approximate the yield spread between AAA-rated and BB-rated bonds.[14] The risk structure of interest rates and CDS prices ought to be tightly aligned.

Figure 10.11 shows the prices of five-year CDS contracts on Greek government debt between 2009 and 2010 as well as the spread between yields on Greek and German government bonds. As the strongest economy in the eurozone, German bonds are the natural candidate to play the role of the "risk-free benchmark." As expected, the credit spread and the CDS prices move almost in lockstep.

You can see in Figure 10.11 that both the credit spread and CDS price started to increase dramatically toward the end of 2009. As perceptions of Greece's credit risk increased, so did the price of insuring its debt. Ultimately, in what amounted to the largest-ever sovereign default, lenders agreed in 2012 to reduce Greece's debt by around $130 billion.

CDS contracts trade on corporate as well as on sovereign debt. While CDSs were conceived as a form of bond insurance, it wasn't long before investors realized that they could be used to speculate on the financial health of particular companies. For example, an investor in early 2008 who predicted the imminent financial crisis might have purchased CDS contracts on mortgage bonds as well as the debt of financial firms and would have profited as their CDS prices spiked in September. In fact, hedge fund manager John Paulson famously did just this. His bearish bets in 2007–2008 on commercial banks and Wall Street firms as well as on some riskier mortgage-backed securities made his funds more than $15 billion, bringing him a personal payoff of more than $3.7 billion.

The nearby box discusses the role of credit default swaps in the financial crisis of 2008–2009.

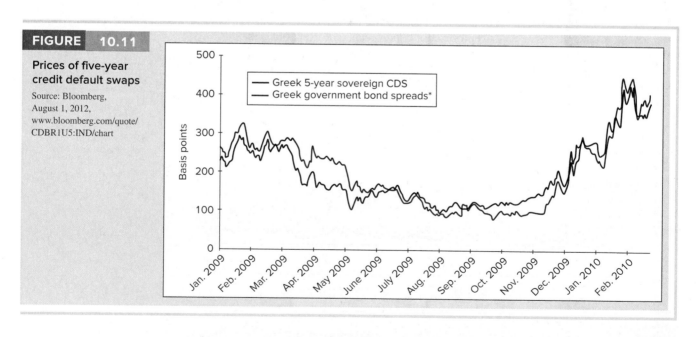

FIGURE 10.11

Prices of five-year credit default swaps

Source: Bloomberg, August 1, 2012, www.bloomberg.com/quote/CDBR1U5:IND/chart

---

[14] We say "approximately" because there are some differences between highly rated bonds and bonds synthetically enhanced with credit default swaps. For example, the term of the swap may not match the maturity of the bond. Tax treatment of coupon payments versus swap payments may differ, as may the liquidity of the bonds. Finally, some CDSs may entail one-time up-front payments as well as annual premiums.

On the MARKET FRONT

CREDIT DEFAULT SWAPS, SYSTEMIC RISK, AND THE FINANCIAL CRISIS OF 2008–2009

The credit crisis of 2008–2009, when lending among banks and other financial institutions effectively seized up, was in large measure a crisis of transparency. The biggest problem was a widespread lack of confidence in the financial standing of counterparties to a trade. If one institution could not be confident that another would remain solvent, it would understandably be reluctant to offer it a loan. When doubt about the credit exposure of customers and trading partners spiked to levels not seen since the Great Depression, the market for loans dried up.

Credit default swaps were particularly cited for fostering doubts about counterparty reliability. By August 2008, $63 trillion of such swaps were reportedly outstanding. (By comparison, U.S. gross domestic product in 2008 was about $14 trillion.) As the subprime-mortgage market collapsed and the economy entered a deep recession, the potential obligations on these contracts ballooned to levels previously considered unimaginable, and the ability of CDS sellers to honor their commitments was in doubt. For example, the huge insurance firm AIG alone had sold more than $400 billion of CDS contracts on subprime mortgages and other loans and was days from insolvency. But AIG's insolvency would have triggered the insolvency of other firms that had relied on its promise of protection against loan defaults. These in turn might have triggered further defaults. In the end, the government felt compelled to rescue AIG to prevent a chain reaction of insolvencies.

Counterparty risk and lax reporting requirements made it effectively impossible to tease out firms' exposures to credit risk. One problem was that CDS positions did not have to be accounted for on balance sheets. And the possibility of one default setting off a sequence of further defaults meant that lenders were exposed to the default of an institution with which they did not even directly trade. Such knock-on effects create *systemic risk*, in which the entire financial system can freeze up. With the ripple effects of bad debt extending in ever-widening circles, it can seem imprudent to lend to anyone.

In the aftermath of the credit crisis, the Dodd-Frank Act called for new regulation and reforms. One reform is the creation of a central clearinghouse for credit derivatives such as CDS contracts. Such a system fosters transparency and allows the clearinghouse to replace traders' offsetting long and short positions with a single net position. It also requires daily recognition of gains or losses through a margin or collateral account. If losses mount, positions have to be unwound before growing to unsustainable levels. Allowing traders to accurately assess counterparty risk, and limiting such risk through margin accounts and the extra backup of the clearinghouse, can go a long way in limiting systemic risk.

10.6 THE YIELD CURVE

Return to Figure 10.1 again, and you will see that while yields to maturity on bonds of similar maturities are reasonably close, yields do differ. Bonds with shorter maturities generally offer lower yields to maturity than longer-term bonds. The graphical relationship between the yield to maturity and the term to maturity is called the **yield curve.** The relationship also is called the **term structure of interest rates** because it relates yields to maturity to the term (maturity) of each bond. The yield curve may be found at several websites, for example, *The Wall Street Journal Online* or Yahoo! Finance. Four such sets of curves are reproduced in Figure 10.12. Figure 10.12 illustrates that a wide range of yield curves may be observed in practice. Panel A is an essentially flat yield curve. Panel B is an upward-sloping curve, and Panel C is a downward-sloping, or "inverted," yield curve. Finally, the yield curve in Panel D is hump-shaped, first rising and then falling. Rising yield curves are most commonly observed. We will see why momentarily.

Why should bonds of differing maturity offer different yields? The two most plausible possibilities have to do with expectations of future rates and risk premiums. We will consider each of these arguments in turn.

yield curve

A graph of yield to maturity as a function of term to maturity.

term structure of interest rates

The relationship between yields to maturity and terms to maturity across bonds.

The Expectations Theory

Suppose everyone in the market believes that while the current one-year interest rate is 8%, the interest rate on one-year bonds next year will rise to 10%. What would this belief imply about the proper yield to maturity on two-year bonds issued today?

It is easy to see that an investor who buys the one-year bond and rolls the proceeds into another one-year bond in the following year will earn, on average, about 9% per year. This value is just the average of the 8% earned this year and the 10% expected for next year. More

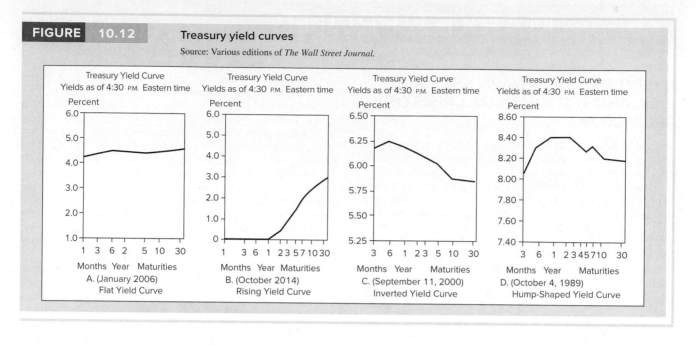

FIGURE   10.12   **Treasury yield curves**

Source: Various editions of *The Wall Street Journal*.

precisely, the investment will grow by a factor of 1.08 in the first year and 1.10 in the second year, for a total two-year growth factor of $1.08 \times 1.10 = 1.188$. This corresponds to an annual compound growth rate of 8.995% (because $1.08995^2 = 1.188$).

For two-year bonds to be competitive with the strategy of rolling over one-year bonds, they also must offer an average annual return of 8.995% over the two-year holding period. This is illustrated in Figure 10.13. The current short-term rate of 8% and the expected value of next year's short-term rate, 10%, are depicted above the time line. The two-year rate that provides the same expected two-year total return is below the time line. In this example, therefore, the yield curve will be upward-sloping; while one-year bonds offer an 8% yield to maturity, two-year bonds offer an 8.995% yield.

expectations hypothesis

The theory that yields to maturity are determined solely by expectations of future short-term interest rates.

This notion is the essence of the **expectations hypothesis,** which asserts that the slope of the yield curve is attributable to expectations of changes in short-term rates. Relatively high yields on long-term bonds reflect expectations of future increases in rates, while relatively low yields on long-term bonds (a downward-sloping or inverted yield curve) reflect expectations of falling short-term rates.

One of the implications of the expectations hypothesis is that expected holding-period returns on bonds of all maturities ought to be about equal. Even if the yield curve is upward-sloping (so that two-year bonds offer higher yields to maturity than one-year bonds), this does not necessarily mean investors expect higher rates of return on the two-year bonds. As we've seen, the higher initial yield to maturity on the two-year bond is necessary to compensate investors for the fact that interest rates the next year will be even higher. Over the two-year period, and indeed over any holding period, this theory predicts that holding-period returns will be equalized across bonds of all maturities.

FIGURE   10.13

Returns to two two-year investment strategies

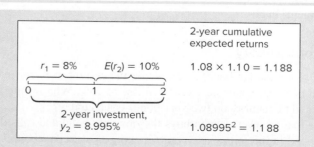

2-year cumulative expected returns

$r_1 = 8\%$ $E(r_2) = 10\%$ $1.08 \times 1.10 = 1.188$

0   1   2

2-year investment,
$y_2 = 8.995\%$ $1.08995^2 = 1.188$

Suppose we buy the one-year zero-coupon bond with a current yield to maturity of 8%. If its face value is $1,000, its price will be $925.93, providing an 8% rate of return over the coming year. Suppose instead that we buy the two-year zero-coupon bond at its yield of 8.995%. Its price today is $1,000/(1.08995)^2 = $841.76. After a year passes, the zero will have a remaining maturity of only one year; based on the forecast that the one-year yield next year will be 10%, it then will sell for $1,000/1.10 = $909.09. The expected rate of return over the year is thus ($909.09 − $841.76)/ $841.76 = .08, or 8%, precisely the same return provided by the one-year bond. This makes sense: If risk considerations are ignored when pricing the two bonds, they ought to provide equal expected rates of return.

In fact, advocates of the expectations hypothesis commonly invert this analysis to *infer* the market's expectation of future short-term rates. They note that we do not directly observe the expectation of next year's rate, but we *can* observe yields on bonds of different maturities. Suppose, as in this example, we see that one-year bonds offer yields of 8% and two-year bonds offer yields of 8.995%. Each dollar invested in the two-year zero would grow after two years to $1 × 1.08995^2 = $1.188. A dollar invested in the one-year zero would grow by a factor of 1.08 in the first year and, then, if reinvested or "rolled over" into another one-year zero in the second year, would grow by an additional factor of $1 + r_2$. Final proceeds would be $1 × 1.08 × (1 + r_2)$.

The final proceeds of the rollover strategy depend on the interest rate that actually transpires in year 2. However, we can solve for the second-year interest rate that makes the expected payoff of these two strategies equal. This "break-even" value is called the **forward rate** for the second year, f_2, and is derived as follows:

$$1.08995^2 = 1.08 \times (1 + f_2)$$

which implies that $f_2 = .10$, or 10%. Notice that the forward rate equals the market's expectation of the year-2 short rate. Hence, we conclude that if the expected total return of a long-term bond equals that of rolling over a short-term bond, the forward rate equals the expected short-term interest rate. This is why the theory is called the expectations hypothesis.

More generally, we obtain the forward rate by equating the return on an *n*-period zero-coupon bond with that of an $(n − 1)$-period zero-coupon bond rolled over into a one-year bond in year *n*:

$$(1 + y_n)^n = (1 + y_{n-1})^{n-1} (1 + f_n) \tag{10.3}$$

The actual total returns on the two *n*-year strategies will be equal if the short-term interest rate in year *n* turns out to equal f_n.

forward rate

The inferred short-term rate of interest for a future period that makes the expected total return of a long-term bond equal to that of rolling over short-term bonds.

Suppose that two-year maturity bonds offer yields to maturity of 6% and three-year bonds have yields of 7%. What is the forward rate for the third year? We could compare these two strategies as follows:

1. Buy a three-year bond. Total proceeds per dollar invested will be

$$\$1 \times (1.07)^3 = \$1.2250$$

2. Buy a two-year bond. Reinvest all proceeds in a one-year bond in the third year, which will provide a return in that year of r_3. Total proceeds per dollar invested will be the result of two years' growth of invested funds at 6% plus the final year's growth at rate r_3:

$$\$1 \times (1.06)^2 \times (1 + r_3) = \$1.1236 \times (1 + r_3)$$

The forward rate is the rate in year 3 that makes the total return on these strategies equal:

$$1.2250 = 1.1236 \times (1 + f_3)$$

We conclude that the forward rate for the third year satisfies $(1 + f_3) = 1.0902$, so that f_3 is 9.02%.

While the expectations hypothesis gives us a tool to infer expectations of future market interest rates, it tells us nothing of what underlying considerations generated those expectations. Ultimately, interest rates reflect investors' expectations of the state of the macroeconomy. Not surprisingly, then, forward rates and the yield curve have proven themselves to be useful inputs for economic forecasts. The slope of the yield curve is one of the more important components of the index of leading economic indicators used to predict the course of economic activity. Inverted yield curves in particular, which imply falling interest rates, turn out to be among the best indicators of a coming recession.

The Liquidity Preference Theory

The expectations hypothesis starts from the assertion that bonds are priced so that "buy and hold" investments in long-term bonds provide the same returns as rolling over a series of short-term bonds. However, the risks of long- and short-term bonds are not equivalent.

We've seen that longer-term bonds are subject to greater interest rate risk than short-term bonds. As a result, investors in long-term bonds might require a risk premium to compensate them for bearing this risk. In this case, the yield curve will be upward-sloping even in the absence of expectations of future increases in rates. The source of the upward slope is investor demand for higher expected returns on assets that are perceived as riskier.

liquidity preference theory

The theory that investors demand a risk premium on long-term bonds.

This viewpoint is called the **liquidity preference theory** of the term structure. Its name reflects the fact that shorter-term bonds have more "liquidity" than longer-term bonds in the sense that they offer greater price certainty and trade in more active markets with lower bid–ask spreads. Their preference for greater liquidity makes them willing to hold shorter-term bonds even if their expected returns are lower than those of longer-term bonds.

liquidity premium

The yield spread demanded by investors as compensation for the greater risk of longer-term bonds.

We can think of a **liquidity premium** as resulting from the extra compensation investors demand for holding longer-term bonds with greater price risk. We measure it as the spread between the forward rate of interest and the expected short rate:

$$f_n = E(r_n) + \text{Liquidity premium} \tag{10.4}$$

In the absence of a liquidity premium, the forward rate would equal the expectation of the future short rate. But, generally, we expect the forward rate to be higher to compensate investors for the lower liquidity of longer-term bonds.

Advocates of the liquidity preference theory also note that borrowers seem to prefer to issue long-term bonds. This allows them to lock in an interest rate on their borrowing for long periods, and thus they may be willing to pay higher yields on these issues. In sum, bond buyers demand higher rates on longer-term bonds, and bond issuers are willing to pay higher rates on those bonds. As a result, the yield curve generally slopes upward.

According to the liquidity preference theory, forward rates of interest will exceed the market's expectations of future interest rates. Even if rates are expected to remain unchanged, the yield curve will slope upward because of the liquidity premium. That upward slope would be mistakenly attributed to expectations of rising rates if one were to use the pure expectations hypothesis to interpret the yield curve.

EXAMPLE 10.17

Liquidity Premiums and the Yield Curve

Suppose that the short-term rate of interest is currently 8% and that investors expect it to remain at 8% next year. In the absence of a liquidity premium, with no expectation of a change in yields, the yield to maturity on two-year bonds also would be 8%, the yield curve would be flat, and the forward rate would be 8%. But what if investors demand a risk premium to invest in two-year rather than one-year bonds? If the liquidity premium is 1%, then the forward rate would be 8% + 1% = 9%, and the yield to maturity on the two-year bond would be determined by

$$(1 + y_2)^2 = 1.08 \times 1.09 = 1.1772$$

implying that $y_2 = .085 = 8.5\%$. Here, the yield curve is upward-sloping due solely to the liquidity premium embedded in the price of the longer-term bond.

Suppose that the expected value of the interest rate for year 3 remains at 8% but that the liquidity premium for that year is also 1%. What would be the yield to maturity on three-year zeros? What would this imply about the slope of the yield curve?

A Synthesis

Of course, we do not need to make an either/or choice between expectations and risk premiums. Both affect the yield curve, and both should be considered in interpreting it.

Figure 10.14 shows two possible yield curves. In Panel A, rates are expected to rise over time. This fact, together with a liquidity premium, makes the yield curve steeply upward-sloping. In Panel B, rates are expected to fall, which by itself would make the yield curve slope downward. However, the liquidity premium lends something of an upward slope. The net effect of these two opposing factors is a "hump-shaped" curve.

These two examples make it clear that the combination of varying expectations and liquidity premiums can result in a wide array of yield-curve profiles. For example, an upward-sloping curve does not in and of itself imply expectations of higher future interest rates, because the slope can result either from expectations or from risk premiums. A curve that is more steeply sloped than usual might signal expectations of higher rates, but even this inference is perilous.

Figure 10.15 presents yield spreads between 90-day T-bills and 10-year T-bonds since 1970. The figure shows that the yield curve is generally upward-sloping in that the longer-term bonds usually offer higher yields to maturity, despite the fact that rates could not have been expected to increase throughout the entire period. This tendency is the empirical basis for the liquidity premium doctrine that at least part of the upward slope in the yield curve must be due to a risk premium.

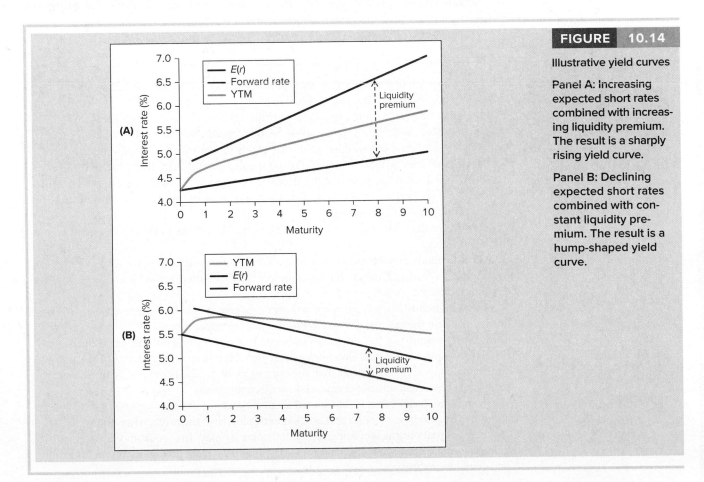

FIGURE 10.14

Illustrative yield curves

Panel A: Increasing expected short rates combined with increasing liquidity premium. The result is a sharply rising yield curve.

Panel B: Declining expected short rates combined with constant liquidity premium. The result is a hump-shaped yield curve.

FIGURE 10.15

Term spread: Yields on 10-year versus 90-day Treasury securities

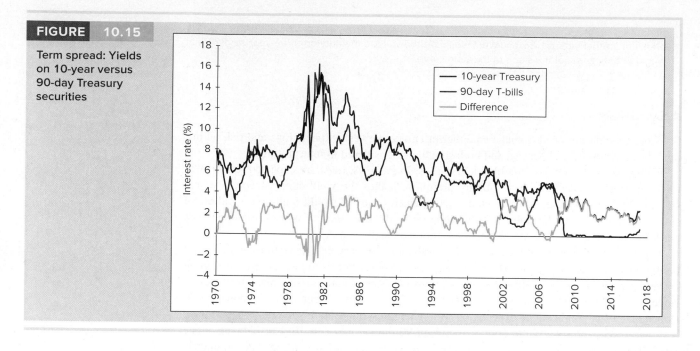

FIGURE 10.15

Term spread: Yields on 10-year versus 90-day Treasury securities

Because the yield curve normally has an upward slope due to risk premiums, a downward-sloping yield curve is taken as a strong indication that yields are more likely than not to fall. The prediction of declining interest rates is in turn often interpreted as a signal of a coming recession. Short-term rates exceeded long-term ones in each of the seven recessions since 1970. For this reason, it is not surprising that the slope of the yield curve is one of the key components of the index of leading economic indicators.

SUMMARY

- Debt securities are distinguished by their promise to pay a fixed or specified stream of income to their holders. The coupon bond is a typical debt security.
- Treasury notes and bonds have original maturities greater than one year. They are issued at or near par value, with their prices quoted net of accrued interest.
- Callable bonds should offer higher promised yields to maturity to compensate investors for the fact that they will not realize full capital gains should the interest rate fall and the bonds be called away from them at the stipulated call price. Bonds often are issued with a period of call protection. In addition, discount bonds selling significantly below their call price offer implicit call protection.
- Put bonds give the bondholder rather than the issuer the choice to terminate or extend the life of the bond.
- Convertible bonds may be exchanged, at the bondholder's discretion, for a specified number of shares of stock. Convertible bondholders "pay" for this option by accepting a lower coupon rate on the security.
- Floating-rate bonds pay a fixed premium over a reference short-term interest rate. Risk is limited because the rate paid is tied to current market conditions.
- The yield to maturity is the single discount rate that equates the present value of a security's cash flows to its price. Bond prices and yields are inversely related. For premium bonds, the coupon rate is greater than the current yield, which is greater than the yield to maturity. These inequalities are reversed for discount bonds.
- The yield to maturity often is interpreted as an estimate of the average rate of return to an investor who purchases a bond and holds it until maturity. However, when future rates are uncertain, actual returns including reinvested coupons may diverge from yield to maturity. Related measures are yield to call, realized compound yield, and expected (versus promised) yield to maturity.

- Treasury bills are U.S. government-issued zero-coupon bonds with original maturities of up to one year. Treasury STRIPS are longer-term default-free zero-coupon bonds. Prices of zero-coupon bonds rise exponentially over time, providing a rate of appreciation equal to the interest rate. The IRS treats this price appreciation as imputed taxable interest income to the investor.
- When bonds are subject to potential default, the stated yield to maturity is the maximum possible yield to maturity that can be realized by the bondholder. In the event of default, however, that promised yield will not be realized. To compensate bond investors for default risk, bonds must offer default premiums, that is, promised yields in excess of those offered by default-free government securities. If the firm remains healthy, its bonds will provide higher returns than government bonds. Otherwise, the returns may be lower.
- Bond safety often is measured using financial ratio analysis. Bond indentures offer safeguards to protect the claims of bondholders. Common indentures specify sinking fund requirements, collateralization, dividend restrictions, and subordination of future debt.
- Credit default swaps provide insurance against the default of a bond or loan. The swap buyer pays an annual premium to the swap seller but collects a payment equal to lost value if the loan later goes into default.
- The term structure of interest rates is the relationship between time to maturity and term to maturity. The yield curve is a graphical depiction of the term structure. The forward rate is the break-even interest rate that would equate the total return on a rollover strategy to that of a longer-term zero-coupon bond.
- The expectations hypothesis holds that forward interest rates are unbiased forecasts of future interest rates. The liquidity preference theory, however, argues that long-term bonds will carry a risk premium known as a liquidity premium. A positive liquidity premium can cause the yield curve to slope upward even if no increase in short rates is anticipated.

KEY TERMS

KEY FORMULAS

Price of a coupon bond:

$$\text{Price} = \text{Coupon} \times \frac{1}{r}\left[1 - \frac{1}{(1+r)^T}\right] + \text{Par value} \times \frac{1}{(1+r)^T}$$

$$= \text{Coupon} \times \text{Annuity factor}(r, T) + \text{Par value} \times \text{PV factor}(r, T)$$

Forward rate of interest: $1 + f_n = \dfrac{(1 + y_n)^n}{(1 + y_{n-1})^{n-1}}$

Liquidity premium: Forward rate − Expected short rate

PROBLEM SETS

 Select problems are available in McGraw-Hill's *Connect*. Please see the Supplements section of the book's frontmatter for more information.

1. Define the following types of bonds: *(LO 10-1)*
   a. Catastrophe bond.
   b. Eurobond.
   c. Zero-coupon bond.
   d. Samurai bond.
   e. Junk bond.
   f. Convertible bond.
   g. Serial bond.
   h. Equipment obligation bond.
   i. Original-issue discount bond.
   j. Indexed bond.

2. What is the option embedded in a callable bond? A puttable bond?   *(LO 10-1)*

3. What would be the likely effect on a bond's yield to maturity of: *(LO 10-5)*
   a. An increase in the issuing firm's times-interest-earned ratio?
   b. An increase in the issuing firm's debt-equity ratio?
   c. An increase in the issuing firm's quick ratio?

4. A coupon bond paying semiannual interest is reported as having an ask price of 117% of its $1,000 par value. If the last interest payment was made one month ago and the coupon rate is 6%, what is the invoice price of the bond?   *(LO 10-1)*

5. A zero-coupon bond with face value $1,000 and maturity of five years sells for $746.22.   *(LO 10-2)*
   a. What is its yield to maturity?
   b. What will happen to its yield to maturity if its price falls immediately to $730?

6. Why do bond prices go down when interest rates go up? Don't bond investors like to receive high interest rates?   *(LO 10-2)*

7. Two bonds have identical times to maturity and coupon rates. One is callable at 105, the other at 110. Which should have the higher yield to maturity? Why?   *(LO 10-4)*

8. Consider a bond with a 10% coupon and with yield to maturity = 8%. If the bond's yield to maturity remains constant, then in one year will the bond price be higher, lower, or unchanged? Why?   *(LO 10-2)*

9. A bond with an annual coupon rate of 4.8% sells for $970. What is the bond's current yield?   *(LO 10-2)*

10. An investor believes that a bond may temporarily increase in credit risk. Which of the following would be the most liquid method of exploiting this?   *(LO 10-5)*
    a. The purchase of a credit default swap.
    b. The sale of a credit default swap.
    c. The short sale of the bond.

11. Which of the following *most accurately* describes the behavior of credit default swaps?   *(LO 10-5)*
    a. When credit risk increases, swap premiums increase.
    b. When credit and interest rate risk increases, swap premiums increase.
    c. When credit risk increases, swap premiums increase, but when interest rate risk increases, swap premiums decrease.

12. You buy an eight-year maturity bond that has a 6% current yield and a 6% coupon (paid annually). In one year, promised yields to maturity have risen to 7%. What is your holding-period return?   *(LO 10-3)*

13. The stated yield to maturity and realized compound yield to maturity of a (default-free) zero-coupon bond are always equal. Why?   *(LO 10-6)*

14. Which security has a higher *effective* annual interest rate?   *(LO 10-6)*
    a. A three-month T-bill with face value of $100,000 currently selling at $97,645.
    b. A coupon bond selling at par and paying a 10% coupon semiannually.

15. Treasury bonds paying an 8% coupon rate with *semiannual* payments currently sell at par value. What coupon rate would they have to pay in order to sell at par if they paid their coupons *annually*?   *(LO 10-2)*

16. Consider a bond paying a coupon rate of 10% per year semiannually when the market interest rate is only 4% per half-year. The bond has three years until maturity.   *(LO 10-6)*
    a. Find the bond's price today and six months from now after the next coupon is paid.
    b. What is the total rate of return on the bond?

17. A 20-year maturity bond with par value $1,000 makes semiannual coupon payments at a coupon rate of 8%. Find the bond equivalent and effective annual yield to maturity of the bond if the bond price is: *(LO 10-2)*
    a. $950
    b. $1,000
    c. $1,050

18. Redo the previous problem using the same data, but now assume that the bond makes its coupon payments annually. Why are the yields you compute lower in this case?   *(LO 10-2)*

19. Return to Table 10.1, showing the cash flows for TIPS bonds.
    a. What is the nominal rate of return on the bond in year 2?
    b. What is the real rate of return in year 2?
    c. What is the nominal rate of return on the bond in year 3?
    d. What is the real rate of return in year 3?   *(LO 10-6)*

20. Fill in the table below for the following zero-coupon bonds, all of which have par values of $1,000.   *(LO 10-2)*

Price	Maturity (years)	Yield to Maturity
$400	20	(a)
$500	20	(b)
$500	10	(c)
(d)	10	10%
(e)	10	8%
$400	(f)	8%

21. A bond has a par value of $1,000, a time to maturity of 10 years, and a coupon rate of 8% with interest paid annually. If the current market price is $800, what will be the percentage capital gain of this bond over the next year if its yield to maturity remains unchanged?   *(LO 10-3)*

22. A bond with a coupon rate of 7% makes semiannual coupon payments on January 15 and July 15 of each year. *The Wall Street Journal* reports the ask price for the bond on January 30 at 100.125. What is the invoice price of the bond? The coupon period has 182 days.   *(LO 10-1)*

23. A bond has a current yield of 9% and a yield to maturity of 10%. Is the bond selling above or below par value? Explain.   *(LO 10-2)*

24. Is the coupon rate of the bond in the previous problem more or less than 9%?   *(LO 10-2)*

25. Consider a bond with a settlement date of February 22, 2018, and a maturity date of March 15, 2026. The coupon rate is 5.5%.   *(LO 10-1)*
    a. If the yield to maturity of the bond is 5.34% (bond equivalent yield, semiannual compounding), what is the list price of the bond on the settlement date?
    b. What is the accrued interest on the bond?
    c. What is the invoice price of the bond?

Templates and spreadsheets are available in Connect

26. Now suppose the bond in the previous question is selling for 102.   *(LO 10-2)*
    a. What is the bond's yield to maturity?
    b. What would the yield to maturity be at a price of 102 if the bond paid its coupons only once per year?

27. A 10-year bond of a firm in severe financial distress has a coupon rate of 14% and sells for $900. The firm is currently renegotiating the debt, and it appears that the lenders will allow the firm to reduce coupon payments on the bond to one-half the originally contracted amount. The firm can handle these lower payments. What are the stated and expected yields to maturity of the bonds? The bond makes its coupon payments annually.   *(LO 10-5)*

28. A two-year bond with par value $1,000 making annual coupon payments of $100 is priced at $1,000. What is the yield to maturity of the bond? What will be the realized compound yield to maturity if the one-year interest rate next year turns out to be (*a*) 8%, (*b*) 10%, (*c*) 12%?   *(LO 10-6)*

29. Suppose that today's date is April 15. A bond with a 10% coupon paid semiannually every January 15 and July 15 is quoted as selling at an ask price of 101.25. If you buy the bond from a dealer today, what price will you pay for it?   *(LO 10-1)*

30. Assume that two firms issue bonds with the following characteristics. Both bonds are issued at par.

	ABC Bonds	XYZ Bonds
Issue size	$1.2 billion	$150 million
Maturity	10 years*	20 years
Coupon	9%	10%
Collateral	First mortgage	General debenture
Callable	Not callable	In 10 years
Call price	None	110
Sinking fund	None	Starting in 5 years

*Bond is extendable at the discretion of the bondholder for an additional 10 years.

Ignoring credit quality, identify four features of these issues that might account for the lower coupon on the ABC debt. Explain.   *(LO 10-4)*

31. A large corporation issued both fixed- and floating-rate notes five years ago, with terms given in the following table: *(LO 10-4)*

	9% Coupon Notes	Floating-Rate Note
Issue size	$250 million	$280 million
Maturity	20 years	15 years
Current price (% of par)	93	98
Current coupon	9%	5%
Coupon adjusts	Fixed coupon	Every year
Coupon reset rule	—	1-year T-bill rate + 2%
Callable	10 years after issue	10 years after issue
Call price	106	102.50
Sinking fund	None	None
Yield to maturity	9.9%	—
Price range since issued	$85–$112	$97–$102

a. Why is the price range greater for the 9% coupon bond than the floating-rate note?
b. What factors could explain why the floating-rate note is not always sold at par value?
c. Why is the call price for the floating-rate note not of great importance to investors?

   d. Is the probability of call for the fixed-rate note high or low?
   e. If the firm were to issue a fixed-rate note with a 15-year maturity, callable after five years at 106, what coupon rate would it need to offer to issue the bond at par value?
   f. Why is an entry for yield to maturity for the floating-rate note not appropriate?

32. A 30-year maturity, 8% coupon bond paying coupons semiannually is callable in five years at a call price of $1,100. The bond currently sells at a yield to maturity of 7% (3.5% per half-year).   *(LO 10-4)*
   a. What is the yield to call?
   b. What is the yield to call if the call price is only $1,050?
   c. What is the yield to call if the call price is $1,100 but the bond can be called in two years instead of five years?

33. A newly issued 20-year maturity, zero-coupon bond is issued with a yield to maturity of 8% and face value $1,000. Find the imputed interest income in the first, second, and last year of the bond's life.   *(LO 10-3)*

34. A newly issued 10-year maturity, 4% coupon bond making *annual* coupon payments is sold to the public at a price of $800. What will be an investor's taxable income from the bond over the coming year? The bond will not be sold at the end of the year. The bond is treated as an original-issue discount bond.   *(LO 10-3)*

35. Fincorp. issues two bonds with 20-year maturities. Both bonds are callable at $1,050. The first bond is issued at a deep discount with a coupon rate of 4% and a price of $580 to yield 8.4%. The second bond is issued at par value with a coupon rate of 8.75%.   *(LO 10-2)*
   a. What is the yield to maturity of the par bond? Why is it higher than the yield of the discount bond?
   b. If you expect rates to fall substantially in the next two years, which bond would you prefer to hold?
   c. In what sense does the discount bond offer "implicit call protection"?

36. Under the expectations hypothesis, if the yield curve is upward-sloping, the market must expect an increase in short-term interest rates. True/false/uncertain? Why?   *(LO 10-7)*

37. The yield curve is upward-sloping. Can you conclude that investors expect short-term interest rates to rise? Why or why not?   *(LO 10-7)*

38. Assume you have a one-year investment horizon and are trying to choose among three bonds. All have the same degree of default risk and mature in 10 years. The first is a zero-coupon bond that pays $1,000 at maturity. The second has an 8% coupon rate and pays the $80 coupon once per year. The third has a 10% coupon rate and pays the $100 coupon once per year.   *(LO 10-3)*
   a. If all three bonds are now priced to yield 8% to maturity, what are their prices?
   b. If you expect their yields to maturity to be 8% at the beginning of next year, what will their prices be then?
   c. What is your rate of return on each bond during the one-year holding period?

39. Under the liquidity preference theory, if inflation is expected to be falling over the next few years, long-term interest rates will be higher than short-term rates. True/false/uncertain? Why?   *(LO 10-7)*

40. The yield curve for default-free zero-coupon bonds is currently as follows:

Maturity (years)	YTM
1	10%
2	11
3	12

   a. What are the implied one-year forward rates?   *(LO 10-7)*
   b. Assume that the pure expectations hypothesis of the term structure is correct. If market expectations are accurate, what will be the yield to maturity on one-year zero-coupon bonds next year?   *(LO 10-7)*

c. What will be the yield to maturity on two-year zeros?   *(LO 10-7)*

d. If you purchase a two-year zero-coupon bond now, what is the expected total rate of return over the next year? (*Hint:* Compute the current and expected future prices.) Ignore taxes.   *(LO 10-6)*

e. What if you purchase a three-year zero-coupon bond?   *(LO 10-6)*

41. The yield to maturity on one-year zero-coupon bonds is 8%. The yield to maturity on two-year zero-coupon bonds is 9%.   *(LO 10-7)*

a. What is the forward rate of interest for the second year?

b. If you believe in the expectations hypothesis, what is your best guess as to the expected value of the short-term interest rate next year?

c. If you believe in the liquidity preference theory, is your best guess as to next year's short-term interest rate higher or lower than in (*b*)?

42. The following table contains spot rates and forward rates for three years. However, the labels got mixed up. Can you identify which row of the interest rates represents spot rates and which one the forward rates?   *(LO 10-7)*

	Year:	1	2	3
Spot rates or forward rates?		10%	12%	14%
Spot rates or forward rates?		10%	14.0364%	18.1078%

Challenge

43. Consider the following $1,000 par value zero-coupon bonds:

Bond	Years until Maturity	Yield to Maturity
A	1	5%
B	2	6
C	3	6.5
D	4	7

According to the expectations hypothesis, what is the market's expectation of the yield curve one year from now? Specifically, what are the expected values of next year's yields on bonds with maturities of (*a*) 1 year; (*b*) 2 years; (*c*) 3 years?   *(LO 10-7)*

44. A newly issued bond pays its coupons once a year. Its coupon rate is 5%, its maturity is 20 years, and its yield to maturity is 8%.   *(LO 10-6)*

a. Find the holding-period return for a one-year investment period if the bond is selling at a yield to maturity of 7% by the end of the year.

b. If you sell the bond after one year when its yield is 7%, what taxes will you owe if the tax rate on interest income is 40% and the tax rate on capital gains income is 30%? The bond is subject to original-issue discount (OID) tax treatment.

c. What is the after-tax holding-period return on the bond?

d. Find the realized compound yield *before taxes* for a two-year holding period, assuming that (i) you sell the bond after two years, (ii) the bond yield is 7% at the end of the second year, and (iii) the coupon can be reinvested for one year at a 3% interest rate.

e. Use the tax rates in part (*b*) to compute the *after-tax* two-year realized compound yield. Remember to take account of OID tax rules.

CFA Problems

1. The following multiple-choice problems are based on questions that appeared in past CFA examinations.
   a. A bond with a call feature: *(LO 10-4)*
      (1) Is attractive because the immediate receipt of principal plus premium produces a high return.
      (2) Is more apt to be called when interest rates are high because the interest saving will be greater.
      (3) Will usually have a higher yield to maturity than a similar noncallable bond.
      (4) None of the above.
   b. In which *one* of the following cases is the bond selling at a discount?   *(LO 10-2)*
      (1) Coupon rate is greater than current yield, which is greater than yield to maturity.
      (2) Coupon rate, current yield, and yield to maturity are all the same.
      (3) Coupon rate is less than current yield, which is less than yield to maturity.
      (4) Coupon rate is less than current yield, which is greater than yield to maturity.
   c. Consider a five-year bond with a 10% coupon selling at a yield to maturity of 8%. If interest rates remain constant, one year from now the price of this bond will be: *(LO 10-3)*
      (1) Higher.
      (2) Lower.
      (3) The same.
      (4) Par.
   d. Which of the following statements is *true*?   *(LO 10-7)*
      (1) The expectations hypothesis indicates a flat yield curve if anticipated future short-term rates exceed current short-term rates.
      (2) The basic conclusion of the expectations hypothesis is that the long-term rate is equal to the anticipated short-term rate.
      (3) The liquidity hypothesis indicates that, all other things being equal, longer maturities will have higher yields.
      (4) The liquidity preference theory states that a rising yield curve necessarily implies that the market anticipates increases in interest rates.

2. On May 30, 2018, Janice Kerr is considering the newly issued 10-year AAA corporate bonds shown in the following exhibit: *(LO 10-3)*

Description	Coupon	Price	Callable	Call Price
Sentinal, due May 30, 2028	4.00%	100	Noncallable	NA
Colina, due May 30, 2028	4.20%	100	Currently callable	102

   a. Suppose that market interest rates decline by 100 basis points (i.e., 1%). Contrast the effect of this decline on the price of each bond.
   b. Should Kerr prefer the Colina over the Sentinal bond when rates are expected to rise or to fall?

3. A convertible bond has the following features. What is its conversion premium?   *(LO 10-4)*

Coupon	5.25%
Maturity	June 15, 2028
Market price of bond	$77.50
Market price of underlying common stock	$28.00
Annual dividend	$1.20
Conversion ratio	20.83 shares

4. *a.* Explain the likely impact on the offering yield of adding a call feature to a proposed bond issue.

   b. Explain the likely impact on the bond's expected life of adding a call feature to a proposed bond issue.

   c. Cite one advantage and one disadvantage of investing in callable bonds rather than non-callable bonds.   *(LO 10-4)*

5. Bonds of Zello Corporation with a par value of $1,000 sell for $960, mature in five years, and have a 7% annual coupon rate paid semiannually.   *(LO 10-6)*

   a. Calculate the:

      (1) Current yield.

      (2) Yield to maturity.

      (3) Horizon yield (also called realized compound return) for an investor with a three-year holding period and a reinvestment rate of 6% over the period. At the end of three years the 7% coupon bonds with two years remaining will sell to yield 7%.

   b. Cite *one* major shortcoming for *each* of the following fixed-income yield measures:

      (1) Current yield.

      (2) Yield to maturity.

      (3) Horizon yield (also called realized compound return).

WEB *master*

1. Go to the website of Standard & Poor's at **www.standardandpoors.com.** Look for *Rating Services (Find a Rating).* Find the ratings on bonds of at least 10 companies. Try to choose a sample with a wide range of ratings. Then go to a website such as **finance .google.com** or **finance.yahoo.com** and obtain, for each firm, as many of the financial ratios tabulated in Table 10.3 as you can find. What is the relationship between bond rating and these ratios? Can you tell from your sample which of these ratios are the more important determinants of bond rating?

2. The FINRA operates the TRACE (Trade Reporting and Compliance Engine) system, which reports over-the-counter secondary market trades of fixed-income securities. Find the "TRACE Fact Book" at **www.finra.org/industry/trace/trace-fact-book**. Find the data tables and locate the table with information on corporate bond issues, excluding convertible bonds. For each of the last three years, calculate the following:

   a. The percentage of bonds that were publicly traded and the percentage that were privately traded.

   b. The percentage of bonds that were investment grade and the percentage that were high-yield.

   c. The percentage of bonds that had fixed coupon rates and the percentage that had floating rates.

   d. Repeat the calculations using the information for convertible bond issues.

SOLUTIONS TO CONCEPT *checks*

10.1 The callable bond will sell at the *lower* price. Investors will not be willing to pay as much if they know that the firm retains a valuable option to reclaim the bond for the call price if interest rates fall.

10.2 At a semiannual interest rate of 3%, the bond is worth $40 × Annuity factor(3%, 60) + $1,000 × PV factor(3%, 60) = $1,276.76, which results in a capital gain of $276.76. This exceeds the capital loss of $189.29 (= $1,000 − $810.71) when the semiannual interest rate increased from 4% to 5%.

10.3 Yield to maturity exceeds current yield, which exceeds coupon rate. Take as an example the 8% coupon bond with a yield to maturity of 10% per year (5% per half-year). Its price is $810.71, and therefore its current yield is 80/810.71 = 0.0987, or 9.87%, which is higher than the coupon rate but lower than the yield to maturity.

10.4 The current price of the bond can be derived from the yield to maturity. Using your calculator, set $n = 40$ (semiannual periods); PMT = $45 per period; FV = $1,000; $i = 4\%$ per semiannual period. Calculate present value as $1,098.96. Now we can calculate yield to call. The time to call is five years, or 10 semiannual periods. The price at which the bond will be called is $1,050. To find yield to call, we set $n = 10$ (semiannual periods); PMT = $45 per period; FV = $1,050; PV = $1,098.96. Calculate the semiannual yield to call as 3.72%, or 7.44% bond equivalent yield.

10.5 Price = $70 × Annuity factor(8%, 1) + $1,000 × PV factor(8%, 1) = $990.74

$$\text{Rate of return to investor} = \frac{\$70 + (\$990.74 - \$982.17)}{\$982.17} = .080 = 8\%$$

10.6 By year-end, remaining maturity is 29 years. If the yield to maturity were still 8%, the bond would still sell at par and the holding-period return would be 8%. At a higher yield, price and return will be lower. Suppose the yield to maturity is 8.5%. With annual payments of $80 and a face value of $1,000, the price of the bond is $946.70 ($n = 29$; $i = 8.5\%$; PMT = $80; FV = $1,000). The bond initially sold at $1,000 when issued at the start of the year. The holding-period return is

$$\text{HPR} = \frac{80 + (946.70 - 1,000)}{1,000} = .0267 = 2.67\%$$

which is less than the initial yield to maturity of 8%.

10.7 At the lower yield, the bond price will be $631.67 [($n = 29$, $i = 7\%$, FV = $1,000, PMT = $40)]. Therefore, total after-tax income is:

Coupon	$40 × (1 − 0.38) =	$24.80
Imputed interest	($553.66 − $549.69) × (1 − 0.38) =	2.46
Capital gains	($631.67 − $553.66) × (1 − 0.20) =	62.41
Total income after taxes:		$89.67

Rate of return = 89.67/549.69 = .163 = 16.3%

10.8 The yield to maturity on two-year bonds is 8.5%. The forward rate for the third year is $f_3 = 8\% + 1\% = 9\%$. We obtain the yield to maturity on three-year zeros from

$$(1 + y_3)^3 = (1 + y_2)^2(1 + f_3) = 1.085^2 \times 1.09 = 1.2832$$

Therefore, $y_3 = .0867 = 8.67\%$. We note that the yield on one-year bonds is 8%, on two-year bonds is 8.5%, and on three-year bonds is 8.67%. The yield curve is upward-sloping due solely to the liquidity premium.

Managing Bond Portfolios

Learning Objectives

LO 11-1 Analyze the features of a bond that affect the sensitivity of its price to interest rates.

LO 11-2 Compute the duration of bonds, and use duration to measure interest rate sensitivity.

LO 11-3 Show how convexity affects the response of bond prices to changes in interest rates.

LO 11-4 Formulate fixed-income immunization strategies for various investment horizons.

LO 11-5 Analyze the choices to be made in an actively managed bond portfolio.

I n this chapter, we turn to various strategies that bond managers can pursue, making a distinction between passive and active strategies. Rather than attempting to beat the market by exploiting superior information or insight, a *passive investment strategy* seeks to maintain an appropriate risk-return balance given market opportunities. One special case of passive management for fixed-income portfolios is an immunization strategy that attempts to insulate the portfolio from interest rate risk.

An *active investment strategy* attempts to achieve returns that are more than commensurate with risk. In the context of bond portfolios, this style of management can take two forms. Active managers use interest rate forecasts to predict movements in the entire bond market, or they employ some form of intramarket analysis to identify particular sectors of the market (or particular securities) that are relatively mispriced.

Because interest rate risk is crucial to formulating both active and passive strategies, we begin our discussion with an analysis of the sensitivity of bond prices to interest rate fluctuations. This sensitivity is measured by the duration of the bond, and we devote considerable attention to what determines bond duration. We discuss several passive investment strategies, and show how duration-matching techniques can be used to immunize the holding-period return of a portfolio from interest rate risk. After examining a broad range of applications of the duration measure, we consider refinements in the way that interest rate sensitivity is measured, focusing on the concept of bond convexity.

Duration is important in formulating active investment strategies as well, and we next explore several of these strategies. We conclude the chapter with a discussion of active fixed-income strategies. These include policies based on interest rate forecasting as well as intramarket analysis that seeks to identify relatively attractive sectors or securities within the fixed-income market.

11.1 INTEREST RATE RISK

You know already that there is an inverse relationship between bond prices and yields and that interest rates can fluctuate substantially. As interest rates rise and fall, bondholders experience capital losses and gains. These gains or losses make fixed-income investments risky, even if the coupon and principal payments are guaranteed, as in the case of Treasury obligations.

Why do bond prices respond to interest rate fluctuations? In a competitive market, all securities must offer investors fair expected rates of return. If a bond is issued with a 6% coupon when competitive yields are 6%, then it will sell at par value. If the market rate rises to 7%, however, who would pay par value for a bond offering only a 6% coupon? The bond price must fall until its expected return increases to the competitive level of 7%. Conversely, if the market rate falls to 5%, the 6% coupon on the bond is attractive compared to yields on alternative investments. Investors eager for that return will respond by bidding up the bond price until the total rate of return for investors who purchase at that higher price is no better than the market rate.

Interest Rate Sensitivity

The sensitivity of bond prices to changes in market interest rates is obviously of great concern to investors. To gain some insight into the determinants of interest rate risk, turn to Figure 11.1, which presents the percentage changes in price corresponding to changes in yield to maturity for four bonds that differ according to coupon rate, initial yield to maturity, and time to maturity. All four bonds illustrate that bond prices decrease when yields rise and that the price curve is convex, meaning that decreases in yields have bigger impacts on price than increases in yields of equal magnitude. We summarize these observations in the following two propositions:

1. *Bond prices and yields are inversely related: As yields increase, bond prices fall; as yields fall, bond prices rise.*
2. *An increase in a bond's yield to maturity results in a smaller price change than a decrease in yield of equal magnitude.*

Now compare the interest rate sensitivity of bonds A and B, which are identical except for maturity. Figure 11.1 shows that bond B, which has a longer maturity than bond A, exhibits greater sensitivity to interest rate changes. This illustrates another general property:

3. *Prices of long-term bonds tend to be more sensitive to interest rate changes than prices of short-term bonds.*

This is not surprising. If rates increase, for example, the bond is less valuable as its cash flows are discounted at a now-higher rate. The impact of the higher discount rate will be greater as that rate is applied to more-distant cash flows.

While bond B has six times the maturity of bond A, it has less than six times the interest rate sensitivity. Although interest rate sensitivity generally increases with maturity, it does so less than proportionally as bond maturity increases. Therefore, our fourth property is that:

4. *The sensitivity of bond prices to changes in yields increases at a decreasing rate as maturity increases. In other words, interest rate risk is less than proportional to bond maturity.*

FIGURE   11.1   Change in bond price as a function of change in yield to maturity

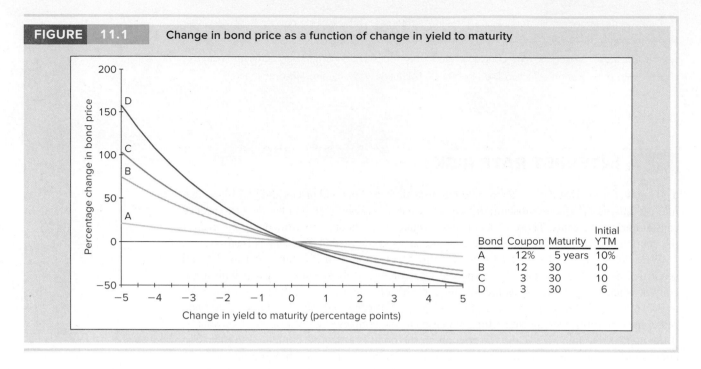

Bond	Coupon	Maturity	Initial YTM
A	12%	5 years	10%
B	12	30	10
C	3	30	10
D	3	30	6

Bonds B and C, which are alike in all respects except for coupon rate, illustrate another point. The lower-coupon bond exhibits greater sensitivity to changes in interest rates. This turns out to be a general property of bond prices:

5. *Interest rate risk is inversely related to the bond's coupon rate. Prices of low-coupon bonds are more sensitive to changes in interest rates than prices of high-coupon bonds.*

Finally, bonds C and D are identical except for the yield to maturity at which the bonds currently sell. Yet bond C, with a higher yield to maturity, is less sensitive to changes in yields. This illustrates our final property:

6. *The sensitivity of a bond's price to a change in its yield is inversely related to the yield to maturity at which the bond currently is selling.*

The first five of these general properties were described by Malkiel (1962) and are sometimes known as Malkiel's bond pricing relationships. The last property was demonstrated by Homer and Leibowitz (1972).

These six propositions confirm that maturity is a major determinant of interest rate risk. However, they also show that maturity alone is not sufficient to measure interest rate sensitivity. For example, bonds B and C in Figure 11.1 have the same maturity, but the higher coupon bond has less price sensitivity to interest rate changes. Obviously, we need to know more than a bond's maturity to quantify its interest rate risk.

To see why bond characteristics such as coupon rate or yield to maturity affect interest rate sensitivity, let's start with a simple numerical example.

Table 11.1 gives bond prices for 8% annual coupon bonds at different yields to maturity and times to maturity. The shortest term bond falls in value by less than 1% when the interest rate increases from 8% to 9%. The 10-year bond falls by 6.4% and the 20-year bond by more than 9%.

Now look at a similar computation using a zero-coupon bond rather than the 8% coupon bond. The results are shown in Table 11.2.

For maturities beyond one year, the price of the zero-coupon bond falls by a greater proportional amount than the price of the 8% coupon bond. The greater sensitivity of zero-coupon

TABLE 11.1	Prices of 8% annual coupon bonds		
Bond's Yield to Maturity	**T = 1 Year**	**T = 10 Years**	**T = 20 Years**
8%	1,000.00	1,000.00	1,000.00
9%	990.83	935.82	908.71
Percent change in price*	−0.92%	−6.42%	−9.13%

*Equals value of bond at a 9% yield to maturity minus value of bond at (the original) 8% yield, divided by the value at 8% yield.

TABLE 11.2	Prices of zero-coupon bonds		
Bond's Yield to Maturity	**T = 1 Year**	**T = 10 Years**	**T = 20 Years**
8%	925.93	463.19	214.55
9%	917.43	422.41	178.43
Percent change in price*	−0.92%	−8.80%	−16.84%

*Equals value of bond at a 9% yield to maturity minus value of bond at (the original) 8% yield, divided by the value at 8% yield.

bonds to interest rate movements suggests that in some sense they must represent a longer-term investment than an equal-time-to-maturity coupon bond.

In fact, this insight about the effective maturity of a bond can be made mathematically precise. To start, note that the times to maturity of the two bonds in this example are incomplete measures of the long- or short-term nature of the bonds. The 8% bond makes many coupon payments, most of which come years before the bond's maturity date. Each payment may be considered to have its own "maturity." In this sense, it is often useful to view a coupon bond as a "portfolio" of coupon payments. The *effective* maturity of the bond would then be measured as some sort of average of the maturities of *all* the cash flows. The zero-coupon bond, by contrast, makes only one payment at maturity, so its time to maturity is well defined.

A high-coupon rate bond has a higher fraction of its value tied to coupons rather than payment of par value, and so the portfolio is more heavily weighted toward the earlier, short-maturity payments, which give it lower "effective maturity." This explains Malkiel's fifth rule, that price sensitivity falls with coupon rate.

Similar logic explains our sixth rule, that price sensitivity falls with yield to maturity. A higher yield reduces the present value of all of the bond's payments, but more so for more distant payments. Therefore, at a higher yield, a higher proportion of the bond's value is due to its earlier payments, so effective maturity is lower. The overall sensitivity of the bond price to changes in yields is thus lower.

Duration

To deal with the concept of the "maturity" of a bond that makes many payments, we need a measure of the average maturity of the bond's promised cash flows. Frederick Macaulay (1938) called the effective maturity concept the *duration* of the bond. **Macaulay's duration** equals the weighted average of the times to each coupon or principal payment. The weights are related to the "importance" of each payment to the value of the bond. Specifically, the weight for each payment time is the proportion of the total value of the bond accounted for by that payment, that is, the present value of the payment divided by the bond price.

We define the weight, w_t, associated with the cash flow made at time t (denoted CF_t) as

$$w_t = \frac{CF_t/(1+y)^t}{\text{Bond price}}$$

Macaulay's duration

A measure of the effective maturity of a bond, defined as the weighted average of the times until each payment, with weights proportional to the present value of the payment.

where y is the bond's yield to maturity. The numerator on the right-hand side of this equation is the present value of the cash flow occurring at time t, while the denominator is the present value of all the bond's payments. These weights sum to 1 because the sum of the cash flows discounted at the yield to maturity equals the bond price.

Using these values to calculate the weighted average of the times until the receipt of each of the bond's payments, we obtain Macaulay's formula for duration, denoted D.

$$D = \sum_{t=1}^{T} t \times w_t \qquad\qquad \textbf{(11.1)}$$

If we write out each term in the summation sign, we can express duration as:

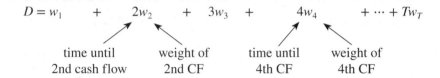

$$D = w_1 \quad + \quad 2w_2 \quad + \quad 3w_3 \quad + \quad 4w_4 \quad + \cdots + Tw_T$$

time until   weight of   time until   weight of
2nd cash flow   2nd CF   4th CF   4th CF

An example of how to apply Equation 11.1 appears in Spreadsheet 11.1, where we derive the durations of an 8% coupon and zero-coupon bond, each with three years to maturity. We assume that the yield to maturity on each bond is 10%. The present value of each payment is discounted at 10% for the number of years shown in column B. The weight associated with each payment time (column E) equals the present value of the payment (column D) divided by the bond price (the sum of the present values in column D).

The numbers in column F are the products of time to payment and payment weight. Each of these products corresponds to one of the terms in Equation 11.1. According to that equation, we can calculate the duration of each bond by adding the numbers in column F.

The duration of the zero-coupon bond is exactly equal to its time to maturity, three years. This makes sense for, with only one payment, the average time until payment must be the bond's maturity. The three-year coupon bond, in contrast, has a shorter duration of 2.7774 years.

While the top panel of the spreadsheet in Spreadsheet 11.1 presents numbers for our particular example, the bottom panel presents the formulas we actually entered in each cell. The inputs in the spreadsheet—specifying the cash flows the bond will pay—are given in columns B and C. In column D we calculate the present value of each cash flow using a discount rate of 10%, in column E we calculate the weights for Equation 11.1, and in column F we compute the product of time until payment and payment weight. Each of these terms corresponds to one of the terms in Equation 11.1. The sum of these terms, reported in cells F9 and F14, is therefore the duration of each bond. Using the spreadsheet, you can easily answer several "what if" questions such as the one in Concept Check 11.1.

CONCEPT check   11.1   Suppose the interest rate decreases to 9%. What will happen to the price and duration of each bond in Spreadsheet 11.1?

Duration is a key concept in bond portfolio management for at least three reasons. First, it is a simple summary measure of the effective average maturity of the portfolio. Second, it turns out to be an essential tool in immunizing portfolios from interest rate risk. We will explore this application in the next section. Third, duration is a measure of the interest rate sensitivity of a bond portfolio, which we explore here.

We have already seen that price sensitivity to interest rate movements generally increases with maturity. Duration enables us to quantify this relationship. It turns out that when interest

SPREADSHEET   11.1

Calculation of the duration of two bonds using Excel spreadsheet

	A	B	C	D	E	F
1	Interest rate:	10%				
2						
3		Time until		Payment		Column (B)
4		Payment		Discounted		×
5		(Years)	Payment	at 10%	Weight*	Column (E)
6	A. 8% coupon bond	1	80	72.727	0.0765	0.0765
7		2	80	66.116	0.0696	0.1392
8		3	1080	811.420	0.8539	2.5617
9	Sum:			950.263	1.0000	2.7774
10						
11	B. Zero-coupon bond	1	0	0.000	0.0000	0.0000
12		2	0	0.000	0.0000	0.0000
13		3	1000	751.315	1.0000	3.0000
14	Sum:			751.315	1.0000	3.0000
15						
16	*Weight = Present value of each payment (column D) divided by bond price					

	A	B	C	D	E	F
1	Interest rate:	0.1				
2						
3		Time until		Payment		Column (B)
4		Payment		Discounted		×
5		(Years)	Payment	at 10%	Weight	Column (E)
6	A. 8% coupon bond	1	80	=C6/(1+$B$1)^B6	=D6/D$9	=E6*B6
7		2	80	=C7/(1+$B$1)^B7	=D7/D$9	=E7*B7
8		3	1080	=C8/(1+$B$1)^B8	=D8/D$9	=E8*B8
9	Sum:			=SUM(D6:D8)	=D9/D$9	=SUM(F6:F8)
10						
11	B. Zero-coupon	1	0	=C11/(1+$B$1)^B11	=D11/D$14	=E11*B11
12		2	0	=C12/(1+$B$1)^B12	=D12/D$14	=E12*B12
13		3	1000	=C13/(1+$B$1)^B13	=D13/D$14	=E13*B13
14	Sum:			=SUM(D11:D13)	=D14/D$14	=SUM(F11:F13)

Ⴝ

Spreadsheets are available in Connect

rates change, the percentage change in a bond's price is proportional to its duration. Specifically, the proportional change in a bond's price can be related to the change in its yield to maturity, *y*, according to the rule

$$\frac{\Delta P}{P} = -D \times \left[\frac{\Delta(1+y)}{1+y}\right] \qquad (11.2)$$

The proportional price change equals the proportional change in (1 plus the bond's yield) times the bond's duration. Therefore, bond price volatility is proportional to the bond's duration, and duration becomes a natural measure of interest rate exposure.[1] This relationship is key to interest rate risk management.

Practitioners commonly use Equation 11.2 in a slightly different form. They define **modified duration** as $D^* = D/(1+y)$ and rewrite Equation 11.2 as

$$\frac{\Delta P}{P} = -D^*\Delta y \qquad (11.3)$$

The percentage change in bond price is just the product of modified duration and the change in the bond's yield to maturity.

modified duration

Macaulay's duration divided by 1 + yield to maturity. Measures interest rate sensitivity of bond.

---

[1]Actually, as we will see later, Equation 11.2 is only approximately valid for large changes in the bond's yield. The approximation becomes exact as one considers smaller, or localized, changes in yields.

A bond with maturity of 30 years has a coupon rate of 8% (paid annually) and a yield to maturity of 9%. Its price is $897.26, and its duration is 11.37 years. What will happen to the bond price if the bond's yield to maturity increases to 9.1%?

Equation 11.3 tells us that an increase of 0.1% in the bond's yield to maturity ($\Delta y = .001$ in decimal terms) will result in a price change of

$$\Delta P = -(D^*\Delta y) \times P$$
$$= -\frac{11.37}{1.09} \times .001 \times \$897.26 = -\$9.36$$

To confirm the relationship between duration and the sensitivity of bond price to interest rate changes, let's compare the price sensitivity of the three-year coupon bond in Spreadsheet 11.1, which has a duration of 2.7774 years, to the sensitivity of a zero-coupon bond with maturity and duration of 2.7774 years. Both should have equal interest rate exposure if duration is a useful measure of price sensitivity.

The three-year bond sells for $950.263 at the initial interest rate of 10%. If the bond's yield increases by 1 basis point (1/100 of a percent) to 10.01%, its price will fall to $950.0231, a percentage decline of .0252%. The zero-coupon bond has a maturity of 2.7774 years. At the initial interest rate of 10%, it sells at a price of $1,000/1.10^{2.7774} = $767.425. When the interest rate increases, its price falls to $1,000/1.1001^{2.7774} = $767.2313, for an identical .0252% capital loss. We conclude that equal-duration assets are equally sensitive to interest rate movements.

Incidentally, this example also confirms the validity of Equation 11.2. The equation predicts that the proportional price change of the two bonds should have been $-2.7774 \times .0001/1.10 = .000252$, or .0252%, just as we found from direct computation.

a. In Concept Check 11.1, you calculated the price and duration of a three-year maturity, 8% coupon bond at an interest rate of 9%. Now suppose the interest rate increases to 9.05%. What is the new value of the bond, and what is the percentage change in the bond's price?
b. Calculate the percentage change in the bond's price predicted by the duration formula in Equation 11.2 or 11.3. Compare this value to your answer for (a).

The equations for the durations of coupon bonds are tedious, and spreadsheets like Spreadsheet 11.1 are cumbersome to modify for different maturities and coupon rates. Fortunately, spreadsheet programs such as Excel come with built-in functions for duration. Moreover, these functions easily accommodate bonds that are between coupon payment dates. Spreadsheet 11.2 illustrates how to use Excel to compute duration. The spreadsheets use many of the same conventions as the bond pricing spreadsheets described in Chapter 10.

We can use the spreadsheet to reconfirm the duration of the 8% coupon bond examined in Panel A of Spreadsheet 11.1. The settlement date (i.e., today's date) and maturity date are entered in cells B2 and B3 of Spreadsheet 11.2 using Excel's date function, DATE(year, month, day). For this three-year maturity bond, we don't have a specific settlement date. We arbitrarily set the settlement date to January 1, 2000, and use a maturity date precisely three years later. The coupon rate and yield to maturity are entered as decimals in cells B4 and B5, and the payment periods per year are entered in cell B6. Macaulay and modified duration appear in cells B9 and B10. Cell B9 shows that the duration of the bond is indeed 2.7774 years. The modified duration of the bond is 2.5249, which equals 2.7774/1.10.

Consider a 9% coupon, 8-year maturity bond with annual payments selling at a yield to maturity of 10%. Use Spreadsheet 11.2 to confirm that the bond's duration is 5.97 years. What would its duration be if the bond paid its coupon semiannually? Why intuitively does duration fall?

SPREADSHEET 11.2

Using Excel functions to compute duration

	A	B	C
1	Inputs		Formula In column B
2	Settlement date	1/1/2000	=DATE(2000,1,1)
3	Maturity date	1/1/2003	=DATE(2003,1,1)
4	Coupon rate	0.08	0.08
5	Yield to maturity	0.10	0.10
6	Coupons per year	1	1
7			
8	Outputs		
9	Macaulay duration	2.7774	=DURATION(B2,B3,B4,B5,B6)
10	Modified duration	2.5249	=MDURATION(B2,B3,B4,B5,B6)

Spreadsheets are available in Connect

What Determines Duration?

Malkiel's bond price relations, which we laid out in the previous section, characterize the determinants of interest rate sensitivity. Duration allows us to quantify that sensitivity. For example, if we wish to speculate on interest rates, duration tells us how strong a bet we are making. Conversely, if we wish to remain "neutral" on rates, and simply match the interest rate sensitivity of a chosen bond market index, duration allows us to measure that sensitivity and mimic it in our own portfolio. For these reasons, it is crucial to understand the determinants of duration and convenient to have formulas to calculate the duration of some commonly encountered securities. Therefore, in this section, we present several "rules" that summarize most of its important properties. These rules are also illustrated in Figure 11.2, which contains plots of durations of bonds of various coupon rates, yields to maturity, and times to maturity.

We have already established:

Rule 1: The duration of a zero-coupon bond equals its time to maturity.

We also have seen that the three-year coupon bond has a lower duration than the three-year zero because coupons early in the bond's life reduce the bond's weighted-average time until payments. This illustrates another general property:

Rule 2: With time to maturity and yield to maturity held constant, a bond's duration and interest rate sensitivity are higher when the coupon rate is lower.

This property corresponds to Malkiel's fifth bond pricing relationship and is attributable to the impact of early coupons on the average maturity of a bond's payments. The lower these coupons, the less weight these early payments have on the weighted-average maturity of all the bond's payments. In other words, a lower fraction of the total value of the bond is tied up in the (earlier) coupon payments whose values are relatively insensitive to yields rather than the (later and more yield-sensitive) repayment of par value. Compare the plots in Figure 11.2 of the durations of the 3% coupon and 15% coupon bonds, each with identical yields of 15%. The plot of the duration of the 15% coupon bond lies below the corresponding plot for the 3% coupon bond.

Rule 3: With the coupon rate held constant, a bond's duration and interest rate sensitivity generally increase with time to maturity. Duration always increases with maturity for bonds selling at par or at a premium to par.

This property of duration corresponds to Malkiel's third relationship and is fairly intuitive. What is surprising is that duration need not always increase with time to maturity. For some deep discount bonds, such as the 3% coupon bond selling to yield 15% in Figure 11.2, duration may eventually fall with increases in maturity. For virtually all traded bonds, however, it is safe to assume that duration increases with maturity.

FIGURE   **11.2**   **Duration as a function of maturity**

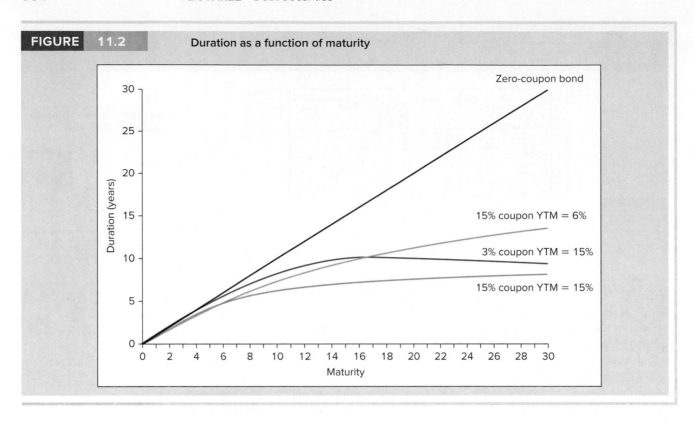

Notice in Figure 11.2 that the maturity and duration of the zero-coupon bond are equal. For all the coupon bonds, however, duration increases by less than a year for each year's increase in maturity, and duration is less than maturity.

Figure 11.2 shows that the two 15% coupon bonds have different durations when they sell at different yields to maturity. The lower-yield bond has longer duration. This makes sense, because at lower yields the more distant payments have relatively greater present values and thereby account for a greater share of the bond's total value. Thus, in the weighted-average calculation of duration, the distant payments receive greater weights, which results in a higher duration measure. This establishes

Rule 4: With other factors held constant, the duration and interest rate sensitivity of a coupon bond are higher when the bond's yield to maturity is lower.

Rule 4, which is the sixth bond pricing relationship noted above, applies to coupon bonds. For zeros, duration equals time to maturity, regardless of the yield to maturity.

Finally, we present an algebraic rule for the duration of a perpetuity. This rule is derived from and is consistent with the formula for duration given in Equation 11.1, but it is far easier to use for infinitely lived bonds.

Rule 5: The duration of a level perpetuity is

$$\text{Duration of perpetuity} = \frac{1+y}{y} \qquad \textbf{(11.4)}$$

For example, at a 15% yield, the duration of a perpetuity that pays $100 once a year forever is $1.15/.15 = 7.67$ years, while at a 6% yield it is $1.06/.06 = 17.67$ years.

TABLE 11.3 Duration of annual coupon bonds (initial yield to maturity = 6%)

Maturity (years)	Coupon Rate			
	2%	4%	6%	8%
1	1.000	1.000	1.000	1.000
5	4.786	4.611	4.465	4.342
10	8.961	8.281	7.802	7.445
20	15.170	13.216	12.158	11.495
Infinite (perpetuity)	17.667	17.667	17.667	17.667

Equation 11.4 makes it obvious that maturity and duration can differ substantially. The maturity of the perpetuity is infinite, while the duration of the instrument at a 15% yield is only 7.67 years. The present value-weighted cash flows early on in the life of the perpetuity dominate the computation of duration. Figure 11.2 shows that as their maturities become ever longer, the durations of the two coupon bonds with yields of 15% both converge to the duration of the perpetuity with the same yield, 7.67 years.

Durations can vary widely among traded bonds. Table 11.3 presents durations for several bonds, all paying annual coupons and yielding 6% per year. Duration decreases as coupon rates increase and increases with time to maturity. According to Table 11.3 and Equation 11.2, if the interest rate were to increase from 6% to 6.1%, the 6% coupon, 20-year bond would fall in value by about 1.15% (= −12.158 × .1%/1.06) while the 8% coupon, five-year bond would fall by only .41% (= −4.342 × .1%/1.06). Notice also from Table 11.3 that duration is independent of coupon rate only for perpetuities.

Show that the duration of a perpetuity increases as the interest rate decreases, in accordance with Rule 4.

CONCEPT check   11.4

11.2 PASSIVE BOND MANAGEMENT

Passive managers take bond prices as fairly set and seek to control only the risk of their fixed-income portfolios. Generally, there are two ways of viewing this risk. Some institutions, such as banks, are concerned with protecting the portfolio's current net worth or net market value against interest rate fluctuations. Risk-based capital guidelines for commercial banks and thrift institutions require the setting aside of additional capital as a buffer against potential losses in market value, for example, due to interest rate fluctuations. The amount of capital required is directly related to the losses that may be incurred. Other investors, such as pension funds, may have an investment goal to be reached after a given number of years. These investors are more concerned with protecting the future values of their portfolios.

What is common to all investors, however, is interest rate risk. The net worth of the firm and its ability to meet future obligations fluctuate with interest rates. **Immunization** and dedication techniques refer to strategies that investors use to shield their net worth from interest rate risk.

immunization

A strategy to shield net worth from interest rate movements.

Immunization

Many banks and thrift institutions have a natural mismatch between the maturities of assets and liabilities. For example, bank liabilities are primarily the deposits owed to customers; these liabilities are short term and consequently have low duration. Assets largely comprise commercial and consumer loans or mortgages, which have longer duration. Their values are

On the MARKET FRONT

PENSION FUNDS LOSE GROUND DESPITE BROAD MARKET GAINS

With the S&P 500 providing a 16% rate of return, 2012 was a good year for the stock market, and this performance helped boost the balance sheets of U.S. pension funds. Yet despite the increase in the value of their assets, the total estimated pension deficit of 400 large U.S. companies *rose* by nearly $80 billion, and many of these firms entered 2013 needing to shore up their pension funds with billions of dollars of additional cash. Ford Motor Company alone predicted that it would contribute $5 billion to its fund.*

How did this happen? Blame the decline in interest rates during the year that were in large part the force behind the stock market gains. As rates fell, the present value of pension obligations to retirees rose even faster than the value of the assets backing those promises. It turns out that the value of pension liabilities is more sensitive to interest rate changes than is the value of the typical assets held in those funds. So even though falling rates tend to pump up asset returns, they pump up liabilities even more. In other words, the duration of fund investments is shorter than the duration of its obligations. This duration mismatch makes funds vulnerable to interest rate declines.

Why don't funds better match asset and liability durations? One reason is that fund managers are often evaluated based on their performance relative to standard bond market indexes. Those indexes tend to have far shorter durations than pension fund liabilities. So to some extent, managers may be keeping their eyes on the wrong ball, one with the wrong interest rate sensitivity.

*These estimates appear in Mike Ramsey and Vipal Monga, "Low Rates Force Companies to Pour Cash into Pensions," *The Wall Street Journal,* February 3, 2013.

---

correspondingly more sensitive than deposits to interest rate fluctuations. When interest rates increase unexpectedly, banks can suffer decreases in net worth—their assets fall in value by more than their liabilities.

Similarly, a pension fund may have a mismatch between the interest rate sensitivity of the assets held in the fund and the present value of its liabilities—the promise to make payments to retirees. The nearby box illustrates the dangers that pension funds face when they neglect the interest rate exposure of *both* assets and liabilities. It points out that when interest rates change, the present value of the fund's liabilities change. For example, in some recent years pension funds lost ground despite the fact that they enjoyed excellent investment returns. As interest rates fell, the value of their liabilities grew even faster than the value of their assets. The conclusion: Funds should match the interest rate exposure of assets and liabilities so that the value of assets will track the value of liabilities whether rates rise or fall. In other words, the financial manager might want to *immunize* the fund against interest rate volatility.

Pension funds are not alone in this concern. Any institution with a future fixed obligation might consider immunization a reasonable risk management policy. Insurance companies, for example, also pursue immunization strategies. In fact, the tactic of immunization was introduced by F. M. Redington (1952), an actuary for a life insurance company. The idea is that duration-matched assets and liabilities let the asset portfolio meet the firm's obligations despite interest rate movements.

Consider, for example, an insurance company that issues a guaranteed investment contract, or GIC, for $10,000. (GICs are essentially zero-coupon bonds issued by the insurance company to its customers. They are popular products for individuals' retirement-savings accounts.) If the GIC has a five-year maturity and a guaranteed interest rate of 8%, the insurance company promises to pay $10,000 \times (1.08)^5 = $14,693.28 in five years.

Suppose that the insurance company chooses to fund its obligation with $10,000 of 8% *annual* coupon bonds, selling at par value, with six years to maturity. As long as the market interest rate stays at 8%, the company has fully funded the obligation, as the present value of the obligation exactly equals the value of the bonds.

Table 11.4, Panel A, shows that if interest rates remain at 8%, the accumulated funds from the bond will grow to exactly the $14,693.28 obligation. Over the five-year period, the year-end coupon income of $800 is reinvested at the prevailing 8% market interest rate. At the end of the period, the bonds can be sold for $10,000; they still will sell at par value because the

TABLE 11.4 Terminal value of a six-year maturity bond portfolio after five years (all proceeds reinvested)

Payment Number	Years Remaining until Obligation	Accumulated Value of Invested Payment	
A. Rates remain at 8%			
1	4	$800 \times (1.08)^4 =$	1,088.39
2	3	$800 \times (1.08)^3 =$	1,007.77
3	2	$800 \times (1.08)^2 =$	933.12
4	1	$800 \times (1.08)^1 =$	864.00
5	0	$800 \times (1.08)^0 =$	800.00
Sale of bond	0	$10,800/1.08 =$	10,000.00
			14,693.28
B. Rates fall to 7%			
1	4	$800 \times (1.07)^4 =$	1,048.64
2	3	$800 \times (1.07)^3 =$	980.03
3	2	$800 \times (1.07)^2 =$	915.92
4	1	$800 \times (1.07)^1 =$	856.00
5	0	$800 \times (1.07)^0 =$	800.00
Sale of bond	0	$10,800/1.07 =$	10,093.46
			14,694.05
C. Rates increase to 9%			
1	4	$800 \times (1.09)^4 =$	1,129.27
2	3	$800 \times (1.09)^3 =$	1,036.02
3	2	$800 \times (1.09)^2 =$	950.48
4	1	$800 \times (1.09)^1 =$	872.00
5	0	$800 \times (1.09)^0 =$	800.00
Sale of bond	0	$10,800/1.09 =$	9,908.26
			14,696.02

Note: The sale price of the bond portfolio equals the portfolio's final payment ($10,800) divided by $1 + r$, because the time to maturity of the bonds will be one year at the time of sale.

coupon rate still equals the market interest rate. Total income after five years from reinvested coupons and the sale of the bond is precisely $14,693.28.

If interest rates change, however, two offsetting influences will affect the ability of the fund to grow to the targeted value of $14,693.28. If interest rates rise, the fund will suffer a capital loss, impairing its ability to satisfy the obligation. However, at a higher interest rate, reinvested coupons will grow at a faster rate, offsetting the capital loss. In other words, fixed-income investors face two offsetting types of interest rate risk: *price risk* and *reinvestment rate risk*. Increases in interest rates cause capital losses but at the same time increase the rate at which reinvested income will grow. If the portfolio duration is chosen appropriately, these two effects will cancel out exactly. When portfolio duration equals the investor's horizon date, the accumulated value of the investment fund at the horizon date will be unaffected by interest rate fluctuations. *For a horizon equal to the portfolio's duration, price risk and reinvestment risk are precisely offsetting.* The obligation is immunized.

In our example, the duration of the six-year maturity bonds used to fund the GIC is just about five years. You can confirm this using either Spreadsheet 11.1 or 11.2. The duration of the (zero-coupon) GIC is also five years. Because the assets and liabilities have equal duration, the insurance company is immunized against interest rate fluctuations. To confirm this, let's check that the bond can generate enough income to pay off the obligation in five years regardless of interest rate movements.

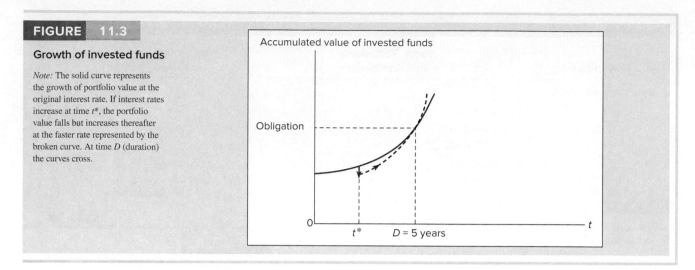

Panels B and C of Table 11.4 illustrate two possible interest rate scenarios: Rates either fall to 7% or increase to 9%. In both cases, the annual coupon payments are reinvested at the new interest rate, which is assumed to change before the first coupon payment, and the bond is sold in year 5 to help satisfy the obligation of the GIC.

Panel B shows that if interest rates fall to 7%, the total funds will accumulate to $14,694.05, providing a small surplus of $0.77. If rates increase to 9% as in Panel C, the fund accumulates to $14,696.02, providing a small surplus of $2.74.

Several points are worth highlighting. First, duration matching balances the difference between the accumulated value of the coupon payments (reinvestment rate risk) and the sale value of the bond (price risk). That is, when interest rates fall, the coupons grow less than in the base case, but the higher value of the bond offsets this. When interest rates rise, the value of the bond falls, but the coupons more than make up for this loss because they are reinvested at the higher rate. Figure 11.3 illustrates this case. The solid curve traces the accumulated value of the bonds if interest rates remain at 8%. The dashed curve shows that value if interest rates happen to increase. The initial impact is a capital loss, but this loss eventually is offset by the now-faster growth rate of reinvested funds. At the five-year horizon date, equal to the bond's duration, the two effects just cancel, leaving the company able to satisfy its obligation with the accumulated proceeds from the bond.

We can also analyze immunization in terms of present as opposed to future values. Table 11.5, Panel A, shows the initial balance sheet for the insurance company's GIC. Both

TABLE 11.5 Market value balance sheets

A. Interest rate = 8%

Assets		Liabilities	
Bonds	$10,000.00	Obligation	$10,000.00

B. Interest rate = 7%

Assets		Liabilities	
Bonds	$10,476.65	Obligation	$10,476.11

C. Interest rate = 9%

Assets		Liabilities	
Bonds	$ 9,551.41	Obligation	$ 9,549.62

Notes: Value of bonds = 800 × Annuity factor(r, 6) + 10,000 × PV factor(r, 6).

Value of obligation $= \dfrac{14,693.28}{(1 + r)^5} = 14{,}693.28 \times$ PV factor(r, 5).

assets and the obligation have market values of $10,000, so the plan is just fully funded. Panels B and C show that whether the interest rate increases or decreases, the value of the bonds funding the GIC and the present value of the company's obligation change by virtually identical amounts. Regardless of the interest rate change, the plan remains fully funded, with the surplus in Panels B and C just about zero. The duration-matching strategy has ensured that both assets and liabilities react equally to interest rate fluctuations.

Figure 11.4 is a graph of the present values of the bond and the single-payment obligation as a function of the interest rate. At the current rate of 8%, the values are equal, and the obligation is fully funded by the bond. Moreover, the two present value curves are tangent at $y = 8\%$. As interest rates change, the change in value of both the asset and the obligation are equal, so the obligation remains fully funded. For greater changes in the interest rate, however, the present value curves diverge. This reflects the fact that the fund actually shows a small surplus at market interest rates other than 8%.

Why is there *any* surplus in the fund? After all, we claimed that a duration-matched asset and liability mix would make the investor indifferent to interest rate shifts. Actually, such a claim is valid for only *small* changes in the interest rate, because as bond yields change, so too does duration. (Recall Rule 4 for duration.) In fact, while the duration of the bond in this example is equal to five years at a yield to maturity of 8%, the duration rises to 5.02 years when the bond yield falls to 7% and drops to 4.97 years at $y = 9\%$. That is, the bond and the obligation were not duration-matched *across* the interest rate shift, so the position was not exactly immunized.

This example highlights the importance of **rebalancing** immunized portfolios. As interest rates and asset durations continually change, managers must adjust the portfolio to realign its duration with the duration of the obligation. Moreover, even if interest rates do not change, asset durations *will* change solely because of the passage of time. Recall from Figure 11.2 that duration generally decreases less rapidly than maturity as time passes, so even if an obligation is immunized at the outset, the durations of the asset and liability will fall at different rates. Without rebalancing, durations will become unmatched. Therefore, immunization is a passive strategy only in the sense that it does not involve attempts to identify undervalued securities. Immunization managers still must proactively update and monitor their positions.

rebalancing

Realigning the proportions of assets in a portfolio as needed.

An insurance company must make a payment of $19,487 in seven years. The market interest rate is 10%, so the present value of the obligation is $10,000. The company's portfolio manager wishes to fund the obligation using three-year zero-coupon bonds and perpetuities paying annual coupons. (We focus on zeros and perpetuities to keep the algebra simple.) How can the manager immunize the obligation?

Immunization requires that the duration of the portfolio of assets equal the duration of the liability. We can proceed in four steps:

Step 1. Calculate the duration of the liability, which in this case is simple to compute. It is a single-payment obligation with maturity and duration of seven years.

Step 2. Calculate the duration of the asset portfolio, which is the weighted average of the durations of each component asset, with weights proportional to the funds placed in each asset. The duration of the zero-coupon bond is simply its maturity, 3 years. The duration of the perpetuity is $1.10/.10 = 11$ years. Therefore, if the fraction of the portfolio invested in the zero is called w, and the fraction invested in the perpetuity is $(1 - w)$, the portfolio duration is

$$\text{Asset duration} = w \times 3 \text{ years} + (1 - w) \times 11 \text{ years}$$

Step 3. Find the asset mix that sets the duration of assets equal to the seven-year duration of liabilities. This requires us to solve for w in the following equation

$$w \times 3 \text{ years} + (1 - w) \times 11 \text{ years} = 7 \text{ years}$$

EXAMPLE 11.2

Constructing an Immunized Portfolio

(continued)

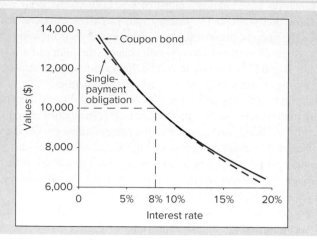

FIGURE 11.4

Immunization. The coupon bond fully funds the obligation at an interest rate of 8%. Moreover, the present value curves are tangent at 8%, so the obligation will remain fully funded even if rates change by a small amount.

EXAMPLE 11.2

Constructing an Immunized Portfolio (concluded)

This implies that $w = 1/2$. The manager should invest half the portfolio in the zero and half in the perpetuity. This will result in an asset duration of seven years.

Step 4.   Fully fund the obligation. Because the obligation has a present value of $10,000, and the fund will be invested equally in the zero and the perpetuity, the manager must purchase $5,000 of the zero-coupon bond and $5,000 of the perpetuity. Note that the face value of the zero will be $5,000 $\times$ 1.10^3 = $6,655$.

Even if a position is immunized, however, the portfolio manager still cannot rest. This is because of the need to rebalance as interest rates fluctuate. Moreover, even if rates do not change, the passage of time also will affect duration and require rebalancing. Let's continue Example 11.2 and see how the portfolio manager can maintain an immunized position.

EXAMPLE 11.3

Rebalancing

Suppose that a year has passed, and the interest rate remains at 10%. The portfolio manager of Example 11.2 needs to reexamine her position. Is the position still fully funded? Is it still immunized? If not, what actions are required?

First, examine funding. The present value of the obligation will have grown to $11,000, as it is one year closer to maturity. The manager's funds also have grown to $11,000: The zero-coupon bonds have increased in value from $5,000 to $5,500 with the passage of time, while the perpetuity has paid its annual $500 coupons and remains worth $5,000. Therefore, the obligation is still fully funded.

The portfolio weights must be changed, however. The zero-coupon bond now has a duration of 2 years, while the perpetuity duration remains at 11 years. The obligation is now due in 6 years. The weights must now satisfy the equation

$$w \times 2 + (1 - w) \times 11 = 6$$

which implies that $w = 5/9$. To rebalance the portfolio and maintain the duration match, the manager now must invest a total of $11,000 \times 5/9 = $6,111.11$ in the zero-coupon bond. This requires that the entire $500 coupon payment be invested in the zero, with an additional $111.11 of the perpetuity sold and invested in the zero-coupon bond.

Of course, rebalancing the portfolio entails transaction costs as assets are bought or sold. In practice, managers strike a compromise between the desire for perfect immunization, which requires continual rebalancing, and the need to control trading costs, which dictates less frequent rebalancing.

Immunization

The Excel immunization model allows you to analyze any number of time-period or holding-period immunization examples. The model is built using the Excel-supplied formulas for bond duration. In these calculations, the coupon period is assumed to be annual.

Spreadsheets are available in Connect

	A	B	C	D	E	F	G	H
1			Holding Period Immunization					
2								
3	YTM	0.0800	Mar Price	1000.00				
4	Coupon rate	0.0800						
5	Maturity	6			Duration	4.993		
6	Par value	1000.00						
7	Holding period	5						
8	Duration	4.9927						
9								
10								
11	If rates increase by 200 basis points				If rates increase by 100 basis points			
12	Rate	0.1000			Rate	0.0900		
13	FV of CPS	488.41			FV of CPS	478.78		
14	Sales price	981.82			Sales price	990.83		
15	Total	1470.23			Total	1469.60		
16	IRR	0.0801			IRR	0.0800		
17								
18								
19								
20	If rates decrease by 200 basis points				If rates decrease by 100 basis points			
21	Rate	0.0600			Rate	0.0700		
22	FV of CPS	450.97			FV of CPS	460.06		
23	Sales price	1018.87			Sales price	1009.35		
24	Total	1469.84			Total	1469.40		
25	IRR	0.0801			IRR	0.0800		

Excel Questions

1. When rates increase by 100 basis points, what is the change in the future sales price of the bond? The value of reinvested coupons?

2. What if rates increase by 200 basis points?

3. What is the relation between price risk and reinvestment rate risk as we consider larger changes in bond yields?

CONCEPT check 11.5

Look again at Example 11.3. What would have been the immunizing weights in the second year if the interest rate had fallen to 8%?

Cash Flow Matching and Dedication

The problems associated with immunization seem to have a simple solution. Why not simply buy a zero-coupon bond with face value equal to the projected cash outlay? This is **cash flow matching,** which automatically immunizes a portfolio from interest rate risk because the cash flow from the bond and the obligation exactly offset each other.

Cash flow matching on a multiperiod basis is referred to as a **dedication strategy.** In this case, the manager selects either zero-coupon or coupon bonds with total cash flows that match a series of obligations. The advantage of dedication is that it is a once-and-for-all approach to eliminating interest rate risk. Once the cash flows are matched, there is no need for rebalancing.

Cash flow matching is not widely pursued, however, probably because of the constraints it imposes on bond selection. Immunization/dedication strategies are appealing to firms that do not wish to bet on general movements in interest rates, yet these firms may want to immunize

cash flow matching

Matching cash flows from a fixed-income portfolio with those of an obligation.

dedication strategy

Multiperiod cash flow matching.

using bonds they believe are undervalued. Cash flow matching places so many constraints on bond selection that it can make it impossible to pursue a dedication strategy using only "underpriced" bonds. Firms looking for underpriced bonds exchange exact and easy dedication for the possibility of achieving superior returns from their bond portfolios.

Sometimes, cash flow matching is not even possible. To cash flow match for a pension fund that is obligated to pay out a perpetual flow of income to current and future retirees, the pension fund would need to purchase fixed-income securities with maturities ranging up to hundreds of years. Such securities do not exist, making exact dedication infeasible. Immunization is easy, however. If the interest rate is 8%, for example, the duration of the pension fund obligation is $1.08/.08 = 13.5$ years (see Rule 5 in Section 11.1). Therefore, the fund can immunize its obligation by purchasing zero-coupon bonds with maturity of 13.5 years and a market value equal to that of the pension liabilities.

CONCEPT check 11.6

a. Suppose that this pension fund is obligated to pay out $800,000 per year in perpetuity. What should be the maturity and face value of the zero-coupon bond it purchases to immunize its obligation?

b. Now suppose the interest rate immediately increases to 8.1%. How should the fund rebalance to remain immunized against further interest rate shocks? Ignore transaction costs.

CONCEPT check 11.7

How would an increase in trading costs affect the attractiveness of dedication versus immunization?

11.3 CONVEXITY

Duration clearly is a key tool in bond portfolio management. Yet, the duration rule for the impact of interest rates on bond prices is only an approximation. Equation 11.3, which we repeat here, states that the percentage change in the value of a bond approximately equals the product of modified duration times the change in the bond's yield:

$$\frac{\Delta P}{P} = -D^*\Delta y$$

In other words, the percentage price change is directly proportional to the change in the bond's yield. If this were *exactly* so, however, a graph of the percentage change in bond price as a function of the change in its yield would plot as a straight line, with slope equal to $-D^*$. Yet we know from Figure 11.1, and more generally from Malkiel's five bond pricing relationships (specifically Relationship 2), that the relationship between bond prices and yields is *not* linear. The duration rule is a good approximation for small changes in bond yield, but it is less accurate for larger changes.

Figure 11.5 illustrates this point. Like Figure 11.1, this figure presents the percentage change in bond price in response to a change in the bond's yield to maturity. The curved line is the percentage price change for a 30-year maturity, 8% coupon bond, selling at an initial yield to maturity of 8%. The straight line is the percentage price change predicted by the duration rule: The modified duration of the bond at its initial yield is 11.26 years, so the straight line is a plot of $-D^*\Delta y = -11.26 \times \Delta y$. The two plots are tangent at the initial yield. Thus, for small changes in the bond's yield to maturity, the duration rule is quite accurate. However, for larger changes, there is progressively more "daylight" between the two plots, demonstrating that the duration rule becomes progressively less accurate.

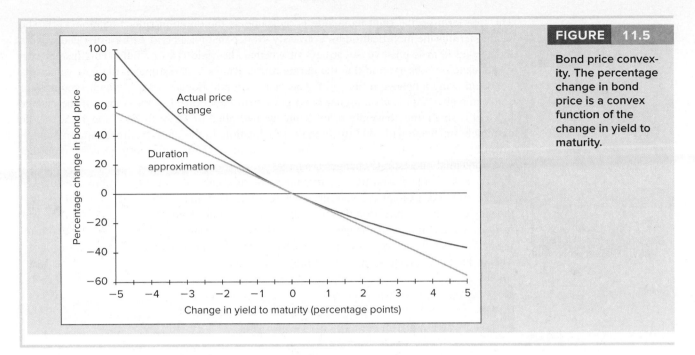

FIGURE 11.5

Bond price convexity. The percentage change in bond price is a convex function of the change in yield to maturity.

Figure 11.5 shows that the duration approximation (the straight line) always understates the value of the bond; it underestimates the increase in bond price when the yield falls, and it overestimates the decline in price when the yield rises. This is due to the curvature of the true price-yield relationship. Curves with shapes such as that of the price-yield relationship are said to be convex, and the curvature of the price-yield curve is called the **convexity** of the bond.

convexity

The curvature of the price-yield relationship of a bond.

We measure convexity as the rate of change of the slope of the price-yield curve, expressed as a fraction of the bond price.[2] As a practical matter, you can view bonds with higher convexity as exhibiting higher curvature in the price-yield relationship. The convexity of noncallable bonds, such as that in Figure 11.5, is positive: The slope increases (i.e., becomes less negative) at higher yields.

Convexity allows us to improve the duration approximation for bond price changes. Accounting for convexity, Equation 11.3 can be modified as follows:[3]

$$\frac{\Delta P}{P} = -D^* \Delta y + \frac{1}{2} \times \text{Convexity} \times (\Delta y)^2 \qquad \textbf{(11.5)}$$

---

[2]If you have taken a calculus class, you will recognize that Equation 11.3 for modified duration can be written as $dP/P = -D^* dy$. Thus, $-D^* = 1/P \times dP/dy$ is the slope of the price-yield curve expressed as a fraction of the bond price. Similarly, the convexity of a bond equals the second derivative (the rate of change of the slope) of the price-yield curve divided by bond price: Convexity $= 1/P \times d^2 P/dy^2$. The formula for the convexity of a bond with a maturity of n years making annual coupon payments is

$$\text{Convexity} = \frac{1}{P \times (1 + y)^2} \sum_{t=1}^{n} \left[\frac{CF_t}{(1 + y)^t} (t^2 + t) \right]$$

where CF_t is the cash flow paid to the bondholder at date t; CF_t represents either a coupon payment before maturity or final coupon plus par value at the maturity date.

[3]To use the convexity rule, you must express interest rates as decimals rather than percentages.

The first term on the right-hand side is the same as the duration rule, Equation 11.3. The second term is the modification for convexity. Notice that for a bond with positive convexity, the second term is positive, regardless of whether the yield rises or falls. This insight corresponds to our observation that the duration rule always underestimates the new value of a bond following a change in its yield. The more accurate Equation 11.5, which accounts for convexity, always predicts a higher bond price than Equation 11.3. Of course, if the change in yield is small, the convexity term, which is multiplied by $(\Delta y)^2$ in Equation 11.5, will be extremely small and will add little to the approximation. In this case, the linear approximation given by the duration rule will be sufficiently accurate. Thus, convexity is more important when potential interest rate changes are large.

Convexity is the reason that the immunization examples we considered above resulted in small errors. For example, if you turn back to Table 11.5 and Figure 11.4, you will see that the single-payment obligation that was funded with a coupon bond of the same duration was well immunized for small changes in yields. However, for larger yield changes, the two pricing curves diverged a bit, implying that such changes in yields would result in small surpluses. This is due to the greater convexity of the coupon bond.

EXAMPLE 11.4

Convexity

The bond in Figure 11.5 has a 30-year maturity, an 8% coupon, and sells at an initial yield to maturity of 8%. Because the coupon rate equals yield to maturity, the bond sells at par value, or $1,000. The modified duration of the bond at its initial yield is 11.26 years, and its convexity is 212.4, which can be calculated using the formula in footnote 2. (You can find a spreadsheet to calculate the convexity of a 30-year bond in Connect. See also the nearby Excel Application.) If the bond's yield increases from 8% to 10%, the bond price will fall to $811.46, a decline of 18.85%. The duration rule, Equation 11.3, would predict a price decline of

$$\frac{\Delta P}{P} = -D^* \Delta y = -11.26 \times .02 = -.2252 = -22.52\%$$

which is considerably more than the bond price actually falls. The duration-with-convexity rule, Equation 11.5, is far more accurate:

$$\frac{\Delta P}{P} = -D^* \Delta y + \frac{1}{2} \times \text{Convexity} \times (\Delta y)^2$$

$$= -11.26 \times .02 + \frac{1}{2} \times 212.4 \times (.02)^2 = -.1827 = -18.27\%$$

which is far closer to the exact change in bond price. (Notice that when we use Equation 11.5, we must express interest rates as decimals rather than percentages. The change in rates from 8% to 10% is represented as $\Delta y = .02$.)

If the change in yield were smaller, say, 0.1%, convexity would matter less. The price of the bond actually would fall to $988.85, a decline of 1.115%. Without accounting for convexity, we would predict a price decline of

$$\frac{\Delta P}{P} = -D^* \Delta y = -11.26 \times .001 = -.01126 = -1.126\%$$

Accounting for convexity, we get almost the precisely correct answer:

$$\frac{\Delta P}{P} = -11.26 \times .001 + \frac{1}{2} \times 212.4 \times (.001)^2 = -.01115 = -1.115\%$$

Nevertheless, the duration rule is quite accurate in this case, even without accounting for convexity.

Why Do Investors Like Convexity?

Convexity is generally considered a desirable trait. Bonds with greater curvature gain more in price when yields fall than they lose when yields rise. For example, in Figure 11.6 bonds A and B have the same duration at the initial yield. The plots of their proportional price changes as a function of interest rate changes are tangent, meaning that their sensitivities to changes in yields at that point are equal. However, bond A is more convex than bond B. It enjoys greater price increases and smaller price decreases when interest rates fluctuate by larger amounts.

Convexity

The Convexity spreadsheet allows you to calculate bond convexity. You can specify yield to maturity and coupon and allow for short maturities by setting later cash flows equal to zero and setting the last cash flow equal to principal plus final coupon payment.

Spreadsheets are
available in Connect

	A	B	C	D	E	F	G	H
1								
2								
3								
4			Time (t)	Cash flow	PV(CF)	t + t^2	(t + t^2) × PV(CF)	
5								
6	Coupon	3	1	3	2.871	2	5.742	
7	YTM	0.045	2	3	2.747	6	16.483	
8	Maturity	10	3	3	2.629	12	31.547	
9	Price	$88.13	4	3	2.516	20	50.314	
10			5	3	2.407	30	72.221	
11			6	3	2.304	42	96.755	
12			7	3	2.204	56	123.451	
13			8	3	2.110	72	151.888	
14			9	3	2.019	90	181.684	
15			10	103	66.325	110	7295.701	
16								
17			Sum:		88.13092273		8025.785	
18								
19				Convexity:			83.392425	

Excel Questions

1. Calculate the convexity of a "bullet" fixed-income portfolio, that is, a portfolio with a single cash flow. Suppose a single $1,000 cash flow is paid in year 5.

2. Now calculate the convexity of a "ladder" fixed-income portfolio, that is, a portfolio with equal cash flows over time. Suppose the security makes $100 cash flows in each of years 1–9, so that its duration is close to the bullet in Question 1.

3. Do ladders or bullets have greater convexity?

If interest rates are volatile, this is an attractive asymmetry that increases the expected return on the bond because bond A will benefit more from rate decreases and suffer less from rate increases. Of course, if convexity is desirable, it will not be available for free: Investors will have to pay more for (equivalently, accept lower yields on) bonds with greater convexity.

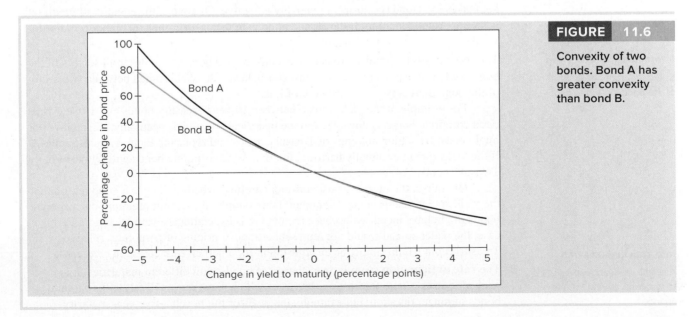

FIGURE 11.6

Convexity of two bonds. Bond A has greater convexity than bond B.

11.4   ACTIVE BOND MANAGEMENT

Sources of Potential Profit

Broadly speaking, there are two sources of potential value in active bond management. The first is interest rate forecasting, that is, anticipating movements across the entire spectrum of the fixed-income market. If interest rate declines are forecast, managers will increase portfolio duration; if increases seem likely, they will shorten duration. The second source of potential profit is identification of relative mispricing within the fixed-income market. An analyst might believe, for example, that the default premium on one bond is unnecessarily large and the bond is underpriced.

These techniques will generate abnormal returns only if the analyst's information or insight is superior to that of the market. You can't profit from knowledge that rates are about to fall if everyone else in the market already knows this. In that case, the anticipated lower future rates will be built into bond prices in the sense that long-duration bonds already sell at higher prices, reflecting the anticipated fall in future short rates. If you do not have information before the market does, you will be too late to act—prices will have already responded to the news. You know this from our discussion of market efficiency.

For now we simply repeat that valuable information is differential information. And it is worth noting that interest rate forecasters have a notoriously poor track record.

Homer and Leibowitz (1972) have developed a popular taxonomy of active bond portfolio strategies. They characterize portfolio rebalancing activities as one of four types of *bond swaps*. In the first two swaps, the investor typically believes the yield relationship between bonds or sectors is only temporarily out of alignment. Until the aberration is eliminated, gains can be realized on the underpriced bond during a period of realignment called the *workout period*.

substitution swap

Exchange of one bond for a bond with similar attributes but more attractively priced.

1. The **substitution swap** is an exchange of one bond for a nearly identical substitute. The substituted bonds should be of essentially equal coupon, maturity, quality, call features, sinking fund provisions, and so on. A substitution swap would be motivated by a belief that the market has temporarily mispriced the two bonds, with a discrepancy representing a profit opportunity.

   An example of a substitution swap would be a sale of a 20-year maturity, 6% coupon Toyota bond that is priced to provide a yield to maturity of 6.05% coupled with a purchase of a 6% coupon Honda bond with the same time to maturity that yields 6.15%. If the bonds have about the same credit risk, there is no apparent reason for the Honda bonds to provide a higher yield. Therefore, the higher yield actually available in the market makes the Honda bond seem relatively attractive. Of course, the equality of credit risk is an important condition. If the Honda bond is in fact riskier, then its higher promised yield does not represent a bargain.

intermarket spread swap

Switching from one segment of the bond market to another.

2. The **intermarket spread swap** is an exchange of two bonds from different sectors of the bond market. It is pursued when an investor believes the yield spread between two sectors of the bond market is temporarily out of line.

   For example, if the yield spread between 10-year Treasury bonds and 10-year Baa-rated corporate bonds is now 3%, and the historical spread has been only 2%, an investor might consider selling holdings of Treasury bonds and replacing them with corporates. If the yield spread eventually narrows, the Baa-rated corporate bonds will outperform the Treasury bonds.

   Of course, the investor must consider carefully whether there is a good reason that the yield spread seems out of alignment. For example, the default premium on corporate bonds might have increased because the market is expecting a severe recession. In this case, the wider spread would not represent attractive pricing of corporates relative to Treasuries but would simply be an adjustment for a perceived increase in credit risk.

rate anticipation swap

A switch made in response to forecasts of interest rate changes.

3. The **rate anticipation swap** is an exchange of bonds with different maturities. It is pegged to interest rate forecasting. Investors who believe rates will fall will swap into bonds of longer duration. For example, the investor might sell a five-year maturity

Treasury bond, replacing it with a 25-year maturity Treasury bond. The new bond has the same lack of credit risk as the old one, but it has longer duration.

4. The **pure yield pickup swap** is an exchange of a shorter-duration bond for a longer-duration bond. This swap is pursued not in response to perceived mispricing but as a means of increasing return by holding higher-yielding, longer-maturity bonds. The investor is willing to bear the interest rate risk this strategy entails.

   A yield pickup swap can be illustrated using the Treasury bond listings in Figure 10.1 in the previous chapter. You can see from that figure that longer-term T-bonds offered higher yields to maturity than shorter ones. The investor who swaps the shorter-term bond for the longer one will earn a higher rate of return as long as the yield curve does not shift upward during the holding period. Of course, if it does, the longer-duration bond will suffer a greater capital loss.

We can add a fifth swap, called a **tax swap,** to this list. This refers to a swap to exploit some tax advantage. For example, an investor may swap from one bond that has decreased in price to another similar bond if realization of capital losses is advantageous for tax purposes.

pure yield pickup swap

Moving to higher yield bonds, usually with longer maturities.

tax swap

Swapping two similar bonds; motivated by a reduction in total tax obligations.

Horizon Analysis

One form of interest rate forecasting, which we encountered in the last chapter, is called **horizon analysis.** The analyst selects a particular investment period and predicts bond yields at the end of that period. Given the predicted yield to maturity at the end of the investment period, the bond price can be calculated. The coupon income earned over the period is then added to the predicted capital gain or loss to obtain a forecast of the total return on the bond over the holding period.

horizon analysis

Forecast of bond returns based on a prediction of the yield curve at the end of the investment horizon as well as the interest rate on reinvested coupon income.

EXAMPLE 11.5

Horizon Analysis

A 20-year maturity bond with a 10% coupon rate (paid annually) currently sells at a yield to maturity of 9%. A portfolio manager with a two-year horizon needs to forecast the total return on the bond over the coming two years. In two years, the bond will have an 18-year maturity. The analyst forecasts that two years from now 18-year bonds will sell at yields to maturity of 8% and that coupon payments can be reinvested in short-term securities over the coming two years at a rate of 7%.

To calculate the two-year return on the bond, the analyst would perform the following calculations:

1. Current price = $100 × Annuity factor(9%, 20 years) = $1,000 × PV factor(9%, 20 years)
   = $1,091.29
2. Forecast price = $100 × Annuity factor(8%, 18 years) + $1,000 × PV factor(8%, 18 years)
   = $1,187.44
3. The future value of reinvested coupons will be ($100 × 1.07) + $100 = $207

4. The two-year return is $\dfrac{\$207 + (\$1,187.44 - \$1,091.29)}{\$1,091.29} = .278$, or 27.8%

The annualized rate of return over the two-year period would then be $1.278^{1/2} - 1 = .13$, or 13%.

What will be the rate of return in Example 11.5 if the manager forecasts that in two years the yield to maturity on 18-year maturity bonds will be 10% and that the reinvestment rate for coupons will be 8%?

CONCEPT **11.8**
check

An Example of a Fixed-Income Investment Strategy

To demonstrate a reasonable, active fixed-income portfolio strategy, we discuss here the policies of a large fixed-income manager, as explained in a speech by its manager of fixed-income investments. The company believes big bets on general marketwide interest movements are unwise. Instead, it concentrates on exploiting numerous instances of perceived *relative* minor pricing misalignments *within* the fixed-income sector. The firm takes as a benchmark the

Barclays Aggregate Bond Index, which includes the vast majority of publicly traded bonds with maturities greater than one year. Any deviation from this passive or neutral position must be justified by active analysis. The firm considers a neutral portfolio duration to be equal to that of the index.

The firm is willing to make only limited bets on interest rate movements. It explains that when it is neutral on the direction of interest rates, it sets portfolio duration equal to that of the index. If its economic forecasts imply interest rate changes, it will alter portfolio duration. However, to prevent fixed-income performance from being dominated by the accuracy of just a single aspect of its research effort, it limits the degree to which it will modify interest rate exposure. It rarely allows the duration of its portfolios to differ from that of the Aggregate Index by more than one year.

The company expends most of its effort in exploiting numerous but minor inefficiencies in bond prices that result from lack of attention by its competitors. Its analysts follow about 1,000 securities, attempting to identify specific securities and/or industries that are attractive or unattractive. These two activities would be characterized as substitution swaps and inter-market spread swaps in the Homer–Leibowitz scheme.

The company realizes that market opportunities will arise, if at all, only in sectors of the bond market that present the least competition from other analysts. For this reason, it tends to focus on relatively more complicated bond issues in the belief that extensive research efforts give the firm a comparative advantage in that sector. Finally, the company does not take unnecessary risks. If there do not appear to be enough seemingly attractive bonds, funds are placed in Treasury securities as a "neutral" parking space until new opportunities are identified.

To summarize the key features of this sort of strategy, we make the following observations:

1. The firm has a respect for market prices. It believes that only minor mispricing usually can be detected. It works toward meaningful abnormal returns by combining numerous *small* profit opportunities, not by hoping for the success of one big bet.

2. To have value, information cannot already be reflected in market prices. A large research staff must focus on market niches that appear to be neglected by others.

3. Interest rate movements are extremely hard to predict, and attempts to time the market can wipe out all the profits of intramarket analysis.

SUMMARY

- Even default-free bonds such as Treasury issues are subject to interest rate risk. Longer-term bonds generally are more sensitive to interest rate shifts than short-term bonds. A measure of the average life of a bond is Macaulay's duration, defined as the weighted average of the times until each payment made by the security, with weights proportional to the present value of the payment.

- Modified duration is a direct measure of the sensitivity of a bond's price to a change in its yield. The proportional change in a bond's price approximately equals the negative of modified duration times the change in the bond's yield.

- Immunization strategies are an important type of passive bond portfolio management. Such strategies attempt to render the individual or firm immune from movements in interest rates. This may take the form of immunizing net worth or, instead, immunizing the future accumulated value of a bond portfolio.

- Immunization of a fully funded plan is accomplished by matching the durations of assets and liabilities. To maintain an immunized position as time passes and interest rates change, the portfolio must be periodically rebalanced.

- Convexity refers to the curvature of a bond's price-yield relationship. Accounting for convexity can substantially improve on the accuracy of the duration approximation for the response of bond prices to changes in yields.

- A more direct form of immunization is dedication or cash flow matching. If a portfolio is perfectly matched in cash flow to those of projected liabilities, rebalancing will be unnecessary.

- Active bond management can be decomposed into interest rate forecasting techniques and intermarket spread analysis. One popular taxonomy classifies active strategies as substitution swaps, intermarket spread swaps, rate anticipation swaps, and pure yield pickup swaps.

KEY TERMS

cash flow matching, 341	intermarket spread swap, 346	rate anticipation swap, 346
convexity, 343		rebalancing, 339
dedication strategy, 341	Macaulay's duration, 329	substitution swap, 346
horizon analysis, 347	modified duration, 331	tax swap, 347
immunization, 335	pure yield pickup swap, 347	

KEY EQUATIONS

Macaulay's duration: $D = \sum_{t=1}^{T} t \times w_t$

Modified duration and bond price risk: $\dfrac{\Delta P}{P} = -D \times \left[\dfrac{\Delta(1+y)}{1+y}\right] = -D^* \times \Delta y$

Duration of perpetuity $= \dfrac{1+y}{y}$

Bond price risk including convexity: $\dfrac{\Delta P}{P} = -D^*\Delta y + \dfrac{1}{2} \times \text{Convexity} \times (\Delta y)^2$

PROBLEM SETS

 Select problems are available in McGraw-Hill's Connect. Please see the Supplements section of the book's frontmatter for more information.

1. How can a perpetuity, which has an infinite maturity, have a duration as short as 10 or 20 years? *(LO 11-1)*

2. You predict that interest rates are about to fall. Which bond will give you the highest capital gain? *(LO 11-1)*
   a. Low coupon, long maturity
   b. High coupon, short maturity
   c. High coupon, long maturity
   d. Zero coupon, long maturity

3. The historical yield spread between AAA bonds and Treasury bonds widened dramatically during the financial crisis. *(LO 11-4)*
   a. If you believed the spread would soon return to more typical historical levels, what should you have done?
   b. This would be an example of what sort of bond swap?

4. A bond currently sells for $1,050, which gives it a yield to maturity of 6%. Suppose that if the yield increases by 25 basis points, the price of the bond falls to $1,025. What is the modified duration of this bond? *(LO 11-2)*

5. Macaulay's duration is less than modified duration except for: *(LO 11-2)*
   a. Zero-coupon bonds.
   b. Premium bonds.
   c. Bonds selling at par value.
   d. None of the above.

6. Is the decrease in a bond's price corresponding to an increase in its yield to maturity more or less than the price increase resulting from a decrease in yield of equal magnitude? *(LO 11-3)*

7. Short-term interest rates are more volatile than long-term rates. Despite this, the rates of return of long-term bonds are more volatile than returns on short-term securities. How can these two empirical observations be reconciled? *(LO 11-1)*

8. *a.* Find the duration of a 6% coupon bond making *annual* coupon payments if it has three years until maturity and a yield to maturity of 6%.

   b. What is the duration if the yield to maturity is 10%?   *(LO 11-2)*

9. A nine-year bond has a yield of 10% and a duration of 7.194 years. If the bond's yield changes by 50 basis points, what is the percentage change in the bond's price?   *(LO 11-2)*

10. A pension plan is obligated to make disbursements of $1 million, $2 million, and $1 million at the end of each of the next three years, respectively. Find the duration of the plan's obligations if the interest rate is 10% annually.   *(LO 11-2)*

11. If the plan in the previous problem wants to fully fund and immunize its position, how much of its portfolio should it allocate to one-year zero-coupon bonds and perpetuities, respectively, if these are the only two assets funding the plan?   *(LO 11-4)*

12. You own a fixed-income asset with a duration of five years. If the level of interest rates, which is currently 8%, goes down by 10 basis points, how much do you expect the price of the asset to go up (in percentage terms)?   *(LO 11-2)*

13. Rank the interest rate sensitivity of the following pairs of bonds.   *(LO 11-1)*

    a. Bond A is a 6% coupon, 20-year maturity bond selling at par value.
    Bond B is a 6% coupon, 20-year maturity bond selling below par value.

    b. Bond A is a 20-year, noncallable coupon bond with a coupon rate of 6%, selling at par.
    Bond B is a 20-year, callable bond with a coupon rate of 7%, also selling at par.

14. Long-term Treasury bonds currently are selling at yields to maturity of nearly 6%. You expect interest rates to fall. The rest of the market thinks that they will remain unchanged over the coming year. In each question, choose the bond that will provide the higher capital gain if you are correct. Briefly explain your answer.   *(LO 11-2)*

    a. (1) A Baa-rated bond with coupon rate 6% and time to maturity 20 years.
    (2) An Aaa-rated bond with coupon rate 6% and time to maturity 20 years.

    b. (1) An A-rated bond with coupon rate 4% and maturity 20 years, callable at 105.
    (2) An A-rated bond with coupon rate 6% and maturity 20 years, callable at 105.

    c. (1) A 4% coupon T-bond with maturity 20 years and YTM = 6%.
    (2) A 7% coupon T-bond with maturity 20 years and YTM = 6%.

15. You will be paying $10,000 a year in tuition expenses at the end of the next two years. Bonds currently yield 8%.   *(LO 11-2)*

    a. What is the present value and duration of your obligation?

    b. What maturity zero-coupon bond would immunize your obligation?

    c. Suppose you buy a zero-coupon bond with value and duration equal to your obligation. Now suppose that rates immediately increase to 9%. What happens to your net position, that is, to the difference between the value of the bond and that of your tuition obligation?

    d. What if rates fall to 7%?

16. Pension funds pay lifetime annuities to recipients. If a firm remains in business indefinitely, the pension obligation will resemble a perpetuity. Suppose, therefore, that you are managing a pension fund with obligations to make perpetual payments of $2 million per year to beneficiaries. The yield to maturity on all bonds is 16%.   *(LO 11-4)*

    a. If the duration of 5-year maturity bonds with coupon rates of 12% (paid annually) is four years and the duration of 20-year maturity bonds with coupon rates of 6% (paid annually) is eight years, how much of each of these coupon bonds (in market value) will you want to hold to both fully fund and immunize your obligation?

    b. What will be the *par value* of your holdings in the 20-year coupon bond?

17. Frank Meyers, CFA, is a fixed-income portfolio manager for a large pension fund. A member of the Investment Committee, Fred Spice, is very interested in learning about the management of fixed-income portfolios. Spice has approached Meyers with several questions. Specifically, Spice would like to know how fixed-income managers position portfolios to capitalize on their expectations of future interest rates.

Meyers decides to illustrate fixed-income trading strategies to Spice using a fixed-rate bond and note. Both bonds have semiannual coupon periods. Unless otherwise stated, all interest rate (yield curve) changes are parallel. The characteristics of these securities are shown in the following table. He also considers a nine-year floating-rate bond (floater) that pays a floating rate semiannually and is currently yielding 5%.

Characteristics of Fixed-Rate Bond and Fixed-Rate Note		
	Fixed-Rate Bond	**Fixed-Rate Note**
Price	107.18	100.00
Yield to maturity	5.00%	5.00%
Time to maturity (years)	18	8
Modified duration (years)	6.9848	3.5851

Spice asks Meyers about how a fixed-income manager would position his portfolio to capitalize on expectations of increasing interest rates. Which of the following would be the most appropriate strategy? *(LO 11-5)*
a. Shorten his portfolio duration.
b. Buy fixed-rate bonds.
c. Lengthen his portfolio duration.

18. Spice asks Meyers (see previous problem) to quantify price changes from changes in interest rates. To illustrate, Meyers computes the value change for the fixed-rate note in the table. Specifically, he assumes an increase in the level of interest rate of 100 basis points. Using the information in the table, what is the predicted change in the price of the fixed-rate note? *(LO 11-2)*

19. You are managing a portfolio of $1 million. Your target duration is 10 years, and you can choose from two bonds: a zero-coupon bond with maturity five years, and a perpetuity, each currently yielding 5%. *(LO 11-4)*
a. How much of (*i*) the zero-coupon bond and (*ii*) the perpetuity will you hold in your portfolio?
b. How will these fractions change *next year* if target duration is now nine years?

20. Find the duration of a bond with settlement date May 27, 2018, and maturity date November 15, 2027. The coupon rate of the bond is 7%, and the bond pays coupons semi-annually. The bond is selling at a yield to maturity of 8%. You can use Spreadsheet 11.2, available in Connect; link to Chapter 11 material. *(LO 11-2)*

21. What is the duration of the bond in the previous problem if coupons are paid annually? Explain why the duration changes in the direction it does. *(LO 11-2)*

22. You manage a pension fund that will provide retired workers with lifetime annuities. You determine that the payouts of the fund are going to closely resemble level perpetuities of $1 million per year. The interest rate is 10%. You plan to fully fund the obligation using 5-year and 20-year maturity zero-coupon bonds. *(LO 11-2)*
a. How much *market value* of each of the zeros will be necessary to fund the plan if you desire an immunized position?
b. What must be the *face value* of each of the two zeros to fund the plan?

23. Find the convexity of a seven-year maturity, 6% coupon bond selling at a yield to maturity of 8%. The bond pays its coupons annually. (*Hint:* You can use the spreadsheet from this chapter's Excel Application on Convexity, setting cash flows after year 7 equal to zero. The spreadsheet is also available in Connect; link to Chapter 11 material.) *(LO 11-3)*

24. a. Use a spreadsheet to calculate the durations of the two bonds in Spreadsheet 11.1 if the market interest rate increases to 12%. Why does the duration of the coupon bond fall while that of the zero remains unchanged? (*Hint:* Examine what happens to the weights computed in column E.)

KAPLAN
SCHWESER

𝄩
_____
Templates and spreadsheets are available in Connect

𝄩
_____
Templates and spreadsheets are available in Connect

𝄩
_____
Templates and spreadsheets are available in Connect

𝄩
_____
Templates and spreadsheets are available in Connect

b. Use the same spreadsheet to calculate the duration of the coupon bond if the coupon were 12% instead of 8%. Explain why the duration is lower. (Again, start by looking at column E.)   *(LO 11-2)*

25. *a.* Footnote 2 in the chapter presents the formula for the convexity of a bond. Build a spreadsheet to calculate the convexity of the 8% coupon bond in Spreadsheet 11.1 at the initial yield to maturity of 10%.

    b. What is the convexity of the zero-coupon bond?   *(LO 11-3)*

26. A 30-year maturity bond making annual coupon payments with a coupon rate of 12% has duration of 11.54 years and convexity of 192.4. The bond currently sells at a yield to maturity of 8%.   *(LO 11-3)*

    a. Use a financial calculator or spreadsheet to find the price of the bond if its yield to maturity falls to 7%.

    b. What price would be predicted by the duration rule?

    c. What price would be predicted by the duration-with-convexity rule?

    d. What is the percent error for each rule? What do you conclude about the accuracy of the two rules?

    e. Repeat your analysis if the bond's yield to maturity increases to 9%. Are your conclusions about the accuracy of the two rules consistent with parts (*a*)–(*d*)?

27. Currently, the term structure is as follows: One-year bonds yield 7%, two-year zero-coupon bonds yield 8%, three-year and longer maturity zero-coupon bonds all yield 9%. You are choosing between one-, two-, and three-year maturity bonds all paying *annual* coupons of 8%. Which bond will provide the highest rate of return if at year-end the yield curve will be flat at 9%?   *(LO 11-5)*

28. A 30-year maturity bond has a 7% coupon rate, paid annually. It sells today for $867.42. A 20-year maturity bond has a 6.5% coupon rate, also paid annually. It sells today for $879.50. A bond market analyst forecasts that in five years, 25-year maturity bonds will sell at yields to maturity of 8% and that 15-year maturity bonds will sell at yields of 7.5%. Because the yield curve is upward-sloping, the analyst believes that coupons can be invested in short-term securities at a rate of 6%.

    a. Calculate the expected rate of return of the 30-year bond over the five-year period.

    b. What is the expected return of the 20-year bond?   *(LO 11-5)*

Challenge

29. A 12.75-year maturity zero-coupon bond selling at a yield to maturity of 8% has convexity of 150.3 and modified duration of 11.81 years. A 30-year maturity 6% coupon bond making annual coupon payments also selling at a yield to maturity of 8% has nearly identical modified duration—11.79 years—but considerably higher convexity of 231.2.   *(LO 11-3)*

    a. Suppose the yield to maturity on both bonds increases to 9%.

      i. What will be the actual percentage capital loss on each bond?

      ii. What percentage capital loss would be predicted by the duration-with-convexity rule?

    b. Repeat part (*a*), but this time assume the yield to maturity decreases to 7%.

    c. Compare the performance of the two bonds in the two scenarios, one involving an increase in rates, the other a decrease. Based on their comparative investment performance, explain the attraction of convexity.

    d. In view of your answer to (*c*), do you think it would be possible for two bonds with equal duration, but different convexity, to be priced initially at the same yield to maturity if the yields on both bonds always increased or decreased by equal amounts, as in this example? *Hint:* Would anyone be willing to buy the bond with lower convexity under these circumstances?

CFA®
PROBLEMS

CFA Problems

1. Rank the following bonds in order of descending duration. *(LO 11-2)*

Bond	Coupon	Time to Maturity	Yield to Maturity
A	15%	20 years	10%
B	15	15	10
C	0	20	10
D	8	20	10
E	15	15	15

2. Altria has issued bonds that pay annually with the following characteristics: *(LO 11-2)*

Coupon	Yield to Maturity	Maturity	Macaulay Duration
8%	8%	15 years	10 years

a. Calculate modified duration using the information above.
b. Explain why modified duration is a better measure than maturity when calculating the bond's sensitivity to changes in interest rates.
c. Identify the direction of change in modified duration if:
   i. The coupon of the bond were 4%, not 8%.
   ii. The maturity of the bond were 7 years, not 15 years.

3. As part of your analysis of debt issued by Monticello Corporation, you are asked to evaluate two specific bond issues, shown in the table below. *(LO 11-2)*

MONTICELLO CORPORATION BOND INFORMATION

	Bond A (callable)	Bond B (noncallable)
Maturity	2027	2027
Coupon	11.50%	7.25%
Current price	125.75	100.00
Yield to maturity	7.70%	7.25%
Modified duration to maturity	6.20	6.80
Call date	2021	—
Call price	105	—
Yield to call	5.10%	—
Modified duration to call	3.10	—

a. Using the duration and yield information in the table, compare the price and yield behavior of the two bonds under each of the following two scenarios:
   i. Strong economic recovery with rising inflation expectations.
   ii. Economic recession with reduced inflation expectations.
b. Using the information in the table, calculate the projected price change for bond B if the yield-to-maturity for this bond falls by 75 basis points.
c. Describe the shortcoming of analyzing bond A strictly to call or to maturity.

4. One common goal among fixed-income portfolio managers is to earn high incremental returns on corporate bonds versus government bonds of comparable durations. The approach of some corporate-bond portfolio managers is to find and purchase those corporate bonds having the largest initial spreads over comparable-duration government

bonds. John Ames, HFS's fixed-income manager, believes that a more rigorous approach is required.

The following table presents data relating to corporate/government spread relationships (in basis points, bp) at a given date: *(LO 11-5)*

CURRENT AND EXPECTED SPREADS AND DURATIONS OF HIGH-GRADE CORPORATE BONDS (ONE-YEAR HORIZON)

Bond Rating	Initial Spread over Governments	Expected Horizon Spread	Initial Duration	Expected Duration One Year from Now
Aaa	31 bp	31 bp	4 years	3.1 years
Aa	40	50	4	3.1

a. Recommend purchase of *either* Aaa *or* Aa bonds for a one-year investment horizon given a goal of maximizing expected returns.

b. Ames chooses not to rely solely on initial spread relationships. His analytical framework considers a full range of other key variables likely to impact realized incremental returns, including call provisions and potential changes in interest rates. Describe other variables that Ames should include in his analysis, and explain how each of these could cause realized incremental returns to differ from those indicated by initial spread relationships.

5. Noah Kramer, a fixed-income portfolio manager based in the country of Sevista, is considering the purchase of a Sevista government bond. Kramer decides to evaluate two strategies for implementing his investment in Sevista bonds. Table 11.6 gives the details of the two strategies, and Table 11.7 contains the assumptions that apply to both strategies.

Before choosing one of the two bond investment strategies, Kramer wants to analyze how the market value of the bonds will change if an instantaneous interest rate shift occurs immediately after his investment. The details of the shift in the yield curve are shown in Table 11.8. Calculate, for the instantaneous interest rate shift shown in Table 11.8, the percent change in the market value of the bonds that will occur under each strategy. *(LO 11-2)*

6. a. Janet Meer is a fixed-income portfolio manager. Noting that the current shape of the yield curve is flat, she considers the purchase of a newly issued, option-free corporate bond priced at par; the bond is described in Table 11.9. Calculate the duration of the bond.

TABLE 11.6   Investment strategies (amounts are market value invested)

Strategy	5-Year Maturity (Modified Duration = 4.83 Years)	15-Year Maturity (Modified Duration = 14.35 Years)	25-Year Maturity (Modified Duration = 23.81 Years)
I	$5 million	0	$5 million
II	0	$10 million	0

TABLE 11.7   Investment strategy assumptions

Market Value of Bonds	$10 Million
Bond maturities	5 and 25 years or 15 years
Bond coupon rates	0.00%
Target modified duration	15 years

TABLE 11.8 Instantaneous interest rate shift immediately after investment

Maturity	Interest Rate Change
5 years	Down 75 basis points
15	Up 25 bp
25	Up 50 bp

TABLE 11.9 7% option-free bond, maturity = 10 years

	Change in Yields	
	Up 10 Basis Points	Down 10 Basis Points
Price	99.29	100.71
Convexity	35.00	

TABLE 11.10 7.25% option-free bond, maturity = 12 years

Original issue price	Par value, to yield 7.25%
Modified duration (at original price)	7.90
Convexity measure	41.55
Convexity adjustment (for a yield change of 200 basis points)	1.66

b. Meer is also considering the purchase of a second newly issued, option-free corporate bond, which is described in Table 11.10. She wants to evaluate this second bond's price sensitivity to a decline in interest rates. Estimate the percentage price change in the bond price if the yield curve experiences an instantaneous, downward parallel shift of 200 basis points.   *(LO 11-2)*

7. Sandra Kapple presents Maria VanHusen with a description, given in the following exhibit, of the bond portfolio held by the Star Hospital Pension Plan. All securities in the bond portfolio are noncallable U.S. Treasury securities.   *(LO 11-2)*

STAR HOSPITAL PENSION PLAN BOND PORTFOLIO

				Price if Yields Change		
Par Value (U.S. $)	Treasury Security	Market Value (U.S. $)	Current Price	Up 100 Basis Points	Down 100 Basis Points	Modified Duration
$48,000,000	2.375% due 2020	$48,667,680	$101.391	99.245	103.595	2.15
50,000,000	4.75% due 2045	50,000,000	100.000	86.372	116.887	
98,000,000	Total bond portfolio	98,667,680	—	—	—	

a. Calculate the modified duration of each of the following:
   i. The 4.75% Treasury security due 2045. (Use the data on price changes when yields change.)
   ii. The total bond portfolio.
b. VanHusen remarks to Kapple, "If you changed the maturity structure of the bond portfolio to result in a portfolio duration of 5.25, the price sensitivity of that portfolio would be identical to the price sensitivity of a single, noncallable Treasury security that has a duration of 5.25." In what circumstance would VanHusen's remark be correct?

8. The ability to *immunize* a bond portfolio is very desirable for bond portfolio managers in some instances. *(LO 11-4)*
   a. Discuss the components of interest rate risk—that is, assuming a change in interest rates over time, explain the two risks faced by the holder of a bond.
   b. Define *immunization* and discuss why a bond manager would immunize his or her portfolio.
   c. Explain why a duration-matching strategy is a superior technique to a maturity-matching strategy for the minimization of interest rate risk.

9. You are the manager for the bond portfolio of a pension fund. The policies of the fund allow for the use of active strategies in managing the bond portfolio.

   It appears that the economic cycle is beginning to mature, inflation is expected to accelerate, and, in an effort to contain the economic expansion, the central bank is moving toward tighter monetary policy. For each of the situations below, state which one of the two bonds you would prefer. Briefly justify your answer in each case. *(LO 11-5)*
   a. Government of Canada (Canadian pay), 4% due in 2022, and priced at 101.25 to yield 3.50% to maturity;

      or

      Government of Canada (Canadian pay), 4% due in 2032, and priced at 95.75 to yield 4.19% to maturity.
   b. Texas Power and Light Co., 4½% due in 2025, rated AAA, and priced at 85 to yield 7.1% to maturity;

      or

      Arizona Public Service Co., 4.45% due in 2025, rated A–, and priced at 80 to yield 8.1% to maturity.
   c. Commonwealth Edison, 2¾% due in 2024, rated Baa, and priced at 81 to yield 5.2% to maturity;

      or

      Commonwealth Edison, 7⅜% due in 2024, rated Baa, and priced at 114 to yield 5.2% to maturity.
   d. Bank of Montreal (Canadian pay), 3% certificates of deposit due in 2022, rated AAA, and priced at 100 to yield 3% to maturity;

      or

      Bank of Montreal (Canadian pay), floating-rate notes due in 2026, rated AAA.

      Coupon currently set at 2.7% and priced at 100 (coupon adjusted semiannually to 0.5% above the three-month Government of Canada Treasury bill rate).

10. a. Which set of conditions will result in a bond with the greatest price volatility? *(LO 11-1)*
    (1) A high coupon and a short maturity.
    (2) A high coupon and a long maturity.
    (3) A low coupon and a short maturity.
    (4) A low coupon and a long maturity.
    b. An investor who expects declining interest rates would be likely to purchase a bond that has a _____ yield to maturity and a _____ term to maturity. *(LO 11-1)*
    (1) low, long
    (2) high, short
    (3) high, long
    (4) low, short
    c. With a zero-coupon bond: *(LO 11-1)*
    (1) Duration equals the weighted-average term to maturity.
    (2) Term to maturity equals duration.
    (3) Weighted-average term to maturity equals the term to maturity.
    (4) All of the above.

d. As compared with bonds selling at par, deep discount bonds will have: *(LO 11-1)*
   (1) Greater reinvestment risk.
   (2) Greater price volatility.
   (3) Less call protection.
   (4) None of the above.

11. A member of a firm's investment committee is very interested in learning about the management of fixed-income portfolios. He would like to know how fixed-income managers position portfolios to capitalize on their expectations concerning three factors that influence interest rates. Assuming that no investment policy limitations apply, formulate and describe a fixed-income portfolio management strategy for each of the following interest rate factors that could be used to exploit a portfolio manager's expectations about that factor. (*Note:* Three strategies are required, one for each of the listed factors.)   *(LO 11-5)*
   a. Changes in the level of interest rates.
   b. Changes in yield spreads across/between sectors.
   c. Changes in the yield spreads on particular instruments.

12. The following bond swaps could have been made in recent years as investors attempted to increase the total return on their portfolio.
   From the information presented below, identify possible reason(s) that investors may have made each swap.   *(LO 11-5)*

Action		Call	Price	YTM (%)
a. Sell	Baa1 Electric Pwr. 1st mtg. 6.4% due 2023	108.24	95.00	7.71
Buy	Baa1 Electric Pwr. 1st mtg. 2.4% due 2024	105.20	79.00	7.39
b. Sell	Aaa Phone Co. notes 5.5% due 2024	101.50	90.00	7.02
Buy	U.S. Treasury notes 6.5% due 2024	NC	97.15	6.78
c. Sell	Aa1 Apex Bank zero coupon due 2027	NC	45.00	7.51
Buy	Aa1 Apex Bank float rate notes due 2039	103.90	90.00	—
d. Sell	A1 Commonwealth Oil & Gas 1st mtg. 6% due 2029	105.75	72.00	8.09
Buy	U.S. Treasury bond 5.5% due 2035	NC	80.60	7.40
e. Sell	A1 Z mart convertible deb. 3% due 2029	103.90	62.00	6.92
Buy	A2 Lucky Ducks deb. 7.7% due 2035	109.86	75.00	10.43

WEB *master*

1. Use data from **finance.yahoo.com** to answer the following questions. Enter the ticker symbol "S" to locate information for Sprint Corp. Find the company's most recent annual balance sheet in the *Financials* section.
   a. Examine the company's assets and liabilities. What proportion of total assets are current assets? What proportion of total liabilities are current liabilities? Does it seem that there is a good match between the duration of the assets and the duration of the liabilities?
   b. Look at the *Annual Statement of Cash Flows* for Sprint, which is also found in the *Financials* section. Check the *Financing Activities* section to see if the company has issued new debt or reduced its debt outstanding. How much interest did the firm pay during the period?
   c. Repeat the exercise with several other companies of your choice. Try to pick companies in different industries. Do you notice any patterns that might be due to the industrial environments in which the firms operate?

2. Go to **http://www.tipsinc.com/ficalc/calc.tips.** Choose the link for the general-purpose bond calculator. The calculator provides yield to maturity, modified duration, and bond convexity as the bonds' price changes. Experiment by trying different inputs.
   a. What happens to duration and convexity as coupon changes?
   b. What happens to duration and convexity as maturity increases?
   c. What happens to duration and convexity as price increases (holding coupon fixed)?

11.1 Interest rate: 0.09

	(B) Time until Payment (years)	(C) Payment	(D) Payment Discounted at 9%	(E) Weight	Column (B) times Column (E)
A. 8% coupon bond	1	80	73.394	0.0753	0.0753
	2	80	67.334	0.0691	0.1382
	3	1,080	833.958	0.8556	2.5668
Sum:			974.687	1.0000	2.7803
B. Zero-coupon bond	1	0	0.000	0.0000	0.0000
	2	0	0.000	0.0000	0.0000
	3	1,000	772.183	1.0000	3.0000
Sum:			772.183	1.0000	3.0000

The duration of the 8% coupon bond rises to 2.7803 years. Price increases to $974.687. The duration of the zero-coupon bond is unchanged at 3 years, although its price also increases when the interest rate falls.

11.2 *a.* If the interest rate increases from 9% to 9.05%, the bond price falls from $974.687 to $973.445. The percentage change in price is −.127%.

   b. The duration formula would predict a price change of

$$\frac{-2.7802}{1.09} \times .0005 = -.00127 = -.127\%$$

which is the same answer that we obtained from direct computation in part (*a*).

11.3 Use Excel to confirm that DURATION(DATE(2000,1,1), DATE(2008,1,1), .09, .10, 1) = 5.97 years. If you change the last argument of the duration function from 1 to 2 (to allow for semiannual coupons), you will find that DURATION(DATE(2000,1,1), DATE (2008,1,1), .09, .10, 2) = 5.80 years. Duration is lower when coupons are paid semiannually rather than annually because, on average, payments come earlier. Instead of waiting until year-end to receive the annual coupon, investors receive half the coupon midway through the year.

11.4 The duration of a level perpetuity is $(1 + y)/y$ or $1 + 1/y$, which clearly falls as y increases. Tabulating duration as a function of y we get:

y	D
0.01 (i.e., 1%)	101 years
0.02	51
0.05	21
0.10	11
0.20	6
0.25	5
0.40	3.5

11.5 The perpetuity's duration now would be 1.08/.08 = 13.5. We need to solve the following equation for w

$$w \times 2 + (1 - w) \times 13.5 = 6$$

Therefore, $w = .6522$.

11.6 *a.* The present value of the fund's obligation is $800,000/.08 = $10 million. The duration is 13.5 years. Therefore, the fund should invest $10 million in zeros with a 13.5-year maturity. The face value of the zeros will be $10,000,000 × 1.08^{13.5} = $28,263,159.

b. When the interest rate increases to 8.1%, the present value of the fund's obligation drops to 800,000/.081 = $9,876,543. The value of the zero-coupon bond falls by roughly the same amount, to $28,263,159/1.081$^{13.5}$ = $9,875,835. The duration of the perpetual obligation falls to 1.081/.081 = 13.346 years. The fund should sell the zero it currently holds and purchase $9,876,543 in zero-coupon bonds with maturity of 13.346 years.

11.7 Dedication would be more attractive. Cash flow matching eliminates the need for rebalancing and thus saves transaction costs.

11.8 Current price = $1,091.29

Forecast price = $100 × Annuity factor (10%,18 years) + $1,000 × PV factor(10%,18 years) = $1,000

The future value of reinvested coupons will be ($100 × 1.08) + $100 = $208

The two-year return is $= \dfrac{\$208 + (\$1{,}000 - \$1{,}091.29)}{\$1{,}091.29} = .107$, or 10.7%

The annualized rate of return over the two-year period would then be $(1.107)^{1/2} - 1 = .052$, or 5.2%.

Security Analysis

Tell your friends or relatives that you are studying investments and they will ask you, "What stocks should I buy?" This is the question at the heart of security analysis. How do analysts choose the stocks and other securities to hold in their portfolios?

Security analysis requires a wide mix of skills. You need to be a decent economist with a good grasp of both macroeconomics and microeconomics, the former to help you form forecasts of the general direction of the market and the latter to help you assess the relative position of particular industries or firms. You need a good sense of demographic and social trends to help identify industries with bright prospects. You need to be a quick study of the ins and outs of particular industries to choose which specific firms will succeed. You need a good accounting background to analyze the financial statements that firms provide to the public. You also need to have mastered corporate finance because security analysis at its core is the ability to value a firm. In short, a good security analyst will be a generalist, with a grasp of the widest range of financial issues. This is where there is the biggest premium on "putting it all together."

The chapters in Part Four are an introduction to security analysis. We will provide you with a "top-down" approach to the subject, starting with an overview of international, macroeconomic, and industry issues, only then progressing to the analysis of particular firms. These topics form the core of fundamental analysis. After reading these chapters, you will have a good sense of the various techniques used to analyze stocks and the stock market.

12

Macroeconomic and Industry Analysis

Learning Objectives

LO 12-1 Predict the effect of exchange rates as well as monetary, fiscal, and supply-side policies on business conditions.

LO 12-2 Use leading, coincident, and lagging economic indicators to describe and predict the economy's path through the business cycle.

LO 12-3 Predict which industries will be more or less sensitive to business-cycle fluctuations.

LO 12-4 Analyze the effect of industry life cycles and competitive structure on earnings prospects.

fundamental analysis

The analysis of determinants of firm value, such as prospects for earnings and dividends.

The intrinsic value of a stock depends on the dividends and earnings that can be expected from the firm. This is the heart of **fundamental analysis,** that is, the analysis of determinants of value. Ultimately, the business success of the firm determines the dividends it can pay to shareholders and the price it will command in the stock market. Because the prospects of the firm are tied to those of the broader economy, however, valuation analyses must consider the business environment in which the firm operates. For some firms, macroeconomic and industry circumstances might have a greater influence on profits than the firm's relative performance within its industry. In other words, investors need to keep the big economic picture in mind.

Therefore, in analyzing a firm's prospects it often makes sense to start with the broad economic environment, examining the state of the aggregate economy and even the international economy. From there, one considers the implications of the outside environment on the industry in which the firm operates. Finally, the firm's position within the industry is examined.

This chapter examines the broad-based aspects of fundamental analysis—macroeconomic and industry analysis. The following two chapters cover firm-specific analysis. We begin with a discussion of international factors relevant to firm performance and move on to an overview of the significance of the key variables usually used to summarize the state of the economy. We then discuss government macroeconomic policy and the determination of interest rates. We conclude the analysis of the macroeconomic environment with a discussion of business cycles. Next, we move to industry analysis, treating issues concerning the sensitivity of the firm to the business cycle, the typical life cycle of an industry, and strategic issues that affect industry performance.

12.1 THE GLOBAL ECONOMY

A top-down analysis of a firm's prospects must start with the global economy. The international economy might affect a firm's export prospects, the price competition it faces from foreign competitors, or the profits it makes on investments abroad. Table 12.1 shows the importance of the global or broad regional macroeconomy to firms' prospects. For example, economies in southeast Asia such as those in Thailand and Singapore had nearly double the expected GDP growth rate as those in the Eurozone.

Despite the importance of regional macroeconomic conditions, there can be considerable variation in economic performance across countries even within regions. In Europe, for example, the German economy was forecast to expand at a rate of 1.4%, nearly double the projected 0.8% growth rate in Italy.

Perhaps surprisingly, stock market returns do not always align with macroeconomic expectations. This reflects the impact of near market efficiency, where stock returns are driven by performance relative to previous expectations. For example, despite the fact that its predicted economic growth rate was at the top of the pack, the Chinese stock market fell by 16.6% (in U.S. dollar terms), as its expected growth rate fell relative to prior expectations.

These data illustrate that the national economic environment can be a crucial determinant of industry performance. It is far harder for businesses to succeed in a contracting economy than in an expanding one. This observation highlights the role of big-picture macroeconomic analysis as a fundamental part of the investment process.

In addition, political uncertainty can pose considerable economic risks. The sovereign debt crisis offers a compelling illustration of the interplay between politics and economics. In the last decade, the prospects of a bailout for Greece, as well as support for struggling but much larger economies such as Spain, were in large part political issues, but with enormous consequences for the world economy. The exit of the U.K. from the EU was another political battle with big economic implications. Stock markets around the world plummeted on the day the U.K. voted for "Brexit," and the British pound declined by more than 10% against the U.S. dollar. At this level of analysis, it is clear that politics and economics are intimately entwined.

Other political issues that are less sensational but still extremely important to economic growth and investment returns include issues of protectionism and trade policy, the free flow of capital, and the status of a nation's workforce.

One obvious factor that affects the international competitiveness of a country's industries is the exchange rate between that country's currency and other currencies. The **exchange rate** is the rate at which domestic currency can be converted into foreign currency. For example, in mid-2017, it took about 110 Japanese yen to purchase one U.S. dollar. We would say that the exchange rate is ¥110 per dollar or, equivalently, $0.0091 per yen.

As exchange rates fluctuate, the dollar value of goods priced in foreign currency similarly fluctuates. In 1980, the dollar–yen exchange rate was about $0.0045 per yen. Because the exchange rate in 2017 was $0.0091 per yen, a U.S. citizen would have needed about twice as many dollars in 2017 to buy a product selling for ¥10,000 as would have been required in 1980. If the Japanese producer were to maintain a fixed yen price for its product, the price expressed in U.S. dollars would nearly double. This would make Japanese products more expensive to U.S. consumers, however, and result in lost sales. Obviously, appreciation of the yen creates a problem for Japanese producers such as automakers that must compete with U.S. producers.

exchange rate

The rate at which domestic currency can be converted into foreign currency.

TABLE 12.1 Economic performance			
	Stock Market Return, 2016 (%)		Forecasted Growth in GDP, 2017 (%)
	In Local Currency	In U.S. Dollars	
Brazil	42.1	74.4	0.9
Britain	15.2	−3.9	1.1
Canada	19.3	24.6	1.9
China	−10.7	−16.6	6.4
France	5.7	1.9	1.2
Germany	7.8	4.0	1.4
Greece	4.1	0.4	1.2
Hong Kong	1.0	0.9	1.8
India	−5.2	2.0	−0.9
Italy	−8.4	−11.6	0.8
Japan	2.9	5.6	1.0
Mexico	8.4	−12.5	1.9
Russia	28.9	55.4	1.2
Singapore	1.3	−0.2	2.0
South Korea	4.3	1.4	2.5
Spain	−0.9	−4.5	2.3
Thailand	21.4	22.0	3.3
U.S.	14.4	14.4	2.2

Source: *The Economist*, January 7, 2017.

Figure 12.1 shows the change in the purchasing power of the U.S. dollar relative to the purchasing power of several major currencies in the last decade. The ratio of purchasing powers is called the "real" or inflation-adjusted exchange rate. The change in the real exchange rate measures how much more or less expensive foreign goods have become to U.S. citizens, accounting for both exchange-rate fluctuations and inflation differentials across countries. A positive value in Figure 12.1 means that the dollar has gained purchasing power relative to another currency; a negative number indicates a depreciating dollar. Therefore, we see that the U.S. dollar has appreciated in real terms relative to each currency in Figure 12.1, in some cases by substantial amounts. Goods priced in foreign currencies have become less expensive to U.S. consumers; conversely, goods priced in U.S. dollars have become less affordable to consumers abroad.

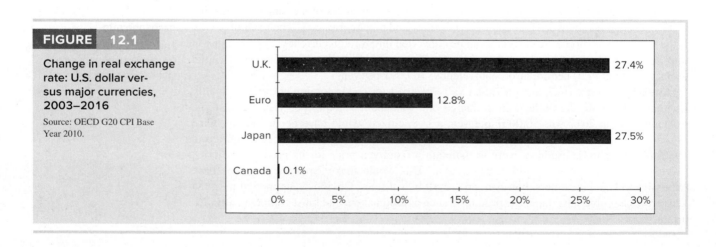

FIGURE 12.1

Change in real exchange rate: U.S. dollar versus major currencies, 2003–2016

Source: OECD G20 CPI Base Year 2010.

12.2   THE DOMESTIC MACROECONOMY

The macroeconomy is the environment in which all firms operate. The importance of the macroeconomy in determining investment performance is illustrated in Figure 12.2, which compares the level of the S&P 500 stock price index to estimates of earnings per share of the S&P 500 companies. The graph shows that stock prices tend to rise along with earnings. While the exact ratio of stock price to earnings per share varies with factors such as interest rates, risk, inflation rates, and other variables, the graph does illustrate that, as a general rule, the ratio has tended to be in the range of 12 to 25. Given "normal" price-to-earnings ratios, we would expect the S&P 500 Index to fall within these boundaries. While the earnings-multiplier rule clearly is not perfect—note the dramatic increase in the P/E multiple during the dot-com boom of the late 1990s—it also seems clear that the level of the broad market and aggregate earnings do trend together.[1] Thus, the first step in forecasting the performance of the broad market is to assess the status of the economy as a whole.

The ability to forecast the macroeconomy can translate into spectacular investment performance. But it is not enough to forecast the macroeconomy well. One must forecast it *better* than one's competitors to earn abnormal profits. In this section, we will review some of the key economic statistics used to describe the state of the macroeconomy.

Gross Domestic Product

Gross domestic product (GDP) is the measure of the economy's total production of goods and services. Rapidly growing GDP indicates an expanding economy with ample opportunity for a firm to increase sales. Another popular measure of the economy's output is *industrial production*. This statistic provides a measure of economic activity more narrowly focused on the manufacturing side of the economy.

gross domestic product (GDP)

The market value of goods and services produced over a period of time.

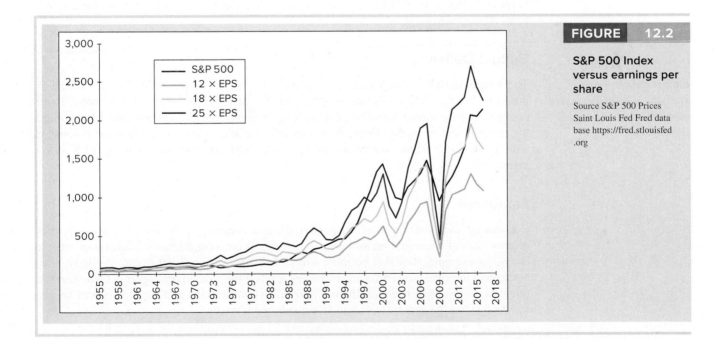

FIGURE   12.2

S&P 500 Index versus earnings per share

Source S&P 500 Prices Saint Louis Fed Fred data base https://fred.stlouisfed.org

---

[1]Figure 12.2 shows that 2009 was another year in which the P/E multiple was much higher than even 25 times earnings. This reflects the fact that earnings in that year, at the height of the deep recession, were dramatically below trend projections. Market prices reflect earnings prospects well into the future, and therefore, they fell by less than earnings in that particular year. As we will see in the next chapter, P/E ratios should be interpreted relative to future, not current, earnings: Stock prices are forward-looking measures of firm value.

Employment

unemployment rate

The ratio of the number of people classified as unemployed to the total labor force.

The **unemployment rate** is the percentage of the total labor force (i.e., those who are either working or actively seeking employment) yet to find work. The unemployment rate measures the extent to which the economy is operating at full capacity. The unemployment rate is a statistic related to workers only, but further insight into the strength of the economy can be gleaned from the employment rate of other factors of production. For example, analysts also look at the factory *capacity utilization rate,* which is the ratio of actual output from factories to potential output.

Inflation

inflation

The rate at which the general level of prices for goods and services is rising.

Inflation is the rate at which the general level of prices is rising. High rates of inflation often are associated with "overheated" economies, that is, economies where the demand for goods and services is outstripping productive capacity, which leads to upward pressure on prices. Most governments walk a fine line in their economic policies. They hope to stimulate their economies enough to maintain nearly full employment but not so much as to bring on inflationary pressures. The perceived trade-off between inflation and unemployment is at the heart of many macroeconomic policy disputes. There is considerable room for disagreement as to the relative costs of inflation versus unemployment as well as the economy's relative vulnerability to these potential problems at any particular time.

Interest Rates

High interest rates reduce the present value of future cash flows, thereby reducing the attractiveness of investment opportunities. For this reason, real interest rates are key determinants of business investment expenditures. Demand for housing and high-priced consumer durables such as automobiles, which are commonly financed, also is highly sensitive to interest rates because interest rates affect interest payments. In Section 12.3 we will examine the determinants of real interest rates.

Budget Deficit

budget deficit

The amount by which government spending exceeds government revenues.

The **budget deficit** of the federal government is the difference between government spending and revenues. Any budgetary shortfall must be offset by government borrowing. Large amounts of government borrowing can force up interest rates by increasing the total demand for credit in the economy. Economists generally believe excessive government borrowing will "crowd out" private borrowing by forcing up interest rates and choking off business investment.

Sentiment

Consumers' and producers' optimism or pessimism concerning the economy are important determinants of economic performance. If consumers have confidence in their future income levels, for example, they will be more willing to spend on big-ticket items. Similarly, businesses will increase production and inventory levels if they anticipate higher demand for their products. In this way, beliefs influence how much consumption and investment will be pursued and affect the aggregate demand for goods and services.

CONCEPT check **12.1**

Consider an economy where the dominant industry is automobile production for both domestic consumption as well as export. Now suppose that auto sales fall in response to an increase in the length of time people use their cars before replacing them. Describe the probable effects of this change on (*a*) GDP, (*b*) unemployment, (*c*) the government budget deficit, and (*d*) interest rates.

12.3 INTEREST RATES

The level of interest rates is among the most important macroeconomic factors guiding investment analysis. Interest rates directly affect returns in the fixed-income market. If your expectation is that rates will increase by more than the consensus view, you will want to shy away from longer-term fixed-income securities. Similarly, increases in interest rates tend to be bad news for the stock market. Unanticipated increases in rates generally are associated with stock market declines. Thus, a superior technique to forecast rates would be of immense value to an investor contemplating the best asset allocation for his or her portfolio.

Unfortunately, forecasting interest rates is one of the most notoriously difficult parts of applied macroeconomics. Nonetheless, we do have a good understanding of the fundamental factors that determine the level of interest rates:

1. The supply of funds from savers, primarily households.
2. The demand for funds from businesses to finance physical investments in plant, equipment, and inventories.
3. The government's net supply and/or demand for funds as modified by actions of the Federal Reserve Bank.
4. The expected rate of inflation.

Although there are many different interest rates economywide (as many as there are types of securities), these rates tend to move together, so economists frequently talk as though there were a single representative rate. We can use this abstraction to gain some insights into what determines the real rate of interest if we consider the supply and demand for funds.

Figure 12.3 shows a downward-sloping demand curve and an upward-sloping supply curve. On the horizontal axis, we measure the quantity of funds, and on the vertical axis, we measure the real rate of interest.

The supply curve slopes up from left to right because the higher the real interest rate, the greater the supply of household savings. The assumption is that at higher real interest rates, households will choose to postpone some current consumption and set aside or invest more of their disposable income for future use.

The demand curve slopes down from left to right because the lower the real interest rate, the more businesses will want to invest in physical capital. Assuming that businesses rank projects by the expected real return on invested capital, firms will undertake more projects the lower the real interest rate on the funds needed to finance those projects.

Equilibrium is at the point of intersection of the supply and demand curves, point E in Figure 12.3.

The government and the central bank (the Federal Reserve) can shift these supply and demand curves either to the right or to the left through fiscal and monetary policies. For example, an increase in the government's budget deficit increases the government's borrowing demand and shifts the demand curve to the right, which causes the equilibrium real

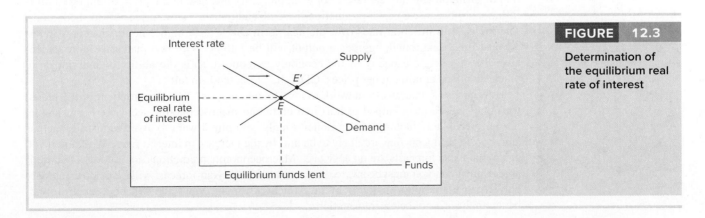

FIGURE 12.3

Determination of the equilibrium real rate of interest

interest rate to rise to point E'. That is, a forecast of higher government borrowing increases expectations of future interest rates. The Fed can offset such a rise through an increase in the money supply, which will increase the supply of loanable funds, and shift the supply curve to the right.

Thus, while the fundamental determinants of the real interest rate are the propensity of households to save and the expected productivity (or we could say profitability) of firms' investment in physical capital, the real rate can be affected as well by government fiscal and monetary policies.

The supply and demand framework illustrated in Figure 12.3 is a reasonable first approximation to the determination of the real interest rate. To obtain the *nominal* interest rate, one needs to add the expected inflation rate to the equilibrium real rate. As we discussed in Section 5.4, the inflation premium is necessary for investors to maintain a given real rate of return on their investments.

While monetary policy can clearly affect nominal interest rates, there is considerable controversy concerning its ability to affect real rates. There is widespread agreement that, in the long run, the ultimate impact of an increase in the money supply is an increase in prices with no permanent impact on real economic activity. A rapid rate of growth in the money supply, therefore, ultimately would result in a correspondingly high inflation rate and nominal interest rate, but it would have no sustained impact on the real interest rate. However, in the shorter run, changes in the money supply may well have an effect on the real interest rate.

12.4   DEMAND AND SUPPLY SHOCKS

demand shock

An event that affects the demand for goods and services in the economy.

supply shock

An event that influences production capacity and costs in the economy.

A useful way to organize your analysis of the factors that might influence the macroeconomy is to classify any impact as a supply or demand shock. A **demand shock** is an event that affects the demand for goods and services in the economy. Examples of positive demand shocks are reductions in tax rates, increases in the money supply, increases in government spending, or increases in foreign export demand. A **supply shock** is an event that influences production capacity and costs. Examples of supply shocks are changes in energy prices; freezes, floods, or droughts that might destroy large quantities of agricultural crops; changes in the educational level of an economy's workforce; or changes in the wage rates at which the labor force is willing to work.

Demand shocks usually are characterized by aggregate output moving in the same direction as interest rates and inflation. For example, a big increase in government spending will tend to stimulate the economy and increase GDP. It also might increase interest rates by increasing the demand for borrowed funds by the government as well as by businesses that might desire to borrow to finance new ventures. Finally, it could increase the inflation rate if the demand for goods and services is raised to a level at or beyond the total productive capacity of the economy.

Supply shocks usually are characterized by aggregate output moving in the opposite direction of inflation and interest rates. For example, a big increase in the price of imported oil is inflationary because costs of production rise and lead to increases in prices of finished goods. The increase in inflation rates over the near term can lead to higher nominal interest rates. Against this background, aggregate output will be falling. With raw materials more expensive, the productive capacity of the economy is reduced, as is the ability of individuals to purchase goods at now-higher prices. GDP, therefore, tends to fall.

How can we relate this framework to investment analysis? You want to identify the industries that will be most helped or hurt in a particular macroeconomic scenario. For example, if you forecast a tightening of the money supply, you might want to avoid industries such as automobile producers that are likely to be hurt by the increase in interest rates. We caution you again that these forecasts are no easy task. Macroeconomic predictions are notoriously unreliable. And again, you must be aware that in all likelihood your forecast will be made using only publicly available information. Any investment advantage you have will be a result only of better analysis—not better information.

12.5 FEDERAL GOVERNMENT POLICY

As the previous section would suggest, the government has two broad classes of macroeconomic tools—those that affect the demand for goods and services and those that affect their supply. For much of postwar history, demand-side policy has been of primary interest. The focus has been on government spending, tax levels, and monetary policy. Since the 1980s, however, increasing attention has also been focused on supply-side economics. Broadly interpreted, supply-side concerns have to do with enhancing the productive capacity of the economy, rather than increasing demand for goods and services. In practice, supply-side economists have focused on the appropriateness of the incentives to work, innovate, and take risks that result from our system of taxation. However, issues such as national policies on education, infrastructure (such as communication and transportation systems), and research and development also are properly regarded as part of supply-side macroeconomic policy.

Fiscal Policy

Fiscal policy refers to the government's spending and tax actions and is part of "demand-side management." Fiscal policy is probably the most direct way either to stimulate or to slow the economy. Decreases in government spending directly reduce the demand for goods and services. Similarly, increases in tax rates immediately siphon income from consumers and result in fairly rapid decreases in consumption.

Ironically, although fiscal policy has the most immediate impact on the economy, the formulation and implementation of such policy is usually painfully slow and involved. This is because fiscal policy requires enormous amounts of compromise between the executive and legislative branches. Tax and spending policy must be initiated and voted on by Congress, which requires considerable political negotiations, and any legislation passed must be signed by the president, requiring more negotiation. Thus, while the impact of fiscal policy is relatively immediate, its formulation is so cumbersome that fiscal policy cannot in practice be used to fine-tune the economy.

Moreover, much of government spending, such as that for Medicare or Social Security, is nondiscretionary, meaning that it is determined by formula rather than policy and cannot be changed in response to economic conditions. This places even more rigidity into the formulation of fiscal policy.

A common way to summarize the net impact of government fiscal policy is to look at the government's budget deficit or surplus, which is simply the difference between revenues and expenditures. A deficit means the government is spending more than it is taking in by way of taxes. The net effect is to increase the demand for goods (via spending) by more than it reduces the demand for goods (via taxes), therefore, stimulating the economy.

fiscal policy

The use of government spending and taxing for the specific purpose of stabilizing the economy.

Monetary Policy

Monetary policy refers to the manipulation of the money supply to affect the macroeconomy and is the other main leg of demand-side policy. Monetary policy works largely through its impact on interest rates. Increases in the money supply lower short-term interest rates, ultimately encouraging investment and consumption demand. Over longer periods, however, most economists believe a higher money supply leads only to a higher price level and does not have a permanent effect on economic activity. Thus, the monetary authorities face a difficult balancing act. Expansionary monetary policy probably will lower interest rates and thereby stimulate investment and some consumption demand in the short run, but these circumstances ultimately will lead only to higher prices. The stimulation/inflation trade-off is implicit in all debate over proper monetary policy.

Fiscal policy is cumbersome to implement but has a fairly direct impact on the economy, while monetary policy is easily formulated and implemented but has a less immediate impact. Monetary policy is determined by the Board of Governors of the Federal Reserve System. Board members are appointed by the president for 14-year terms and are reasonably insulated

monetary policy

Actions taken by the central bank (in the U.S., the Federal Reserve System) to influence the money supply or interest rates.

from political pressure. The board is small enough and often sufficiently dominated by its chairperson that policy can be formulated and modulated relatively easily.

Implementation of monetary policy also is quite direct. The most widely used tool is the open market operation, in which the Fed buys or sells Treasury bonds for its own account. When the Fed buys securities, it simply writes a check, thereby increasing the money supply. (Unlike us, the Fed can pay for the securities without drawing down funds at a bank account.) Conversely, when the Fed sells a security, the money paid for it leaves the money supply. Open market operations occur daily, allowing the Fed to fine-tune its monetary policy.

Other tools at the Fed's disposal are the *discount rate,* which is the interest rate it charges banks on short-term loans, and the *reserve requirement,* which is the fraction of deposits that banks must hold as cash on hand or as deposits with the Fed. Reductions in the discount rate signal a more expansionary monetary policy. Lowering reserve requirements allows banks to make more loans with each dollar of deposits and stimulates the economy by increasing the effective money supply.

While the discount rate is under the direct control of the Fed, it is changed relatively infrequently. The *federal funds rate* is by far the better guide to Federal Reserve policy. The federal funds rate is the interest rate at which banks make short-term, usually overnight, loans to each other. These loans occur because some banks need to borrow funds to meet reserve requirements, while other banks have excess funds. Unlike the discount rate, the fed funds rate is a market rate, meaning that it is determined by supply and demand rather than being set administratively. Nevertheless, the Federal Reserve Board targets the fed funds rate, expanding or contracting the money supply through open market operations as it nudges the fed funds to its targeted value. This is the benchmark short-term U.S. interest rate, and as such it has considerable influence over other interest rates in the U.S. and the rest of the world.

Monetary policy affects the economy in a more roundabout way than fiscal policy. While fiscal policy directly stimulates or dampens the economy, monetary policy works largely through its impact on interest rates. Increases in the money supply lower interest rates, which stimulates investment demand. As the quantity of money in the economy increases, investors will find that their portfolios of assets include too much money. They will rebalance their portfolios by buying securities such as bonds, forcing bond prices up and interest rates down. In the longer run, individuals may increase their holdings of stocks as well and ultimately buy real assets, which stimulates consumption demand directly. The ultimate effect of monetary policy on investment and consumption demand, however, is less immediate than that of fiscal policy.

CONCEPT check **12.2**	Suppose the government wants to stimulate the economy without increasing interest rates. What combination of fiscal and monetary policy might accomplish this goal?

Supply-Side Policies

Fiscal policy and monetary policy are demand-oriented tools that affect the economy by stimulating the total demand for goods and services. The implicit belief is that the economy will not by itself arrive at a full-employment equilibrium and that macroeconomic policy can push the economy toward this goal. In contrast, supply-side policies treat the issue of the productive capacity of the economy. The goal is to create an environment in which workers and owners of capital have the maximum incentive and ability to produce and develop goods.

Supply-side economists also pay considerable attention to tax policy. While demand-siders look at the effect of taxes on consumption demand, supply-siders focus on incentives and marginal tax rates. They argue that lowering tax rates will elicit more investment and improve incentives to work, thereby enhancing economic growth. Some go so far as to claim that reductions in tax rates can lead to increases in tax revenues because the lower tax rates will cause the economy and the revenue tax base to grow by more than the tax rate is reduced.

The Tax Cuts and Jobs Act of 2017 reduced both corporate and personal tax rates. How would demand-side and supply-side economists differ in their interpretations of how this tax change might stimulate the economy?

CONCEPT check 12.3

12.6 BUSINESS CYCLES

We've looked at the tools the government uses to fine-tune the economy, attempting to maintain low unemployment and low inflation. Despite these efforts, economies repeatedly seem to pass through good and bad times. One determinant of the broad asset allocation decision of many analysts is a forecast of whether the macroeconomy is improving or deteriorating. A forecast that differs from the market consensus can have a major impact on investment strategy.

The Business Cycle

The economy recurrently experiences periods of expansion and contraction, although the length and depth of these cycles can be irregular. These recurring patterns of recession and recovery are called **business cycles.** The transition points across cycles are called peaks and troughs. A **peak** is the transition from the end of an expansion to the start of a contraction. A **trough** occurs at the bottom of a recession just as the economy enters a recovery.

As the economy passes through different stages of the business cycle, the relative profitability of different industry groups might be expected to vary. For example, at a trough, as the economy begins to recover from a recession, one would expect that **cyclical industries,** those with above-average sensitivity to the state of the economy, would tend to outperform other industries. Examples of cyclical industries are producers of durable goods, such as automobiles or large household appliances. Because purchases of these goods can be deferred during a recession, sales are particularly sensitive to macroeconomic conditions. Other cyclical industries are producers of capital goods, that is, goods used by other firms to produce their own products. When demand is slack, few companies will be expanding and purchasing capital goods. Therefore, the capital goods industry bears the brunt of a slowdown but does well in an expansion.

In contrast to cyclical firms, **defensive industries** have little sensitivity to the business cycle. These are industries that produce goods for which sales and profits are least sensitive to the state of the economy. Defensive industries include food producers and processors, pharmaceutical firms, and public utilities. These industries will outperform others when the economy enters a recession.

The cyclical/defensive classification corresponds well to the notion of systematic or market risk introduced in our discussion of portfolio theory. When perceptions about the health of the economy become more optimistic, for example, the prices of most stocks will increase as forecasts of profitability rise. Because cyclical firms are most sensitive to such developments, their stock prices will rise the most. These firms tend to have high-beta stocks. In general, then, stocks of cyclical firms will show the best results when economic news is positive, but the worst results when that news is bad. Conversely, defensive firms will have low betas and performance that is less responsive to overall market conditions.

If your assessments of the state of the business cycle were reliably more accurate than those of other investors, choosing between cyclical and defensive industries would be easy. You would choose cyclical industries when you were relatively more optimistic about the economy, and you would choose defensive firms when you were relatively more pessimistic. As we know from our discussion of efficient markets, however, attractive investment choices will rarely be obvious. It is usually not apparent that a recession or expansion has started or ended until several months after the fact. With hindsight, the transitions from expansion to recession and back might seem obvious, but it is often quite difficult to say whether the economy is heating up or slowing down at any moment.

business cycles

Recurring cycles of recession and recovery.

peak

The transition from the end of an expansion to the start of a contraction.

trough

The transition point between recession and recovery.

cyclical industries

Industries with above-average sensitivity to the state of the economy.

defensive industries

Industries with below-average sensitivity to the state of the economy.

Economic Indicators

Given the cyclical nature of the business cycle, it is not surprising that to some extent the cycle can be predicted. The Conference Board publishes a set of cyclical indicators to help forecast, measure, and interpret short-term fluctuations in economic activity. **Leading economic indicators** are those economic series that tend to rise or fall in advance of the rest of the economy. Coincident and lagging indicators, as their names suggest, move in tandem with or somewhat after the broad economy.

Ten series are grouped into a widely followed composite index of leading economic indicators. Similarly, four coincident and seven lagging indicators form separate indexes. The composition of these indexes appears in Table 12.2.

Figure 12.4 graphs the leading and coincident indexes since 1999. The shaded areas in the figure represent periods of recession. The dates at the top of the chart (with format year: month) correspond to peaks and troughs, that is, the turning points between expansions and contractions. While the index of leading indicators consistently turns before the rest of the economy, the lead time is somewhat erratic. Moreover, the lead time for peaks is consistently longer than that for troughs.

The stock market price index is a leading indicator. This is what we would expect, as stock prices are forward-looking predictors of future profitability. Unfortunately, this makes the series of leading indicators much less useful for investment policy—by the time the series predicts an upturn, the market has already made its move. While the business cycle may be somewhat predictable, the stock market may not be. This is just one more manifestation of the efficient market hypothesis.

TABLE 12.2   Indexes of economic indicators

A. Leading indicators
1. Average weekly hours of production workers (manufacturing)
2. Initial claims for unemployment insurance
3. Manufacturers' new orders (consumer goods and materials industries)
4. Institute for Supply Management Index of New Orders
5. New orders for nondefense capital goods
6. New private housing units authorized by local building permits
7. Yield curve: spread between 10-year T-bond yield and federal funds rate
8. Stock prices, 500 common stocks
9. Leading credit index
10. Index of consumer expectations for business conditions

B. Coincident indicators
1. Employees on nonagricultural payrolls
2. Personal income less transfer payments
3. Industrial production
4. Manufacturing and trade sales

C. Lagging indicators
1. Average duration of unemployment
2. Ratio of manufacturing and trade inventories to sales
3. Change in index of labor cost per unit of output
4. Average prime rate charged by banks
5. Commercial and industrial loans outstanding
6. Ratio of consumer installment credit outstanding to personal income
7. Change in consumer price index for services

Source: The Conference Board, *Business Cycle Indicators,* June 2017.

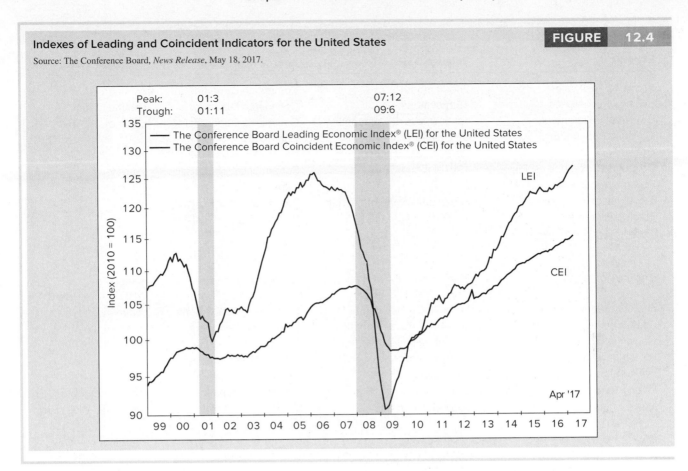

FIGURE 12.4

Indexes of Leading and Coincident Indicators for the United States

Source: The Conference Board, *News Release*, May 18, 2017.

Other leading indicators focus directly on decisions made today that will affect production in the near future. For example, manufacturers' new orders for goods, contracts and orders for plant and equipment, and housing starts all signal a coming expansion in the economy.

A wide range of economic indicators are released to the public on a regular "economic calendar." Table 12.3 lists the public announcement dates and sources for about 20 statistics of interest. These announcements are reported in the financial press, for example, *The Wall Street Journal,* as they are released. They also are available at many sites on the web, for example, at Yahoo!'s site. Figure 12.5 is a short excerpt from a recent Economic Calendar page at **briefing.com.** The page gives a list of the announcements released during the week of June 5, 2017. Notice that recent forecasts of each variable are provided along with the actual value of each statistic. This is useful because, in an efficient market, security prices will already reflect market expectations. The *new* information in the announcement will determine the market response.

Other Indicators

You can find lots of important information about the state of the economy from sources other than the official components of the economic calendar or the components of business-cycle indicators. Table 12.4, which is derived from some suggestions in *Inc.* magazine, contains a few.[2]

---

[2]Gene Sperling and illustrations by Thomas Fuchs, "The Insider's Guide to Economic Forecasting," *Inc.,* August 2003, p. 96.

TABLE 12.3   Economic calendar

Statistic	Release Date*	Source	Website (www.)
Auto and truck sales	2nd of month	Commerce Department	commerce.gov
Business inventories	15th of month	Commerce Department	commerce.gov
Construction spending	1st business day of month	Commerce Department	commerce.gov
Consumer confidence	Last Tuesday of month	Conference Board	conference-board.org
Consumer credit	5th business day of month	Federal Reserve Board	federalreserve.gov
Consumer price index (CPI)	13th of month	Bureau of Labor Statistics	bls.gov
Durable goods orders	26th of month	Commerce Department	commerce.gov
Employment cost index	End of first month of quarter	Bureau of Labor Statistics	bls.gov
Employment record (unemployment, average workweek, nonfarm payrolls)	1st Friday of month	Bureau of Labor Statistics	bls.gov
Existing home sales	25th of month	National Association of Realtors	realtor.org
Factory orders	1st business day of month	Commerce Department	commerce.gov
Gross domestic product	3rd–4th week of month	Commerce Department	commerce.gov
Housing starts	16th of month	Commerce Department	commerce.gov
Industrial production	15th of month	Federal Reserve Board	federalreserve.gov
Initial claims for jobless benefits	Thursdays	Department of Labor	dol.gov
International trade balance	20th of month	Commerce Department	commerce.gov
Index of leading economic indicators	Beginning of month	Conference Board	conference-board.org
Money supply	Thursdays	Federal Reserve Board	federalreserve.gov
New home sales	Last business day of month	Commerce Department	commerce.gov
Producer price index	11th of month	Bureau of Labor Statistics	bls.gov
Productivity and costs	2nd month in quarter (approx. 7th day of month)	Bureau of Labor Statistics	bls.gov
Retail sales	13th of month	Commerce Department	commerce.gov
Survey of purchasing managers	1st business day of month	Institute for Supply Management	ism.ws

*Many of these release dates are approximate.

FIGURE 12.5   Economic calendar at Briefing.com for the week of June 5, 2017

Source: www.briefiing.com/investor/calendars/economic, June 8, 2017.

Last Week   Next Week

Date	(ET)	Release	For	Actual	Briefing.com Forecast	Briefing.com Consensus	Prior	Revised From
Jun 05	08.30	Productivity - Rev.	Q1	0.0%	−0.3%	−0.2%	−0.6%	
Jun 05	08.30	Unit Labor Costs - Rev.	Q1	2.2%	2.5%	2.4%	3.0%	
Jun 05	10.00	Factory Orders	Apr	−0.2%	−0.2%	−0.2%	1.0%	0.2%
Jun 05	10:00	ISM Services	May	56.9	57.6	57.0	57.5	
Jun 07	15.00	Consumer Credit	Apr	56.9	NA	$15.0B	$19.6B	$16.4B
Jun 08	08.30	Initial Claims	03/03	$8.1B	244K	240K	255K	248K
Jun 08	08.30	Continuing Claims	05/27	1917K	NA	NA	1919K	1915K
Jun 08	10.30	Natural Gas Inventories	06/03	106 bcf	NA	NA	81 bcf	
Jun 09	10.00	Wholesale Inventories	Apr		−0.1%	−0.1%	0.2%	

TABLE 12.4 Useful economic indicators

CEO polls **http://businessroundtable.org**	The Business Roundtable surveys CEOs about planned spending, a good measure of their optimism about the economy.
Temp jobs: Search for "Temporary Help Services" at **www.bls.gov**	A useful leading indicator. Businesses often hire temporary workers as the economy first picks up, until it is clear that an upturn is going to be sustained. This series is available at the Bureau of Labor Statistics website.
Walmart sales **http://stock.walmart .com/investors/financial- information/comparable- store-sales/default.aspx**	Walmart sales are a good indicator of the retail sector. It publishes its same-store sales weekly.
Commercial and industrial loans **www.federalreserve.gov**	These loans are used by small and medium-sized firms. Information is published weekly by the Federal Reserve.
Semiconductors **www.semi.org/en/MarketInfo/ Book-to-Bill**	The book-to-bill ratio (i.e., new sales versus actual shipments) indicates whether demand in the technology sector is increasing (ratio > 1) or falling. This ratio is published by Semiconductor Equipment and Materials International.
Commercial structures **www.bea.gov**	Investment in structures is an indicator of businesses' forecasts of demand for their products in the near future. This is one of the series compiled by the Bureau of Economic Analysis as part of its GDP series.

12.7 INDUSTRY ANALYSIS

Industry analysis is important for the same reason that macroeconomic analysis is: Just as it is difficult for an industry to perform well when the macroeconomy is ailing, it is unusual for a firm in a troubled industry to perform well. Similarly, just as we have seen that economic performance can vary widely across countries, performance also can vary widely across industries. Figure 12.6 illustrates the dispersion of industry performance. It shows return on equity (ROE) for several major industry groups in late 2016. ROE ranged from 0.9% for the iron and steel industry to 24.6% for aerospace.

Given this wide variation in profitability, it is not surprising that industry groups exhibit considerable dispersion in their stock market performance. Figure 12.7 presents the stock market performance of several industries for the year ending in June 2017. The spread in performance across industries is remarkable, ranging from a 40.9% gain in airlines to an 8.4% loss in the oil and gas industry. The fact that in this year, 20 of the 22 industries showed a positive return is testament to the influence of broad systematic or market factors on investment performance.

The range of performance demonstrated by these industries was very much available to virtually all investors. Industry-focused exchange-traded funds such as iShares (see Chapter 4) trade like stocks and thus allow even small investors to take a position in each traded industry. Alternatively, one can invest in mutual funds with an industry focus. For example, Fidelity offers more than 40 sector funds, each devoted to a particular industry.

Defining an Industry

While we know what we mean by an industry, it can be difficult in practice to decide where to draw the line between one industry and another. Consider, for example, application software firms. Even within this industry, there is substantial variation by focus and product line. Their differences may result in considerable dispersion in financial performance. Figure 12.8 shows ROE for a sample of the firms included in this industry, and performance did indeed wary widely: from −6.6% for Symantec to 61.6% for Intuit.

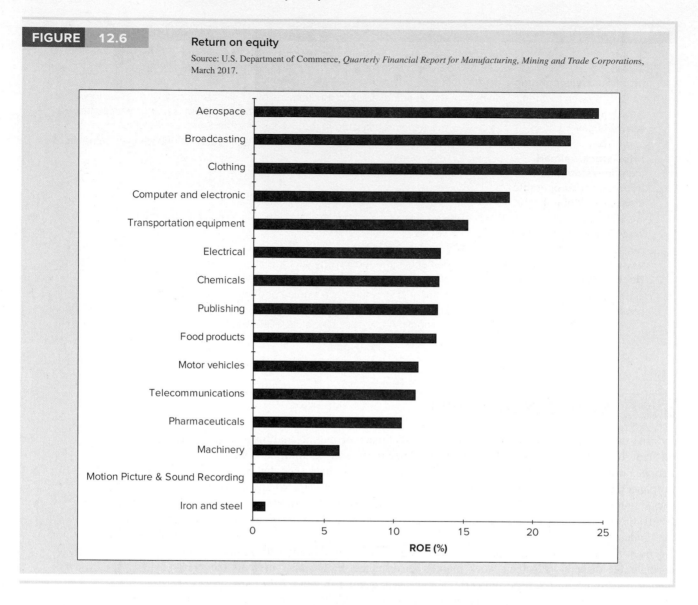

FIGURE	12.6

Return on equity

Source: U.S. Department of Commerce, *Quarterly Financial Report for Manufacturing, Mining and Trade Corporation*s, March 2017.

NAICS codes

Classification of firms into industry groups using numerical codes to identify industries.

A useful way to define industry groups in practice is given by the North American Industry Classification System, or **NAICS, codes.**[3] These are codes assigned to group firms for statistical analysis. The first two digits of the NAICS codes denote very broad industry classifications. For example, Table 12.5 shows that the codes for all construction firms start with 23. The next digits define the industry grouping more narrowly. For example, codes starting with 236 denote *building* construction, 2361 denotes *residential* construction, and 236115 denotes *single-family* construction. The first five digits of NAICS codes are common across all NAFTA countries. The sixth digit is country specific and allows for a finer partition of industries. Firms with the same four-digit NAICS codes are commonly taken to be in the same industry.

Industry classifications are never perfect. For example, both Kohl's and Neiman Marcus might be classified as department stores. Yet the former is a high-volume "value" store, while the latter is a high-margin elite retailer. Are they really in the same industry? Still, these

---

[3]These codes are used for firms operating inside the NAFTA (North American Free Trade Agreement) region, which includes the U.S., Mexico, and Canada. NAICS codes replaced the Standard Industry Classification, or SIC, codes previously used in the U.S.

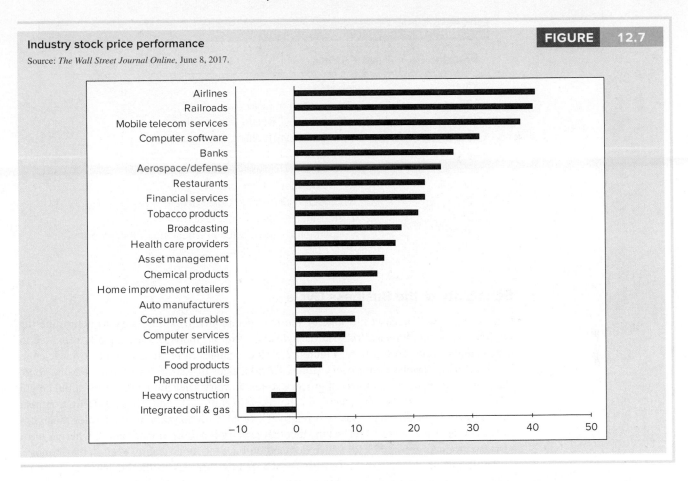

Industry stock price performance

Source: *The Wall Street Journal Online,* June 8, 2017.

FIGURE 12.7

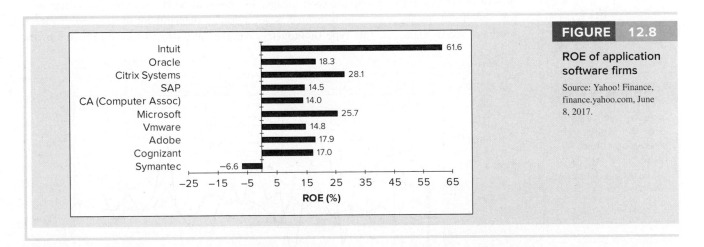

FIGURE 12.8

ROE of application software firms

Source: Yahoo! Finance, finance.yahoo.com, June 8, 2017.

classifications are a tremendous aid in conducting industry analysis because they provide a means of focusing on very broadly or fairly narrowly defined groups of firms.

Several other industry classifications are provided by other analysts; for example, Standard & Poor's reports on the performance of about 100 industry groups. S&P computes stock price indexes for each group, which is useful in assessing past investment performance. The *Value Line Investment Survey* reports on the conditions and prospects of about 1,700 firms, grouped into about 90 industries. Value Line's analysts prepare forecasts of the performance of industry groups as well as of each firm.

TABLE 12.5	Examples of NAICS industry codes
NAICS Code	**NAICS Title**
23	Construction
236	Construction of Buildings
2361	Residential Building Construction
23611	Residential Building Construction
236115	New Single-Family Housing Construction
236116	New Multifamily Housing Construction
236118	Residential Remodelers
2362	Nonresidential Building Construction
23621	Industrial Building Construction
23622	Commercial and Institutional Building Construction

Sensitivity to the Business Cycle

Once the analyst forecasts the state of the macroeconomy, it is necessary to determine the implication of that forecast for specific industries. Not all industries are equally sensitive to the business cycle. To illustrate, Figure 12.9 plots changes in retail sales (year over year) in two industries: jewelry and grocery stores. Clearly, sales of jewelry, which is a luxury good, fluctuate more widely than those of grocery stores. Jewelry sales jumped in 1999 at the height of the dot-com boom but fell steeply in the recessions of 2001 and 2008–2009. In contrast, sales growth in the grocery industry is relatively stable, with no years in which sales meaningfully decline. These patterns reflect the fact that jewelry is a discretionary good, whereas most grocery products are staples for which demand will not fall significantly even in hard times.

Three factors determine the sensitivity of a firm's earnings to the business cycle. First is the sensitivity of sales. Necessities show little sensitivity to business conditions. Examples of industries in this group are food, drugs, and medical services. Other industries with low sensitivity are those for which income is not a crucial determinant of demand. Tobacco products are examples of this type of industry. Another industry in this group is movies,

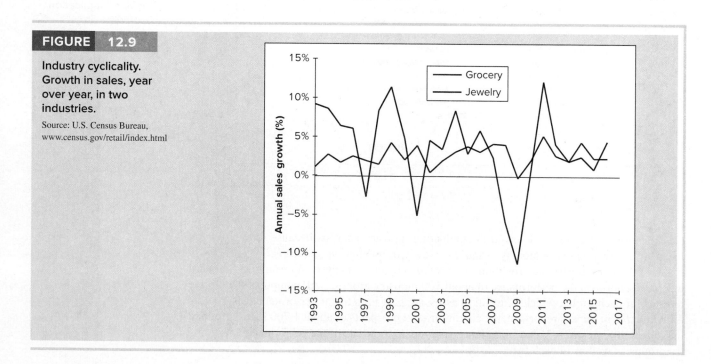

FIGURE 12.9

Industry cyclicality. Growth in sales, year over year, in two industries.

Source: U.S. Census Bureau, www.census.gov/retail/index.html

because consumers tend to substitute movies for more expensive sources of entertainment when income levels are low. In contrast, firms in industries such as machine tools, steel, autos, and transportation are highly sensitive to the state of the economy.

The second factor determining business-cycle sensitivity is operating leverage, which refers to the division between fixed and variable costs. (Fixed costs are those the firm incurs regardless of its production levels. Variable costs are those that rise or fall as the firm produces more or less product.) Profits of firms with greater amounts of variable as opposed to fixed costs will be less sensitive to business conditions. This is because, in economic downturns, these firms can reduce costs as output falls in response to falling sales. Profits for firms with high fixed costs will swing more widely with sales because costs do not move to offset revenue variability. These firms are said to have high operating leverage, as small swings in business conditions can have large impacts on profitability.

The third factor influencing business-cycle sensitivity is financial leverage, which is the use of borrowing. Interest payments on debt must be paid regardless of sales. They are fixed costs that also increase the sensitivity of profits to business conditions. We will have more to say about financial leverage in Chapter 14.

Investors should not always prefer industries with lower sensitivity to the business cycle. Firms in sensitive industries will have high-beta stocks and are riskier. But while they swing lower in downturns, they also swing higher in upturns. As always, the key issue is whether the expected return on the investment is fair compensation for the risks borne.

Sector Rotation

One way that many analysts think about the relationship between industry analysis and the business cycle is the notion of **sector rotation.** The idea is to shift the portfolio more heavily into industry or sector groups that are expected to outperform based on one's assessment of the state of the business cycle.

Figure 12.10 is a stylized depiction of the business cycle. Near the peak of the business cycle, the economy might be overheated with high inflation and interest rates and price pressures on basic commodities. This might be a good time to invest in firms engaged in natural resource extraction and processing such as minerals or petroleum.

Following a peak, when the economy enters a contraction or recession, one would expect defensive industries that are less sensitive to economic conditions, for example, pharmaceuticals, food, and other necessities, to be the best performers. At the height of the contraction, financial firms will be hurt by shrinking loan volume and higher default rates. Toward the end of the recession, however, contractions induce lower inflation and interest rates, which favor financial firms.

sector rotation

An investment strategy that entails shifting the portfolio into industry sectors that are expected to outperform others based on macroeconomic forecasts.

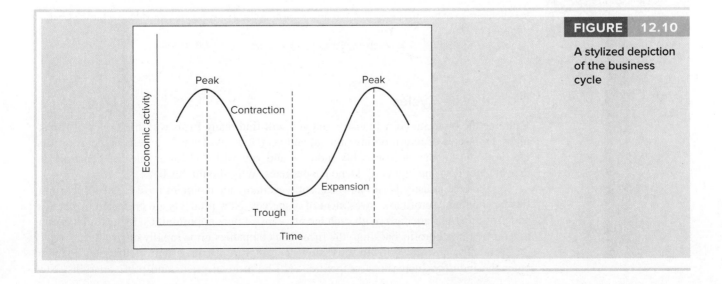

FIGURE 12.10

A stylized depiction of the business cycle

FIGURE 12.11

Sector rotation

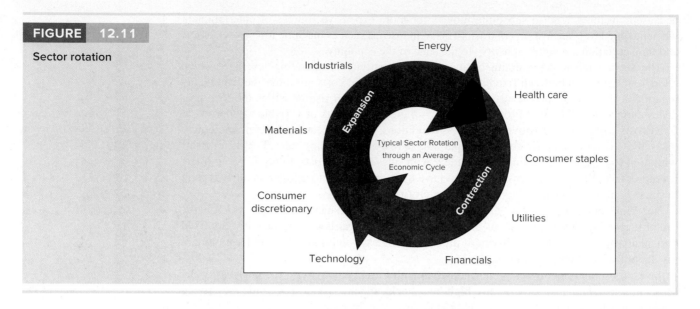

At the trough of a recession, the economy is poised for recovery and subsequent expansion. Firms might thus be spending on purchases of new equipment to meet anticipated increases in demand. This, then, would be a good time to invest in capital goods industries, such as equipment, transportation, or construction.

Finally, in an expansion, the economy is growing rapidly. Cyclical industries such as consumer durables and luxury items will be most profitable in this stage of the cycle. Banks might also do well in expansions because loan volume will be high and default exposure low when the economy is growing rapidly.

Figure 12.11 illustrates sector rotation. When investors are relatively pessimistic about the economy, they will shift into noncyclical industries such as consumer staples or health care. When anticipating an expansion, they will prefer more cyclical industries such as materials and technology.

Be warned, however, that sector rotation, like any other form of market timing, will be successful only if one anticipates the next stage of the business cycle better than other investors. The business cycle depicted in Figure 12.10 is highly stylized. In real life, it is never as clear how long each phase of the cycle will last, nor how extreme it will be. These forecasts are where analysts need to earn their keep.

CONCEPT check 12.4

In which phase of the business cycle would you expect the following industries to enjoy their best performance?

(*a*) Newspapers   (*b*) Machine tools   (*c*) Beverages   (*d*) Timber

---

Industry Life Cycles

Examine the biotechnology industry and you will find many firms with high rates of investment, high rates of return on investment, and very low dividends as a percentage of profits. Do the same for the electric utility industry and you will find lower rates of return, lower investment rates, and higher dividend payout rates. Why should this be?

The biotech industry is still new. Recently available technologies have created opportunities for the highly profitable investment of resources. New products are protected by patents, and profit margins are high. With such lucrative investment opportunities, firms find it advantageous to put all profits back into the firm. The companies grow rapidly on average.

Eventually, however, growth must slow. The high profit rates will induce new firms to enter the industry. Increasing competition will hold down prices and profit margins. New

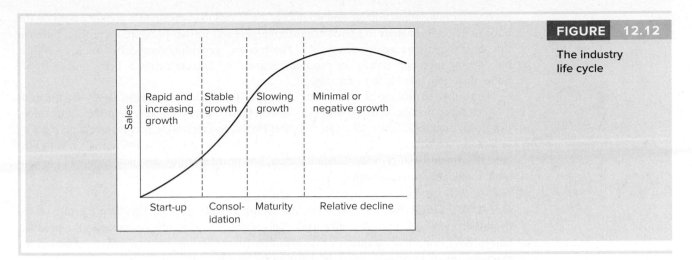

FIGURE 12.12

The industry
life cycle

technologies become proven and more predictable, risk levels fall, and entry becomes even easier. As internal investment opportunities become less attractive, a lower fraction of profits is reinvested in the firm. Cash dividends increase.

Ultimately, in a mature industry, we observe "cash cows," firms with stable dividends and cash flows and little risk. Their growth rates might be similar to that of the overall economy. Industries in early stages of their life cycles offer high-risk/high-potential-return investments. Mature industries offer lower-risk, lower-return combinations.

This analysis suggests that a typical **industry life cycle** might be described by four stages: a start-up stage characterized by extremely rapid growth; a consolidation stage characterized by growth that is less rapid but still faster than that of the general economy; a maturity stage characterized by growth no faster than the general economy; and a stage of relative decline, in which the industry grows less rapidly than the rest of the economy or actually shrinks. This industry life cycle is illustrated in Figure 12.12. Let us turn to an elaboration of each of these stages.

industry life cycle

Stages through which firms typically pass as they mature.

START-UP STAGE The early stages of an industry are often characterized by a new technology or product, such as desktop personal computers in the 1980s, cell phones in the 1990s, or the large touch-screen smartphones introduced in 2007. At this stage, it is difficult to predict which firms will emerge as industry leaders. Some firms will turn out to be wildly successful, and others will fail altogether. Therefore, there is considerable risk in selecting one particular firm within the industry. For example, in the smartphone industry, there continues to be a battle among competing technologies, such as Android versus iPhone.

At the industry level, however, it is clear that sales and earnings will grow at an extremely rapid rate when the new product has not yet saturated its market. For example, in 2000 very few households had smartphones. The potential market for the product therefore was huge. In contrast, consider the market for a mature product such as refrigerators. Almost all households in the U.S. already have refrigerators, so the market for this good is primarily composed of households replacing old ones, which obviously limits the potential growth rate.

CONSOLIDATION STAGE After a product becomes established, industry leaders begin to emerge. For example, by 2015, Apple and Samsung had a combined market share of 35%. The survivors from the start-up stage are more stable, and market share is easier to predict. Therefore, the performance of the surviving firms will more closely track the performance of the overall industry. The industry still grows faster than the rest of the economy as the product penetrates the marketplace and becomes more commonly used.

MATURITY STAGE At this point, the product has reached its potential for use by consumers. Further growth might merely track growth in the general economy. The product has become far more standardized, and producers are forced to compete to a greater extent on the basis of price. This leads to narrower profit margins and further pressure on profits. Firms at this stage sometimes are characterized as "cash cows," providing reasonably stable cash flow but offering little opportunity for profitable expansion. The cash flow is best "milked from" rather than reinvested in the company.

We pointed to desktop personal computers as a start-up industry in the 1980s. By the mid-1990s it was a mature industry, with high market penetration, considerable price competition, low profit margins, and slowing sales. By the 1990s, desktops were progressively giving way to laptops, which were in their own start-up stage. Within a dozen years, laptops had in turn entered a maturity stage, with standardization, low profit margins, and new competition from tablets and large-screen smartphones.

RELATIVE DECLINE   In this stage, the industry might grow at less than the rate of the overall economy, or it might even shrink. This could be due to obsolescence of the product, competition from new products, or competition from new low-cost suppliers; consider, for example, the steady displacement of desktops by laptops.

At which stage in the life cycle are investments in an industry most attractive? Conventional wisdom is that investors should seek firms in high-growth industries. This recipe for success is simplistic, however. If the security prices already reflect the likelihood for high growth, then it is too late to make money from that knowledge. Moreover, high growth and fat profits encourage competition from other producers. The exploitation of profit opportunities brings about new sources of supply that eventually reduce prices, profits, investment returns, and, finally, growth. This is the dynamic behind the progression from one stage of the industry life cycle to another. The famous portfolio manager Peter Lynch makes this point in *One Up on Wall Street.* He says:

> Many people prefer to invest in a high-growth industry, where there's a lot of sound and fury. Not me. I prefer to invest in a low-growth industry. . . . In a low-growth industry, especially one that's boring and upsets people [such as funeral homes or the oil-drum retrieval business], there's no problem with competition. You don't have to protect your flanks from potential rivals . . . and this gives [the individual firm] the leeway to continue to grow. [page 131]

In fact, Lynch uses an industry classification system in a very similar spirit to the life-cycle approach we have described. He places firms in the following six groups:

1. *Slow growers.* Large and aging companies that will grow only slightly faster than the broad economy. These firms have matured from their earlier fast-growth phase. They usually have steady cash flow and pay a generous dividend, indicating that the firm is generating more cash than can be profitably reinvested in the firm.

2. *Stalwarts.* Large, well-known firms like Coca-Cola or Colgate-Palmolive. They grow faster than the slow growers but are not in the very rapid growth start-up stage. They also tend to be in noncyclical industries that are relatively unaffected by recessions.

3. *Fast growers.* Small and aggressive new firms with annual growth rates in the neighborhood of 20% to 25%. Company growth can be due to broad industry growth or to an increase in market share in a more mature industry.

4. *Cyclicals.* These are firms with sales and profits that regularly expand and contract along with the business cycle. Examples are auto companies, steel companies, or the construction industry.

5. *Turnarounds.* These are firms that are in bankruptcy or soon might be. If they can recover from what might appear to be imminent disaster, they can offer tremendous investment returns. A good example of this type of firm would be Chrysler in 1982, when it required a government guarantee on its debt to avoid bankruptcy. The stock price rose fifteenfold in the next five years.

6. *Asset plays.* These are firms that have valuable assets not currently reflected in the stock price. For example, a company may own or be located on valuable real estate that is

worth as much or more than the company's business enterprises. Sometimes the hidden asset can be tax-loss carryforwards. Other times the assets may be intangible. For example, a cable company might have a valuable list of cable subscribers. These assets do not immediately generate cash flow and so may be more easily overlooked by other analysts attempting to value the firm.

Industry Structure and Performance

The maturation of an industry involves regular changes in the firm's competitive environment. As a final topic, we examine the relationship between industry structure, competitive strategy, and profitability. Michael Porter (1980, 1985) has highlighted these five determinants of competition: threat of entry from new competitors, rivalry between existing competitors, price pressure from substitute products, the bargaining power of buyers, and the bargaining power of suppliers.

THREAT OF ENTRY New entrants to an industry put pressure on price and profits. Even if a firm has not yet entered an industry, the potential for it to do so places pressure on prices because high prices and profit margins will encourage entry by new competitors. Therefore, barriers to entry can be a key determinant of industry profitability. Barriers can take many forms. For example, existing firms may already have secure distribution channels for their products based on long-standing relationships with customers or suppliers that would be costly for a new entrant to duplicate. Brand loyalty also makes it difficult for new entrants to penetrate a market and gives firms more pricing discretion. Proprietary knowledge or patent protection also may give firms advantages in serving a market. Finally, an existing firm's experience in a market may give it cost advantages due to the learning that takes place over time.

RIVALRY BETWEEN EXISTING COMPETITORS When there are several competitors in an industry, there will generally be more price competition and lower profit margins as competitors seek to expand their share of the market. Slow industry growth contributes to this competition because expansion must come at the expense of a rival's market share. High fixed costs also create pressure to reduce prices because they put greater pressure on firms to operate near full capacity. Industries producing relatively homogeneous goods also are subject to considerable price pressure because firms cannot compete on the basis of product differentiation.

PRESSURE FROM SUBSTITUTE PRODUCTS Substitute products mean that the industry faces competition from firms in related industries. For example, sugar producers compete with corn syrup producers. Wool producers compete with synthetic fiber producers. The availability of substitutes limits the prices that can be charged to customers.

BARGAINING POWER OF BUYERS If a buyer purchases a large fraction of an industry's output, it will have considerable bargaining power and can demand price concessions. For example, auto producers can put pressure on suppliers of auto parts. This reduces the profitability of the auto parts industry.

BARGAINING POWER OF SUPPLIERS If a supplier of a key input has monopolistic control over the product, it can demand higher prices for the good and squeeze profits out of the industry. One special case of this issue pertains to organized labor as a supplier of a key input to the production process. Labor unions engage in collective bargaining to increase the wages paid to workers. When the labor market is highly unionized, a significant share of the potential profits in the industry can be captured by the workforce.

The key factor determining the bargaining power of suppliers is the availability of substitute products. If substitutes are available, the supplier has little clout and cannot extract higher prices.

SUMMARY

- Macroeconomic policy aims to maintain the economy near full employment without aggravating inflationary pressures. The proper trade-off between these two goals is a source of ongoing debate.
- The traditional tools of macro policy are government spending and tax collection, which constitute fiscal policy, and manipulation of the money supply via monetary policy. Expansionary fiscal policy can stimulate the economy and increase GDP but tends to increase interest rates. Expansionary monetary policy works by lowering interest rates.
- The business cycle is the economy's recurring pattern of expansions and recessions. Leading economic indicators can be used to anticipate the evolution of the business cycle because their values tend to change before those of other key economic variables.
- Industries differ in their sensitivity to the business cycle. More sensitive industries tend to be those producing high-priced durable goods for which the consumer has considerable discretion as to the timing of purchase. Examples are automobiles or consumer durables. Other sensitive industries are those that produce capital equipment for other firms. Operating leverage and financial leverage increase sensitivity to the business cycle.

KEY TERMS

budget deficit, 366	fundamental analysis, 362	monetary policy, 369
business cycles, 371	gross domestic product	NAICS codes, 376
cyclical industries, 371	(GDP), 365	peak, 371
defensive industries, 371	industry life cycle, 381	sector rotation, 379
demand shock, 368	inflation, 366	supply shock, 368
exchange rate, 363	leading economic	trough, 371
fiscal policy, 369	indicators, 372	unemployment rate, 366

PROBLEM SETS

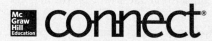

Select problems are available in McGraw-Hill's *Connect*. Please see the Supplements section of the book's frontmatter for more information.

1. What are the differences between bottom-up and top-down approaches to security valuation? What are the advantages of a top-down approach? **(LO 12-1)**

2. Why does it make intuitive sense that the slope of the yield curve is considered a leading economic indicator? **(LO 12-2)**

3. Which one of the following firms would be described as having below-average sensitivity to the state of the economy? **(LO 12-3)**
   a. An asset play firm.
   b. A cyclical firm.
   c. A defensive firm.
   d. A stalwart firm.

4. The price of oil fell dramatically in 2014 and 2015. What sort of macroeconomic shock would this be considered? **(LO 12-1)**

5. How do each of the following affect the sensitivity of profits to the business cycle? **(LO 12-3)**
   a. Financial leverage.
   b. Operating leverage.

6. The present value of a firm's projected cash flows are $15 million. The breakup value of the firm if you were to sell the major assets and divisions separately would be $20 million. This is an example of what Peter Lynch would call a(n): **(LO 12-4)**
   a. Stalwart.
   b. Slow-growth firm.
   c. Turnaround.
   d. Asset play.

7. Define each of the following in the context of a business cycle.   *(LO 12-2)*
   a. Peak.
   b. Contraction.
   c. Trough.
   d. Expansion.

8. Which of the following is consistent with a steeply upwardly sloping yield curve?
   (LO 12-2)
   a. Monetary policy is expansive and fiscal policy is expansive.
   b. Monetary policy is expansive while fiscal policy is restrictive.
   c. Monetary policy is restrictive and fiscal policy is restrictive.

9. Which of the following is *not* a governmental structural policy that supply-side
   economists believe would promote long-term growth in an economy?   *(LO 12-1)*
   a. A redistributive tax system.
   b. Promotion of competition.
   c. Minimal government interference in the economy.

10. What is typically true of corporate dividend payout rates in the early stages of an
    industry life cycle? Why does this make sense?   *(LO 12-4)*

11. If the nominal interest rate is 5% and the inflation rate is 3%, what is the real interest
    rate?   *(LO 12-1)*

12. ATech has fixed costs of $7 million and profits of $4 million. Its competitor, ZTech, is
    roughly the same size and this year earned the same profits, $4 million. But it operates
    with higher fixed costs of $8 million and lower variable costs.   *(LO 12-3)*
    a. Which firm has higher operating leverage?
    b. Which firm will likely have higher profits if the economy strengthens?

13. Choose an industry and identify the factors that will determine its performance in the
    next three years. What is your forecast for performance in that time period?   *(LO 12-3)*

14. What monetary and fiscal policies might be prescribed for an economy in a deep
    recession?   *(LO 12-1)*

15. If you believe the U.S. dollar is about to depreciate more dramatically than do other
    investors, what will be your stance on investments in U.S. auto producers?   *(LO 12-1)*

16. Unlike other investors, you believe the Fed is going to dramatically loosen monetary
    policy. What would be your recommendations about investments in the following
    industries?   *(LO 12-1)*
    a. Gold mining.
    b. Construction.

17. Consider two firms producing smartphones. One uses a highly automated robotics
    process, while the other uses human workers on an assembly line and pays overtime
    when there is heavy production demand.   *(LO 12-3)*
    a. Which firm will have higher profits in a recession?
    b. In a boom?
    c. Which firm's stock will have a higher beta?

18. According to supply-side economists, what will be the long-run impact on prices of a
    reduction in income tax rates? [*Hint:* Think about the wage rate that workers are willing
    to accept.]   *(LO 12-1)*

19. Here are four industries and four forecasts for the macroeconomy. Choose the industry
    that you would expect to perform best in each scenario.   *(LO 12-3)*

    Industries: housing construction, health care, gold mining, steel production.

    Economic Forecasts:

    Deep recession: falling inflation, falling interest rates, falling GDP.

    Superheated economy: rapidly rising GDP, increasing inflation and interest rates.

    Healthy expansion: rising GDP, mild inflation, low unemployment.

    Stagflation: falling GDP, high inflation.

20. For each pair of firms, choose the one that you think would be more sensitive to the business cycle. *(LO 12-3)*
    a. General Autos or General Pharmaceuticals.
    b. Friendly Airlines or Happy Cinemas.

21. In which stage of the industry life cycle would you place the following industries? (*Note:* There is considerable room for disagreement concerning the "correct" answers to this question.) *(LO 12-4)*
    a. Oil well equipment.
    b. Computer hardware.
    c. Computer software.
    d. Genetic engineering.
    e. Railroads.

22. Why do you think the index of consumer expectations for business conditions is a useful leading indicator of the macroeconomy? (See Table 12.2.) *(LO 12-2)*

23. Why do you think the change in the index of labor cost per unit of output is a useful lagging indicator of the macroeconomy? (See Table 12.2.) *(LO 12-2)*

24. You have $5,000 to invest for the next year and are considering three alternatives:
    a. A money market fund with an average maturity of 30 days offering a current annualized yield of 3%.
    b. A two-year CD at a bank offering an interest rate of 4.5%.
    c. A 20-year U.S. Treasury bond offering a yield to maturity of 6% per year.
    What role does your forecast of future interest rates play in your decision? *(LO 12-1)*

25. General Weedkillers dominates the chemical weed control market with its patented product Weed-ex. The patent is about to expire, however. What are your forecasts for changes in the industry? Specifically, what will happen to industry prices, sales, the profit prospects of General Weedkillers, and the profit prospects of its competitors? What stage of the industry life cycle do you think is relevant for the analysis of this market? *(LO 12-4)*

Use the following case in answering Problems 26–28: Institutional Advisors for All Inc. (IAAI) is a consulting firm that primarily advises all types of institutions such as foundations, endowments, pension plans, and insurance companies. IAAI also provides advice to a select group of individual investors with large portfolios. One of the claims the firm makes in its advertising is that IAAI devotes considerable resources to forecasting and determining long-term trends; then it uses commonly accepted investment models to determine how these trends should affect the performance of various investments. The members of the research department of IAAI recently reached some conclusions concerning some important macroeconomic trends. For instance, they have seen an upward trend in job creation and consumer confidence and predict that this should continue for the next few years. Other domestic leading indicators that the research department at IAAI wishes to consider are industrial production, average weekly hours in manufacturing, S&P 500 stock prices, money supply, and the index of consumer expectations.

In light of the predictions for job creation and consumer confidence, the investment advisers at IAAI want to make recommendations for their clients. They use established theories that relate job creation and consumer confidence to inflation and interest rates and then incorporate the forecast movements in inflation and interest rates into established models for explaining asset prices. Their primary concern is to forecast how the trends in job creation and consumer confidence should affect bond prices and how those trends should affect stock prices.

The members of the research department at IAAI also note that stocks have been trending up in the past year, and this information is factored into the forecasts of the overall economy that they deliver. The researchers consider an upward-trending stock market a positive economic indicator in itself; however, they disagree as to the reason this should be the case.

26. The researchers at IAAI have forecast positive trends for both job creation and consumer confidence. Which, if either, of these trends should have a positive effect on stock prices? *(LO 12-1)*

27. Stock prices are useful as a leading indicator. To explain this phenomenon, which of the following is *most* accurate? Stock prices: *(LO 12-2)*
    a. Predict future interest rates as well as future corporate profitability.
    b. Do not predict future interest rates, nor are they correlated with other leading indicators; the usefulness of stock prices as a leading indicator is a mystery.
    c. Reflect the trends in other leading indicators only and do not have predictive power of their own.

28. Which of the domestic series that the IAAI research department listed for use as leading indicators is *least* appropriate? *(LO 12-2)*
    a. Industrial production.
    b. Manufacturing average weekly hours.
    c. Money supply.

Use the following case in answering Problems 29–32: Mary Smith, a CFA candidate, was recently hired for an analyst position at the Bank of Ireland. Her first assignment is to examine the competitive strategies employed by various French wineries.

Smith's report identifies four wineries that are the major players in the French wine industry. Key characteristics of each are cited in Table 12.6. In the body of Smith's report, she includes a discussion of the competitive structure of the French wine industry. She notes that over the past five years, the French wine industry has not responded to changing consumer tastes. Profit margins have declined steadily, and the number of firms representing the industry has decreased from 10 to 4. It appears that participants in the French wine industry must consolidate to survive.

Smith's report notes that French consumers have strong bargaining power over the industry. She supports this conclusion with five key points, which she labels "Bargaining Power of Buyers":

- Many consumers are drinking more beer than wine with meals and at social occasions.
- Increasing sales over the Internet have allowed consumers to better research the wines, read opinions from other customers, and identify which producers have the best prices.
- The French wine industry is consolidating and consists of only 4 wineries today compared to 10 wineries five years ago.
- More than 65% of the business for the French wine industry consists of purchases from restaurants. Restaurants typically make purchases in bulk, buying four to five cases of wine at a time.
- Land where the soil is fertile enough to grow grapes necessary for the wine production process is scarce in France.

After completing the first draft of her report, Smith takes it to her boss, Ron VanDriesen, to review. VanDriesen tells her that he is a wine connoisseur himself and often makes purchases from the South Winery. Smith tells VanDriesen, "In my report I have classified the South Winery as a stuck-in-the-middle firm. It tries to be a cost leader by selling its wine at a price that is slightly below the other firms, but it also tries to differentiate itself from its competitors by producing wine in bottles with curved necks, which increases its cost structure. The end result is that the South Winery's profit margin gets squeezed from both sides." VanDriesen

TABLE 12.6   Characteristics of four major French wineries

	South Winery	North Winery	East Winery	West Winery
Founding date	1750	1903	1812	1947
Generic competitive strategy	?	Cost leadership	Cost leadership	Cost leadership
Major customer market (more than 80% concentration)	France	France	England	U.S.
Production site	France	France	France	France

replies, "I have met members of the management team from the South Winery at a couple of the wine conventions I have attended. I believe that the South Winery could succeed at following both a cost leadership and a differentiation strategy if its operations were separated into distinct operating units, with each unit pursuing a different competitive strategy." Smith makes a note to do more research on generic competitive strategies to verify VanDriesen's assertions before publishing the final draft of her report.

29. If the French home currency were to greatly appreciate in value compared to the English currency, what is the likely impact on the competitive position of the East Winery? *(LO 12-1)*
    a. Make the firm less competitive in the English market.
    b. No impact because the major market for East Winery is England, not France.
    c. Make the firm more competitive in the English market.

30. Which of Smith's points effectively support the conclusion that consumers have strong bargaining power over the industry? *(LO 12-4)*

31. Smith notes in her report that the West Winery might differentiate its wine product on attributes that buyers perceive to be important. Which of the following attributes would be the *most likely* area of focus for the West Winery to create a differentiated product? *(LO 12-4)*
    a. The method of delivery for the product.
    b. The price of the product.
    c. A focus on customers aged 30 to 45.

32. Smith knows that a firm's generic strategy should be the centerpiece of a firm's strategic plan. On the basis of a compilation of research and documents, Smith makes three observations about the North Winery and its strategic planning process:
    i. North Winery's price and cost forecasts account for future changes in the structure of the French wine industry.
    ii. North Winery places each of its business units into one of three categories: build, hold, or harvest.
    iii. North Winery uses market share as the key measure of its competitive position.

    Which of these observation(s) *least* support the conclusion that the North Winery's strategic planning process is guided and informed by its generic competitive strategy? *(LO 12-4)*

Challenge

33. OceanGate sells external hard drives for $200 each. Its total fixed costs are $30 million, and its variable costs per unit are $140. The corporate tax rate is 30%. If the economy is strong, the firm will sell 2 million drives, but if there is a recession, it will sell only half as many. *(LO 12-3)*
    a. What will be the percentage decline in sales if the economy enters a recession?
    b. What will be the percentage decline in profits if the economy enters a recession?
    c. Comparing your answers to (a) and (b), how would you measure the operating leverage of this firm?

CFA Problems

1. As a securities analyst you have been asked to review a valuation of a closely held business, Wigwam Autoparts Heaven, Inc. (WAH), prepared by the Red Rocks Group (RRG). You are to give an opinion on the valuation and to support your opinion by analyzing each part of the valuation. WAH's sole business is automotive parts retailing. The RRG valuation includes a section called "Analysis of the Retail Auto Parts Industry," based completely on the data in Table 12.7 and the following additional information:

    • WAH and its principal competitors each operated more than 150 stores at year-end 2016.
    • The average number of stores operated per company engaged in the retail auto parts industry is 5.3.

TABLE 12.7	Selected retail auto parts industry data									
	2016	**2015**	**2014**	**2013**	**2012**	**2011**	**2010**	**2009**	**2008**	**2007**
Population 18–29 years old (percentage change)	−1.8%	−2.0%	−2.1%	−1.4%	−0.8%	−0.9%	−1.1%	−0.9%	−0.7%	−0.3%
Number of households with income more than $40,000 (percentage change)	6.0	4.0	8.0	4.5	2.7	3.1	1.6	3.6	4.2	2.2
Number of households with income less than $40,000 (percentage change)	3.0	−1.0	4.9	2.3	−1.4	2.5	1.4	−1.3	0.6	0.1
Number of cars 5–15 years old (percentage change)	0.9	−1.3	−6.0	1.9	3.3	2.4	−2.3	−2.2	−8.0	1.6
Automotive aftermarket industry retail sales (percentage change)	5.7	1.9	3.1	3.7	4.3	2.6	1.3	0.2	3.7	2.4
Consumer expenditures on automotive parts and accessories (percentage change)	2.4	1.8	2.1	6.5	3.6	9.2	1.3	6.2	6.7	6.5
Sales growth of retail auto parts companies with 100 or more stores	17.0	16.0	16.5	14.0	15.5	16.8	12.0	15.7	19.0	16.0
Market share of retail auto parts companies with 100 or more stores	19.0	18.5	18.3	18.1	17.0	17.2	17.0	16.9	15.0	14.0
Average operating margin of retail auto parts companies with 100 or more stores	12.0	11.8	11.2	11.5	10.6	10.6	10.0	10.4	9.8	9.0
Average operating margin of all retail auto parts companies	5.5	5.7	5.6	5.8	6.0	6.5	7.0	7.2	7.1	7.2

- The major customer base for auto parts sold in retail stores consists of young owners of old vehicles. These owners do their own automotive maintenance out of economic necessity.   *(LO 12-1)*
    - *a.* One of RRG's conclusions is that the retail auto parts industry as a whole is in the maturity stage of the industry life cycle. Discuss three relevant items of data from Table 12.7 that support this conclusion.
    - *b.* Another RRG conclusion is that WAH and its principal competitors are in the consolidation stage of their life cycle. Cite three items from Table 12.7 that suggest this conclusion. How can WAH be in a consolidation stage while its industry is in a maturity stage?

2. Universal Auto is a large multinational corporation headquartered in the United States. For segment reporting purposes, the company is engaged in two businesses: production of motor vehicles and information processing services.

   The motor vehicle business is by far the larger of Universal's two segments. It consists mainly of domestic U.S. passenger car production, but it also includes small truck manufacturing operations in the United States and passenger car production in other countries. This segment of Universal has had weak operating results for the past several years, including a large loss in 2018. Although the company does not reveal the operating results of its domestic passenger car segments, that part of Universal's business is generally believed to be primarily responsible for the weak performance of its motor vehicle segment.

Idata, the information processing services segment of Universal, was started by Universal about 15 years ago. This business has shown strong, steady growth that has been entirely internal: No acquisitions have been made.

An excerpt from a research report on Universal prepared by Paul Adams, a CFA candidate, states: "Based on our assumption that Universal will be able to increase prices significantly on U.S. passenger cars in 2019, we project a multibillion-dollar profit improvement . . ."   *(LO 12-4)*

a. Discuss the concept of an industrial life cycle by describing each of its four phases.

b. Identify where each of Universal's two primary businesses—passenger cars and information processing—is in such a cycle.

c. Discuss how product pricing should differ between Universal's two businesses, based on the location of each in the industrial life cycle.

3. Adams's research report (see the previous problem) continued as follows: "With a business expansion already under way, the expected profit surge should lead to a much higher price for Universal Auto stock. We strongly recommend purchase."   *(LO 12-3)*

a. Discuss the business-cycle approach to investment timing. (Your answer should describe actions to be taken on both stocks and bonds at different points over a typical business cycle.)

b. Assuming Adams's assertion is correct (that a business expansion is already under way), evaluate the timeliness of his recommendation to purchase Universal Auto, a cyclical stock, based on the business-cycle approach to investment timing.

4. Janet Ludlow is preparing a report on U.S.-based manufacturers in the electric toothbrush industry and has gathered the information shown in Tables 12.8 and 12.9. Ludlow's report concludes that the electric toothbrush industry is in the maturity (i.e., late) phase of its industry life cycle.   *(LO 12-4)*

a. Select and justify three factors from Table 12.8 that support Ludlow's conclusion.

b. Select and justify three factors from Table 12.9 that refute Ludlow's conclusion.

5. The following questions have appeared on CFA examinations.   *(LO 12-1)*

a. Which one of the following statements *best* expresses the central idea of countercyclical fiscal policy?

TABLE 12.8   Ratios for electric toothbrush industry index and broad stock market index

Year	2011	2012	2013	2014	2015	2016
Return on equity						
Electric toothbrush industry index	12.5%	12.0%	15.4%	19.6%	21.6%	21.6%
Market index	10.2	12.4	14.6	19.9	20.4	21.2
Average P/E						
Electric toothbrush industry index	28.5×	23.2×	19.6×	18.7×	18.5×	16.2×
Market index	10.2	12.4	14.6	19.9	18.1	19.1
Dividend payout ratio						
Electric toothbrush industry index	8.8%	8.0%	12.1%	12.1%	14.3%	17.1%
Market index	39.2	40.1	38.6	43.7	41.8	39.1
Average dividend yield						
Electric toothbrush industry index	0.3%	0.3%	0.6%	0.7%	0.8%	1.0%
Market index	3.8	3.2	2.6	2.2	2.3	2.1

TABLE 12.9 Characteristics of the electric toothbrush manufacturing industry

- **Industry sales growth**—Industry sales have grown at 15%–20% per year in recent years and are expected to grow at 10%–15% per year over the next three years.
- **Non-U.S. markets**—Some U.S. manufacturers are attempting to enter fast-growing non-U.S. markets, which remain largely unexploited.
- **Mail order sales**—Some manufacturers have created a new niche in the industry by selling electric toothbrushes directly to customers through mail order. Sales for this industry segment are growing at 40% per year.
- **U.S. market penetration**—The current penetration rate in the United States is 60% of households and will be difficult to increase.
- **Price competition**—Manufacturers compete fiercely on the basis of price, and price wars within the industry are common.
- **Niche markets**—Some manufacturers are able to develop new, unexploited niche markets in the United States based on company reputation, quality, and service.
- **Industry consolidation**—Several manufacturers have recently merged, and it is expected that consolidation in the industry will increase.
- **New entrants**—New manufacturers continue to enter the market.

    (1) Planned government deficits are appropriate during economic booms, and planned surpluses are appropriate during economic recessions.

    (2) The balanced-budget approach is the proper criterion for determining annual budget policy.

    (3) Actual deficits should equal actual surpluses during a period of deflation.

    (4) Government deficits are planned during economic recessions, and surpluses are used to restrain inflationary booms.

  b. Which *one* of the following propositions would a strong proponent of supply-side economics be *most* likely to stress?

    (1) Higher marginal tax rates will lead to a reduction in the size of the budget deficit and lower interest rates because they expand government revenues.

    (2) Higher marginal tax rates promote economic inefficiency and thereby retard aggregate output because they encourage investors to undertake low-productivity projects promising substantial tax-shelter benefits.

    (3) Income redistribution payments will exert little impact on real aggregate supply because they do not consume resources directly.

    (4) A tax reduction will increase the disposable income of households. Thus, the primary impact of a tax reduction on aggregate supply will stem from the influence of the tax change on the size of the budget deficit or surplus.

---

1. This exercise will give you a chance to examine data on some of the leading economic indicators.

  a. Download the data for new privately owned housing units authorized by building permits from **www.census.gov/construction/bps.** Choose the seasonally adjusted data for the United States in an Excel format. Graph the "Total" series.

  b. Search for the last five years of data for manufacturers' new orders of nondefense capital goods from the St. Louis Federal Reserve site at **research.stlouisfed.org.** Graph the data.

  c. Locate data for the average weekly hours of production workers in manufacturing, available at **www.bls.gov/lpc/#tables.** Search for *Hours of Wage and Salary Workers.* (This is part of current employment statistics.) Choose *Manufacturing* as the sector and *Average Weekly Hours* as the measure. Retrieve the report for the past five years. Create a graph of the data that shows the quarterly trend over the last five years.

  d. The data series you retrieved are all leading economic indicators. Based on the tables and your graphs, what is your opinion of where the economy is heading in the near future?

WEB *master*

12.1 The downturn in the auto industry will reduce the demand for the product in this economy. The economy will, at least in the short term, enter a recession. This would suggest that:

a. GDP will fall.

b. The unemployment rate will rise.

c. The government deficit will increase. Income tax receipts will fall, and government expenditures on social welfare programs probably will increase.

d. Interest rates should fall. The contraction in the economy will reduce the demand for credit. Moreover, the lower inflation rate will reduce nominal interest rates.

12.2 Expansionary fiscal policy coupled with expansionary monetary policy will stimulate the economy, with the loose monetary policy keeping down interest rates.

12.3 A traditional demand-side interpretation of the tax cuts is that the resulting increase in after-tax income increases consumption demand and stimulates the economy. A supply-side interpretation is that a reduction in marginal tax rates makes it more attractive for businesses to invest and for individuals to work, thereby increasing economic output.

12.4 a. Newspapers will do best in an expansion when advertising volume is increasing.

b. Machine tools are a good investment at the trough of a recession, just as the economy is about to enter an expansion and firms may need to increase capacity.

c. Beverages are defensive investments, with demand that is relatively insensitive to the business cycle. Therefore, they are good investments if a recession is forecast.

d. Timber is a good investment at a peak period, when natural resource prices are high and the economy is operating at full capacity.

Equity Valuation

Learning Objectives

LO 13-1   Use financial statements and market comparables to estimate firm value.

LO 13-2   Calculate the intrinsic value of a firm using either a constant-growth or multistage dividend discount model.

LO 13-3   Assess the growth prospects of a firm, and relate growth opportunities to the P/E ratio.

LO 13-4   Value a firm using free cash flow models.

Y ou saw in our discussion of market efficiency that finding undervalued securities will never be easy. At the same time, there are enough chinks in the armor of the efficient market hypothesis that the search for such securities should not be dismissed out of hand. Moreover, it is the ongoing search for mispriced securities that maintains a nearly efficient market. Even minor mispricing would allow a stock market analyst to earn his salary.

This chapter describes the ways stock market analysts try to uncover mispriced securities. The models presented are those used by *fundamental analysts,* those analysts who use information concerning the current and prospective profitability of a company to assess its fair market value. Fundamental analysts are different from *technical analysts,* who largely use trading data and trend analysis to uncover trading opportunities.

We start with a discussion of alternative measures of the value of a company. From there, we progress to quantitative tools called *dividend discount models* that security analysts commonly use to measure the value of a firm as an ongoing concern. Next, we turn to price–earnings, or P/E, ratios, explaining why they are of such interest to analysts but also highlighting some of their shortcomings. We explain how P/E ratios are tied to dividend valuation models and, more generally, to the growth prospects of the firm.

We close the chapter with a discussion and extended example of free cash flow models used by analysts to value firms based on forecasts of the cash flows that will be generated from the firm's business endeavors. We apply the several valuation tools covered in the chapter to a real firm and find that there is some disparity in their conclusions—a conundrum that will confront any security analyst—and consider reasons for these discrepancies.

13.1 VALUATION BY COMPARABLES

The purpose of fundamental analysis is to identify stocks that are mispriced relative to some measure of "true" or *intrinsic* value that can be derived from observable financial data. Of course, intrinsic value can only be estimated. In practice, stock analysts use models to estimate the fundamental value of a corporation's stock from observable market data and from the financial statements of the firm and its competitors. These valuation models differ in the specific data they use and in the level of their theoretical sophistication. But, at their heart, most of them use the notion of valuation by comparables: They look at the relationship between price and various determinants of value for similar firms and then extrapolate that relationship to the firm in question.

The Securities and Exchange Commission provides information on U.S. companies at its EDGAR website, **www.sec.gov/edgar.shtml.** The SEC requires all public companies (except foreign companies and companies with less than $10 million in assets and 500 shareholders) to file registration statements, periodic reports, and other forms electronically through EDGAR. Many websites such as **finance.yahoo.com, money.msn.com,** and **finance.google.com** also provide analysis and data derived from the EDGAR reports.

Table 13.1 shows some financial highlights for Apple as well as some comparable data for another giant tech firm, Alphabet, parent company of Google. The price per share of Apple's common stock is $142.71, and the total market value or capitalization of those shares (called *market cap* for short) is $748.7 billion. Under the heading "Valuation," Table 13.1 shows the ratio of Apple's stock price to several benchmarks. Its share price is 13.92 times its (per share) earnings in the most recent 12 months, 5.67 times its recent book value, and 3.43 times its sales. The last valuation ratio, PEG, is the P/E ratio divided by the growth rate of earnings. We would expect more rapidly growing firms to sell at higher multiples of *current* earnings (more on this below), so PEG normalizes the P/E ratio by the growth rate.

These valuation ratios are commonly used to assess the valuation of one firm compared to others in the same industry, and we will consider all of them. The column to the right gives comparable ratios for Alphabet. By two measures, the price/earnings ratio and the price/sales ratio, Apple seems less aggressively priced than Alphabet. On the other hand, both Apple's ratio of market value to **book value,** the net worth of the company as reported on the balance

book value

The net worth of common equity according to a firm's balance sheet.

TABLE 13.1 Financial highlights for Apple and Alphabet (Google)		
	Apple	**Alphabet**
Price per share	142.71	844.04
Common shares outstanding (billion)	5.25	0.70
Market capitalization ($ billion)	748.7	589.0
Latest 12 Months		
Sales ($ billion)	218.12	90.27
EBITDA ($ billion)	69.75	29.86
Net income ($ billion)	45.22	19.48
Earnings per share	8.33	27.88
Valuation		
Price/Earnings	13.92	30.28
Price/Book	5.67	4.20
Price/Sales	3.43	6.52
PEG	1.70	1.32
Profitability		
ROE (%)	34.69	15.02
ROA (%)	11.85	9.41
Operating profit margin (%)	27.15	26.27
Net profit margin (%)	20.73	21.58

Source: Compiled from data available at **finance.yahoo.com,** April 20, 2017.

sheet, and its PEG ratio are higher than Alphabet's. Clearly, rigorous valuation models will be necessary to sort through these sometimes conflicting signals of value.

Limitations of Book Value

Shareholders in a firm are sometimes called "residual claimants," which means that the value of their stake is what is left over when the liabilities of the firm are subtracted from its assets. Shareholders' equity is this net worth. However, the values of both assets and liabilities recognized in financial statements are based on historical—not current—values. For example, the book value of an asset equals the *original* cost of acquisition less some adjustment for depreciation, even if the market price of that asset has changed over time. Moreover, depreciation allowances are used to allocate the original cost of the asset over several years but do not reflect loss of actual value.

Whereas book values are based on historical cost, market values measure *current* values of assets and liabilities. The market value of the shareholders' equity investment equals the difference between the current values of all assets and liabilities. We've emphasized that current values generally will not match historical ones. Equally or even more important, many assets such as the value of a good brand name or specialized expertise developed over many years may not even be included on the financial statements, but they certainly influence market price. Market prices reflect the value of the firm as a going concern.

Can book value represent a "floor" for the stock's price, below which level the market price can never fall? Although Apple's book value per share is considerably less than its market price, other evidence disproves this notion. While it is not common, there are always some firms selling below book value. In 2017, for example, such unfortunate firms included Barclays, Citigroup, Mitsubishi, and Honda.

A better measure of a floor for the stock price is the firm's **liquidation value** per share. This is the amount of money that could be realized by breaking up the firm, selling its assets, repaying its debt, and distributing the remainder to the shareholders. If market capitalization drops below the liquidation value of the firm, the firm becomes attractive as a takeover target. A corporate raider would find it profitable to buy enough shares to gain control and then actually liquidate because the liquidation value exceeds the value of the business as a going concern.

> **liquidation value**
> Net amount that can be realized by selling the assets of a firm and paying off the debt.

Another measure of firm value is the **replacement cost** of assets less liabilities. Some analysts believe the market value of the firm cannot get too far above its replacement cost for long because, if it did, competitors would enter the market. The resulting competitive pressure would drive down profits and the market value of all firms until they fell to replacement cost.

> **replacement cost**
> Cost to replace a firm's assets.

This idea is popular among economists, and the ratio of market price to replacement cost is known as **Tobin's q,** after the Nobel Prize–winning economist James Tobin. In the long run, according to this view, the ratio of market price to replacement cost will tend toward 1, but the evidence is that this ratio can differ significantly from 1 for very long periods of time.

> **Tobin's q**
> Ratio of market value of the firm to replacement cost.

Although focusing on the balance sheet can give some useful information about a firm's liquidation value or its replacement cost, the analyst usually must turn to expected future cash flows for a better estimate of the firm's value as a going concern. We therefore turn to the quantitative models that analysts use to value common stock based on forecasts of future earnings and dividends.

13.2 INTRINSIC VALUE VERSUS MARKET PRICE

The most popular model for assessing the value of a firm as a going concern starts from the observation that the return on a stock investment comprises cash dividends and capital gains or losses. We begin by assuming a one-year holding period and supposing that ABC stock has an expected dividend per share, $E(D_1)$, of $4; that the current price of a share, P_0, is $48; and that the expected price at the end of a year, $E(P_1)$, is $52. For now, don't worry about how you derive your forecast of next year's price. At this point we ask only whether the stock seems attractively priced *today* given your forecast of *next year's* price.

The expected holding-period return is $E(D_1)$ plus the expected price appreciation, $E(P_1) - P_0$, all divided by the current price P_0.

$$\text{Expected HPR} = E(r) = \frac{E(D_1) + [E(P_1) - P_0]}{P_0}$$

$$= \frac{4 + (52 - 48)}{48} = .167 = 16.7\%$$

Note that $E(\ )$ denotes an expected future value. Thus, $E(P_1)$ represents the expectation today of the stock price one year from now. $E(r)$ is referred to as the stock's expected holding-period return. It is the sum of the expected dividend yield, $E(D_1)/P_0$, and the expected rate of price appreciation, the capital gains yield, $[E(P_1) - P_0]/P_0$.

But what is the required rate of return for ABC stock? The capital asset pricing model (CAPM) asserts that when stock market prices are at equilibrium levels, the expected rate of return on a security is $r_f + \beta[E(r_M) - r_f]$. Thus, the CAPM may be viewed as providing an estimate of the rate of return an investor can reasonably expect to earn on a security given its risk as measured by beta. This is the return that investors will require of any other investment with equivalent risk. We will denote this required rate of return as k. If a stock is priced "correctly," it will offer investors a "fair" return, that is, its *expected* return will equal its *required* return. Of course, the goal of a security analyst is to find stocks that are mispriced. For example, an underpriced stock will provide an expected return greater than the required return.

Suppose that $r_f = 6\%$, $E(r_M) - r_f = 5\%$, and the beta of ABC is 1.2. Then the value of k is

$$k = 6\% + 1.2 \times 5\% = 12\%$$

The 16.7% rate of return the investor expects exceeds the required rate based on ABC's beta by a margin of 4.7%. Naturally, the investor will want to include more of ABC stock in the portfolio than a passive strategy would dictate.

intrinsic value

The present value of a firm's expected future net cash flows discounted by the required rate of return.

Another way to see this is to compare the intrinsic value of a share of stock to its market price. The **intrinsic value,** denoted V_0, of a share of stock is defined as the present value of all cash payments to the investor in the stock, including dividends as well as the proceeds from the ultimate sale of the stock, discounted at the appropriate risk-adjusted interest rate, k. Whenever the intrinsic value, or the investor's own estimate of what the stock is really worth, exceeds the market price, the stock is considered undervalued and a good investment. For ABC, using a one-year investment horizon and a forecast that the stock can be sold at the end of the year at price $P_1 = \$52$, the intrinsic value is

$$V_0 = \frac{E(D_1) + E(P_1)}{1 + k} = \frac{\$4 + \$52}{1.12} = \$50$$

Equivalently, at a price of $50, the investor would derive a 12% rate of return—just equal to the required rate of return—on an investment in the stock. However, the actual stock price, $48, is less than intrinsic value. At this price, ABC provides better than a fair rate of return relative to its risk. Using the terminology of the CAPM, it is a positive-alpha stock, and investors will want to buy more of it than they would following a passive strategy.

In contrast, if the intrinsic value turns out to be lower than the current market price, investors should buy less of it than under the passive strategy. It might even pay to go short on ABC stock, as we discussed in Chapter 3.

market capitalization rate

The market-consensus estimate of the appropriate discount rate for a firm's cash flows.

In market equilibrium, the current market price will reflect the intrinsic value estimates of all market participants. This means the individual investor whose V_0 estimate differs from the market price, P_0, in effect must disagree with some or all of the market-consensus estimates of $E(D_1)$, $E(P_1)$, or k. A common term for the market-consensus value of the required rate of return, k, is the **market capitalization rate,** which we use often throughout this chapter.

You expect the price of IBX stock to be $59.77 per share a year from now. Its current market price is $50, and you expect it to pay a dividend one year from now of $2.15 per share.

    a. What are the stock's expected dividend yield, rate of price appreciation, and expected holding-period return?

    b. If the stock has a beta of 1.15, the risk-free rate is 6% per year, and the expected rate of return on the market portfolio is 14% per year, what is the required rate of return on IBX stock?

    c. What is the intrinsic value of IBX stock, and how does it compare to the current market price?

13.3   DIVIDEND DISCOUNT MODELS

Consider an investor who buys a share of Steady State Electronics stock, planning to hold it for one year. The intrinsic value of the share is the present value of the dividend to be received at the end of the first year, D_1, and the expected sales price, P_1. We will henceforth use the simpler notation P_1 instead of $E(P_1)$ to avoid clutter. Keep in mind, though, that future prices and dividends are unknown, and we are dealing with expected values, not certain values. We've already established that

$$V_0 = \frac{D_1 + P_1}{1 + k} \tag{13.1}$$

While this year's dividend is fairly predictable, you might ask how we can estimate P_1, the year-end price. According to Equation 13.1, V_1 (the year-end value) will be

$$V_1 = \frac{D_2 + P_2}{1 + k}$$

If we assume the stock will be selling for its intrinsic value next year, then $V_1 = P_1$, and we can substitute this value for P_1 into Equation 13.1 to find

$$V_0 = \frac{D_1}{1 + k} + \frac{D_2 + P_2}{(1 + k)^2}$$

This equation may be interpreted as the present value of dividends plus sales price for a two-year holding period. Of course, now we need to come up with a forecast of P_2. Continuing in the same way, we can replace P_2 by $(D_3 + P_3)/(1 + k)$, which relates P_0 to the value of dividends plus the expected sales price for a three-year holding period.

More generally, for a holding period of H years, we can write the stock value as the present value of dividends over the H years plus the ultimate sales price, P_H.

$$V_0 = \frac{D_1}{1 + k} + \frac{D_2}{(1 + k)^2} + \cdots + \frac{D_H + P_H}{(1 + k)^H} \tag{13.2}$$

Notice the similarity between this formula and the bond valuation formula developed in Chapter 10. Each relates price to the present value of a stream of payments (coupons in the case of bonds, dividends in the case of stocks) and a final payment (the face value of the bond or the sales price of the stock). The key differences in the case of stocks are the uncertainty of dividends, the lack of a fixed maturity date, and the unknown sales price at the horizon date. Indeed, one can continue to substitute for price indefinitely to conclude

$$V_0 = \frac{D_1}{1 + k} + \frac{D_2}{(1 + k)^2} + \frac{D_3}{(1 + k)^3} + \cdots \tag{13.3}$$

dividend discount model (DDM)

A formula stating that the intrinsic value of a firm equals the present value of all expected future dividends.

Equation 13.3 states the stock price should equal the present value of all expected future dividends into perpetuity. This formula is called the **dividend discount model (DDM)** of stock prices.

It is tempting, but incorrect, to conclude from Equation 13.3 that the DDM focuses exclusively on dividends and ignores capital gains as a motive for investing in stock. Indeed, we assume explicitly in Equation 13.1 that capital gains (as reflected in the expected sales price, P_1) are part of the stock's value. The reason only dividends appear in Equation 13.3 is not that investors ignore capital gains. It is instead that those capital gains will reflect dividend forecasts at the time the stock is sold. That is why in Equation 13.2 we can write the stock price as the present value of dividends plus sales price for *any* horizon date. P_H is the present value at time H of all dividends expected to be paid after the horizon date. That value is then discounted back to today, time 0. The DDM asserts that stock prices are determined ultimately by the cash flows accruing to stockholders, and those are dividends.

The Constant-Growth DDM

Equation 13.3 as it stands is still not very useful because it requires dividend forecasts for every year into the indefinite future. To make the DDM practical, we need to introduce some simplifying assumptions. A useful and common first pass is to assume that dividends are trending upward at a stable growth rate that we will call g. For example, if $g = .05$ and the most recently paid dividend was $D_0 = 3.81$, expected future dividends are

$$D_1 = D_0(1 + g)\ = 3.81 \times 1.05\ \ = 4.00$$
$$D_2 = D_0(1 + g)^2 = 3.81 \times (1.05)^2 = 4.20$$
$$D_3 = D_0(1 + g)^3 = 3.81 \times (1.05)^3 = 4.41 \text{ etc.}$$

Assuming constant growth in Equation 13.3, we can write intrinsic value as

$$V_0 = \frac{D_0(1 + g)}{1 + k} + \frac{D_0(1 + g)^2}{(1 + k)^2} + \frac{D_0(1 + g)^3}{(1 + k)^3} + \cdots$$

This equation can be simplified to

$$V_0 = \frac{D_0(1 + g)}{k - g} = \frac{D_1}{k - g} \tag{13.4}$$

Notice in Equation 13.4 that we calculate intrinsic value by dividing D_1 (not D_0) by $k - g$. If the market capitalization rate for Steady State is 12%, this equation implies that the intrinsic value of a share of Steady State stock is

$$\frac{\$4.00}{.12 - .05} = \$57.14$$

constant-growth DDM

A form of the dividend discount model that assumes dividends will grow at a constant rate.

Equation 13.4 is called the **constant-growth DDM** or the Gordon model, after Myron Gordon, who popularized the model. It should remind you of the formula for the present value of a perpetuity. If dividends were expected not to grow, then the dividend stream would be a simple perpetuity, and the valuation formula for such a nongrowth stock would be $P_0 = D_1/k$.[1] Equation 13.4 generalizes this formula for the case of a *growing* perpetuity. As g increases, the stock price also rises.

EXAMPLE 13.1

Preferred Stock and the DDM

Preferred stock that pays a fixed dividend can be valued using the constant-growth dividend discount model. The growth rate of dividends is simply zero. For example, to value a preferred stock paying a fixed dividend of $2 per share when the discount rate is 8%, we compute

$$V_0 = \frac{\$2}{.08 - 0} = \$25$$

---

[1] Recall from introductory finance that the present value of a $1-per-year perpetuity is $1/k$. For example, if $k = 10\%$, the value of the perpetuity is $\$1/.10 = \$10$. Notice that if $g = 0$ in Equation 13.4, the constant-growth DDM formula is the same as the perpetuity formula.

> **EXAMPLE 13.2**
>
> *The Constant-Growth DDM*
>
> High Flyer Industries has just paid its annual dividend of $3 per share. The dividend is expected to grow at a constant rate of 8% indefinitely. The beta of High Flyer stock is 1, the risk-free rate is 6%, and the market risk premium is 8%. What is the intrinsic value of the stock? What would be your estimate of intrinsic value if you believed that the stock was riskier, with a beta of 1.25?
>
> Because a $3 dividend has just been paid and the growth rate of dividends is 8%, the forecast for the year-end dividend is $3 × 1.08 = $3.24. The market capitalization rate (using the CAPM) is 6% + 1.0 × 8% = 14%. Therefore, the value of the stock is
>
> $$V_0 = \frac{D_1}{k - g} = \frac{\$3.24}{.14 - .08} = \$54$$
>
> If the stock is perceived to be riskier, its value must be lower. At the higher beta, the market capitalization rate is 6% + 1.25 × 8% = 16%, and the stock is worth only
>
> $$\frac{\$3.24}{.16 - .08} = \$40.50$$

The constant-growth DDM is valid only when g is less than k. If dividends were expected to grow forever at a rate faster than k, the value of the stock would be infinite. If an analyst derives an estimate of g that is greater than k, that growth rate must be unsustainable in the long run. The appropriate valuation model to use in this case is a multistage DDM such as those discussed below.

The constant-growth DDM is so widely used by stock market analysts that it is worth exploring some of its implications and limitations. The constant growth rate DDM implies that a stock's value will be greater:

1. The larger its expected dividend per share.
2. The lower the market capitalization rate, k.
3. The higher the expected growth rate of dividends.

Another implication of the constant-growth model is that the stock price is expected to grow at the same rate as dividends. To see this, suppose Steady State stock is selling at its intrinsic value of $57.14, so that $V_0 = P_0$. Then

$$P_0 = \frac{D_1}{k - g}$$

Notice that price is proportional to dividends. Therefore, next year, when the dividends paid to Steady State stockholders are expected to be higher by $g = 5\%$, price also should increase by 5%. To confirm this, we can write

$$D_2 = \$4(1.05) = \$4.20$$
$$P_1 = D_2/(k - g) = \$4.20/(.12 - .05) = \$60.00$$

which is 5% higher than the current price of $57.14. To generalize

$$P_1 = \frac{D_2}{k - g} = \frac{D_1(1 + g)}{k - g} = \frac{D_1}{k - g}(1 + g) = P_0(1 + g)$$

Therefore, the DDM implies that when dividends are growing at a constant rate, the expected rate of price appreciation in any year will equal that constant growth rate, g. For a stock whose market price equals its intrinsic value ($V_0 = P_0$), the expected holding-period return will be

$$E(r) = \text{Dividend yield} + \text{Capital gains yield}$$
$$= \frac{D_1}{P_0} + \frac{P_1 - P_0}{P_0} = \frac{D_1}{P_0} + g \tag{13.5}$$

This formula allows us to infer the market capitalization rate of a stock, for if the stock is selling at its intrinsic value, then $E(r) = k$, implying that $k = D_1/P_0 + g$. By observing the dividend yield, D_1/P_0, and estimating the growth rate of dividends, we can compute k. This equation is also known as the *discounted cash flow (DCF) formula.*

This approach is often used in rate hearings for regulated public utilities. The regulatory agency responsible for approving utility pricing decisions is mandated to allow the firms to charge just enough to cover costs plus a "fair" profit, that is, one that allows a competitive return on the investment the firm has made in its productive capacity. In turn, that return is taken to be the expected return investors require on the stock of the firm. The $D_1/P_0 + g$ formula provides a means to infer that required return.

EXAMPLE 13.3

The Constant-Growth Model

Suppose that Steady State Electronics wins a major contract for its revolutionary computer chip. The very profitable contract will enable it to increase the growth rate of dividends from 5% to 6% without reducing the current dividend from the projected value of $4 per share. What will happen to the stock price? What will happen to future expected rates of return on the stock?

The stock price ought to increase in response to the good news about the contract, and indeed it does. The stock price jumps from its original value of $57.14 to a post-announcement price of

$$\frac{D_1}{k - g} = \frac{\$4}{.12 - .06} = \$66.67$$

Investors who are holding the stock when the good news about the contract is announced will receive a substantial windfall.

On the other hand, at the new price the expected rate of return on the stock is 12%, just as it was before the new contract was announced:

$$E(r) = \frac{D_1}{P_0} + g = \frac{\$4}{\$66.67} + .06 = .12, \text{ or } 12\%$$

This makes sense. Once the news about the contract is reflected in the stock price, the expected rate of return will be consistent with the risk of the stock. Because that risk has not changed, neither should the expected rate of return.

CONCEPT check 13.2

a. IBX's stock dividend at the end of this year is expected to be $2.15, and it is expected to grow at 11.2% per year forever. If the required rate of return on IBX stock is 15.2% per year, what is its intrinsic value?

b. If IBX's current market price is equal to this intrinsic value, what is next year's expected price?

c. If an investor were to buy IBX stock now and sell it after receiving the $2.15 dividend a year from now, what is the expected capital gain (i.e., price appreciation) in percentage terms? What is the dividend yield, and what would be the holding-period return?

Stock Prices and Investment Opportunities

Consider two companies, Cash Cow, Inc., and Growth Prospects, each with expected earnings in the coming year of $5 per share. Both companies could in principle pay out all of these earnings as dividends, maintaining a perpetual dividend flow of $5 per share. If the market capitalization rate were $k = 12.5\%$, both companies would then be valued at $D_1/k = \$5/.125 = \$40$ per share. Neither firm would grow in value, because with all earnings paid out as dividends, and no earnings reinvested in the firm, both companies' capital stock and earnings capacity would remain unchanged over time; earnings[2] and dividends would not grow.

---

[2]Actually, we are referring here to earnings net of the funds necessary to maintain the productivity of the firm's capital, that is, earnings net of "economic depreciation." In other words, the earnings figure should be interpreted as the maximum amount of money the firm could pay out each year in perpetuity without depleting its productive capacity. For this reason, the net earnings number may be quite different from the accounting earnings figure that the firm reports in its financial statements. We will explore this further in the next chapter.

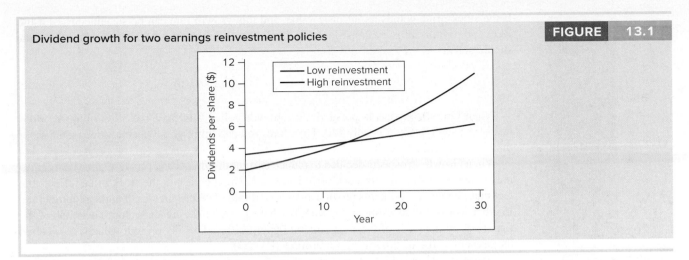

FIGURE   13.1

Dividend growth for two earnings reinvestment policies

Now suppose one of the firms, Growth Prospects, engages in projects that generate a return on investment of 15%, which is greater than the required rate of return, $k = 12.5\%$. It would be foolish for such a company to pay out all of its earnings as dividends. If Growth Prospects retains or plows back some of its earnings into its highly profitable projects, it can earn a 15% rate of return for its shareholders, whereas if it pays out all earnings as dividends, it forgoes the projects, leaving shareholders to invest the dividends in other opportunities at a fair market rate of only 12.5%. Suppose, therefore, Growth Prospects chooses a lower **dividend payout ratio** (the fraction of earnings paid out as dividends), reducing payout from 100% to 40% and maintaining a **plowback ratio** (the fraction of earnings reinvested in the firm) of 60%. The plowback ratio also is referred to as the **earnings retention ratio.**

The dividend of the company, therefore, will be only $2 (40% of $5 earnings) instead of $5. Will the share price fall? No, it will rise! Although dividends initially fall under the earnings reinvestment policy, subsequent growth in the assets of the firm due to reinvested profits will generate growth in future dividends, which will be reflected in today's share price.

Figure 13.1 illustrates the dividend streams generated by Growth Prospects under two dividend policies. A low reinvestment rate plan allows the firm to pay higher initial dividends but results in a lower dividend growth rate. Eventually, a high reinvestment rate plan will provide higher dividends. If the dividend growth generated by the reinvested earnings is high enough, the stock will be worth more under the high reinvestment strategy.

How much growth will be generated? Suppose Growth Prospects starts with plant and equipment of $100 million and is all-equity-financed. With a return on investment or equity (ROE) of 15%, total earnings are ROE × $100 million = .15 × $100 million = $15 million. There are 3 million shares of stock outstanding, so earnings per share are $5, as posited above. If 60% of the $15 million in this year's earnings is reinvested, then the value of the firm's capital stock will increase by .60 × $15 million = $9 million, or by 9%. The percentage increase in the capital stock is the rate at which income was generated (ROE) times the plowback ratio (the fraction of earnings reinvested in more capital), which we will denote as b.

Now endowed with 9% more capital, the company earns 9% more income and pays out 9% higher dividends. The growth rate of the dividends, therefore, is[3]

$$g = \text{ROE} \times b = 15\% \times .60 = 9\%$$

dividend payout ratio

Fraction of earnings paid out as dividends.

plowback ratio or earnings retention ratio

The proportion of the firm's earnings that is reinvested in the business (and not paid out as dividends).

---

[3]We can derive this relationship more generally by noting that with a fixed ROE, earnings (which equal ROE × Book value) will grow at the same rate as the book value of the firm. Abstracting from net new capital raised by the firm, the growth rate of book value equals reinvested earnings/book value. Therefore,

$$g = \frac{\text{Reinvested earnings}}{\text{Book value}} = \frac{\text{Reinvested earnings}}{\text{Total earnings}} \times \frac{\text{Total earnings}}{\text{Book value}} = b \times \text{ROE}$$

If the stock price equals its intrinsic value, and this growth rate can be sustained (i.e., if the ROE and payout ratios are consistent with the long-run capabilities of the firm), then the stock should sell at

$$P_0 = \frac{D_1}{k - g} = \frac{\$2}{.125 - .09} = \$57.14$$

When Growth Prospects pursued a no-growth policy and paid out all earnings as dividends, the stock price was only $40. Therefore, you can think of $40 as the value per share of the assets the company already has in place.

When Growth Prospects decided to reduce current dividends and reinvest some of its earnings in new investments, its stock price increased. The increase in the stock price reflects the fact that planned investments provide an expected rate of return greater than the required rate. In other words, the investment opportunities have positive net present value. The value of the firm rises by the NPV of these investment opportunities. This net present value is also called the **present value of growth opportunities (PVGO).**

present value of growth opportunities (PVGO)

Net present value of a firm's future investments.

Therefore, we can think of the value of the firm as the sum of the value of assets already in place, or the no-growth value of the firm, plus the net present value of the future investments the firm will make, which is the PVGO. For Growth Prospects, PVGO = $17.14 per share:

$$\text{Price} = \text{No-growth value per share} + \text{PVGO}$$
$$P_0 = \frac{E_1}{k} + \text{PVGO}$$
$$\$57.14 = \$40 + \$17.14 \tag{13.6}$$

We know that, in reality, dividend cuts almost always are accompanied by drops in stock prices. Does this contradict our analysis? Not necessarily: Dividend cuts are usually taken as bad news about the future prospects of the firm, and it is the *new information* about the firm—not the reduced dividend per se—that is responsible for the stock price decline.

For example, when J. P. Morgan cut its quarterly dividend from 38 cents to 5 cents a share in 2009, its stock price actually increased by about 5%: The company was able to convince investors that the cut would conserve cash and prepare the firm to weather a severe recession. When investors were convinced that the dividend cut made sense, the stock price actually increased. Similarly, when BP announced in the wake of the massive 2010 Gulf oil spill that it would suspend dividends for the rest of the year, its stock price did not budge. The cut already had been widely anticipated, so it was not new information. These examples show that stock price declines in response to dividend cuts are really a response to the information conveyed by the cut.

It is important to recognize that growth per se is not what investors desire. Growth enhances company value only if it is achieved by investment in projects with attractive profit opportunities (i.e., with ROE > k). To see why, let's now consider Growth Prospects' unfortunate sister company, Cash Cow. Cash Cow's ROE is only 12.5%, just equal to the required rate of return, k. Therefore, the NPV of its investment opportunities is zero. We've seen that following a zero-growth strategy with $b = 0$ and $g = 0$, the value of Cash Cow will be $E_1/k = \$5/.125 = \$40$ per share. Now suppose Cash Cow chooses a plowback ratio of $b = .60$, the same as Growth Prospects' plowback. Then g would rise to

$$g = \text{ROE} \times b = .125 \times .60 = .075$$

but the stock price is still $40:

$$P_0 = \frac{D_1}{k - g} = \frac{\$2}{.125 - .075} = \$40$$

which is no different from the no-growth strategy.

When Cash Cow reduced dividends to free funds for reinvestment, it generated only enough growth to maintain the stock price at its current level. This is not surprising: If the firm's projects yield only what investors can earn on their own, then NPV is zero, and shareholders cannot be made better off by a high reinvestment rate policy. This demonstrates that "growth" is not the same as growth opportunities. To justify reinvestment, the firm must engage in projects with better prospective returns than those shareholders can find elsewhere. Notice also that the PVGO of Cash Cow is zero: $PVGO = P_0 - E_1/k = 40 - 40 = 0$. With $ROE = k$, there is no advantage to plowing funds back into the firm; this shows up as PVGO of zero. In fact, this is why firms with considerable cash flow, but limited investment prospects, are called "cash cows." The cash these firms generate is best taken out of or "milked from" the firm.

Takeover Target is run by entrenched management that insists on reinvesting 60% of its earnings in projects that provide an ROE of 10%, despite the fact that the firm's capitalization rate is $k = 15\%$. The firm's year-end dividend will be \$2 per share, paid out of earnings of \$5 per share. At what price will the stock sell? What is the present value of growth opportunities? Why would such a firm be a takeover target for another firm?

Given current management's investment policy, the dividend growth rate will be

$$g = ROE \times b = 10\% \times .6 = 6\%$$

and the stock price should be

$$P_0 = \frac{\$2}{.15 - .06} = \$22.22$$

The present value of growth opportunities is

$$PVGO = \text{Price per share} - \text{No-growth value per share}$$
$$= \$22.22 - E_1/k = \$22.22 - \$5/.15 = -\$11.11$$

PVGO is *negative*. This is because the net present value of the firm's projects is negative: The rate of return on those assets is less than the opportunity cost of capital.

Such a firm would be subject to takeover, because another firm could buy the firm for the market price of \$22.22 per share and increase the value of the firm by changing its investment policy. For example, if the new management simply paid out all earnings as dividends, the value of the firm would increase to its no-growth value, $E_1/k = \$5/.15 = \$33.33$.

EXAMPLE 13.4

Growth Opportunities

CONCEPT check 13.3

a. Calculate the price of a firm with a plowback ratio of .60 if its ROE is 20%. Current earnings, E_1, will be \$5 per share, and $k = 12.5\%$.

b. What if ROE is 10%, which is less than the market capitalization rate? Compare the firm's price in this instance to that of a firm with the same ROE and E_1 but a plowback ratio of $b = 0$.

Life Cycles and Multistage Growth Models

As useful as the constant-growth DDM formula is, you need to remember that it is based on a simplifying assumption, namely, that the dividend growth rate will be constant forever. In fact, firms typically pass through life cycles with very different dividend profiles in different phases. In early years, there are ample opportunities for profitable reinvestment in the company. Payout ratios are low, and growth is correspondingly rapid. In later years, the firm matures, production capacity is sufficient to meet market demand, competitors enter the market, and attractive opportunities for reinvestment may become harder to find. In this mature phase, with fewer investment opportunities, the firm may choose to pay out a higher fraction of earnings as dividends.

Table 13.2 illustrates this profile. It gives Value Line's forecasts of return on capital, dividend payout ratio, and projected three-year growth rate in earnings per share of a sample of the firms included in the computer software and services industry versus those of East Coast

TABLE 13.2   Financial ratios in two industries

	Ticker	Return on Capital	Payout Ratio	Growth Rate 2017–2020
Computer software				
Adobe Systems	ADBE	15.0	0.0	20.6%
Citrix	CTXS	17.5	0.0	7.6%
Cognizant	CTSH	15.0	0.0	11.1%
Computer Associates	CA	13.5	39.0	9.6%
Intuit	INTU	46.5	28.0	12.2%
Microsoft	MSFT	26.0	52.0	10.2%
Oracle	ORCL	13.5	21.0	10.4%
Red Hat	RHT	14.0	0.0	16.5%
Symantec	SYMC	13.5	18.0	8.1%
SAP	SAP	13.0	36.0	7.7%
Median		14.5	19.5	10.3%
Electric utilities (east coast)				
Dominion Resources	D	7.5	87.0	5.8%
Consolidated Edison	ED	5.5	65.0	3.4%
Duke Energy	DUK	5.0	70.0	3.2%
Eversource	ES	6.5	55.0	8.3%
FirstEnergy	FE	5.0	56.0	2.5%
Nextera Energy	NEE	8.0	64.0	5.9%
Public Service Enterprise	PEG	7.0	59.0	5.9%
South Carolina E & G	SCG	6.0	57.0	6.5%
Southern Company	SO	5.5	70.0	4.8%
Exelon	EXC	6.0	49.0	6.6%
Median		6.0	61.5	5.8%

Source: *Value Line Investment Survey,* February 17, 2017.

electric utilities. (We compare return on capital rather than return on equity because the latter is affected by leverage, which tends to be far greater in the electric utility industry than in the software industry. Return on capital measures operating income per dollar of total long-term financing, regardless of whether the source of the capital supplied is debt or equity. We will return to this issue in the next chapter.)

By and large, software firms have attractive investment opportunities. The median return on capital of these firms is forecast at 14.5%, and the firms have responded with quite high plowback ratios. Several of these firms pay no dividends at all. The high returns on capital and high plowback ratios result in rapid growth. The median growth rate of earnings per share in this group is projected at 10.3%.

In contrast, the electric utilities are more representative of mature firms. Their median return on capital is lower, 6%; dividend payout is higher, 61.5%; and the median growth rate is only 5.8%. We conclude that the higher payouts of the electric utilities reflect their more limited opportunities to reinvest earnings at attractive rates of return.

To value companies with temporarily high growth, analysts use a multistage version of the dividend discount model. For example, a **two-stage dividend discount model (DDM)** allows for an initial high-growth period before the firm settles down to a sustainable growth trajectory. The combined present value of dividends in the initial high-growth period is calculated first. Then, once the firm is projected to settle down to a steady-growth phase, the constant-growth DDM is applied to value the remaining stream of dividends. This approach is useful for any firm with short-term dividend growth, whether high or low, that is not currently on a smooth long-term trend line.

Let's apply the two-stage model to an actual firm. Figure 13.2 is a *Value Line Investment Survey* report on Chevron. Some of the relevant information in 2017 is highlighted.

two-stage dividend discount model (DDM)

Dividend discount model in which dividend growth is assumed to level off to a steady, sustainable rate only at some future date.

Value Line Investment Survey report on Chevron

Source: From *Value Line Investment Survey*, March 3, 2017.

FIGURE 13.2

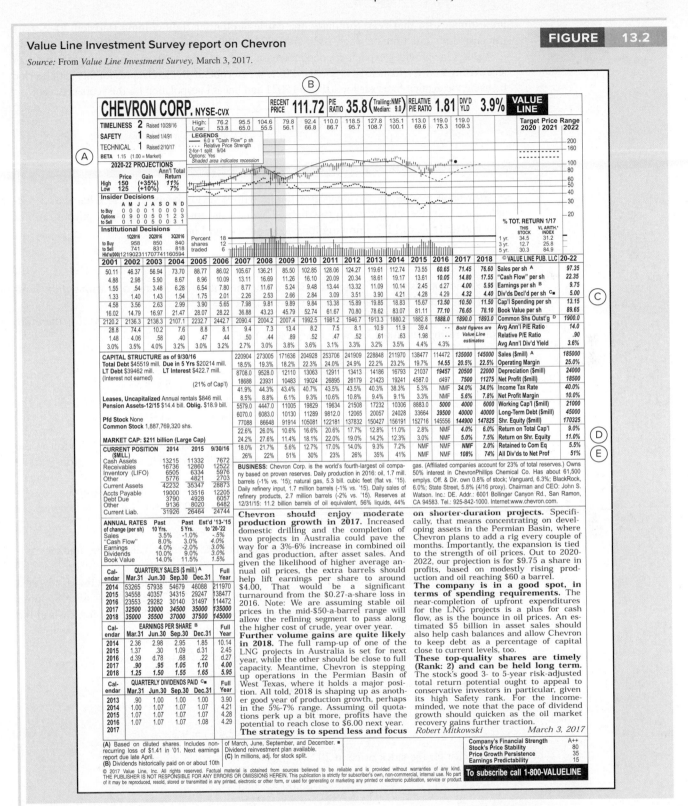

Chevron's beta appears at the circled A, its recent stock price at the B, the per-share dividend payments at the C, the ROE (referred to as "return on shareholder equity") at the D, and the dividend payout ratio (referred to as "all dividends to net profits") at the E. The rows ending at C, D, and E are historical time series. The boldfaced italicized entries under 2018 are estimates for that year. Similarly, the entries in the far right column (labeled 20–22) are forecasts for some time between 2020 and 2022, which we will take to be 2021.

Value Line provides explicit dividend forecasts over the relative short term, with dividends per share rising from $4.40 in 2018 to $5.00 in 2021. We can obtain dividend inputs for this initial period by using the explicit forecasts for 2018 and 2021 and linear interpolation for the years between:

2018	$4.40
2019	$4.60
2020	$4.80
2021	$5.00

Now let us assume the dividend growth rate will be steady beyond 2021. What is a reasonable guess for that steady-state growth rate? Value Line forecasts a dividend payout ratio of 0.51 and an ROE of 11%, implying long-term growth will be

$$g = \text{ROE} \times b = 11\% \times (1 - .51) = 5.39\%$$

Value Line rounds this estimate off to 5.5% (see the entry for "Retained [Earnings] to Common Equity" near the circled D), so we also will set $g = 5.5\%$.

Our estimate of Chevron's intrinsic value using an investment horizon of 2021 is therefore obtained from Equation 13.2, which we restate here:

$$V_{2017} = \frac{D_{2018}}{(1+k)} + \frac{D_{2019}}{(1+k)^2} + \frac{D_{2020}}{(1+k)^3} + \frac{D_{2021} + P_{2021}}{(1+k)^4}$$

$$= \frac{4.40}{(1+k)} + \frac{4.60}{(1+k)^2} + \frac{4.80}{(1+k)^3} + \frac{5.00 + P_{2021}}{(1+k)^4}$$

Here, P_{2021} represents the forecast price at which we can sell our shares of Chevron at the end of 2021, when dividends enter their constant-growth phase. That price, according to the constant-growth DDM, should be

$$P_{2021} = \frac{D_{2022}}{k-g} = \frac{D_{2021}(1+g)}{k-g} = \frac{5.00 \times 1.055}{k - .055}$$

The only variable remaining to be determined to calculate intrinsic value is the market capitalization rate, k.

One way to obtain k is from the CAPM. Observe from the Value Line data that Chevron's beta is 1.15. The risk-free rate on long-term T-bonds in mid-2017 was about 2.4%.[4] Suppose that the market risk premium were forecast at 6%, roughly in line with analyst forecasts at the time. This would imply that the forecast for the market return was

$$\text{Risk-free rate} + \text{Market risk premium} = 2.4\% + 6\% = 8.4\%$$

Therefore, we can solve for the market capitalization rate as

$$k = r_f + \beta\left[E(r_M) - r_f\right]$$
$$= 2.4\% + 1.15(8.4\% - 2.4\%) = 9.3\%$$

Our forecast for the stock price in 2021 is thus

$$P_{2021} = \frac{\$5.00 \times 1.055}{.093 - .055} = \$138.82$$

and today's estimate of intrinsic value is

$$V_{2017} = \frac{4.40}{1.093} + \frac{4.60}{(1.093)^2} + \frac{4.80}{(1.093)^3} + \frac{5.00 + 138.82}{(1.093)^4} = \$112.32$$

---

[4]When valuing long-term assets such as stocks, it is common to treat the long-term Treasury bond, rather than short-term T-bills, as the risk-free asset.

We know from the Value Line report that Chevron's actual price was $111.72 (at the circled B). Our intrinsic value analysis indicates that Chevron was just about fairly priced by the market. Perhaps we need to turn elsewhere in search of a bargain.

But before accepting this conclusion, stop to consider how much confidence you should place in this estimate of intrinsic value. We've had to guess at dividends in the near future, the appropriate discount rate, and the ultimate dividend growth rate. Moreover, we've assumed Chevron will follow a relatively simple two-stage growth process. In practice, the growth of dividends can follow more complicated patterns. Even small errors in these approximations could upset a conclusion.

In particular, it is clear that an overwhelming portion of Chevron's intrinsic value derives from the forecasted 2021 sales price of $138.82. If that sales price is inaccurate, so will be our estimate of intrinsic value. And we have good reason to be skeptical. Even small revisions to this estimate can have huge impacts on the estimate of intrinsic value.

For example, let's suppose we have underestimated Chevron's sustainable growth prospects, and that the actual growth rate in the post-2021 period will be 6% rather than 5.5%. Using this higher estimate in the two-stage dividend discount model increases the estimate of intrinsic value to $127.59, an increase of about 14%. Now Chevron appears to be a bargain. But would you bet your career on a one-half percentage point differential in the growth rate?

The exercise highlights the importance of assessing the sensitivity of your estimate of intrinsic value to changes in underlying assumptions. In the end, your analysis will be no better than your assumptions. Sensitivity analysis will highlight the inputs that need to be most carefully examined. For example, we just found that even small changes in the sustainable growth rate can result in big changes in intrinsic value. On the other hand, reasonable changes in the dividends forecast between 2018 and 2021 have a small impact on intrinsic value.

Confirm that the intrinsic value of Chevron using the same data as in our example, but assuming its sustainable growth rate is 6% is in fact $127.59. (*Hint:* First calculate the discount rate and stock price in 2021. Then calculate the present value of all interim dividends plus the present value of the 2021 sales price.)

CONCEPT check **13.4**

Multistage Growth Models

The two-stage growth model that we just considered for Chevron is a good start toward realism, but clearly we could do even better if our valuation model allowed for more flexible patterns of growth. Multistage growth models allow dividends per share to grow at several different rates as the firm matures. Many analysts use three-stage growth models. They may allow for year-by-year forecasts of dividends for the short term, a final period of sustainable growth, and a transition period in between, during which dividend growth rates taper off from the initial rate to the ultimate sustainable rate. These models are conceptually no harder to work with than a two-stage model, but they require many more calculations and can be tedious to do by hand. It is easy, however, to build an Excel spreadsheet for such a model.

Spreadsheet 13.1 is an example of such a model. Column B contains the inputs we have used so far for Chevron. Column E contains dividend forecasts. In cells E2 through E5 we present the Value Line estimates for the next four years. Value Line's estimate of Chevron's growth rate in 2021 is 5.5%. But that might well be too optimistic as a rate that can be sustained in perpetuity. Suppose a more plausible long-run growth rate is 4%. We assume that dividend growth declines linearly in a transition period from 5.5% in 2021 (cell F6) to its ultimate value of 4% in 2031 (cell F17). Each dividend in the transition period is the previous year's dividend times that year's growth rate. Terminal value once the firm enters a constant-growth stage (cell G17) is computed from the constant-growth DDM. Finally, investor cash flow in each period (column H) equals dividends in each year plus the terminal value in 2032. The present value of these cash flows is computed in cell H19 as $87.01, about 23% below the value we found in the two-stage model. We obtain a lower intrinsic value in this case because we assume the long-run dividend growth rate is 4% rather than the 5.5% rate used in the two-stage model.

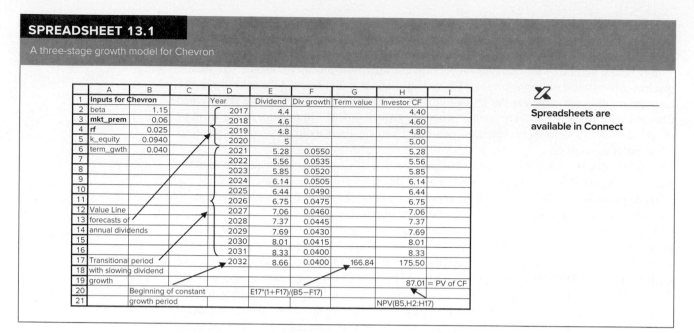

	A	B	C	D	E	F	G	H	I
1	Inputs for Chevron			Year	Dividend	Div growth	Term value	Investor CF	
2	beta	1.15		2017	4.4			4.40	
3	mkt_prem	0.06		2018	4.6			4.60	
4	rf	0.025		2019	4.8			4.80	
5	k_equity	0.0940		2020	5			5.00	
6	term_gwth	0.040		2021	5.28	0.0550		5.28	
7				2022	5.56	0.0535		5.56	
8				2023	5.85	0.0520		5.85	
9				2024	6.14	0.0505		6.14	
10				2025	6.44	0.0490		6.44	
11				2026	6.75	0.0475		6.75	
12	Value Line			2027	7.06	0.0460		7.06	
13	forecasts of			2028	7.37	0.0445		7.37	
14	annual dividends			2029	7.69	0.0430		7.69	
15				2030	8.01	0.0415		8.01	
16				2031	8.33	0.0400		8.33	
17	Transitional period			2032	8.66	0.0400	166.84	175.50	
18	with slowing dividend								
19	growth							87.01	= PV of CF
20		Beginning of constant			E17*(1+F17)/(B5−F17)				
21		growth period						NPV(B5,H2:H17)	

Spreadsheets are available in Connect

13.4   PRICE–EARNINGS RATIOS

The Price–Earnings Ratio and Growth Opportunities

price–earnings multiple

The ratio of a stock's price to its earnings per share.

Much of the real-world discussion of stock market valuation concentrates on the firm's **price–earnings multiple,** the ratio of price per share to earnings per share, commonly called the P/E ratio. In fact, one common approach to valuing a firm is to use an earnings multiplier. The value of the stock is obtained by multiplying projected earnings per share by a forecast of the P/E ratio. This procedure seems simple, but its apparent simplicity is deceptive. First, forecasting earnings is challenging. As we saw in the previous chapter, earnings will depend on international, macroeconomic, and industry as well as firm-specific factors, many of which are highly unpredictable. Second, forecasting the P/E multiple is even more difficult. P/E ratios vary across industries and over time. Nevertheless, our discussion of stock valuation provides some insight into the factors that ought to determine a firm's P/E ratio.

Recall our discussion of growth opportunities, in which we compared two firms, Growth Prospects and Cash Cow, each of which had earnings per share of $5. Growth Prospects reinvested 60% of its earnings in prospects with an ROE of 15%, while Cash Cow paid out all of its earnings as dividends. Cash Cow had a price of $40, giving it a P/E multiple of 40/5 = 8, while Growth Prospects sold for $57.14, giving it a multiple of 57.14/5 = 11.4. This observation suggests the P/E ratio might serve as a useful indicator of expectations of growth opportunities. We can see this explicitly by rearranging Equation 13.6 to

$$\frac{P_0}{E_1} = \frac{1}{k}\left[1 + \frac{\text{PVGO}}{E_1/k}\right] \qquad (13.7)$$

When PVGO = 0, Equation 13.7 shows that $P_0 = E_1/k$. The stock is valued like a nongrowing perpetuity of E_1. The P/E ratio is just $1/k$. However, as PVGO becomes an increasingly dominant contributor to price, the P/E ratio can rise dramatically.

The ratio of PVGO to E/k has a straightforward interpretation. It is the ratio of the component of firm value reflecting growth opportunities to the value of *assets already in place* (which we measure by the no-growth value of the firm, E/k). When future growth opportunities dominate the estimate of total value, the firm will command a high price relative to current earnings. Thus, a high P/E multiple appears to indicate that a firm is endowed with ample growth opportunities.

EXAMPLE 13.5

Google's Growth Opportunities

Google is already a highly profitable firm, but its forward P/E ratio of 23.54 in mid-2017 indicates that it still has substantial growth opportunities. If its market capitalization rate is about 10%, then we can use Equation 13.7 to infer the ratio of the value of its growth opportunities to the present value of its assets in place:

$$\frac{P_0}{E_1} = \frac{1}{k}\left[1 + \frac{PVGO}{E/k}\right] = \frac{1}{.10}\left[1 + \frac{PVGO}{PV(\text{Assets in place})}\right] = 23.54$$

We solve to show that PVGO/PV(Assets in place) = 1.35. So more than half of Google's market value reflects the net present value of its anticipated future investments.

P/E multiples do vary with growth prospects. Between 2001 and 2016, for example, PepsiCo's P/E ratio averaged about 20.2 while Consolidated Edison's average P/E was only 14.7. These numbers do not necessarily imply that Pepsi was overpriced compared to Con Ed. If investors believed Pepsi would grow faster, its higher ratio would be justified. That is, investors might well pay a higher price per dollar of *current earnings* if they expect that earnings stream to grow more rapidly. In fact Pepsi's growth rate has been consistent with its higher P/E multiple. In this period, its earnings per share increased by 192% while Con Ed's earnings grew by only 19%. Figure 13.4 (later in the chapter) shows the EPS history of the two companies.

We conclude that the P/E ratio reflects the market's optimism concerning a firm's growth prospects. Analysts must decide whether they are more or less optimistic than the belief implied by the market multiple. If they are more optimistic, they will recommend buying the stock.

There is a way to make these insights more precise. Look again at the constant-growth DDM formula, $P_0 = D_1/(k - g)$. Now recall that dividends equal the earnings that are *not* reinvested in the firm: $D_1 = E_1(1 - b)$. Recall also that $g = \text{ROE} \times b$. Hence, substituting for D_1 and g, we find that

$$P_0 = \frac{E_1(1 - b)}{k - (\text{ROE} \times b)}$$

implying that the P/E ratio for a firm growing at a long-run sustainable pace is

$$\frac{P_0}{E_1} = \frac{1 - b}{k - (\text{ROE} \times b)} \tag{13.8}$$

It is easy to verify that the P/E ratio increases with ROE. This makes sense, because high ROE projects give the firm good opportunities for growth.[5] We also can verify that the P/E ratio increases for higher plowback, b, as long as ROE exceeds k. This too makes sense. When a firm has good investment opportunities, the market will reward it with a higher P/E multiple if it exploits those opportunities more aggressively by plowing back more earnings into those opportunities.

Remember, however, that growth is not desirable for its own sake. Examine Table 13.3, where we use Equation 13.8 to compute both growth rates and P/E ratios for different combinations of ROE and b. While growth always increases with the plowback ratio (move across the rows in Panel A of Table 13.3), the P/E ratio does not (move across the rows in Panel B). In the top row of Table 13.3, Panel B, the P/E falls as the plowback rate increases. In the middle row, it is unaffected by plowback. In the third row, it increases.

This pattern has a simple interpretation. When the expected ROE is less than the required return, k, investors prefer that the firm pay out earnings as dividends rather than reinvest earnings in the firm at an inadequate rate of return. That is, for ROE lower than k, the value of the firm falls as plowback increases. Conversely, when ROE exceeds k, the firm offers superior investment opportunities, so the value of the firm is enhanced as those opportunities are more fully exploited by increasing the plowback ratio.

[5]Note that Equation 13.8 is a simple rearrangement of the DDM formula, with $\text{ROE} \times b = g$. Because that formula requires that $g < k$, Equation 13.8 is valid only when $\text{ROE} \times b < k$.

TABLE 13.3   Effect of ROE and plowback on growth and the P/E ratio

	Plowback Ratio (*b*)			
	0	**0.25**	**0.50**	**0.75**
A. Growth rate, *g*				
ROE				
10%	0%	2.5%	5.0%	7.5%
12	0	3.0	6.0	9.0
14	0	3.5	7.0	10.5
B. P/E ratio				
ROE				
10%	8.33	7.89	7.14	5.56
12	8.33	8.33	8.33	8.33
14	8.33	8.82	10.00	16.67

Note: Assumption: $k = 12\%$ per year.

Finally, where ROE just equals *k*, the firm offers "break-even" investment opportunities with a fair rate of return. In this case, investors are indifferent between reinvestment of earnings in the firm or elsewhere at the market capitalization rate, because the rate of return in either case is 12%. Therefore, the stock price is unaffected by the plowback ratio.

We conclude that the higher the plowback ratio, the higher the growth rate, but a higher plowback ratio does not necessarily mean a higher P/E ratio. Higher plowback increases P/E only if investments undertaken by the firm offer an expected rate of return higher than the market capitalization rate. Otherwise, increasing plowback hurts investors because more money is sunk into prospects with inadequate rates of return.

Notwithstanding these fine points, P/E ratios commonly are taken as proxies for the expected growth in dividends or earnings. In fact, a common Wall Street rule of thumb is that the growth rate ought to be roughly equal to the P/E ratio. In other words, the ratio of P/E to *g*, often called the **PEG ratio,** should be about 1. Peter Lynch, the famous portfolio manager, puts it this way in his book *One Up on Wall Street:*

PEG ratio

Ratio of P/E multiple to earnings growth rate.

> The P/E ratio of any company that's fairly priced will equal its growth rate. I'm talking here about growth rate of earnings. . . . If the P/E ratio of Coca-Cola is 15, you'd expect the company to be growing at about 15% per year, etc. But if the P/E ratio is less than the growth rate, you may have found yourself a bargain.

Let's try his rule of thumb.

EXAMPLE 13.6

P/E Ratio versus Growth Rate

Assume:

$$r_f = 8\% \text{ (about the value when Peter Lynch was writing)}$$
$$r_M - r_f = 8\% \text{ (about the historical average market risk premium)}$$
$$b = .4 \text{ (a typical value for the plowback ratio in the U.S.)}$$

Therefore, $r_M = r_f +$ Market risk premium $= 8\% + 8\% = 16\%$, and $k = 16\%$ for an average ($\beta = 1$) company. If we also accept as reasonable that ROE = 16% (the same value as the expected return on the stock) we conclude that

$$g = \text{ROE} \times b = 16\% \times .4 = 6.4\%$$

and

$$\text{P/E} = \frac{1 - .4}{.16 - .064} = 6.26$$

(continued)

Thus, the P/E ratio and g are about equal using these assumptions, consistent with the rule of thumb. However, this rule of thumb, like almost all others, will not work in all circumstances. For example, the yield on long-term Treasury bonds today is more like 2.5%, so a comparable forecast of r_M today would be

$$r_f + \text{Market risk premium} = 2.5\% + 8\% = 10.5\%$$

If we continue to focus on a firm with $\beta = 1$, and ROE still is about the same as k, then

$$g = 10.5\% \times .4 = 4.2\%$$

while

$$P/E = \frac{1 - .4}{.105 - .042} = 9.5$$

The P/E ratio and g now diverge, and the PEG ratio is now $9.5/4.2 = 2.3$. Nevertheless, lower-than-average PEG ratios are still widely seen as signaling potential underpricing.

Whatever its shortcomings, the PEG ratio is widely followed. The PEG ratio for the S&P over the last 20 years typically has fluctuated within the range between 1 and 1.5.

ABC stock has an expected ROE of 12% per year, expected earnings per share of $2, and expected dividends of $1.50 per share. Its market capitalization rate is 10% per year.
  a. What are its expected growth rate, its price, and its P/E ratio?
  b. If the plowback rate were 0.4, what would be the firm's expected dividend per share, growth rate, price, P/E, and PEG ratio?

The importance of growth opportunities is most evident in the valuation of start-up firms, for example, in the Internet boom of the late 1990s. Many companies that had yet to turn a profit were valued by the market at billions of dollars. The value of these companies was *exclusively* growth opportunities. For example, the online auction firm eBay had 1998 profits of $2.4 million, far less than the $45 million profit earned by the traditional auctioneer Sotheby's; yet eBay's market value was more than 10 times greater: $22 billion versus $1.9 billion. As it turns out, the market was quite right to value eBay so much more aggressively than Sotheby's. Its operating income in 2016 was $2.3 billion, nearly 20 times that of Sotheby's.

Of course, when company valuation is determined primarily by growth opportunities, those values can be very sensitive to reassessments of such prospects. When the market became more skeptical of the business prospects of most Internet retailers at the close of the 1990s, that is, as it revised the estimates of growth opportunities downward, their stock prices plummeted.

As perceptions of future prospects wax and wane, share price can swing wildly. Growth prospects are intrinsically difficult to tie down; ultimately, however, those prospects drive the value of the most dynamic firms in the economy.

The nearby box contains a simple valuation analysis. Facebook's 2012 IPO was among the most highly anticipated in decades, and there was widespread speculation about the price at which it would eventually trade in the stock market. There was considerable disparity among analysts about what the stock would be worth. The points of contention in their analysis turned on two key questions. First, what was a reasonable projection for the growth rate of Facebook's profits? Second, what multiple of earnings was appropriate to translate an earnings forecast into a price forecast? These are precisely the questions addressed by our stock valuation models.

FACEBOOK'S IPO

As Facebook's IPO drew near, valuation estimates by professional analysts were surprisingly disparate, ranging from as little as $50 billion to as much as $125 billion.

Disputes over fair value turned on a few key questions: Just how fast would the company be able to grow? How much profit would it be able to derive from advertising? And what earnings multiple would the market be willing to pay for that profit stream?

Everyone believed that Facebook had many years of rapid growth before it, but even so, its growth rate had already begun to slow compared to its early years. While revenue grew 88% in 2011 and net income grew 65%, that increase was nevertheless considerably below the 154% increase in revenue from 2009 to 2010.

The president of IPOdesktop.com, which analyzes IPOs for investors, estimated Facebook's value at no more than $50 billion.* Even that value, at the low end of the range of most analysts, seemed generous in some respects: It would have been 50 times Facebook's 2011 profits of $1 billion, and a P/E multiple

of 50 was more than triple the market's average price-to-earnings ratio at the time.

However, many higher estimates were also offered. For example, an analyst at Wedge Partners believed the value could top $100 billion. If Facebook traded at 15 to 18 times next year's EBITDA (expected earnings before interest, taxes, and certain noncash charges), it would result in a stock valuation of around $89 billion. But if Facebook could generate faster growth in ad spending, it could justify a multiple as high as 20 times earnings, implying a $110 billion valuation. By comparison, more mature companies such as Microsoft or Google traded at 7 to 10 times EBITDA. IPOdesktop was unconvinced, pointing out that at a $100 billion valuation, Facebook would be worth about half as much as Google, even though Google's sales and profits were 10 times that of Facebook.

In the end, based on its IPO price, the market valued Facebook at about $90 billion.

*The valuation estimates cited in this box appeared in Randall Smith, "Facebook's $100 Billion Question," *The Wall Street Journal*, February 3, 2012.

P/E Ratios and Stock Risk

One important implication of any stock valuation model is that (holding all else equal) riskier stocks will have lower P/E multiples. We can see this in the context of the constant-growth model by examining the formula for the P/E ratio (Equation 13.8):

$$\frac{P}{E} = \frac{1 - b}{k - g}$$

Riskier firms will have higher required rates of return (i.e., higher values of k). Therefore, their P/E multiples will be lower. This is true even outside the context of the constant-growth model. For *any* expected earnings and dividend stream, the present value of those cash flows will be lower when the stream is perceived to be riskier. Hence the stock price and the ratio of price to earnings will be lower.

Of course, many small, risky, start-up companies have very high P/E multiples. This does not contradict our claim that P/E multiples should fall with risk: Instead, it is evidence of the market's expectations of high growth rates for those companies. This is why we said that high-risk firms will have lower P/E ratios *holding all else equal*. Given a growth projection, the P/E multiple will be lower when risk is perceived to be higher.

Pitfalls in P/E Analysis

No description of P/E analysis is complete without mentioning some of its pitfalls. First, consider that the denominator in the P/E ratio is accounting earnings, which are influenced by somewhat arbitrary accounting rules such as the use of historical cost in depreciation and inventory valuation. In times of high inflation, historic cost depreciation and inventory costs will tend to underrepresent true economic values because the replacement cost of both goods and capital equipment will rise with the general level of prices. As Figure 13.3 demonstrates, P/E ratios generally have been inversely related to the inflation rate. In part, this reflects the market's assessment that earnings in high inflation periods are of "lower quality," artificially distorted by inflation, and warranting lower P/E ratios.

Earnings management is the practice of using flexibility in accounting rules to manipulate the apparent profitability of the firm. We will have much to say on this topic in the next chapter on interpreting financial statements. One version of earnings management is the

earnings management

The practice of using flexibility in accounting rules to manipulate the apparent profitability of the firm.

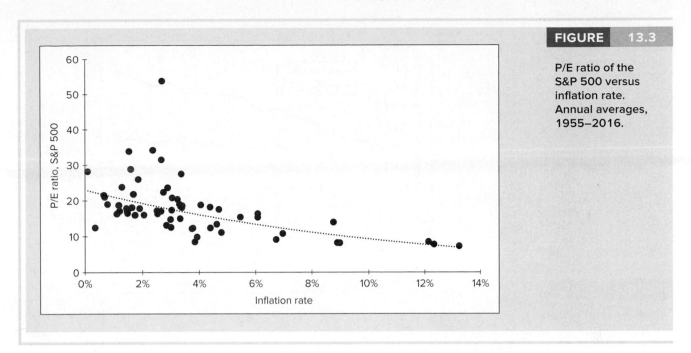

FIGURE   13.3

P/E ratio of the
S&P 500 versus
inflation rate.
Annual averages,
1955–2016.

reporting of "pro forma earnings." These measures are sometimes called *operating earnings,* a term with no precise generally accepted definition.

Pro forma earnings are calculated ignoring certain expenses, for example, restructuring charges or write-downs of assets from continuing operations. Firms argue that ignoring these expenses gives a clearer picture of the underlying profitability of the firm.

But when there is too much leeway for choosing what to exclude it becomes hard for investors or analysts to interpret the numbers or to compare them across firms. The lack of standards gives firms considerable leeway to manage earnings.

Even generally accepted accounting principles (GAAP) allow firms considerable discretion to manage earnings. For example, in the late 1990s, Kellogg took restructuring charges, which are supposed to be one-time events, nine quarters in a row. Were these really one-time events, or were they more appropriately treated as ordinary expenses? Given the available leeway in reporting earnings, the justified P/E multiple becomes difficult to gauge.

Another confounding factor in the use of P/E ratios is related to the business cycle. We were careful in deriving the DDM to define earnings as being net of *economic* depreciation, that is, the maximum flow of income that the firm could pay out without depleting its productive capacity. Yet reported earnings are computed in accordance with GAAP and need not correspond to economic earnings. Beyond this problem, notions of a normal or justified P/E ratio, as in Equation 13.7 or 13.8, assume implicitly that earnings rise at a constant rate, or, put another way, on a smooth trend line. In contrast, reported earnings can fluctuate dramatically around a trend line over the course of the business cycle.

Another way to make this point is to note that the "normal" P/E ratio predicted by Equation 13.8 is the ratio of today's price to the trend value of future earnings, E_1. This is called the *forward P/E.* The P/E ratio reported in the financial pages of the newspaper, by contrast, is the ratio of price to the most recent *past* accounting earnings and is called the *trailing P/E.* Current earnings can differ considerably from their trend values. Because ownership of stock conveys the right to future as well as current earnings, the ratio of price to current earnings can vary substantially over the business cycle.

Because the market values the entire stream of future dividends generated by the company, when earnings are temporarily depressed, the P/E ratio should tend to be high—that is, the denominator of the ratio responds more sensitively to the business cycle than the numerator does. Conversely, when earnings are temporarily high, the P/E ratio will fall, as price increases less dramatically than earnings.

Earnings growth for
two companies

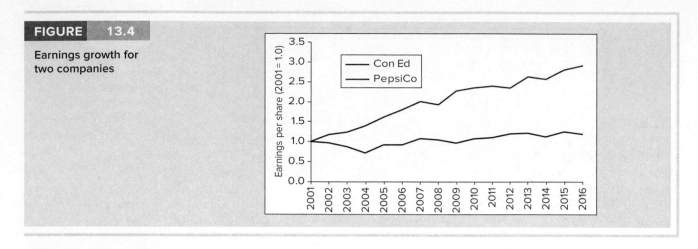

Price–earnings ratios

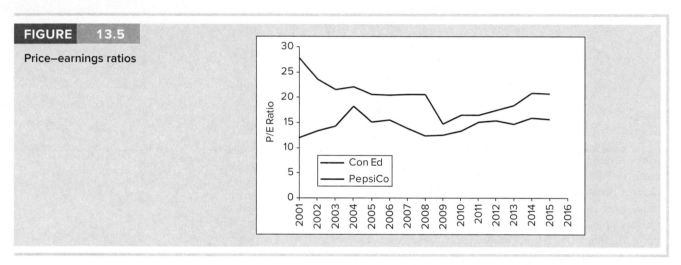

Figure 13.4 graphs the earnings per share of PepsiCo and Consolidated Edison since 2001, and Figure 13.5 plots their P/E ratios. When earnings depart from the trend line, the P/E ratio does in fact move in the opposite direction. For example, when Con Ed's earnings fell in 2001–2003, its P/E ratio rose. Similarly, when Pepsi's earnings per share increased at an above-trend rate of 17% between 2008 to 2009, its P/E fell.

These examples show why analysts must be careful in using P/E ratios. There is no way to say a P/E ratio is overly high or low without referring to the company's long-run growth prospects, as well as to current earnings per share relative to the long-run trend line.

Nevertheless, Figures 13.4 and 13.5 demonstrate a clear relationship between P/E ratios and growth. Despite short-run fluctuations, Pepsi's EPS clearly trended upward over the period. Its compound rate of growth in the 2001–2016 period was 7.4%. Con Edison's earnings grew far less rapidly, with a compound growth rate of 1.2%. Pepsi's growth prospects are reflected in its consistently higher P/E multiple.

Combining P/E Analysis and the DDM

Some analysts use P/E ratios in conjunction with earnings forecasts to estimate the price of stock at an investor's horizon date. The Chevron analysis in Figure 13.2 shows that Value Line forecast a P/E ratio for 2021 of 14. EPS for 2021 was forecast at $9.75, implying a price in 2021 of $14 \times \$9.75 = \$136.50$. Given this forecast, we would compute Chevron's intrinsic value as

$$V_{2017} = \frac{4.40}{(1.093)} + \frac{4.60}{(1.093)^2} + \frac{4.80}{(1.093)^3} + \frac{5.00 + 136.50}{(1.093)^4} = \$110.70$$

Other Comparative Valuation Ratios

The price–earnings ratio is an example of a comparative valuation ratio. Such ratios are used to assess the valuation of one firm versus another based on a fundamental indicator such as earnings. For example, an analyst might compare the P/E ratios of two firms in the same industry to test whether the market is valuing one firm "more aggressively" than the other. Other such comparative ratios are commonly used.

PRICE-TO-BOOK RATIO   This is the ratio of price per share divided by book value per share. As we noted earlier in this chapter, some analysts view book value as a useful measure of fundamental value and therefore treat the ratio of price to book value as an indicator of how aggressively the market values the firm.

PRICE-TO-CASH-FLOW RATIO   Earnings as reported on the income statement can be affected by the company's choice of accounting practices and thus are commonly viewed as subject to some imprecision and even manipulation. In contrast, cash flow—which tracks cash actually flowing into or out of the firm—is less affected by accounting decisions. As a result, some analysts prefer to use the ratio of price to cash flow per share rather than price to earnings per share. Some analysts use operating cash flow when calculating this ratio; others prefer free cash flow, that is, operating cash flow net of new investment.

PRICE-TO-SALES RATIO   Many start-up firms have no earnings. As a result, the P/E ratio for these firms is meaningless. The price-to-sales ratio (the ratio of stock price to the annual sales per share) is sometimes taken as a valuation benchmark for these firms. Of course, price-to-sales ratios can vary markedly across industries because profit margins vary widely.

BE CREATIVE   Sometimes a standard valuation ratio will simply not be available, and you will have to devise your own. In the 1990s, some analysts valued retail Internet firms based on the number of hits their websites received. In retrospect, they valued these firms using too generous "price-to-hits" ratios. Nevertheless, in a new investment environment, these analysts used the information available to them to devise the best valuation tools they could.

Figure 13.6 presents the behavior of these valuation measures for the S&P 500. While the levels of these ratios differ considerably, for the most part they track each other fairly closely, with upturns and downturns at the same times.

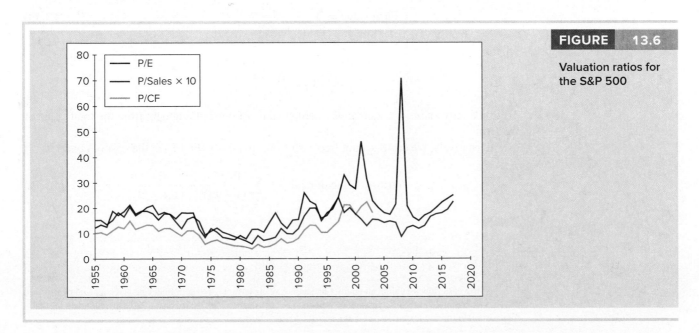

FIGURE 13.6

Valuation ratios for the S&P 500

13.5 FREE CASH FLOW VALUATION APPROACHES

An alternative approach to the dividend discount model values the firm using free cash flow, that is, cash flow available to the firm or the equityholders net of capital expenditures. This approach is particularly useful for firms that pay no dividends, for which the dividend discount model would be difficult to implement. But free cash flow models are valid for any firm, and can provide useful insights about firm value beyond the DDM.

One approach starts by discounting the *free cash flow* for the *firm* (FCFF) at the weighted-average cost of capital to find the value of the whole firm. Subtracting the value of debt then results in the value of equity. Another approach is to focus from the start on the free cash flow to *equityholders* (FCFE), discounting those directly at the cost of equity to obtain the market value of equity.

The free cash flow to the firm is the after-tax cash flow generated by the firm's operations, net of investments in capital and net working capital. It includes cash flows available to both debt- and equityholders[6] and equals:

$$\text{FCFF} = \text{EBIT}(1 - t_c) + \text{Depreciation} - \text{Capital expenditures} - \text{Increase in NWC} \quad \textbf{(13.9)}$$

where

$$\begin{aligned}
\text{EBIT} &= \text{Earnings before interest and taxes} \\
t_c &= \text{The corporate tax rate} \\
\text{NWC} &= \text{Net working capital}
\end{aligned}$$

Alternatively, we can focus on cash flow available to equityholders. This will differ from free cash flow to the firm by after-tax interest expenditures, as well as by cash flow associated with net issuance or repurchase of debt (i.e., principal repayments minus proceeds from issuance of new debt).

$$\text{FCFE} = \text{FCFF} - \text{Interest expense} \times (1 - t_c) + \text{Increases in net debt} \quad \textbf{(13.10)}$$

A free cash flow to the firm valuation model discounts year-by-year cash flows plus an estimate of terminal value, V_T. In Equation 13.11, we use the constant-growth model to estimate terminal value. The appropriate discount rate is the weighted-average cost of capital.

$$\text{Firm value} = \sum_{t=1}^{T} \frac{\text{FCFF}_t}{(1 + \text{WACC})^t} + \frac{V_T}{(1 + \text{WACC})^T} \quad \textbf{(13.11)}$$

where

$$V_T = \frac{\text{FCFF}_{T+1}}{\text{WACC} - g}$$

To find equity value, we subtract the market value of outstanding debt from the total value of the firm.

Alternatively, we can discount free cash flows to *equity* (FCFE) at the cost of *equity*, k_E,

$$\text{Intrinsic value of equity} = \sum_{t=1}^{T} \frac{\text{FCFE}_t}{(1 + k_E)^t} + \frac{E_T}{(1 + k_E)^T} \quad \textbf{(13.12)}$$

where

$$E_T = \frac{\text{FCFE}_{T+1}}{k_E - g}$$

---

[6] This is firm cash flow assuming all-equity financing. Any tax advantage to debt financing is recognized by using an after-tax cost of debt in the computation of weighted-average cost of capital. This issue is discussed in any introductory corporate finance text.

SPREADSHEET 13.2

Free cash flow valuation of Chevron

	A	B	C	D	E	F	G	H	I	J	K	L	M
1			2017	2018	2019	2020	2021						
2	A. Input data												
3	P/E		17.90	16.93	15.95	14.98	14.00						
4	Cap spending/shr		10.50	11.50	12.05	12.60	13.15						
5	LT Debt ($M)		40,000	40,000	41,667	43.333	45,000						
6	Shares (million)		1,890	1,893	1,895	1,898	1,900						
7	EPS		4.00	5.95	7.22	8.48	9.75						
8	Working Capital		4,000	6,000	11,000	16,000	21,000						
9													
10	B. Cash flow calculations												
11	Profits ($M, after tax)		7,500	11,275	13,683	16,092	18,500						
12	Interest ($M, after tax)		728	728	758	789	819			=(1-tax_rate) × r_debt × LT Debt			
13	Chg Working Cap ($M)			2,000	5,000	5,000	5,000						
14	Depreciation ($M)		20,500	22,000	22,667	23,333	24,000						
15	Cap Spending ($M)			21,770	22,841	23,913	24,985						
16								Terminal value					
17	FCFF ($M)			10,234	9,267	11,301	13,334	357,373					
18	FCFE ($M)			9,506	10,175	12,179	14,182	300,371		assumes fixed debt ratio after 2020			
19													
20	C. Discount rate calculations												
21	Current beta	1.15								from Value Line			
22	Unlevered beta	0.963								current beta /[1+(1-tax)*debt/equity)]			
23	Terminal growth	0.04											
24	Tax_rate	0.35											
25	r_debt	0.028								YTM in 2017 on Moody's Aa2 rated LT debt			
26	Risk-free rate	0.025											
27	Market risk prem	0.06											
28	MV equity		134,250				259,000			Row 3 × Row 11			
29	Debt/Value		0.23	0.21	0.19	0.17	0.15			linear trend from initial to final value			
30	Levered beta		1.150	1.129	1.109	1.090	1.072			unlevered beta × [1+(1-tax)*debt/equity]			
31	k_equity		0.094	0.093	0.092	0.090	0.089	0.089		from CAPM and levered beta			
32	WACC		0.077	0.077	0.078	0.078	0.079	0.079		(1-t)*r_debt*D/V+k_equity*(1-D/V)			
33	PV factor for FCFF		1.000	0.928	0.861	0.799	0.741	0.741		Discount each year at WACC			
34	PV factor for FCFE		1.000	0.915	0.838	0.769	0.706	0.706		Discount each year at k_equity			
35													
36	D. Present values									Intrinsic val	Equity val	Intrin/share	
37	PV(FCFF)			9,501	7,983	9,028	9,875	264,657		301,044	261,044	138.12	
38	PV(FCFE)			8,699	8,531	9,364	10,010	212,004		248,607	248,607	131.54	

* 2017 P/E ratio is from Yahoo! Finance. Final input is from Value Line, and intermediate values are interpolated.

Spreadsheets are available in Connect

As in the dividend discount model, free cash flow models use a terminal value to avoid adding the present values of an infinite sum of cash flows. That terminal value may simply be the present value of a constant-growth perpetuity (as in the formulas above), or it may be based on a multiple of EBIT, book value, earnings, or free cash flow. As a general rule, estimates of intrinsic value depend critically on terminal value.

Spreadsheet 13.2 presents a free cash flow valuation of Chevron using the data supplied by Value Line in Figure 13.2. We start with the free cash flow to the firm approach given in Equation 13.9. Panel A of the spreadsheet lays out values supplied by Value Line. (Entries for middle years are interpolated from beginning and final values.) Panel B calculates free cash flow. The sum of after-tax profits in row 11 plus after-tax interest payments in row 12 [that is, interest expense $\times (1 - t_c)$] equals $EBIT(1 - t_c)$.[7] In row 13 we subtract the change in net working capital, in row 14 we add back depreciation, and in row 15 we subtract capital expenditures. The result in row 17 is the free cash flow to the firm, FCFF, for each year between 2018 and 2021.

To find the present value of these cash flows, we will discount at WACC, which is calculated in panel C. WACC is the weighted average of the after-tax cost of debt and the cost of equity in each year. When computing WACC, we must account for the change in leverage forecast by Value Line. To compute the cost of equity, we will use the CAPM as in our earlier

---

[7] Throughout the spreadsheet, we use a corporate tax rate of 35%. At the time of this valuation exercise, early 2017, it seems plausible that the market did not yet expect the reduction in the corporate tax rate to 21% that occurred at the end of the year. Indeed, one common explanation for the stock price run-up in the latter half of the year was an emerging recognition of the likelihood of tax cuts. Similarly, the spreadsheet uses depreciation estimates as of early 2017, before depreciation tax rules were changed at the end of the year.

(dividend discount model) valuation exercise but account for the fact that equity beta will decline each year as the firm reduces leverage.[8]

A reasonable approximation to Chevron's cost of debt, which was rated Aa2 by Moody's in 2017, is the yield to maturity on comparably rated long-term debt, approximately 2.8% (cell B25). Chevron's debt-to-value ratio (assuming its debt is selling near par value) is computed in row 29. In 2017, the ratio was 0.23. Based on Value Line forecasts, it will fall to 0.15 by 2021. We interpolate the debt-to-value ratio for the intermediate years. WACC is computed in row 32. WACC increases slightly over time as the debt-to-value ratio steadily declines between 2017 and 2021. The present value factor for cash flows accruing in each year is the previous year's factor divided by (1 + WACC) for that year. The present value of each cash flow (row 37) is the free cash flow times the cumulative discount factor.

The terminal value of the firm (cell H17) is computed from the constant-growth model as $FCFF_{2021} \times (1 + g)/(WACC_{2021} - g)$, where g (cell B23) is the assumed value for the steady growth rate.[9] We assume in the spreadsheet that $g = .04$.[10] Terminal value is also discounted back to 2017 (cell H37), and the intrinsic value of the firm is thus found as the sum of discounted free cash flows between 2018 and 2021 plus the discounted terminal value. Finally, the value of debt in 2017 is subtracted from firm value to arrive at the intrinsic value of equity in 2017 (cell K37), and value per share is calculated in cell L37 as equity value divided by number of shares in 2017.

The free cash flow to equity approach yields a similar intrinsic value for the stock. FCFE (row 18) is obtained from FCFF by subtracting after-tax interest expense and net debt repurchases. The cash flows are then discounted at the equity rate. Like WACC, the cost of equity changes each period as leverage changes. The present value factor for equity cash flows is presented in row 34. Equity value is reported in cell J38, which is put on a per-share basis in cell L38.

Spreadsheet 13.2 is available in Connect.

Comparing the Valuation Models

In principle, the free cash flow approach is fully consistent with the dividend discount model and should provide the same estimate of intrinsic value if one can extrapolate to a period in which the firm begins to pay dividends growing at a constant rate. This was demonstrated in two famous papers by Modigliani and Miller (1958, 1961). However, in practice, you will find that values from these models may differ, sometimes substantially. This is due to the fact that in practice, analysts are always forced to make simplifying assumptions. For example, how long

---

[8]Call β_L the firm's equity beta at the initial level of leverage as provided by Value Line. Equity betas reflect both business risk and financial risk. When a firm changes its capital structure (debt/equity mix), it changes financial risk, and therefore equity beta changes. How should we recognize the change in financial risk? As you may remember from an introductory corporate finance class, you must first unleverage beta. This leaves us a beta that reflects only business risk. We use the following formula in cell B22 to find unleveraged beta, β_U, (where D/E is the firm's current debt-equity ratio):

$$\beta_U = \frac{\beta_L}{1 + (D/E)(1 - t_c)}$$

Then, we re-leverage beta in row 30 in each any particular year using the forecast capital structure (which reintroduces the financial risk associated with that year's capital structure):

$$\beta_L = \beta_U[1 + (D/E)(1 - t_c)]$$

[9]Over the 2017–2021 period, Value Line predicts that Chevron will retire a small fraction of its outstanding debt. The implied debt repurchases are a use of cash and reduce the cash flow available to equity. Such repurchases cannot be sustained indefinitely, however, for debt outstanding would eventually be run down to zero. Therefore, in our estimate of terminal value, we compute the final cash flow assuming that by 2021, Chevron will begin *issuing* enough debt to maintain its debt-to-value ratio unchanged. This approach is consistent with the assumption of constant growth and constant discount rates after 2021. To maintain consistency with the assumption that debt will grow at the same rate as the rest of the firm, in the numerator in cell H18, we subtract the actual growth of debt in the most recent year and add back the change in debt that would have taken place if debt had grown at the long-run growth rate.

[10]This is the same terminal growth rate that we used in the three-stage dividend discount model, Spreadsheet 13.1. In the long run a firm can't grow forever at a rate higher than the aggregate economy. So by the time we assert that growth is in a stable stage, it seems reasonable that the growth rate should not be significantly greater than that of the overall economy (although it can be less if the firm is in a declining industry).

will it take the firm to enter a constant-growth stage? How should depreciation best be treated? What is the best estimate of ROE? Answers to questions like these can have a big impact on value, and it is not always easy to maintain consistent assumptions across the models.

We have now valued Chevron using several approaches, with estimates of intrinsic value as follows:

Model	Intrinsic Value
Two-stage dividend discount model	$112.32
DDM with earnings multiple terminal value	110.70
Three-stage DDM	87.01
Free cash flow to the firm	138.12
Free cash flow to equity	131.54
Market price in 2017	111.72

What should we make of these differences? The three-stage dividend discount model is the most conservative of the estimates, primarily because (in contrast to the two-stage model) we assume the dividend growth rate declines from its 2021 level of 5.5% to a lower long-run value of 4%. The two-stage model estimate of intrinsic value as well as the earnings multiplier model pretty much match market price, although we caution you not to conclude that this is a common outcome. Finally, the free cash flow valuations exceed market price. So there is considerable dispersion in our signals about whether the market valuation of Chevron is too high or too low.

There is a larger lesson here. Models are all unavoidably simplified versions of the real world. The hard part in using them well is not in performing the calculations. The real challenge is ensuring that your inputs make sense. We've already mentioned the importance of sensitivity analysis. You also need to think more broadly about reality tests. Is the sustainable growth rate plausible? Is the date at which the firm is assumed to settle down to a trend growth trajectory reasonable? Are the final values for ROE and plowback consistent and credible? These questions require good judgment rather than just technical skills.

On balance, therefore, this valuation exercise suggests that obvious conclusions are not going to be common. While applying these models is easy, establishing proper inputs is not. This should not be surprising. In even a moderately efficient market, finding profit opportunities will be more involved than analyzing Value Line data for a few hours. The models are nevertheless extremely useful to analysts. They provide ballpark estimates of intrinsic value. More than that, they force rigorous thought about underlying assumptions and highlight the variables with the greatest impact on value and the greatest payoff to further analysis.

The Problem with DCF Models

Our estimates of Chevron's intrinsic value are all based on discounted cash flow (DCF) models, in which we calculate the present value of forecast cash flows and a terminal sales price at some future date. It is clear from our calculations that most of the action in these models is in the terminal value and that this value can be highly sensitive to even small changes in some input values (see, for example, Concept Check 13.4). Therefore, you must recognize that DCF valuation estimates are almost always going to be imprecise. Growth opportunities and future growth rates are especially hard to pin down.

For this reason, many value investors employ a hierarchy of valuation. They view the most reliable components of value as the items on the balance sheet for which estimate of market value are readily available. Real estate, plant, and equipment would fall in this category.

A somewhat less reliable component of value is the economic profit on assets already in place. For example, a company such as Intel earns a far higher ROE on its investments in chip-making facilities than its cost of capital. The present value of these "economic profits," or economic value added,[11] is a major component of Intel's market value. This component of

---

[11] We discuss economic value added in greater detail in the next chapter.

value is less certain than its balance sheet assets, however, because there is always a concern that new competitors will enter the market, force down prices and profit margins, and reduce the return on Intel's investments. Thus, one needs to carefully assess the barriers to entry that protect Intel's pricing and profit margins. We reviewed some of these barriers in the last chapter, where we discussed the role of industry analysis, market structure, and competitive position (see Section 12.7).

Finally, the least reliable components of value are growth opportunities, the purported ability of firms like Intel to invest in positive-NPV ventures that contribute to high market valuations today. Value investors don't deny that such opportunities exist, but they are skeptical that precise values can be attached to them and, therefore, tend to be less willing to make investment decisions that turn on the value of those opportunities.

13.6   THE AGGREGATE STOCK MARKET

The most popular approach to valuing the overall stock market is the earnings multiplier approach applied at the aggregate level. The first step is to forecast corporate profits for the coming period. Then we derive an estimate of the earnings multiplier, the aggregate P/E ratio, based on a forecast of long-term interest rates. The product of the two forecasts is the estimate of the end-of-period level of the market.

The forecast of the P/E ratio of the market is sometimes derived from a graph similar to that in Figure 13.7, which plots the *earnings yield* (earnings per share divided by price per share, the reciprocal of the P/E ratio) of the S&P 500 and the yield to maturity on 10-year Treasury bonds. The two series clearly move in tandem over time and suggest that one might use this relationship and the current yield on 10-year Treasury bonds to forecast the earnings yield on the S&P 500. Given that earnings yield, a forecast of earnings could be used to predict the level of the S&P in some future period. Let's consider a simple example of this procedure.

EXAMPLE 13.7 *Forecasting the* *Aggregate Stock Market*	In mid-2017, the S&P 500 was at 2,400. The forecast for 12-month forward earnings per share for the S&P 500 portfolio was about $126. The 10-year Treasury-bond yield at this time was about 2.25%, but the yield curve was upward sloping, so a plausible forecast for its value next year would be higher, perhaps 2.5%. As a first approach, we might posit that the spread between the earnings yield and the Treasury yield, which was around 2.4% in 2017, will remain at that level by the end of the year. Given the assumed Treasury yield, this would imply an earnings yield for the S&P of 4.9% and a P/E ratio of 1/.049 = 20.41. Our forecast for the level of the S&P Index would then be 20.41 × 126 = 2,571, which would imply a one-year capital gain on the index of 171/2,400 = 7.1%. Of course, there is uncertainty regarding all three inputs into this analysis: the actual earnings on the S&P 500 stocks, the level of Treasury yields at year-end, and the spread between the Treasury yield and the earnings yield. One would wish to perform sensitivity or scenario analysis to examine the impact of changes in all of these variables. To illustrate, consider Table 13.4, which shows a simple scenario analysis treating possible effects of variation in the Treasury-bond yield. The scenario analysis shows that the forecast level of the stock market varies inversely and with dramatic sensitivity to interest rate changes.

TABLE 13.4 S&P 500 index forecasts under various scenarios

	Pessimistic Scenario	Most Likely Scenario	Optimistic Scenario
Treasury bond yield	3.0%	2.5%	2.0%
Earnings yield	5.4%	4.9%	4.4%
Resulting P/E ratio	18.52	20.41	22.73
EPS forecast	126	126	126
Forecast for S&P 500	2,333	2,571	2,864

Note: The forecast for the earnings yield on the S&P 500 equals the Treasury-bond yield plus 2.4%. The P/E ratio is the reciprocal of the forecast earnings yield.

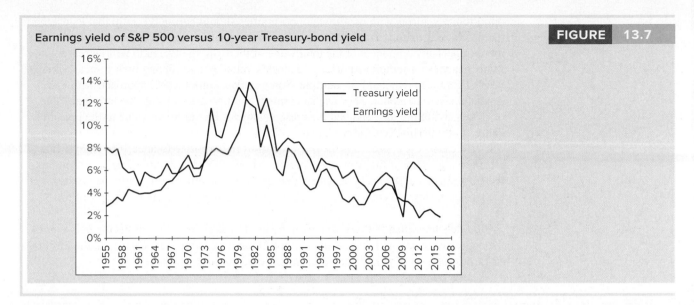

FIGURE **13.7**

Earnings yield of S&P 500 versus 10-year Treasury-bond yield

Some analysts use an aggregate version of the dividend discount model rather than an earnings multiplier approach. All of these models, however, rely heavily on forecasts of such macroeconomic variables as GDP, interest rates, and the rate of inflation, which are difficult to predict accurately.

Because stock prices reflect expectations of future dividends, which are tied to the economic fortunes of firms, it is not surprising that the performance of a broad-based stock index like the S&P 500 is taken as a leading economic indicator, that is, a predictor of the performance of the aggregate economy. Stock prices are viewed as embodying consensus forecasts of economic activity and are assumed to move up or down in anticipation of movements in the economy. The government's index of leading economic indicators, which is taken to predict the progress of the business cycle, is made up in part of recent stock market performance. However, the predictive value of the market is far from perfect. A well-known joke, often attributed to Paul Samuelson, is that the market has forecast eight of the last five recessions.

- One approach to firm valuation is to focus on the firm's book value, either as it appears on the balance sheet or adjusted to reflect the current replacement cost of assets or the liquidation value. Another approach is to focus on the present value of expected future dividends.

- The dividend discount model holds that the price of a share of stock should equal the present value of all future dividends per share, discounted at an interest rate commensurate with the risk of the stock.

- The constant-growth version of the DDM asserts that if dividends are expected to grow at a constant rate forever, then the intrinsic value of the stock is given by the formula

$$V_0 = \frac{D_1}{k - g}$$

- The constant-growth version of the DDM is simplistic in its assumption of a constant value of g. There are more sophisticated multistage versions of the model for more complex environments. When the constant-growth assumption is reasonably satisfied, however, the formula can be inverted to infer the market capitalization rate for the stock:

$$k = \frac{D_1}{P_0} + g$$

- Stock market analysts devote considerable attention to a company's price–earnings ratio. The P/E ratio is a useful measure of the market's assessment of the firm's growth

SUMMARY

opportunities. Firms with no growth opportunities should have a P/E ratio that is just the reciprocal of the capitalization rate, k. As growth opportunities become a progressively more important component of the total value of the firm, the P/E ratio will increase.

- Many analysts form their estimates of a stock's value by multiplying their forecast of next year's EPS by a predicted P/E multiple. Some analysts mix the P/E approach with the dividend discount model. They use an earnings multiplier to forecast the terminal value of shares at a future date and add the present value of that terminal value to the present value of all interim dividend payments.

- The free cash flow approach is the one used most in corporate finance. The analyst first estimates the value of the firm as the present value of expected future free cash flows to the entire firm and then subtracts the value of all claims other than equity. Alternatively, the free cash flows to equity can be discounted at a rate appropriate to the risk of the stock.

- The models presented in this chapter can be used to explain or to forecast the behavior of the aggregate stock market. The key macroeconomic variables that determine the level of stock prices in the aggregate are interest rates and corporate profits.

KEY TERMS

book value, 394
constant-growth DDM, 398
dividend discount model (DDM), 397
dividend payout ratio, 401
earnings management, 412
earnings retention ratio, 401
intrinsic value (of a firm), 396

liquidation value, 395
market capitalization rate, 396
PEG ratio, 410
plowback ratio, 401
present value of growth opportunities (PVGO), 402

price–earnings multiple, 408
replacement cost, 395
Tobin's q, 395
two-stage dividend discount model (DDM), 404

KEY FORMULAS

Intrinsic value: $V_0 = \dfrac{D_1}{1 + k} + \dfrac{D_2}{(1 + k)^2} + \cdots + \dfrac{D_H + P_H}{(1 + k)^H}$

Constant-growth DDM: $V_0 = \dfrac{D_1}{k - g}$

Growth opportunities: $\text{Price} = \dfrac{E_1}{k} + \text{PVGO}$

Determinant of *P/E* ratio: $\dfrac{P_0}{E_1} = \dfrac{1}{k}\left(1 + \dfrac{\text{PVGO}}{E_1/k}\right)$

Free cash flow to the firm:

$\quad\quad \text{FCFF} = \text{EBIT}(1 - t_c) + \text{Depreciation} - \text{Capital expenditures} - \text{Increases in NWC}$

Free cash flow to equity:

$\quad\quad \text{FCFE} = \text{FCFF} - \text{Interest expense} \times (1 - t_c) + \text{Increase in net debt}$

PROBLEM SETS

Select problems are available in McGraw-Hill's *Connect*. Please see the Supplements section of the book's frontmatter for more information.

1. In what circumstances would you choose to use a dividend discount model rather than a free cash flow model to value a firm?   *(LO 13-4)*

2. In what circumstances is it most important to use multistage dividend discount models rather than constant-growth models?   *(LO 13-2)*

3. If a security is underpriced (i.e., intrinsic value > price), then what is the relationship between its market capitalization rate and its expected rate of return? *(LO 13-2)*

4. Deployment Specialists pays a current (annual) dividend of $1 and is expected to grow at 20% for two years and then at 4% thereafter. If the required return for Deployment Specialists is 8.5%, what is the intrinsic value of its stock? *(LO 13-2)*

5. Jand, Inc., currently pays a dividend of $1.22, which is expected to grow indefinitely at 5%. If the current value of Jand's shares based on the constant-growth dividend discount model is $32.03, what is the required rate of return? *(LO 13-2)*

6. A firm pays a current dividend of $1, which is expected to grow at a rate of 5% indefinitely. If the current value of the firm's shares is $35, what is the required return applicable to the investment based on the constant-growth dividend discount model (DDM)? *(LO 13-2)*

7. Tri-coat Paints has a current market value of $41 per share with earnings of $3.64. What is the present value of its growth opportunities (PVGO) if the required return is 9%? *(LO 13-2)*

8. A firm has current assets that could be sold for their book value of $10 million. The book value of its fixed assets is $60 million, but they could be sold for $90 million today. The firm has total debt with a book value of $40 million, but interest rate declines have caused the market value of the debt to increase to $50 million. What is this firm's market-to-book ratio? *(LO 13-1)*

9. The market capitalization rate for Admiral Motors Company is 8%. Its expected ROE is 10% and its expected EPS is $5. If the firm's plowback ratio is 60%, what will be its P/E ratio? *(LO 13-2)*

10. Miltmar Corporation will pay a year-end dividend of $4, and dividends thereafter are expected to grow at the constant rate of 4% per year. The risk-free rate is 4%, and the expected return on the market portfolio is 12%. The stock has a beta of 0.75. What is the intrinsic value of the stock? *(LO 13-2)*

11. Sisters Corp. expects to earn $6 per share next year. The firm's ROE is 15% and its plowback ratio is 60%. If the firm's market capitalization rate is 10%, what is the present value of its growth opportunities? *(LO 13-3)*

12. Eagle Products' EBIT is $300, its tax rate is 21%, depreciation is $20, capital expenditures are $60, and the planned increase in net working capital is $30. What is the free cash flow to the firm? *(LO 13-4)*

13. FinCorp's free cash flow to the firm is reported as $205 million. The firm's interest expense is $22 million. Assume the corporate tax rate is 21% and the net debt of the firm increases by $3 million. What is the market value of equity if the FCFE is projected to grow at 3% indefinitely and the cost of equity is 12%? *(LO 13-4)*

14. A common stock pays an annual dividend per share of $2.10. The risk-free rate is 7% and the risk premium for this stock is 4%. If the annual dividend is expected to remain at $2.10, what is the value of the stock? *(LO 13-2)*

15. The risk-free rate of return is 5%, the required rate of return on the market is 10%, and High-Flyer stock has a beta coefficient of 1.5. If the dividend per share expected during the coming year, D_1, is $2.50 and $g = 4\%$, at what price should a share sell? *(LO 13-2)*

16. Explain why the following statements are true/false/uncertain. *(LO 13-3)*
    a. With all else held constant, a firm will have a higher P/E if its beta is higher.
    b. P/E will tend to be higher when ROE is higher (assuming plowback is positive).
    c. P/E will tend to be higher when the plowback rate is higher.

17. a. Computer stocks currently provide an expected rate of return of 16%. MBI, a large computer company, will pay a year-end dividend of $2 per share. If the stock is selling at $50 per share, what must be the market's expectation of the growth rate of MBI dividends?
    b. If dividend growth forecasts for MBI are revised downward to 5% per year, what will happen to the price of MBI stock?
    c. What (qualitatively) will happen to the company's price–earnings ratio? *(LO 13-3)*

18. Even Better Products has come out with an even better product. As a result, the firm projects an ROE of 20%, and it will maintain a plowback ratio of 0.30. Its earnings this year will be $2 per share. Investors expect a 12% rate of return on the stock.   *(LO 13-3)*
    a. At what price and P/E ratio would you expect the firm to sell?
    b. What is the present value of growth opportunities?
    c. What would be the P/E ratio and the present value of growth opportunities if the firm planned to reinvest only 20% of its earnings?

19. a. MF Corp. has an ROE of 16% and a plowback ratio of 50%. If the coming year's earnings are expected to be $2 per share, at what price will the stock sell? The market capitalization rate is 12%.
    b. What price do you expect MF shares to sell for in three years?   *(LO 13-2)*

20. The market consensus is that Analog Electronic Corporation has an ROE of 9% and a beta of 1.25. It plans to maintain indefinitely its traditional plowback ratio of 2/3. This year's earnings were $3 per share. The annual dividend was just paid. The consensus estimate of the coming year's market return is 14%, and T-bills currently offer a 6% return.   *(LO 13-3)*
    a. Find the price at which Analog stock should sell.
    b. Calculate the P/E ratio.
    c. Calculate the present value of growth opportunities.
    d. Suppose your research convinces you Analog will announce momentarily that it will immediately reduce its plowback ratio to 1/3. Find the intrinsic value of the stock.
    e. The market is still unaware of this decision. Explain why V_0 no longer equals P_0 and why V_0 is greater or less than P_0.

21. The FI Corporation's dividends per share are expected to grow indefinitely by 5% per year.   *(LO 13-3)*
    a. If this year's year-end dividend is $8 and the market capitalization rate is 10% per year, what must the current stock price be according to the dividend discount model?
    b. If the expected earnings per share are $12, what is the implied value of the ROE on future investment opportunities?
    c. How much is the market paying per share for growth opportunities (that is, for an ROE on future investments that exceeds the market capitalization rate)?

22. The stock of Nogro Corporation is currently selling for $10 per share. Earnings per share in the coming year are expected to be $2. The company has a policy of paying out 50% of its earnings each year in dividends. The rest is retained and invested in projects that earn a 20% rate of return per year. This situation is expected to continue indefinitely.   *(LO 13-3)*
    a. Assuming the current market price of the stock reflects its intrinsic value as computed using the constant-growth DDM, what rate of return do Nogro's investors require?
    b. By how much does its value exceed what it would be if all earnings were paid as dividends and nothing was reinvested?
    c. If Nogro were to cut its dividend payout ratio to 25%, what would happen to its stock price?
    d. What if Nogro eliminated the dividend?

23. The risk-free rate of return is 8%, the expected rate of return on the market portfolio is 15%, and the stock of Xyrong Corporation has a beta coefficient of 1.2. Xyrong pays out 40% of its earnings in dividends, and the latest earnings announced were $10 per share. Dividends were just paid and are expected to be paid annually. You expect that Xyrong will earn an ROE of 20% per year on all reinvested earnings forever.   *(LO 13-2)*
    a. What is the intrinsic value of a share of Xyrong stock?
    b. If the market price of a share is currently $100, and you expect the market price to be equal to the intrinsic value one year from now, what is your expected one-year holding-period return on Xyrong stock?

24. The MoMi Corporation's cash flow from operations before interest and taxes was $2 million in the year just ended, and it expects that this will grow by 5% per year forever. To make this happen, the firm will have to invest an amount equal to 20% of pretax cash flow each year. The tax rate is 21%. Depreciation was $200,000 in the year just ended and is expected to grow at the same rate as the operating cash flow. The appropriate market capitalization rate for the unleveraged cash flow is 12% per year, and the firm currently has debt of $4 million outstanding. Use the free cash flow approach to value the firm's equity.   *(LO 13-4)*

25. For each of the following scenarios, recalculate the intrinsic value of Chevron using the three-stage growth model of Spreadsheet 13.1 (available in Connect; link to Chapter 13 material). Treat each scenario independently.   *(LO 13-2)*
    a. The terminal growth rate will be 5%.
    b. Chevron's actual beta is 1.0.
    c. The market risk premium is 6.5%.

Templates and spreadsheets are available in Connect

26. For each of the following scenarios, recalculate the intrinsic value of Chevron's shares using the free cash flow model of Spreadsheet 13.2 (available in Connect; link to Chapter 13 material). Treat each scenario independently.   *(LO 13-4)*
    a. The terminal growth rate will be 3%.
    b. Chevron's current stock market beta (cell B21) is 1.25.
    c. The market risk premium (cell B27) is 6.5%.

Templates and spreadsheets are available in Connect

Challenge

27. Chiptech, Inc., is an established computer chip firm with several profitable existing products as well as some promising new products in development. The company earned $1 per share last year and just paid out a dividend of $0.50 per share. Investors believe the company plans to maintain its dividend payout ratio at 50%. ROE equals 20%. Everyone in the market expects this situation to persist indefinitely.   *(LO 13-2)*
    a. What is the market price of Chiptech stock? The required return for the computer chip industry is 15%, and the company has just gone ex-dividend (i.e., the next dividend will be paid a year from now, at $t = 1$).
    b. Suppose you discover that Chiptech's competitor has developed a new chip that will eliminate Chiptech's current technological advantage in this market. This new product, which will be ready to come to the market in two years, will force Chiptech to reduce the prices of its chips to remain competitive. This will decrease ROE to 15%, and, because of falling demand for its product, Chiptech will decrease the plowback ratio to 0.40. The plowback ratio will be decreased at the end of the second year, at $t = 2$: The annual year-end dividend for the second year (paid at $t = 2$) will be 60% of that year's earnings. What is your estimate of Chiptech's intrinsic value per share? (*Hint:* Carefully prepare a table of Chiptech's earnings and dividends for each of the next three years. Pay close attention to the change in the payout ratio in $t = 2$.)
    c. No one else in the market perceives the threat to Chiptech's market. In fact, you are confident that no one else will become aware of the change in Chiptech's competitive status until the competitor firm publicly announces its discovery near the end of year 2. What will be the rate of return on Chiptech stock in the coming year (i.e., between $t = 0$ and $t = 1$)?
    d. What will be the rate of return in the second year (between $t = 1$ and $t = 2$)?
    e. What will be the rate of return in the third year (between $t = 2$ and $t = 3$)? (*Hint:* Pay attention to when the *market* catches on to the new situation. A table of dividends and market prices over time might help.)

CFA Problems

1. At Litchfield Chemical Corp. (LCC), a director of the company said that the use of dividend discount models by investors is "proof" that the higher the dividend, the higher the stock price. *(LO 13-2)*

   a. Using a constant-growth dividend discount model as a basis of reference, evaluate the director's statement.

   b. Explain how an increase in dividend payout would affect each of the following (holding all other factors constant):
      i. Sustainable growth rate.
      ii. Growth in book value.

2. Phoebe Black's investment club wants to buy the stock of either NewSoft, Inc. or Capital Corp. In this connection, Black prepared the following table. You have been asked to help her interpret the data, based on your forecast for a healthy economy and a strong stock market over the next 12 months. *(LO 13-2)*

	NewSoft, Inc.	Capital Corp.	S&P 500 Index
Current price	$30	$32	
Industry	Computer software	Capital goods	
P/E ratio (current)	25	14	16
P/E ratio (5-year average)	27	16	16
Price/book ratio (current)	10	3	3
Price/book ratio (5-year average)	12	4	2
Beta	1.5	1.1	1.0
Dividend yield	0.3%	2.7%	2.8%

   a. Newsoft's shares have higher price–earnings (P/E) and price–book value (P/B) ratios than those of Capital Corp. (The price–book ratio is the ratio of market value to book value.) Briefly discuss why the disparity in ratios may not indicate that NewSoft's shares are overvalued relative to the shares of Capital Corp. Answer the question in terms of the two ratios, and assume that there have been no extraordinary events affecting either company.

   b. Using a constant-growth dividend discount model, Black estimated the value of NewSoft to be $28 per share and the value of Capital Corp. to be $34 per share. Briefly discuss weaknesses of this dividend discount model, and explain why this model may be less suitable for valuing NewSoft than for valuing Capital Corp.

   c. Recommend and justify a more appropriate dividend discount model for valuing NewSoft's common stock.

3. Peninsular Research is initiating coverage of a mature manufacturing industry. John Jones, CFA, head of the research department, gathered the following fundamental industry and market data to help in his analysis: *(LO 13-3)*

Forecast industry earnings retention rate	40%
Forecast industry return on equity	25%
Industry beta	1.2
Government bond yield	6%
Equity risk premium	5%

a. Compute the price-to-earnings (P_0/E_1) ratio for the industry based on this fundamental data.

b. Jones wants to analyze how fundamental P/E ratios might differ among countries. He gathered the following economic and market data:

Fundamental Factors	Country A	Country B
Forecast growth in real GDP	5%	2%
Government bond yield	10%	6%
Equity risk premium	5%	4%

Determine whether each of these fundamental factors would cause P/E ratios to be generally higher for Country A or higher for Country B.

4. Janet Ludlow's firm requires all its analysts to use a two-stage DDM and the CAPM to value stocks. Using these measures, Ludlow has valued QuickBrush Company at $63 per share. She now must value SmileWhite Corporation.   *(LO 13-2)*

a. Calculate the required rate of return for SmileWhite using the information in the following table:

	December 2017	
	QuickBrush	**SmileWhite**
Beta	1.35	1.15
Market price	$45.00	$30.00
Intrinsic value	$63.00	?

Note: Risk-free rate = 4.50%; expected market return = 14.50%.

b. Ludlow estimates the following EPS and dividend growth rates for SmileWhite:

First three years:	12% per year
Years thereafter:	9% per year

Estimate the intrinsic value of SmileWhite using the table above and the two-stage DDM. Dividends per share in 2017 were $1.72.

c. Recommend QuickBrush or SmileWhite stock for purchase by comparing each company's intrinsic value with its current market price.

d. Describe *one* strength of the two-stage DDM in comparison with the constant-growth DDM. Describe *one* weakness inherent in all DDMs.

5. Rio National Corp. is a U.S.-based company and the largest competitor in its industry. Tables 13.5–13.8 present financial statements and related information for the company. Table 13.9 presents relevant industry and market data.

   The portfolio manager of a large mutual fund comments to one of the fund's analysts, Katrina Shaar: "We have been considering the purchase of Rio National Corp. equity shares, so I would like you to analyze the value of the company. To begin, based on Rio National's past performance, you can assume that the company will grow at the same rate as the industry."   *(LO 13-2)*

a. Calculate the value of a share of Rio National equity on December 31, 2018, using the constant-growth model and the capital asset pricing model.

b. Calculate the sustainable growth rate of Rio National on December 31, 2018. Use 2018 beginning-of-year balance sheet values.

TABLE 13.5 Rio National Corp. summary year-end balance sheets (U.S. $ millions)

	2018	2017
Cash	$ 13.00	$ 5.87
Accounts receivable	30.00	27.00
Inventory	209.06	189.06
Current assets	$252.06	$221.93
Gross fixed assets	474.47	409.47
Accumulated depreciation	(154.17)	(90.00)
Net fixed assets	$320.30	$319.47
Total assets	$572.36	$541.40
Accounts payable	$ 25.05	$ 26.05
Notes payable	0.00	0.00
Current portion of long-term debt	0.00	0.00
Current liabilities	$ 25.05	$ 26.05
Long-term debt	240.00	245.00
Total liabilities	$265.05	$271.05
Common stock	160.00	150.00
Retained earnings	147.31	120.35
Total shareholders' equity	$307.31	$270.35
Total liabilities and shareholders' equity	$572.36	$541.40

TABLE 13.6 Rio National Corp. summary income statement for the year ended December 31, 2018 (U.S. $ millions)

Revenue	$300.80
Total operating expenses	(173.74)
Operating profit	$127.06
Gain on sale	4.00
Earnings before interest, taxes, depreciation & amortization (EBITDA)	$131.06
Depreciation and amortization	(71.17)
Earnings before interest & taxes (EBIT)	$59.89
Interest	(16.80)
Income tax expense	(12.93)
Net income	$ 30.16

TABLE 13.7 Rio National Corp. supplemental notes for 2018

Note 1: Rio National had $75 million in capital expenditures during the year.

Note 2: A piece of equipment that was originally purchased for $10 million was sold for $7 million at year-end, when it had a net book value of $3 million. Equipment sales are unusual for Rio National.

Note 3: The decrease in long-term debt represents an unscheduled principal repayment; there was no new borrowing during the year.

Note 4: On 1 January 2018, the company received cash from issuing 400,000 shares of common equity at a price of $25 per share.

Note 5: A new appraisal during the year increased the estimated market value of land held for investment by $2 million, which was not recognized in 2018 income.

TABLE 13.8 Rio National Corp. common equity data for 2018	
Dividends paid (U.S. $ millions)	$3.20
Weighted-average shares outstanding during 2018	16,000,000
Dividend per share	$0.20
Earnings per share	$1.89
Beta	1.80

Note: The dividend payout ratio is expected to be constant.

TABLE 13.9 Industry and market data, December 31, 2018	
Risk-free rate of return	4.00%
Expected rate of return on market index	9.00%
Median industry price–earnings (P/E) ratio	19.90
Expected industry earnings growth rate	12.00%

6. While valuing the equity of Rio National Corp. (from the previous problem), Katrina Shaar is considering the use of either free cash flow to the firm (FCFF) or free cash flow to equity (FCFE) in her valuation process.   *(LO 13-4)*
   a. State two adjustments that Shaar should make to FCFF to obtain free cash flow to equity.
   b. Shaar decides to calculate Rio National's FCFE for the year 2018, starting with net income. Determine for each of the five supplemental notes given in Table 13.7 whether an adjustment should be made to net income to calculate Rio National's free cash flow to equity for the year 2018, and the dollar amount of any adjustment.
   c. Calculate Rio National's free cash flow to equity for the year 2018.

7. Shaar (from the previous problem) has revised slightly her estimated earnings growth rate for Rio National and, using normalized (underlying trend) EPS, which is adjusted for temporary impacts on earnings, now wants to compare the current value of Rio National's equity to that of the industry, on a growth-adjusted basis. Selected information about Rio National and the industry is given in Table 13.10.

   Compared to the industry, is Rio National's equity overvalued or undervalued on a P/E-to-growth (PEG) basis, using normalized (underlying) earnings per share? Assume that the risk of Rio National is similar to the risk of the industry.   *(LO 13-3)*

8. Helen Morgan, CFA, has been asked to use the dividend discount model to determine the value of Sundanci, Inc. Morgan anticipates that Sundanci's earnings and dividends will grow at 32% for two years and 13% thereafter.

TABLE 13.10 Rio National Corp. vs. industry	
Rio National	
Estimated earnings growth rate	11.00%
Current share price	$25.00
Normalized (underlying trend) EPS for 2018	$ 1.71
Weighted-average shares outstanding during 2018	16,000,000
Industry	
Estimated earnings growth rate	12.00%
Median price–earnings (P/E) ratio	19.90

TABLE 13.11   Sundanci actual 2018 and forecast 2019 financial statements for fiscal years ending May 31 ($ million, except per-share data)

Income Statement	2018	2019
Revenue	$ 474	$ 598
Depreciation	20	23
Other operating costs	368	460
Income before taxes	$ 86	$ 115
Taxes	26	35
Net income	$ 60	$ 80
Dividends	18	24
Earnings per share	$0.714	$0.952
Dividend per share	$0.214	$0.286
Common shares outstanding (millions)	84.0	84.0

Balance Sheet	2018	2019
Current assets	$ 201	$ 326
Net property, plant, and equipment	474	489
Total assets	$ 675	$ 815
Current liabilities	$ 57	$ 141
Long-term debt	0	0
Total liabilities	$ 57	$ 141
Shareholders' equity	618	674
Total liabilities and equity	$ 675	$ 815
Capital expenditures	34	38

TABLE 13.12   Selected financial information

Required rate of return on equity	14%
Growth rate of industry	13%
Industry P/E ratio	26

Calculate the current value of a share of Sundanci stock by using a two-stage dividend discount model and the data from Tables 13.11 and 13.12.   *(LO 13-2)*

9. To continue with Sundanci, Abbey Naylor, CFA, has been directed to determine the value of Sundanci's stock using the free cash flow to equity (FCFE) model. Naylor believes that Sundanci's FCFE will grow at 27% for two years and 13% thereafter. Capital expenditures, depreciation, and working capital are all expected to increase proportionately with FCFE.   *(LO 13-4)*

a. Calculate the FCFE per share for the year 2019 using the data from Table 13.11.
b. Calculate the current value of a share of Sundanci stock based on the two-stage FCFE model.
c. i. Describe one limitation of the two-stage DDM model that is addressed by using the two-stage FCFE model.
    ii. Describe one limitation of the two-stage DDM model that is *not* addressed by using the two-stage FCFE model.

10. Christie Johnson, CFA, has been assigned to analyze Sundanci using the constant-dividend-growth price–earnings (P/E) ratio model. Johnson assumes that Sundanci's earnings and dividends will grow at a constant rate of 13%. *(LO 13-2)*

   a. Calculate the P/E ratio based on information in Tables 13.11 and 13.12 and on Johnson's assumptions for Sundanci.

   b. Identify, within the context of the constant-dividend-growth model, how each of the following factors would affect the P/E ratio.

   - Risk (beta) of Sundanci.

   - Estimated growth rate of earnings and dividends.

   - Market risk premium.

---

1. Choose 10 firms that interest you and download their financial statements from **finance.yahoo.com.**

   a. For each firm, find the return on equity (ROE), the number of shares outstanding, the dividends per share, and the net income. Record them in a spreadsheet.

   b. Calculate the total amount of dividends paid (dividends per share × number of shares outstanding), the dividend payout ratio (total dividends paid/net income), and the plowback ratio (1 − dividend payout ratio).

   c. Compute the sustainable growth rate, $g = b \times \text{ROE}$, where b equals the plowback ratio.

   d. Plot P/E ratios against growth rates in a scatter diagram. Is there a relationship between the two?

   e. Using data from financial statements, find or calculate the ratios of price-to-book, price-to-sales, and price-to-cash flow from operations for each firm in your sample. Use a line chart to plot these three ratios on the same set of axes. What relationships do you see among the three series?

   f. For each firm, compare the three-year growth rate of earnings per share with the growth rate you calculated above. Is the actual rate of earnings growth correlated with the sustainable growth rate you calculated?

2. Now calculate the intrinsic value of three of the firms you selected in the previous question. Make reasonable judgments about the market risk premium and the risk-free rate, or find estimates from the Internet.

   a. What is the required return on each firm based on the CAPM? You can get the beta of each firm from its *Statistics* page.

   b. Try using a two-stage growth model, making reasonable assumptions about how future growth rates will differ from current growth rates. Compare the intrinsic values derived from the two-stage model to the intrinsic values you find assuming a constant-growth rate. Which estimate seems more reasonable for each firm?

3. Now choose one of your firms and look up other firms in the same industry. Perform a "Valuation by Comparables" analysis by looking at the price/earnings, price/book value, price/sales, and price/operating cash flow ratios of the firms relative to each other and to the industry average. Which of the firms seem to be overvalued? Which seem to be undervalued? Can you think of reasons to be wary of your conclusions?

4. The actual expected return on a stock based on estimates of future dividends and future price can be compared to the "required" or equilibrium return given its risk. If the expected return is greater than the required return, the stock may be an attractive investment.

   a. First calculate the expected holding-period return (HPR) on Target Corporation's stock based on its current price, its expected price, and its expected dividend.

      i. Get information for Target (enter TGT under quote search). From the *Analyst Opinion* page, find the range for estimated target price for the next fiscal year.

      ii. Collect information about today's price and the dividend rate. What is the company's expected dividend in dollars for the next fiscal year?

      iii. Use these inputs to calculate the range of Target's HPR for the next year.

    b. Calculate the required return based on the capital asset pricing model (CAPM).

        i. Use a risk-free rate from Yahoo's *Market Data* page.

        ii. Use the beta coefficient shown in the *Statistics* page.

        iii. Calculate the historical return on a broad-based market index of your choice. You may use any time period that you deem appropriate. Your goal is to derive an estimate of the expected return on the market index for the coming year.

        iv. Use the data you've collected as inputs for the CAPM to find the required rate of return for Target Corporation.

    c. Compare the expected HPR you calculated in part (*a*) to the required CAPM return you calculated in part (*b*). What is your best judgment about the stock's current status—do you think it is selling at an appropriate price?

SOLUTIONS TO

CONCEPT
checks

13.1 *a.* Dividend yield = $2.15/$50 = 4.3%

    Capital gains yield = (59.77 − 50)/50 = 19.54%

    Total return = 4.3% + 19.54% = 23.84%

    b. $k = 6\% + 1.15(14\% − 6\%) = 15.2\%$

    c. $V_0 = (\$2.15 + \$59.77)/1.152 = \$53.75$, which exceeds the market price. This would indicate a "buy" opportunity.

13.2 *a.* $D_1/(k − g) = \$2.15/(.152 − .112) = \$53.75$

    b. $P_1 = P_0(1 + g) = \$53.75(1.112) = \$59.77$

    c. The expected capital gain equals $59.77 − $53.75 = $6.02, for a percentage gain of 11.2%. The dividend yield is $D_1/P_0 = 2.15/53.75 = 4\%$, for a holding-period return of 4% + 11.2% = 15.2%.

13.3 *a.* $g = \text{ROE} \times b = .20 \times .60 = .12$

    $P_0 = 2/(.125 − .12) = 400$

    b. When the firm invests in projects with ROE less than *k,* its stock price falls. If $b = .60$, then $g = 10\% \times .60 = 6\%$ and $P_0 = \$2/(.125 − .06) = \$30.77$. In contrast, if $b = 0$, then $P_0 = \$5/.125 = \$40$.

13.4 Intrinsic value is

$$V_{2017} = \frac{4.40}{1.093} + \frac{4.60}{(1.093)^2} + \frac{4.80}{(1.093)^3} + \frac{5.00 + P_{2021}}{(1.093)^4}$$

To estimate P_{2021} in this equation, use the constant-growth dividend discount model.

$$P_{2021} = \frac{5.00 \times (1 + g)}{k − g} = \frac{5.00 \times 1.06}{.093 − .006} = \$160.61$$

Therefore, $V_{2017} = \$127.59$.

13.5 *a.* ROE = 12%

    $b = \$.50/\$2.00 = .25$

    $g = \text{ROE} \times b = 12\% \times .25 = 3\%$

    $P_0 = D_1/(k − g) = \$1.50/(.10 − .03) = \$21.43$

    $P_0/E_1 = 21.43/\$2 = 10.71$

    b. If $b = .4$, then $.4 \times \$2 = \$.80$ would be reinvested and the remainder of earnings, or $1.20, would be paid as dividends.

    $g = 12\% \times .4 = 4.8\%$

    $P_0 = D_1/(k − g) = \$1.20/(.10 − .048) = \$23.08$

    $P_0/E_1 = \$23.08/\$2.00 = 11.54$

    PEG = 11.54/4.8 = 2.4

Financial Statement Analysis

Learning Objectives

LO 14-1 Interpret a firm's income statement, balance sheet, and statement of cash flows, and calculate standard measures of a firm's operating efficiency, leverage, and liquidity.

LO 14-2 Calculate and interpret performance measures such as economic value added and rates of return on assets, capital, and equity.

LO 14-3 Use ratio decomposition analysis to show how profitability depends on efficient use of assets, profit margin, and leverage.

LO 14-4 Identify possible sources of biases in conventional accounting data.

I n the previous chapter, we explored equity valuation techniques. These techniques take as inputs the firm's dividends and earnings prospects. While the valuation analyst is interested in economic earnings streams, only financial accounting data are readily available. What can we learn from a company's accounting data that can help us estimate the intrinsic value of its common stock? In this chapter, we show how investors can use financial data as inputs into stock valuation analysis.

We start by reviewing the basic sources of such data: the income statement, the balance sheet, and the statement of cash flows. We note the difference between economic and accounting earnings. While economic earnings are more important for issues of valuation, they can at best be estimated, so, in practice, analysts always begin their study of the firm using accounting data. We next show how they use financial ratios to explore the sources of a firm's profitability and evaluate the "quality" of its earnings in a systematic fashion. We also examine the impact of debt policy on various financial ratios.

Finally, we conclude with a discussion of the challenges you will encounter when using financial statement analysis as a tool in uncovering mispriced securities. Some of these issues arise from differences in firms' accounting procedures. Others are due to inflation-induced distortions in accounting numbers.

income statement

A financial statement showing a firm's revenues and expenses during a specified period.

14.1 THE MAJOR FINANCIAL STATEMENTS

The Income Statement

The **income statement** summarizes the profitability of the firm over a period of time, such as a year. It presents revenues generated during the operating period, the expenses incurred during that same period, and the company's net earnings or profits, which are simply the difference between revenues and expenses.

Firms incur four broad classes of expenses: cost of goods sold, which is the direct cost attributable to producing the product sold by the firm; general and administrative expenses, which correspond to overhead expenses, salaries, advertising, and other costs of operating the firm that are not directly attributable to production; interest expense on the firm's debt; and taxes on earnings owed to federal and local governments.

Table 14.1 presents an income statement for Home Depot (HD). At the top are the company's revenues. Next come operating expenses, that is, the costs incurred in the course of generating these revenues, including a depreciation allowance. The difference between operating revenues and operating costs is called *operating income*. Income (or expenses) from other, primarily nonrecurring, sources is then added to obtain earnings before interest and taxes (EBIT), which is what the firm would have earned if not for obligations to its creditors and the tax authorities. EBIT is a measure of the profitability of the firm's operations abstracting from any interest burden attributable to debt financing. The income statement then goes on to subtract net interest expense from EBIT to arrive at taxable income.[1] Finally, the income tax due the government is subtracted to arrive at net income, the "bottom line" of the income statement.

TABLE 14.1   Home Depot's income statement

	$ Million	Percent of Revenue
Operating revenues		
Net sales	94,595	100.0
Operating expenses		
Cost of goods sold	62,282	65.8
Selling, general, & admininstrative expenses	15,159	16.0
Other	1,754	1.9
Depreciation	1,973	2.1
Total operating expenses	81,168	85.8
Earnings before interest and taxes	13,427	14.2
Interest expense	936	1.0
Taxable income	12,491	13.2
Taxes	4,534	4.8
Net income	7,957	8.4
Allocation of net income		
Dividends	3,404	3.6
Addition to retained earnings	4,553	4.8

Note: Sums subject to rounding error.

Source: Home Depot Annual Report, year ending January 2017.

[1]The Tax Cuts and Jobs Act of 2017 limits the interest expense that can be deducted for the purpose of calculating taxable income. Until 2021, the deduction for net interest expense is limited to 30% of EBITDA (earnings before interest, taxes, depreciation and amortization). Starting in 2022, the limit is 30% of EBIT. Neither limit is binding on most firms, so we will generally assume that all of a firm's net interest expense is deductible.

Analysts also commonly prepare a *common-size income statement,* in which all items on the income statement are expressed as a percentage of total revenue. This makes it easier to compare firms of different sizes. The right-hand column of Table 14.1 is HD's common-size income statement.

In the previous chapter, we saw that stock valuation models require a measure of **economic earnings**—the sustainable cash flow that can be paid out to stockholders without impairing the productive capacity of the firm. In contrast, **accounting earnings** are affected by several conventions regarding the valuation of assets such as inventories (e.g., LIFO versus FIFO treatment) and by the way some expenditures such as capital investments are recognized over time (as depreciation expenses). We will discuss problems with some of these accounting conventions in greater detail later in the chapter. In addition to these accounting issues, as the firm makes its way through the business cycle, its earnings will rise above or fall below the trend line that might more accurately reflect sustainable economic earnings. This introduces an added complication in interpreting net income figures. One might wonder how closely accounting earnings approximate economic earnings and, correspondingly, how useful accounting data might be to investors attempting to value the firm.

In fact, financial statements clearly convey considerable information: stock prices respond vigorously when firms announce earnings greater than market analysts or investors had anticipated.

economic earnings

The real flow of cash that a firm could pay out without impairing its productive capacity.

accounting earnings

Earnings of a firm as reported on its income statement.

The Balance Sheet

While the income statement provides a measure of profitability over a period of time, the **balance sheet** provides a "snapshot" of the financial condition of the firm at a particular time. The balance sheet is a list of the firm's assets and liabilities at that moment. The difference in assets and liabilities is the net worth of the firm, also called *stockholders' equity* or, equivalently, *shareholders' equity.* Like income statements, balance sheets are reasonably standardized in presentation.

Table 14.2 is HD's balance sheet. The first section lists the firm's assets. Current assets are presented first. These are cash and other items such as accounts receivable or inventories that will be converted into cash within one year. Next comes a listing of long-term or "fixed" assets. *Tangible fixed assets* are items such as buildings, equipment, or vehicles. HD also has several intangible assets such as a respected brand name and expertise. But accountants generally are reluctant to include these assets on the balance sheet, as they are so hard to value. However, when one firm purchases another for a premium over its book value, that difference is called *goodwill* and is listed on the balance sheet as an *intangible fixed asset.* HD lists goodwill at $2,093 million.[2]

The liability and shareholders' equity section is arranged similarly. Listed first are short-term or "current" liabilities, such as accounts payable, accrued taxes, and debts due within one year. Long-term debt and other liabilities due in more than a year follow. The difference between total assets and total liabilities is shareholders' equity. This is the net worth or book value of the firm.

Shareholders' equity is divided into par value of stock, capital surplus (additional paid-in capital), and retained earnings, although this division is usually unimportant. Briefly, par value plus capital surplus represents the proceeds realized from the sale of stock to the public. Conversely, when the firm repurchases stock from the public, this is treated as a "negative share issuance," and shareholders' equity falls. These repurchased shares are held in the company's treasury and are, therefore, known as **treasury stock.** The shares held by investors are said to be **issued** and **outstanding.** Home Depot's par value plus paid-in capital is negative, −$31,186 million, signifying that the firm has spent more repurchasing previously

balance sheet

An accounting statement of a firm's financial position at a particular time.

treasury stock

Stock that has been repurchased by the company and is held in its treasury.

issued shares

Shares that have been issued by the company.

outstanding shares

Shares that have been issued by the company and are held by investors.

[2]Firms are required to test their goodwill assets for "impairment" each year. If it becomes apparent that the value of the acquired firm is less than its purchase price, that amount must be charged off as an expense. For example, in 2012 Hewlett-Packard wrote off $8.8 billion on its earlier purchase of the software company Autonomy Corp. amid charges that Autonomy had overstated its profitability prior to the purchase. AOL Time Warner set a record when it recognized an impairment of $99 billion in 2002 following the January 2001 merger of Time Warner with AOL.

TABLE 14.2 Home Depot's balance sheet

Assets	$ Million	Percent of Total Assets	Liabilities and Shareholders' Equity	$ Million	Percent of Total Assets
Current assets			Current liabilities		
Cash and marketable securities	2,538	5.9%	Debt due for repayment	1,252	2.9%
Receivables	2,029	4.7%	Accounts payable	11,212	26.1%
Inventories	12,549	29.2%	Other current liabilities	1,669	3.9%
Other current assets	608	1.4%	Total current liabilities	14,133	32.9%
Total current assets	17,724	41.3%	Long-term debt	22,349	52.0%
Fixed assets			Other long-term liabilities	1,855	4.3%
Tangible fixed assets			Deferred long-term liability charges	296	0
Property, plant, and equipment	21,914	51.0%	Total liabilities	38,633	89.9%
Other long-term assets	1,235	2.9%	Shareholders' equity:		
Total tangible fixed assets	23,149	53.9%	Common stock and other paid-in capital	−31,186	−72.6%
Intangible fixed assets			Retained earnings	35,519	82.7%
Goodwill	2,093	4.9%	Total shareholders' equity	4,333	10.1%
Total fixed assets	25,242	58.7%	Total liabilities and shareholders' equity	42,966	100.0%
Total assets	42,966	100.0%			

Source: Home Depot Annual Report, year ending January 2017.

Note: Column sums subject to rounding error.

issued stock than it originally raised by selling that stock. Of course, considerable sums have been reinvested in the business on the shareholders' behalf; the buildup of equity from profits plowed back into the firm shows up as retained earnings in Table 14.2.

The entries in the left columns of the balance sheet in Table 14.2 present the dollar value of each asset. To make it easier to compare firms of different sizes, analysts often present each item on the balance sheet as a percentage of total assets. This is called a *common-size balance sheet* and is presented in the right columns.

The Statement of Cash Flows

statement of cash flows

A financial statement showing a firm's cash receipts and cash payments during a specified period.

The income statement and balance sheets are based on accrual methods of accounting, which means revenues and expenses are recognized at the time of a sale even if no cash has yet been exchanged. In contrast, the **statement of cash flows** summaries the firm's net cash transactions. For example, if goods are sold now, with payment due in 60 days, the income statement will treat the revenue as generated when the sale occurs, and the balance sheet will be immediately augmented by accounts receivable, but the statement of cash flows is concerned with when the bill is paid and the cash is in hand.

Table 14.3 is the statement of cash flows for HD. The first entry listed under "Cash provided by operations" is net income. The following entries modify that figure for components of income that have been recognized but for which cash has not yet changed hands. For example, HD's accounts receivable increased by $138 million. This portion of its income was claimed on the income statement, but the cash had not yet been collected. Increases in accounts receivable are in effect an investment in working capital and, therefore, reduce the cash flows realized from operations. Similarly, increases in accounts payable mean expenses have been recognized, but cash has not yet left the firm. Any payment delay increases the company's net cash flows in this period.

TABLE 14.3 Home Depot's statement of cash flows

	$ Million
Cash provided by operations	
Net income	$7,957
Adjustments to net income	
Depreciation	1,973
Changes in working capital	
Decrease (increase) in receivables	(138)
Decrease (increase) in inventories	(769)
Increase (decrease) in other current liabilities	654
Other	106
Total adjustments	$1,826
Cash provided by operations	$9,783
Cash flows from investments	
Gross investment in tangible fixed assets	−1,621
Investments in other assets	38
Cash provided by (used for) investments	($1,583)
Cash provided by (used for) financing activities	
Additions to (reductions in) long-term debt	$2,274
Net issues (repurchases of) shares	(6,662)
Dividends	(3,404)
Other	(78)
Cash provided by (used for) financing activities	($7,870)
Net increase in cash	$330

Source: Home Depot Annual Report, year ending January 2017.

Another major difference between the income statement and the statement of cash flows involves depreciation, which accounts for a substantial addition in the adjustment section of the statement of cash flows. In most countries, including the U.S. until 2018, the depreciation expense on the income statement is used to "smooth" large capital expenditures over time by recognizing them over a period of many years rather than at the time of purchase. In contrast, the statement of cash flows recognizes the cash implication of a capital expenditure when it occurs. Therefore, it adds back the depreciation "expense" that was used to compute net income; instead, it acknowledges a capital expenditure when it is paid. It does so by reporting cash flows separately for operations, investing, and financing activities. This way, large cash flows such as those for big investments can be recognized without affecting the measure of cash flow provided by operations.

The Tax Cuts and Jobs Act of 2017 allows new capital expenditures to be fully depreciated in the year of purchase, at least until 2023. After that, capital expenditures will again be recognized over time, with depreciation allowances spread over several years. Capital investments put in place before the passage of the Act will continue to be depreciated over time, as they were before the Act was signed into law.

The second section of the statement of cash flows is HD's accounting of cash flows from investing activities. For example, HD used $1,621 million of cash investing in tangible fixed assets. These entries are investments in the assets necessary for the firm to maintain or enhance its productive capacity.

Finally, the last section of the statement lists the cash flows realized from financing activities. Issuance of securities contributes positive cash flows, while redemption of outstanding securities uses cash. For example, HD expended $6,662 million to repurchase shares of its stock, which was a use of cash. Its dividend payments, $3,404 million, also used cash. In total, HD's financing activities absorbed $7,870 million of cash.

To summarize, HD's operations generated a cash flow of $9,783 million. The company laid out $1,583 million to pay for new investments, and financing activities used another $7,870 million. HD's cash holdings therefore changed by $9,783 − $1,583 − $7,870 = $330 million. This is reported on the last line of Table 14.3.

The statement of cash flows provides important evidence on the well-being of a firm. If a company cannot pay its dividends and maintain the productivity of its capital stock out of cash flow from operations, for example, and it must resort to borrowing to meet these demands, this is a serious warning that the firm cannot maintain payout at its current level in the long run. The statement of cash flows will reveal this developing problem when it shows that cash flow from operations is inadequate and that borrowing is being used to maintain dividend payments at unsustainable levels.

14.2   MEASURING FIRM PERFORMANCE

In Chapter 1, we pointed out that a natural goal of the firm is to maximize value but that various agency problems, or conflicts of interest, may impede that goal. How can we measure how well the firm is actually performing? Financial analysts have come up with a mind-numbing list of financial ratios that measure many aspects of firm performance. Before getting lost in the trees, therefore, let's first pause to consider what sorts of ratios may be related to the ultimate objective of added value.

Two broad activities are the responsibility of a firm's financial managers: investment decisions and financing decisions. Investment, or capital budgeting, decisions pertain to the firm's *use* of capital: the business activities in which it is engaged. Here, our concern is the profitability of those projects. How should profitability be measured? How does the acceptable level of profitability depend on risk and the opportunity cost of the funds used to pay for the firm's many projects? In contrast, financial decisions pertain to the firm's *sources* of capital. Is there a sufficient supply of financing to meet projected needs for growth? Does the financing plan rely too heavily on borrowed funds? Is there sufficient liquidity to deal with unexpected cash needs?

These questions suggest that we organize the ratios we choose to examine along the lines given in Figure 14.1. The figure shows that when evaluating the firm's investment activities, we will ask two broad sets of questions: How efficiently does the firm deploy its assets, and how profitable are its sales? In turn, aspects of both efficiency and profitability can be measured with several ratios: Efficiency is typically assessed using turnover ratios, while the profitability of sales is commonly measured with various profit margins. When evaluating financing decisions, we look at both leverage and liquidity, and we will see that aspects of each of these two concepts also can be measured with an array of statistics.

The next section shows how to calculate and interpret some of these key financial ratios and shows how many of them are related.

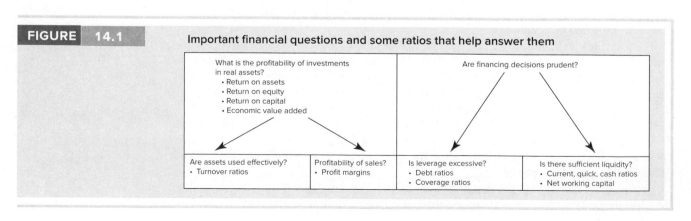

FIGURE   14.1   Important financial questions and some ratios that help answer them

14.3 PROFITABILITY MEASURES

Big firms naturally earn greater profits than smaller ones. Therefore, most profitability measures focus on earnings per dollar employed. The most common measures are return on assets, return on capital, and return on equity.

Return on Assets

Return on assets (ROA) equals EBIT as a fraction of the firm's total assets.[3]

return on assets (ROA)

Earnings before interest and taxes divided by total assets.

$$ROA = \frac{EBIT}{Total\ assets}$$

The numerator of this ratio may be viewed as total operating income of the firm. Therefore, ROA tells us operating income earned per dollar deployed in the firm.

Return on Capital

Whereas ROA compares EBIT to total assets, **return on capital (ROC)** expresses EBIT as a fraction of long-term capital, that is, shareholders' equity plus long-term debt. It measures operating earnings per dollar of long-term capital invested in the firm.

return on capital (ROC)

EBIT divided by long-term capital.

$$ROC = \frac{EBIT}{Long\text{-}term\ capital}$$

Return on Equity

Whereas ROA and ROC measure profitability relative to funds raised by both debt and equity financing, **return on equity (ROE)** focuses only on the profitability of equity investments. It equals net income realized by shareholders per dollar they have invested in the firm.

return on equity (ROE)

The ratio of net profits to common equity.

$$ROE = \frac{Net\ income}{Shareholders'\ equity}$$

We saw in Chapter 13 that return on equity (ROE) is one of the two basic factors in determining a firm's growth rate of earnings. Sometimes it is reasonable to assume that future ROE will approximate its past value, but a high ROE in the past does not necessarily imply a firm's future ROE will be high. It can be dangerous to accept historical values as indicators of future values. Data from the recent past may provide information regarding future performance, but your focus should be on the future.

Not surprisingly, ROA and ROE are linked, but as we will see next, the relationship between them is affected by the firm's financial policies.

Financial Leverage and ROE

ROE is affected by the firm's debt–equity mix as well as the interest rate on its debt. An example will show why. Suppose Nodett is all-equity-financed and has total assets of $100 million. Assume it pays corporate taxes of approximately 20% of taxable earnings. (The exact corporate tax rate is currently 21%.)

Table 14.4 shows Nodett's sales, earnings before interest and taxes, and net profits under three scenarios representing phases of the business cycle. It also shows two of the most commonly used profitability measures: operating ROA, which equals EBIT/total assets, and ROE, which equals net profits/equity.

---

[3]ROA sometimes is computed using EBIT × (1 − Tax rate) in the numerator. Sometimes it is computed using after-tax operating income, that is: Net income + Interest × (1 − Tax rate). Sometimes, it even is calculated using just net income in the numerator, although this definition ignores altogether the income the firm has generated for debt investors. Unfortunately, definitions of many key financial ratios are not fully standardized.

TABLE 14.4 Nodett's profitability over the business cycle

Scenario	Sales ($ million)	EBIT ($ million)	ROA (% per year)	Net Profit ($ million)	ROE (% per year)
Bad year	$ 80	$ 5	5%	$ 4	4%
Normal year	100	10	10	8	8
Good year	120	15	15	12	12

Somdett is an otherwise identical firm to Nodett, but it has financed $40 million of its $100 million of assets with debt bearing an interest rate of 8%. It pays annual interest expenses of $3.2 million. Table 14.5 shows how Somdett's ROE differs from Nodett's.

Annual sales, EBIT, and therefore ROA for both firms are the same in each of the three scenarios; in other words, business risk for the two companies is identical. But their financial risk differs: Although Nodett and Somdett have the same ROA in each scenario, Somdett's ROE exceeds that of Nodett in normal and good years and is lower in bad years.

We can summarize the exact relationship among ROE, ROA, and leverage in the following equation:[4]

$$ROE = (1 - \text{Tax rate})\left[ROA + (ROA - \text{Interest rate})\frac{\text{Debt}}{\text{Equity}}\right] \qquad \textbf{(14.1)}$$

This result makes sense: If ROA exceeds the borrowing rate, the firm earns more on its money than it pays out to creditors. The surplus earnings are available to the firm's owners, the equityholders, which increases ROE. If, on the other hand, ROA is less than the interest rate paid on debt, then ROE will decline by an amount that depends on the debt/equity ratio.

EXAMPLE 14.1

Leverage and ROE

To illustrate the application of Equation 14.1, look at Table 14.5. In a normal year, Nodett has an ROE of 8%, which is (1 − tax rate), or 0.8, times its ROA of 10%. However, Somdett, which borrows at an interest rate of 8% and maintains a debt/equity ratio of ⅔, has an ROE of 9.07%. The calculation using Equation 14.1 is

$$ROE = .8[10\% + (10\% - 8\%)⅔]$$
$$= .8(10\% + ⁴/₃\%) = 9.07\%$$

Somdett's debt makes a positive contribution to ROE in this scenario because the firm's ROA exceeds the interest rate on the debt.

Table 14.5 shows that financial leverage increases the risk of the equityholder returns. ROE on Somdett is worse than that of Nodett in bad years, but it is better in good years. The presence of debt makes Somdett's ROE more sensitive to the business cycle than Nodett's. Even though the two companies have equal business risk (reflected in their identical EBIT in all three scenarios), Somdett's stockholders carry greater financial risk than Nodett's because all of the firm's business risk is absorbed by a smaller base of equity investors.

---

[4] The derivation of Equation 14.1 is as follows:

$$ROE = \frac{\text{Net profit}}{\text{Equity}} = \frac{\text{EBIT} - \text{Interest} - \text{Taxes}}{\text{Equity}} = \frac{(1 - \text{Tax rate})(\text{EBIT} - \text{Interest})}{\text{Equity}}$$

$$= (1 - \text{Tax rate})\frac{(\text{ROA} \times \text{Assets} - \text{Interest rate} \times \text{Debt})}{\text{Equity}}$$

$$= (1 - \text{Tax rate})\left[\text{ROA} \times \frac{(\text{Equity} + \text{Debt})}{\text{Equity}} - \text{Interest rate} \times \frac{\text{Debt}}{\text{Equity}}\right]$$

$$= (1 - \text{Tax rate})\left[\text{ROA} + (\text{ROA} - \text{Interest rate})\frac{\text{Debt}}{\text{Equity}}\right]$$

		Nodett		Somdett	
Scenario	EBIT ($ million)	Net Profit ($ million)	ROE (%)	Net Profit* ($ million)	ROE† (%)
Bad year	$ 5	$4	4%	$1.44	2.40%
Normal year	10	8	8	5.44	9.07
Good year	15	12	12	9.44	15.73

TABLE 14.5 Impact of financial leverage on ROE

*Somdett's after-tax profits equal $(1 - .2)(\text{EBIT} - \$3.2 \text{ million})$.

†Somdett's equity is only $60 million, so ROE = net profit/$60 million.

Even if financial leverage increases the expected ROE of Somdett relative to Nodett (as it seems to in Table 14.5), this does not imply that Somdett's share price will be higher. Financial leverage increases the risk of the firm's equity as surely as it raises the expected ROE, and the higher discount rate will offset the higher expected earnings.

> **CONCEPT check 14.1**
>
> Mordett is a company with the same assets as Nodett and Somdett but a debt/equity ratio of 1 and an interest rate of 9%. What would its net profit and ROE be in a bad year, a normal year, and a good year?

Economic Value Added

While it is common to use profitability measures such as ROA, ROC, or ROE to evaluate performance, profitability is really not enough. A firm should be viewed as successful only if the return on its projects is better than the rate investors could expect to earn for themselves (on a risk-adjusted basis) in the capital market. Plowing back funds into the firm increases share value only if the firm earns a higher rate of return on the reinvested funds than the opportunity cost of capital, that is, the market capitalization rate. To account for this opportunity cost, we might measure the success of the firm using the *difference* between the return on assets, ROA, and the opportunity cost of capital. **Economic value added (EVA)** is the spread between ROA and the cost of capital multiplied by the capital invested in the firm. It therefore measures the dollar value of the firm's return in excess of its opportunity cost. Another term for EVA (the term coined by Stern Stewart, a consulting firm that has promoted the concept) is **residual income.**

economic value added (EVA) or residual income
A measure of the dollar value of a firm's return in excess of its opportunity cost.

> **EXAMPLE 14.2**
>
> *Economic Value Added*
>
> In 2016, Walmart had a weighted-average cost of capital (WACC) of 4.59% (based on its cost of debt, its capital structure, its equity beta, and estimates derived from the CAPM for the cost of equity). Walmart's return on assets was 7.14%, fully 2.55% greater than the opportunity cost of capital on its investments in plant, equipment, and know-how. In other words, each dollar invested by Walmart earned about 2.55 cents more than the return that investors could have anticipated by investing in equivalent-risk stocks. Walmart earned this superior rate of return on a capital base of $123.97 billion. Its economic value added, that is, its return in excess of opportunity cost, was therefore $(.0714 - .0459) \times \$123.97 = \$3.16$ billion.

Table 14.6 shows EVA for a small sample of firms.[5] The EVA leader in this sample was Apple. But you should notice that EVA is affected by firm size. For example, the difference between Home Depot's ROA and its cost of capital was $19.76\% - 8.05\% = 11.71\%$, which was considerably greater than the spread for Apple. Yet Apple had the higher EVA because its

[5]Actual EVA estimates reported by Stern Stewart differ from the values in Table 14.6 because of adjustments to the accounting data involving issues such as treatment of research and development expenses, taxes, advertising expenses, and depreciation. The estimates in Table 14.6 are designed to show the logic behind EVA but must be taken as imprecise. We calculate WACC using the corporate tax rate of 35% that prevailed in 2017.

	Ticker	EVA ($ billion)	Capital ($ billion)	ROA (%)	Cost of Capital (%)
Apple	AAPL	5.28	220.07	11.85	9.45
Home Depot	HD	3.27	27.93	19.76	8.05
Walmart	WMT	3.16	123.97	7.14	4.59
Microsoft	MSFT	2.26	164.37	9.41	8.04
Intel	INTC	0.60	91.28	8.78	8.12
Walt Disney	DIS	0.44	63.15	9.75	9.05
AT&T	T	−2.35	250.28	4.07	5.01
Honda	HMC	−4.10	124.56	2.13	5.42

TABLE 14.6   Economic value added, 2016

Source: Authors' calculations using data from **finance.yahoo.com,** April 19, 2017.

margin was applied to a much larger capital base. At the other extreme, Honda earned less than its opportunity cost on a large capital base, which resulted in a large negative EVA.

Notice that even the EVA "losers" in Table 14.6 had positive profits. For example, by conventional standards, Honda was solidly profitable with an ROA of 2.13%. But its cost of capital was higher, 5.42%. By this standard, Honda did not cover its opportunity cost of capital, and its EVA was negative. EVA treats the opportunity cost of capital as a real cost that should be deducted from revenues to arrive at a more meaningful "bottom line." A firm that is generating accounting profits but is not covering its opportunity cost might be able to redeploy its capital to better uses. Therefore, a growing number of firms calculate EVA and tie managers' compensation to it.

14.4   RATIO ANALYSIS

Decomposition of ROE

To understand the factors affecting a firm's ROE, including its trend over time and its performance relative to competitors, analysts often "decompose" ROE into the product of a series of ratios. Each component ratio is in itself meaningful, and the process serves to focus the analyst's attention on the separate factors influencing performance. This decomposition of ROE is often called the **DuPont system.**

DuPont system

Decomposition of profitability measures into component ratios.

One useful decomposition of ROE is

$$\text{ROE} = \underbrace{\frac{\text{Net profit}}{\text{Equity}}}_{} = \underbrace{\frac{\text{Net profit}}{\text{Pretax profit}}}_{(1)} \times \underbrace{\frac{\text{Pretax profit}}{\text{EBIT}}}_{(2)} \times \underbrace{\frac{\text{EBIT}}{\text{Sales}}}_{(3)} \times \underbrace{\frac{\text{Sales}}{\text{Assets}}}_{(4)} \times \underbrace{\frac{\text{Assets}}{\text{Equity}}}_{(5)} \quad \textbf{(14.2)}$$

Table 14.7 shows these ratios for Nodett and Somdett in each of the three economic scenarios. Let us first focus on factors 3 and 4. Notice that their product gives us the firm's ROA = EBIT/Assets.

Factor 3 is known as the firm's operating **profit margin,** or **return on sales,** which equals operating profit per dollar of sales. In an average year, Nodett's margin is 0.10, or 10%; in a bad year, it is 0.0625, or 6.25%; and in a good year, it is 0.125, or 12.5%.

Factor 4, the ratio of sales to total assets, is known as **total asset turnover.** It indicates the efficiency of the firm's use of assets in the sense that it measures the annual sales generated by each dollar of assets. In a normal year, Nodett's ATO is 1 per year, meaning that sales of $1 per year were generated per dollar of assets. In a bad year, this ratio declines to 0.8 per year, and in a good year, it rises to 1.2 per year.

profit margin or return on sales

The ratio of operating profits per dollar of sales (EBIT divided by sales).

total asset turnover (ATO)

The annual sales generated by each dollar of assets (sales/ assets).

TABLE 14.7 Ratio decomposition analysis for Nodett and Somdett

	ROE	(1) Net Profit / Pretax Profit	(2) Pretax Profit / EBIT	(3) EBIT / Sales (Margin)	(4) Sales / Assets (Turnover)	(5) Assets / Equity	(6) Compound Leverage Factor (2) × (5)
Bad year							
Nodett	0.040	0.8	1.000	0.0625	0.800	1.000	1.000
Somdett	0.024	0.8	0.360	0.0625	0.800	1.667	0.600
Normal year							
Nodett	0.080	0.8	1.000	0.100	1.000	1.000	1.000
Somdett	0.091	0.8	0.680	0.100	1.000	1.667	1.133
Good year							
Nodett	0.120	0.8	1.000	0.125	1.200	1.000	1.000
Somdett	0.157	0.8	0.787	0.125	1.200	1.667	1.311

Comparing Nodett and Somdett, we see that factors 3 and 4 do not depend on a firm's financial leverage. The firms' ratios equal each other in each scenario. Similarly, factor 1, the ratio of net income after taxes to pretax profit, is the same for both firms. We call this the tax-burden ratio. Its value reflects both the government's tax code and the policies pursued by the firm in trying to minimize its tax burden. In our example, it does not change over the business cycle, remaining a constant 0.8.

While factors 1, 3, and 4 are not affected by a firm's capital structure, factors 2 and 5 are. Factor 2 is the ratio of pretax profits to EBIT. The firm's pretax profits are greatest when there are no interest payments to be made to debtholders. In fact, another way to express this ratio is

$$\frac{\text{Pretax profits}}{\text{EBIT}} = \frac{\text{EBIT} - \text{Interest expense}}{\text{EBIT}}$$

We call this factor the *interest-burden (IB) ratio*. It takes on its highest possible value, 1, for Nodett, which has no financial leverage and no interest expense. The higher the degree of financial leverage, the lower the IB ratio. Nodett's IB ratio does not vary over the business cycle. It is fixed at 1, reflecting the absence of interest payments. For Somdett, however, because interest expense is a fixed dollar amount while EBIT varies, the IB ratio varies from a low of 0.36 in a bad year to a high of 0.787 in a good year.

A closely related statistic to the interest-burden ratio is the **interest coverage ratio,** or **times interest earned.** The ratio is defined as

$$\text{Interest coverage} = \frac{\text{EBIT}}{\text{Interest expense}}$$

A high coverage ratio indicates that annual earnings are significantly greater than annual interest obligations. It is widely used by both lenders and borrowers in determining the firm's debt capacity and is a major determinant of the firm's bond rating.

Factor 5, the ratio of assets to equity, is a measure of the firm's degree of financial leverage. It is called the **leverage ratio** and is equal to 1 plus the debt/equity ratio.[6] In our numerical example in Table 14.7, Nodett has a leverage ratio of 1, while Somdett's is 1.667.

From our discussion of Equation 14.1, we know that financial leverage helps boost ROE only if ROA is greater than the interest rate on the firm's debt. How is this fact reflected in the

interest coverage ratio or times interest earned

A financial leverage measure arrived at by dividing earnings before interest and taxes by interest expense.

leverage ratio

Measure of debt to total capitalization of a firm.

---

[6] $\dfrac{\text{Assets}}{\text{Equity}} = \dfrac{\text{Equity} + \text{Debt}}{\text{Equity}} = 1 + \dfrac{\text{Debt}}{\text{Equity}}$

ratios of Table 14.7? The answer is that the full impact of leverage in this framework equals the product of the interest burden and leverage ratios (that is, factors 2 and 5, in Table 14.7). This product is called the compound leverage factor, and it is shown in Column 6. Nodett's compound leverage factor equals 1 in all three scenarios. But Somdett's is greater than 1 in normal years (1.134) and in good years (1.311), indicating a positive contribution of financial leverage to ROE. It is less than 1 in bad years, reflecting the fact that when ROA falls below the interest rate, ROE falls with increased use of debt.

We can summarize all of these relationships as follows:

$$\text{ROE} = \text{Tax burden} \times \text{Interest burden} \times \text{Margin} \times \text{Turnover} \times \text{Leverage}$$

Because

$$\text{ROA} = \text{Margin} \times \text{Turnover} \qquad\qquad \textbf{(14.3)}$$

and

$$\text{Compound leverage factor} = \text{Interest burden} \times \text{Leverage}$$

we can decompose ROE equivalently as follows:

$$\text{ROE} = \text{Tax burden} \times \text{ROA} \times \text{Compound leverage factor}$$

Equation 14.3 shows that ROA is the *product* of margin and turnover. High values of one of these ratios are often accompanied by low values of the other. For example, Walmart has low profit margins but high turnover, while Tiffany has high margins but low turnover. Firms would love to have high values for both margin and turnover, but this generally will not be possible: Retailers with high markups will sacrifice sales volume, while those with low turnover need high margins just to remain viable. Therefore, comparing these ratios in isolation usually is meaningful only in evaluating firms following similar strategies in the same industry.

Figure 14.2 shows evidence of the turnover-profit margin trade-off. Industries with high turnover such as groceries or retail apparel tend to have low profit margins, while industries with high margins such as utilities tend to have low turnover. The two curved lines in the figure trace out turnover-margin combinations that result in an ROA of either 3% or 10%. You can see that most industries lie inside this range, so ROA across industries demonstrates far less variation than either turnover or margin taken in isolation.

EXAMPLE 14.3

Margin vs. Turnover

Consider two firms with the same ROA of 10% per year. The first is a discount chain and the second is a gas and electric utility.

As Table 14.8 shows, the discount chain has a "low" profit margin of 2% and achieves a 10% ROA by "turning over" its assets five times per year. The capital-intensive utility, on the other hand, has a "low" asset turnover ratio (ATO) of only 0.5 times per year and achieves its 10% ROA through its higher, 20%, profit margin. The point here is that a "low" margin or ATO ratio need not indicate a troubled firm. Each ratio must be interpreted in light of industry norms.

CONCEPT check 14.2

Do a ratio decomposition analysis for the Mordett corporation of Concept Check 14.1, preparing a table similar to Table 14.7.

TABLE 14.8   Differences between profit margin and asset turnover across industries

	Margin	×	ATO	=	ROA
Supermarket chain	2%		5.0		10%
Utility	20%		0.5		10%

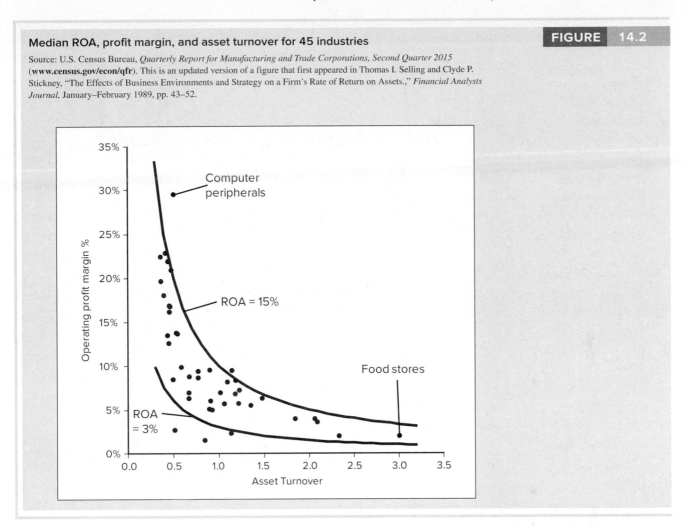

Median ROA, profit margin, and asset turnover for 45 industries

Source: U.S. Census Bureau, *Quarterly Report for Manufacturing and Trade Corporations, Second Quarter 2015* (**www.census.gov/econ/qfr**). This is an updated version of a figure that first appeared in Thomas I. Selling and Clyde P. Stickney, "The Effects of Business Environments and Strategy on a Firm's Rate of Return on Assets.," *Financial Analysts Journal,* January–February 1989, pp. 43–52.

FIGURE 14.2

Turnover and Asset Utilization

It is often helpful in understanding a firm's ratio of sales to assets to compute comparable efficiency-of-utilization, or turnover, ratios for subcategories of assets. For example, fixed-asset turnover would be

$$\frac{\text{Sales}}{\text{Fixed assets}}$$

This ratio measures sales per dollar of the firm's money tied up in fixed assets.

To illustrate how you can compute this and other ratios from a firm's financial statements, consider Growth Industries, Inc. (GI). GI's income statement and opening and closing balance sheets for the years 2015–2017 appear in Table 14.9. (We use a corporate tax rate of 40% in this example; the current tax rate of 21% was not put into effect until 2018.)

GI's total asset turnover in 2017 was 0.303, which was below the industry average of 0.4. To understand better why GI underperformed, we compute asset utilization ratios separately for fixed assets, inventories, and accounts receivable.

GI's sales in 2017 were $144 million. Its only fixed assets were plant and equipment, which were $216 million at the beginning of the year and $259.2 million at year's end. Average fixed assets for the year were, therefore, $237.6 million [($216 million + $259.2 million)/2]. GI's fixed-asset turnover for 2017 was $144 million per year/$237.6 million = .606 per year. In other words, for every dollar of fixed assets, there was $0.606 in sales during 2017.

Notice that when a financial ratio includes one item from the income statement, which covers a period of time, and another from the balance sheet, which is a "snapshot" at a

TABLE 14.9 Growth Industries financial statements ($ thousand)

	2014	2015	2016	2017
Income statements				
Sales revenue		$100,000	$120,000	$144,000
Cost of goods sold (including depreciation)		55,000	$ 66,000	$ 79,200
Depreciation		15,000	18,000	21,600
Selling and administrative expenses		15,000	18,000	21,600
Operating income		$ 30,000	$ 36,000	$ 43,200
Interest expense		10,500	19,095	34,391
Taxable income		$ 19,500	$ 16,905	$ 8,809
Income tax (40% rate)		7,800	6,762	3,524
Net income		$ 11,700	$ 10,143	$ 5,285
Balance sheets (end of year)				
Cash and marketable securities	$ 50,000	$ 60,000	$ 72,000	$ 86,400
Accounts receivable	25,000	30,000	36,000	43,200
Inventories	75,000	90,000	108,000	129,600
Net plant and equipment	150,000	180,000	216,000	259,200
Total assets	$300,000	$360,000	$432,000	$518,400
Accounts payable	$ 30,000	$ 36,000	$ 43,200	$ 51,840
Short-term debt	45,000	87,300	141,957	214,432
Long-term debt (8% bonds maturing in 2030)	75,000	75,000	75,000	75,000
Total liabilities	$150,000	$198,300	$260,157	$341,272
Shareholders' equity (1 million shares outstanding)	$150,000	$161,700	$171,843	$177,128
Other data				
Market price per common share at year-end		$ 93.60	$ 61.00	$ 21.00

particular time, common practice is to take the average of the beginning and end-of-year balance sheet figures. Thus, in computing the fixed-asset turnover ratio, you divide sales (from the income statement) by average fixed assets (from the balance sheet).

GI's fixed-asset turnover ratio for 2015 through 2017 and the 2017 industry average are:

2015	2016	2017	2017 Industry Average
0.606	0.606	0.606	0.700

GI's fixed-asset turnover has been stable over time and below the industry average.

inventory turnover ratio

Cost of goods sold divided by average inventory.

Another widely followed turnover ratio is the **inventory turnover ratio,** which is the ratio of cost of goods sold per dollar of inventory. We use the cost of goods sold (instead of sales revenue) in the numerator to maintain consistency with inventory, which is valued at cost. This ratio measures the speed with which inventory is turned over.

In 2015, GI's cost of goods sold (less depreciation) was $40 million, and its average inventory was $82.5 million [($75 million + $90 million)/2]. Its inventory turnover therefore was 0.485 per year ($40 million/$82.5 million). In 2016 and 2017, inventory turnover remained the same and continued below the industry average of 0.5 per year. In other words, GI was burdened with a higher level of inventories relative to production than its competitors. This higher investment in working capital in turn resulted in a higher level of assets per dollar of sales or profits and a lower ROA than its competitors.

Another aspect of efficiency surrounds management of accounts receivable, which is often measured by **days sales in receivables,** that is, the average level of accounts receivable expressed as a multiple of daily sales. It is computed as average accounts receivable/sales × 365 and may be interpreted as the number of days' worth of sales tied up in accounts receivable. You can also think of it as the average lag between the date of sale and the date payment is received, and it is therefore also called the **average collection period.**

For GI in 2017, this number was 100.4 days:

$$\frac{(\$36 \text{ million} + \$43.2 \text{ million})/2}{\$144 \text{ million}} \times 365 = 100.4 \text{ days}$$

The industry average was 60 days. This statistic tells us that GI's average receivables per dollar of sales exceeds that of its competitors. Again, this implies a higher required investment in working capital and ultimately a lower ROA.

In summary, these ratios show us that GI's poor total asset turnover relative to the industry is in part caused by lower-than-average fixed-asset turnover and inventory turnover and higher-than-average days receivables. This suggests GI may have excess plant capacity as well as poor inventory and receivables management practices.

Liquidity Ratios

Leverage is one measure of the safety of a firm's debt. Debt ratios compare the firm's indebtedness to various measures of its assets, and coverage ratios compare measures of earning power against the cash flow needed to satisfy debt obligations. But leverage is not the only determinant of financial prudence. You also want to know that a firm can lay its hands on cash either to pay its scheduled obligations or to meet unforeseen obligations. **Liquidity** is the ability to convert assets into cash at short notice. Liquidity is commonly measured using the current ratio, quick ratio, and cash ratio.

1. **Current ratio:** current assets/current liabilities. This ratio measures the ability of the firm to pay off its current liabilities by liquidating its current assets (that is, turning them into cash). It indicates the firm's ability to avoid insolvency in the short run. GI's current ratio in 2015, for example, was $(60 + 30 + 90)/(36 + 87.3) = 1.46$. In other years, it was:

2015	2016	2017	2017 Industry Average
1.46	1.17	0.97	2.0

This represents an unfavorable time trend and poor standing relative to the industry. This troublesome pattern is not surprising given the working capital burden resulting from GI's subpar performance with respect to receivables and inventory management.

2. **Quick ratio:** (cash + marketable securities + receivables)/current liabilities. This ratio is also called the **acid test ratio.** It has the same denominator as the current ratio, but its numerator includes only cash, cash equivalents such as marketable securities, and receivables. The quick ratio is a better measure of liquidity than the current ratio for firms whose inventory is not readily convertible into cash. GI's quick ratio shows the same disturbing trends as its current ratio:

2015	2016	2017	2017 Industry Average
0.73	0.58	0.49	1.0

3. **Cash ratio.** A company's receivables are less liquid than its holdings of cash and marketable securities. Therefore, in addition to the quick ratio, analysts also compute a firm's cash ratio, defined as

$$\text{Cash ratio} = \frac{\text{Cash} + \text{Marketable securities}}{\text{Current liabilities}}$$

days sales in receivables or average collection period
Accounts receivable per dollar of daily sales.

liquidity
The ability to convert assets into cash at short notice.

current ratio
Current assets/current liabilities.

quick ratio or acid test ratio
A measure of liquidity similar to the current ratio except for exclusion of inventories.

cash ratio
Another liquidity measure. Ratio of cash and marketable securities to current liabilities.

GI's cash ratios are:

2015	2016	2017	2017 Industry Average
0.487	0.389	0.324	0.70

GI's liquidity ratios have fallen dramatically over this period, and by 2017, they are far below the industry average. The decline in the liquidity ratios combined with the decline in coverage ratio (you can confirm that times interest earned also has fallen over this period) suggest that its credit rating has been declining as well and, no doubt, GI is considered a relatively poor credit risk in 2017.

Market Price Ratios

market-to-book-value ratio

Market price of a share divided by book value per share.

The **market-to-book-value ratio** (P/B) equals the market price of a share of the firm's common stock divided by its *book value,* that is, shareholders' equity per share. Some analysts consider the stock of a firm with a low market-to-book ratio to be a "safer" investment, seeing the book value as a "floor" supporting the market price. These analysts presumably view book value as the level below which market price will not fall because the firm always has the option to liquidate, or sell, its assets for their book values. However, this view is questionable. In fact, some firms do sometimes sell for less than book value. For example, we've already seen that in mid-2017 shares in Honda, Mitsubishi, and Barclays sold for less than book value. Nevertheless, a low market-to-book-value ratio is seen by some as providing a "margin of safety," and some analysts will screen out or reject high P/B firms in their stock selection process.

A better interpretation of the price-to-book ratio is as a measure of growth opportunities. Recall from the previous chapter that we may view the two components of firm value as assets in place and growth opportunities. As the next example illustrates, firms with greater growth opportunities will tend to exhibit higher multiples of market price to book value.

EXAMPLE 14.4

Price-to-Book and Growth Opportunities

Consider two firms, both of which have book value per share of $10, a market capitalization rate of 15%, and a plowback ratio of 0.60.

Bright Prospects has an ROE of 20%, which is well in excess of the market capitalization rate; this ROE implies that the firm is endowed with ample growth opportunities. With ROE = .20, Bright Prospects will earn .20 × 10 = $2 per share this year. With its plowback ratio of .60, it pays out a dividend of $D_1 = (1 - .6) \times \$2 = \$.80$, has a growth rate of $g = b \times ROE = .60 \times .20 = .12$, and a stock price of $D_1/(k - g) = \$.80/(.15 - .12) = \$26.67$. Its P/B ratio is 26.67/10 = 2.667.

In contrast, Past Glory has an ROE of only 15%, just equal to the market capitalization rate. It therefore will earn .15 × 10 = $1.50 per share this year and will pay a dividend of $D_1 = .4 \times \$1.50 = \$.60$. Its growth rate is $g = b \times ROE = .60 \times .15 = .09$, and its stock price is $D_1/(k - g) = \$.60/(.15 - .09) = \$10$. Its P/B ratio is $10/$10 = 1. Not surprisingly, a firm that earns just the required rate of return on its investments will sell for book value, and no more.

We conclude that the price-to-book-value ratio is determined in large part by growth prospects.

---

price–earnings ratio (P/E)

The ratio of a stock's price to its earnings per share. Also referred to as the P/E multiple.

Another measure used to place firms along a growth versus value spectrum is the **price–earnings ratio (P/E).** In fact, we saw in the last chapter that the ratio of the present value of growth opportunities to the value of assets in place largely determines the P/E multiple. While low P/E stocks allow you to pay less per dollar of *current* earnings, the high P/E stock may still be a better bargain if its earnings are expected to grow quickly enough.[7]

---

[7]Remember, though, P/E ratios reported in the financial press are based on *past* earnings, while price is determined by the firm's prospects of *future* earnings. Therefore, reported P/E ratios may reflect variation in current earnings around a trend line.

Many analysts nevertheless believe that low P/E stocks are more attractive than high P/E stocks. And in fact, low P/E stocks have generally been positive-alpha investments using the CAPM as a return benchmark. But an efficient market adherent would discount this track record, arguing that such a simplistic rule could not really generate abnormal returns and that the CAPM may not be a good benchmark for returns in this case.

In any event, the important points to keep in mind are that ownership of the stock conveys the right to future as well as current earnings and, therefore, that a high P/E ratio may best be interpreted as a signal that the market views the firm as enjoying attractive growth opportunities.

Before leaving the P/B and P/E ratios, it is worth pointing out an important relationship between them.

$$\text{ROE} = \frac{\text{Earnings}}{\text{Book value}} = \frac{\text{Market price}}{\text{Book value}} \div \frac{\text{Market price}}{\text{Earnings}} \qquad \textbf{(14.4)}$$
$$= \text{P/B ratio} \div \text{P/E ratio}$$

Rearranging terms, we find that a firm's P/E ratio equals its price-to-book ratio divided by ROE:

$$\frac{P}{E} = \frac{\text{P/B}}{\text{ROE}}$$

Wall Street often distinguishes between "good firms" and "good investments." A good firm may be highly profitable, with a high ROE. But if its stock price is bid up to a level commensurate with this ROE, its P/B ratio will also be high, and the stock price may be a relatively large multiple of earnings, thus reducing its attractiveness as an investment. The high ROE of the *firm* does not by itself imply that the *stock* is a good investment. Conversely, troubled firms with low ROEs can be good investments if their prices are low enough.

Table 14.10 summarizes the ratios reviewed in this section.

> **CONCEPT check 14.3**
>
> What were GI's ROE, P/E, and P/B ratios in 2017? How do they compare to these industry average ratios: ROE = 8.64%, P/E = 8, and P/B = .69? How does GI's earnings yield in 2017 compare to the industry average?

Choosing a Benchmark

We have discussed how to calculate the principal financial ratios. To evaluate the performance of a given firm, however, you need a benchmark to which you can compare its ratios. One obvious benchmark is the ratio for the same company in earlier years. For example, Figure 14.3 shows Home Depot's return on assets, profit margin, and asset turnover ratio for the last few years. You can see there that HD's ROA has increased dramatically since 2009, driven by simultaneous increases in both profit margin and turnover.

It is also helpful to compare financial ratios to those of other firms in the same industry. Financial ratios for industries are published by the U.S. Department of Commerce (see Table 14.11), Dun & Bradstreet, the Risk Management Association (RMA), and others, and many ratios are available on the web, for example, on the Yahoo! Finance site.

Table 14.11 presents ratios for a sample of major industry groups to give you a feel for some of the differences across industries. Some ratios such as asset turnover or total debt ratio reflect persistent characteristics of a firm or its industry and tend to be relatively stable. For example, asset turnover in drug development and production companies will be consistently lower than in the clothing industry. However, other ratios, for example, return on assets or equity, are more sensitive to current business conditions.

TABLE 14.10	Summary of key financial ratios

Leverage ratios:

Interest burden

$$\frac{\text{EBIT} - \text{Interest expense}}{\text{EBIT}}$$

Interest coverage (Times interest earned)

$$\frac{\text{EBIT}}{\text{Interest expense}}$$

Leverage

$$\frac{\text{Assets}}{\text{Equity}} = 1 + \frac{\text{Debt}}{\text{Equity}}$$

Compound leverage factor

Interest burden × Leverage

Asset utilization:

Total asset turnover

$$\frac{\text{Sales}}{\text{Average total assets}}$$

Fixed-asset turnover

$$\frac{\text{Sales}}{\text{Average fixed assets}}$$

Inventory turnover

$$\frac{\text{Cost of goods sold}}{\text{Average inventories}}$$

Days sales in receivables

$$\frac{\text{Average accounts receivables}}{\text{Annual sales}} \times 365$$

Liquidity:

Current ratio

$$\frac{\text{Current assets}}{\text{Current liabilities}}$$

Quick ratio

$$\frac{\text{Cash} + \text{Marketable securities} + \text{Receivables}}{\text{Current liabilities}}$$

Cash ratio

$$\frac{\text{Cash} + \text{Marketable securities}}{\text{Current liabilities}}$$

Profitability ratios:

Return on assets

$$\frac{\text{EBIT}}{\text{Average total assets}}$$

Return on equity

$$\frac{\text{Net income}}{\text{Average stockholders' equity}}$$

Return on sales (Profit margin)

$$\frac{\text{EBIT}}{\text{Sales}}$$

Market price ratios:

Market-to-book

$$\frac{\text{Price per share}}{\text{Book value per share}}$$

Price–earnings ratio

$$\frac{\text{Price per share}}{\text{Earnings per share}}$$

Earnings yield

$$\frac{\text{Earnings per share}}{\text{Price per share}}$$

14.5 AN ILLUSTRATION OF FINANCIAL STATEMENT ANALYSIS

In her 2017 annual report to the shareholders of Growth Industries, Inc., the president wrote: "2017 was another successful year for Growth Industries. As in 2016, sales, assets, and operating income all continued to grow at a rate of 20%."

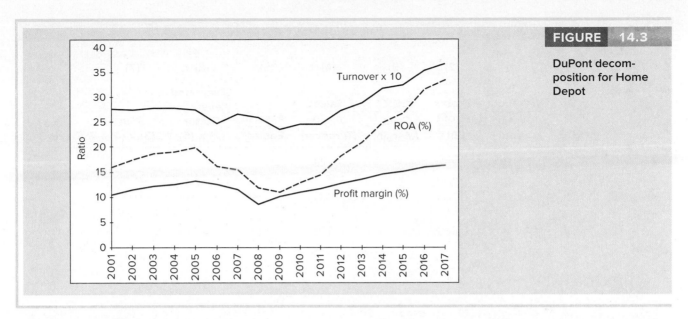

FIGURE 14.3

DuPont decomposition for Home Depot

TABLE 14.11 Financial ratios for major industry groups

	LT Debt Assets	Interest Coverage	Current Ratio	Quick Ratio	Asset Turnover	Profit Margin (%)	Return on Assets (%)	Return on Equity (%)	Payout Ratio
All manufacturing	0.26	3.11	1.26	0.85	0.63	6.76	4.28	13.04	0.54
Food products	0.25	6.87	1.52	0.97	0.91	8.92	8.09	13.05	0.44
Clothing	0.25	7.36	1.17	0.36	2.07	5.49	11.39	22.28	0.23
Aerospace	0.23	5.70	1.15	0.47	0.71	9.29	6.62	24.59	1.01
Chemicals	0.32	2.29	1.12	0.83	0.39	10.11	3.97	13.20	0.66
Drugs	0.33	2.18	1.05	0.81	0.32	11.85	3.76	10.52	0.86
Machinery	0.23	2.43	1.32	0.86	0.65	5.03	3.28	6.11	1.22
Electrical	0.21	4.51	1.12	0.74	0.54	7.74	4.19	13.29	0.74
Motor vehicles	0.14	4.50	1.04	0.74	1.25	3.24	4.06	11.70	0.54
Computer and electronic	0.27	3.10	1.21	0.98	0.42	9.83	4.12	18.27	0.27

Source: *U.S. Department of Commerce, Quarterly Financial Report for Manufacturing, Mining and Trade Corporations,* March 2017. Available at http://www2.census.gov/econ/qfr/current/qfr_pub.pdf.

Is she right?

We can evaluate her statement by conducting a full-scale ratio analysis of Growth Industries. Our purpose is to assess GI's performance in the recent past, to evaluate its future prospects, and to determine whether its market price reflects its intrinsic value.

Table 14.12 shows some key financial ratios we can compute from GI's financial statements. The president is certainly right about the growth in sales, assets, and operating income. Inspection of GI's key financial ratios, however, contradicts her first sentence: 2017 was not another successful year for GI—it appears to have been another miserable one.

ROE has been declining steadily from 7.51% in 2015 to 3.03% in 2017. A comparison of GI's 2017 ROE to the 2017 industry average of 8.64% makes the deteriorating time trend especially alarming. The low and falling market-to-book-value ratio and the falling

TABLE 14.12   Key financial ratios of Growth Industries, Inc.

Year	ROE	(1) Net Profit / Pretax Profit	(2) Pretax Profit / EBIT	(3) EBIT / Sales (Margin)	(4) Sales / Assets (Turnover)	(5) Assets / Equity	(6) Compound Leverage Factor (2) × (5)	(7) ROA (3) × (4)	P/E	P/B
2015	7.51%	0.6	0.650	30%	0.303	2.117	1.376	9.09%	8	0.58
2016	6.08	0.6	0.470	30	0.303	2.375	1.116	9.09	6	0.35
2017	3.03	0.6	0.204	30	0.303	2.723	0.556	9.09	4	0.12
Industry average	8.64	0.6	0.800	30	0.400	1.500	1.200	12.00	8	0.69

price–earnings ratio indicate that investors are less and less optimistic about the firm's future profitability.

The fact that ROA has not been declining, however, tells us that the source of the declining time trend in GI's ROE must be due to financial leverage. And, in fact, as GI's leverage ratio climbed from 2.117 in 2015 to 2.723 in 2017, its interest-burden ratio worsened from 0.650 to 0.204—with the net result that the compound leverage factor fell from 1.376 to 0.556.

The rapid increase in short-term debt from year to year and the concurrent increase in interest expense make it clear that, to finance its 20% growth rate in sales, GI has incurred sizable amounts of short-term debt at high interest rates. The firm is paying rates of interest greater than the ROA it is earning on the investment financed with the new borrowing. As the firm has expanded, its situation has become ever more precarious.

In 2017, for example, the average interest rate on short-term debt was 20% versus an ROA of 9.09%. (You can calculate the interest rate on GI's short-term debt using the data in Table 14.9 as follows: The balance sheet shows us that the coupon rate on its long-term debt was 8% and its par value was $75 million. Therefore the interest paid on the long-term debt was .08 × $75 million = $6 million. Total interest paid in 2017 was $34,391,000, so the interest paid on the short-term debt must have been $34,391,000 – $6,000,000 = $28,391,000. This is 20% of GI's short-term debt at the start of the year.)

GI's problems become clear when we examine its statement of cash flows in Table 14.13. The statement is derived from the income statement and balance sheet data in Table 14.9. GI's cash flow from operations is falling steadily, from $12,700,000 in 2015 to $6,725,000 in 2017. The firm's investment in plant and equipment, by contrast, has increased greatly. Net plant and equipment (i.e., net of depreciation) rose from $150,000,000 in 2014 to $259,200,000 in 2017. This near doubling of capital assets makes the decrease in cash flow from operations all the more troubling.

The source of the difficulty is GI's enormous amount of short-term borrowing. In a sense, the company is being run as a pyramid scheme. It borrows more and more each year to maintain its 20% growth rate in assets and income. However, the new assets are not generating enough cash flow to support the extra interest burden of the debt, as the falling cash flow from operations indicates. Eventually, when the firm loses its ability to borrow further, its growth will be at an end.

At this point, GI stock might be an attractive investment. Its market price is only 12% of its book value, and with a P/E ratio of 4, its earnings yield is 25% per year. GI is a likely candidate for a takeover by another firm that might replace GI's management and build shareholder value through a radical change in policy.

TABLE 14.13 Growth Industries statement of cash flows ($ thousand)

	2015	2016	2017
Cash flow from operating activities			
Net income	$ 11,700	$ 10,143	$ 5,285
Depreciation	15,000	18,000	21,600
Decrease (increase) in accounts receivable	(5,000)	(6,000)	(7,200)
Decrease (increase) in inventories	(15,000)	(18,000)	(21,600)
Increase in accounts payable	6,000	7,200	8,640
Cash provided by operations	$ 12,700	$ 11,343	$ 6,725
Cash flow from investing activities			
Investment in plant and equipment*	$(45,000)	$(54,000)	$(64,800)
Cash flow from financing activities			
Dividends paid[†]	$ 0	$ 0	$ 0
Short-term debt issued	42,300	54,657	72,475
Change in cash and marketable securities[‡]	$ 10,000	$ 12,000	$ 14,400

*Gross investment equals increase in net plant and equipment plus depreciation.

[†]We can conclude that no dividends are paid because stockholders' equity increases each year by the full amount of net income, implying a plowback ratio of 1.

[‡] Equals cash flow from operations plus cash flow from investment activities plus cash flow from financing activities. Note that this equals the yearly change in cash and marketable securities on the balance sheet.

You have the following information for IBX Corporation for the years 2018 and 2021 (all figures are in $ millions):

	2021	2018
Net income	$ 253.7	$ 239.0
Pretax income	411.9	375.6
EBIT	517.6	403.1
Average assets	4,857.9	3,459.7
Sales	6,679.3	4,537.0
Shareholders' equity	2,233.3	2,347.3

What is the trend in IBX's ROE, and how can you account for it in terms of tax burden, margin, turnover, and financial leverage?

14.6 COMPARABILITY PROBLEMS

Financial statement analysis gives us a good amount of ammunition for evaluating a company's performance and future prospects. But comparing financial results of different companies is not so simple. There is more than one acceptable way to represent various items of revenue and expense according to generally accepted accounting principles (GAAP). This means two firms may have exactly the same economic income yet very different accounting incomes.

Interpreting a single firm's performance over time is even more complicated when inflation distorts the dollar measuring rod. Comparability problems are especially acute in this case because the impact of inflation on reported results often depends on the particular method the firm adopts to account for inventories and depreciation. Earnings and financial ratios must be adjusted to a uniform standard before attempting to compare financial results across firms and over time. Other important potential sources of noncomparability include the capitalization of leases and other expenses, the treatment of pension costs, and allowances for reserves.

Inventory Valuation

There are two commonly used ways to value inventories: **LIFO** (last-in, first-out) and **FIFO** (first-in, first-out). We can explain the difference using a numerical example.

Suppose Generic Products, Inc. (GPI), has a constant inventory of 1 million units of generic goods. The inventory turns over once per year, meaning the ratio of cost of goods sold to inventory is 1.

The LIFO system calls for valuing the million units used up during the year at the current cost of production, so that the last goods produced are considered the first ones to be sold. They are valued at today's cost. The FIFO system assumes that the units used up or sold are the ones that were added to inventory first, and goods sold therefore are valued at original cost.

If the price of generic goods has been constant, say at the level of $1, the book value of inventory and the cost of goods sold would be the same, $1 million under both systems. But suppose the price of generic goods rises by 10 cents per unit during the year as a result of inflation.

Under LIFO, the last goods produced are assumed to be sold at the current cost of $1.10; the goods remaining are the previously produced goods, at a cost of only $1. Therefore, LIFO accounting would result in a cost of goods sold of $1.1 million, while the end-of-year balance sheet value of the 1 million units in inventory remains $1 million. You can see that, although LIFO accounting accurately measures the cost of goods sold today, it understates the current value of the remaining inventory in an inflationary environment.

In contrast, under FIFO accounting, the cost of goods sold would be $1 million, and the end-of-year balance sheet value of the inventory is $1.1 million. The result is that the LIFO firm has both a lower reported profit and a lower balance sheet value of inventories than the FIFO firm.

LIFO results in a more realistic estimate of economic earnings (that is, real sustainable cash flow), because it uses up-to-date prices to evaluate the cost of goods sold. However, it induces balance sheet distortions when it values investment in inventories at original cost. This practice results in an upward bias in ROE because the investment base on which return is earned is undervalued.

Depreciation

Another source of problems is the measurement of depreciation, which is a key factor in computing earnings. The accounting and economic measures of depreciation can differ markedly. According to the *economic* definition, depreciation is the amount of operating cash flow that the firm must reinvest to sustain its real cash flow at the current level.

The *accounting* measurement is quite different. Accounting depreciation is the portion of the original acquisition cost of an asset that is allocated to each period over an arbitrarily specified life of the asset. This is the figure reported in financial statements.

Assume, for example, that a firm buys machines with a useful economic life of 20 years at $100,000 apiece. In its financial statements, however, the firm can depreciate the machines over 10 years using the straight-line method, for $10,000 per year in depreciation. Thus, after 10 years, a machine will be fully depreciated on the books, even though it remains a productive asset that will not need replacement for another 10 years.

In computing accounting earnings, this firm will overestimate depreciation in the first 10 years of the machine's economic life and underestimate it in the last 10 years. This will cause reported earnings to be understated compared with economic earnings in the first 10 years and overstated in the last 10 years.

Depreciation comparability problems add one more wrinkle. A firm can use different depreciation methods for tax purposes than for other reporting purposes. Most firms use accelerated depreciation methods for tax purposes and straight-line depreciation in published financial statements. There also are differences across firms in their estimates of the depreciable life of plant, equipment, and other assets. Under current U.S. tax law, firms may depreciate the full cost of a capital investment in the year it is put into use, but this is not the case in most countries.

Another complication arises from inflation. Because conventional depreciation is based on the historical cost rather than on the current replacement cost of assets, measured depreciation in periods of inflation is understated relative to replacement cost, and *real* economic income (sustainable cash flow) is correspondingly overstated.

For example, suppose Generic Products, Inc., has a machine with a three-year useful life that originally cost $3 million. Annual straight-line depreciation is $1 million, regardless of what happens to the replacement cost of the machine. Suppose inflation in the first year turns out to be 10%. Then the true annual depreciation expense is $1.1 million in current terms, while conventionally measured depreciation remains fixed at $1 million per year. Accounting income therefore overstates *real* economic income.

Inflation and Interest Expense

While inflation can cause distortions in the measurement of a firm's inventory and depreciation costs, it has perhaps an even greater effect on the calculation of *real* interest expense. Nominal interest rates include an inflation premium that compensates the lender for inflation-induced erosion in the real value of principal. From the perspective of both lender and borrower, therefore, part of what is conventionally measured as interest expense should be treated more properly as repayment of principal.

Suppose Generic Products has debt outstanding with a face value of $10 million at an interest rate of 10% per year. Interest expense as conventionally measured is $1 million per year. However, suppose inflation during the year is 6%, so that the real interest rate is approximately 4%. Then $0.6 million of what appears as interest expense on the income statement is really an inflation premium, or compensation for the anticipated reduction in the real value of the $10 million principal; only $0.4 million is *real* interest expense. The $0.6 million reduction in the purchasing power of the outstanding principal may be thought of as repayment of principal, rather than as an interest expense. Real income of the firm is, therefore, understated by $0.6 million.

EXAMPLE 14.5

Inflation and Real Income

Mismeasurement of real interest means that inflation results in an underestimate of real income. The effects of inflation on the reported values of inventories and depreciation that we have discussed work in the opposite direction.

In a period of rapid inflation, companies ABC and XYZ have the same *reported* earnings. ABC uses LIFO inventory accounting, has relatively fewer depreciable assets, and has more debt than XYZ. XYZ uses FIFO inventory accounting. Which company has the higher *real* income and why?

CONCEPT check 14.5

Fair Value Accounting

Many major assets and liabilities are not traded in financial markets and do not have easily observable values. For example, we cannot simply look up the values of employee stock options, health care benefits for retired employees, or buildings and other real estate. While the true financial status of a firm may depend critically on these values, which can swing widely over time, common practice has been to simply value them at historic cost. Proponents

fair value or mark-to-market accounting

Use of current market values rather than historic cost in the firm's financial statements.

of **fair value accounting,** also known as **mark-to-market accounting,** argue that financial statements would give a truer picture of the firm if they better reflected the current market values of all assets and liabilities.

The Financial Accounting Standards Board's Statement No. 157 on fair value accounting places assets in one of three "buckets." Level 1 assets are traded in active markets and therefore should be valued at their market price. Level 2 assets are not actively traded, but their values still may be estimated using observable market data on similar assets. These assets can be "marked to a matrix" of comparable securities. Level 3 assets are hardest to value. Here, it is difficult even to identify other assets that are similar enough to serve as benchmarks for their market values; one has to resort to pricing models to estimate their intrinsic values. Rather than mark to market, these values are often called "mark to model," although they are also disparagingly known as mark-to-make-believe, as the estimates are so prone to manipulation by creative use of model inputs. Since 2012, firms have been required to disclose more about the methods and assumptions used in their valuation models and to describe the sensitivity of their valuation estimates to changes in methodology.

Critics of fair value accounting argue that it relies too heavily on estimates. Such estimates potentially introduce considerable noise in firms' accounts and can induce profit volatility as fluctuations in asset valuations are recognized. Even worse, subjective valuations may offer management a tempting tool to manipulate earnings or the apparent financial condition of the firm at opportune times. As just one example, Bergstresser, Desai, and Rauh (2006) find that firms make more aggressive assumptions about returns on defined benefit pension plans (which lowers the computed present value of pension obligations) during periods in which executives are actively exercising their stock options.

A contentious debate over the application of fair value accounting to troubled financial institutions erupted in 2008 when values of financial securities such as subprime mortgage pools and derivative contracts backed by these pools came into question as trading in these instruments dried up. Without well-functioning markets, estimating (much less observing) market values was, at best, a precarious exercise.

Many observers feel that mark-to-market accounting exacerbated the financial meltdown by forcing banks to excessively write down asset values; others, that a failure to mark would have been tantamount to willfully ignoring reality and abdicating the responsibility to redress problems at nearly or already insolvent banks. The nearby box discusses the debate.

Quality of Earnings and Accounting Practices

Many firms make accounting choices that present their financial statements in the best possible light. The different choices that firms can make give rise to the comparability problems we have discussed. As a result, earnings statements for different companies may be more or less rosy presentations of true "economic earnings"—sustainable cash flow that can be paid to shareholders without impairing the firm's productive capacity. Analysts commonly evaluate the **quality of earnings** reported by a firm. This concept refers to the realism and conservatism of the earnings number, in other words, the extent to which we might expect the reported level of earnings to be sustained.

Examples of the accounting choices that influence quality of earnings are:

quality of earnings

The realism and sustainability of reported earnings.

- *Allowance for bad debt.* Most firms sell goods using trade credit and must make an allowance for bad debt. An unrealistically low allowance overstates the payments the firm is likely to receive and therefore reduces the quality of reported earnings. Look for a rising average collection period on accounts receivable as evidence of potential problems with future collections.

- *Nonrecurring items.* Some items that affect earnings should not be expected to recur regularly. These include asset sales, effects of accounting changes, effects of exchange rate movements, or unusual investment income. For example, in years with large equity returns, some firms enjoy large capital gains on securities held. These contribute to that year's earnings but should not be expected to repeat regularly. They would be considered a "low-quality" component of earnings. Similarly, gains in corporate pension plans can generate large, but one-time, contributions to reported earnings.

On the MARKET FRONT

MARK-TO-MARKET ACCOUNTING: CURE OR DISEASE?

As banks and other institutions holding mortgage-backed securities revalued their portfolios throughout 2008, their net worth fell along with the value of those securities. The losses on these securities were painful enough but, in addition, they led to knock-on effects that only increased the banks' woes. For example, banks are required to maintain adequate levels of capital relative to assets. If capital reserves decline, a bank may be forced to shrink until its remaining capital is once again adequate compared to its asset base. But such shrinkage may require the bank to cut back on its lending, which restricts its customers' access to credit. It may also have to sell some of its assets; and if many banks attempt to shrink their portfolios at once, waves of forced sales may put further pressure on prices, resulting in additional write-downs and reductions to capital in a self-feeding cycle. Critics of mark-to-market accounting therefore conclude that it acted to exacerbate the problems of an already reeling economy.

Advocates, however, contend that the critics confuse the message with the messenger. Mark-to-market accounting makes transparent losses that have already been incurred, but it does not cause those losses. But the critics retort that when markets are faltering, market prices may be unreliable. If trading activity has largely broken down, and assets can be sold only at fire-sale prices, then those prices may no longer be indicative of fundamental value. Markets cannot be efficient if they are not even functioning. In the turmoil surrounding the defaulted mortgages weighing down bank portfolios, one of the early proposals of then–Treasury Secretary Henry Paulson was for the government to buy bad assets at "hold to maturity" prices based on estimates of intrinsic value in a normally functioning market. In the same spirit, in April 2009, FASB granted financial firms more leeway to put off write-downs on assets deemed to be only "temporarily impaired."

Waiving write-down requirements may best be viewed as thinly veiled regulatory forbearance. Regulators know that losses have been incurred and that capital has been impaired. But by allowing firms to carry assets on their books at model rather than market prices, the unpleasant implications of that fact for capital adequacy may be politely ignored for a time. Even so, if the goal is to avoid forced sales in a distressed market, transparency may nevertheless be the best policy. Better to acknowledge losses and explicitly modify capital regulations to help institutions recover their footing in a difficult economy than to deal with losses by ignoring them. After all, why bother preparing financial statements if they are allowed to obscure the true condition of the firm?

Before abandoning fair value accounting, it would be prudent to consider the alternative. Traditional historic-cost accounting, which would allow firms to carry assets on the books at their original purchase price, has even less to recommend it. It would leave investors without an accurate sense of the condition of shaky institutions and, by the same token, lessen the pressure on those firms to get their houses in order. Dealing with losses must surely first require acknowledging them.

- *Earnings smoothing.* In 2003, Freddie Mac was the subject of an accounting scandal, with the disclosure that it had improperly reclassified mortgages held in its portfolio in an attempt to *reduce* its current earnings. Why would it take such actions? Because later, if earnings turned down, Freddie could "release" earnings by reversing these transactions and thereby create the appearance of steady earnings growth. Similarly, in the four quarters ending in October 2012, the four largest U.S. banks released $18.2 billion in reserves, which accounted for nearly one-quarter of their pretax income.[8] Such "earnings" are clearly not sustainable over the long term and therefore must be considered low quality.

- *Revenue recognition.* Under GAAP accounting, a firm is allowed to recognize a sale before it is paid. This is why firms have accounts receivable. But sometimes it can be hard to know when to recognize sales. For example, suppose a computer firm signs a contract to provide products and services over a five-year period. Should the revenue be booked immediately or spread out over five years? A more extreme version of this problem is called "channel stuffing," in which firms "sell" large quantities of goods to customers but give them the right to later either refuse delivery or return the product. The revenue from the "sale" is booked now, but the likely returns are not recognized until they occur (in a future accounting period). Hewlett-Packard argued in 2012 that it was led to overpay for its acquisition of Autonomy Corp. when Autonomy artificially enhanced its financial performance using channel stuffing. For example, Autonomy apparently sold software valued at more than £4 billion to Tikit Group; it booked the entire deal as revenue, but would not be paid for the software until Tikit actually sold software to its clients.[9] Thus, several

[8]Michael Rapoport, "Bank Profit Spigot to Draw Scrutiny," *The Wall Street Journal,* October 11, 2012.

[9]Ben Worthen, Paul Sonne, and Justin Scheck, "Long Before H-P Deal, Autonomy's Red Flags," *The Wall Street Journal,* November 26, 2012.

years' worth of only tentative future sales was recognized in 2010. HP paid about $11.1 billion for Autonomy. Only one year later, it wrote down that investment by $8.8 billion.

If you see accounts receivable increasing far faster than sales, or becoming a larger percentage of total assets, beware of these practices. Given the latitude firms have in how they recognize revenue, many analysts choose instead to concentrate on cash flow, which is far harder for a company to manipulate.

- *Off-balance-sheet assets and liabilities.* Suppose that one firm guarantees the outstanding debt of another firm, perhaps a firm in which it has an ownership stake. That obligation ought to be disclosed as a *contingent liability* because it may require payments down the road. But these obligations may not be reported as part of the firm's outstanding debt. Before its bankruptcy in 2001, Enron became notorious for this practice. Although it had guaranteed the debts of other companies, it failed to recognize these potential liabilities on its balance sheet. To the contrary, it obscured that exposure behind the veil of paper firms—its so-called special-purpose entities (SPEs).

  You need to keep your eye on other off-balance sheet items as well. A primary example is leasing. Airlines, for example, may show no aircraft on their balance sheets but have long-term leases that are virtually equivalent to debt-financed ownership. However, if the leases are treated as operating rather than as capital leases, they may appear only as footnotes to the financial statements.

International Accounting Conventions

The examples cited above illustrate some of the problems that analysts can encounter when attempting to interpret financial data. Even greater problems arise in the interpretation of the financial statements of foreign firms. This is because these firms do not follow GAAP guidelines. Accounting practices in various countries differ to greater or lesser extents from U.S. standards. Here are some of the major issues that you should be aware of when using the financial statements of foreign firms.

RESERVING PRACTICES   Many countries allow firms considerably more discretion in setting aside reserves for future contingencies than is typical in the United States. Because additions to reserves result in a charge against income, reported earnings are subject to managerial discretion.

DEPRECIATION   In the United States, firms typically maintain separate sets of accounts for tax and reporting purposes. For example, accelerated depreciation (or even immediate expensing) is used for tax purposes, while straight-line depreciation is used for reporting purposes. In contrast, most other countries do not allow dual sets of accounts, and most firms in foreign countries use accelerated depreciation to minimize taxes despite the fact that it results in lower reported earnings. This makes reported earnings of foreign firms lower than they would be if the firms were allowed to follow the U.S. practice.

INTANGIBLES   Treatment of intangibles can vary widely. Are they amortized or expensed? If amortized, over what period? Such issues can have a large impact on reported profits.

The effect of different country practices can be substantial. Figure 14.4 compares average P/E ratios for several countries as reported and restated on a common basis. While P/E multiples have changed considerably since this study was published, these results illustrate how different accounting rules can have a big impact on these ratios.

international financial reporting standards (IFRS)

A principles-based set of accounting rules adopted by about 100 countries around the world, including the European Union.

Some of the differences between U.S. and European accounting standards arise from different philosophies regarding regulating accounting practice. GAAP accounting in the U.S. is "rules-based," with detailed, explicit, and lengthy rules governing almost any circumstance that can be anticipated. In contrast, the **international financial reporting standards (IFRS)** used in the European Union as well as in about 100 other countries, such as Australia, Canada, Brazil, India, and China, are "principles-based," setting out general approaches for the preparation of financial statements. While IFRS rules are more flexible, firms must be prepared to demonstrate that their accounting choices are consistent with IFRS principles.

FIGURE 14.4

Adjusted versus
reported price–
earnings ratios

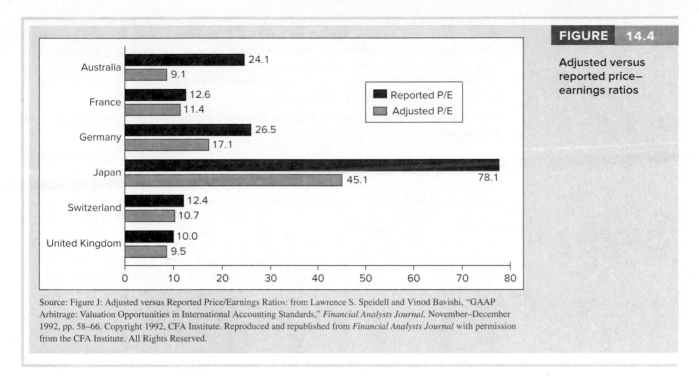

For some years, the SEC worked to bring U.S. accounting standards more in line with international rules. In 2007, the SEC began allowing foreign firms to issue securities in the U.S. if their financial statements were prepared using IFRS. Subsequently, it went even further when it proposed allowing large U.S. multinational firms to report earnings using IFRS rather than GAAP, and announced that it hoped to eventually adopt IFRS more broadly. But after many years of protracted negotiations, it become clear by 2014 that the SEC's plan to move to IFRS had stalled. While the SEC and International Accounting Standards Board (IASB) continue to collaborate on accounting rules, there is little immediate prospect for a single global accounting standard that will include the United States.

14.7 VALUE INVESTING: THE GRAHAM TECHNIQUE

No presentation of fundamental security analysis would be complete without a discussion of the ideas of Benjamin Graham, the greatest of the investment "gurus." Until the evolution of modern portfolio theory in the latter half of the twentieth century, Graham was the single most important thinker, writer, and teacher in the field of investment analysis. His influence on investment professionals, among them, his now equally famous student Warren Buffett, remains very strong.

Graham's magnum opus is *Security Analysis,* written with Columbia Professor David Dodd in 1934. Its message is similar to the ideas presented in this chapter. Graham believed careful analysis of a firm's financial statements could turn up bargain stocks. Over the years, he developed many different rules for determining the most important financial ratios and the critical values for judging a stock to be undervalued. Through many editions, his book has had a profound influence on investment professionals. It has been so influential and successful, in fact, that widespread adoption of Graham's techniques has led to elimination of the very bargains they are designed to identify.

In a 1976 seminar Graham said[10]

I am no longer an advocate of elaborate techniques of security analysis in order to find superior value opportunities. This was a rewarding activity, say, forty years ago, when our textbook

[10]Graham's full interview is reproduced in *Financial Analysts Journal,* Vol. 32, No. 5 (September/October, 1976), pp. 20–23.

"Graham and Dodd" was first published; but the situation has changed a good deal since then. In the old days any well-trained security analyst could do a good professional job of selecting under-valued issues through detailed studies; but in the light of the enormous amount of research now being carried on, I doubt whether in most cases such extensive efforts will generate sufficiently superior selections to justify their cost. To that very limited extent I'm on the side of the "efficient market" school of thought now generally accepted by the professors.

Nonetheless, in that same seminar, Graham suggested a simplified approach to identifying bargain stocks:

My first, more limited, technique confines itself to the purchase of common stocks at less than their working-capital value, or net current-asset value, giving no weight to the plant and other fixed assets, and deducting all liabilities in full from the current assets. We used this approach extensively in managing investment funds, and over a thirty-odd-year period we must have earned an average of some 20% per year from this source. For awhile, however, after the mid-1950s, this brand of buying opportunity became very scarce because of the pervasive bull market. But it has returned in quantity since the 1973–1974 decline. In January 1976 we counted over 100 such issues in the Standard & Poor's *Stock Guide*—about 10% of the total. I consider it a foolproof method of systematic investment—once again, not on the basis of individual results but in terms of the expectable group outcome.

SUMMARY

- The primary focus of the security analyst should be the firm's real economic earnings rather than its reported earnings. Accounting earnings as reported in financial statements can be a noisy estimate of real economic earnings, although empirical studies confirm that reported earnings convey considerable information concerning a firm's prospects.
- ROE is affected by the firm's degree of financial leverage. An increase in the debt/equity ratio will increase ROE if the firm's return on assets is greater than the interest rate on its debt.
- It is often helpful to decompose a firm's ROE into the product of several accounting ratios and to analyze their separate behavior over time or across companies within an industry. A useful breakdown is

$$\text{ROE} = \frac{\text{Net profits}}{\text{Pretax profits}} \times \frac{\text{Pretax profits}}{\text{EBIT}} \times \frac{\text{EBIT}}{\text{Sales}} \times \frac{\text{Sales}}{\text{Assets}} \times \frac{\text{Assets}}{\text{Equity}}$$

- Other accounting ratios that have a bearing on a firm's profitability and/or risk are fixed-asset turnover, inventory turnover, days sales in receivables, and the current, quick, and interest-coverage ratios.
- Two ratios that make use of the market price of the firm's common stock in addition to its financial statements are the ratios of market-to-book value and price to earnings. Analysts sometimes take low values for these ratios as a margin of safety or a sign that the stock is a bargain.
- A major problem in the use of data obtained from a firm's financial statements is compa-rability. Firms have a great deal of latitude in how they choose to compute various items of revenue and expense. Accounting earnings and financial ratios must be adjusted to a uniform standard before comparing financial results.
- Comparability problems can be acute when inflation is high. Inflation can create distor-tions in accounting for inventories, depreciation, and interest expense.
- Fair value or mark-to-market accounting attempts to value assets at current market value rather than historical cost. This policy is controversial because in many instances it is difficult to ascertain true market value, and critics contend that it makes financial state-ments unduly volatile. Advocates argue that financial statements should reflect the best estimate of current asset values.
- International financial reporting standards have become progressively accepted throughout the world. They differ from traditional U.S. GAAP procedures in that they are principles-based rather than rules-based.

KEY FORMULAS

ROE and leverage: $\text{ROE} = (1 - \text{Tax rate})\left[\text{ROA} + (\text{ROA} - \text{Interest rate})\dfrac{\text{Debt}}{\text{Equity}}\right]$

DuPont formula: $\text{ROE} = \dfrac{\text{Net profit}}{\text{Pretax profit}} \times \dfrac{\text{Pretax profit}}{\text{EBIT}} \times \dfrac{\text{EBIT}}{\text{Sales}} \times \dfrac{\text{Sales}}{\text{Assets}} \times \dfrac{\text{Assets}}{\text{Equity}}$

Another DuPont formula: $\text{ROA} = \text{Margin} \times \text{Turnover}$

PROBLEM SETS

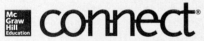

Select problems are available in McGraw-Hill's *Connect.* Please see the Supplements section of the book's frontmatter for more information.

1. Use the following financial statements of Heifer Sports Inc. in Table 14.14 to find Heifer's: *(LO 14-1)*
    a. Inventory turnover ratio.
    b. Debt/equity ratio.
    c. Cash flow from operating activities.
    d. Average collection period.
    e. Asset turnover ratio.
    f. Interest coverage ratio.
    g. Operating profit margin.
    h. Return on equity.
    i. P/E ratio.
    j. Compound leverage ratio.
    k. Net cash provided by operating activities.

2. Use the following cash flow data for Rocket Transport to find Rocket's: *(LO 14-1)*
    a. Net cash provided by or used in investing activities.
    b. Net cash provided by or used in financing activities.
    c. Net increase or decrease in cash for the year.

Cash dividend	$ 80,000
Purchase of bus	33,000
Interest paid on debt	25,000
Sales of old equipment	72,000
Repurchase of stock	55,000
Cash payments to suppliers	95,000
Cash collections from customers	300,000

3. The Crusty Pie Co., which specializes in apple turnovers, has a return on sales higher than the industry average, yet its ROA is the same as the industry average. How can you explain this?   *(LO 14-3)*

4. The ABC Corporation has a profit margin on sales below the industry average, yet its ROA is above the industry average. What does this imply about its asset turnover?   *(LO 14-3)*

5. A company's current ratio is 2. If the company uses cash to retire notes payable due within one year, would this transaction increase or decrease the current ratio? What about the asset turnover ratio?   *(LO 14-1)*

6. Cash flow from investing activities *excludes:*   *(LO 14-1)*
    a. Cash paid for acquisitions.
    b. Cash received from the sale of fixed assets.
    c. Inventory increases due to a new (internally developed) product line.
    d. All of the above.

TABLE 14.14   Heifer Sports financial statements

Income statement	2018	
Sales	$5,500,000	
Cost of goods sold	2,850,000	
Depreciation	280,000	
Selling & administrative expenses	1,500,000	
EBIT	$ 870,000	
Interest expense	130,000	
Taxable income	$ 740,000	
Taxes	330,000	
Net income	$ 410,000	

Balance sheet, year-end	2018	2017
Assets		
Cash	$ 50,000	$ 40,000
Accounts receivable	660,000	690,000
Inventory	490,000	480,000
Total current assets	$1,200,000	$1,210,000
Fixed assets	3,100,000	2,800,000
Total assets	$4,300,000	$4,010,000
Liabilities and shareholders' equity		
Accounts payable	$ 340,000	$ 450,000
Short-term debt	480,000	550,000
Total current liabilities	$ 820,000	$1,000,000
Long-term bonds	2,520,000	2,200,000
Total liabilities	$3,340,000	$3,200,000
Common stock	$ 310,000	$ 310,000
Retained earnings	650,000	500,000
Total shareholders' equity	$ 960,000	810,000
Total liabilities and shareholders' equity	$4,300,000	$4,010,000

7. Cash flow from operating activities *includes:* **(LO 14-1)**
   a. Inventory increases resulting from acquisitions.
   b. Inventory changes due to changing exchange rates.
   c. Interest paid to bondholders.
   d. Dividends paid to stockholders.

8. Recently, Galaxy Corporation lowered its allowance for doubtful accounts by reducing bad debt expense from 2% of sales to 1% of sales. Ignoring taxes, what are the immediate effects on (*a*) operating income and (*b*) operating cash flow? **(LO 14-1)**

Use the following case in answering Problems 9–11: Hatfield Industries is a large manufacturing conglomerate based in the United States with annual sales in excess of $300 million. Hatfield is currently under investigation by the Securities and Exchange Commission (SEC) for accounting irregularities and possible legal violations in the presentation of the company's financial statements. A due-diligence team from the SEC has been sent to Hatfield's corporate headquarters for an audit. The team finds that:

- Management has been involved in ongoing negotiations with the local labor union, of which approximately 40% of its full-time labor force are members. Labor officials are seeking increased wages and pension benefits, which Hatfield's management states is not possible at this time due to decreased profitability and a tight cash flow situation. Labor officials have accused Hatfield's management of manipulating the company's financial statements to justify not granting any wage concessions.
- All new equipment obtained over the past several years has been established on Hatfield's books as operating leases, although past acquisitions of similar equipment were nearly always classified as capital leases. Financial statements of industry peers indicate that capital leases for this type of equipment are the norm. The SEC wants Hatfield's management to provide justification for this apparent deviation from "normal" accounting practices.
- Inventory on Hatfield's books has been steadily increasing for the past few years in comparison to sales growth. Management credits improved operating efficiencies in its production methods that have contributed to boosts in overall production. The SEC wonders whether Hatfield may have manipulated its inventory accounts.

The SEC due-diligence team is not necessarily searching for evidence of fraud but of possible manipulation of accounting standards for the purpose of misleading shareholders and other interested parties. Initial review of Hatfield's financial statements indicates that, at a minimum, certain practices have resulted in low-quality earnings.

9. Labor officials believe that the management of Hatfield is attempting to understate its net income to avoid making any concessions in the labor negotiations. Which of the following actions by management will *most likely* result in low-quality earnings? **(LO 14-4)**
   a. Lengthening the life of a depreciable asset to lower the depreciation expense.
   b. Lowering the discount rate used in the valuation of the company's pension obligations.
   c. The recognition of revenue at the time of delivery rather than when payment is received.

10. Hatfield has begun recording all new equipment leases on its books as operating leases, a change from its consistent past use of capital leases, in which the present value of lease payments is classified as a debt obligation. What is the *most likely* motivation behind Hatfield's change in accounting methodology? Hatfield is attempting to: **(LO 14-4)**
    a. Improve its leverage ratios and reduce its perceived leverage.
    b. Reduce its cost of goods sold and increase its profitability.
    c. Increase its operating margins relative to industry peers.

11. The SEC due-diligence team is searching for the reason behind Hatfield's inventory buildup relative to its sales growth. One way to identify a deliberate manipulation of financial results by Hatfield is to search for: *(LO 14-4)*

    a. A decline in inventory turnover.

    b. Receivables that are growing faster than sales.

    c. A delay in the recognition of expenses.

12. Use the DuPont system and the following data to find return on equity. *(LO 14-3)*

- Leverage ratio   2.2
- Total asset turnover   2.0
- Net profit margin   5.5%
- Dividend payout ratio   31.8%

13. A firm has an ROE of 3%, a debt/equity ratio of 0.5, a tax rate of 20%, and pays an interest rate of 6% on its debt. What is its operating ROA? *(LO 14-2)*

14. A firm has a tax burden ratio of 0.75, a leverage ratio of 1.25, an interest burden of 0.6, and a return on sales of 10%. The firm generates $2.40 in sales per dollar of assets. What is the firm's ROE? *(LO 14-3)*

15. An analyst gathers the following information about Meyer, Inc.:

- Meyer has 1,000 shares of 8% cumulative preferred stock outstanding, with a par value of $100 and liquidation value of $110.
- Meyer has 20,000 shares of common stock outstanding, with a par value of $20.
- Meyer had retained earnings at the beginning of the year of $5,000,000.
- Net income for the year was $70,000.
- This year, for the first time in its history, Meyer paid no dividends on preferred or common stock.

    What is the book value per share of Meyer's common stock? *(LO 14-1)*

16. Here are data on two firms: *(LO 14-2)*

	Equity ($ million)	Debt ($ million)	ROC (%)	Cost of capital (%)
Acme	100	50	17	9
Apex	450	150	15	10

    a. Which firm has the higher economic value added?

    b. Which has higher economic value added per dollar of invested capital?

CFA Problems

1. Jones Group has been generating stable after-tax return on equity (ROE) despite declining operating income. Explain how it might be able to maintain its stable after-tax ROE. *(LO 14-3)*

2. Which of the following *best* explains a ratio of "net sales to average net fixed assets" that *exceeds* the industry average? *(LO 14-3)*

    a. The firm added to its plant and equipment in the past few years.

    b. The firm makes less efficient use of its assets than other firms.

    c. The firm has a lot of old plant and equipment.

    d. The firm uses straight-line depreciation.

3. Use the financial statements for Chicago Refrigerator Inc. (see Tables 14.15 and 14.16) to compute ratios *a* through *h* for 2019. *(LO 14-2)*
   a. Quick ratio.
   b. Return on assets.
   c. Return on common shareholders' equity.
   d. Earnings per share of common stock.
   e. Profit margin.
   f. Times interest earned.
   g. Inventory turnover.
   h. Leverage ratio.

4. Janet Ludlow is a recently hired analyst. After describing the electric toothbrush indus-try, her first report focuses on two companies, QuickBrush Company and SmileWhite Corporation, and concludes:

   QuickBrush is a more profitable company than SmileWhite, as indicated by the 40% sales growth and substantially higher margins it has produced over the last few years. SmileWhite's sales and earnings are growing at a 10% rate and produce much lower margins. We do not think SmileWhite is capable of growing faster than its recent growth rate of 10% whereas QuickBrush can sustain a 30% long-term growth rate. *(LO 14-3)*
   a. Criticize Ludlow's analysis and conclusion that QuickBrush is more profitable, as defined by return on equity (ROE), than SmileWhite and that it has a higher sustain-able growth rate. Use only the information provided in Tables 14.17 and 14.18. Sup-port your criticism by calculating and analyzing:
      • The five components that determine ROE.
      • The two ratios that determine sustainable growth: ROE and plowback.
   b. Explain how QuickBrush has produced an average annual earnings per share (EPS) growth rate of 40% over the last two years with an ROE that has been declining. Use only the information provided in Table 14.17.

5. The information in the following table comes from the 2017 financial statements of QuickBrush Company and SmileWhite Corporation:

Notes to the 2017 Financial Statements		
	QuickBrush	**SmileWhite**
Goodwill	The company amortizes goodwill over 20 years.	The company amortizes goodwill over 5 years.
Property, plant, and equipment	The company uses a straight-line depreciation method over the economic lives of the assets, which range from 5 to 20 years for buildings.	The company uses an accelerated depreciation method over the economic lives of the assets, which range from 5 to 20 years for buildings.
Accounts receivable	The company uses a bad-debt allowance of 2% of accounts receivable.	The company uses a bad-debt allowance of 5% of accounts receivable.

   Determine which company has the higher quality of earnings by discussing *each* of the *three* notes. *(LO 14-4)*

6. Scott Kelly is reviewing MasterToy's financial statements to estimate its sustainable growth rate. Using the information presented in Table 14.19: *(LO 14-3)*
   a. Identify and calculate the components of the DuPont formula.
   b. Calculate the ROE for 2019 using the components of the DuPont formula.
   c. Calculate the sustainable growth rate for 2019 from the firm's ROE and plowback ratios.

TABLE 14.15 Chicago Refrigerator Inc. balance sheet, as of December 31 ($ thousand)

	2018	2019
Assets		
Current assets		
Cash	$ 683	$ 325
Accounts receivable	1,490	3,599
Inventories	1,415	2,423
Prepaid expenses	15	13
Total current assets	$3,603	$6,360
Property, plant, equipment, net	1,066	1,541
Other	123	157
Total assets	$4,792	$8,058
Liabilities		
Current liabilities		
Notes payable to bank	$ —	$ 875
Current portion of long-term debt	38	115
Accounts payable	485	933
Estimated income tax	588	472
Accrued expenses	576	586
Customer advance payment	34	963
Total current liabilities	$1,721	$3,945
Long-term debt	122	179
Other liabilities	81	131
Total liabilities	$1,924	$4,255
Shareholders' equity		
Common stock, $1 par value 1,000,000 shares authorized; 550,000 and 829,000 outstanding, respectively	$ 550	$ 829
Preferred stock, Series A 10%; $25.00 par value; 25,000 authorized; 20,000 and 18,000 outstanding, respectively	500	450
Additional paid-in capital	450	575
Retained earnings	1,368	1,949
Total shareholders' equity	$2,868	$3,803
Total liabilities and shareholders' equity	$4,792	$8,058

TABLE 14.16 Chicago Refrigerator Inc. income statement, years ending December 31 ($ thousand)

	2018	2019
Net sales	$7,570	$12,065
Other income, net	261	345
Total revenues	$7,831	$12,410
Cost of goods sold	$4,850	$ 8,048
General administrative and marketing expenses	1,531	2,025
Interest expense	22	78
Total costs and expenses	$6,403	$10,151
Net income before tax	$1,428	$ 2,259
Income tax	628	994
Net income	$ 800	$ 1,265

TABLE 14.17	Quickbrush Company financial statements: Yearly data ($000 except per-share data)		

Income statement	December 2017	December 2018	December 2019
Revenue	$3,480	$5,400	$7,760
Cost of goods sold	2,700	4,270	6,050
Selling, general, and admin. expense	500	690	1,000
Depreciation and amortization	30	40	50
Operating income (EBIT)	$ 250	$ 400	$ 660
Interest expense	0	0	0
Income before taxes	$ 250	$ 400	$ 660
Income taxes	60	110	215
Income after taxes	$ 190	$ 290	$ 445
Diluted EPS	$ 0.60	$ 0.84	$ 1.18
Average shares outstanding (000)	317	346	376

Financial statistics	December 2017	December 2018	December 2019	3-Year Average
COGS as % of sales	77.59%	79.07%	77.96%	78.24%
General & admin. as % of sales	14.37	12.78	12.89	13.16
Operating margin (%)	7.18	7.41	8.51	
Pretax income/EBIT (%)	100.00	100.00	100.00	
Tax rate (%)	24.00	27.50	32.58	

Balance sheet	December 2017	December 2018	December 2019
Cash and cash equivalents	$ 460	$ 50	$ 480
Accounts receivable	540	720	950
Inventories	300	430	590
Net property, plant, and equipment	760	1,830	3,450
Total assets	$2,060	$3,030	$5,470
Current liabilities	$ 860	$1,110	$1,750
Total liabilities	$ 860	$1,110	$1,750
Stockholders' equity	1,200	1,920	3,720
Total liabilities and equity	$2,060	$3,030	$5,470
Market price per share	$21.00	$30.00	$45.00
Book value per share	$ 3.79	$ 5.55	$ 9.89
Annual dividend per share	$ 0.00	$ 0.00	$ 0.00

7. The DuPont formula defines the net return on shareholders' equity as a function of the following components: *(LO 14-3)*

- Operating margin.
- Asset turnover.
- Interest burden.
- Financial leverage.
- Income tax rate.

TABLE 14.18   Smilewhite Corporation financial statements: Yearly data ($000 except per share data)

Income statement	December 2017	December 2018	December 2019
Revenue	$104,000	$110,400	$119,200
Cost of goods sold	72,800	75,100	79,300
Selling, general, and admin. expense	20,300	22,800	23,900
Depreciation and amortization	4,200	5,600	8,300
Operating income (EBIT)	$ 6,700	$ 6,900	$ 7,700
Interest expense	600	350	350
Income before taxes	$ 6,100	$ 6,550	$ 7,350
Income taxes	2,100	2,200	2,500
Income after taxes	$ 4,000	$ 4,350	$ 4,850
Diluted EPS	$ 2.16	$ 2.35	$ 2.62
Average shares outstanding (000)	1,850	1,850	1,850

Financial statistics	December 2017	December 2018	December 2019	3-Year Average
COGS as % of sales	70.00%	68.00%	66.53%	68.10%
General & admin. as % of sales	19.52	20.64	20.05	20.08
Operating margin (%)	6.44	6.25	6.46	
Pretax income/EBIT (%)	91.04	94.93	95.45	
Tax rate (%)	34.43	33.59	34.01	

Balance sheet	December 2017	December 2018	December 2019
Cash and cash equivalents	$ 7,900	$ 3,300	$ 1,700
Accounts receivable	7,500	8,000	9,000
Inventories	6,300	6,300	5,900
Net property, plant, and equipment	12,000	14,500	17,000
Total assets	$ 33,700	$ 32,100	$ 33,600
Current liabilities	$ 6,200	$ 7,800	$ 6,600
Long-term debt	9,000	4,300	4,300
Total liabilities	$ 15,200	$ 12,100	$ 10,900
Stockholders' equity	18,500	20,000	22,700
Total liabilities and equity	$ 33,700	$ 32,100	$ 33,600
Market price per share	$ 23.00	$ 26.00	$ 30.00
Book value per share	$ 10.00	$ 10.81	$ 12.27
Annual dividend per share	$ 1.42	$ 1.53	$ 1.72

Using *only* the data in Table 14.20:
- *a.* Calculate each of the five components listed above for 2016 and 2019, and calculate the return on equity (ROE) for 2016 and 2019, using all of the five components.
- *b.* Briefly discuss the impact of the changes in asset turnover and financial leverage on the change in ROE from 2016 to 2019.

TABLE 14.19 Mastertoy, Inc.: Actual 2018 and estimated 2019 financial statements for fiscal year ending December 31 ($ million, except per-share data)

	2018	2019
Income statement		
Revenue	$4,750	$5,140
Cost of goods sold	2,400	2,540
Selling, general, and administrative	1,400	1,550
Depreciation	180	210
Goodwill amortization	10	10
Operating income	$ 760	$ 830
Interest expense	20	25
Income before taxes	$ 740	$ 805
Income taxes	265	295
Net income	$ 475	$ 510
Earnings per share	$ 1.79	$ 1.96
Average shares outstanding (millions)	265	260
Balance sheet		
Cash	$ 400	$ 400
Accounts receivable	680	700
Inventories	570	600
Net property, plant, and equipment	800	870
Intangibles	500	530
Total assets	$2,950	$3,100
Current liabilities	$ 550	$ 600
Long-term debt	300	300
Total liabilities	$ 850	$ 900
Stockholders' equity	2,100	2,200
Total liabilities and equity	$2,950	$3,100
Book value per share	$ 7.92	$ 8.46
Annual dividend per share	0.55	0.60

TABLE 14.20 Income statements and balance sheets

	2016	2019
Income statement data		
Revenues	$542	$979
Operating income	$ 38	$ 76
Depreciation and amortization	3	9
Interest expense	3	0
Pretax income	$ 32	$ 67
Income taxes	13	37
Net income after tax	$ 19	$ 30
Balance sheet data		
Fixed assets	$ 41	$ 70
Total assets	245	291
Working capital	123	157
Total debt	16	0
Total shareholders' equity	159	220

WEB *master*

1. Go to **finance.yahoo.com** to find information about Vulcan Materials Company (VMC), Southwest Airlines (LUV), Honda Motor Company (HMC), Nordstrom, Inc. (JWN), and Abbott Laboratories (ABT). Download the most recent income statement and balance sheet for each company.

   a. Calculate the operating profit margin (operating profit/sales) and the asset turnover (sales/assets) for each firm.

   b. Calculate the return on assets directly (ROA = Operating profit/Total assets), and then confirm it by calculating ROA = Operating margin × Asset turnover.

   c. In what industries do these firms operate? Do the ratios make sense when you consider the industry types?

   d. For the firms that have relatively low ROAs, does the source of the problem seem to be the operating profit margin, the asset turnover, or both?

   e. Calculate the return on equity (ROE = Net income/Equity) for each firm. For the two firms with the lowest ROEs, perform a DuPont analysis to isolate the source(s) of the problem.

2. Answer the following questions for these two toy and game companies: Mattel (MAT) and Hasbro (HAS). You can find the relevant information at **finance.yahoo.com.**

   a. Retrieve the latest annual balance sheet for each company. Calculate the common-size percentages for the balance sheet in the new column.

   b. Compare the firms' investments in accounts receivable; inventory; and net plant, property, and equipment. Which firm has more invested in these items on a percentage basis?

   c. Compare the firms' investments in current liabilities and long-term liabilities. Does one firm have a significantly higher burden in either of these areas?

   d. Analyze the firms' capital structures by examining the debt ratios and the percentages of preferred and common equity. How much do the firms' capital structures differ from each other?

3. Select a company of interest to you and link to its annual cash flow statement under the company's *Financials* tab. Answer the following questions about the firm's cash flow activities.

   a. Did the firm have positive or negative cash flow from operations?

   b. Did the firm invest in or sell off long-term investments?

   c. What were the major sources of financing for the firm?

   d. What was the net change in cash?

   e. Did exchange rates have any effect on the firm's cash flows?

   Now answer these questions:

   f. How liquid is the firm?

   g. How well is the firm using its assets?

   h. How effectively is the firm using leverage?

   i. Is the firm profitable?

SOLUTIONS TO
CONCEPT
checks

14.1   A debt/equity ratio of 1 implies that Mordett will have $50 million of debt and $50 million of equity. Interest expense will be .09 × $50 million, or $4.5 million per year. Mordett's net profits and ROE over the business cycle will therefore be:

Scenario	EBIT	Nodett Net Profits	Nodett ROE	Mordett Net Profits*	Mordett ROE†
Bad year	$5M	$4M	4%	$0.4M	0.8%
Normal year	10	8	8	4.4	8.8
Good year	15	12	12	8.4	16.8%

*Mordett's after-tax profits are given by: (1 − .2)(EBIT − $4.5 million).

†Mordett's equity is only $50 million, so ROE = net profits/$50 million.

14.2 Ratio decomposition analysis for Mordett Corporation:

Year	ROE	(1) Net Profit / Pretax Profit	(2) Pretax Profit / EBIT	(3) EBIT / Sales (Margin)	(4) Sales / Assets (Turnover)	(5) Assets / Equity	(6) Compound Leverage Factor (2) × (5)
a. Bad year							
Nodett	0.040	0.8	1.000	0.0625	0.800	1.000	1.000
Somdett	0.024	0.8	0.360	0.0625	0.800	1.667	0.600
Mordett	0.008	0.8	0.100	0.0625	0.800	2.000	0.200
b. Normal year							
Nodett	0.080	0.8	1.000	0.100	1.000	1.000	1.000
Somdett	0.091	0.8	0.680	0.100	1.000	1.667	1.134
Mordett	0.088	0.8	0.550	0.100	1.000	2.000	1.100
c. Good year							
Nodett	0.120	0.8	1.000	0.125	1.200	1.000	1.000
Somdett	0.157	0.8	0.787	0.125	1.200	1.667	1.311
Mordett	0.168	0.8	0.700	0.125	1.200	2.000	1.400

14.3 GI's ROE was 3.03%, computed as follows:

$$\text{ROE} = \frac{\$5,285}{.5(\$171,843 + \$177,128)} = .0303, \text{ or } 3.03\%$$

Its P/E ratio was $21/$5.285 = 4, and its P/B ratio was $21/$177 = .12. Its earnings yield was 25% compared with an industry average of 12.5%.

Note that in our calculations the P/E does not equal (P/B)/ROE because (following common practice) we have computed ROE with *average* shareholders' equity in the denominator and P/B with *end*-of-year shareholders' equity in the denominator.

14.4 IBX ratio analysis:

ROE increased despite a decline in operating margin and a decline in the tax burden ratio because of increased leverage and turnover. Note that ROA declined from 11.65% in 2018 to 10.65% in 2021.

Year	ROE	(1) Net Profit / Pretax Profit	(2) Pretax Profit / EBIT	(3) EBIT / Sales (Margin)	(4) Sales / Assets (Turnover)	(5) Assets / Equity	(6) Compound Leverage Factor (2) × (5)	(7) ROA (3) × (4)
2021	11.4%	0.616	0.796	7.75%	1.375	2.175	1.731	10.65%
2018	10.2	0.636	0.932	8.88	1.311	1.474	1.374	11.65

14.5 LIFO accounting results in lower reported earnings than does FIFO. Fewer assets to depreciate result in lower reported earnings because there is less bias associated with the use of historic cost. More debt results in lower reported earnings because the inflation premium in the interest rate is treated as part of interest.

Derivative Markets

Horror stories about large losses incurred by high-flying traders in derivatives markets periodically become a staple of the evening news. Indeed, there were some amazing losses to report in the last decade: several totaling hundreds of millions of dollars, and a few amounting to more than a billion. Among the most notorious of these were the loss of $7.2 billion in equity futures contracts by Société Générale in January 2008 and the loss of more than $100 billion on positions in credit derivatives by American International Group that resulted in a massive government bailout in September 2008. In the wake of these debacles, some venerable institutions have gone under, notable among them Barings Bank, which once helped the U.S. finance the Louisiana Purchase and the British Empire finance the Napoleonic Wars.

These stories, while important, fascinating, and even occasionally scandalous, often miss the point. Derivatives, when misused, can indeed provide a quick path to insolvency. Used properly, however, they are potent tools for risk management and control. In fact, you will discover in these chapters that one firm was sued for *failing* to use derivatives to hedge price risk. One article in *The Wall Street Journal* on hedging applications using derivatives was entitled "Index Options Touted as Providing Peace of Mind." Hardly material for bankruptcy court or the *National Enquirer*.

Derivatives provide a means to control risk that is qualitatively different from the techniques traditionally considered in portfolio theory. In contrast to the mean-variance analysis we discussed in Parts Two and Three, derivatives allow investors to change the *shape* of the probability distribution of investment returns. An entirely new approach to risk management follows from this insight.

The following chapters will explore how derivatives can be used as parts of a well-designed portfolio strategy. We will examine some popular portfolio strategies utilizing these securities and take a look at how derivatives are valued.

Learning Objectives

LO 15-1 Calculate the profit to various option positions as a function of ultimate security prices.

LO 15-2 Formulate option strategies to modify portfolio risk-return attributes.

LO 15-3 Identify embedded options in various securities and determine how option characteristics affect the prices of those securities.

Derivative securities, or simply *derivatives,* play a large and increasingly important role in financial markets. These are securities whose prices are determined by, or "derive from," the prices of other securities.

Options and futures contracts are both derivative securities. Their payoffs depend on the value of other securities. Swap contracts, which we will discuss in Chapter 17, also are derivatives. Because the values of derivatives depend on the values of other securities, they can be powerful tools for both hedging and speculation. We will investigate these applications in the next three chapters, beginning in this chapter with options.

Trading of standardized options on a national exchange started in 1973 when the Chicago Board Options Exchange (CBOE) began listing call options. These contracts were almost immediately a great success,

crowding out the previously existing over-the-counter options market.

Options contracts now are traded on several exchanges. They are written on common stock, stock indexes, foreign exchange, agricultural commodities, precious metals, and interest rates. In addition, the over-the-counter market also has enjoyed a tremendous resurgence in recent years as its trading in custom-tailored options has exploded. Popular and potent for modifying portfolio characteristics, options have become essential tools that every portfolio manager must understand.

This chapter is an introduction to options markets. It explains how puts and calls work and examines their investment characteristics. Popular option strategies are considered next. Finally, we will examine a range of securities with embedded options such as callable or convertible bonds.

15.1 THE OPTION CONTRACT

A **call option** gives its holder the right to purchase an asset for a specified price, called the **exercise or strike price,** on or before some specified expiration date. For example, a July 7 call option on shares of Microsoft with exercise price $72 entitles its owner to purchase Microsoft for a price of $72 at any time up to and including the expiration date in July. The holder of the call is not required to exercise it. She will exercise her option to buy only if Microsoft's share price exceeds the strike price. If the share price remains below the strike price, the option will be left unexercised. If not exercised before the expiration date, a call option simply expires and becomes valueless. Therefore, if the stock price is greater than the exercise price on the expiration date, the call value equals the difference between the stock price and the exercise price; but if the stock price is less than the exercise price, the call expires worthless. The *net profit* on the call is the value of the option minus the price originally paid to purchase it.

The purchase price of the option is called the **premium.** It represents the compensation the call buyer pays for the ability to exercise only when exercise is desirable.

Sellers of call options, who are said to *write* calls, receive premium income now as payment against the possibility they will be required at some later date to deliver the asset in return for an exercise price less than the market value of the asset. If the option is left to expire worthless, the call writer clears a profit equal to the premium collected when the option was initially sold. But if the call is exercised, the option writer's profit is the premium income *minus* the difference between the value of the stock that must be delivered and the exercise price that is paid for those shares. If that difference is larger than the initial premium, the writer will incur a loss.

call option

The right to buy an asset at a specified exercise price on or before a specified expiration date.

exercise or strike price

Price set for calling (buying) an asset or putting (selling) an asset.

premium

Purchase price of an option.

Consider the July 2017 expiration call option on a share of Microsoft with an exercise price of $72 selling on June 2, 2017, for $1.15. Until the expiration date, the call holder may exercise the option to buy shares of Microsoft for $72. Because the stock price on June 2 is only $71.75, it clearly would not make sense at the moment to exercise the option to buy at $72. Indeed, if Microsoft remains below $72 by the expiration date, the call will be left to expire worthless. On the other hand, if Microsoft is selling above $72 at expiration, the call holder will find it optimal to exercise. For example, if Microsoft sells for $73 on July 7, the option will be exercised, as it will give its holder the right to pay $72 for a stock worth $73. The value of each option on the expiration date would then be

EXAMPLE 15.1

Profits and Losses on a Call Option

$$\text{Value at expiration} = \text{Stock price} - \text{Exercise price} = \$73 - \$72 = \$1$$

Despite the $1 payoff at expiration, the call holder still realizes a loss of $0.15 on the investment because the initial purchase price was $1.15:

$$\text{Profit} = \text{Final value} - \text{Original investment} = \$1.00 - \$1.15 = -\$.15$$

Nevertheless, exercise of the call is optimal at expiration if the stock price exceeds the exercise price because the exercise proceeds will offset at least part of the purchase price. The call buyer will clear a profit if Microsoft is selling above $73.15 at the expiration date. At that stock price, the net proceeds from exercise will just cover the original cost of the call.

A **put option** gives its holder the right to *sell* an asset for a specified exercise or strike price on or before some expiration date. A July expiration put on Microsoft with an exercise price of $72 entitles its owner to sell Microsoft stock to the put writer for $72 even if the market price of Microsoft is less than that amount. Whereas profits on call options increase when the asset price rises, profits on put options increase when the asset price *falls.* A put will be exercised only if the price of the underlying asset is less than the exercise price, that is, only if its holder can deliver for the exercise price an asset with a lower market value. (One doesn't need to own the shares of Microsoft to exercise the put option. Upon exercise, the investor's broker purchases the necessary shares of Microsoft at the market price and immediately delivers, or

put option

The right to sell an asset at a specified exercise price on or before a specified expiration date.

"puts them," to an option writer for the exercise price. The owner of the put profits by the difference between the exercise price and market price.)

EXAMPLE 15.2 *Profits and Losses on a Put Option*	Now consider the July 2017 expiration put option on Microsoft with an exercise price of $72, selling on June 2 for $1.32. It entitled its owner to *sell* a share of Microsoft for $72 at any time until July 7. If the holder of the put buys a share of Microsoft and immediately exercises the right to sell it at $72, the exercise proceeds will be $72 − $71.75 = $.25. Obviously, an investor who pays $1.32 for the put has no intention of exercising it immediately. If, on the other hand, Microsoft is selling for $70 at expiration, the put will turn out to be a profitable investment. Its value at expiration will be Value at expiration = Exercise price − Stock price = $72 − $70 = $2 and the investor's profit will be $2 − $1.32 = $.68. This is a holding period return of $.68/$1.32 = .515 or 51.5%—over only 35 days! Obviously, put option sellers on June 2 (who are on the other side of the transaction) did not consider this outcome very likely.

---

in the money

An option where exercise would generate a positive cash flow.

out of the money

An option which, if exercised, would produce a negative cash flow. Out-of-the-money options are therefore never exercised.

at the money

An option where the exercise price equals the asset price.

An option is described as **in the money** when its exercise would produce a positive cash flow. Therefore, a call option is in the money when the asset price exceeds the exercise price, and a put option is in the money when the asset price is less than the exercise price. Conversely, a call is **out of the money** when the exercise price exceeds the asset value; no one would exercise the right to pay the exercise price for a stock with a market value less than that amount. A put option is out of the money when the exercise price is less than the asset price. Options are **at the money** when the exercise price and asset price are equal.

Options Trading

Some options trade on over-the-counter (OTC) markets. The OTC market offers the advantage that the terms of the option contract—the exercise price, expiration date, and number of shares committed—can be tailored to the needs of the traders. The costs of establishing an OTC option contract, however, are relatively high. Today, most option trading occurs on organized exchanges.

Options contracts traded on exchanges are standardized by allowable expiration dates and exercise prices for each listed option. Each stock option contract provides for the right to buy or sell 100 shares of stock (except when stock splits occur after the contract is listed and the contract is adjusted for the terms of the split).

Standardization of the terms of listed option contracts means all market participants trade in a limited and uniform set of securities. This increases the depth of trading in any particular option, which lowers trading costs and increases market liquidity.

Most options trading in the U.S. initially took place on the Chicago Board Options Exchange. However, by 2003 the electronic International Securities Exchange had displaced the CBOE as the largest options market.

Figure 15.1 is a small sample of listed stock option quotations for Microsoft on June 2, 2017. The most recent price for the company's stock was $71.75 per share.[1] Figure 15.1 includes options with exercise prices of $70, $72, and $74. These values also are called the *strike prices*.

These exercise or strike prices bracket the stock price.[2] If the stock price moves outside the range of exercise prices of the existing set of options, new options with appropriate exercise prices may be offered. Therefore, at any time, both in-the-money and out-of-the-money options will be listed, as in this figure.

---

[1]Occasionally, this price may not match the closing price listed for the stock on the stock market page. This is because some NYSE stocks also trade on exchanges that close after the NYSE, and the stock pages may reflect the more recent closing price. The options exchanges, however, close with the NYSE, so the closing NYSE stock price is appropriate for comparison with the closing option price.

[2]If a stock splits, the terms of the option—such as the exercise price—are adjusted to offset the impact of the split.

Microsoft (MSFT)		Underlying stock price = $71.75	
Expiration	Strike	Call	Put
June 16, 2017	70	2.02	0.24
June 16, 2017	72	0.67	0.90
June 16, 2017	74	0.13	2.37
July 7, 2017	70	2.40	0.58
July 7, 2017	72	1.15	1.32
July 7, 2017	74	0.42	2.59

FIGURE 15.1

Options on Microsoft, June 2, 2017

Source: *The Wall Street Journal Online*, June 2, 2017.

Figure 15.1 shows both call and put options listed for each exercise price and expiration date. When we compare the prices of call options with the same expiration date but different exercise prices, we see that the value of the call is lower when the exercise price is higher. This makes sense, for the right to purchase a share is not as valuable when the purchase price is higher. Thus, the July expiration call option with strike price of $70 sells for $2.40, while the $74 exercise price July call sells for only $0.42. Conversely, put options are worth *more* when the exercise price is higher: You would rather have the right to sell shares for $74 than for $70, and this is reflected in the prices of the puts. The July expiration put option with strike price $74 sells for $2.59, while the $70 exercise price July put sells for only $0.58.

Not infrequently, you will find some options that go an entire day without trading. Because trading in any particular option can be sporadic, it is not unusual to find option prices that appear out of line with other prices. You might see, for example, two calls with different exercise prices that seem to sell for the same price. This discrepancy arises because the last trades for these options may have occurred at different times during the day. At any moment, the call with the lower exercise price must be worth more, and the put less, than an otherwise-identical call or put with a higher exercise price.

Expirations of most exchange-traded options tend to be fairly short, ranging up to only several months. For larger firms and several stock indexes, however, longer-term options are traded with expirations ranging up to three years. These options are called LEAPS (for Long-term Equity AnticiPation Securities).

CONCEPT check 15.1

a. What will be the proceeds and net profits to an investor who purchases the July 2017 expiration Microsoft calls with exercise price $72 if the stock price at option expiration is $70? What if the stock price at expiration is $74?

b. Now answer part (*a*) for an investor who purchases the July expiration put option with exercise price $72.

American and European Options

An **American option** allows its holder to exercise the right to purchase (if a call) or sell (if a put) the underlying asset on or *before* the expiration date. **European options** allow for exercise of the option only on the expiration date. American-style options, because they allow more leeway than their European-style counterparts, generally will be more valuable. Most traded options in the U.S. are American style. Foreign currency options and some stock-index options are notable exceptions to this rule, however.

American option

Can be exercised on or before its expiration.

European option

Can be exercised only at expiration.

The Option Clearing Corporation

The Option Clearing Corporation (OCC), the clearinghouse for options trading, is jointly owned by the exchanges on which stock options are traded. The OCC places itself between options traders, becoming the effective buyer of the option from the writer and the effective writer of the option to the buyer. All individuals, therefore, deal only with the OCC, which effectively guarantees contract performance.

When an option holder exercises an option, the OCC arranges for a member firm with clients who have written that option to make good on the option obligation. The member firm selects from among its clients who have written that option to fulfill the contract. The selected client must deliver 100 shares of stock at a price equal to the exercise price for each call option contract written or must purchase 100 shares at the exercise price for each put option contract written.

Because the OCC guarantees contract performance, it requires option writers to post margin to guarantee that they can fulfill their obligations. The margin required is determined in part by the amount by which the option is in the money, because "moneyness" indicates the potential obligation of the option writer. Out-of-the-money options require less margin from the writer, for expected payouts are lower. When the required margin exceeds the posted margin, the writer will receive a margin call. The *holder* of the option need not post margin because the holder will exercise the option only if it is advantageous to do so. Once the option is purchased, no further money is at risk.

Margin requirements also depend on whether the underlying asset is held in portfolio. For example, a call option writer owning the stock against which the option is written can satisfy the margin requirement simply by allowing a broker to hold that stock in the brokerage account. The stock is then guaranteed to be available for delivery should the call option be exercised.

Other Listed Options

Options on assets other than stocks also are widely traded. These include options on market indexes and industry indexes, on foreign currency, and even on the futures prices of agricultural products, gold, silver, fixed-income securities, and stock indexes. We will discuss these in turn.

INDEX OPTIONS An index option is a call or put based on a stock market index such as the S&P 500. Index options are traded on several broad-based indexes as well as on several industry-specific indexes. We discussed many of these indexes in Chapter 2.

Options contracts on many foreign stock indexes also trade. For example, options on the Nikkei Stock Index of Japanese stocks trade on the Singapore as well as the Chicago Mercantile Exchange. Options on European indexes such as the Financial Times Share Exchange (FTSE 100) trade on the NYSE-Euronext exchange. The Chicago Board Options Exchange also lists options on industry indexes such as the oil or high-tech industries.

In contrast to stock options, index options do not require that the call writer actually "deliver the index" upon exercise or that the put writer "purchase the index." Instead, a cash settlement procedure is used. The payoff that would accrue upon exercise of the option is calculated, and the option writer simply pays that amount to the option holder. The payoff is equal to the difference between the exercise price of the option and the value of the index. For example, if the S&P index is at 2,480 when a call option on the index with exercise price 2,470 is exercised, the holder of the call receives a cash payment equal to the difference, 2,480 − 2,470, times the contract multiplier of $100, or $1,000 per contract.

Options on the S&P 100 contract, often called the OEX after its ticker symbol, the S&P 500 Index (the SPX), and the Dow Jones Industrials (the DJX), are by far the most actively traded contracts on the CBOE. Together, these contracts dominate CBOE volume.

FUTURES OPTIONS Futures options give their holders the right to buy or sell a specified futures contract, using as a futures price the exercise price of the option. Although the delivery process is slightly complicated, the terms of futures options contracts are designed in effect to allow the option to be written on the futures price itself. The option holder receives upon exercise the difference between the current futures price and the exercise price of the option. Thus, if the futures price is, say, $37, and the call has an exercise price of $35, the holder who exercises the call option on the futures gets a payoff of $2.

FOREIGN CURRENCY OPTIONS A currency option offers the right to buy or sell a specified quantity of foreign currency for a specified number of U.S. dollars. Contracts are quoted in cents or fractions of a cent per unit of foreign currency.

There is an important difference between currency options and currency *futures* options. The former provide payoffs that depend on the difference between the exercise price and the exchange rate at expiration. The latter provide payoffs that depend on the difference between the exercise price and the exchange rate *futures price*. Because exchange rates and exchange rate futures prices generally are not equal, the options and futures options contracts will have different values, even with identical expiration dates and exercise prices. Trading volume in currency futures options dominates by far trading in currency options.

INTEREST RATE OPTIONS Options also are traded on Treasury notes and bonds, Treasury bills, and government bonds of other major economies such as the U.K. or Japan. Options on several interest rates also trade. Among them are contracts on Treasury bond, Treasury note, federal funds, LIBOR, and British and euro-denominated yields.

15.2　VALUES OF OPTIONS AT EXPIRATION

Call Options

Recall that a call option gives the right to purchase a security at the exercise price. If you hold a call on FinCorp stock with an exercise price of $80, and FinCorp is now selling at $90, you can exercise your option to purchase the stock at $80 and simultaneously sell the shares at the market price of $90, clearing $10 per share. Yet if the shares sell below $80, you can sit on the option and do nothing, realizing no further gain or loss. The value of the call option at expiration equals

$$\text{Payoff to call holder at expiration} = \begin{cases} S_T - X & \text{if } S_T > X \\ 0 & \text{if } S_T \leq X \end{cases}$$

where S_T is the value of the stock at the expiration date and X is the exercise price. This formula emphasizes the option property because the payoff cannot be negative. The call is exercised only if S_T exceeds X. If S_T is less than X, the option expires with zero value. The loss to the option holder in this case equals the price originally paid. More generally, the *profit* to the option holder is the option payoff minus the original purchase price.

The value at expiration of the call with exercise price $80 is given by the following schedule:

Stock price	$60	$70	$80	$90	$100
Option value	0	0	0	10	20

For stock prices at or below $80, the option expires worthless. Above $80, the option is worth the excess of the stock price over $80. The option's value increases by one dollar for each dollar increase in the stock price. This relationship is depicted in Figure 15.2.

The solid line is the value of the call at expiration. The net *profit* equals the gross payoff less the initial price of the call. Suppose the call cost $14. Then the profit to the call holder would be the dashed (bottom) line of Figure 15.2. At option expiration, the investor suffers a loss of $14 if the stock price is less than or equal to $80.

Profits do not become positive until the stock price at expiration exceeds $94. At that price the payoff to the call, $S_T - X = \$94 - \$80 = \$14$, equals the cost paid to acquire it. Hence, the call holder shows a profit only if the stock price is higher.

Conversely, the writer of the call incurs losses if the stock price is high. In that scenario, the writer will be obligated to deliver a stock worth S_T for only X dollars.

$$\text{Payoff to call writer} = \begin{cases} -(S_T - X) & \text{if } S_T > X \\ 0 & \text{if } S_T \leq X \end{cases}$$

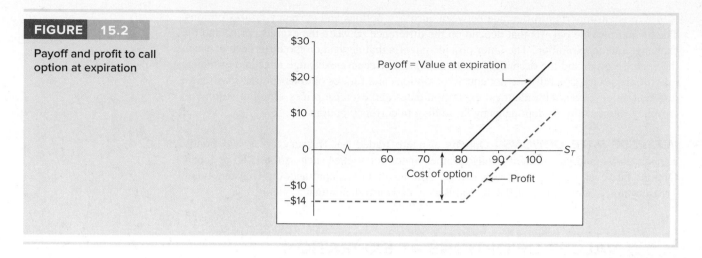

FIGURE 15.2

Payoff and profit to call option at expiration

The call writer, who is exposed to losses if the stock price increases, is willing to bear this risk in return for the option premium.

Figure 15.3 shows the payoff and profit diagrams for the call writer. These are the mirror images of the corresponding diagrams for call holders. The break-even point for the option writer also is $94. The (negative) payoff at that point just offsets the premium originally received when the option was written.

Put Options

A put option conveys the right to sell an asset at the exercise price. In this case, the holder will not exercise unless the asset price is *less* than the exercise price. For example, if FinCorp shares fall to $70, a put option with exercise price $80 can be exercised to give a $10 payoff. The holder would purchase a share for $70 and simultaneously deliver it to the put option writer for the exercise price of $80.

The value of a put option at expiration is

$$\text{Payoff to put holder} = \begin{cases} 0 & \text{if } S_T \geq X \\ X - S_T & \text{if } S_T < X \end{cases}$$

The solid line in Figure 15.4 plots the payoff at expiration on a FinCorp put with an exercise price of $80. If the stock price at option expiration is above $80, the put has no value, as the right to sell the shares at $80 would not be exercised. Below a price of $80, the put value at expiration increases by $1 for each dollar the stock price falls. The dashed line plots the put option owner's profit at expiration, net of the initial cost of the put.

FIGURE 15.3

Payoff and profit to call writers at expiration

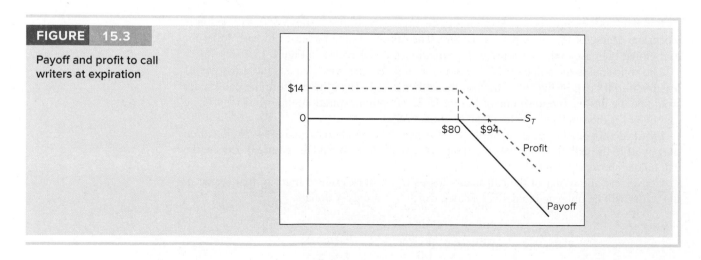

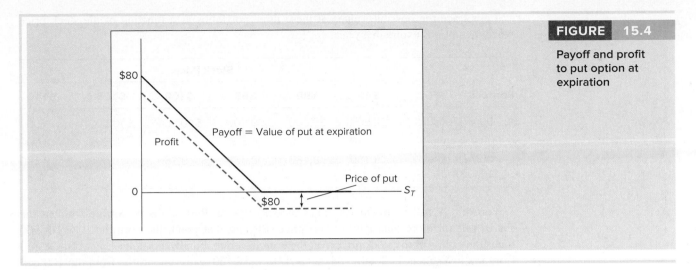

FIGURE 15.4

Payoff and profit to put option at expiration

Writing puts *naked* (i.e., writing a put without an offsetting short position in the stock) exposes the writer to losses if the market falls. Writing naked, deep out-of-the-money puts was once considered an attractive way to generate income: as long as the market did not fall sharply before the option expiration, the option premium could be collected without the put holder ever exercising the option against the writer. Because the put would remain out of the money unless the market fell sharply, the strategy was not viewed as overly risky. However, in the wake of the market crash of October 1987, such put writers suffered huge losses. Participants now perceive much greater risk to this strategy.

Consider these four option strategies: (i) buy a call; (ii) write a call; (iii) buy a put; (iv) write a put.
a. For each strategy, plot both the payoff and profit diagrams as a function of the final stock price.
b. Why might one characterize both buying calls and writing puts as "bullish" strategies? What is the difference between them?
c. Why might one characterize both buying puts and writing calls as "bearish" strategies? What is the difference between them?

CONCEPT check **15.2**

Options versus Stock Investments

Purchasing call options is a bullish strategy; that is, the calls provide profits when stock prices increase. Purchasing puts, in contrast, is a bearish strategy. Symmetrically, writing calls is bearish, while writing puts is bullish. Because option values depend on the price of the underlying stock, the purchase of options may be viewed as a substitute for direct purchase or sale of a stock. Why might an option strategy be preferable to direct stock transactions? We can begin to answer this question by comparing the values of option versus stock positions in FinCorp.

Suppose you believe the stock will increase in value from its current level, which we assume is $90. You know your analysis could be incorrect, however, and the share price also could fall. Suppose a one-year maturity call option with exercise price of $90 sells for $10 and the interest rate is 2%. Consider the following three strategies for investing a sum of $9,000. Suppose the firm will not pay any dividends until after the options expire.

Strategy *A:* Invest entirely in stock. Buy 100 shares, each selling for $90.

Strategy *B:* Invest entirely in at-the-money call options. Buy 900 calls, each selling for $10. (This would require 9 contracts, each for 100 shares.)

Strategy *C:* Purchase 100 call options for $1,000. Invest the remaining $8,000 in one-year T-bills, to earn 2% interest.

Let's trace the possible values of these three portfolios as a function of the stock price when the options expire in a year.

	Stock Price					
Portfolio	$85	$90	$95	$100	$105	$110
A: 100 shares stock	$8,500	$9,000	$9,500	$10,000	$10,500	$11,000
B: 900 call options	0	0	4,500	9,000	13,500	18,000
C: 100 calls plus $8,000 in T-bills	8,160	8,160	8,660	9,160	9,660	10,160

Portfolio A will be worth 100 times the share price. Portfolio B is worthless unless the shares sell for more than the exercise price. Beyond that point, the portfolio is worth 900 times the excess of the stock price over the exercise price. Finally, portfolio C is worth $8,160 from the investment in T-bills ($8,000 × 1.02 = $8,160) plus any profits from the 100 call options. Remember that each of these portfolios involves the same $9,000 initial investment. The rates of return on these three portfolios are as follows:

	Stock Price					
Portfolio	$85	$90	$95	$100	$105	$110
A: 100 shares stock	−5.56%	0.0%	5.56%	11.11%	16.67%	22.22%
B: 900 call options	−100.0	−100.0	−50.00	0.0	50.0	100.0
C: 100 calls plus $8,000 in T-bills	−9.33	−9.33	−3.78	1.78	7.33	12.89

These rates of return are graphed in Figure 15.5.

Comparing the returns of portfolios B and C to those of the simple investment in stock represented by portfolio A, we see that options offer two interesting features. First, an option offers leverage. Compare the returns of portfolios B and A. When the stock fares poorly, ending anywhere below $90, the value of portfolio B falls precipitously to zero—a rate of return of negative 100%. Conversely, modest increases in the rate of return on the stock result in disproportionate increases in the option rate of return. For example, a 4.8% increase in the stock price from $105 to $110 would increase the rate of return on the call from 50% to 100%.

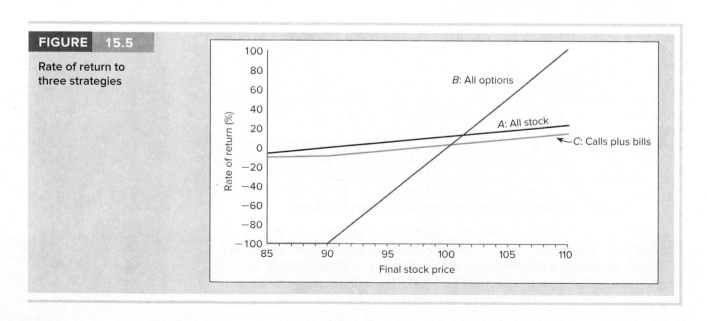

FIGURE 15.5

Rate of return to three strategies

An Excel model based on the FinCorp example discussed in the text is shown below. The model allows you to use any variety of options, stock, and lending or borrowing with a set investment amount and demonstrates the investment flexibility of options.

	A	B	C	D	E	F	G	H
1	Current stock price	90						
2	Exercise price	90						
3	Interest rate	0.02						
4	Investment budget	9000						
5	Call price	10						
6								
7			Dollar value of portfolio as a function of FinCorp price					
8	**Portfolio**		**$85**	**$90**	**$95**	**$100**	**$105**	**$110**
9	Portfolio A: All stock		$8,500	$9,000	$9,500	$10,000	$10,500	$11,000
10	Portfolio B: All call options		0	0	4,500	9,000	13,500	18,000
11	Portfolio C: Call plus bills		8,160	8,160	8,660	9,160	9,660	10,160
12								
13								
14			Rate of return as a function of FinCorp price					
15	**Portfolio**		**$85**	**$90**	**$95**	**$100**	**$105**	**$110**
16	Portfolio A: All stock		−5.6%	0.00%	5.6%	11.1%	16.7%	22.2%
17	Portfolio B: All call options		−100.0%	−100.0%	−50.0%	0.0%	50.0%	100.0%
18	Portfolio C: Call plus bills		−9.33%	−9.33%	−3.78%	1.78%	7.33%	12.89%

Excel Questions

1. Plot the rate of return to the call-plus-bills strategy using a diagram like that in Figure 15.5 but now assuming the investor uses an in-the-money call option with a strike price of $80. Assume the calls sell for $15. The higher cost for these calls compared to the at-the-money calls will result in less money being placed in T-bills because the investment budget is still $9,000.

2. Compare the plots of rate of return for the strategies using at-the-money calls (as in Figure 15.5) and your solution to Question 1. Which strategy is riskier?

In this sense, calls are a levered investment on the stock. Their values respond more than proportionately to changes in the stock value.

Figure 15.5 vividly illustrates this point. For stock prices above $90, the slope of the all-option portfolio is far steeper than that of the all-stock portfolio, reflecting its greater proportional sensitivity to the value of the underlying security. The leverage factor is the reason that investors (illegally) exploiting inside information commonly choose options as their investment vehicle.

The potential insurance value of options is the second interesting feature, as portfolio *C* shows. The T-bill-plus-option portfolio cannot be worth less than $8,160 after six months, as the option can always be left to expire worthless. The worst possible rate of return on portfolio *C* is −9.33%, compared to a (theoretically) worst possible rate of return on the stock of −100%. Of course, this insurance comes at a price: When the share price rises above $90, portfolio *C* underperforms portfolio *A,* the all-stock portfolio, by about 9.33 percentage points.

This simple example makes an important point. While options can be used by speculators as effectively leveraged stock positions, as in portfolio *B,* they also can be used by investors who desire to tailor their risk exposures in creative ways, as in portfolio *C.* For example, the call-plus-T-bills strategy of portfolio *C* provides a rate of return profile quite unlike that of the stock alone. The absolute limitation on downside risk is a novel and attractive feature of this strategy. In the next section, we will discuss several option strategies that provide other novel risk profiles that might be attractive to hedgers and other investors.

15.3 OPTION STRATEGIES

An unlimited variety of payoff patterns can be achieved by combining puts and calls with various exercise prices. Below we explain the motivation and structure of some of the more popular strategies.

TABLE 15.1	Payoff to protective put strategy	
	$S_T \leq X$	$S_T > X$
Stock	S_T	S_T
Put	$X - S_T$	0
Total	X	S_T

PROTECTIVE PUT Imagine you would like to invest in a stock but you are unwilling to bear potential losses beyond some given level. Investing in the stock alone seems risky to you because in principle you could lose all the money you invest. You might consider instead investing in stock and purchasing a put option on the stock.

Table 15.1 shows the total value of your portfolio at option expiration. Whatever happens to the stock price, you are guaranteed a payoff at least equal to the put option's exercise price because the put gives you the right to sell the share for the exercise price even if the stock price is below that value.

Figure 15.6 illustrates the payoff and profit to this **protective put** strategy. The solid line in Figure 15.6C is the total payoff. The dashed line is displaced downward by the cost of establishing the position, $S_0 + P$. Notice that potential losses are limited.

protective put

An asset combined with a put option that guarantees minimum proceeds equal to the put's exercise price.

FIGURE   15.6

Value of a protective put position at expiration

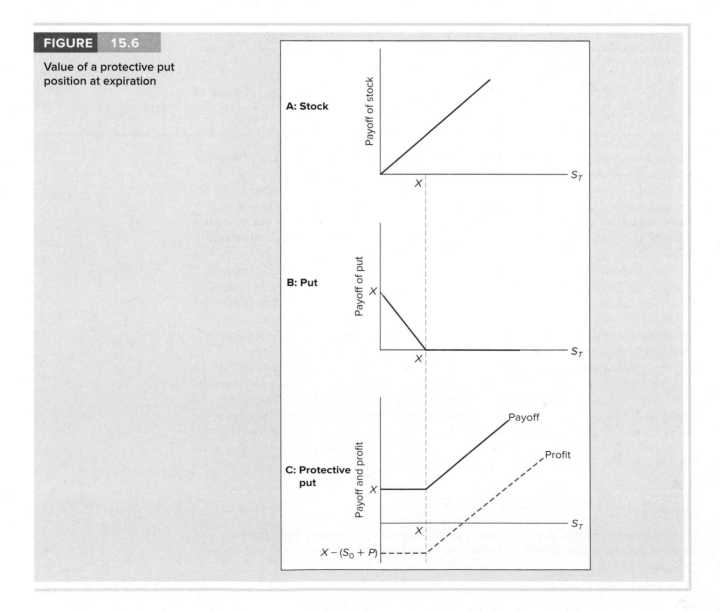

EXAMPLE 15.3

Protective Put

Suppose the strike price is $X = \$90$ and the stock is selling for $87 at option expiration. Then the value of your total portfolio is $90: The stock is worth $87 and the value of the expiring put option is

$$X - S_T = \$90 - \$87 = \$3$$

Another way to look at it is that you are holding the stock and a put contract giving you the right to sell it for $90. Even if $S_T < \$90$, you can still sell the stock for $90 by exercising the put. On the other hand, if the stock price is above $90, say, $94, then the right to sell a share at $90 is worthless. You allow the put to expire unexercised, ending up with a share of stock worth $S_T = \$94$.

It is instructive to compare the profit on the protective put strategy with that of the stock investment. For simplicity, consider an at-the-money protective put, so that $X = S_0$. Figure 15.7 compares the profits for the two strategies. The profit on the stock is zero if the stock price remains unchanged, and $S_T = S_0$. It rises or falls by $1 for every dollar swing in the ultimate stock price. The profit on the protective put is negative and equal to the cost of the put if S_T is below S_0. The profit on the protective put increases one for one with increases in the stock price once the stock price exceeds X.

Figure 15.7 makes it clear that the protective put offers some insurance against stock price declines in that it limits losses. Therefore, protective put strategies provide a form of *portfolio insurance.* The cost of the protection is that, if the stock price increases, your profit is reduced by the cost of the put, which turned out to be unneeded.

This example also shows that despite the common perception that "derivatives mean risk," derivative securities can be used effectively for **risk management**. In fact, such risk management is becoming accepted as part of the fiduciary responsibility of financial managers. Indeed, in a highly cited court case, *Brane v. Roth,* a company's board of directors was successfully sued for failing to use derivatives to hedge the price risk of grain held in storage. Such hedging might have been accomplished using protective puts.

The claim that derivatives are best viewed as risk management tools may seem surprising in light of the credit crisis of the last few years. The crisis was immediately precipitated when the highly risky positions that many financial institutions had established in credit derivatives blew up in 2007–2008, resulting in large losses and government bailouts. Still, the same characteristics that make derivatives potent tools to increase risk also make them highly effective in managing risk, at least when used properly. Derivatives have aptly been compared to power tools: very useful in skilled hands but also very dangerous when not handled with care.

risk management
Strategies to limit the risk of a portfolio.

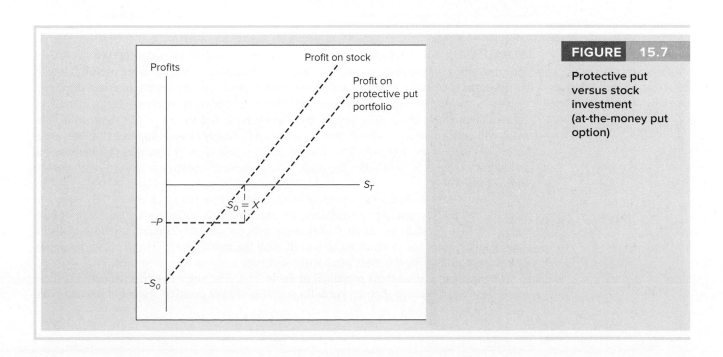

FIGURE   15.7

Protective put versus stock investment (at-the-money put option)

	$S_T \leq X$	$S_T > X$
Payoff of stock	S_T	S_T
− Payoff of call	−0	−($S_T − X$)
Total	S_T	X

TABLE 15.2 Payoff to a covered call

covered call

Writing a call on an asset together with buying the asset.

COVERED CALLS   A **covered call** position is the purchase of a share of stock coupled with the sale of a call option on that stock. The written option is "covered" because the potential obligation to deliver the stock can be satisfied using the stock held in the portfolio. Writing an option without an offsetting stock position is called by contrast *naked option writing*. The payoff to a covered call, presented in Table 15.2, equals the stock value minus the payoff of the written call.

The solid line in Figure 15.8C illustrates the payoff pattern. You see that the total position is worth S_T when the stock price at time T is below X and rises to a maximum of X when S_T exceeds X. In essence, the sale of the call option means the call writer has sold the claim to any stock value above X in return for the initial premium (the call price). Therefore, at expiration, the position is worth at most X. The dashed line is the net profit.

Writing covered call options has been a popular investment strategy among institutional investors. Consider the managers of a fund invested largely in stocks. They might find it appealing to write calls on some or all of the stock in order to boost income by the premiums collected. Although they thereby forfeit potential capital gains should the stock price rise above the exercise price, if they view X as the price at which they plan to sell the stock anyway, then the call may be viewed as enforcing a kind of "sell discipline." The written call guarantees the stock sale will occur as planned.

EXAMPLE 15.4

Covered Call

Assume a pension fund holds 1,000 shares of GXX stock, with a current price of $130 per share. Suppose the portfolio manager intends to sell all 1,000 shares if the share price hits $140, and a call expiring in 90 days with an exercise price of $140 currently sells for $5. By writing 10 GXX call contracts (100 shares each) the fund can pick up $5,000 in extra income. The fund would lose its share of profits from any movement of GXX stock above $140 per share, but given that it would have sold its shares at $140, it would not have realized those profits anyway.

---

straddle

A combination of a call and a put, each with the same exercise price and expiration date.

STRADDLE   A long **straddle** is established by buying both a call and a put on a stock, each with the same exercise price, X, and the same expiration date, T. Straddles are useful strategies for investors who believe a stock will move a lot in price but are uncertain about the direction of the move. For example, suppose you believe an important court case that will make or break a company is about to be settled, and the market is not yet aware of the situation. The stock will either double in value if the case is settled favorably or will drop by half if the settlement goes against the company. The straddle position will do well regardless of the outcome because its value is highest when the stock price makes either extreme upward or downward moves from X.

The worst-case scenario for a straddle is no movement in the stock price. If S_T equals X, both the call and the put expire worthless, and the investor's outlay for the purchase of both options is lost. Straddle positions therefore are bets on volatility. Investors who establish a straddle must view the stock as more volatile than the market does. They collect the option premiums now, hoping the stock price will not change much before expiration.

The payoff to a straddle is presented in Table 15.3. The solid line of Figure 15.9C illustrates this payoff. Notice that the portfolio payoff is always positive, except at the one point

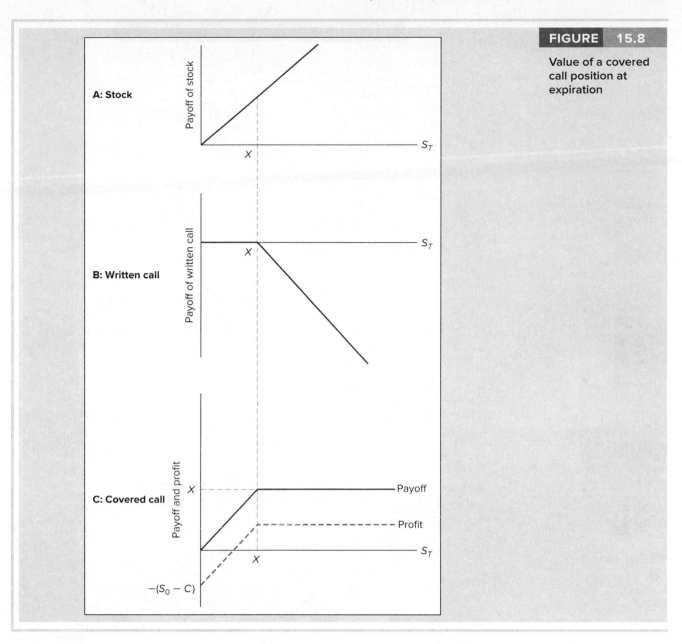

FIGURE   15.8

Value of a covered
call position at
expiration

where the portfolio has zero value, $S_T = X$. You might wonder why all investors don't pursue such a no-lose strategy. To see why, remember that the straddle requires that both the put and the call be purchased. The value of the portfolio at expiration, while never negative, still must exceed the initial outlay for a straddle investor to clear a profit.

The dashed line of Figure 15.9C is the profit to the straddle. The profit line lies below the payoff line by the initial cost of the straddle, $P + C$. The final stock price must depart from X by this amount for the straddle to provide a profit.

Strips and *straps* are variations of straddles. A strip is two puts and one call on a security with the same exercise price and expiration date. A strap is two calls and one put.

Graph the profit and payoff diagrams for strips and straps.   **CONCEPT** **15.3**
                                                                                 c h e c k

TABLE 15.3 Payoff to a straddle

	$S_T \leq X$	$S_T > X$
Payoff of call	0	$S_T - X$
+Payoff of put	$+(X - S_T)$	$+0$
Total	$X - S_T$	$S_T - X$

FIGURE 15.9

Payoff and profit to a straddle at expiration

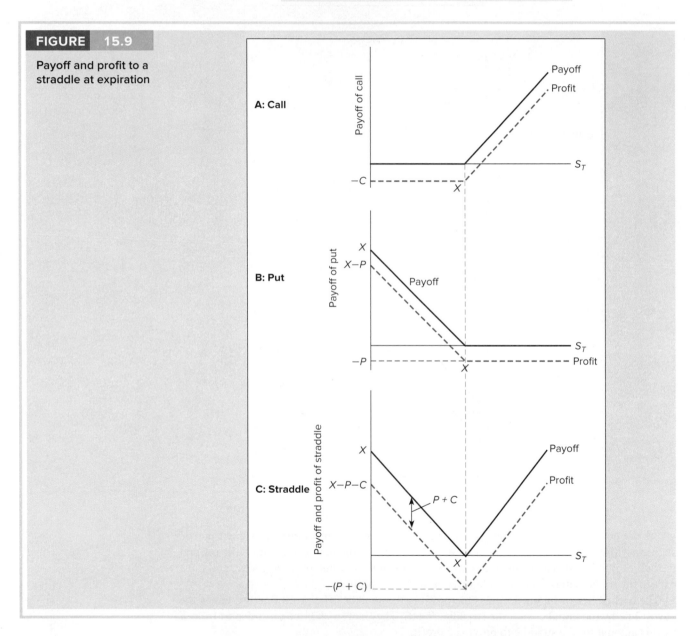

SPREADS   A **spread** is a combination of two or more call options (or two or more puts) on the same stock with differing exercise prices or times to expiration. Some options are bought, while others are sold, or written. A *money spread* involves the purchase of one option and the simultaneous sale of another with a different exercise price. A *time spread* refers to the sale and purchase of options with differing expiration dates.

Consider a money spread in which one call option is bought at an exercise price X_1, while another call with identical expiration date, but higher exercise price, X_2, is written. The payoff will be the difference in the value of the call held and the value of the call written, as in Table 15.4.

spread

A combination of two or more call options or put options on the same asset with differing exercise prices or times to expiration.

TABLE 15.4   Payoff to a bullish spread

	$S_T \leq X_1$	$X_1 < S_T \leq X_2$	$S_T > X_2$
Payoff of first call, exercise price = X_1	0	$S_T - X_1$	$S_T - X_1$
−Payoff of second call, exercise price = X_2	−0	−0	$-(S_T - X_2)$
Total	0	$S_T - X_1$	$X_2 - X_1$

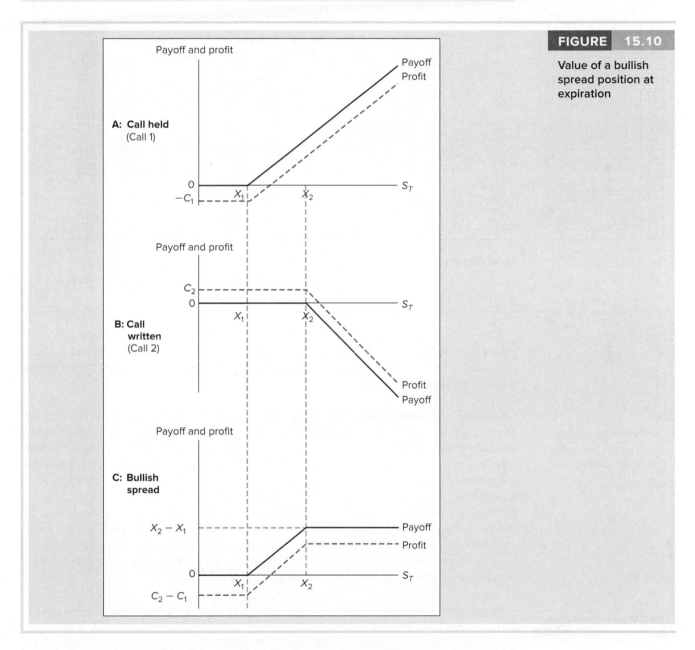

FIGURE   15.10

Value of a bullish spread position at expiration

There are now three instead of two outcomes to distinguish: the lowest-price region, where S_T is below both exercise prices; a middle region, where S_T is between the two exercise prices; and a high-price region, where S_T exceeds both exercise prices. Figure 15.10 illustrates the payoff and profit to this strategy, which is called a *bullish spread* because the payoff either increases or is unaffected by stock price increases.

𝒵

Spreadsheets are available in Connect

Using spreadsheets to analyze combinations of options is very helpful. Once the basic models are built, it is easy to extend the analysis to different bundles of options. The Excel model "Spreads and Straddles" shown below can be used to evaluate the profitability of different strategies.

	A	B	C	D	E	F	G	H	I	J	K	L
1					Spreads and Straddles							
2												
3	Stock Prices											
4	Beginning Market Price	116.5										
5	Ending Market Price	130						X 110 Straddle			X 120 Straddle	
6								Ending	Profit		Ending	Profit
7	Buying Options:							Stock Price	-15.40		Stock Price	-24.00
8	Call Options Strike	Price	Payoff	Profit	Return %			50	24.60		50	36.00
9	110	22.80	20.00	-2.80	-12.28%			60	14.60		60	26.00
10	120	16.80	10.00	-6.80	-40.48%			70	4.60		70	16.00
11	130	13.60	0.00	-13.60	-100.00%			80	-5.40		80	6.00
12	140	10.30	0.00	-10.30	-100.00%			90	-15.40		90	-4.00
13								100	-25.40		100	-14.00
14	Put Options Strike	Price	Payoff	Profit	Return %			110	-35.40		110	-24.00
15	110	12.60	0.00	-12.60	-100.00%			120	-25.40		120	-34.00
16	120	17.20	0.00	-17.20	-100.00%			130	-15.40		130	-24.00
17	130	23.60	0.00	-23.60	-100.00%			140	-5.40		140	-14.00
18	140	30.50	10.00	-20.50	-67.21%			150	4.60		150	-4.00
19								160	14.60		160	6.00
20	Straddle	Price	Payoff	Profit	Return %			170	24.60		170	16.00
21	110	35.40	20.00	-15.40	-43.50%			180	34.60		180	26.00
22	120	34.00	10.00	-24.00	-70.59%			190	44.60		190	36.00
23	130	37.20	0.00	-37.20	-100.00%			200	54.60		200	46.00
24	140	40.80	10.00	-30.80	-75.49%			210	64.60		210	56.00
25												

Excel Question

1. Use the data in this spreadsheet to plot the profit on a bullish spread (see Figure 15.10) with $X_1 = 120$ and $X_2 = 130$.

One motivation for a bullish spread might be that the investor thinks one option is overpriced relative to another. For example, an investor who believes an $X = \$50$ call is cheap compared to an $X = \$55$ call might establish the spread, even without a strong desire to take a bullish position in the stock.

collar

An options strategy that brackets the value of a portfolio between two bounds.

COLLARS A **collar** is an options strategy that brackets the value of a portfolio between two bounds. Suppose that an investor currently is holding a large position in Eagle Corp., which is currently selling at $70 per share. A lower bound of $60 can be placed on the value of the portfolio by buying a protective put with exercise price $60. This protection, however, requires that the investor pay the put premium. To raise the money to pay for the put, the investor might write a call option, say, with exercise price $80. The call might sell for roughly the same price as the put, meaning that the net outlay for the two options positions is approximately zero. Writing the call limits the portfolio's upside potential. Even if the stock price moves above $80, the investor will do no better than $80, because at a higher price the stock will be called away. Thus, the investor obtains the downside protection represented by the exercise price of the put by selling her claim to any upside potential beyond the exercise price of the call.

EXAMPLE 15.5

Collars

A collar would be appropriate for an investor who has a target wealth goal in mind but is unwilling to risk losses beyond a certain level. Suppose you are contemplating buying a house for $160,000. You might set this figure as your goal. Your current wealth may be $140,000, and you are unwilling to risk losing more than $20,000. A collar established by (1) purchasing 2,000 shares of stock currently selling at $70 per share, (2) purchasing 2,000 put options (i.e., 20 option contracts) with exercise price $60, and (3) writing 2,000 calls with exercise price $80 would give you a good chance to realize the $20,000 capital gain without risking a loss of more than $20,000.

15.4   OPTIONLIKE SECURITIES

Even if you never intend to trade an option directly, you would still need to appreciate their properties. This is because many financial instruments and agreements have features that convey implicit or explicit options to one or more parties. To value and use these securities correctly, you must understand their embedded options.

Callable Bonds

You know from Chapter 10 that many corporate bonds are issued with call provisions entitling the issuer to buy the bonds back from the bondholders at a specified call price. This provision conveys a call option to the issuer, where the exercise price is the price at which the bond can be repurchased. A callable bond is therefore essentially a combination of a *straight bond* (a bond with no option features such as callability or convertibility) held by the investor and a call option held by the bond-issuing firm.

Investors must receive some compensation for implicitly writing the call option to the bond issuer. If the callable bond were issued with the same coupon rate as a straight bond, we would expect it to sell at a discount to the straight bond. To sell callable bonds at par, firms must issue them with coupon rates higher than the coupons on straight debt. The higher coupons are the investor's compensation for the option retained by the issuer. Coupon rates usually are selected so that the newly issued bond will sell at par value.

Figure 15.11 illustrates this optionlike property. The horizontal axis is the value of a straight bond with otherwise identical terms as the callable bond. The dashed 45-degree line represents the value of straight debt. The solid line is the value of the callable bond, and the dotted line is the value of the call option retained by the firm. A callable bond's potential for capital gains is limited by the firm's option to repurchase at the call price.

The option inherent in callable bonds actually is more complex than an ordinary call option because usually it may be exercised only after some initial period of *call protection*. The price at which the bond is callable also may change over time. Unlike exchange-listed options, these

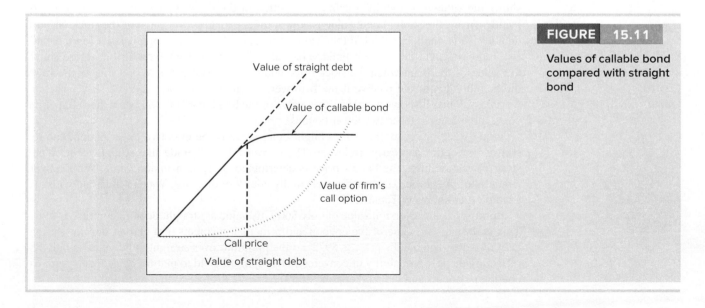

FIGURE   15.11

Values of callable bond compared with straight bond

features are defined in the initial bond covenants and will depend on the needs of the issuing firm and its perception of the market's tastes.

> **CONCEPT check**   **15.6**   Suppose the period of call protection is extended. How will this affect the coupon rate the company must offer to issue the bonds at par value?

Convertible Securities

Convertible bonds and convertible preferred stock convey options to the holder of the security rather than to the issuing firm. A convertible security typically gives its holder the right to exchange each bond or share of preferred stock for a fixed number of shares of common stock, regardless of the market prices of the securities at the time.

> **CONCEPT check**   **15.7**   Should a convertible bond issued at par value have a higher or lower coupon rate than a nonconvertible bond issued at par?

To illustrate, a bond with a conversion ratio of 10 allows its holder to convert one bond of par value $1,000 into 10 shares of common stock. Alternatively, we say the conversion price is $100: To receive 10 shares of stock, the investor sacrifices bonds with face value $1,000 or $100 of face value per share. If the present value of the bond's scheduled payments is less than 10 times the value of one share of stock, it may pay to convert; that is, the conversion option is in the money. A bond worth $950 with a conversion ratio of 10 could be converted profitably if the stock were selling above $95, as the value of the 10 shares received for each bond surrendered would exceed $950. Most convertible bonds are issued "deep out of the money." That is, the issuer sets the conversion ratio so that conversion will not be profitable unless there is a substantial increase in stock prices and/or decrease in bond prices from the time of issue.

A bond's conversion value equals the value it would have if you converted it into stock immediately. Clearly, a bond must sell for at least its conversion value. If it did not, you could purchase the bond, convert it immediately, and clear a riskless profit. This situation could never persist, for all investors would pursue such a strategy and quickly bid up the price of the bond.

The straight bond value or "bond floor" is the value the bond would have if it were not convertible into stock. The bond must sell for more than its straight bond value because a convertible bond has more value; it is in fact a straight bond *plus* a valuable call option. Therefore, the convertible bond has two lower bounds on its market price: the conversion value and the straight bond value.

Figure 15.12 illustrates the optionlike properties of the convertible bond. Figure 15.12A shows the value of the straight debt as a function of the stock price of the issuing firm. For healthy firms, the straight debt value is almost independent of the value of the stock because default risk is small. However, if the firm is close to bankruptcy (stock prices are low), default risk increases, and the straight bond value falls. The vertical intercept in the figure shows the value of the bond when the stock price equals zero. You can interpret this as the value the bondholders would receive if the firm were to enter bankruptcy and the shares become worthless. Panel B shows the conversion value of the bond. Panel C compares the value of the convertible bond to these two lower bounds.

When stock prices are low, the straight bond value is the effective lower bound, and the conversion option is nearly irrelevant. The convertible will trade like straight debt. When stock prices are high, the bond's price is determined by its conversion value. With conversion all but guaranteed, the bond is essentially equity in disguise. We can illustrate with two examples, as shown in Table 15.5.

Bond A has a conversion value of only $600. Its value as straight debt, in contrast, is $967. This is the present value of the coupon and principal payments at a market rate for straight debt of 8.5%. The bond's price is $972, so the premium over straight bond value is only $5, reflecting the low probability of conversion. Its reported yield to maturity based on scheduled coupon payments and the market price of $972 is 8.42%, close to that of straight debt.

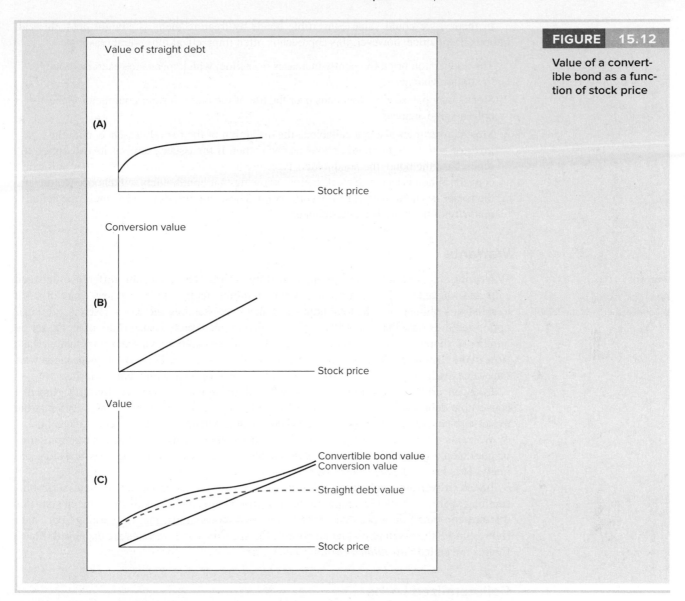

FIGURE   15.12

Value of a convertible bond as a function of stock price

The conversion option on bond B is in the money. Conversion value is $1,250, and the bond's price, $1,255, reflects its value as equity (plus $5 for the protection the bond offers against stock price declines). The bond's reported yield is 4.76%, far below the comparable yield on straight debt. The big yield sacrifice is attributable to the far greater value of the conversion option.

TABLE 15.5 Two convertible bonds

	Bond A	Bond B
Annual coupon	$80	$80
Maturity date	10 years	10 years
Quality rating	Baa	Baa
Conversion ratio	20	25
Stock price	$30	$50
Conversion value	$600	$1,250
Market yield on 10-year Baa-rated bonds	8.5%	8.5%
Value as straight debt	$967	$967
Actual bond price	$972	$1,255
Reported yield to maturity	8.42%	4.76%

In theory, we could value convertible bonds by treating them as straight debt plus call options. In practice, however, this approach is often impractical for several reasons:

1. The conversion price frequently increases over time, which means the exercise price for the option changes.

2. Stocks may pay several dividends over the life of the bond, further complicating the option value analysis.

3. Most convertibles also are callable at the discretion of the firm. In essence, both the investor and the issuer hold options on each other. If the issuer exercises its call option to repurchase the bond, the bondholders typically have a month during which they still can convert. When issuers use a call option, knowing that bondholders will choose to convert, the issuer is said to have *forced a conversion*. These conditions together mean the actual maturity of the bond is indeterminate.

Warrants

warrant

An option issued by the firm to purchase shares of the firm's stock.

Warrants are essentially call options issued by a firm. The important difference between calls and warrants is that exercise of a warrant requires the firm to issue a new share of stock to satisfy its obligation—the total number of shares outstanding increases. Exercise of a call option requires only that the writer of the call deliver an already-issued share of stock, so the number of shares outstanding remains fixed. Also unlike call options, warrants provide a cash flow to the firm when the warrant holder pays the exercise price. These differences mean warrant values will differ somewhat from the values of call options with identical terms.

Like convertible debt, warrant terms may be tailored to meet the needs of the firm. Also like convertible debt, warrants generally are protected against stock splits and dividends in that the exercise price and the number of warrants held are adjusted to offset the effects of the split.

Warrants often are issued in conjunction with another security. Bonds, for example, may be packaged together with a warrant "sweetener," frequently a warrant that may be sold separately. This is called a *detachable warrant*.

Issues of warrants and convertible securities create the potential for an increase in outstanding shares of stock if exercise occurs. Exercise obviously would affect financial statistics that are computed on a per-share basis, so annual reports must include earnings per share figures under the assumption that all convertible securities and warrants are exercised. These figures are called *fully diluted earnings per share*.[3]

Collateralized Loans

Many loan arrangements require that the borrower put up collateral to guarantee the loan will be paid back. In the event of default, the lender takes possession of the collateral. A *nonrecourse loan* gives the lender no recourse beyond the right to the collateral. That is, the lender may not sue the borrower for further payment if the collateral turns out not to be valuable enough to repay the loan.[4]

This arrangement gives an implicit call option to the borrower. Assume the borrower is obligated to pay back L dollars at the maturity of the loan. The collateral will be worth S_T dollars at maturity. (Its value today is S_0.) The borrower has the option to wait until the loan is due and repay it only if the collateral is worth more than L dollars. If the collateral is worth less than L, the borrower can default, discharging the obligation by forfeiting the collateral, which is worth only S_T.

Another way of describing the loan is to view the borrower as turning over the collateral to the lender but retaining the right to reclaim it by paying off the loan. In effect, the borrower

---

[3]Exercise of a convertible bond need not reduce earnings per share (EPS). Diluted EPS will be less than undiluted EPS when interest saved (per share) on the converted bonds is less than the prior EPS.

[4]In reality, of course, defaulting on a loan is not so simple. Losses of reputation are involved as well as considerations of ethical behavior. This is a description of a pure nonrecourse loan where both parties agree from the outset that only the collateral backs the loan and that default is not to be taken as a sign of bad faith if the collateral is insufficient to repay the loan.

turns over collateral but keeps an option to "repurchase" it for L dollars at maturity if L turns out to be less than S_T. This is a call option.

A third way to look at a collaterized loan is to assume the borrower will repay the L dollars with certainty but also retains the option to sell the collateral to the lender for L dollars, even if S_T is less than L. In this case, the sale of the collateral would generate the cash necessary to satisfy the loan. The ability to "sell" the collateral for L dollars represents a put option, which guarantees the borrower can raise enough money to satisfy the loan simply by turning over the collateral.

Figure 15.13 illustrates these different ways of viewing the loan. Figure 15.13A is the value of the payment to be received by the lender, which equals the minimum of S_T or L. Panel B shows that this amount can be expressed as S_T minus the payoff of the call implicitly written by the lender and held by the borrower. Panel C shows it also can be viewed as a receipt of L dollars minus the proceeds of a put option.

Leveraged Equity and Risky Debt

Investors holding stock in incorporated firms are protected by limited liability, which means that if the firm cannot pay its debts, the firm's creditors may attach only the firm's assets and may not sue the corporation's equityholders for further payment. In effect, any time the corporation borrows money, the maximum possible collateral is the total of the firm's assets. If

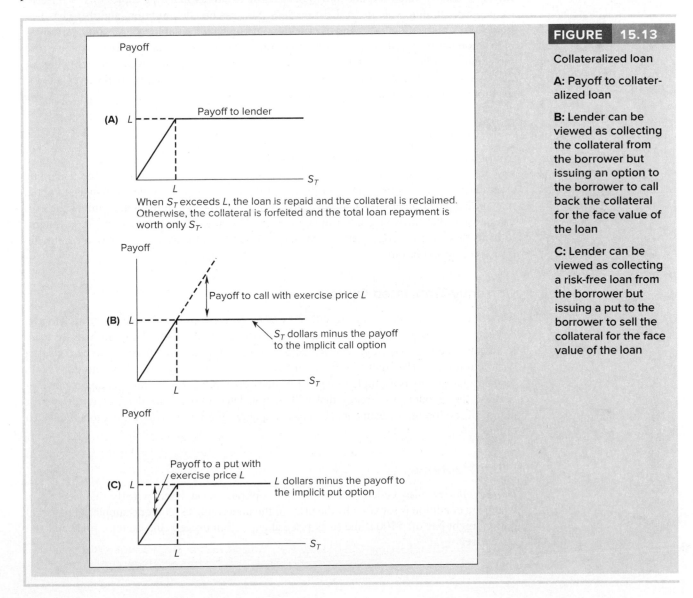

FIGURE   15.13

Collateralized loan

A: Payoff to collateralized loan

B: Lender can be viewed as collecting the collateral from the borrower but issuing an option to the borrower to call back the collateral for the face value of the loan

C: Lender can be viewed as collecting a risk-free loan from the borrower but issuing a put to the borrower to sell the collateral for the face value of the loan

the firm declares bankruptcy, we can interpret this as an admission that the firm's assets are insufficient to satisfy the claims against it. The corporation may discharge its obligations by transferring ownership of the firm's assets to the creditors.

Just as is true for nonrecourse collateralized loans, the required payment to the creditors represents the exercise price of the implicit option, while the value of the firm is the underlying asset. The equityholders have a put option to transfer their ownership claims on the firm to the creditors in return for the face value of the firm's debt.

Alternatively, we may view the equityholders as retaining a call option. They have implicitly transferred their ownership claim to the firm to the creditors but have retained the right to reacquire it by paying off the loan. Hence, the equityholders have an implicit option to "buy back" the firm for a specified price.

The significance of this observation is that analysts can value corporate bonds using option-pricing techniques. The default premium required of risky debt in principle can be estimated using option valuation models. We will consider some of these models in the next chapter.

15.5 EXOTIC OPTIONS

Investors clearly value the portfolio strategies that options make possible; this is reflected in the heavy trading volume in these markets. Success breeds imitation, and there has been tremendous innovation in the range of option instruments available to investors. Part of this innovation has occurred in the market for customized options, which now trade in active over-the-counter markets. Many of these options have terms that would have been highly unusual 25 years ago; they therefore are called *exotic options*. In this section, we will survey a few of the more interesting variants of these new instruments.

Asian Options

You already have been introduced to American and European options. *Asian options* are options with payoffs that depend on the average (rather than final) price of the underlying asset during at least some portion of the life of the option. For example, an Asian call option may have a payoff equal to the average stock price over the last three months minus the exercise price if that difference is positive, or zero otherwise. These options may be of interest to firms that wish to hedge a profit stream that depends on the average price of a commodity over some period of time.

Currency-Translated Options

Currency-translated options have either asset or exercise prices denominated in a foreign currency. A good example of such an option is the *quanto*, which allows an investor to fix in advance the exchange rate at which an investment in a foreign currency can be converted back into dollars. The right to translate a fixed amount of foreign currency into dollars at a given exchange rate is a simple foreign exchange option. Quantos are more complex however, because the amount of currency that will be translated into dollars depends on the performance of the foreign investment. Therefore, a quanto in effect provides a *random number* of options.

Digital Options

Digital options, also called *binary* or "bet" options, have fixed payoffs that depend on whether a condition is satisfied by the price of the underlying asset. For example, a binary call option might pay off $100 if the stock price at expiration exceeds the exercise price and zero otherwise.

- A call option is the right to buy an asset at an agreed-upon exercise price. A put option is the right to sell an asset at a given exercise price.
- Calls are worth more when the exercise price is lower, while puts are worth more when the exercise price is higher. Both options are generally worth more when the time until expiration is longer.
- American-style options allow exercise on or before the exercise date. European-style options allow exercise only on the expiration date. Most traded options are American in nature.
- Options are traded on stocks, stock indexes, foreign currencies, fixed-income securities, and several futures contracts.
- Options can be used either to lever up an investor's exposure to an asset price or to provide insurance against volatility of asset prices. Popular option strategies include covered calls, protective puts, straddles, and spreads.
- Many commonly traded securities embody option characteristics. Examples of these securities are callable bonds, convertible bonds, and warrants. Other arrangements, such as collateralized loans and limited-liability borrowing, can be analyzed as conveying implicit options to one or more parties.

SUMMARY

			KEY TERMS
American option, 477	exercise price, 475	risk management, 485	
at the money, 476	in the money, 476	spread, 488	
call option, 475	out of the money, 476	straddle, 486	
collar, 490	premium, 475	strike price, 475	
covered call, 486	protective put, 484	warrant, 494	
European option, 477	put option, 475		

KEY FORMULAS

$$\text{Payoff to call option} = \begin{cases} S_T - X & \text{if } S_T > X \\ 0 & \text{if } S_T \leq X \end{cases}$$

$$\text{Payoff to put option} = \begin{cases} 0 & \text{if } S_T > X \\ X - S_T & \text{if } S_T \leq X \end{cases}$$

PROBLEM SETS

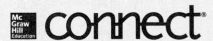 Select problems are available in McGraw-Hill's *Connect.* Please see the Supplements section of the book's frontmatter for more information.

1. We said that options can be used either to scale up or reduce overall portfolio risk. What are some examples of risk-increasing and risk-reducing options strategies? Explain each. *(LO 15-2)*

2. Why do you think the most actively traded options tend to be the ones that are near the money? *(LO 15-1)*

3. The following price quotations are for exchange-listed options on Primo Corporation common stock.

Company	Strike	Expiration	Call	Put
Primo 61.12	55	Feb	7.25	0.48

With transaction costs ignored, how much would a buyer have to pay for one call option contract? *(LO 15-1)*

4. Turn back to Figure 15.1, which lists the prices of various Microsoft options. Use the data in the figure to calculate the payoff and the profits for investments in each of the following June 2017 expiration options, assuming that the stock price on the expiration date is $71. *(LO 15-1)*

   a. Call option, $X = 70$.
   b. Put option, $X = 70$.
   c. Call option, $X = 72$.
   d. Put option, $X = 72$.

5. You purchase one Microsoft July $72 put contract for a premium of $1.32. What is your maximum possible profit? (See Figure 15.1.)   *(LO 15-1)*

6. An investor buys a call at a price of $4.50 with an exercise price of $40. At what stock price will the investor break even on the purchase of the call?   *(LO 15-1)*

7. You establish a straddle on Fincorp using September call and put options with a strike price of $80. The call premium is $7.00 and the put premium is $8.50.   *(LO 15-2)*
   a. What is the most you can lose on this position?
   b. What will be your profit or loss if Fincorp is selling for $88 in September?
   c. At what stock prices will you break even on the straddle?

8. The following diagram shows the value of a put option at expiration:

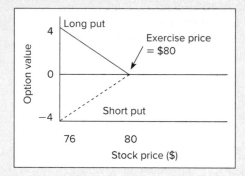

Ignoring transaction costs, which of the following statements about the value of the put option at expiration is *true?*   *(LO 15-1)*
   a. The expiration value of the short position in the put is $4 if the stock price is $76.
   b. The expiration value of the long position in the put is −$4 if the stock price is $76.
   c. The long put has a positive expiration value when the stock price is below $80.
   d. The value of the short position in the put is zero for stock prices equaling or exceeding $76.

9. You are a portfolio manager who uses options positions to customize the risk profile of your clients. In each case, what strategy is best given your client's objective?   *(LO 15-2)*
   a. • Performance to date: Up 16%.
      • Client objective: Earn at least 15%.
      • Your scenario: Good chance of large stock price gains or large losses between now and end of year.
         i. Long straddle.
         ii. Long bullish spread.
         iii. Short straddle.
   b. • Performance to date: Up 16%.
      • Client objective: Earn at least 15%.
      • Your scenario: Good chance of large stock price losses between now and end of year.
         i. Long put options.
         ii. Short call options.
         iii. Long call options.

10. An investor purchases a stock for $38 and a put for $0.50 with a strike price of $35. The investor sells a call for $0.50 with a strike price of $40.   *(LO 15-1)*
   a. What is the maximum profit and loss for this position?
   b. Draw the profit and loss diagram for this strategy as a function of the stock price at expiration.

11. Imagine that you are holding 5,000 shares of stock, currently selling at $40 per share. You are ready to sell the shares but would prefer to put off the sale until next year due to tax reasons. If you continue to hold the shares until January, however, you face the risk that the stock will drop in value before year-end. You decide to use a collar to limit downside risk without laying out a good deal of additional funds. January call options with a strike price of $45 are selling at $2, and January puts with a strike price of $35 are selling at $3. What will be the value of your portfolio in January (net of the proceeds from the options) if the stock price ends up at (*a*) $30? (*b*) $40? (*c*) $50?

(*d*) Compare these proceeds to what you would realize if you simply continued to hold the shares. **(LO 15-2)**

12. Suppose you think AppX stock is going to appreciate substantially in value in the next year. Say the stock's current price, S_0, is $100, and the call option expiring in one year has an exercise price, X, of $100 and is selling at a price, C, of $10. With $10,000 to invest, you are considering three alternatives:
    a. Invest all $10,000 in the stock, buying 100 shares.
    b. Invest all $10,000 in 1,000 options (10 contracts).
    c. Buy 100 options (one contract) for $1,000 and invest the remaining $9,000 in a money market fund paying 4% interest annually.

Rate of return on investment

	Price of Stock 1 Year from Now			
	$80	$100	$110	$120
a. All stocks (100 shares)				
b. All options (1,000 shares)				
c. Bills + 100 options				

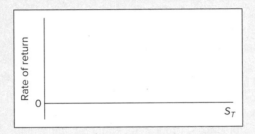

What is your rate of return for each alternative for four stock prices one year from now? Summarize your results in the table and diagram below. **(LO 15-1)**

13. The common stock of the P.U.T.T. Corporation has been trading in a narrow price range for the past month, and you are convinced it is going to break far out of that range in the next three months. You do not know whether it will go up or down, however. The current price of the stock is $100 per share, the price of a three-month call option with an exercise price of $100 is $10, and a put with the same expiration date and exercise price costs $7. **(LO 15-2)**
    a. What would be a simple options strategy to exploit your conviction about the stock price's future movements?
    b. How far would the price have to move in either direction for you to make a profit on your initial investment?

14. The common stock of the C.A.L.L. Corporation has been trading in a narrow range around $50 per share for months, and you believe it is going to stay in that range for the next three months. The price of a three-month put option with an exercise price of $50 is $4, and a call with the same expiration date and exercise price sells for $7. **(LO 15-2)**
    a. What would be a simple options strategy using a put and a call to exploit your conviction about the stock price's future movement?
    b. What is the most money you can make on this position?
    c. How far can the stock price move in either direction before you lose money?
    d. How can you create a position involving a put, a call, and riskless lending that would have the same payoff structure as the stock at expiration? The stock will pay no dividends in the next three months.
    e. What is the net cost of establishing that position now?

15. Joseph Jones, a manager at Computer Science, Inc. (CSI), received 10,000 shares of company stock as part of his compensation package. The stock currently sells at $40 a share. Joseph would like to defer selling the stock until the next tax year. In January, however, he will need to sell all his holdings to provide for a down payment on his new house. Joseph is worried about the price risk involved in keeping his shares. At current

prices, he would receive $40,000 for the stock. If the value of his stock holdings falls below $35,000, his ability to come up with the necessary down payment would be jeopardized. On the other hand, if the stock value rises to $45,000, he would be able to maintain a small cash reserve even after making the down payment. Joseph considers three investment strategies:

a. Strategy A is to write January call options on the CSI shares with strike price $45. These calls are currently selling for $3 each.

b. Strategy B is to buy January put options on CSI with strike price $35. These options also sell for $3 each.

c. Strategy C is to establish a zero-cost collar by writing the January calls and buying the January puts.

Evaluate each of these strategies with respect to Joseph's investment goals. What are the advantages and disadvantages of each? Which would you recommend?   *(LO 15-2)*

16. a. A butterfly spread is the purchase of one call at exercise price X_1, the sale of two calls at exercise price X_2, and the purchase of one call at exercise price X_3. X_1 is less than X_2, and X_2 is less than X_3 by equal amounts, and all calls have the same expiration date. Graph the payoff diagram to this strategy.

b. A vertical combination is the purchase of a call with exercise price X_2 and a put with exercise price X_1, with X_2 greater than X_1. Graph the payoff to this strategy.   *(LO 15-2)*

17. A bearish spread is the purchase of a call with exercise price X_2 and the sale of a call with exercise price X_1, with X_2 greater than X_1. Graph the payoff to this strategy and compare it to Figure 15.10.   *(LO 15-2)*

18. You think there is great upward potential in the stock market and would like to participate in the upward move if it materializes. However, you are not able to afford substantial stock market losses and so cannot run the risk of a stock market collapse, which you recognize is also possible. Your investment adviser therefore suggests a protective put position: Buy shares in a market-index stock fund *and* put options on those shares with three months until expiration and exercise price of $1,950. The stock index is currently at $2,250. However, your uncle suggests you instead buy a three-month call option on the index fund with exercise price $2,100 and buy three-month T-bills with face value $2,100.   *(LO 15-2)*

a. On the same graph, draw the *payoffs* to each of these strategies as a function of the stock fund value in three months. (*Hint:* Think of the options as being on one "share" of the stock index fund, with the current price of each share of the index equal to $2,250.)

b. Which portfolio must require a greater initial outlay to establish? (*Hint:* Does either portfolio provide a final payoff that is always at least as great as the payoff of the other portfolio?)

c. Suppose the market prices of the securities are as follows:

Stock fund	$2,250
T-bill (face value $2,100)	2,025
Call (exercise price $2,100)	260
Put (exercise price $1,950)	15

Make a table of profits realized for each portfolio for the following values of the stock price in three months: $S_T = $0, $1,750, $2,000, $2,250, and $2,400. Graph the profits to each portfolio as a function of S_T on a single graph.

d. Which strategy is riskier? Which should have a higher beta?

19. Use the spreadsheet from the Excel Application boxes on spreads and straddles (available in Connect; link to Chapter 15 material) to answer these questions.   *(LO 15-1)*

a. Plot the payoff and profit diagrams to a straddle position with an exercise (strike) price of $130. Assume the options are priced as they are in the Excel Application.

b. Plot the payoff and profit diagrams to a spread position with exercise (strike) prices of $120 and $130. Assume the options are priced as they are in the Excel Application.

20. In what ways is owning a corporate bond similar to writing a put option? A call option?   *(LO 15-3)*

21. An executive compensation scheme might provide a manager a bonus of $1,000 for every dollar by which the company's stock price exceeds some cutoff level. In what way is this arrangement equivalent to issuing the manager call options on the firm's stock?   *(LO 15-3)*

22. Consider the following options portfolio: You write a June 2017 expiration call option on Microsoft with exercise price $72. You also write a June expiration Microsoft put option with exercise price $70.   *(LO 15-2)*

    a. Graph the payoff of this portfolio at option expiration as a function of the stock price at that time.

    b. What will be the profit/loss on this position if Microsoft is selling at $70 on the option expiration date? What if it is selling at $74? Use option prices from Figure 15.1 to answer this question.

    c. At what two stock prices will you just break even on your investment?

    d. What kind of "bet" is this investor making; that is, what must this investor believe about the stock price in order to justify this position?

23. Consider the following portfolio. You *write* a put option with exercise price $90 and *buy* a put with the same expiration date with exercise price $95.   *(LO 15-2)*

    a. Plot the value of the portfolio at the expiration date of the options.

    b. Now, plot the profit of the portfolio. *Hint:* Which option must cost more?

24. A put option with strike price $60 trading on the Acme options exchange sells for $2. To your amazement, a put on the firm with the same expiration selling on the Apex options exchange but with strike price $62 also sells for $2. If you plan to hold the options position until expiration, devise a zero-net-investment arbitrage strategy to exploit the pricing anomaly. Draw the profit diagram at expiration for your position.   *(LO 15-1)*

25. You buy a share of stock, write a one-year call option with $X = 10, and buy a one-year put option with $X = 10. Your net outlay to establish the entire portfolio is $9.50. What is the payoff of your portfolio? What must be the risk-free interest rate? The stock pays no dividends.   *(LO 15-1)*

Challenge

26. Joe Finance has just purchased a stock-index fund, currently selling at $2,400 per share. To protect against losses, Joe plans to purchase an at-the-money European put option on the fund for $120, with exercise price $2,400, and three-month time to expiration. Sally Calm, Joe's financial adviser, points out that Joe is spending a lot of money on the put. She notes that three-month puts with strike prices of $2,340 cost only $90, and suggests that Joe use the cheaper put.   *(LO 15-2)*

    a. Analyze Joe's and Sally's strategies by drawing the *profit* diagrams for the stock-plus-put positions for various values of the stock fund in three months.

    b. When does Sally's strategy do better? When does it do worse?

    c. Which strategy entails greater systematic risk?

27. You write a call option with $X = 50 and buy a call with $X = 60. The options are on the same stock and have the same expiration date. One of the calls sells for $3; the other sells for $9.   *(LO 15-2)*

    a. Draw the *payoff* graph for this strategy at the option expiration date.

    b. Draw the *profit* graph for this strategy.

    c. What is the break-even point for this strategy?

    d. Is the investor bullish or bearish on the stock?

28. Devise a portfolio using only call options and shares of stock with the following value (payoff) at the option expiration date. If the stock price is currently $53, what kind of bet is the investor making?   *(LO 15-2)*

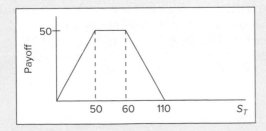

29. Some agricultural price support systems have guaranteed farmers a minimum price for their output.   *(LO 15-3)*
    a. Describe the program provisions as an option.
    b. What is the asset?
    c. What is the exercise price?

CFA Problems

1. Which one of the following statements about the value of a call option at expiration is *false*?   *(LO 15-1)*
    a. A short position in a call option will result in a loss if the stock price exceeds the exercise price.
    b. The value of a long position equals zero or the stock price minus the exercise price, whichever is higher.
    c. The value of a long position equals zero or the exercise price minus the stock price, whichever is higher.
    d. A short position in a call option has a zero value for all stock prices equal to or less than the exercise price.

2. Donna Donie, CFA, has a client who believes the common stock price of TRT Materials (currently $58 per share) could move substantially in either direction in reaction to an expected court decision involving the company. The client currently owns no TRT shares, but asks Donie for advice about implementing a strangle strategy to capitalize on the possible stock price movement. A strangle is a portfolio of a put and a call with different exercise prices but the same expiration date. Donie gathers the following TRT option price data: *(LO 15-2)*

Characteristic	Call Option	Put Option
Price	$5	$4
Strike price	$60	$55
Time to expiration	90 days from now	90 days from now

    a. Recommend whether Donie should choose a long strangle strategy or a short strangle strategy to achieve the client's objective.
    b. Calculate, at expiration for the appropriate strangle strategy in part (*a*), the:
        i. Maximum possible loss per share.
        ii. Maximum possible gain per share.
        iii. Break-even stock price(s).

3. A member of an investment committee interested in learning more about fixed-income investment procedures recalls that a fixed-income manager recently stated that derivative instruments could be used to control portfolio duration, saying, "A futures-like position can be created in a portfolio by using put and call options on Treasury bonds."   *(LO 15-3)*
    a. Identify the options market exposure or exposures that create a "futures-like position" similar to being long Treasury-bond futures. Explain why the position you created is similar to being long Treasury-bond futures.
    b. Explain in which direction and why the exposure(s) you identified in part (*a*) would affect portfolio duration.
    c. Assume that a pension plan's investment policy requires the fixed-income manager to hold portfolio duration within a narrow range. Identify and briefly explain circumstances or transactions in which the use of Treasury-bond futures would be helpful in managing a fixed-income portfolio when duration is constrained.

4. Suresh Singh, CFA, is analyzing a convertible bond. The characteristics of the bond and the underlying common stock are given in the nearby table.
    Compute the bond's: *(LO 15-3)*
    a. Conversion value.
    b. Market conversion price.

Convertible Bond Characteristics	
Par value	$1,000
Annual coupon rate (annual pay)	6.5%
Conversion ratio	22
Market price	105% of par value
Straight value	99% of par value

Underlying Stock Characteristics	
Current market price	$40 per share
Annual cash dividend	$1.20 per share

5. Rich McDonald, CFA, is evaluating his investment alternatives in Ytel Incorporated by analyzing a Ytel convertible bond and Ytel common equity. Characteristics of the two securities are given in the following exhibit: *(LO 15-3)*

Characteristics	Convertible Bond	Common Equity
Par value	$1,000	—
Coupon (annual payment)	4%	—
Current market price	$980	$35 per share
Straight bond value	$925	—
Conversion ratio	25	—
Conversion option	At any time	—
Dividend	—	$0
Expected market price in 1 year	$1,125	$45 per share

a. Calculate, based on the exhibit, the
   i. Current market conversion price for the Ytel convertible bond.
   ii. Expected one-year rate of return for the Ytel convertible bond.
   iii. Expected one-year rate of return for the Ytel common equity.

   One year has passed and Ytel's common equity price has increased to $51 per share. Also, over the year, the yield to maturity on Ytel's nonconvertible bonds of the same maturity increased, while credit spreads remained unchanged.

b. Name the two components of the convertible bond's value. Indicate whether the value of each component should decrease, stay the same, or increase in response to the:
   i. Increase in Ytel's common equity price.
   ii. Increase in bond yield.

WEB *master*

1. Use data from **finance.yahoo.com** to answer the following questions. In the *Get Quotes* box, enter stock symbol "GE" for General Electric. Go to the S&P Stock Reports section for GE.
   a. Locate the 52-week range for GE.
   b. At what price did GE last trade?
   c. Click on the link to *Options* on the left side of the Yahoo! Finance screen. Choose an expiration date three months in the future, and then choose *one* of the call options listed by selecting an exercise (strike) price. What is the last price (premium) shown for the call option?

    d. Is the call option in the money?

    e. Draw a graph that shows the payoff and the profit to the holder of this call option over a range of prices, including the prices you found in the 52-week range of the S&P Stock Report.

    f. Repeat the steps for a put option on GE with the same expiration date and the same strike price.

2. Go to **www.nasdaq.com** and select Facebook (FB) in the quote section. Once you have the information quote, request the information on *Option Chain*. Use options with times to expiration of about one month and two months that are as close as possible to at-the-money.

    a. What are the prices for the puts and calls with one-month expiration?

    b. What would be the cost of a straddle using these options?

    c. At expiration, what would be the break-even stock prices for the straddle?

    d. What would be the percentage increase or decrease in the stock price required to break even?

    e. What are the prices for the put and call with two-months' time until expiration?

    f. What would be the cost of a straddle using the later expiration date? At expiration, what would be the break-even stock prices for the straddle?

    g. What would be the percentage increase or decrease in the stock price required to break even?

SOLUTIONS TO

CONCEPT
checks

15.1 *a.* Proceeds = $S_T - X = S_T - \$72$ if this value is positive; otherwise, the call expires worthless. Profit = Proceeds − Price of call option = Proceeds − $1.15.

	$S_T = \$70$	$S_T = \$74$
Proceeds	$0	$2
Profits	−1.15	0.85

b. Proceeds = $X - S_T = \$72 - S_T$ if this value is positive; otherwise, the put expires worthless. Profit = Proceeds − Price of put option = Proceeds − $1.32.

	$S_T = \$70$	$S_T = \$74$
Proceeds	$2	$0
Profits	+0.68	−1.32

15.2 *a.*

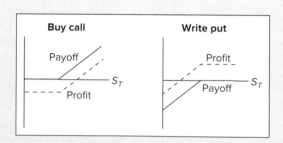

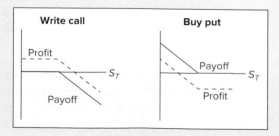

  b. The payoffs and profits to both buying calls and writing puts generally are higher when the stock price is higher. In this sense, both positions are bullish. Both involve potentially taking delivery of the stock. However, the call holder will *choose* to take delivery when the stock price is high, while the put writer *is obligated* to take delivery when the stock price is low.

  c. The payoffs and profits to both writing calls and buying puts generally are higher when the stock price is lower. In this sense, both positions are bearish. Both involve potentially making delivery of the stock. However, the put holder will *choose* to make delivery when the stock price is low, while the call writer *is obligated* to make delivery when the stock price is high.

15.3

Payoff to a Strip

	$S_T \leq X$	$S_T > X$
2 Puts	$2(X - S_T)$	0
1 Call	0	$S_T - X$

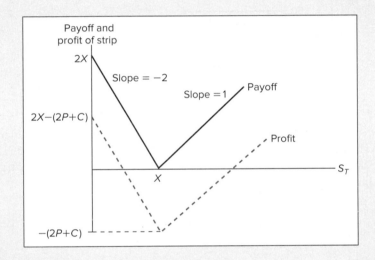

Payoff to a Strap

	$S_T \leq X$	$S_T > X$
1 Put	$X - S_T$	0
2 Calls	0	$2(S_T - X)$

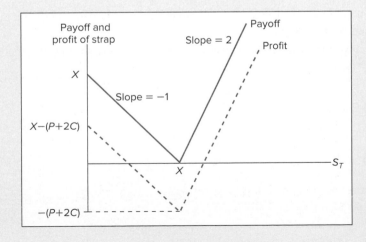

15.4   The payoff table on a per-share basis is as follows:

	$S_T < 60$	$60 < S_T < 80$	$S_T > 80$
Buy put ($X = 60$)	$60 - S_T$	0	0
Buy one share	S_T	S_T	S_T
Write call ($X = 80$)	0	0	$-(S_T - 80)$
Total	60	S_T	80

The graph of the payoff follows. If you multiply the per-share values by 2,000, you will see that the collar provides a minimum payoff of $120,000 (representing a maximum loss of $20,000) and a maximum payoff of $160,000 (which is the cost of the house).

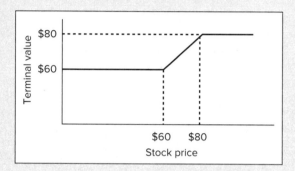

15.5   The covered call strategy would consist of a straight bond with a call written on the bond. The payoff value of the covered call position at option expiration as a function of the value of the straight bond is given in the following figure, and is virtually identical to the value of the callable bond in Figure 15.11.

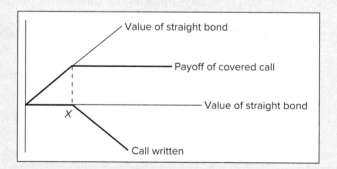

15.6   The call option is less valuable as call protection is expanded. Therefore, the coupon rate need not be as high.

15.7   Lower. Investors will accept a lower coupon rate in return for the conversion option.

Option Valuation

Learning Objectives

LO 16-1 Identify the features of an option that affect its market value.

LO 16-2 Compute an option value in two-scenario and binomial models of the economy.

LO 16-3 Compute the Black-Scholes value and implied volatility of an option.

LO 16-4 Derive the proper relationship between call and put prices.

LO 16-5 Compute the hedge ratio of an option, and use that ratio to manage risk.

I n the previous chapter, we examined option markets and strategies. We ended by noting that many securities contain embedded options that affect both their values and their risk-return characteristics. In this chapter, we turn our attention to option valuation. Most option-valuation models require considerable background in statistics. Still, many of their ideas and insights can be demonstrated in simple examples, and we will concentrate on these.

We start with a discussion of the factors that ought to affect option prices. After this qualitative discussion, we present a simple "two-state" quantitative option valuation model and show how we can generalize it into a useful and accurate pricing tool. Next, we move on to one particular option valuation formula, the famous Black-Scholes model. Option-pricing models allow us to "back out" market estimates of stock price volatility, and we will examine these measures of implied volatility.

Next we turn to some of the more important applications of option-pricing theory in risk management. Finally, we take a brief look at some of the empirical evidence on option pricing and the implications of that evidence concerning the limitations of the Black-Scholes model.

16.1 OPTION VALUATION: INTRODUCTION

Intrinsic and Time Values

Consider a call option that is out of the money at the moment, with the stock price below the exercise price. This does not mean the option is valueless. Even though immediate exercise would be unprofitable, the call still has value because there is always a chance the stock price will rise above the exercise price by the expiration date. If not, the worst that can happen is that the option will expire with zero value.

intrinsic value (of an option)

The value an option would have if it were about to expire.

time value (of an option)

Difference between an option's price and its intrinsic value.

The value $S_0 - X$ is sometimes called the **intrinsic value** of an in-the-money call option because it gives the payoff that could be obtained by immediate exercise. Intrinsic value is set equal to zero for out-of-the-money or at-the-money options. The difference between the actual call price and the intrinsic value is commonly called the **time value** of the option.

Time value is an unfortunate choice of terminology because it may confuse the option's time value with the time value of money. Time value in the options context simply refers to the difference between the option's price and the value it would have if it were expiring immediately. It is the part of the option's value that may be attributed to the time to expiration.

Most of an option's time value typically is a type of "volatility value." As long as the option holder can choose not to exercise, the payoff cannot be worse than zero, and there is always a chance it may be positive. The volatility value lies in the right *not* to exercise if doing so would be unprofitable. The option to exercise a call, as opposed to the obligation to exercise, provides insurance against poor stock price performance.

As the stock price increases substantially, it becomes more likely that the call option will be exercised by expiration. In this case, with exercise all but assured, the volatility value becomes minimal. As the stock price gets ever larger, the option value approaches the "adjusted" intrinsic value—the stock price minus the present value of the exercise price, $S_0 - PV(X)$.

Why should this be? If you *know* the option will be exercised and the stock will be purchased for X dollars, it is as though you own the stock already. You almost certainly will own it shortly. You just haven't paid for it yet. You will pay the exercise price, for the stock so the value of your prospective payment is the present value of X, and the present value of your net payoff is $S_0 - PV(X)$.[1]

Figure 16.1 illustrates the call option valuation function. The value curve shows that when the stock price is low, the option is nearly worthless because there is almost no chance that it will be exercised. When the stock price is very high, the option value approaches adjusted intrinsic value. In the midrange case, where the option is approximately at the money, the option curve diverges from the straight lines corresponding to adjusted intrinsic value. This is because, while exercise today would have a negligible (or negative) payoff, the volatility value of the option is quite high in this region.

The call option always increases in value with the stock price. The slope is greatest, however, when the option is deep in the money. In this case, exercise is all but assured, and the option price increases one-for-one with the stock price.

Determinants of Option Values

We can identify at least six factors that should affect the value of a call option: the stock price, the exercise price, the volatility of the stock price, the time to expiration, the interest rate, and the dividend rate of the stock. The call's value should increase with the stock price and decrease with the exercise price because its payoff, if exercised, equals $S_T - X$. The expected payoff increases with the difference $S_0 - X$.

---

[1]This discussion presumes the stock pays no dividends until after option expiration. If the stock does pay dividends before expiration, then there *is* a reason you would care about getting the stock now rather than at expiration—getting it now entitles you to the interim dividend payments. In this case, the adjusted intrinsic value must subtract the value of the dividends the stock will pay out before the call is exercised. Adjusted intrinsic value would more generally be defined as $S_0 - PV(X) - PV(D)$, where D represents dividends to be paid before option expiration.

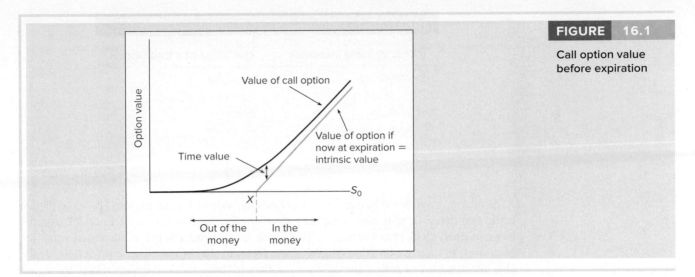

FIGURE 16.1

Call option value before expiration

Call option values also increase with the volatility of the underlying stock price. To see why, compare a situation where possible stock prices at expiration may range from $10 to $50 to one where they range only from $20 to $40. In both cases, the expected stock price is $30. Suppose the exercise price on a call option is also $30. What are the option payoffs?

High-Volatility Scenario

Stock price	$10	$20	$30	$40	$50
Option payoff	0	0	0	10	20

Low-Volatility Scenario

Stock price	$20	$25	$30	$35	$40
Option payoff	0	0	0	5	10

If each outcome is equally likely, with probability 0.2, the expected payoff to the option under high-volatility conditions will be $6, but under the low-volatility conditions, the expected payoff is half as much, only $3.

Although the expected stock price in each scenario is $30, the average option payoff is greater in the high-volatility scenario. The source of this extra value is the limited loss an option holder can suffer, or the volatility value of the call. No matter how far below $30 the stock price drops, the option holder will get zero. Extremely poor stock price performance is no worse for the call option holder than moderately poor performance.

When the stock performs well, however, the call will expire in the money, and it will be more profitable the higher the stock price. Thus, extremely good stock outcomes can improve the option payoff without limit, but extremely poor outcomes cannot worsen the payoff below zero. This asymmetry means volatility in the underlying stock price increases the expected payoff to the option.[2]

Should a put option increase in value with the volatility of the stock? Illustrate with an example.

CONCEPT check 16.1

[2]You should be careful interpreting the relationship between volatility and option value. Neither the focus of this analysis on total (as opposed to systematic) volatility nor the conclusion that options buyers seem to like volatility contradicts modern portfolio theory. In conventional discounted cash flow analysis, we find the discount rate appropriate for a *given* distribution of future cash flows. Greater risk implies a higher discount rate and lower present value. Here, however, the cash flow from the *option* depends on the volatility of the *stock*. The option value increases not because traders like risk but because the expected cash flow to the option holder increases along with the volatility of the underlying asset.

TABLE 16.1 Determinants of call option values	
If This Variable Increases	**The Value of a Call Option**
Stock price, S	Increases
Exercise price, X	Decreases
Volatility, σ	Increases
Time to expiration, T	Increases
Interest rate, r_f	Increases
Dividend payouts	Decreases

Similarly, longer time to expiration increases the value of a call option. For more distant expiration dates, there is more time for unpredictable future events to affect prices, and the range of likely stock prices increases. This has an effect similar to that of increased volatility. Moreover, as time to expiration lengthens, the present value of the exercise price falls, which also benefits the call option holder. As a corollary to this issue, call option values are higher when interest rates rise (holding the stock price constant), because higher interest rates also reduce the present value of the exercise price.

Finally, the firm's dividend payout policy affects option values. High dividend payouts put a drag on growth of the stock price. For any expected total rate of return on the stock, a higher dividend yield must imply a lower expected rate of capital gain. This drag decreases the potential payoff from the call option, thereby lowering its value. Table 16.1 summarizes these relationships.

CONCEPT check 16.2

Prepare a table like Table 16.1 for the determinants of put option values. How should put values respond to increases in S, X, T, σ, r_f, and dividend payout?

16.2 BINOMIAL OPTION PRICING

Two-State Option Pricing

A complete understanding of commonly used option valuation formulas is difficult without a substantial mathematics background. Nevertheless, we can develop valuable insight into option valuation by considering a simple special case. Assume a stock price can take only two possible values at option expiration: The stock will either increase to a given higher price or decrease to a given lower price. Although this simplification may seem extreme, it provides a useful introduction to more complicated and realistic models. Moreover, this approach can be extended to describe far more reasonable specifications of stock price behavior. In fact, several major financial firms employ extensions of this simple model to value options and securities with optionlike features.

Suppose the stock now sells at $100, and the price will either increase by a factor of $u = 1.2$ to $120 ($u$ stands for "up") or fall by a factor of $d = .9$ to $90 ($d$ stands for "down") by year-end. A call option on the stock might specify an exercise price of $110 and a time to expiration of one year. The interest rate is 10%. At year-end, the payoff to the call will be either zero, if the stock falls, or $10, if the stock price increases.

These possibilities are illustrated by the following "value trees":

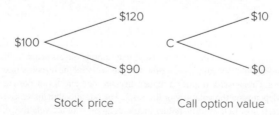

Stock price   Call option value

Now compare this payoff to that of a portfolio consisting of one share of the stock and borrowing of $81.82 at the interest rate of 10%. The payoff of this portfolio also depends on the stock price at year-end.

Value of stock at year-end	$ 90	$ 120
−Repayment of loan with interest	−90	−90
Total	$ 0	$ 30

We know the cash outlay to establish the portfolio is $18.18: $100 for the stock less the $81.82 proceeds from borrowing. Therefore, the portfolio's value tree is

The final payoff of this portfolio is exactly three times that of the call option for either value of the stock price. Because the portfolio replicates the payoff of the three calls, we call it a *replicating portfolio*. Moreover, because their payoffs are the same, the three calls and the replicating portfolio must have the same value. Therefore,

$$3C = \$18.18$$

so each call should sell at $C = \$6.06$. Thus, given the stock price, exercise price, interest rate, and volatility of the stock price (as represented by the spread between the up or down movements), we can derive the fair value for the call option.

The notion of replication is behind most option-pricing formulas. For more complex price distributions for stocks, the replication technique is correspondingly more complex, but the principles remain the same.

One way to view the role of replication is to note that, in this example, a portfolio made up of one share of stock and three call options written is perfectly hedged: Its year-end value is independent of the ultimate stock price:

Stock price	$90	$120
−Obligations from 3 calls written	−0	−30
Net payoff	$90	$ 90

The investor has formed a riskless portfolio with a payout of $90. Its value must be the present value of $90 discounted at the risk-free rate, or $90/1.10 = $81.82. The value of the portfolio, which equals $100 from the stock held long minus 3C from the three calls written, therefore, should equal $81.82. Hence, $100 − 3C = $81.82, or C = $6.06.

The ability to create a perfect hedge is the key to this argument. The hedge locks in the end-of-year payout, which therefore can be discounted using the *risk-free* interest rate. To find the value of the option in terms of the value of the stock, we do not need to know the option's or the stock's beta or expected rate of return. When a perfect hedge can be established, the final stock price does not affect the investor's payoff, so the stock's risk and return parameters have no bearing.

The hedge ratio in this example is one share of stock to three calls, or one-third. This ratio has an easy interpretation: It is the ratio of the range of the values of the option to those of the stock across the two possible outcomes. The stock, which originally sells for $S_0 = \$100$, will be worth either $d \times \$100 = \$90$ or $u \times \$100 = \$120$, for a range of \$30. If the stock price increases, the call will be worth $C_u = \$10$, whereas if the stock price decreases, the call will be worth $C_d = 0$, for a range of \$10. The ratio of ranges, \$10/\$30, is one-third, which is the hedge ratio.

The hedge ratio equals the ratio of ranges because the option and stock are perfectly correlated in this two-state example. Because they are perfectly correlated, a perfect hedge requires that they be held in a fraction determined only by relative volatility.

We can generalize the hedge ratio for other two-state option problems as

$$H = \frac{C_u - C_d}{uS_0 - dS_0}$$

where C_u or C_d refers to the call option's value when the stock goes up or down, respectively, and uS_0 and dS_0 are the stock prices in the two states. The hedge ratio, H, is the ratio of the swings in the possible end-of-period values of the option and the stock. If the investor writes one option and holds H shares of stock, the value of the portfolio will be unaffected by the stock price. In this case, option pricing is easy: Simply set the value of the hedged portfolio equal to the present value of the known payoff.

Using our example, the option-pricing technique would proceed as follows:

1. Given the possible end-of-year stock prices, $uS_0 = \$120$ and $dS_0 = \$90$, and the exercise price of \$110, calculate that $C_u = \$10$ and $C_d = \$0$. The stock price range is \$30, while the option price range is \$10.
2. Find that the hedge ratio is $\$10/\$30 = \frac{1}{3}$.
3. Find that a portfolio made up of $\frac{1}{3}$ share with one written option would have an end-of-year value of \$30 with certainty.
4. Show that the present value of \$30 with a one-year interest rate of 10% is \$27.27.
5. Set the value of the hedged position equal to the present value of the certain payoff:

$$\frac{1}{3}S_0 - C_0 = \$27.27$$
$$\$33.33 - C_0 = \$27.27$$

6. Solve for the call's value, $C_0 = \$6.06$.

What if the option were overpriced, perhaps selling for \$6.50? Then you can make arbitrage profits. Here is how:

	Initial Cash Flow	Cash Flow in One Year for Each Possible Stock Price	
		$S_1 = \$90$	$S_1 = \$120$
1. Write 3 options	\$ 19.50	\$ 0	\$−30
2. Purchase 1 share	−100	90	120
3. Borrow \$80.50 at 10% interest; repay in 1 year	80.50	−88.55	−88.55
Total	\$ 0	\$ 1.45	\$ 1.45

Although the net initial investment is zero, the payoff in one year is positive and riskless. If the option were underpriced, one would simply reverse this arbitrage strategy: Buy the option, and sell the stock short to eliminate price risk. Notice, by the way, that the present value of the profit to this arbitrage strategy equals three times the amount by which the option is overpriced. The present value of the risk-free profit of \$1.45 at a 10% interest rate is \$1.32. With three options written in the strategy above, this translates to a profit of \$0.44 per option, exactly the amount by which the option was overpriced: \$6.50 versus the "fair value" of \$6.06.

Suppose the call option had been underpriced, selling at $5.50. Formulate the arbitrage strategy to exploit the mispricing, and show that it provides a riskless cash flow in one year of $0.6167 per option purchased. Compare the present value of this cash flow to the option mispricing.

Generalizing the Two-State Approach

Although the two-state stock price model seems simplistic, we can generalize it to incorporate more realistic assumptions. To start, suppose we were to break up the year into two six-month segments and then assert that over each half-year segment the stock price could take on two values. In this example, we will say it can increase 10% (i.e., $u = 1.10$) or decrease 5% (i.e., $d = 0.95$). A stock initially selling at $100 could follow the following possible paths over the course of the year:

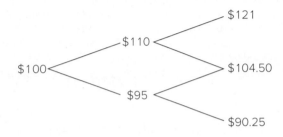

The midrange value of $104.50 can be attained by two paths: an increase of 10% followed by a decrease of 5%, or a decrease of 5% followed by an increase of 10%.

There are now three possible end-of-year values for the stock and three for the option:

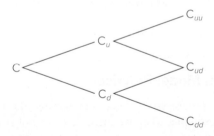

Using methods similar to those we followed above, we could value C_u from knowledge of C_{uu} and C_{ud}, then value C_d from knowledge of C_{du} and C_{dd}, and finally value C from knowledge of C_u and C_d. And there is no reason to stop at six-month intervals. We could next break the year into 4 three-month units, or 12 one-month units, or 365 one-day units, each of which would be posited to have a two-state process. Although the calculations become quite numerous and correspondingly tedious, they are easy to program into a computer, and such computer programs are used widely by participants in the options market.

Suppose that the risk-free interest rate is 5% per six-month period and we wish to value a call option with exercise price $110 on the stock described in the two-period price tree just above. We start by finding the value of C_u. From this point, the call can rise to an expiration-date value of $C_{uu} = \$11$ (because at this point the stock price is $u \times u \times S_0 = \$121$) or fall to a final value of $C_{ud} = 0$ (because at this point the stock price is $u \times d \times S_0 = \$104.50$, which is less than the $110 exercise price). Therefore, the hedge ratio at this point is

$$H = \frac{C_{uu} - C_{ud}}{uuS_0 - udS_0} = \frac{\$11 - 0}{\$121 - \$104.5} = \frac{2}{3}$$

(continued)

EXAMPLE 16.1

Binomial Option Pricing

Thus, the following portfolio will be worth $209 at option expiration regardless of the ultimate stock price:

	$udS_0 = \$104.50$	$uuS_0 = \$121$
Buy 2 shares at price $uS_0 = \$110$	$209	$242
Write 3 calls at price C_u	0	−33
Total	$209	$209

The portfolio must have a current market value equal to the present value of $209:

$$2 \times \$110 - 3C_u = \$209/1.05 = \$199.047$$

Solve to find that $C_u = \$6.984$.

Next we find the value of C_d. It is easy to see that this value must be zero. If we reach this point (corresponding to a stock price of $95), the stock price at option expiration will be either $104.50 or $90.25; in both cases, the option will expire out of the money. (More formally, we could note that with $C_{ud} = C_{dd} = 0$, the hedge ratio is zero, and a portfolio of *zero* shares will replicate the payoff of the call!)

Finally, we solve for C by using the values of C_u and C_d. The following Concept Check leads you through the calculations that show the option value to be $4.434.

**CONCEPT
check   16.4**

Show that the initial value of the call option in Example 16.1 is $4.434.
  a. Confirm that the spread in option values is $C_u - C_d = \$6.984$.
  b. Confirm that the spread in stock values is $uS_0 - dS_0 = \$15$.
  c. Confirm that the hedge ratio is .4656 shares purchased for each call written.
  d. Demonstrate that the value in one period of a portfolio comprising .4656 shares and one call written is riskless.
  e. Calculate the present value of this payoff.
  f. Solve for the option value.

Making the Valuation Model Practical

As we break the year into progressively finer subintervals, the range of possible year-end stock prices expands. For example, when we increase the number of subperiods to three, the number of possible stock prices increases to four, as in the following stock price tree:

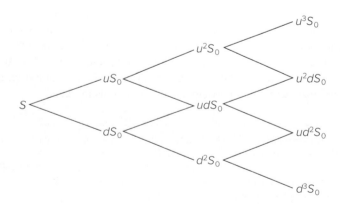

Thus, by allowing for an ever-greater number of subperiods, we can overcome one of the apparent limitations of the valuation model: that the number of possible end-of-period stock prices is small.

Notice that extreme outcomes such as u^3S_0 or d^3S_0 will be relatively rare, as they require either three consecutive increases or decreases in the three subintervals. More moderate, or midrange, results such as u^2dS_0 can be arrived at by more than one path; any combination of two price increases and one decrease will result in stock price u^2dS_0. There are three of these paths: *uud, udu, duu*. In contrast, only one path, *uuu*, results in a stock price of u^3S_0. Thus, midrange values are more likely. As we make the model more realistic and break up the option maturity into more and more subperiods, the probability distribution for the final stock price begins to resemble the familiar bell-shaped curve, with highly unlikely extreme outcomes and far more likely midrange outcomes. The exact probability of each outcome is given by the binomial probability distribution, so this multiperiod approach to option pricing is called the **binomial model.**

But we still need to answer an important practical question. Before the binomial model can be used to value actual options, we need a way to choose reasonable values for u and d. The spread between up and down movements in the price of the stock reflects the volatility of its rate of return, so the choice for u and d should depend on that volatility. Call σ your estimate of the standard deviation of the stock's continuously compounded annualized rate of return and Δt the length of each subperiod. To make the standard deviation of the stock in the binomial model match your estimate of σ, it turns out that you can set $u = \exp(\sigma\sqrt{\Delta t})$ and $d = \exp(-\sigma\sqrt{\Delta t})$.[3] You can see that the proportional difference between u and d increases with annualized volatility as well as the duration of the subperiod. This makes sense, as both higher σ and longer holding periods make future stock prices more uncertain. The following example illustrates how to use this calibration.

binomial model

An option valuation model predicated on the assumption that stock prices can move to only two values over any short time period.

> Suppose you are using a three-period model to value a one-year option on a stock with volatility (i.e., annualized standard deviation) of $\sigma = 0.30$. With a time to expiration of $T = 1$ year, and $n = 3$ subperiods, you would calculate $\Delta t = T/n = \frac{1}{3}$, $u = \exp(\sigma\sqrt{\Delta t}) = \exp(.30\sqrt{\frac{1}{3}}) = 1.189$ and $d = \exp(-\sigma\sqrt{\Delta t}) = \exp(-.30\sqrt{\frac{1}{3}}) = .841$. Given the probability of an up movement, you could then work out the probability of any final stock price. For example, suppose the probability that the stock price increases is 0.554 and the probability that it decreases is 0.446.[4] Then the probability of stock prices at the end of the year would be as follows:

EXAMPLE 16.2

Calibrating u and d to Stock Volatility

Event	Possible Paths	Probability	Final Stock Price
3 down movements	*ddd*	$0.446^3 = 0.089$	$59.48 = 100 \times 0.841^3$
2 down and 1 up	*ddu, dud, udd*	$3 \times 0.446^2 \times 0.554 = 0.330$	$84.10 = 100 \times 1.189 \times 0.841^2$
1 down and 2 up	*uud, udu, duu*	$3 \times 0.446 \times 0.554^2 = 0.411$	$118.89 = 100 \times 1.189^2 \times 0.841$
3 up movements	*uuu*	$0.554^3 = 0.170$	$168.09 = 100 \times 1.189^3$

> We plot this probability distribution in Figure 16.2, Panel A. Notice that the two middle end-of-period stock prices are, in fact, more likely than either extreme.
> Now we can extend Example 16.2 by breaking up the option maturity into ever-shorter subintervals. As we do, the stock price distribution becomes increasingly plausible, as we demonstrate in Example 16.3.

---

[3]Notice that $d = 1/u$. This is the most common, but not the only, way to calibrate the model to empirical volatility. For alternative methods, see Robert L. McDonald, *Derivatives Markets*, 3rd ed. (Boston: Pearson/Addison-Wesley, 2013), chap. 11, sec. 11.3.

[4]Using this probability, the continuously compounded expected rate of return on the stock is .10. In general, the formula relating the probability of an upward movement with the annual expected rate of return, r, is $p = \dfrac{\exp(r\Delta t) - d}{u - d}$.

FIGURE **16.2**

Probability distributions for final stock price: possible outcomes and associated probabilities. In each panel, the stock's expected annualized, continuously compounded rate of return is 10% and its standard deviation is 30%.

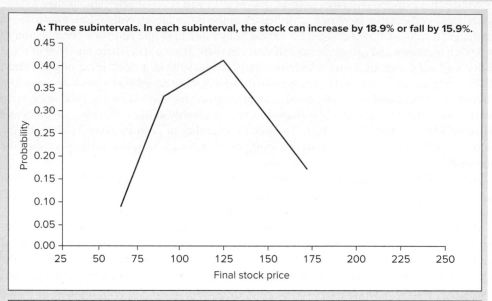

A: Three subintervals. In each subinterval, the stock can increase by 18.9% or fall by 15.9%.

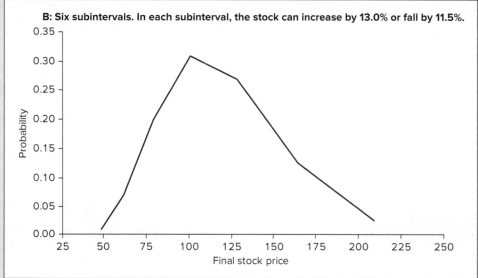

B: Six subintervals. In each subinterval, the stock can increase by 13.0% or fall by 11.5%.

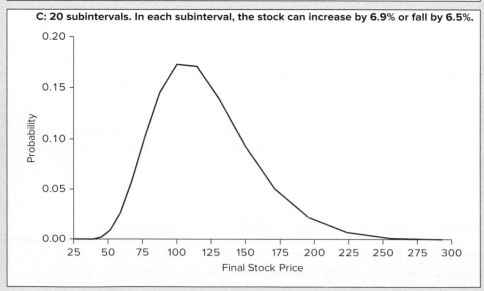

C: 20 subintervals. In each subinterval, the stock can increase by 6.9% or fall by 6.5%.

EXAMPLE 16.3

Increasing the Number of Subperiods

In Example 16.2, we broke up the year into 3 subperiods. Let's also look at the cases of 6 and 20 subperiods.

Subperiods, n	$\Delta t = T/n$	$u = \exp(\sigma\sqrt{\Delta t})$	$d = \exp(-\sigma\sqrt{\Delta t})$
3	0.333	$\exp(0.173) = 1.189$	$\exp(-0.173) = 0.841$
6	0.167	$\exp(0.123) = 1.130$	$\exp(-0.095) = 0.885$
20	0.050	$\exp(0.067) = 1.069$	$\exp(-0.067) = 0.935$

We plot the resulting probability distributions in Panels B and C of Figure 16.2.[5]

Notice that the right tail of the distribution in Panel C is noticeably longer than the left tail. In fact, as the number of intervals increases, the distribution progressively approaches the skewed lognormal (rather than the symmetric normal) distribution. Even if the stock price were to decline in *each* subinterval, it can never drop below zero. But there is no corresponding upper bound on its potential performance. This asymmetry gives rise to the skewness of the distribution.

Eventually, as we divide the option maturity into an ever-greater number of subintervals, each node of the event tree corresponds to a smaller and smaller time interval. The possible stock price movement within each time interval is correspondingly small. As those many intervals pass, the end-of-period stock price more and more closely resembles a lognormal distribution.[6] Thus, the apparent oversimplification of the two-state model can be overcome by progressively subdividing any period into many subperiods.

At any node, one still can set up a portfolio that is perfectly hedged over the next time interval. Then, at the end of that interval, on reaching the next node, a new hedge ratio can be computed and the portfolio composition revised to remain hedged over the coming small interval. By continuously revising the hedge position, the portfolio remains hedged and earns a riskless rate of return over each interval. This is called *dynamic hedging,* the continued updating of the hedge ratio as time passes. As the dynamic hedge becomes ever finer, the resulting option valuation procedure becomes more precise. The nearby box offers further refinements on the use of the binomial model.

> **CONCEPT check 16.5**
>
> In the table in Example 16.3, u and d both get closer to 1 (u is smaller and d is larger) as the time interval Δt shrinks. Why does this make sense? Does the fact that u and d are each closer to 1 mean that the total volatility of the stock over the remaining life of the option is lower?

16.3   BLACK-SCHOLES OPTION VALUATION

While the binomial model we have described is extremely flexible, it requires a computer to be useful in actual trading. An option-pricing *formula* would be easier to use than the algorithm involved in the binomial model. It turns out that such a formula can be derived

---

[5]We adjust the probabilities of up versus down movements using the formula in footnote 4 to make the distributions in Figure 16.2 comparable. In each panel, p is chosen so that the stock's expected annualized, continuously compounded rate of return is 10%.

[6]Actually, more complex considerations enter here. The limit of this process is lognormal only if we assume also that stock prices move continuously, by which we mean that over small time intervals only small price movements can occur. This rules out rare events such as sudden, extreme price moves in response to dramatic information (like a takeover attempt). For a treatment of this type of "jump process," see John C. Cox and Stephen A. Ross, "The Valuation of Options for Alternative Stochastic Processes," *Journal of Financial Economics* 3 (January–March 1976), pp. 145–166; or Robert C. Merton, "Option Pricing When Underlying Stock Returns Are Discontinuous," *Journal of Financial Economics* 3 (January–March 1976), pp. 125–144.

On the MARKET FRONT

A RISK-NEUTRAL SHORTCUT

We pointed out earlier in the chapter that the binomial-model valuation approach is arbitrage-based. We can value the option by replicating it with shares of stock plus borrowing. The ability to replicate the option means that its price relative to the stock and the interest rate must be based only on the technology of replication, and *not* on risk preferences. It cannot depend on risk aversion or the capital asset pricing model or any other model of equilibrium risk-return relationships.

This insight—that the pricing model must be independent of risk aversion—leads to a very useful shortcut to valuing options. Imagine a *risk-neutral economy*, that is, an economy in which all investors are risk-neutral. This hypothetical economy must value options the same as our real one, because risk aversion cannot affect the valuation formula.

In a risk-neutral economy, investors would not demand risk premiums and would therefore value all assets by discounting expected payoffs at the risk-free rate of interest. Therefore, a security such as a call option would be valued by discounting its expected cash flow at the risk-free rate: $C = \dfrac{"E"(CF)}{1 + r_f}$. We put the expectation operator in quotation marks to signify that this is not the true expectation but the expectation that would prevail in the hypothetical risk-neutral economy. To be consistent, we must calculate this expected cash flow using the expected rate of return the stock *would* have in the risk-neutral economy, *not* using its actual expected rate of return. But if we can successfully maintain consistency, the value derived for the hypothetical economy should match the one in our own.

How do we compute the expected cash flow from the option in the risk-neutral economy? Because there are no risk premiums, the stock's expected rate of return must equal the risk-free rate. Call p the probability that the stock price increases. Then p must be chosen to equate the expected rate of increase of the stock price to the risk-free rate (we ignore dividends here):

$$"E"(S_1) = p(uS) + (1 - p)dS = (1 + r_f)S$$

This implies that $p = \dfrac{1 + r_f - d}{u - d}$. We call p a *risk-neutral probability* to distinguish it from the true or "objective" probability. To illustrate, in our two-state example at the beginning of Section 16.2, we had $u = 1.2$, $d = .9$, and $r_f = .10$. Given these values,

$$p = \frac{1 + .10 - .9}{1.2 - .9} = \frac{2}{3}.$$

Now let's see what happens if we use the discounted cash flow formula to value the option in the risk-neutral economy. We continue to use the two-state example from Section 16.2. We find the present value of the option payoff using the risk-neutral probability and discount at the risk-free interest rate:

$$C = \frac{"E"(CF)}{1 + r_f} = \frac{p\, C_u + (1 - p)\, C_d}{1 + r_f} = \frac{\tfrac{2}{3} \times 10 + \tfrac{1}{3} \times 0}{1.10} = 6.06$$

This answer exactly matches the value we found using our no-arbitrage approach!

We repeat: This is not truly an expected discounted value.

- The *numerator* is not the true expected cash flow from the option because we use the risk-neutral probability, p, rather than the true probability.

- The *denominator* is not the proper discount rate for option cash flows because we do not account for the risk.

- In a sense these two "errors" cancel out. But this is not just luck: We are *assured* to get the correct result because the no-arbitrage approach implies that risk preferences cannot affect the option value. Therefore, the value computed for the risk-neutral economy *must* equal the value that we obtain in our economy.

When we move to the more realistic multiperiod model, the calculations are more cumbersome, but the idea is the same. Footnote 4 shows how to relate p to any expected rate of return and volatility estimate. Simply set the expected rate of return on the stock equal to the risk-free rate, use the resulting probability to work out the expected payoff from the option, discount at the risk-free rate, and you will find the option value. These calculations are not difficult to program in Excel.

---

if one is willing to make just two more assumptions: that both the risk-free interest rate and stock price volatility are constant over the life of the option. In this case, as the time to expiration is divided into ever more subperiods, the distribution of the stock price at expiration progressively approaches the lognormal distribution, as suggested by Figure 16.2. When the stock price distribution is actually lognormal, we can derive an exact option-pricing formula.

The Black-Scholes Formula

Black-Scholes pricing formula

A formula to value an option that uses the stock price, the risk-free interest rate, the time to expiration, and the standard deviation of the stock return.

Financial economists searched for years for a workable option-pricing model before Black and Scholes (1973) and Merton (1973) derived a formula for the value of a call option. Now widely used by options market participants, the **Black-Scholes pricing formula** for a European-style call option is

$$C_0 = S_0 e^{-\delta T} N(d_1) - X e^{-rT} N(d_2) \tag{16.1}$$

where

$$d_1 = \frac{\ln(S_0/X) + (r - \delta + \sigma^2/2)T}{\sigma\sqrt{T}}$$

$$d_2 = d_1 - \sigma\sqrt{T}$$

and where

C_0 = Current call option value.

S_0 = Current stock price.

$N(d)$ = The probability that a random draw from a standard normal distribution will be less than d. This equals the area under the normal curve up to d, as in the shaded area of Figure 16.3. In Excel, this function is called NORMSDIST(d) or NORM.S.DIST(d).

X = Exercise price.

e = The base of the natural log function, approximately 2.71828. In Excel, e^x can be evaluated using the function EXP(x).

δ = Annual dividend yield of underlying stock. (We assume for simplicity that the stock pays a continuous income flow, rather than discrete periodic payments, such as quarterly dividends.)

r = Risk-free interest rate, expressed as a decimal (the annualized continuously compounded rate[7] on a safe asset with the same maturity as the expiration date of the option, which is to be distinguished from r_f, the discrete period interest rate).

T = Time remaining until expiration of option (in years).

ln = Natural logarithm function. In Excel, $\ln(x)$ can be calculated using the built-in function LN(x).

σ = Standard deviation of the annualized continuously compounded rate of return of the stock, expressed as a decimal, not a percent.

Notice a surprising feature of Equation 16.1: The option value does not depend on the expected rate of return on the stock. In a sense, this information is already built into the formula with inclusion of the stock price, which itself reflects the stock's risk and return characteristics. This version of the Black-Scholes formula is predicated on the assumption that the underlying asset has a constant dividend (or income) yield.

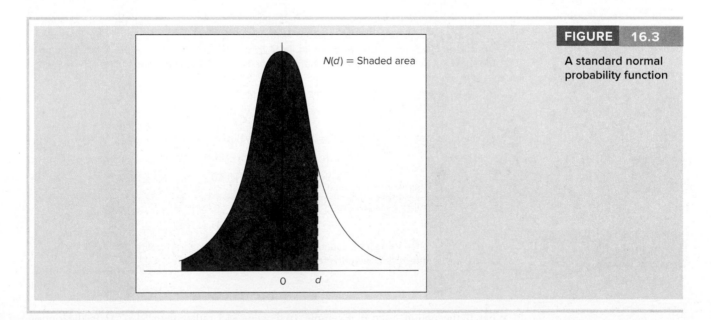

FIGURE 16.3

A standard normal probability function

$N(d)$ = Shaded area

---

[7]See Chapter 5, Section 5.1, for a review of continuous compounding.

Although the Black-Scholes formula can be intimidating, we can explain it at a somewhat intuitive level. Consider a nondividend-paying stock, for which $\delta = 0$. Then $S_0 e^{-\delta T} = S_0$.

The trick is to view the $N(d)$ terms (loosely) as risk-adjusted probabilities that the call option will expire in the money. First, look at Equation 16.1 assuming both $N(d)$ terms are close to 1, that is, when there is a very high probability that the option will be exercised. Then the call option value is equal to $S_0 - Xe^{-rT}$, which is what we called earlier the adjusted intrinsic value, $S_0 - PV(X)$. This makes sense; if exercise is certain, we have a claim on a stock with current value S_0 and an obligation with present value $PV(X)$, or with continuous compounding, Xe^{-rT}.

Now look at Equation 16.1 assuming the $N(d)$ terms are close to zero, meaning the option almost certainly will not be exercised. Then the equation confirms that the call is worth nothing. For middle-range values of $N(d)$ between 0 and 1, Equation 16.1 tells us that the call value can be viewed as the present value of the call's potential payoff adjusting for the probability of in-the-money expiration.

How do the $N(d)$ terms serve as risk-adjusted probabilities? This question quickly leads us into advanced statistics. Notice, however, that d_1 and d_2 both increase as the stock price increases. Therefore, $N(d_1)$ and $N(d_2)$ also increase with higher stock prices. This is the property we would desire of our "probabilities." For higher stock prices relative to exercise prices, future exercise is more likely.

EXAMPLE 16.4

*Black-Scholes Call
Option Valuation*

You can use the Black-Scholes formula fairly easily. Suppose you want to value a call option under the following circumstances:

Stock price	$S_0 = 100$
Exercise price	$X = 95$
Interest rate	$r = .10$ (10% per year)
Dividend yield	$\delta = 0$
Time to expiration	$T = .25$ (one-quarter year)
Standard deviation	$\sigma = .50$ (50% per year)

First calculate

$$d_1 = \frac{\ln(100/95) + (.10 - 0 + .5^2/2).25}{.5\sqrt{0.25}} = .43$$

$$d_2 = .43 - .5\sqrt{.25} = .18$$

Next find $N(d_1)$ and $N(d_2)$. The normal distribution function is tabulated and can be found in many statistics textbooks. A table of $N(d)$ is provided as Table 16.2. The normal distribution function $N(d)$ is also provided in any spreadsheet program. In Microsoft Excel, for example, the function name is NORMSDIST or NORM.S.DIST. Using either Excel or Table 16.2 (using interpolation for .43), we find that

$$N(.43) = .6664$$

$$N(.18) = .5714$$

Finally, remember that with $\delta = 0$, $S_0 e^{-\delta T} = S_0$. Thus, the value of the call option is

$$C = 100 \times .6664 - 95 e^{-.10 \times .25} \times .5714$$

$$= 66.64 - 52.94 = \$13.70$$

**CONCEPT
check**   **16.6**

Calculate the call option value if the standard deviation of the stock's rate of return is 0.6 instead of 0.5. Confirm that the option is worth more using this higher volatility.

What if the option price in Example 16.4 were $15 rather than $13.70? Is the option mispriced? Maybe, but before betting your career on that, you may want to reconsider the

TABLE 16.2   Cumulative normal distribution

d	N(d)	d	N(d)	d	N(d)	d	N(d)	d	N(d)	d	N(d)
−3.00	0.0013	−1.58	0.0571	−0.76	0.2236	0.06	0.5239	0.88	0.8106	1.70	0.9545
−2.95	0.0016	−1.56	0.0594	−0.74	0.2297	0.08	0.5319	0.90	0.8159	1.72	0.9573
−2.90	0.0019	−1.54	0.0618	−0.72	0.2358	0.10	0.5398	0.92	0.8212	1.74	0.9591
−2.85	0.0022	−1.52	0.0643	−0.70	0.2420	0.12	0.5478	0.94	0.8264	1.76	0.9608
−2.80	0.0026	−1.50	0.0668	−0.68	0.2483	0.14	0.5557	0.96	0.8315	1.78	0.9625
−2.75	0.0030	−1.48	0.0694	−0.66	0.2546	0.16	0.5636	0.98	0.8365	1.80	0.9641
−2.70	0.0035	−1.46	0.0721	−0.64	0.2611	0.18	0.5714	1.00	0.8414	1.82	0.9656
−2.65	0.0040	−1.44	0.0749	−0.62	0.2676	0.20	0.5793	1.02	0.8461	1.84	0.9671
−2.60	0.0047	−1.42	0.0778	−0.60	0.2743	0.22	0.5871	1.04	0.8508	1.86	0.9686
−2.55	0.0054	−1.40	0.0808	−0.58	0.2810	0.24	0.5948	1.06	0.8554	1.88	0.9699
−2.50	0.0062	−1.38	0.0838	−0.56	0.2877	0.26	0.6026	1.08	0.8599	1.90	0.9713
−2.45	0.0071	−1.36	0.0869	−0.54	0.2946	0.28	0.6103	1.10	0.8643	1.92	0.9726
−2.40	0.0082	−1.34	0.0901	−0.52	0.3015	0.30	0.6179	1.12	0.8686	1.94	0.9738
−2.35	0.0094	−1.32	0.0934	−0.50	0.3085	0.32	0.6255	1.14	0.8729	1.96	0.9750
−2.30	0.0107	−1.30	0.0968	−0.48	0.3156	0.34	0.6331	1.16	0.8770	1.98	0.9761
−2.25	0.0122	−1.28	0.1003	−0.46	0.3228	0.36	0.6406	1.18	0.8810	2.00	0.9772
−2.20	0.0139	−1.26	0.1038	−0.44	0.3300	0.38	0.6480	1.20	0.8849	2.05	0.9798
−2.15	0.0158	−1.24	0.1075	−0.42	0.3373	0.40	0.6554	1.22	0.8888	2.10	0.9821
−2.10	0.0179	−1.22	0.1112	−0.40	0.3446	0.42	0.6628	1.24	0.8925	2.15	0.9842
−2.05	0.0202	−1.20	0.1151	−0.38	0.3520	0.44	0.6700	1.26	0.8962	2.20	0.9861
−2.00	0.0228	−1.18	0.1190	−0.36	0.3594	0.46	0.6773	1.28	0.8997	2.25	0.9878
−1.98	0.0239	−1.16	0.1230	−0.34	0.3669	0.48	0.6844	1.30	0.9032	2.30	0.9893
−1.96	0.0250	−1.14	0.1271	−0.32	0.3745	0.50	0.6915	1.32	0.9066	2.35	0.9906
−1.94	0.0262	−1.12	0.1314	−0.30	0.3821	0.52	0.6985	1.34	0.9099	2.40	0.9918
−1.92	0.0274	−1.10	0.1357	−0.28	0.3897	0.54	0.7054	1.36	0.9131	2.45	0.9929
−1.90	0.0287	−1.08	0.1401	−0.26	0.3974	0.56	0.7123	1.38	0.9162	2.50	0.9938
−1.88	0.0301	−1.06	0.1446	−0.24	0.4052	0.58	0.7191	1.40	0.9192	2.55	0.9946
−1.86	0.0314	−1.04	0.1492	−0.22	0.4129	0.60	0.7258	1.42	0.9222	2.60	0.9953
−1.84	0.0329	−1.02	0.1539	−0.20	0.4207	0.62	0.7324	1.44	0.9251	2.65	0.9960
−1.82	0.0344	−1.00	0.1587	−0.18	0.4286	0.64	0.7389	1.46	0.9279	2.70	0.9965
−1.80	0.0359	−0.98	0.1635	−0.16	0.4365	0.66	0.7454	1.48	0.9306	2.75	0.9970
−1.78	0.0375	−0.96	0.1685	−0.14	0.4443	0.68	0.7518	1.50	0.9332	2.80	0.9974
−1.76	0.0392	−0.94	0.1736	−0.12	0.4523	0.70	0.7580	1.52	0.9357	2.85	0.9978
−1.74	0.0409	−0.92	0.1788	−0.10	0.4602	0.72	0.7642	1.54	0.9382	2.90	0.9981
−1.72	0.0427	−0.90	0.1841	−0.08	0.4681	0.74	0.7704	1.56	0.9406	2.95	0.9984
−1.70	0.0446	−0.88	0.1894	−0.06	0.4761	0.76	0.7764	1.58	0.9429	3.00	0.9986
−1.68	0.0465	−0.86	0.1949	−0.04	0.4841	0.78	0.7823	1.60	0.9452	3.05	0.9989
−1.66	0.0485	−0.84	0.2005	−0.02	0.4920	0.80	0.7882	1.62	0.9474		
−1.64	0.0505	−0.82	0.2061	0.00	0.5000	0.82	0.7939	1.64	0.9495		
−1.62	0.0526	−0.80	0.2119	0.02	0.5080	0.84	0.7996	1.66	0.9515		
−1.60	0.0548	−0.78	0.2177	0.04	0.5160	0.86	0.8051	1.68	0.9535		

valuation analysis. First, like all models, the Black-Scholes formula is based on some simplifying abstractions that make the formula only approximately valid.

Some of the important assumptions underlying the formula are the following:

1. The stock will pay a constant, continuous dividend yield until the option expiration date.
2. Both the interest rate, r, and variance rate, σ^2, of the stock are constant (or in slightly more general versions of the formula, both are *known* functions of time, so any changes are perfectly predictable).
3. Stock prices are continuous, meaning that sudden extreme jumps, such as those in the aftermath of an announcement of a takeover attempt, are ruled out.

Variants of the Black-Scholes formula have been developed to deal with many of these limitations.

Second, even within the context of the Black-Scholes model, you must be sure of the accuracy of the parameters used in the formula. Four of these—S_0, X, T, and r—are straightforward. The stock price, exercise price, and time to expiration are readily determined. The interest rate used is the money market rate for a maturity equal to that of the option, and the dividend yield is usually reasonably predictable, at least over short horizons.

The last input, though, the standard deviation of the stock return, is not directly observable. It must be estimated from historical data, from scenario analysis, or from the prices of other options, as we will describe momentarily. Because the standard deviation can only be estimated, it is always possible that discrepancies between an option price and its Black-Scholes value simply reflect error in the estimation of the stock's volatility.

implied volatility

The standard deviation of stock returns that is consistent with an option's market value.

In fact, market participants often give the option valuation problem a different twist. Rather than calculating a Black-Scholes option value for a given stock standard deviation, they ask instead: What standard deviation would be necessary for the option price that I actually observe to be consistent with the Black-Scholes formula? This is called the **implied volatility** of the option, the volatility level for the stock implied by the option price. Investors can then judge whether they think the actual stock standard deviation exceeds the implied volatility. If it does, the option is considered a good buy; if actual volatility seems greater than the implied volatility, the option's fair price would exceed the observed price.

Another variation is to compare two options on the same stock with equal expiration dates but different exercise prices. The option with the higher implied volatility would be considered relatively expensive because a higher standard deviation is required to justify its price. The analyst might consider buying the option with the lower implied volatility and writing the option with the higher implied volatility.

The Black-Scholes call option valuation formula, as well as the implied volatility, is easily calculated using an Excel spreadsheet, as in Spreadsheet 16.1. The model inputs are provided in column B, and the outputs are given in column E. The formulas for d_1 and d_2 are provided in the spreadsheet, and the Excel formula NORMSDIST(d_1) or NORM.S.DIST(d_1) is used to calculate $N(d_1)$. Cell E6 contains the Black-Scholes call option formula.

To compute an implied volatility, we can use the Goal Seek command from the What-If Analysis menu (which may be found under the Data tab) in Excel. (See Figure 16.4 for an

SPREADSHEET 16.1

Spreadsheet to calculate Black-Scholes call-option values

Spreadsheets are available in Connect

	A	B	C	D	E	F	G	H	I	J
1	INPUTS			OUTPUTS			FORMULA FOR OUTPUT IN COLUMN E			
2	Standard deviation (annual)	0.2783		d1	0.0029		(LN(B5/B6)+(B4–B7+.5*B2^2)*B3)/(B2*SQRT(B3))			
3	Expiration (in years)	0.5		d2	–0.1939		E2–B2*SQRT(B3)			
4	Risk-free rate (annual)	0.06		N(d1)	0.5012		NORMSDIST(E2)			
5	Stock price	100		N(d2)	0.4231		NORMSDIST(E3)			
6	Exercise price	105		B/S call value	7.0000		B5*EXP(–B7*B3)*E4–B6*EXP(–B4*B3)*E5			
7	Dividend yield (annual)	0		B/S put value	8.8967		B6*EXP(–B4*B3)*(1–E5)–B5*EXP(–B7*B3)*(1–E4)			

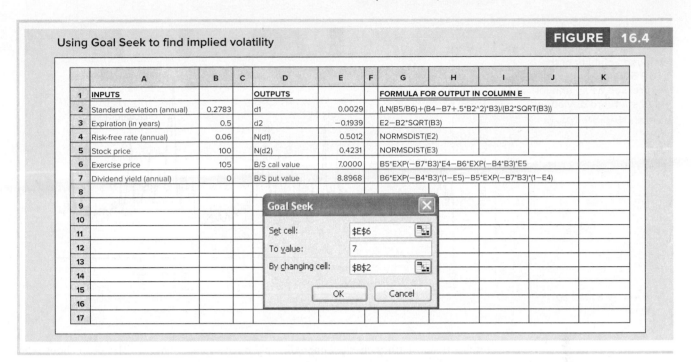

FIGURE 16.4

Using Goal Seek to find implied volatility

	A	B	C	D	E	F	G	H	I	J	K
1	INPUTS			OUTPUTS			FORMULA FOR OUTPUT IN COLUMN E				
2	Standard deviation (annual)	0.2783		d1	0.0029		(LN(B5/B6)+(B4−B7+.5*B2^2)*B3)/(B2*SQRT(B3))				
3	Expiration (in years)	0.5		d2	−0.1939		E2−B2*SQRT(B3)				
4	Risk-free rate (annual)	0.06		N(d1)	0.5012		NORMSDIST(E2)				
5	Stock price	100		N(d2)	0.4231		NORMSDIST(E3)				
6	Exercise price	105		B/S call value	7.0000		B5*EXP(−B7*B3)*E4−B6*EXP(−B4*B3)*E5				
7	Dividend yield (annual)	0		B/S put value	8.8968		B6*EXP(−B4*B3)*(1−E5)−B5*EXP(−B7*B3)*(1−E4)				
8											
9											
10											
11											
12											
13											
14											
15											
16											
17											

Goal Seek

Set cell: $E$6

To value: 7

By changing cell: $B$2

OK   Cancel

illustration.) Goal Seek asks us to change the value of one cell to make the value of another cell (called the *target cell*) equal to a specific value. For example, if we observe a call option selling for $7 with other inputs as given in the spreadsheet, we can use Goal Seek to change the value in cell B2 (the standard deviation of the stock) to force the option value in cell E6 equal to $7. The target cell, E6, is the call price, and the spreadsheet manipulates cell B2. When you click *OK*, the spreadsheet finds that a standard deviation equal to 0.2783 is consistent with a call price of $7; therefore, 27.83% would be the call's implied volatility if the option were selling at $7.

CONCEPT check 16.7

Consider the call option in Example 16.4. If it sells for $15 rather than the value of $13.70 found in the example, is its implied volatility more or less than 0.5? Use Spreadsheet 16.1 (available in Connect) to find its implied volatility at this price.

The Chicago Board Options Exchange regularly computes the implied volatility of major stock indexes. Figure 16.5 is a graph of the implied (30-day) volatility of the S&P 500. During periods of turmoil, implied volatility can spike quickly. Notice the peaks in January 1991 (Gulf War), in August 1998 (collapse of Long-Term Capital Management), on September 11, 2001, in 2002 (buildup to invasion of Iraq), and, most dramatically, during the credit crisis of 2008. Because implied volatility correlates with crisis, it is sometimes called an "investor fear gauge."

A futures contract on the implied volatility of the S&P 500 has traded on the CBOE Futures Exchange since 2004. The payoff of the contract depends on market implied volatility at the expiration of the contract. The ticker symbol of the contract is VIX.

Figure 16.5 also reveals an awkward empirical fact. While the Black-Scholes formula is derived assuming that stock volatility is constant, the time series of implied volatilities consistent with that formula is in fact far from constant. This contradiction reminds us that the Black-Scholes model (like all models) is a simplification that does not capture all aspects of real markets. In this particular context, extensions of the pricing model that allow stock volatility to evolve randomly over time would be desirable, and, in fact, many extensions of the model along these lines have been developed.[8]

[8]Influential articles on this topic are Hull and White (1987), Wiggins (1987), and Heston (1993). For a review, see Ghysels, Harvey, and Renault (1996).

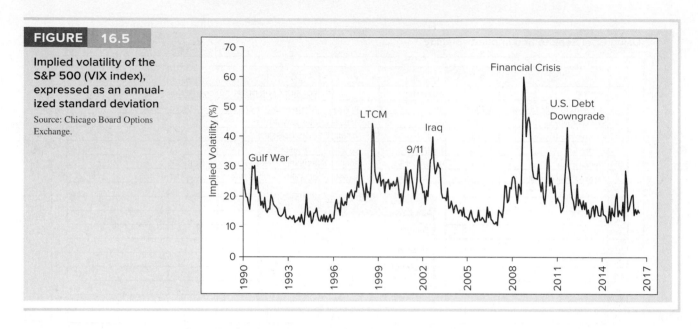

Implied volatility of the S&P 500 (VIX index), expressed as an annualized standard deviation

Source: Chicago Board Options Exchange.

The fact that volatility changes unpredictably means that it can be difficult to choose the proper volatility input to use in any option-pricing model. A considerable amount of research has been devoted to techniques to predict changes in volatility. These techniques, which are known as *ARCH* and *stochastic volatility models,* posit that changes in volatility are partially predictable and that by analyzing recent levels and trends in volatility, one can improve predictions of future volatility.[9]

The Put-Call Parity Relationship

So far, we have focused on the pricing of call options. In many important cases, put prices can be derived simply from the prices of calls. This is because prices of European put and call options are linked together in an equation known as the put-call parity relationship. Therefore, once you know the value of a call, finding the value of the put is easy.

Suppose you buy a call option and write a put option, each with the same exercise price, X, and the same expiration date, T. At expiration, your payoff equals the payoff on the purchased call minus the payoff on the written put. The payoff on each option will depend on whether the ultimate stock price, S_T, exceeds the exercise price at contract expiration.

	$S_T \leq X$	$S_T > X$
Payoff on call held	0	$S_T - X$
− Payoff on put written	$-(X - S_T)$	0
Total	$S_T - X$	$S_T - X$

Figure 16.6 plots the payoff. Compare the payoff to that of a portfolio made up of the stock plus a borrowing position, where the money to be paid back will grow, with interest, to X dollars at the maturity of the loan. Such a position is a *levered* equity position in which $PV(X) = Xe^{-rT}$ dollars is borrowed today (so that X will be repaid at maturity), and S_0 dollars is invested in the stock. The total payoff of the levered equity position is $S_T - X$, the same as that of the option strategy. Thus, the long call–short put position replicates the levered equity position. Again, we see that option trading provides leverage.

[9]For an introduction to these models, see Alexander (2001).

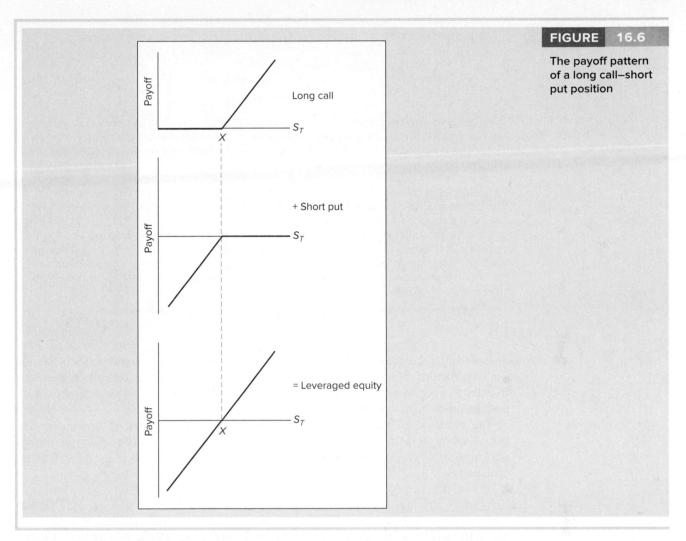

FIGURE 16.6

The payoff pattern of a long call–short put position

Because the option portfolio has a payoff identical to that of the levered equity position, the costs of establishing them must be equal. The net cash outlay necessary to establish the option position is $C - P$: The call is purchased for C, while the written put generates income of P. Likewise, the levered equity position requires a net cash outlay of $S_0 - Xe^{-rT}$, the cost of the stock less the proceeds from borrowing. Equating these costs, we conclude

$$C - P = S_0 - Xe^{-rT} \tag{16.2}$$

Equation 16.2 is called the **put-call parity relationship** because it represents the proper relationship between put and call prices. If the parity relationship is ever violated, an arbitrage opportunity arises.

put-call parity relationship

An equation representing the proper relationship between put and call prices.

Suppose you observe the following data for a certain stock.

Stock price	$110
Call price (six-month maturity, $X = \$105$)	14
Put price (six-month maturity, $X = \$105$)	5
Risk-free interest rate	5% continuously compounded rate

EXAMPLE 16.5

Put-Call Parity

(continued)

Put-Call Parity
(concluded)

We use these data in the put-call parity relationship to see if parity is violated.

$$C - P \stackrel{?}{=} S_0 - Xe^{-rT}$$
$$14 - 5 \stackrel{?}{=} 110 - 105e^{-.05 \times .5}$$
$$9 \stackrel{?}{=} 7.59$$

This result, a violation of parity (9 does not equal 7.59), indicates mispricing and leads to an arbitrage opportunity. You can buy the relatively cheap portfolio (the stock plus borrowing position represented on the right-hand side of Equation 16.2) and sell the relatively expensive portfolio (the long call–short put position corresponding to the left-hand side, that is, you write a call and buy a put).

Let's examine the payoff to this strategy. In six months, the stock will be worth S_T. You borrowed the present value of the exercise price, $105, and must pay back the loan with interest, resulting in a cash outflow of $105. The written call will result in a cash outflow of $S_T - \$105$ if S_T exceeds $105. The purchased put pays off $105 - S_T$ if the stock price is below $105.

Table 16.3 summarizes the outcome. The immediate cash inflow is $1.41, precisely equal to the mispricing of the option. In six months, the various positions provide exactly offsetting cash flows: The $1.41 inflow is realized risklessly without any offsetting outflows. This is an arbitrage opportunity that investors will pursue on a large scale until buying and selling pressure restores the parity condition expressed in Equation 16.2.

Equation 16.2 actually applies only to options on stocks that pay no dividends before the expiration date of the option. It also applies only to European options, as the cash flow streams from the two portfolios represented by the two sides of Equation 16.2 will match only if each position is held until expiration.

The extension of the parity condition for European call options on dividend-paying stocks is, however, straightforward. Problem 32 at the end of the chapter leads you through the extension of the parity relationship. The more general formulation of the put-call parity condition is

$$P = C - S_0 + PV(X) + PV(\text{dividends}) \tag{16.3}$$

where PV(dividends) is the present value of the dividends that will be paid by the stock during the life of the option. If the stock does not pay dividends, Equation 16.3 becomes identical to Equation 16.2.

Notice that this generalization would apply as well to European options on assets other than stocks. Instead of using dividend income in Equation 16.3, we would let any income paid out by the underlying asset play the role of the stock dividends. For example, European put and call options on bonds would satisfy the same parity relationship, except that the bond's coupon income would replace the stock's dividend payments in the parity formula.

Let's see how well parity works using the data in Figure 15.1 (from the previous chapter) on the Microsoft options. The July 7 expiration call with exercise price $72 and time to

TABLE 16.3   Arbitrage strategy

		Cash Flow in Six Months	
Position	**Immediate Cash Flow**	$S_T < 105$	$S_T \geq 105$
Buy stock	−110	S_T	S_T
Borrow $Xe^{-rT} = \$102.41$	+102.41	−105	−105
Sell call	+14	0	$-(S_T - 105)$
Buy put	−5	$105 - S_T$	0
Total	1.41	0	0

expiration of 35 days costs $1.15, while the corresponding put option costs $1.32. Microsoft was selling for $71.75, and the annualized short-term interest rate on this date was 0.6%. Microsoft was not expected to pay a dividend prior to option expiration. According to parity, we should find that

$$P = C + PV(X) - S_0 + PV(\text{dividends})$$
$$1.32 = 1.15 + 72e^{-.006 \times (35/365)} - 71.75 + 0$$
$$1.32 = 1.15 + 71.96 - 71.75 + 0$$
$$1.32 = 1.36$$

So parity is violated by about $0.04 per share. Is this a big enough difference to exploit? Almost certainly not. You have to weigh the potential profit against the trading costs of the call, put, and stock. More important, given the fact that options may trade relatively infrequently, this deviation from parity might not be "real" but may instead be attributable to "stale" (i.e., out-of-date) price quotes at which you cannot actually trade.

Put Option Valuation

As we saw in Equation 16.3, we can use the put-call parity relationship to value put options once we know the call option value. Sometimes, however, it is easier to work with a put option valuation formula directly. The Black-Scholes formula for the value of a European put option is[10]

$$P = Xe^{-rT}[1 - N(d_2)] - S_0e^{-\delta T}[1 - N(d_1)] \qquad \textbf{(16.4)}$$

> **EXAMPLE 16.6**
>
> *Black-Scholes Put Option Valuation*
>
> Using data from the Black-Scholes call option in Example 16.4, we find that a European put option on that stock with identical exercise price and time to expiration is worth
>
> $$\$95e^{-.10 \times .25}(1 - .5714) - \$100(1 - .6664) = \$6.35$$
>
> Notice that this value is consistent with put-call parity:
>
> $$P = C + PV(X) - S_0 + PV(\text{Div}) = 13.70 + 95e^{-.10 \times .25} - 100 + 0 = 6.35$$
>
> As we noted traders can do, we might then compare this formula value to the actual put price as one step in formulating a trading strategy.

Equation 16.4 is valid for European puts. Most listed put options are American-style, however, and offer the opportunity of early exercise. Because an American option allows its owner to exercise at any time before the expiration date, it must be worth at least as much as the corresponding European option. However, while Equation 16.4 describes only the lower bound on the true value of the American put, in many applications the approximation is very accurate.

16.4 USING THE BLACK-SCHOLES FORMULA

Hedge Ratios and the Black-Scholes Formula

In the last chapter, we considered two investments in FinCorp stock: 100 shares or 900 call options. We saw that the call option position was more sensitive to swings in the stock price

---

[10]This formula is consistent with the put-call parity relationship and in fact can be derived from it. If you want to try, remember to take present values using continuous compounding, and use the fact that when a stock pays a continuous flow of income in the form of a constant dividend yield, δ, the present value of that dividend flow is $S_0(1 - e^{-\delta T})$. (Notice that $e^{-\delta T}$ approximately equals $1 - \delta T$, so the value of the dividend flow is approximately $\delta T S_0$.)

hedge ratio or delta

The number of shares of stock required to hedge the price risk of holding one option.

than the all-stock position. To analyze the overall exposure to a stock price more precisely, however, it is necessary to quantify these relative sensitivities. We can summarize the overall exposure of portfolios of options with various exercise prices and times to expiration using the hedge ratio. An option's **hedge ratio** is the change in the option price for a $1 increase in the stock price. A call option, therefore, has a positive hedge ratio, and a put option has a negative hedge ratio. The hedge ratio is commonly called the option's **delta.**

If you graph the option value as a function of the stock price, as in Figure 16.7, the hedge ratio is simply the slope of the value function evaluated at the current stock price. For example, suppose the slope of the curve at $S_0 = \$120$ equals .60. As the stock increases in value by $1, the call increases by approximately $0.60, as the figure shows.

For every call option written, 0.60 shares of stock would be needed to hedge the investor's portfolio. If you write 10 options and hold six shares of stock, a $1 increase in stock price will result in a gain of $6 on the stock holdings, while the loss on the 10 options written will be 10 × $.60, an equivalent $6. The stock price movement leaves your total wealth unaltered, which is what a hedged position is intended to do.

Black-Scholes hedge ratios are particularly easy to compute. The hedge ratio for a call is $N(d_1)$, while the hedge ratio for a put is $N(d_1) - 1$. We defined $N(d_1)$ as part of the Black-Scholes formula in Equation 16.1. Recall that $N(d)$ stands for the area under the standard normal curve up to d. Therefore, the call option hedge ratio must be positive and less than 1.0, while the put option hedge ratio is negative and has smaller absolute value than 1.0.

Figure 16.7 shows that the slope of the call option valuation function is less than 1, approaching 1 only as the stock price becomes extremely large. This tells us that option values change less than one-for-one with changes in stock prices. Why should this be? Suppose an option is so far in the money that you are absolutely certain it will be exercised. In that case, every $1 increase in the stock price would increase the option value by $1. But if there is a chance the call option will expire out of the money, even after a moderate stock price gain, a $1 increase in the stock price will not necessarily increase the ultimate payoff to the call; therefore, the call price will not respond by a full $1.

The fact that hedge ratios are less than 1 does not contradict our earlier observation that options offer leverage and are sensitive to stock price movements. Although *dollar* movements in option prices are less than dollar movements in the stock price, the *rate of return* volatility of options is nevertheless greater than stock return volatility because options sell at lower prices. In our example, with the stock selling at $120, and a hedge ratio of 0.6, an option with exercise price $120 may sell for $5. If the stock price increases to $121, the call price would be expected to increase by only $0.60, to $5.60. The percentage increase in the option value is $.60/$5 = 12%, however, while the percentage stock price increase is only $1/$120 = .83%. The ratio of the percent changes is 12%/.83% = 14.4. For every 1% increase in the stock price,

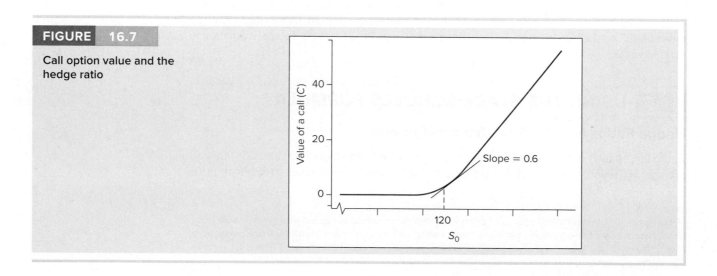

FIGURE 16.7

Call option value and the hedge ratio

the option price increases by 14.4%. This ratio, the percent change in option price per percent change in stock price, is called the **option elasticity.**

The hedge ratio is an essential tool in portfolio management and control. An example will show why.

option elasticity

The percent change in option price per percent change in stock price.

EXAMPLE 16.7

Portfolio Hedge Ratios

Consider two portfolios, one holding 750 FinCorp calls and 200 shares of FinCorp stock and the other holding 800 shares of FinCorp. Which portfolio has greater dollar exposure to FinCorp price movements? You can answer this question easily using the hedge ratio.

Each option changes in value by H dollars for each dollar change in stock price, where H stands for the hedge ratio. Thus, if H equals 0.6, the 750 options are equivalent to 450 shares (= .6 × 750) in terms of the response of their value to FinCorp stock price movements. The first portfolio has less dollar sensitivity to stock price change because the 450 share-equivalents of the options plus the 200 shares actually held are less than the 800 shares held in the second portfolio.

This is not to say, however, that the first portfolio is less sensitive to the stock's rate of return. As we noted in discussing option elasticities, the first portfolio may be worth less than the second, so despite its lower sensitivity in terms of its dollar value, it might have greater rate-of-return sensitivity.

CONCEPT check   16.8

What is the elasticity of a put option currently selling for $4 with exercise price $120 and hedge ratio −0.4 if the stock price is currently $122?

Portfolio Insurance

In Chapter 15, we showed that protective put strategies offer a sort of insurance policy on an asset. The protective put has proven to be extremely popular with investors. Even if the asset price falls, the put conveys the right to sell the asset for the exercise price, which is a way to lock in a minimum portfolio value. With an at-the-money put ($X = S_0$), the maximum possible loss is the cost of the put. The asset can be sold for X, which equals its original price, so even if the asset price falls, the investor's net loss is just the cost of the put. If the asset value increases, however, the upside potential is unlimited. Figure 16.8 graphs the profit or loss on a protective put position as a function of the change in the value of the underlying asset.

While the protective put is a simple and convenient way to achieve **portfolio insurance,** that is, to limit the worst-case portfolio rate of return, there are practical difficulties in trying to insure a portfolio of stocks. First, unless the investor's portfolio corresponds to a standard market index for which puts are traded, a put option on the portfolio will not be available. And if index puts are used to protect a nonindexed portfolio, tracking error can result. For example,

portfolio insurance

Portfolio strategies that limit investment losses while maintaining upside potential.

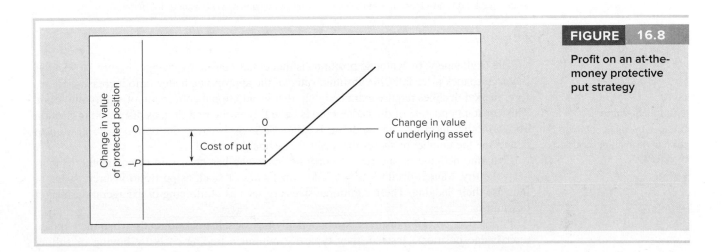

FIGURE   16.8

Profit on an at-the-money protective put strategy

if the portfolio falls in value while the market index rises, the put will fail to provide the intended protection. Moreover, the maturities of traded options may not match the investor's horizon. Therefore, rather than using option strategies, investors may use trading strategies that mimic the payoff to a protective put option.

Here is the general idea. Even if a put option on the desired portfolio with the desired expiration date does not exist, a theoretical option-pricing model (such as the binomial or Black-Scholes model) can be used to determine how that option's price *would* respond to the portfolio's value if it did trade. For example, if stock prices were to fall, the put option would increase in value. The option model could quantify this relationship. The net exposure of the (hypothetical) protective put portfolio to swings in stock prices is the sum of the exposures of the two components of the portfolio: the stock and the put.

We can create "synthetic" protective put positions by holding a quantity of stocks with the same net exposure to market swings as the hypothetical protective put position. The key to this strategy is the option delta, that is, the change in the price of the protective put option per change in the value of the underlying stock portfolio.

EXAMPLE 16.8	Suppose a portfolio is currently valued at $100 million. An at-the-money put option on the portfolio might have a hedge ratio or delta of −0.6, meaning the option's value swings $0.60 for every dollar change in portfolio value, but in an opposite direction. Suppose the stock portfolio falls in value by 2%. The profit on a hypothetical protective put position (if the put existed) would be as follows (in millions of dollars):
Synthetic Protective Puts	

Loss on stocks:	2% of $100 = $2.00
+Gain on put:	.6 × $2.00 = 1.20
Net loss	$0.80

We create the synthetic option position by selling a proportion of shares equal to the put option's delta (i.e., selling 60% of the shares) and placing the proceeds in risk-free T-bills. The rationale is that the hypothetical put option would have offset 60% of any change in the stock portfolio's value, so one must reduce portfolio risk directly by selling 60% of the equity and putting the proceeds into a risk-free asset. Total return on a synthetic protective put position with $60 million in risk-free investments such as T-bills and $40 million in equity is:

Loss on stocks:	2% of $40 = $.80
+Loss on bills:	0
Net loss	$.80

The synthetic and actual protective put positions have equal returns. We conclude that if you sell a proportion of shares equal to the put option's delta and place the proceeds in cash equivalents, your exposure to the stock market will equal that of the desired protective put position.

The challenge with synthetic positions is that deltas constantly change. Figure 16.9 shows that as the stock price falls, the absolute value of the appropriate hedge ratio increases. Therefore, market declines require extra hedging, that is, additional conversion of equity into cash. This constant updating of the hedge ratio is called **dynamic hedging,** as discussed in Section 16.2. Another term for such hedging is *delta hedging,* because the option delta is used to determine the number of shares that needs to be bought or sold.

Dynamic hedging is one reason portfolio insurance has been said to contribute to market volatility. Market declines trigger additional sales of stock as portfolio insurers strive to increase their hedging. These additional sales are seen as reinforcing or exaggerating market downturns.

In practice, portfolio insurers do not actually buy or sell stocks directly when they update their hedge positions. Instead, they typically minimize trading costs by buying or selling

dynamic hedging

Constant updating of hedge positions as market conditions change.

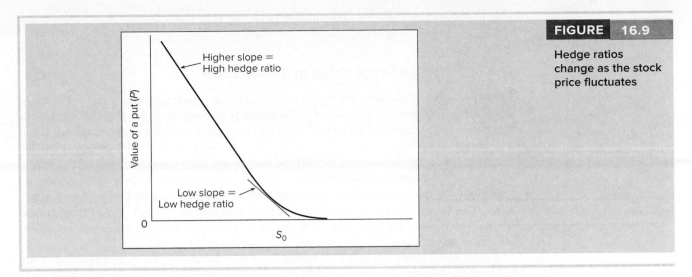

FIGURE 16.9

Hedge ratios change as the stock price fluctuates

stock-index futures as a substitute for sale of the stocks themselves. As you will see in the next chapter, stock prices and index future prices usually are very tightly linked by cross-market arbitrageurs so that futures transactions can be used as reliable proxies for stock transactions. Instead of selling equities based on the put option's delta, insurers will sell an equivalent number of futures contracts.[11]

Several portfolio insurers suffered great setbacks during the market "crash" of October 19, 1987, when the S&P 500 fell more than 20%. A description of what happened then should help you appreciate the complexities of applying a seemingly straightforward hedging concept.

1. Market volatility at the crash was much greater than ever encountered before. Put option deltas computed from historical volatility estimates were too low; insurers underhedged, held too much equity, and suffered excessive losses.

2. Prices moved so fast that insurers could not keep up with the necessary rebalancing. They were "chasing deltas" that kept getting away from them. The futures market saw a "gap" opening, where the opening price was nearly 10% below the previous day's close. Prices dropped before insurers could update their hedge ratios.

3. Execution problems were severe. First, current market prices were unavailable, with trade execution and the price quotation system hours behind, which made computation of correct hedge ratios impossible. Moreover, trading in stocks and stock futures ceased during some periods. The continuous rebalancing capability that is essential for a viable insurance program vanished during the precipitous market collapse.

4. Futures prices traded at steep discounts to their proper levels compared to reported stock prices, thereby making the sale of futures (as a proxy for equity sales) to increase hedging seem expensive. While you will see in the next chapter that stock-index futures prices should have exceeded the value of the stock index, futures on October 19 sold far below the stock-index level. When some insurers gambled that the futures price would recover to its expected premium over the stock index and chose to defer sales, they remained underhedged. As the market fell farther, their portfolios experienced substantial losses.

While most observers believe that the portfolio insurance industry will never recover from the market crash, dynamic hedges are still widely used to hedge potential losses from options positions. For example, when Microsoft ended its employee stock option program in 2003, and J. P. Morgan purchased many already-issued options from Microsoft employees, it was

---

[11]Notice, however, that the use of index futures reintroduces the problem of tracking error between the portfolio and the market index.

widely expected that Morgan would protect its options position by selling shares in Microsoft using a delta hedging strategy.

Option Pricing and the Crisis of 2008–2009

Merton[12] shows how option-pricing models can provide insight into the financial crisis of 2008–2009. The key to understanding his argument is to recognize that when banks lend to or buy the debt of firms with limited liability, they implicitly write a put option to the borrower. To see why, consider the payoff to the lender when the loan comes due for repayment. If the borrower has sufficient assets to pay off the loan, it will do so, and the lender will be fully repaid. But if the borrower has insufficient assets, it can declare bankruptcy and discharge its obligations by transferring ownership of the firm to its creditors. The borrower's ability to satisfy a loan by transferring ownership is equivalent to the right to "sell" itself to the creditor for the face value of the loan. This arrangement is therefore just like a put option on the firm with exercise price equal to the stipulated loan repayment.

Figure 16.10 shows the payoff to the lender at loan maturity (time T) as a function of the value of the borrowing firm, V_T, when the loan, with face value L, comes due. If $V_T \geq L$, the lender is paid off in full. But if $V_T < L$, the lender gets the firm, which is worth less than the promised payment L.

We can write the payoff in a way that emphasizes the implicit put option:

$$\text{Payoff} = \begin{cases} L \\ V_T \end{cases} = L - \begin{cases} 0 & \text{if } V_T \geq L \\ L - V_T & \text{if } V_T < L \end{cases} \tag{16.5}$$

Equation 16.5 shows that the payoff on the loan equals L (when the firm has sufficient assets to pay off the debt) *minus* the payoff of a put option on the value of the firm (V_T) with an exercise price of L. Therefore, we may view risky lending as a combination of safe lending, with a guaranteed payoff of L, with a short position in a put option on the borrower.

When firms sell credit default swaps (CDSs; see Chapter 10), the implicit put option is even clearer. Here, the CDS seller agrees to make up any losses due to the insolvency of a bond issuer. If the bond issuer goes bankrupt, leaving assets of only V_T for the creditors, the CDS seller is obligated to make up the difference, $L - V_T$. This is in essence a pure put option.

Now think about the exposure of these implicit put writers to changes in the financial health of the underlying firm. The value of a put option on V_T appears in Figure 16.11. When the firm is financially strong (i.e., V is far greater than the present value of L), the slope of the curve is nearly zero, implying that there is little exposure of the implicit put writer (either the

FIGURE 16.10

A risky loan. The payoff to the lender may be viewed as L, the face value of the loan, minus the proceeds to a put option on the value of the firm with exercise price L.

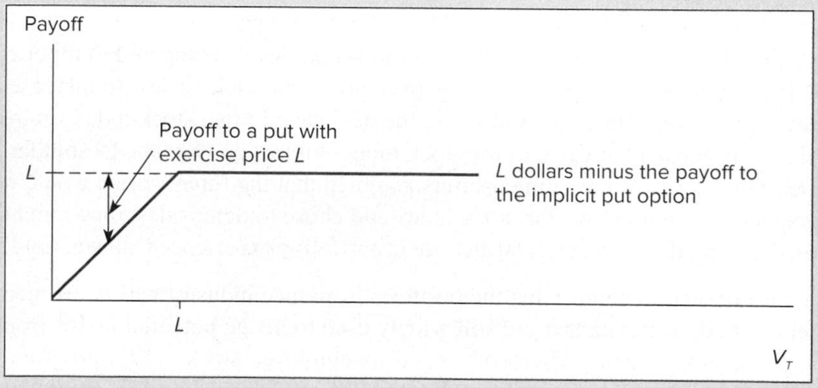

Payoff

Payoff to a put with exercise price L

L dollars minus the payoff to the implicit put option

L

V_T

---

[12]This material is based on a lecture given by Robert Merton at MIT in March 2009. You can find the lecture online at **http://techtv.mit.edu/videos/16527-observations-on-the-science-of-finance-in-the-practice-of-finance.**

FIGURE **16.11**

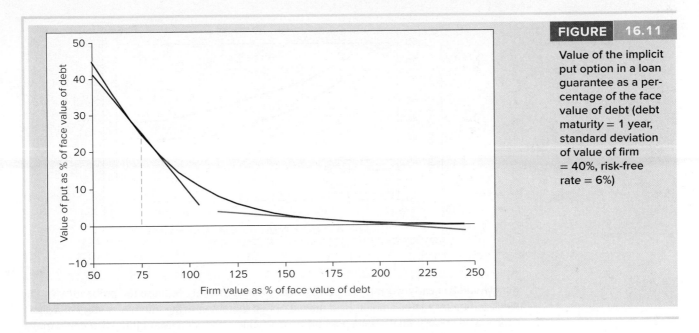

Value of the implicit put option in a loan guarantee as a percentage of the face value of debt (debt maturity = 1 year, standard deviation of value of firm = 40%, risk-free rate = 6%)

lender or the CDS writer) to the value of the borrowing firm. For example, when firm value is 1.75 times the value of the debt, the lighter line drawn tangent to the put value curve has a slope of only −0.040. But if there is a big shock to the economy, and firm value falls, not only does the value of the implicit put rise, but its slope is now steeper, implying that exposure to further shocks is now greater. When firm value is only 75% of the value of the loan, the slope of the line tangent to the put value valuation curve increases by a multiple of about 16, to −0.644. You can see how as you get closer to the edge of the cliff, it gets easier and easier to slide right off.

We often hear people say that a shock to asset values of the magnitude of the financial crisis was a 10-sigma event, by which they mean that such an event was so extreme that it would be 10 standard deviations away from an expected outcome, making it virtually inconceivable. But this analysis shows that standard deviation may be a moving target, increasing dramatically as the firm weakens. As the economy falters and put options go further into the money, their sensitivity to further shocks increases, increasing the risk that even worse losses may be around the corner. The built-in instability of risk exposures makes a scenario like the crisis more plausible and should give us pause when we discount an extreme scenario as "almost impossible."

16.5 EMPIRICAL EVIDENCE

There have been an enormous number of empirical tests of the Black-Scholes option-pricing model. For the most part, the results of the studies have been positive in that the model generates option values close to the actual prices at which options trade. Still, some regular empirical failures have been noted.

The biggest problem concerns volatility. If the model were accurate, the implied volatility of all options on a particular stock with the same expiration date would be equal—after all, the underlying asset and expiration date are the same for each option, so the volatility inferred from each also ought to be the same. But, in fact, when one actually plots implied volatility as a function of exercise price, the typical results appear as in Figure 16.12, which treats S&P 500 Index options as the underlying asset. Implied volatility steadily falls as the exercise price rises. Clearly, the Black-Scholes model is missing something.

Rubinstein (1994) was one of the first to suggest that the problem with the model has to do with fears of a market crash like that of October 1987. The idea is that deep out-of-the-money

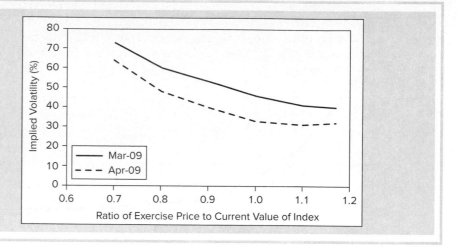

Implied volatility as a function of option "moneyness," that is, ratio of exercise price to asset price, on two dates

Source: *The CBOE Skew Index*, Chicago Board Options Exchange, 2010.

puts would be nearly worthless if stock prices evolve smoothly because the probability of the stock falling by a large amount (and the put option thereby moving into the money) in a short time would be very small. But a possibility of a sudden large downward jump that could move the puts into the money, as in a market crash, would impart greater value to these options. Thus, the market might price these options as though there is a bigger chance of a large drop in the stock price than would be consistent with the Black-Scholes assumptions. The result of the higher option price is a greater implied volatility derived from the Black-Scholes model.

Interestingly, Rubinstein points out that prior to the 1987 market crash, plots of implied volatility like the one in Figure 16.12 were relatively flat, consistent with the notion that the market was then less attuned to fears of a crash. However, postcrash plots have been consistently downward sloping, exhibiting a shape often called the *option smirk*. When we use option-pricing models that allow for more general stock price distributions, including large downward jumps and random changes in volatility, they generate downward-sloping implied volatility curves similar to those shown in Figure 16.12.[13]

SUMMARY

- Option values may be viewed as the sum of intrinsic value plus time or "volatility" value. The volatility value is the right to choose not to exercise if the stock price moves against the holder. Thus, option holders cannot lose more than the cost of the option regardless of stock price performance.
- Call options are more valuable when the exercise price is lower, when the stock price is higher, when the interest rate is higher, when the time to expiration is greater, when the stock's volatility is greater, and when dividends are lower.
- Options may be priced relative to the underlying stock price using a simple two-period, two-state pricing model. As the number of periods increases, the model can approximate more realistic stock price distributions. The Black-Scholes formula may be seen as a limiting case of the binomial option model, as the holding period is divided into progressively smaller subperiods.
- The put-call parity theorem relates the prices of put and call options. If the relationship is violated, arbitrage opportunities will result. Specifically, the relationship that must be satisfied is

$$P = C - S_0 + PV(X) + PV(\text{dividends})$$

[13]For an extensive discussion of these more general models, see R. L. McDonald, *Derivatives Markets*, 3rd ed. (Boston: Pearson Education, Addison-Wesley, 2013).

where X is the exercise price of both the call and the put options and $PV(X)$ is the present value of the claim to X dollars to be paid at the expiration date of the options.

- The implied volatility of an option is the standard deviation of stock returns consistent with an option's market price. It can be backed out of an option-pricing model by finding the stock volatility that makes the model's estimate of the option's value equal to the observed price.

- The hedge ratio (or option delta) is the number of shares of stock required to hedge the price risk involved in writing one option. Hedge ratios are near zero for deep out-of-the-money call options and approach one for deep in-the-money calls.

- Although option deltas are less than one, call options have elasticities greater than one. The rate of return on a call (as opposed to the dollar return) responds more than one-for-one with stock price movements.

- Portfolio insurance can be obtained by purchasing a protective put option on an equity position. When the appropriate put is not traded, portfolio insurance entails a dynamic hedge strategy where a fraction of the equity portfolio equal to the desired put option's delta is sold, with proceeds placed in risk-free securities.

- Empirically, implied volatilities derived from the Black-Scholes formula tend to be lower on options with higher exercise prices. This may be evidence that the option prices reflect the possibility of a sudden dramatic decline in stock prices. Such "crashes" are inconsistent with the Black-Scholes assumptions.

KEY TERMS

binomial model, 515
Black-Scholes pricing
  formula, 518
delta, 528
dynamic hedging, 530

hedge ratio, 528
implied volatility, 522
intrinsic value
  (of an option), 508
option elasticity, 529

portfolio insurance, 529
put-call parity
  relationship, 525
time value (of an
  option), 508

KEY FORMULAS

Binomial model: $u = \exp(\sigma\sqrt{\Delta t}); \; d = \exp(-\sigma\sqrt{\Delta t}); \; p = \dfrac{\exp(r\Delta t) - d}{u - d}$

Put-call parity: $P = C + PV(X) - S_0 + PV(\text{Dividends})$

Black-Scholes formula: $C_0 = S_0 e^{-\delta T} N(d_1) - X e^{-rT} N(d_2)$

$$d_1 = \frac{\ln(S_0/X) + (r - \delta + \sigma^2/2)T}{\sigma\sqrt{T}}$$

$$d_2 = d_1 - \sigma\sqrt{T}$$

Delta (or hedge ratio): $H = \dfrac{\text{Change in option value}}{\text{Change in stock value}}$

PROBLEM SETS

connect Select problems are available in McGraw-Hill's *Connect*. Please see the Supplements section of the book's frontmatter for more information.

1. A call option with a strike price of $50 on a stock selling at $55 costs $6.50. What are the call option's intrinsic and time values? *(LO 16-1)*

2. A put option on a stock with a current price of $33 has an exercise price of $35. The price of the corresponding call option is $2.25. According to put-call parity, if the effective annual risk-free rate of interest is 4% and there are three months until expiration, what should be the price of the put? *(LO 16-4)*

3. A call option on Jupiter Motors stock with an exercise price of $75 and one-year expiration is selling at $3. A put option on Jupiter stock with an exercise price of $75 and one-year expiration is selling at $2.50. If the risk-free rate is 8% and Jupiter pays no dividends, what should the stock price be? *(LO 16-4)*

4. We showed in the text that the value of a call option increases with the volatility of the stock. Is this also true of put option values? Use the put-call parity relationship as well as a numerical example to demonstrate your answer. *(LO 16-4)*

5. In each of the following questions, you are asked to compare two options with parameters as given. The risk-free interest rate for *all* cases should be assumed to be 6%. Assume the stocks on which these options are written pay no dividends. *(LO 16-1)*

   a.

Put	T	X	σ	Price of Put
A	0.5	50	0.20	10
B	0.5	50	0.25	10

   Which put option is written on the stock with the lower price?
   (1) A
   (2) B
   (3) Not enough information

   b.

Put	T	X	σ	Price of Put
A	0.5	50	0.2	10
B	0.5	50	0.2	12

   Which put option must be written on the stock with the lower price?
   (1) A
   (2) B
   (3) Not enough information

   c.

Call	S	X	σ	Price of Call
A	50	50	0.20	12
B	55	50	0.20	10

   Which call option must have the lower time to expiration?
   (1) A
   (2) B
   (3) Not enough information

   d.

Call	T	X	S	Price of Call
A	0.5	50	55	10
B	0.5	50	55	12

   Which call option is written on the stock with higher volatility?
   (1) A
   (2) B
   (3) Not enough information

e.

Call	T	X	S	Price of Call
A	0.5	50	55	10
B	0.5	55	55	7

Which call option is written on the stock with higher volatility?

(1) A

(2) B

(3) Not enough information

6. Reconsider the determination of the hedge ratio in the two-state model (Section 16.2), where we showed that one-third share of stock would hedge one option. What would be the hedge ratio for each of the following exercise prices: (*a*) $120; (*b*) $110; (*c*) $100; (*d*) $90? What do you conclude about the hedge ratio as the option becomes progressively more in the money? *(LO 16-5)*

7. Show that Black-Scholes call option hedge ratios increase as the stock price increases. Consider a one-year option with exercise price $50 on a stock with annual standard deviation 20%. The T-bill rate is 3% per year. Find $N(d_1)$ for stock prices (*a*) $45, (*b*) $50, and (*c*) $55. *(LO 16-3)*

8. We will derive a two-state put option value in this problem. Data: $S_0 = 100$; $X = 110$; $1 + r = 1.10$. The two possibilities for S_T are 130 and 80. *(LO 16-2)*

    a. Show that the range of *S* is 50 while that of *P* is 30 across the two states. What is the hedge ratio of the put?

    b. Form a portfolio of three shares of stock and five puts. What is the (nonrandom) payoff to this portfolio?

    c. What is the present value of the portfolio?

    d. Given that the stock currently is selling at 100, show that the value of the put must be 10.91.

9. *a.* Calculate the value of a *call* option on the stock in the previous problem with an exercise price of 110.

    b. Verify that the put-call parity relationship is satisfied by your answers to both Problems 8 and 9. (Do not use continuous compounding to calculate the present value of *X* in this example, because the interest rate is quoted as an effective per-period rate.) *(LO 16-2)*

Use the following case in answering Problems 10–15.

Mark Washington, CFA, is an analyst with BIC. One year ago, BIC analysts predicted that the U.S. equity market would most likely experience a slight downturn and suggested delta-hedging the BIC portfolio. As predicted, the U.S. equity markets did indeed experience a downturn of approximately 4% over a 12-month period. However, portfolio performance for BIC was disappointing, lagging its peer group by nearly 10%. Washington has been told to review the options strategy to determine why the hedged portfolio did not perform as expected.

10. Which of the following *best* explains a delta-neutral portfolio? A delta-neutral portfolio is hedged against: *(LO 16-5)*

    a. Small price changes in the underlying asset.

    b. Small price decreases in the underlying asset.

    c. All price changes in the underlying asset.

11. After discussing the concept of a delta-neutral portfolio, Washington determines that he needs to further explain the concept of delta. Washington draws the value of an option as a function of the underlying stock price. If you draw such a diagram, delta is the: *(LO 16-5)*

    a. Slope in the option price diagram.

    b. Curvature of the option price graph.

    c. Level in the option price diagram.

12. Washington considers a put option that has a delta of −0.65. If the price of the underlying asset decreases by $6, then what is the best estimate of the change in option price? *(LO 16-5)*

13. BIC owns 51,750 shares of Smith & Oates. The shares are currently priced at $69. A call option on Smith & Oates with a strike price of $70 is selling at $3.50 and has a delta of 0.69. What is the number of call options necessary to create a delta-neutral hedge? *(LO 16-5)*

14. Return to the previous problem. Will the number of call options written for a delta-neutral hedge increase or decrease if the stock price falls? *(LO 16-5)*

15. Which of the following statements regarding the goal of a delta-neutral portfolio is *most* accurate? One example of a delta-neutral portfolio is to combine a: *(LO 16-5)*
    a. Long position in a stock with a short position in call options so that the value of the portfolio does not change with changes in the value of the stock.
    b. Long position in a stock with a short position in a call option so that the value of the portfolio changes with changes in the value of the stock.
    c. Long position in a stock with a long position in call options so that the value of the portfolio does not change with changes in the value of the stock.

16. Use the Black-Scholes formula to find the value of a call option on the following stock:

    Time to expiration = 6 months

    Standard deviation = 50% per year

    Exercise price = $50

    Stock price = $50

    Interest rate = 3%

    Dividend = 0

    (LO 16-3)

17. Find the Black-Scholes value of a put option on the stock in the previous problem with the same exercise price and expiration as the call option.   *(LO 16-3)*

18. Recalculate the value of the option in Problem 16, successively substituting one of the changes below while keeping the other parameters as in Problem 16:
    a. Time to expiration = 3 months
    b. Standard deviation = 25% per year
    c. Exercise price = $55
    d. Stock price = $55
    e. Interest rate = 5%

    Consider each scenario independently. Confirm that the option value changes in accordance with the prediction of Table 16.1.   *(LO 16-3)*

19. What would be the Excel formula in Spreadsheet 16.1 for the Black-Scholes value of a straddle position?   *(LO 16-3)*

20. Would you expect a $1 increase in a call option's exercise price to lead to a decrease in the option's value of more or less than $1?   *(LO 16-1)*

21. All else being equal, is a put option on a high-beta stock worth more than one on a low-beta stock? The firms have identical firm-specific risk.   *(LO 16-1)*

22. All else being equal, is a call option on a stock with a lot of firm-specific risk worth more than one on a stock with little firm-specific risk? The betas of the stocks are equal.   *(LO 16-1)*

23. All else being equal, will a call option with a high exercise price have a higher or lower hedge ratio than one with a low exercise price?   *(LO 16-5)*

24. Should the rate of return of a call option on a long-term Treasury bond be more or less sensitive to changes in interest rates than the rate of return of the underlying bond?   *(LO 16-1)*

25. If the stock price falls and the call price rises, then what has happened to the call option's implied volatility?   *(LO 16-1)*

26. If the time to expiration falls and the put price rises, then what has happened to the put option's implied volatility?   *(LO 16-1)*

Templates and spreadsheets are available in Connect

Templates and spreadsheets are available in Connect

Templates and spreadsheets are available in Connect

27. According to the Black-Scholes formula, what will be the hedge ratio (delta) of a call option as the stock price becomes infinitely large? Explain briefly.   *(LO 16-5)*

28. According to the Black-Scholes formula, what will be the hedge ratio (delta) of a put option for a very small exercise price?   *(LO 16-5)*

29. The hedge ratio (delta) of an at-the-money call option on IBM is 0.4. The hedge ratio of an at-the-money put option is −0.6. What is the hedge ratio of an at-the-money straddle position on IBM?   *(LO 16-5)*

30. Consider a six-month expiration European call option with exercise price $105. The underlying stock sells for $100 a share and pays no dividends. The risk-free rate is 5%. What is the implied volatility of the option if the option currently sells for $8? Use Spreadsheet 16.1 (available in Connect; link to Chapter 16 material) to answer this question.   *(LO 16-3)*

Templates and spreadsheets are available in Connect

   a. Go to the *Data* tab of the spreadsheet and select *Goal Seek* from the *What-If* menu. The dialog box will ask you for three pieces of information. In that dialog box, you should *set cell* E6 *to value* 8 *by changing cell* B2. In other words, you ask the spreadsheet to find the value of standard deviation (which appears in cell B2) that forces the value of the option (in cell E6) equal to $8. Then click *OK*, and you should find that the call is now worth $8, and the entry for standard deviation has been changed to a level consistent with this value. This is the call's implied standard deviation at a price of $8.
   b. What happens to implied volatility if the option is selling at $9? Why?
   c. What happens to implied volatility if the option price is unchanged at $8 but the time until option expiration is lower, say, only four months? Why?
   d. What happens to implied volatility if the option price is unchanged at $8 but the exercise price is lower, say, only $100? Why?
   e. What happens to implied volatility if the option price is unchanged at $8 but the stock price is lower, say, only $98? Why?

31. These three put options all are written on the same stock. One has a delta of −0.9, one a delta of −0.5, and one a delta of −0.1. Assign deltas to the three puts by filling in the table below.   *(LO 16-5)*

Put	X	Delta
A	10	
B	20	
C	30	

32. In this problem, we derive the put-call parity relationship for European options on stocks that pay dividends before option expiration. For simplicity, assume that the stock makes one dividend payment of $D per share at the expiration date of the option.   *(LO 16-4)*
   a. What is the value of the stock-plus-put position on the expiration date of the option?
   b. Now consider a portfolio consisting of a call option and a zero-coupon bond with the same expiration date as the option and with face value $(X + D)$. What is the value of this portfolio on the option expiration date? You should find that its value equals that of the stock-plus-put portfolio, regardless of the stock price.
   c. What is the cost of establishing the two portfolios in parts (a) and (b)? Equate the cost of these portfolios, and you will derive the put-call parity relationship, Equation 16.3.

33. A collar is established by buying a share of stock for $50, buying a six-month put option with exercise price $45, and writing a six-month call option with exercise price $55. Based on the volatility of the stock, you calculate that for an exercise price of $45 and maturity of six months, $N(d_1) = 0.60$, whereas for the exercise price of $55, $N(d_1) = 0.35$.   *(LO 16-5)*
   a. What will be the gain or loss on the collar if the stock price increases by $1?
   b. What happens to the delta of the portfolio if the stock price becomes very large?
   c. What happens to the delta of the portfolio if the stock price becomes very small?

34. You are very bullish (optimistic) on stock EFG, much more so than the rest of the market. In each question, choose the portfolio strategy that will give you the biggest dollar profit if your bullish forecast turns out to be correct. Explain your answer.   *(LO 16-5)*
    a. *Choice A:* $100,000 invested in calls with $X = 50$.
       Choice B: $100,000 invested in EFG stock.
    b. *Choice A:* 10 call options contracts (for 100 shares each), with $X = 50$.
       Choice B: 1,000 shares of EFG stock.

35. You are attempting to value a call option with an exercise price of $100 and one year to expiration. The underlying stock pays no dividends, its current price is $100, and you believe it has a 50% chance of increasing to $120 and a 50% chance of decreasing to $80. The risk-free rate of interest is 10%. Calculate the call option's value using the two-state stock price model.   *(LO 16-2)*

36. Consider an increase in the volatility of the stock in the previous problem. Suppose that if the stock increases in price, it will increase to $130, and that if it falls, it will fall to $70. Show that the value of the call option is higher than the value derived using the original assumptions.   *(LO 16-2)*

37. *a.* Return to Example 16.1. Use the binomial model to value a one-year European put option with exercise price $110 on the stock in that example.
    b. Show that your solution for the put price satisfies put-call parity.   *(LO 16-2)*

Challenge

38. Imagine you are a provider of portfolio insurance. You are establishing a four-year program. The portfolio you manage is currently worth $100 million, and you promise to provide a minimum return of 0%. The equity portfolio has a standard deviation of 25% per year, and T-bills pay 5% per year. Assume for simplicity that the portfolio pays no dividends (or that all dividends are reinvested).   *(LO 16-5)*
    a. What fraction of the portfolio should be placed in bills? What fraction in equity?
    b. What should the manager do if the stock portfolio falls by 3% on the first day of trading?

39. You would like to be holding a protective put position on the stock of XYZ Co. to lock in a guaranteed minimum value of $100 at year-end. XYZ currently sells for $100. Over the next year, the stock price will either increase by 10% or decrease by 10%. The T-bill rate is 5%. Unfortunately, no put options are traded on XYZ Co.   *(LO 16-5)*
    a. Suppose the desired put option were traded. How much would it cost to purchase?
    b. What would have been the cost of the protective put portfolio?
    c. What portfolio position in stock and T-bills will ensure you a payoff equal to the payoff that would be provided by a protective put with $X = \$100$? Show that the payoff to this portfolio and the cost of establishing the portfolio match those of the desired protective put.

40. Suppose you are attempting to value a one-year maturity option on a stock with volatility (i.e., annualized standard deviation) of $\sigma = 0.40$. What would be the appropriate values for u and d if your binomial model is set up using the following?   *(LO 16-2)*
    a. One period of one year.
    b. Four subperiods, each three months.
    c. Twelve subperiods, each one month.

41. You build a binomial model with one period and assert that over the course of a year, the stock price will either rise by a factor of 1½ or fall by a factor of ⅔. What is your implicit assumption about the volatility of the stock's rate of return over the next year?   *(LO 16-2)*

42. Use the put-call parity relationship to demonstrate that an at-the-money European call option on a nondividend-paying stock must cost more than an at-the-money put option. Show that the prices of the put and call will be equal if $X = S_0(1 + r)^T$.   *(LO 16-4)*

43. Return to Problem 35. Value the call option using the risk-neutral shortcut described in the On the Market Front box. Confirm that your answer matches the value you get using the two-state approach.   *(LO 16-2)*

44. *a.* Return to Problem 37. What will be the payoff to the put, P_u, if the stock goes up?
    b. What will be the payoff, P_d, if the stock price falls?
    c. Value the put option using the risk-neutral shortcut described in the On the Market Front box. Confirm that your answer matches the value you get using the two-state approach. *(LO 16-2)*

CFA Problems

1. Ken Webster manages a $400 million equity portfolio benchmarked to the S&P 500 Index. Webster believes the market is overvalued when measured by several traditional fundamental/economic indicators. He is therefore concerned about potential losses but recognizes that the S&P 500 Index could nevertheless move above its current 1,766 level. Webster is considering the following *option collar* strategy:
   - Protection for the portfolio can be attained by purchasing S&P 500 Index puts with a strike price of 1,760.
   - The puts can be approximately financed by selling an equal number of call options with strike price 1,800.
   - Because the combined delta of the purchased put and written call positions (see the following table) is smaller in absolute value than −1, (that is, −.44 −.30 = −.74), the options will not lose more than the underlying portfolio will gain if the market advances.

   The information in the following table describes the two options used to create the collar. *(LO 16-5)*

Characteristics	1,800 Call	1,760 Put
Option price	$34.10	$32.20
Option implied volatility	22%	24%
Option's delta	0.30	−0.44

   Notes:
   Ignore transaction costs.
   S&P 500 historical 30-day volatility = 23%.
   Time to option expiration = 30 days.

   a. Describe the potential returns of the combined portfolio (the underlying portfolio plus the option collar) if after 30 days the S&P 500 Index has:
      i. Risen approximately 5% to 1,854.
      ii. Remained at 1,766 (no change).
      iii. Declined by approximately 5% to 1,682.
      (No calculations are necessary.)
   b. Discuss the effect on the hedge ratio (delta) of *each* option as the S&P 500 approaches the level of *each* of the potential outcomes listed in part (*a*).
   c. Evaluate the pricing of each of the following in relation to the volatility data provided:
      i. The put.
      ii. The call.

2. Michael Weber, CFA, is analyzing several aspects of option valuation, including the determinants of the value of an option, the characteristics of various models used to value options, and the potential for divergence of calculated option values from observed market prices. *(LO 16-1)*
   a. What is the expected effect on the value of a call option on common stock if (i) the volatility of the underlying stock price decreases; (ii) the time to expiration of the option increases?
   b. Using the Black-Scholes option-pricing model, Weber calculates the price of a three-month call option and notices the option's calculated value is different from its market price. With respect to Weber's use of the Black-Scholes option-pricing model,

(i) discuss why the calculated value of an out-of-the-money European option may differ from its market price; (ii) discuss why the calculated value of an American option may differ from its market price.

3. A stock index is currently trading at 50. Paul Tripp, CFA, wants to value two-year index options using the binomial model. In any year, the stock will either increase in value by 20% or fall in value by 20%. The annual risk-free interest rate is 6%. No dividends are paid on any of the underlying securities in the index. *(LO 16-2)*
   a. Construct a two-period binomial tree for the value of the stock index.
   b. Calculate the value of a European call option on the index with an exercise price of 60.
   c. Calculate the value of a European put option on the index with an exercise price of 60.
   d. Confirm that your solutions for the values of the call and the put satisfy put-call parity.

WEB *master*

1. Use information from **finance.yahoo.com** to answer the following questions.
   a. What is Coke's current price?
   b. Now enter the ticker "KO" (for Coca-Cola) and find the *Analyst Opinion* tab. What is the mean 12-month target price for Coke? Based on this forecast, would at-the-money calls or puts have the higher expected profit?
   c. What is the spread between the high and low target stock prices, expressed as a percentage of Coke's current stock price? How (qualitatively) should the spread be related to the price at which Coke options trade?
   d. Calculate the implied volatility of the call option closest to the money with time to expiration of about three months. You can use Spreadsheet 16.1 (available in Connect) to calculate implied volatility using the Goal Seek command.
   e. Now repeat the exercise for Pepsi (ticker: PEP). What would you expect to be the relationship between the high versus low target price spread and the implied volatility of the two companies? Are your expectations consistent with actual option prices?
   f. Suppose you believe that the volatility of KO is going to increase from currently anticipated levels. Would its call options be overpriced or underpriced? What about its put options?
   g. Could you take positions in both puts and calls on KO in such a manner as to speculate on your volatility beliefs without taking a stance on whether the stock price is going to increase or decrease? Would you buy or write each type of option?
   h. How would your relative positions in puts and calls be related to the delta of each option?

2. Calculating implied volatility can be difficult if you don't have a spreadsheet handy. Fortunately, many tools are available on the web to perform the calculation; for example, **www .option-price.com** contains several option calculators, including one for implied volatility.

   Using daily price data, calculate the annualized standard deviation of the daily percentage change in a stock price. For the same stock, use these websites to find the implied volatility. Option price data can be retrieved from **www.cboe.com.**

   Recalculate the standard deviation using three months, six months, and nine months of daily data. Which of the calculations most closely approximates implied volatility? What time frame does the market seem to use for assessing stock price volatility?

SOLUTIONS TO CONCEPT *checks*

16.1 Yes. Consider the same scenarios as for the call.

High-Volatility Scenario					
Stock price	$10	$20	$30	$40	$50
Put payoff	20	10	0	0	0

Low-Volatility Scenario					
Stock price	$20	$25	$30	$35	$40
Put payoff	10	5	0	0	0

The low-volatility scenario yields a lower expected payoff.

16.2

If This Variable Increases . . .	The Value of a Put Option
S	Decreases
X	Increases
σ	Increases
T	Increases/uncertain*
r_f	Decreases
Dividend payouts	Increases

*For American puts, increase in time to expiration *must* increase value. One can always choose to exercise early if this is optimal; the longer expiration date simply expands the range of alternatives open to the option holder, thereby making the option more valuable. For a European put, where early exercise is not allowed, longer time to expiration can have an indeterminate effect. Longer maturity increases volatility value because the final stock price is more uncertain, but it reduces the present value of the exercise price that will be received if the put is exercised. The net effect on put value is ambiguous.

16.3 Because the option now is underpriced, we want to reverse our previous strategy.

	Initial Cash Flow	Cash Flow in One Year for Each Possible Stock Price	
		$S = \$90$	$S = \$120$
Buy three options	−$16.50	$ 0	$ 30
Short-sell one share; repay in one year	100	−90	−120
Lend $83.50 at 10% interest rate	−83.50	91.85	91.85
Total	$ 0	$ 1.85	$ 1.85

The riskless cash flow in one year per option is $1.85/3 = $.6167, and the present value is $.6167/1.10 = $.56, precisely the amount by which the option is underpriced.

16.4 a. $C_u - C_d = \$6.984 - 0 = \$6.984$
  b. $uS_0 - dS_0 = \$110 - \$95 = \$15$
  c. $6.984/15 = .4656$
  d.

Action Today (Time 0)	Value in Next Period as Function of Stock Price	
	$dS_0 = \$95$	$uS_0 = \$110$
Buy 0.4656 shares at price $S_0 = \$100$	$44.232	$51.216
Write one call at price C_0	0	−6.984
Total	$44.232	$44.232

The portfolio must have a market value equal to the present value of $44.232.
  e. $44.232/1.05 = $42.126
  f. $.4656 \times \$100 - C_0 = \$42.126$
    $C_0 = \$46.56 - \$42.126 = \$4.434$

16.5 When Δt shrinks, there should be lower possible dispersion in the stock price by the end of the subperiod because each shorter subperiod offers less time in which new information can move stock prices. However, as the time interval shrinks, there will be a correspondingly greater number of these subperiods until option expiration.

Thus, *total* volatility over the remaining life of the option will be unaffected. In fact, take another look at Figure 16.2. There, despite the fact that *u* and *d* each get closer to 1 as the number of subintervals increases and the length of each subinterval falls, the total volatility of the stock return until option expiration is unaffected.

16.6 Because $\sigma = .6$, $\sigma^2 = .36$.

$$d_1 = \frac{\ln(100/95) + (.10 + .36/2).25}{.6\sqrt{.25}} = .4043$$

$$d_2 = d_1 - .6\sqrt{.25} = .1043$$

Using Table 16.2 and interpolation, or a spreadsheet function,

$$N(d_1) = .6570$$
$$N(d_2) = .5415$$
$$C = 100 \times .6570 - 95e^{-.10 \times .25} \times .5415 = 15.53$$

16.7 Implied volatility exceeds 0.5. Given a standard deviation of 0.5, the option value is $13.70. A higher volatility is needed to justify the actual $15 price. Using Spreadsheet 16.1 and Goal Seek, we find the implied volatility is 0.5714, or 57.14%.

16.8 A $1 increase in stock price is a percentage increase of $1/122 = 0.82\%$. The put option will *fall* by $(.4 \times \$1) = \$.40$, a percentage decrease of $\$.40/\$4 = 10\%$. Elasticity is $-10/.82 = -12.2$.

Futures Markets and Risk Management

Learning Objectives

LO 17-1 Calculate the profit on futures positions as a function of current and eventual futures prices.

LO 17-2 Formulate futures market strategies for hedging or speculative purposes.

LO 17-3 Compute the futures price appropriate to a given price on the underlying asset.

LO 17-4 Design arbitrage strategies to exploit futures market mispricing.

LO 17-5 Determine how swaps can be used to mitigate interest rate risk.

Futures and forward contracts are like options in that they specify the purchase or sale of some underlying asset at some future date. The key difference is that the holder of an option is not compelled to buy or sell and will not do so unless the trade is advantageous. A futures or forward contract, however, carries the obligation to go through with the agreed-upon transaction.

A forward contract is not an investment in the strict sense that funds are paid for an asset. It is only a commitment today to transact in the future. Forward arrangements are part of our study of investments, however, because they offer a powerful means to hedge other investments and modify portfolio characteristics.

Forward markets for future delivery of various commodities go back at least to ancient Greece. Organized *futures markets,* though, are a relatively modern development, dating only to the 19th century. Futures markets replace informal forward contracts with standardized, exchange-traded securities.

While futures markets have their roots in agricultural products and commodities, the markets today are dominated by trading in financial futures such as those on stock indexes, interest rate–dependent securities such as government bonds, and foreign exchange. The markets themselves also have changed, with trading today largely taking place in electronic markets.

This chapter describes the workings of futures markets and the mechanics of trading in these markets. We show how futures contracts are useful investment vehicles for both

17.1 THE FUTURES CONTRACT

To see how futures and forwards work and how they might be useful, consider the portfolio diversification problem facing a farmer growing a single crop, let's say wheat. The entire planting season's revenue depends critically on the volatile crop price. The farmer can't easily diversify his position because virtually his entire wealth is tied up in the crop.

The miller who must purchase wheat for processing faces a risk management problem that is the mirror image of the farmer's. He is subject to profit uncertainty because of the unpredictable cost of the wheat.

forward contract

An arrangement calling for future delivery of an asset at an agreed-upon price.

Both parties can hedge their risk by entering into a **forward contract** calling for the farmer to deliver the wheat when harvested at a price agreed upon now, regardless of the market price at harvest time. No money need change hands at this time. All that is required is that each party be willing to lock in the ultimate delivery price. The forward contract protects each from price fluctuations.

Futures markets formalize and standardize forward contracting. Buyers and sellers do not have to rely on a chance matching of their interests; they can trade in a centralized market. The futures exchange also standardizes the types of contracts that may be traded: It establishes contract size, the acceptable grade of commodity, contract delivery dates, and so forth. While standardization eliminates much of the flexibility available in informal forward contracting, it offers the offsetting advantage of liquidity because many traders will concentrate on the same small set of contracts. Futures contracts also differ from forward contracts in that they call for a daily settling up of any gains or losses on the contract. By contrast, no money changes hands in forward contracts until the delivery date.

In a centralized market, buyers and sellers can trade through brokers without searching for trading partners. The standardization of contracts and the depth of trading in each contract allows futures positions to be liquidated easily rather than personally renegotiated with the other party to the contract. Because the exchange guarantees the performance of each party, costly credit checks on other traders are not necessary. Instead, each trader simply posts a good-faith deposit, called the *margin,* to guarantee contract performance.

The Basics of Futures Contracts

futures price

The agreed-upon price to be paid on a futures contract at maturity.

The futures contract calls for delivery of a commodity at a specified delivery or maturity date, for an agreed-upon price, called the **futures price,** to be paid at contract maturity. The contract specifies precise requirements for the commodity. For agricultural commodities, the exchange sets allowable grades (e.g., No. 2 hard winter wheat or No. 1 soft red wheat). The place and means of delivery of the commodity are specified as well. Delivery of agricultural commodities is made by transfer of warehouse receipts issued by approved warehouses. For financial futures, delivery may be made by wire transfer; for index futures, delivery may be accomplished by a cash settlement procedure such as those used for index options. (Although the futures contract technically calls for delivery of an asset, delivery rarely occurs. Instead, parties to the contract much more commonly close out their positions before contract maturity, taking gains or losses in cash. We will show you how this is done later in the chapter.)

Because the futures exchange specifies all the terms of the contract, the traders need bargain only over the futures price. The trader taking the **long position** commits to purchasing the commodity on the delivery date. The trader who takes the **short position** commits to delivering the commodity at contract maturity. The trader in the long position is said to "buy" a contract; the short-side trader "sells" a contract. The words *buy* and *sell* are figurative only, because a contract is not really bought or sold like a stock or bond; it is entered into by mutual agreement. At the time the contract is entered into, no money changes hands.

Figure 17.1 shows prices for a sample of futures contracts as they appear in *The Wall Street Journal*. The boldface heading lists in each case the commodity, the exchange where the futures contract is traded in parentheses, the contract size, and the pricing unit. For example, the first contract listed under "Agriculture Futures" is for corn, traded on the Chicago Board of Trade (CBT). Each contract calls for delivery of 5,000 bushels, and prices in the entry are quoted in cents per bushel.

The next several rows detail price data for contracts expiring on various dates. The July maturity corn contract, for example, opened during the day at a futures price of 381 cents per bushel. The highest futures price during the day was 385, the lowest was 376.75, and the settlement price (a representative trading price during the last few minutes of trading) was 377. The settlement price fell by 4 cents from the previous trading day. Finally, open interest, or the number of outstanding contracts, was 452,077. Similar information is given for each maturity date.

The trader holding the long position, that is, the person who will purchase the good, profits from price increases. Suppose that when the contract matures, the price of corn turns out to be 382 cents per bushel. The long position trader who entered the contract at the futures price of 377 cents on June 15 (the date of *The Wall Street Journal* listing) earns a profit of 5 cents per bushel: The eventual price is 5 cents higher than the originally agreed-upon futures price. As each contract calls for delivery of 5,000 bushels, the profit to the long position equals $5,000 \times \$.05 = \$250$ per contract. Conversely, the short position loses 5 cents per bushel. The short position's loss equals the long position's gain.

To summarize, at maturity

$$\text{Profit to long} = \text{Spot price at maturity} - \text{Original futures price}$$

$$\text{Profit to short} = \text{Original futures price} - \text{Spot price at maturity}$$

where the spot price is the actual market price of the commodity when the contract matures.

The futures contract, therefore, is a *zero sum game,* with losses and gains to all positions netting out to zero. Every long position is offset by a short position. The aggregate profits to futures trading, summing over all investors, also must be zero, as is the net exposure to changes in the commodity price.

Figure 17.2, Panel A, is a plot of the profits realized by an investor who enters the long side of a futures contract as a function of the price of the asset on the maturity date. Notice that profit is zero when the ultimate spot price, P_T, equals the initial futures price, F_0. Profit per unit of the underlying asset rises or falls one-for-one with changes in the final spot price. Unlike the payoff of a call option, the payoff of the long futures position can be negative: This will be the case if the spot price falls below the original futures price. Unlike the holder of a call, who has an *option* to buy, the long futures position trader cannot simply walk away from the contract. Also unlike options, there is no need to distinguish gross payoffs from the net profits on futures contracts. This is because the futures contract is not purchased; it is simply a contract that is agreed to by two parties. The futures price adjusts to make the value of either side of the contract equal to zero.

The distinction between futures and options is highlighted by comparing Panel A of Figure 17.2 to the payoff and profit diagrams for an investor in a call option with exercise price, *X,* chosen equal to the futures price, F_0 (see Panel C). The futures investor is exposed to considerable losses if the asset price falls. In contrast, the investor in the call cannot lose more than the cost of the option.

long position

The futures trader who commits to purchasing the asset.

short position

The futures trader who commits to delivering the asset.

FIGURE 17.1

Futures listings for June 15, 2017

Source: From *The Wall Street Journal,* June 15, 2017.

Futures Contracts

Metal & Petroleum Futures

	Open	Contract High	hi lo	Contract Low	Settle	Chg	Open Interest
Copper-High (CMX)-25,000 lbs.; $ per lb.							
June	2.5800	2.5800		2.5625	**2.5705**	−0.0225	1,053
July	2.5990	2.6050		2.5605	**2.5735**	−0.0230	83,015
Gold (CMX)-100 troy oz.; $ per troy oz.							
June	1269.40	1278.00		1256.80	**1272.80**	7.00	1,551
Aug	1268.40	1284.20		1259.00	**1275.90**	7.30	345,745
Oct	1272.30	1287.20		1263.00	**1279.50**	7.30	10,913
Dec	1275.50	1290.00		1266.20	**1282.90**	7.30	80,269
Feb'18	1279.30	1291.00		1272.70	**1286.30**	7.30	10,331
Dec	1295.00	1303.20		1295.00	**1303.10**	7.00	5,920
Palladium (NYM)-50 troy oz.; $ per troy oz.							
June	862.80	869.50		862.80	**863.30**	−2.95	82
July	865.60	871.55		852.35	**857.60**	−3.75	45
Aug	858.50	863.50		858.50	**856.15**	−3.75	2
Sept	858.90	871.25		847.55	**853.80**	−3.75	34,111
Dec	843.90	857.10		837.00	**843.50**	−0.45	1,729
March'18	839.30	843.00	▲	835.00	**832.15**	−0.45	122
June	839.00	839.00	▲	839.00	**828.15**	−0.45	16
Platinum (NYM)-50 troy oz.; $ per troy oz.							
June	925,40	926.80		925.40	**950.70**	27.70	48
July	925.00	955.50		923.30	**951.90**	27.70	52,791
Silver (CMX)-5,000 troy oz.; $ per troy oz.							
June	16.840	17,180		16.840	**17.107**	0.369	28
July	16.820	17,365		16.790	**17.136**	0.369	100,533
Crude Oil, Light Sweet (NYM)-1,000 bbls.; $ per bbl.							
July	45.94	46.49		44.55	**44.73**	−1.73	209,102
Aug	46.13	46.68		44.74	**44.93**	−1.74	442,660
Sept	46.38	46.85		44.96	**45.14**	−1.75	274,042
Dec	46.90	47.37		45.59	**45.82**	−1.63	311,431
June'18	47.74	47.95		46.49	**46.74**	−1.36	121,798
Dec	48.00	48.24		46.90	**47.21**	−1.10	150,760
NY Harbor ULSD (NYM)-42,000 gal.; $ per gal.							
July	1.4412	1.4550		1.4062	**1.4102**	−.0375	81,641
Aug	1.4500	1.4618		1.4139	**1.4180**	−.0368	84,147
Gasoline-NY RBOB (NYM)-42,000 gal.; $ per gal.							
July	1.4856	1.4959		1.4292	**1.4327**	−.0668	97,511
Aug	1.4811	1.4953		1.4281	**1.4315**	−.0625	85,745
Natural Gas (NYM)-10,000 MMBtu.; $ per MMBtu.							
July	2.962	2.989		2.916	**2.933**	−.033	186,368
Aug	2.990	3.007		2.936	**2.953**	−.036	208,648
Sept	2.970	2.989		2.922	**2.937**	−.035	180,592
Oct	2.997	3.013		2.949	**2.962**	−.038	185,021
Jan'18	3.301	3.303		3.249	**3.263**	−.033	109,540
April	2.881	2.887		2.854	**2.856**	−.026	85,557

Agriculture Futures

	Open	Contract High	hi lo	Contract Low	Settle	Chg	Open Interest
Corn (CBT)-5,000 bu.; cents per bu.							
July	381.00	385.00		376.75	**377.00**	−4.00	452,077
Sept	388.50	392.75		384.25	**385.00**	−3.50	409,284
Oats (CBT)-5,000 bu.; cents per bu.							
July	254.00	256.25		252.50	**255.50**	2.25	4,211
Dec	241.75	243.75	▲	241.50	**242.75**	2.00	1,890
Soybeans (CBT)-5,000 bu.; cents per bu.							
July	932.00	939.00		931.00	**931.75**	−.75	248,150
Nov	938.25	945.25		937.50	**939.00**	---	284,651
Soybean Meal (CBT)-100 tons; $ per ton.							
July	301.20	304.20		301.20	**301.80**	.30	129,154
Dec	307.00	309.20		306.70	**307.70**	.80	135,043
Soybean Oil (CBT)-60,000 lbs.; cents per lb.							
July	32.09	32.28		31.96	**32.09**	---	126,008
Dec	32.50	32.71		32.40	**32.56**	.03	141,285
Rough Rice (CBT)-2,000 cwt.; $ per cwt.							
July	1124.50	1126.00		1086.00	**1103.00**	−22.50	5,163
Sept	1153.00	1153.00		1108.00	**1130.50**	−23.00	3,819
Wheat (CBT)-5,000 bu.; cents per bu.							
July	445.00	452.25		441.75	**443.00**	−2.00	154,696
Sept	459.00	466.50		456.00	**457.25**	−2.00	144,177
Wheat (KC)-5,000 bu.; cents per bu.							
July	457.25	468.00		455.00	**457.50**	.50	108,082
Sept	474.00	484.75		472.25	**475.00**	.75	78,968
Wheat (MPLS)-5,000 bu.; cents per bu.							
July	627.00	645.75	▲	623.25	**627.50**	−.50	24.255
Sept	634.25	651.50	▲	630.50	**634.50**	---	26,710
Cattle-Feeder (CME)-50,000 lbs.; cents per lb.							
Aug	149.100	149.400		145.550	**146.125**	−3.825	32,577
Sept	148.800	149.000		145.200	**145.700**	−4.000	9,864
Cattle-Live (CME)-40,000 lbs.; cents per lb.							
June	126.875	127.000		124.500	**124.500**	−3.000	12,798
Aug	120.300	120.425		117.875	**117.875**	−3.000	190,817
Hogs-Lean (CME)-40,000 lbs.; cents per lb.							
June	82.775	83.050	▲	82.700	**83.000**	.225	11,366
Aug	80.850	81.000		79.700	**80.400**	.175	86,145
Lumber (CME)-110,000 bd.ft., $ per 1,000 bd.ft.							
July	368.90	370.00		365.60	**368.00**	−.90	2.342
Sept	354.50	359.80		354.80	**357.60**	−.90	1,200
Milk (CME)-200,000 lbs.; cents per lb.							
June	16.34	16.36		16.30	**16.31**	---	5,097
July	16.70	16.70		16.50	**16.61**	−.06	4,344
Cocoa (ICE-US)-10 metric tons; $ per ton.							
July	2,017	2,043		2,001	**2,040**	18	15,136
Sept	2,048	2,077		2,033	**2,075**	19	120,024
Coffee (ICE-US)-37,500 lbs.; cents per lb.							
July	126.50	127.90		125.30	**125.55**	−.85	44,764
Sept	128.25	130.00	▼	127.55	**127.75**	−.90	97,731
Sugar-World (ICE-US)-112,000 lbs.; cents per lb.							
July	13.74	13.81	▼	13.36	**13.62**	−.17	212,475
Oct	13.97	13.99	▼	13.61	**13.85**	−.17	349,542
Sugar-Domestic (ICE-US)-112,000 lbs.; cents per lb.							
Sept	27.76	27.76		27.75	**27.67**	.03	1,964
Nov	27.39	27.39		27.39	**27.44**	−.04	1,279
Cotton (ICE-US)-50,000 lbs.; cents per lb.							
July	74.47	74.83		73.40	**73.50**	−.98	45,003
Dec	71.82	72.00		70.86	**70.95**	−.87	155,910
Orange Juice (ICE-US)-15,000 lbs.; cents per lb.							
July	141.05	141.50		139.00	**140.25**	−.80	6,044
Sept	138.45	139.55		137.40	**138.05**	−1.40	4,087

Interest Rate Futures

	Open	Contract High	hi lo	Contract Low	Settle	Chg	Open Interest
Treasury Bonds (CBT)-$100,000; pts 32nds of 100%							
June	155–130	157–130		155–120	**156–290**	1-19.0	3,304
Sept	153–310	156–050		153–290	**155–200**	1-19.0	730,435
Treasury Notes (CBT)-$100,000; pts 32nds of 100%							
June	126–180	127–175		126–180	**127–035**	16.0	48,739
Sept	126–110	127–080		125–105	**126–295**	17.5	1,131,656
5 Yr. Treasury Notes (CBT)-$100,000; pts 32nds of 100%							
June	118–225	119–057		118–217	**118–292**	7.5	49,887
Sept	118–065	118–247		118–060	**118–150**	8.0	1,123,645
2 Yr. Treasury Notes (CBT)-$200,000; pts 32nds of 100%							
June	108–085	108–130		108–085	**108–095**	1.2	11,027
Sept	108–030	108–092		108–030	**108–052**	1.7	1,174,,311
30 Day Federal Funds (CBT)-$5,000,000; 100-daily avg.							
June	98.968	98.975	▼	98.960	**98.963**	−.005	78,380
July	98.860	98.875	▼	98.850	**98.855**	−.005	457,474
10 Yr. Del. Int. Rate Swaps (CBT)-$100,000; pts 32nds of 100%							
June	93.391	94.500	▲	93.391	**94.141**	.578	12,681
Sept	102.531	103.313	▲	102.203	**102.984**	.625	16,446
1 Month Libor (CME)-$3,000,000; pts of 100%							
June	98.7900	98.8000	▼	98.7900	**98.7900**	−.0075	9,528
July	98.7900	98.7900	▼	98.7900	**98.7875**	−.0050	3,147
Eurodollar (CME)-$1,000,000; pts of 100%							
June	98.7275	98.7500		98.7250	**98.7275**	−.0025	1,493,523
Sept	98.6400	98.7000		98.6400	**98.6700**	.0250	1,407,477
Dec	98.5600	98.6300		98.5550	**98.5900**	.0300	1,724,980
Dec'18	98.2300	98.3500	▲	98.2250	**98.2900**	.0550	1,397,044

Currency Futures

	Open	Contract High	hi lo	Contract Low	Settle	Chg	Open Interest
Japanese Yen (CME)-¥12,500,000; $ per 100¥							
June	.9086	.9192		.9064	**.9129**	−.0033	145,801
Sept	.9124	.9228		.9102	.9166	−.0033	63,409
Canadian Dollar (CME)-CAD 100,000; $ per CAD							
June	.7554	.7597		.7536	**.7549**	-.0011	143,138
Sept	.7566	.7609		.7548	**.7561**	-.0011	56,254
British Pound (CME)-£62,500; $ per £							
June	1.2754	1.2821		1.2724	**1.2748**	−.0008	177,546
Sept	1.2787	1.2856		1.2761	**1.2784**	−.0008	89,873
Swiss Franc (CME)-CHF 125,000; $ per CHF							
June	1.0326	1.0376		1.0274	**1.0292**	−.0038	38,989
Sept	1.0387	1.0437		1.0336	**1.0353**	−.0038	16,045
Australian Dollar (CME)-AUD 100,000; $ per AUD							
June	.7534	.7636	▲	.7532	**.7591**	.0052	105,593
July	.7531	.7631		.7530	**.7587**	.0051	507
Aug	.7530	.7628		.7527	**.7585**	.0052	316
Sept	.7525	.7625		.7523	**.7581**	.0052	28,292
Dec	.7520	.7620		.7518	**.7572**	.0050	224
Mexican Peso (CME)-MXN 500,000; $ per MXN							
June	0.5536	0.5582		0.5531	**0.5560**	.00027	106,536
Euro (CME)-€125,000; $ per €							
June	1.1212	1.1299		1.1196	**1.1219**	.0003	326,182
Sept	1.1267	1.1354		1.1251	**1.1274**	.0004	143,565

Index Futures

	Open	Contract High	hi lo	Contract Low	Settle	Chg	Open Interest
Mini DJ Industrial Average (CBT)-$5 x index							
June	21322	21388		21289	**21371**	49	40,827
Sept	21282	21346	▲	21246	**21327**	47	102,619
S&P 500 Index (CME)-$250 x index							
June	2443.00	2443.00		2429.00	**2437.20**	-2.80	72,284
Sept	2437.10	2442.10		2427.00	**2435.30**	-2.70	33,603
Mini S&P 500 (CME)-$50 x index							
June	2440.25	2440.50		2427.75	**2437.25**	-2.75	1,023,610
Sept	2438.25	2443.25		2425.25	**2435.25**	-2.75	2,433,721
Mini S&P Midcap 400 (CME)-$100 x index							
June	1768.60	1773.60		1754.40	**1761.50**	-8.10	16,422
Sept	1770.30	1774.10		1754.30	**1762.10**	-8.00	81,233
Mini Nasdaq 100 (CME)-$20 x index							
June	5752.3	5780.0		5680.0	**5725.3**	-26.0	159,624
Sept	5762.3	5789.0		5687.0	**5732.8**	-26.5	287,790
Mini Russell 2000 (ICE-US)-$100 x index							
June	1428.30	1430.00		1410.00	**1416.30**	-11.10	164,216
Sept	1427.20	1429.70		1409.80	**1416.30**	-10.90	493,530
Mini Russell 1000 (ICE-US)-$100 x index							
June	1353.70	1353.70		1345.80	**1351.30**	-1.60	2,724
Sept	1352.70	1352.70		1345.10	1350.60	-1.00	7,716
U.S. Dollar Index (ICE-US)-$1,000 x index							
June	97.01	97.11		96.31	**96.31**	-.02	63,508
Sept	96.73	96.81		96.02	**96.59**	-.09	20,603

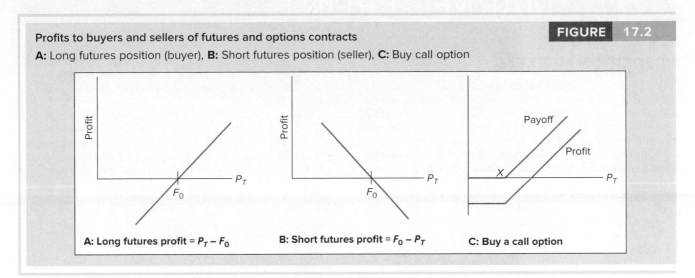

FIGURE 17.2

Profits to buyers and sellers of futures and options contracts
A: Long futures position (buyer), **B:** Short futures position (seller), **C:** Buy call option

A: Long futures profit = $P_T - F_0$ B: Short futures profit = $F_0 - P_T$ C: Buy a call option

Figure 17.2, Panel B, is a plot of the profits realized by an investor who enters the short side of a futures contract. It is the mirror image of the profit diagram for the long position.

> **CONCEPT check 17.1**
>
> *a.* Compare the profit diagram in Figure 17.2, Panel B, to the payoff diagram for a long position in a put option. Assume the exercise price of the option equals the initial futures price.
> *b.* Compare the profit diagram in Figure 17.2, Panel B, to the payoff diagram for an investor who writes a call option.

Existing Contracts

Futures and forward contracts are traded on a wide variety of goods in four broad categories: agricultural commodities, metals and minerals (including energy commodities), foreign currencies, and financial futures (fixed-income securities and stock market indexes). In addition to indexes on broad stock indexes, the electronic OneChicago market lists so-called **single stock futures** on some actively traded individual stocks and narrowly based indexes.

Table 17.1 offers a sample of contracts trading in 2017. While the table includes many contracts, the large and ever-growing array of markets makes this list necessarily incomplete. The nearby box discusses some comparatively fanciful futures markets in which payoffs may be tied to the winner of presidential elections, the box office receipts of a particular movie, or anything else in which participants are willing to take positions.

Outside the futures markets, a well-developed network of banks and brokers has established a forward market in foreign exchange. Whereas in futures markets, contract size and delivery dates are set by the exchanges, participants in over-the-counter forward markets may negotiate for delivery of any quantity of goods at any time. The forward market in foreign exchange is huge, with more than $5 trillion of currency trading hands each day.

single stock futures
A futures contract on the shares of an individual company.

17.2 TRADING MECHANICS

The Clearinghouse and Open Interest

Until about 20 years ago, most futures trades in the United States occurred among floor traders in the "trading pit" for each contract. Today, however, trading is overwhelmingly conducted through electronic networks.

On the MARKET FRONT

PREDICTION MARKETS

If you find S&P 500 or T-bond contracts a bit dry, perhaps you'd be interested in futures contracts with payoffs that depend on the winner of the next presidential election, or the severity of the next influenza season, or the host city of the 2028 Olympics. You can now find "futures markets" in these events and many others.

For example, both Iowa Electronic Markets (**http://tippie.biz .uiowa.edu/iem**) and *PredictIt* (**www.predictlt.org**) maintain presidential futures markets. In September 2016, you could have purchased a contract that would pay off $1 in November if Hillary Clinton won the presidential race but nothing if she lost. The contract price (expressed as a percentage of face value) therefore may be viewed as the probability of a Clinton victory, at least according to the consensus view of market participants at the time. If you believed in September that the probability of a Clinton victory was 55%, you would have been prepared to pay up to $.55 for the contract. Alternatively, if you had wished to bet against Clinton, you could have sold the contract. Similarly, you could have bet on (or against) a Donald Trump victory using his contract. (When there are only two relevant parties, betting on one is equivalent to betting against the other, but in other elections, such as primaries where there are several viable candidates, selling one candidate's contract is not the same as buying another's.)

The accompanying figure shows the price of Democratic and Republican contracts from November 2014 through Election Day. The price clearly tracks each party's perceived prospects. You can see Clinton's price rise to above $.90 in the week just before the election as the polls increasingly suggested she would win. Her price then declined substantially when the FBI announced it was reopening its investigation into her e-mail server. By the day before the election, with the investigation again apparently closed, her price had rebounded to $.80: Her victory seemed nearly inevitable—at least until the votes were counted.

Interpreting prediction market prices as probabilities actually requires a caveat. Because the contract payoff is risky, the price of the contract may reflect a risk premium. Therefore, to be precise, these probabilities are actually risk-neutral probabilities (see Chapter 16). In practice, however, it seems unlikely that the risk premium associated with these contracts is substantial.

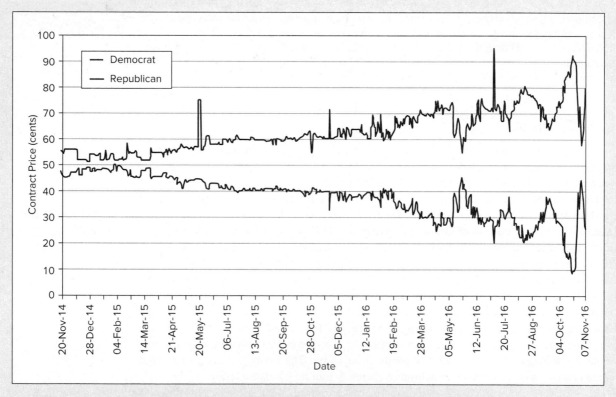

Prediction markets for the 2016 presidential election. Contract on each party pays $1 if the party wins the election. Price is in cents.

Source: Iowa Electronic Markets, downloaded November 16, 2016.

TABLE 17.1 Sample of futures contracts

Foreign Currencies	Agricultural	Metals and Energy	Interest Rate Futures	Equity Indexes
British pound	Corn	Copper	Eurodollars	Dow Jones Industrials
Canadian dollar	Oats	Aluminum	Euroyen	S&P Midcap 400
Japanese yen	Soybeans	Gold	Euro-denominated	NASDAQ 100
Euro	Soybean meal	Platinum	bond	NYSE Index
Swiss franc	Soybean oil	Palladium	Euroswiss	Russell 2000 Index
Australian dollar	Wheat	Silver	Sterling	Nikkei 225 (Japanese)
Mexican peso	Barley	Crude oil	British gov't bond	FTSE Index (British)
Brazilian real	Palm oil	Heating oil	German gov't bond	CAC Index (French)
New Zealand dollar	Canola	Gas oil	Italian gov't bond	DAX Index (German)
	Rye	Natural gas	Canadian gov't bond	All ordinary (Australian)
	Cattle	Gasoline	Treasury bonds	Toronto 35 (Canadian)
	Milk	Propane	Treasury notes	Titans 30 (Italian)
	Hogs	Commodity index	Treasury bills	Dow Jones Euro STOXX 50
	Pork bellies	Electricity	LIBOR	Industry indexes, e.g.,
	Cocoa	Weather	EURIBOR	banking
	Coffee	Kerosene	Interest rate swaps	natural resources
	Cotton	Fuel oil	Federal funds rate	chemical
	Orange juice	Iron ore	Bankers' acceptance	health care
	Sugar		S&P 500 Index	technology
	Lumber			retail
	Rice			utilities
				telecom

Once a trade is agreed to, the **clearinghouse** enters the picture. Rather than having the long and short traders hold contracts with each other, the clearinghouse becomes the seller of the contract for the long position and the buyer of the contract for the short position. The clearinghouse delivers the commodity to the long position and pays for delivery from the short; consequently, its position nets to zero. This arrangement makes the clearinghouse the trading partner of each trader, both long and short. The clearinghouse, bound to perform on its side of each contract, is the only party that can be hurt by the failure of any trader to honor the obligations of the contract. This arrangement is necessary because a futures contract calls for future performance, which cannot be as easily guaranteed as an immediate stock transaction.

Figure 17.3, Panel A, shows what would happen in the absence of the clearinghouse. The long position would be obligated to pay the futures price to the short position, and the short position would be obligated to deliver the commodity. Panel B shows how the clearinghouse becomes an intermediary, acting as the trading partner for each side of the contract. The clearinghouse's position is neutral, as it takes a long and a short position for each transaction.

The clearinghouse makes it possible for traders to liquidate positions easily. If you are currently long and want to undo your position, you simply instruct your broker to enter the short side of a contract. This is called a *reversing trade*. The exchange nets out your long and short positions, reducing your net position to zero. Your zero net position eliminates the need to fulfill at maturity either the original long or reversing short position.

The *open interest* on the contract is the number of contracts outstanding. (Long and short positions are not counted separately, meaning that open interest can be defined as either the number of long or short contracts outstanding. The clearinghouse's position nets out to zero, and so it is not counted in the computation of open interest.) When contracts begin trading,

clearinghouse

Established by exchanges to facilitate trading. The clearinghouse interposes itself as an intermediary between two traders.

FIGURE 17.3   Trading with and without a clearinghouse

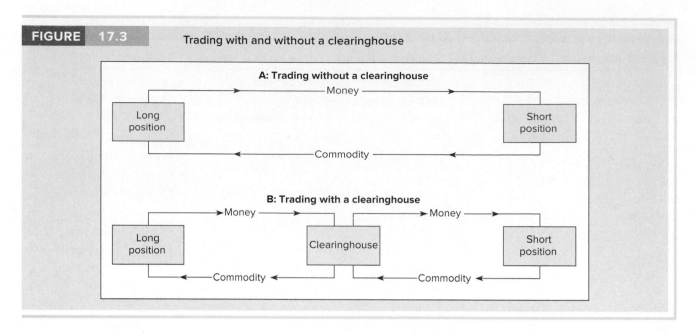

---

open interest is zero. As time passes, open interest increases as progressively more contracts are entered.

There are many apocryphal stories about futures traders who wake up to discover a small mountain of wheat or corn on their front lawn. But the truth is that futures contracts rarely result in actual delivery of the underlying asset. Traders establish long or short positions in contracts that will benefit from a rise or fall in the futures price and almost always close out those positions before the contract expires. The fraction of contracts that result in actual delivery is estimated to range from less than 1% to 3%, depending on the commodity and activity in the contract. In the unusual case of actual deliveries of commodities, they occur via regular channels of supply, usually via warehouse receipts.

You can see the typical pattern of open interest in Figure 17.1. In the gold contract, for example, the June delivery contracts are close to maturity and open interest is small; most contracts have been reversed already. The August maturity contract has significantly greater open interest. Finally, the most distant maturity contracts have less open interest, as they have been available only recently and few participants have yet traded. For other contracts such as natural gas futures, for which the nearest maturity is still more than a month away, open interest is still quite high in the nearest contract.

Marking to Market and the Margin Account

The total profit or loss realized by the long trader who buys a contract at time 0 and closes, or reverses, it at time t is just the change in the futures price over the period, $F_t - F_0$. Symmetrically, the short trader earns $F_0 - F_t$.

marking to market

The daily settlement of obligations on futures positions.

The process by which profits or losses accrue to traders is called **marking to market.** At initial execution of a trade, each trader establishes a margin account. The margin is a security account consisting of cash or near-cash securities, such as Treasury bills, that ensures the trader will be able to satisfy the obligations of the futures contract. Because both parties to the contract are exposed to losses, both must post margin. To illustrate, return to the July corn contract listed in Figure 17.1. If the initial required margin on corn, for example, is 10%, the trader must post $1,885 per contract for the margin account. This is 10% of the value of the contract ($3.77 per bushel × 5,000 bushels per contract).

Because the initial margin may be satisfied by posting interest-earning securities, the requirement does not impose a significant opportunity cost of funds on the trader. The initial margin is usually set between 5% and 15% of the total value of the contract. Contracts written on assets with more volatile prices require higher margins.

On any day that contracts trade, futures prices may rise or fall. Instead of waiting until the maturity date for traders to realize all gains and losses, the clearinghouse requires all positions to recognize profits as they accrue daily. If the futures price of corn rises from 377 to 379 cents per bushel, for example, the clearinghouse credits the margin account of the long position for 5,000 bushels times 2 cents per bushel, or $100 per contract. Conversely, for the short position, the clearinghouse takes this amount from the margin account for each contract held. Therefore, as futures prices change, proceeds accrue to the trader's account immediately.

Marking to market is the major way in which futures and forward contracts differ, besides contract standardization. Futures follow this pay- (or receive-) as-you-go method. Forward contracts are simply held until maturity, and no funds are transferred until that date.

What must be the net inflow or outlay from marking to market for the clearinghouse?

CONCEPT check 17.2

If a trader accrues sustained losses from daily marking to market, the margin account may fall below a critical value called the **maintenance margin.** If the value of the account falls below this value, the trader receives a *margin call,* requiring that the margin account be replenished or the position be reduced to a size commensurate with the remaining funds. Margins and margin calls safeguard the position of the clearinghouse. Positions are closed out before the margin account is exhausted—the trader's losses are covered, and the clearinghouse is not put at risk.

maintenance margin
An established value below which a trader's margin may not fall. Reaching the maintenance margin triggers a margin call.

Suppose the maintenance margin is 5% while the initial margin was 10% of the value of the corn, or $1,885. Then a margin call will go out when the original margin account has fallen about in half, or by $943. Each 1-cent decline in the corn price results in a $50 loss to the long position. Therefore, the futures price need fall only by 19 cents to trigger a margin call.

EXAMPLE 17.1

Maintenance Margin

On the contract maturity date, the futures price will equal the spot price of the commodity. As a maturing contract calls for immediate delivery, the futures price on that day must equal the spot price—the cost of the commodity from the two competing sources is equalized in a competitive market.[1] You may obtain delivery of the commodity either by purchasing it directly in the spot market or by entering the long side of a maturing futures contract.

A commodity available from two sources (the spot and futures markets) must be priced identically, or else investors will rush to purchase it from the cheap source in order to sell it in the high-priced market. Such arbitrage activity could not persist without prices adjusting to eliminate the arbitrage opportunity. Therefore, the futures price and the spot price must converge at maturity. This is called the **convergence property.**

For an investor who establishes a long position in a contract now (time 0) and holds that position until maturity (time T), the sum of all daily settlements will equal $F_T - F_0$, where F_T stands for the futures price at contract maturity. Because of convergence, however, the futures price at maturity, F_T, equals the spot price, P_T, so total futures profits also may be expressed as $P_T - F_0$. Thus, we see that profits on a futures contract held to maturity perfectly track changes in the value of the underlying asset.

convergence property
The convergence of futures prices and spot prices at the maturity of the futures contract.

---

[1] Small differences between the spot and futures prices at maturity may persist because of transportation costs, but this is a minor factor.

EXAMPLE 17.2

Marking to Market and Futures Contract Profits

Assume the five-day maturity futures price for silver is $16.10 per ounce and that over the next five days, the futures price evolves as follows:

Day	Futures Price
0 (today)	$16.10
1	16.20
2	16.25
3	16.18
4	16.18
5 (maturity)	16.21

The daily mark-to-market settlements for each contract held by the long positions will be as follows:

Day	Profit (loss) per Ounce	× 5,000 Ounces/Contract = Daily Proceeds
1	$16.20 − $16.10 = $0.10	$500
2	16.25 − 16.20 = 0.05	250
3	16.18 − 16.25 = −0.07	−350
4	16.18 − 16.18 = 0	0
5	16.21 − 16.18 = 0.03	150
		Sum = $550

The profit on day 1 is the increase in the futures price from the previous day, or ($16.20 − $16.10) per ounce. Because each silver contract on the Commodity Exchange calls for purchase and delivery of 5,000 ounces, the profit per contract is 5,000 times $.10, or $500. On day 3, when the futures price falls, the long position's margin account will be debited by $350. By day 5, the sum of all daily proceeds is $550. This is exactly equal to 5,000 times the difference between the final futures price of $16.21 and the original futures price of $16.10. Because the final futures price equals the spot price on that date, the sum of all the daily proceeds (per ounce of silver held long) equals $P_T − F_0$.

Cash versus Actual Delivery

Most futures markets call for delivery of an actual commodity, such as a particular grade of wheat or a specified amount of foreign currency, if the contract is not reversed before maturity. For agricultural commodities, where quality of the delivered good may vary, the exchange sets quality standards as part of the futures contract. In some cases, contracts may be settled with higher- or lower-grade commodities. In these cases, a premium or discount is applied to the delivered commodity to adjust for the quality differences.

cash settlement

The cash value of the underlying asset (rather than the asset itself) is delivered to satisfy the contract.

Some futures contracts call for **cash settlement.** An example is a stock-index futures contract where the underlying asset is an index such as the Standard & Poor's 500 Index. Delivery of every stock in the index clearly would be impractical. Hence, the contract calls for "delivery" of a cash amount equal to the value of the index on the maturity date. The sum of all the daily settlements from marking to market results in the long position realizing total profits or losses of $S_T − F_0$, where S_T is the value of the stock index on the maturity date T, and F_0 is the original futures price. Cash settlement closely mimics actual delivery, except the cash value of the asset rather than the asset itself is delivered.

More concretely, the most widely traded contract on the S&P 500 Index, the so-called E-Mini, calls for delivery of $50 times the value of the index. $50 is therefore called the contract multiplier.[2] At maturity, the index might list at 2,000, a market value–weighted index of

---

[2]There is another contract on the S&P 500 with a multiplier of $250. This so-called "big contract" was originally more widely traded. Today, however, the all-electronic E-Mini dominates trading (compare open interest of the two S&P contracts in Figure 17.1), so we will use its $50 multiplier in all of our examples.

the prices of all 500 stocks in the index. Instead of delivering the index, the cash settlement contract calls for the short side to deliver $50 × 2,000, or $100,000 cash. This yields exactly the same profit as would result from directly purchasing 50 units of the index for $100,000 and then delivering it for $50 times the original futures price.

Regulations

Futures markets are regulated by the federal Commodity Futures Trading Commission (CFTC). The CFTC sets capital requirements for member firms of the futures exchanges, authorizes trading in new contracts, and oversees maintenance of daily trading records.

The futures exchange may set limits on the amount by which futures prices may change from one day to the next. For example, if the price limit on silver contracts is $1, and silver futures close today at $16.10 per ounce, trades in silver tomorrow may vary only between $15.10 and $17.10 per ounce. The exchange may increase or reduce these price limits in response to perceived changes in the price volatility of the contract. Price limits often are eliminated as contracts approach maturity, usually in the last month of trading.

Price limits traditionally are viewed as a means to limit violent price fluctuations. This reasoning seems dubious, however. Suppose an international monetary crisis overnight drives up the spot price of silver to $25. No one would sell silver futures at prices for future delivery as low as $16.10. Instead, the futures price would rise each day by the $1 limit, although the quoted price would represent only an unfilled bid order—no contracts would trade at the low quoted price. After several days of limit moves of $1 per day, the futures price would finally reach its equilibrium level, and trading would resume. This process means no one could unload a position until the price reached its equilibrium level. This example shows that price limits offer no real protection against fluctuations in equilibrium prices.

Taxation

Because of the mark-to-market procedure, investors do not have control over the tax year in which they realize gains or losses. Instead, price changes are realized gradually, with each daily settlement. Therefore, taxes are paid at year-end on cumulated profits or losses regardless of whether the position has been closed out. As a general rule, 60% of futures gains or losses are treated as long term and 40% as short term.

17.3   FUTURES MARKET STRATEGIES

Hedging and Speculation

Hedging and speculating are two polar uses of futures markets. A speculator uses a futures contract to profit from movements in futures prices; a hedger, to protect against price movements.

If speculators believe prices will increase, they will take a long position for expected profits. Conversely, they exploit expected price declines by taking a short position.

Suppose you believe that crude oil prices are going to increase. You might purchase crude oil futures. Each contract calls for delivery of 1,000 barrels of oil, so for every dollar increase in the price of crude, the long position gains $1,000 and the short position loses that amount.

EXAMPLE 17.3

Speculating with Oil Futures

Conversely, suppose you think that prices are heading lower and therefore sell a contract. If crude oil prices fall, then your short position gains $1,000 for every dollar that prices decline.

If the futures price for delivery in February is $52 and crude oil is selling for $53 at the contract maturity date, the long side will profit by $1,000 per contract purchased. The short side will lose an identical amount on each contract sold. On the other hand, if oil has fallen to $51, the long side will lose, and the short side will gain, $1,000 per contract.

Why would a speculator buy a futures contract? Why not buy the underlying asset directly? One reason lies in transaction costs, which are far smaller in futures markets.

Another reason is the leverage futures trading provides. Recall that futures contracts require traders to post considerably less margin than the value of the asset underlying the contract. Therefore, they allow speculators to achieve much greater leverage than is available from direct trading in a commodity.

EXAMPLE 17.4

Futures and Leverage

Suppose the initial margin requirement for the oil contract is 10%. At a current futures price of $52, and contract size of 1,000 barrels, this would require margin of $.10 \times \$52 \times 1,000 = \$5,200$. A $1 increase in oil prices represents an increase of 1.92%, and results in a $1,000 gain on the contract for the long position. This is a percentage gain of 19.2% in the $5,200 posted as margin, precisely 10 times the percentage increase in the oil price. The 10-to-1 ratio of percentage changes reflects the leverage inherent in the futures position because the contract was established with an initial margin of one-tenth the value of the underlying asset.

Hedgers, by contrast, use futures to insulate themselves against price movements. A firm planning to sell oil, for example, might wish to protect its revenue against price fluctuations. To hedge the total revenue derived from the sale, the firm enters a short position in oil futures. As the following example illustrates, this locks in its total proceeds (i.e., revenue from the sale of the oil plus proceeds from its futures position).

EXAMPLE 17.5

Hedging with Oil Futures

Consider an oil distributor planning to sell 100,000 barrels of oil in February that wishes to hedge against a possible decline in oil prices. Because each contract calls for delivery of 1,000 barrels, it would sell 100 contracts. Any decrease in prices would then generate a profit on the contracts that would offset the lower sales revenue from the oil.

To illustrate, suppose that the only three possible prices for oil in February are $51, $52, and $53 per barrel. The revenue from the oil sale will be 100,000 times the price per barrel. The profit on each contract sold will be 1,000 times any decline in the futures price. At maturity, the convergence property ensures that the final futures price will equal the spot price of oil. Therefore, the profit on the 100 contracts sold will equal $100,000 \times (F_0 - P_T)$, where P_T is the oil price on the delivery date and F_0 is the original futures price, $52.

Now consider the firm's overall position. The total revenue in February can be computed as follows:

	Oil Price in February, P_T		
	$51	**$52**	**$53**
Revenue from oil sale: $100,000 \times P_T$	$5,100,000	$5,200,000	$5,300,000
+ Profit on futures: $100,000 \times (F_0 - P_T)$	100,000	0	−100,000
Total proceeds	$5,200,000	$5,200,000	$5,200,000

The revenue from the oil sale plus the proceeds from the contracts equals the current futures price, $52 per barrel. The variation in the price of the oil is precisely offset by the profits or losses on the futures position. For example, if oil falls to $51 a barrel, the short futures position generates $100,000 profit, just enough to bring total revenues to $5,200,000. The total is the same as if one were to arrange today to sell the oil in February at the futures price.

Figure 17.4 illustrates the nature of the hedge in Example 17.5. The upward-sloping line is the revenue from the sale of oil. The downward-sloping line is the profit on the futures contract. The horizontal line is the sum of sales revenue plus futures profits. This line is flat, as the hedged position is independent of oil prices.

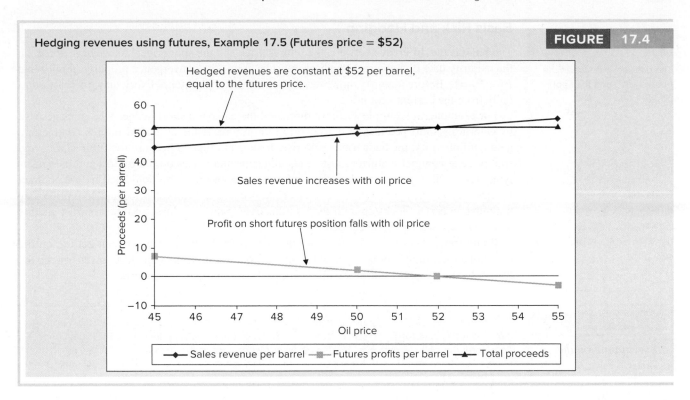

Hedging revenues using futures, Example 17.5 (Futures price = $52)

FIGURE 17.4

To generalize Example 17.5, note that oil will sell for P_T per barrel at the maturity of the contract. The profit per barrel on the futures will be $F_0 - P_T$. Therefore, total revenue is $P_T + (F_0 - P_T) = F_0$, which is independent of the eventual oil price.

The oil distributor in this example engaged in a *short hedge*, taking a short futures position to offset risk in the sales price of a particular asset. A *long hedge* is the analogous hedge for someone who wishes to eliminate the risk of an uncertain purchase price. For example, a petrochemical firm planning to purchase oil may be afraid that prices might rise by the time of the purchase. As the following Concept Check illustrates, the firm might *buy* oil futures to lock in the net purchase price at the time of the transaction.

CONCEPT check 17.3

Suppose as in Example 17.5 that oil will be selling in February for $51, $52, or $53 per barrel. Consider a firm that plans to buy 100,000 barrels of oil in February. Show that if the firm buys 100 oil contracts, its net expenditures will be hedged and equal to $5,200,000.

Exact futures hedging may be impossible for some goods because the necessary futures contract is not traded. For example, a portfolio manager might want to hedge the value of a diversified, actively managed portfolio for a period of time. However, futures contracts are listed only on indexed portfolios. Nevertheless, because returns on the manager's diversified portfolio will have a high correlation with returns on broad-based indexed portfolios, an effective hedge may be established by selling index futures contracts. Hedging a position using futures on another asset is called *cross-hedging*.

CONCEPT check 17.4

What are the sources of risk to an investor who uses stock-index futures to hedge an actively managed stock portfolio? How might you estimate the magnitude of that risk?

Basis Risk and Hedging

basis

The difference between the futures price and the spot price.

The **basis** is the difference between the futures price and the spot price.[3] As we have noted, on the maturity date of a contract, the basis must be zero: The convergence property implies that $F_T - P_T = 0$. Before maturity, however, the futures price for later delivery may differ substantially from the current spot price.

For example, in Example 17.5, we discussed the case of a short hedger who manages risk by entering a short position to deliver oil in the future. If the asset and futures contract are held until maturity, the hedger bears no risk. Risk is eliminated because the futures price and spot price at contract maturity must be equal: Gains and losses on the futures and the underlying asset will exactly cancel. If the contract and asset are to be liquidated before contract maturity, however, the hedger bears **basis risk,** because the futures price and spot price may not move in perfect lockstep until then. In this case, gains and losses on the contract and the asset may not exactly offset each other.

basis risk

Risk attributable to uncertain movements in the spread between a futures price and a spot price.

Some speculators try to profit from movements in the basis. Rather than betting on the direction of the futures or spot prices per se, they bet on changes in the difference between the two. A long spot–short futures position will profit when the basis narrows.

EXAMPLE 17.6

Speculating on the Basis

Consider an investor holding 100 ounces of gold, who is short one gold futures contract. Suppose that gold today sells for $1,191 an ounce, and the futures price for June delivery is $1,196 an ounce. Therefore, the basis is currently $5. Tomorrow, the spot price might increase to $1,194, while the futures price increases to $1,198.50, so the basis narrows to $4.50. The investor's gains and losses are as follows:

Gain on holdings of gold (per ounce): $1,194 − $1,191 = $3.00
Loss on gold futures position (per ounce): $1,198.50 − $1,196 = $2.50

The investor gains $3 per ounce on the gold holdings but loses $2.50 an ounce on the short futures position. The net gain is the decrease in the basis, or $0.50 an ounce.

---

spread (futures)

Taking a long position in a futures contract of one maturity and a short position in a contract of a different maturity, both on the same asset.

A related strategy is a **spread,** where the investor takes a long position in a futures contract of one maturity and a short position in a contract on the same commodity but with a different maturity. Profits accrue if the difference in futures prices between the two contracts changes in the hoped-for direction, that is, if the futures price on the contract held long increases by more (or decreases by less) than the futures price on the contract held short. Like basis strategies, spread positions aim to exploit movements in relative prices rather than to profit from movements in the general level of prices.

EXAMPLE 17.7

Speculating on the Spread

Consider an investor who holds a September maturity contract long and a June contract short. If the September futures price increases by 5 cents while the June futures price increases by 4 cents, the net gain will be 5 cents − 4 cents, or 1 cent.

17.4 FUTURES PRICES

Spot-Futures Parity

There are at least two ways to obtain an asset at some date in the future. One way is to purchase it now and store it until the horizon date. The other is to take a long futures position that calls for purchase of the asset on the date in question. As each strategy leads to an equivalent

---

[3] Usage of the word *basis* is somewhat loose. It sometimes is used to refer to the futures-spot difference, $F - P$, and other times it is used to refer to the spot-futures difference, $P - F$. We will consistently call the basis $F - P$.

result, namely, the ultimate acquisition of the asset, you would expect their costs to be equal. Therefore, there should be a predictable relationship between the current price of the asset, including the costs of holding and storing it, and the futures price.

To illustrate, consider a futures contract on gold. This is a particularly simple case: Explicit storage costs for gold are minimal, gold provides no income flow for its owners (in contrast to stocks or bonds that make dividend or coupon payments), and gold is not subject to the seasonal price patterns that characterize most agricultural commodities. Two strategies that will ensure possession of the gold at some future date T are:

Strategy A: Buy the gold now, paying the current or "spot" price, S_0, and hold it until time T, when its spot price will be S_T.

Strategy B: Initiate a long futures position, and invest enough money now to pay the futures price when the contract matures.

Strategy B requires an immediate investment of the *present value* of the futures price in a riskless security such as Treasury bills, that is, an investment of $F_0/(1 + r_f)^T$ dollars, where r_f is the interest rate on T-bills. Examine the cash flow streams of the following two strategies.[4]

	Action	Initial Cash Flow	Cash Flow at Time T
Strategy A:	Buy gold	$-S_0$	S_T
Strategy B:	Enter long futures position	0	$S_T - F_0$
	Invest $F_0/(1 + r_f)^T$ in bills	$-F_0/(1 + r_f)^T$	F_0
	Total for strategy B	$-F_0/(1 + r_f)^T$	S_T

The initial cash flow of strategy A is negative, reflecting the cash outflow necessary to purchase the gold at the current spot price, S_0. At time T, the gold will be worth S_T.

Strategy B involves an initial investment equal to the present value of the futures price. By time T, the investment will grow to F_0. In addition, the profits to the long position at time T will be $S_T - F_0$. The sum of the two components of strategy B will be S_T dollars, exactly the amount needed to purchase the gold at time T.

Each strategy results in an identical value of S_T dollars at T. Therefore, the cost, or initial cash outflow, required by these strategies also must be equal; it follows that

$$F_0/(1 + r_f)^T = S_0$$

or

$$F_0 = S_0(1 + r_f)^T \qquad \textbf{(17.1)}$$

Equation 17.1 tells us the relationship between the current price and the futures price of the gold. The interest rate in this case may be viewed as the "cost of carrying" the gold from the present to time T. The cost in this case represents the time-value-of-money opportunity cost—instead of investing in the gold, you could have invested risklessly in Treasury bills to earn interest income.

---

[4]We ignore the margin requirement on the futures contract and treat the cash flow involved in establishing the futures position as zero for the two reasons mentioned above: First, the margin is small relative to the amount of gold controlled by one contract; second, and more important, the margin requirement may be satisfied with interest-bearing securities. For example, the investor merely needs to transfer Treasury bills already owned into the brokerage account. There is no time-value-of-money cost.

Suppose that gold currently sells for $1,200 an ounce. If the risk-free interest rate is 0.1% per month, a six-month maturity futures contract should have a futures price of

$$F_0 = S_0(1 + r_f)^T = \$1,200(1.001)^6 = \$1,207.22$$

If the contract has a 12-month maturity, the futures price should be

$$F_0 = \$1,200(1.001)^{12} = \$1,214.48$$

If Equation 17.1 does not hold, investors can earn arbitrage profits. For example, suppose the six-month maturity futures price in Example 17.8 were $1,210 rather than the "appropriate" value of $1,207.22 that we just derived. The arbitrage entails a long position in strategy A (buy the gold) and a short position in strategy B (sell the futures contract and borrow enough to pay for the gold purchase).

Action	Initial Cash Flow	Cash Flow at Time T (6 months)
Borrow $1,200, repay with interest at time T	+$1,200	$-\$1,200(1.001)^6 = \$1,207.22$
Buy gold for $1,200	−1,200	S_T
Enter short futures position ($F_0 = \$1,210$)	0	$1,210 - S_T$
Total	$ 0	$2.78

The net initial investment of this strategy is zero. Moreover, its cash flow at time T is positive and riskless: The total payoff at time T will be $2.78 regardless of the price of gold. The profit is precisely equal to the mispricing of the futures contract, $1,210 rather than $1,207.22. Risk has been eliminated because profits and losses on the futures and gold positions exactly offset each other. The portfolio is perfectly hedged.

Such a strategy produces an arbitrage profit—a riskless profit requiring no initial net investment. If such an opportunity existed, all market participants would rush to take advantage of it. The results? The price of gold would be bid up, and/or the futures price offered down, until Equation 17.1 is satisfied. A similar analysis applies to the possibility that F_0 is less than $1,207.22. In this case, you simply reverse the above strategy to earn riskless profits. We conclude, therefore, that in a well-functioning market in which arbitrage opportunities are competed away, $F_0 = S_0(1 + r_f)^T$.

 **17.5**

Return to the arbitrage strategy just laid out. What would be the three steps of the strategy if F_0 were too low, say, $1,206? Work out the cash flows of the strategy now and at time T in a table like the one above. Confirm that your profits equal the mispricing of the contract.

The arbitrage strategy can be represented more generally as follows:

Action	Initial Cash Flow	Cash Flow at Time T
1. Borrow S_0	$+S_0$	$-S_0(1 + r_f)^T$
2. Buy gold for S_0	$-S_0$	S_T
3. Enter short futures position	0	$F_0 - S_T$
Total	0	$F_0 - S_0(1 + r_f)^T$

The initial cash flow is zero by construction: The money necessary to purchase the gold in step 2 is borrowed in step 1, and the futures position in step 3, which is used to hedge the

The Spot-Futures Parity spreadsheet allows you to calculate futures prices corresponding to a spot price for different maturities, interest rates, and income yields. You can use the spreadsheet to see how prices of more distant contracts will fluctuate with spot prices and the cost of carry.

You can learn more about this spreadsheet by using the version available in Connect.

Spreadsheets are available in Connect

	A	B	C	D	E
1					
2		Spot-Futures Parity and Time Spreads			
3					
4	Spot price	100			
5	Income yield (%)	2		Futures prices versus maturity	
6	Interest rate (%)	1.5			
7	Today's date	10/05/2017		Spot price	100.00
8	Maturity date 1	10/11/2017		Futures 1	99.75
9	Maturity date 2	10/07/2018		Futures 2	99.42
10	Maturity date 3	10/09/2018		Futures 3	99.33
11					
12	Time to maturity 1	0.50			
13	Time to maturity 2	1.17			
14	Time to maturity 3	1.33			

Excel Questions

1. Experiment with different values for both income yield and interest rate. What happens to the size of the time spread (the difference in futures prices for the long- versus short-maturity contracts) if the interest rate increases by 2%?

2. What happens to the time spread if the income yield increases by 2%?

3. What happens to the spread if the income yield equals the interest rate?

---

value of the gold, does not require an initial outlay. Moreover, the total cash flow at time T is riskless because it involves only terms that are already known when the contract is entered. This situation could not persist, as all investors would try to cash in on the arbitrage opportunity. Ultimately, prices would change until the time T cash flow was reduced to zero, at which point F_0 would equal $S_0(1 + r_f)^T$. This result is called the **spot-futures parity theorem or cost-of-carry relationship;** it gives the normal or theoretically correct relationship between spot and futures prices.

We can easily extend the parity theorem to the case where the underlying asset provides a flow of income to its owner. For example, consider a futures contract on a stock index such as the S&P 500. In this case, the underlying asset (i.e., the stock portfolio indexed to the S&P 500 index) pays a dividend yield to the investor. If we denote the dividend yield as d, then the net cost of carry is only $r_f - d$; the forgone interest earnings on the wealth tied up in the stock are offset by the flow of dividends from the stock. The net opportunity cost of holding the stock is the forgone interest less the dividends received. Therefore, in the dividend-paying case, the spot-futures parity relationship is[5]

$$F_0 = S_0(1 + r_f - d)^T \tag{17.2}$$

where d is the dividend yield on the stock. Problem 10 at the end of the chapter leads you through a derivation of this result.

spot-futures parity theorem or cost-of-carry relationship

Describes the theoretically correct relationship between spot and futures prices. Violation of the parity relationship gives rise to arbitrage opportunities.

---

[5] This relationship is only approximate in that it assumes the dividend is paid just before the maturity of the contract.

Notice that when the dividend yield is less than the risk-free rate, Equation 17.2 implies that futures prices will exceed spot prices and by greater amounts for longer times to contract maturity. But when $d > r_f$, as is the case today for the S&P 500, the income yield on the stock actually exceeds the forgone (risk-free) interest that could be earned on the money invested; in this event, the futures price will be less than the current stock price, again by greater amounts for longer maturities. You can confirm that this is so by examining the S&P listings in Figure 17.1. In contrast, the NASDAQ index comprises lower-dividend firms, and as a result, $d < r_f$. Here, the more distant contract has the *higher* futures price.

Although dividends of individual securities may fluctuate unpredictably, the annualized dividend yield of a broad-based index such as the S&P 500 is fairly stable, recently in the neighborhood of a bit more than 2% per year. The yield is seasonal, however, with regular peaks and troughs, so the dividend yield for the relevant months must be the one used. Figure 17.5 illustrates the yield pattern for the S&P 500. Some months, such as January or April, have consistently low yields, while others, such as May, have consistently high ones.

The arbitrage strategy just described should convince you that these parity relationships are more than just theoretical results. Any violations of the parity relationship give rise to arbitrage opportunities that can provide large profits to traders. We will see shortly that index arbitrage in the stock market is a tool used to exploit violations of the parity relationship for stock-index futures contracts.

EXAMPLE 17.9 *Stock-Index Futures Pricing*	Suppose that the risk-free interest rate is 0.1% per month, the dividend yield on the stock index is 0.2% per month, and the stock index is currently 2,400. The net cost of carry is therefore negative, .1% − .2% = −.1% per month. Equation 17.2 tells us that a three-month contract should have a futures price of $2,400(1 − .001)^3 = 2,392.81$, while a six-month contract should have a futures price of $2,400(1 − .001)^6 = 2,385.64$. If the index rises to 2,410, both futures prices will rise commensurately: The three-month futures price will rise to $2,410(1 − .001)^3 = 2,402.78$, while the six-month futures price will rise to $2,410(1 − .001)^6 = 2,395.58$.

Spreads

Just as we can predict the relationship between spot and futures prices, there are similar ways to determine the proper relationships among futures prices for contracts of different maturity dates. Equation 17.2 shows that the futures price is in part determined by time to maturity.

FIGURE **17.5** **S&P 500 dividend yield, annualized**	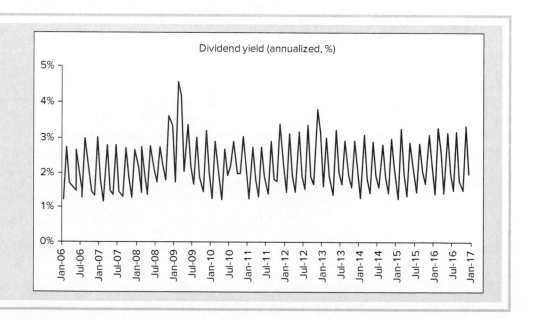

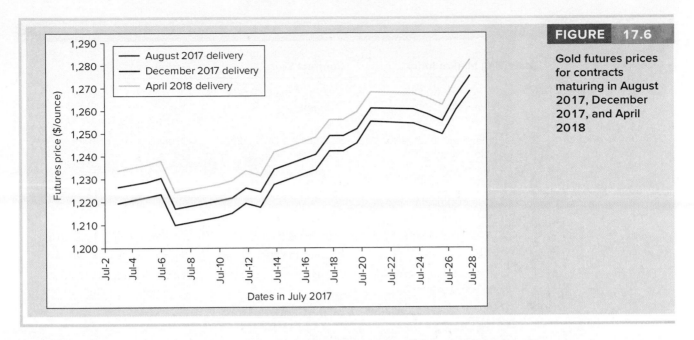

FIGURE 17.6

Gold futures prices for contracts maturing in August 2017, December 2017, and April 2018

If $r_f < d$, as was true of S&P 500 stock-index futures in 2017, then the futures price will be lower on longer-maturity contracts. For futures on assets like gold, which pay no "dividend yield," we can set $d = 0$ and conclude that F must increase as time to maturity increases.

Equation 17.2 implies that futures prices for different maturity dates should all move in unison, for all are linked to the same spot price through the parity relationship. Figure 17.6 plots futures prices on gold for three maturity dates. It is apparent that the prices move in virtual lockstep and that the more distant delivery dates command higher futures prices, as predicted by Equation 17.2.

17.5 FINANCIAL FUTURES

Although futures markets have their origins in agricultural commodities, today's market is dominated by contracts on financial assets. We review the most important of these contracts in this section: stock-index futures, foreign exchange futures, and interest rate futures.

Stock-Index Futures

Futures trade actively on stock market indexes such as the Standard & Poor's 500. In contrast to most futures contracts, which call for delivery of a specified asset, these contracts are settled by a cash amount equal to the value of the stock index in question on the contract maturity date times a multiplier that scales the size of the contract. This cash settlement duplicates the profits that would arise with actual delivery.

Contracts trade on several stock indexes. Table 17.2 lists some contracts on major indexes, showing under "Contract Size" the multiplier used to calculate contract settlements. An S&P 500 E-Mini contract with an initial futures price of 2,400 and a final index value of 2,420, for example, would result in a profit for the long side of $50 × (2,420 − 2,400) = $1,000. The S&P contract by far dominates the market in stock-index futures.

The broad-based U.S. stock market indexes are all highly correlated. Table 17.3 presents a correlation matrix for four of them. The correlation between the Dow Jones Industrial Average and the S&P 500, both of which are dominated by large firms, is 0.96, indicating almost perfect correlation. But the other correlations are also quite high. The NASDAQ Composite Index, which is dominated by technology firms, has correlation of 0.925 with the S&P 500

TABLE 17.2 Sample of stock-index futures

Contract	Underlying Market Index	Contract Size	Exchange
S&P 500 (E-Mini)	Standard & Poor's 500 Index, a value-weighted arithmetic average of 500 stocks	$50 times the S&P 500 Index	Chicago Mercantile Exchange
Dow Jones Industrials (DJIA Mini)	Price-weighted arithmetic average of 30 blue-chip stocks	$5 times the Dow Jones Industrial Average	Chicago Board of Trade
NASDAQ 100 (Mini)	Value-weighted arithmetic average of 100 of the largest over-the-counter stocks	$20 times the OTC index	Chicago Mercantile Exchange
Russell 2000 (Mini)	Index of 2,000 smaller firms	$100 times the index	Intercontinental Exchange, ICE
Nikkei 225	Nikkei 225 stock average	$5 times the Nikkei Index	Chicago Mercantile Exchange
FTSE 100	Financial Times–Stock Exchange Index of 100 U.K. firms	£10 times the FTSE Index	London International Financial Futures Exchange (Euronext)
CAC 40	Index of 40 of the largest French firms	10 euros times the index	Euronext Paris
DAX 30	Index of 30 of the largest German firms	25 euros times the index	Eurex
Hang Seng	Value-weighted index of largest firms in Hong Kong	50 Hong Kong dollars times the index	Hong Kong Exchange

TABLE 17.3 Correlations among major U.S. stock market indexes, monthly returns, January 2012–June 2016

	S&P 500	DJIA	NASDAQ	Russell 2000
S&P 500	1.000			
DJIA	0.960	1.000		
NASDAQ	0.925	0.836	1.000	
Russell 2000	0.808	0.790	0.788	1.000

Source: Authors' calculations.

and 0.836 with the Dow. The Russell 2000 Index of smaller-capitalization firms has somewhat smaller correlations with the other three indexes, but even these are close to 0.800.

CREATING SYNTHETIC STOCK POSITIONS   One reason stock-index futures are so popular is that they can substitute for holdings in the underlying stocks themselves. Index futures let investors participate in broad market movements without actually buying or selling large numbers of stocks.

Because of this, we say futures represent "synthetic" holdings of the market position. Instead of holding the market directly, the investor takes a long futures position in the index. Such a strategy is attractive because the transaction costs involved in establishing and liquidating futures positions are much lower than what would be required to take actual spot positions. Investors who wish to buy and sell market positions frequently find it much cheaper and easier to play the futures market.

One way to market time is to shift between Treasury bills and broad-based stock market holdings. Timers attempt to shift from bills into the market before market upturns and to shift back into bills to avoid market downturns, thereby profiting from broad market movements. Market timing of this sort, however, can result in huge trading costs with the frequent purchase and sale of many stocks. An attractive alternative is to invest in Treasury bills and hold varying amounts of market-index futures contracts, for which trading costs are far lower.

The strategy works like this: When timers are bullish, they will establish many long futures positions that they can liquidate quickly and cheaply when expectations turn bearish. Rather than shifting back and forth between T-bills and stocks, traders buy and hold T-bills and adjust only the futures position. (Recall strategies A and B of the preceding section where we showed that a T-bill plus futures position resulted in a payoff equal to the stock price.) This strategy minimizes transaction costs.

INDEX ARBITRAGE Whenever the actual futures price differs from its parity value, there is an opportunity for profit. This is why the parity relationships are so important. **Index arbitrage** is an investment strategy that exploits divergences between the actual futures price on a stock market index and its theoretically correct parity value.

In principle, index arbitrage is simple. If the futures price is too high, short the futures contract and buy the stocks in the index. If it is too low, buy futures and short the stocks. You can perfectly hedge your position and should earn arbitrage profits equal to the mispricing of the contract.

Although it is simple in theory, index arbitrage can be difficult to implement. The problem lies in buying the stocks in the index. Selling or purchasing shares in all 500 stocks in the S&P 500 is difficult for two reasons. The first is transaction costs, which may outweigh any profits to be made from the arbitrage. Second, index arbitrage calls for the purchase or sale of shares of 500 different firms simultaneously—and any lags in the execution of such a strategy can destroy the effectiveness of a plan to exploit short-lived price discrepancies.

Arbitrageurs need to trade an entire portfolio of stocks quickly and simultaneously if they hope to exploit temporary disparities between the futures price and its corresponding stock index. For this they need a coordinated trading program; hence the term **program trading,** which refers to coordinated purchases or sales of entire portfolios of stocks. Such strategies can be executed using electronic trading, which enables traders to send coordinated buy or sell programs to the floor of the stock exchange over computer lines. (See Chapter 3 for a discussion of electronic trading.)

index arbitrage

Strategy that exploits divergences between actual futures prices and their theoretically correct parity values to make a riskless profit.

program trading

Coordinated buy orders and sell orders of entire portfolios, often to achieve index arbitrage objectives.

Foreign Exchange Futures

Exchange rates between currencies vary continually and often substantially. This variability can be a source of concern for anyone involved in international business. A U.S. exporter who sells goods in England, for example, will be paid in British pounds, and the dollar value of those pounds depends on the exchange rate at the time payment is made. Until that date, the U.S. exporter is exposed to foreign exchange rate risk. This risk can be hedged through currency futures or forward markets. For example, if you know you will receive £100,000 in 60 days, you can sell those pounds forward today in the forward market and lock in an exchange rate equal to today's forward price.

The forward market in foreign exchange is relatively informal. It is simply a network of banks and brokers that allows customers to enter forward contracts to trade currency in the future at a currently agreed-upon rate of exchange. The bank market in currencies is among the largest in the world, and most large traders with sufficient creditworthiness execute their trades here rather than in futures markets. Contracts in these markets are not standardized in a formal market setting. Instead, each is negotiated separately. Moreover, there is no marking to market as would occur in futures markets. Forward contracts call for execution only at the maturity date.

For currency futures, however, there are formal markets established by the Chicago Mercantile Exchange (International Monetary Market), the London International Financial

FIGURE 17.7

Foreign exchange rates

Source: June 15, 2017, *The Wall Street Journal*, page B9.

Currencies

U.S.-dollar foreign-exchange rates in late New York trading

Country/currency	Wed in US$	per US$	US$vs, YTD chg (%)	Country/currency	Wed in US$	per US$	US$vs, YTD chg (%)
Americas				**Thailand** baht	.02949	33.910	−5.3
Argentina peso	.0629	15.9027	0.2	**Vietnam** dong	.00004404	22705	−0.3
Brazil real	.3053	3.2756	0.6	**Europe**			
Canada dollar	.7549	1.3248	−1.4	**Czech Rep.** koruna	.04287	23.324	−9.2
Chile peso	.001512	661.30	−1.3	**Denmark** krone	.1509	6.6281	−6.2
Colombia peso	.0003418	2925.50	−2.5	**Euro area** euro	1.1219	.8914	−6.2
Ecuador US dollar	1	1	unch	**Hungary** forint	.003666	272.81	−7.3
Mexico peso	.0558	17.9195	−13.6	**Iceland** krona	.009954	100.46	−11.1
Peru new sol	.3052	3.277	−2.3	**Norway** krone	.1187	8.4236	−2.6
Uruguay peso	.03534	28.3000	−3.6	**Poland** zloty	.2673	3.7413	−10.6
Venezuela b. fuerte	.100150	9.9851	−0.1	**Russia** ruble	.01740	57.461	−6.2
				Sweden krona	.1149	8.7034	−4.4
Asia-Pacific				**Switzerland** franc	1.0298	.9711	−4.7
Australian dollar	.7589	1.3177	−5.1	**Turkey** lira	.2867	3.4882	−1.0
China yuan	.1472	6.7917	−2.2	**Ukraine** hryvina	.0385	25.9985	−4.0
Hong Kong dollar	.1282	7.7980	0.5	**UK** pound	1.2753	.7841	−3.2
India rupee	.01558	64.172	−5.6	**Middle East/Africa**			
Indonesia rupiah	.0000753	13285	−1.8	**Bahrain** dinar	2.6515	.3772	−0.01
Japan yen	.009126	109.58	−6.3	**Eqypt** pound	.0556	17.9985	−0.7
Kazakhstan tenge	.003159	316.58	−5.1	**Israel** shekel	.2839	3.5219	−8.5
Macau pataca	.1244	8.0357	1.5	**Kuwait** dinar	3.2957	.3034	−0.7
Malaysia ringgit	.2349	4.2580	−5.1	**Oman** sulrial	2.5972	.3850	0.02
New Zealand dollar	.7268	1.3759	−4.7	**Qatar** rial	.2729	3.664	0.7
Pakistan rupee	.00954	104.805	0.4	**Saudi Arabia** riyal	.2667	3.7501	−0.02
Philippines peso	.0202	49.415	−0.4	**South Africa** rand	.0792	12.6249	−7.8
Singapore dollar	.7270	1.3755	−5.0				
South Korea won	.0008929	1119.94	−7.3		Close	Net Chg %Chg YTD%Chg	
Sri Lanka rupee	.0065479	152.72	2.9				
Taiwan dollar	.03318	30.142	−7.1	**WSJ Dollar Index**	88.12	−0.19-0.22	−5.19

Sources: Tulett Preborn, WSJ Market Data Group

Futures Exchange, and other exchanges. Here, contracts are standardized by size, and daily marking to market is observed. Moreover, there are standard clearing arrangements that allow traders to enter or reverse positions easily.

Figure 17.7 reproduces *The Wall Street Journal* listing of foreign exchange rates. The listing gives the number of U.S. dollars required to purchase some unit of foreign currency, so-called *direct quotes,* and then the amount of foreign currency needed to purchase $1, *indirect quotes.* By custom, some exchange rates (the British pound or the euro) are typically quoted using indirect rates, for example, $1.2753/£, but most currencies are quoted using indirect rates, for example, ¥109.58/$. The quotes in Figure 17.7 are spot rates, that is, exchange rates for immediate delivery.

Figure 17.1 included listings for currency futures contracts. The futures listings employ exclusively direct quotes (the number of dollars needed to purchase a given unit of foreign currency). The futures contracts specify the size of each contract and the maturity date. There are also very active forward markets in foreign currency. In forward markets, traders can negotiate to deliver any quantity of currency on any delivery date that is mutually agreeable to both sides of the contract.

Interest Rate Futures

The major U.S. interest rate contracts are on Eurodollars, Treasury bills, Treasury notes, and Treasury bonds. These contracts allow traders to hedge against interest rate risk in a wide spectrum of maturities from very short (T-bills) to long term (T-bonds). In addition, futures contracts tied to interest rates in Europe, Japan, the United Kingdom, and several other countries actively trade. Figure 17.1 shows listings of some of these contracts.

The Treasury contracts call for delivery of a Treasury bond, bill, or note. Should interest rates rise, the market value of the security at delivery will be less than the original futures price, and the deliverer will profit. Hence, the short position in the interest rate futures contract gains when interest rates rise and bond prices fall.

Similarly, Treasury bond futures can be useful hedging vehicles for bond dealers or underwriters. Consider, for example, these problems:

1. A fixed-income manager holds a bond portfolio on which considerable capital gains have been earned. She foresees an increase in interest rates but is reluctant to sell her portfolio and replace it with a lower-duration mix of bonds because such rebalancing would result in large trading costs as well as realization of capital gains for tax purposes. Still, she would like to hedge her exposure to interest rate increases.

2. A corporation plans to issue bonds to the public, but it cannot issue the bonds for another three months because of the lags inherent in SEC registration. It would like to hedge the uncertainty surrounding the yield at which it eventually will be able to sell the bonds.

3. A pension fund will receive a large cash inflow next month that it plans to invest in long-term bonds. It is concerned that interest rates may fall by the time it can make the investment and would like to lock in the yield currently available on long-term issues.

In each of these cases, the investment manager wishes to hedge interest rate changes. To illustrate the procedures that might be followed, we will focus on the first example and suppose that the portfolio manager has a $10 million bond portfolio with a modified duration of nine years.[6] If, as feared, market interest rates increase and the bond portfolio's yield also rises, say by 10 basis points (.10%), the fund will suffer a capital loss. Recall from Chapter 11 that the capital loss in percentage terms will be the product of modified duration, D^*, and the change in the portfolio yield. Therefore, the loss will be

$$D^* \times \Delta y = 9 \times .10\% = .9\%$$

or $90,000. This establishes that the sensitivity of the value of the unprotected portfolio to changes in market yields is $9,000 per one-basis-point change in the yield. Market practitioners call this ratio the **price value of a basis point (PVBP)**. The PVBP represents the sensitivity of the dollar value of the portfolio to changes in interest rates. Here, we've shown that

$$PVBP = \frac{\text{Change in portfolio value}}{\text{Predicted change in yield}} = \frac{\$90,000}{10 \text{ basis points}} = \$9,000 \text{ per basis point}$$

price value of a basis point (PVBP)

The change in the value of a fixed-income security resulting from a one-basis-point change in its yield to maturity.

One way to hedge this risk is to take an offsetting position in an interest rate futures contract, for example, the Treasury bond contract. The bond nominally calls for delivery of $100,000 par value T-bonds with 6% coupons and 20-year maturity. In practice, the contract delivery terms are fairly complicated because many bonds with different coupon rates and maturities may be substituted to settle the contract. However, we will assume that the bond to be delivered on the contract already is known and has a modified duration of 10 years. Finally, suppose that the futures price currently is $90 per $100 par value. Because the contract requires delivery of $100,000 par value of bonds, the contract multiplier is $1,000.

Given these data, we can calculate the PVBP for the futures contract. If the yield on the delivery bond increases by 10 basis points, the bond value will fall by $D^* \times .1\% = 10 \times .1\% = 1\%$. The futures price also will decline 1%, from 90 to 89.10.[7] Because the contract multiplier is $1,000, the gain on each short contract will be $1,000 \times .90 = $900. Therefore, the PVBP for one futures contract is $900/10-basis-point change, or $90 for a change in yield of 1 basis point.

---

[6] Recall that modified duration, D^*, is related to duration, D, by the formula $D^* = D/(1 + y)$, where y is the bond's yield to maturity. If the bond pays coupons semiannually, then y should be measured as a semiannual yield. For simplicity, we will assume annual coupon payments and treat y as the effective annual yield to maturity.

[7] This assumes the futures price will be exactly proportional to the bond price, which ought to be nearly true.

Now we can easily calculate the hedge ratio as follows:

$$H = \frac{\text{PVBP of portfolio}}{\text{PVBP of hedge vehicle}} = \frac{\$90,000}{\$90 \text{ per contract}} = 100 \text{ contracts}$$

Therefore, 100 T-bond futures contracts will serve to offset the portfolio's exposure to interest rate fluctuations.

CONCEPT
check   **17.6**

Suppose the bond portfolio is twice as large, $20 million, but that its modified duration is only 4.5 years. Show that the proper hedge position in T-bond futures is the same as the value just calculated, 100 contracts.

Although the hedge ratio is easy to compute, the hedging problem in practice is more difficult. For example, we assumed in our example that the yields on the T-bond contract and the bond portfolio would move perfectly in unison. Although interest rates on various fixed-income instruments do tend to vary in tandem, there is considerable slippage across sectors of the fixed-income market.

cross-hedging

Hedging a position in one asset by establishing an offsetting position in a related, but different, asset.

This problem highlights the fact that most hedging activity is in fact **cross-hedging**, meaning that the hedge vehicle is a different asset from the one to be hedged. To the extent that there is slippage between prices or yields of the two assets, the hedge will not be perfect. Nevertheless, even cross-hedges can eliminate a large fraction of the total risk of the unprotected portfolio.

17.6   SWAPS

foreign exchange swap

An agreement to exchange a sequence of payments denominated in one currency for payments in another currency at an exchange rate agreed to today.

interest rate swaps

Contracts between two parties to trade cash flows corresponding to different interest rates.

Swaps are multiperiod extensions of forward contracts. For example, rather than agreeing to exchange British pounds for U.S. dollars at an agreed-upon forward price at one single date, a **foreign exchange swap** would call for an exchange of currencies on several future dates. For example, the parties might exchange $1.4 million for £1 million in each of the next five years. Similarly, **interest rate swaps** call for the exchange of a series of cash flows proportional to a given interest rate for a corresponding series of cash flows proportional to a floating interest rate.[8] One party might exchange a variable cash flow equal to $1 million times a short-term interest rate for $1 million times a fixed interest rate of 4% for each of the next seven years.

The swap market is a huge component of the derivatives market, with around $400 trillion in interest rate and exchange rate swap agreements outstanding. We will illustrate how these contracts work using a simple interest rate swap as an example.

EXAMPLE 17.10

Interest Rate Swap

Consider the manager of a large portfolio that currently includes $100 million par value of long-term bonds paying an average coupon rate of 7%. The manager believes that interest rates are about to rise. As a result, he would like to sell the bonds and replace them with either short-term or floating-rate issues. However, it would be exceedingly expensive in terms of transaction costs to replace the portfolio every time the forecast for interest rates is updated. A cheaper and more flexible way to modify the portfolio is for the manager to "swap" the $7 million a year in interest income the portfolio currently generates for an amount of money that is tied to the short-term interest rate. That way, if rates do rise, so will the portfolio's interest income.

A swap dealer might advertise its willingness to exchange, or "swap," a cash flow based on the LIBOR rate for one based on a fixed rate of 7%. (The LIBOR, or London InterBank Offered Rate, is the interest rate at which banks borrow from each other in the Eurodollar market. It is the most commonly used short-term interest rate in the swap market.) The portfolio manager would then enter into a

---

[8] Interest rate swaps have nothing to do with the Homer-Leibowitz bond swap taxonomy described in Chapter 11.

swap agreement with the dealer to *pay* 7% on **notional principal** of $100 million and *receive* payment of the LIBOR rate.[9] In other words, the manager swaps a payment of .07 × $100 million for a payment of LIBOR × $100 million. The manager's *net* cash flow from the swap agreement is therefore (LIBOR − .07) × $100 million. The swap arrangement does not mean that a loan has been made. The participants have agreed only to exchange a fixed cash flow for a variable one.

Now consider the net cash flow to the manager's portfolio in three interest rate scenarios:

	LIBOR Rate		
	6.5%	7.0%	7.5%
Interest income from bond portfolio (= 7% of $100 million bond portfolio)	$7,000,000	$7,000,000	$7,000,000
Cash flow from swap [= (LIBOR − 7%) × notional principal of $100 million]	(500,000)	0	500,000
Total (= LIBOR × $100 million)	$6,500,000	$7,000,000	$7,500,000

The total income on the overall position—bonds plus swap agreement—equals the LIBOR rate in each scenario times $100 million. The manager has, in effect, converted a fixed-rate bond portfolio into a synthetic floating-rate portfolio.

EXAMPLE 17.10

Interest Rate Swap (concluded)

notional principal
Principal amount used to calculate swap payments.

Swaps and Balance Sheet Restructuring

Example 17.10 illustrates why interest rate swaps have tremendous appeal to fixed-income managers. These contracts allow managers to quickly, cheaply, and anonymously restructure the balance sheet. Suppose a corporation that has issued fixed-rate debt believes that interest rates are likely to fall; it might prefer to have issued floating-rate debt. In principle, it could issue floating-rate debt and use the proceeds to buy back the outstanding fixed-rate debt. It is faster and easier to convert the outstanding fixed-rate debt into synthetic floating-rate debt by entering a swap to receive a fixed interest rate (offsetting its fixed-rate coupon obligation) and pay a floating rate.

Conversely, a bank that pays current market interest rates to its depositors, and thus is exposed to increases in rates, would enter a swap to receive a floating rate and pay a fixed rate on some amount of notional principal. This swap position, added to its floating-rate deposit liability, would result in a net liability of a fixed stream of cash. The bank might then be able to invest in long-term fixed-rate loans without encountering interest rate risk.

As a final example, consider a fixed-income portfolio manager who wishes to switch back and forth between a fixed- or floating-rate profile quickly and cheaply as the forecast for the interest rate changes. A manager who holds a fixed-rate portfolio can transform it into a synthetic floating-rate portfolio by entering a pay fixed–receive floating swap and can later transform it back by entering the opposite side of a similar swap.

The Swap Dealer

What about the swap dealer? Why is the dealer, which is typically a financial intermediary such as a bank, willing to take on the opposite side of the swaps desired by the participants in these hypothetical swaps?

---

[9] The participants to the swap do not loan each other money. They agree only to exchange a fixed cash flow for a variable cash flow that depends on the short-term interest rate. This is why the principal is described as *notional*. The notional principal is simply a way to describe the size of the swap agreement. In this example, the parties to the swap exchange a 7% fixed rate for the LIBOR rate; the difference between LIBOR and 7% is multiplied by notional principal to determine the dollar value of the cash that must be exchanged.

Interest rate swap. Company A has issued a fixed-rate 7% coupon bond. It enters a swap to pay LIBOR and receive 6.95%. Company B has issued a floating-rate bond paying the LIBOR rate. It enters a swap to receive LIBOR and pay 7.05%.

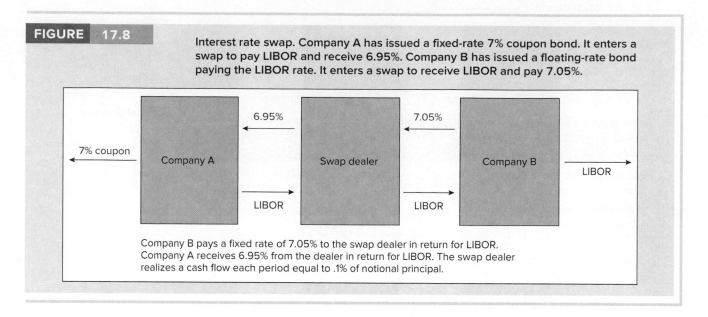

Company B pays a fixed rate of 7.05% to the swap dealer in return for LIBOR.
Company A receives 6.95% from the dealer in return for LIBOR. The swap dealer
realizes a cash flow each period equal to .1% of notional principal.

Consider a dealer who takes on one side of a swap, let's say paying LIBOR and receiving a fixed rate. The dealer will search for another trader in the swap market who wishes to receive a fixed rate and pay LIBOR. For example, company A may have issued a 7% coupon fixed-rate bond that it wishes to convert into synthetic floating-rate debt, while company B may have issued a floating-rate bond tied to LIBOR that it wishes to convert into synthetic fixed-rate debt. The dealer will enter a swap with company A in which it pays a fixed rate and receives LIBOR and will enter another swap with company B in which it pays LIBOR and receives a fixed rate. When the two swaps are combined, the dealer's position is effectively neutral on interest rates, paying LIBOR on one swap and receiving it on another. Similarly, the dealer pays a fixed rate on one swap and receives it on another. The dealer becomes little more than an intermediary, funneling payments from one party to the other.[10] The dealer finds this activity profitable because it charges a bid–asked spread on the transaction.

This rearrangement is illustrated in Figure 17.8. Company A has issued 7% fixed-rate debt (the leftmost arrow in the figure) but enters a swap to pay the dealer LIBOR and receive a 6.95% fixed rate. Therefore, the company's net payment is 7% + (LIBOR − 6.95%) = LIBOR + .05%. It has thus transformed its fixed-rate debt into synthetic floating-rate debt. Conversely, company B has issued floating-rate debt paying LIBOR (the rightmost arrow) but enters a swap to pay a 7.05% fixed rate in return for LIBOR. Therefore, its net payment is LIBOR + (7.05% − LIBOR) = 7.05%. It has transformed its floating-rate debt into synthetic fixed-rate debt. The bid–asked spread, the source of the dealer's profit, is 0.10% of notional principal each year.

A pension fund holds a portfolio of money market securities that the manager believes are paying excellent yields compared to comparable short-term securities. However, the manager believes that interest rates are about to fall. What type of swap will allow the fund to continue to hold its portfolio of short-term securities while at the same time benefiting from a decline in rates?

---

[10]Actually, things are a bit more complicated. The dealer is more than just an intermediary because it bears the credit risk that one or the other of the parties to the swap might default on the obligation. Referring to Figure 17.8, if firm A defaults on its obligation, for example, the swap dealer still must maintain its commitment to firm B. As a guarantor, the dealer does more than simply pass through cash flows to the other swap participants.

- Forward contracts are arrangements that call for the future delivery of an asset at a currently agreed-upon price. The long trader is obligated to purchase the good, and the short trader is obligated to deliver it. If the price at the maturity of the contract exceeds the forward price, the long side benefits by virtue of acquiring the good at the contract price.

- A futures contract is similar to a forward contract, differing most importantly in the aspects of standardization and marking to market, which is the process by which gains and losses on futures contract positions are settled daily. In contrast, forward contracts call for no cash exchanges until contract maturity.

- Futures contracts are traded on organized exchanges that standardize the size of the contract, the grade of the deliverable asset, the delivery date, and the delivery location. Traders negotiate only the contract price. This standardization creates increased liquidity in the marketplace and means buyers and sellers can easily find many traders for a desired purchase or sale.

- The clearinghouse steps in between each pair of traders, acting as the short position for each long and as the long position for each short, so traders need not be concerned about the performance of the trader on the opposite side of the contract. Traders are required to post margins to guarantee their own performance on the contracts.

- The long position's gain or loss on a contract held between time 0 and t is $F_t - F_0$. Because $F_T = P_T$ at maturity, the long's profit if the contract is held until maturity is $P_T - F_0$, where P_T is the spot price at time T and F_0 is the original futures price. The gain or loss to the short position is $F_0 - P_T$.

- Futures contracts may be used for hedging or speculating. Speculators use the contracts to take a stand on the ultimate price of an asset. Short hedgers take short positions in contracts to offset any gains or losses on the value of an asset already held in inventory. Long hedgers take long positions in futures contracts to offset gains or losses in the purchase price of a good.

- The spot-futures parity relationship states that the equilibrium futures price on an asset providing no service or payments (such as dividends) is $F_0 = P_0(1 + r_f)^T$. If the futures price deviates from this value, then market participants can earn arbitrage profits.

- If the asset provides services or payments with yield d, the parity relationship becomes $F_0 = P_0(1 + r_f - d)^T$. This model is also called the cost-of-carry model, because it states that the futures price must exceed the spot price by the net cost of carrying the asset until maturity date T.

- Futures contracts calling for cash settlement are traded on various stock-market indexes. The contracts may be mixed with Treasury bills to construct artificial equity positions, which makes them potentially valuable tools for market timers. Market-index contracts also are used by arbitrageurs who attempt to profit from violations of the parity relationship.

- Interest rate futures allow for hedging against interest rate fluctuations in several different markets. The most actively traded contract is for Treasury bonds.

- The interest rate swap market is a major component of the fixed-income market. In these arrangements, parties trade the cash flows of different securities without actually exchanging any securities directly. This is a useful tool to manage the interest rate exposure of a portfolio.

SUMMARY

KEY TERMS

basis, 558
basis risk, 558
cash settlement, 554
clearinghouse, 551
convergence property, 553
cost-of-carry relationship, 561
cross-hedging, 568
foreign exchange swap, 568
forward contract, 546

futures price, 546
index arbitrage, 565
interest rate swaps, 568
long position, 547
maintenance margin, 553
marking to market, 552
notional principal, 569
price value of a basis point
  (PVBP), 567

program trading, 565
short position, 547
single stock futures, 549
spot-futures parity theorem,
  561
spread (futures), 558

KEY FORMULAS   Spot futures parity: $F_0 = (1 + r_f - d)^T$

PROBLEM SETS

 **Select problems are available in McGraw-Hill's** *Connect.* **Please see the Supplements section of the book's frontmatter for more information.**

1. On January 1, you sold one February maturity S&P 500 Index futures contract at a futures price of 2,400. If the futures price is 2,450 at contract maturity, what is your profit? The contract multiplier is $50.   *(LO 17-1)*

2. The current level of the S&P 500 is 2,400. The dividend yield on the S&P 500 is 2%. The risk-free interest rate is 1%. What should be the price of a one-year maturity futures contract?   *(LO 17-3)*

3. A one-year gold futures contract is selling for $1,247. Spot gold prices are $1,200 and the one-year risk-free rate is 2%.   *(LO 17-4)*
   a. According to spot-futures parity, what should be the futures price?
   b. What risk-free strategy can investors use to take advantage of the futures mispricing, and what will be the profits on the strategy?

4. You purchase a Treasury-bond futures contract with an initial margin requirement of 15% and a futures price of $115,098. The contract is traded on a $100,000 underlying par value bond. If the futures price falls to $108,000, what will be the percentage loss on your position?   *(LO 17-1)*

5. a. Turn to Figure 17.1 and locate the E-Mini contract on the Standard & Poor's 500 Index. If the margin requirement is 10% of the futures price times the multiplier of $50, how much must you deposit with your broker to trade the June contract?
   b. If the June futures price were to increase to 2,460, what percentage return would you earn on your net investment if you entered the long side of the contract at the price shown in the figure?
   c. If the June futures price falls by 1%, what is the percentage gain or loss on your net investment?   *(LO 17-1)*

6. Why might individuals purchase futures contracts rather than the underlying asset?   *(LO 17-2)*

7. What is the difference in cash flow between short-selling an asset and entering a short futures position?   *(LO 17-1)*

8. Suppose the value of the S&P 500 Stock Index is currently $2,400.   *(LO 17-3)*
   a. If the one-year T-bill rate is 3% and the expected dividend yield on the S&P 500 is 2%, what should the one-year maturity futures price be?
   b. What if the T-bill rate is less than the dividend yield, for example, 1%?

9. It is now January. The current annual interest rate is 3% . The June futures price for gold is $1,246.30, while the December futures price is $1,251. Is there an arbitrage opportunity here? If so, how would you exploit it?   *(LO 17-4)*

10. Consider a stock that will pay a dividend of D dollars in one year, which is when a futures contract matures. Consider the following strategy: Buy the stock, short a futures contract on the stock, and borrow S_0 dollars, where S_0 is the current price of the stock.   *(LO 17-3)*
    a. What are the cash flows now and in one year? (*Hint:* Remember the dividend the stock will pay.)
    b. Show that the equilibrium futures price must be $F_0 = S_0(1 + r) - D$ to avoid arbitrage.
    c. Call the dividend yield $d = D/S_0$, and conclude that $F_0 = S_0(1 + r - d)$.

11. a. A single stock futures contract on a nondividend-paying stock with current price $150 has a maturity of one year. If the T-bill rate is 3%, what should the futures price be?
    b. What should the futures price be if the maturity of the contract is three years?
    c. What if the interest rate is 5% and the maturity of the contract is three years?   *(LO 17-3)*

12. The Excel Applications box in the chapter (available in Connect; link to Chapter 17 material) shows how to use the spot-futures parity relationship to find a "term structure of futures prices," that is, futures prices for various maturity dates. *(LO 17-3)*

    a. Suppose that today is January 1, 2018. Assume the interest rate is 1% per year and a stock index currently at 2,400 pays a dividend yield of 2%. Find the futures price for contract maturity dates of February 14, 2018, May 21, 2018, and November 18, 2018.

    b. What happens to the term structure of futures prices if the dividend yield is lower than the risk-free rate? For example, what if the interest rate is 3%?

13. OneChicago has just introduced a new single stock futures contract on the stock of Brandex, a company that currently pays no dividends. Each contract calls for delivery of 1,000 shares of stock in one year. The T-bill rate is 4% per year. *(LO 17-3)*

    a. If Brandex stock now sells at $120 per share, what should the futures price be?

    b. If the Brandex stock price drops by 3%, what will be the change in the futures price and the change in the investor's margin account?

    c. If the margin on the contract is $12,000, what is the percentage return on the investor's position?

14. The multiplier for a futures contract on the stock-market index is $50. The maturity of the contract is one year, the current level of the index is 2,000, and the risk-free interest rate is 0.5% per month. The dividend yield on the index is 0.2% per month. Suppose that after one month, the stock index is at 2,010. *(LO 17-1)*

    a. Find the cash flow from the mark-to-market proceeds on the contract. Assume that the parity condition always holds exactly.

    b. Find the one-month holding-period return if the initial margin on the contract is $10,000.

15. Suppose the S&P 500 Index portfolio pays a dividend yield of 2% annually. The index currently is 2,000. The T-bill rate is 3%, and the S&P futures price for delivery in one year is $2,030. Construct an arbitrage strategy to exploit the mispricing and show that your profits one year hence will equal the mispricing in the futures market. *(LO 17-4)*

16. a. How should the parity condition (Equation 17.2) for stocks be modified for futures contracts on Treasury bonds? What should play the role of the dividend yield in that equation?

    b. In an environment with an upward-sloping yield curve, should T-bond futures prices on more distant contracts be higher or lower than those on near-term contracts?

    c. Confirm your intuition by examining Figure 17.1. *(LO 17-3)*

17. Desert Trading Company has issued $100 million worth of long-term bonds at par at a fixed rate of 7%. The firm then enters into an interest rate swap where it pays LIBOR and receives a fixed 6% on notional principal of $100 million. What is the firm's effective interest rate on its borrowing? *(LO 17-5)*

18. What type of interest rate swap would be appropriate for a speculator who believes interest rates soon will fall? *(LO 17-5)*

19. The margin requirement on the S&P 500 futures contract is 10%, and the stock index is currently 2,000. Each contract has a multiplier of $50. *(LO 17-1)*

    a. How much margin must be put up for each contract sold?

    b. If the futures price falls by 1% to 1,980, what will happen to the margin account of an investor who holds one contract?

    c. What will be the investor's percentage return based on the amount put up as margin?

20. The multiplier for a futures contract on a certain stock market index is $50. The maturity of the contract is one year, the current level of the index is 2,000, and the risk-free interest rate is 0.2% per *month*. The dividend yield on the index is 0.1% per month. Suppose that *after one month*, the stock index is at 2,040. *(LO 17-1)*

    a. Find the cash flow from the mark-to-market proceeds on the contract. Assume that the parity condition always holds exactly.

    b. Find the holding-period return if the initial margin on the contract is $5,000.

Templates and spreadsheets are available in Connect

21. You are a corporate treasurer who will purchase $1 million of bonds for the sinking fund in three months. You believe rates soon will fall and would like to repurchase the company's sinking fund bonds, which currently are selling below par, in advance of requirements. Unfortunately, you must obtain approval from the board of directors for such a purchase, and this can take up to two months. *(LO 17-2)*
    a. What action can you take in the futures market to hedge any adverse movements in bond yields and prices until you actually can buy the bonds?
    b. Will you be long or short? Why?

22. A manager is holding a $1 million bond portfolio with a modified duration of eight years. She would like to hedge the risk of the portfolio by short-selling Treasury bonds. The modified duration of T-bonds is 10 years. How many dollars' worth of T-bonds should she sell to minimize the risk of her position? *(LO 17-2)*

23. A corporation plans to issue $10 million of 10-year bonds in three months. At current yields the bonds would have modified duration of eight years. The T-note futures contract is selling at $F_0 = 100$ and has modified duration of six years. How can the firm use this futures contract to hedge the risk surrounding the yield at which it will be able to sell its bonds? Both the bond and the contract are at par value. *(LO 17-2)*

Challenge

24. The S&P 500 Index is currently at 2,000. You manage a $10 million indexed equity portfolio. The S&P 500 futures contract has a multiplier of $50. *(LO 17-2)*
    a. If you are temporarily bearish on the stock market, how many contracts should you sell to fully eliminate your exposure over the next six months?
    b. If T-bills pay 2% per six months and the semiannual dividend yield is 1%, what is the parity value of the futures price?
    c. Show that if the contract is fairly priced, the total risk-free proceeds on the hedged strategy in part (*a*) provide a return equal to the T-bill rate.

25. a. How would your hedging strategy in the previous problem change if, instead of holding an indexed portfolio, you hold a portfolio of only one stock with a beta of 0.6?
    b. How many contracts would you now choose to sell? Would your hedged position be riskless?
    c. What would be the beta of the hedged position? *(LO 17-2)*

26. A corporation has issued a $10 million issue of floating-rate bonds on which it pays an interest rate 1% over the LIBOR rate. The bonds are selling at par value. The firm is worried that rates are about to rise, and it would like to lock in a fixed interest rate on its borrowings. The firm sees that dealers in the swap market are offering swaps of LIBOR for 7%. *(LO 17-5)*
    a. What swap arrangement will convert the firm's borrowings to a synthetic fixed-rate loan?
    b. What interest rate will it pay on that synthetic fixed-rate loan?

27. The one-year futures price on a particular stock-index portfolio is 2,240, the stock index currently is 2,200, the one-year risk-free interest rate is 3%, and the year-end dividend that will be paid on a $2,200 investment in the index portfolio is $22. *(LO 17-4)*
    a. By how much is the contract mispriced?
    b. Formulate a zero-net-investment arbitrage portfolio, and show that you can lock in riskless profits equal to the futures mispricing.
    c. Now assume (as is true for small investors) that if you short-sell the stocks in the market index, the proceeds of the short sale are kept with the broker and you do not receive any interest income on the funds. Is there still an arbitrage opportunity (assuming you don't already own the shares in the index)? Explain.
    d. Given the short-sale rules, what is the no-arbitrage *band* for the stock-futures price relationship? That is, given a stock index of 2,200, how high and how low can the futures price be without giving rise to arbitrage opportunities?

CFA Problems

1. The open interest on a futures contract at any given time is the total number of outstanding: *(LO 17-1)*
   a. Contracts.
   b. Unhedged positions.
   c. Clearinghouse positions.
   d. Long and short positions.

2. In futures trading, the minimum level to which an equity position may fall before requiring additional margin is *most accurately* termed the: *(LO 17-1)*
   a. Initial margin.
   b. Variation margin.
   c. Cash flow margin.
   d. Maintenance margin.

3. A silver futures contract requires the seller to deliver 5,000 ounces of silver. Jerry Harris sells one July silver futures contract at a price of $28 per ounce, posting a $6,000 initial margin. If the required maintenance margin is $2,500, what is the *first* price per ounce at which Harris would receive a maintenance margin call? *(LO 17-1)*

4. In each of the following cases, discuss how you, as a portfolio manager, could use financial futures to protect a portfolio. *(LO 17-2)*
   a. You own a large position in a relatively illiquid bond that you want to sell.
   b. You have a large gain on one of your long Treasuries and want to sell it, but you would like to defer the gain until the next accounting period, which begins in four weeks.
   c. You will receive a large contribution next month that you hope to invest in long-term corporate bonds on a yield basis as favorable as is now available.

5. Futures contracts and options contracts can be used to modify risk. Identify the fundamental distinction between a futures contract and an option contract, and briefly explain the difference in the manner that futures and options modify portfolio risk. *(LO 17-2)*

6. Joan Tam, CFA, believes she has identified an arbitrage opportunity for a commodity as indicated by the information given in the following exhibit: *(LO 17-4)*

Commodity Price and Interest Rate Information	
Spot price for commodity	$120
Futures price for commodity expiring in one year	$125
Interest rate for one year	8%

   a. Describe the transactions necessary to take advantage of this specific arbitrage opportunity.
   b. Calculate the arbitrage profit.

7. Several Investment Committee members have asked about interest rate swap agreements and how they are used in the management of domestic fixed-income portfolios. *(LO 17-5)*
   a. Define an interest rate swap, and briefly describe the obligation of each party involved.
   b. Cite and explain two examples of how interest rate swaps could be used by a fixed-income portfolio manager to control risk or improve return.

8. Janice Delsing, a U.S.-based portfolio manager, manages an $800 million portfolio ($600 million in stocks and $200 million in bonds). In reaction to anticipated short-term

market events, Delsing wishes to adjust the allocation to 50% stocks and 50% bonds through the use of futures. Her position will be held only until "the time is right to restore the original asset allocation." Delsing determines a financial futures-based asset allocation strategy is appropriate. The stock futures index multiplier is $50, and the denomination of the bond futures contract is $100,000. Other information relevant to a futures-based strategy is given in the following exhibit: *(LO 17-2)*

Information for Futures-Based Strategy	
Bond portfolio modified duration	5 years
Bond portfolio yield to maturity	7%
Price value of basis point (PVBP) of bond futures	$97.85
Stock-index futures price	1,378
Stock portfolio beta	1.0

  a. Describe the financial futures-based strategy needed, and explain how the strategy allows Delsing to implement her allocation adjustment. No calculations are necessary.
  b. Compute the number of each of the following needed to implement Delsing's asset allocation strategy:
   i. Bond futures contracts.
   ii. Stock-index futures contracts.
 9. Maria VanHusen, CFA, suggests that forward contracts on fixed-income securities can be used to protect the value of the Star Hospital Pension Plan's bond portfolio against the possibility of rising interest rates. VanHusen prepares the following example to illustrate how such protection would work:

  • A 10-year bond with a face value of $1,000 is issued today at par value. The bond pays an annual coupon.
  • An investor intends to buy this bond today and sell it in six months.
  • The six-month risk-free interest rate today is 5% (annualized).
  • A six-month forward contract on this bond is available, with a forward price of $1,024.70.
  • In six months, the price of the bond, including accrued interest, is forecast to fall to $978.40 as a result of a rise in interest rates.   *(LO 17-2)*

  a. Should the investor buy or sell the forward contract to protect the value of the bond against rising interest rates during the holding period?
  b. Calculate the value of the forward contract for the investor at the maturity of the forward contract if VanHusen's bond price forecast turns out to be accurate.
  c. Calculate the change in value of the combined portfolio (the underlying bond and the appropriate forward contract position) six months after contract initiation.

WEB *master*

 1. Suppose that you want to create a spread position using S&P 500 futures contracts. Go to **www.cmegroup.com** and listed under Equity Index Products, select *S&P 500*. Click on *Contract Specifications* at the top of the product listing. Review the contract's specifications. Click on the *Contract Months* link to see the contracts that are available for trading. Note the code for one contract that expires in approximately three months and the code for another that expires in approximately nine months.
 2. Assume that you bought the three-month contract and sold the nine-month contract about two months ago. *The Wall Street Journal Online* provides a comprehensive list of current and historical prices (under the *Market Data* tab). Specifically, navigate to the

Commodities & Futures tab and then the *Index* tab. Choose the S&P 500 Index, and click on the *Chart* icon. From here you can move your mouse over any day and retrieve the closing price on that day. Choose a trading date that occurred two months ago and note the price. Find the closing prices for the two contracts that you selected.

3. Return to the CME listings and find the closing prices of the two contracts on today's date. Assume that you close your positions in both contracts.

4. Using the beginning and ending prices for the futures contracts that you bought and sold, calculate the return you earned on the spread position during the two-month period, before commissions.

17.1 *a.* The payoff on the put looks like that on the short futures contract when the asset price falls below X or F_0, but when the asset price rises above F_0, the futures payoff turns negative whereas the value of the put cannot fall below zero. The put (which must be purchased) gives you upside potential if the asset price falls but limits downside risk, whereas the futures gives you both upside and downside exposure.

b. The payoff on the written call looks like that on the short futures contract when the asset price rises above F_0, but when the asset price falls, the futures payoff is positive, whereas the payoff on the written call is never positive. The written call gives you downside exposure, but your upside potential is limited to the premium you received for the option.

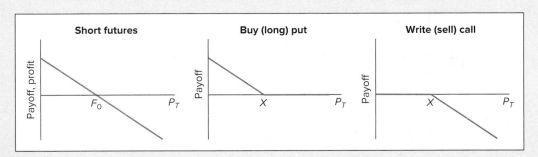

17.2 The clearinghouse has a zero net position in all contracts. Its long and short positions are offsetting, so that net cash flow from marking to market must be zero.

17.3

	Oil Price in February, P_T		
	$51	**$52**	**$53**
Cash flow to purchase oil: $-100{,}000 \times P_T$	$-\$5{,}100{,}000$	$-\$5{,}200{,}000$	$-\$5{,}300{,}000$
$+$ Profit on long futures: $100{,}000 \times (P_T - F_0)$	$-100{,}000$	0	$+100{,}000$
Total cash flow	$-\$5{,}200{,}000$	$-\$5{,}200{,}000$	$-\$5{,}200{,}000$

17.4 The risk would be that the index and the portfolio do not move perfectly together. Thus, risk involving the spread between the futures price and the portfolio value could persist even if the index futures price were set perfectly relative to index itself. You can measure this risk using the index model introduced in Chapter 7. If you regress the excess return of the active portfolio on that of the index portfolio, the regression R-square will equal the proportion of the variance of the active portfolio's return that could have been hedged using the index futures contract. You can also measure the risk of the imperfectly hedged position using the standard error of the regression, which tells you the standard deviation of the residuals in the index model. Because these are the components of the risky returns that are independent of the market index, this standard deviation measures the variability of the portion of the active portfolio's return that *cannot* be hedged using the index futures contract.

17.5 The future price, $1,206 is $1.22 below the parity value of $1,207.22. The cash flow to the following strategy is riskless and equal to this mispricing.

Action	Initial Cash Flow	Time-T Cash Flow
Lend $1,200	−$1,200	$1,200(1.001)^6 = \$1,207.22$
Sell gold short	+1,200	$-S_T$
Long futures	0	$S_T - \$1,206$
Total	$0	$1.22 risklessly

17.6 The price value of a basis point is still $9,000, as a one-basis-point change in the interest rate reduces the value of the $20 million portfolio by $.01\% \times 4.5 = .045\%$. Therefore, the number of futures needed to hedge the interest rate risk is the same as for a portfolio half the size with double the modified duration.

17.7 The manager would like to hold on to the money market securities because of their attractive relative pricing compared to other short-term assets. However, there is an expectation that rates will fall. The manager can hold this *particular* portfolio of short-term assets and still benefit from the drop in interest rates by entering a swap to pay a short-term interest rate and receive a fixed interest rate. The resulting synthetic fixed-rate portfolio will increase in value if rates do fall.

Active Investment Management

PART

6

Passive investment, or indexing, is the preferred strategy for investors who believe markets are essentially efficient. While administration of passive portfolios requires efficient organization and trading structure, there is no need for security analysis or portfolio strategy. In contrast, active managers believe that markets are not efficient and that bargains can be found in security markets by application of asset valuation and portfolio theory.

Earlier in the text we asked how to effectively exploit security mispricing—how to balance superior expected returns with the increased risk from reduced diversification. In a market economy, we look to incentives: How will portfolio managers behave when evaluated using standard performance measures? They will choose portfolios that are expected to provide them with the best evaluation. Superior results, in turn, will lead to increased assets under management and higher profits. Accordingly, Chapter 18 discusses performance evaluation and techniques to achieve superior performance.

Investing across borders is conceptually a simple extension of efficient diversification. However, this pursuit entails exposure to political risk and the impact of uncertain exchange rates on investment performance. These issues, unique to international investing, are addressed in Chapter 19.

Chapter 20 covers hedge funds, probably the most active of active managers. It also focuses on some of the special problems encountered in evaluation of hedge fund performance.

Investments originate with a savings plan that diverts funds from consumption to investment. Taxes and inflation complicate the relationship between how much you save and what you will be able to achieve with your accumulating investment fund. Chapter 21 introduces a framework to formulate an effective household savings/investment plan.

Professional management of active investment begins with a contractual relationship between a client and a portfolio manager. The economic needs of clients must be articulated and their objectives translated into an operational financial plan. For this purpose, the CFA Institute has laid out a broad framework for active investment management. Chapter 22 familiarizes you with this framework.

Chapter 18

Evaluating Investment Performance

Learning Objectives

LO 18-1 Compute raw and risk-adjusted rates of return, and use them to evaluate investment performance.

LO 18-2 Determine which risk-adjusted performance measure is appropriate in a variety of investment contexts.

LO 18-3 Apply style analysis to assess portfolio strategy.

LO 18-4 Decompose portfolio returns into components attributable to asset allocation choices versus security selection choices.

LO 18-5 Assess the presence and value of market-timing ability.

Most financial assets are managed by professional investors, who thus at least indirectly allocate the lion's share of capital across firms. Efficient allocation therefore depends on the quality of these professionals and the ability of financial markets to direct capital to the best stewards. Therefore, if capital markets are to be reasonably efficient, investors must be able to measure the performance of their asset managers.

How can we evaluate investment performance? It turns out that even an average portfolio return is not as straightforward to measure as it might seem. In addition, adjusting average returns for risk presents a host of other problems. In the end, performance evaluation is far from trivial.

We begin this chapter with the measurement of portfolio returns. From there we move on to conventional approaches to risk adjustment. We consider the situations in which each of the standard risk-adjusted performance measures will be of most interest to investors and show how style analysis may be viewed as a generalization of the index model and the alpha statistic that it generates.

Performance measurement becomes far more difficult when managers change portfolio composition during the measurement period, so we also examine the complications posed by changes in the risk characteristics of the portfolio. One particular way in which this may occur is when managers attempt to time the broad market and adjust portfolio beta in anticipation of

market movements. Market timing raises a wide
range of issues in performance evaluation.

We close the chapter with a look at performance attribution techniques. These are tools

used to decompose managers' performance
into results that can be attributed to security
selection, sector selection, and asset allocation decisions.

18.1 THE CONVENTIONAL THEORY OF PERFORMANCE EVALUATION

Average Rates of Return

We defined the holding-period return (HPR) in Section 5.1 of Chapter 5 and explained the difference between the arithmetic and geometric average. We begin with a brief review.

Suppose we evaluate the performance of a portfolio over a period of 20 years. The *arithmetic average* return is the sum of the 20 annual returns divided by 20. In contrast, the *geometric average* is the constant annual return over the 20 years that would provide the same total cumulative return over the entire investment period. Therefore, the geometric average, r_G, is defined by

$$(1 + r_G)^{20} = (1 + r_1)(1 + r_2) \cdots (1 + r_{20})$$

The right-hand side of this equation is the compounded final value of a $1 investment earning the 20 annual rates of return. The left-hand side is the compounded value of a $1 investment earning r_G *each* year. We solve for $1 + r_G$ as

$$1 + r_G = [(1 + r_1)(1 + r_2) \cdots (1 + r_{20})]^{1/20}$$

Each return has an equal weight in the geometric average. For this reason, the geometric average is referred to as a **time-weighted average.**

time-weighted average

An average (often a geometric average) of the period-by-period holding-period returns of an investment.

Time-Weighted Returns versus Dollar-Weighted Returns

To set the stage for the more subtle issues that follow, let's start with a trivial example. Consider a stock paying a dividend of $2 annually that currently sells for $50. You purchase the stock today, collect the $2 dividend, and then sell the stock for $53 at year-end. Your rate of return is

$$\frac{\text{Total proceeds}}{\text{Initial investment}} = \frac{\text{Income + Capital gain}}{50} = \frac{2 + 3}{50} = .10, \text{ or } 10\%$$

Another way to derive the rate of return that is useful in the more difficult multiperiod case is to set up the investment as a discounted cash flow problem. Call r the rate of return that equates the present value of all cash flows from the investment with the initial outlay. In our example, the stock is purchased for $50 and generates cash flows at year-end of $2 (dividend) plus $53 (sale of stock). Therefore, we solve $50 = (2 + 53)/(1 + r)$ to find again that $r = .10$, or 10%.

When we consider investments over a period during which cash was added to or withdrawn from the portfolio, measuring the rate of return becomes more difficult. To continue our example, suppose that you purchase a second share of the same stock at the end of the first year, and hold both shares until the end of year 2, at which point you sell your shares for $54 each.

Total cash outlays are shown below.

Time	Outlay
0	$50 to purchase first share
1	$53 to purchase second share a year later

	Proceeds
1	$2 dividend from initially purchased share
2	$4 dividend from the two shares held in the second year, plus
	$108 received from selling both shares at $54 each

Using the discounted cash flow (DCF) approach, we can solve for the average return over the two years by equating the present values of the cash inflows and outflows:

$$50 + \frac{53}{1+r} = \frac{2}{1+r} + \frac{112}{(1+r)^2}$$

dollar-weighted rate of return

The internal rate of return on an investment.

resulting in $r = 7.117\%$. This is the internal rate of return on the investment, and is called the **dollar-weighted rate of return** because performance when more funds are invested has a greater impact on the average return.[1]

The time-weighted (geometric average) return is 7.81%:

$$r_1 = \frac{2 + (53 - 50)}{50} = .10 = 10\% \quad r_2 = \frac{2 + (54 - 53)}{53} = .0566 = 5.66\%$$
$$r_G = (1.10 \times 1.0566)^{1/2} - 1 = .0781 = 7.81\%$$

The dollar-weighted average is less than the time-weighted average in this example because the return in the second year, when more money was invested, is lower.

CONCEPT Check 18.1

Shares of XYZ Corp. pay a $2 dividend at the end of every year on December 31. An investor buys two shares of the stock on January 1 at a price of $20 each, sells one of those shares for $22 a year later on the next January 1, and sells the second share an additional year later for $19. Find the dollar- and time-weighted rates of return on the two-year investment.

Adjusting Returns for Risk

Evaluating performance based on average return alone is not very useful because returns must be adjusted for risk before they can be compared meaningfully. The simplest and most popular way to make the adjustment is to compare rates of return with those of other investment funds with similar risk characteristics. For example, high-yield bond portfolios are grouped into one **comparison universe,** growth-stock equity funds are grouped into another, and so on. Then the (usually time-weighted) average returns of each fund within the universe are ordered, and each portfolio manager receives a percentile ranking of relative performance within the comparison group. For example, the manager with the ninth-best performance in a universe of 100 funds would be the 90th percentile manager: Her performance was better than 90% of all competing funds over the evaluation period.

comparison universe

The set of portfolio managers with similar investment styles that is used to assess relative performance.

These relative rankings are usually displayed in a chart similar to that in Figure 18.1. The chart summarizes performance rankings over four periods: 1 quarter, 1 year, 3 years, and 5 years. The top and bottom lines of each box are drawn at the rate of return of the 95th and 5th percentile managers. The three dashed lines correspond to the rates of return of the 75th,

---

[1] Excel's function XIRR calculates IRR. The function provides the IRR between any two dates given a starting value, cash flows at various dates in between (with additions given as negative numbers, and withdrawals as positive values), and a final value on the closing date.

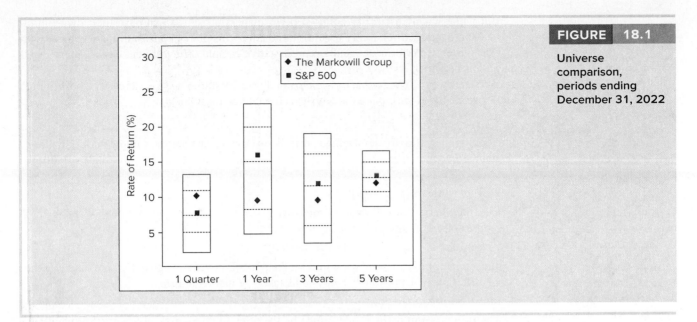

FIGURE 18.1

Universe comparison, periods ending December 31, 2022

50th (median), and 25th percentile managers. The diamond is drawn at the average return of a particular fund and the square is drawn at the return of a benchmark index, such as the S&P 500. The placement of the diamond within the box is an easy-to-read representation of the performance of the fund relative to the comparison universe.

This comparison of performance with other managers of similar investment style is a useful first step in evaluating performance. However, such rankings can be misleading. Within a particular universe, some managers may concentrate on particular subgroups, so that portfolio characteristics are not truly comparable. For example, within the equity universe, one manager may concentrate on high-beta or aggressive growth stocks. Similarly, within fixed-income universes, durations can vary across managers.

A more fundamental problem with the comparison universe methodology is that the benchmark performance is not an investable strategy available to a passive investor. When we evaluate the performance of investment professionals and implicitly ask if they have justified their fees, we would like to compare their performance to what would have been available to a passive investor. This is why market index portfolios, many of which are available as mutual funds or ETFs, are natural benchmarks. But the median fund in Figure 18.1 cannot be known in advance, and passive investors have no way to earn the median return. They can, however, easily earn the return on an index. Therefore, the return of the median fund in the comparison universe is an unsatisfactory benchmark for performance.

These considerations suggest that a more precise means for risk adjustment is desirable.

Risk-Adjusted Performance Measures

Methods of risk-adjusted performance evaluation using mean-variance criteria came on stage simultaneously with the capital asset pricing model. Jack Treynor,[2] William Sharpe,[3] and Michael Jensen[4] recognized immediately the implications of the CAPM for rating the performance of managers. Within a short time, academicians were in command of a battery of performance measures, and a bounty of scholarly investigation of mutual fund performance was pouring from ivory towers. Shortly thereafter, agents emerged who were willing to supply rating services to portfolio managers and their clients.

---

[2] Jack L. Treynor, "How to Rate Management Investment Funds," *Harvard Business Review* 43 (January–February 1966).

[3] William F. Sharpe, "Mutual Fund Performance," *Journal of Business* 39 (January 1966).

[4] Michael C. Jensen, "The Performance of Mutual Funds in the Period 1945–1964," *Journal of Finance,* May 1968; and "Risk, the Pricing of Capital Assets, and the Evaluation of Investment Portfolios," *Journal of Business,* April 1969.

But while widely used, risk-adjusted performance measures each have their own limitations. Moreover, their reliability requires quite a long history of consistent management with a steady level of performance and a representative sample of investment environments: bull as well as bear markets.

We start by cataloging some possible risk-adjusted performance measures for a portfolio, P, and examine the circumstances in which each might be most relevant.

1. *Sharpe ratio:* $(\bar{r}_P - \bar{r}_f)/\sigma_P$

   The **Sharpe ratio** divides average portfolio excess return over the sample period by the standard deviation of returns over that period. It measures the reward to (total) volatility trade-off.[5]

2. *Treynor measure:* $(\bar{r}_P - \bar{r}_f)/\beta_P$

   Like the Sharpe ratio, **Treynor's measure** gives excess return per unit of risk, but it focuses on systematic risk instead of total risk.

3. *Jensen's alpha:* $\alpha_P = \bar{r}_P - [\bar{r}_f + \beta_P(\bar{r}_M - \bar{r}_f)]$

   Jensen's alpha is the average return on the portfolio over and above that predicted by the CAPM, given the portfolio's beta and the average market return.[6]

4. *Information ratio:* $\alpha_P/\sigma(e_P)$

   The **information ratio** divides alpha by the nonsystematic risk of the portfolio, called "tracking error" in the industry. It measures abnormal return per unit of risk that in principle could be diversified away by holding a market index portfolio. (We should note that industry jargon tends to be a little loose concerning this topic. Some define the information ratio as excess return—rather than alpha—per unit of nonsystematic risk, using *appraisal ratio* to refer to the ratio of alpha to nonsystematic risk. Unfortunately, terminology in the profession is not fully uniform, and you may well encounter both of these definitions of the information ratio. We will consistently define it as we have done here, specifically as the ratio of alpha to the standard deviation of residual returns.)

Each performance measure has some appeal. But as Concept Check 18.2 shows, these competing measures do not necessarily provide consistent assessments of performance, because the risk measures used to adjust returns differ substantially. Therefore, we need to consider the circumstances in which each of these measures is appropriate.

Sharpe ratio

Ratio of excess return to standard deviation.

Treynor's measure

Ratio of excess return to beta.

Jensen's alpha

The alpha of an investment; the difference between the portfolio return and the return on a combination of the market index and bills with the same beta as the portfolio.

information ratio

Ratio of alpha to the standard deviation of the residual.

CONCEPT check **18.2**

Consider the following data for a particular sample period:

	Portfolio *P*	Market Index, *M*
Average return	35%	28%
Beta	1.20	1.00
Standard deviation	42%	30%
Tracking error (nonsystematic risk), $\sigma(e)$	18%	0

Calculate the following performance measures for portfolio *P* and the market index: Sharpe, Jensen (alpha), Treynor, information ratio. The T-bill rate during the period was 6%. By which measures did portfolio *P* outperform the market?

---

[5] We place bars over r_f as well as r_P to denote the fact that because the risk-free rate may not be constant over the measurement period, we are taking a sample average, just as we do for r_P. Equivalently, we may simply compute sample average *excess* returns.

[6] In many cases performance evaluation assumes a multifactor market. For example, when the Fama-French three-factor model is used, Jensen's alpha will be: $\alpha_P = \bar{r}_P - r_f - \beta_P(\bar{r}_M - r_f) - s_P\bar{r}_{SMB} - h_P\bar{r}_{HML}$ where s_P is the loading on the SMB portfolio and h_P is the loading on the HML portfolio.

The Sharpe Ratio for Overall Portfolios

Earlier chapters of this text help to determine the criteria for the investor's optimal risky portfolio. If preferences can be summarized by a mean-variance utility function, we arrive at a relatively simple criterion: Investors seek the risky portfolio with the highest possible Sharpe ratio.

The Sharpe ratio is the slope of the capital allocation line, and investors will naturally seek the portfolio that provides the greatest slope, that is, the greatest increase in expected return for each unit increase in volatility. We focus on total volatility rather than systematic risk because we are looking at the full portfolio rather than a small component of it. The benchmark for acceptable performance is the Sharpe ratio of the market index, since the investor can easily opt for a passive strategy by investing in an indexed equity mutual fund. The actively managed portfolio therefore must offer a higher Sharpe ratio than the market index if it is to be an acceptable candidate for the investor's optimal risky portfolio.

THE M^2 MEASURE AND THE SHARPE RATIO While the Sharpe ratio can be used to rank portfolio performance, its numerical value is not easy to interpret. Comparing the ratios for portfolios M and P in Concept Check 18.2, you should have found that $S_P = .69$ and $S_M = .73$. This suggests that portfolio P underperformed the market index. But is a difference of 0.04 in the Sharpe ratio economically meaningful? We often compare rates of return, but these values are difficult to interpret.

An equivalent representation of Sharpe's ratio was proposed by Graham and Harvey, and later popularized by Leah Modigliani of Morgan Stanley and her grandfather Franco Modigliani, past winner of the Nobel Prize in Economics.[7] Their approach has been dubbed the M^2 measure (for Modigliani-squared). Like the Sharpe ratio, M^2 focuses on total volatility as a measure of risk, but its risk adjustment leads to an easy-to-interpret differential return relative to the benchmark index.

To compute M^2, we imagine that an active portfolio, $P,$ is mixed with a position in T-bills so that the resulting "adjusted" portfolio matches the volatility of a passive market index such as the S&P 500. For example, if the active portfolio has 1½ times the standard deviation of the index, you would mix it with T-bills using proportions of 1/3 in bills and 2/3 in the active portfolio. The resulting adjusted portfolio, which we call P^*, would then have the same standard deviation as the index. (If the active portfolio had *lower* standard deviation than the index, it would be leveraged by borrowing money and investing the proceeds in the portfolio.) Because the market index and portfolio P^* have the same standard deviation, we may compare their performance simply by comparing returns. This is the M^2 measure for portfolio P:

$$M^2_P = r_{P^*} - r_M \qquad (18.1)$$

Consider the performance of portfolio P and the market index portfolio, $M,$ from Concept Check 18.2. Portfolio P had the higher return, but it also had higher risk, with the result that its Sharpe ratio was less than the market's. In Figure 18.2, we plot the average return and volatility of each portfolio and draw the capital allocation line for each. Portfolio P's CAL is less steep than the CML, consistent with its lower Sharpe ratio.

EXAMPLE 18.1

M^2 Measure

The adjusted portfolio P^* is formed by mixing bills with portfolio P. We use weights 30/42 = .714 in P and $1 - .714 = .286$ in T-bills. By construction, the adjusted portfolio has exactly the same standard deviation as the market index: 30/42 × 42% = 30%. Despite its equal volatility, its average return is only (.286 × 6%) + (.714 × 35%) = 26.7%, which is less than that of the market index.

You can see in Figure 18.2 that portfolio P^* is formed by moving down portfolio P's capital allocation line (by mixing P with T-bills) until we reduce the standard deviation by just enough to match that of the market index. M^2 is the vertical distance between points M and P^*. The M^2 of Portfolio P is therefore 26.7% − 28% = −1.3%; the negative M^2 is consistent with the inferior Sharpe ratio.[8]

---

[7] John R. Graham and Campbell R. Harvey, "Grading the Performance of Market Timing Newsletters," *Financial Analysts Journal* 53 (November/December 1997), pp. 54–66; and Franco Modigliani and Leah Modigliani, "Risk-Adjusted Performance," *Journal of Portfolio Management,* Winter 1997, pp. 45–54.

[8] M^2 is positive when the portfolio's Sharpe ratio exceeds the market's. Letting R denote excess returns and S denote Sharpe measures, the geometry of Figure 18.2 implies that $R_{P^*} = S_P\sigma_M$, and therefore that $M^2 = r_{P^*} - r_M = R_{P^*} - R_M = S_P\sigma_M - S_M\sigma_M = (S_P - S_M)\sigma_M$. M^2 and the Sharpe ratio therefore always rank order portfolios identically.

FIGURE   **18.2**

M^2 of portfolio P

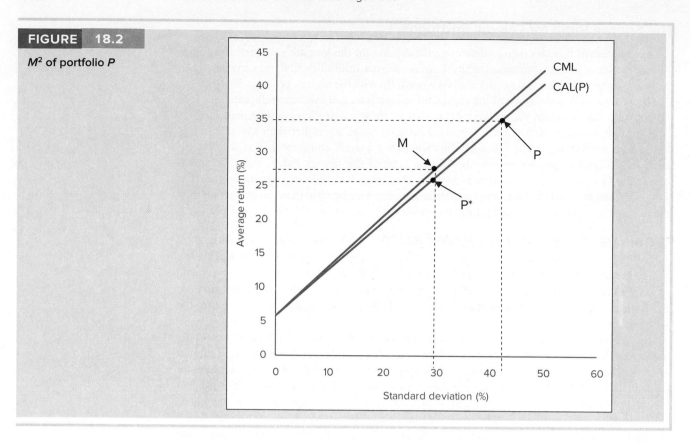

The Treynor Ratio

In many circumstances, you have to select funds or portfolios that will be mixed together to form the investor's overall risky portfolio. For example, the manager in charge of a large pension plan might parcel out the total assets to several portfolio managers. Consider CalPERS (the California Public Employee Retirement System), which had a portfolio of about $350 billion in early 2018. Like many large plans, it uses a *funds of funds* approach, allocating the endowment among a number of professional managers (funds). How should you compare performance across candidate managers in this context?

When employing a number of managers, nonsystematic risk will be largely diversified away, so systematic risk becomes the relevant measure of risk. The appropriate performance metric when evaluating potential *components* of the full risky portfolio is now the Treynor measure: This reward-to-risk ratio divides expected excess return by *systematic* risk (i.e., by beta).

Suppose the relevant data for two portfolios and the market index are given in Table 18.1. Portfolio Q has an alpha of 3.5% while that of portfolio U is 3%. It might appear that you would prefer portfolio Q, but this turns out not to be the case. To see why, turn to Figure 18.3. As in Figure 18.2, we plot portfolios on a return-risk graph, but now measure risk using beta.

TABLE 18.1   Portfolio performance

	Portfolio Q	Portfolio U	Market Index, M
Beta	1.25	0.8	1.0
Excess return ($\bar{r} - \bar{r}_f$)	16%	11%	10%
Alpha*	3.5%	3%	0

*Alpha = Excess return − (Beta × Market excess return)
  $= (\bar{r} - r_f) - \beta(\bar{r}_M - \bar{r}_f) = \bar{r} - [\bar{r}_f + \beta(\bar{r}_M - \bar{r}_f)]$

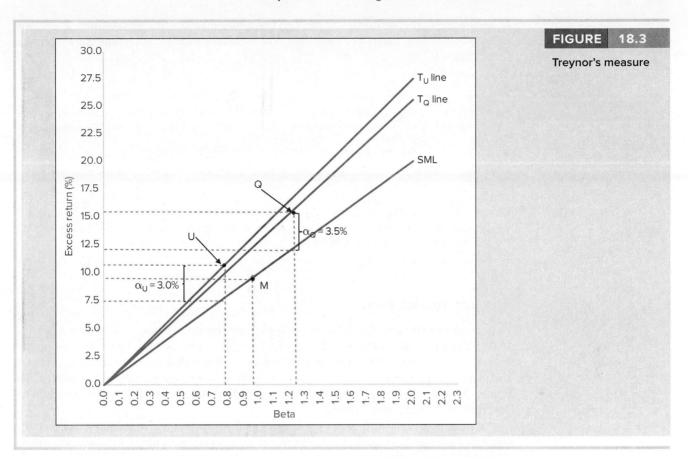

FIGURE **18.3**

Treynor's measure

The SML is the black line from the origin (where both zero excess return and beta are zero) through point M. Its slope is the Treynor ratio of the market index, the increase in excess return per unit of beta provided by portfolios that mix the market index with T-bills.

The line from the origin through point Q shows us all the beta-excess return combinations that can be achieved by mixing bills with portfolio Q. The slope of this line, giving the trade-off between excess return and beta, is portfolio Q's excess return divided by its beta; this is the portfolio's Treynor ratio. Therefore, we call it the T_Q-line. Similarly, the T_U-line goes from the origin through point U.

As always, the investor wants the portfolio that provides the best risk-return trade-off. When we measure risk using beta, that will be the portfolio that provides the T-line with the steepest slope, or equivalently, the portfolio with the highest Treynor ratio. Therefore, we see that despite its lower alpha, portfolio U actually will be preferred to portfolio Q. For any level of risk (beta), it provides the greater excess return.

We can measure the advantage of each portfolio compared to the market index using a measure similar to M-square. We will again combine portfolios with T-bills to match market risk so that we can directly compare rates of return. Here, however, we use beta to measure risk, so we will form adjusted portfolios designed to match the beta of the market index (which, of course, is 1). We form the adjusted portfolio Q^* by mixing Q with T-bills in proportions w_Q and $(1 - w_Q)$. We seek portfolio proportions that will make the beta of Q^* equal to 1. Therefore, we choose w_Q to satisfy

$$\beta_{Q^*} = w_Q \times \beta_Q + (1 - w_Q) \times \beta_{\text{bills}} = w_Q \times 1.25 + (1 - w_Q) \times 0 = 1.0$$

which implies that $w_Q = .8$.

Because the systematic risk of the adjusted portfolio is constructed to match the market's, we can meaningfully compare their excess returns. The excess return on Q^* is $.8 \times 16 + .2 \times 0 = 12.8\%$, which beats the market by 2.8%. This measure is analogous to the

M-square measure, but it extends the Treynor rather than the Sharpe measure. Therefore, we will call it the *T*-square or T^2 measure. The following example computes the T^2 measure for portfolio *U*.

<table>
<tr>
<td>

EXAMPLE 18.2

Equalizing Beta and the T-Square Measure

</td>
<td>

Portfolio *U* has a beta of 0.8, which is less than the market beta of 1. Therefore we will need to use leverage to increase systematic risk to the level of the market index. We choose w_U to satisfy:

$$\beta_{U^*} = w_U \times \beta_U + (1 - w_U) \times \beta_{\text{bills}} = w_U \times .8 + (1 - w_U) \times 0 = 1.0$$

which implies that $w_U = 1.25$. So the adjusted portfolio U^* entails *borrowing* at the risk-free rate, with all proceeds invested in portfolio *U*.

The excess return on the adjusted portfolio U^* is $1.25 \times 11 - .25 \times 0 = 13.75\%$, which beats the market's excess return by 3.75%. Portfolio *U*'s higher *T*-square measure compared to portfolio *Q* is consistent with the steeper slope it displayed in Figure 18.3. We can use either the *T*-square or the Treynor measure to rank portfolios when beta is the relevant measure of risk.

</td>
</tr>
</table>

The Information Ratio

Here is another situation that calls for yet another performance criterion. Consider a pension fund with a largely passive and well-diversified position—for example, a portfolio that resembles an indexed equity fund. Now the fund decides to add a position in an active portfolio to its current position. For example, a university might employ a hedge fund as a possible addition to its core positions in more traditional portfolios that were established primarily with concerns of diversification in mind.

As we saw in Chapter 6, when the hedge fund (or another active position) is optimally combined with the baseline indexed portfolio, the improvement in the Sharpe measure will be determined by its information ratio $\alpha_H/\sigma(e_H)$, according to

$$S_P^2 = S_M^2 + \left[\frac{\alpha_H}{\sigma(e_H)} \right]^2 \tag{18.2}$$

Equation 18.2 tells us that the appropriate performance measure for the hedge fund, *H*, is its information ratio (IR). If you are looking for active managers to add to a currently indexed position, you will want to select potential candidates with the best information ratios.

The information ratio is yet another version of a reward-to-risk ratio. In this context, the reward is the alpha of the active position. It is the expected return on that incremental portfolio over and above the risk premium that would normally correspond to its systematic risk. On the other hand, the incremental position tilts the total risky portfolio away from the passive index, and therefore exposes it to risk that could in principle be diversified. The information ratio quantifies the trade-off between alpha and diversifiable risk.

We can summarize the preceding discussion with the following table, which shows the definition of the various performance measures and the situations in which each is the relevant performance measure.

Performance Measure	Definition	Application
Sharpe	$\dfrac{\text{Excess return}}{\text{Standard deviation}}$	When choosing among portfolios competing for the overall risky portfolio
Treynor	$\dfrac{\text{Excess return}}{\text{Beta}}$	When ranking many portfolios that will be mixed to form the overall risky portfolio
Information ratio	$\dfrac{\text{Alpha}}{\text{Residual standard deviation}}$	When evaluating a portfolio to be mixed with the benchmark portfolio

Performance Measurement

The following performance measurement spreadsheet computes all the performance measures discussed in this section. You can see how relative ranking differs according to the criterion selected. This Excel model is available in Connect or through your course instructor.

Spreadsheets are available in Connect

	A	B	C	D	E	F	G	H	I	J	K
1	**Performance Measurement**								**LEGEND**		
2									Enter data		
3									Value calculated		
4									See comment		
5											
6					Non-						
7		Average	Standard	Beta	systematic	Sharpe's	Treynor's	Jensen's	M2	T2	Information
8	**Fund**	Return	Deviation	Coefficient	Risk	Measure	Measure	Measure	Measure	Measure	Ratio
9	Alpha	28.00%	27.00%	1.7000	5.00%	0.8148	0.1294	−0.0180	−0.0015	−0.0106	−0.3600
10	Omega	31.00%	26.00%	1.6200	6.00%	0.9615	0.1543	0.0232	0.0235	0.0143	0.3867
11	Omicron	22.00%	21.00%	0.8500	2.00%	0.7619	0.1882	0.0410	−0.0105	0.0482	2.0500
12	Millennium	40.00%	33.00%	2.5000	27.00%	1.0303	0.1360	−0.0100	0.0352	−0.0040	−0.0370
13	Big Value	15.00%	13.00%	0.9000	3.00%	0.6923	0.1000	−0.0360	−0.0223	−0.0400	−1.2000
14	Momentum Watcher	29.00%	24.00%	1.4000	16.00%	0.9583	0.1643	0.0340	0.0229	0.0243	0.2125
15	Big Potential	15.00%	11.00%	0.5500	1.50%	0.8182	0.1636	0.0130	−0.0009	0.0236	0.8667
16	S & P Index Return	20.00%	17.00%	1.0000	0.00%	0.8235	0.1400	0.0000	0.0000	0.0000	0.0000
17	T-Bill Return	6.00%		0.0000							
18											
19	**Ranking By Sharpe's Measure**				Non-						
20		Average	Standard	Beta	systematic	Sharpe's	Treynor's	Jensen's	M2	T2	Information
21	**Fund**	Return	Deviation	Coefficient	Risk	Measure	Measure	Measure	Measure	Measure	Ratio

Excel Questions

1. Examine the performance measures of the funds included in the spreadsheet. Rank performance and determine whether the rankings are consistent using each measure. What explains these results?

2. Which fund would you choose if you were considering investing the entire risky portion of your portfolio? What if you were considering adding a small position in one of these funds to a portfolio currently invested in the market index?

The Role of Alpha in Performance Measures

Given the central role of alpha in the index model, the CAPM, and other models of risk versus return, you may be surprised that we have not encountered a situation in which alpha is the criterion used to choose one fund over another. But don't conclude from this that alpha does not matter! With some algebra, we can derive the relationship between the performance measures discussed so far and the alpha of the portfolio. The following table shows these relationships. In all cases, you can see that it is impossible to outperform the passive market index unless the fund is expected to generate a positive alpha. Because superior performance requires positive alpha, it is the most widely used performance measure.

	Treynor (T_p)	Sharpe* (S_p)	Information Ratio
Relation to alpha	$\dfrac{E(r_p) - r_f}{\beta_p} = \dfrac{\alpha_p}{\beta_p} + T_M$	$\dfrac{E(r_p) - r_f}{\sigma_p} = \dfrac{\alpha_p}{\sigma_p} + \rho S_M$	$\dfrac{\alpha_p}{\sigma(e_p)}$
Improvement compared to market index	$T_p - T_M = \dfrac{\alpha_p}{\beta_p}$	$S_p - S_M = \dfrac{\alpha_p}{\sigma_p} - (1 - \rho)S_M$	$\dfrac{\alpha_p}{\sigma(e_p)}$

*ρ denotes the correlation coefficient between portfolio P and the market, and is less than 1.

However, while positive alpha is *necessary,* it is not sufficient to guarantee that a portfolio will outperform the index: Taking advantage of mispricing means departing from full diversification, which entails a cost in terms of nonsystematic risk. A mutual fund can achieve a positive alpha, yet, at the same time, its volatility may increase to a level at which its Sharpe ratio will actually fall.

Implementing Performance Measurement: An Example

To illustrate some of the calculations underlying portfolio evaluation, let's look at the performance of portfolio P over the last 12 months. Table 18.2 shows its excess return in each month as well as those of an alternative portfolio Q, and the market index portfolio M. The bottom two rows in Table 18.2 provide the sample average and standard deviation of each portfolio. From these, and regressions of P and Q on M, we can compute the necessary performance statistics. These appear in Table 18.3.

The performance statistics in Table 18.3 show that portfolio Q is more aggressive than P, in the sense that its beta is significantly higher (1.40 versus 0.70). At the same time, P's lower residual standard deviation shows that it is better diversified than Q (2.02% versus 9.81%). Both portfolios outperformed the benchmark market index, as is evident from their higher Sharpe ratios (and thus positive M^2) and their positive alphas.

Which portfolio is more attractive based on reported performance? If P or Q represents the entire investment fund, Q would be preferable on the basis of its higher Sharpe measure (0.49 vs. 0.43) and better M^2 (2.66% vs. 2.16%). For the second scenario, where P and Q are competing for a role as one of a number of subportfolios, Q also dominates because its Treynor measure is higher (5.38 vs. 3.97). However, as an active portfolio to be mixed with the index portfolio, P is preferred because its information ratio [IR $= \alpha/\sigma(e)$] is higher (0.81 vs. 0.54).

TABLE 18.2 Excess returns for portfolios P and Q and the market index M over 12 months

Month	Portfolio P	Portfolio Q	Index M
1	3.58%	2.81%	2.20%
2	−4.91	−1.15	−8.41
3	6.51	2.53	3.27
4	11.13	37.09	14.41
5	8.78	12.88	7.71
6	9.38	39.08	14.36
7	−3.66	−8.84	−6.15
8	5.56	0.83	2.74
9	−7.72	0.85	−15.27
10	7.76	12.09	6.49
11	−4.01	−5.68	−3.13
12	0.78	−1.77	1.41
Average	2.77	7.56	1.64
Standard deviation	6.45	15.55	8.84

TABLE 18.3 Performance statistics

	Portfolio P	Portfolio Q	Portfolio M
Sharpe ratio	0.43	0.49	0.19
M^2	2.16	2.66	0.00
SCL regression statistics			
Alpha	1.63	5.26	0.00
Beta	0.70	1.40	1.00
Treynor	3.97	5.38	1.64
T^2	2.34	3.74	0.00
$\sigma(e)$	2.02	9.81	0.00
Information ratio	0.81	0.54	0.00
R-square	0.91	0.64	1.00

THE MAGELLAN FUND AND MARKET EFFICIENCY: ASSESSING THE PERFORMANCE OF MONEY MANAGERS

Fidelity's Magellan Fund outperformed the S&P 500 in 11 of the 13 years ending in 1989, when its manager, Peter Lynch, retired. Is such performance consistent with the efficient market hypothesis? Casual statistical analysis would suggest not.

If outperforming the market were like flipping a fair coin, as would be the case if all securities were fairly priced, then the odds of an arbitrarily selected manager producing 11 out of 13 winning years would be only about 0.95%, or 1 in 105. The Magellan Fund, however, is not a randomly selected fund. Instead, it is the fund that emerged after a 13-year "contest" as a clear winner. Given that we have chosen to focus on the winner of a money management contest, should we be surprised to find performance far above the mean? Clearly not.

Once we select a fund precisely because it has outperformed all other funds, the proper benchmark for predicted performance is no longer a standard index such as the S&P 500. The benchmark must be the expected performance of the best-performing fund out of a sample of randomly selected funds.

Consider as an analogy a coin-flipping contest. If 50 contestants were to flip a coin 13 times, and the winner were to flip 11 heads out of 13, we would not consider that evidence that the winner's coin was biased. Instead, we would recognize that with 50 contestants, the probability is greater than 40% that the individual who emerges as the winner would, in fact, flip heads 11 or more times. (In contrast, a coin chosen at random that resulted in 11 out of 13 heads would be highly suspect!)

How then ought we evaluate the performance of those managers who show up in the financial press as (recently) superior performers. We know that after the fact some managers will have been lucky. When is the performance of a manager so good that even after accounting for selection bias—the selection of the ex post winner—we still cannot account for such performance by chance?

SELECTION BIAS AND PERFORMANCE BENCHMARKS

Consider this experiment. Allow 50 money managers to flip a coin 13 times, and record the maximum number of heads realized by any of the contestants. (If markets are efficient, the coin will have the same probability of turning up heads as that of a money manager beating the market.) Now repeat the contest, and again record the winning number of heads. Repeat this experiment 10,000 times. When we are done, we can compute the frequency distribution of the winning number of heads over the 10,000 trials.

The table (column 1) presents the results of such an experiment simulated on a computer. The table shows that in 9.2% of

PROBABILITY DISTRIBUTION OF NUMBER OF SUCCESSFUL YEARS OUT OF THIRTEEN FOR THE BEST-PERFORMING MONEY MANAGER

Winning Years	Managers in Contest			
	50	100	250	500
8	0.1%	0%	0%	0%
9	9.2	0.9	0	0
10	47.4	31.9	5.7	0.2
11	34.8	51.3	59.7	42.3
12	7.7	14.6	31.8	51.5
13	0.8	1.2	2.8	5.9
Mean winning years of best performer	10.43	10.83	11.32	11.63

the contests, the winning number of heads was 9; in 47.4% of the trials, 10 heads would be enough to emerge as the best manager. Interestingly, in 43.3% of the trials, the winning number of heads was 11 or more out of 13.

Viewed in this context, the performance of Magellan is still impressive but somewhat less surprising. The simulation shows that out of a sample of 50 managers, chance alone would provide a 43.3% probability that *someone* would beat the market at least 11 out of 13 years. Averaging over all 10,000 trials, the mean number of winning years necessary to emerge as most reliable manager over the 13-year contest was 10.43.

Therefore, once we recognize that Magellan is not a fund chosen at random, but a fund that came to our attention precisely because it turned out to perform so well, the frequency with which it beat the market is no longer high enough to be considered a violation of market efficiency. Indeed, using the conventional 5% confidence level, we could not reject the hypothesis that the consistency of its performance was due to chance.

The other columns in the table present the frequency distributions of the winning number of successful coin flips (analogously, the number of years in which the best-performing manager beats an efficient market) for other possible sample sizes. Not surprisingly, as the pool of managers increases, the predicted best performance steadily gets better. By providing as a benchmark the probability distribution of the best performance, rather than the average performance, the table tells us how many grains of salt to add to reports of the latest investment guru.

SOURCE: Alan J. Marcus, "The Magellan Fund and Market Efficiency." *The Journal of Portfolio Management,* Fall 1990, pp. 85–86.

Thus, the example illustrates that the right way to evaluate a portfolio depends in large part on how the portfolio fits into the investor's overall investment plan.

This analysis is based on 12 months of data only, a period too short to lend statistical significance to the conclusions. Nevertheless, the analysis illustrates what one might wish to do with more extensive data. A model that calculates these performance measures is available in Connect.

Selection Bias and Portfolio Evaluation

A warning: Regardless of the performance criterion, some funds will outperform their benchmarks in any year and others will underperform. The good performers are likely to attract more interest from the financial press and potential investors. But beware of focusing on these above-average performers and extrapolating their track records into the future.

When we address the performance of mutual funds selected *because* they have been successful, we need to be highly cautious in evaluating their track records. In particular, we need to recognize that even if all managers were equally skilled, a few "winners" would emerge by sheer chance each period. With thousands of funds in operation, the best-performing funds will have been wildly successful, even if these results reflect luck rather than skill. The nearby box addresses the problems that can arise when a sample of funds is selected based in part of past performance.

Another manifestation of selection bias arises when we limit a sample of funds to those for which returns are available over an entire sample period. This practice implies that we exclude from consideration all funds that were closed down over the sample period. The ensuing bias is called **survivorship bias.** It turns out that when even a small number of funds have failed, the upward bias in the performance of surviving funds can be substantial. Most mutual fund databases now include failed funds so that samples can be protected from survivorship bias.

survivorship bias

Upward bias in average fund performance due to the failure to account for failed funds over the sample period.

18.2   STYLE ANALYSIS

The index model regression can be viewed as a way to measure and describe facets of a portfolio manager's investment style. Portfolios with high betas are called cyclical or aggressive because they are more responsive to economywide developments. Low beta portfolios are described as defensive. Multifactor models generalize this idea, describing the portfolio's exposure to several risk factors or segments of the market. Each of these exposures can be viewed as an implicit sort of asset allocation decision.

Style analysis was introduced by William Sharpe as a tool to systematically measure the exposures of managed portfolios.[9] The popularity of the concept was boosted by a well-known study[10] concluding that 91.5% of the variation in returns of 82 mutual funds could be explained by the funds' asset allocation to bills, bonds, and stocks. While later studies have taken issue with the exact interpretation of these results, there is widespread agreement that asset allocation is responsible for a high proportion of the variation in investment performance across funds.

Sharpe's idea was to regress fund returns on indexes representing a range of asset classes. The regression coefficient on each index would then measure the fund's implicit allocation to that "style." Because funds are typically barred from short positions, the regression coefficients are constrained to be either zero or positive and to sum to 100%, so as to represent a complete asset allocation. The *R*-square of the regression would then measure the percentage of return variability attributable to style choice rather than to security selection. The intercept measures the average return from security selection of the fund portfolio. It therefore tracks the average success of security selection over the sample period.

To illustrate Sharpe's approach, we use monthly returns on Fidelity's Magellan Fund during the famous manager Peter Lynch's tenure between October 1986 and September 1991, with results shown in Table 18.4. While seven asset classes are included in this analysis (of which six are represented by stock indexes and one is the T-bill alternative), the regression coefficients are positive for only three, namely, large capitalization stocks, medium cap stocks, and high P/E (growth) stocks. These portfolios alone explain 97.5% of the variance of Magellan's returns. In other words, a tracking portfolio made up of the three style portfolios,

---

[9] William F. Sharpe, "Asset Allocation: Management Style and Performance Evaluation," *Journal of Portfolio Management,* Winter 1992, pp. 7–19.

[10] Gary Brinson, Brian Singer, and Gilbert Beebower, "Determinants of Portfolio Performance," *Financial Analysts Journal,* May/June 1991.

TABLE 18.4 Style analysis for Fidelity's Magellan Fund	
Style Portfolio	**Regression Coefficient**
T-bill	0
Small cap	0
Medium cap	35
Large cap	61
High P/E (growth)	5
Medium P/E	0
Low P/E (value)	0
Total	100
R-square	97.5

Source: Authors' calculations. Return data for Magellan obtained from finance.yahoo.com/funds and return data for style portfolios obtained from the Web page of Professor Kenneth French: mba.tuck.dartmouth.edu/pages/faculty/ken.french/data_library.html.

with weights as given in Table 18.4, would explain the vast majority of Magellan's variation in monthly performance. We conclude that the fund returns are well represented by three style portfolios.

The proportion of return variability *not* explained by asset allocation can be attributed to security selection within asset classes, as well as timing that shows up as periodic changes in allocation. For Magellan, residual variability was $100 - 97.5 = 2.5\%$. This sort of result is commonly interpreted as evidence against the importance of security selection, but such a conclusion misses the important role of the intercept in this regression. (The *R*-square of the regression can be 100%, and yet the intercept can be positive due to consistently superior stock selection.) For Magellan, the intercept was 32 basis points per month, providing a cumulative abnormal return over the five-year period of 19.19%. The superior performance of Magellan in this period is displayed in Figure 18.4, which plots the combined impact of the intercept plus monthly residuals relative to both the tracking portfolio composed of the individual style portfolios as well as relative to the simple CAPM benchmark provided by the security market line.

Of course, Magellan's consistently positive residual returns (reflected in the steadily increasing plot of cumulative return difference) is hardly common. Figure 18.5 shows the frequency distribution of average residuals across 636 mutual funds. The distribution has the familiar bell shape with a slightly negative mean of -0.074% per month.

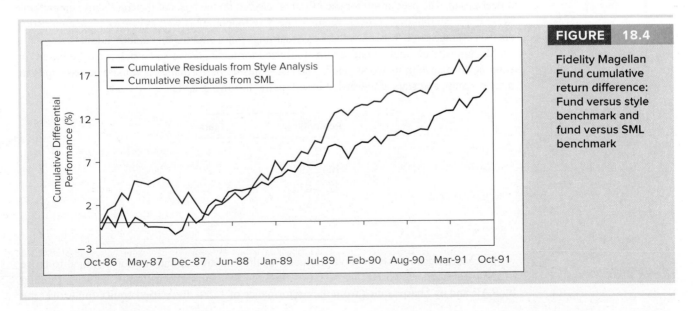

FIGURE 18.4

Fidelity Magellan Fund cumulative return difference: Fund versus style benchmark and fund versus SML benchmark

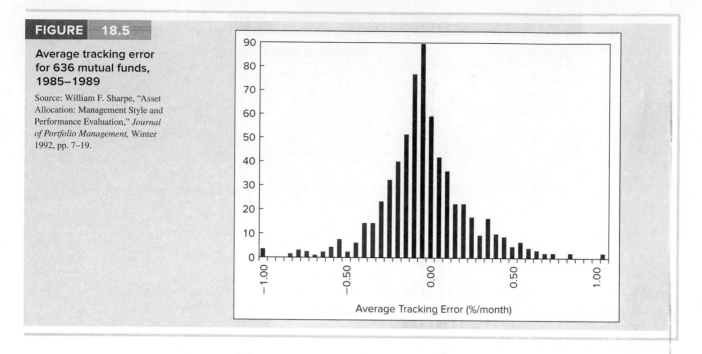

FIGURE **18.5**

**Average tracking error
for 636 mutual funds,
1985–1989**

Source: William F. Sharpe, "Asset
Allocation: Management Style and
Performance Evaluation," *Journal
of Portfolio Management,* Winter
1992, pp. 7–19.

Style analysis has become very popular in the investment management industry and has spawned quite a few variations on Sharpe's methodology. Many portfolio managers use websites that help investors identify their style and stock selection performance.

18.3 MORNINGSTAR'S RISK-ADJUSTED RATING

The commercial success of Morningstar, Inc., the premier source of information on mutual funds, has made its *Risk Adjusted Rating* (RAR) among the most widely used performance measures. The Morningstar five-star rating is coveted by the managers of the thousands of funds covered by the service.

Morningstar calculates a number of RAR performance measures that are similar, although not identical, to the standard mean-variance measures (see Chapter 4 for a more detailed discussion). The most distinct measure, the Morningstar Star Rating, is based on comparison of each fund to a peer group. The peer group for each fund is selected on the basis of the fund's investment universe (e.g., international, growth versus value, fixed-income) as well as portfolio characteristics such as average price-to-book value, price–earnings ratio, and market capitalization.

Morningstar computes fund returns (adjusted for loads) as well as a risk measure based on fund performance in its worst years. The risk-adjusted performance is ranked across funds in a style group, and stars are awarded based on the following table:

Percentile	Stars
0–10	1
10–32.5	2
32.5–67.5	3
67.5–90	4
90–100	5

The Morningstar RAR method produces results that are similar but not identical to those of the mean/variance-based Sharpe ratios. Figure 18.6 demonstrates the fit between ranking by RAR and by Sharpe ratios from the performance of 1,286 diversified equity funds over the

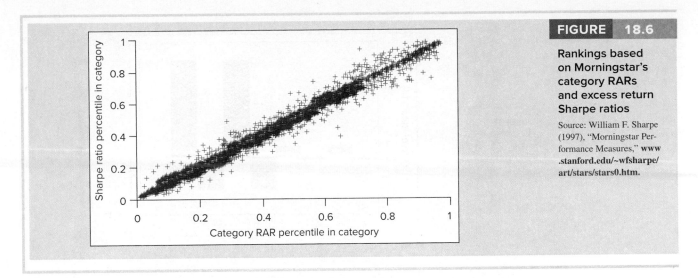

FIGURE   18.6

Rankings based on Morningstar's category RARs and excess return Sharpe ratios

Source: William F. Sharpe (1997), "Morningstar Performance Measures," **www .stanford.edu/~wfsharpe/ art/stars/stars0.htm.**

period 1994–1996. Sharpe (1997) notes that this period is characterized by high dispersion of returns that contribute to a good fit.

18.4 PERFORMANCE MEASUREMENT WITH CHANGING PORTFOLIO COMPOSITION

One potential problem with risk-adjustment techniques is that they all assume that portfolio risk, whether measured by standard deviation or beta, is constant over the relevant time period. This isn't necessarily so. For example, if a manager attempts to increase portfolio beta when she thinks the market is about to go up and to decrease beta when she's pessimistic, both the standard deviation and the beta of the portfolio will change over time. Variation in risk can wreak havoc with our performance measures, as illustrated by the following example.

Suppose that the Sharpe measure of the market index is 0.4. In the first year, the portfolio manager executes a low-risk strategy and realizes an (annualized) mean excess return of 1% and standard deviation of 2%. This makes for a Sharpe ratio of 0.5, which beats the passive strategy. Over the next year, the manager decides that a *high*-risk strategy is optimal and achieves an annual mean excess return of 9% and standard deviation of 18%. Here, again, the Sharpe ratio is 0.5. Over the two-year period, our manager consistently maintains a better-than-passive Sharpe measure.

Figure 18.7 shows a pattern of (annualized) quarterly returns that are consistent with our description of the manager's strategy of two years. In the first four quarters the excess returns are −1%, 3%, −1%, and 3%, making for an average of 1% and standard deviation of 2%. In the next four quarters the excess returns are −9%, 27%, −9%, and 27%, making for an average of 9% and standard deviation of 18%. Thus, *both* years exhibit a Sharpe measure of 0.5. However, the mean and standard deviation of the eight quarterly returns are 5% and 13.42%, respectively, making for a Sharpe measure of only 0.37, apparently inferior to the passive strategy!

EXAMPLE 18.3

Changing Portfolio Risk

What happened in Example 18.3? The shift of the mean from the first four quarters to the next was not recognized as a shift in strategy. Instead, the difference in mean returns in the two years added to the *appearance* of volatility in portfolio returns. The active strategy with shifting means appears riskier than it really is and biases the estimate of the Sharpe measure downward. We conclude that for actively managed portfolios it is necessary to keep track of portfolio composition and changes in both portfolio mean and risk. We will see another example of this problem next, when we turn to market timing.

FIGURE   18.7

Portfolio returns: Returns in last four quarters are more variable than in the first four

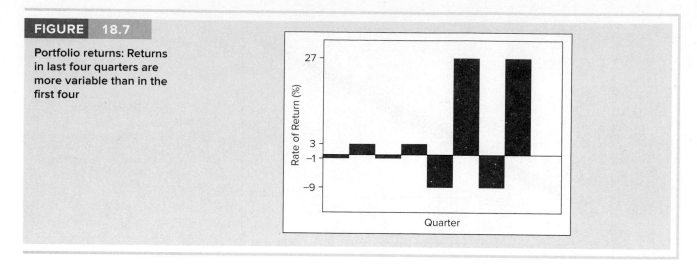

18.5   MARKET TIMING

market timing

A strategy that moves funds between the risky portfolio and cash, based on forecasts of relative performance.

A potentially important driver of variation in portfolio risk is **market timing.** In its pure form, market timing involves shifting funds between a market-index portfolio and a safe asset, depending on whether the market index is expected to outperform the safe asset. In practice, most managers do not shift fully between T-bills and the market. How can we account for partial shifts into the market when it is expected to perform well?

To simplify, suppose that an investor holds only the market-index portfolio and T-bills. If the weight of the market were constant, say, 0.6, then portfolio beta would also be constant, and the security characteristic line (SCL) would plot as a straight line with slope 0.6, as in Figure 18.8, Panel A. If, however, the investor could correctly time the market and shift funds into it in periods when the market does well, the SCL would plot as in Figure 18.8, Panel B. If bull and bear markets can be predicted, the investor will shift more into the market when the market is more likely to go up. The portfolio beta and the slope of the SCL will be higher when r_M is higher, resulting in the curved line that appears in Figure 18.8, Panel B.

FIGURE   18.8

Characteristic lines.
Panel A: No market timing, beta is constant. *Panel B:* Market timing, beta steadily increases with expected market excess return. *Panel C:* Market timing with only two values of beta.

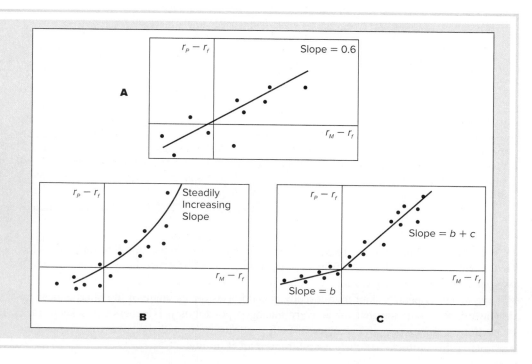

Treynor and Mazuy were the first to propose estimating such a line by adding a squared term to the usual linear index model:[11]

$$r_P - r_f = a + b(r_M - r_f) + c(r_M - r_f)^2 + e_P$$

where r_P is the portfolio return, and a, b, and c are estimated by regression analysis. If c turns out to be positive, we have evidence of timing ability, because this last term will make the characteristic line steeper as $r_M - r_f$ is larger. Treynor and Mazuy estimated this equation for a number of mutual funds, but found little evidence of timing ability.

A similar but simpler methodology was proposed by Henriksson and Merton.[12] These authors suggested that the beta of the portfolio takes only two values: a large value if the market is expected to do well and a small value otherwise. Under this scheme the portfolio character-istic line appears as shown in Figure 18.8, Panel C. Such a line appears in regression form as

$$r_P - r_f = a + b(r_M - r_f) + c(r_M - r_f)D + e_P$$

where D is a dummy variable that equals one when $r_M > r_f$ and zero otherwise. Hence the beta of the portfolio is b in bear markets and $b + c$ in bull markets. Again, a positive value of c implies market timing ability. They also found little evidence of such ability.

To illustrate how you might implement a test for market timing, return to Table 18.2, which contains 12 months of excess returns for two managed portfolios, P and Q, and the market index, M. Regress the excess returns of each portfolio on the excess returns of M and the square of these returns as in the following specifications:

$$r_P - r_f = a_P + b_P(r_M - r_f) + c_P(r_M - r_f)^2 + e_P$$
$$r_Q - r_f = a_Q + b_Q(r_M - r_f) + c_Q(r_M - r_f)^2 + e_Q$$

You will derive the following statistics. The numbers in parentheses are included for com-parison: They are the regression estimates from the single-variable regression reported in Table 18.3.

	Portfolio	
Estimate	**P**	**Q**
Alpha (*a*)	1.77 (1.63)	−2.29 (5.26)
Beta (*b*)	0.70 (0.70)	1.10 (1.40)
Timing (*c*)	0.00	0.10
R-square	0.91 (0.91)	0.98 (0.64)

Portfolio P shows no evidence of attempted timing: Its timing coefficient, c, is estimated to be zero. It is not clear whether this is because no attempt was made at timing or because any effort to time the market was in vain and served only to increase portfolio variance unnecessarily.

The results for portfolio Q, however, reveal that timing has, in all likelihood, been attempted. Here the coefficient, c, is positive, with an estimated value of 0.10. The evidence thus suggests successful timing, offset by unsuccessful stock selection (negative a). Note that the estimate of alpha, a, is now −2.29% as opposed to the 5.26% estimate derived from the regression equation that did not allow for the possibility of timing activity.

[11] Jack L. Treynor and Kay Mazuy, "Can Mutual Funds Outguess the Market?" *Harvard Business Review* 43 (July–August 1966).

[12] Roy D. Henriksson and R. C. Merton, "On Market Timing and Investment Performance. II. Statistical Procedures for Evaluating Forecast Skills," *Journal of Business* 54 (October 1981).

This example illustrates the inadequacy of conventional performance evaluation techniques that assume constant mean returns and constant risk. The market timer constantly moves into and out of the market, thereby shifting both beta and mean return. So timing presents another instance in which portfolio composition and risk vary, complicating the effort to evaluate performance. Whereas the expanded regression captures this possibility, the simple SCL does not. The important point for performance evaluation is that expanded regressions can capture many of the effects of portfolio composition change that would confound more conventional mean-variance measures.

The Potential Value of Market Timing

Suppose we define perfect market timing as the ability to tell (with certainty) at the beginning of each year whether the S&P 500 portfolio will outperform the strategy of rolling over one-month T-bills throughout the year. Accordingly, at the beginning of each year, the market timer shifts all funds into either cash equivalents (T-bills) or equities (the S&P portfolio), whichever is predicted to do better. Beginning with $1 on December 31, 1926, how would the perfect timer end a 90-year experiment on December 31, 2016, in comparison with investors who kept their funds in either equity or T-bills for the entire period?

Table 18.5 presents summary statistics for each of the three passive strategies, computed from the historical annual returns of bills and equities. From the returns on stocks and bills, we calculate wealth indexes of the all-bills and all-equity investments and show terminal values for these investors at the end of 2016. The return for the perfect timer in each year is the *maximum* of the return on stocks and the return on bills.

The first row in Table 18.5 shows that the terminal value of investing $1 in bills over the 90 years (1926–2016) is $20, while the terminal value of the same initial investment in equities is $5,143. We argued in Chapter 5 that as impressive as the difference in terminal values is, it is best interpreted as no more than fair compensation for the risk borne by equity investors. The *annual* difference in returns is just about 8.23%, which doesn't seem as dramatic.

Now observe that the terminal value of the perfect timer is $617,929, a 120-fold increase over the already large terminal value of the all-equity strategy! In fact, this result is even better than it looks, because the return to the market timer is truly risk-free. This is the classic case where a large standard deviation (13.38%) has nothing to do with risk. Because the timer never delivers a return below the risk-free rate, the standard deviation is a measure of *good* surprises only.

The positive skew of the timer's distribution (0.73, compared with the negative skew of equities) is a manifestation of the fact that the extreme values are all positive. Other indications of this stellar performance are the minimum and maximum returns—the minimum return for the timer equals zero (in 1940) and the maximum return, 56.38%, is that of equities (in 1933). All negative returns on equities (as low as −44% in 1931) were avoided by the timer.

TABLE 18.5	Performance of bills, equities, and perfect (annual) market timers. (Initial investment = $1)		
	Bills	**Equities**	**Perfect Timer**
Terminal value	$20	$5,143	$617,929
Arithmetic average	3.43%	11.66%	16.51%
Standard deviation	3.15%	19.97%	13.38%
Geometric average	3.38%	9.96%	15.97%
Maximum	14.71%	56.38%	56.38%
Minimum*	−0.02%	−43.73%	0.00%
Skew	1.02	−0.42	0.73
Kurtosis	0.94	0.10	−0.15

*A negative rate on "bills" was observed in 1940. The Treasury security used in the data series in these early years was actually not a T-bill but a T-bond with 30 days to maturity.

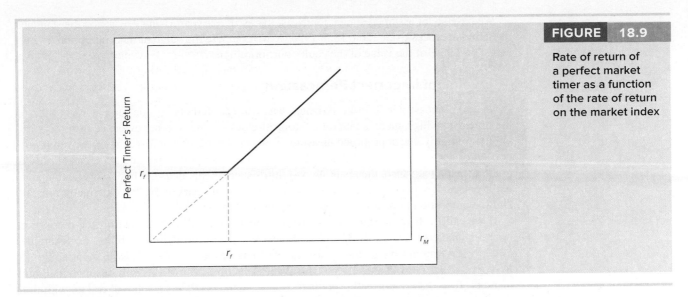

FIGURE 18.9

Rate of return of a perfect market timer as a function of the rate of return on the market index

Valuing Market Timing as a Call Option

The key to valuing market timing ability is to recognize that perfect foresight is equivalent to holding a call option on the equity portfolio—but without having to pay for it! The perfect timer invests 100% in either the safe asset or the equity portfolio, whichever will provide the higher return. The rate of return is *at least* the risk-free rate. This is shown in Figure 18.9.

To see the value of information as an option, suppose that the market index currently is at S_0 and that a call option on the index has an exercise price of $X = S_0(1 + r_f)$. If the market outperforms bills over the coming period, S_T will exceed X; otherwise it will be less than X. Now look at the payoff to a portfolio consisting of this option and S_0 dollars invested in bills:

	$S_T < X$	$S_T \geq X$
Bills	$S_0(1 + r_f)$	$S_0(1 + r_f)$
Call	0	$S_T - X$
Total	$S_0(1 + r_f)$	S_T

The portfolio pays the risk-free return when the market is bearish (i.e., the market return is less than the risk-free rate), and it pays the market return when the market is bullish and outperforms bills. Such a portfolio is a perfect market timer.[13]

Because the ability to predict the better-performing investment is equivalent to acquiring a (free) call option on the market and adding it to a position in bills, we can use option-pricing models to assign a dollar value to perfect timing ability. This value would constitute the fair fee that a perfect timer could charge investors for its services.

The exercise price of the perfect-timer call option on $1 of the equity portfolio is the final value of the T-bill investment. Using continuous compounding, this is $1 \times e^{rT}$. When you use this exercise price in the Black-Scholes formula for the value of the call option, the formula simplifies considerably to[14]

$$\text{MV(Perfect timer per \$ of assets)} = C = 2N(\tfrac{1}{2}\, \sigma_M \sqrt{T}) - 1 \qquad \textbf{(18.3)}$$

---

[13] The analogy between market timing and call options, and the valuation formulas that follow from it, were developed in Robert C. Merton, "On Market Timing and Investment Performance: An Equilibrium Theory of Value for Market Forecasts," *Journal of Business*, July 1981.

[14] Substitute $S_0 = \$1$ for the current value of the equity portfolio and $X = \$1 \times e^{rT}$ in Equation 16.1 of Chapter 16, and you will obtain Equation 18.3.

We have so far assumed annual forecasts, that is, $T = 1$ year. Using $T = 1$, and the standard deviation of stocks from Table 18.5, 19.97%, we compute the value of this call option as 7.95 cents, or 7.95% of the value of the equity portfolio.[15]

The Value of Imperfect Forecasting

A weather forecaster in Tucson, Arizona, who *always* predicts no rain may be right 90% of the time. But a high success rate for a "stopped-clock" strategy is not evidence of forecasting ability. Similarly, the appropriate measure of market forecasting ability is not the overall proportion of correct forecasts. If the market is up two days out of three and a forecaster *always* predicts market advance, the resulting two-thirds success rate does not imply forecasting ability. We need to separately examine the proportion of bull markets ($r_M > r_f$) correctly forecast *and* the proportion of bear markets ($r_M < r_f$) correctly forecast.

If we call P_1 the proportion of the correct forecasts of bull markets and P_2 the proportion for bear markets, then $P_1 + P_2 - 1$ is the correct measure of timing ability. For example, a forecaster who always guesses correctly will have $P_1 = P_2 = 1$, and will show ability of $P_1 + P_2 - 1 = 1$ (100%). An analyst who always bets on a bear market will mispredict all bull markets ($P_1 = 0$), will correctly "predict" all bear markets ($P_2 = 1$), and will end up with timing ability of $P_1 + P_2 - 1 = 0$.

CONCEPT Check **18.3**	What is the market-timing score of someone who flips a fair coin to predict the market?

Merton shows that the value of imperfect market timing is equal to a portion of a call option. The value of an imperfect timer is simply the value of the perfect-timing call times our measure of timing ability, $P_1 + P_2 - 1$.[16]

$$\text{MV}(\text{Imperfect timer}) = (P_1 + P_2 - 1) \times C = (P_1 + P_2 - 1)\left[2N(\tfrac{1}{2}\sigma_M\sqrt{T}) - 1\right] \quad \textbf{(18.4)}$$

The incredible potential payoff to accurate timing versus the relative scarcity of billionaires suggests that market timing is far from a trivial exercise and that very imperfect timing is the most we can hope for.

18.6 PERFORMANCE ATTRIBUTION PROCEDURES

Rather than focus on risk-adjusted returns, practitioners often want simply to ascertain which decisions resulted in superior or inferior performance. Superior investment performance depends on an ability to be in the "right" securities at the right time. Such timing and selection ability may be considered broadly, such as being in equities as opposed to fixed-income securities when the stock market is performing well. Or it may be defined at a more detailed level, such as choosing the relatively better-performing stocks within a particular industry.

Portfolio managers continually make broad-brush asset allocation decisions as well as more detailed sector and security allocation decisions within asset classes. Performance attribution studies attempt to decompose overall performance into discrete components that may be identified with a particular level of the portfolio selection process.

Attribution analysis starts from the broadest asset allocation choices and progressively focuses on ever-finer details of portfolio choice. The difference between a managed portfolio's performance and that of a benchmark portfolio then may be expressed as the sum

---

[15] This is less than the historical-average excess return of perfect timing shown in Table 18.5, reflecting the fact that the actual value of timing is sensitive to fat tails in the distribution of returns, whereas Black-Scholes assumes a lognormal distribution.

[16] Notice that Equation 24.5 implies that an investor with a value of $P = 0$ who attempts to time the market would add zero value. The shifts across markets would be no better than a random decision concerning asset allocation.

of the contributions to performance of a series of decisions made at the various levels of the portfolio construction process. For example, one common attribution system decomposes performance into three components: (1) broad asset market allocation choices across equity, fixed-income, and money markets; (2) industry (sector) choice within each market; and (3) security choice within each sector.

The attribution method explains the difference in returns between a managed portfolio, *P*, and a selected benchmark portfolio, *B*, called the **bogey.** The bogey is designed to measure the returns the portfolio manager would earn if he or she were to follow a completely passive strategy. "Passive" in this context has two attributes. First, it means that the allocation of funds across broad asset classes is set in accord with a notion of "usual," or neutral, allocation across sectors. This would be considered a passive asset-market allocation. Second, it means that *within* each asset class, the portfolio manager holds an indexed portfolio, such as the S&P 500 index for the equity sector. In such a manner, the passive strategy used as a performance benchmark rules out asset allocation as well as security selection decisions. Any departure of the manager's return from the passive benchmark must be due to either asset allocation bets (departures from the neutral allocation across markets) or security selection bets (departures from the passive index within asset classes).

bogey
The benchmark portfolio an investment manager is compared to for performance evaluation.

While we have already discussed in earlier chapters the justification for indexing within sectors, it is worth briefly explaining the determination of the neutral allocation of funds across the broad asset classes. Weights that are designated as "neutral" will depend on the risk tolerance of the investor and must be determined in consultation with the client. For example, risk-tolerant clients may place a large fraction of their portfolio in the equity market, perhaps directing the fund manager to set neutral weights of 75% equity, 15% bonds, and 10% cash equivalents. Any deviation from these weights must be justified by a belief that one or another market will either over- or underperform its usual risk–return profile. In contrast, more risk-averse clients may set neutral weights of 45%/35%/20% for the three markets. Therefore, their portfolios in normal circumstances will be exposed to less risk than that of the risk-tolerant client. Only intentional bets on market performance will result in departures from this profile.

To illustrate, consider the attribution results for a hypothetical portfolio. The portfolio invests in stocks, bonds, and money market securities. An attribution analysis appears in Tables 18.6 through 18.9. The portfolio return over the month is 5.34%.

In Table 18.6, the neutral weights have been set at 60% equity, 30% fixed income, and 10% cash (money market securities). The bogey portfolio, comprised of investments in each index with the 60/30/10 weights, returned 3.97%. The managed portfolio's performance is positive and equal to its actual return less the return of the bogey: 5.34 − 3.97 = 1.37%. The next step is to allocate the 1.37% excess return to the separate decisions that contributed to it.

TABLE 18.6 Performance of the managed portfolio

Bogey Performance and Excess Return		
Component	Benchmark Weight	Return of Index during Month (%)
Equity (S&P 500)	0.60	5.81
Bonds (Barclays Aggregate Index)	0.30	1.45
Cash (money market)	0.10	0.48
Bogey = (0.60 × 5.81) + (0.30 × 1.45) + (0.10 × 0.48) = 3.97%		
Return of managed portfolio		5.34%
−Return of bogey portfolio		3.97
Excess return of managed portfolio		1.37%

TABLE 18.7 Performance attribution

A. Contribution of Asset Allocation to Performance

Market	(1) Actual Weight in Market	(2) Benchmark Weight in Market	(3) Active or Excess Weight	(4) Index Return (%)	(5) = (3) × (4) Contribution to Performance (%)
Equity	0.70	0.60	0.10	5.81	0.5810
Fixed-income	0.07	0.30	−0.23	1.45	−0.3335
Cash	0.23	0.10	0.13	0.48	0.0624
Contribution of asset allocation					0.3099

B. Contribution of Selection to Total Performance

Market	(1) Portfolio Performance (%)	(2) Index Performance (%)	(3) Excess Performance (%)	(4) Portfolio Weight	(5) = (3) × (4) Contribution (%)
Equity	7.28	5.81	1.47	0.70	1.03
Fixed-income	1.89	1.45	0.44	0.07	0.03
Contribution of selection within markets					1.06

Asset Allocation Decisions

Table 18.7 shows that in this month, the manager established asset allocation weights of 70% in equity, 7% in fixed income, and 23% in cash equivalents. To isolate the effect of this departure from neutral asset allocation, we compare the performance of a hypothetical portfolio that would have been invested in a passive index for each market with weights 70/7/23 versus one invested in each index using the benchmark 60/30/10 weights. This return difference measures the effect of the shift away from the benchmark weights without allowing for any effects attributable to active management of the securities selected within each market.

Superior performance relative to the bogey is achieved by overweighting investments in markets that turn out to perform well and by underweighting those in poorly performing markets. The contribution of asset allocation to superior performance equals the sum over all markets of the excess weight (sometimes called the *active weight* in the industry) in each market times the return of the index for each market.

Panel A of Table 18.7 demonstrates that asset allocation contributed 31 basis points to the portfolio's overall excess return of 137 basis points. The major factor contributing to superior performance in this month is the heavy weighting on equity in a month when the equity market has an excellent return of 5.81%.

Sector and Security Selection Decisions

If 0.31% of the excess performance (Table 18.7, Panel A) can be attributed to advantageous asset allocation *across* markets, the remaining 1.06% must be attributable to sector selection and security selection *within* each market. Table 18.7, Panel B, details the contribution of the managed portfolio's sector and security selection to total performance.

Panel B shows that the equity component of the managed portfolio has a return of 7.28% versus a return of 5.81% for the S&P 500. The fixed-income return is 1.89% versus 1.45% for the Barclays Aggregate Bond Index. The superior performance in both equity and fixed-income markets weighted by the portfolio proportions invested in each market sums to the 1.06% contribution to performance attributable to sector and security selection.

The performance attribution spreadsheet develops the attribution analysis presented in this section. The model can be used to analyze the performance of mutual funds and other managed portfolios.

Spreadsheets are
available in Connect

	A	B	C	D	E	F
1	**Performance Attribution**					
2						
3						
4	**Bogey**					
5	**Portfolio**		**Benchmark**	**Return on**	**Portfolio**	
6	**Component**	**Index**	**Weight**	**Index**	**Return**	
7	Equity	S&P 500	0.60	5.8100%	3.4860%	
8	Bonds	Barclays Index	0.30	1.4500%	0.4350%	
9	Cash	Money Market	0.10	0.4800%	0.0480%	
10			Return on Bogey		3.9690%	
11						
12		**Managed**				
13		**Portfolio**	**Portfolio**	**Actual**	**Portfolio**	
14		**Component**	**Weight**	**Return**	**Return**	
15		Equity	0.70	7.2800%	5.0960%	
16		Bonds	0.07	1.8900%	0.1323%	
17		Cash	0.23	0.4800%	0.1104%	
18			Return on Managed		5.3387%	
19			Excess Return		1.3697%	

You can find this Excel model in Connect.

Excel Questions

1. What would happen to the contribution of asset allocation to overall performance if the actual weights had been 75/12/13 instead of 70/7/23? Explain your result.

2. What would happen to the contribution of security selection to overall performance if the actual return on the equity portfolio had been 8.28% instead of 7.28% and the return on the bond portfolio had been .89% instead of 1.89%? Explain your result.

Table 18.8 documents the decisions that led to the superior equity market performance. The first three columns detail the allocation of funds within the equity market compared to their representation in the S&P 500. Column (4) shows the rate of return of each sector. The contribution of each sector's allocation presented in column (5) equals the product of the difference in the sector weight and the sector's performance.

Good performance (a positive contribution) derives from overweighting well-performing sectors such as consumer noncyclicals. The excess return of the equity component of the portfolio attributable to sector allocation alone is 1.29%. Table 18.7, Panel B, column (3), shows that the equity component of the portfolio outperformed the S&P 500 by 1.47%. We conclude that the effect of security selection *within* sectors must have contributed an additional 1.47% − 1.29%, or 0.18%, to the performance of the equity component of the portfolio.

A similar sector analysis can be applied to the fixed-income portion of the portfolio, but we do not show those results here.

Summing Up Component Contributions

In this particular month, all facets of the portfolio selection process were successful. Table 18.9 details the contribution of each aspect of performance. Asset allocation across the major security markets contributes 31 basis points. Sector and security allocation within those markets contributes 106 basis points, for total excess portfolio performance of 137 basis points.

TABLE 18.8 Sector selection within the equity market

	(1)	(2)	(3)	(4)	(5) = (3) × (4)
	Beginning of Month Weights (%)				
Sector	**Portfolio**	**S&P 500**	**Active Weight (%)**	**Sector Return (%)**	**Sector Allocation Contribution**
Basic materials	1.96	8.3	−6.34	6.9	−0.4375
Business services	7.84	4.1	3.74	7.0	0.2618
Capital goods	1.87	7.8	−5.93	4.1	−0.2431
Consumer cyclical	8.47	12.5	−4.03	8.8	0.3546
Consumer noncyclical	40.37	20.4	19.97	10.0	1.9970
Credit sensitive	24.01	21.8	2.21	5.0	0.1105
Energy	13.53	14.2	−0.67	2.6	−0.0174
Technology	1.95	10.9	−8.95	0.3	−0.0269
Total					1.2898

TABLE 18.9 Portfolio attribution: summary

		Contribution (basis points)
1. Asset allocation		31
2. Selection		
a. Equity excess return (basis points)		
i. Sector allocation	129	
ii. Security selection	18	
	147 × 0.70 (portfolio weight) =	102.9
b. Fixed-income excess return	44 × 0.07 (portfolio weight) =	3.1
Total excess return of portfolio		137.0

The sector and security allocation of 106 basis points can be partitioned further. Sector allocation within the equity market results in excess performance of 129 basis points, and security selection within sectors contributes 18 basis points. (The total equity excess performance of 147 basis points is multiplied by the 70% weight in equity to obtain contribution to portfolio performance.) Similar partitioning could be done for the fixed-income sector.

CONCEPT check 18.4

a. Suppose the benchmark weights in Table 18.7 had been set at 70% equity, 25% fixed-income, and 5% cash equivalents. What would have been the contributions of the manager's asset allocation choices?

b. Suppose the S&P 500 return is 5%. Compute the new value of the manager's security selection choices.

- The simplest performance measure compares average return to that on a benchmark such as an appropriate market index or even the median return of funds in a comparison universe. Alternative measures of the average return include the arithmetic and geometric average and time-weighted versus dollar-weighted returns.
- The appropriate risk-adjusted performance measure depends on the role of the portfolio to be evaluated. Appropriate performance measures are as follows:
  - Sharpe: When the portfolio represents the entire investment fund.
  - Treynor: When the portfolio represents one subportfolio of many.
  - Information ratio: When the portfolio represents an active portfolio to be optimally mixed with the passive portfolio.
  - Jensen (alpha): All of these measures require a positive alpha for the portfolio to be considered attractive.
- Style analysis uses a multiple regression model where the factors are category (style) portfolios such as bills, bonds, and stocks. The coefficients on the style portfolios indicate an implicit asset allocation that matches the risk exposures of the managed portfolio. The difference in returns between the managed portfolio and the matching portfolio measures performance relative to similar-style funds.
- Shifting mean and risk of actively managed portfolios make it difficult to assess performance. An important example of this problem arises when portfolio managers attempt to time the market, resulting in ever-changing portfolio betas.
- A simple way to measure timing and selection success simultaneously is to estimate an expanded security characteristic line for which the slope (beta) coefficient is allowed to increase as the market return increases. Another way to evaluate timers is based on the implicit call option embedded in their performance.
- Common attribution procedures decompose portfolio performance to asset allocation, sector selection, and security selection decisions. Performance is assessed by calculating departures of portfolio composition from a benchmark or neutral portfolio.

bogey, 601
comparison universe, 582
dollar-weighted rate of
   return, 582

information ratio, 584
Jensen's alpha, 584
market timing, 596
Sharpe ratio, 584

survivorship bias, 592
time-weighted average, 581
Treynor's measure, 584

Geometric time-weighted return: $1 + r_G = [(1 + r_1)(1 + r_2) \cdots (1 + r_n)]^{1/n}$

Sharpe ratio: $S_P = \dfrac{r_P - r_f}{\sigma_P}$

M^2 of portfolio P given its Sharpe ratio: $M^2 = \sigma_M(S_P - S_M)$

Treynor's measure: $T_P = \dfrac{r_P - r_f}{\beta_P}$

Jensen's alpha: $\alpha_P = \bar{r}_P - [\bar{r}_f + \beta_P(\bar{r}_M - \bar{r}_f)]$

Information ratio: $\dfrac{\alpha_P}{\sigma(e_P)}$

PROBLEM SETS   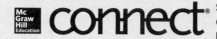   Select problems are available in McGraw-Hill's
Connect. Please see the Supplements section of the
book's frontmatter for more information.

1. A household savings-account spreadsheet shows the following entries for the first day of
   each month:

Month	Additions	Withdrawals	Value
January			148,000
February	2,500		
March	4,000		
April	1,500		
May	13,460		
June		23,000	
July	3,000		
August			198,000

   Calculate the household's monthly dollar-weighted average return for this period.
   (LO 18-1)

2. Is it possible for a positive alpha to be associated with inferior performance? Explain.
   (LO 18-2)

3. We know that the geometric average (time-weighted return) on a risky investment is
   always lower than the corresponding arithmetic average. Can the internal rate of return
   (IRR; the dollar-weighted return) similarly be ranked relative to these other two averages?
   (LO 18-1)

4. Suppose the value of your portfolio will either double or fall with equal probability in
   any particular year.
   a. What is the expected value of the portfolio after one year?
   b. What is the expected value of the arithmetic average return on the portfolio?
   c. What is the expected value of the geometric average rate of return?
   d. In light of the answer to part (*a*), would you consider the arithmetic or geometric
   return more informative for performance evaluation?   *(LO 18-1)*

5. Consider the rate of return of stocks ABC and XYZ.

Year	r_{ABC}	r_{XYZ}
1	20%	30%
2	12	12
3	14	18
4	3	0
5	1	−10

   a. Calculate the arithmetic average return on these stocks over the sample period.
   b. Which stock has greater dispersion around the mean return?
   c. Calculate the geometric average returns of each stock. What do you conclude?
   d. If you were equally likely to earn a return of 20%, 12%, 14%, 3%, or 1% in each year
   (these are the five annual returns for stock ABC), what would be your expected rate
   of return?
   e. What if the five possible outcomes were those of stock XYZ?
   f. Given your answers to parts (*d*) and (*e*), which measure of average return, arithmetic
   or geometric, appears more useful for predicting future performance?   *(LO 18-1)*

6. XYZ's stock price and dividend history are as follows:

Year	Beginning-of-Year Price	Dividend Paid at Year-End
2017	$100	$4
2018	120	4
2019	90	4
2020	100	4

An investor buys three shares of XYZ at the beginning of 2017, buys another two shares at the beginning of 2018, sells one share at the beginning of 2019, and sells all four remaining shares at the beginning of 2020.

a. What are the arithmetic and geometric average time-weighted rates of return for the investor?

b. What is the dollar-weighted rate of return? (*Hint:* Carefully prepare a chart of cash flows for the *four* dates corresponding to the turns of the year for January 1, 2017, to January 1, 2020. If your calculator cannot calculate IRR, you will have to use trial and error or a spreadsheet program.)   *(LO 18-1)*

7. A manager buys three shares of stock today and then sells one of those shares each year for the next three years. His actions and the price history of the stock are summarized below. The stock pays no dividends.

Time	Price	Action
0	$ 90	Buy 3 shares
1	100	Sell 1 share
2	100	Sell 1 share
3	100	Sell 1 share

a. Calculate the time-weighted geometric average return on this portfolio.

b. Calculate the time-weighted arithmetic average return on this portfolio.

c. Calculate the dollar-weighted average return on this portfolio.   *(LO 18-1)*

8. Based on current dividend yields and expected capital gains, the expected rates of return on portfolios A and B are 12% and 16%, respectively. The beta of A is 0.7, while that of B is 1.4. The T-bill rate is currently 5%, whereas the expected rate of return of the S&P 500 index is 13%. The standard deviation of portfolio A is 12% annually, that of B is 31%, and that of the S&P 500 index is 18%.

a. If you currently hold a market-index portfolio, would you choose to add either of these portfolios to your holdings? Explain.

b. If instead you could invest *only* in T-bills and *one* of these portfolios, which would you choose?   *(LO 18-2)*

9. Consider the two (excess return) index-model regression results for stocks A and B. The risk-free rate over the period was 6%, and the market's average return was 14%. Performance is measured using an index model regression on excess returns.

	Stock A	Stock B
Index model regression estimates	$1\% + 1.2(r_M - r_f)$	$2\% + 0.8(r_M - r_f)$
R-square	0.576	0.436
Residual standard deviation, $\sigma(e)$	10.3%	19.1%
Standard deviation of excess returns	21.6%	24.9%

a. Calculate the following statistics for each stock:
   i. Alpha
   ii. Information ratio
   iii. Sharpe ratio
   iv. Treynor's measure

    b. Which stock is the best choice under the following circumstances?

      i. This is the only risky asset to be held by the investor.

      ii. This stock will be mixed with the rest of the investor's portfolio, currently composed solely of holdings in the market-index fund.

      iii. This is one of many stocks that the investor is analyzing to form an actively managed stock portfolio.   **(LO 18-2)**

10. Evaluate the market timing and security selection abilities of four managers whose performances are plotted in the accompanying diagrams.   **(LO 18-5)**

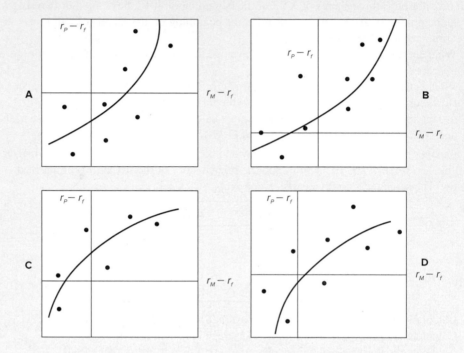

11. Consider the following information regarding the performance of a money manager in a recent month. The table represents the actual return of each sector of the manager's portfolio in column 1, the fraction of the portfolio allocated to each sector in column 2, the benchmark or neutral sector allocations in column 3, and the returns of sector indices in column 4.

	Actual Return	Actual Weight	Benchmark Weight	Index Return
Equity	2%	0.70	0.60	2.5% (S&P 500)
Bonds	1	0.20	0.30	1.2 (Barclay's Aggregate)
Cash	0.5	0.10	0.10	0.5

    a. What was the manager's return in the month? What was her overperformance or underperformance?

    b. What was the contribution of security selection to relative performance?

    c. What was the contribution of asset allocation to relative performance? Confirm that the sum of selection and allocation contributions equals her total "excess" return relative to the bogey. **(LO 18-4)**

12. A global equity manager is assigned to select stocks from a universe of large stocks throughout the world. The manager will be evaluated by comparing her returns to the return on the MSCI World Market Portfolio, but she is free to hold stocks from various

countries in whatever proportions she finds desirable. Results for a given month are contained in the following table:

Country	Weight in MSCI Index	Manager's Weight	Manager's Return in Country	Return of Stock Index for That Country
U.K.	0.15	0.30	20%	12%
Japan	0.30	0.10	15	15
U.S.	0.45	0.40	10	14
Germany	0.10	0.20	5	12

 a. Calculate the total value added of all the manager's decisions this period.
 b. Calculate the value added (or subtracted) by her *country* allocation decisions.
 c. Calculate the value added from her stock selection ability within countries.
 d. Confirm that the sum of the contributions to value added from her country allocation plus security selection decisions equals total over- or underperformance.   *(LO 18-4)*

13. Conventional wisdom says that one should measure a manager's investment performance over an entire market cycle. What arguments support this convention? What arguments contradict it?   *(LO 18-2)*

14. Does the use of universes of managers with similar investment styles to evaluate relative investment performance overcome the statistical problems associated with instability of beta or total variability?   *(LO 18-2)*

15. During a particular year, the T-bill rate was 6%, the market return was 14%, and a portfolio manager with beta of 0.5 realized a return of 10%.
 a. Evaluate the manager based on the portfolio alpha.
 b. Reconsider your answer to part (*a*) in view of the empirical finding that the security market line is too flat (see Chapter 7). Now how do you assess the manager's performance?   *(LO 18-2)*

16. Bill Smith is evaluating the performance of four large-cap equity portfolios: Funds *A*, *B*, *C*, and *D*. As part of his analysis, Smith computed the Sharpe ratio and Treynor's measure for all four funds. Based on his finding, the ranks assigned to the four funds are as follows:

Fund	Treynor Measure Rank	Sharpe Ratio Rank
A	1	4
B	2	3
C	3	2
D	4	1

The difference in rankings for Funds *A* and *D* is most likely due to:
 a. A lack of diversification in Fund *A* as compared to Fund *D*.
 b. Different benchmarks used to evaluate each fund's performance.
 c. A difference in risk premiums.   *(LO 18-2)*

Use the following information to answer Problems 17 through 20: Primo Management Co. is looking at how best to evaluate the performance of its managers. Primo has been hearing more and more about benchmark portfolios and is interested in trying this approach. As such, the company hired Sally Jones, CFA, as a consultant to educate the managers on the best methods for constructing a benchmark portfolio, how to choose the best benchmark, whether the style of the fund under management matters, and what they should do with their global funds in terms of benchmarking.

For the sake of discussion, Jones put together some comparative two-year performance numbers that relate to Primo's current domestic funds under management and a potential benchmark.

	Weight		Return	
Style Category	Primo	Benchmark	Primo	Benchmark
Large-cap growth	0.60	0.50	17%	16%
Mid-cap growth	0.15	0.40	24	26
Small-cap growth	0.25	0.10	20	18

As part of her analysis, Jones also takes a look at one of Primo's global funds. In this particular portfolio, Primo is invested 75% in Dutch stocks and 25% in British stocks. The benchmark is invested 50% in Dutch and and 50% in British stocks. On average, the British stocks outperformed the Dutch stocks. The euro appreciated 6% versus the U.S. dollar over the holding period while the pound depreciated 2% versus the dollar. In terms of the local return, Primo outperformed the benchmark with the Dutch investments, but underperformed the index with respect to the British stocks.

17. What is the within-sector selection effect for each individual sector? *(LO 18-4)*

18. Calculate the amount by which the Primo portfolio out-(under-)performed the market over the period, as well as the contribution to performance of the pure sector allocation and security selection decisions. *(LO 18-4)*

19. If Primo decides to use return-based style analysis, will the R^2 of the regression equation of a passively managed fund be higher or lower than that of an actively managed fund? *(LO 18-3)*

20. Which of the following statements about Primo's global fund is most correct? Primo appears to have a positive currency allocation effect as well as
   a. A negative market allocation effect and a positive security allocation effect.
   b. A negative market allocation effect and a negative security allocation effect.
   c. A positive market allocation effect and a negative security allocation effect. *(L 18-5)*

21. Kelli Blakely is a portfolio manager for the Miranda Fund, a core large-cap equity fund. The market proxy and benchmark for performance measurement purposes is the S&P 500. Although the Miranda portfolio generally mirrors the asset class and sector weightings of the S&P, Blakely is allowed a significant amount of leeway in managing the fund. However, her portfolio holds only stocks found in the S&P 500 and cash.

   Blakely was able to produce exceptional returns last year (as outlined in the table below) through her market timing and security selection skills. At the outset of the year, she became extremely concerned that the combination of a weak economy and geopolitical uncertainties would negatively impact the market. Taking a bold step, she changed her market allocation. For the entire year her asset class exposures averaged 50% in stocks and 50% in cash. The S&P's allocation between stocks and cash during the period was a constant 97% and 3%, respectively. The risk-free rate of return was 2%.

One-Year Trailing Returns		
	Miranda Fund	S&P 500
Return	10.2%	−22.5%
Standard deviation	37%	44%
Beta	1.10	1.00

   a. What are the Sharpe ratios for the Miranda Fund and the S&P 500?
   b. What are the M^2 measures for Miranda and the S&P 500?
   c. What is the Treynor's measure for the Miranda Fund and the S&P 500?
   d. What is the Jensen measure for the Miranda Fund? *(LO 18-2)*

22. Go to Kenneth French's data library site at **http://mba.tuck.dartmouth.edu/pages/ faculty/ken.french/data_library.html**. Select two industry portfolios of your choice and download 36 months of data. Download other data from the site as needed to perform the following tasks.

   a. Compare the portfolio's performance to that of the market index on the basis of the Sharpe, Jensen, Treynor measures as well as the information ratio. Plot the monthly values of alpha plus residual return.

   b. Now use the Fama-French (FF) three-factor model (see Chapter 7) as the return benchmark. Compute plots of alpha plus residual return using the FF model. How does performance change using this benchmark instead of the market index? *(LO 18-2)*

CFA Problems

1. You and a prospective client are considering the measurement of investment performance, particularly with respect to international portfolios for the past five years. The data you discussed are presented in the following table:

International Manager or Index	Total Return	Country and Security Return	Currency Return
Manager A	−6.0%	2.0%	−8.0%
Manager B	−2.0	−1.0	−1.0
International Index	−5.0	0.2	−5.2

   a. Assume that the data for manager A and manager B accurately reflect their investment skills and that both managers actively manage currency exposure. Briefly describe one strength and one weakness for each manager.

   b. Recommend and justify a strategy that would enable your fund to take advantage of the strengths of each of the two managers while minimizing their weaknesses. *(LO 18-4)*

2. Carl Karl, a portfolio manager for the Alpine Trust Company, has been responsible since 2020 for the City of Alpine's Employee Retirement Plan, a municipal pension fund. Alpine is a growing community, and city services and employee payrolls have expanded in each of the past 10 years. Contributions to the plan in fiscal 2025 exceeded benefit payments by a three-to-one ratio.

   The plan board of trustees directed Karl five years ago to invest for total return over the long term. However, as trustees of this highly visible public fund, they cautioned him that volatile or erratic results could cause them embarrassment. They also noted a state statute that mandated that not more than 25% of the plan's assets (at cost) be invested in common stocks.

   At the annual meeting of the trustees in November 2025, Karl presented the following portfolio and performance report to the board:

ALPINE EMPLOYEE RETIREMENT PLAN

Asset Mix as of 9/30/25	At Cost (millions)		At Market (millions)	
Fixed-income assets:				
Short-term securities	$ 4.5	11.0%	$ 4.5	11.4%
Long-term bonds and mortgages	26.5	64.7	23.5	59.5
Common stocks	10.0	24.3	11.5	29.1
	$41.0	100.0%	$39.5	100.0%

INVESTMENT PERFORMANCE

	Annual Rates of Return for Periods Ending 9/30/25	
	5 Years	1 Year
Total Alpine Fund:		
Time-weighted	8.2%	5.2%
Dollar-weighted (internal)	7.7%	4.8%
Assumed actuarial return	6.0%	6.0%
U.S. Treasury bills	7.5%	11.3%
Large sample of pension funds (average 60% equities, 40% fixed income)	10.1%	14.3%
Common stocks—Alpine Fund	13.3%	14.3%
Alpine portfolio beta coefficient	0.90	0.89
Standard & Poor's 500 stock index	13.8%	21.1%
Fixed-income securities—Alpine Fund	6.7%	1.0%
Broad Investment Grade bond index	4.0%	−11.4%

Karl was proud of his performance and was chagrined when a trustee made the following critical observations:

    a. "Our one-year results were terrible, and it's what you've done for us lately that counts most."

    b. "Our total fund performance was clearly inferior compared to the large sample of other pension funds for the last five years. What else could this reflect except poor management judgment?"

    c. "Our common stock performance was especially poor for the five-year period."

    d. "Why bother to compare your returns to the return from Treasury bills and the actuarial assumption rate? What your competition could have earned for us or how we would have fared if invested in a passive index (which doesn't charge a fee) are the only relevant measures of performance."

    e. "Who cares about time-weighted return? If it can't pay pensions, what good is it?" Appraise the merits of each of these statements and give counterarguments that Mr. Karl can use. *(LO 18-1)*

3. The Retired Fund is an open-ended mutual fund composed of $500 million in U.S. bonds and U.S. Treasury bills. This fund has had a portfolio duration (including T-bills) of between three and nine years. Retired has shown first-quartile performance over the past five years, as measured by an independent fixed-income measurement service. However, the directors of the fund would like to measure the market timing skill of the fund's sole bond investor manager. An external consulting firm has suggested the following three methods:

    a. Method I examines the value of the bond portfolio at the beginning of every year, then calculates the return that would have been achieved had that same portfolio been held throughout the year. This return would then be compared with the return actually obtained by the fund.

    b. Method II calculates the average weighting of the portfolio in bonds and T-bills for each year. Instead of using the actual bond portfolio, the return on a long-bond market index and T-bill index would be used. For example, if the portfolio on average was 65% in bonds and 35% in T-bills, the annual return on a portfolio invested 65% in a long-bond index and 35% in T-bills would be calculated. This return is compared with the annual return that would have been generated using the indexes and the manager's actual bond/T-bill weighting for each quarter of the year.

    c. Method III examines the net bond purchase activity (market value of purchases less sales) for each quarter of the year. If net purchases were positive (negative) in any quarter, the performance of the bonds would be evaluated until the net purchase activity became negative (positive). Positive (negative) net purchases would be viewed as a bullish (bearish) view taken by the manager. The correctness of this view would be measured.

Critique *each* method with regard to market-timing measurement problems. *(LO 18-1)*

Use the following data to solve CFA Problems 4 and 5: The administrator of a large pension fund wants to evaluate the performance of four portfolio managers. Each portfolio manager invests only in U.S. common stocks. Assume that during the most recent five-year period, the average annual total rate of return including dividends on the S&P 500 was 14%, and the average nominal rate of return on government Treasury bills was 8%. The following table shows risk and return measures for each portfolio:

Portfolio	Average Annual Rate of Return	Standard Deviation	Beta
P	17%	20%	1.1
Q	24	18	2.1
R	11	10	0.5
S	16	14	1.5
S&P 500	14	12	1.0

4. What is the Treynor performance measure for portfolio P? *(LO 18-2)*
5. What is the Sharpe performance measure for portfolio Q? *(LO 18-2)*
6. An analyst wants to evaluate portfolio X, consisting entirely of U.S. common stocks, using both the Treynor and Sharpe measures of portfolio performance. The following table provides the average annual rate of return for portfolio X, the market portfolio (as measured by the S&P 500), and U.S. Treasury bills during the past eight years:

	Average Annual Rate of Return	Standard Deviation of Return	Beta
Portfolio X	10%	18%	0.60
S&P 500	12	13	1.00
T-bills	6	N/A	N/A

a. Calculate the Treynor and Sharpe measures for both portfolio X and the S&P 500. Briefly explain whether portfolio X underperformed, equaled, or outperformed the S&P 500 on a risk-adjusted basis using both the Treynor's measure and the Sharpe ratio.
b. On the basis of the performance of portfolio X relative to the S&P 500 calculated in part (a), briefly explain the reason for the conflicting results when using Treynor's measure versus the Sharpe ratio. *(LO 18-2)*

7. Assume you invested in an asset for two years. The first year you earned a 15% return, and the second year you earned a negative 10% return. What was your annual geometric return? *(LO 18-1)*

8. A portfolio of stocks generates a −9% return in 2017, a 23% return in 2018, and a 17% return in 2019. What is the annualized return (geometric mean) for the entire period? *(LO 18-1)*

9. A two-year investment of $2,000 results in a cash flow of $150 at the end of the first year and another cash flow of $150 at the end of the second year, in addition to the return of the original investment. What is the IRR on the investment? *(LO 18-1)*

10. In measuring the performance of a portfolio, the time-weighted rate of return is superior to the dollar-weighted rate of return because:
a. When the rate of return varies, the time-weighted return is higher.
b. The dollar-weighted return assumes all portfolio deposits are made on day 1.
c. The dollar-weighted return can only be estimated.
d. The time-weighted return is unaffected by the timing of portfolio contributions and withdrawals. *(LO 18-1)*

11. A pension fund portfolio begins with $500,000 and earns 15% the first year and 10% the second year. At the beginning of the second year, the sponsor contributed another $500,000. What were the time-weighted and dollar-weighted rates of return? *(LO 18-1)*

12. During the annual review of Acme's pension plan, several trustees questioned their investment consultant about various aspects of performance measurement and risk assessment.
    a. Comment on the appropriateness of using each of the following benchmarks for performance evaluation:
       - Market index.
       - Benchmark normal portfolio.
       - Median of the manager universe.
    b. Distinguish among the following performance measures:
       - The Sharpe ratio.
       - Treynor's measure.
       - Jensen's alpha.
         i. Describe how each of the three performance measures is calculated.
         ii. State whether each measure assumes that the relevant risk is systematic, unsystematic, or total. Explain how each measure relates excess return and the relevant risk. *(LO 18-2)*

13. Trustees of the Pallor Corp. pension plan ask consultant Donald Millip to comment on the following statements. What should his response be?
    a. Median manager benchmarks are statistically unbiased measures of performance over long periods of time.
    b. Median manager benchmarks are unambiguous and are therefore easily replicated by managers wishing to adopt a passive/indexed approach.
    c. Median manager benchmarks are not appropriate in all circumstances because the median manager universe encompasses nonuniform investment styles. *(LO 18-1)*

14. James Chan is reviewing the performance of the global equity managers of the Jarvis University endowment fund. Williamson Capital is currently the endowment fund's only large-capitalization global equity manager. Performance data for Williamson Capital are shown in Table 18.10.

TABLE 18.10 Williamson Capital performance data, 2007–2018

Average annual rate of return	22.1%
Beta	1.2
Standard deviation of returns	16.8%

Chan also presents the endowment fund's investment committee with performance information for Joyner Asset Management, which is another large-capitalization global equity manager. Performance data for Joyner Asset Management are shown in Table 18.11. Performance data for the relevant risk-free asset and market index are shown in Table 18.12.

TABLE 18.11 Joyner Asset Management performance data, 2007–2018

Average annual rate of return	24.2%
Beta	0.8
Standard deviation of returns	20.2%

TABLE 18.12 Risk-free asset and market index performance data, 2007–2018

Risk-Free Asset	
Average annual rate of return	5.0%
Market Index	
Average annual rate of returns	18.9%
Standard deviation of returns	13.8%

a. Calculate the Sharpe ratio and Treynor's measure for both Williamson Capital and Joyner Asset Management.

b. The investment committee notices that using the Sharpe ratio versus Treynor's measure produces different performance rankings of Williamson and Joyner. Explain why these criteria may result in different rankings. *(LO 18-2)*

Morningstar has an extensive ranking system for mutual funds, including a screening program that allows you to select funds based on a number of factors. Open the Morningstar website at **www.morningstar.com** and click on the *Funds* link. Select the *Mutual Fund Quickrank* link in the Performance section. (Free registration is required to access the site.) Use the Quickrank screener to find a list of large growth stock funds with the highest one-year returns. Repeat the process to find the funds with the highest three-year returns. What fraction of funds appears on both lists?

Select three of the funds that appear on both lists. For each fund, click on the ticker symbol to get its Morningstar report and look in the Ratings & Risk section.

1. What is the fund's standard deviation?

2. What is the fund's Sharpe ratio?

3. What is the fund's Treynor's ratio?

4. What is the standard index? What is the best-fit index?

5. What are the beta and alpha coefficients using both the standard index and the best-fit index? How do these compare to the fund's parameters?

6. Look at the Management section of the report. Was the same manager in place for the entire 10-year period?

7. Are any of these funds of interest to you? How might your screening choices differ if you were choosing funds for various clients?

18.1

Time	Action	Cash Flow
0	Buy two shares	−40
1	Collect dividends; then sell one of the shares	4 + 22
2	Collect dividend on remaining share, then sell it	2 + 19

a. Dollar-weighted return:

$$-40 + \frac{26}{1+r} + \frac{21}{(1+r)^2} = 0$$

$$r = .1191, \text{ or } 11.91\%$$

b. Time-weighted return:

The rates of return on the stock in the two years were:

$$r_1 = \frac{2 + (22 - 20)}{20} = .20$$

$$r_2 = \frac{2 + (19 - 22)}{22} = -.0455$$

Arithmetic time-weighted return: $(r_1 + r_2)/2 = .0773$, or 7.73%

Geometric time-weighted return: $[(1 + r_1)(1 + r_2)]^{1/2} - 1 = .0702 = 7.02\%$

18.2 Sharpe: $(\bar{r} - \bar{r}_f)/\sigma$

$$S_P = (35 - 6)/42 = .69$$
$$S_M = (28 - 6)/30 = .733$$

Alpha: $\bar{r} - [\bar{r}_f + \beta(\bar{r}_M - \bar{r}_f)]$

$$\alpha_P = 35 - [6 + 1.2(28 - 6)] = 2.6$$
$$\alpha_M = 0$$

Treynor: $(\bar{r} - \bar{r}_f)/\beta$

$$T_P = (35 - 6)/1.2 = 24.2$$
$$T_M = (28 - 6)/1.0 = 22$$

Information ratio: $\alpha/\sigma(e)$

$$I_P = 2.6/18 = .144$$
$$I_M = 0$$

Therefore, portfolio P outperformed the market according to the Jensen and Treynor measures, but had an inferior Sharpe measure.

18.3 The timer will guess bear or bull markets completely randomly. One-half of all bull markets will be preceded by a correct forecast and similarly for bear markets. Hence $P_1 + P_2 - 1 = \frac{1}{2} + \frac{1}{2} - 1 = 0$.

18.4 First compute the new bogey performance as $(.70 \times 5.81) + (.25 \times 1.45) + (.05 \times .48) = 4.45$.

a. Contribution of asset allocation to performance:

Market	(1) Actual Weight in Market	(2) Benchmark Weight in Market	(3) Active or Excess Weight	(4) Market Return (%)	(5) = (3) × (4) Contribution to Performance (%)
Equity	0.70	0.70	0.00	5.81	0.00
Fixed-income	0.07	0.25	−0.18	1.45	−0.26
Cash	0.23	0.05	0.18	0.48	0.09
Contribution of asset allocation					−0.17

b. Contribution of selection to total performance:

Market	(1) Portfolio Performance (%)	(2) Index Performance (%)	(3) Excess Performance (%)	(4) Portfolio Weight	(5) = (3) × (4) Contribution (%)
Equity	7.28	5.00	2.28	0.70	1.60
Fixed-income	1.89	1.45	0.44	0.07	0.03
Contribution of selection within markets					1.63

International Diversification

Learning Objectives

LO 19-1 Understand the special issues that affect the efficacy of international diversification.

LO 19-2 Formulate hedge strategies to offset the currency risk involved in international investments.

LO 19-3 Implement international investment strategies.

LO 19-4 Understand the components of political risk in an international setting

LO 19-5 Decompose investment returns into contributing factors such as country, currency, and stock selection.

Although we in the United States customarily use a broad index of U.S. equities as the market-index portfolio, the practice is increasingly inappropriate. U.S. equities represent only about 40% of world equities and a far smaller fraction of total world wealth. In this chapter, we look beyond domestic markets to survey issues of international and extended diversification.

In one sense, international investing may be viewed as no more than a straightforward generalization of our earlier treatment of portfolio selection, with a larger menu of assets from which to construct a portfolio. Similar issues of diversification, security analysis, security selection, and asset allocation face the investor. On the other hand, international investments pose problems not encountered in domestic markets. Among these are the presence of exchange rate risk, restrictions on capital flows across national boundaries, an added dimension of political risk and country-specific regulations, and differing informational transparency in different countries. Therefore, in this chapter we review the major topics covered in the rest of the book, emphasizing their international aspects.

We begin with a brief description of international equity markets, pointing out the wide range of venues available to investors. We then turn to the central concepts of portfolio theory—risk and diversification. We will see how exchange rate fluctuations add another element to the uncertainty surrounding rates of return. However, global diversification offers opportunities for improving portfolio risk–return trade-offs. International investing also entails a range of political risks. We consider several of these risks as well as sources of information pertaining to them. Finally, we show how active asset allocation can be generalized to incorporate country and currency choices in addition to traditional domestic asset class choices and demonstrate performance attribution in an international context.

19.1 GLOBAL MARKETS FOR EQUITIES

You can easily invest today in the capital markets of nearly 100 countries and obtain up-to-date data about your investments in each of them. In 2017, more than 20 countries had stock markets with market capitalization above $100 billion.

U.S. investors have several avenues through which they can invest internationally. The most obvious method, which is available in practice primarily to larger institutional investors, is to purchase securities directly in the capital markets of other countries. However, even small investors can take advantage of several investment vehicles with an international focus.

Shares of several foreign firms are traded in U.S. markets either directly or in the form of American depositary receipts (ADRs). A U.S. financial institution such as a bank will purchase shares of a foreign firm in that firm's country and then issue claims to those shares in the United States. Each ADR is then a claim on a given number of the shares of stock held by the bank. Some stocks trade in the U.S. both directly and as ADRs.

There is also a wide array of mutual funds with an international focus. In addition to single-country funds, there are several open-end mutual funds with an international focus. For example, Fidelity offers funds with investments concentrated overseas, generally in Europe, in the Pacific Basin, and in developing economies in an emerging opportunities fund. Vanguard, consistent with its indexing philosophy, offers separate index funds for Europe, the Pacific Basin, and emerging markets. Finally, as noted in Chapter 4, there are many exchange-traded funds known as iShares or WEBS (World Equity Benchmark Shares) that are country-specific index products.

U.S. investors also can trade derivative securities based on prices in foreign security markets. For example, they can trade options and futures on the Nikkei stock index of 225 stocks traded on the Tokyo stock exchange or on FTSE (Financial Times Share Exchange) indexes of U.K. and European stocks.

The investments industry commonly distinguishes between "developed" and "emerging" markets. A typical emerging economy still is undergoing industrialization, is growing faster than developed economies, and has capital markets that usually entail greater risk. We use the FTSE[1] criteria, which emphasize capital market conditions, to classify markets as emerging or developed.

Developed Countries

To appreciate the myopia of an exclusive investment focus on U.S. stocks and bonds, consider the data in Table 19.1 for a sample of developed countries. The United States accounts for only 40.6% of world stock market capitalization. Clearly, active investors can attain better risk–return trade-offs by extending their search for attractive securities abroad. Developed countries accounted for about 70% of world gross domestic product in 2015 and 78.6% of world market capitalization.

The United States is by far the largest economy, measured either by GDP or the size of the stock market. However, Switzerland is the leader in GDP per capita, and Hong Kong has the

---

[1]FTSE Index Company, the sponsor of the British FTSE (Financial Times Share Exchange) stock market index, uses 14 specific criteria to classify markets as "developed" or "emerging."

TABLE 19.1 Market capitalization and GDP of developed countries, 2015

	Market Capitalization ($ billions)	Percent of World (%)	GDP ($ billions)	GDP per Capita ($)	Market Cap as % of GDP
United States	$25,068	40.6%	$ 17,947	$ 55,837	139.7%
Japan	4,895	7.9	4,123	32,477	118.7
Hong Kong	3,185	5.2	310	42,423	1,027.6
United Kingdom	2,781	4.4	2,849	43,734	97.6
France	2,088	3.4	2,422	36,248	86.2
Germany	1,716	2.8	3,356	41,219	51.1
Canada	1,593	2.6	1,551	43,249	102.8
Switzerland	1,519	2.5	665	80,215	228.6
Korea	1,231	2.0	1,378	27,222	89.4
Australia	1,187	1.9	1,340	56,328	88.6
Spain	787	1.3	1,199	25,832	65.7
Netherlands	728	1.2	753	44,433	96.8
Italy	587	1.0	1,815	29,847	27.5
Belgium	415	0.7	454	40,231	91.3
Mexico	402	0.7	1,144	9,009	35.2
Israel	244	0.4	296	35,330	82.4
Norway	194	0.3	388	74,735	49.9
Chile	190	0.3	240	13,384	79.2
Turkey	189	0.3	718	9,130	26.3
Poland	138	0.2	475	12,494	29.0
Ireland	128	0.2	238	51,290	53.8
Austria	96	0.2	374	43,439	25.7
New Zealand	74	0.1	174	37,808	42.8
Portugal	60	0.1	199	19,223	30.1
Luxembourg	47	0.1	58	101,450	81.6
Greece	42	0.1	195	18,036	21.6
Hungary	18	0.0	121	12,259	14.7
Slovenia	6	0.0	43	20,713	14.1
All developed countries	49,609	78.6	44,823		110.7
World	63,150	100.0	63,982		98.7

Source: The World Bank, data.worldbank.org.

largest stock market compared to GDP. On average, the total stock market capitalization in these countries is about the same magnitude as annual GDP, but there is tremendous variation in these numbers. Capitalization as a fraction of GDP for the countries toward the bottom of the list, with smaller capital markets, is generally far lower than for those countries near the top. This suggests widespread differences in economic structure even across developed nations.

Emerging Markets

For a passive strategy, one could argue that a portfolio of equities of just the six countries with the largest capitalization would make up over 70% (in 2015) of the world portfolio and may be sufficiently diversified. However, this argument will not hold for active portfolios that seek to tilt investments toward promising assets. Active portfolios will naturally include many stocks or indexes of emerging markets.

Surely, active portfolio managers do not want to neglect stocks in markets such as China, with an average GDP growth rate in the last five years of 15%. Table 19.2 shows data from the largest emerging markets. These markets make up 21% of the world GDP. Per capita GDP in these emerging markets is quite variable, ranging from $1,582 (India) to $52,889 (Singapore). Market capitalization as a percent of GDP in these countries is still below 70%, suggesting that these capital markets can grow significantly over the coming years, even without spectacular growth in GDP.

Market Capitalization and GDP

A contemporary view of economic development[2] holds that an important requirement for economic advancement is a developed code of business laws, institutions, and regulations that allows citizens to legally own, capitalize, and trade capital assets. As a corollary, we expect that development of equity markets will serve as a catalyst for enrichment of the population.

Figure 19.1 depicts the relationship between per capita GDP and market capitalization (where both variables have been transformed to $\log_{10}$ scale). The positive slope of the

TABLE 19.2   Market capitalization of stock exchanges in emerging markets

	Market Capitalization ($ billions)	Percent of World (%)	GDP ($ billions)	GDP per Capita (%)	Market Cap as % of GDP
China	$8,188	13.3%	$ 10,866	7,925%	75.4%
India	1,516	2.5	2,074	1,582	73.1
South Africa	736	1.2	313	5,692	235.3
Singapore	640	1.0	293	52,889	218.6
Brazil	491	0.8	1,775	8,539	27.6
Russia	393	0.6	1,326	9,057	29.7
Malaysia	383	0.6	296	9,766	129.3
Indonesia	353	0.6	862	3,346	41.0
Thailand	349	0.6	395	5,816	88.2
Philippines	239	0.4	292	2,899	81.8
Colombia	86	0.1	292	6,056	29.4
Peru	57	0.1	192	6,122	29.4
Argentina	56	0.1	583	13,432	9.6
Sri Lanka	21	0.0	82	3,926	25.3
Cyprus	3	0.0	19	22,957	13.9
All emerging markets	13,510	21.9	19,660.6		68.7

Source: The World Bank, data.worldbank.org.

[2]A highly influential paper in this literature is Rafael La Porta, Florencia Lopez-de-Silanes, Andrei Shleifer, and Robert W. Vishny, "Law and Finance," *Journal of Political Economy* 106 (December 1998), pp. 1113–1155.

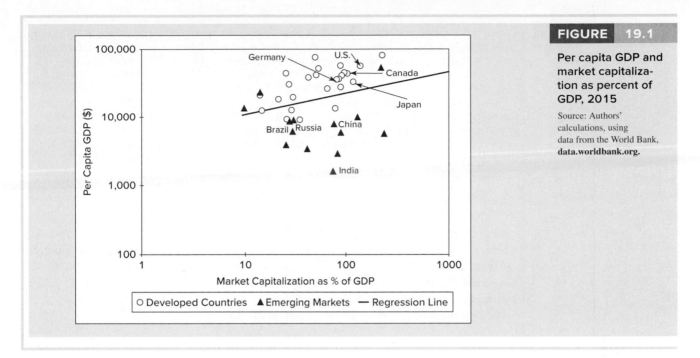

FIGURE 19.1

Per capita GDP and market capitalization as percent of GDP, 2015

Source: Authors' calculations, using data from the World Bank, **data.worldbank.org.**

regression line through the scatter shows that, on average, countries with larger capital markets also tend to have higher levels of per capita GDP. The slope of the line is 0.32, which implies that every percentage point increase in total market capitalization predicts an increase of 0.32% in per capita GDP.[3] Even so, we observe that most of the observations for the developed countries (the circles) lie above the regression line while most of the observations for the emerging markets (the triangles) lie below. This may be evidence that legal, regulatory, and economic institutions in the more advanced economies also contribute to productivity.

Home-Country Bias

We know that purely passive investment strategies would call for risky portfolios that are indexed to a broad market portfolio. In the international context, that market portfolio would include stock markets from all nations, and the market index would be a broadly diversified world portfolio.

Despite this, it is clear that investors everywhere tend to overweight investments in their home countries (relative to representation in the world portfolio) and underweight investments in foreign assets. For example, referring back to Table 19.1, a purely indexed U.S. investor would hold about 41% of the total equity portfolio in U.S. securities with the remaining 59% invested abroad. Yet in practice, U.S. investors hold a large majority of their equity investments in U.S. firms. This pattern is mirrored in the behavior of investors around the world and is commonly called *home-country bias*.

19.2 EXCHANGE RATE RISK AND INTERNATIONAL DIVERSIFICATION

Exchange Rate Risk

When a U.S. investor invests abroad, the dollar-denominated return depends on two factors: first, the performance of the investment in the local currency, and second, the exchange rate at which that investment can be brought back into dollars. We illustrate with the following example.

---

[3]This simple single-variable regression is not put forward as a causal model but simply as a way to describe the relation between per capita GDP and the size of markets.

EXAMPLE 19.1

Exchange Rate Risk

Consider an investment in risk-free British government bills paying 10% annual interest in British pounds. While these U.K. bills would be the risk-free asset to a British investor, this is not the case for a U.S. investor. Suppose, for example, the current exchange rate is $1.40 per pound and the U.S. investor starts with $14,000. That amount can be exchanged for £10,000 and invested at a riskless 10% rate in the United Kingdom to provide £11,000 in one year.

What happens if the dollar–pound exchange rate varies over the year? Say that during the year, the pound depreciates by 10% relative to the dollar, so that by year-end only $1.26 is required to purchase £1. The £11,000 can be exchanged at the year-end exchange rate for only $13,860 (= £11,000 × $1.26/£), resulting in a loss of $140 relative to the initial $14,000 investment. Despite the positive 10% pound-denominated return, the dollar-denominated return is negative 1%.

We can generalize from Example 19.1. The $14,000 is exchanged for $14,000/$E_0$ pounds, where E_0 denotes the original exchange rate ($1.40/£). The U.K. investment grows to $(14,000/E_0)[1 + r_f(\text{UK})]$ British pounds, where $r_f(\text{UK})$ is the risk-free rate in the United Kingdom. The pound proceeds ultimately are converted back to dollars at the subsequent exchange rate E_1, for total dollar proceeds of $14,000(E_1/E_0)[1 + r_f(\text{UK})]$. Therefore, the dollar-denominated return on the investment in British bills is

$$1 + r(\text{US}) = [1 + r_f(\text{UK})]E_1/E_0 \tag{19.1}$$

We see in Equation 19.1 that the dollar-denominated return equals the pound-denominated return times the exchange rate "return." For a U.S. investor, the investment in British bills is a combination of a safe investment in the United Kingdom and a risky investment in the performance of the pound relative to the dollar. Here, the pound fared poorly, falling from a value of $1.40 to only $1.26. The loss on the pound more than offset the earnings on the British bill.

Figure 19.2 illustrates this point. It presents rates of return on stock market indexes in several countries for 2016. The top bar in each pair depicts returns in local currencies, while the bottom bar depicts returns in U.S. dollars, adjusted for exchange rate movements. It's clear that exchange rate fluctuations over this period had large effects on dollar-denominated returns in several countries.

CONCEPT check 19.1

Using the data in Example 19.1, calculate the rate of return in dollars to a U.S. investor holding the British bill if the year-end exchange rate is: (*a*) $E_1 = \$1.40/£$; (*b*) $E_1 = \$1.54/£$.

exchange rate risk

The uncertainty in asset returns due to movements in the exchange rates between the U.S. dollar and foreign currency.

Exchange rate risk arises from uncertainty in exchange rate fluctuations. The investor in safe U.K. bills in Example 19.1 still bears the risk of the U.K./U.S. exchange rate. We can assess the magnitude of exchange rate risk by examining historical rates of change in various exchange rates and their correlations.

Table 19.3, Panel A, presents the annualized standard deviation of monthly percent changes in the exchange rates of six major currencies against the U.S. dollar over the period 2011–2016. The data show that currency volatility can be quite high. With the exception of the Chinese RMB, the standard deviation of the percent changes in the exchange rate was around three-quarters that of the return on the S&P 500, with annualized values ranging from 7.47% (Canadian dollar) to 10.01% (Swiss franc). The annualized standard deviation of returns on U.S. large stocks for the same period was 12%. An active investor who believes that a foreign stock is underpriced but has no information about any mispricing of its currency should consider hedging the currency risk exposure when tilting the portfolio toward that stock.

On the other hand, exchange rate risk may be mostly diversifiable. This is evident both from the low correlation between exchange rate changes and the return on the S&P 500 shown in the second line of Table 19.3, Panel A, as well as the low correlation coefficients among currency pairs that appear in Panel B.

Stock market returns, 2016

Source: *The Economist*, January 7, 2017.

FIGURE 19.2

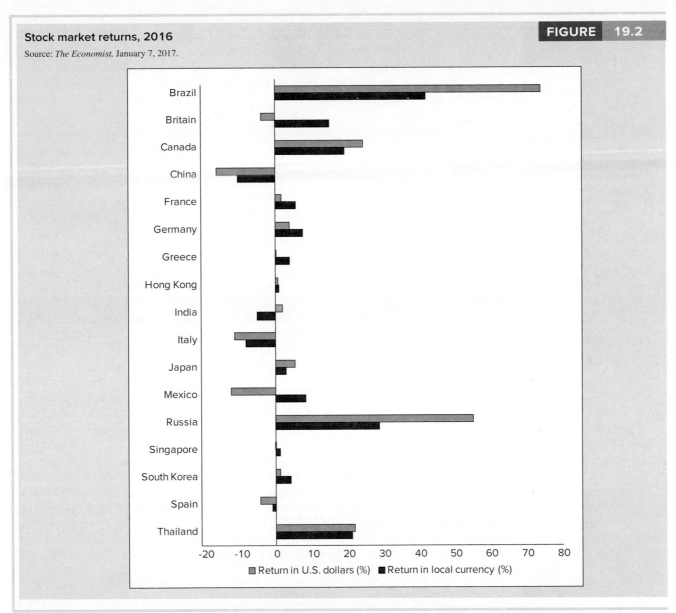

■ Return in U.S. dollars (%)   ■ Return in local currency (%)

TABLE 19.3 Exchange rate volatility, 2011–2016

A. Monthly Change in Exchange Rate against U.S. Dollar

	Euro (€)	U.K. (£)	Switzerland (SFr)	Japan (¥)	China (RMB)	Canada (C$)
Standard deviation (annualized)	8.19%	8.72%	10.01%	9.47%	2.60%	7.47%
Correlation with S&P 500	−0.095	−0.090	−0.042	0.134	−0.373	−0.453

B. Correlation Matrix of Monthly Changes in Exchange Rate against U.S. Dollar

	Euro (€)	U.K. (£)	Switzerland (SFr)	Japan (¥)	China (RMB)	Canada (C$)
Euro (€)	1.00					
U.K. (£)	0.56	1.00				
Switzerland (SFr)	0.43	0.28	1.00			
Japan (¥)	0.20	0.23	0.28	1.00		
China (RMB)	−0.05	0.27	0.09	−0.10	1.00	
Canada (C$)	0.46	0.44	0.14	0.14	0.29	1.00

Source: Authors' calculations using data downloaded from Datastream.

Investors can hedge exchange rate risk using a forward or futures contract in foreign exchange. Recall that such contracts entail delivery or acceptance of one currency for another at a stipulated exchange rate. To illustrate, recall Example 19.1. In this case, to hedge her exposure to the British pound, the U.S. investor would agree to deliver pounds for dollars at a fixed exchange rate, thereby eliminating the risk involved with the eventual conversion of the pound investment back into dollars.

EXAMPLE 19.2

Hedging Exchange Rate Risk

The U.S. investor in Example 19.1 could have assured a riskless dollar-denominated return by arranging to deliver the £11,000 at the forward exchange rate of $F_0 = \$1.33/£$. In this case, the riskless U.S. return would have been 4.5%:

$$[1 + r_f(UK)]F_0/E_0$$

$$= (1.10)1.33/1.40$$

$$= 1.045$$

Here are the steps to lock in the dollar-denominated returns. The futures contract entered in the second step exactly offsets the exchange rate risk incurred in step 1. Notice that the total cash flow at year-end is riskless and represents a 4.5% increase over the initial investment of $14,000.

Initial Transaction	End-of-Year Proceeds in Dollars
Exchange $14,000 for £10,000 and invest at 10% in the United Kingdom.	£11,000 × E_1
Enter a contract to deliver £11,000 for dollars at the (forward) exchange rate $1.33/£.	£11,000(1.33 − E_1)
Total	£11,000 × $1.33/£ = $14,630

The hedge underlying Example 19.2 is the same strategy at the heart of the spot-futures parity relationship, first discussed in Chapter 17. In both instances, futures or forward markets are used to eliminate the risk of holding another asset. The U.S. investor can lock in a riskless dollar-denominated return either by investing in U.K. bills and hedging exchange rate risk or by investing in riskless U.S. assets. Because investments in two riskless strategies must provide equal returns, we conclude that $[1 + r_f(UK)]F_0/E_0 = 1 + r_f(US)$, which can be rearranged to

$$\frac{F_0}{E_0} = \frac{1 + r_f(US)}{1 + r_f(UK)} \tag{19.2}$$

interest rate parity relationship or covered interest arbitrage relationship

The spot-futures exchange rate relationship that precludes arbitrage opportunities.

This relationship is called the **interest rate parity relationship** or **covered interest arbitrage.**

Consider the intuition behind this parity result. If $r_f(US)$ is greater than $r_f(UK)$, money invested in the United States will grow at a faster rate than money invested in the United Kingdom. If this is so, why wouldn't all investors decide to invest their money in the United States? One important reason is that the dollar may be depreciating relative to the pound. Although dollar investments in the United States grow faster than pound investments in the United Kingdom, each dollar is worth progressively fewer pounds as time passes. This will exactly offset the advantage of the higher U.S. interest rate.

To complete the argument, we need only determine how a depreciating dollar will be reflected in Equation 19.2. If the dollar is depreciating, meaning that progressively more dollars are required to purchase each pound, then the forward exchange rate, F_0 (which equals the dollars required to purchase 1 pound for delivery in the future), must exceed E_0, the current exchange rate.

That is exactly what Equation 19.2 tells us: When $r_f(US)$ exceeds $r_f(UK)$, F_0 must exceed E_0. The depreciation of the dollar embodied in the ratio of F_0 to E_0 exactly compensates for the difference in interest rates available in the two countries. Of course, the argument also works in reverse: If $r_f(US)$ is less than $r_f(UK)$, then F_0 will be less than E_0.

EXAMPLE 19.3

Covered Interest Arbitrage

What if the interest rate parity relationship were violated? Suppose r_f(US) is 4.5% but the futures price is $1.30/£ instead of $1.33/£. You could adopt the following strategy to reap arbitrage profits. In this example, let E_1 denote the exchange rate that will prevail in one year. E_1 is, of course, a random variable from the perspective of today's investors.

Action	Initial Cash Flow (in $)	Cash Flow in One Year (in $)
1. Borrow 1 British pound in London. Repay in one year.	$ 1.40	$-E_1(1.10)$
2. Convert the pound to $1.40 and lend in the United States.	−1.40	1.40(1.045)
3. Enter a contract to purchase 1.10 pounds at a (futures) price of $F_0 = \$1.30/£$	0	$1.10(E_1 - 1.30)$
Total	$ 0	$.033

In step 1, you borrow 1 pound in the United Kingdom (worth $1.40 at the current exchange rate) and, after one year, repay the pound borrowed with interest. Because the loan is made in the United Kingdom at the U.K. interest rate, you would repay 1.10 pounds, which would be worth $E_1(1.10)$ dollars. The U.S. loan in step 2 is made at the U.S. interest rate of 4.5%. The futures position in step 3 results in receipt of 1.10 pounds, for which you would first pay F_0 (i.e., 1.30) dollars each and later convert into dollars at exchange rate E_1.

The exchange rate risk here is exactly offset between the pound obligation in step 1 and the futures position in step 3. The profit from the strategy is, therefore, riskless and requires no net investment. This is an arbitrage opportunity.

CONCEPT check 19.2

What are the arbitrage strategy and associated profits if the initial future price is $F_0 = \$1.35/\text{pound}$?

Ample empirical evidence bears out this theoretical relationship. For example, on August 28, 2017, the three-month dollar-dominated LIBOR rate was 1.318%, while the British pound LIBOR rate was 0.773%. With a higher interest rate in the U.S. than in the U.K., the forward exchange rate should have exceeded the spot exchange rate. The spot exchange rate was $1.2936/£. Using Equation 19.2, we find that interest rate parity implies that the forward exchange rate for delivery in three months should have been $1.2936 \times (1.01318/1.00773)^{3/12}$ = $1.3006/£. The actual forward rate was $1.2967/£, which was so close to the parity value that transaction costs would have prevented arbitrageurs from profiting from the discrepancy.

DIRECT VERSUS INDIRECT QUOTES   The exchange rate in Example 19.1 is expressed as dollars per pound. This is an example of what is termed a *direct* exchange rate quote. The euro–dollar exchange rate is also typically expressed as a direct quote. In contrast, exchange rates for other currencies such as the Japanese yen or Swiss franc are typically expressed as *indirect* quotes, that is, as units of foreign currency per dollar, for example, 110 yen per dollar. For currencies expressed as indirect quotes, depreciation of the dollar would result in a *decrease* in the quoted exchange rate ($1 buys fewer yen); in contrast, dollar depreciation versus the pound would show up as a *higher* exchange rate (more dollars are required to buy £1). When the exchange rate is quoted as foreign currency per dollar, the domestic and foreign exchange rates in Equation 19.2 must be switched: In this case the equation becomes

$$F_0(\text{foreign currency}/\$) = \frac{1 + r_f(\text{foreign})}{1 + r_f(\text{U.S.})} \times E_0(\text{foreign currency}/\$)$$

For example, if the interest rate in the U.S. is higher than in Japan, the dollar commands a lower exchange rate in the forward market than in the spot market.

Imperfect Exchange Rate Risk Hedging

Unfortunately, perfect exchange rate hedging usually is not so easy. In our example, we knew exactly how many pounds to sell in the forward or futures market because the pound-denominated return in the United Kingdom was riskless. If the U.K. investment had not been in bills, but instead had been in risky U.K. equity, we would have known neither the ultimate value in pounds of our U.K. investment nor how many pounds to sell forward. The hedging opportunity offered by foreign exchange forward contracts would thus be imperfect.

To summarize, the generalization of Equation 19.1 for unhedged investments is that

$$1 + r(\text{US}) = [1 + r(\text{foreign})]E_1/E_0 \tag{19.3}$$

where $r(\text{foreign})$ is the possibly risky return earned in the currency of the foreign investment and exchange rates are direct quotes (\$ per unit of foreign currency). You can set up a perfect hedge only in the special case that $r(\text{foreign})$ is actually known. In that case, you must sell in the forward or futures market an amount of foreign currency equal to $[1 + r(\text{foreign})]$ for each unit of that currency you purchase today.

CONCEPT check	**19.3**	How many pounds would the investor in Example 19.1 (who is planning to invest £10,000 in the U.K.) need to sell forward to hedge exchange rate risk if: (*a*) $r(\text{UK}) = 20\%$; and (*b*) $r(\text{UK}) = 30\%$?

Investment Risk in International Markets

While active-strategy managers engage in both individual-market asset allocation as well as security selection, we will restrict our focus to market-index portfolios across countries, keeping us on the side of an enhanced passive strategy. Nevertheless, our analysis illustrates the essential features of extended active management as well.

As we pointed out in Chapter 5, estimates of mean returns are extremely unreliable without very long data series. Little can be learned about average rates of return from periods as short as 5 or even 10 years. This is because estimates of expected return essentially depend on only the initial and final stock price (which fully determine the average rate of increase). Long sample periods are intrinsically necessary for precise estimates of expected return. However, over such long periods, the mean of the return distribution can change. This is a difficult hurdle for empirical research to clear.

In contrast, estimates of volatility can be informed by return variation *within* the sample period. Increasing the frequency of observations therefore can increase the accuracy of risk estimates, meaning that precise estimates are feasible even with relatively short sample periods.

Therefore, we will focus largely on the risk of international investments, where we are more confident in our empirical estimates. We will use monthly data on country index returns for the five years ending in October 2016.

Table 19.4 shows key statistics for the investment risk of various equity indexes during this period. The indexes include most of the world's largest equity markets as well as markets from regions with smaller and less developed capital markets. The first pair of columns show the standard deviation of monthly returns measured both in local currency as well as translated into U.S. dollars, thus reflecting the impact of exchange rate movements in each month.[4]

The U.S. equity market (here taken to be the S&P 500) had the lowest volatility in terms of U.S. dollar-denominated returns over this period, but Canada had the lowest volatility in local currency. Its higher dollar-denominated volatility reflects the added risk attributable to

---

[4]Currency-translated returns are not available for the regional indexes. We compute the dollar-denominated return on the MSCI World portfolio as the weighted average of the dollar-denominated returns of the individual country indexes in Table 19.4 where weights are based on the proportion of each country in the World portfolio from Table 19.1. While this sample is not the complete World portfolio, it accounts for over 95% of world market capitalization.

| **TABLE 19.4** | Stock market volatility using both local and dollar-denominated returns |

	Standard Deviation of Monthly Returns		Correlation with Dollar-Denominated MSCI World	
	Local Currency	**Dollar-Denominated**	**Local Currency**	**Dollar-Denominated**
S&P 500	0.032	0.032	0.958	0.905
Nikkei	0.060	0.044	0.696	0.796
FTSE	0.038	0.044	0.863	0.855
Shanghai	0.071	0.072	0.254	0.545
Euronext	0.045	0.048	0.837	0.856
Hang Seng	0.052	0.052	0.653	0.777
Toronto	0.025	0.037	0.711	0.401
Swiss	0.044	0.039	0.726	0.845
India	0.045	0.065	0.614	0.603
Korea	0.035	0.051	0.693	0.743
MSCI-Arabian	0.047		0.494	
MSCI-Latin America	0.070		0.725	
MSCI World	0.035	0.034	0.952	1.000
Mean	0.045	0.048	0.701	0.733
Median	0.045	0.046	0.703	0.786

Source: Authors' calculations using returns downloaded from Datastream.

exchange rate movements. But in general, the impact of exchange rate movements on the volatility of dollar-denominated returns is minimal. The mean volatility of dollar-denominated returns is not much higher than that of local returns. (The mean and median estimates reported in Table 19.4 are computed only over the individual country indexes.)

Correlations with the MSCI World index, shown in the next pair of columns, are also broadly similar for local and dollar-denominated returns. Not surprisingly, given the prominence of the U.S. in the World portfolio and the prominence of its economy in the world economy, the U.S. has the highest correlation with the World index. Similarly, the FTSE index (U.K.) and Euronext index (E.U.), both of which measure returns in large and developed economies, also have very high correlations with the World index, approximately 0.85 using either dollar-denominated or local currency returns. The Shanghai index is notable for its low local-currency correlation with the rest of the world.

Table 19.5 shows results for index model regressions of each country's index against the MSCI World portfolio. The betas of each index against the World portfolio appear in the first pair of columns. The beta of the U.S. against the World portfolio is less than 1, as is the median beta of the other indexes in the sample. Betas computed from dollar-denominated returns are on average higher than those using local returns but, with the exception of China, not substantially so.

We do not report country-index alphas in this table because results over five years are such unreliable forecasts of future performance. As we noted above, this is a common problem in using an historical sample to estimate expected returns (as opposed to risk measures). It is why many decades of data are commonly used to estimate "normal" returns on the broad market index. Nevertheless, in this sample period, we can report that the median alpha in local currency was only 1 basis point, almost precisely zero. The dollar generally appreciated over this period, so the average dollar-denominated alpha was negative, −32 basis points per month.

The second pair of columns in Table 19.5 show the residual standard deviation for each country index. As discussed in Chapter 6, the regression residual in each month is the portion of the country return that is independent of the return on the World portfolio. The entries in these

TABLE 19.5 Index model regressions of country indexes against the MSCI World index using both local and dollar-denominated returns

	Beta against MSCI World		Residual Standard Deviation (of monthly returns)	
	Local Currency	**Dollar-Denominated**	**Local Currency**	**Dollar-Denominated**
S&P 500	0.885	0.847	0.009	0.014
Nikkei	1.207	1.022	0.043	0.027
FTSE	0.955	1.095	0.019	0.023
Shanghai	0.521	1.150	0.069	0.061
Euronext	1.089	1.195	0.025	0.025
Hang Seng	0.975	1.186	0.039	0.033
Toronto	0.512	0.428	0.018	0.033
Swiss	0.919	0.954	0.030	0.021
India	0.804	1.140	0.036	0.052
Korea	0.692	1.109	0.025	0.034
MSCI-Arabian	0.667		0.041	
MSCI-Latin America	1.473		0.049	
World	1.000		0.000	
Mean	0.856	1.013	0.031	0.032
Median	0.902	1.102	0.028	0.030

Source: Authors' calculations using returns downloaded from Datastream.

columns are therefore estimates of the standard deviation of "country-specific returns." The results are consistent with the other risk measures. The U.S. has by far the lowest country-specific risk, reflecting its prominence in the World portfolio, and China has the highest, consistent with its lower correlation with the World portfolio. Indexes for the countries in the Arab world and Latin America have above-average nonsystematic risk despite the fact that these indexes already enjoy some diversification across the countries included in each region. Average country-specific risk is essentially the same regardless of whether returns are measured in local or foreign currency. By and large, country-specific risk is meaningful. Even the U.S. value of 1.4% per month is not trivial. The message is that international diversification is potentially valuable.

By and large, the results in Table 19.4 and Table 19.5 indicate that investment risk is pretty much the same regardless of whether we use local currency or dollar-denominated returns. Therefore, we will focus largely on local returns when we turn to the potential for international diversification in the next section.

International Diversification

In Chapter 6, we looked at the risk of equally weighted portfolios composed of different numbers of U.S. stocks chosen at random and saw the efficacy of naïve diversification. Figure 19.3 presents the results of a similar exercise, but one in which diversification includes stocks from around the world. You can see that extending the universe of investable assets to foreign stocks allows even greater opportunities for risk reduction.

Of course, as emphasized in the nearby box, the benefits from diversification depend on the correlation structure among securities. The box notes that international correlations have increased over time. Table 19.6 shows correlation pairs (using local currency returns) for our sample of country and regional indexes from a recent five-year period. This correlation matrix can be used to construct the minimum-variance portfolio, which provides a better estimate of the potential benefits from diversification than the naïve (i.e., equally weighted) diversification exercise conducted in Figure 19.3.

INVESTORS' CHALLENGE: MARKETS SEEM TOO LINKED

It's one of the golden rules of investing: Reduce risk by diversifying your money into a variety of holdings—stock funds, bonds, commodities—that don't move in lockstep with one another. And it's a rule that's getting tougher to obey.

According to recent research, an array of investments whose prices used to rise and fall independently are now increasingly correlated. For example, the MSCI EAFE index, which measures emerging markets, currently shows 0.96 correlation to the S&P, up from just 0.32 six years ago.

For investors, that poses a troubling issue: how to maintain a portfolio diversified enough so all the pieces don't tank at once.

The current correlation trend doesn't mean investors should go out and ditch their existing investments. It's just that they may not be "getting the same diversification" they thought if the investment decisions were made some time ago, says Mr. Ezrati, chief economist at money-management firm Lord Abbett & Co. He adds that over long periods of time, going back decades, sometimes varied asset classes tend to converge.

One explanation for today's higher correlation is increased globalization, which has made the economies of various countries more interdependent. International stocks, even with their higher correlations at present, deserve some allocation in a long-term investor's holdings, says Jeff Tjornehoj, an analyst at data firm Lipper Inc. Mr. Tjornehoj is among those who believe these correlations are a temporary phenomenon and expects that the diversity will return some time down the line—a year or few years.

SOURCE: Shefali Anand, "Investors Challenge: Markets Seem Too Linked," *The Wall Street Journal*, June 2, 2006, p. C1.

FIGURE 19.3

International diversification. Portfolio standard deviation as a percentage of the average standard deviation of a one-stock portfolio

Source: B. Solnik, "Why Not Diversify Internationally Rather Than Domestically?" *Financial Analysts Journal*, July/August 1974, pp. 48–54. Copyright 1995, CFA Institute. Reproduced and republished from *Financial Analysts Journal* with permission from the CFA Institute.

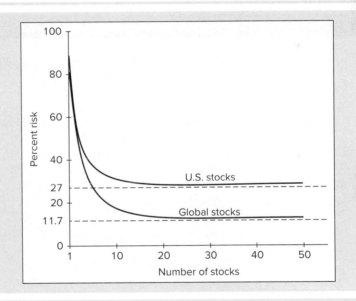

Table 19.7 shows portfolio volatility using equal weights for each country or regional index (column 1), using minimum variance weights (column 2), or using minimum variance weights without allowing short sales (column 3). The equally weighted portfolio is in the spirit of Figure 19.3. Even naïve diversification provides considerable benefit: The standard deviation of the portfolio is 3.3%, which is only 70% of the average of the individual country standard deviations. But we can reduce volatility considerably from this level. The minimum variance portfolio has a standard deviation of only 1.9% when we allow short sales, and 2.4% when we do not. We see here ample evidence for the potential of international diversification to substantially reduce portfolio risk.

What about efficient diversification that achieves the best risk–return trade-off? This is harder to assess because, as we have pointed out several times, sample average returns do not provide reliable estimates of expected returns. However, as an alternative to historical returns, we can estimate expected returns from an international version of the CAPM.

TABLE 19.6	Correlation matrix of returns using local currency returns, 2011–2016												
	S&P 500	Nikkei	FTSE	Shanghai	Euronext	Hang Seng	Toronto	Swiss	India	Korea	Arabian	Latin Am.	World
S&P 500	1.000	0.684	0.832	0.231	0.790	0.555	0.633	0.697	0.562	0.621	0.461	0.677	0.958
Nikkei	0.684	1.000	0.644	0.341	0.621	0.484	0.377	0.636	0.511	0.513	0.283	0.473	0.696
FTSE	0.832	0.644	1.000	0.233	0.844	0.651	0.649	0.724	0.588	0.627	0.353	0.716	0.863
Shanghai	0.231	0.341	0.233	1.000	0.232	0.590	0.231	0.113	0.153	0.360	0.199	0.277	0.254
Euronext	0.790	0.621	0.844	0.232	1.000	0.535	0.559	0.730	0.455	0.578	0.339	0.558	0.837
Hang Seng	0.555	0.484	0.651	0.590	0.535	1.000	0.615	0.393	0.548	0.711	0.486	0.753	0.653
Toronto	0.633	0.377	0.649	0.231	0.559	0.615	1.000	0.484	0.521	0.543	0.442	0.674	0.711
Swiss	0.697	0.636	0.724	0.113	0.730	0.393	0.484	1.000	0.339	0.485	0.272	0.355	0.726
India	0.562	0.511	0.588	0.153	0.455	0.548	0.521	0.339	1.000	0.566	0.266	0.624	0.614
Korea	0.621	0.513	0.627	0.360	0.578	0.711	0.543	0.485	0.566	1.000	0.478	0.692	0.693
Arabian	0.461	0.283	0.353	0.199	0.339	0.486	0.442	0.272	0.266	0.478	1.000	0.472	0.494
Latin Am.	0.677	0.473	0.716	0.277	0.558	0.753	0.674	0.355	0.624	0.692	0.472	1.000	0.725
World	0.958	0.696	0.863	0.254	0.837	0.653	0.711	0.726	0.614	0.693	0.494	0.725	1.000

Source: Authors' calculations using returns downloaded from Datastream.

TABLE 19.7	Composition and volatility of internationally diversified portfolios		
	Equally Weighted Portfolio	Minimum Variance Portfolio	Minimum Variance Portfolio (no short sales)
A. Weights			
S&P 500	0.083	0.318	0.114
Nikkei	0.083	−0.034	0.000
FTSE	0.083	0.207	0.000
Shanghai	0.083	0.051	0.024
Euronext	0.083	−0.149	0.000
Hang Seng	0.083	−0.103	0.000
Toronto	0.083	0.696	0.742
Swiss	0.083	−0.107	0.000
India	0.083	0.046	0.000
Korea	0.083	0.308	0.109
Arabian	0.083	0.044	0.012
Latin Am.	0.083	−0.276	0.000
B. Volatility			
Standard deviation	0.033	0.019	0.024

Source: Authors' calculations using returns downloaded from Datastream.

Table 19.8 presents such estimates using the MSCI World index as the market portfolio and assuming a risk-free rate of 2% and market risk premium of 8%. Given these expected returns, the standard deviations in Table 19.4, and the correlation matrix in Table 19.6, we can generate the efficient frontier. The results appear in Figure 19.4.

The frontier in Figure 19.4 is drawn without allowing for short sales. This reflects the constraints on shorting imposed on many institutional traders. Even with this restriction, however, the benefits of international diversification are evident. The U.S. portfolio (the S&P 500) appears as the solid dot and is located substantially below the capital allocation line, despite the fact that its weight in the tangency portfolio is nearly 50%. The CAL supported by the U.S. index has a Sharpe ratio (based on monthly returns) of 0.185, considerably lower

TABLE 19.8	Expected rates of return using local-currency betas against the MSCI World portfolio and an international CAPM

	Beta	Expected Return (%)
S&P 500	0.885	9.1%
Nikkei	1.207	11.7
FTSE	0.955	9.6
Shanghai	0.521	6.2
Euronext	1.089	10.7
Hang Seng	0.975	9.8
Toronto	0.512	6.1
Swiss	0.919	9.3
India	0.804	8.4
Korea	0.692	7.5
MSCI—Arabian	0.667	7.3
MSCI—Latin America	1.473	13.8
World	1.000	10.0

Source: Betas calculated by authors using returns downloaded from Datastream. Expected returns are derived from the CAPM, assuming a risk-free rate of 2% and market risk premium of 8%.

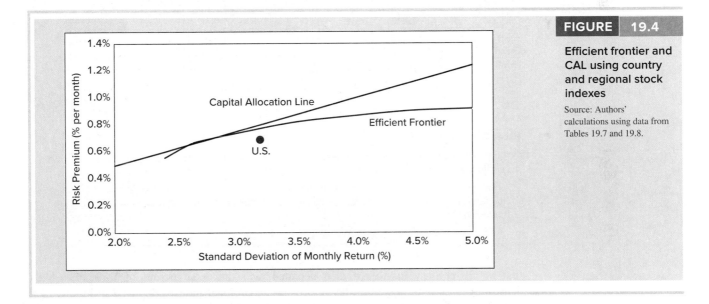

FIGURE 19.4

Efficient frontier and CAL using country and regional stock indexes

Source: Authors' calculations using data from Tables 19.7 and 19.8.

than the Sharpe ratio of the tangency portfolio, which is 0.248. Thus, a U.S. investor who foregoes international equity markets is giving up ample opportunities to improve the risk–return trade-off of his risky portfolio.

Are Benefits from International Diversification Preserved in Bear Markets?

Some studies suggest that correlation in country portfolio returns increases during periods of turbulence in capital markets.[5] If so, benefits from diversification would be lost exactly when they are needed the most. For example, a study by Roll of the crash of October 1987 shows

[5]F. Longin and B. Solnik, "Is the Correlation in International Equity Returns Constant: 1960–1990?" *Journal of International Money and Finance* 14 (1995), pp. 3–26; and Eric Jacquier and Alan Marcus, "Asset Allocation Models and Market Volatility," *Financial Analysts Journal* 57 (March–April 2001), pp. 16–30.

This Excel model provides an efficient frontier analysis similar to that in Chapter 6. In Chapter 6 the frontier was focused on diversification within the U.S., whereas this model examines the returns on international exchange-traded funds and enables us to analyze the benefits of international diversification. The Excel spreadsheet is available in Connect or through your course instructor.

	A	B	C	D	E	F	G	H	I	J
58		Bordered Covariance Matrix for Target Return Portfolio								
59			EWD	EWH	EWI	EWJ	EWL	EWP	EWW	SP 500
60	Weights		0.00	0.00	0.08	0.38	0.02	0.00	0.00	0.52
61		0.0000	0.00	0.00	0.00	0.00	0.00	0.00	0.00	0.00
62		0.0000	0.00	0.00	0.00	0.00	0.00	0.00	0.00	0.00
63		0.0826	0.00	0.00	4.63	3.21	0.55	0.00	0.00	7.69
64		0.3805	0.00	0.00	3.21	98.41	1.82	0.00	0.00	53.79
65		0.0171	0.00	0.00	0.55	1.82	0.14	0.00	0.00	2.09
66		0.0000	0.00	0.00	0.00	0.00	0.00	0.00	0.00	0.00
67		0.0000	0.00	0.00	0.00	0.00	0.00	0.00	0.00	0.00
68		0.5198	0.00	0.00	7.69	53.79	2.09	0.00	0.00	79.90
69		1.0000	0.00	0.00	16.07	157.23	4.59	0.00	0.00	143.47
70										
71	Port Variance	321.36								
72	Port S.D.	17.93								
73	Port Mean	12.00								
74										
75										
76						Weights				
77	Mean	St. Dev	EWD	EWH	EWI	EWJ	EWL	EWP	EWW	SP 500
78	6	21.89	0.02	0.00	0.00	0.71	0.00	0.02	0.00	0.26
79	9	19.66	0.02	0.00	0.02	0.53	0.02	0.00	0.00	0.41
80	12	17.93	0.00	0.00	0.08	0.38	0.02	0.00	0.00	0.52
81	15	16.81	0.00	0.00	0.14	0.22	0.02	0.00	0.00	0.62
82	18	16.46	0.00	0.00	0.19	0.07	0.02	0.00	0.00	0.73
83	21	17.37	0.00	0.00	0.40	0.00	0.00	0.00	0.00	0.60
84	24	21.19	0.00	0.00	0.72	0.00	0.00	0.00	0.00	0.28
85	27	26.05	0.00	0.00	1.00	0.00	0.00	0.00	0.00	0.00
86										
87										

Excel Questions

1. Find three points on the efficient frontier corresponding to three different expected returns. What are the portfolio standard deviations corresponding to each expected return?

2. Now assume that the correlation between the S&P 500 and the other country indexes is cut in half. Find the new standard deviations corresponding to each of the three expected returns. Are they higher or lower? Why?

that all 23 country indexes studied declined over the crash period of October 12–26.[6] This correlation is reflected in the movements of regional indexes depicted in Figure 19.5. Roll found that the beta of a country index on the world index (estimated prior to the crash) was the best predictor of that index's response to the October crash of the U.S. stock market. This suggests a common factor underlying the movement of stocks around the world. This model predicts that a macroeconomic shock would affect all countries and that while diversification can mitigate risk, it cannot eliminate exposure to such broad-based events.

The 2008 crash of stock markets around the world allows us to test Roll's prediction. The data in Figure 19.6 include average monthly rates of return for both the 10-year period 1999–2008 and the crisis period corresponding to the last four months of 2008, as well as the beta on the U.S. market and monthly standard deviation for several portfolios. The graph shows that both beta against the U.S. and the country-index standard deviation help explain the difference between crisis period returns and overall period averages. Market behavior during the 1987 crisis, that is, larger correlations in extreme bad times, repeated itself in the crisis of 2008, vindicating Roll's prediction.

[6]Richard Roll, "The International Crash of October 1987," *Financial Analysts Journal,* September–October 1988.

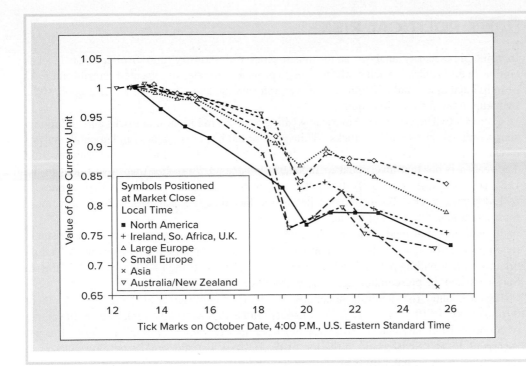

FIGURE 19.5

Regional indexes around the crash, October 14–October 26, 1987

Source: From Richard Roll, "The International Crash of October 1987," *Financial Analysts Journal,* September–October 1988. Copyright 1995, CFA Institute. Reproduced from *Financial Analysts Journal* with permission from the CFA Institute.

FIGURE 19.6

Beta and standard deviation of portfolios against deviation of monthly return over September–December 2008 from average return over 1999–2008

Source: Authors' calculations.

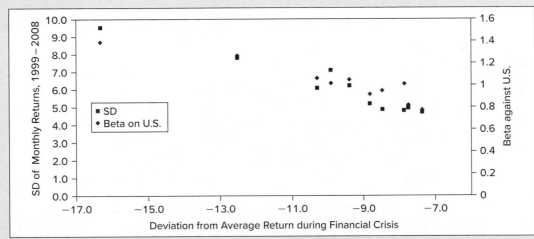

Market	Average Monthly Return 1999–2008	2008: Sept.–Dec.	Deviation from Average	Beta on U.S.	SD
USA	−0.47	−8.31	−7.84	1	4.81
World largest six (non–U.S.) markets	−0.16	−7.51	−7.35	0.77	4.71
EU developed markets	−0.05	−10.34	−10.29	1.06	6.08
Other Europe developed markets	−0.14	−7.59	−7.73	0.82	4.95
Australia + Far East	−0.10	−9.29	−9.38	1.04	6.21
Emerging Far East + South Africa	−0.20	−9.70	−9.90	1.01	7.10
Emerging Latin America	−0.80	−11.72	−12.52	1.27	7.83
Emerging markets in Europe	−0.90	−15.43	−16.32	1.38	9.54
World minus U.S. (48 countries by cap)	−0.01	−8.79	−8.81	0.91	5.19
World portfolio (by country cap)	−0.15	−8.60	−8.45	0.94	4.88

19.3 POLITICAL RISK

In principle, security analysis at the macroeconomic, industry, and firm-specific level is similar in all countries. Such analysis aims to provide estimates of expected returns and risks of individual assets and portfolios. However, information about assets in a foreign country is by nature more difficult to acquire.

Consider two investors: an American wishing to invest in Indonesian stocks and an Indonesian wishing to invest in U.S. stocks. While each would have to conduct fundamental analysis of each foreign company, the task would be much more difficult for the American investor. The reason is not that investment in Indonesia is *necessarily* riskier than investment in the U.S. You can easily find U.S. stocks that are, in the final analysis, riskier than a number of Indonesian stocks. The difference lies in the fact that U.S. financial markets are more transparent than those of Indonesia.

political risk

Possibility of expropriation of assets, changes in tax policy, restrictions on the exchange of foreign currency for domestic currency, or other changes in the business climate of a country.

In addition, **political risk** varies dramatically across countries, and its assessment requires expertise in each nation's economic, legal, tax, and political environment. A leading organization providing political risk assessment for investors is the PRS Group (Political Risk Services), and the presentation here follows the PRS methodology.[7]

PRS's country-risk analysis generates a country composite risk rating on a scale of 0 (most risky) to 100 (least risky). To illustrate, Table 19.9 shows the rank of a small sample of countries from the January 2015 issue of PRS's *International Country Risk Guide*. It is not surprising to find Switzerland at the top of the low-risk list and small emerging markets at the bottom, with Somalia (ranked 140) closing the list. What may be surprising is the fairly mediocre ranking of the United States (ranked 27).

TABLE 19.9 Composite risk ratings for January 2014 and January 2015

Rank	Country	Risk Rating, 2015	Risk Rating, 2014
1	Switzerland	89.8	89.5
6	Canada	83.0	82.3
6	Germany	83.0	85.3
10	Qatar	82.3	82.0
19	Japan	79.5	81.5
27	United States	77.3	75.3
47	China, Peoples' Rep.	72.0	73.3
59	Spain	69.5	69.3
68	Brazil	68.0	69.3
77	Indonesia	67.0	65.5
90	Russia	64.5	69.5
97	Turkey	63.3	59.3
118	Haiti	60.8	58.8
126	Pakistan	58.3	61.3
132	Venezuela	54.8	54.3
138	Liberia	49.3	52.8
139	Syria	41.3	42.0
140	Somalia	37.5	37.5

Source: *International Country Risk Guide,* January 2015, The PRS Group, Inc.

[7]You can find more information on the website **www.prsgroup.com.** We are grateful to the PRS Group for supplying data and guidance.

The composite risk rating is a weighted average of three measures: political risk, financial risk, and economic risk. Political risk is measured on a scale of 100–0, while financial risk and economic risk are each measured on a scale of 50–0. The three measures are added and divided by 2 to obtain the composite rating. The variables used by PRS to determine the composite risk rating from the three measures are shown in Table 19.10.

Table 19.11 shows the three risk measures for 11 countries in order of the January 2015 ranking of composite risk. The table shows that the United States was among the best performers in terms of political risk. But it was at the bottom of this (admittedly short) list in terms of financial risk. The surprisingly poor performance of the U.S. in this dimension was probably due to its large government and balance-of-trade deficits, which put pressure on its exchange rate. Exchange rate stability, foreign trade imbalance, and foreign indebtedness all enter PRS's computation of financial risk.

Finally, Table 19.12 shows ratings of political risk by each of its 12 components. The U.S. does well in corruption risk (variable F) and democratic accountability (variable K). China does well in government stability (variable A) but poorly in democratic accountability (variable K).

TABLE 19.10	Variables used in PRS's political risk score

Political Risk Variables	Financial Risk Variables	Economic Risk Variables
Government stability	Foreign debt (% of GDP)	GDP per capita
Socioeconomic conditions	Foreign debt service (% of exports)	Real annual GDP growth
Investment profile	Current account (% of exports)	Annual inflation rate
Internal conflicts	Net liquidity (months of import cover)	Budget balance (% of GDP)
External conflicts	Exchange rate stability	Current account balance (% GDP)
Corruption		
Military in politics		
Religious tensions		
Law and order		
Ethnic tensions		
Democratic accountability		
Bureaucracy quality		

TABLE 19.11	Country risk rankings by category, 2015

Country	Political	Financial	Economic	Composite
Pakistan	48.5	37.5	30.5	58.3
Turkey	53.0	37.5	36.0	63.3
Russia	56.5	35.5	37.0	64.5
India	61.0	43.0	33.5	68.8
China, Peoples' Rep.	56.5	47.5	40.0	72.0
United States	82.5	32.5	39.5	77.3
United Kingdom	84.0	35.5	38.0	78.8
Qatar	73.5	42.5	48.5	82.3
Canada	85.0	39.0	42.0	83.0
Germany	84.5	38.0	43.5	83.0
Switzerland	88.0	46.5	45.0	89.8

Source: *International Country Risk Guide,* January 2015, The PRS Group, Inc.

TABLE 19.12   Political risk points by component, January 2015

This table lists the total points for each of the following political risk components out of the maximum points indicated. The final column shows the overall political risk rating (the sum of the points awarded to each component).

A	Government stability	12	G	Military in politics	6
B	Socioeconomic conditions	12	H	Religious tensions	6
C	Investment profile	12	I	Law and order	6
D	Internal conflict	12	J	Ethnic tensions	6
E	External conflict	12	K	Democratic accountability	6
F	Corruption	6	L	Bureaucracy quality	4

Country	A	B	C	D	E	F	G	H	I	J	K	L	Risk Rating
Pakistan	6.0	5.5	7.0	6.0	9.0	2.0	1.5	1.0	3.0	1.0	4.5	2.0	48.5
Turkey	7.5	6.0	6.0	7.0	7.0	2.5	2.0	4.0	3.0	2.0	4.0	2.0	53.0
Russia	9.0	5.5	7.5	7.5	7.0	1.5	4.0	5.5	3.0	3.0	2.0	1.0	56.5
China, Peoples' Rep.	9.0	7.0	6.0	7.0	8.0	2.0	3.0	4.0	3.5	3.5	1.5	2.0	56.5
India	8.5	5.0	7.5	6.5	9.0	2.5	4.0	2.5	4.0	2.5	6.0	3.0	61.0
Qatar	10.5	8.0	10.0	9.5	8.5	4.0	4.0	4.0	5.0	6.0	2.0	2.0	73.5
United States	7.5	9.5	12.0	10.0	9.5	4.5	4.0	5.5	5.0	5.0	6.0	4.0	82.5
United Kingdom	7.5	9.5	11.5	10.0	9.5	5.0	6.0	6.0	5.0	4.0	6.0	4.0	84.0
Germany	8.5	9.0	11.0	10.5	10.5	5.0	6.0	5.0	5.0	4.0	6.0	4.0	84.5
Canada	7.5	8.5	12.0	10.0	11.0	5.0	6.0	6.0	5.5	3.5	6.0	4.0	85.0
Switzerland	9.0	10.5	11.5	12.0	10.5	5.0	6.0	4.5	5.0	4.0	6.0	4.0	88.0

Source: *International Country Risk Guide,* January 2015, The PRS Group, Inc.

Each monthly issue of the *International Country Risk Guide* of the PRS Group includes great detail and holds some 250 pages. Other organizations compete in supplying such evaluations. The result is that today's investor can become well equipped to properly assess the risk involved in international investing.

19.4   INTERNATIONAL INVESTING AND PERFORMANCE ATTRIBUTION

Because many security markets may be less efficient than those in highly developed economies such as the U.S., international investing offers greater opportunities for active managers. International investing calls for specialization in additional fields of analysis: currency, country and worldwide industry prospects, as well as a greater universe for stock selection.

Constructing a Benchmark Portfolio of Foreign Assets

Europe, Australasia, Far East (EAFE) index

A widely used index of non-U.S. stocks computed by MSCI.

Active (as well as passive) international investing requires a benchmark portfolio (called the *bogey*). One widely used international market index is the MSCI World index. MSCI also computes variants on this index that exclude some large markets such as the United States. Another popular non-U.S. index is the **Europe, Australasia, Far East (EAFE) index** of large and mid-cap securities in 21 developed markets, also computed by MSCI. Other indexes of world equity performance are published by Capital International Indices, Salomon Brothers, Credit Suisse First Boston, and Goldman Sachs. Portfolios designed to mirror or even replicate the country, currency, and company representation of these indexes would be the obvious generalization of the purely domestic passive equity strategy.

An issue that sometimes arises in the international context is the appropriateness of market-capitalization weighting schemes in the construction of international indexes. Capitalization weighting is far and away the most common approach. However, some argue that it might not be the best weighting scheme in an international context. This is in part because different countries have differing proportions of their corporate sector organized as publicly traded firms.

Table 19.13 shows market-capitalization weights versus GDP weights for countries in the EAFE index. These data reveal substantial disparities between the relative sizes of market capitalization and GDP. The countries with smaller stock markets (toward the bottom of the table) tend to have a much smaller share of EAFE total market capitalization than they do of EAFE GDP. For example, while Portugal accounts for 0.5% of total EAFE GDP, it represents only 0.1% of the market cap of the index. At the other extreme, Hong Kong accounts for only 0.7% of GDP, but it represents 6.5% of total EAFE market cap. These disparities indicate that a greater proportion of economic activity is conducted by publicly traded firms in Hong Kong than in the other EAFE countries.

Some argue that it would be more appropriate to weight international indexes by GDP rather than by market capitalization. The justification for this view is that an internationally diversified portfolio should purchase shares in proportion to the broad asset base of each country, and GDP might be a better measure of the weight of a country in the international economy than the value of its outstanding stocks. Others have even suggested weights proportional to the import share of various countries. The argument is that investors who wish to hedge the price of imported goods might choose to hold securities in foreign firms in proportion to the goods imported from those countries.

TABLE 19.13 Weighting schemes for EAFE countries, 2015

	% of EAFE Market Capitalization	% of EAFE GDP
United States	50.8%	43.1%
Japan	9.9	9.9
Hong Kong	6.5	0.7
United Kingdom	5.6	6.8
France	4.2	5.8
Germany	3.5	8.1
Canada	3.2	3.7
Switzerland	3.1	1.6
Sweden	2.6	1.2
Australia	2.4	3.2
Spain	1.6	2.9
Netherlands	1.5	1.8
Singapore	1.3	0.7
Italy	1.2	4.4
Belgium	0.8	1.1
Norway	0.4	0.9
Denmark	0.4	0.7
Finland	0.3	0.6
Ireland	0.3	0.6
Austria	0.2	0.9
New Zealand	0.2	0.4
Portugal	0.1	0.5
Greece	0.1	0.5

Source: Authors' calculations using data from Tables 19.1 and 19.2.

Performance Attribution

We can measure the contribution of each of the following decisions to portfolio performance following a procedure similar to the performance attribution techniques introduced in Chapter 18.

1. **Currency selection** measures the contribution to total portfolio performance attributable to exchange rate fluctuations relative to the investor's benchmark currency, which we will take to be the U.S. dollar. We might use a benchmark like the EAFE index to compare a portfolio's currency selection for a particular period to that of a passive benchmark. The benchmark for currency selection would be the weighted average of the appreciation of the currencies represented in the EAFE portfolio using as weights the fraction of that portfolio invested in each currency.

2. **Country selection** measures the contribution to portfolio performance attributable to investing in the better-performing stock markets of the world. It can be assessed from the weighted average of the equity *index* returns of each country using as weights the share of the manager's portfolio in each country. We use index returns to abstract from the effect of security selection within countries. To measure the contribution of country selection, we compare the manager's weighted average to the weighted average of a benchmark passive allocation, for example, the share of each country in the EAFE portfolio.

3. **Stock selection** ability may, as in Chapter 18, be measured as the weighted average of equity returns *in excess of the equity index* in each country. Here, we would use local currency returns and use as weights the investments in each country.

4. **Cash/bond selection** may be measured as the excess return derived from weighting bonds and bills differently from some benchmark weights.

Table 19.14 provides an example of how to measure the contribution of the decisions an international portfolio manager might make.

currency selection

Asset allocation in which the investor chooses among investments denominated in different currencies.

country selection

Asset allocation in which the investor chooses among investments in different countries.

stock selection

Choice of specific stocks within a country's equity market.

cash/bond selection

Choice between money market and longer-term bonds.

TABLE 19.14 Example of performance attribution: International

	EAFE Weight	Return on Equity Index	Currency Appreciation $E_1/E_0 - 1$	Manager's Weight	Manager's Return
Europe	0.30	10%	10%	0.35	8%
Australasia	0.10	5	−10	0.10	7
Far East	0.60	15	30	0.55	18

Overall performance (dollar return = local return + currency appreciation)

EAFE: $0.30(10 + 10) + 0.10(5 − 10) + 0.60(15 + 30) = 32.5\%$

Manager: $0.35(8 + 10) + 0.10(7 − 10) + 0.55(18 + 30) = 32.4\%$

Loss of 0.10% relative to EAFE

Currency selection

EAFE: $(0.30 \times 10\%) + (0.10 \times (−10\%)) + (0.60 \times 30\%) = 20\%$ appreciation

Manager: $(0.35 \times 10\%) + (0.10 \times (−10\%)) + (0.55 \times 30\%) = 19\%$ appreciation

Loss of 1% relative to EAFE

Country selection

EAFE: $(0.30 \times 10\%) + (0.10 \times 5\%) + (0.60 \times 15\%) = 12.5\%$

Manager: $(0.35 \times 10\%) + (0.10 \times 5\%) + (0.55 \times 15\%) = 12.25\%$

Loss of 0.25% relative to EAFE

Stock selection

$(8\% − 10\%)0.35 + (7\% − 5\%)0.10 + (18\% − 15\%)0.55 = 1.15\%$

Contribution of 1.15% relative to EAFE

Sum of attributions (equal to overall performance)

Currency (−1%) + country (−.25%) + selection (1.15%) = −0.10%

SUMMARY

- U.S. assets are only a part of the world portfolio. International capital markets offer important opportunities for portfolio diversification with enhanced risk–return characteristics.
- Exchange rate risk imparts an extra source of uncertainty to investments denominated in foreign currencies. Much of that risk can be hedged in foreign exchange futures or forward markets, but a perfect hedge is not feasible unless the foreign currency rate of return is known.
- Returns in different countries are far from perfectly correlated. Therefore, there is a benefit from international diversification. The minimum variance global portfolio has considerably lower volatility than almost any individual country index, including that of the U.S. More importantly, single-country stock indexes, again including those of the U.S., plot considerably inside the efficient frontier constructed when foreign equity markets are added to the investment menu. Therefore, international investing offers ample opportunities to improve the risk-reward trade-off.
- International investing entails an added dimension of political risk, including uncertainty about government and social stability, democratic accountability, macroeconomic conditions, international trade, and legal protections afforded individuals, businesses, and investors. Several services now exist that sell information about political risk to interested parties.
- Several world market indexes can form a basis for passive international investing. Active international management can be partitioned into currency selection, country selection, stock selection, and cash/bond selection.

KEY TERMS

cash/bond selection, 638
country selection, 638
covered interest arbitrage
 relationship, 624

currency selection, 638
Europe, Australasia, Far
 East (EAFE) index, 636
exchange rate risk, 622

interest rate parity
 relationship, 624
political risk, 634
stock selection, 638

KEY EQUATIONS

Interest rate parity (covered interest arbitrage) for direct ($/foreign currency) exchange rates:

$$F_0 = E_0 \frac{1 + r_f(\text{U.S.})}{1 + r_f(\text{foreign})}$$

Interest rate parity for indirect (foreign currency/$) exchange rates:

$$F_0 = E_0 \frac{1 + r_f(\text{foreign})}{1 + r_f(\text{U.S.})}$$

PROBLEM SETS

Select problems are available in McGraw-Hill's *Connect.* Please see the Supplements section of the book's frontmatter for more information.

1. Do you agree with the following claim? "U.S. companies with global operations can give you international diversification." Think about both business risk and foreign exchange risk. *(LO 19-1)*

2. In Figure 19.2, we provide stock market returns in both local and dollar-denominated terms. Which of these is more relevant? What does this have to do with whether the foreign exchange risk of an investment has been hedged?   *(LO 19-1)*

3. Suppose a U.S. investor wishes to invest in a British firm currently selling for £40 per share. The investor has $10,000 to invest, and the current exchange rate is $2/£.
   a. How many shares can the investor purchase?
   b. Fill in the table below for dollar-denominated rates of return after one year in each of the nine scenarios (three possible share prices denominated in pounds times three possible exchange rates).

Price per Share (£)	Pound-Denominated Return (%)	Dollar-Denominated Return for Year-End Exchange Rate		
		$1.80/£	$2/£	$2.20/£
£35				
£40				
£45				

   c. When is the dollar-denominated return equal to the pound-denominated return?   *(LO 19-2)*

4. If each of the nine outcomes in Problem 3 is equally likely, find the standard deviation of both the pound- and dollar-denominated rates of return.   *(LO 19-2)*

5. Now suppose the investor in Problem 3 also sells forward £5,000 at a forward exchange rate of $2.10/£.
   a. Recalculate the dollar-denominated returns for each scenario.
   b. What happens to the standard deviation of the dollar-denominated return? Compare it to both its old value and the standard deviation of the pound-denominated return.   *(LO 19-2)*

6. Calculate the contribution to total performance from currency, country, and stock selection for the manager in the example below. All exchange rates are expressed as units of foreign currency that can be purchased with 1 U.S. dollar.   *(LO 19-5)*

	EAFE Weight	Return on Equity Index	E_1/E_0	Manager's Weight	Manager's Return
Europe	0.30	20%	0.9	0.35	18%
Australasia	0.10	15	1.0	0.15	20
Far East	0.60	25	1.1	0.50	20

7. If the current exchange rate is $1.35/£, the one-year forward exchange rate is $1.45/£, and the interest rate on British government bills is 3% per year, what risk-free dollar-denominated return can be locked in by investing in the British bills?   *(LO 19-2)*

8. If you were to invest $10,000 in the British bills of Problem 7, how would you lock in the dollar-denominated return?   *(LO 19-2)*

9. Much of this chapter was written from the perspective of a U.S. investor. But suppose you are advising an investor living in a small country (choose one to be concrete). How might the lessons of this chapter need to be modified for such an investor?   *(LO 19-3)*

A common misconception is that investors can earn excess returns by investing in foreign bonds with higher interest rates than are available in the U.S. Interest rate parity implies that any such interest rate differentials will be offset by premiums or discounts in the forward or futures market for foreign currency.

Interest rates on government bonds in the U.S., U.K., Japan, Germany, and Australia can be found at **www.bloomberg.com/markets/rates/index.html.**

Spot exchange rates on international currencies can be found at **www.bloomberg.com/markets/currencies/fxc.html.**

Forward exchange rates on currency futures contracts can be found at **www.cmegroup.com/trading/fx/index.html.**

1. Select one of these countries and record the yield on a short-term government security from the Bloomberg website. Also make note of the U.S. Treasury yield on an instrument with the same (or closest possible) maturity.

2. Record the spot exchange rate from the Bloomberg site and the futures contract exchange rate from the CME website for the date closest to the maturity of the investment you chose in the previous question.

3. Calculate the rate of return available on the foreign government security, converting the foreign currency transactions into dollars at the current and forward exchange rates.

4. How well does interest rate parity seem to hold? Are there bargains to be found in other currencies? What factors might account for interest rate parity violations?

CFA Problems

1. You are a U.S. investor who purchased British securities for £2,000 one year ago when the British pound cost U.S.$1.50. What is your total return (denominated in U.S. dollars) if the value of the securities is now £2,400 and the pound is worth $1.45? No dividends or interest were paid during this period. *(LO 19-1)*

2. The correlation coefficient between the returns on a broad index of U.S. stocks and the returns on indexes of the stocks of other industrialized countries is mostly _____, and the correlation coefficient between the returns on various broad indexes of U.S. stocks is mostly _____.
   a. less than 0.8; greater than 0.8.
   b. greater than 0.8; less than 0.8.
   c. less than 0; greater than 0.
   d. greater than 0; less than 0. *(LO 19-1)*

3. An investor in the common stock of companies in a foreign country may wish to hedge against the _____ of the investor's home currency and can do so by _____ the foreign currency in the forward market.
   a. depreciation; selling.
   b. appreciation; purchasing.
   c. appreciation; selling.
   d. depreciation; purchasing. *(LO 19-1)*

4. John Irish, CFA, is an independent investment adviser who is assisting Alfred Darwin, the head of the Investment Committee of General Technology Corporation, to establish a new pension fund. Darwin asks Irish about international equities and whether the Investment Committee should consider them as an additional asset for the pension fund.
   a. Explain the rationale for including international equities in General's equity portfolio. Identify and describe three relevant considerations in formulating your answer.
   b. List three possible arguments against international equity investment and briefly discuss the significance of each.

c. To illustrate several aspects of the performance of international securities over time, Irish shows Darwin the accompanying graph of investment results experienced by a U.S. pension fund in the recent past. Compare the performance of the U.S. dollar and non-U.S. dollar equity and fixed-income asset categories, and explain the significance of the result of the account performance index relative to the results of the four individual asset class indexes.   **(LO 19-3)**

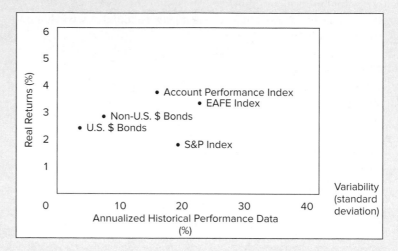

5. You are a U.S. investor considering purchase of one of the following securities. Assume that the currency risk of the Canadian government bond will be hedged, and the six-month discount on Canadian dollar forward contracts is −0.75% versus the U.S. dollar.

Bond	Maturity	Coupon	Price
U.S. government	6 months	6.50%	100.00
Canadian government	6 months	7.50%	100.00

Calculate the expected price change required in the Canadian government bond that would result in the two bonds having equal total returns in U.S. dollars over a six-month horizon. Assume that the yield on the U.S. bond is expected to remain unchanged.   **(LO 19-2)**

6. A global manager plans to invest $1 million in U.S. government cash equivalents for the next 90 days. However, she is also authorized to use non-U.S. government cash equivalents, as long as the currency risk is hedged to U.S. dollars using forward currency contracts.

a. What rate of return will the manager earn if she invests in money market instruments in either Canada or Japan and hedges the dollar value of her investment? Use the data in the following tables.

b. What must be the approximate value of the 90-day interest rate available on U.S. government securities? **(LO 19-2)**

Interest Rates (APR): 90-Day Cash Equivalents	
Japanese government	2.52%
Canadian government	6.74%

Exchange Rates: U.S. Dollars per Unit of Foreign Currency		
	Spot	90-Day Forward
Japanese yen	0.0119	0.0120
Canadian dollar	0.7284	0.7269

7. The Windsor Foundation, a U.S.-based, not-for-profit charitable organization, has a diversified investment portfolio of $100 million. Windsor's board of directors is considering an initial investment in emerging market equities. Robert Houston, treasurer of the foundation, has made the following comments:

   a. "For an investor holding only developed market equities, the existence of stable emerging market currencies is one of several preconditions necessary for that investor to realize strong emerging market performance."

   b. "Local currency depreciation against the dollar has been a frequent occurrence for U.S. investors in emerging markets. U.S. investors have consistently seen large percentages of their returns erased by currency depreciation. This is true even for long-term investors."

   c. "Historically, the addition of emerging market stocks to a U.S. equity portfolio such as the S&P 500 index has reduced volatility; volatility has also been reduced when emerging market stocks are combined with an international portfolio such as the MSCI EAFE index."

   Discuss whether *each* of Houston's comments is correct or incorrect.   *(LO 19-3)*

8. After much research on the developing economy and capital markets of the country of Otunia, your firm, GAC, has decided to include an investment in the Otunia stock market in its Emerging Markets Commingled Fund. However, GAC has not yet decided whether to invest actively or by indexing. Your opinion on the active versus indexing decision has been solicited. The following is a summary of the research findings:

   Otunia's economy is fairly well-diversified across agricultural and natural resources, manufacturing (both consumer and durable goods), and a growing finance sector. Transaction costs in securities markets are relatively large in Otunia because of high commissions and government "stamp taxes" on securities trades. Accounting standards and disclosure regulations are quite detailed, resulting in wide public availability of reliable information about companies' financial performance.

   Capital flows into and out of Otunia, and foreign ownership of Otunia securities, is strictly regulated by an agency of the national government. The settlement procedures under these ownership rules often cause long delays in settling trades made by nonresidents. Senior finance officials in the government are working to deregulate capital flows and foreign ownership, but GAC's political consultant believes that isolationist sentiment may prevent much real progress in the short run.

   a. Briefly discuss aspects of the Otunia environment that favor investing actively, and aspects that favor indexing.

   b. Recommend whether GAC should invest in Otunia actively or by indexing. Justify your recommendation based on the factors identified in part (*a*).   *(LO 19-4)*

19.1 $1 + r(US) = [1 + r_f(UK)] \times (E_1/E_0)$

   a. $1 + r(US) = 1.1 \times (1.40/1.40) = 1.10$. Therefore, $r(US) = 10\%$.
   b. $1 + r(US) = 1.1 \times (1.54/1.40) = 1.21$. Therefore, $r(US) = 21\%$.

19.2

	Initial Cash Flow (in $)	Cash Flow in One Year (in $)
1. Lend 1 British pound in London. Collect interest and principal in one year.	−$ 1.40	$E_1(1.10)$
2. Borrow $1.40 in the United States. Repay in one year.	1.40	−1.40(1.045)
3. Enter a contract to sell 1.10 pounds at a (futures) price of $F_0 = \$1.35/\pounds$	0	$1.10(1.35 - E_1)$
Total	$ 0	$.022

   In this case, the futures exchange rate was above its parity value. So you sold the futures contract instead of buying one.

19.3   You would like to sell forward the number of pounds you will end up with at the end
       of the year. This value cannot be known with certainty, however, unless the rate of
       return of the pound-denominated investment is known.
       a. $10,000 \times 1.20 = 12,000$ pounds.
       b. $10,000 \times 1.30 = 13,000$ pounds.

19.4   *Country selection:*

$$(0.40 \times 10\%) + (0.20 \times 5\%) + (0.40 \times 15\%) = 11\%$$

This is a loss of 1.5% (11% versus 12.5%) relative to the EAFE passive benchmark.
Currency selection:

$$(0.40 \times 10\%) + (0.20 \times (-10\%)) + (0.40 \times 30\%) = 14\%$$

This is a loss of 6% (14% versus 20%) relative to the EAFE benchmark.

Hedge Funds

Learning Objectives

LO 20-1 Identify directional versus nondirectional or market-neutral investment strategies.

LO 20-2 Formulate "pure plays" on seemingly misaligned security prices, and identify the risks that are hedged using these strategies as well as the risks that remain.

LO 20-3 Cite the various difficulties entailed in evaluating hedge fund investment performance.

LO 20-4 Interpret incentive fees charged by hedge funds as implicit options and value them using option-pricing methods.

W hile mutual funds are still the dominant form of investing in securities markets for most individuals, hedge funds enjoyed far greater growth rates in the last two decades. Assets under hedge fund management increased from around $200 billion in 1997 to over $3 trillion in 2017. Like mutual funds, hedge funds allow private investors to pool assets to be invested by a fund manager. Unlike mutual funds, however, they are commonly organized as private partnerships and thus not subject to many SEC regulations. They typically are open only to wealthy or institutional investors.

Hedge funds touch on virtually every issue discussed in the earlier chapters of the text, including liquidity, security analysis, market efficiency, portfolio analysis, hedging, and option pricing. For example, these funds often bet on relative mispricing of specific securities but hedge broad market exposure. This sort of pure "alpha-seeking" behavior requires a procedure for optimally mixing a hedge fund position with a more traditional portfolio. Other funds engage in aggressive market timing; their risk profiles can shift rapidly and substantially, raising difficult questions for performance evaluation. Many hedge funds take extensive derivatives positions. Even those funds that do not trade derivatives charge incentive fees that resemble the payoff to a call option; an option-pricing background therefore is necessary to interpret both hedge fund strategies and costs. In short, hedge funds raise the full range of issues that one might confront in active portfolio management.

We begin with a survey of various hedge fund orientations. We devote considerable attention to the classic "market-neutral" or hedged strategies that historically gave hedge funds their name. We move on to evidence on hedge fund performance, and the difficulties in evaluating that performance. Finally, we consider the implications of their unusual fee structure for investors in and managers of such funds.

20.1 HEDGE FUNDS VERSUS MUTUAL FUNDS

hedge fund

A private investment pool, open to wealthy or institutional investors, that is largely exempt from SEC regulation and therefore can pursue more speculative policies than mutual funds.

Like mutual funds, the basic idea behind a **hedge fund** is investment pooling. Investors buy shares in these funds, which then invest the pooled assets on their behalf. The net asset value of each share represents the value of the investor's stake in the portfolio. In this regard, hedge funds operate much like mutual funds. However, there are important differences between the two.

TRANSPARENCY Mutual funds are subject to the Securities Act of 1933 and the Investment Company Act of 1940 (designed to protect unsophisticated investors), which require transparency and predictability of strategy. They periodically must provide the public with information on portfolio composition. In contrast, hedge funds usually are set up as limited liability partnerships or limited liability companies and provide minimal information about portfolio composition and strategy to their investors only.

INVESTORS Hedge funds traditionally are open only to "accredited" investors, in practice usually defined by minimum net worth and income requirements. They do not advertise to the general public, although the recent trend is to market as well to ever-smaller and less sophisticated investors. Minimum investments are often between $500,000 and $1 million.

INVESTMENT STRATEGIES Mutual funds lay out their general investment approach (e.g., large, value-stock orientation versus small-cap growth orientation) in their prospectus. They face pressure to avoid *style drift* (departures from their stated investment orientation), especially given the importance of retirement funds such as 401(k) plans to the industry and the demand of such plans for predictable strategies. Most mutual funds promise to limit their use of short-selling and leverage, and their use of derivatives is highly restricted. Some so-called 130/30 funds, serving primarily institutional clients, have prospectuses that explicitly allow for more active short-selling and derivatives positions, but even these have less flexibility than hedge funds.[1]

In contrast, hedge funds may effectively partake in any investment strategy and may act opportunistically as conditions evolve. For this reason, it would be a mistake to view hedge funds as anything remotely like a uniform asset class. Hedge funds by design are empowered to invest in a wide range of investments, with various funds focusing on derivatives, distressed firms, currency speculation, convertible bonds, emerging markets, merger arbitrage, and so on. Other funds may jump from one asset class to another as perceived investment opportunities shift.

lock-up period

Period in which investors cannot redeem investments in the hedge fund.

LIQUIDITY Hedge funds often impose **lock-up periods,** that is, periods as long as several years in which investments cannot be withdrawn. Many also employ redemption notices requiring investors to provide notice weeks or months in advance of their desire to redeem funds. These restrictions limit the liquidity of investors but in turn enable the funds to invest in illiquid assets where returns may be higher, without worrying about meeting unanticipated demands for redemptions.

---

[1]These are funds that may sell short up to 30% of the value of their portfolios, using the proceeds of the sale to increase their positions in invested assets. So for every $100 in net assets, the fund could sell short $30, investing the proceeds to increase its long positions to $130. This gives rise to the 130/30 moniker.

COMPENSATION STRUCTURE　Hedge funds also differ from mutual funds in their fee structure. Whereas mutual funds assess management fees equal to a fixed percentage of assets, for example, between 0.5% and 1.25% annually for typical equity funds, hedge funds charge a management fee, usually between 1% and 2% of assets, *plus* a substantial *incentive fee* equal to a fraction of any investment profits beyond some benchmark. The incentive fee is often 20%. The threshold return to earn the incentive fee is often a money market rate such as LIBOR. Indeed, some observers only half-jokingly characterize hedge funds as "a compensation scheme masquerading as an asset class."

20.2　HEDGE FUND STRATEGIES

Table 20.1 presents a list of most of the common investment themes found in the hedge fund industry. The list contains a wide diversity of styles and suggests how hard it can be to speak generically about hedge funds as a group. We can, however, divide hedge fund strategies into two general categories: directional and nondirectional.

directional strategy

Speculation that one market sector will outperform other sectors.

Directional versus Nondirectional Strategies

Directional strategies are easy to understand. They are simply bets that one sector or another will outperform other sectors of the market.

In contrast, **nondirectional strategies** are usually designed to exploit temporary misalignments in security valuations. For example, if the yield on corporate bonds seems abnormally high compared to that on Treasury bonds, the hedge fund would buy corporates and short-sell Treasury securities. Notice that the fund is *not* betting on broad movements in the entire bond market: It buys one type of bond and sells another. By taking a long corporate–short Treasury

nondirectional strategy

A position designed to exploit temporary misalignments in relative pricing; typically involves a long position in one security hedged with a short position in a related security.

TABLE 20.1	Hedge fund styles*
Convertible arbitrage	Hedged investing in convertible securities, typically long convertible bonds and short stock.
Dedicated short bias	Net short position, usually in equities, as opposed to pure short exposure.
Emerging markets	Goal is to exploit market inefficiencies in emerging markets. Typically establish long positions in assets because short-selling is not feasible in many of these markets.
Equity market neutral	Commonly uses long-short hedges. Typically controls for industry, sector, size, and other exposures, and establishes market-neutral positions designed to exploit some market inefficiency. Commonly involves leverage.
Event driven	Attempts to profit from situations such as mergers, acquisitions, restructuring, bankruptcy, or reorganization.
Fixed-income arbitrage	Attempts to profit from price anomalies in related interest rate securities. Includes interest-rate swap arbitrage, U.S. versus non-U.S. government bond arbitrage, yield-curve arbitrage, and mortgage-backed arbitrage.
Global macro	Involves long and short positions in capital or derivative markets across the world. Portfolio positions reflect views on broad market conditions and major economic trends.
Long-short equity hedge	Equity-oriented positions on either side of the market (i.e., long or short), depending on outlook. *Not* meant to be market neutral. May establish a concentrated focus regionally (e.g., U.S. or Europe) or on a specific sector (e.g., tech or health care stocks). Derivatives may be used to hedge positions.
Managed futures	Uses financial, currency, or commodity futures. May make use of technical trading rules or a less-structured judgmental approach.
Multistrategy	Opportunistic choice of strategy depending on outlook.
Fund of funds	Fund allocates its cash to several other hedge funds to be managed.

*Credit Suisse maintains one of the most comprehensive databases on hedge fund performance. It categorizes hedge funds into these 11 different investment styles.

market neutral

A strategy designed to exploit relative mispricing within a market, but which is hedged to avoid taking a stance on the direction of the broad market.

position, the fund hedges its interest rate exposure while making a bet on the *relative* valuation across the two sectors. The idea is that when yield spreads converge back to their "normal" relationship, the fund will profit from the realignment regardless of the general trend in the level of interest rates. In this respect, it strives to be **market neutral,** or hedged with respect to the direction of interest rates, which gives rise to the term *hedge fund.*

Nondirectional strategies are sometimes further divided into *convergence* or *relative value* positions. The difference between them is a specific time horizon at which the mispricing ought to be resolved. An example of a convergence strategy would be index arbitrage to exploit mispricing of a futures contract that must be corrected by the time the contract matures. In contrast, the corporate versus Treasury spread we just discussed would be a relative value strategy, because there is no obvious horizon during which the yield spread would "correct" from unusual levels.

EXAMPLE 20.1

Market-Neutral Positions

We can illustrate a market-neutral position with a strategy used extensively by several hedge funds, which observed that newly issued or "on-the-run" 30-year Treasury bonds regularly sell at higher prices (lower yields) than 29½-year bonds with almost identical duration. The yield spread presumably is a premium due to the greater liquidity of the on-the-run bonds. Hedge funds, which have relatively low liquidity needs, therefore buy the 29½-year bond and sell the 30-year bond. This is a hedged, or market-neutral, position that will generate a profit when the yields on the two bonds converge, as typically happens when the 30-year bonds age, are no longer the most liquid on-the-run bond, and are no longer priced at a premium.

This strategy should generate profits regardless of the general direction of interest rates. It will return a profit as long as the 30-year bonds underperform the 29½-year bonds, as they should when the liquidity premium dissipates. Because the pricing discrepancies between these two securities almost necessarily *must* disappear at a given date, this strategy is an example of convergence arbitrage. While the convergence date in this application is not quite as definite as the maturity of a futures contract, one can be sure that the currently on-the-run T-bonds will lose that status by the time the Treasury next issues 30-year bonds.

Long-short positions such as in Example 20.1 are characteristic of hedged strategies. They are designed to *isolate* a bet on some mispricing without taking on market exposure. Profits are made regardless of broad market movements once prices "converge" or return to their "proper" levels. Hence, use of short positions and derivatives is part and parcel of the industry.

A more complex long-short strategy is *convertible bond arbitrage.* Noting that a convertible bond may be viewed as a straight bond plus a call option on the underlying stock, the market-neutral strategy in this case involves a position in the bond offset by an opposite position in the stock. For example, if the convertible is viewed as underpriced, the fund will buy it and offset its resultant exposure to declines in the stock price by shorting the stock.

pure plays

Bets on particular mispricing across two or more securities, with extraneous sources of risk such as general market exposure hedged away.

Although these market-neutral positions are hedged, they are *not* risk-free arbitrage strategies. Rather, they should be viewed as **pure plays,** that is, bets on *particular* (perceived) mispricing between two sectors or securities, with extraneous sources of risk such as general market exposure hedged away. Moreover, because the funds often operate with considerable leverage, returns can be quite volatile.

CONCEPT Check 20.1

Classify each of the following strategies as directional or nondirectional.

a. The fund buys shares in the India Investment Fund, a closed-end fund that is selling at a discount to net asset value, and sells the MSCI India Index Swap.

b. The fund buys shares in Petrie Stores and sells Toys "R" Us, which is a major component of Petrie's balance sheet.

c. The fund buys shares in Generic Pharmaceuticals, betting that it will be acquired at a premium by Pfizer.

Statistical Arbitrage

Statistical arbitrage is a version of a market-neutral strategy, but one that merits its own discussion. It differs from pure arbitrage in that it does not exploit risk-free positions based on unambiguous mispricing (such as index arbitrage). Instead, it uses quantitative and often automated trading systems that seek out many temporary and modest misalignments in prices among securities. By taking relatively small positions in many of these opportunities, the law of averages would make the probability of profiting from the collection of apparently positive-value bets very high, ideally almost a "statistical certainty." Of course, this strategy presumes that the fund's modeling techniques can actually identify reliable, if small, market inefficiencies. The law of averages guarantees profits only if the expected return is positive!

Statistical arbitrage often involves trading in hundreds of securities a day with holding periods that can be measured in minutes or less. Such rapid and heavy trading requires extensive use of quantitative tools such as automated trading and mathematical algorithms to identify profit opportunities and efficient diversification across positions. These strategies try to profit from the smallest of perceived mispricing opportunities and require the fastest trading technology and the lowest possible trading costs. They would not be possible without the algorithmic trading tools discussed in Chapter 3.

A particular form of statistical arbitrage is **pairs trading,** in which stocks are paired up based on an analysis of either fundamental similarities or market exposures (betas). The general approach is to pair up similar companies whose returns are highly correlated but where one company seems to be priced more aggressively than the other.[2] Market-neutral positions can be formed by buying the relatively cheap firm and selling the expensive one. Many such pairs comprise the hedge fund's overall portfolio. Each pair may have an uncertain outcome, but with many such matched pairs, the presumption is that the large number of long-short bets will provide a very high probability of a positive abnormal return. More general versions of pairs trading allow for positions in clusters of stocks that may be relatively mispriced.

Statistical arbitrage is commonly associated with **data mining,** which refers to sorting through huge amounts of historical data to uncover systematic patterns in returns that can be exploited by traders. The risk of data mining, and statistical arbitrage in general, is that historical relationships may break down when fundamental economic conditions change or, indeed, that the apparent patterns in the data may be due to pure chance. Enough analysis applied to enough data is sure to produce apparent patterns that do not reflect real relationships that can be counted on to persist in the future.

statistical arbitrage

Use of quantitative systems to uncover many perceived misalignments in relative pricing and ensure profit by diversifying across these small bets.

pairs trading

Stocks are paired up based on underlying similarities, and long-short positions are established to exploit any relative mispricing between each pair.

data mining

Sorting through large amounts of historical data to uncover patterns that can be exploited.

20.3   PORTABLE ALPHA

An important implication of the market-neutral pure play is the notion of **portable alpha.** Suppose you wish to speculate on a stock that you think is underpriced, but you think that the market is about to fall. Even if you are right about the stock being *relatively* underpriced, it still might decline in response to declines in the broad market. You would like to separate the stock-specific bet from the exposure to the broad market that arises because the stock's beta is positive. The solution is to buy the stock and eliminate the market exposure by selling enough index futures to drive beta to zero. This long stock–short futures strategy gives you a pure play or, equivalently, a *market-neutral* position on the stock.

More generally, you might wish to separate asset allocation from security selection. The idea is to invest wherever you can "find alpha." You would then hedge the systematic risk of that investment to isolate its alpha from the asset market where it was found. Finally, you establish exposure to desired market sectors by using passive products such as indexed mutual

portable alpha or alpha transfer

A strategy in which you invest in positive alpha positions, then hedge the systematic risk of that investment, and, finally, establish market exposure where you want it using passive indexes.

---

[2]Rules for deciding relative "aggressiveness" of pricing may vary. In one approach, a computer scans for stocks whose prices historically have tracked very closely but have recently diverged. If the differential in cumulative return typically dissipates, the fund will buy the recently underperforming stock and sell the outperforming one. In other variants, pricing aggressiveness may be determined by evaluating the stocks based on the ratio of price to some measure of intrinsic value.

funds, ETFs, or index futures. In other words, you create portable alpha that can be mixed with an exposure to whatever sector of the market you choose. This procedure is also called **alpha transfer,** because you transfer alpha from the sector where you find it to the asset class in which you ultimately establish exposure. Finding alpha requires skill. By contrast, beta, or market exposure, is a standardized "commodity" that can be supplied cheaply through index funds or ETFs and does not provide value added.

An Example of a Pure Play

Suppose you manage a $2.5 million portfolio. You believe that the alpha of the portfolio is positive, $\alpha > 0$, but also that the market is about to fall, that is, that $r_M < 0$. You would therefore try to establish a pure play on the perceived mispricing.

The return on the portfolio over the next month may be described by Equation 20.1, which states that the portfolio return will equal its "fair" CAPM return (the first two terms on the right-hand side), plus firm-specific risk reflected in the "residual," e, plus an alpha that reflects perceived mispricing:

$$r_{\text{portfolio}} = r_f + \beta(r_M - r_f) + e + \alpha \tag{20.1}$$

To be concrete, suppose that $\beta = 1.20$, $\alpha = 0.02$, $r_f = 0.01$, the current value of the S&P 500 Index is $S_0 = 2,000$, and, for simplicity, that the portfolio pays no dividends. You want to capture the positive alpha of 2% per month, but you don't want the positive beta that the stock entails because you are worried about a market decline. So you choose to hedge your exposure by selling S&P 500 futures contracts.

Assume you hedge your position using the E-Mini S&P 500 contract with multiplier of $50. Because the portfolio has a beta of 1.20, your stock position can be hedged for one month by selling 30 futures contracts:[3]

$$\text{Hedge ratio} = \frac{\$2,500,000}{2,000 \times \$50} \times 1.20 = 30 \text{ contracts}$$

The dollar value of your portfolio after one month will be

$$\$2,500,000 \times \left(1 + r_{\text{portfolio}}\right) = \$2,500,000 \left[1 + .01 + 1.20(r_M - .01) + .02 + e\right]$$
$$= \$2,545,000 + \$3,000,000 \times r_M + \$2,500,000 \times e$$

The dollar proceeds from your futures position will be:

$$30 \times \$50 \times (F_0 - F_1) \qquad \text{Mark-to-market on 30 contracts sold}$$
$$= \$1,500 \times \left[S_0(1.01) - S_1\right] \qquad \text{Substitute for futures price, } F_0, \text{from parity relationship}$$
$$= \$1,500 \times S_0\left[1.01 - (1 + r_M)\right] \qquad \text{Because } S_1 = S_0(1 + r_M) \text{ when no dividends are paid}$$
$$= \$1,500 \times \left[S_0(.01 - r_M)\right] \qquad \text{Simplify}$$
$$= \$30,000 - \$3,000,000 \times r_M \qquad \text{Because } S_0 = 2,000$$

The total value of the stock plus futures position at month's end will be the sum of the portfolio value plus the futures proceeds, which equals

$$\text{Hedged proceeds} = \$2,575,000 + \$2,500,000 \times e \tag{20.2}$$

The dollar exposure to the market from your futures position precisely offsets your exposure from the stock portfolio: you have reduced beta to zero. Your investment is $2.5 million and the expected value of your hedged payoff is $2,575,000, so your total monthly rate of return is 3% plus the remaining nonsystematic risk (the second term of Equation 20.2). The "fair" or equilibrium expected rate of return on such a zero-beta position is the risk-free rate, 1%, so you have preserved the portfolio's alpha of 2%, while eliminating its market exposure.

This is an idealized example of a pure play. In particular, it simplifies by assuming a known and fixed portfolio beta, but it illustrates that the goal is to speculate on the specific

---

[3]We simplify here by assuming that the maturity of the futures contract precisely equals the hedging horizon, in this case, one month. If the contract maturity were longer, one would have to slightly reduce the hedge ratio in a process called "tailing the hedge."

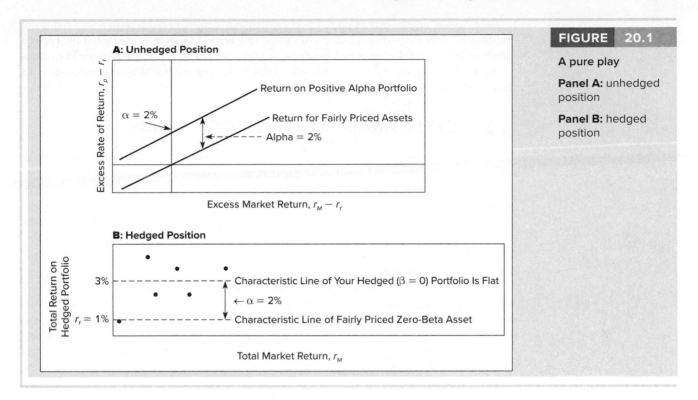

stock while hedging out the undesired market exposure. Once this is accomplished, you can establish any desired exposure to other sources of systematic risk by buying indexes or entering index futures contracts in those markets. Thus, you have made alpha portable.

Figure 20.1 is a graphical analysis of this pure play. Panel A shows the excess returns to betting on a positive-alpha stock portfolio "naked," that is, unhedged. Your *expected* return is better than an equilibrium return given your risk, but because of your market exposure you still can lose if the market declines. Panel B shows the characteristic line for the position with systematic risk hedged out. There is no market exposure.

A warning: Even market-neutral positions are still bets, and they can go wrong. This is not true arbitrage because your profits still depend on whether your analysis (your perceived alpha) is correct. Moreover, you can be done in by simple bad luck, that is, your analysis may be correct but a bad realization of idiosyncratic risk (negative values of e in Equation 20.1 or 20.2) can still result in losses.

What would be the dollar value and rate of return on the market-neutral position if the value of the residual turns out to be −4%? If the market return in that month is 5%, where would the plot of the strategy return lie in each panel of Figure 20.1?

CONCEPT Check   20.2

An apparently market-neutral bet misfired badly in 1998. While the 30- versus 29½-year maturity T-bond strategy (see Example 20.1) worked well over several years, it blew up when Russia defaulted on its debt, triggering massive investment demand for the safest, most liquid assets that drove up the price of the 30-year Treasury relative to its 29½-year counterpart. The big losses that ensued illustrate that even the safest bet—one based on convergence arbitrage—carries risks. Although the T-bond spread had to converge eventually, and in fact it did several weeks later, Long Term Capital Management (LTCM) and other hedge funds suffered large losses on their positions when the spread widened temporarily. The ultimate convergence came too late for LTCM, which was also facing massive losses on its other positions and had to be bailed out.[4]

EXAMPLE 20.2

The Risks of Pure Plays

---

[4]This timing problem is a common one for active managers. We saw other examples of this issue when we discussed limits to arbitrage in Chapter 9. More generally, when security analysts think they have found a mispriced stock, they usually acknowledge that it is hard to know how long it will take for price to converge to intrinsic value.

Even market-neutral bets can result in considerable volatility because most hedge funds use considerable leverage. Most incidents of relative mispricing are fairly minor, and the hedged nature of long-short strategies makes overall volatility low. The hedge funds respond by scaling up their bets. This amplifies gains when their bets work out but also amplifies losses. In the end, the volatility of the funds is not small.

20.4 STYLE ANALYSIS FOR HEDGE FUNDS

While the classic hedge fund strategy may have focused on market-neutral opportunities, as the market has evolved, the freedom to use derivatives contracts and short positions means that hedge funds can in effect follow any investment strategy. While many hedge funds pursue market-neutral strategies, a quick glance at the range of investment styles in Table 20.1 should convince you that many, if not most, funds pursue directional strategies. In these cases, the fund makes an outright bet, for example, on currency movements, the outcome of a take-over attempt, or the performance of an investment sector. These funds are most certainly not hedged, despite their name.

In Chapter 18, we introduced style analysis, which uses regression analysis to measure the exposure of a portfolio to various factors or asset classes. The betas on a series of factors measure the fund's exposure to each source of systematic risk. A market-neutral fund will have no sensitivity to an index for that market. In contrast, directional funds will exhibit significant betas, often called *loadings* in this context, on whatever factors the fund tends to bet on. Observers attempting to identify investment style can use these factor loadings to impute exposures to a range of variables.

We present a simple style analysis for the hedge fund indexes in Table 20.2. The four systematic factors we consider are

- *Interest rates*—the return on long-term U.S. Treasury bonds.
- *Equity markets*—the return on the S&P 500.
- *Credit conditions*—the difference in the return on Baa-rated bonds over Treasury bonds.
- *Foreign exchange*—the percentage change in the value of the U.S. dollar against a basket of foreign currencies.

The excess returns on hedge fund index i in month t may be statistically described by

$$R_{it} = \alpha_i + \beta_{i1} \text{Factor} 1_t + \cdots + \beta_{i4} \text{Factor} 4_t + e_{it} \tag{20.3}$$

The betas (equivalently, factor loadings) measure the sensitivity to each factor. As usual, the residual, e_{it}, measures "nonsystematic" risk that is uncorrelated with the set of explanatory factors, and the intercept, α_i, measures average performance of fund i net of the impact of these systematic factors.

Table 20.2 presents factor exposure estimates for 13 hedge fund indexes. The results confirm that most funds are in fact directional with very clear exposures to one or more of the four factors. Moreover, the estimated factor betas seem reasonable in terms of the funds' stated style. For example:

- The equity market–neutral funds have uniformly low and statistically insignificant factor betas, as one would expect of a market-neutral posture.
- Dedicated short bias funds exhibit substantial negative betas on the S&P index.
- Distressed-firm funds have significant exposure to credit conditions (more positive credit spreads in this table indicate better economic conditions) as well as to the S&P 500. This exposure arises because restructuring activities often depend on access to borrowing, and successful restructuring depends on the state of the economy.
- Global macro funds show negative exposure to a stronger U.S. dollar, which would make the dollar value of foreign investments less valuable.

We conclude that, by and large, most hedge funds are making very explicit directional bets on a wide array of economic factors.

TABLE 20.2   Style analysis for a sample of hedge fund indexes

Funds Group*	Alpha	S&P 500	Long T-Bond	Credit Conditions	U.S. Dollar
All funds	0.0052	0.2718	0.0189	0.1755	−0.1897
	3.3487	5.0113	0.3064	2.0462	−2.1270
Market neutral	0.0014	0.1677	−0.0163	0.3308	−0.5097
	0.1990	0.6917	−0.0589	0.8631	−1.2790
Short bias	0.0058	−0.9723	0.1310	0.3890	−0.2630
	1.3381	−6.3684	0.7527	1.6113	−1.0476
Event driven	0.0071	0.2335	−0.0000	0.2056	−0.1165
	5.1155	4.7858	−0.0002	2.6642	−0.1520
Risk arbitrage	0.0034	0.1498	0.0130	−0.0006	−0.2130
	3.0678	3.8620	0.0442	−0.0097	−3.3394
Distressed	0.0068	0.2080	0.0032	0.2521	−0.1156
	5.7697	4.9985	0.0679	3.8318	−1.6901
Emerging markets	0.0082	0.3750	0.2624	0.4551	−0.2169
	2.8867	3.7452	2.2995	2.8748	−1.3173
Fixed-income arb	0.0018	0.1719	0.2284	0.5703	−0.1714
	1.0149	2.8139	3.2806	5.9032	−1.7063
Convertible arb	0.0005	0.2477	0.2109	0.5021	−0.0972
	0.2197	3.1066	2.3214	3.9825	−0.7414
Global macro	0.0079	0.0746	0.0593	0.1492	−0.2539
	3.5217	0.9437	0.6587	1.1938	−1.9533
Long-short equity	0.0053	0.4442	−0.0070	0.0672	−0.1471
	2.5693	6.1425	−0.0850	0.5874	−1.2372
Managed futures	0.0041	0.2565	−0.2991	−0.5223	−0.2703
	0.8853	1.5944	−1.6310	−2.0528	−1.0217
Multistrategy	0.0075	0.2566	−0.0048	0.1781	−0.1172
	4.2180	4.1284	−0.0684	1.8116	−1.1471

*Fund definitions given in Table 20.1.

Note: Top line of each entry is the estimate of the factor beta. Lower line is the *t*-statistic for that estimate.
Source: Authors' calculations. Hedge fund returns are on indexes computed by Credit Suisse/Tremont Index, LLC.

Analyze the betas of the fixed-income arbitrage index in Table 20.2. Based on these results, are these funds typically market neutral? If not, do their factor exposures make sense in terms of the markets in which they operate?

CONCEPT Check   20.3

20.5 PERFORMANCE MEASUREMENT FOR HEDGE FUNDS

Table 20.3 shows basic performance data for a collection of hedge fund indexes computed from the standard index model with the S&P 500 used as the market benchmark. The model is estimated using monthly returns over the five-year period ending in September 2016. We

TABLE 20.3 Index-model regressions for hedge fund indexes*

	Beta	Serial Correlation	Alpha (%/month)	Sharpe Ratio
Hedge fund composite	0.232	−0.031	−0.17%	0.116
Convertible Arbitrage	0.088	0.151	0.12%	0.238
Dedicated Short Bias	−0.955	−0.113	0.14%	−0.268
Emerging Markets	0.497	−0.069	−0.22%	0.157
Equity Market Neutral	0.169	−0.203	−0.08%	0.097
Event Driven	0.313	0.067	−0.31%	0.054
Fixed Income Arbitrage	0.020	0.104	0.10%	0.244
Global Macro	0.125	−0.094	−0.29%	−0.102
Long/Short Equity	0.501	−0.117	−0.26%	0.195
Managed Futures	−0.071	0.000	0.21%	0.037
Multi-Strategy	0.063	0.123	0.23%	0.448
Average across funds	0.089	−0.017	−0.05%	0.111
S&P 500	1.000	−0.145	0.00%	0.306

*Monthly data, October 2011–September 2016.

Source: Authors' calculations using data downloaded from Credit Suisse, *Hedge Fund Indexes,* hedgeindex.com, October 2016.

report for each index the beta relative to the S&P 500, the serial correlation of returns, the Sharpe ratio, and the alpha. Betas tend to be considerably less than 1; not surprisingly, the beta of the short bias index is large and negative.

By and large, hedge fund performance in this period was not impressive. The average alpha across indexes was slightly negative, and the average Sharpe ratio was less than that of the S&P 500. In earlier periods, however, particularly before 2010, hedge funds seemed to substantially outperform passive indexes. Regardless of this variability in outcome, several factors make hedge fund performance difficult to evaluate, and these are important to consider.

Liquidity and Hedge Fund Performance

Recall that one of the more important extensions of the CAPM is a version that allows for the possibility of a return premium for investors willing to hold less liquid assets. Hedge funds tend to hold more illiquid assets than other institutional investors such as mutual funds. They can do so because of restrictions such as the lock-up provisions that commit investors to keep their investment in the fund for some period of time. Therefore, it is important to control for liquidity when evaluating performance. If it is ignored, what may be no more than compensation for illiquidity may appear to be true alpha, that is, risk-adjusted abnormal returns.

Aragon (2007) demonstrates that hedge funds with lock-up restrictions do tend to hold less liquid portfolios. Moreover, once he controlled for lock-ups or other share restrictions (such as redemption notice periods), the apparently positive average alpha of those funds turned insignificant. Aragon's work suggests that part of any "alpha" exhibited by hedge funds may in fact be an equilibrium liquidity premium rather than a sign of stock-picking ability, in other words, a "fair" reward for providing liquidity to other investors.

Whereas Aragon focuses on the average level of liquidity, Sadka (2009) addresses the liquidity *risk* of hedge funds. He shows that exposure to unexpected declines in market liquidity is an important determinant of hedge fund returns, and that the spread in average returns across the funds with the highest and lowest liquidity exposure may be as much as 6% annually. Hedge fund performance may therefore reflect significant compensation for liquidity risk. Figure 20.2, constructed from data reported in his study, is a scatter diagram relating average

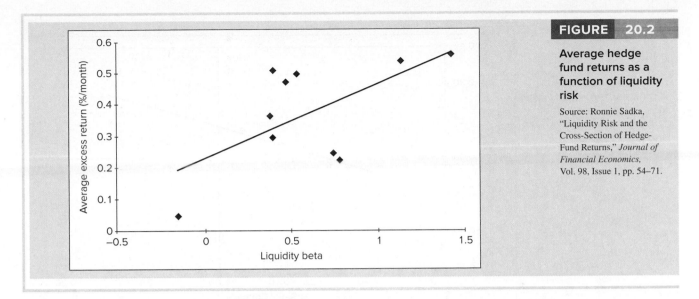

FIGURE   20.2

Average hedge fund returns as a function of liquidity risk

Source: Ronnie Sadka, "Liquidity Risk and the Cross-Section of Hedge-Fund Returns," *Journal of Financial Economics*, Vol. 98, Issue 1, pp. 54–71.

return for the hedge funds in each style group of Table 20.2 to the liquidity-risk beta for that group.[5] Average return clearly rises with exposure to changes in market liquidity.

One symptom of illiquid assets is serial correlation in returns. Positive serial correlation means that positive returns are more likely to be followed by positive than by negative returns. Such a pattern is often taken as an indicator of less liquid markets for the following reason: When accurate and timely prices are not available because an asset is not actively traded, the hedge fund must estimate net asset value and the rate of return. But such procedures are at best imperfect and, as demonstrated by Getmansky, Lo, and Makarov (2004), tend to result in serial correlation in prices as firms either smooth out their value estimates or only gradually mark prices to true market values. Positive serial correlation is therefore often interpreted as evidence of liquidity problems; in nearly efficient markets with frictionless trading, we would expect serial correlation or other predictable patterns in prices to be minimal.[6]

Hasanhodzic and Lo (2007) find that hedge fund returns tend to exhibit significant serial correlation. This symptom of smoothed prices has two important implications. First, it lends further support to the hypothesis that hedge funds are holding less liquid assets and that part of their average returns may reflect liquidity premiums. Second, it implies that their performance measures are upward-biased, because any smoothing in the estimates of portfolio value will reduce total volatility (thereby increasing the Sharpe ratio) as well as covariances and therefore betas with systematic factors (thereby increasing risk-adjusted alphas).

In fact, Figure 20.3 shows that both the alphas and the Sharpe ratios of the hedge fund indexes in Table 20.3 increase with the serial correlation of returns. These results are consistent with the fund-specific results of Hasanhodzic and Lo and suggest that price smoothing may account for some part of the apparently superior risk-adjusted hedge fund performance they find for their sample period.

Performance can be even more difficult to interpret if a hedge fund takes advantage of illiquid markets to manipulate returns by purposely misvaluing illiquid assets. In this regard, it is worth noting that, on average, hedge funds report average returns in December that are substantially greater than their average returns in other months (Agarwal, Daniel, and Naik, 2011). The pattern is stronger for lower-liquidity funds and for funds that are near or beyond

---

[5]Just as the market beta of a stock measures sensitivity of returns to changes in overall market performance as reflected in the return on a broad market index, the liquidity beta measures sensitivity to changes in market liquidity. Because liquidity risk is nondiversifiable, stocks with greater liquidity betas should compensate investors with higher expected rates of return.

[6]Of course, in any particular sample period, the point estimate of serial correlation may be positive or negative. With long data series, we find that serial correlations generally are in fact small.

FIGURE 20.3

Hedge funds with higher serial correlation in returns, an indicator of illiquid portfolio holdings, exhibit both higher Sharpe ratios (Panel A) and higher alphas (Panel B)

Source: Prepared using data in Table 20.3.

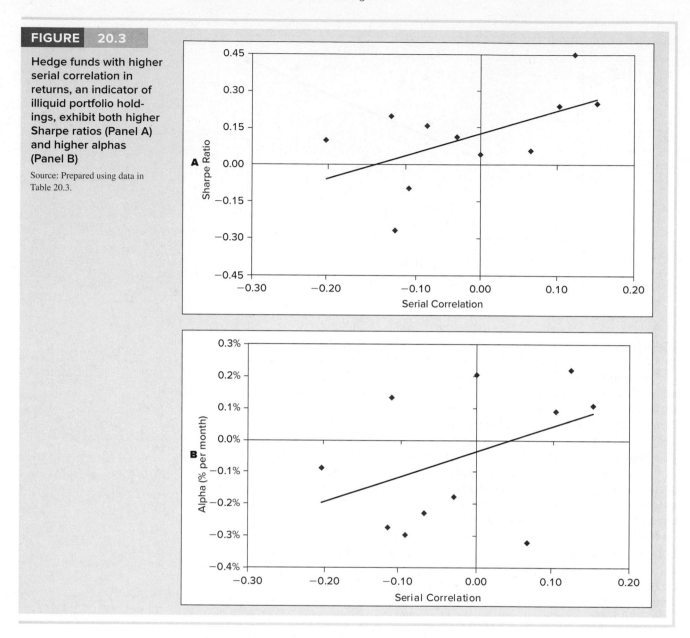

FIGURE 20.3

Hedge funds with higher serial correlation in returns, an indicator of illiquid portfolio holdings, exhibit both higher Sharpe ratios (Panel A) and higher alphas (Panel B)

Source: Prepared using data in Table 20.3.

the threshold return at which performance incentive fees kick in. It appears that funds use their discretion in valuing assets to move returns to December when that will enhance their annual incentive fees.

It also appears that some hedge funds attempt to manipulate their measured performance by buying additional shares in stocks they already own in an effort to push up their prices (Ben-David, Franzoni, Landier, and Moussawi, 2013). The buying takes place just before market close at the end of the month when hedge fund performance is reported. Moreover, the effort is concentrated in less liquid stocks where the price impact would be expected to be greater. If, as these papers suggest, funds take advantage of illiquid markets to manage returns, then accurate performance measurement becomes almost impossible.

Hedge Fund Performance and Selection Bias

We already know that survivorship bias (when only successful funds remain in a database) can affect the estimated performance of a sample of mutual funds. The same problems, as well as related ones, apply to hedge funds. **Backfill bias** arises because hedge fund operators

backfill bias

Bias in the average returns of a sample of funds induced by including past returns on funds that entered the sample only if they happened to be successful.

may not report returns on all funds to database publishers. Funds started with seed capital will eventually open to the public and therefore enter standard databases only if their past performance is deemed sufficiently successful to attract clients. Therefore, the prior performance of funds that find their way into the sample may not be representative of typical performance. **Survivorship bias** arises when unsuccessful funds that cease operation stop reporting returns and leave a database, leaving behind only the successful funds. Malkiel and Saha (2005) find that attrition rates for hedge funds are far higher than for mutual funds—in fact, commonly more than double the attrition rate of mutual funds—making this an important issue to address. Estimates of survivorship bias in various studies are typically substantial, in the range of 2% to 4%.[7]

survivorship bias

Bias in the average returns of a sample of funds induced by excluding past returns on funds that left the sample because they happened to be unsuccessful.

Hedge Fund Performance and Changing Factor Loadings

In Chapter 18, we pointed out that an important assumption underlying conventional performance evaluation is that the portfolio manager maintains a reasonably stable risk profile. But hedge funds are designed to be opportunistic and have considerable flexibility to change that profile. This too can make performance evaluation tricky. And if the risk profile changes systematically with the expected return on the market, performance evaluation is even more difficult.

To see why, look at Figure 20.4, which illustrates the characteristic line of a perfect market timer (see Chapter 18, Section 18.6) who engages in no security selection but moves funds from T-bills into the market portfolio only when the market will outperform bills. The characteristic line is nonlinear, with a slope of 0 when the market underperforms T-bills, and a slope of 1 when it outperforms. But a naïve attempt to estimate a regression equation from this pattern would result in a fitted line with a slope between 0 and 1 and a positive alpha. Neither statistic accurately describes the fund.

As we noted in Chapter 18, and as is evident from Figure 20.4, an ability to conduct perfect market timing is much like obtaining a call option on the underlying portfolio without having to pay for it. Similar nonlinearities would arise if the fund actually buys or writes options. Figure 20.5, Panel A, illustrates the case of a fund that holds a stock portfolio and writes put options on it, and Panel B illustrates the case of a fund that holds a stock portfolio and writes call options. In both cases, the characteristic line is steeper when portfolio returns are poor— in other words, the fund has greater sensitivity to the market when it is falling than when it is rising. This is the opposite profile that would arise from timing ability, which is much like acquiring rather than writing options.[8]

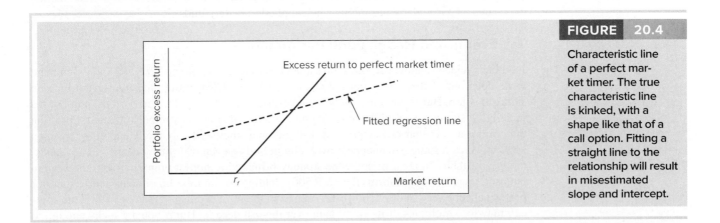

FIGURE   20.4

Characteristic line of a perfect market timer. The true characteristic line is kinked, with a shape like that of a call option. Fitting a straight line to the relationship will result in misestimated slope and intercept.

---

[7]For example, Malkiel and Saha (2005) estimate the bias at 4.4%, Amin and Kat (2003) find a bias of about 2%, and Fung and Hsieh (2000) find a bias of about 3.6%.

[8]But the fund that writes options would at least receive fair compensation for the unattractive shape of its characteristic line in the form of the premium received when it writes the options.

Characteristic lines of stock portfolio with written options

Panel A: Buy stock, write put. Here, the fund writes fewer puts than the number of shares it holds.

Panel B: Buy stock, write calls. Here, the fund writes fewer calls than the number of shares it holds.

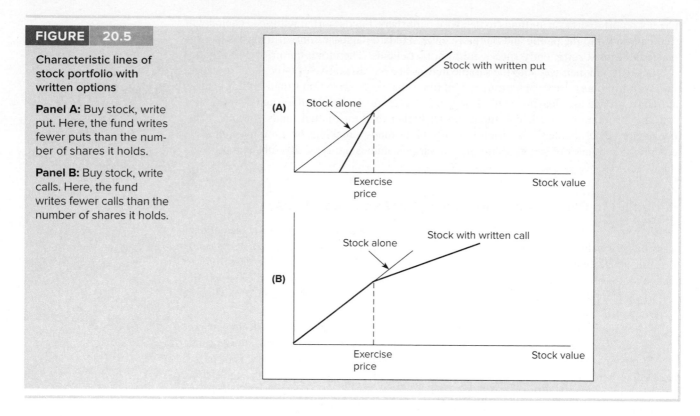

Figure 20.6 presents evidence on these sorts of nonlinearities. A nonlinear regression line is fitted to the scatter diagram of returns on hedge fund indexes plotted against returns on the S&P 500. The fitted lines in each panel suggest that these funds have higher down-market betas (higher slopes) than up-market betas. This is precisely what investors presumably do *not* want: higher market sensitivity when the market is weak. This is evidence that these funds may be *writing* options, either explicitly or implicitly through dynamic trading strategies[9] (see Chapter 16, Section 16.4, for a discussion of such dynamic strategies).

Just as hedge fund betas may be unstable, so may be other aspects of their risk profile, for example, total volatility of returns. Because they have great discretion to use leverage and to trade in derivatives, these funds have tremendous capacity to alter their risk exposures. The bottom line is that conventional performance evaluation methods, which assume fixed market exposures, is particularly hazardous when applied to hedge funds.

Tail Events and Hedge Fund Performance

Imagine a hedge fund whose entire investment strategy is to hold an S&P 500 Index fund and write deep out-of-the-money put options on the index. Clearly the fund manager brings no skill to his job. But if you knew only his investment results over limited periods, and not his underlying strategy, you might be fooled into thinking that he is extremely talented. For if the put options are written sufficiently out-of-the-money, they will only rarely end up imposing a loss, and such a strategy can appear over long periods—even over many years—to be consistently profitable. In most periods, the strategy brings in a modest premium from the written puts and therefore outperforms the S&P 500, yielding the impression of consistently superior performance. Every so often, however, such as in the market crash of October 1987, the strategy may lose multiples of its entire gain over the last decade. But if you are lucky enough to avoid these rare but extreme *tail events* (so named because they fall in the far-left tail of the probability distribution), the strategy might appear to be gilded.

The evidence in Figure 20.6 indicating that some hedge funds are at least implicitly option writers should make us nervous about taking their measured performance at face value. The

[9]Not all the hedge fund categories exhibited this sort of pattern. Many showed effectively symmetric up- and down-market betas. However, Figure 20.6, Panel A, shows that the asymmetry affects hedge funds taken as a group.

Monthly returns on hedge fund indexes versus return on S&P 500, five years ending September 2016

Source: Constructed from data downloaded from **www.hedgeindex.com** and **finance.yahoo.com**.

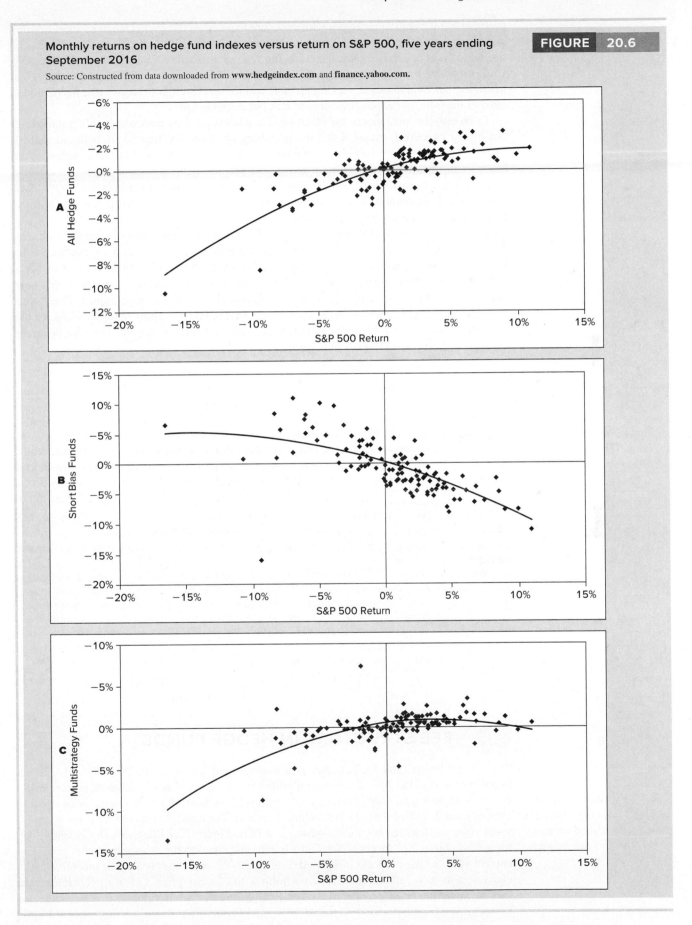

FIGURE   20.6

problem in interpreting strategies with exposure to extreme tail events (such as short options positions) is that these events by definition occur very infrequently, so it can take *decades* of results to fully appreciate their true risk and reward attributes. Nassim Taleb (2004, 2007) who is a hedge fund operator himself, makes the case that many hedge funds are analogous to our hypothetical manager, racking up fame and fortune through strategies that make money *most* of the time, but expose investors to rare but extreme losses.

Taleb uses the metaphor of the black swan to discuss the importance of highly improbable, but highly impactful, events. Until the discovery of Australia, Europeans believed that all swans were white: They had never encountered swans that were not. In their experience, the black swan was outside the realm of reasonable possibility, in statistical jargon, an extreme outlier relative to their sample of observations. Taleb argues that the world is filled with black swans, deeply important developments that simply could not have been predicted from the range of accumulated experience to date.

While we can't predict which black swans to expect, we nevertheless know that one may be making an appearance at any moment. The October 1987 crash, when the market fell by more than 20% in one day, or the financial crisis of 2008–2009 might be viewed as black swans—events that had never taken place before, ones that most market observers would have dismissed as impossible and certainly not worth modeling, but with high impact. These sorts of events seemingly come out of the blue, and they caution us to show humility when we use past experience to evaluate the future risk of our actions. With this in mind, consider again the example of Long-Term Capital Management.

EXAMPLE 20.3

Tail Events and Long-Term Capital Management

In the late 1990s, Long-Term Capital Management (LTCM) was widely viewed as the most successful hedge fund in history. It had consistently provided double-digit returns to its investors, and it had earned hundreds of millions of dollars in incentive fees for its managers. The firm used sophisticated computer models to estimate correlations across assets and believed that its capital was almost 10 times the annual standard deviation of its portfolio returns, presumably enough to withstand any "possible" shock to capital (at least, assuming normal distributions!). But in the summer of 1998, things went badly. On August 17, 1998, Russia defaulted on its sovereign debt and threw capital markets into chaos. LTCM's *one-day* loss on August 21 was $550 million (approximately nine times its estimated *monthly* standard deviation). Total losses in August were about $1.3 billion, despite the fact that LTCM believed that most of its positions were market-neutral relative value trades. Losses accrued on virtually all of its positions, flying in the face of the presumed diversification of the overall portfolio.

How did this happen? The answer lies in the massive flight to quality and, even more so, to liquidity that was set off by the Russian default. LTCM was typically a seller of liquidity (holding less liquid assets, selling more liquid assets with lower yields, and earning the yield spread) and suffered huge losses. This was a different type of shock from those that appeared in its historical sample/modeling period. In the liquidity crisis that engulfed asset markets, the unexpected commonality of liquidity risk across asset classes previously believed to be uncorrelated became obvious. Losses that seemed statistically impossible on past experience had in fact come to pass; LTCM fell victim to a black swan.

20.6   FEE STRUCTURE IN HEDGE FUNDS

incentive fee

A fee charged by hedge funds equal to a share of any investment returns beyond a stipulated benchmark performance.

The typical hedge fund fee structure is a management fee of 1% to 2% of assets plus an **incentive fee** equal to 20% of investment profits beyond a stipulated benchmark performance, annually. Incentive fees are effectively call options on the portfolio with a strike price equal to current portfolio value times (1 + benchmark return). The manager gets the fee if the portfolio value rises sufficiently, but loses nothing if it falls. Figure 20.7 illustrates the incentive fee for a fund with a 20% incentive fee and a hurdle rate equal to the money market rate, r_f. The current value of the portfolio is denoted S_0 and the year-end value is S_T. The incentive fee is equivalent to 0.20 call options on the portfolio with exercise price $S_0(1 + r_f)$. Therefore, we can use an option pricing model like Black-Scholes to estimate its value.

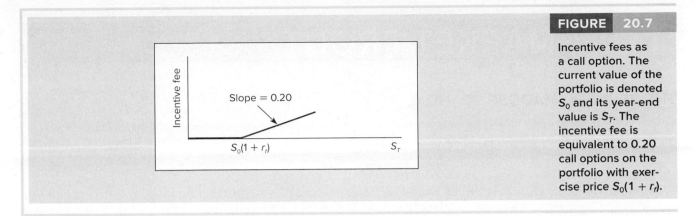

FIGURE 20.7

Incentive fees as a call option. The current value of the portfolio is denoted S_0 and its year-end value is S_T. The incentive fee is equivalent to 0.20 call options on the portfolio with exercise price $S_0(1 + r_f)$.

Suppose the standard deviation of a hedge fund's annual rate of return is 30% and the incentive fee is 20% of any investment return over the risk-free money market rate. If the portfolio currently has a net asset value of $100 per share, and the effective annual risk-free rate is 5% (or 4.88% expressed as a continuously compounded rate), then the implicit exercise price on the incentive fee is $105. The Black-Scholes value of a call option with $S_0 = 100$, $X = 105$, $\sigma = 0.30$, $r = 0.0488$, $T = 1$ year is $11.92, just a shade below 12% of net asset value. Because the incentive fee is worth 20% of the call option, its value is just about 2.4% of net asset value. Together with a typical management fee of 2% of net asset value, the investor in the fund pays annual fees with a total value of 4.4% of assets under management.

EXAMPLE 20.4

Black-Scholes Valuation of Incentive Fees

The major complication to this description of the typical compensation structure is the **high water mark.** If a fund experiences losses, it may not be able to charge an incentive fee unless and until it recovers to its previous higher value. With large losses, this may be difficult. High water marks therefore give managers an incentive to shut down funds that have performed poorly and likely contribute to the high attrition rate for funds noted above.

A notable fraction of the hedge fund universe is invested in **funds of funds,** which are hedge funds that invest in one or more other hedge funds. Funds of funds are also called *feeder funds,* because they feed assets from the original investor to the ultimate hedge fund. They market themselves as providing investors the capability to diversify across funds and also as providing the due diligence involved in screening funds for investment worthiness. In principle, this can be a valuable service because many hedge funds are opaque and feeder funds may have greater insight than typical outsiders.

However, when Bernard Madoff was arrested in December 2008 after admitting to a $65 billion Ponzi scheme, it emerged that many large feeder funds were among his biggest clients and that their "due diligence" may have been, to put it mildly, lacking. At the head of the list was Fairfield Greenwich Advisors, with exposure reported at $7.5 billion, but several other feeder funds and asset management firms around the world were also on the hook for amounts greater than $1 billion. In the end, it appears that some funds had in effect become little more than marketing agents for Madoff. More generally, Brown, Gregoriou, and Pascalau (2011) conclude that highly diversified funds of funds actually exhibit *greater* tail risk, which they attribute to the difficulty of performing timely due diligence on the large number of funds under management. The nearby box presents further discussion of the Madoff affair.

Optionality can have a big impact on expected fees in funds of funds. This is because a fund of funds pays an incentive fee to each underlying fund that outperforms its benchmark, even if the aggregate performance of the fund of funds is poor. In this case, diversification can hurt you (Brown, Goetzmann, and Liang, 2004)!

high water mark

The previous value of a portfolio that must be reattained before a hedge fund can charge incentive fees.

funds of funds

Hedge funds that invest in other hedge funds.

Suppose a fund of funds is established with $1 million invested in each of three hedge funds. For simplicity, we will ignore the asset-value-based portion of fees (the management fee) and focus only on the incentive fee. Suppose that the hurdle rate for the incentive fee is a zero return, so each fund

(continued)

EXAMPLE 20.5

Incentive Fees in Funds of Funds

THE BERNARD MADOFF SCANDAL

Bernard Madoff seemed like one of the great success stories in the annals of finance. His asset management firm, Bernard L. Madoff Investment Securities, reported to its clients that their investments of around $20 billion had grown to about $65 billion in 2008. But that December, Madoff reportedly confessed to his two sons that he had for years been operating a Ponzi scheme. A Ponzi scheme is an investment fraud in which a manager collects funds from clients, claims to invest those funds on their behalf, reports extremely favorable investment returns, but in fact uses the funds for his own purposes. (The schemes are named after Charles Ponzi, whose success with this scheme in the early 1900s made him notorious throughout the United States.) Early investors who ask to redeem their investments are paid back with the funds coming in from new investors rather than with true earnings. The scheme can continue as long as new investors provide enough funds to cover the redemption requests of the earlier ones—and these inflows are attracted both by the superior returns "earned" by early investors and their apparent ability to redeem funds as requested.

As a highly respected member of the Wall Street establishment, Madoff was in a perfect position to perpetrate such a fraud. He was a pioneer in electronic trading and had served as chairman of the NASDAQ stock market. Aside from its trading operations, Bernard L. Madoff Investment Securities LLC also acted as a money manager, and it claimed to achieve highly consistent annual returns, between 10% and 12% in good markets as well as bad. Its strategy was supposedly based on option hedging strategies, but Madoff was never precise about his approach. Still, his stature on Wall Street and the prestige of his client list seemed to testify to his legitimacy. Moreover, he played hard-to-get with new investors, and it appeared that one needed connections to join the fund,

which only increased its appeal. The scheme seems to have operated for decades, but in the 2008 stock market downturn several large clients requested redemptions totaling around $7 billion. With less than $1 billion of assets left in the firm, the scheme collapsed.

Not everyone was fooled, and, in retrospect, several red flags should have aroused suspicion. For example, some institutional investors shied away from the fund, objecting to its unusual opacity. Given the magnitude of the assets supposedly under management, the option hedging trades purportedly at the heart of Madoff's investment strategy should have dominated options market trading volume, yet there was no evidence of their execution. Moreover, Madoff's auditor, a small firm with only three employees (including only one active accountant!), seemed grossly inadequate to audit such a large and complex operation. In addition, Madoff's fee structure was highly unusual. Rather than acting as a hedge fund that would charge a percentage of assets plus incentive fees, he claimed to profit instead through trading commissions on the account—if true, this would have been a colossal price break to clients. Finally, rather than placing assets under management with a custodial bank as most funds do, Madoff claimed to keep the funds in house, which meant that no one could independently verify their existence. In 2000, the SEC received a letter from an industry professional named Harry Markopolos concluding that "Madoff Securities is the world's largest Ponzi scheme," but Madoff continued to operate unimpeded.

The scandal raised several questions. How much help did Madoff receive from others? Exactly how much money was lost? Most of the "lost" funds represented fictitious profits that had never actually been earned, but some money was returned to early investors. How much was skimmed off to support Madoff's lifestyle? And perhaps most important, why didn't the red flags and early warnings prompt a more aggressive response from regulators?

EXAMPLE 20.5

Incentive Fees in Funds of Funds

(concluded)

charges an incentive fee of 20% of total return (if positive). The following table shows the performance of each underlying fund over a year, the gross rate of return, and the return realized by the fund of funds net of the incentive fee. Funds 1 and 2 have positive returns, and therefore earn an incentive fee, but Fund 3 has terrible performance, so its incentive fee is zero.

	Fund 1	Fund 2	Fund 3	Fund of Funds
Start of year (millions)	$1.00	$1.00	$1.00	$3.00
End of year (millions)	$1.20	$1.40	$0.25	$2.85
Gross rate of return	20%	40%	−75%	−5%
Incentive fee (millions)	$0.04	$0.08	$0.00	$0.12
End of year, net of fee	$1.16	$1.32	$0.25	$2.73
Net rate of return	16%	32%	−75%	−9%

Even though the return on the aggregate portfolio of the fund of funds is *negative* 5%, it still pays incentive fees of $0.12 for every $3 invested because incentive fees are paid on the first two well-performing funds. The incentive fees amount to 4% of net asset value. As demonstrated in the last column, this reduces the rate of return earned by investors in the fund of funds from −5% to −9%.

The idea behind funds of funds is to spread risk across several different funds. However, investors need to be aware that these funds of funds may operate with considerable leverage, on top of the leverage of the primary funds in which they invest, which can make returns highly volatile. Moreover, if the various hedge funds in which these funds of funds invest have similar investment styles, the diversification benefits of spreading investments across several funds may be illusory—but the extra layer of steep management fees paid to the manager of the fund of funds certainly is not.[10]

---

[10]One small silver lining: While funds of funds pay incentive fees to each of the underlying funds, the incentive fees they charge their own investors tend to be lower, typically around 10% rather than 20%.

- Like mutual funds, hedge funds pool the assets of several clients and manage the pooled assets on their behalf. However, hedge funds differ from mutual funds with respect to disclosure, investor base, flexibility and predictability of investment orientation, regulation, and fee structure.
- Directional funds take a stance on the performance of broad market sectors. Nondirectional funds establish market-neutral positions on relative mispricing. However, even these hedged positions still present idiosyncratic risk.
- Statistical arbitrage is the use of quantitative systems to uncover many perceived misalignments in relative pricing and ensure profits by averaging over all of these small bets. It often uses data-mining methods to uncover past patterns that form the basis for the established investment positions.
- Portable alpha is a strategy in which one invests in positive-alpha positions, then hedges the systematic risk of that investment, and, finally, establishes market exposure where desired by using passive indexes or futures contracts.
- Performance evaluation of hedge funds is complicated by survivorship bias, by the potential instability of risk attributes, by the existence of liquidity premiums, and by unreliable market valuations of infrequently traded assets.
- Performance evaluation is particularly difficult when the fund engages in option positions. Tail events make it hard to assess the true performance of positions involving options without extremely long histories of returns.
- Hedge funds typically charge investors both a management fee and an incentive fee equal to a percentage of profits beyond some threshold value. The incentive fee is akin to a call option on the portfolio.
- Funds of hedge funds pay the incentive fee to each underlying fund that beats its hurdle rate, even if the overall performance of the portfolio is poor.

SUMMARY

alpha transfer, 649	high water mark, 661	portable alpha, 649	**KEY TERMS**
backfill bias, 656	incentive fee, 660	pure plays, 648	
data mining, 649	lock-up period, 646	statistical arbitrage, 649	
directional strategy, 647	market neutral, 648	survivorship bias, 657	
funds of funds, 661	nondirectional strategy, 647		
hedge fund, 646	pairs trading, 649		

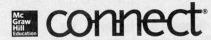 Select problems are available in McGraw-Hill's *Connect*. Please see the Supplements section of the book's frontmatter for more information.

PROBLEM SETS

1. Would a market-neutral hedge fund be a good candidate for an investor's entire retirement portfolio? If not, would there be a role for the hedge fund in the overall portfolio of such an investor? *(LO 20-1)*
2. A fund manages a $3.6 billion equity portfolio with a beta of 0.6. If the S&P contract multiplier is $50 and the index is currently at 2,400, how many contracts should the fund sell to make its overall position market neutral? *(LO 20-2)*

3. A hedge fund charges an incentive fee of 20% of any investment returns above the T-bill rate, which currently is 2% but is subject to a high water mark. In the first year, the fund suffers a loss of 8%. What rate of return must it earn in the second year to be eligible for an incentive fee?   *(LO 20-4)*

4. Which of the following is *most* accurate in describing the problems of survivorship bias and backfill bias in the performance evaluation of hedge funds?   *(LO 20-3)*

   a. Survivorship bias and backfill bias both result in upwardly biased hedge fund index returns.

   b. Survivorship bias and backfill bias both result in downwardly biased hedge fund index returns.

   c. Survivorship bias results in upwardly biased hedge fund index returns, but backfill bias results in downwardly biased hedge fund index returns.

5. Which of the following would be the *most* appropriate benchmark to use for hedge fund evaluation?   *(LO 20-3)*

   a. A multifactor model.

   b. The S&P 500.

   c. The risk-free rate.

6. With respect to hedge fund investing, the net return to an investor in a fund of funds would be lower than that earned from an individual hedge fund because of: *(LO 20-4)*

   a. Both the extra layer of fees and the higher liquidity offered.

   b. No reason; funds of funds earn returns that are equal to those of individual hedge funds.

   c. The extra layer of fees only.

7. Which of the following hedge fund types is *most likely* to have a return that is closest to risk free?   *(LO 20-1)*

   a. A market-neutral hedge fund.

   b. An event-driven hedge fund.

   c. A long-short hedge fund.

8. How might the incentive fee of a hedge fund affect the manager's proclivity to take on high-risk assets in the portfolio?   *(LO 20-4)*

9. Why is it harder to assess the performance of a hedge fund portfolio manager than that of a typical mutual fund manager?   *(LO 20-3)*

10. Is statistical arbitrage true arbitrage? Explain.   *(LO 20-2)*

11. A hedge fund with $1 billion of assets charges a management fee of 2% and an incentive fee of 20% of returns over a money market rate, which currently is 5%. Calculate total fees, both in dollars and as a percent of assets under management, for portfolio returns of: *(LO 20-4)*

    a. −5%.

    b. 0.

    c. 5%.

    d. 10%.

12. A hedge fund with net asset value of $62 per share currently has a high water mark of $66. Is the value of its incentive fee more or less than it would be if the high water mark were $67?   *(LO 20-4)*

13. Reconsider the hedge fund in the previous problem. Suppose it is January 1, the standard deviation of the fund's annual returns is 50%, and the risk-free rate is 4%. The fund has an incentive fee of 20%, but its current high water mark is $66, and net asset value is $62.   *(LO 20-4)*

    a. What is the value of the annual incentive fee according to the Black-Scholes formula?

    b. What would the annual incentive fee be worth if the fund had no high water mark and it earned its incentive fee on its total return?

c. What would the annual incentive fee be worth if the fund had no high water mark and it earned its incentive fee on its return in excess of the risk-free rate? (Treat the risk-free rate as a continuously compounded value to maintain consistency with the Black-Scholes formula.)

d. Recalculate the incentive fee value for part (b) now assuming that an increase in fund leverage increases volatility to 60%.

14. Log in to Connect, link to Chapter 20, and find there a spreadsheet containing monthly values of the S&P 500 Index. Suppose that in each month you had written an out-of-the-money put option on one unit of the index with an exercise price 5% lower than the current value of the index.   *(LO 20-3)*

Templates and spreadsheets are available in Connect

a. What would have been the average value of your gross monthly payouts on the puts over the 10-year period October 1977–September 1987? The standard deviation?

b. Now extend your sample by one month to include October 1987, and recalculate the average payout and standard deviation of the put-writing strategy.

c. What do you conclude about tail risk in naked put writing?

15. Suppose a hedge fund follows the following strategy: Each month it holds $100 million of an S&P 500 Index fund and writes out-of-the-money put options on $100 million of the index with exercise price 5% lower than the current value of the index. Suppose the premium it receives for writing each put is $0.25 million, roughly in line with the actual value of the puts.   *(LO 20-3)*

Templates and spreadsheets are available in Connect

a. Calculate the Sharpe ratio the fund would have realized in the period October 1982–September 1987. Compare its Sharpe ratio to that of the S&P 500. Use the data from the previous problem (available in Connect), and assume the monthly risk-free interest rate over this period was 0.7%.

b. Now calculate the Sharpe ratio the fund would have realized if we extend the sample period by one month to include October 1987.

c. What do you conclude about performance evaluation and tail risk for funds pursuing optionlike strategies?

16. The following is part of the computer output from a regression of monthly returns on Waterworks stock against the S&P 500 Index. A hedge fund manager believes that Waterworks is underpriced, with an alpha of 2% over the coming month.   *(LO 20-2)*

Beta	R-square	Standard Deviation of Residuals
0.75	0.65	0.06 (i.e., 6% monthly)

a. If he holds a $6 million portfolio of Waterworks stock and wishes to hedge market exposure for the next month using one-month maturity S&P 500 futures contracts, how many contracts should he enter? Should he buy or sell contracts? The S&P 500 currently is at 2,000 and the contract multiplier is $50.

b. What is the standard deviation of the monthly return of the hedged portfolio?

c. Assuming that monthly returns are approximately normally distributed, what is the probability that this market-neutral strategy will lose money over the next month? Assume the risk-free rate is 0.5% per month.

Challenge

17. Return to the previous problem.   *(LO 20-2)*

a. Suppose you hold an equally weighted portfolio of 100 stocks with the same alpha, beta, and residual standard deviation as Waterworks. Assume the residual returns (the e terms in Equations 20.1 and 20.2) on each of these stocks are independent of each other. What is the residual standard deviation of the portfolio?

b. Recalculate the probability of a loss on a market-neutral strategy involving equally weighted, market-hedged positions in the 100 stocks over the next month.

18. Return to Problem 16. Now suppose that the manager misestimates the beta of Water-works stock, believing it to be 0.50 instead of 0.75. The standard deviation of the monthly market rate of return is 5%.   **(LO 20-2)**

    a. What is the standard deviation of the (now imperfectly) hedged portfolio?

    b. What is the probability of incurring a loss over the next month if the monthly market return has an expected value of 1% and a standard deviation of 5%? Compare your answer to the probability you found in Problem 16.

    c. What would be the probability of a loss using the data in Problem 17 if the manager similarly misestimated beta as 0.50 instead of 0.75? Compare your answer to the probability you found in part (b).

    d. Why does the misestimation of beta matter so much more for the 100-stock portfolio than it does for the one-stock portfolio?

19. Here are data on three hedge funds. Each fund charges its investors an incentive fee of 20% of total returns. Suppose initially that a fund of funds (FF) manager buys equal amounts of each of these funds and also charges its investors a 20% incentive fee. For simplicity, assume also that management fees other than incentive fees are zero for all funds.   **(LO 20-4)**

	Hedge Fund 1	Hedge Fund 2	Hedge Fund 3
Start of year value (millions)	$100	$100	$100
Gross portfolio rate of return	20%	10%	30%

    a. Compute the rate of return after incentive fees to an investor in the fund of funds.

    b. Suppose that instead of buying shares in each of the three hedge funds, a stand-alone (SA) hedge fund purchases the same *portfolio* as the three underlying funds. The total value and composition of the SA fund is therefore identical to the one that would result from aggregating the three hedge funds. Consider an investor in the SA fund. After paying 20% incentive fees, what would be the value of the investor's portfolio at the end of the year?

    c. Confirm that the investor's rate of return in SA is higher than in FF by an amount equal to the extra layer of fees charged by the fund of funds.

    d. Now suppose that the return on the portfolio held by hedge fund 3 was −30% rather than +30%. Recalculate your answers to parts (a) and (b).

    e. Will either FF or SA charge an incentive fee in the scenario in part (d)? Why then does the investor in FF still do worse than the investor in SA?

WEB *master*

Log on to **https://lab.credit-suisse.com/#/en/home** a site run by Credit Suisse, which maintains a database of the performance of more than 2,000 hedge funds and produces indexes of investment performance for several hedge fund classes. Look for the link to *All Hedge Indexes*. Under the *Download* tab, choose *Performance* (free registration is required for access to this part of the website). Select *Broad Hedge Fund Indices* and then *Download Historical Performance* to obtain historical monthly rates of return on each of the hedge fund subclasses (e.g., market neutral, event driven, dedicated short bias, and so on).

1. Download the most recent five years of monthly returns for each subclass and download returns on the S&P 500 for the same period from **finance.yahoo.com.**

2. Calculate the beta of the equity market–neutral and dedicated short bias funds. Do the results seem reasonable in terms of the orientation of these funds?

3. Look at the year-by-year performance of indexes for several hedge fund classes. How does the variability of performance results in different years compare to that of the S&P 500?

20.1 *a.* Nondirectional. The shares in the fund and the short position in the index swap constitute a hedged position. The hedge fund is betting that the discount on the closed-end fund will shrink and that it will profit regardless of the general movements in the Indian market.

b. Nondirectional. The value of both positions is driven by the value of Toys "R" Us. The hedge fund is betting that the market is undervaluing Petri relative to Toys "R" Us and that as the *relative* values of the two positions come back into alignment, it will profit regardless of the movements in the underlying shares.

c. Directional. This is an outright bet on the price that Generic Pharmaceuticals will eventually command at the conclusion of the predicted takeover attempt.

20.2 The expected rate of return on the position (in the absence of any knowledge about idiosyncratic risk reflected in the residual) is 3%. If the residual turns out to be −4%, then the position will lose 1% of its value over the month or $25,000 and fall to $2,475,000. (Alternatively, in Equation 20.2, set $e = -.04$ and verify that the hedged proceeds are $2,475,000.) The excess return on the market in this month over T-bills would be 5% − 1% = 4%, while the excess return on the hedged strategy would be −1% −1% = −2%, so the strategy would plot in Panel A as the point (4%, −2%). In Panel B, which plots *total* returns on the market and the hedge position, the strategy would plot as the point (5%, −1%).

20.3 Fixed-income arbitrage portfolios show positive exposure to the long bond and to the credit spread. This pattern suggests that these are *not* hedged arbitrage portfolios but in fact are directional portfolios.

Learning Objectives

LO 21-1 Analyze and design lifetime savings plans.

LO 21-2 Account for inflation in formulating savings and investment plans.

LO 21-3 Account for taxes in formulating savings and investment plans.

LO 21-4 Understand tax shelters.

LO 21-5 Show how adverse selection and moral hazard affect markets such as those for insurance or annuity products.

A good deal of investment management in practice revolves around the individual's lifetime savings and investment plan. We all confront many real-world complications such as taxes and tax shelters, Social Security, insurance, and inflation. In this chapter, we illustrate the *principles* of managing personal savings in a complex environment in which taxes and inflation interact, rather than provide a detailed analysis of an (ever-changing) tax code.

Saving for retirement, purchasing a home, and paying for the education of children are the three major financial challenges for many households. Inflation and taxes make the task of gearing investment to accomplish these objectives complex. The long-term nature of savings intertwines the power of compounding with inflation and tax effects. Appropriate

investment strategy also must address adequate insurance coverage for contingencies such as death, disability, and property damage.

We start with the long-term goal of formulating a retirement plan. We investigate the effect of inflation on the savings plan and examine how tax shelters may be integrated into it. The framework developed here may be adapted to the tax codes of many countries. Next we incorporate Social Security and show how to generalize the savings plan to meet other objectives such as purchasing a home and financing children's education. Finally, we discuss uncertainty about longevity and other contingencies. Understanding the spreadsheets we develop along the way will enable you to devise savings/investment plans for yourself and others and adapt them to a changing environment.

21.1 SAVING FOR THE LONG RUN

Our objective in this chapter is to quantify the essentials of savings/investment plans and adapt them to the presence of both inflation and taxes. In the next chapter we describe the framework that the CFA Institute has established to help financial advisers communicate with and involve client households in structuring their savings/investment plans. As a first step, we set up a spreadsheet for a simple retirement plan, ignoring saving for other objectives.

Before we dive in, a brief word on what we mean by saving. Economists think of saving as a way to smooth out the lifetime consumption stream; you save when you have high earnings in order to support consumption in low-income years. In a "global" sense, the concept implies that you save for retirement so that consumption during the retirement years will not be too low relative to consumption during the saving years. In a "local" sense, smoothing consumption implies that you might finance a large purchase such as a car, rather than buy it for cash. Clearly, local consumption smoothing is of second-order importance; that is, how you purchase durable goods has little effect on the overall savings plan, except for very large expenditures such as buying a home or sending children to college. We begin with a savings plan that ignores even large expenditures and later discuss how to integrate these needs.

A Hypothetical Household

Imagine you are now 30 years old and have already completed your formal education, accumulated some work experience, and are planning the rest of your economic life. Your goal is to retire at age 65 with a remaining life expectancy of an additional 25 years. Later on, we will further assume that you have two young children and plan to finance their college education.

For starters, we assume you desire to obtain a (level) annuity for your 25-year retirement period; we postpone discussion of planning for the uncertain time of death. (You may well live to over 100; what then?) Suppose your gross income this year was $50,000, and you expect income to increase at 7% per year. We initially ignore the impact of inflation and taxes. You intend to steadily save 15% of income and invest in safe government bonds that will yield 6% over the entire period. Proceeds from your investments will be automatically reinvested at the same 6% until retirement. Upon retirement, your savings will be used to purchase a 25-year annuity (using the same 6% interest rate) to finance a steady consumption annuity. Let's examine the consequences of this framework.

The Retirement Annuity

We can easily obtain your **retirement annuity** from Spreadsheet 21.1, where we have hidden some age lines. All of the spreadsheets in the chapter are available in Connect.

Let's see how this spreadsheet was constructed. To view the formulas used in an Excel spreadsheet, click on the "Formulas" tab on the command ribbon and choose "Show Formulas." The formula view of Spreadsheet 21.1 is shown in the lower panel (numbers are user inputs).

Inputs in row 2 include the number of retirement years (cell A2 = 25); the income growth rate (cell B2 = .07); nominal portfolio rate of return (cell D2 = .06); age (column A); and income at age 30 (B4 = 50,000). Column B computes income in future years using the growth rate in cell B2; column C computes annual savings by applying the savings rate (cell C2) to income; and column E computes consumption as the difference between income and savings: column B − column C. Cumulative savings appear in column D. To obtain the value in D6, for example, multiply cell D5 by 1 plus the assumed rate of return in cell D2 (the ROR) and then add current savings from column C. Finally, C40 shows the sum of savings over the lifetime, and E40 converts cumulative savings (including interest) at age 65 to a 25-year annuity using the financial function PMT from Excel's function menu: PMT(rate, nper, PV, FV).

We observe that your retirement fund will accumulate approximately $2.5 million (cell D39) by age 65. This hefty sum shows the power of compounding because your contributions to the savings account were only $1.1 million (C40). This fund will yield an annuity

retirement annuity

Stream of level cash flows available for consumption during one's retirement years.

SPREADSHEET 21.1

The savings plan

Z

Spreadsheets are available
in Connect

	A	B	C	D	E
1	Retirement Years	Income Growth	Savings Rate	ROR	
2	25	0.07	0.15	0.06	
3	Age	Income	Savings	Cumulative Savings	Consumption
4	30	50,000	7,500	7,500	42,500
5	31	53,500	8,025	15,975	45,475
9	35	70,128	10,519	61,658	59,608
19	45	137,952	20,693	308,859	117,259
29	55	271,372	40,706	943,477	230,666
39	65	533,829	80,074	2,457,518	453,755
40	Total	7,445,673	1,116,851	Retirement Annuity	192,244

	A	B	C	D	E
1	Retirement Years	Income Growth	Savings Rate	ROR	
2	25	0.07	0.15	0.06	
3	Age	Income	Savings	Cumulative Savings	Consumption
4	30	50000	=B4*$C$2	=C4	=B4-C4
5	31	=B4*(1+$B$2)	=B5*$C$2	=D4*(1+$D$2)+C5	=B5-C5
39	65	=B38*(1+$B$2)	=B39*$C$2	=D38*(1+$D$2)+C39	=B39-C39
40	Total	=SUM(B4:B39)	=SUM(C4:C39)	Retirement Annuity	=PMT($D$2,$A$2,-$D$39,0,0)

of \$192,244 per year (E40) for your 25-year retirement, which seems quite attractive, except that the standard of living you'll have to get accustomed to in your retirement years is much lower than your consumption at age 65 (E39). In fact, if you unhide the hidden lines, you'll see that upon retirement, you'll have to make do with what you used to consume at age 51. This may not worry you much because, with your children having flown the coop and the mortgage paid off, you may be able to maintain the luxury to which you recently became accustomed. But your projected well-being is deceptive: Get ready to account for inflation and taxes.

CONCEPT Check 21.1

If you project an ROR of only 5%, what savings rate would you need to provide the same retirement annuity?

21.2 ACCOUNTING FOR INFLATION

Inflation puts a damper on your plans in two ways: First, it erodes the purchasing power of the cumulative dollars you have so far saved. Second, the *real* dollars you earn on your portfolio each year depend on the *real* interest rate, which is approximately equal to the nominal rate minus inflation. Because an appropriate savings plan must generate an acceptable *real* annuity, we must recast the entire plan in real dollars. We will assume your income still is forecast to grow at a 7% rate, but now you recognize that part of income growth is due to inflation, which is running at 3% per year.

A Real Savings Plan

To convert nominal dollars to real dollars we need to calculate the price level in future years relative to today's prices. The "deflator" (or relative price level) for a given year is that year's price level divided by today's. It equals the dollars required at that future date to provide the same purchasing power as \$1 today (at age 30). For an inflation rate of $i = 3\%$, the deflator for age 35 is $(1 + i)^5$, or in Excel notation, $(1 + i)\text{^}5 = 1.03\text{^}5 = 1.16$. By age 65, the deflator is 2.81. Thus, even with a moderate rate of inflation, nominal dollars will lose a lot of purchasing power over long horizons. We also can compute the *real* rate of return (rROR) from the nominal ROR of 6% using Equation 5.7 from Chapter 5: rROR = (ROR − i)/(1 + i) = 3/1.03 = 2.91%.

Spreadsheet 21.2, with the formula view below it, reworks Spreadsheet 21.1 to account for inflation. In addition to the rate of inflation (cell C2) and the real rate of return (F2), the major addition to this sheet is the price level deflator (column C). Instead of nominal consumption, we present **real consumption** (column F), calculated by dividing nominal consumption (column B − column D) by the price deflator, column C.

The numbers have changed considerably. Gone is the luxurious retirement we anticipated earlier. At age 65 and beyond, with a real annuity of $49,668 (cell F40), you will have to revert to a standard of living equal to that you attained at age 34; this is less than a third of your real consumption in your last working year, at age 65. The reason is that the retirement fund of $2.5 million (E39) is worth only $873,631 in today's purchasing power (E39/C39). Such is the effect of inflation. If you wish to do better than that, you must save more.

In our initial plan (Spreadsheet 21.1), we envisioned consuming a level, nominal annuity in retirement. This is an inappropriate goal once we account for inflation because it would imply a declining real standard of living starting at age 65. Its purchasing power at age 65 in terms of current dollars would be $68,320 (i.e., $192,244/1.03^{35}), and at age 90 only $32,630. (Check this!)

It is tempting to contemplate solving the problem of an inadequate retirement annuity by increasing the assumed rate of return on investments. However, this can be accomplished only by investing in riskier assets with higher expected returns. Much of this text elaborates on how to do so efficiently; yet it also emphasizes that while taking on risk will give you an *expectation* of a better retirement, it implies as well the possibility of doing a lot worse. At age 30, you should be able to tolerate some risk to the retirement annuity for the simple reason that if things go wrong, you can change course, increase your savings rate, and work harder. As you get older, this option progressively fades, and assuming more risk becomes less of a viable option. For most investors, therefore, the right approach is to stick with a conservative assumed ROR and make the effort to balance the standard of living before and after retirement.

Therefore, the only variable under your control in this spreadsheet is the rate of saving. To improve retirement lifestyle relative to the preretirement years, without jeopardizing its safety, you will have to reduce consumption during the saving years—there is no free lunch.

real consumption

Nominal consumption divided by the price deflator.

If you project a rate of inflation of 4%, what nominal ROR on investments would you need to maintain the same real retirement annuity as in Spreadsheet 21.2?

CONCEPT Check 21.2

SPREADSHEET 21.2

A real retirement plan

	A	B	C	D	E	F
1	Retirement Years	Income Growth	Rate of Inflation	Savings Rate	ROR	rROR
2	25	0.07	0.03	0.15	0.06	0.0291
3	Age	Income	Deflator	Saving	Cumulative Savings	rConsumption
4	30	50,000	1.00	7,500	7,500	42,500
5	31	53,500	1.03	8,025	15,975	44,150
9	35	70,128	1.16	10,519	61,658	51,419
19	45	137,952	1.56	20,693	308,859	75,264
29	55	271,372	2.09	40,706	943,477	110,167
39	65	533,829	2.81	80,074	2,457,518	161,257
40	Total	7,445,673		1,116,851	Real Annuity	49,668

	A	B	C	D	E	F
1	Retirement Years	Income Growth	Rate of Inflation	Savings Rate	ROR	rROR
2	25	0.07	0.03	0.15	0.06	=(E2-C2)/(1+C2)
3	Age	Income	Deflator	Savings	Cumulative Savings	rConsumption
4	30	50000	1	=B4*$D$2	=D4	=(B4-D4)/C4
5	31	=B4*(1+$B$2)	=C4*(1+$C$2)	=B5*$D$2	=E4*(1+$E$2)+D5	=(B5-D5)/C5
39	65	=B38*(1+$B$2)	=C38*(1+$C$2)	=B39*$D$2	=E38*(1+$E$2)+D39	=(B39-D39)/C39
40	Total	=SUM(B4:B39)		=SUM(D4:D39)	Real Annuity	=PMT($F$2,$A$2,-$E$39/$C$39,0,0)

Spreadsheets are available in Connect

**Spreadsheets are
available in Connect**

	A	B	C	D	E	F
1	Retirement Years	Income Growth	Rate of Inflation	Savings Rate	ROR	rROR
2	25	0.07	0.03	0.1	0.06	0.0291
3	Age	Income	Deflator	Savings	Cumulative Savings	rConsumption
4	30	50,000	1.00	5,000	5,000	45,000
5	31	53,500	1.03	5,511	10,811	46,592
9	35	70,128	1.16	8,130	44,351	53,480
19	45	137,952	1.56	21,492	260,927	74,751
29	55	271,372	2.09	56,819	947,114	102,471
39	65	533,829	2.81	150,212	2,964,669	136,331
40	Total	7,445,673		1,572,466	**Real Annuity**	59,918

	A	B	C	D	E	F
1	Retirement Years	Income Growth	Rate of Inflation	Savings Rate	ROR	rROR
2	25	0.07	0.03	0.1	0.06	=(E2-C2)/(1+C2)
3	Age	Income	Deflator	Savings	Cumulative Savings	rConsumption
4	30	50000	1	=B4*C4*$D$2	=D4	=(B4-D4)/C4
5	31	=B4*(1+$B$2)	=C4*(1+$C$2)	=B5*C5*$D$2	=E4*(1+$E$2)+D5	=(B5-D5)/C5
39	65	=B38*(1+$B$2)	=C38*(1+$C$2)	=B39*C39*$D$2	=E38*(1+$E$2)+D39	=(B39-D39)/C39
40	Total	=SUM(B4:B39)		=SUM(D4:D39)	**Real Annuity**	=PMT($F$2,$A$2,-$E$39/$C$39,0,0)

An Alternative Savings Plan

In Spreadsheet 21.2, we saved a constant fraction of income. But since real income grows over time (nominal income is expected to grow at 7% while inflation is only 3%), we might consider deferring our savings toward future years when real income is higher. By applying a higher savings rate to future (higher) real income, we are able to reduce the current savings rate. In Spreadsheet 21.3, we use a base savings rate of 10% (lower than the savings rate in the previous spreadsheet), but we increase it by 3% per year. Saving in each year therefore equals a fixed savings rate times annual income (column B), times the exponential growth factor 1.03^t. By saving a larger fraction of income in later years, when real income is larger, you create a smoother profile of real consumption.

Spreadsheet 21.3 shows that with an *initial* savings rate of 10%, compared with the unchanging 15% rate in the previous spreadsheet, you can achieve a retirement annuity of $59,918, larger than the $49,668 annuity in the previous plan.

Notice that real consumption in the early years is greater than with the previous plan. What you have done is to postpone some saving until your income is higher. At first blush, this plan is preferable: It allows for a more comfortable consumption of 90% of income at the outset when your real income is lower, and a consistent increase in standard of living during your earning years, all without significantly affecting the retirement annuity. But this program has one serious downside: By postponing the bulk of your savings to a later age, you come to depend on your health, longevity, and, more ominously *(and without possibility of insurance)*, on a successful future career. Put differently, this plan achieves comfort by increasing risk, making this choice a matter of risk tolerance.

Suppose you like the plan of tilting saving toward later years, but worry about the increased risk of postponing the bulk of your saving to later years. Is there anything you can do to mitigate the risk?

21.3   ACCOUNTING FOR TAXES

flat tax

A tax code that taxes all income (possibly above some exemption) at a fixed rate.

To initiate our discussion of taxes, let's assume that you are subject to a **flat tax** rate of 25% on taxable income less one exemption, currently $15,000 but indexed to future changes in consumer prices. This is similar to several proposals for a simplified U.S. tax code that have

SPREADSHEET 21.4

Saving with a simple tax code

	A	B	C	D	E	F	G	H
1	Retirement Years	Income Growth	Rate of Inflation	Exemption Now	Tax Rate	Savings Rate	ROR	rROR
2	25	0.07	0.03	15000	0.25	0.15	0.06	0.0291
3	Age	Income	Deflator	Exemption	Taxes	Savings	Cumulative Savings	rConsumption
4	30	50,000	1.00	15,000	8,750	6,188	6,188	35,063
5	31	53,500	1.03	15,450	9,605	6,584	13,143	36,224
9	35	70,128	1.16	17,389	13,775	8,453	50,188	41,319
19	45	137,952	1.56	23,370	31,892	15,909	245,334	57,864
29	55	271,372	2.09	31,407	69,943	30,214	733,467	81,773
39	65	533,829	2.81	42,208	148,611	57,783	1,874,346	116,365
40	Total				1,884,163	834,226	Real Annuity=	37,882
41	**RETIREMENT**							
42	Age	Nom Withdraw	Deflator	Exemption	Taxes		Funds Left	rConsumption
43	66	109,792	2.90	43,474	17,247		1,877,014	31,931
47	70	123,572	3.26	48,931	15,743		1,853,382	33,056
52	75	143,254	3.78	56,724	12,200		1,721,015	34,656
57	80	166,071	4.38	65,759	6,047		1,422,954	36,503
62	85	192,521	5.08	76,232	0		883,895	37,882
67	90	223,185	5.89	88,374	0		0	37,882
68	Total	4,002,944			203,199			

	A	B	C	D	E	F	G	H
1	Retirement Years	Income Growth	Rate of Inflation	Exemption Now	Tax Rate	Savings Rate	ROR	rROR
2	25	0.07	0.03	15000	0.25	0.15	0.06	=(G2-C2)/(1+C2)
3	Age	Income	Deflator	Exemption	Taxes	Savings	Cumulative Savings	rConsumption
4	30	50000	1	=$D$2*C4	=(B4-D4)*$E$2	=(B4-E4)*$F$2	=F4	=(B4-E4-F4)/C4
5	31	=B4*(1+$B$2)	=C4*(1+$C$2)	=$D$2*C5	=(B5-D5+G4*$G$2)*$E$2	=(B5-E5)*$F$2	=G4*(1+$G$2)+F5	=(B5-E5-F5)/C5
39	65	=B38*(1+$B$2)	=C38*(1+$C$2)	=$D$2*C39	=(B39-D39+G38*$G$2)*$E$2	=(B39-E39)*$F$2	=G38*(1+$G$2)+F39	=(B39-E39-F39)/C39
40	Total				=SUM(E4:E39)	=SUM(F4:F39)	Real Annuity	=PMT($H$2,$A$2,-$G$39/$C$39,0,0)
41	**RETIREMENT**							
42	Age	Nom Withdraw	Deflator	Exemption	Taxes		Funds Left	rConsumption
43	66	=$H$40*C43	=C39*(1+$C$2)	=$D$2*C43	=MAX(0,(G39*$G$2-D43)*$E$2)		=G39*(1+$G$2)-B43	=(B43-E43)/C43
44	67	=$H$40*C44	=C43*(1+$C$2)	=$D$2*C44	=MAX(0,(G43*$G$2-D44)*$E$2)		=G43*(1+$G$2)-B44	=(B44-E44)/C44
67	90	=$H$40*C67	=C66*(1+$C$2)	=$D$2*C67	=MAX(0,(G66*$G$2-D67)*$E$2)		=G66*(1+$G$2)-B67	=(B67-E67)/C67
68	Total	=SUM(B43:B67)			=SUM(E43:E67)			

Ⅹ
Spreadsheets are available in Connect

been floated from time to time. An important feature of this (and the existing) tax code is that the tax rate is levied on nominal income and applies as well to investment income. To adapt our spreadsheet to this simple tax code, we must add columns for taxes and after-tax income. The tax-adjusted plan is shown in Spreadsheet 21.4. It adapts the savings plan of Spreadsheet 21.2, that is, saving 15% of nominal income.

The top panel of the sheet deals with the earning years. Column D adjusts the exemption (D2) by the price level (column C). Column E applies the tax rate (cell E2) to taxable income (column B − column D). The savings rate (F2) is applied to after-tax income (column B − column E), allowing us to calculate cumulative savings (column G) and real consumption (column H). The formula view shows the detailed construction.

As you might have expected, real consumption is lower in the presence of taxes, as are savings and therefore, the retirement fund. The retirement fund provides for a real, before-tax annuity of only $37,882, compared with $49,668 absent taxes in Spreadsheet 21.2.

The bottom panel of the sheet shows the further reduction in real consumption due to taxes paid during the retirement years. While you do not pay taxes on the cumulative savings in the retirement plan (you did that already as the savings accrued interest), you do pay taxes on interest earned by the fund while you are drawing it down. These taxes are quite significant and further deplete the fund and its net-of-tax earning power. For this reason, your consumption annuity is lower in the early years when your fund has not yet been depleted and taxable interest income is higher.

In the end, despite a handsome income that grows at a real rate of almost 4%, an aggressive savings rate of 15%, and a modest rate of inflation, you will be able to achieve only a modest (but at least low-risk) real retirement income. This is a reality with which most people must struggle. Whether to sacrifice more of today's standard of living through an increased rate of saving, or take some risk in the form of saving a real annuity and/or invest in a risky portfolio with a higher expected return, is a question of preference and risk tolerance.

tax shelters

Means by which to postpone payment of tax liabilities for as long as possible.

21.4   THE ECONOMICS OF TAX SHELTERS

Tax shelters range from the simple to the mind-bogglingly complex, yet they all have one common objective: to postpone payment of tax liabilities for as long as possible. We know already that this isn't a minor issue. Postponement implies a smaller present value of tax payment, and a tax paid with a long delay can have present value near zero. However, the advantage of delay also depends on how tax rates are projected to change over time. If the tax rate on retirement income is higher than during earning years, the value of a tax deferral may be questionable; on the other hand, if the tax rate will decline, deferral is even more advantageous.

A Benchmark Tax Shelter

Postponing tax payments is the only attainable objective because, whenever you have taxable income, a tax liability is created that can (almost) never be erased.[1] For this reason, a benchmark tax shelter *postpones* all taxes on savings and the income on those savings. We will assume that taxes on your entire savings account will be paid during retirement, as you draw down the retirement fund. This sort of shelter is actually equivalent to the tax treatment of Individual Retirement Accounts (IRAs) which we discuss later, so we will describe this structure as having an "IRA style."

To examine the impact of an IRA-style structure (assuming you shelter all your savings) in a situation comparable to the nonsheltered flat-tax scenario, we maintain the same consumption level as in Spreadsheet 21.4 (flat tax with no shelter) but now input the new, sheltered savings plan in Spreadsheet 21.5. This focuses the entire effect of the tax shelter onto retirement consumption.

SPREADSHEET 21.5

Saving with a flat tax and an IRA-style tax shelter

Spreadsheets are available in Connect

	A	B	C	D	E	F	G	H
1	Retirement Years	Income Growth	Rate of Inflation	Exemption Now	Tax Rate	Savings Rate	ROR	rROR
2	25	0.07	0.03	15000	0.25	0.15	0.06	0.0291
3	Age	Income	Deflator	Exemption	Taxes	Savings	Cumulative Savings	rConsumption
4	30	50,000	1.00	15,000	5,016	9,922	9,922	35,063
5	31	53,500	1.03	15,450	5,465	10,724	21,242	36,224
9	35	70,128	1.16	17,389	7,628	14,600	83,620	41,319
19	45	137,952	1.56	23,370	16,695	31,106	438,234	57,864
29	55	271,372	2.09	31,407	34,952	65,205	1,393,559	81,773
39	65	533,829	2.81	42,208	71,307	135,087	3,762,956	116,365
40	Total				944,536	1,773,854	**Real Annuity**	**76,052**
41	**RETIREMENT**							
42	Age	Nom Withdraw	Deflator	Exemption	Taxes		Funds Left	rConsumption
43	66	220,420	2.90	43,474	44,236		3,768,313	60,789
47	70	248,085	3.26	48,931	49,789		3,720,867	60,789
52	75	287,598	3.78	56,724	57,719		3,455,127	60,789
57	80	333,405	4.38	65,759	66,912		2,856,737	60,789
62	85	386,508	5.08	76,232	77,569		1,774,517	60,789
67	90	448,068	5.89	88,374	89,924		0	60,789
68	Total	8,036,350			1,612,828			

	A	B	C	D	E	F	G	H
1	Retirement Years	Income Growth	Rate of Inflation	Exemption Now	Tax Rate	Savings Rate	ROR	rROR
2	25	0.07	0.03	15000	0.25	0.15	0.06	=(G2-C2)/(1+C2)
3	Age	Income	Deflator	Exemption	Taxes	Savings	Cumulative Savings	rConsumption
4	30	50000	1	=$D$2*C4	=(H4*C4-D4)*$E$2	=B4-E4-H4*C4	=F4	35062.5
5	31	=B4*(1+$B$2)	=C4*(1+$C$2)	=$D$2*C5	=(H5*C5-D5)*$E$2	=B5-E5-H5*C5	=G4*(1+$G$2)+F5	36223.77
39	65	=B38*(1+$B$2)	=C38*(1+$C$2)	=$D$2*C39	=(H39*C39-D39)*$E$2	=B39-E39-H39*C39	=G38*(1+$G$2)+F39	116364.98
40	Total				=SUM(E4:E39)	=SUM(F4:F39)	**Real Annuity**	=PMT($H$2,$A$2,-$G$39/$C$39,0,0)
41	**RETIREMENT**							
42	Age	Nom Withdraw	Deflator	Exemption	Taxes		Funds Left	rConsumption
43	66	=$H$40*C43	=C39*(1+$C$2)	=$D$2*C43	=MAX(0,(B43-D43)*$E$2)		=G39*(1+$G$2)-B43	=(B43-E43)/C43
44	67	=$H$40*C44	=C43*(1+$C$2)	=$D$2*C44	=MAX(0,(B44-D44)*$E$2)		=G43*(1+$G$2)-B44	=(B44-E44)/C44
67	90	=$H$40*C67	=C66*(1+$C$2)	=$D$2*C67	=MAX(0,(B67-D67)*$E$2)		=G66*(1+$G$2)-B67	=(B67-E67)/C67
68	Total	=SUM(B43:B67)			=SUM(E43:E67)			

---

[1]Bankruptcy or death can erase some tax liabilities, though. We will avoid dealing with these unhappy outcomes.

In this sheet, we input desired real consumption (column H, copied from Spreadsheet 21.4). Taxes (column E) are then calculated by applying the tax rate (E2) to nominal consumption less the exemption (H × C − D). Thus, savings are the residual from nominal income (B) minus taxes (E), minus nominal consumption (H × C). The retirement panel shows that you pay taxes on all withdrawals—all funds in the retirement account are subject to tax.

The results are interesting. Total lifetime taxes paid with the IRA tax shelter amount to $2.5 million, a lot more than $2.1 million without the shelter. The reason is that the tax shelter allows for larger savings that increase lifetime income to $3.7 million compared with only $1.9 million without the shelter. Because in this comparison, income and consumption during the earnings years are as before, the entire net gain from the shelter is pushed to the retirement years. Thus, the real annuity (pretax) during retirement increases from $37,882 to $76,052.

With the IRA-style tax shelter, all your taxes are due during retirement. Is the trade-off between exemption and tax rate different from the circumstance where you have no shelter?	**CONCEPT** Check **21.4**

The Effect of the Progressive Nature of the Tax Code

Because of the exemption, the flat tax is somewhat progressive: Taxes as a fraction of income increase along with income. For very high incomes, the marginal tax rate (25%) is only slightly higher than the average rate. With income of $50,000 at the outset, the average tax rate is 17.5% ($.25 \times 35,000/50,000$), and it grows steadily as income grows. In general, with a flat tax, the ratio of the average to marginal rate equals the ratio of taxable to gross income. This ratio becomes 0.89 at age 45, at which point the average tax rate is above 22%. The current U.S. tax code, with multiple income brackets, is much more progressive than our assumed structure.

In Spreadsheet 21.6 we work with a more **progressive tax** structure that is closer to the U.S. federal tax code augmented with an average state tax. Our hypothetical tax schedule is described in Table 21.1.

We have seen that taxes on income during the earning period have a greater effect because of the time value of money; early tax payments (during earning years) have a larger effect than later payments during retirement years. In a progressive tax environment, this effect is magnified if your retirement income (withdrawal from the retirement fund) is lower than income during the earning years.

Spreadsheet 21.6, which continues to maintain the same income and consumption during the earning years, differs from Spreadsheet 21.4 only in that column E replaces the flat tax

progressive tax

Taxes are an increasing fraction of income.

SPREADSHEET 21.6

Saving with a progressive tax

	A	B	C	D	E	F	G	H
1	Retirement Years	Income Growth	Rate of Inflation	Exemption Now	Tax rates in	Savings Rate	ROR	rROR
2	25	0.07	0.03	10000	Table 21.1	0.15	0.06	0.0291
3	Age	Income	Deflator	Exemption	Taxes	Savings	Cumulative Savings	rConsumption
4	30	50,000	1.00	10,000	8,000	6,300	6,300	35,700
5	31	53,500	1.03	10,300	8,716	6,718	13,396	36,958
9	35	70,128	1.16	11,593	12,489	8,646	51,310	42,262
19	45	137,952	1.56	15,580	32,866	15,763	248,018	57,333
29	55	271,372	2.09	20,938	76,587	29,218	731,514	79,076
39	65	533,829	2.81	28,139	186,335	52,124	1,833,644	104,970
40	Total		Total	632,759	2,116,533	799,371	**Real Annuity**	37,059
41	**RETIREMENT**							
42	Age	Nom Withdraw	Deflator	Exemption	Taxes		Fund Left	rConsumption
43	66	107,408	2.90	28,983	16,207		1,836,254	31,467
47	70	120,889	3.26	32,620	15,371		1,813,134	32,347
52	75	140,143	3.78	37,816	13,083		1,683,643	33,599
57	80	162,464	4.38	43,839	8,831		1,392,054	35,045
62	85	188,341	5.08	50,821	1,757		864,701	36,714
67	90	218,338	5.89	58,916	0		0	37,059
68	Total	3,916,018			**227,675**			

Spreadsheets are available in Connect

TABLE 21.1	Income tax schedule used for the progressive tax

Taxable Income* Over	But Not Over	The Tax Is	of the Amount Over
$ 0	$ 50,000	$ 0 + 20%	$ 0
50,000	150,000	10,000 + 30%	50,000
150,000	. . .	40,000 + 40%	150,000

*Current exemption with this code is assumed to be $10,000; that is, taxable income = income − 10,000. The exemption and tax brackets are continuously adjusted for inflation.

with the tax schedule of Table 21.1. Surprisingly, the effect on consumption in both earning and retirement years is small. This is due to two offsetting effects. The higher tax rate applied to the high incomes of the later earning years increases the tax bite. At the same time, the lower income and corresponding lower tax bracket during both early earning and retirement years dampen that effect. The bottom line is that a roughly typical life cycle of earnings mitigates the difference between flat and progressive tax schedules.

Spreadsheet 21.7 augments the progressive tax code with our benchmark (IRA-style) tax shelter that allows you to pay taxes on consumption (minus an exemption) and accumulate a tax liability to be paid during your retirement years. The construction of this spreadsheet is identical to Spreadsheet 21.5, with the only difference being the tax structure built into column E. We copied the real preretirement consumption stream from Spreadsheet 21.6 to focus the effect of the tax shelter on the standard of living during the retirement years. Spreadsheet 21.7 shows that the lower tax bracket during the retirement years allows you to pay lower taxes over the life of the plan and significantly increases retirement consumption. The use of the IRA-style tax shelter increases the retirement annuity by an average of $32,000 a year, a better improvement than we obtained from the shelter with the flat tax.

The effectiveness of the shelter also has a sort of hedge quality. If you become fortunate and strike it rich, the tax shelter will be less effective because your tax bracket will be higher at retirement. However, mediocre or worse outcomes will result in low marginal rates upon retirement, making the shelter more effective and the tax bite lower.

CONCEPT Check	21.5	Are you indifferent between an increase in the low-income-bracket tax rate versus an equal increase in the high-bracket tax rates?

SPREADSHEET 21.7

The benchmark (IRA) tax shelter with a progressive tax code

Spreadsheets are available in Connect

	A	B	C	D	E	F	G	H
1	Retirement Years	Income Growth	Rate of Inflation	Exemption Now	Tax rates in	Savings Rate	ROR	rROR
2	25	0.07	0.03	10000	Table 21.1	0.15	0.06	0.0291
3	Age	Income	Deflator	Exemption	Taxes	Savings	Cumulative Savings	rConsumption
4	30	50,000	1.00	10,000	5,140	9,160	9,160	35,700
5	31	53,500	1.03	10,300	5,553	9,880	19,590	36,958
9	35	70,128	1.16	11,593	7,480	13,654	77,112	42,262
19	45	137,952	1.56	15,580	14,749	33,880	434,916	57,333
29	55	271,372	2.09	20,938	32,920	72,885	1,455,451	79,076
39	65	533,829	2.81	28,139	66,100	172,359	4,125,524	104,970
40	Total			632,759	879,430	2,036,474	Real Annuity	83,380
41	**RETIREMENT**							
42	Age	Nom Withdraw	Deflator	Exemption	Taxes		Funds Left	rConsumption
43	66	241,658	2.90	28,983	49,311		4,131,398	66,366
47	70	271,988	3.26	32,620	55,500		4,079,381	66,366
52	75	315,309	3.78	37,816	64,340		3,788,036	66,366
57	80	365,529	4.38	43,839	74,588		3,131,989	66,366
62	85	423,749	5.08	50,821	86,467		1,945,496	66,366
67	90	491,241	5.89	58,916	100,239		0	66,366
68	Total	8,810,670	Total		1,797,848			

21.5 A MENU OF TAX SHELTERS

Defined Benefit Plans

The Employee Retirement Income Security Act (ERISA) of 1974 sets out rules that govern the management of one of two types of employee pension funds: a "defined benefit" retirement plan, or a "defined contribution" retirement plan.

Defined benefit plans vary in their particulars, but in general they amount to an annuity that replaces a certain percentage of employee income upon retirement. An employer that offers a defined benefit plan must dedicate and manage a stand-alone fund that promises to pay retired employees (those who have served the required number of years to qualify for pension payouts) a specified (or "defined") amount of income for their lifetimes. Corporations are responsible for investing sufficient funds to ensure that the projected cash flows from these investments will cover the payouts owed to employees. Thus, the corporation bears the risk that arises when the pension fund is invested in risky assets.

defined benefit plan
A pension fund that promises a specified level of income to vested retired employees.

The government plays a dual role in this pension coverage: First, it exempts from taxes contributions to defined benefit funds as well as earnings on pension fund assets. Second, the government has established the Pension Benefit Guarantee Corporation (PBGC) to guarantee a portion of the pension benefits promised to vested employees if the sponsoring firm defaults and has underfunded the pension plan. Because corporations filing for bankruptcy may renege on their promises of benefits, their risk is limited. In contrast, employees bear potentially catastrophic risk from corporate bankruptcy, only partially mitigated by PBGC benefits that are often far smaller than promised defined benefits. This arrangement may encourage sponsoring corporations to opt for higher expected return but riskier investment strategies in the pension fund, as they are able to off-load a good portion of investment risk onto their employees and the government.

Defined Contribution Plans

Defined contribution plans are better known as 401(k) (private-sector) plans or 403(b) (not-for-profit) plans from the relevant paragraphs of the ERISA legislation that enabled them (the two are essentially identical and we will refer to all of them as 401(k) plans).

In a **401(k) plan,** the employer sets up an account for each employee with an administrator, usually an investment management company such as Fidelity or Vanguard. The employee contributes a fraction of wages, and the employer likewise contributes a fraction of wages to the account. Like wages, this type of compensation is tax deductible to the firm. It is a tax-efficient form of employee compensation because both the contributed funds and investment earnings are shielded from individual taxes until later in life. To limit lost tax revenue, the government limits annual employee contributions. In 2018, the maximum allowed contribution was $18,500 until the age of 50 and $24,500 for those aged 50 and over.

401(k) plans
Defined contribution pension plans wherein the employer matches a portion of the employee's contribution up to a set percentage.

An immediate implication of the employer match is that 401(k) employees should contribute at least the amount that maximizes the employer's matching contributions, even if this calls for borrowing to pay for consumption needs.

Individual Retirement Accounts

Individual Retirement Accounts (IRAs) were set up by Congress in 1984 to increase the incentives to save for retirement. The limited scope of these accounts is an important feature. Currently, annual contributions are limited (in 2018) to $5,500. Workers 50 years of age and older can increase annual contributions by up to another $1,000. IRAs are somewhat illiquid (as are most shelters), in that there is a 10% penalty on withdrawals prior to age 59½. However, allowances for early withdrawal with no penalty for qualified reasons such as (one-time) purchase of a home or higher education expenses substantially mitigate the problem.

As far as retirees are concerned, 401(k) plans and IRAs are in most respects identical; employees can use both, combining the benefits from each. Hence, from this point on, we refer to them both simply as retirement "accounts" or retirement "plans."

The IRS allows you to choose two very different schedules of tax shelters for your retirement accounts: One is called *traditional* (introduced first) and the other, *Roth* (after the congressman who proposed it). The choice between them is not trivial.

traditional retirement account

Contributions to the account and investment earnings are tax sheltered until retirement.

TRADITIONAL RETIREMENT PLANS Contributions to **traditional retirement accounts** are tax deductible, as are the earnings in the account until retirement. In principle, if you were able to contribute all your savings to a traditional account, your savings plan would be identical to our benchmark tax shelter (Spreadsheets 21.5 and 21.7), with the effectiveness of tax mitigation depending on your marginal tax rate upon retirement.

Roth account

Contributions are not tax sheltered, but investment earnings are never taxed.

ROTH RETIREMENT PLANS A **Roth account** is a variation on the traditional tax shelter, with both a drawback and an advantage. Contributions to Roth plans are *not* tax deductible. However, earnings on the accumulating funds in the Roth account are tax-free, and unlike a traditional plan, no taxes are paid upon withdrawals of savings during retirement. The trade-off is not easy to evaluate. To gain insight and illustrate how to analyze the trade-off, we contrast Roth with traditional plans under the currently more realistic, progressive tax code.

Roth Accounts with the Progressive Tax Code

As we have noted, a traditional plan is identical to the benchmark tax shelter set up under two alternative tax codes in Spreadsheets 21.5 and 21.7. We saw that, as a general rule, the effectiveness of a tax shelter depends on the progressivity of the tax code: Lower tax rates during retirement favor the postponement of tax obligations until one's retirement years. With a Roth plan, you pay no taxes at all on withdrawals during the retirement phase. The question is whether this advantage is sufficient to compensate for the nondeductibility of contributions, which is the primary advantage of the traditional plan.

To evaluate the trade-off, Spreadsheet 21.8 modifies Spreadsheet 21.7 (progressive tax) to conform to the features of a Roth plan; that is, we eliminate deductibility of contributions and taxes during the retirement phase. We keep consumption during the earning years the same as they were in the benchmark (traditional) tax shelter to compare the standard of living in retirement afforded by a Roth tax shelter.

Table 21.2 demonstrates the difference between the two types of shelters. In both cases, lifetime income and real consumption during the earning years, as well as the progressive

---

SPREADSHEET 21.8

Roth plan with a progressive tax

Z

Spreadsheets are available in Connect

	A	B	C	D	E	F	G	H
3	Retirement Years	Income Growth	Rate of Inflation	Exemption Now	Tax Rates in	Savings Rate	ROR	rROR
4	25	0.07	0.03	10000	Table 21.1	0.15	0.06	0.0291
5	Age	Income	Deflator	Exemption	Taxes	Savings	Cumulative Savings	rConsumption
6	30	50,000	1.00	10,000	8,000	6,300	6,300	35,700
7	31	53,500	1.03	10,300	8,640	6,793	13,471	36,958
11	35	70,128	1.16	11,593	11,764	9,370	52,995	42,262
21	45	137,952	1.56	15,580	28,922	19,707	278,528	57,333
31	55	271,372	2.09	20,938	64,661	41,143	883,393	79,076
41	65	533,829	2.81	28,139	145,999	92,460	2,432,049	104,970
42	Total	7,445,673		632,759	1,752,425	1,163,478	**Real Annuity**	**49,153**
43	**RETIREMENT**							
44	Age	Nom Withdraw	Deflator	Exemption	Taxes		Funds Left	rConsumption
45	66	142,460	2.90	28,983	0		2,435,512	49,153
49	70	160,340	3.26	32,620	0		2,404,847	49,153
54	75	185,879	3.78	37,816	0		2,233,096	49,153
59	80	215,484	4.38	43,839	0		1,846,348	49,153
64	85	249,805	5.08	50,821	0		1,146,895	49,153
69	90	289,593	5.89	58,916	0		0	49,153
70	Total	5,194,003			0			

TABLE 21.2 Traditional vs. Roth plan tax shelters under a progressive tax code		
	Traditional Plan	**Roth Plan**
Lifetime labor income	**$7,445,673**	**$7,445,673**
Taxes ($):		
Earning years	$ 879,430	$ 1,752,425
Retirement years	1,797,848	0
Total paid over lifetime	**$2,677,278**	**$1,752,425**
Lifetime average tax rate (%)	35.96%	23.54%
Retirement annuity:		
Before-tax	$ 83,380	$ 49,153
After-tax	66,366	49,153

tax scheme, are identical. The only difference is which plan you choose, traditional or Roth. Hence the first line of Table 21.2, lifetime labor income, is fixed at $7.4 million. But the shelter works differently in each case. The traditional plan shelters more income during the earning years, resulting in total taxes of only $879,430, compared with $1.75 million under the Roth plan. In the retirement years, however, the Roth plan entails no taxes, while the traditional plan results in taxes of just under $1.8 million. Lifetime taxes are $2.7 million using the traditional account compared with only $1.75 million for the Roth plan. Despite this, the larger accumulation in the traditional IRA account results in a larger retirement fund ($4.1 million compared with $2.4 million) and a larger real after-tax retirement annuity of $66,366. The bottom line is that the traditional plan is more effective for this middle-income family.

The explanation of why the traditional plan is better in this example also indicates when the Roth plan may be preferred. If your income (and therefore your tax rate) is higher in your working years, then the tax shield of the traditional plan will be more valuable, as was the case for the investor in Spreadsheet 21.8. However, if you believe that tax rates across the board will increase in the future, you may prefer the Roth plan, for which retirement income is entirely tax exempt. Another advantage of Roth plans has to do with IRA contribution limits: Limits on Roth contributions apply to after-tax rather than to pretax dollars, allowing more funds to be funneled into your retirement account than are allowed in the traditional plans.

Notice in Table 21.2 that the lifetime average tax rate for saving with a traditional plan is 35.96%. This is a result of a large accumulation of earnings on savings that are taxed on retirement and shows the importance of early accumulation. Despite the higher lifetime taxes, this tax shelter ends up with larger after-tax real consumption during retirement. The lifetime average tax rate is not a good measure of the effect of taxes on lifetime consumption, because it does not fully account for the timing of tax collections. In the circumstances we postulated (a long period with middle-class earnings levels), the tax savings with Roth trumps the traditional plan.

Suppose all taxpayers were like you, and the IRS wished to raise a fixed tax revenue. Is the traditional or Roth plan the better choice?

CONCEPT
C h e c k
21.6

Risky Investments and Capital Gains as Tax Shelters

So far we have limited our examples to assume safe investments that yield a sure 6%. This number, coupled with the inflation assumption (3%), determined the results of various savings rules given the appropriate tax configuration. Clearly, the 6% return and 3% inflation assumptions are not hard numbers, and you must consider the implications of other possible scenarios over the life of the savings plan. The spreadsheets we developed make scenario analysis quite easy. Once you set up a spreadsheet with a contemplated savings plan, you can vary the inputs for ROR (the nominal rate of return) and inflation and record the implications for each scenario. The probabilities of possible deviations from the expected numbers and your risk tolerance will dictate which savings plan provides you with sufficient security of obtaining your goals. This sensitivity analysis will be even more important when you consider risky investments.

The tax shelters we described allow you to invest in a broad array of securities and mutual funds, and you can invest your nonsheltered savings in any asset. Which portfolio to choose is a matter of risk versus return. That said, taxes lend importance to the otherwise largely irrelevant aspect of cash dividends and interest income versus capital gains.

Under current U.S. tax law, interest income is taxed at the same rate as other earned income. However, most dividend and long-term capital gains income is subject to lower tax rates: 0% for low-to-moderate-income investors, 15% for middle-to-upper-income investors, and 20% for the highest-income households (e.g., taxable income in 2018 higher than $479,000 for married couples filing a joint return).[2] However, you pay the applicable rate on capital gains only when you sell the security. Thus, investing in nondividend-paying securities provides an implicit partial tax shelter. Investment in a low- or no-dividend portfolio therefore may be the efficient vehicle for investors who are investing more than the IRA contribution limit. Another advantage of such portfolios is that you can sell securities that have lost value to realize capital losses and thereby reduce your tax bill in any given year. This virtue of risky securities is called the *tax-timing option.*

The average dividend yield on the S&P 500 stocks is only a bit above 2%, and other indexes (such as NASDAQ) bear an even lower yield. This means that you can easily construct a well-diversified portfolio with a very low dividend yield. Such a portfolio allows you to utilize the tax advantage of capital gains versus dividends. Spreadsheet 21.9 adapts Spreadsheet 21.6 (progressive tax with no shelter) to a no-dividend portfolio of stocks, maintaining the same preretirement consumption stream, holding the ROR at 6%, and assuming 15% a capital gains tax rate. Real retirement consumption, averaging $45,105, is almost identical to that supported by a Roth plan (Spreadsheet 21.8).[3]

SPREADSHEET 21.9

Saving with no-dividend stocks under a progressive tax

Spreadsheets are available in Connect

	A	B	C	D	E	F	G	H
3	Retirement Years	Income Growth	Rate of Inflation	Exemption Now	Tax rates in	Savings Rate	ROR	rROR
4	**25**	0.07	0.03	10000	Table 21.1	0.15	0.06	0.0291
5	Age	Income	Deflator	Exemption	Taxes	Savings	Cumulative Savings	rConsumption
6	30	50,000	1.00	10,000	8,000	6,300	6,300	35,700
7	31	53,500	1.03	10,300	8,640	6,793	13,471	36,958
11	35	70,128	1.16	11,593	11,764	9,370	52,995	42,262
21	45	137,952	1.56	15,580	28,922	19,707	278,528	57,333
31	55	271,372	2.09	20,938	64,661	41,143	883,393	79,076
41	65	533,829	2.81	28,139	145,999	92,460	2,432,049	104,970
42	Total				1,752,425	1,163,478	**Real Annuity**	**49,153**
43	**RETIREMENT**				Tax Rate	Capital Gains		
44	Age	Nom Withdraw	Deflator	Cum Cap Gains	on Exemption	Taxes	Funds Left	rConsumption
45	66	142,460	2.90	1,340,186	28,983	6,799	2,435,512	46,808
49	70	160,340	3.26	1,561,124	32,620	10,178	2,404,847	46,033
54	75	185,879	3.78	1,660,844	37,816	14,598	2,233,096	45,293
59	80	215,484	4.38	1,503,386	43,839	19,338	1,846,348	44,742
64	85	249,805	5.08	995,489	50,821	24,535	1,146,895	44,326
69	90	289,593	5.89	1,500	58,916	30,626	0	43,955
70	Total				1,056,691	445,850		

[2]High-income investors (e.g., married couples with over $250,000 of taxable income) also face an additional tax surcharge of 3.8% on their investment earnings.

[3]In Spreadsheet 21.9 we did not take full advantage of the tax code. You can defer capital gains longer by specifying the particular shares you sell so that you sell first new shares with little capital gains and old shares last.

Sheltered versus Unsheltered Savings

Suppose your desired level of savings is double the amount you are able to shelter. At the same time you wish to invest equal amounts in stocks and bonds. Where should you keep the stocks and where the bonds? You will be surprised by how many investors make the costly mistake of holding the stocks in a tax-protected account and the bonds in an unsheltered account. Most of the return from bonds is in the form of taxable interest payments, while stocks already provide some tax shelter.

Recall that tax shelters enhance the retirement annuity via two elements: (1) tax deferral on contributions and (2) tax deferral on the investment income earned on savings. The effectiveness of each element depends on the tax rate on withdrawals. Traditional plans contain both of these advantages; Roth plans provide only the second, but with the offsetting advantage that the tax rate on withdrawals is zero. Therefore, we need to analyze the stock–bond shelter question separately for each type of retirement plan. Table 21.3 shows the trade-offs for a Roth plan. The difference is apparent by comparing the taxes in each column. With stocks inside and bonds outside the shelter you pay taxes early and at the ordinary income rate. When you remove stocks from and move bonds into the shelter, you pay taxes later at the lower capital gains rate.

When you use a traditional plan, contributions are tax deferred regardless of whether you purchase stocks or bonds, so we need to compare only taxes on income from savings and withdrawal. Table 21.4 shows the trade-off for a traditional plan.

The advantage ends up being the same as with the Roth plan. By removing stocks from and moving bonds into the shelter, you gain the deferral on the bond interest during the savings phase. During the retirement phase you gain the difference between the ordinary income and the capital gains rate on the gains from the stocks.

Does the rationale of sheltering bonds rather than stocks apply to preferred stocks? **CONCEPT Check 21.7**

TABLE 21.3 Investing Roth plan contributions in stocks and bonds

Phase	Asset	Stocks Inside; Bonds Outside	Stocks Outside; Bonds Inside
Savings	Bonds	Taxed upon accrual	No taxes
	Stocks	No taxes	Taxes deferred
Withdrawal*	Bonds	No taxes	No taxes
	Stocks	No taxes	Taxed at capital gains rate

*Because the retirement annuity is similar in both plans, taxes on this annuity are ignored.

TABLE 21.4 Investing stocks and bonds in traditional plans

Phase	Asset	Stocks Inside; Bonds Outside	Stocks Outside; Bonds Inside
Savings	Bonds	Taxed on accrual	Taxes deferred
	Stocks	Tax deferred	Taxes deferred
Withdrawal*	Bonds	No taxes	Taxed at marginal rate
	Stocks	Taxed at marginal rate	Taxed at capital gains rate

*Because the retirement annuity is similar in both plans, taxes on this annuity are ignored.

21.6 SOCIAL SECURITY

Social Security

Federally mandated pension plan established to provide minimum retirement benefits to all workers.

Social Security (SS) is a cross between a pension and an insurance plan. It is regressive in that employees pay a proportional (currently 6.2%) tax on gross wages only up to an income cap of $128,400 (in 2018). Employers match employees' contributions and therefore also pay a 6.2% Social Security tax directly to the federal government. There is also a Medicare tax of 1.45% assessed on both employee and employer; this tax is not subject to an income cap. On the other hand, SS is progressive in the way it allocates benefits: low-income individuals receive a relatively larger replacement of preretirement income upon retirement.

SS payments are made throughout one's entire working life, but only the highest 35 years of contributions count for the determination of benefits. Benefits are in the form of a lifetime real annuity based on a retirement age of 67, although you can retire earlier (as of age 62) or later (up to age 70) and draw a smaller or larger annuity, respectively.[4]

One reason SS is projected to face fiscal difficulties in future years is the increased longevity of the population and the rising proportion of retirees in the overall population. The projected large deficits in future Social Security budgets will require financial reform. Increasing the retirement age in line with increased longevity would not constitute a reduction in the present value of expected benefits to plan participants and therefore would seem a reasonable solution to deficits arising from growing life expectancy.

CONCEPT Check 21.8

Part of your retirement expenditures will be paid for with your Social Security benefits. Part will come from your retirement savings. Compare the risks surrounding the income stream that will be generated from each of these sources.

21.7 LARGE PURCHASES

Sending a child to a private college can cost a family well in excess of $50,000 a year for four years. Even a state college can cost more than $30,000 a year. Many families will send two or more children to college, creating a need to finance large expenditure. Other large expenditures such as a second home (we deal with the primary residence in the next section) or an expensive vehicle present similar problems, albeit on a smaller scale.

The question is whether planned, large outflows during the working years require a major innovation in our planning tools. The answer is no. All you need to do is add a column to your spreadsheet for extra-consumption expenditures that come out of savings. As long as cumulative savings do not turn negative as the outflows take place, the only effect to consider is the reduction in the retirement annuity that results from these expenditures. To respond to a lower-than-desired retirement annuity you have four options: (1) Increase the savings rate, (2) live with a smaller retirement annuity, (3) do away with or reduce the magnitude of the expenditure item, or (4) increase expected ROR by taking on more risk. Recall though, that in Section 21.2, we suggested option 4 isn't viable for many investors.

The situation is a little more complicated when the extra-consumption expenditures create negative cumulative savings in the retirement plan. In principle, one can simply borrow to finance these expenditures (as is common for large purchases such as automobiles). Again, the primary variable of interest is the retirement annuity. The problem, however, is that if you arrive at a negative savings level quite late in your savings plan, you will be betting the farm on the success of the plan in later years. Pushing risk into later years, other things equal, is more dangerous because you will have little time to recover from any setback.

An illuminating example requires adding only one column to Spreadsheet 21.2, as shown in Spreadsheet 21.10. Column G adds the extra-consumption expenditures. We use as input

---

[4]Retirement age for individuals born before 1960 is 66. For a complete listing of retirement ages, go to **www.socialsecurity.gov**.

SPREADSHEET 21.10

Financing children's education

	A	B	C	D	E	F	G
1	Retirement Years	Income Growth	Rate of Inflation	Savings Rate	ROR	rROR	Extra-Cons
2	25	0.07	0.03	0.15	0.06	0.0291	40,000
3	Age	Income	Deflator	Savings	Cumulative Savings	rConsumption	Expenditures
4	30	50,000	1.00	7,500	7,500	42,500	0
5	31	53,500	1.03	8,025	15,975	44,150	0
9	35	70,128	1.16	10,519	61,658	51,419	0
19	45	137,952	1.56	20,693	308,859	75,264	0
22	48	168,997	1.70	25,349	375,099	84,378	68,097
23	49	180,826	1.75	27,124	354,588	87,654	70,140
24	50	193,484	1.81	29,023	260,397	91,058	144,489
25	51	207,028	1.86	31,054	158,252	94,595	148,824
26	52	221,520	1.92	33,228	124,331	98,268	76,644
27	53	237,026	1.97	35,554	88,401	102,084	78,943
28	54	253,618	2.03	38,043	131,748	106,049	0
29	55	271,372	2.09	40,706	180,359	110,167	0
39	65	533,829	2.81	80,074	1,090,888	161,257	0
40	Total			1,116,851	Real Annuity	22,048	

𝕏

Spreadsheets are available in Connect

(cell G2) a hypothetical $40,000 cost of one college year per child. We assume your first child will be college-bound when you are 48 years old and the second when you are 50. The expenditures in column G are inflated by the price level in column C and subtracted from cumulative savings in column E.

The real retirement annuity prior to this extra-consumption expenditure was $49,688, but "after-children," it falls to $22,048. The expenditure of $320,000 in today's dollars lowers your lifetime real consumption by 25 × ($49,688 − $22,048) = $690,514 because of the loss of interest on the funds that would have been saved. If you change the input in G2 to $25,000 (a reasonable cost estimate for many public colleges), the retirement annuity falls to $32,405, a loss of "only" 35% in the standard of living.

Another tax shelter comes in the form of a "529 plan" that allows for tax-exempt saving for higher education (see, for example, **www.saveforcollege.com**). These plans are similar to Roth plans in that they are funded with after-tax dollars, but investment earnings are not taxed. Deployment of such plans can reduce the impact of children's education on lifetime consumption.

What, if anything, should you do about the risk of a rapid increase in college tuition?	CONCEPT Check	**21.9**

21.8 HOME OWNERSHIP: THE RENT-VERSUS-BUY DECISION

Many people dream of owning a home and for good reason. In addition to the natural desire for roots that goes with owning your home, a house is an important hedge for most families. Dwelling is the largest long-term consumption item, and fluctuations in the cost of dwelling are responsible for the largest consumption risk they face. Dwelling costs, in turn, are subject to general price inflation, as well as to significant fluctuations specific to geographic location.

However, homes are illiquid assets, and transaction costs in buying/selling a house are high. Therefore, purchasing a home that isn't expected to be a long-term residence for the owner may well be a speculative investment with inferior expected returns.

With all this in mind, it is evident that investment in a home enters the savings plan in two ways. First, during the working years the cash down payment and mortgage payments should be treated just like any other large, extra-consumption expenditure as discussed earlier. Second, home ownership affects your retirement plan because if you own your home free and clear by the time you retire, you will need a smaller annuity to get by; moreover, the value of the house is part of retirement (and bequest) wealth.

CONCEPT **21.10**
Check
Should you have any preference for fixed- versus variable-rate mortgages?

21.9 UNCERTAIN LONGEVITY AND OTHER CONTINGENCIES

Perhaps the most daunting uncertainty in our life is the time it will end. This uncertainty has economic implications. Old age is hard enough without worrying about expenses. Yet the amount of money you may need to save is at least proportional to longevity. Not knowing how much you will need, plus a healthy degree of risk aversion, requires saving a lot more than necessary just to insure against the fortune of longevity.

life annuity

An annuity that lasts for your entire life.

One solution to this problem is to invest in a life annuity to supplement Social Security benefits. When you own a **life annuity** that pays until you die, the provider bears the risk of the time of death. To survive, the provider must earn a rate of return commensurate with risk. Except for wars and natural disasters, however, an individual's time of death is a unique, nonsystematic risk. It would appear, then, that the cost of a life annuity should be a simple calculation of interest rates applied to life expectancy from mortality tables. Unfortunately, adverse selection upsets this approach.

adverse selection

The tendency for any proposed deal to attract the type of party who would make the deal a losing proposition to the offering party.

Adverse selection is the tendency for any proposed contract (deal) to attract the type of party who would make the contract a losing proposition to the offering party. A good example of adverse selection arises in health care. Suppose that Blue Cross offers health coverage where you choose your doctor and Blue Cross pays 80% of the costs. Another HMO covers 100% of the cost but charges a fixed fee per treatment. If HMOs were to price the services on the basis of a survey of the average health care needs in the population at large, they would be in for an unpleasant surprise. People who need frequent and more expensive care would prefer the fixed-fee HMO plan over the cost-sharing Blue Cross plan. The adverse selection in this case is that higher-need individuals will choose the plan that provides more complete coverage. The individuals that the HMO most wants *not* to insure are most likely to sign up for coverage. Hence, to stay in business, HMOs must expect their patients to have greater than average needs, and price the policy on this basis.

Providers of life annuities can expect a good dose of adverse selection as well, as people with the longest life expectancies will be their most enthusiastic customers. Therefore, it is advantageous to acquire these annuities at a younger age, before either individuals or insurers learn much about their particular life expectancies. The Social Security trust does not face adverse selection because virtually the entire population is forced into the purchase regardless of their health status.

Unfortunately we also must consider untimely death or disability of a member of the household. These require an appropriate amount of life and disability insurance, particularly in the early stage of the life cycle. The appropriate coverage should be thought of in the context of a retirement annuity. Coverage should replace at least the most essential part of the retirement annuity.

CONCEPT **21.11**
Check
Insurance companies offer life insurance on your children. Does it make economic sense to buy such insurance?

21.10 MATRIMONY, BEQUEST, AND INTERGENERATIONAL TRANSFERS

In the context of a retirement plan, we think of risk in terms of safety first. The imperative to avoid disastrous outcomes makes mean-variance analysis inadequate. We touched on this issue in the context of (1) raising the ROR by tilting toward riskier investments, (2) avoiding savings plans that rely too heavily on savings in later years, and (3) acquiring life insurance and life annuities.

One sort of insurance the market cannot supply is wage insurance. If we could obtain wage insurance, a savings plan would be a lot easier to formulate. **Moral hazard** is the reason for this void in the marketplace. Moral hazard is the tendency for a party to a contract (deal) to change behavior in a way that makes the deal less attractive to the other party. For example, a person who buys wage insurance would have an incentive to consume leisure at the expense of work effort. Moral hazard is also why insuring items for more than their market or intrinsic value is prohibited. If your warehouse were insured for lots more than its value, you might have less incentive to prevent fires, an obvious moral hazard.

In contrast, marriage provides a form of co-insurance that extends also to the issue of longevity. A married couple has a greater probability that at least one will survive to an older age, giving greater incentive to save for a longer life. Put differently, saving for a longer life has a smaller probability of going to waste.

Bequest is another motive for saving. When you save for members of the next generation (or beyond), you double the planning horizon, and by considering later generations as well, you can make it effectively infinite. This has implications for the composition of the savings portfolio. For example, the common argument that you should gradually shift out of stocks and into bonds as you age is less salient when bequest motives are in play.

Having discussed marriage co-insurance and bequest, we cannot fail to mention that despite the virtues of saving for the longest term, many individuals overshoot the mark. When a person saves for old age and passes on before taking full advantage of the nest egg, the estate is called an "involuntary, intergenerational transfer." Data show that such transfers are widespread. This suggests that people make too little use of the market for life annuities. Hopefully you will not be one of them, both because you will live to a healthy old age and because you'll have a ball spending your never-expiring annuity.

moral hazard

The phenomenon whereby one party to a contract has an incentive to change behavior in a way that makes the contract less attractive to the other party.

SUMMARY

- The major objective of a savings plan is to provide for adequate retirement income.
- Even moderate inflation will affect the purchasing power of the retirement annuity. Therefore, the plan must be cast in terms of real consumption and retirement income.
- From a standpoint of smoothing consumption, it is advantageous to save a fixed or rising fraction of real income. However, postponement of savings to later years increases the risk surrounding retirement consumption.
- The traditional-style tax shelter defers taxes on both contributions and investment earnings.
- The progressive tax code sharpens the importance of taxes during the retirement years. High tax rates during retirement reduce the effectiveness of the tax shelter.
- A Roth-style tax shelter does not shield contributions but eliminates taxes during retirement. Savers who anticipate high retirement income (and taxes) must examine whether this shelter is more beneficial than a traditional account.
- 401(k) plans are similar to traditional Individual Retirement Accounts but allow matched contributions by employers. This benefit should not be forgone.
- Capital gains can be postponed and later taxed at a lower rate. Therefore, investment in low-dividend stocks is a natural tax shelter. Investments in interest-bearing securities should be sheltered first.
- Social Security benefits are an important component of retirement income. Social Security taxes are generally regressive, but benefits are progressive.
- Home ownership can be viewed in part as a hedge against increases in rental cost.
- Uncertain longevity and other contingencies can be managed using life annuities and appropriate insurance coverage.

KEY TERMS

adverse selection, 684
defined benefit plan, 677
flat tax, 672
401(k) plans, 677
life annuity, 684

moral hazard, 685
progressive tax, 675
real consumption, 671
retirement annuity, 669
Roth account, 678

Social Security, 682
tax shelters, 674
traditional retirement
  account, 678

PROBLEM SETS

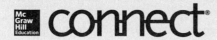

Select problems are available in McGraw-Hill's *Connect*. Please see the Supplements section of the book's frontmatter for more information.

1. A ship owner is attempting to insure an old vessel for twice its current market value. Is this an adverse selection or moral hazard issue? *(LO 21-5)*

2. The same ship owner advertises a tariff whereby the freight charged per pound for all cargo will be the same. What kind of cargo can the ship owner expect to attract? *(LO 21-5)*

3. What type of investors would be interested in a target date retirement fund? Why? *(LO 21-1)*

4. What is the insurance aspect of the Social Security annuity? *(LO 21-1)*

5. Why does a progressive tax code produce a retirement annuity for a middle-class household that is similar to that which would follow from a flat tax? *(LO 21-3)*

6. With no taxes or inflation (Spreadsheet 21.1), what would be your retirement annuity if you increase the savings rate by 1%? *(LO 21-1)*

7. With a 3% inflation rate (Spreadsheet 21.2), by how much would your retirement annuity grow if you increase the savings rate by 1%? Is the benefit greater in the face of inflation? *(LO 21-2)*

8. What savings rate from real income (Spreadsheet 21.3) will produce the same retirement annuity as a 15% savings rate from nominal income? *(LO 21-2)*

9. Under the flat tax (Spreadsheet 21.4), will a 1% increase in ROR offset a 1% increase in the tax rate? *(LO 21-3)*

10. With a traditional tax shelter (Spreadsheet 21.5), compare the effect on real consumption during retirement of a 1% increase in the rate of inflation to a 1% increase in the tax rate. *(LO 21-4)*

11. With a progressive tax (Spreadsheet 21.6), compare the effects of an increase of 1% in the lowest tax bracket to an increase of 1% in the highest tax bracket. *(LO 21-4)*

12. Verify that the traditional tax shelter with a progressive tax (Spreadsheet 21.7) acts as a hedge. Compare the effect of a decline of 2% in the ROR to an increase of 2% in ROR. *(LO 21-4)*

13. What is the trade-off between ROR and the rate of inflation with a Roth plan under a progressive tax (Spreadsheet 21.8)? *(LO 21-3)*

14. Suppose you could defer capital gains tax to the last year of your retirement (Spreadsheet 21.9). Would it be worthwhile given the progressivity of the tax code? *(LO 21-3)*

15. Project your Social Security benefits with the parameters of Section 21.6. *(LO 21-1)*

16. Using Spreadsheet 21.10, assess the present value of a 1% increase in college tuition as a fraction of the present value of labor income. *(LO 21-4)*

17. Give another example of adverse selection. *(LO 21-5)*

18. In addition to expected longevity, what traits might affect an individual's demand for a life annuity? *(LO 21-5)*

19. Give another example of a moral hazard problem. *(LO 21-5)*

WEB *master*

Visit the AARP's Financial Planning and Retirement website at **www.aarp.org.** Find the link to *Tools* (under *Take Action*) and then to *Retirement Calculator* under *Money Tools*. The calculator allows you to enter information about your retirement plans, your current level of assets, expected benefits from other sources, and your spouse's financial data and needs. Use the AARP Retirement Planning Calculator to enter your specific data and assumptions.

1. On the Results page, do you have a projected excess of funds or a shortfall of funds at the end of the retirement period? Can you meet your goals by following your current financial path?

Templates and spreadsheets are available in Connect

2. Look at the list of parameters toward the bottom of the page. Which one would be the easiest for you to change to make your goals attainable? Some people might choose to work longer, some to spend less in retirement, and so on. Choose the combination of factors that would work best for you, and then recalculate to see the new results. Can you come up with a plan that has a combination of factors that offer you an acceptable level of comfort?

SOLUTIONS TO
CONCEPT
checks

21.1 When ROR falls by 1% to 5%, the retirement annuity falls from $192,244 to $149,855 (i.e., by 22.45%). To restore this annuity, the savings rate must rise by 4.24 percentage points to 19.24%. With this savings rate, the entire loss of 1% in ROR falls on consumption during the earning years.

21.2 Intuition suggests you need to keep the real rate (2.91%) constant, that is, increase the nominal rate to 7% (confirm this). However, this will not be sufficient because the nominal income growth of 7% (column B) has a lower real growth when inflation is higher. Result: You must increase the real ROR to compensate for a lower growth in real income, ending with a nominal rate of 7.67%.

21.3 There are two components to the risk of relying on future labor income: disability/death and career failure/unemployment. You can insure the first component but not the second.

21.4 The qualitative result is the same. However, with no shelter you are worse off early and hence also lose the earning power of the additional tax bills.

21.5 No, an increase in the low-bracket tax rate applies to your entire taxable income, while an increase in the high-bracket tax rate applies only to a fraction of your taxable income.

21.6 Using the same inputs as in Spreadsheet 21.8, the Roth plan will generate less taxes yet still result in a smaller real retirement annuity. The reason is the timing of the taxes. The timing issue does not affect the stream of tax revenues to the IRS because at any point in time, taxpayers are distributed over all ages. In this case, the IRS can replace all Roth plans with traditional ones and lower the tax rates. The IRS will collect similar revenue each year, and retirees will enjoy higher real retirement annuities.

21.7 No, in terms of cash income, preferred stocks are more similar to bonds.

21.8 Your projected retirement fund is risky because of uncertainty about future labor income and future real returns on savings. The projected Social Security real annuity is risky because of political uncertainty about future benefits. It's hard to judge which risk is greater.

21.9 You need an investment that pays more when tuition is higher. Some states now offer "tuition futures" contracts that allow you to lock in the price of future tuition expenditures.

21.10 A fixed-rate mortgage is the lower-risk, higher-expected-cost option. Homeowners with greater risk tolerance might opt for a variable-rate mortgage, which is expected to average a lower rate over the life of the mortgage.

21.11 In the old days, children were more than a bundle of joy; they also provided a hedge for old-age income. Under such circumstance, insuring children would make economic sense. These days, children may well be a financial net expenditure, ruling out insurance on economic grounds. Other nonfinancial considerations are a matter of individual preference.

Investors and the Investment Process

Learning Objectives

LO 22-1 Specify investment objectives of individual and institutional investors.

LO 22-2 Identify constraints on individual and institutional investors.

LO 22-3 Develop investment policy statements consistent with a client's objectives and constraints.

Translating the aspirations and circumstances of diverse households into appropriate investment decisions is a daunting task. Financial advisers must translate often vague and non-quantitative concerns into concrete investment decisions.

The task is equally difficult for institutions, most of which have many stakeholders and often are regulated by various authorities. The investment process is not easily reduced to a simple or mechanical algorithm.

While many principles of investments are quite general and apply to virtually all investors, some issues are peculiar to the specific investor. Tax bracket, age, risk tolerance, wealth, job prospects, and uncertainties make each investor's circumstances somewhat unique. In this chapter we focus on a process by which investors systematically can review their particular objectives, constraints, and circumstances.

Along the way, we survey some of the major classes of institutional investors and examine the special issues they must confront.

There is no unique "correct" investment process, but some approaches are better than others. It can be helpful to take one high-quality approach as a useful case study. For this reason, we examine the approach suggested by the CFA Institute. The CFA Institute is one of the most important professional organizations for finance practitioners. It confers the Chartered Financial Analyst designation on those who meet its requirements, which include both work experience and a set of three exams. There are currently more than 150,000 CFA charterholders employed in about 150 countries. (The "On the Market Front" box on page 691 describes how to become a CFA charterholder.) Dozens of countries have adopted the CFA Institute's Global Investment Performance Standards.

The CFA curriculum thus influences the training of the highest-level and most respected investment managers around the world.

The CFA Institute has created a framework to help professionals develop and explain financial policy to individual and institutional clients. This chapter presents the CFA Institute's approach. As you read about it, concentrate on the methodology underlying its approach to the investment process.

The basic framework divides the investment process into four stages: specifying objectives, specifying constraints, formulating policy, and monitoring and updating the portfolio. We start with an overview of the investment process and a description of major types of investors, both individual and institutional. We then turn to the objectives and constraints peculiar to each investor class and consider some of the investment policies that each can choose.

22.1 THE INVESTMENT MANAGEMENT PROCESS

The CFA Institute divides the process of investment management into elements that constitute a dynamic feedback loop: planning, execution, and feedback. Figure 22.1 and Table 22.1 describe the steps in that process. *Planning* is focused largely on establishing the inputs necessary for decision making. These include data about the client as well as the capital market, leading to broad policy guidelines (strategic asset allocation). *Execution* fleshes out the details of optimal asset allocation and security selection. Finally, *feedback* is the process of adapting to changes in expectations and objectives as well as to changes in portfolio composition that result from changes in market prices.

The result of this analysis can be summarized in an *investment policy statement* (IPS) addressing the topics specified in Table 22.2. In the next sections we elaborate on the steps leading to an IPS. We start with the planning phase, the top panel of Table 22.1.

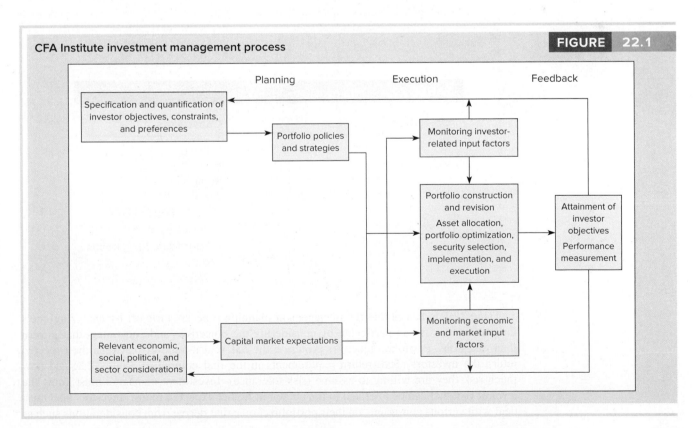

FIGURE 22.1

CFA Institute investment management process

TABLE 22.1   Components of the investment management process

I. Planning
  A. Identifying and specifying the investor's objectives and constraints
  B. Creating the *investment policy statement* [See Table 22.2.]
  C. Forming capital market expectations
  D. Creating the strategic asset allocation (Target, minimum, and maximum asset-class weights)
II. Execution: Portfolio construction and revision
  A. Asset allocation (including tactical) and portfolio optimization (combining assets to meet risk and return objectives)
  B. Security selection
  C. Implementation and execution
III. Feedback
  A. Monitoring (investor, economic, and market input factors)
  B. Rebalancing
  C. Performance evaluation

Source: John L. Maginn, Donald L. Tuttle, Dennis W. McLeavey, and Jerald E. Pinto, "The Portfolio Management Process and the Investment Policy Statement," in *Managing Investment Portfolios: A Dynamic Process,* 3rd ed. (CFA Institute, 2007) and correspondence with Tom Robinson, head of educational content.

TABLE 22.2   Components of the investment policy statement (IPS)

1. Brief client description
2. Purpose of establishing policies and guidelines
3. Duties and investment responsibilities of parties involved
4. Statement of investment goals, objectives, and constraints [See Table 22.3.]
5. Schedule for review of investment performance and the IPS
6. Performance measures and benchmarks
7. Any considerations in developing strategic asset allocation
8. Investment strategies and investment styles
9. Guidelines for rebalancing

TABLE 22.3   Determination of portfolio policies

Objectives	Constraints
Return requirements	Liquidity
Risk tolerance	Horizon
	Regulations
	Taxes
	Unique needs, such as:
	Ethical concerns
	Specific hedging needs
	Age
	Wealth

Table 22.1 indicates that the management planning process starts off by analyzing one's investment clients—in particular, by considering the objectives and constraints that govern their decisions. Portfolio objectives center on the risk-return trade-off between the expected return the investors need (return requirements in the first column of Table 22.3) and how much risk they are willing to assume (risk tolerance). Investment managers must know the level of risk that can be tolerated in the pursuit of higher expected return. Investors also must deal with various constraints on their portfolio choice that derive from considerations such as

liquidity needs, regulations, or tax concerns. The second column of Table 22.3 lists the more important constraints.

In the next sections, we explore some of these objectives and constraints.

22.2 INVESTOR OBJECTIVES

Individual Investors

The basic factors affecting an individual investor's objectives usually arise from that investor's stage in the life cycle. The first significant investment decision for most individuals concerns education, which is an investment in "human capital." The major asset most people have during their early working years is the earning power derived from their skills. For these people, the financial risk due to illness or injury is far greater than that associated with the rate of return on their portfolios of financial assets. At this point in the life cycle, the most important financial decisions concern insurance against the possibility of disability or death.

As one ages and accumulates savings to provide for consumption during retirement, the composition of wealth shifts from human capital toward financial capital. At this point, portfolio choices become progressively more important. In middle age, most investors will be willing to take on a meaningful amount of portfolio risk to increase their expected rates of return. As retirement draws near, however, risk tolerance seems to diminish.

Questionnaire results confirm that attitudes shift away from risk tolerance and toward risk aversion as investors near retirement age. (See the questionnaire in the nearby box for an example.) With age, individuals lose the potential to recover from a disastrous investment performance. When they are young, they can respond to a loss by working harder and saving more of their income. But as retirement approaches, there is less time to recover, hence the shift to safe assets.

Professional Investors

Professional investors provide investment management services for a fee. Some are employed directly by wealthy individual investors. Most professional investors, however, either pool and manage the funds of many individual investors or serve institutional investors.

On the MARKET FRONT

WHAT LEVEL OF RISK IS RIGHT FOR YOU?

No risk, no reward. Most people intuitively understand that they have to bear some risk to achieve an acceptable return on their investment portfolios.

But how much risk is right for you? If your investments turn sour, you may put at jeopardy your ability to retire, to pay for your kid's college education, or to weather an unexpected need for cash. These worst-case scenarios focus our attention on how to manage our exposure to uncertainty.

Assessing—and quantifying—risk aversion is, to put it mildly, difficult. It requires confronting at least these two big questions.

First, how much investment risk can you afford to take? If you have a steady high-paying job, for example, you have greater ability to withstand investment losses. Conversely, if you are close to retirement, you have less ability to adjust your lifestyle in response to bad investment outcomes.

Second, you need to think about your personality and decide how much risk you can tolerate. At what point will you be unable to sleep at night?

To help clients quantify their risk aversion, many financial firms have designed quizzes to help people determine whether they are conservative, moderate, or aggressive investors. These quizzes try to get at clients' attitudes toward risk and their capacity to absorb investment losses.

Here is a sample of the sort of questions these quizzes tend to pose to shed light on an investor's risk tolerance.

MEASURING YOUR RISK TOLERANCE

Circle the letter that corresponds to your answer.

1. The stock market fell by more than 30% in 2008. If you had been holding a substantial stock investment in that year, would you have:

   a. Sold off the remainder of your investment before it had the chance to fall further.

   b. Stayed the course with neither redemptions nor purchases.

   c. Bought more stock, reasoning that the market is now cheaper and therefore offers better deals.

2. The value of one of the funds in your 401(k) plan (your primary source of retirement savings) increased 30% last year. What will you do?

   a. Move your funds into a money market account in case the price gains reverse.

   b. Sit tight and do nothing.

   c. Put more of your assets into that fund, reasoning that its value is clearly trending upward.

3. Would you describe your non-investment sources of income (for example, your salary) as:

   a. Highly uncertain

   b. Moderately stable

   c. Highly stable

4. At the end of the month, do you find yourself:

   a. Short of cash and impatiently waiting for your next paycheck.

   b. Not overspending your salary, but not saving very much.

   c. With a comfortable surplus of funds to put into your savings account.

5. You are 30 years old and enrolling in your company's retirement plan, and you need to allocate your contributions across three funds: a money market account, a bond fund, and a stock fund. Which of these allocations sounds best to you?

   a. Invest everything in a safe money-market fund.

   b. Split your money evenly between the bond fund and stock fund.

   c. Put everything into the stock fund, reasoning that by the time you retire the year-to-year fluctuations in stock returns will have evened out.

6. You are a contestant on *Let's Make a Deal* and have just won $1,000. But you can exchange the winnings for two random payoffs. One is a coin flip with a payoff of $2,500 if the coin comes up heads. The other is a flip of two coins with a payoff of $6,000 if both coins come up heads. Will you:

   a. Keep the $1,000 in cash.

   b. Choose the single coin toss.

   c. Choose the double coin toss.

7. Suppose you have the opportunity to invest in a start-up firm. If the firm is successful, you will multiply your investment by a factor of 10. But if it fails, you will lose everything. You think the odds of success are around 20%. How much would you be willing to invest in the start-up?

   a. Nothing

   b. 2 months' salary

   c. 6 months' salary.

8. Now imagine that to buy into the start-up you will need to borrow money. Would you be willing to take out a $10,000 loan to make the investment?

   a. No

   b. Maybe

   c. Yes

SCORING YOUR RISK TOLERANCE

For each question, give yourself one point if you answered (*a*), two points if you answered (*b*), and three points for a (*c*). The higher your total score, the greater is your risk tolerance, or equivalently, the lower is your risk aversion.

PERSONAL TRUSTS   A **personal trust** is established when an individual confers legal title to property to another person or institution, which then manages that property for one or more beneficiaries. The holder of the title is called the *trustee*. The trustee is usually a bank, a lawyer, or an investment professional. Investment of a trust is subject to state trust laws and *prudent investor rules* that limit the types of allowable trust investment.

The objectives of personal trusts normally are more limited in scope than those of the individual investor. Because of their fiduciary responsibility, personal trust managers typically are expected to invest with more risk aversion than individual investors. Certain asset classes, such as options and futures contracts, for example, and some strategies, such as short-selling or buying on margin, are ruled out.

personal trust

An interest in an asset held by a trustee for the benefit of another person.

MUTUAL FUNDS   **Mutual funds** are firms that manage pools of individual investor money. They invest in accordance with their objectives and issue shares that entitle investors to a pro rata portion of the income generated by the funds.

The return requirement and risk tolerance across mutual funds are highly variable because funds segment the investor market. Various funds appeal to distinct investor groups and will adopt a return requirement and risk tolerance that fit a particular market niche. For example, "income" funds cater to the conservative investor, while "growth" funds target more risk-tolerant ones. Tax-free bond funds segment the market by tax bracket.

A mutual fund's objectives are spelled out in its prospectus. We discussed mutual funds in detail in Chapter 4.

mutual fund

A firm pooling and managing funds of investors.

PENSION FUNDS   There are two basic types of pension plans: *defined contribution* and *defined benefit*. Defined contribution plans are in effect savings accounts established by the firm for its employees. The employer contributes funds to the plan, but the employee bears all the risk of the fund's investment performance. These plans are called defined contribution because the firm's only obligation is to make the stipulated contributions to the employee's retirement account. The employee is responsible for directing the management of the assets, usually by selecting among several investment funds in which the assets can be placed. Therefore, objectives for defined contribution plans are similar to those that would pertain to each individual investor. These plans were discussed in Chapter 21.

In defined benefit plans, by contrast, the employer has an obligation to provide a specified annual retirement benefit. That benefit is defined by a formula that typically takes into account years of service and the level of salary or wages. For example, the employer may pay the retired employee a yearly amount equal to 2% of the employee's final annual salary for each year of service. A 30-year employee would then receive an annual benefit equal to 60% of his or her final salary. The payments are an obligation of the employer, and the assets in the pension fund provide collateral for the promised benefits. If the investment performance of the assets is poor, the firm is obligated to make up the shortfall by contributing additional assets to the fund. Therefore, in contrast to defined contribution plans, the risk surrounding investment performance in defined benefit plans is borne by the firm.

The pension fund sponsor, the corporation that sets up the fund, appoints a pension fund manager. While its presumed constituency is the group of retirees covered by the fund, the sponsoring firm still exerts influence over the fund manager. The pension actuary retained by the fund must sign off on the expected rate of return assumed for the asset portfolio. This is used as the discount rate to compute the present value of fund obligations, which determines whether the pension liabilities are deemed to be adequately funded or additional funds need to be endowed by the sponsor to meet these liabilities. For example, if the actuary assumes a rate of return of 10%, then the firm must contribute $385.54 now for every $1,000 of pension liabilities due in 10 years, because $385.54 \times 1.10^{10} = \$1,000$.

If a pension fund's *actual* rate of return exceeds the actuarial *assumed* rate, the firm's shareholders reap the gain, because the excess return can be used to reduce future contributions. If the plan's actual rate of return falls short of the assumed rate, however, the firm will have to increase future contributions. Because the sponsoring firm's shareholders bear the risk in a defined benefit pension plan, the objective of the plan will be consistent with the objective of the firm's shareholders. Thus, a potential conflict of interest arises: Although the fund in principle should be run for the benefit of the retirees, because the pension plan manager and actuary are retained and compensated by the sponsor, the interests of shareholders may, in practice, be treated as paramount.

Life Insurance Companies

Life insurance companies generally invest to hedge their liabilities, which are defined by the policies they write. The company can reduce risk by investing in assets that will return more in the event the insurance policy coverage becomes more expensive.

For example, if the company writes a policy that pays a death benefit linked to the consumer price index, then the company is subject to inflation risk. It might search for assets expected to return more when the rate of inflation rises, thus hedging the price-index linkage of the policy.

There are as many objectives as there are distinct types of insurance policies. Until the 1970s, only two types of life insurance policies were available for individuals: whole-life and term.

A *whole-life insurance policy* combines a death benefit with a kind of savings plan that provides for a gradual buildup of cash value that the policyholder can withdraw later in life, usually at retirement. *Term insurance,* on the other hand, provides death benefits only, with no buildup of cash value.

The interest rate embedded in the schedule of cash value accumulation promised under the whole-life policy is a fixed rate. One way life insurance companies try to hedge this liability is by investing in long-term bonds. Often the insured individual has the right to borrow at a prespecified fixed interest rate against the cash value of the policy.

During the high-interest-rate years of the 1970s and early 1980s, many older whole-life policies allowed policyholders to borrow at rates as low as 4% or 5% per year; some holders borrowed heavily against the cash value to invest in assets paying double-digit yields. Other actual and potential policyholders abandoned whole-life policies and took out term insurance, which accounted for more than half the volume of new sales of individual life policies.

In response to these developments, the insurance industry came up with two new policy types: variable life and universal life. A *variable life policy* entitles the insured to a fixed death benefit plus a cash value that can be invested in the policyholder's choice of mutual funds. A *universal life policy* allows policyholders to increase or reduce either the insurance premium (the annual fee paid on the policy) or the death benefit (the cash amount paid to beneficiaries in the event of death) according to their changing needs. Furthermore, the interest rate on the cash value component changes with market interest rates. The great advantage of variable and universal life insurance policies is that earnings on the cash value are not taxed until the money is withdrawn.

Non-Life-Insurance Companies

Non-life-insurance companies such as property and casualty insurers have investable funds primarily because they pay claims *after* they collect policy premiums. Typically, they are conservative in their attitude toward risk.

A common thread in the objectives of pension plans and insurance companies is the need to hedge predictable long-term liabilities. Investment strategies typically call for hedging these liabilities with bonds of various maturities.

Banks

Most bank investments are loans to businesses and consumers, and most of their liabilities are accounts of depositors. As investors, banks try to match the risk of assets to liabilities while earning a profitable spread between the lending and borrowing rates.

Most liabilities of banks and thrift institutions are checking accounts, time or savings deposits, and certificates of deposit (CDs). Checking account funds may be withdrawn at any time, so they are of the shortest maturity. Time or savings deposits are of various maturities. Some time deposits may extend as long as seven years, but, on average, they are of fairly short maturity. CDs are bonds of various maturities that the bank issues to investors. While the range of maturities is from 90 days to 10 years, the average is about 1 year.

In the past, a large part of the loan portfolio of savings and loan (S&L) institutions was in home mortgages, with typical maturities of 15 to 30 years. Today, the bulk of thrifts' portfolios are business loans. The maturities of these loans typically are less than those of mortgages but still generally exceed the maturities of sources of financing. Thus, profits are exposed to interest rate risk. When rates rise, thrifts have to pay higher rates to depositors, while the income from their longer-term investments is relatively fixed.

Banks earn profit from the interest rate spread between loans extended (the bank's assets) and deposits and CDs (the bank's liabilities), as well as from fees for services. Managing bank assets calls for balancing the loan portfolio with the portfolio of deposits and CDs. A bank can increase the interest rate spread by lending to riskier borrowers and by increasing the proportion of longer-term loans. However, both of these policies increase risk. Bank capital regulations now are risk-based, so higher-risk strategies will elicit higher capital requirements as well as the possibility of greater regulatory interference in the bank's affairs.

As we noted in Chapter 2, most long-term fixed-rate mortgages today are securitized into pass-through certificates and held as securities in the portfolios of mutual funds, pension funds, and other institutional investors. Mortgage originators typically sell a portion of the mortgages they originate to pass-through agencies such as Fannie Mae or Freddie Mac rather than holding them in a portfolio. They earn their profits on mortgage origination and servicing fees. The trend away from maintaining portfolio holdings of long-term mortgages also has reduced interest rate risk.

Endowment Funds

Endowment funds are held by organizations chartered to use their money for specific nonprofit purposes. They are financed by gifts from one or more sponsors and are typically managed by educational, cultural, and charitable organizations or by independent foundations established solely to carry out the fund's specific purposes. Generally, the investment objectives of an endowment fund are to produce a steady flow of income subject to only a moderate degree of risk. Trustees of an endowment fund, however, can specify other objectives as circumstances dictate.

endowment funds
Portfolios operated for the benefit of a nonprofit entity.

> Describe several distinguishing characteristics of endowment funds that differentiate them from pension funds.

CONCEPT check 22.1

Table 22.4 summarizes the objectives governing these classes of investors.

TABLE 22.4 Matrix of objectives

Type of Investor	Return Requirement	Risk Tolerance
Individual and personal trusts	Life cycle (education, children, retirement)	Life cycle (younger are more risk tolerant)
Mutual funds	Variable, depending on fund clientele	Variable
Pension funds	Assumed actuarial rate	Depends on proximity of payouts
Endowment funds	Determined by current income needs and need for asset growth to maintain real value	Generally conservative
Life insurance companies	Should exceed new money rate by sufficient margin to meet expenses and profit objectives; actuarial rates also important	Conservative
Non-life-insurance companies	Match to contingent liabilities	Conservative
Banks	Maintain positive interest spread	Variable

22.3 INVESTOR CONSTRAINTS

Even with identical attitudes toward risk, different households and institutions might choose different investment portfolios because of their differing circumstances. These circumstances include tax status, requirements for liquidity or a flow of income from the portfolio, or various regulatory restrictions. These circumstances impose *constraints* on investor choice. Together, objectives and constraints determine investment policy.

Some constraints arise from an investor's particular circumstances. For example, if a family has children about to enter college, there will be a high demand for liquidity because cash will be needed to pay tuition bills. Other times, however, constraints are imposed externally. For example, banks and trusts are subject to legal limitations on the types of assets they may hold in their portfolios. Finally, some constraints are self-imposed. For example, *social investing* means that investors will not hold shares of firms involved in ethically objectionable activities. Some criteria that have been used to judge firms as ineligible for a portfolio are involvement in countries with human rights abuses, production of tobacco or weapons and participation in polluting activities.

Five common types of constraints are described below.

Liquidity

liquidity

The speed and ease with which an asset can be converted to cash.

Liquidity is the speed and ease with which an asset can be sold and still fetch a fair price, or conversely, the price discount necessary to achieve an immediate sale. It is a relationship between the time dimension (how long it will take to sell) and the price dimension (the discount from intrinsic value) of an investment asset.

When an actual concrete measure of liquidity is necessary, one thinks of the discount when an immediate sale is unavoidable.[1] Cash and money market instruments such as Treasury bills and commercial paper, where the bid–ask spread is a small fraction of 1%, are the most liquid assets, and real estate is among the least liquid. Office buildings and manufacturing structures in extreme cases can suffer a 50% liquidity discount.

Both individual and institutional investors must consider how likely they are to require cash at short notice. From this likelihood, they establish the minimum level of liquid assets they need in the investment portfolio.

Investment Horizon

investment horizon

The planned liquidation date of the portfolio.

This is the planned liquidation date of the investment. Examples of an individual's **investment horizon** could be the time to fund a college education or the retirement date for a wage earner. For a university or hospital endowment, an investment horizon could relate to the time to fund a major construction project. Horizon dates must be considered when investors choose between assets of various maturities. For example, the maturity date of a bond might make it a more attractive investment if it coincides with a date on which cash is needed. This idea is analogous to the matching principle from corporate finance: Strive to match financing maturity to the economic life of the financed asset.

Regulations

prudent investor rule

The fiduciary responsibility of a professional investor.

Professional and institutional investors are constrained by regulations. First and foremost is the **prudent investor rule.** That is, professional investors who manage other people's money have a fiduciary responsibility to restrict investment to assets that would have been approved by a prudent investor. The law is purposefully nonspecific. The asset manager must stand

---

[1] In many cases, it is impossible to know the liquidity of an asset with certainty until it is put up for sale. In more active markets, however, the liquidity of the traded assets can be observed from the bid–ask spread, that is, the difference between the "bid" quote (the lower price available when someone wishes to sell an asset) and the "ask" quote (the higher price a buyer would have to pay to acquire the asset).

ready to defend an investment policy in a court of law, and interpretation may differ according to the standards of the times.

In 2016, the Department of Labor ruled that under ERISA (the Employee Retirement Security Act of 1974), advisers who work with tax-advantaged retirement savings are to be held to a *fiduciary standard,* meaning that they are required to work in the best interest of their clients. Previously, they were required to offer only "suitable" guidance, meaning that investment choices needed to be acceptable, but not necessarily defensible as the best choice for the client. For example, a client's money might be placed in a "suitable" mutual fund even if cheaper funds with nearly identical investment profiles were available. This new rule is meant to reduce conflicts of interest between advisers and clients. The new ruling has not yet been fully implemented, and in light of recent political pushback, its timetable (and ultimate survival) is not yet clear.

Also, specific regulations apply to various institutional investors. For instance, U.S. mutual funds are subject to regulations that put upper bounds on the allowed use of leverage or investments in illiquid securities and lower bounds on some measures of diversification.

Sometimes, "self-imposed" regulations also affect the investment choice. We have noted several times, for example, that mutual funds describe their investment policies in a prospectus. These policy guidelines amount to constraints on the ability to choose portfolios freely.

Tax Considerations

Tax consequences are central to investment decisions. The performance of any investment strategy should be measured by its rate of return *after* taxes. For household and institutional investors who face significant tax rates, tax sheltering and deferral of tax obligations may be pivotal in their investment strategy.

Unique Needs

Virtually every investor faces special circumstances. Imagine husband-and-wife aeronautical engineers holding high-paying jobs in the same aerospace corporation. The entire human capital of that household is tied to a single player in a rather cyclical industry. This couple would need to hedge the risk of a deterioration in the economic well-being of the aerospace industry.

Similar issues would confront an executive on Wall Street who owns an apartment near work. Because the value of the home in that part of Manhattan probably depends on the vitality of the securities industry, the individual is doubly exposed to the vagaries of the stock market. Because both job and home already depend on the fortunes of Wall Street, the purchase of a typical diversified stock portfolio would actually increase the exposure to the stock market.

These examples illustrate that the job, or more generally, human capital, is often an individual's biggest "asset," and the unique risk profile that results from employment can play a big role in determining a suitable investment portfolio.

Other unique needs of individuals often center around their stage in the life cycle, as previously discussed. Retirement, housing, and children's education constitute three major demands for funds, and investment policy will depend in part on the proximity of these expenditures.

Institutional investors also face unique needs. For example, pension funds will differ in their investment policy, depending on the average age of plan participants. Another example of a unique need for an institutional investor would be a university whose trustees allow the administration to use only cash income from the endowment fund. This constraint would translate into a preference for high-dividend-paying assets.

A particular constraint for mutual funds arises from investor response to the fund's performance. When a mutual fund earns an unsatisfactory rate of return, investors often redeem their shares—they withdraw money from the fund. The mutual fund then contracts. The reverse happens when a mutual fund earns an unusually high return: Investment success will lead to a growth in its asset base.

Pension funds are heavily regulated by the Employee Retirement Income Security Act of 1974 (ERISA). This law revolutionized savings for retirement in the United States and remains a major piece of social legislation. Thus, for pension funds, regulatory constraints are relatively important. Also, mature pension funds are required to pay out more than young funds and hence need more liquidity.

When new contributions exceed payouts, as is the case for many endowment funds, the fund does not need to liquidate assets, or even use dividend income, to finance payouts. In this case, liquidity is not an overriding concern.

Life insurance companies are subject to complex regulation. The corporate tax rate, which currently is 21%, also applies to insurance company investment income, so taxes are an important concern.

Property and casualty insurance, like term life insurance, is written on a short-term basis. Most policies must be renewed annually, which means property and casualty insurance companies are subject to short-term horizon constraints.

The short horizon constraint for banks comes from the interest rate risk component of the interest rate spread (i.e., the risk of interest rate increases that banks face when financing long-term assets with short-term liabilities). Risk-based capital regulations, which mandate higher capital requirements for riskier investment portfolios, also impose constraints on bank portfolio choice.

Table 22.5 presents a matrix of constraints for various investors. As you would expect, liquidity and tax constraints for individuals are variable because of wealth and age differentials.

TABLE 22.5   Matrix of constraints

Type of Investor	Liquidity	Horizon	Regulatory	Taxes
Individuals	Variable	Life cycle	None	Variable
Personal trusts	Variable	Life cycle	Prudent investor laws	Variable
Mutual funds	Usually low	Short	Little	None
Pension funds	Young, low; mature, high	Long	ERISA	None
Endowment funds	Low	Long	Little	None
Life insurance companies	Low	Long	Complex	Yes
Non-life-insurance companies	High	Short	Little	Yes
Banks	Low	Short	Risk-based capital requirements	Yes

CONCEPT
check   **22.2**

a. Think about the financial circumstances of your closest relative in your parents' generation (for example, your parents' household if you are fortunate enough to have them around). Write down the objectives and constraints for their investment decisions.

b. Now consider the financial situation of your closest friend or relative who is in his or her 30s. Write down the objectives and constraints that would fit his or her investment decision.

c. How much of the difference between the two statements is due to the age of the investors?

22.4 INVESTMENT POLICIES

Once objectives and constraints are determined, an investment policy that suits the investor can be formulated. That policy must reflect an appropriate risk-return profile as well as needs for liquidity, income generation, and tax positioning. Institutional investors such as pension plans and endowments often must issue formal statements of their investment policy. These policy statements should be based on, and often make explicit, the objectives and constraints of the investment fund.

The investment policy statement serves as a strategic guide to the planning and implementation of an investment program.[2] When implemented successfully, the IPS anticipates issues related to governance of the investment program, planning for appropriate asset allocation, implementing an investment program with internal and/or external managers, monitoring the results, risk management, and appropriate reporting. The IPS also establishes accountability for the various entities that may work on behalf of an investor. Perhaps most importantly, the IPS serves as a policy guide that can offer an objective course of action to be followed during periods of disruption when emotional or instinctive responses might otherwise motivate less prudent actions.

The nearby box suggests desirable components of an investment policy statement for use with individual and/or high-net-worth investors. Not every component will be appropriate for every investor or every situation, and there may be other components that are desirable for inclusion reflecting unique investor circumstances.

The following is an example of a portion of a policy statement for a defined benefit pension plan.

The investment plan should emphasize production of adequate levels of real return as its primary return objective, giving special attention to the inflation-related aspects of the plan. To the extent consistent with appropriate control of portfolio risk, investment action should seek to maintain or increase the surplus of plan assets relative to benefit liabilities over time. Five-year periods, updated annually, shall be employed in planning for investment decision making; the plan's actuary shall update the benefit liabilities breakdown by country every three years.

The orientation of investment planning shall be long term in nature. In addition, minimal liquidity reserves shall be maintained so long as annual company funding contributions and investment income exceed annual benefit payments to retirees and the operating expenses of the plan. The plan's actuary shall update plan cash flow projections annually. Plan administration shall ensure compliance with all laws and regulations related to maintenance of the plan's tax-exempt status and with all requirements of the Employee Retirement Income Security Act (ERISA).

The most important portfolio decision an investor makes is the proportion of the total investment fund allocated to risky as opposed to safe assets. This choice is the most fundamental means of controlling investment risk.

---

[2]This material is adapted from documents of the CFA Institute that were made available to the authors in draft form. They may differ from the final published documents.

It follows that the first decision an investor must make is the asset allocation decision. Asset allocation refers to the allocation of the portfolio across major asset categories such as:

1. Money market assets (cash equivalents).
2. Fixed-income securities (primarily bonds).
3. Stocks.
4. Non-U.S. stocks and bonds.
5. Real estate.
6. Precious metals and other commodities.

Only after the broad asset classes to be held in the portfolio are determined can one sensibly choose the specific securities to purchase.

Investors who have relatively high degrees of risk tolerance will choose asset allocations more concentrated in higher-risk investment classes, such as equity, to obtain higher expected rates of return. More conservative investors will choose asset allocations with a greater weight in bonds and cash equivalents.

Asset allocation also will depend on expectations for capital market performance in the coming period. (Look back at Figure 22.1 and Table 22.1, and you will see that the CFA Institute classifies this part of the planning process as the formation of "capital market expectations.") Given the risk-return positioning of the investor and the set of expectations, an optimal asset mix may be formed (see Panel II, Execution, in Table 22.1).

Top-Down Policies for Institutional Investors

Individual investors need not concern themselves with organizational efficiency. But professional investors with large amounts to invest must structure asset allocation activities to decentralize some of the decision making.

Common features of large organizations are the investment committee and the asset universe. The investment committee includes top management officers, senior portfolio managers, and senior security analysts. The committee determines investment policies and verifies that portfolio managers and security analysts are operating within the bounds of specified policies. A major responsibility of the investment committee is to translate the objectives and constraints of the company into an **asset universe,** an approved list of assets for each of the company's portfolios.

asset universe

Approved list of assets in which a portfolio manager may invest.

The investment committee has responsibility for broad asset allocation. While the investment manager might have some leeway to tilt the portfolio toward or away from one or another asset class, the investment committee establishes the benchmark allocation that largely determines the risk characteristics of the portfolio. The task of choosing specific securities from the approved universe is more fully delegated to the investment manager.

Figure 22.2 illustrates the stages of the portfolio choice process for Palatial Investments, a hypothetical firm that invests internationally. The first two stages are asset allocation choices. The broadest choice is in the weighting of the portfolio between U.S. and Japanese securities. Palatial has chosen a weight of 75% in the United States and 25% in Japan. The allocation of the portfolio across asset classes may now be determined. For example, 15% of the U.S. portfolio is invested in cash equivalents, 40% in fixed income, and 45% in equity. The asset-class weights are, in general, a policy decision of the investment committee, although the investment manager might have some authority to alter the asset allocation to limited degrees based on her expectations concerning the investment performance of various asset classes. Finally, security selection within each country is determined by the portfolio manager from the approved universe. For example, 45% of funds held in the U.S. equity market will be placed in IBM, 35% in GE, and 20% in ExxonMobil. (We show only three securities in the figure because of space limitations. Obviously a $1 billion fund will hold securities of many more firms.)

These ever-finer decisions determine the proportion of each individual security in the overall portfolio. As an example, consider the proportion of Palatial's portfolio invested in ExxonMobil, 6.75%. This fraction results from the following decisions: First, the United States receives a weight of 75% of the overall portfolio, and equities comprise 45% of the U.S. component of the portfolio. These are asset allocation choices. ExxonMobil comprises 20% of the U.S. equity component of the portfolio. This is a security selection choice. Therefore, ExxonMobil's weight in the overall portfolio is $.75 \times .45 \times .20 = .0675$, or 6.75%. If the entire portfolio is $1 billion, $67,500,000 will be invested in ExxonMobil. If ExxonMobil is selling for $90 a share, 750,000 shares must be purchased. The bottom line in Figure 22.2 shows the percentage of the overall portfolio held in each asset.

This example illustrates a top-down approach that is consistent with the needs of large organizations. The top managers set the overall policy of the portfolio by specifying asset allocation guidelines. Lower-level portfolio managers fill in the details with their security selection decisions.

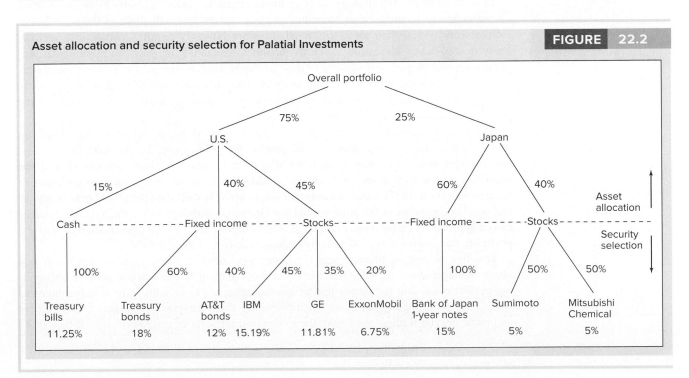

FIGURE 22.2

Asset allocation and security selection for Palatial Investments

Active versus Passive Policies

One choice that must be confronted by all investors, individual as well as institutional, is the degree to which the portfolio will be actively versus passively managed. Recall that passive management is based on the belief that security prices usually are close to "fair" levels. Instead of spending time and other resources attempting to "beat the market," that is, to find mispriced securities with unusually attractive risk-return characteristics, the investor simply assumes that she will be fairly compensated for the risk she is willing to take on and selects a portfolio consistent with her risk tolerance.[3]

Passive management styles can be applied to both the security selection and the asset allocation decisions. With regard to asset allocation, passive management simply means that the manager does not depart from his or her "normal" asset-class weightings in response to changing expectations about the performance of different markets. Those "normal" weights are based on the investor's risk and return objectives, as discussed earlier. For example, an asset allocation for a 45-year-old investor of 65% equity, 25% bonds, and 10% cash equivalents would be considered fairly conventional. A purely passive manager would not depart from these weights in response to forecasts of market performances. The weighting scheme would be adjusted only in response to changes in risk tolerance as age and wealth change over time.

Next consider passive security selection. Imagine that you must choose a portfolio of stocks without access to any special information about security values. This would be the case if you believed that anything you know about a stock is already known by the rest of the investors in the market and therefore is already reflected in the stock price. If you cannot predict which stocks will be winners, you should broadly diversify your portfolio to avoid putting all your eggs in one basket. A natural course of action for such an investor would be to choose a portfolio with "a little bit of everything."

This reasoning leads one to look for a portfolio that is invested across the entire security market. We saw in Chapter 4 that some mutual fund operators have established index funds that follow just such a strategy. These funds hold each stock or bond in proportion to its representation in a particular index, such as the Standard & Poor's 500 stock price index or the Barclays Capital Aggregate Bond Index. Holding an indexed portfolio represents purely passive security selection in that the investor's return simply duplicates the return of the overall market without making a bet on one or another stock or sector of the market.

In contrast to passive strategies, active management assumes an ability to outguess other investors and to identify either securities or asset classes that will shine in the near future. Active security selection for institutional investors typically requires two layers: security analysis and asset allocation. Security analysts specialize in particular industries and companies and prepare assessments of their particular market niches. The portfolio managers then sift through the reports of many analysts. They use forecasts of market conditions to make asset allocation decisions and use the security analysts' recommendations to choose the particular securities to include within each asset class.

The choice between active and passive strategies need not be all-or-nothing. One can pursue both active security selection and passive asset allocation, for example. In this case, the manager would maintain fixed asset allocation targets but would actively choose the securities within each asset class. Or one could pursue active asset allocation and passive security selection. In this case, the manager might actively shift the allocation between equity and bond components of the portfolio but hold indexed portfolios within each sector. Another mixed approach is called a *passive core* strategy. In this case, the manager indexes *part* of the portfolio, the passive core, and actively manages the rest of the portfolio.

Is active or passive management the better approach? It might seem at first blush that active managers have the edge because active management is necessary to achieve outstanding performance. But remember that active managers start out with some disadvantages as well. They incur significant costs when preparing their analyses of markets and securities and incur heavier trading costs from the more rapid turnover of their portfolios. If they don't

---

[3]We discussed arguments for passive management in previous chapters.

uncover information or insights currently unavailable to other investors (not a trivial task in a nearly efficient market), then all of this costly activity will be wasted, and they will underperform a passive strategy. In fact, low-cost passive strategies have performed surprisingly well in the last few decades, as we saw in Chapters 4 and 8.

CONCEPT check 22.3

Classify the following statements according to where each fits in the objective-constraints-policies framework.

  a. Invest 5% in bonds and 95% in stocks.
  b. Do not invest more than 10% of the budget in any one security.
  c. Shoot for an average rate of return of 10%.
  d. Make sure there will be $95,000 in cash in the account on December 31, 2035.
  e. If the market is bearish, reduce the investment in stocks to 80%.
  f. As of next year, we will be in a higher tax bracket.
  g. Our new president believes pension plans should take no risk whatsoever with the pension fund.
  h. Our acquisition plan will require large sums of cash to be available at any time.

22.5 MONITORING AND REVISING INVESTMENT PORTFOLIOS

Choosing the investment portfolio requires the investor to set objectives, acknowledge constraints, determine asset-class proportions, and perform security analysis. Is the process ever finished and behind us? By the time we have completed all of these steps, many of the inputs we have used will be out of date. Moreover, our circumstances as well as our objectives change over time. Therefore, the investment process requires that we continually monitor and update our portfolios. This is the task of rebalancing, part of the feedback process described earlier in Table 22.1 and Figure 22.1.

Moreover, even when circumstances do not change, our portfolios necessarily will. Suppose you currently hold 1,000 shares of ExxonMobil, selling at $90 a share, and 1,000 shares of Microsoft, selling at $70. If the price of ExxonMobil falls to $80 a share, while that of Microsoft rises to $75, the fractions of your portfolio allocated to each security change without your taking any direct action. The value of your investment in ExxonMobil is now lower, and the value of the Microsoft investment is higher. Unless you are happy with this reallocation of investment proportions, you will need to take some action to restore the portfolio weights to desired levels.

Asset allocation also will change over time, as the investment performance of different asset classes diverges. If the stock market outperforms the bond market, the proportion of your portfolio invested in stocks will increase while the proportion invested in bonds will decrease. If you are uncomfortable with this shift in the asset mix, you must rebalance the portfolio by selling some of the stocks and purchasing bonds.

Therefore, investing is a *dynamic process,* meaning that you must continually update and reevaluate your decisions over time.

SUMMARY

• The CFA Institute has developed a systematic framework for the translation of investor goals to investment strategy. Its three main parts are objectives, constraints, and policy. Investor objectives include the return requirement and risk tolerance, reflecting the overriding concern of investment with the risk-return trade-off. Investor constraints include liquidity requirements, investment horizon, regulatory concerns, tax obligations, and the unique needs of various investors. Investment policies specify the portfolio manager's asset allocation and security selection decisions.

- Major institutional investors include pension funds, mutual funds, life insurance companies, non-life-insurance companies, banks, and endowment funds. For individual investors, life-cycle concerns are the most important factor in setting objectives, constraints, and policies.
- Major asset classes include cash (money market assets), fixed-income securities (bonds), and stocks. Other relevant asset classes are real estate, precious metals, and collectibles. Asset allocation refers to the investment proportions allocated to each asset class. An active asset allocation strategy calls for the production of frequent market forecasts and the adjustment of asset allocation according to these forecasts.
- Active security selection requires security analysis and portfolio choice. Analysis of individual securities is required to choose securities that will make up a coherent portfolio and outperform a passive benchmark.
- Perhaps the most important feature of the investment process is that it is dynamic. Portfolios must be continually monitored and updated. The frequency and timing of various decisions are in themselves important decisions. Successful investment management requires management of these dynamic aspects.

KEY TERMS

asset universe, 700	investment horizon, 696	personal trust, 693
endowment funds, 695	liquidity, 696	prudent investor rule, 696
	mutual fund, 693	

PROBLEM SETS

Select problems are available in McGraw-Hill's *Connect*. Please see the Supplements section of the book's frontmatter for more information.

1. You are being interviewed for a job as a portfolio manager at an investment counseling partnership. As part of the interview, you are asked to demonstrate your ability to develop investment portfolio policy statements for the clients listed below:

    a. A pension fund described as a mature defined benefit plan, with the workforce having an average age of 54, no unfunded pension liabilities, and wage cost increases forecast at 5% annually.

    b. A university endowment fund described as conservative, with investment returns being utilized along with gifts and donations to help meet annual expenses. The spending rate is 5% per year and inflation in costs is expected at 3% annually.

    c. A life insurance company described as specializing in annuities; policy premium rates are based on a minimum annual accumulation rate of 7% in the first year of the policy and a 4% minimum annual accumulation rate in the next five years.

    List and discuss separately for *each* client described above the objectives and constraints that will determine the portfolio policy you would recommend for that client. *(LO 22-3)*

CFA Problems

1. You are P. J. Walter, CFA, a managing partner of a prestigious investment counseling firm that specializes in individual rather than institutional accounts. The firm has developed a national reputation for its ability to blend modern portfolio theory and traditional portfolio methods.

    Dr. and Mrs. A. J. Mason have been referred to your firm and to you in particular. At your first meeting on June 2, 2018, Dr. Mason explained that he is an electrical engineer and long-time professor at the Essex Institute. He is also an inventor, and, after 30 years of teaching, the rights to one of his patented inventions, the "inverse thermothrocle valve," have just been acquired by a new electronics company, ACS, Inc.

In anticipation of the potential value of his invention, Dr. Mason had followed his accountant's advice and established a private corporation, wholly owned by the Masons, to hold the title to the inverse thermothrocle valve patent. It was this corporation that ACS acquired from the Masons for $1 million in cash, payable at the closing on June 7, 2018. In addition, ACS has agreed to pay royalties to Dr. Mason or his heirs based on its sales of systems that utilize the inverse thermothrocle valve.

Because ACS has no operating record, it is difficult for either the company or Dr. Mason to forecast future sales and royalties. While all parties are optimistic about prospects for success, they are also mindful of the risks associated with any new firm, especially those exposed to the technological obsolescence of the electronics industry. The management of ACS has indicated to Dr. Mason that he might expect royalties of as much as $100,000 in the first year of production and maximum royalties of as much as $500,000 annually thereafter.

During your counseling meeting, Mrs. Mason expressed concern for the proper investment of the $1,000,000 initial payment. She pointed out that Dr. Mason has invested all of their savings in his inventions. Thus, they will have only their Social Security retirement benefits and a small pension from the Essex Institute to provide for their retirement. Dr. Mason will be 65 in 2022. His salary from the Essex Institute is $75,000 per year. Additionally, he expects to continue earning $10,000 to $25,000 annually from consulting and speaking engagements.

The Masons have two daughters and a son, all of whom are married and have families of their own. Dr. and Mrs. Mason are interested in helping with the education of their grandchildren and have provided in their wills for their estate to be divided among their children and grandchildren.

In the event that the royalty payments from ACS meet the projections cited above, Mrs. Mason is interested in providing a scholarship fund in the name of Dr. Mason for the benefit of enterprising young engineers attending the Essex Institute. The scholarship fund ranks third in priority, behind the provision for the Masons' retirement and for the education of their grandchildren.

In your discussions with Dr. and Mrs. Mason, you have stressed the importance of identifying investment objectives and constraints and having an appropriate investment policy. Identify and describe an appropriate set of investment objectives and investment constraints for Dr. and Mrs. Mason, and prepare a comprehensive investment policy statement based on these investment objectives and constraints.   *(LO 22-1, 22-2)*

2. Your client says, "With the unrealized gains in my portfolio, I have almost saved enough money for my daughter to go to college in eight years, but educational costs keep going up." Based on this statement alone, which one of the following appears to be least important to your client's investment policy?   *(LO 22-2)*
   a. Time horizon.
   b. Purchasing power risk.
   c. Liquidity.
   d. Taxes.

3. The aspect least likely to be included in the investment policy statement is: *(LO 22-3)*
   a. Identifying an investor's objectives, constraints, and preferences.
   b. Organizing the management process itself.
   c. Implementing strategies regarding the choice of assets to be used.
   d. Procedures for monitoring market conditions, relative values, and investor circumstances.

4. A clearly written investment policy statement is critical for: *(LO 22-3)*
   a. Mutual funds.
   b. Individuals.
   c. Pension funds.
   d. All investors.

5. The investment policy statement of an institution must be concerned with all of the following *except:*   *(LO 22-3)*
   a. Its obligations to its clients.
   b. The level of the market.
   c. Legal regulations.
   d. Taxation.

6. Under the provisions of a typical corporate defined benefit pension plan, the employer is responsible for: *(LO 22-2)*
   a. Paying benefits to retired employees.
   b. Investing in conservative fixed-income assets.
   c. Counseling employees in the selection of asset classes.
   d. Maintaining an actuarially determined, fully funded pension plan.

7. Which of the following statements reflects the importance of the asset allocation decision to the investment process? The asset allocation decision: *(LO 22-3)*
   a. Helps the investor decide on realistic investment goals.
   b. Identifies the specific securities to include in a portfolio.
   c. Determines most of the portfolio's returns and volatility over time.
   d. Creates a standard by which to establish an appropriate investment time horizon.

8. You are a portfolio manager and senior executive vice president of Advisory Securities Selection, Inc. Your firm has been invited to meet with the trustees of the Wood Museum Endowment Funds. Wood Museum is a privately endowed charitable institution that is dependent on the investment return from a $25 million endowment fund to balance the budget. The treasurer of the museum has recently completed the budget that indicates a need for cash flow of $3 million in 2019, $3.2 million in 2020, and $3.5 million in 2021 from the endowment fund to balance the budget in those years. Currently, the entire endowment portfolio is invested in Treasury bills and money market funds because the trustees fear a financial crisis. The trustees do not anticipate any further capital contributions to the fund.

   The trustees are all successful businesspeople, and they have been critical of the fund's previous investment advisers because they did not follow a logical decision-making process. In fact, several previous managers have been dismissed because of their inability to communicate with the trustees and their preoccupation with the fund's relative performance rather than the cash flow needs.

   Advisory Securities Selection, Inc., has been contacted by the trustees because of its reputation for understanding and relating to the client's needs. The trustees have asked you, as a prospective portfolio manager for the Wood Museum Endowment Fund, to prepare a written report in response to the following questions. Your report will be circulated to the trustees before the initial interview on June 15, 2019.

   Explain in detail how each of the following relates to the determination of either investor objectives or investor constraints that can be used to determine the portfolio policies for this three-year period for the Wood Museum Endowment Fund.   *(LO 22-1, 22-2)*
   a. Liquidity requirements.
   b. Return requirements.
   c. Risk tolerance.
   d. Time horizon.
   e. Tax considerations.
   f. Regulatory and legal considerations.
   g. Unique needs and circumstances.

9. Mrs. Mary Atkins, age 66, has been your firm's client for five years, since the death of her husband, Dr. Charles Atkins. Dr. Atkins had built a successful newspaper business that he sold two years before his death to Merit Enterprises, a publishing and broadcasting conglomerate, in exchange for Merit common stock. The Atkinses have no children, and their wills provide that upon their deaths the remaining assets shall be used to create a fund for the benefit of Good Samaritan Hospital, to be called the Atkins Endowment Fund.

Good Samaritan is a 180-bed, not-for-profit hospital with an annual operating budget of $12.5 million. In the past, the hospital's operating revenues have often been sufficient to meet operating expenses and occasionally even generate a small surplus. In recent years, however, rising costs and declining occupancy rates have caused Good Samaritan to run a deficit. The operating deficit has averaged $300,000 to $400,000 annually over the last several years. Existing endowment assets (that is, excluding the Atkins's estate) of $7.5 million currently generate approximately $375,000 of annual income, up from less than $200,000 five years ago. This increased income has been the result of somewhat higher interest rates, as well as a shift in asset mix toward more bonds. To offset operating deficits, the Good Samaritan Board of Governors has determined that the endowment's current income should be increased to approximately 6% of total assets (up from 5% currently). The hospital has not received any significant additions to its endowment assets in the past five years.

Identify and describe an appropriate set of investment objectives and constraints for the Atkins Endowment Fund to be created after Mrs. Atkins's death. *(LO 22-1, 22-2)*

10. Several discussion meetings have provided the following information about one of your firm's new advisory clients, a charitable endowment fund recently created by means of a one-time $10 million gift:

Objectives

Return requirement. Planning is based on a minimum total return of 8% per year, including an initial current income component of $500,000 (5% on beginning capital). Realizing this current income target is the endowment fund's primary return goal. (See "unique needs" below.)

Constraints

Time horizon. Perpetuity, except for requirement to make an $8,500,000 cash distribution on June 30, 2020. (See "unique needs.")

Liquidity needs. None of a day-to-day nature until 2020. Income is distributed annually after year-end. (See "unique needs.")

Tax considerations. None; this endowment fund is exempt from taxes.

Legal and regulatory considerations. Minimal, but the prudent investor rule applies to all investment actions.

Unique needs, circumstances, and preferences. The endowment fund must pay out to another tax-exempt entity the sum of $8,500,000 in cash on June 30, 2020. The assets remaining after this distribution will be retained by the fund in perpetuity. The endowment fund has adopted a "spending rule" requiring a first-year current income payout of $500,000; thereafter, the annual payout is to rise by 3% in real terms. Until 2020, annual income in excess of that required by the spending rule is to be reinvested. After 2020, the spending rate will be reset at 5% of the then-existing capital.

Based on this information, do the following: *(LO 22-3)*

a. Formulate an appropriate investment policy statement for the endowment fund.
b. Identify and briefly explain three major ways in which your firm's initial asset allocation decisions for the endowment fund will be affected by the client's circumstances.

11. You have been named as investment adviser to a foundation established by Dr. Walter Jones with an original contribution consisting entirely of the common stock of Jomedco, Inc. Founded by Dr. Jones, Jomedco manufactures and markets medical devices invented by the doctor and collects royalties on other patented innovations.

All of the shares that made up the initial contribution to the foundation were sold at a public offering of Jomedco common stock, and the $5 million proceeds will be delivered to the foundation within the next week. At the same time, Mrs. Jones will receive $5 million in proceeds from the sale of her stock in Jomedco.

Dr. Jones's purpose in establishing the Jones Foundation was to "offset the effect of inflation on medical school tuition for the maximum number of worthy students."

You are preparing for a meeting with the foundation trustees to discuss investment policy and asset allocation.   *(LO 22-1, 22-2, 22-3)*

a. Define and give examples that show the differences between an investment objective, an investment constraint, and investment policy.

b. Identify and describe an appropriate set of investment objectives and investment constraints for the Jones Foundation.

c. Based on the investment objectives and investment constraints identified in part *(b)*, prepare a comprehensive investment policy statement for the Jones Foundation to be recommended for adoption by the trustees.

WEB *master*

The proper asset allocation for an investor planning for retirement changes dramatically over time. Investors who do *not* periodically update their asset allocation are exposed to poor performance that can significantly delay their retirement. This is exactly what occurred in 2008 to many investors planning for retirement who had not reallocated their portfolios away from stocks and into more conservative securities over the years, as they should have.

Go to **money.cnn.com** and under the *Personal Finance* tab, select *Calculators*. Then choose the Asset Allocation calculator in the *Investing* category. Calculate an asset allocation for the following two scenarios:

A. Need the money: 20+ years

How much risk: As much as possible

How flexible: If I miss my goal . . . OK

During market sell-offs: See an opportunity to buy

B. Need the money: 3–5 years

How much risk: Not much at all

How flexible: I can't afford to miss my target

During market sell-offs: Do nothing

1. What is the ratio of stock to bonds in each scenario? Notice the dramatic shift from risky assets to safe assets. How would this change have impacted an investor during the stock market crash of 2008?

2. Explain the impact on an investor planning to retire in 3–5 years if the investor had maintained asset allocation A and not asset allocation B during the 2008 stock market crash.

3. How frequently do you think investors should examine their asset allocation? What else should investors review on a periodic basis in addition to asset allocation?

SOLUTIONS TO
CONCEPT
checks

22.1 A convenient and effective way to organize the answer to this question is to cast it in the context of the investment policy statement framework.

Risk: Endowment funds have no "safety nets" such as the ones that pension funds enjoy in the event of difficulty, either in the form of corporate assets to fall back on or a call on public assistance, such as from the Pension Benefit Guaranty Corporation. Moreover, endowment fund cash flows may be highly erratic due to the uncertain timing of income from gifts and/or bequests, while pension fund cash flows tend to be very predictable and steady. These differences suggest the typical endowment fund will adopt a more conservative risk-bearing posture than will the typical pension fund, both to asset-class exposures and to the type of security content of such exposures.

Return: Because investment-related spending usually is limited to "income yield," endowment funds often focus their return goals on the matter of current spendable income; pension funds, in contrast, tend to adopt total return approaches, at least until a plan matures. Although inflation protection should be of great importance to both types of funds, endowment funds appear to be less concerned with real return production than are pension funds, perhaps because of their common emphasis on "income now" in setting return goals.

Time horizon: Theoretically, an endowment fund is a perpetuity, while a pension fund may have a finite life span. Therefore, an endowment fund should operate with a very long-term view of investment. However, such funds in practice tend to adopt shorter horizons than are typical of pension funds (just as they typically assume less risk). The pressure they may face to emphasize income production in the near term is the probable reason for this behavior.

Liquidity: Endowment funds, particularly those that use gifts and bequests to supplement their investment income, often have fairly large liquidity reserves—both to protect against fluctuations in their cash flows and to reflect their generally conservative outlooks—while, except for very mature plans, pension funds tend to require minimum liquidity reserves. Endowment funds also frequently maintain substantial liquid holdings to provide for known future cash payout requirements, such as for new buildings.

Taxes: Here, although differing in detail, the situations of the two forms of institutions are very much the same. In the United States, tax considerations are normally of minimal importance in both cases.

Regulatory/legal: Endowment fund investment is carried out under state governance, while pension fund investment, in the United States, is carried out under federal law, specifically under ERISA. The difference is significant. Endowment funds operate under the prudent investor rule, whereby each investment must be judged on its own merits apart from any other portfolio holdings, while pension plans operate under a broader context for investment—each security being judged in terms of the portfolio as a whole—and an ERISA-mandated diversification requirement that often leads to wider asset-class exposures.

Unique circumstances: Endowment funds often are faced with unique situations that sometimes affect pension fund management, including the scrutiny of such special-interest groups as trustees, alumni, faculty, student organizations, local community pressure groups, etc., each with separate and often incompatible constraints and goals that may need to be accommodated in policy setting and/or in investment content. Similarly, endowment funds may be subjected to considerable pressure for socially responsible investing, for example, divestment from tobacco, arms, or some energy firms, that can have an important investment impact by restricting the available universe of investment securities, mandating participation or nonparticipation in certain industries, sectors, or countries, or otherwise changing investment action from what it would otherwise have been. In pension fund investment, ERISA mandates that no other interests be put ahead of the interests of the beneficiaries in determining investment actions.

22.2 Identify the elements that are life-cycle driven in the two schemes of objectives and constraints.

22.3 *a.* Policy, asset allocation.
   b. Constraint, regulation.
   c. Objective, return requirement.
   d. Constraint, horizon.
   e. Policy, market timing.
   f. Constraint, taxes.
   g. Objectives, risk tolerance.
   h. Constraint, liquidity.

Appendix A

References

Affleck-Graves, John, and Richard R. Mendenhall. "The Relation between the Value Line Enigma and Post-Earnings-Announcement Drift." *Journal of Financial Economics* 31 (February 1992), pp. 75–96.

Agarwal, Vikas; Naveen D. Daniel; and Narayan Y. Naik. "Why Is Santa So Kind to Hedge Funds? The December Return Puzzle!" March 29, 2007, http://ssrn.com/abstract=891169.

Alexander, C. *Market Models.* Chichester, England: Wiley, 2001.

Alexander, Sidney. "Price Movements in Speculative Markets: Trends or Random Walks, No. 2." In *The Random Character of Stock Market Prices,* ed. Paul Cootner. Cambridge, MA: MIT Press, 1964.

Amihud, Yakov, and Haim Mendelson. "Asset Pricing and the Bid-Ask Spread." *Journal of Financial Economics* 17 (December 1986), pp. 223–50.

⎯⎯⎯ "Liquidity, Asset Prices, and Financial Policy." *Financial Analysts Journal* 47 (November–December 1991), pp. 56–66.

Amin, G., and H. Kat. "Stocks, Bonds and Hedge Funds: Not a Free Lunch!" *Journal of Portfolio Management* 29 (Summer 2003), pp. 113–20.

Aragon, George O. "Share Restrictions and Asset Pricing: Evidence from the Hedge Fund Industry." *Journal of Financial Economics* 83 (2007), pp. 33–58.

Arbel, Avner. "Generic Stocks: An Old Product in a New Package." *Journal of Portfolio Management,* Summer 1985, pp. 4–13.

Arbel, Avner, and Paul J. Strebel. "Pay Attention to Neglected Firms." *Journal of Portfolio Management,* Winter 1983, pp. 37–42.

Arnott, Robert. "Orthodoxy Overwrought." *Institutional Investor,* December 18, 2006.

Asness, Cliff. "The Value of Fundamental Indexing." *Institutional Investor,* October 16, 2006, pp. 94–99.

Ben-David, Itzhak; Francesco Franzoni; Augustin Landier; and Rabih Moussawi. "Do Hedge Funds Manipulate Stock Prices?" *Journal of Finance* 68 (December 2013), pp. 2383–2434.

Ball, R., and P. Brown. "An Empirical Evaluation of Accounting Income Numbers." *Journal of Accounting Research* 9 (1968), pp. 159–78.

Banz, Rolf. "The Relationship between Return and Market Value of Common Stocks." *Journal of Financial Economics* 9 (March 1981), pp. 3–18.

Barber, B.; R. Lehavy; M. McNichols; and B. Trueman. "Can Investors Profit from the Prophets? Security Analysts Recommendations and Stock Returns." *Journal of Finance* 56 (April 2001), pp. 531–63.

Barber, Brad, and Terrance Odean. "Trading Is Hazardous to Your Wealth: The Common Stock Investment Performance of Individual Investors." *Journal of Finance* 55 (2000), pp. 773–806.

⎯⎯⎯ "Boys Will Be Boys: Gender, Overconfidence, and Common Stock Investment." *Quarterly Journal of Economics* 16 (2001), pp. 262–92.

Barberis, Nicholas, and Richard Thaler. "A Survey of Behavioral Finance." In *The Handbook of the Economics of Finance,* ed. G. M. Constantinides, M. Harris, and R. Stulz. Amsterdam: Elsevier, 2003.

Basu, Sanjoy. "The Investment Performance of Common Stocks in Relation to Their Price-Earnings Ratios: A Test of the Efficient Market Hypothesis." *Journal of Finance* 32 (June 1977), pp. 663–82.

⎯⎯⎯ "The Relationship between Earnings Yield, Market Value, and Return for NYSE Common Stocks: Further Evidence." *Journal of Financial Economics* 12 (June 1983), pp. 129–56.

Battalio, R. H., and R. Mendenhall. "Earnings Expectation, Investor Trade Size, and Anomalous Returns around Earnings Announcements." *Journal of Financial Economics* 77 (2005), pp. 289–319.

Benveniste, Lawrence, and William Wilhelm. "Initial Public Offerings: Going by the Book." *Journal of Applied Corporate Finance* 10 (March 1997), pp. 98–108.

Bergstresser, D.; M. Desai; and J. Rauh. "Earnings Manipulation, Pension Assumptions, and Managerial Investment Decisions." *Quarterly Journal of Economics* 121 (2006), pp. 157–95.

Berk, J. B., and R. C. Green. "Mutual Fund Flows and Performance in Rational Markets." *Journal of Political Economy* 112 (2004), pp. 1269–95.

Bernard, V., and J. Thomas. "Evidence That Stock Prices Do Not Fully Reflect the Implications of Current Earnings for Future Earnings." *Journal of Accounting and Economics* 13 (1990), pp. 305–40.

Bernard, Victor L., and Jacob K. Thomas. "Post-Earnings-Announcement Drift: Delayed Price Response or Risk Premium?" *Journal of Accounting Research* 27 (1989), pp. 1–36.

Bernhard, Arnold. *Value Line Methods of Evaluating Common Stocks.* New York: Arnold Bernhard, 1979.

Black, Fischer. "Yes, Virginia, There Is Hope: Tests of the Value Line Ranking System." Graduate School of Business, University of Chicago, 1971.

Black, Fischer; Michael C. Jensen; and Myron Scholes. "The Capital Asset Pricing Model: Some Empirical Tests." In *Studies in the Theory of Capital Markets,* ed. Michael C. Jensen. New York: Praeger, 1972.

Black, Fischer, and Myron Scholes. "The Pricing of Options and Corporate Liabilities."

Journal of Political Economy 81 (May–June 1973), pp. 637–59.

Black, Fischer, Charles Smithson, Richard Mason, Mark Rubinstein, Kenneth Leong, Alan White, John Hull, Ron Dembo, Mark Garman, and Greg Bentley. *"From Black-Scholes to Black Holes: New Frontiers in Options."* London: *Risk* Magazine, 1992.

Blake, Christopher; Edwin J. Elton; and Martin J. Gruber. "The Performance of Bond Mutual Funds." *Journal of Business* 66 (July 1993), pp. 371–404.

Blume, Marshall E., and Robert F. Stambaugh. "Biases in Computed Returns: An Application to the Size Effect." *Journal of Finance Economics,* 1983, pp. 387–404.

Bogle, John C. "Investing in the 1990s: Remembrance of Things Past, and Things Yet to Come." *Journal of Portfolio Management,* Spring 1991, pp. 5–14.

_____ *Bogle on Mutual Funds.* Burr Ridge, IL: Irwin, 1994.

Bollen, Nicolas P. B., and Jeffrey A. Busse. "Short-Term Persistence in Mutual Fund Performance." *Review of Financial Studies* 19 (2004), pp. 569–97.

Brav, Alon; Christopher Geczy; and Paul A. Gompers. "Is the Abnormal Return Following Equity Issuances Anomalous?" *Journal of Financial Economics* 56 (2000), pp. 209–49.

Brennan, Michael. "Taxes, Market Valuation and Corporate Financial Policy." *National Tax Journal,* 1970.

Brinson, G.; C. R. Hood; and G. Beebower. "Determinants of Portfolio Performance." *Financial Analysts Journal,* July–August 1986.

Brinson, Gary; Brian Singer; and Gilbert Beebower. "Determinants of Portfolio Performance." *Financial Analysts Journal,* May–June 1991.

Brock, William; Josef Lakonishok; and Blake LeBaron. "Simple Technical Trading Rules and the Stochastic Properties of Stock Returns." *Journal of Finance* 47 (December 1992), pp. 1731–64.

Brown, David, and Robert H. Jennings. "On Technical Analysis." *Review of Financial Studies* 2 (1989), pp. 527–52.

Brown, Lawrence D., and Michael Rozeff. "The Superiority of Analysts' Forecasts as Measures of Expectations: Evidence from Earnings." *Journal of Finance,* March 1978.

Brown, S. J.; W. N. Goetzmann; and B. Liang. "Fees on Fees in Funds of Funds." *Journal*

of Investment Management 2 (2004), pp. 39–56.

Brown, Stephen J.; Greg N. Gregoriou; and Razvan Pascalau. "Diversification in Funds of Hedge Funds: Is It Possible to Overdiversify?" *Review of Asset Pricing Studies* 2 (2012), pp. 89–110.

Busse, J. A., and T. C. Green. "Market Efficiency in Real Time." *Journal of Financial Economics* 65 (2002), pp. 415–37.

Campbell, John Y., and Robert Shiller. "Stock Prices, Earnings and Expected Dividends." *Journal of Finance* 43 (July 1988), pp. 661–76.

Cao, Jie; Jason C. Hsu; Zhanbing Xiao; and Xintong Zhan. "Smart Beta, 'Smarter' Flows," (2018), Available at SSRN: https://ssrn.com/abstract=2962479.

Carhart, Mark. "On Persistence in Mutual Fund Performance." *Journal of Finance* 52 (1997), pp. 57–82.

Chen, Nai-fu; Richard Roll; and Stephen Ross. "Economic Forces and the Stock Market." *Journal of Business* 59 (1986), pp. 383–403.

Chen, Y.; W. E. Ferson; and H. Peters. "Measuring the Timing Ability and Performance of Bond Mutual Funds." *Journal of Financial Economics* 98 (2010), pp. 72–89.

Chopra, Navin; Josef Lakonishok; and Jay R. Ritter. "Measuring Abnormal Performance: Do Stocks Overreact?" *Journal of Financial Economics* 31 (1992), pp. 235–68.

Chordia, Tarun; Avanidhar Subrahmanyam; and Qing Tong. "Have Capital Market Anomalies Attenuated in the Recent Era of High Liquidity and Trading Activity?" *Journal of Accounting and Economics* 58 (August 2014), pp. 41–58.

Clarke, Roger, and Mark P. Kritzman. *Currency Management: Concepts and Practices.* Charlottesville: Research Foundation of the Institute of Chartered Financial Analysts, 1996.

Clayman, Michelle. "In Search of Excellence: The Investor's Viewpoint." *Financial Analysts Journal,* May–June 1987.

Connolly, Robert. "An Examination of the Robustness of the Weekend Effect." *Journal of Financial and Quantitative Analysis* 24 (June 1989), pp. 133–69.

Conrad, Jennifer, and Gautam Kaul. "Time-Variation in Expected Returns." *Journal of Business* 61 (October 1988), pp. 409–25.

Copeland, Thomas E., and David Mayers. "The Value Line Enigma (1965–1978):

A Case Study of Performance Evaluation Issues." *Journal of Financial Economics,* November 1982.

Coval, Joshua D., and Tyler Shumway. "Do Behavioral Biases Affect Prices?" *Journal of Finance* 60 (February 2005), pp. 1–34.

Cremers, Martijn; Antti Petajisto; and Eric Zitzewitz. "Should Benchmark Indices Have Alpha? Revisiting Performance Evaluation." *Critical Finance Review* 2 (2013), pp. 1–48.

Davis, James L.; Eugene F. Fama; and Kenneth R. French. "Characteristics, Covariances, and Average Returns, 1929 to 1997." *Journal of Finance* 55 (2000), pp. 389–406.

De Bondt, W. F. M., and R. H. Thaler. "Does the Stock Market Overreact?" *Journal of Finance* 40 (1985), pp. 793–805.

_____ "Further Evidence on Investor Overreaction and Stock Market Seasonality." *Journal of Finance* 42 (1987), pp. 557–81.

_____ "Do Security Analysts Overreact?" *American Economic Review* 80 (1990), pp. 52–57.

_____ "Financial Decision Making in Markets and Firms." In *Handbooks in Operations Research and Management Science, Vol. 9: Finance,* ed. R. A. Jarrow, V. Maksimovic, and W. T. Ziemba. Amsterdam: Elsevier, 1995.

Del Guercio, Diane, and Jonathan Reuter. "Mutual Fund Performance and the Incentive to Generate Alpha." *Journal of Finance* 69 (2014), pp. 1673–1704.

DeLong, J. Bradford; Andrei Schleifer; Lawrence Summers; and Robert Waldmann. "Noise Trader Risk in Financial Markets." *Journal of Political Economy* 98 (August 1990), pp. 704–38.

DeMarzo, Peter M.; Ron Kaniel; and Ilan Kremer. "Diversification as a Public Good: Community Effects in Portfolio Choice." *Journal of Finance* 59 (August 2004), pp. 1677–1716.

de Soto, Hernando. *The Mystery of Capital: Why Capitalism Triumphs in the West and Fails Everywhere Else.* New York: Basic Books, 2000.

Dimson, E.; P. R. Marsh; and M. Staunton. *Millennium Book II: 101 Years of Investment Returns.* London: ABN-Amro and London Business School, 2001.

Douglas, George W. "Risk in Equity Markets: An Empirical Appraisal of Market Efficiency." *Yale Economic Essays* IX (Spring 1969).

Dunn, Patricia, and Rolf D. Theisen. "How Consistently Do Active Managers Win?" *Journal of Portfolio Management* 9 (Summer 1983), pp. 47–53.

Errunza, Vihang, and Etienne Losq. "International Asset Pricing under Mild Segmentation: Theory and Test." *Journal of Finance* 40 (March 1985), pp. 105–24.

Fama, Eugene. "The Behavior of Stock Market Prices." *Journal of Business* 38 (January 1965), pp. 34–105.

_____ "Market Efficiencies, Long-Term Returns, and Behavioral Finance." *Journal of Financial Economics* 49 (September 1998), pp. 283–306.

Fama, Eugene, and Marshall Blume. "Filter Rules and Stock Market Trading Profits." *Journal of Business* 39 (Supplement, January 1966), pp. 226–41.

Fama, Eugene F., and Kenneth R. French. "Permanent and Temporary Components of Stock Prices." *Journal of Political Economy* 96 (1988), pp. 246–73.

_____ "Dividend Yields and Expected Stock Returns." *Journal of Financial Economics* 22 (October 1988), pp. 3–25.

_____ "Business Conditions and Expected Returns on Stocks and Bonds." *Journal of Financial Economics* 25 (November 1989), pp. 3–22.

_____ "The Cross Section of Expected Stock Returns." *Journal of Finance* 47 (June 1992), pp. 427–65.

_____ "Common Risk Factors in the Returns on Stocks and Bonds." *Journal of Financial Economics* 33 (1993), pp. 3–56.

_____ "Multifactor Explanations of Asset Pricing Anomalies." *Journal of Finance* 51 (1996), pp. 55–84.

_____ "The Equity Premium." *Journal of Finance* 57 (April 2002), pp. 637–60.

_____ "Luck versus Skill in the Cross-Section of Mutual Fund Returns." *Journal of Finance* 65 (2010), pp. 1915–47.

Fama, Eugene, and James MacBeth. "Risk, Return and Equilibrium: Empirical Tests." *Journal of Political Economy* 81 (March 1973).

Fisher, Irving. *The Theory of Interest: As Determined by Impatience to Spend Income and Opportunity to Invest It.* New York: Augustus M. Kelley, 1965, originally published in 1930.

Flannery, Mark J., and Christopher M. James. "The Effect of Interest Rate Changes on the Common Stock Returns of Financial Institutions." *Journal of Finance* 39 (September 1984), pp. 1141–54.

Foster, George; Chris Olsen; and Terry Shevlin. "Earnings Releases, Anomalies, and the Behavior of Security Returns." *The Accounting Review* 59 (October 1984).

French, Kenneth. "Stock Returns and the Weekend Effect." *Journal of Financial Economics* 8 (March 1980), pp. 55–69.

Froot, K. A., and E. M. Dabora. "How Are Stock Prices Affected by the Location of Trade?" *Journal of Financial Economics* 53 (1999), pp. 189–216.

Fung, William, and David Hsieh. "Empirical Characteristics of Dynamic Trading Strategies: The Case of Hedge Funds." *Review of Financial Studies* 10 (1997), pp. 275–302.

_____ "Performance Characteristics of Hedge Funds and CTA Funds: Natural versus Spurious Biases." *Journal of Financial and Quantitative Analysis* 35 (2000), pp. 291–307.

Gervais, S., and T. Odean. "Learning to Be Overconfident." *Review of Financial Studies* 14 (2001), pp. 1–27.

Geske, Robert, and Richard Roll. "On Valuing American Call Options with the Black-Scholes European Formula." *Journal of Finance* 39 (June 1984), pp. 443–56.

Getmansky, Mila; Andrew W. Lo; and Igor Makarov. "An Econometric Model of Serial Correlation and Illiquidity in Hedge Fund Returns." *Journal of Financial Economics* 74 (2004), pp. 529–609.

Ghysels, E.; A. Harvey; and E. Renault. "Stochastic Volatility." In *Statistical Methods in Finance*, eds. C. Rao and G. Maddala. Amsterdam: Elsevier Science, North-Holland Series in Statistics and Probability, 1996.

Gibbons, Michael, and Patrick Hess. "Day of the Week Effects and Asset Returns." *Journal of Business* 54 (October 1981), pp. 579–98.

Givoly, Dan, and Dan Palmon. "Insider Trading and Exploitation of Inside Information: Some Empirical Evidence." *Journal of Business* 58 (1985), pp. 69–87.

Goetzmann, William N., and Roger G. Ibbotson. "Do Winners Repeat?" *Journal of Portfolio Management*, Winter 1994, pp. 9–18.

Graham, J. R., and C. R. Harvey. "Grading the Performance of Market Timing Newsletters." *Financial Analysts Journal* 53 (November–December 1997), pp. 54–66.

_____ "Expectations of Equity Risk Premia, Volatility and Asymmetry from a Corporate Finance Perspective." 2001, available at SSRN, http://ssrn.com/abstract=292623.

Grieves, Robin, and Alan J. Marcus. "Riding the Yield Curve: Reprise." *Journal of Portfolio Management*, Winter 1992.

Grinblatt, Mark, and Bing Han. "Prospect Theory, Mental Accounting, and Momentum." *Journal of Financial Economics* 78 (November 2005), pp. 311–39.

Grinblatt, Mark, and Sheridan Titman. "Mutual Fund Performance: An Analysis of Quarterly Portfolio Holdings." *Journal of Business* 62 (1989), pp. 393–416.

Grossman, Sanford J., and Joseph E. Stiglitz. "On the Impossibility of Informationally Efficient Markets." *American Economic Review* 70 (June 1980), pp. 393–408.

Hasanhodzic, Jasmina, and Andrew W. Lo. "Can Hedge Fund Returns Be Replicated? The Linear Case." *Journal of Investment Management* 5 (2007), pp. 5–45.

Haugen, Robert A. *The New Finance: The Case against Efficient Markets.* Englewood Cliffs, NJ: Prentice Hall, 1995.

Henriksson, Roy D. "Market Timing and Mutual Fund Performance: An Empirical Investigation." *Journal of Business* 57 (January 1984).

Heston, S. L. "A Closed-Form Solution for Options with Stochastic Volatility with Applications to Bonds and Currency Options." *Review of Financial Studies* 6 (1993), pp. 327–43.

Hirshleifer, David. "Investor Psychology and Asset Pricing." *Journal of Finance* 56 (August 2001), pp. 1533–97.

Homer, Sidney, and Martin L. Leibowitz. *Inside the Yield Book: New Tools for Bond Market Strategy.* Englewood Cliffs, NJ: Prentice Hall, 1972.

Hull, J. C., and A. White. "The Pricing of Options on Assets with Stochastic Volatilities." *Journal of Finance* 42 (1987), pp. 281–300.

Ibbotson, Roger G. "Price Performance of Common Stock New Issues." *Journal of Financial Economics* 2 (September 1975).

Ibbotson, Roger; Richard C. Carr; and Anthony W. Robinson. "International Equity and Bond Returns." *Financial Analysts Journal*, July–August 1982.

Ibbotson, R. G., and L. B. Siegel. "The World Market Wealth Portfolio." *Journal of Portfolio Management*, Winter 1983.

Ibbotson, R. G.; L. B. Siegel; and K. Love. "World Wealth: Market Values and

Returns." *Journal of Portfolio Management,* Fall 1985.

Jacquier, Eric, and Alan Marcus. "Asset Allocation Models and Market Volatility." *Financial Analysts Journal* 57 (March–April 2001), pp. 16–30.

Jaffe, Jeffrey F. "Special Information and Insider Trading." *Journal of Business* 47 (July 1974), pp. 410–28.

_____ "Gold and Gold Stocks as Investments for Institutional Portfolios." *Financial Analysts Journal* 45 (March–April 1989), pp. 53–59.

Jagannathan, R.; E. R. McGrattan; and A. Scherbina. "The Declining U.S. Equity Premium." *Federal Reserve Bank of Minneapolis Quarterly Review* 24 (Fall 2000), pp. 3–19.

Jagannathan, Ravi, and Zhenyu Wang. "The Conditional CAPM and the Cross-Section of Expected Returns." *Staff Report 208,* Federal Reserve Bank of Minneapolis, 1996.

Jegadeesh, N.; J. Kim; S. D. Krische; and C. M. Lee. "Analyzing the Analysts: When Do Recommendations Add Value?" *Journal of Finance* 59 (June 2004), pp. 1083–1124.

Jegadeesh, Narasimhan. "Evidence of Predictable Behavior of Security Returns." *Journal of Finance* 45 (September 1990), pp. 881–98.

Jegadeesh, Narasimhan, and Sheridan Titman. "Returns to Buying Winners and Selling Losers: Implications for Stock Market Efficiency." *Journal of Finance* 48 (March 1993), pp. 65–91.

Jensen, Michael C. "The Performance of Mutual Funds in the Period 1945–1964." *Journal of Finance,* May 1968.

_____ "Risk, the Pricing of Capital Assets, and the Evaluation of Investment Portfolios." *Journal of Business* 42 (April 1969), pp. 167–247.

Kahneman, D., and A. Tversky. "Subjective Probability: A Judgment of Representativeness." *Cognitive Psychology* 3 (1972), pp. 430–54.

_____ "On the Psychology of Prediction." *Psychology Review* 80 (1973), pp. 237–51.

Keim, Donald B. "Size Related Anomalies and Stock Return Seasonality: Further Empirical Evidence." *Journal of Financial Economics* 12 (June 1983), pp. 13–32.

Keim, Donald B., and Robert F. Stambaugh. "Predicting Returns in the Stock and Bond Markets." *Journal of Financial Economics* 17 (1986), pp. 357–90.

Kendall, Maurice. "The Analysis of Economic Time Series, Part I: Prices." *Journal of the Royal Statistical Society* 96 (1953), pp. 11–25.

Kopcke, Richard W., and Geoffrey R. H. Woglom. "Regulation Q and Savings Bank Solvency—The Connecticut Experience." In *The Regulation of Financial Institutions,* Federal Reserve Bank of Boston Conference Series, No. 21, 1979.

Kosowski, R.; A. Timmermann; R. Wermers; and H. White. "Can Mutual Fund 'Stars' Really Pick Stocks? New Evidence from a Bootstrap Analysis." *Journal of Finance* 61 (December 2006), pp. 2551–95.

Kothari, S. P.; Jay Shanken; and Richard G. Sloan. "Another Look at the Cross-Section of Expected Stock Returns." *Journal of Finance* 50 (March 1995), pp. 185–224.

Kotlikoff, Laurence J., and Avia Spivack. "The Family as an Incomplete Annuities Market." *Journal of Political Economy* 89, no. 2 (April 1981), pp. 372–91.

Kotlikoff, Laurence J., and Lawrence H. Summers. "The Role of Intergenerational Transfers in Aggregate Capital Accumulation." *Journal of Political Economy* 89, no. 4 (August 1981), pp. 706–32.

Lakonishok, Josef; Andrei Shleifer; and Robert W. Vishny. "Contrarian Investment, Extrapolation, and Risk." *Journal of Finance* 50 (1995), pp. 1541–78.

Lamont, O. A., and R. H. Thaler. "Can the Market Add and Subtract? Mispricing in Tech Carve-Outs." *Journal of Political Economy* 111 (2003), pp. 227–68.

La Porta, Raphael. "Expectations and the Cross-Section of Stock Returns." *Journal of Finance* 51 (December 1996), pp. 1715–42.

Latane, H. A., and C. P. Jones. "Standardized Unexpected Earnings—1971–1977." *Journal of Finance,* June 1979.

Lease, R.; W. Lewellen; and G. Schlarbaum. "Market Segmentation: Evidence on the Individual Investor." *Financial Analysts Journal* 32 (1976), pp. 53–60.

Lee, C. M.; A. Shleifer; and R. H. Thaler. "Investor Sentiment and the Closed-End Fund Puzzle." *Journal of Finance* 46 (March 1991), pp. 75–109.

Lehmann, Bruce. "Fads, Martingales and Market Efficiency." *Quarterly Journal of Economics* 105 (February 1990), pp. 1–28.

Levy, Robert A. "The Predictive Significance of Five-Point Chart Patterns." *Journal of Business* 44 (July 1971), pp. 316–23.

Liebowitz, Martin L., and Alfred Weinberger. "Contingent Immunization—Part I: Risk Control Procedure." *Financial Analysts Journal* 38 (November–December 1982).

Lo, Andrew W., and Craig MacKinlay. "Stock Market Prices Do Not Follow Random Walks: Evidence from a Simple Specification Test." *Review of Financial Studies* 1 (Spring 1988), pp. 41–66.

Loeb, T. F. "Trading Cost: The Critical Link between Investment Information and Results." *Financial Analysts Journal,* May–June 1983.

Longin, F., and B. Solnik. "Is the Correlation in International Equity Returns Constant: 1960–1990?" *Journal of International Money and Finance* 14 (1995), pp. 3–26.

Lynch, Peter, with John Rothchild. *One Up on Wall Street.* New York: Penguin Books, 1989.

Macaulay, Frederick. *Some Theoretical Problems Suggested by the Movements of Interest Rates, Bond Yields, and Stock Prices in the United States since 1856.* New York: National Bureau of Economic Research, 1938.

Malkiel, Burton G. "Expectations, Bond Prices, and the Term Structure of Interest Rates." *Quarterly Journal of Economics* 76 (May 1962), pp. 197–218.

_____ "Returns from Investing in Equity Mutual Funds: 1971–1991." *Journal of Finance* 50 (June 1995), pp. 549–72.

Malkiel, Burton G., and Atanu Saha. "Hedge Funds: Risk and Return." *Financial Analysts Journal* 61 (2005), pp. 80–88.

Malmendier, U., and G. Tate. "Who Makes Acquisitions? CEO Overconfidence and the Market's Reaction." *Journal of Financial Economics* 89 (July 2008) pp. 20–43.

Marcus, Alan J. "The Magellan Fund and Market Efficiency." *Journal of Portfolio Management* 17 (Fall 1990), pp. 85–88.

Mayers, David. "Nonmarketable Assets and Capital Market Equilibrium under Uncertainty." In *Studies in the Theory of Capital Markets,* ed. M. C. Jensen. New York: Praeger, 1972.

McDonald, Robert L. *Derivative Markets,* 2nd ed. Boston: Addison-Wesley, 2005.

McLean, R. David, and Jeffrey E. Pontiff. "Does Academic Research Destroy Stock Return Predictability." *Journal of Finance* 71 (2016), pp. 5–32.

Merton, Robert C. "Theory of Rational Option Pricing." *Bell Journal of Economics and Management Science* 4 (Spring 1973), pp. 141–83.

_____ "On Market Timing and Investment Performance: An Equilibrium Theory of Value for Market Forecasts." *Journal of Business* 54 (July 1981).

_____ "A Simple Model of Capital Market Equilibrium with Incomplete Information." *Journal of Finance* 42 (1987), pp. 483–510.

Miller, Merton H., and Myron Scholes. "Rate of Return in Relation to Risk: A Re-examination of Some Recent Findings." In *Studies in the Theory of Capital Markets,* ed. Michael C. Jensen. New York: Praeger, 1972.

Modigliani, Franco, and Leah Modigliani. "Risk-Adjusted Performance." *Journal of Portfolio Management,* Winter 1997, pp. 45–54.

Modigliani, Franco, and M. Miller. "The Cost of Capital, Corporation Finance, and the Theory of Investment." *American Economic Review,* June 1958.

_____ "Dividend Policy, Growth, and the Valuation of Shares." *Journal of Business,* October 1961.

Morrell, John A. "Introduction to International Equity Diversification." In *International Investing for U.S. Pension Funds,* Institute for Fiduciary Education, London/ Venice, May 6–13, 1989.

Niederhoffer, Victor, and Patrick Regan. "Earnings Changes, Analysts' Forecasts, and Stock Prices." *Financial Analysts Journal,* May–June 1972.

Norby, W. C. "Applications of Inflation-Adjusted Accounting Data." *Financial Analysts Journal,* March–April 1983.

Odean, T. "Are Investors Reluctant to Realize Their Losses?" *Journal of Finance* 53 (1998), pp. 1775–98.

Patel, J. M., and M. A. Wolfson. "The Intraday Speed of Adjustment of Stock Prices to Earnings and Dividend Announcements." *Journal of Financial Economics* 13 (June 1984), pp. 223–52.

Perold, André. "Fundamentally Flawed Indexing." HBS mimeo, January 2007.

Perry, Kevin, and Robert A. Taggart. "The Growing Role of Junk Bonds in Corporate Finance." *Continental Bank Journal of Applied Corporate Finance* 1 (Spring 1988).

Pontiff, Jeffrey. "Closed-End Fund Premia and Returns Implications for Financial Market Equilibrium." *Journal of Financial Economics* 37 (1995), pp. 341–70.

_____ "Costly Arbitrage: Evidence from Closed-End Funds." *Quarterly Journal of Economics* 111 (November 1996), pp. 1135–51.

Porter, Michael E. *Competitive Strategy: Techniques for Analyzing Industries and Competitors.* New York: Free Press, 1980.

_____ *Competitive Advantage: Creating and Sustaining Superior Performance.* New York: Free Press, 1985.

Poterba, James M., and Lawrence Summers. "Mean Reversion in Stock Market Prices: Evidence and Implications." *Journal of Financial Economics* 22 (1988), pp. 27–59.

Rau, P. R.; O. Dimitrov; and M. Cooper. "A Rose.com by Any Other Name." *Journal of Finance* 56 (2001), pp. 2371–88.

Ready, Mark J. "Profits from Technical Trading Rules." *Financial Management* 31 (Autumn 2002), pp. 43–62.

Redington, F. M. "Review of the Principle of Life-Office Valuations." *Journal of the Institute of Actuaries* 78 (1952), pp. 286–340.

Reinganum, Marc R. "The Anomalous Stock Market Behavior of Small Firms in January: Empirical Tests for Tax-Loss Effects." *Journal of Financial Economics* 12 (June 1983), pp. 89–104.

_____ "The Anatomy of a Stock Market Winner." *Financial Analysts Journal,* March–April 1988, pp. 272–84.

Rendleman, Richard J., Jr.; Charles P. Jones; and Henry A. Latané. "Empirical Anomalies Based on Unexpected Earnings and the Importance of Risk Adjustments." *Journal of Financial Economics* 10 (November 1982), pp. 269–87.

Ritter, Jay R. "The Buying and Selling Behavior of Individual Investors at the Turn of the Year." *Journal of Finance* 43 (July 1988), pp. 701–17.

Roberts, Harry. "Stock Market 'Patterns' and Financial Analysis: Methodological Suggestions." *Journal of Finance* 14 (March 1959), pp. 11–25.

Roll, Richard. "A Critique of the Capital Asset Theory Tests: Part I: On Past and Potential Testability of the Theory." *Journal of Financial Economics* 4 (1977).

_____ "The International Crash of October 1987." *Financial Analysts Journal,* September–October 1988.

Ross, Stephen A. "Return, Risk and Arbitrage." In *Risk and Return in Finance,* ed. I. Friend and J. Bicksler. Cambridge, MA: Ballinger, 1976.

_____ "Neoclassical Finance, Alternative Finance and the Closed End Fund Puzzle." *European Financial Management* 8 (2002), pp. 129–37, ssrn.com/abstract= 313444.

Rubinstein, Mark. "Implied Binomial Trees." *Journal of Finance* 49 (July 1994), pp. 771–818.

Sadka, Ronnie. "Liquidity Risk and the Cross-Section of Hedge-Fund Returns." *Journal of Financial Economics* 98 (October 2010), pp. 54–71.

Samuelson, Paul. "The Judgment of Economic Science on Rational Portfolio Management." *Journal of Portfolio Management* 16 (Fall 1989), pp. 4–12.

Schleifer, Andrei. *Inefficient Markets.* New York: Oxford University Press, 2000.

Schleifer, Andrei, and Robert Vishny. "Equilibrium Short Horizons of Investors and Firms." *American Economic Review* 80 (May 1990), pp. 148–53.

_____ "The Limits of Arbitrage." *Journal of Finance* 52 (March 1997), pp. 35–55.

Seyhun, H. Nejat. "Insiders' Profits, Costs of Trading and Market Efficiency." *Journal of Financial Economics* 16 (1986), pp. 189–212.

Sharpe, William F. "A Simplified Model for Portfolio Analysis." *Management Science* IX (January 1963), pp. 277–93.

_____ "Mutual Fund Performance." *Journal of Business* 39 (January 1966).

_____ "Asset Allocation: Management Style and Performance Evaluation." *Journal of Portfolio Management,* Winter 1992, pp. 7–19.

Shefrin, Hersh. *Beyond Greed and Fear.* Boston: Harvard Business School Press, 2002.

Shefrin, Hersh, and Meir Statman. "The Disposition to Sell Winners Too Early and Ride Losers Too Long: Theory and Evidence." *Journal of Finance* 40 (July 1985), pp. 777–90.

Shefrin, Hersh and Meir Statman. "Explaining Investor Preference for Cash Dividends," *Journal of Financial Economics* 13 (1984), pp. 253–282.

Shefrin, Hersh and Meir Statman. "Behavioral Portfolio Theory," *Journal of Financial and Quantitative Analysis* 35 (June, 2000), pp. 127–151.

Shiller, Robert. "Do Stock Prices Move Too Much to Be Justified by Subsequent

Changes in Dividends?" *American Economic Review* 71 (June 1981).

Solnik, B. *International Investing,* 4th ed. Reading, MA: Addison-Wesley, 1999.

Solnik, Bruno, and A. De Freitas. "International Factors of Stock Price Behavior." CESA Working Paper, February 1986 (cited in Bruno Solnik, *International Investments.* Reading, MA: Addison-Wesley, 1988).

Speidell, Lawrence S., and Vinod Bavishi. "GAAP Arbitrage: Valuation Opportunities in International Accounting Standards." *Financial Analysts Journal,* November–December 1992, pp. 58–66.

Statman, Meir. "Behavioral Finance." *Contemporary Finance Digest* 1 (Winter 1997), pp. 5–22.

Statman, Meir. "What Is Behavioral Finance?" *Handbook of Finance,* vol. II, chap. 9 (2008), pp. 79–84.

Statman, Meir; Kenneth L. Fisher; and Deniz Anginer. "Affect in a Behavioral Asset-Pricing Model." *Financial Analysts Journal* 64 (2008), pp. 20–29.

Stickel, Scott E. "The Effect of Value Line Investment Survey Rank Changes on Common Stock Prices." *Journal of Financial Economics* 14 (1986), pp. 121–44.

Taleb, Nassim N. *Fooled by Randomness: The Hidden Role of Chance in Life and in the Markets.* New York: TEXERE (Thomson), 2004.

_____ *The Black Swan: The Impact of the Highly Improbable.* New York: Random House, 2007.

Thaler, Richard H. *The Winner's Curse.* Princeton, NJ: Princeton University Press, 1992.

_____ *Advances in Behavioral Finance.* New York: Russell Sage Foundation, 1993.

Tobin, James. "Liquidity Preference as Behavior toward Risk." *Review of Economic Studies* XXVI (February 1958), pp. 65–86.

Treynor, Jack L. "How to Rate Management Investment Funds." *Harvard Business Review* 43 (January–February 1965).

Treynor, Jack, and Fischer Black. "How to Use Security Analysis to Improve Portfolio Selection." *Journal of Business* 46 (January 1973).

Treynor, Jack L., and Kay Mazuy. "Can Mutual Funds Outguess the Market?" *Harvard Business Review* 43 (July–August 1966).

Trippi, Robert R., and Duane Desieno. "Trading Equity Index Futures with Neural Networks." *Journal of Portfolio Management* 19 (Fall 1992).

Trippi, Robert R.; Duane Desieno; and Efraim Turban, eds. *Neural Networks in Finance and Investing.* Chicago: Probus, 1993.

Wallace, A. "Is Beta Dead?" *Institutional Investor* 14 (July 1980), pp. 22–30.

Wermers, R. R. "Mutual Fund Performance: An Empirical Decomposition into Stock-Picking Talent, Style, Transaction Costs, and Expenses." *Journal of Finance* 55 (2000), pp. 1655–1703.

Whaley, Robert E. "Valuation of American Call Options on Dividend-Paying Stocks: Empirical Tests." *Journal of Financial Economics* 10 (1982), pp. 29–58.

Wiggins, J. B. "Option Values under Stochastic Volatilities." *Journal of Financial Economics* 19 (1987), pp. 351–72.

Womack, K. L. "Do Brokerage Analysts' Recommendations Have Investment Value?" *Journal of Finance* 51 (March 1996), pp. 137–67.

Appendix B

References to CFA Questions

Each end-of-chapter CFA question is reprinted with permission from the CFA Institute, Charlottesville, Virginia.[1] Following is a list of the CFA questions in the end-of-chapter material and the exams/study guides from which they were taken and updated.

Chapter 2

CFA 1. 1986 Level II CFA Study Guide, © 1986.

Chapter 5

CFA 1–3. 1998 Level I CFA Study Guide, © 1998.

CFA 4–6. 1991 Level I CFA Study Guide, © 1991.

CFA 7–11. 1993 Level I CFA Study Guide, © 1993.

Chapter 6

CFA 1. 1998 Level I CFA Study Guide, © 1998.

CFA 2. 2001 Level III CFA Study Guide, © 2001.

CFA 3. 2001 Level II CFA Study Guide, © 2001.

CFA 4–6. 1982 Level III CFA Study Guide, © 1982.

CFA 7. 2000 Level II CFA Study Guide, © 2000.

Chapter 7

CFA 1. 1998 Level I CFA Study Guide, © 1998.

CFA 2. 2000 Level II CFA Study Guide, © 2000.

CFA 3. 2002 Level II CFA Study Guide, © 2002.

CFA 4. 2001 Level II CFA Study Guide, © 2001.

CFA 5–14. Various CFA exams.

Chapter 8

CFA 1–5. 1993 Level I CFA Study Guide, © 1993.

CFA 6. 1998 Level I CFA Study Guide, © 1998.

CFA 7. 1981 Level I CFA Study Guide, © 1981.

CFA 8. 1989 Level III CFA Study Guide, © 1989.

CFA 9. 1996 Level III CFA Study Guide, © 1996.

CFA 10. 1996 Level III CFA Study Guide, © 1996.

CFA 11. 1996 Level III CFA Study Guide, © 1996.

Chapter 9

CFA 1. 2000 Level III CFA Study Guide, © 2000.

CFA 2. 2001 Level III CFA Study Guide, © 2001.

CFA 3. 2004 Level III CFA Study Guide, © 2004.

CFA 4. 2003 Level III CFA Study Guide, © 2003.

CFA 5. 2002 Level III CFA Study Guide, © 2002.

Chapter 10

CFA 1. From various CFA exams.

CFA 2. 1999 Level II CFA Study Guide, © 1999.

CFA 3. 1992 Level II CFA Study Guide, © 1992.

CFA 4. 1993 Level I CFA Study Guide, © 1993.

CFA 5. 1994 Level I CFA Study Guide, © 1994.

Chapter 11

CFA 1. 1985 Level I CFA Study Guide, © 1985.

CFA 2. 1985 Level I CFA Study Guide, © 1985.

CFA 3. 1992 Level II CFA Study Guide, © 1992.

CFA 4. 1983 Level III CFA Study Guide, © 1983.

CFA 5. 2001 Level II CFA Study Guide, © 2001.

CFA 6. 2003 Level II CFA Study Guide, © 2003.

CFA 7. 2004 Level II CFA Study Guide, © 2004.

CFA 8–9. 1983 Level III CFA Study Guide, © 1983.

CFA 10. From various CFA exams.

CFA 11–12. 1983 Level III CFA Study Guide, © 1983.

Chapter 12

CFA 1. 1995 Level II CFA Study Guide, © 1995.

CFA 2. 1993 Level II CFA Study Guide, © 1993.

CFA 3. 1993 Level II CFA Study Guide, © 1993.

CFA 4. 1998 Level II CFA Study Guide, © 1998.

CFA 5. From various CFA exams.

Chapter 13

CFA 1. 1995 Level II CFA Study Guide, © 1995.

CFA 2. 1987 Level I CFA Study Guide, © 1987.

CFA 3. 2001 Level II CFA Study Guide, © 2001.

CFA 4. 1994 Level II CFA Study Guide, © 1994.

[1]The CFA Institute does not endorse, promote, review, or warrant the accuracy of the product or services offered by McGraw-Hill Education.

CFA 5.   2003 Level I CFA
         Study Guide, © 2003.
CFA 6.   2003 Level I CFA
         Study Guide, © 2003.
CFA 7.   2003 Level II CFA
         Study Guide, © 2003.
CFA 8.   2001 Level II CFA
         Study Guide, © 2001.
CFA 9.   2001 Level II CFA
         Study Guide, © 2001.
CFA 10. 2001 Level II CFA
         Study Guide, © 2001.

Chapter 14

CFA 1.   2002 Level II CFA
         Study Guide, © 2002.
CFA 2.   1988 Level I CFA
         Study Guide, © 1988.
CFA 3.   1998 Level II CFA
         Study Guide, © 1998.
CFA 4.   1987 Level I CFA
         Study Guide, © 1987.
CFA 5.   1998 Level II CFA
         Study Guide, © 1998.
CFA 6.   1999 Level II CFA
         Study Guide, © 1999.
CFA 7.   1998 Level II CFA
         Study Guide, © 1998.

Chapter 15

CFA 1.   1984 Level III CFA
         Study Guide, © 1984.
CFA 2.   2000 Level II CFA
         Study Guide, © 2000.
CFA 3.   1984 Level III CFA
         Study Guide, © 1984.
CFA 4.   2001 Level II CFA
         Study Guide, © 2001.
CFA 5.   2002 Level II CFA
         Study Guide, © 2002.

Chapter 16

CFA 1.   2000 Level I CFA
         Study Guide, © 2000.
CFA 2.   2000 Level I CFA
         Study Guide, © 2000.
CFA 3.   2000 Level II CFA
         Study Guide, © 2000.

Chapter 17

CFA 1–3. 1998 Level I CFA
         Study Guide, © 1998.
CFA 4.   1982 Level III CFA
         Study Guide, © 1982.
CFA 5.   1986 Level III CFA
         Study Guide, © 1986.
CFA 6.   2000 Level II CFA
         Study Guide, © 2000.
CFA 7.   1993 Level I CFA
         Study Guide, © 1993.
CFA 8.   2000 Level III
         Study Guide, © 2000.
CFA 9.   2004 Level II CFA
         Study Guide, © 2004.

Chapter 18

CFA 1.   1995 Level II CFS
         Study Guide, © 1995.
CFA 2.   2001 Level II CFS
         Study Guide, © 2001.
CFA 3.   2001 Level II CFS
         Study Guide, © 2001.
CFA 4.   2001 Level II CFS
         Study Guide, © 2001.
CFA 5.   2004 Level II CFS
         Study Guide, © 2004.
CFA 6.   2004 Level II CFS
         Study Guide, © 2004.
CFA 7.   2001 Level II CFS
         Study Guide, © 2001.
CFA 8.   1993 Level I CFS
         Study Guide, © 1993.

CFA 9.   2003 Level I CFS
         Study Guide, © 2003.
CFA 10. 2003 Level I CFS
         Study Guide, © 2003.
CFA 11. 2003 Level II CFS
         Study Guide, © 2003.

Chapter 19

CFA 1–3. From various Level I CFA
         Study Guides.
CFA 4.   1986 Level III CFS
         Study Guide, © 1986.
CFA 5.   1991 Level II CFS
         Study Guide, © 1991.
CFA 6.   1995 Level II CFS
         Study Guide, © 1995.
CFA 7.   2003 Level III CFS
         Study Guide, © 2003.
CFA 8.   1998 Level II CFS
         Study Guide, © 1998.

Chapter 22

CFA 1.   1984 Level II CFA
         Study Guide, © 1984.
CFA 2.   1988 Level I CFA
         Study Guide, © 1988.
CFA 3.   1988 Level I CFA
         Study Guide, © 1988.
CFA 4.   From various CFA exams.
CFA 5.   From various CFA exams.
CFA 6.   1981 Level II CFA
         Study Guide, © 1981.
CFA 7.   1985 Level III CFA
         Study Guide, © 1985.
CFA 8.   1988 Level I CFA
         Study Guide, © 1988.
CFA 9.   1982 Level III CFA
         Study Guide, © 1982.
CFA 10–11. From various CFA exams.

Note: **Bold** type indicates key terms and their definitions. Page numbers followed by *n* indicate source notes or footnotes.